WHITE COLLAR CRIME: CASES, MATERIALS, AND PROBLEMS

WHITE COLLAR CRIME: CASES, MATERIALS, AND PROBLEMS

SECOND EDITION

J. Kelly Strader
Professor of Law
Southwestern Law School

Sandra D. Jordan
Professor of Law
Charlotte School of Law

2009

ISBN: 978-1-4224-2741-5

Strader, J. Kelly.
White collar crime : cases, materials, and problems / J. Kelly Strader, Sandra D. Jordan. -- 2nd ed.
p. cm.
Includes bibliographical references and index.
ISBN 978-1-4224-2395-0 (hardbound : alk. paper)
1. White collar crimes--United States--Cases.
    2. Business enterprises--Corrupt practices--Case studies. I. Jordan, Sandra D. II. Title.
KF9350.S78 2009
345.73'0268--dc22 2009017935

Editorial Offices
744 Broad Street, Newark, NJ 07102 (973) 820-2000
201 Mission St., San Francisco, CA 94105-1831 (415) 908-3200
www.lexisnexis.com

MATTHEW◆BENDER

(2009–Pub.3193)

Dedications

J.K.S.

To Hal and my parents

S.D.J.

To Mom, Byron, Nedra and B.J.

PREFACE

Our background and goals

With this book, we hope to put to good use our many years of practicing in the area of white collar crime and of teaching and writing about the subject. Professor Jordan served for nearly 10 years as an Assistant United States Attorney for the Western District of Pennsylvania, eventually heading the White Collar Crimes Unit of the United States Attorney's Office. From 1988 to 1991, she was a member of the prosecution team in the Iran-Contra investigation, one of the most significant tests of executive powers and congressional immunity in recent times. Professor Strader has practiced white collar criminal defense since his days with the New York City law firm of Morvillo, Abramowitz, Grand, Iason, Anello and Bohrer, P.C. His cases include major Wall Street prosecutions in areas such as securities fraud, mail and wire fraud, RICO, perjury, obstruction of justice, and tax fraud.

Based upon our academic and practice experiences, we have endeavored to write a problem-based casebook that provides a topical, informative, and thought-provoking perspective on this rapidly evolving area of the law. We also believe that the study of white collar law and practice raises unique issues of criminal law and justice policy, and serves as an excellent vehicle for deepening our understanding of criminal justice issues in general. For the second edition, we have emphasized the text's focus on practice problems. We have more than doubled the number of these exercises, and hope that they prove both fun and useful for students and teachers alike.

Coverage

This casebook focuses on the substance and procedure of federal white collar and corporate crime. The book is intended for use in two-, three-, or four-unit courses in White Collar Crime, Federal Criminal Law, Corporate Crime, and related subjects. The book is organized as follows:

- Chapters 1 and 2 (Overview of White Collar Crime and Corporate and Individual Liability) introduce themes and concepts discussed throughout the text.

- Chapters 3–14 cover the substantive law of white collar and corporate crime. Chapters 3 and 4 address at length the crimes of conspiracy and mail and wire fraud, the building blocks of most white collar crime prosecutions. Chapters 5–14 address specific types of fraud (securities fraud, computer fraud, and tax fraud), political corruption (bribery, gratuities, and extortion), the "cover-up" crimes (false statements, perjury, and obstruction of justice), financial crimes (currency transaction reporting and money laundering), and the RICO statute.

- Chapters 15–17 (Internal Investigations and Compliance Programs, The Grand Jury, and Self-Incrimination — Witness Testimony and Document Production), cover the principal practical and procedural issues that arise in white collar investigations and prosecutions.

- Chapters 18–20 address the consequences of white collar offenses — civil fines, criminal penalties, and forfeitures.

Selection of materials

Throughout the text, our goal has been to provide the leading cases in each area, focusing, where possible, on United States Supreme Court opinions. This goal is

PREFACE

challenging, given the lightening speed at which this area of the law changes. The rapid evolution of federal sentencing law is only the most recent example of how quickly the law in this area evolves. We have done our best to provide both foundational cases and the most recent significant cases.

In the introductory material to each of the substantive crime chapters, we have included an overview of the law and the statutory elements. (The statutes themselves, along with other supplemental materials, are included in the casebook supplement.) Because our goal is to teach principally through the study of the cases, we have tried to edit the cases judiciously* and to keep the case notes to a minimum. We also include a number of concurring and dissenting opinions, both because these opinions help elucidate the issues and because in close cases today's dissent may be tomorrow's majority.

Finally, we intersperse practice problems throughout the casebook. The problems focus on substantive law, procedural issues, and ethical dilemmas that arise in white collar practice. The text is designed to be used flexibly, and thus lends itself both to comprehensive study of the black letter law and to a problem-based approach.

A special request

Any book of this length will contain errors. If you find any errors, or have any comments or suggestions, kindly let us know. Please contact Kelly Strader ((213) 738-6753, kstrader@swlaw.edu, Southwestern Law School, 3050 Wilshire Blvd, Los Angeles, CA 90010), or Sandra D. Jordan, ((704) 971-8589, sjordan@charlottelaw.edu, Charlotte School of Law, 2145 Suttle Avenue, Charlotte, NC 28208).

---

* We indicate lengthy omissions with centered asterisks, and short omissions with ellipses. We generally have not indicated the omission of citations and footnotes. With respect to footnotes, we have retained the cases' original note numbers. The footnotes that we have written are indicated by letters rather than numbers.

Acknowledgments

J.K.S.

This book would not have been possible without the support of Southwestern Law School's Faculty Development Program. I would also like to thank Mark Cammack, Leo Romero, Karen Smith, and Ken Williams, for giving generously of their time to read various of the book's chapters; my mentors at Morvillo, Abramowitz, Grand, Iason, Anello & Bohrer; my research assistants, especially Christopher DeClue, Matthew Mann, and Peter Schoettler; and my family for their patience.

S.D.J.

This project is the end result of many months of effort, thought, and revision. Several of my colleagues generously offered their suggestions support and, vast legal experience as they read through some of the earlier drafts of the chapters. Thanks to my current and former colleagues who had a role in this publication. Robert B. Harper, Charles DeMonaco, Paul Hull, Robert J. Bondi, and Welsh White all spent time reviewing drafts, making suggestions, or offering valuable insight into the substance of our topics. My research assistants were invaluable and I especially want to commend them for their hard work: Sarah Beatty, Erin VanValkenburg, Melanie Jones, Maryam Shad, and Jake Lifson. Thanks to all of you. Finally, I appreciate all of the support provided for this project by the University of Charlotte School of Law.

TABLE OF CONTENTS

TABLE OF CONTENTS

TABLE OF CONTENTS

TABLE OF CONTENTS

TABLE OF CONTENTS

TABLE OF CONTENTS

TABLE OF CONTENTS

TABLE OF CONTENTS

TABLE OF CONTENTS

TABLE OF CONTENTS

TABLE OF CONTENTS

TABLE OF CONTENTS

TABLE OF CONTENTS

TABLE OF CONTENTS

TABLE OF CONTENTS

Chapter 1

OVERVIEW OF WHITE COLLAR CRIME

[A]   INTRODUCTORY NOTES

Over the past several decades, white collar crime has captured the attention of law makers, law enforcement, and the general public. This development has largely been due to a number of high profile investigations and prosecutions, including:

- *Corporate and financial fraud,* leading to the bankruptcy of major corporations and the destabilization of the U.S. financial system.[a]
- *Political corruption investigations and prosecutions* of members of the United States Congress, high-ranking members of the executive branch of the U.S. government, state governors, and many others.[b]
- *Individual crimes* committed by high profile defendants.[c]

All these events have produced substantial debate about the nature of white collar

---

[a] In the 1990s, the savings and loan fraud prosecutions of, among others, mogul Charles Keating, and the money laundering prosecution of Bank of Credit and Commerce International (BCCI) made headlines. *See* Christian Berthelsen, *Keating Pleads Guilty to 4 Counts of Fraud,* N.Y. Times, Apr. 7, 1999, at C2; United States v. BCCI Holdings (Luxembourg), S.A., 961 F. Supp. 287 (D.D.C. 1997). In the early 20th century, major companies failed as a result of fraud, including Enron, WorldCom, HealthSouth, Adelphia, and many others. *See* United States v. Livesay, 525 F.3d 1081 (11th Cir. 2008) (describing $1.4 billion HealthSouth fraud scheme); John R. Emshwiller, *Executives on Trial: Enron Ex-Official Pleads Guilty to Fraud, Agrees to Aid Probe,* Wall St. J., Aug. 2, 2004, at C3; Ken Belson, *Ex-Chief of WorldCom Is Found Guilty in $11 Billion Fraud,* Wall St. J., Mar. 16, 2005, at A1; Jane Sasseen & David Polek, *White-Collar Crime: Who Does Time?,* Bus. Wk., Feb. 6, 2006, at 60. (80-year-old John Rigas, Adelphia's founder and former CEO, received a 15-year sentence).

[b] *See, e.g.,* Douglas Belkin and David Kesmodel, *Illinois Outs Governor,* Wall St. J., Jan. 29, 2009, at A1 (former Illinois governor Rod R. Blagojevich alleged to have used his office to extract bribes); United States v. Libby, 432 F. Supp. 2d 26 (D.D.C. 2006) (case against "Scooter" Libby, Chief of Staff for former Vice President Dick Cheney, for obstructing investigation into leak of identity of covert CIA agent); *In re* Espy, 145 F.3d 1365 (D.C. Cir. 1998) (special prosecutor appointed to investigate alleged receipt of illegal gifts by U.S. Secretary of Agriculture); United States v. Myers, 692 F.2d 823 (2d Cir. 1982) (the "Abscam" case against members of Congress); United States v. Mandel, 591 F.2d 1347 (4th Cir. 1979) (case against former Maryland governor); United States v. Isaacs, 493 F.2d 1124 (7th Cir. 1974) (case against former Illinois governor).

[c] These include both high profile financial figures and celebrities. For example, investment banker Bernard Madoff pleaded guilty to fraud in connection with a Ponzi scheme that cost investors approximately $65 billion. *See* Diana B. Henriques and Jack Healy, *Madoff Jailed After Pleading Guilty to Fraud,* N.Y. Times, March 13, 2009, at A1. In the 1980s, insider trading investigations and prosecutions ensnared many high profile individuals, including Wall Street guru Ivan Boesky and "junk bond" king Michael Milken. *See* United States v. Milken, 759 F. Supp. 109 (S.D.N.Y. 1990); FMC Corp. v. Boesky, 852 F.2d 981, 982 n.1 (7th Cir. 1988).

Celebrities convicted of white collar crimes include actor Wesley Snipes and businesswoman and media figure Martha Stewart. *See* John J. Tigue Jr. and Jeremy H. Temkin, *Tax Litigation Issues: The Wesley Snipes Trial,* 239 N.Y. L.J. 3, col. 1 (May 15, 2008) (Snipes convicted of tax crimes); United States v. Stewart, 305 F. Supp. 2d 368 (S.D.N.Y. 2004) (Stewart convicted of cover-up crimes in connection with securities fraud investigation).

crime and about methods for combating that crime.

There is little doubt that white collar crime causes enormous harm. For example, when fraudulent practices led the savings and loan industry to collapse, thousands of investors lost their life savings. When corporations used fraudulent accounting practices to overstate their earnings, over expanded, and then collapsed, both investors and employees suffered. When public officials committed bribery and other crimes, the public's trust in government was severely undermined. Criminal justice policy therefore must effectively address white collar crime.

This chapter highlights some of the principal issues of law and policy that arise in white collar investigations and prosecutions. Although white collar crimes exist under both state and federal law, most of the significant white collar prosecutions occur at the federal level, and it is upon federal law that this text focuses. Before turning to themes in federal white collar crime, the section below sets the parameters for the study of white collar crime.

[B] THE DEFINITION OF "WHITE COLLAR CRIME"[d]

As seen below, there are many definitions of "white collar crime." This text defines the term in a way that comports with the practices of prosecutors and defenders of those charged with such crime.

[1] The Development of the Term "White Collar Crime"

The term "white collar crime" was coined in 1939 by criminologist and sociologist Edwin Sutherland. Sutherland distinguished white collar crime from "common" or "street" crime. Sutherland wrote that "[w]hite collar crime may be defined approximately as a crime committed by a person of respectability and high social status in the course of his occupation," and as crime committed by organizations such as corporations. Edwin H. Sutherland, *White Collar Crime: The Uncut Version* 7 (1983).

In seeking to explore the determinants of crime, Sutherland used the study of "white collar crime" to question the assumption that a person's social status or class determines that person's propensity to commit crime. Sutherland's thesis was that, contrary to popular belief, crime is not primarily caused by social circumstances, nor is it primarily perpetrated by those of low socio-economic status.

Although historically important, Sutherland's definition is not particularly helpful for studying white collar crime today. It is difficult to draw a principled distinction, for example, between tax fraud committed by a corporate executive and tax fraud committed by a "blue collar" worker.

Nor does a status-based definition comport with white collar cases. For example, the crime of "insider trading" occurs when a person buys or sells stock based upon stolen secret information; "insider trading" is a classic white collar crime. Yet, the United States Supreme Court first addressed insider trading in *United States v. Chiarella*, 445 U.S. 222 (1980), where the defendant was not a corporate executive

---

[d] This section is adapted from J. Kelly Strader, *The Judicial Politics of White Collar Crime*, 50 Hastings L.J. 1199 (1999). Copyright © 1999 J. Kelly Strader.

but a "markup man" for a printing company. In fact, many "white collar" defendants, particularly in cases involving crimes such as bank embezzlement and government benefits fraud, do not look much different from defendants in common crime cases. Sutherland's sociologically-oriented definition thus fails to provide a workable framework for a substantive legal discussion of the *types* of crimes that lawyers and academics speak of as "white collar offenses." Indeed, in this sense, the term "white collar" crime is a misnomer.

Perhaps the most useful definition of "white collar crime" comes from the way the term is used by those who practice in the field. In common usage, "white collar crime" is best identified by what it does not include. As used in this text, "white collar crime" does *not* include:

1. *Crimes that necessarily involve the use or threat of physical force, either against the victim or the victim's property.*

Whether a crime is "white collar" may sometimes depend upon the criminal means used, rather than upon the crime's statutory definition. For example, under the Hobbs Act, 18 U.S.C. § 1951, the crime of extortion may sometimes be "white collar" (for example, when the defendant threatens the victim with economic harm), and sometimes not (for example, when the defendant threatens the victim with the use of physical force).

2. *Offenses directly related to the possession, sale, or distribution of controlled substances.*

Many narcotics offenses do not involve the use of force. They are excluded from "white collar crime," however, because (a) there is a common perception that the "drug culture" often has a violent context, and (b) criminal investigations and prosecutions of these offenses are typically handled by specialized agencies, such as the United States Drug Enforcement Agency.

3. *Crime directly related to organized crime activities.*

Organized crime can be non-violent and, on the surface, conducted by "legitimate" businesses. It is excluded from "white collar crime," however, because (a) it often has a violent context, and (b) it is investigated and prosecuted by specialized law enforcement departments.

4. *Crime directly related to certain national policy-driven areas such as immigration and civil rights.*

Once again, these areas are considered specialized areas by law enforcement. Each raises particular policy-driven issues specific to its context.

5. *Common theft crimes and "vice" crimes.*

Ordinary theft crimes and "vice" crimes are generally considered common street crimes and not "white collar" offenses. This generalization does not apply to one type of theft crime — fraud — which is criminalized in a wide variety of white collar contexts. *See, e.g.,* Chapters 4 (Mail and Wire Fraud) and 5 (Securities Fraud), *infra*.

After excluding (1) crimes of violence, (2) narcotics offenses, (3) organized crime cases, (4) national policy crimes, and (5) common theft crimes and vice crimes, what remains is a broad, common-sense definition of white collar crime. White collar offenses are nonviolent offenses that lead either to economic harm (for example, mail and wire fraud, securities fraud, and financial crimes) or to harm to the government's ability to function effectively and without conflicts of interest (for example, bribery, extortion, perjury, false statements, obstruction of justice, and currency transaction violations). Such offenses encompass both simple cases of individual fraud and political corruption and wide-spread financial fraud and bribery and extortion schemes. This definition removes the pure socio-economic focus of "white collar crime," but comports with the views of criminal law practitioners and the general public concerning the distinction between white collar and non-white collar crime.

[2]   The Overlap Between White Collar and Common Crime

By defining "white collar crime" according to the type of criminal activity — or, more accurately, by excluding types of criminal activities from the term "white collar crime" — the focus shifts from the characteristics of the defendant to the characteristics of the crime. Often, this distinction works relatively easily; securities fraud and tax fraud, for example, are "paper" crimes that are "white collar" by nature.

Some crimes, however, and some issues in white collar cases do not observe these neat categories. For example, some of the most important Supreme Court cases interpreting federal conspiracy statutes have arisen in the white collar crime context, and a conspiracy count is often included in a white collar indictment. Governing legal principles in these cases, however, apply to any federal conspiracy case, whether the case involves white collar or common crime. As noted above, the crime of extortion includes some offenses that are "white collar" offenses and others that are not. Also, the "cover-up" offenses of perjury, false statements, and obstruction of justice fall within the definition of "white collar" offenses used here, and often arise in white collar cases. When such charges arise in cases of violent crime, they lose their "white collar" association. Finally, the broad-ranging criminal provisions of the federal racketeering ("RICO") and money laundering statutes are most often used outside the white collar context, but of course can also apply in the white collar context. Again, though, governing legal principles remain the same in the white collar and non-white collar contexts.

[3]   Corporate Crime and White Collar Crime

Corporate crime has been very much in the headlines in recent years, and there is no indication that the government will retreat from its aggressive enforcement of white collar crime statutes. Corporate or business crime is economic in nature, and can be considered a subset of white collar criminal activity. Criminal conduct that takes place within the context of the corporation is often committed for the benefit of the organization for economic reasons. In addition, corporate offenses can be committed by individuals on behalf of an organization or for personal benefit. Both of these types of offenses fall within the category of corporate crime, but they are also a part of the broader concept of white collar crime for the reasons stated in this introduction.

[4]   "Civil" vs. "Criminal" Cases

It is important to note that some civil cases are properly included within the category of "white collar" cases. This is so because the rules established in civil cases arising under such statutes as the securities laws and RICO also govern in criminal cases. Thus, a number of the chapters below include civil cases — initiated either by the government or by private parties — that establish principles applicable in criminal cases as well.

[5]   "Substantive" vs. "Procedural" White Collar Cases

This text focuses both on the substance of white collar crime and on the procedure of white collar investigations and prosecutions. The vast majority of criminal procedure issues that arise in white collar cases mirror issues that arise in common crime cases. Some procedural issues, however, merit special attention in the white collar context. For example, the production of documents to the government by entities such as corporations raises unique issues under the Fifth Amendment's Self-Incrimination Clause. In addition, because white collar investigations typically are conducted by grand juries, issues relating to grand jury proceedings should be included within the category of "white collar" cases.

[C]   RECURRING ISSUES IN WHITE COLLAR INVESTIGATIONS AND PROSECUTIONS

Apart from its timeliness, the study of white collar crime presents an opportunity to study criminal law and procedure within a particular context. Studying the processes of enacting white collar crimes and prosecuting those crimes thus allows us to address critical criminal justice issues, such as the criminalization of economic regulations, the constitutional impact of "over-criminalization," and the balance between federal and state/local law enforcement.

Further, white collar investigations raise interesting and important strategic and ethical issues for prosecutors and defense counsel. Issues relating to the representation of witnesses before grand juries, pre-indictment negotiations between prosecutors and defense counsel, parallel civil and criminal proceedings, and other issues often arise in white collar matters. These issues are discussed in cases and notes throughout this text, and are also addressed in many of the practice problems contained in the chapters that follow.

[1]   Criminalization

The fundamental question in criminal law is determining when it is appropriate to deem conduct "criminal." When should society subject a defendant to the full force of criminal penalties rather than to civil and/or administrative remedies? This issue is particularly acute when the matters at hand involve the regulation of economic activities. Some have argued that it is often not appropriate to criminalize complex economic and business activities, for two reasons: (a) Such activities are morally ambiguous and may not deserve the full condemnation of the criminal law; and (b) Criminal statutes designed to cover such matters are often flawed, in large part because economic crimes are difficult to define. As you read the materials in this text, consider whether these criticisms are justified.[e]

[a]   Distinguishing Civil and Criminal Liability

With respect to the increased criminalization of certain areas of the law, including economic regulations, consider the following excerpt written by Professor John Coffee in 1991:

> [T]he dominant development in substantive federal criminal law over the last decade has been the disappearance of any clearly definable line between civil and criminal law. [T]his blurring of the border between tort and crime predictably will result in injustice, and ultimately will weaken the efficacy of the criminal law as an instrument of social control. [T]o define the proper sphere of the criminal law, one must explain how its purposes and methods differ from those of tort law. Although it is easy to identify distinguishing characteristics of the criminal law — *e.g.*, the greater role of intent in the criminal law, the relative unimportance of actual harm to the victim, the special character of incarceration as a sanction, and the criminal law's greater reliance on public enforcement — none of these is ultimately decisive.
>
> Rather, the factor that most distinguishes the criminal law is its operation as a system of moral education and socialization. The criminal law is obeyed not simply because there is a legal threat underlying it, but because the public perceives its norms to be legitimate and deserving of compliance. Far more than tort law, the criminal law is a system for public communication of values. As a result, the criminal law often and necessarily displays a deliberate disdain for the utility of the criminalized conduct to the defendant.
>
> Thus, while tort law seeks to balance private benefits and public costs, criminal law does not (or does so only by way of special affirmative defenses), possibly because balancing would undercut the moral rhetoric of the criminal law. Characteristically, tort law prices, while criminal law prohibits.

John C. Coffee, Jr., *Does "Unlawful" Mean "Criminal"?: Reflections on the Disappearing Tort/Crime Distinction in American Law*, 71 B.U. L. Rev. 193, 193–194 (1991).

According to Professor Coffee, what are the principal purposes of the criminal law? As we study white collar crime in different contexts, it will be helpful to ask

---

[e] For the views of one of the earliest and most influential critics of overcriminalization, see Sanford Kadish, *Some Observations on the Use of Criminal Sanctions to Enforce Economic Regulations*, 30 U. Chi. L. Rev. 423 (1963). Many others have explored this topic. *See, e.g.*, J. Kelly Strader, *White Collar Crime and Punishment — Reflections on Michael, Martha, and Milberg Weiss*, 15 Geo. Mason L. Rev. 45 (2007) ("gray area" financial fraud cases should be pursued using civil and administrative remedies unless there is overwhelming evidence of actual harm); Sara Sun Beale, *The Many Faces of Overcriminalization: From Morals and Mattress Tags to Overfederalization*, 54 Am. U. L. Rev. 747, 748 (2005) ("a good deal of so-called regulatory or 'white collar crime' should fall outside the ambit of the criminal law, to be dealt with by other bodies of specialized civil law"); Erik Luna, *The Overcriminalization Phenomenon*, 54 Am. U. L. Rev. 703, 743–744 (2005) (the expansion of federal criminal law is "contrary to the principles of limited government and narrow congressional powers, looking instead like the usurpation of a de facto police power by federal lawmakers").

whether the particular criminal statute — or particular criminal prosecution — serves those goals. When reading any particular case in this text, consider whether the conduct at issue merits criminal sanctions and, if so, what purposes criminal sanctions serve.

[b]   The Effects of Over-Criminalization

The difficulty in clearly drawing the boundaries of white collar crimes is a theme that runs throughout the materials in this text. For example, in the securities business, it is often the job of brokers and analysts to gain as much information as they can about the companies in which they are trading stock. But when a broker trades on "inside information," a term that has proven notoriously difficult to define (*see* Chapter 5, *below*), the trading may constitute securities fraud. And when analyzing the criminal application of an antitrust statute, the United States Supreme Court in *United States v. United States Gypsum Co.*, 438 U.S. 422, 441 (1978), noted that the statute does not always distinguish criminal conduct from the "gray zone of socially acceptable and economically justifiable business conduct."

The difficulty in separating criminal from non-criminal acts is not limited to the business context. For example, as discussed in more detail in Chapter 9 below, Congress and the Supreme Court have had difficulty distinguishing legitimate political campaign fundraising from the crime of extortion "under color of official right." *See McCormick v. United States*, 500 U.S. 257, 272 (1991) (expressing concern that an overly broad reading of the federal extortion statute could lead to criminalization of routine political fundraising activities). As you cover the materials in this book, consider whether criminal sanctions may actually have negative consequences in some instances.

[2]   Due Process

The difficulty in defining white collar crimes also raises issues relating to the fairness of the criminal justice system. As Professor John Coffee has written, "the federal law of 'white collar' crime now seems to be judge-made to an unprecedented degree, with courts deciding on a case-by-case, retrospective basis whether conduct falls within often vaguely defined legislative prohibitions." Coffee, *supra*, at 198. Such statutes run the risks of reaching conduct that Congress did not intend to criminalize, failing to provide fair notice to potential defendants, and failing to provide sufficient guidance to prosecutors. (Copies of the relevant statutes are included in the statutory appendix.)

[3]   Prosecutorial Discretion

White collar investigations and prosecutions raise complex issues of prosecutorial discretion. Prosecutors have the discretion to decide (a) whether the facts merit criminal charges, (b) whether to seek criminal penalties when civil and/or administrative proceedings have been or may be brought, (c) what criminal statutes to use in bringing a case, (d) what theories to charge when using those statutes, and/or (e) whom to charge in the case.

This broad discretion provides prosecutors with substantial powers in the white collar crime arena. As Professor Ellen Podgor has noted:

Prosecutors have an array of crimes for proceeding against those engaged in white collar criminality. In many instances the involved activity fits the elements of more than one offense. Conduct will be mail fraud, tax fraud, a false statement, perjury, and also be violations of the Travel Act and RICO. A prosecutor, who in some instances may be a relatively inexperienced attorney, will be deciding which of these offenses will be used from the arsenal of possible charges to proceed against the defendant.

Ellen S. Podgor, *Corporate and White Collar Crime: Simplifying the Ambiguous*, 31 Am. Crim. L. Rev. 391, 400 (1994).

Apart from deciding which offenses to charge, a prosecutor may have the discretion to apply a white collar statute in a novel way. Precisely because many white collar criminal statutes are so broad-reaching, these statutes call upon prosecutors to exercise discretion when applying the statutes to new situations and to particular defendants. In addition, prosecutors identify the amount of loss or the number and identity of victims, factors that may contribute heavily to a defendant's sentence. These decisions thus give prosecutors tremendous leverage relating to plea bargaining, restitution, and sentencing.

Courts have traditionally declined to supervise the exercise of prosecutorial discretion, absent some egregious showing such as racial bias. Does reliance upon the exercise of sound prosecutorial discretion solve the problem of vagueness in white collar criminalization?

[4]   Enforcement Barriers

White collar crime often occurs behind closed doors, causing harm of which the victim may not even be aware. Apart from the difficulty of detection, these crimes also often are highly complex, and require substantial resources and expertise to investigate and prosecute. The government continually struggles to make white collar criminal law enforcement more efficient and effective. Important questions arise as to whether the more effective way to achieve these goals is to enact more laws and/or to devote more resources to the effort to fight white collar crime.

[5]   Federalism

[a]   Over-Federalization?

Under our constitutional system, criminal law enforcement is primarily left to the states; historically only about five percent of all criminal cases are brought at the federal level. *See Report of the ABA Task Force on the Federalization of Criminal Law* 4 (1998). In recent decades, however, Congress has enacted an ever-broader array of criminal statutes; over 40 percent of all federal crimes have been enacted since 1970. *Id.*

Federal white collar criminalization is a significant part of a broader trend to federalize criminal law. Apart from the increased burdens on the federal judicial system, what are the implications of this development for our federal system of government? Consider the following excerpt by Professor Kathleen Brickey:

The original role of federal criminal law was auxiliary to that of the states. Federal law addressed matters of substantial federal concern that were beyond the reach of the states. The evolution of a national police power paralleled the rise of economic regulation. Increased economic regulation inspired a Congress enamored with commerce-based jurisdiction to add more and more crimes to the books. Thus, as economic regulation ascended, criminal law flourished as well. But somewhere along the line, federal criminal law lost its compass. Congress, disregarding the auxiliary nature of federal law enforcement, placed federal criminal law on an evolutionary collision course with state criminal law. Thus, instead of complementing state criminal law, federal law began competing with it.

Federal duplication of state criminal law unduly burdens the federal justice system, which is ill-equipped to supplant local law enforcement. The federal government's assumption of a major responsibility for maintaining local law and order is not only harmful to the federal justice system. It is also harmful to the states. When the government preempts local prosecutions in areas of overlapping jurisdiction, it interferes with a state's ability to exercise discretion in a way that is responsive to local concerns. Excessive use of federal jurisdiction diminishes the prestige of local law enforcement authorities and thus may interfere with their development of responsibility for and capacity to handle complex matters or detract from the distinctive role states play as "laboratories of change."

Kathleen F. Brickey, *Criminal Mischief: The Federalization of American Criminal Law*, 46 Hastings L.J. 1135, 1172–1174 (1995). *See also* Adam H. Kurland, *First Principles of American Federalism and the Nature of Federal Criminal Jurisdiction*, 45 Emory L.J. 1 (1996); Sara Sun Beale, *Too Many and Yet Too Few: New Principles to Define the Proper Limits for Federal Criminal Jurisdiction*, 46 Hastings L.J. 979 (1995).

What has caused this trend towards "over-federalization"? In 1998, the American Bar Association's Criminal Justice Section issued a report prepared by the bi-partisan Task Force of the Federalization of Criminal Law. That report stated:

The Task Force was told explicitly by more than one source that many of these new federal laws are passed not because federal prosecution of these crimes is necessary but because federal crime legislation in general is thought to be politically popular. Put another way, it is not considered politically wise to vote against crime legislation, even if it is misguided, unnecessary, and even harmful.

The Task Force believes that the Congressional appetite for new crimes regardless of their merit is not only misguided and ineffectual, but has serious adverse consequences, some of which have already occurred and some of which can be confidently predicted.

Report of the ABA Task Force, supra, at 1–2. This text provides repeated opportunities to study the increased role of the federal government in the criminal law in matters ranging from routine fraud prosecutions to state and local political corruption cases.

[b]   Jurisdiction

There must be a jurisdictional basis for any federal criminal prosecution. In most white collar cases, jurisdiction exists under the Commerce Clause of the United States Constitution. U.S. Const. art. I, § 8, cl. 3. That clause provides that

Congress may "regulate Commerce with Foreign Nations, and among the several states, and with the Indian Tribes." After years of reading the Commerce Clause broadly, the Supreme Court employed a more restrictive reading in *United States v. Lopez*, 514 U.S. 549, 554–555 (1995). In that case, the Court voided a non-white collar federal statute because the proscribed activity (relating to the possession of firearms on school grounds) did not meet the requirement of "substantially affect[ing] interstate commerce." It is rare, however, for a white collar statute to be voided on jurisdictional grounds. Note also that some white collar statutes rely upon the postal power (mail fraud) and the taxing power (tax fraud) for their jurisdictional basis.

[D] WHITE COLLAR CRIME AND GENERAL CRIMINAL LAW

The study of white collar crime provides a valuable opportunity to gain a more in-depth understanding of how substantive criminal law operates. In common crime cases, the primary issue is often one of identity — have the police caught the right person? In white collar cases, on the other hand, the issues are usually far more complex. First, because of the vagueness of many white collar statutes, the primary issue is often whether the defendant's admitted conduct even constitutes a crime. Second, the defendant's culpable mental state, or mens rea, is more frequently the principal issue in white collar cases than in non-white collar cases. For example, in a business fraud case, the government must prove that the defendant had the purpose to defraud, as opposed to an intent merely to engage in an aggressive but legal business practice.

[1] Mens Rea

The required proof of mens rea is a key issue in most white collar cases. Initially, in many contexts, the required level of mens rea may not be clear from the criminal statute at issue. Further, defining precisely what a particular level of mens rea really means is often a difficult task.

[a] Strict Liability

Recall that the vast majority of crimes require proof of both the criminal act and the criminal intent. But what if a criminal statute fails on its face to require proof of mens rea? Should such a requirement be read into the statute? In *United States v. United States Gypsum Co.*, 438 U.S. 422 (1978), the United States Supreme Court examined whether intent is an element of a criminal antitrust charge under the Sherman Act, 15 U.S.C. § 1. That statute proscribes certain anticompetitive business practices, such as price-fixing, and can be enforced in both civil and criminal proceedings. In *United States Gypsum*, the trial judge instructed the jury that "the law presumes that a person intends the necessary and natural consequences of his acts. Therefore, if the effect of the exchanges of pricing information was to raise, fix, maintain, and stabilize prices, then the parties to them are presumed, as a matter of law, to have intended that result." The defendant was convicted, and on appeal, challenged this jury instruction.

The Supreme Court reversed. The Court noted that "the instructions given by the trial judge provided that the [defendants'] *purpose* was essentially irrelevant if the jury found that the *effect* of verification was to raise, fix, maintain, or stabilize prices." The instructions thus imposed strict liability if the actus reus of the crime was present. The Court concluded "a defendant's state of mind or intent is an element of a criminal antitrust offense which must be established by evidence and inferences drawn therefrom and cannot be taken from the trier of fact through reliance on a legal presumption of wrongful intent from proof of an effect on prices. . . . [I]ntent generally remains an indispensable element of a criminal offense. This is as true in a sophisticated criminal antitrust case as in one involving any other criminal offense." Absent clear Congressional intent to impose strict liability, the Court held, criminal intent must be proven in any criminal case.

The Court in *United States Gypsum* decided that a criminal violation of the Sherman Act is not a "strict liability" offense. As seen in the next chapter, however, the Court has approved of strict liability criminal offenses in other contexts.

[b]   Recklessness and Negligence

In *United States Gypsum*, the Court stated that, "[i]n dealing with the kinds of business decisions upon which the antitrust laws focus, the concepts of recklessness[f] and negligence[g] have no place." Yet, as we will see in the chapters below, Congress has adopted statutes that indeed impose criminal liability based upon reckless and negligent conduct. Can you determine why the Court found these standards inappropriate to a charge of price-fixing?

[c]   Purpose vs. Knowledge

Once it had decided that proof of mens rea is required in a criminal prosecution under the Sherman Act, the Court in *United States Gypsum* turned to the task of defining the required level of mens rea. Relying upon the Model Penal Code ("MPC"), the Court identified four possible levels: purpose,[h] knowledge,[i] recklessness, and negligence. Concluding that recklessness and negligence set the bar too low, the court stated that:

> Our question instead is whether a criminal violation of the antitrust laws requires . . . a demonstration that the disputed conduct was undertaken

---

[f] Model Penal Code § 2.02(c) provides:

A person acts recklessly . . . when he consciously disregards a substantial and unjustifiable risk that the material element exists or will result from his conduct. The risk must be of such a nature and degree that, considering the nature and purpose of the actor's conduct and the circumstances known to him, its disregard involves a gross deviation from the standard of conduct that a law-abiding person would observe in the actor's situation.

[g] Model Penal Code § 2.02(d) provides:

A person acts negligently . . . when he should be aware of a substantial and unjustifiable risk that the material element exists or will result from his conduct. The risk must be of such a nature and degree that the actor's failure to perceive it, considering the nature and purpose of his conduct and the circumstances known to him, involves a gross deviation from the standard of care that a reasonable person would observe in the actor's situation.

[h] Model Penal Code § 2.02(a) provides:

"A person acts purposely . . . when . . . it is his conscious object to engage in the [proscribed] conduct or to cause [the proscribed] result. . . . "

[i] Model Penal Code § 2.02(b) provides:

"A person acts knowingly . . . when (i) if the element involves the nature of his conduct, he is aware that his conduct is of that nature; and (ii) if the element involves a result of his conduct, he is aware that it is practically certain that his conduct will cause such a result."

with the 'conscious object' [i.e., purpose] of producing such effects, or whether it is sufficient that the conduct is shown to have been undertaken with knowledge that the proscribed effects would most likely follow. While the difference between these formulations is a narrow one, we conclude that action undertaken with knowledge of its probable consequences- . . . can be a sufficient predicate for a finding of criminal liability under the antitrust laws.

According to the Court, at least when anticompetitive effects are shown, knowledge is the required mens rea; the Court declined to require proof that the defendants acted with "purpose." As a practical matter, what is the difference?

[d]   "Specific" vs. "General" Intent

The Model Penal Code and the *United States Gypsum* opinion both reject the old common law distinction between specific and general intent — terms with varying definitions that have produced more confusion than clarity. As a general matter, if the term "specific intent" appears in a case, it is probably used to mean "purpose" as employed by the MPC. The MPC provides that a defendant acted "purposefully" when the defendant acted with the "conscious object to engage in the [proscribed] conduct or to cause [the proscribed] result." Model Penal Code § 2.02(2)(a)(i).

[e]   "Willfulness"

Some white collar statutes require proof that the defendant acted "willfully." The interpretation of this term varies according to the context. In the realm of tax fraud, for example, the Supreme Court stated in *Cheek v. United States*, 498 U.S. 192, 201 (1991), that "[w]illfulness . . . requires the Government to prove that the law imposed a duty on the defendant, that the defendant knew of this duty, and that he voluntarily and intentionally violated that duty." This unusually high burden of proof defies the usual maxim that "ignorance of the law is no excuse." The Court concluded that the extraordinary complexity of the federal tax code justifies this high level of proof. The Court reached a similar result when interpreting the currency transaction reporting statutes. *Ratzlaf v. United States*, 510 U.S. 135 (1994).[j] In other contexts, however, "willfulness" may mean "purpose" or even "knowledge." Care should be taken to identify precisely how courts have interpreted the term "willfulness" under the particular statute.

[2]   The Rule of Lenity

The defendants in *United States Gypsum* were prosecuted under a statute that, on its face, did not require that the government prove any level of mens rea in order to obtain a criminal conviction. In interpreting Section 1 of the Sherman Act to require proof of a culpable mental state, the Court relied upon the rule of "lenity." The Supreme Court has defined lenity as "the familiar rule that, 'where there is ambiguity in a criminal statute, doubts are to be resolved in favor of the defendant.'" *Adamo Wrecking Co. v. United States*, 434 U.S. 275, 285 (1978),

---

[j] As discussed in Chapter 14 below, Congress later amended the applicable statute to overturn the *Ratzlaf* result.

quoting United States v. Bass, 404 U.S. 336, 348 (1971). As you read the materials in this text, consider whether lenity provides a meaningful safeguard when construing ambiguous statutes.

[E] THE "HARM" FROM WHITE COLLAR CRIME

Does white collar criminal activity cause the sort of harm that might even warrant criminalization? As one scholar has written with respect to white collar crimes, "the harms they cause are often diffuse; and the victims they affect are frequently hard to identify." Stuart P. Green, *Moral Ambiguity in White Collar Criminal Law*, 18 Notre Dame J.L. Ethics & Pub. Pol'y 501, 501 (2004). The indeterminacy of harm is an issue that does not often arise in connection with common crime, where the injury to person or property is usually readily apparent.

By contrast, enforcement of some white collar crimes arguably causes more harm than it prevents. In *United States Gypsum*, for example, the United States Supreme Court suggested that an overly broad reading of the Sherman Act might result in "overdeterrence" that would prevent business people from engaging in beneficial activities. The uncertainty over the "harm" caused by white collar crime underscores the problematic nature of white collar criminalization. Professor William Stuntz, for example, has argued that prosecutors' emphasis on white collar crime is not justified by the harm that such crime causes:

> White-collar criminal prosecutions were a small feature of law enforcement, state and federal, before about 1970. They are still a small feature of local prosecutors' dockets, but they play a large role indeed in many U.S. Attorneys' offices. This large growth in white-collar prosecutions, like the explosion in drug enforcement, has taken place in Republican and Democratic administrations alike, and now appears to be a permanent feature of federal criminal practice.

> What explains it? The phenomenon was partly prompted by Edwin Sutherland's skillful propagandizing: Sutherland spent years making exaggerated claims about the high cost of the frauds of the wealthy. . . . But it is hard to credit the popularity of white-collar criminal enforcement to the perceived cost of white-collar crimes. The best study of those crimes and the criminals who commit them concluded that many are fairly small-time frauds that cost their victims a few thousand dollars or less. More importantly, frauds do not impose the biggest costs that more traditional street crime imposes: fear of violence, and the attendant inability to travel about one's neighborhood in peace. Plus, white-collar cases are more costly to investigate and prosecute than street crime, partly because of the nature of the evidence the government must gather, and partly because white-collar defendants are so often represented by counsel even while the investigation is going forward. Sutherland's fulminations notwithstanding, street crime is and always has been more socially costly and more easily punished than its white-collar counterpart.

William J. Stuntz, *Race, Class, and Drugs*, 98 Colum. L. Rev. 1795, 1839–1840 (1998).

Do you agree that, because street crime involves the fear of violence, it "is and always has been more socially costly" than white collar crime? What are the social costs of white collar crime?

If you were a prosecutor with limited resources, whom would you pursue — a person who repeatedly and intentionally murdered a number of victims, or a corporate executive whose workplace practices had caused a similar number of employees to be killed?

Would you pursue a burglar who had stolen thousands of dollars worth of property from hundreds of homes, or a savings and loan executive who had defrauded a similar number of victims out of an equivalent sum of money? Why?

Chapter 2

CORPORATE AND INDIVIDUAL LIABILITY

[A] INTRODUCTORY NOTES

Any study of white collar crime must incorporate a comprehensive understanding of the scope of individual and corporate liability for criminal activity. Legal entities such as corporations may be held criminally liable even if the individuals who acted on behalf of the entity are not charged with any crime. Further, individuals acting solely on behalf of entities may be liable even if those individuals were acting solely to benefit the corporation.

Criminal prosecution of corporations has become much more frequent in recent years, reflecting a government shift in priorities and resources. Highly publicized scandals focused public attention on corporate governance and accounting practices and on the harm that corporate malfeasance causes to shareholders and other individuals. The ensuing public outcry often leads legislatures and prosecutors to respond swiftly to such scandals. For example, public outrage at the corporate accounting scandals of the early 21st century resulted in the hasty passage of the Sarbanes-Oxley Act of 2002. This law exposes corporations, employees, and officers to expanded criminal sanctions and has resulted in closer scrutiny of individual wrongdoers within corporate entities. As noted in Chapter 1, *supra*, a number of corporations and individuals have been prosecuted as a result of high profile corporate scandals.

The scope of corporate liability has evolved over many decades, and runs the gamut from administrative and civil sanctions to strict criminal liability. Because of the unique nature of artificial entities such as corporations, corporate liability is subject to considerable public policy debate. Corporations lack the most fundamental aspects of criminal liability: artificial entities alone cannot commit criminal acts or possess criminal mental states. Thus, criminal liability is imputed to corporations through the acts of their employees and agents. Over the years, courts have struggled with the concept of convicting and sentencing abstract entities such as corporations, partly because punishing a corporation in reality punishes innocent shareholders and deprives them of their property.

[B] CORPORATE CRIMINAL LIABILITY

This chapter will review the basic principles of corporate criminal liability and some of the considerations that persuade a prosecutor to charge a corporation and/or various individuals within the corporate setting. Corporations can be held liable for acts of employees under two different legal approaches: respondeat superior and the Model Penal Code (MPC). This section discusses each of these approaches.

[1]   Respondeat Superior

In the federal court system, the doctrine of respondeat superior applies to corporate criminal investigations, and the requirements are often incorporated into the statutory language. Courts use a three-prong test to determine whether an agent's acts can be imputed to the corporation. The essence of the respondeat superior doctrine imposes liability on corporations for acts committed by corporate agents acting (1) on behalf of the corporation, (2) to benefit the corporation, and (3) within the scope of the agent's authority. As will be seen, determining the presence of these criteria is often a difficult task.

*   *   *

A frequent issue that arises in corporate investigations is whether the agent was acting within the scope of the agent's employment. Proof of this fact is necessary for a corporation to be convicted under the respondeat superior theory of criminal liability. In the next case, the court discusses the sufficiency of the evidence on the "scope of employment."

UNITED STATES v. AUTOMATED MEDICAL LABORATORIES, INC.
770 F.2d 399 (4th Cir. 1985)

SNEEDEN, CIRCUIT JUDGE:

The defendant, Automated Medical Laboratories, Inc. ("AML"), appeals its conviction of one count of conspiracy, in violation of 18 U.S.C. § 371, and three counts of making and using false documents in a matter within the jurisdiction of a federal agency, in violation of 18 U.S.C. § 1001. AML was convicted of these four counts following a jury trial in March 1984 in the United States District Court for the Eastern District of Virginia. AML was fined $250.00 for each count, for a total fine of $1000.00. AML argues that its convictions should be reversed because several instances of prosecutorial misconduct denied it a fundamentally fair trial and because the evidence adduced at trial was insufficient to sustain its convictions. We disagree with these contentions and consequently affirm AML's conviction on all counts.

On December 12, 1983, a grand jury indicted AML, along with one of its wholly-owned subsidiaries, Richmond Plasma Corporation ("RPC"), and three individuals, Hugo Partucci, Noberto Queris, and Pedro Ramos, for engaging in a conspiracy that included falsification of logbooks and records required to be maintained in connection with the commercial enterprise of producing blood plasma. The indictment alleged that the falsification of logbooks and records was engaged in to conceal from the Food and Drug Administration ("FDA") various violations of federal regulations governing the plasmapheresis process and facilities. The remainder of the eight-count indictment alleged specific violations of the false statements statute, 18 U.S.C. § 1001, with regard to particular logbooks or records at the RPC facility. AML was named as a defendant in six of the seven substantive counts plus the conspiracy count. RPC was found guilty on all counts.

The three individuals indicted — Partucci, Queris, and Ramos — were all involved, at various times, in the management or oversight of RPC. Queris was the manager of RPC from 1979 to 1980. In 1980, Ramos succeeded Queris as manager of RPC. Hugo Partucci was a regional manager and "Responsible Head" for several of AML's plasmapheresis facilities between 1972 and 1979. Queris pleaded guilty to one substantive count prior to trial. Ramos was found guilty of one substantive count. Partucci was not present at trial, having apparently left for his native country, Argentina, about six months before the indictment was returned.

AML, a Florida corporation with its main office in Miami, owns and operates several medically-related businesses, such as kidney dialysis centers, facilities for the manufacture and sale of the cancer drug Interferon, and plasmapheresis facilities. AML's primary line of business, however, is the collection and sale of plasma through its eight commercial plasmapheresis centers. Each center, including RPC, is separately incorporated and wholly-owned by AML.

AML had experienced difficulties with RPC dating back to 1977. The FDA closed RPC twice, once in 1977 and again in late 1978, because of problems with overbleeding of donors (removing more blood from a given donor than is allowed by federal regulations) and incomplete recordkeeping. Following the first closing, the manager and responsible head for RPC were changed. Partucci became responsible head for RPC and was charged with assuring compliance with FDA regulations. Partucci, although technically employed by the Orlando Plasma Center, another AML subsidiary, operated as a regional manager for AML and was responsible for assuring compliance with FDA regulations. Partucci was responsible for assuring compliance at RPC and at least two other plasma centers.

At some point, apparently in 1978, Partucci and Edgar Nugent, an Executive Vice President at AML, established a special office for the specific purpose of assuring compliance with federal regulations at AML plasma centers. The compliance office, headed by Partucci, operated from the Orlando Center. By late 1978, the compliance office included Partucci, Claudia Hayes, and Mary Jo Lawton. Another AML employee, Robert Curry, sometimes accompanied them on inspection trips. The members of the compliance "team" conducted periodic inspections at various AML centers to discover and correct any deficiencies in compliance with FDA regulations. Contrary to AML's later characterizations of their responsibilities, the members of the compliance team clearly drew their authority from AML, not from the Orlando Center where their office was located. Thus, they functioned as agents of AML.

The compliance team often conducted inspections in advance of FDA inspections. Some of the deficiencies, particularly at RPC, were severe enough, however, that the compliance team members began to instruct plasma center employees to falsify and fabricate records to conceal these deficiencies — a practice apparently engaged in on the basis of Partucci's instructions. During the time that RPC was closed in late 1978 and early 1979, the compliance team, sometimes with Queris and Curry, visited RPC to prepare for the FDA inspection prior to its reopening. Faced with numerous problems, the compliance team, Queris, and Curry instructed RPC employees to falsify various records or falsified the records themselves.

Partucci left AML in December of 1979; but, even after his departure, the practice of falsifying records continued. Several RPC employees testified at trial that they were instructed by the compliance team, Queris, or Curry to falsify various records. . . .

After Partucci's departure, members of the compliance team began to report to Mili Lamas, a vice-president at AML. Sometime in March or April of 1980, Queris informed Lamas of the entire history of unlawful practices at RPC. In mid-March 1980, Lois Keith, an AML employee, travelled from the Miami office to the RPC offices, where she discovered a whole blood weight log that had been falsified. Keith telephoned Lamas to inform Lamas of her discovery. Several days later, Lamas met with Keith, Lawton, and Hayes to discuss the falsification of the weight log. Lamas informed them that AML's attorney would notify the FDA of the problem. Unbeknownst to Lamas, however, or anyone else at AML or RPC, several RPC employees had gone to the FDA in mid-March 1980 to report the long-standing and pervasive falsification practices at RPC.

The FDA began an inspection of RPC in March of 1980. By the end of that March, an initial FDA inspection report had been prepared. The investigation was concluded by June of 1980 and a final report prepared by October 1980. From that point until March 1982, various levels of the FDA reviewed what had been recommended. In March of 1982, the FDA referred the matter to the Department of Justice recommending criminal prosecution. The Department of Justice referred it to the U.S. Attorney's office in Richmond in mid-March 1982. An indictment was returned by the grand jury on December 12, 1983. An eight-day jury trial was held in March 1984 resulting in the conviction of AML on four of seven counts.

*   *   *

AML's final argument is that there is insufficient evidence to support its conviction, and thus the district court should have granted AML's motion for a judgment of acquittal. AML asserts that there is no evidence that any officer or director at AML knowingly and willfully participated in or authorized the unlawful practices at RPC, essentially arguing that the Government failed to prove that AML had the requisite intent to violate 18 U.S.C. § 1001. AML further maintains that the Government failed to prove the "element" that its agents' criminal acts were undertaken primarily to benefit AML.

In *United States v. Basic Construction Co.*, 711 F.2d 570 (4th Cir. 1983), this Court rejected the argument that the Government had to prove "that the corporation, presumably as represented by its upper level officers and managers, had an intent separate from that of its lower level employees to violate the antitrust laws." *Basic Construction* involved a criminal prosecution under section 1 of the Sherman Act, for bid rigging in state road paving contracts. The conviction of Basic Construction Company, affirmed by the Court, was based on evidence showing that the bid rigging activities were perpetrated by two relatively minor officials and were done without the knowledge of high level corporate officers. Basic introduced evidence indicating that it had a longstanding, well known, and strictly enforced policy against bid rigging. The Court, citing with approval several cases from other circuits, summarized the rule on corporate criminal liability as follows:

> These cases hold that a corporation may be held criminally responsible for antitrust violations committed by its employees if they were acting within the scope of their authority, or apparent authority, and for the benefit of the corporation even if . . . such acts were against corporate policy or express instructions.

Thus, AML may be held criminally liable for the unlawful practices at RPC if its agents were acting within the scope of their employment, which includes a determination of whether the agents were acting for the benefit of the corporation.

The term "scope of employment" has been broadly defined to include acts on the corporation's behalf in performance of the agent's general line of work. *United States v. Hilton Hotels Corporation*, 467 F.2d 1000, 1004 (9th Cir. 1972). To be acting within the scope of his employment, an agent must be "performing acts of the kind which he is authorized to perform, and those acts must be motivated — at least in part — by an intent to benefit the corporation." It is clear that the agents of AML — Partucci, Lawton, Hayes, and Curry — were acting within the scope of their employment. AML had specifically assigned to these individuals the responsibility for assuring compliance by its plasmapheresis centers with FDA regulations. In instructing other employees regarding compliance with applicable regulations, Partucci and the others were acting within the scope of their authority or certainly within their apparent authority. The fact that many of their actions were unlawful and contrary to corporate policy does not absolve AML of legal responsibility for their acts.

The basic purpose of requiring that an agent have acted with the intent to benefit the corporation, however, is to insulate the corporation from criminal liability for actions of its agents which be *inimical* to the interests of the corporation or which may have been undertaken solely to advance the interests of that agent or of a party other than the corporation. It would seem entirely possible, therefore, for an agent to have acted for his own benefit while also acting for the benefit of the corporation.

In light of the foregoing principles, we believe that the jury could reasonably have concluded from the evidence presented at trial that Partucci and other agents of AML acted, at least in part, with the intent of benefiting AML by their unlawful acts. AML attempts to make much of the testimony regarding Partucci's ambitious nature and his desire to ascend the corporate ladder at AML, arguing that he instigated the unlawful practices at RPC to benefit himself, not AML. We are not persuaded by this argument. Partucci was clearly acting in part to benefit AML since his advancement within the corporation depended on AML's well-being and its lack of difficulties with the FDA. At any rate, regardless of Partucci's motivation, the other members of the compliance team appear to have been acting for the benefit of AML.

When viewed in light of the proper principles governing corporate criminal liability, the evidence presented at trial is more than sufficient to sustain AML's conviction on all counts. It is well-established that a jury verdict must be affirmed if there is sufficient evidence, viewed in the light most favorable to the Government, from which a rational jury could have found guilt beyond reasonable doubt. Numerous Government witnesses testified regarding the unlawful actions of and instructions given by Partucci, Lawton, Hayes, and Curry — all agents of AML. Based on our review of the record, we find that there was sufficient evidence to support the jury's verdict. The conviction of AML is AFFIRMED.

NOTES AND QUESTIONS

1. *Respondeat superior.* What is the precise legal test for respondeat superior? Respondeat superior is a civil law tort doctrine. Is it appropriate to apply a civil law concept to the criminal law? How difficult is it for a corporation to avoid criminal liability under this standard?

2. *Debate over corporate criminal liability.* Courts and commentators have argued that corporate criminal liability is overly broad, principally because of the

absence of any requirement that the corporation itself possessed a mens rea. Critics also argue that it is not appropriate to apply standards of civil law to criminal matters. Federal courts have rejected these grounds and have imposed corporate liability based on three main arguments: liability is necessary to ensure that corporations adequately supervise their agents and employees; corporate liability encourages corporations to develop general policies to deter wrongdoing; and corporate liability appropriately places responsibility on the entity that benefits from the wrongdoing rather than solely upon the individual wrongdoer.

3. *Scope of authority.* What evidence can be shown to establish that an employee is acting within the scope of employment? Suppose that an employee does not have the express authority to bind the corporation. Will that establish that the employee was not acting within the scope of employment?

4. *Modern doctrine revisited.* The modern doctrine of corporate criminal liability states that a corporation is liable for the actions of its agents whenever such agents act within the scope of their employment and at least in part to benefit the corporation. Should it matter where the employee fits within the corporate hierarchy? Should it matter whether the corporation had policies in place to deter wrongdoing?

*   *   *

In the next case, the employee was acting in violation of corporate compliance policies. Should a corporation be liable because of the acts of an employee who violated explicit corporate policy?

UNITED STATES v. HILTON HOTELS
467 F.2d 1000 (9th Cir. 1972)

This is an appeal from a conviction under an indictment charging a violation of section 1 of the Sherman Act, 15 U.S.C. § 1.

Operators of hotels, restaurants, hotel and restaurant supply companies, and other businesses in Portland, Oregon, organized an association to attract conventions to their city. To finance the association, members were asked to make contributions in predetermined amounts. Companies selling supplies to hotels were asked to contribute an amount equal to one per cent of their sales to hotel members. To aid collections, hotel members, including appellant, agreed to give preferential treatment to suppliers who paid their assessments, and to curtail purchases from those who did not.

The jury was instructed that such an agreement by the hotel members, if proven, would be a per se violation of the Sherman Act. Appellant argues that this was error.

*   *   *

Appellant's president testified that it would be contrary to the policy of the corporation for the manager of one of its hotels to condition purchases upon payment of a contribution to a local association by the supplier. The manager of appellant's Portland hotel and his assistant testified that it was the hotel's policy to purchase supplies solely on the basis of price, quality, and service. They also testified that on two occasions they told the hotel's purchasing agent that he was to take no part in the boycott. The purchasing agent confirmed the receipt of these instructions, but admitted that, despite them, he had threatened a supplier with loss of the hotel's business unless the supplier paid the association assessment. He testified that he violated his instructions because of anger and personal pique toward the individual representing the supplier.

Based upon this testimony, appellant requested certain instructions bearing upon the criminal liability of a corporation for the unauthorized acts of its agents. These requests were rejected by the trial court. The court instructed the jury that a corporation is liable for the acts and statements of its agents "within the scope of their employment," defined to mean "in the corporation's behalf in performance of the agent's general line of work," including "not only that which has been authorized by the corporation, but also that which outsiders could reasonably assume the agent would have authority to do." The court added: "A corporation is responsible for acts and statements of its agents, done or made within the scope of their employment, even though their conduct may be contrary to their actual instructions or contrary to the corporation's stated policies." Appellant objects only to the court's concluding statement.

Congress may constitutionally impose criminal liability upon a business entity for acts or omissions of its agents within the scope of their employment. *United States v. A & P Trucking Co.*, 358 U.S. 121, 125–26 (1958); *New York Central & Hudson R.R. Co. v. United States*, 212 U.S. 481 (1909); *cf. United States v. Illinois Central R.R. Co.*, 303 U.S. 239 (1938). Such liability may attach without proof that the conduct was within the agent's actual authority, and even though it may have been contrary to express instructions. . . .

The intention to impose such liability is sometimes express, *New York Central & Hudson R.R. Co. v. United States*, *supra*, 212 U.S. 481, but it may also be implied. The text of the Sherman Act does not expressly resolve the issue. For the reasons that follow, however, we think the construction of the Act that best achieves its purpose is that a corporation is liable for acts of its agents within the scope of their authority even when done against company orders. . . .

*   *   *

Legal commentators have argued forcefully that it is inappropriate and ineffective to impose criminal liability upon a corporation, as distinguished from the human agents who actually perform the unlawful acts. . . . But it is the legislative judgment that controls, and "the great mass of legislation calling for corporate criminal liability suggests a widespread belief on the part of legislators that such liability is necessary to effectuate regulatory policy." ALI Model Penal Code, Comment on § 2.07. Moreover, the strenuous efforts of corporate defendants to avoid conviction, particularly under the Sherman Act, strongly suggests that Congress is justified in its judgment that exposure of the corporate entity to potential conviction may provide a substantial spur to corporate action to prevent violations by employees. . . .

*   *   *

Complex business structures, characterized by decentralization and delegation of authority, commonly adopted by corporations for business purposes, make it difficult to identify the particular corporate agents responsible for Sherman Act violations. At the same time, it is generally true that high management officials, for whose conduct the corporate directors and stockholders are the most clearly responsible, are likely to have participated in the policy decisions underlying Sherman Act violations, or at least to have become aware of them.

Violations of the Sherman Act are a likely consequence of the pressure to maximize profits that is commonly imposed by corporate owners upon managing agents and, in turn, upon lesser employees. In the face of that pressure, generalized directions to obey the Sherman Act, with the probable effect of foregoing profits, are the least likely to be taken seriously. And if a violation of the Sherman Act occurs, the corporation, and not the individual agents, will have realized the profits from the illegal activity. In sum, identification of the particular agents responsible for a Sherman Act violation is especially difficult, and their conviction and punishment is peculiarly ineffective as a deterrent. At the same time, conviction and punishment of the business entity itself is likely to be both appropriate and effective.

For these reasons we conclude that as a general rule a corporation is liable under the Sherman Act for the acts of its agents in the scope of their employment, even though contrary to general corporate policy and express instructions to the agent. . . .

Affirmed.

NOTES AND QUESTIONS

1. *Relevance of corporate profit.* The Ninth Circuit upheld the conviction of Hilton Hotels partly because a corporation, rather than its employees, profits from the illegal activity. In addition, the court reasoned that it is often difficult to identify the particular agent who engaged in the activity. Do you agree with either of these rationales as a basis for holding a large, complex organization criminally liable based on the acts of a few individuals? Why or why not?

2. *New York Central.* The seminal case applying the tort doctrine of respondeat superior to criminal actions against corporations was *New York Central & Hudson River Railroad v. United States*, 212 U.S. 481 (1909). In *New York Central*, a railroad company and its employee were both convicted of violating the Elkins Act, regulating the rates common carriers could charge. The Supreme Court rejected the two primary arguments on appeal: the conviction should be reversed because it would harm or punish the innocent shareholders, and the conviction was improper because there was no evidence that the actions leading to the offense were authorized by the board of directors. In extending the tort doctrine of respondeat superior, the Court stated that "to give [corporations] immunity from all punishment because of the old and exploded doctrine that a corporation cannot commit a crime would virtually take away the only means of effectually controlling the subject matter [of the Elkins Act] and correcting the abuses. . . . " *Id.* at 496.

At the time of the *New York Central* decision, the finding that a corporation was criminally liable meant the imposition of monetary fines against the corporation. Today, a criminal conviction might also mean forfeitures, debarment (suspension from doing business with the government), a corporate death penalty (Arthur Andersen accounting firm dissolved after indictment for obstruction of justice in connection with the Enron investigation), and quite possibly the conviction of the key officers who could also be sent to prison.

The result in the Arthur Andersen case –in which Enron's Big Five accounting firm was indicted for obstruction of justice and soon thereafter ceased to exist (*see* Chapter 11, Obstructive of Justice, *infra* at § 11.D) – reinvigorated critics who question the legal theory that holds a corporation liable for the acts of individual employees. Consider the following points:

1. Civil, not criminal, sanctions should be the primary approach to corporate misbehavior. First, criminal prosecution causes more collateral damage to innocent individuals. Second, a corporation is not deterred by the primary criminal sanctions of going to jail or feeling shame.

2. The judicial rationale for indicting corporations is outdated. Originally, the Court in *New York Central* applied criminal sanctions to corporations because of the lack of alternatives. Today, the significant expansion of civil and regulatory sanctions makes this rationale moot.

3. Federal prosecutors held too much power over Andersen because the criminal conviction automatically disbarred it from practicing before the SEC. This sort of ultimate power is tantamount to controlling the life and death of the entity.

4. The federal standard of respondeat superior is too broad and dangerous. In its current state, the doctrine allows for conviction of the corporation regardless of whether the employee was a low-level employee or a high-level officer, and regardless of whether the behavior was condoned or prohibited by management.

Elizabeth K. Ainslie, *Indicting Corporations Revisited: Lessons of the Arthur Andersen Prosecution*, 43 Am. Crim. L. Rev. 107 (2006). Are these criticisms justified? Why or why not?

3. *Internal corporate policies and compliance programs.* Should a corporation be held criminally liable where the corporate policies specifically prohibit the behavior? This question is important because corporate compliance programs may affect charging and sentencing decisions. Corporations have instituted compliance programs in an effort to insulate the corporation from criminal scrutiny. If a compliance program cannot be a shield for a criminal investigation, then does this dissuade corporations from instituting and following such programs? To what extent should such programs be relevant at the time of sentencing? *See United States v. Portac, Inc.*, 869 F.2d 1288 (9th Cir. 1989) (the company was convicted despite the fact that the supervisor had instructed the employees that the company did not permit violations of law in its business practices). *See* Chapter 15, Internal Investigations and Compliance Programs, *infra*.

[2]   Model Penal Code

Many state courts have adopted an alternative approach to corporate criminal liability based on the Model Penal Code (MPC) formulation. Section 2.07(1) of the MPC provides that a corporation may be convicted of a crime where:

(a) The offense is a violation or the offense is defined by a statute other than the Code in which a legislative purpose to impose liability on corporations plainly appears and the conduct is performed by an agent of the corporation acting on behalf of the corporation within the scope of the agent's office or employment . . . ; or

(b) The offense consists of an omission to discharge a specific duty of affirmative performance imposed on corporations by law; or

(c) The commission of the offense was authorized, requested, commanded, performed, or recklessly tolerated by the board of directors or by a high managerial agent acting on behalf of the corporation within the scope of the agent's office or employment.

In states where clear standards for corporate liability have not been established, courts have considered the respective merits of respondeat superior and MPC Section 2.07. As you read the next case, consider the key differences between the MPC approach and the respondeat superior approach to corporate criminal accountability.

COMMONWEALTH v. BENEFICIAL FINANCE CO.
275 N.E.2d 33 (Mass. 1971)

SPIEGEL, JUSTICE.

We have before us appeals emanating from 2 separate series of indictments and 2 separate jury trials of various individual and corporate defendants. . . .

These cases have become generally known as the "small loans" cases. In each case the defendants were charged with various offences under numerous indictments returned in 1964 by a special grand jury. The offences charged were offering or paying, or soliciting or receiving, bribes, or conspiring to do so. These indictments were presented to the special grand jury as a result of an investigation developed by the Massachusetts Crime Commission (Commission). The Commission was specifically created by the Legislature "to investigate and study as a basis for legislative action the existence and extent of organized crime within the Commonwealth and corrupt practices in government at state and local levels."

[The court then detailed the extensive trial and pre-trial history in these protracted proceedings. The agents of the various companies skirted the law and charged illegal interest rates by bribing public officials. The court instructed the jury that it should apply the common law standard of respondeat superior. The defendants argued that the court erred and should have directed the jury to use the MPC formulation, requiring that the jury find that a high level corporate agent had authorized or recklessly tolerated the bribery scheme.]

*   *   *

THE SUFFICIENCY OF THE EVIDENCE

The Corporate Defendants,

Having concluded that the evidence was sufficient to establish that the defendants Pratt and Woodcock were part of a conspiracy joined in by Farrell, Glynn and Barber to bribe Hanley and Garfinkle, we turn to the question of whether there was sufficient evidence to support a finding that Beneficial, Household, and Liberty were parties to the conspiracy. Each of the corporate defendants raised this issue by means of a motion for a directed verdict. In view of the fact that this issue is discussed extensively in the briefs of the respective corporate defendants as well as in the Commonwealth's brief, and because the legal principles involved permeate these cases, in this part of the opinion we discuss at length the applicable legal standards concerning the extent to which a corporation may be held criminally responsible for the acts of its directors, officers and agents. We then summarize the evidence admitted against the respective corporations and apply the appropriate legal standard to the evidence.

* * *

The defendants and the Commonwealth have proposed differing standards upon which the criminal responsibility of a corporation should be predicated. The defendants argue that a corporation should not be held criminally liable for the conduct of its servants or agents unless such conduct was performed, authorized, ratified, adopted or tolerated by the corporations' directors, officers or other "high managerial agents" who are sufficiently high in the corporate hierarchy to warrant the assumption that their acts in some substantial sense reflect corporate policy. This standard is that adopted by the American Law Institute Model Penal Code, approved in May, 1962. Section 2:07 of the Code provides that, except in the case of regulatory offences and offences consisting of the omission of a duty imposed on corporations by law, a corporation may be convicted of a crime if "the commission of the offence was authorized, requested, commanded, performed or recklessly tolerated by the board of directors or by a high managerial agent acting in behalf of the corporation within the scope of his office or employment." The section proceeds to define "high managerial agent" as "an officer of a corporation . . . or any other agent . . . having duties of such responsibility that his conduct may fairly be assumed to represent the policy of the corporation."

The Commonwealth, on the other hand, argues that the standard applied by the judge in his instructions to the jury was correct. These instructions, which prescribe a somewhat more flexible standard than that delineated in the Model Penal Code, state in part, as follows:

> [T]he Commonwealth must prove beyond a reasonable doubt that there existed between the guilty individual or individuals and the corporation which is being charged with the conduct of the individuals, such a relationship that the acts and the intent of the individuals were the acts and intent of the corporation. . . .

> It does not mean that the Commonwealth must prove that the individual who acted criminally was a member of the corporation's board of directors, or that he was a high officer in the corporation, or that he held any office at all. If the Commonwealth did prove that an individual for whose act it seeks to hold a corporation criminally liable was an officer of the corporation, the jury should consider that. But more important than that, it should consider what the authority of that person was as such officer in relation to the corporation. The mere fact that he has a title is not enough to make the corporation liable for his criminal conduct. The Commonwealth must prove that the individual for whose conduct it seeks to charge the corporation criminally was placed in a position by the corporation where he had enough power, duty, responsibility and authority to act for and in behalf of the corporation to handle the particular business or operation or project of the corporation in which he was engaged at the time that he committed the criminal act, with power of decision as to what he would or would not do while acting for the corporation, and that he was acting for and in behalf of

the corporation in the accomplishment of that particular business or operation or project, and that he committed a criminal act while so acting. . . .

You will note from what I said that it is not necessary that the Commonwealth prove that an individual had any particular office or any office at all or that he had any particular title or any title at all. It isn't the title that counts. It isn't the name of the office that counts, but it's the position in which the corporation placed that person with relation to its business, with regard to the powers and duties and responsibilities and authority which it gave to him which counts. If it placed him in a position with such power, duty, authority, and responsibility that it can be found by you that, when he acted in the corporation's business, the corporation was acting, then you may find the corporation equally guilty of the criminal acts which he commits and of the intent which he holds, if you first find that the individual was guilty of the crime.

Now, this test doesn't depend upon the power, duty, the responsibility, or the authority which the individual has with reference to the entire corporation business. The test should be applied to his position with relation to the particular operation or project in which he is serving the corporation.

The difference between the judge's instructions to the jury and the Model Penal Code lies largely in the latter's reference to a "high managerial agent" and in the Code requirement that to impose corporate criminal liability, it at least must appear that its directors or high managerial agent "authorized . . . or recklessly tolerated" the allegedly criminal acts. The judge's instructions focus on the authority of the corporate agent in relation to the particular corporate business in which the agent was engaged. The Code seems to require that there be authorization or reckless inaction by a corporate representative having some relation to framing corporate policy, or one "having duties of such responsibility that his conduct may fairly be assumed to represent the policy of the corporation." Close examination of the judge's instructions reveals that they preserve the underlying corporate policy rationale of the Code by allowing the jury to infer "corporate policy" from the position in which the corporation placed the agent in commissioning him to handle the particular corporate affairs in which he was engaged at the time of the criminal act. We need not deal with the Model Penal Code in greater detail. Although we give it careful consideration as a scholarly proposal, it has not been enacted in Massachusetts and does not purport to be a restatement of existing law. . . . The judge correctly charged the jury on the basis of decided cases, rather than on the basis of a proposed model code.

It may also be observed that the judge's standard is somewhat similar to the traditional common law rule of respondeat superior. However, in applying this rule to a criminal case, the judge added certain requirements not generally associated with that common law doctrine. He further qualified the rule of respondeat superior by requiring that the conduct for which the corporation is being held accountable be performed on behalf of the corporation. . . .

The judge's instructions, as a whole and in context, required a greater quantum of proof in the practical application of this standard than is required in a civil case. In focusing on the "kinship" between the authority of an individual and the act he committed, the judge emphasized that the jury must be satisfied "beyond a reasonable doubt" that the act of the individual "constituted" the act of the corporation. Juxtaposition of the traditional criminal law requirement of ascertaining guilt beyond a reasonable doubt (as opposed to the civil law standard of the preponderance of the evidence), with the rule of respondeat superior, fully justifies application of the standard enunciated by the judge to a criminal prosecution against a corporation for a crime requiring specific intent.

The foregoing is especially true in view of the particular circumstances of this case. In order to commit the crimes charged in these indictments, the defendant corporations either had to offer to pay money to a public official or conspire to do so. The disbursal of funds is an act peculiarly within the ambit of corporate activity. These corporations by the very nature of their business are constantly dealing with the expenditure and collection of moneys. It could hardly be expected that any of the individual defendants would conspire to pay, or would pay, the substantial amount of money here involved, namely $25,000, out of his own pocket. The jury would be warranted in finding that the disbursal of such an amount of money would come from the corporate treasury. A reasonable inference could therefore be drawn that the payment of such money by the corporations was done as a matter of corporate policy and as a reflection of corporate intent, thus comporting with the underlying rationale of the Model Penal Code, and probably with its specific requirements.

Moreover, we do not think that the Model Penal Code standard really purports to deal with the evidentiary problems which are inherent in establishing the quantum of proof necessary to show that the directors or officers of a corporation authorize, ratify, tolerate, or participate in the criminal acts of an agent when such acts are apparently performed on behalf of the corporation. Evidence of such authorization or ratification is too easily susceptible of concealment. As is so trenchantly stated by the judge: "Criminal acts are not usually made the subject of votes of authorization or ratification by corporate Boards of Directors; and the lack of such votes does not prevent the act from being the act of the corporation."

It is obvious that criminal conspiratorial acts are not performed within the glare of publicity, nor would we expect a board of directors to meet officially and record on the corporate records a delegation of authority to initiate, conduct or conclude proceedings for the purpose of bribing a public official. Of necessity, the proof of authority to so act must rest on all the circumstances and conduct in a given situation and the reasonable inferences to be drawn therefrom.

Additional factors of importance are the size and complexity of many large modern corporations which necessitate the delegation of more authority to lesser corporate agents and employees. As the judge pointed out: "There are not enough seats on the Board of Directors, nor enough offices in a corporation, to permit the corporation engaged in widespread operations to give such a title or office to every person in whom it places the power, authority, and responsibility for decision and action." This latter consideration lends credence to the view that the title or position of an individual in a corporation should not be conclusively determinative in ascribing criminal responsibility. In a large corporation, with many numerous and distinct departments, a high ranking corporate officer or agent may have no authority or involvement in a particular sphere of corporate activity, whereas a lower ranking corporate executive might have much broader power in dealing with a matter peculiarly within the scope of his authority. Employees who are in the lower echelon of the corporate hierarchy often exercise more responsibility in the everyday operations of the corporation than the directors or officers. Assuredly, the title or office that the person holds may be considered, but it should not be the decisive criterion upon which to predicate corporate responsibility. . . .

To permit corporations to conceal the nefarious acts of their underlings by using the shield of corporate armor to deflect corporate responsibility, and to separate the subordinate from the executive, would be to permit "endocratic" corporations to inflict widespread public harm without hope of redress. It would merely serve to ignore the scramble and realities of the market place. This we decline to do. We believe that stringent standards must be adopted to discourage any attempt by "endocratic" corporations' executives to place the sole responsibility for criminal acts on the shoulders of their subordinates. . . .

Considering everything we have said above, we are of [the] opinion that the quantum of proof necessary to sustain the conviction of a corporation for the acts of its agents is sufficiently met if it is shown that the corporation has placed the agent in a position where he has enough authority and responsibility to act for and in behalf of the corporation in handling the *particular* corporate business operation or project in which he was engaged at the time he committed the criminal act. The judge properly instructed the jury to this effect and correctly stated that this standard does not depend upon the responsibility or authority which the agent has with respect to the entire corporate business, but only to his position with relation to the particular business in which he was serving the corporation. . . .

All judgments affirmed.

NOTES AND QUESTIONS

1. *Beneficial under the MPC.* Under the facts of *Beneficial*, could the jury have found liability under the MPC? Why or why not?

2. *Lenient rule.* The *Beneficial* court rejected the MPC's requirement of high managerial approval. The court stated that the MPC standard was too lenient because "[e]vidence of such authorization or ratification is too easily susceptible of concealment." The court also found that requiring high managerial approval would simply allow large organizations to avoid liability by delegating decision making to lower-level employees and hiding behind various levels of management. Do you agree with this position?

3. *Respondeat superior.* Other courts and commentators view the respondeat superior rule as more relaxed than the MPC rule. The respondeat superior theory includes those corporate agents who are not only high level, such as managers, supervisors, and executives, but also entry level, line employees. Is a rule that allows a subordinate employee to bind the corporation fundamentally fair? Why or why not? What is the basis for this extension of criminal liability? What if the actor is an independent contractor?

Consider the application of *Beneficial* to the following case. In *Commonwealth v. Angelo Todesca Corp.*, 842 N.E.2d 930 (Mass. 2006), the employee, a driver for the defendant trucking company, struck and killed a police officer while backing up without a functioning back-up alarm. The jury found the company guilty of vehicular homicide as a result of the incident. The appeals court reversed the conviction, but the Massachusetts Supreme Judicial Court reinstated the conviction based on *Beneficial*. The court found that a corporation could be held criminally liable even if the conduct was not " 'performed, authorized, ratified, adopted or tolerated by' corporate officials or managers." *Angelo*, 842 N.E.2d at 937. Instead, all that was required was " '(1) that an individual committed a criminal offense; (2) that at the time of committing the offense, the individual 'was engaged in some particular corporate business or project'; and (3) that the individual had been vested by the corporation with the authority to act for it, and on its behalf, in carrying out that particular corporate business or project when the offense occurred.' " *Id.* (quoting *Commonwealth v. Angelo Todesca Corp.*, 818 N.E.2d 608, 613 (Mass. App. Ct. 2004)). Is this outcome fair and appropriate? Why or why not?

4. *Who benefits?* A corporate agent can act to benefit both himself or herself and the corporation. If the employee is stealing from the corporation, will that action defeat a charge that the employee is acting within the scope of employment? Why or why not?

5. *Overly broad liability?* Are theories of corporate prosecution partly responsible for the recent trend of aggressive prosecutions against corporations? *See* Preet Bharara, *Corporations Cry Uncle and Their Employees Cry Foul: Rethinking Prosecutorial Pressure on Corporate Defendants*, 44 Am. Crim. L. Rev. 53 (2007). The author argues that overly broad rules, such as vicarious liability for corporations, are to blame for the recent trend of overly aggressive prosecutions and the negative effect that such prosecutions have on individual employees. For example, a corporation may be subject to liability for the acts of one low-level employee who had no authorization to act and who was not acting to benefit the corporation. *Id.* at 61–70. Corporations are extremely vulnerable because simply being indicted may mean a corporate death sentence. (*See* Chapter 20, Forfeitures, *infra.*) Note that, despite the broad scope of corporate liability, prosecution of corporations is actually infrequent.

6. *Forbidden acts.* Should the principal be held liable for the acts of an agent in situations where the action was expressly forbidden by the principal? *See United States v. Potter*, 463 F.3d 9, 26 (2006) (principal may be liable for actions of an agent even if it is established that the act was forbidden by the principal). Under this theory, what can the principal do to insulate itself from criminal liability?

*   *   *

Some state jurisdictions, such as New York, follow the MPC theory of corporate criminal liability. As you read this case, consider how the result might have been different had the case arisen in a jurisdiction that adhered to the respondeat superior theory of corporate criminal liability.

<h2 style="text-align:center">PEOPLE v. LESSOFF & BERGER</h2>
608 N.Y.S.2d 54 (N.Y. Sup. Ct. 1994)

MICHAEL R. JUVILER, JUSTICE.

This is a written version of an oral decision on a motion to dismiss the indictment. The defendant Lessoff is a lawyer whose office is in Manhattan. The co-defendant is the law partnership in which the defendant Lessoff is a partner. The issue is whether a law partnership may be indicted for crimes of fraud, and if so, whether a partnership may be indicted if only one partner is involved in the alleged crimes.

The evidence before the Grand Jury showed that the defendant Lessoff referred clients in personal-injury accident cases to a radiologist in Brooklyn for examination and report. The indictment, as clarified by a bill of particulars, alleges that Lessoff instructed the radiologist to change MRI reports to delete references to nontraumatic damage and to abnormalities or injuries predating the accidents.

The crimes alleged are insurance fraud, for soliciting the doctor to change the MRI findings with intent to defraud insurers; falsifying business records, the MRI reports at the radiologist's office; and attempted grand larceny, an attempt by false pretenses to gain money in a lawsuit against the New York City Transit Authority. At the time of the crimes charged in the indictment, the doctor, unknown to the defendant Lessoff, was working undercover with the District Attorney's Office during the Grand Jury investigation and was secretly recording his telephone conversations with Lessoff. The indictment alleges ten separate transactions involving ten separate clients of Lessoff and the partnership. At all times Lessoff was acting in the name of the law firm. There is no evidence implicating anyone else in the firm in the alleged crimes.

For reasons not relevant to this decision, counts relating to three of the transactions have been dismissed for lack of evidence, and counts for seven transactions have been sustained, except that some counts have been reduced to attempts to commit the crimes.

The partnership defendant has moved to dismiss the entire indictment on the ground that the evidence before the Grand Jury shows, at most, culpable involvement by only one partner, the defendant Lessoff.

The plain language of Penal Law § 10.00(7) authorizes an indictment of the partnership on such facts. That section provides that a "person" — which includes a person charged with a crime — means, "where appropriate," "a partnership." Similarly, the section defining the crime of insurance fraud, Penal Law § 176.00(3), provides that a "person" chargeable with the crime of insurance fraud includes any "*firm, association* or corporation"; under the Partnership Law, a partnership is "an *association* of two or more persons to carry on as co-owners a business for profit." § 10(1) (emphasis added). Unmistakably, therefore, the Penal Law applies to a law "firm," whether it be a partnership or a professional corporation, and the law firm may be charged if one partner has committed a crime in the name of the law firm, as alleged in this case. Presumably, if there is a conviction of a partnership, the sentence can be a fine, a conditional discharge, or an unconditional discharge, as for a corporation.

The background of these Penal Law provisions confirms this interpretation. The quoted language was adopted as part of the Penal Law after federal criminal statutes had been construed by the Supreme Court of the United States to apply to partnerships, without reference to individual responsibility. *United States v. A & P Trucking Co.*, 358 U.S. 121, 126–27, had held that "a partnership can violate each of the statutes here in question quite apart from the participation and knowledge of the partners as individuals."

Application of the Penal Law to a partnership when only one partner is alleged to have been culpable may be harsh, but it is rational. It is analogous to the criminal responsibility of a corporation for conduct of a "high managerial agent." And it is consistent with the settled principle in torts that a partnership is responsible for conversion of funds by one partner, even if the other partners are unaware of the misconduct.

Criminal liability for one partner's frauds is particularly appropriate in the case of a law partnership. Not only do law partners, as any partners, benefit financially from the fruits of one partner's fraudulent conduct committed in the name of the firm, but there is a strong public interest in regulating the ethics of the legal profession. *Cf. People v. Smithtown General Hospital*, 399 N.Y.S.2d 993 (Sup. Ct. Suffolk Co.) (public regulation of hospitals in the public interest supports criminal prosecution of a hospital partnership even without evidence of culpability of individual partners).

The partnership's motion to dismiss the indictment is denied.

NOTES AND QUESTIONS

1. *High managerial agents.* In contrast to the respondeat superior approach to corporate criminal liability used in the federal system, many states have adopted language that limits liability to those criminal acts committed by or approved by "high managerial agents." Model Penal Code § 2.07(1)(c). High managerial agents are defined as "officer[s], of a corporation or an unincorporated association, or, in the case of a partnership, a partner, or any other agent of a corporation or association having duties of such responsibility that his conduct may fairly be assumed to represent the policy of the corporation or association." *Id.* § 2.07(4)(c). The MPC imposes criminal liability on a corporation in two types of situations: (a) where the employee behavior was authorized or recklessly tolerated by the board of directors or by a high managerial agent acting on behalf of the corporation within the scope of his or her office or employment, or (b) where such liability is imposed by statute. Thus, the MPC section sets forth a more restrictive test for corporate liability than does respondeat superior.

2. *Key differences.* What are the key differences between the MPC approach and respondeat superior? Which one is preferable, given the current enforcement climate and the aggressive approach of the Department of Justice to corporate criminal liability?

3. *Partnerships and high managerial agents.* As this case demonstrated, the concept of "high managerial agent" extends beyond the traditional corporate setting to include other entities, such as partnerships. The court noted that public policy supports this conclusion because the public has a special interest in regulating the ethics of lawyers and because the law firm itself benefited from the fraud. Despite the fact that the criminal activities were the result of only one partner, the court noted that the statute authorized prosecution of a "person," defined to include a "partnership." Would the same result occur if the culpable actor had been a law firm associate? Why or why not?

[C] CORPORATE MENS REA

[1]   Criminal Intent

In the next case, the court assessed the proof required for corporate criminal liability. As you read the case, consider the scope of corporate criminal liability under both respondeat superior and the Model Penal Code.

STATE v. CHAPMAN DODGE CENTER
428 So. 2d 413 (La. 1983)

Chapman Dodge Center, Inc., a Baton Rouge Dodge dealership, closed its doors because of financial difficulty on September 12, 1980. Shortly thereafter the district attorney's office began receiving complaints from Dodge customers that they had not received their permanent license plates for their cars because the dealership had neither registered the cars purchased, nor paid the sales tax due. The usual practice was for the customer to pay the amount due for sales tax to the car dealer who, in turn, would register the car with the state and tender the tax. After a car is registered and the tax paid, the state issues a permanent license plate. In the meantime, the dealership is authorized to give the customer a temporary plate that is valid for 35 days. Dodge customers were being stopped for expired temporary license plates since they had not received their permanent tags.

Chapman Dodge had been in financial trouble for about a year prior to its closing. Aside from the general economic situation, Chapman's difficulties were due in great part to Chapman's financial relationship to the financially troubled Chrysler Corporation. According to the trial record, at the time Chapman closed, Chrysler Corporation owed between $250,000 and $400,000 to Chapman Dodge. In addition, Chrysler Credit Corporation, a subsidiary of Chrysler Motors, had $140,000 of Chapman's money "on reserve" for potential losses on loans Chrysler Credit made to Chapman customers.

After Chapman Dodge closed its doors, Chrysler Credit Corporation took possession of Chapman Dodge. On the premises, employees of Chrysler Credit Corporation found between 180 and 190 registration forms for purchased cars which had not been filed with the state and for which no sales tax had been paid. Since Chrysler Credit Corporation owned the mortgages on 159 of these cars, it paid the sales taxes due on them (approximately $68,000) in order to register the cars and the chattel mortgages with the state.

The defendant, John Swindle, personally paid the sales taxes (about $11,000) on the remaining cars which had not been financed by Chrysler Credit Corporation. The defendant did so after he was notified by the district attorney's office that the taxes were due. The defendant's attorney in Mississippi, however, testified that he advised the defendant that Chrysler Credit Corporation should be responsible for all taxes due since it had possession of all of Chapman Dodge's assets, and was therefore responsible for discharging Chapman's tax liability.

The original bill of information charged 159 counts of theft, but was later amended to 20 counts with a reservation to prosecute the remaining 139 at a later time. Defendant John Swindle testified that he was the sole owner of Barony Corporation, a holding company for several food service corporations. Barony Corporation owned a subsidiary called Center Management which was formed to hold automobile dealerships when Swindle expanded his operations to include that business. Chapman Dodge was one of four dealerships owned by Center Management. Center Management, after acquiring the necessary funding, then purchased Chapman Dodge. Subsequently Chapman Dodge endorsed the notes Center Management had signed in obtaining financing. Each month a check was sent by Chapman Dodge to Center Management to cover the payment due by Center Management on the notes.

The evidence showed that the defendant, a resident of Jackson, Mississippi, was seldom at the dealership more than twice a month. It was Donald Barrett that was in charge of the daily operations of Chapman Dodge as general manager. All department managers were responsible to Barrett, who in turn answered to Swindle. According to the testimony of James Duvall, Chapman Dodge's accountant, he and Barrett made the decisions as to which bills were to be paid.

Swindle testified that when the dealership was showing continued financial trouble, he discussed this matter with James Duvall. Since the dealership was behind in paying withholding taxes, as well as sales taxes, he ordered Duvall to pay all of the taxes owed, particularly the federal withholdings. When the dealership was closed, Swindle asked Barrett if all the taxes had been paid. The record shows that in the presence of Johnilyn Smith, an administrative assistant to Swindle, and Frank Peel, a business associate of Swindle, Barrett stated that *all* taxes had been paid. Barrett testified that he did not say *all* the taxes had been paid, only that the *federal* taxes had been paid. On cross-examination however Barrett stated that he "may" have said that all the taxes were paid.

The defendant received no indication that the sales taxes were not paid until a week or ten days after closing the dealership when the district attorney contacted Chapman Dodge's lawyer. Duvall testified that he was instructed by Donald Barrett to retain the sales tax money. Donald Barrett however testified that he had told James Duvall in June of 1980 to pay only those obligations necessary to keep the dealership open; but that he never told Duvall to retain the contracts and sales taxes on the purchased vehicles.

Donald Barrett was originally indicted on the theft charges along with John Swindle and Chapman Dodge. Both he and James Duvall were granted "use" immunity in order to compel their testimony against Chapman Dodge and John Swindle. Duvall was granted immunity at the preliminary examination. Barrett was granted immunity when his counsel invoked his privilege against compulsory self-incrimination when he was called to testify at the trial. Barrett stated on cross-examination that the district attorney's office had told him three weeks earlier that he would not be prosecuted if he testified for the state.

OPINION ON SWINDLE

John Swindle was charged with the crime of theft. The jury, however, apparently found that the elements of theft had not been proven by the state and returned a verdict of the lesser included offense of unauthorized use of a movable.

In the instant case, the state has failed to prove any intent on the part of Swindle, fraudulent or otherwise. . . .

OPINION ON CHAPMAN DODGE

The question of the criminal liability of the corporate defendant in this cause is a more difficult proposition involving fundamental issues of the nature of criminal responsibility. These issues have not been generally considered with respect to corporations in this jurisdiction. Certainly our law contemplates corporate criminal defendants. Louisiana law delineates a number of acts the commission or omission of which creates corporate criminal responsibility.

The problem of what criminal liability a corporation should bear for the unauthorized acts of its officers and managers is indeed a grave and troubling one. Recent allegations of corporate responsibility for large train derailments and massive pollution of water sources underscore the importance of this troubling topic. Certainly there is civil responsibility under such circumstances. The question is whether a corporation should be criminally responsible in the absence of a specific statute which defines and describes the corporate act, prohibits that act, and establishes a specific punishment therefor.

Criminal liability in our system of justice has always been founded upon the simultaneous existence of two distinct elements namely: (1) actus reus, and (2) mens rea. The existence of only one of these elements does not make one criminally liable. Both must be present to invoke the sanctions society has placed on what is termed "criminal conduct." Certainly one cannot be held criminally liable for simply thinking of a criminal act without the act occurring. A somewhat more difficult, but logically consistent idea, is that an act, committed without the required criminal intent or mens rea, is not criminally punishable. We do not criminally punish those that do not know what they are doing — such as the insane. Neither do we punish those who, while aware of what they are doing, have no control over their actions — the victims of threats or coercion. We do not impose criminal liability on those who act without criminal intent for the simple reason that such an imposition would not achieve the main goal of our criminal law: deterrence.

Given these basic ruminations on the topic of criminal intent, we should now consider the nature of a corporation. Our Civil Code in Article 427 defines a corporation as:

> . . . an intellectual body, created by law, composed of individuals united under a common name, the members of which succeed each other, so that the body continues always the same, notwithstanding the change of the individuals which compose it, and which, for certain purposes, *is considered as a natural person.* (Emphasis added.)

The corporation as a fictitious person is capable of entering into contracts, owning property and making and receiving donations. In short, it is capable of doing virtually anything that a natural person is capable of doing.

A corporation by the very nature of its operation is dependent upon people to carry out its business. Some of these people may rightfully be regarded as the "mind" of the corporation. This group, known as the board of directors, is responsible for the direction that the corporation takes in its business activity. Plans for the corporation, developed by the board of directors, are transmitted to the officers of the corporation and through them to the employees. This latter group may be regarded as the "hands" of the corporation. But here our analogy to the human form must end. For unlike ordinary human hands, corporate "hands" have minds of their own and are capable of self direction.

When a corporation is accused of committing a crime which requires intent, it must be determined who within the corporate structure had the intent to commit the crime. If the crime was the product of a board of directors' resolution authorizing its employees to commit specific criminal acts, then intent on the part of the corporation is manifest. However, a more difficult question arises if the crime is actually committed by an employee of the corporation not authorized to perform such an act. Holding a corporation criminally responsible for the acts of an employee may be inconsistent with basic notions of criminal intent, since such a posture would render a corporate entity responsible for actions which it theoretically had no intent to commit.

Common law jurisdictions hold corporations criminally liable for the acts of low-ranking employees. In such jurisdictions, corporate criminal liability is based on an extension of the tort doctrine of vicarious liability. The theme of vicarious criminal liability, however, is varied. Some jurisdictions impose criminal liability where there has been an act or an authorization to act by a managerial officer, some where there has been an act committed within the scope of the actor's employment, and still others where there has been an act done which benefits the corporation. These varied applications notwithstanding, common law jurisdictions have found corporations liable for forms of homicide, theft, extortion — in short, virtually every crime other than rape and carnal knowledge.

Although this merger of tort and criminal law doctrine has found wide acceptance, it has also generated significant theoretical problems. Admittedly, tort law and criminal law are cousins, causing concern as to whether their relationship is within the prohibited degree such that a union of the two might produce unwanted offspring. It should be remembered that the main function of the law of torts is compensation and to a much lesser degree, deterrence.

Tort law attempts to distribute the loss of a harmful occurrence. Causation is the important ingredient therein. Holding a corporation vicariously liable for the torts of its employees dovetails with the idea of compensating the victim. The corporation is in a more likely position to compensate.

On the other hand, as mentioned earlier, the primary function of criminal law is to deter future criminal liability. To impose such liability on another party who had no part in the act and, as in the case of most corporate crimes, no intent to commit such an act, seems at first glance to be contrary to the purpose of our criminal legal system. . . .

The instant defendant is a closely held holding corporation which is accused of a basic "Ten Commandment Crime" — theft — and convicted of a lesser included offense. Thus the finder of fact in effect determined that the defendant corporation kept the money in question with fraudulent intent, but with the intent to eventually return the funds. The evidence further indicates that "retention" of the funds was not specifically authorized by the board of directors or by the president or any other officer of the corporation. The record does not indicate, moreover, that any of these entities had any real knowledge of that action. Of course the corporation, its board of directors, its parent corporations and its president are for all practical purposes the same entity — the individual defendant Swindle. Furthermore, as discussed earlier, the evidence preponderates that it was a party other than Swindle who determined to "retain the funds."

Thus, the facts of this case can be narrowed to a fine point. In so doing, however, broad questions of a complex nature are visited upon us. While recognizing the potential disservice to the jurisprudence we are nevertheless unable, within the confines of this appeal, to resolve these extremely complex issues. We simply determine that under the circumstances of this case, criminal intent has not been adequately established. We determine that under the circumstances of this case, there was insufficient intent shown in the trial court to withstand a *Jackson v. Virginia*, [443 U.S. 307 (1979),] analysis, and therefore this corporate defendant may not be found criminally responsible. We hold that since this record reveals no evidence of complicity by the officers or the board of directors, explicit or tacit, that the actions of these managers and/or employees were insufficient to cause this corporate entity to be guilty of the offense of an unauthorized use of a movable. We thus reverse as to both defendants and order their discharge.

Reversed and discharged as to both defendants.

LEMMON, JUSTICE, dissenting in part.

The evidence supports a conclusion that a high managerial agent, in whom the corporation had vested the authority to manage its day-to-day business operations, knowingly committed a criminal offense on behalf of the corporation and for its benefit while acting in the scope of his employment. The corporation should therefore be held criminally liable. *See* Model Penal Code § 2.07(1)(c).

NOTES AND QUESTIONS

1. *Employee immunity.* In order to prosecute Chapman Dodge and Swindle, the government offered immunity from prosecution to two of the company's employees. Swindle had little day-to-day interaction with the business dealings of Chapman Dodge. His conviction was reversed because there was insufficient evidence of a criminal intent on his behalf. The court noted that there might have been evidence sufficient for civil liability, but not for criminal liability. Do you agree that the evidence was insufficient to hold the corporation and/or Swindle criminally liable? Why or why not?

2. *Principles of Federal Prosecution of Business Organizations.* The Department of Justice issued its revised Principles of Federal Prosecution of Business Organizations, which are incorporated for the first time in the United States Attorneys' Manual (USAM) and are binding on all federal prosecutors. USAM § 9-28.300. (The memorandum announcing the new policy is available at http://www.usdoj.gov/dag/readingroom/dag-memo-08282008.pdf.) These principles are set forth and discussed in Chapter 15, Internal Investigations and Compliance Programs, *infra* at § 15[C][2].

3. *Discretion to proceed civilly.* If you were a prosecutor, what would be the principal considerations for deciding whether to pursue an investigation against a corporation criminally rather than civilly? If you were defense counsel, how would you persuade the prosecutor that your client's matter should be resolved civilly rather than criminally?

[2]   New Models of Corporate Criminal Liability

As the preceding materials show, applying the concept of mens rea to artificial entities such as corporations raises complex issues. This is particularly true in the context of a large national or multinational corporation. Even in a jurisdiction that applies respondeat superior, courts often look for some sort of corporate acquiescence to, or conscious avoidance of knowledge of, wrongdoing by corporate employees or agents.

One controversial doctrine, known as "collective knowledge," collects all of the knowledge of individual corporate agents and then attributes this knowledge to the organization. This doctrine is beneficial in cases where there is no individual corporate agent who possesses the mental state necessary for the offense. The first case to discuss this doctrine was the First Circuit decision in *United States v. Bank of New England, N.A.*, 821 F.2d 844 (1st Cir. 1987). In that decision, the court held that the corporation was criminally liable based upon the "collective knowledge" of all the employees within the corporation. The Bank of New England failed to file Currency Transaction Reports (CTRs) triggered by 31 separate cash withdrawals made by a customer over the course of a year. The government charged the Bank with violations of 31 U.S.C. § 5322, which attached when a financial institution "willfully" failed to file the required reports. The court acknowledged the difficulty of establishing willfulness "since it is a state of mind; it is usually established by drawing reasonable inferences from the available facts." *Id.*

The evidence established that individual employees each possessed one component of the required knowledge. The court assembled the individual knowledge and held that this equated with collective knowledge attributable to the Bank:

> Regarding the Bank's specific intent to violate the reporting obligation, [the teller] testified that head teller knew that [the customer's] transactions were reportable, but, on one occasion deliberately chose not to file a CTR on him because he was a "good customer." In addition, the jury heard testimony that bank employees regarded [the customer's] transactions as unusual, speculated that he was a bookie, and suspected that he was structuring his transactions to avoid the Act's reporting requirements. An internal Bank memo, written after an investigation of the [customer's] transactions, concluded that a "person managing the branch would have to have known that something strange was going on." Given the suspicions aroused . . . and the abundance of information indicating that his transactions were reportable, the jury could have concluded that the failure by Bank personnel to, at least, inquire about the reportability . . . constituted flagrant indifference to the obligations imposed by the Act.

821 F.2d 844, 857 (1st Cir. 1987).

Since that decision, most commentators have rejected this doctrine as being overly broad and inconsistent with principles of criminal accountability. Do you agree with this view? Why or why not?

NOTES AND QUESTIONS

1. *Willful blindness.* Does the theory of collective knowledge in corporate cases suggest a similarity to the willful blindness concept used in drug cases? For example, a person may be asked to take a package from a well-known drug source country to another country for a huge fee. Although the courier may not have actual knowledge of the package's contents — and declines to inquire — the courier likely has constructive knowledge that the package contains drugs. Willful blindness has also been called the "ostrich" approach — burying one's head in the sand to avoid knowledge. MPC § 2.02(7) states:

> Requirement of Knowledge Satisfied by Knowledge of High Probability. When knowledge of the existence of a particular fact is an element of an offense, such knowledge is established if a person is aware of a high probability of its existence, unless he actually believes that it does not exist.

Should this type of criminal liability be applied to the corporate and white collar arena? Why or why not? *See* Chapter 3, Conspiracy, *infra.*

2. *Reality of government threats.* Consider the obligations of the corporation in today's business climate. Besides the regulatory requirements, corporations are faced with tremendous challenges in order to conduct business in multiple jurisdictions. Considering the government's aggressive approach to corporate liability, corporations must confront not only the possibility of civil regulations, but also the risk of criminal prosecutions. How does the possibility of criminal prosecution affect the day-to-day business practices of the corporation?

3. *Viability of the collective knowledge doctrine.* Although the collective knowledge doctrine is subject to substantial criticism, courts continue to apply the doctrine. In *In re Worldcom, Inc. Sec. Litig.*, 352 F. Supp. 2d 472, 497 (S.D.N.Y. 2005), the Court held that the defendant, Arthur Andersen, was not entitled to summary judgment. Andersen claimed that there was no evidence of scienter, but the Court held that "the 'core requirement' in proving an auditor's scienter is proof that the defendant 'lacked a genuine belief that the information disclosed was accurate and complete in all material respects.'" *Id.* at 495 (quoting *McLean v. Alexander*, 599 F.2d 1190, 1198 (3d Cir. 1979)). Furthermore, the Court relied on *Bank of New England* to say that "[t]o carry their burden of showing that a corporate defendant acted with scienter, plaintiffs in securities fraud cases need not prove that any one individual employee of a corporate defendant also acted with scienter. Proof of a corporation's collective knowledge and intent is sufficient." *Id.* at 497.

In a revival of the collective knowledge theory, the Second Circuit allowed the plaintiffs to replead their case to establish collective scienter. *Teamsters Local 445 Freight Div. Pension Fund v. Dynex Capital Inc.*, 531 F.3d 190 (2d Cir. 2008). In that case, the court stated:

> Although there are circumstances in which a plaintiff may plead the requisite scienter against a corporate defendant without successfully pleading scienter against a specifically named individual, the plaintiff here has failed to do so. . . .
>
> When the defendant is a corporate entity, . . . the pleaded facts must create a strong inference that *someone* whose intent could be imputed to the corporation acted with the requisite scienter. In most cases, the most

straightforward way to raise such an inference for a corporate defendant will be to plead it for an individual defendant. But it is possible to raise the required inference with regard to a corporate defendant without doing so with regard to a specific individual defendant.

Id. at 192, 195. The Second Circuit dismissed the complaint, with leave to replead to allow the plaintiff to assert sufficient allegations of scienter. *Id.* at 197.

4. *Criticism of corporate criminal liability.* The widespread criticism on the scope of criminal liability for corporations is summarized by the observation of District Judge Gerald E. Lynch:

> If a corporation is criminally liable for the unauthorized acts of mid-level managers, the corporation will often not have a viable defense, despite legitimate questions about the justice of punishing it. . . . Such defendants are increasingly relegated to making their most significant moral and factual arguments to prosecutors, as a matter of "policy" or "prosecutorial discretion," rather than making them to judges, as a matter of law, or to juries, as a matter of factual guilt or innocence."

Gerald E. Lynch, *The Role of Criminal Law in Policing Corporate Misconduct*, 60 Law & Contemp. Probs. 23, 59 (1997).

Do you agree with this position? In the post-Enron world of corporate investigations, should the law reconsider the application of the century-old *New York Central* decision allowing respondeat superior to be a basis for criminal, as opposed to civil, corporate liability? Is vicarious liability at odds with basic principles of criminal law? *See* Andrew Weissmann and David Newman, *Rethinking Criminal Corporate Liability*, 82 Ind. L.J. 411 (2007).

[D] INDIVIDUAL LIABILITY WITHIN THE CORPORATE SETTING

[1]   The Responsible Corporate Officer Doctrine

Individuals within a corporation can not only subject their employer to criminal liability, but can also be individually accountable for their conduct. The *Park* decision is a major case addressing the liability of the CEO of a large retail chain. As you read this case, consider what, if anything, Park could have done to avoid criminal liability under the facts.

UNITED STATES v. PARK
421 U.S. 658 (1975)

Mr. CHIEF JUSTICE BURGER delivered the opinion of the Court.

We granted certiorari to consider whether the jury instructions in the prosecution of a corporate officer under § 301(k) of the Federal Food, Drug, and Cosmetic Act, 21 U.S.C. § 331(k), were appropriate under *United States v. Dotterweich*, 320 U.S. 277 (1943).

Acme Markets, Inc., is a national retail food chain with approximately 36,000 employees, 874 retail outlets, 12 general warehouses, and four special warehouses. Its headquarters, including the office of the president, respondent Park, who is chief executive officer of the corporation, are located in Philadelphia, Pa. In a five-count information filed in the United States District Court for the District of Maryland, the Government charged Acme and respondent with violations of the Federal Food, Drug and Cosmetic Act. Each count of the information alleged that the defendants had received food that had been shipped in interstate commerce and that, while the food was being held for sale in Acme's Baltimore warehouse following shipment in interstate commerce, they caused it to be held in a building accessible to rodents and to be exposed to contamination by rodents. These acts were alleged to have resulted in the food's being adulterated within the meaning of 21 U.S.C. §§ 342(a)(3) and (4), in violation of 21 U.S.C. § 331(k).

Acme pleaded guilty to each count of the information. Respondent pleaded not guilty. The evidence at trial demonstrated that in April 1970 the Food and Drug Administration (FDA) advised respondent by letter of insanitary conditions in Acme's Philadelphia warehouse. In 1971 the FDA found that similar conditions existed in the firm's Baltimore warehouse. An FDA consumer safety officer testified concerning evidence of rodent infestation and other insanitary conditions discovered during a 12-day inspection of the Baltimore warehouse in November and December 1971. He also related that a second inspection of the warehouse had been conducted in March 1972. On that occasion the inspectors found that there had been improvement in the sanitary conditions, but that "there was still evidence of rodent activity in the building and in the warehouses and we found some rodent-contaminated lots of food items."

The Government also presented testimony by the Chief of Compliance of the FDA's Baltimore office, who informed respondent by letter of the conditions at the Baltimore warehouse after the first inspection. There was testimony by Acme's Baltimore division vice president, who had responded to the letter on behalf of Acme and respondent and who described the steps taken to remedy the insanitary conditions discovered by both inspections. The Government's final witness, Acme's vice president for legal affairs and assistant secretary, identified respondent as the president and chief executive officer of the company and read a bylaw prescribing the duties of the chief executive officer. He testified that respondent functioned by delegating "normal operating duties," including sanitation, but that he retained "certain things, which are the big, broad, principles of the operation of the company," and had "the responsibility of seeing that they all work together."

At the close of the Government's case in chief, respondent moved for a judgment of acquittal on the ground that "the evidence in chief has shown that Mr. Park is not personally concerned in this Food and Drug violation." The trial judge denied the motion, stating that *United States v. Dotterweich*, 320 U.S. 277 (1943), was controlling.

Respondent was the only defense witness. He testified that, although all of Acme's employees were in a sense under his general direction, the company had an "organizational structure for responsibilities for certain functions" according to which different phases of its operation were "assigned to individuals who, in turn, have staff and departments under them." He identified those individuals responsible for sanitation, and related that upon receipt of the January 1972 FDA letter, he had conferred with the vice president for legal affairs, who informed him that the Baltimore division vice president "was investigating the situation immediately and would be taking corrective action and would be preparing a summary of the corrective action to reply to the letter." Respondent stated that he did not "believe there was anything [he] could have done more constructively than what [he] found was being done."

On cross-examination, respondent conceded that providing sanitary conditions for food offered for sale to the public was something that he was "responsible for in the entire operation of the company," and he stated that it was one of many phases of the company that he assigned to "dependable subordinates." Respondent was asked about and, over the objections of his counsel, admitted receiving, the April 1970 letter addressed to him from the FDA regarding insanitary conditions at Acme's Philadelphia warehouse.[1] He acknowledged that, with the exception of the division vice president, the same individuals had responsibility for sanitation in both Baltimore and Philadelphia. Finally, in response to questions concerning the Philadelphia and Baltimore incidents, respondent admitted that the Baltimore problem indicated the system for handling sanitation "wasn't working perfectly" and that as Acme's chief executive officer he was responsible for "any result which occurs in our company."

At the close of the evidence, respondent's renewed motion for a judgment of acquittal was denied. The relevant portion of the trial judge's instructions to the jury challenged by respondent is set out in the margin.[2] Respondent's counsel objected to the instructions on the ground that they failed fairly to reflect our decision in *United States v. Dotterweich, supra,* and to define "responsible relationship." The trial judge overruled the objection. The jury found respondent guilty on all counts of the information, and he was subsequently sentenced to pay a fine of $50 on each count.

The Court of Appeals reversed the conviction and remanded for a new trial. That court viewed the Government as arguing "that the conviction may be predicated solely upon a showing that . . . [respondent] was the President of the offending corporation," and it stated that as "a general proposition, some act of commission or omission is an essential element of every crime." It reasoned that, although our decision in *United States v. Dotterweich, supra,* 320 U.S. at 281, had construed the statutory provisions under which respondent was tried to dispense with the traditional element of "awareness of some wrongdoing," the Court had not

---

[1] The April 1970 letter informed respondent of the following "objectionable conditions" in Acme's Philadelphia warehouse:

1. Potential rodent entry ways were noted via ill fitting doors and door in irrepair at Southwest corner of warehouse; at dock at old salvage room and at receiving and shipping doors which were observed to be open most of the time.

2. Rodent nesting, rodent excreta pellets, rodent stained bale bagging and rodent gnawed holes were noted among bales of flour stored in warehouse.

3. Potential rodent harborage was noted in discarded paper, rope, sawdust and other debris piled in corner of shipping and receiving dock near bakery and warehouse doors. Rodent excreta pellets were observed among bags of sawdust (or wood shavings).

"In order to find the Defendant guilty on any count of the Information, you must find beyond a reasonable doubt on each count. . . .

"[T]hat John R. Park held a position of authority in the operation of the business of Acme Markets, Incorporated. . . .

"The individual is or could be liable under the statute, even if he did not consciously do wrong. However, the fact that the Defendant is pres[id]ent and is a chief executive officer of the Acme Markets does not require a finding of guilt. Though, he need not have personally participated in the situation, he must have had a responsible relationship to the issue. The issue is, in this case, whether the Defendant, John R. Park, by virtue of his position in the company, had a position of authority and responsibility in the situation out of which these charges arose."

construed them as dispensing with the element of "wrongful action." The Court of Appeals concluded that the trial judge's instructions "might well have left the jury with the erroneous impression that Park could be found guilty in the absence of 'wrongful action' on his part," and that proof of this element was required by due process. It held, with one dissent, that the instructions did not "correctly state the law of the case," and directed that on retrial the jury be instructed as to "wrongful action," which might be "gross negligence and inattention in discharging . . . corporate duties and obligations or any of a host of other acts of commission or omission which would 'cause' the contamination of food." . . .

We granted certiorari because of an apparent conflict among the Courts of Appeals with respect to the standard of liability of corporate officers under the Federal Food, Drug, and Cosmetic Act as construed in *United States v. Dotterweich, supra*, and because of the importance of the question to the Government's enforcement program. We reverse. . . .

The question presented by the Government's petition for certiorari in *United States v. Dotterweich, supra*, and the focus of this Court's opinion, was whether "the manager of a corporation, as well as the corporation itself, may be prosecuted under the Federal Food, Drug, and Cosmetic Act of 1938 for the introduction of misbranded and adulterated articles into interstate commerce." In *Dotterweich*, a jury had disagreed as to the corporation, a jobber purchasing drugs from manufacturers and shipping them in interstate commerce under its own label, but had convicted *Dotterweich*, the corporation's president and general manager. The Court of Appeals reversed the conviction on the ground that only the drug dealer, whether corporation or individual, was subject to the criminal provisions of the Act, and that where the dealer was a corporation, an individual connected therewith might be held personally only if he was operating the corporation "as his 'alter ego.'"

In reversing the judgment of the Court of Appeals and reinstating Dotterweich's conviction, this Court looked to the purposes of the Act and noted that they "touch phases of the lives and health of the people which, in the circumstances of modern industrialism, are largely beyond self-protection." It observed that the Act is of "a now familiar type" which "dispenses with the conventional requirement for criminal conduct — awareness of some wrongdoing. In the interest of the larger good it puts the burden of acting at hazard upon a person otherwise innocent but standing in responsible relation to a public danger."

Central to the Court's conclusion that individuals other than proprietors are subject to the criminal provisions of the Act was the reality that "the only way in which a corporation can act is through the individuals who act on its behalf." The Court also noted that corporate officers had been subject to criminal liability under the Federal Food and Drugs Act of 1906, and it observed that a contrary result under the 1938 legislation would be incompatible with the expressed intent of Congress to "enlarge and stiffen the penal net" and to discourage a view of the Act's criminal penalties as a "license fee for the conduct of an illegitimate business."

At the same time, however, the Court was aware of the concern which was the motivating factor in the Court of Appeals' decision that literal enforcement "might operate too harshly by sweeping within its condemnation any person however remotely entangled in the proscribed shipment." A limiting principle, in the form of "settled doctrines of criminal law" defining those who "are responsible for the commission of a misdemeanor," was available. In this context, the Court concluded, those doctrines dictated that the offense was committed "by all who . . . have . . . a responsible share in the furtherance of the transaction which the statute outlaws."

The Court recognized that, because the Act dispenses with the need to prove "consciousness of wrongdoing," it may result in hardship even as applied to those who share "responsibility in the business process resulting in" a violation. It regarded as "too treacherous" an attempt "to define or even to indicate by way of illustration the class of employees which stands in such a responsible relation." The question of responsibility, the Court said, depends "on the evidence produced at the trial and its submission — assuming the evidence warrants it — to the jury under appropriate guidance." The Court added: "In such matters the good sense of prosecutors, the wise guidance of trial judges, and the ultimate judgment of juries must be trusted."

The rule that corporate employees who have "a responsible share in the furtherance of the transaction which the statute outlaws" are subject to the criminal provisions of the Act was not formulated in a vacuum. Cases under the Federal Food and Drugs Act of 1906 reflected the view both that knowledge or intent were not required to be proved in prosecutions under its criminal provisions, and that responsible corporate agents could be subjected to the liability thereby imposed. Moreover, the principle had been recognized that a corporate agent, through whose act, default, or omission the corporation committed a crime, was himself guilty individually of that crime. The principle had been applied whether or not the crime required "consciousness of wrongdoing," and it had been applied not only to those corporate agents who themselves committed the criminal act, but also to those who by virtue of their managerial positions or other similar relation to the actor could be deemed responsible for its commission.

In the latter class of cases, the liability of managerial officers did not depend on their knowledge of, or personal participation in, the act made criminal by the statute. Rather, where the statute under which they were prosecuted dispensed with "consciousness of wrongdoing," an omission or failure to act was deemed a sufficient basis for a responsible corporate agent's liability. It was enough in such cases that, by virtue of the relationship he bore to the corporation, the agent had the power to prevent the act complained of.

The rationale of the interpretation given the Act in *Dotterweich*, as holding criminally accountable the persons whose failure to exercise the authority and supervisory responsibility reposed in them by the business organization resulted in the violation complained of, has been confirmed in our subsequent cases. Thus, the Court has reaffirmed the proposition that "the public interest in the purity of its food is so great as to warrant the imposition of the highest standard of care on distributors." In order to make "distributors of food the strictest censors of their merchandise," the Act punishes "neglect where the law requires care, or inaction where it imposes a duty." "The accused, if he does not will the violation, usually is in a position to prevent it with no more care than society might reasonably expect and no more exertion than it might reasonably exact from one who assumed his responsibilities." Similarly, in cases decided after *Dotterweich*, the Courts of Appeals have recognized that those corporate agents vested with the responsibility, and power commensurate with that responsibility, to devise whatever measures are necessary to ensure compliance with the Act bear a "responsible relationship" to, or have a "responsible share" in, violations.

Thus *Dotterweich* and the cases which have followed reveal that in providing sanctions which reach and touch the individuals who execute the corporate mission — and this is by no means necessarily confined to a single corporate agent or employee — the Act imposes not only a positive duty to seek out and remedy violations when they occur but also, and primarily, a duty to implement measures that will insure that violations will not occur. The requirements of foresight and vigilance imposed on responsible corporate agents are beyond question demanding, and perhaps onerous, but they are no more stringent than the public has a right to expect of those who voluntarily assume positions of authority in business enterprises whose services and products affect the health and well-being of the public that supports them.

The Act does not, as we observed in *Dotterweich*, make criminal liability turn on "awareness of some wrongdoing" or "conscious fraud." The duty imposed by Congress on responsible corporate agents is, we emphasize, one that requires the highest standard of foresight and vigilance, but the Act, in its criminal aspect, does not require that which is objectively impossible. The theory upon which responsible corporate agents are held criminally accountable for "causing" violations of the Act permits a claim that a defendant was "powerless" to prevent or correct the violation to "be raised defensively at a trial on the merits." *United States v. Wiesenfield Warehouse Co.*, 376 U.S. 86, 91 (1964). If such a claim is made, the defendant has the burden of coming forward with evidence, but this does not alter the Government's ultimate burden of proving beyond a reasonable doubt the defendant's guilt, including his power, in light of the duty imposed by the Act, to prevent or correct the prohibited condition. Congress has seen fit to enforce the accountability of responsible corporate agents dealing with products which may affect the health of consumers by penal sanctions cast in rigorous terms, and the obligation of the courts is to give them effect so long as they do not violate the Constitution.

We cannot agree with the Court of Appeals that it was incumbent upon the District Court to instruct the jury that the Government had the burden of establishing "wrongful action" in the sense in which the Court of Appeals used that phrase. The concept of a "responsible relationship" to, or a "responsible share" in, a violation of the Act indeed imports some measure of blameworthiness; but it is equally clear that the Government establishes a prima facie case when it introduces evidence sufficient to warrant a finding by the trier of the facts that the defendant had, by reason of his position in the corporation, responsibility and authority either to prevent in the first instance, or promptly to correct, the violation complained of, and that he failed to do so. The failure thus to fulfill the duty imposed by the interaction of the corporate agent's authority and the statute furnishes a sufficient causal link. The considerations which prompted the imposition of this duty, and the scope of the duty, provide the measure of culpability.

Turning to the jury charge in this case, it is of course arguable that isolated parts can be read as intimating that a finding of guilt could be predicated solely on respondent's corporate position. But this is not the way we review jury instructions, because "a single instruction to a jury may not be judged in artificial isolation, but must be viewed in the context of the overall charge."

Reading the entire charge satisfies us that the jury's attention was adequately focused on the issue of respondent's authority with respect to the conditions that formed the basis of the alleged violations. Viewed as a whole, the charge did not permit the jury to find guilt solely on the basis of respondent's position in the corporation; rather, it fairly advised the jury that to find guilt it must find respondent "had a responsible relation to the situation," and "by virtue of his position . . . had . . . authority and responsibility" to deal with the situation. The situation referred to could only be "food . . . held in unsanitary conditions in a warehouse with the result that it consisted, in part, of filth or . . . may have been contaminated with filth."

Moreover, in reviewing jury instructions, our task is also to view the charge itself as part of the whole trial. "Often isolated statements taken from the charge, seemingly prejudicial on their face, are not so when considered in the context of the entire record of the trial." The record in this case reveals that the jury could not have failed to be aware that the main issue for determination was not respondent's position in the corporate hierarchy, but rather his accountability, because of the responsibility and authority of his position, for the conditions which gave rise to the charges against him.

We conclude that, viewed as a whole and in the context of the trial, the charge was not misleading and contained an adequate statement of the law to guide the jury's determination.

*   *   *

Reversed.

Mr. JUSTICE STEWART, with whom Mr. JUSTICE MARSHALL and Mr. JUSTICE POWELL join, dissenting.

Although agreeing with much of what is said in the Court's opinion, I dissent from the opinion and judgment, because the jury instructions in this case were not consistent with the law as the Court today expounds it.

As I understand the Court's opinion, it holds that in order to sustain a conviction under § 301(k) of the Federal Food, Drug, and Cosmetic Act the prosecution must at least show that by reason of an individual's corporate position and responsibilities, he had a duty to use care to maintain the physical integrity of the corporation's food products. A jury may then draw the inference that when the good is found to be in such condition as to violate the statute's prohibitions, that condition was "caused" by a breach of the standard of care imposed upon the responsible official. This is the language of negligence, and I agree with it.

To affirm this conviction, however, the Court must approve the instructions given to the members of the jury who were entrusted with determining whether the respondent was innocent or guilty. Those instructions did not conform to the standards that the Court itself sets out today.

*   *   *

As the Court today recognized, the *Dotterweich* case did not deal with what kind of conduct must be proved to support a finding of criminal guilt under the Act. *Dotterweich* was concerned, rather, with the statutory definition of "person" — with what kind of corporate employees were even "subject to the criminal provisions of the Act." The Court held that those employees with "a responsible relation" to the violative transaction or condition were subject to the Act's criminal provisions, but all that the Court had to say with respect to the kind of conduct that can constitute criminal guilt was that the Act "dispenses with the conventional requirement for criminal conduct — awareness of some wrongdoing."

*   *   *

The *Dotterweich* case stands for two propositions, and I accept them both. First, "any person" within the meaning of 21 U.S.C. § 333 may include any corporate officer or employee "standing in responsible relation" to a condition or transaction forbidden by the Act. Second, a person may be convicted of a criminal offense under the Act even in the absence of "the conventional requirement for criminal conduct — awareness of some wrongdoing." But before a person can be convicted of a criminal violation of this Act, a jury must find — and must be clearly instructed that it must find — evidence beyond a reasonable doubt that he engaged in wrongful conduct amounting at least to common-law negligence. There were no such instructions, and clearly, therefore, no such finding in this case.

For these reasons, I cannot join the Court in affirming Park's criminal conviction.

NOTES AND QUESTIONS

1. *Mens rea and actus reus.* What level of mens rea did Park possess? What actus reus did he commit? Given the proof adduced on those essential elements of criminal liability, why did the Court affirm Park's criminal conviction?

2. Dotterweich *and strict liability.* The Court in *Park* relied heavily on its opinion in *Dotterweich.* In that case, the defendant was the president and general manager of a pharmaceutical company that shipped adulterated and misbranded products in interstate commerce. He was convicted of violating the Food, Drug, and Cosmetic Act. The Court upheld the conviction based on proof that Dotterweich had a "responsible share in the furtherance of the transaction." *Dotterweich*, 320 U.S. at 284. *Dotterweich* involved a strict liability offense where the public welfare was threatened. Is strict liability appropriate in this setting? Why or why not?

3. *Modern business practices.* Modern business involves complex relationships among subsidiaries, partnerships, and other entities. One glaring recent example of corporate wrongdoing was the Enron collapse and the related demise of the Arthur Andersen accounting firm. The public favors individual accountability in these settings. In such cases, how much proof should the government be required to adduce concerning an executive's knowledge of the wrongdoing?

4. *Whistleblower liability.* In *Armstrong v. Trans-Service Logistics, Inc.*, 2005 Ohio App. LEXIS 2565 (Ohio Ct. App. 2005), an employee sued his employer and supervisors under the Ohio "whistleblower" statute and under a common law theory of wrongful retaliatory discharge. The plaintiff was fired after he reported to government officials that meat was being shipped at an unsafe temperature. The Ohio Court of Appeals held that Ohio's "whistleblower" statute did not provide for individual liability of the entity's managers. However, it held that there could still be individual liability under a common law wrongful retaliatory discharge claim. This decision relied in part on *Park*'s holding that, if the defendant's position within the corporation gave him the responsibility or authority to prevent or

correct the violation, this was prima facie evidence to support a finding of individual liability. The court also found the policy rationale of *Park* and *Dotterweich* compelling, and held that the health concerns of unsafe food shipment supported liability.

PROBLEM

2-1. David acquired a wastewater treatment facility. The facility treated water for various municipalities. During his association with the facility, David changed the name several times, eventually calling it Crystal Clear Processing Corp. (CCP). David moved CCP's operations to a new location and controlled the finances. His name did not appear on the corporate records and he did not have a formal association with CCP. David maintained an office at CCP, where he negotiated the purchase of a new treatment plant, guided the employees in marketing CCP, and controlled the expenses. CCP employed 50 people.

In an effort to secure another contract for the city of Water's Edge, the general manager Klark acquired a special carbon filtration system. Although this system was to be used as a final step in water treatment, and was not intended to be used on untreated water, CCP used it as the sole treatment process. The salesperson who sold the filtration system told Klark and David that the system would not function properly unless it was preceded by a more comprehensive filtration system. David inspected the carbon filtration system on at least one occasion, and did not install an additional filtration system.

CCP began to "treat" the water in the Water's Edge community. CCP began to discharge untreated water into the municipality's sewage facility. Based on this conduct, CCP was charged with violating federal law, requiring the pretreatment of water under the Clean Water Act. Each count alleged that David committed the violations as the responsible corporate officer. The provision of the Clean Water Act under which David was charged applies to "any person who negligently violates the pretreatment requirements." The law defines a person as an "individual, corporation, partnership, association" and a person is further defined as "any responsible corporate officer."

    a.   *David comes to you seeking legal advice to defend against the charges. David tells you that he was never formally designated as a corporate officer of CCP and that he never exercised sufficient control over the operations to come under the law's parameters. What additional information do you need to know in order to defend him?*

    b.   *You are the prosecutor in this case. Do you have sufficient information to establish that David had a mens rea to commit a crime? What additional information do you need to proceed with prosecution?*

    c.   *Is Klark criminally liable for the conduct in the processing of the water for Water's Edge? What theories would apply to Klark?*

In *Dotterweich* and *Park*, the Court upheld strict liability for responsible corporate officers in connection with certain public welfare offenses that Congress designated as strict liability offenses for such officers. In the next case, the defendant argued that he was not a "responsible corporate officer" under the statute at issue.

[2]   High Profile Prosecutions

The 21st century has already seen a number of high profile prosecutions of corporate executives, including those of Enron and WorldCom. One notable successful prosecution was that of Bernard J. Ebbers, former chief executive officer of WorldCom, a telecommunications giant before its collapse in 2002. On March 15, 2005, a jury convicted Ebbers of securities fraud, conspiracy, and seven counts of filing false reports with regulators. Ebbers was sentenced to 25 years in prison, effectively a life sentence. *See* Carrie Johnson, *Ebbers Gets 25-Year Sentence For Role in WorldCom Fraud*, Wash. Post, July 14, 2005, at A1 ("The fraud at WorldCom ultimately topped $11 billion and led to the country's biggest bankruptcy filing, in July 2002."). The Second Circuit affirmed Ebbers's conviction and sentence. *United States v. Ebbers*, 458 F.3d 110 (2d Cir. 2006). As one commentator noted, Ebbers' conviction showed that "juries are willing to hold the top officers of major corporations responsible" for corporate wrongdoing. Kurt Eichenwald, *When the Top Seat is the Hot Seat*, N.Y. Times, Mar. 16, 2005, at C1.

In many of the recent corporate scandals, chief executives have claimed that they are not liable for corporate wrongdoing because they did not intend to commit a crime. These executives have claimed that they simply relied on the assurances of managers and on the advice of attorneys and accountants. To support this claim, the executives have often minimized their own roles in their corporations. *See id.*

Before WorldCom's collapse in 2002, Ebbers' story was an inspiring tale of entrepreneurship. Ebbers, who came from a modest background and had little formal education, rose to become the chief executive of a "global telecommunications titan." Ken Belson, *Ex-Chief of WorldCom Is Found Guilty in $11 Billion Fraud*, N.Y. Times, Mar. 16, 2005, at A1. In 2002, however, WorldCom experienced an $11 billion collapse. In June of 2002, WorldCom's internal auditors unmasked massive fraud; the auditors discovered $3.8 billion in expenses that had been improperly characterized, resulting in inflated revenue for the company. The day after the auditors' announcement, the SEC initiated a civil investigation. At the same time, the FBI and U.S. Attorney's Office in the Southern District of New York started a criminal investigation. In July 2002, the company filed for bankruptcy, and in the same month, prosecutors filed complaints against WorldCom officers.

According to prosecutors, Bernard Ebbers knew that WorldCom could not meet Wall Street's forecasts for the company. Ebbers therefore instructed his employees to alter the corporation's books, starting as early as 2000. WorldCom's chief financial officer, Scott D. Sullivan, testified at Ebbers' trial that Ebbers had directed Sullivan to doctor the books to hide WorldCom's slowing sales. Sullivan had pled guilty to his role in the fraud, and testified against Ebbers in the hope of getting a more lenient sentence. *See* Kathleen F. Brickey, *Symposium: White Collar Criminal Law in Comparative Perspective: The Sarbanes-Oxley Act of 2002: Enron's Legacy*, 8 Buff. Crim. L. Rev. 221, 266 (2004) (detailing the charging process in the WorldCom case and the importance in securing Sullivan's cooperation).

Bernard Ebbers' counsel faced a tough case. Prosecutors had not offered Ebbers any real plea bargain, so defense counsel had little choice but to go to trial. Also, with Scott Sullivan pleading guilty to the fraud, the defense could not argue that fraud had not occurred or that these actions did not rise to the level of fraud. Instead, the defense was left with the assertion that Ebbers was not complicit in the fraud.

Ebbers' attorney, Reid H. Weingarten, sought to portray Ebbers as a "coach" rather than as someone intimately involved with the company's day-to-day operations. Weingarten attempted to use Sullivan's plea bargain to question Sullivan's credibility. In his closing statement, Weingarten asserted that Ebbers had no reason to lie: Ebbers was already wealthy, and put money into the company during the fraud years instead of pulling money out. Despite all of these attempts by defense counsel, Ebbers' testimony that he was unaware of the fraud did not convince the jury. Do you think that juries often accept such defense arguments? Why or why not?

In addition, the Enron prosecutions resulted in convictions of some of the key actors. Former Enron President Jeffrey Skilling was convicted on 19 out of 28 counts, including conspiracy, securities fraud, making false statements to auditors, and one insider trading count; he was acquitted on the other nine. He was sentenced to 24 years and 4 months in prison, and hefty fines were imposed. Former Enron CEO Kenneth Lay was convicted on all six counts, including conspiracy, wire fraud, and securities fraud. He was also convicted at a separate bench trial of bank fraud and on three counts of making false statements to banks. Lay died before sentencing, and his conviction was vacated. *See* Kate Murphy, *Judge Throws Out Kenneth Lay's Conviction*, N.Y. Times, Oct. 18, 2006, at C1. What does the Enron investigation and prosecution teach us about the feasibility of using the criminal laws to reach corporate wrongdoing?

PROBLEMS

2.2. The Gado corporation is engaged in providing the local school districts with a variety of supplies during the school year. Sarah Steady is an account manager. Sarah handles all of the orders for the corporation and she negotiates the best prices in order to secure the most advantageous account. She handles the orders for the entire school district. Sarah wants to impress the boss and she negotiates a deal with a competing vendor to coordinate the bidding process so that each of them is the low bidder on certain contracts. That way, both of them will see an increase in the level of their business. Assume that this activity is a violation of federal law. *Evaluate the corporate accountability under both the MPC and respondeat superior in the following scenarios*:

a. Sarah is a low-level employee and she acted on her own without any direction from corporate executives.

b. The Gado corporation did not benefit from Sarah's conduct. The evidence is that Gado was awarded as many contracts as it would have received without Sarah's conduct. She engaged in this wrongdoing to benefit only herself.

c. Gado instructed all of its employees not to violate any laws and Sarah had received this mandatory internal corporate training.

d. Sarah only intended to benefit herself, but Gado benefited from Sarah's conduct because it was awarded more business than it would have received otherwise.

2.3. Harvey is the manager of Harvey's Cars, a car dealership located in Oklahoma. The dealership was a subsidiary of General Autos, located in Texas. Harvey sold cars under a licensing agreement with General Autos. Harvey ran the dealership's day-to-day operations. He had authority to hire and fire employees and to sign and process all payroll checks. General Autos was running its spring sale campaign and offered customers the option of receiving rebate checks when they purchased certain current model cars. The rebate campaign applied to all of General Autos' dealerships. The rebate checks were issued from the corporate offices of General Autos once the sale was completed and they were sent to each of the participating dealerships for them to forward to the qualifying customer. This procedure was designed to allow for the dealership to have additional contact with the customer in order to provide additional goods and services.

Harvey's Cars was in financial trouble because it was not meeting its quarterly goals. Harvey began to neglect to advise certain customers that their car purchase would qualify for the national rebate being offered by General Autos. In addition, he falsely told certain customers that their particular car was not covered by the rebate or that the program had expired at the end of the month. Because the rebates applied to all of these purchases, when Harvey processed the paperwork, he included the rebate request in the submission to General Autos and forwarded it with all of the other documentation. Assume that the government seeks to charge General Autos with fraud based upon Harvey's acts.

Assume the role of the prosecution and defense in this case. (a) Assume that the jurisdiction has not yet determined whether to follow the respondeat superior or the MPC approach to corporate criminal liability. Argue for the adoption of the approach that best supports your case. (b) Argue for and against General Autos' liability under each approach.

Chapter 3

CONSPIRACY

[A] INTRODUCTORY NOTES

[1] The Importance of a Conspiracy Charge

Conspiracy is an inchoate offense that is frequently charged in federal and state criminal cases. In the simplest terms, a conspiracy exists whenever two or more people agree to commit a criminal offense. Some modern statutes also require that the government prove an "overt act" in furtherance of the conspiracy. Because white collar crimes often involve multiple actors, a conspiracy charge is common in white collar cases.

The crime of conspiracy is the principal avenue for punishing uncompleted criminal conduct in white collar cases.[a] Under federal law, conspiracy does not merge with the crimes that are the objects of the conspiracy. Thus, if the criminal objectives are achieved, the co-conspirators generally may be punished both for the crime of conspiracy and for the object crimes.

As noted by Justice Jackson in his oft-cited concurring opinion in *Krulewitch v. United States*, 336 U.S. 440, 446 (1949), conspiracy is a controversial crime. The boundaries of the crime are notoriously unclear; as Justice Jackson wrote, conspiracy is "so vague that it almost defies definition." *Id.* Thus, prosecutors have tremendous discretion in deciding when to bring a conspiracy charge. In addition, as discussed in the cases below, a conspiracy charge provides the prosecutor with substantial strategic and tactical advantages.

[2] Advantages of a Conspiracy Charge

Including a conspiracy charge in a white collar case places the prosecution at an advantage, and the defense at a disadvantage, in several important ways. Most importantly, a conspiracy charge enables the government to bring together at a single trial all defendants who were allegedly part of the conspiracy, including minor participants against whom the evidence may not be strong.

As to venue, the government may bring the conspiracy case in any district where the agreement was entered into or where any co-conspirator committed any act in furtherance of the conspiracy. It may advantage the government to bring the

---

[a] There is no general provision in the federal criminal code that criminalizes attempts to commit crimes. Some specific federal criminal statutes do impose inchoate liability under the terms of the statutes themselves. For example, the federal obstruction of justice statute criminalizes "endeavors" to obstruct justice. *See* 18 U.S.C. § 1503, discussed in Chapter 11, Extortion, *infra.* And the criminal tax evasion statute applies to "[a]ny person who willfully attempts in any manner to evade or defeat any tax." 26 U.S.C. § 7201, discussed in Chapter 12, Tax Fraud, *infra.*

case in a venue that is convenient for the government and/or inconvenient for the defense.

A conspiracy charge also gives the government important evidentiary advantages. First, a conspiracy charge typically expands the scope of relevant evidence. Thus, evidence as to any co-conspirators' acts in furtherance of the conspiracy may be admissible. Second, as discussed in § [E][2] below, co-conspirator statements made during and in furtherance of a conspiracy are admissible under the "co-conspirators exception" to the hearsay rule.

A defendant charged with conspiracy also faces possible expanded liability. As noted above, the defendant can be found guilty both of the conspiracy and of the conspiracy's object crimes. And, as discussed in § [F] below, the defendant may also be vicariously liable for substantive offenses committed by other co-conspirators.

Finally, including a conspiracy charge may also extend the statute of limitations, which does not begin to run until the conspiratorial goals are achieved or abandoned. Even if the limitations period for some or all of the conspiracy's object crimes has expired, all co-conspirators may be liable for the *crime of conspiracy* so long as any co-conspirator committed an overt act within five years of the indictment.

[3]   Federal Conspiracy Statutes

Federal law contains both a general conspiracy provision and more specific conspiracy provisions. The general conspiracy law is set forth at § 371 of the criminal code, 18 U.S.C. § 371. Federal law also contains distinct provisions that criminalize conspiring to commit certain types of offenses, such as narcotics, antitrust, and racketeering offenses (*see, e.g.*, 21 U.S.C. § 846; 15 U.S.C. §§ 1, 2; 18 U.S.C. § 1962(d)). Also, the Sarbanes-Oxley Act, passed in response to financial scandals of the early 21st century, includes a conspiracy statute specifically applicable to a number of white collar crimes, including mail and wire fraud and certain financial crimes. (18 U.S.C. § 1349). Most federal conspiracy charges arise under § 371, and it is upon that statute that this chapter focuses.

[4]   The Elements of Conspiracy

[a]   Section 371

Section 371 makes it a crime for "two or more persons to conspire either to commit any offense against the United States, or to defraud the United States, or any agency thereof in any manner or for any purpose." Specifically, under § 371, the government must show that:

(1) An agreement existed

(a) to commit an offense against the United States, *and/or*

(b) to defraud the United States;

(2) Two or more persons were parties to that agreement (the "plurality" requirement);

(3) The defendant intended

    (a) to enter into the agreement, *and*

    (b) that the object offense or fraud come to pass; *and*

    (4) A co-conspirator committed an "overt act" in furtherance of the offense.

The precise level of intent, or mens rea, required for conspiracy is the subject of § [B] below.

[b]   The "Plurality" Requirement

Because so many white collar cases arise in the corporate context, complex issues may arise as to whether the plurality requirement has been satisfied. In general, several principles govern. First, two or more corporations, or a corporation and its subsidiary, are capable of conspiring with one another. Thus, a conspiracy may exist solely between or among artificial entities. Second, courts generally hold that a corporation can conspire with its own agents, provided that there are at least two agents/co-conspirators. *See, e.g., United States v. Hartley*, 678 F.2d 961, 972 (11th Cir. 1982). The latter rule does not apply, however, where the alleged co-conspirators are (1) the corporation and (2) a sole stockholder who completely controls the corporation. *See United States v. Stevens*, 909 F.2d 431, 431 (11th Cir. 1990). Third, a corporation may be vicariously liable under respondeat superior for a conspiracy entered into by its agents.

Finally, special rules apply to antitrust law, which focuses on unlawful business combinations. Thus, under Section 1 of the Sherman Act, 15 U.S.C. § 1, a conspiracy cannot be comprised of a corporation and its wholly-owned subsidiary, or a corporation and its agents who are acting on behalf of the corporation. *See, e.g., Copperweld Corp. v. Independence Tube Corp.*, 467 U.S. 752, 769–771 (1984).

[c]   The Overt Act Requirement

Under the common law, the actus reus of conspiracy was the agreement itself. Many modern conspiracy statutes follow the same approach.[b] Some statutes, including § 371, also require that the government prove an "overt act" in furtherance of the conspiracy. This requirement serves to corroborate the conspiratorial intent that is at the heart of the crime.

The overt act requirement is not hard to meet. Any act by a co-conspirator that occurs during the conspiracy and in furtherance of the conspiracy will qualify. Significantly, the overt act need not meet the test required for the actus reus of attempt at common law; the overt act need not constitute a "substantial step" towards nor be "dangerously proximate" to the criminal objective. Thus, a conspiracy prosecution rarely fails for lack of an overt act.

Co-conspirators are considered to be agents of each other. An overt act by one co-conspirator will therefore meet the proof requirement for all co-conspirators who are members of the conspiracy at the time the act is committed or who join later. *See Salinas v. United States*, 522 U.S. 52 (1997).

---

[b] *See, e.g.*, 18 U.S.C. § 1962(d) (RICO conspiracy), discussed in the Chapter 14, RICO, *infra*.

[5]   Sentencing

The maximum sentence under § 371 is five years. As with all federal crimes, however, the actual sentence will depend on the application of the federal sentencing guidelines to the facts of the case. *See* Chapter 19, Sentencing, *infra.* In conspiracy cases, the sentences are tied to those for the substantive offenses, and thus will vary considerably from case to case.

[B]   MENS REA

As noted in the case below, conspiracy is often difficult to prove because it is primarily a mental crime that usually must be demonstrated by circumstantial evidence. In particular, a defendant must both knowingly and intentionally enter into an agreement to achieve illegal objectives, and intend to achieve those objectives. The case below involves proof of mens rea in a two-person conspiracy to commit "insider trading."[c] As you read the case, try to identify precisely the level of criminal intent that the government is required to adduce.

UNITED STATES v. SVOBODA
347 F.3d 471 (2d Cir. 2003)

Scullin, Chief District Judge.

After a thirteen-day jury trial, Robles was convicted of one count of conspiracy to commit securities and tender offer fraud. On appeal, Robles principally contends that the district court erred in giving a conscious avoidance instruction with respect to the conspiracy charge. For the reasons set forth below, we affirm.

I. BACKGROUND

At trial, the government sought to prove that Robles and his long-time friend Richard Svoboda[4] engaged in a conspiracy to commit securities and tender offer fraud for profit between approximately November 1994 and December 1997. During that period, Svoboda was employed in Dallas, Texas, as a "credit policy officer" at Nations Bank, a financial institution engaged, *inter alia*, in commercial lending. As a credit policy officer, Svoboda was charged with structuring and approving loans to corporate clients. In the course of his duties at Nations Bank, Svoboda was privy to confidential information about Nations Bank's clients, such as earnings information and merger and acquisition plans. Svoboda testified that he obtained confidential information about certain securities and tender offers through his position at Nations Bank; that he passed the information to Robles,

---

[c] As discussed more fully in Chapter 5, Securities Fraud, *infra*, illegal insider trading occurs when a person trades on the basis of important, secret information that is not available to the general public. Many of the trades in this case involved "tender offers." A tender offer is an announcement by one company that it intends to buy the stock of another (the "target" company) at a specified price above the prevailing market price for the stock. Upon the public announcement of such an offer, the price of the target company's stock generally rises. Thus, in this case, the defendants learned secret information (for example, that company A was going to announce a tender offer for company B), bought stock in company B before the tender offer was announced, and then sold the stock after the announcement, reaping substantial profits.

[4] Svoboda was originally indicted along with Robles but later entered into a plea agreement with the government in which he agreed, *inter alia*, to testify against Robles at trial.

who, in turn, used the insider information to make trades; and that he and Robles shared the profits realized from their illicit trading. Svoboda further testified that he and Robles discussed and agreed upon the details of the above-described scheme and that Robles was fully aware that he was trading on the basis of unlawfully obtained insider information. Robles, however, took the stand in his own defense and denied knowledge of the unlawful source of Svoboda's information.

At the close of evidence, the government requested a conscious avoidance instruction; i.e., an instruction to the effect that the government could satisfy its obligation to prove Robles' knowledge of the unlawful source of the information by proving that he deliberately avoided acquiring that knowledge. Over Robles' objection, the district court granted the government's request and included a conscious avoidance instruction in the jury charge.[5]

II. DISCUSSION

A. The Conscious Avoidance Instruction

The instant case requires us to determine whether and under what circumstances the doctrine of conscious avoidance may be employed in a conspiracy prosecution. Robles' principal contention on appeal is that the conscious avoidance doctrine cannot be employed in the course of establishing a conspiratorial agreement between two persons. We disagree.

1. Proof of a conspiratorial agreement

Robles was convicted of conspiracy to engage in insider trading under 18 U.S.C. § 371, the general federal conspiracy statute, which provides that:

> [i]f two or more persons conspire either to commit any offense against the United States, or to defraud the United States, or any agency thereof in any manner or for any purpose, and one or more of such persons do any act to effect the object of the conspiracy, each shall be fined under this title or imprisoned not more than five years, or both.

18 U.S.C. § 371. A conspiracy conviction under § 371 requires proof of three essential elements: (1) an agreement among two or more persons, the object of which is an offense against the United States; (2) the defendant's knowing and willful joinder in that conspiracy; and (3) commission of an overt act in furtherance of the conspiracy by at least one of the alleged coconspirators.

---

[5] The district court instructed the jury as follows:

In determining whether the defendant acted knowingly, you may consider whether the defendant deliberately closed his eyes to what would otherwise have been obvious to him. If you find, beyond a reasonable doubt, that the defendant acted with a conscious purpose to avoid learning the truth, that he was trading on the basis of insider information, then this element may be satisfied.

However, guilty knowledge may not be established by demonstrating that the defendant was merely negligent, foolish or mistaken. If you find that the defendant was aware of a high probability that he was trading on the basis of insider information, and that the defendant acted with a deliberate disregard of the facts, you may find that the defendant acted knowingly. However, if you find that the defendant actually believed that he was not receiving insider information, he may not be convicted.

"The gist of conspiracy is, of course, agreement." *United States v. Beech-Nut Nutrition Corp.*, 871 F.2d 1181, 1191 (2d Cir.1989). "A conspiracy need not be shown by proof of an explicit agreement but can be established by showing that the parties have a tacit understanding to carry out the prohibited conduct." *United States v. Samaria*, 239 F.3d 228, 234 (2d Cir.2001). In either case, "the evidence must be sufficient to permit the jury to infer that the defendant and other alleged coconspirators entered into a joint enterprise with consciousness of its general nature and extent." *Beech-Nut Nutrition Corp.*, 871 F.2d at 1191.

Conspiracies are secretive by their very nature, and it is thus well-settled that the elements of a conspiracy may be proved by circumstantial evidence. In certain conspiracy prosecutions, the government often seeks to prove that a particular defendant joined a preexisting conspiracy. In other cases, the question is whether a conspiracy existed at all and, if so, whether a particular defendant was a party to the alleged conspiratorial agreement. In either case, the fundamental legal question is the same: whether the evidence establishes beyond a reasonable doubt that a particular defendant entered into an agreement with others with knowledge of the criminal purpose of the scheme and with the specific intent to aid in the accomplishment of those unlawful ends.

2. The conscious avoidance doctrine

"The conscious avoidance doctrine provides that a defendant's knowledge of a fact required to prove the defendant's guilt may be found when the jury is persuaded that the defendant consciously avoided learning that fact while aware of a high probability of its existence." *Samaria*, 239 F.3d at 239. "In such circumstances, a conscious avoidance instruction to the jury permits a finding of knowledge even where there is no evidence that the defendant possessed actual knowledge."

3. The application of the conscious avoidance doctrine in the conspiracy context

Relying on dictum in one of our opinions, *United States v. Reyes*, 302 F.3d 48, 54 (2d Cir.2002), Robles contends that "the doctrine of conscious avoidance cannot be used at all in the context of a two-person conspiracy." We disagree. . . .

In *Reyes*, we upheld the defendant's conviction by the jury, overturning the district court's grant of a directed verdict. The defendant was in the business of selling auto parts. The jury found him guilty of engaging in the transportation and sale of stolen airbags and conspiracy to do the same. There was evidence that the defendant, when being interviewed by an FBI agent, said he was aware that the bags were stolen, making "an analogy to . . . when you see a friend using drugs, you see what's happening, but you turn the other way." *Reyes*, 302 F.3d at 52. In analyzing the sufficiency of the evidence to support the conviction, we found that the evidence was sufficient to prove that the defendant knew the airbags were stolen, or in any event "thought the airbags were stolen, but deliberately avoided confirming that fact." *Reyes*, 302 F.3d at 56. We further found that evidence supported the defendant's intentional participation in the conspiracy.

Prior to analyzing the evidence, our opinion discoursed on the nature of the conscious avoidance doctrine and observed, "[We] do not permit the doctrine to be used to prove intent to participate in a conspiracy." *Id.* at 54. This observation played no role in the decision.

Robles relies on this sentence for his argument. His argument is essentially that conspiracy by definition requires the participation of two or more conspirators, both of whom must intend to participate. If intent to participate may not be proved by reliance on conscious avoidance, then in a case of only two conspirators where the prosecution must rely on the doctrine of conscious avoidance to prove intent to participate on the part of one, the necessary proof of intent to participate by at least two conspirators will be lacking. . . .

When *Reyes* states that conscious avoidance cannot prove intent to participate, we do not understand it to mean that conscious avoidance cannot be used to prove any aspect of intent to participate; it simply means that just as actual knowledge of the illegal purpose of a conspiracy is insufficient to prove a defendant's joinder in a conspiracy, so conscious avoidance of such knowledge is also insufficient. There must be further proof that the defendant joined in the illegal agreement with the intent of helping it succeed in its criminal purpose.

In sum, we can see no reason why the factfinder may not rely on conscious avoidance to satisfy at least the knowledge component of intent to participate in a conspiracy. Moreover, we firmly reject Robles' contention that a conscious avoidance charge may not be used in a two-person conspiracy. Whether the conspiracy is among two members or more, a defendant's conscious avoidance of knowledge of its illegal purpose may substitute for knowledge of the illegal purpose.[9] . . .

4. Factual predicate for the conscious avoidance instruction

Having found no doctrinal obstacle to employing a conscious avoidance instruction in the context of a two-person conspiracy, we now turn to the question of whether the facts in the instant case support such an instruction. . . .

A conscious avoidance instruction "may only be given if (1) the defendant asserts the lack of some specific aspect of knowledge required for conviction, . . . and (2) the appropriate factual predicate for the charge exists, i.e., the evidence is such that a rational juror may reach [the] conclusion beyond a reasonable doubt . . . that [the defendant] was aware of a high probability [of the fact in dispute] and consciously avoided confirming that fact[.]" *Ferrarini*, 219 F.3d at 154. The second prong of this test thus has two components — there must be evidence that the defendant (1) was aware of a high probability of the disputed fact and (2) deliberately avoided confirming that fact. . . .

Here, the first prerequisite is easily met, as Robles denied knowledge of the unlawful source of Svoboda's investment advice. The second prerequisite is also easily met. First, the source of Svoboda's information was suspicious — Robles knew that Svoboda was a credit officer at Nations Bank and would thus be privy to confidential financial information. Second, the timing of Robles' trades was suspi-

---

[9] Significantly, Robles *does not* challenge the sufficiency of the evidence supporting his conspiracy conviction. Accordingly, we assume, for purposes of this appeal, that the evidence was, in fact, sufficient to establish beyond a reasonable doubt (1) Robles' knowledge that he was trading on inside information and (2) his active participation in the charged scheme. We have no difficulty concluding that this evidence provides a proper evidentiary foundation, as a matter of law, to infer the existence of an agreement to violate federal securities laws.

cious — for example, some of Robles' trades occurred as little as a day before a tender offer announcement. Third, the success of the trades was suspicious — Robles realized large returns, up to 400%, on trades based on Svoboda's advice. These facts suggest a high probability that Svoboda's tips were based on inside information and that any lack of actual knowledge on Robles' part was due to a conscious effort to avoid confirming an otherwise obvious fact. We therefore find that there was a sufficient factual predicate in the instant case to warrant a conscious avoidance instruction.

*   *   *

For the foregoing reasons, the judgment of the district court is hereby AFFIRMED.

NOTES AND QUESTIONS

1. *Appellate practice.* Many of the cases in this text raise issues of appellate practice in addition to substantive legal issues. In this case, what precisely are the defendant's arguments? Is he raising issues of law? Of fact? What is the standard of appellate review for these issues?

2. *"Specific intent."* As the court discussed in *Svoboda,* the government must prove two levels of mens rea in a conspiracy case: (1) the intent to agree, with knowledge of the illegal nature of the conspiracy; and (2) the intent that the object offense(s) be committed. *See United States v. United States Gypsum Co.,* 438 U.S. 422, 444 n.20 (1978). At least on the second prong, conspiracy is generally considered to be a "specific intent" crime. Such intent corresponds to the level of mens rea that the Model Penal Code terms "purposefulness;" that is, a conscious desire to achieve the criminal result. Why is this high level of mens rea required in conspiracy cases?

3. *Conscious avoidance.* What is the conscious avoidance doctrine? What is the basis for the defendant's argument that it should not have been applied in his case? Of course, the conscious avoidance doctrine is not limited to conspiracy cases, but generally applies when proof of knowledge is an element of a crime. Why do courts allow proof of "knowledge" based upon evidence that concededly may not show actual knowledge?

4. *Mens rea and jurisdiction.* Must the government prove mens rea as to the jurisdictional element of a conspiracy case? Assume, for example, that the defendants conspire to harm an undercover agent who, unbeknownst to them, is a federal agent. Are the defendants guilty of conspiring to commit the crime of assaulting a federal officer? Would the purposes of conspiracy law be served in such a case? *See United States v. Feola,* 420 U.S. 671 (1975).

5. *Inconsistent verdicts.* In a conspiracy case, the government must show that two or more persons agreed to enter into a conspiracy. Suppose that, in a two person conspiracy, the jury acquits one of the alleged coconspirators but convicts the other. May the conviction stand? Most circuit courts answer in the affirmative. *See, e.g., United States v. Valles-Vallencia,* 811 F.2d 1232 (9th Cir. 1986), *amended by* 823 F.2d 381 (9th Cir. 1987). *Cf. United States v. Powell,* 469 U.S. 57 (1984) (affirming conviction of defendant who was acquitted of narcotics charges but convicted of using a telephone to commit those charges). Can you explain these results?

[C]   THE "OFFENSE CLAUSE" AND THE "DEFRAUD CLAUSE"

Section 371 makes it a crime for "two or more persons to conspire either to commit any offense against the United States, or to defraud the United States, or any agency thereof in any manner or for any purpose." Thus, the statute defines two distinct offenses: conspiring to violate United States law, and conspiring to "defraud" the United States. The following case deals with the scope of the "offense clause," and the relationship between the "offense clause" and the "defraud clause."

UNITED STATES v. ARCH TRADING CO.
987 F.2d 1087 (4th Cir. 1993)

NIEMEYER, CIRCUIT JUDGE:

On August 2, 1990, Iraq invaded Kuwait. On that same day President Bush invoked the emergency powers provided to him by Congress and issued executive orders prohibiting United States persons from, among other things, traveling to Iraq and dealing with the government of Iraq and its agents. In the present appeal, Arch Trading Company, Inc., a Virginia corporation, challenges its convictions for various crimes arising from violations of these prohibitions. The company was convicted of conspiring to commit an offense against the United States, in violation of 18 U.S.C. § 371.

Arch Trading contends principally that the indictment charging it with conspiracy to *commit an offense* under § 371 was defective because in the circumstances the company could only have been charged with conspiracy *to defraud.* . . .

I.

In November 1988 Arch Trading entered into a $1.9 million contract with Agricultural Supplies Company, a "quasi-governmental body owned by the government of Iraq" (Agricultural of Iraq), to ship to Iraq and install there laboratory equipment, including a "virology fermenter" and a "bacteriology machine," purportedly for veterinary use. . . .

From April 1990 through July 1990 Arch Trading acquired the equipment and related chemicals and arranged for their delivery to Iraq. By early August 1990, five of a planned six shipments had arrived in Iraq, but none had been installed. The sixth shipment, which was never actually delivered, was en route. On August 2, 1990, when Iraq invaded Kuwait, President Bush, issued Executive Order No. 12722 prohibiting United States persons from, among other things, exporting goods, technology, or services to Iraq; performing any contract in support of an industrial, commercial or governmental project in Iraq; and engaging in any transaction related to travel to Iraq by United States persons. At Arch Trading's request, that same day the Treasury Department's OFAC faxed a copy of the Executive Order to Arch Trading's offices. A week later the President issued a slightly more detailed order.

Notwithstanding the prohibitions of the first executive order, two executives of Arch Trading immediately attempted to enter Iraq via Cyprus to install the laboratory equipment that had already been delivered. When that effort failed,

Arch Trading retained a Jordanian firm, Biomedical Technologies, Inc., to perform the installation. One of the Arch Trading executives who had earlier attempted to enter Iraq later joined Biomedical employees in Baghdad to help coordinate the installation, which was accomplished between October 24 and November 2, 1990. The travel expenses of both the Arch Trading executive and the Biomedical Technologies employees were reimbursed by Arch Trading, on authority of its president, Kamal Sadder, and upon completion of the installation, Biomedical Technologies was paid a bonus. . . .

Arch Trading's dealings with Iraq ultimately came to the attention of the United States Customs Service during an investigation into a shipment unrelated to this case. In late July 1990, customs agents discovered a personal computer at Dulles International Airport in Washington, D.C., that Arch Trading was shipping to Baghdad, Iraq, without proper documentation. During the course of the investigation the government questioned Arch Trading executives and subsequently executed a search warrant which led to the indictment and conviction in this case. This appeal followed.

II.

Arch Trading contends that it was improperly charged under 18 U.S.C. § 371. That section criminalizes conspiracies of two sorts: conspiracies *to commit an offense* against the United States and conspiracies *to defraud* the United States. Arch Trading was charged with, and convicted of, conspiring to commit an "offense" against the United States government. It asserts, however, it could only have been charged, if at all, with having conspired to "defraud" the United States, because violations of executive orders and regulations do not constitute an "offense." Arch Trading argues that the conspiracy count must therefore be dismissed, relying on *United States v. Minarik*, 875 F.2d 1186, 1193–94 (6th Cir.1989).

We reject this argument because we do not agree that violation of an executive order cannot constitute an offense as that term is used in 18 U.S.C. § 371. While it may be that executive orders cannot alone establish crimes, when such orders are duly authorized by an act of Congress and Congress specifies a criminal sanction for their violation, the consequence is different. In this case the International Emergency Economic Powers Act (IEEPA), 50 U.S.C. § 1701, *et seq.*, authorized the President to issue executive orders proscribing conduct, and 50 U.S.C. § 1705(b) makes criminal the disobedience of an order issued under the Act.[2] There is no question that violation of a federal criminal statute may properly be charged under the "offense" clause. We therefore hold that when Congress provides criminal sanctions for violations of executive orders that it empowers the President to issue, such violation constitutes an "offense" for the purposes of 18 U.S.C. § 371.

While Arch Trading's conduct could arguably have been charged also as a conspiracy "to defraud," the two prongs of § 371 are not mutually exclusive. Because of the broad interpretation which has been given the "defraud" clause,

---

[2] 50 U.S.C. § 1705(b) provides:

> Whoever willfully violates any license, order, or regulation issued under this chapter shall, upon conviction, be fined not more than $50,000, or, if a natural person, may be imprisoned for not more than ten years, or both; and any officer, director, or agent of any corporation who knowingly participates in such violation may be punished by a like fine, imprisonment, or both.

§ 371's two clauses overlap considerably. The wide breadth of the "defraud" clause has long been established:

> To conspire to defraud the United States means to cheat the government out of property or money, but it also means to interfere with or obstruct one of its lawful functions by deceit, craft or trickery, or at least by means that are dishonest. It is not necessary that the government shall be subjected to property or pecuniary loss by the fraud, but only that its legitimate official actions and purpose shall be defeated by misrepresentation, chicane, or the overreaching of those charged with carrying out the governmental intention.

Hammerschmidt v. United States, 265 U.S. 182, 188 (1924).

Because of this overlap, given conduct may be proscribed by both of the section's clauses. In such a situation, the fact that a particular course of conduct is chargeable under one clause does not render it immune from prosecution under the other. When both prongs of § 371 apply to the conduct with which a particular defendant is charged, the government enjoys considerable latitude in deciding how to proceed. *See United States v. Jones*, 976 F.2d 176, 183 (4th Cir.1992) ("[F]aced with two equally applicable penal statutes, there is nothing wrong with the government's decision [absent an improper purpose] to prosecute under one and not the other"). Convictions under the "defraud" clause for conspiracies *to commit particular offenses* are commonly upheld. Conversely, convictions under the "offense" clause for conspiracy to engage in conduct which would defraud the United States are also proper. Many courts have even found it permissible to list both prongs of § 371 in a single indictment count rather than specifying whether the alleged conspiracy was one to defraud or one to commit an offense.

The case upon which Arch Trading primarily relies, *United States v. Minarik*, is in no way inconsistent with our conclusions. In *Minarik*, the Sixth Circuit found that the prosecution had "used the defraud clause in a way that created great confusion about the conduct claimed to be illegal." *Minarik*, 875 F.2d at 1196. In light of the prejudice to the defendant that resulted from the confusion in that case, the Sixth Circuit reversed the defendant's conviction. *Id.* at 1186, 1193–96. As that court has since stressed, however, *Minarik* did not hold that the two clauses of § 371 are mutually exclusive, but only that in the case then before the court confusion prejudicial to the defendant had arisen from the government's choice of proceeding under the "defraud" clause. In cases such as the present one, however, where the defense will not be unfairly burdened by invocation of either clause, the prosecution may frame the indictment at its discretion.

In short, the evidence in this case against Arch Trading would have supported conviction under either the "offense" or the "defraud" clause, and absent an improper motive, which is not alleged here, the government's choice of invoking the offense clause was an appropriate exercise of discretion.

* * *

Affirmed.

Notes and Questions

1. *The "defraud" clause.* According to the court in *Arch Trading*, what is the scope of the defraud clause? When would a conspiracy to defraud not also be a conspiracy to commit an offense against the United States? In other words, does the defraud clause add anything to the statute? If so, what?

The defraud clause only applies when there is a sufficiently close connection between the criminal objective and the United States government. In *Tanner v. United States*, 483 U.S. 107 (1987), for example, the defendants defrauded a private corporation that received aid from the federal government. The Supreme Court held that, because the aid did not remain subject to government supervision, the federal aid did not provide a sufficient tie to the federal government to form the basis for a defraud clause conviction. In essence, the facts were not sufficient to show an intent to defraud the United States. *Id.* at 128–132.

2. *Choosing between the two theories.* When can the government proceed under the offense clause? Under the defraud clause? Can it use both theories in support of a single conspiracy charge? In what circumstances? Conversely, if both theories apply to the facts of a particular case, are there times when the government must choose one theory or the other? When?

3. *Punishment.* A conspiracy to commit an offense is punished as a felony where the object crime was a felony, and as a misdemeanor where the object crime was a misdemeanor. Conspiracies to defraud the United States, however, are punished as felonies. Why should this be so?

Problem

3-1. Defendant was a partner in a produce distribution business, Wholesale Foods Company, Inc. (Wholesale). Wholesale bought produce from the growers and sold it, almost exclusively, to Retail Foods Co. (Retail). Almost 90 percent of Retail's purchases were from Wholesale. Over the last five years, there was a sharp rise in the price of organic produce. At the same time, the overall prices of non-organic produce remained relatively constant.

Because of the price increase, Defendant decided last year to begin distributing organic produce, even though Defendant had no experience with the regulations governing such produce. In a scheme to turn a quick profit, Defendant agreed with Nick Barracuda, a produce grower, for Barracuda to deliver to Defendant non-organic produce fraudulently labeled as organic. Barracuda also had no previous experience with regulations governing organic produce. Defendant then sold this mislabeled produce to Retail. The difference between the actual value of non-organic produce sold and the price charged was $4.2 million.

Federal laws and regulations require accuracy in labeling organic produce sold in interstate commerce. The United States Department of Agriculture has the function of enforcing these standards, which Retail violated because of Defendant's and Barracuda's misrepresentations. Intentional violations of the regulations may be subject to criminal sanctions.

Defendant and Barracuda were charged with one count of violating 18 U.S.C. § 371. The indictment alleged, in the alternative, that the defendants conspired to defraud the United States and conspired to commit an offense against the United

States. Barracuda agreed to plead guilty and to testify against Defendant. By means of a general verdict, the jury convicted Defendant.

Defendant appeals the conviction. How should the court rule? Why?

[D] SCOPE OF THE CONSPIRACY

Under federal joinder rules, one defendant may be tried with another defendant only when the evidence shows that both defendants participated in "the same act or transaction or in the same series of acts or transactions." Fed. R. Crim. P. 8(b). Because the scope of a conspiracy is not always clear, defendants often argue that they were not part of the conspiracy charged by the government and thus cannot be jointly tried with the other defendants. In effect, the argument is that, instead of one grand conspiracy, there were two or more conspiracies constituting different crimes. Thus, the defendants argue, they should be tried at a separate trial for the smaller conspiracy rather than at a single trial for the grand conspiracy.

The following is the leading United States Supreme Court case on the issue of when the government has sufficiently pleaded and proven a single, overarching conspiracy. Note that, to prevail, the defendant must prove both that the government failed to prove a single conspiracy and that the error was prejudicial.

KOTTEAKOS v. UNITED STATES
328 U.S. 750 (1946)

MR. JUSTICE RUTLEDGE delivered the opinion of the Court.

The only question is whether petitioners have suffered substantial prejudice from being convicted of a single general conspiracy by evidence which the government admits proved not one conspiracy but some eight or more different ones of the same sort executed through a common key figure, Simon Brown. Petitioners were convicted under the general conspiracy section of the Criminal Code of conspiring to violate the provisions of the National Housing Act. . . .

The indictment named thirty-two defendants, including the petitioners.[1] The gist of the conspiracy, as alleged, was that the defendants had sought to induce various financial institutions to grant credit, with the intent that the loans or advances would then be offered to the Federal Housing Administration for insurance upon applications containing false and fraudulent information.

Of the thirty-two persons named in the indictment nineteen were brought to trial[3] and the names of thirteen were submitted to the jury.[4] Two were acquitted; the jury disagreed as to four; and the remaining seven, including petitioners, were found guilty.

Simon Brown, who pleaded guilty, was the common and key figure in all of the transactions proven. He was president of the Brownie Lumber Company. Having had experience in obtaining loans under the National Housing Act, he undertook to

---

[1] Four other persons were alleged to be conspirators but were not made defendants.

[3] As to four, a severance was granted. The indictment was nol-prossed as to one, and eight others pleaded guilty.

[4] One pleaded guilty during trial. The indictment was nol-prossed as to another, and a severance was ordered for a third. Verdicts of acquittal were directed as to three others.

act as broker in placing for others loans for modernization and renovation, charging a five per cent commission for his services. Brown knew, when he obtained the loans, that the proceeds were not to be used for the purposes stated in the applications.

In May, 1939, petitioner Lekacos told Brown that he wished to secure a loan in order to finance opening a law office, to say the least a hardly auspicious professional launching. Brown made out the application, as directed by Lekacos, to state that the purpose of the loan was to modernize a house belonging to the estate of Lekacos' father. Lekacos obtained the money. Later in the same year Lekacos secured another loan through Brown, the application being in the names of his brother and sister-in-law. Lekacos also received part of the proceeds of a loan for which one Gerakeris, a defendant who pleaded guilty, had applied.

In June, 1939, Lekacos sent Brown an application for a loan signed by petitioner Kotteakos. It contained false statements. Brown placed the loan, and Kotteakos thereafter sent Brown applications on behalf of other persons. Two were made out in the names of fictitious persons. The proceeds were received by Kotteakos and petitioner Regenbogen, his partner in the cigarette and pinball machine business. Regenbogen, together with Kotteakos, had indorsed one of the applications. Kotteakos also sent to Brown an application for a loan in Regenbogen's name. This was for modernization of property not owned by Regenbogen. The latter, however, repaid the money in about three months after he received it.

The evidence against the other defendants whose cases were submitted to the jury was similar in character. They too had transacted business with Brown relating to National Housing Act loans. But no connection was shown between them and petitioners, other than that Brown had been the instrument in each instance for obtaining the loans. In many cases the other defendants did not have any relationship with one another, other than Brown's connection with each transaction. As the Circuit Court of Appeals said, there were "at least eight, and perhaps more, separate and independent groups, none of which had any connection with any other, though all dealt independently with Brown as their agent." As the government puts it, the pattern was "that of separate spokes meeting at a common center," though we may add without the rim of the wheel to enclose the spokes.

The proof therefore admittedly made out a case, not of a single conspiracy, but of several, notwithstanding only one was charged in the indictment. The Court of Appeals aptly drew analogy in the comment, "Thieves who dispose of their loot to a single receiver — a single 'fence' — do not by that fact alone become confederates: they may, but it takes more than knowledge that he is a 'fence' to make them such." It stated that the trial judge "was plainly wrong in supposing that upon the evidence there could be a single conspiracy; and in the view he took of the law, he should have dismissed the indictment." Nevertheless the appellate court held the error not prejudicial, saying among other things that "especially since guilt was so manifest, it was 'proper' to join the conspiracies," and "to reverse the conviction would be a miscarriage of justice." This is indeed the government's entire position. It does not now contend that there was no variance in proof from the single conspiracy charged in the indictment. Admitting that separate and distinct conspiracies were shown, it urges that the variance was not prejudicial to the petitioners.

* * *

If, when all is said and done, the conviction is sure that the error did not influence the jury, or had but very slight effect, the verdict and the judgment should stand, except perhaps where the departure is from a constitutional norm or a specific command of Congress. But if one cannot say, with fair assurance, after pondering all that happened without stripping the erroneous action from the whole, that the judgment was not substantially swayed by the error, it is impossible to conclude that substantial rights were not affected. The inquiry cannot be merely whether there was enough to support the result, apart from the phase affected by the error. It is rather, even so, whether the error itself had substantial influence. If so, or if one is left in grave doubt, the conviction cannot stand.

*   *   *

The government's theory seems to be, in ultimate logical reach, that the error presented by the variance is insubstantial and harmless, if the evidence offered specifically and properly to convict each defendant would be sufficient to sustain his conviction, if submitted in a separate trial. For reasons we have stated and in view of the authorities cited, this is not and cannot be the test. But in apparent support of its view the government argues that there was no prejudice here because the results show that the jury exercised discrimination as among the defendants whose cases were submitted to it. As it points out, the jury acquitted some, disagreed as to others, and found still others guilty. From this it concludes that the jury was not confused and, apparently, reached the same result as would have been reached or would be likely, if the convicted defendants had been or now should be tried separately.

One difficulty with this is that the trial court itself was confused in the charge which it gave to guide the jury in deliberation. The court instructed:

> The indictment charges but one conspiracy, and to convict each of the defendants of a conspiracy, the government would have to prove, and you would have to find, that each of the defendants was a member of that conspiracy. You cannot divide it up. It is one conspiracy, and the question is whether or not each of the defendants or which of the defendants, are members of that conspiracy.

On its face, as the Court of Appeals said, this portion of the charge was plainly wrong in application to the proof made; and the error pervaded the entire charge, not merely the portion quoted. The jury could not possibly have found, upon the evidence, that there was only one conspiracy. The trial court was of the view that one conspiracy was made out by showing that each defendant was linked to Brown in one or more transactions, and that it was possible on the evidence for the jury to conclude that all were in a common adventure because of this fact and the similarity of purpose presented in the various applications for loans.

This view, specifically embodied throughout the instructions, obviously confuses the common purpose of a single enterprise with the several, though similar, purposes of numerous separate adventures of like character. It may be that, notwithstanding the misdirection, the jury actually understood correctly the purport of the evidence, as the government now concedes it to have been; and came to the conclusion that the petitioners were guilty only of the separate conspiracies in which the proof shows they respectively participated. But, in the face of the misdirection and in the circumstances of this case, we cannot assume that the lay triers of fact were so well informed upon the law or that they disregarded the permission expressly given to ignore that vital difference.

As we have said, the error permeated the entire charge, indeed the entire trial. Not only did it permit the jury to find each defendant guilty of conspiring with thirty-five other potential co-conspirators, or any less number as the proof might turn out for acquittal of some, when none of the evidence would support such a conviction, as the proof did turn out in fact. It had other effects. One was to prevent the court from giving a precautionary instruction such as would be appropriate, perhaps, required, in cases where related but separate conspiracies are tried together, namely, that the jury should take care to consider the evidence relating to each conspiracy separately from that relating to each other conspiracy charged. The court here was careful to caution the jury to consider each defendant's case separately, in determining his participation in "the scheme" charged. But this obviously does not, and could not, go to keeping distinct conspiracies distinct, in view of the court's conception of the case.

Moreover, the effect of the court's misconception extended also to the proof of overt acts. Carrying forward his premise that the jury could find one conspiracy on the evidence, the trial judge further charged that, if the jury found a conspiracy, "then the acts or the statements of any of those whom you so find to be conspirators between the two dates that I have mentioned, may be considered by you in evidence as against all of the defendants whom you so find to be members of the conspiracy." The instructions in this phase also declared: "It is not necessary, as a matter of law, that an overt act be charged against each defendant. It is sufficient if the conspiracy be established and the defendant be found to be a member of the conspiracy — it is sufficient to allege overt acts on the part of any others who may have been members of the conspiracy, if those acts were done in furtherance of, and for the purpose of accomplishing the conspiracy."

On those instructions it was competent not only for the jury to find that all of the defendants were parties to a single common plan, design and scheme, where none was shown by the proof, but also for them to impute to each defendant the acts and statements of the others without reference to whether they related to one of the schemes proven or another, and to find an overt act affecting all in conduct which admittedly could only have affected some. We do not understand how it can be concluded, in the face of the instruction, that the jury considered and was influenced by nothing else.

* * *

Numbers are vitally important in trial, especially in criminal matters. Guilt with us remains individual and personal, even as respects conspiracies. It is not a matter of mass application. There are times when of necessity, because of the nature and scope of the particular federation, large numbers of persons taking part must be tried together or perhaps not at all, at any rate as respects some. When many conspire, they invite mass trial by their conduct. Even so, the proceedings are exceptional to our tradition and call for use of every safeguard to individualize each defendant in his relation to the mass. Wholly different is it with those who join together with only a few, though many others may be doing the same and though some of them may line up with more than one group.

Criminal they may be, but it is not the criminality of mass conspiracy. They do not invite mass trial by their conduct. Nor does our system tolerate it. That way lies the drift toward totalitarian institutions. True, this may be inconvenient for prosecution. But our government is not one of mere convenience or efficiency. It too has a stake, with every citizen, in his being afforded our historic individual protections, including those surrounding criminal trials. About them we dare not become careless or complacent when that fashion has become rampant over the earth.

Here toleration went too far. We do not think that either Congress intended to authorize the government to string together, for common trial, eight or more separate and distinct crimes, conspiracies related in kind though they might be, when the only nexus among them lies in the fact that one man participated in all. Leeway there must be for [cases] where proof may not accord with exact specifications in indictments. Otherwise criminal conspirators never could be brought to halt. But if the practice here followed were to stand, we see nothing to prevent its extension to a dozen, a score, or more conspiracies and at the same time to scores of men involved, if at all, only separately in them. The dangers for transference of guilt from one to another across the line separating conspiracies, subconsciously or otherwise, are so great that no one really can say prejudice to substantial right has not taken place. The line must be drawn somewhere.

*   *   *

Accordingly the judgments are reversed and the causes are remanded for further proceedings in conformity with this opinion.

Reversed.

MR. JUSTICE DOUGLAS, with whom MR. JUSTICE REED agrees, dissenting.

It is clear that there was error in the charge. An examination of the record in *Berger v. United States*, 295 U.S. 78 (1935), shows that the same erroneous instructions were in fact given in that case. But I do not think the error "substantially injured" the defendants in this case any more than it did in the *Berger* case.

Whether injury results from the joinder of several conspiracies depends on the special circumstances of each case. Situations can easily be imagined where confusion on the part of the jury is likely by reason of the sheer number of conspirators and the complexities of the facts which spell out the series of conspiracies. The evidence relating to one defendant may be used to convict another.

Those possibilities seem to be non-existent here. Nothing in the testimony of the other defendants even remotely implicated petitioners in the other frauds. Nothing in the evidence connected petitioners with the other defendants, except Brown, in the slightest way. On the record no implication of guilt by reason of a mass trial can be found. The dangers which petitioners conjure up are abstract ones.

Moreover, the true picture of the case is not thirty-two defendants engaging in eight or more different conspiracies which were lumped together as one. The jury convicted only four persons in addition to petitioners. The other defendants and the evidence concerning them were in effect eliminated from the case. We have then a case of two closely related conspiracies involving petitioners and two additional conspiracies in which petitioners played no part — but all of the same character and revolving around the same central figure, Brown. And the strong and irresistible inference that the jury was not confused is bolstered by their failure to convict six of the thirteen defendants on trial before them.

*   *   *

NOTES AND QUESTIONS

1. *Advantages of a "mass" trial.* Why would the government choose to bring a case like *Kotteakos* rather than bringing a number of separate trials? Would it not be simpler and more straightforward to bring separate trials? If you were the prosecutor in the case, how would you structure such a case? Why?

2. *Reversible error.* Even if the defendant shows that the case was improperly charged and tried as a single conspiracy, is a reversal necessarily required? What was the basis for the government's argument that the conviction should have been affirmed in *Kotteakos*? Why did the Court reject the argument? Although the Court in *Kotteakos* reversed the conviction, most defendants fail to obtain a reversal even if the appeals court finds that multiple conspiracies were improperly charged as a single conspiracy. If you were the trial judge in a similar case, what would your incentives be when confronted with such arguments?

3. *Mandatory vs. discretionary severance.* Rule 8(b) provides that defendants may be joined if the government sufficiently alleges that they participated in "the same act or transaction or in the same series of acts or transactions." If a defendant has been misjoined, then the trial judge *must* sever that defendant's trial under Rule 8(b).

Even if joinder is proper under Rule 8(b), a trial judge has the *discretion* to grant the defendant a separate trial under Fed. R. Crim. P. 14, in the interest of fairness. A judge might grant such an order, for example, as to a minor defendant, where there is substantial evidence that is only admissible against the principal defendants. Defendants in conspiracy trials frequently bring Rule 14 motions, but such motions rarely succeed. Why do you think this is so?

4. *Wheels and chains.* What if an alleged co-conspirator knows of the existence of other participants, but does not know their identities? Is that sufficient? In *Blumenthal v. United States*, 332 U.S. 539 (1947), defendants were charged with conspiracy to sell whiskey at illegal prices. The alleged conspiracy was comprised of the owner of the whiskey, two distributors, and two salespeople. The salespeople argued that they did not know each other or the owner, and could not have conspired with each other or the owner. The Court rejected the argument, finding it sufficient that the salespeople knew that they were selling portions of one large lot of whiskey and thus that others were involved. The *Blumenthal*-type conspiracy is often charged in narcotics cases, and has come to be known as a "chain" conspiracy.

In a "chain" conspiracy case — as compared with a *Kotteakos*-type "wheel" conspiracy case — the government seeks to show that each participant in the conspiracy constituted a "link." The various links can be charged as part of a single conspiracy so long as each link was aware of the other links' existence. In both types of conspiracies, the government must prove that each co-conspirator knew that the other conspirators existed but need not prove that each co-conspirator knew the identities of the other co-conspirators. "Wheel" and "chain" analysis is often used in white collar cases. In many cases, large conspiracies may be too complex to fit neatly within either category.

PROBLEM

3-2. Larson was an associate at a large New York law firm. After a couple of years with the firm, Larson decided to leave the practice of law and to become a securities broker. To that end and while still at the firm, Larson began to observe "new matter" memos, confidential documents that were circulated among attorneys at the law firm announcing new business. In this way, Larson was able to determine when companies were involved in transactions that had the strong potential to affect stock prices. Larson discussed this information with acquaintances in the securities industry in order to curry their favor.

In violation of federal securities laws, Larson personally gave confidential "new matter" information to Bond, a principal at a major securities firm. Bond used this information to trade on stocks, at a substantial profit. Larson also gave the information to Larson's friend Asher, who worked at a different securities firm. Asher gave the information to Asher's boss, Thompson. Thompson also traded in the stock of the companies discussed, again making a substantial profit. Thompson and Larson were casual acquaintances, but the two never discussed the "new matter" information.

Larson, Asher, Bond, and Thompson were indicted for conspiracy to commit insider trading in violation of the federal securities laws. Larson and Asher agreed to plead guilty, and to testify against Bond and Thompson.

At trial, Larson admitted giving the stolen, secret information directly to Bond and to Asher, but denied ever speaking directly with Thompson. Asher admitted getting the information and passing along both the substance of the tips and the source (Larson) to Thompson, though Thompson denied hearing the source of the information.

There is no evidence that Bond and Thompson ever discussed the information from Larson. Larson did testify that Larson was visiting Bond at Bond's office one day, and that Thompson happened to be there paying a social visit to Bond. According to Larson, Thompson said to Larson, "What are you doing here? Shouldn't you be at the law firm?"

At the end of the government's case, Bond and Thompson moved to dismiss the conspiracy count or, in the alternative, to sever their trials. How should the court rule? Why?

[E] DURATION OF A CONSPIRACY

Because the crime of conspiracy essentially rests on a meeting of the minds, it can only begin when the agreement is formed and, if the statute requires, when an overt act is committed. Determining when a conspiracy ends, however, is more complicated. The first case below deals with the issue of when a conspiracy terminates.

[1] Defining the Termination Point

UNITED STATES v. JIMENEZ RECIO
537 U.S. 270 (2003)

JUSTICE BREYER delivered the opinion of the Court.

We here consider the validity of a Ninth Circuit rule that a conspiracy ends automatically when the object of the conspiracy becomes impossible to achieve — when, for example, the Government frustrates a drug conspiracy's objective by seizing the drugs that its members have agreed to distribute. In our view, conspiracy law does not contain any such "automatic termination" rule.

I.

In *United States v. Cruz*, 127 F.3d 791, 795 (9th Cir 1997), the Ninth Circuit, following the language of an earlier case, *United States v. Castro*, 972 F.2d 1107, 1112 (9th Cir. 1992), wrote that a conspiracy terminates when " 'there is affirmative evidence of abandonment, withdrawal, disavowal *or defeat of the object of the conspiracy*' " (emphasis added). It considered the conviction of an individual who, the Government had charged, joined a conspiracy (to distribute drugs) after the Government had seized the drugs in question. The Circuit found that the Government's seizure of the drugs guaranteed the "defeat" of the conspiracy's objective, namely, drug distribution. The Circuit held that the conspiracy had terminated with that "defeat," *i.e.*, when the Government seized the drugs. Hence the individual, who had joined the conspiracy after that point, could not be convicted as a conspiracy member.

In this case the lower courts applied the *Cruz* rule to similar facts: On November 18, 1997, police stopped a truck in Nevada. They found, and seized, a large stash of illegal drugs. With the help of the truck's two drivers, they set up a sting. The Government took the truck to the drivers' destination, a mall in Idaho. The drivers paged a contact and described the truck's location. The contact said that he would call someone to get the truck. And three hours later, the two defendants, Francisco Jimenez Recio and Adrian Lopez-Meza, appeared in a car. Jimenez Recio drove away in the truck; Lopez-Meza drove the car away in a similar direction. Police stopped both vehicles and arrested both men.

A federal grand jury indicted Jimenez Recio, Lopez-Meza, and the two original truck drivers, charging them with having conspired, together and with others, to possess and to distribute unlawful drugs. . . . [A jury convicted the defendants.]

Jimenez Recio and Lopez-Meza appealed [their convictions]. They pointed out that, given *Cruz*, the jury had to find that they had joined the conspiracy before the Nevada stop, and they claimed that the evidence was insufficient at both trials to warrant any such jury finding. The Ninth Circuit panel . . . agreed. The Government sought certiorari. It noted that the Ninth Circuit's holding in this case was premised upon the legal rule enunciated in *Cruz*. And it asked us to decide the rule's validity, *i.e.*, to decide whether "a conspiracy ends as a matter of law when the government frustrates its objective." We agreed to consider that question.

II.

In *Cruz*, the Ninth Circuit held that a conspiracy continues " 'until there is affirmative evidence of abandonment, withdrawal, disavowal or defeat of the object of the conspiracy.' " 127 F.3d at 795 (quoting *Castro*, 972 F.2d at 1112). The critical portion of this statement is the last segment, that a conspiracy ends once there has been "defeat of [its] object." The Circuit's holdings make clear that the phrase means that the conspiracy ends through "defeat" when the Government intervenes, making the conspiracy's goals impossible to achieve, even if the conspirators do not know that the Government has intervened and are totally unaware that the conspiracy is bound to fail. In our view, this statement of the law is incorrect. A conspiracy does not automatically terminate simply because the Government, unbeknownst to some of the conspirators, has "defeat[ed]" the conspiracy's "object."

Two basic considerations convince us that this is the proper view of the law. First, the Ninth Circuit's rule is inconsistent with our own understanding of basic conspiracy law. The Court has repeatedly said that the essence of a conspiracy is "an agreement to commit an unlawful act." *Iannelli v. United States*, 420 U.S. 770, 777 (1975). That agreement is "a distinct evil," which "may exist and be punished whether or not the substantive crime ensues." *Salinas v. United States*, 522 U.S. 52, 65 (1997). The conspiracy poses a "threat to the public" over and above the threat of the commission of the relevant substantive crime — both because the "[c]ombination in crime makes more likely the commission of [other] crimes" and because it "decreases the probability that the individuals involved will depart from their path of criminality." *Callanan v. United States*, 364 U.S. 587, 593–594 (1961). Where police have frustrated a conspiracy's specific objective but conspirators (unaware of that fact) have neither abandoned the conspiracy nor withdrawn, these special conspiracy-related dangers remain. *Cf.* 2 W. LaFave & A. Scott, Substantive Criminal Law § 6.5, p. 85 (1986) ("[i]mpossibility" does not terminate conspiracy because "criminal combinations are dangerous apart from the danger of attaining the particular objective"). So too remains the essence of the conspiracy — the agreement to commit the crime. That being so, the Government's defeat of the conspiracy's objective will not necessarily and automatically terminate the conspiracy.

Second, the view we endorse today is the view of almost all courts and commentators but for the Ninth Circuit. No other Federal Court of Appeals has adopted the Ninth Circuit's rule. Three have explicitly rejected it. . . .

The *Cruz* majority argued that the more traditional termination rule threatened "endless" potential liability. To illustrate the point, the majority posited a sting in which police instructed an arrested conspirator to go through the "telephone directory . . . [and] call all of his acquaintances" to come and help him, with the Government obtaining convictions of those who did so. The problem with this example, however, is that, even though it is not necessarily an example of entrapment itself, it draws its persuasive force from the fact that it bears certain resemblances to entrapment. The law independently forbids convictions that rest upon entrapment. And the example fails to explain why a different branch of the law, conspiracy law, should be modified to forbid entrapment-like behavior that falls outside the bounds of current entrapment law. At the same time, the *Cruz* rule would reach well beyond arguable police misbehavior, potentially threatening the use of properly run law enforcement sting operations. . . .

III.

We conclude that the Ninth Circuit's conspiracy-termination law holding set forth in *Cruz* is erroneous in the manner discussed. We reverse the present judgment insofar as it relies upon that holding.

NOTES AND QUESTIONS

1. *Why have the crime of conspiracy?* According to the Court in *Jimenez Recio*, what particular danger does the crime of conspiracy address? Does prosecution of the defendants in this case fulfill those aims? Why? According to the Court, what would the problem be for law enforcement if the Ninth Circuit's approach had prevailed? Are the Court's concerns valid? Why?

2. *Duration of a conspiracy.* A conspiracy begins upon the agreement and, where required, the commission of an overt act in furtherance of the conspiracy. According to the Court, when exactly does a conspiracy end?

[2]　The Implications of Termination

Determining when a conspiracy ends may have important implications for the defendant. For example, the end of a conspiracy will trigger the running of the statute of limitations. In addition, a conspiracy charge provides important evidentiary advantages to the prosecution, including an expanded application of relevancy and the admissibility of co-conspirators' statements.[d] Those advantages will not apply to evidence of acts that occurred after the conspiracy ended. The next case deals with the admissibility of a co-conspirator's statement. Pay particular attention to Justice Jackson's concurring opinion, which contains perhaps the most often-cited critique of modern conspiracy law.

KRULEWITCH v. UNITED STATES
336 U.S. 440 (1949)

MR. JUSTICE BLACK delivered the opinion of the Court.

A federal district court indictment charged in three counts that petitioner and a woman defendant had (1) induced and persuaded another woman to go on October 20, 1941, from New York City to Miami, Florida, for the purpose of prostitution, in violation of 18 U.S.C. § 399 [now § 2422]; (2) transported or caused her to be transported from New York to Miami for that purpose, in violation of 18 U.S.C. § 398 [now § 2421]; and (3) conspired to commit those offenses in violation of 18 U.S.C. § 88 [now § 371]. Tried alone, the petitioner was convicted on all three counts of the indictment. The Court of Appeals affirmed. We granted certiorari limiting our review to consideration of alleged error in admission of certain hearsay testimony against petitioner over his timely and repeated objections.

The challenged testimony was elicited by the Government from its complaining witness, the person whom petitioner and the woman defendant allegedly induced to go from New York to Florida for the purpose of prostitution. The testimony narrated the following purported conversation between the complaining witness

---

[d] A "co-conspirator statement" would normally be considered hearsay and would be inadmissible. Recall that "hearsay" includes a statement that is (a) made out of court by one person (the "declarant"), (b) repeated in court by another person (the witness), and (c) offered for its truth. Such statements are generally inadmissible because they are unreliable and because the declarant is not available for cross-examination. Rule 801(d)(2)(E) of the Federal Rules of Evidence, however, provides that such a statement may be admissible under the "co-conspirators' exception" if the party offering the statement shows that it was "made by the coconspirator of a party during the course of and in furtherance of the conspiracy." This exception exists both because co-conspirators are considered agents who adopt each other's statements, and because prosecutors need leeway in proving what is essentially a mental crime.

and petitioner's alleged coconspirator, the woman defendant.

> "She asked me, she says, 'You didn't talk yet?' And I says, 'No.' And she says, 'Well, don't,' she says, 'until we get you a lawyer.' And then she says, 'Be very careful what you say.' And I can't put it in exact words. But she said, 'It would be better for us two girls to take the blame than Kay [the defendant] because he couldn't stand it, he couldn't stand to take it.' "

The time of the alleged conversation was more than a month and a half after October 20, 1941, the date the complaining witness had gone to Miami. Whatever original conspiracy may have existed between petitioner and his alleged coconspirator to cause the complaining witness to go to Florida in October, 1941, no longer existed when the reported conversation took place in December, 1941. For on this latter date the trip to Florida had not only been made — the complaining witness had left Florida, had returned to New York, and had resumed her residence there. Furthermore, at the time the conversation took place, the complaining witness, the alleged coconspirator, and the petitioner had been arrested. They apparently were charged in a United States District Court of Florida with the offense of which petitioner was here convicted.

It is beyond doubt that the central aim of the alleged conspiracy — transportation of the complaining witness to Florida for prostitution — had either never existed or had long since ended in success or failure when and if the alleged coconspirator made the statement attributed to her. The statement plainly implied that petitioner was guilty of the crime for which he was on trial. It was made in petitioner's absence and the Government made no effort whatever to show that it was made with his authority. The testimony thus stands as an unsworn, out-of-court declaration of petitioner's guilt. This hearsay declaration, attributed to a coconspirator, was not made pursuant to and in furtherance of objectives of the conspiracy charged in the indictment, because if made, it was after those objectives either had failed or had been achieved. Under these circumstances, the hearsay declaration attributed to the alleged coconspirator was not admissible on the theory that it was made in furtherance of the alleged criminal transportation undertaking.

Although the Government recognizes that the chief objective of the conspiracy — transportation for prostitution purposes — had ended in success or failure before the reported conversation took place, it nevertheless argues for admissibility of the hearsay declaration as one in furtherance of a continuing subsidiary objective of the conspiracy. Its argument runs this way. Conspirators about to commit crimes always expressly or implicitly agree to collaborate with each other to conceal facts in order to prevent detection, conviction and punishment. Thus the argument is that even after the central criminal objectives of a conspiracy have succeeded or failed, an implicit subsidiary phase of the conspiracy always survives, the phase which has concealment as its sole objective. . . .

We cannot accept the Government's contention. There are many logical and practical reasons that could be advanced against a special evidentiary rule that permits out-of-court statements of one conspirator to be used against another. But however cogent these reasons, it is firmly established that where made in furtherance of the objectives of a going conspiracy, such statements are admissible as exceptions to the hearsay rule. This prerequisite to admissibility, that hearsay statements by some conspirators to be admissible against others must be made in furtherance of the conspiracy charged, has been scrupulously observed by federal courts. The Government now asks us to expand this narrow exception to the hearsay rule and hold admissible a declaration, not made in furtherance of the alleged criminal transportation conspiracy charged, but made in furtherance of an alleged implied but uncharged conspiracy aimed at preventing detection and punishment. . . . The rule contended for by the Government could have far-reaching results. For under this rule plausible arguments could generally be made in conspiracy cases that most out-of-court statements offered in evidence tended to shield coconspirators. We are not persuaded to adopt the Government's implicit conspiracy theory which in all criminal conspiracy cases would create automatically a further breach of the general rule against the admission of hearsay evidence.

It is contended that the statement attributed to the alleged coconspirator was merely cumulative evidence, that without the statement the case against petitioner was so strong that we should hold the error harmless. In *Kotteakos v. United States*, 328 U.S. 750 (1946), we said that error should not be held harmless under the harmless error statute if upon consideration of the record the court is left in grave doubt as to whether the error had substantial influence in bringing about a verdict. We have such doubt here. The Florida District Court grand jury failed to indict. After indictment in New York petitioner was tried four times with the following results: mistrial; conviction; mistrial; conviction with recommendation for leniency. The revolting type of charges made against this petitioner by the complaining witness makes it difficult to believe that a jury convinced of a strong case against him would have recommended leniency. There was corroborative evidence of the complaining witness on certain phases of the case. But as to all vital phases, those involving the sordid criminal features, the jury was compelled to choose between believing the petitioner or the complaining witness. The record persuades us that the jury's task was difficult at best. We cannot say that the erroneous admission of the hearsay declaration may not have been the weight that tipped the scales against petitioner.

Reversed.

MR. JUSTICE JACKSON, concurring in the judgment and opinion of the Court.

This case illustrates a present drift in the federal law of conspiracy which warrants some further comment because it is characteristic of the long evolution of that elastic, sprawling and pervasive offense. Its history exemplifies the "tendency of a principle to expand itself to the limit of its logic." The unavailing protest of courts against the growing habit to indict for conspiracy in lieu of prosecuting for the substantive offense itself, or in addition thereto, suggests that loose practice as to this offense constitutes a serious threat to fairness in our administration of justice.

The modern crime of conspiracy is so vague that it almost defies definition.[3] Despite certain elementary and essential elements, it also, chameleon-like, takes on a special coloration from each of the many independent offenses on which it may be overlaid. It is always "predominantly mental in composition" because it consists primarily of a meeting of minds and an intent.

---

[3] Albert J. Harno, *Intent in Criminal Conspiracy*, 89 U. Pa. L. Rev. 624: "In the long category of crimes there is none, not excepting criminal attempt, more difficult to confine within the boundaries of definitive statement than conspiracy." An English author — Wright, The Law of Criminal Conspiracies, p. 11 — gives up with the remark: "But no intelligible definition of 'conspiracy' has yet been established."

*   *   *

It is not intended to question that the basic conspiracy principle has some place in modern criminal law, because to unite, back of a criminal purpose, the strength, opportunities and resources of many is obviously more dangerous and more difficult to police than the efforts of a lone wrongdoer. However, even when appropriately invoked, the looseness and pliability of the doctrine present inherent dangers which should be in the background of judicial thought wherever it is sought to extend the doctrine to meet the exigencies of a particular case.

*   *   *

A recent tendency has appeared in this Court to expand this elastic offense and to facilitate its proof. In *Pinkerton v. United States*, 328 U.S. 640, it sustained a conviction of a substantive crime where there was no proof of participation in or knowledge of it, upon the novel and dubious theory that conspiracy is equivalent in law to aiding and abetting.

*   *   *

Of course, it is for prosecutors rather than courts to determine when to use a scatter-gun to bring down the defendant, but there are procedural advantages from using it which add to the danger of unguarded extension of the concept.

An accused, under the Sixth Amendment, has the right to trial "by an impartial jury of the State and district wherein the crime shall have been committed." The leverage of a conspiracy charge lifts this limitation from the prosecution and reduces its protection to a phantom, for the crime is considered so vagrant as to have been committed in any district where any one of the conspirators did any one of the acts, however innocent, intended to accomplish its object. The Government may, and often does, compel one to defend at a great distance from any place he ever did any act because some accused confederate did some trivial and by itself innocent act in the chosen district. Circumstances may even enable the prosecution to fix the place of trial in Washington, D. C., where a defendant may lawfully be put to trial before a jury partly or even wholly made up of employees of the Government that accuses him.

When the trial starts, the accused feels the full impact of the conspiracy strategy. Strictly, the prosecution should first establish prima facie the conspiracy and identify the conspirators, after which evidence of acts and declarations of each in the course of its execution are admissible against all. But the order of proof of so sprawling a charge is difficult for a judge to control. As a practical matter, the accused often is confronted with a hodgepodge of acts and statements by others which he may never have authorized or intended or even known about, but which help to persuade the jury of existence of the conspiracy itself. In other words, a conspiracy often is proved by evidence that is admissible only upon assumption that conspiracy existed. The naive assumption that prejudicial effects can be overcome by instructions to the jury all practicing lawyers know to be unmitigated fiction. . . .

The trial of a conspiracy charge doubtless imposes a heavy burden on the prosecution, but it is an especially difficult situation for the defendant. The hazard from loose application of rules of evidence is aggravated where the Government institutes mass trials. Moreover, in federal practice there is no rule preventing conviction on uncorroborated testimony of accomplices, as there are in many jurisdictions, and the most comfort a defendant can expect is that the court can be induced to follow the "better practice" and caution the jury against "too much reliance upon the testimony of accomplices." *Caminetti v. United States*, 242 U.S. 470, 495 (1917).

A co-defendant in a conspiracy trial occupies an uneasy seat. There generally will be evidence of wrongdoing by somebody. It is difficult for the individual to make his own case stand on its own merits in the minds of jurors who are ready to believe that birds of a feather are flocked together. If he is silent, he is taken to admit it and if, as often happens, co-defendants can be prodded into accusing or contradicting each other, they convict each other. There are many practical difficulties in defending against a charge of conspiracy which I will not enumerate.

Against this inadequately sketched background, I think the decision of this case in the court below introduced an ominous expansion of the accepted law of conspiracy. The prosecution was allowed to incriminate the defendant by means of the prostitute's recital of a conversation with defendant's alleged co-conspirator, who was not on trial. The conversation was said to have taken place after the substantive offense was accomplished, after the defendant, the co-conspirator and the witness had all been arrested, and after the witness and the other two had a falling out. The Court of Appeals sustained its admission upon grounds stated as follows: "We think that implicit in a conspiracy to violate the law is an agreement among the conspirators to conceal the violation after as well as before the illegal plan is consummated."

* * *

I do not see the slightest warrant for judicially introducing a doctrine of implied crimes or constructive conspiracies. . . .

There is, of course, strong temptation to relax rigid standards when it seems the only way to sustain convictions of evildoers. But statutes authorize prosecution for substantive crimes for most evil-doing without the dangers to the liberty of the individual and the integrity of the judicial process that are inherent in conspiracy charges. We should disapprove the doctrine of implied or constructive crime in its entirety and in every manifestation. And I think there should be no straining to uphold any conspiracy conviction where prosecution for the substantive offense is adequate and the purpose served by adding the conspiracy charge seems chiefly to get procedural advantages to ease the way to conviction.

Although a reversal after four trials is, of course, regrettable, I cannot overlook the error as a harmless one. But I should concur in reversal even if less sure that prejudice resulted, for it is better that the crime go unwhipped of justice than that this theory of implied continuance of conspiracy find lodgment in our law, either by affirmance or by tolerance. Few instruments of injustice can equal that of implied or presumed or constructive crimes. The most odious of all oppressions are those which mask as justice.

NOTES AND QUESTIONS

1. *The hearsay rule.* What did Justice Jackson mean when he said that "a conspiracy often is proved by evidence that is admissible only upon assumption that conspiracy existed"? Note that the government may adduce co-conspirator statements even before the conspiracy has been proven beyond a reasonable doubt

at trial, so long as it has established that (a) a conspiracy existed by a preponderance of the evidence and (b) the defendant and declarant were members of the conspiracy when the statement was made. And under *Bourjaily v. United States*, 483 U.S. 171 (1987), the trial court may use a co-conspirator's statement to decide whether the government has made such a showing.

Most courts require, however, that the government adduce further proof — in addition to the co-conspirator's statement — of the existence of the conspiracy. *See, e.g., United States v. Silverman*, 861 F.2d 571 (9th Cir. 1988).

2. *The advantages of a conspiracy charge.* In his concurring opinion, Justice Jackson identified several ways in which a conspiracy charge advantages the government: (a) co-conspirator liability under the *Pinkerton* doctrine (discussed more fully below); (b) flexible venue rules; (c) the admissibility of co-conspirator statements; and (d) the tactical advantages flowing from the joining of multiple defendants at a single trial. Another advantage, discussed in the *Kotteakos* case, is the broadened scope of relevant evidence in a conspiracy case. Can you specify exactly how these factors may assist the government in a conspiracy case? Are these advantages unfair to defendants? Why or why not?

3. *Statute of limitations.* A conspiracy charge can extend the limitations period for bringing the charge in some cases. The five-year limitations period for conspiracy does not begin to run until the commission of the last overt act, even if the criminal objectives have all been achieved and even if charges for object offenses would be time-barred. Thus, all co-conspirators may be charged with the crime of conspiracy if at least one co-conspirator committed an overt act within five years of the indictment.

What flexibility does a prosecutor have in alleging the *starting point* of a conspiracy? Would it be appropriate for a prosecutor, in order to extend the limitations period, to allege that the conspiracy began even after the agreement was formed and an overt act that was committed? Similarly, how much discretion should a prosecutor have in picking the last overt act?

4. *Is conspiracy necessary?* As seen by Justice Jackson's opinion, conspiracy is a controversial crime that has been deemed by some to be unnecessary. *See* Phillip E. Johnson, *The Unnecessary Crime of Conspiracy*, 61 Cal. L. Rev. 1137 (1973). Nonetheless, the crime remains deeply rooted in both federal and state penal codes. Why is this so? Does the Court's opinion in *Krulewitch* provide the answer?

5. *Withdrawal.*

a. *The test for withdrawal.* Even if a conspiracy has not been concluded, an individual co-conspirator may withdraw from the conspiracy. In *United States v. United States Gypsum Co.*, 438 U.S. 422, 464–465 (1978), the Supreme Court held that an effective withdrawal requires that a co-conspirator commit "affirmative acts inconsistent with the object of the conspiracy and communicated in a manner reasonably calculated to reach coconspirators." The defendant need not notify law enforcement or otherwise attempt to prevent the crime from occurring. If the defendant continued to benefit from the conspiracy even after attempting to withdraw, however, the withdrawal will not be effective.

b. *The effects of withdrawal.* Although the withdrawal will not affect the co-conspirator's liability for the crime of conspiracy, it may nonetheless have important consequences for that person: (i) the statute of limitations will begin to run as of the withdrawal date for that co-conspirator; (ii) most courts hold that the co-conspirator will not be liable for the crimes of other co-conspirators under the *Pinkerton* doctrine (discussed below); and (iii) co-conspirator statements made after the withdrawal will not be admissible against a conspirator who had withdrawn.

[F] VICARIOUS LIABILITY

The crime of conspiracy under federal law provides a form of vicarious liability that is somewhat different from traditional aiding and abetting liability. Recall that, in general terms, an accessory can be liable for the crime committed by the principal when the accessory has (1) aided, abetted, or encouraged the principal's commission of the crime, and (2) acted with the purpose to aid and abet and with the purpose that the object crime be committed. In reading this case, be sure to identify the ways in which "*Pinkerton*" liability is different from aiding and abetting liability.

PINKERTON v. UNITED STATES
328 U.S. 640 (1946)

MR. JUSTICE DOUGLAS delivered the opinion of the Court.

Walter and Daniel Pinkerton are brothers who live a short distance from each other on Daniel's farm. They were indicted for violations of the Internal Revenue Code. The indictment contained ten substantive counts and one conspiracy count. The jury found Walter guilty on nine of the substantive counts and on the conspiracy count. It found Daniel guilty on six of the substantive counts and on the conspiracy count. Walter was fined $500 and sentenced generally on the substantive counts to imprisonment for thirty months. On the conspiracy count he was given a two year sentence to run concurrently with the other sentence. Daniel was fined $1,000 and sentenced generally on the substantive counts to imprisonment for thirty months. On the conspiracy count he was fined $500 and given a two year sentence to run concurrently with the other sentence. The judgments of conviction were affirmed by the Circuit Court of Appeals.

* * *

It is contended that there was insufficient evidence to implicate Daniel in the conspiracy. But we think there was enough evidence for submission of the issue to the jury.

There is, however, no evidence to show that Daniel participated directly in the commission of the substantive offenses on which his conviction has been sustained, although there was evidence to show that these substantive offenses were in fact committed by Walter in furtherance of the unlawful agreement or conspiracy existing between the brothers. The question was submitted to the jury on the theory that each petitioner could be found guilty of the substantive offenses, if it was found at the time those offenses were committed petitioners were parties to an unlawful conspiracy and the substantive offenses charged were in fact committed in furtherance of it.[6]

---

[6] Daniel was not indicted as an aider or abettor, nor was his case submitted to the jury on that theory.

Daniel relies on *United States v. Sall*, 116 F.2d 745 (3d Cir. 1940). That case held that participation in the conspiracy was not itself enough to sustain a conviction for the substantive offense even though it was committed in furtherance of the conspiracy. The court held that, in addition to evidence that the offense was in fact committed in furtherance of the conspiracy, evidence of direct participation in the commission of the substantive offense or other evidence from which participation might fairly be inferred was necessary.

We take a different view. We have here a continuous conspiracy. There is here no evidence of the affirmative action on the part of Daniel which is necessary to establish his withdrawal from it. *Hyde v. United States*, 225 U.S. 347 (1912). As stated in that case, "having joined in an unlawful scheme, having constituted agents for its performance, scheme and agency to be continuous until full fruition be secured, until he does some act to disavow or defeat the purpose he is in no situation to claim the delay of the law. As the offense has not been terminated or accomplished, he is still offending. And we think, consciously offending, offending as certainly, as we have said, as at the first moment of his confederation, and consciously through every moment of its existence." *Id.* at 369. And so long as the partnership in crime continues, the partners act for each other in carrying it forward. It is settled that "an overt act of one partner may be the act of all without any new agreement specifically directed to that act." *United States v. Kissel*, 218 U.S. 601, 608 (1910). Motive or intent may be proved by the acts or declarations of some of the conspirators in furtherance of the common objective. The governing principle is the same when the substantive offense is committed by one of the conspirators in furtherance of the unlawful project. The criminal intent to do the act is established by the formation of the conspiracy. Each conspirator instigated the commission of the crime. The unlawful agreement contemplated precisely what was done. It was formed for the purpose. The act done was in execution of the enterprise. The rule which holds responsible one who counsels, procures, or commands another to commit a crime is founded on the same principle. That principle is recognized in the law of conspiracy when the overt act of one partner in crime is attributable to all. An overt act is an essential ingredient of the crime of conspiracy. . . . If that can be supplied by the act of one conspirator, we fail to see why the same or other acts in furtherance of the conspiracy are likewise not attributable to the others for the purpose of holding them responsible for the substantive offense.

A different case would arise if the substantive offense committed by one of the conspirators was not in fact done in furtherance of the conspiracy, did not fall within the scope of the unlawful project, or was merely a part of the ramifications of the plan which could not be reasonably foreseen as a necessary or natural consequence of the unlawful agreement. But as we read this record, that is not this case.

Affirmed.

MR. JUSTICE RUTLEDGE, dissenting in part.

The judgment concerning Daniel Pinkerton should be reversed. In my opinion it is without precedent here and is a dangerous precedent to establish.

Daniel and Walter, who were brothers living near each other, were charged in several counts with substantive offenses, and then a conspiracy count was added naming those offenses as overt acts. The proof showed that Walter alone committed the substantive crimes. There was none to establish that Daniel participated in them, aided and abetted Walter in committing them, or knew that he had done so. Daniel in fact was in the penitentiary, under sentence for other crimes, when some of Walter's crimes were done.

There was evidence, however, to show that over several years Daniel and Walter had confederated to commit similar crimes concerned with unlawful possession, transportation, and dealing in whiskey, in fraud of the federal revenues. On this evidence both were convicted of conspiracy. Walter also was convicted on the substantive counts on the proof of his committing the crimes charged. Then, on that evidence without more than the proof of Daniel's criminal agreement with Walter and the latter's overt acts, which were also the substantive offenses charged, the court told the jury they could find Daniel guilty of those substantive offenses. They did so.

I think this ruling violates both the letter and the spirit of what Congress did when it separately defined the three classes of crime, namely, (1) completed substantive offenses; (2) aiding, abetting or counseling another to commit them; and (3) conspiracy to commit them. Not only does this ignore the distinctions Congress has prescribed shall be observed. It either convicts one [person] for another's crime or punishes the [person] convicted twice for the same offense.

The gist of conspiracy is the agreement; that of aiding, abetting or counseling is in consciously advising or assisting another to commit particular offenses, and thus becoming a party to them; that of substantive crime, going a step beyond mere aiding, abetting, counseling to completion of the offense.

These general differences are well understood. But when conspiracy has ripened into completed crime, or has advanced to the stage of aiding and abetting, it becomes easy to disregard their differences and loosely to treat one as identical with the other, that is, for every purpose except the most vital one of imposing sentence. And thus the substance, if not the technical effect, of double jeopardy or multiple punishment may be accomplished. Thus also may one be convicted of an offense not charged or proved against him, on evidence showing he committed another. . . .

Daniel has been held guilty of the substantive crimes committed only by Walter on proof that he did no more than conspire with him to commit offenses of the same general character. There was no evidence that he counseled, advised or had knowledge of those particular acts or offenses. There was, therefore, none that he aided, abetted or took part in them. There was only evidence sufficient to show that he had agreed with Walter at some past time to engage in such transactions generally. As to Daniel this was only evidence of conspiracy, not of substantive crime.

The Court's theory seems to be that Daniel and Walter became general partners in crime by virtue of their agreement and because of that agreement without more on his part Daniel became criminally responsible as a principal for everything Walter did thereafter in the nature of a criminal offense of the general sort the agreement contemplated, so long as there was not clear evidence that Daniel had withdrawn from or revoked the agreement. Whether or not his commitment to the penitentiary had that effect, the result is a vicarious criminal responsibility as broad as, or broader than, the vicarious civil liability of a partner for acts done by a co-partner in the course of the firm's business.

Such analogies from private commercial law and the law of torts are dangerous, in my judgment, for transfer to the criminal field. Guilt there with us remains personal, not vicarious, for the more serious offenses. It should be kept so. The effect of Daniel's conviction in this case, to repeat, is either to attribute to him Walter's guilt or to punish him twice for the same offense, namely, agreeing with Walter to engage in crime. Without the agreement Daniel was guilty of no crime on this record. With it and no more, so far as his own conduct is concerned, he was guilty of two. [Daniel's conviction for Walter's substantive crimes should be reversed.]

NOTES AND QUESTIONS

1. *Vicarious liability.* The federal aiding and abetting statute, now codified at 18 U.S.C. § 2, provides that "[w]hoever commits an offense against the United States or aids, abets, counsels, commands, induces or procures its commission, is punishable as a principal." As the majority states in note 6, Daniel was not charged on this theory. Review the dissent's comments concerning aiding and abetting. Could Daniel Pinkerton have been liable as an aider and abetter? Why or why not?

2. *Conspiracy and substantive offenses.* As noted above, under federal law, the crime of conspiracy does not merge with substantive offenses. Thus, it is critical to distinguish between liability for (a) the crime of conspiracy itself and (b) liability for substantive offenses. Was Daniel Pinkerton's liability for the crime of conspiracy the principal issue in the case? Why or why not?

3. *The merits of the* Pinkerton *rule.* Why does Justice Rutledge object to the outcome in *Pinkerton*? Exactly what was Daniel's role in the crimes committed by Walter? Is it fair to hold Daniel liable? Note that the Model Penal Code and a number of states have rejected *Pinkerton* liability. Can you explain why? What are the advantages of the doctrine?

PROBLEM

3-3. Associate worked for a personal injury law firm, and conducted a jury trial in January, Year 00. Concerned that the trial had gone poorly, Associate spoke with Partner at the law firm about paying a juror $10,000. Partner approved, and Investigator made the payment on January 30, Year 00. This payment constituted an illegal bribe. In addition, without Associate's knowledge, Partner approved a separate $20,000 bribe to another juror in the same case the following week.

In July, Year 00, Partner asked Investigator to pay $5,000 to bribe a witness in a trial that Partner would be conducting the following October. Investigator paid the bribe on October 1, Year 00. In September, Year 00, Associate left the law firm to take another job. Other than social engagements with friends at the law firm, Associate had no further dealings with the law firm after that time.

Nearly five years later, on August 15, Year 05, Associate, Partner, and Investigator were each indicted on charges of (1) conspiring to obstruct justice under 18 U.S.C. § 1503, (2) obstruction for the $10,000 payment, (3) obstruction for the $20,000 payment, and (4) obstruction for the $5,000 payment. Investigator and Partner pleaded guilty and agreed to cooperate with the government. At Associate's trial, the government introduced the July, Year 00, conversation between Partner and Investigator. Associate was convicted of all charges.

Associate has appealed the four convictions. Assuming that the substance of the obstruction charges was proven beyond a reasonable doubt, should the defendant prevail as to any or all of the charges? Why or why not?

Chapter 4

MAIL AND WIRE FRAUD

[A] INTRODUCTORY NOTES

[1] Breadth of the Mail and Wire Fraud Statutes

The mail and wire fraud statutes, 18 U.S.C. §§ 1341, 1343, have long been among federal prosecutors' favorite tools for fighting white collar crime.[a] On their face, the statutes are relatively straightforward. Subject to qualifications discussed below, the statutes merely require the government to prove that the defendant engaged in a scheme to defraud, and that the scheme involved the use of the United States mails, a private courier, or interstate wires. Because of their breadth and simplicity, the mail and wire fraud statutes may be used in a wide range of circumstances:

- To prosecute traditional financial fraud schemes, ranging from complex interstate schemes to ordinary fraud cases;
- To prosecute private employees who have breached their fiduciary duties to their employers;
- To prosecute public officials who have abused their positions of public trust;
- To prosecute cases that are primarily focused on other substantive crimes; for example, mail and wire fraud may be the basis for charges arising out of the same acts that form the basis for securities fraud, bank fraud, and other specific charges; and
- As predicate crimes that form the basis for charges under the federal racketeering (RICO) and money laundering statutes discussed later in this text.

The very flexibility of the mail and wire fraud statutes raises important law enforcement policy issues. Because the statutes reach ordinary fraud cases that would normally be prosecuted at the state level, they pose significant questions concerning the role of federal law enforcement. Also, the statutes broadly criminalize breaches of fiduciary duties, and have triggered debate over the role of the criminal law in regulating every day economic activity. *See* John C. Coffee Jr., *Hush!: The Criminal Status of Confidential Information after* McNally *and* Carpenter *and the Enduring Problem of Overcriminalization*, 26 Am. Crim. L. Rev. 121 (1988). Finally, the statutes raise vagueness concerns under the Due Process Clause, including issues of notice and abuse of prosecutorial discretion. These themes recur throughout the materials in this chapter.

---

[a] The mail fraud statute was first enacted in 1872, and has been amended many times; the current version is based upon amendments enacted in 1948.

[2]   The Statutory Elements

The language of the mail and wire fraud statutes does not provide much guidance to courts. Therefore, the statutes have been subject to substantial judicial interpretation. Under the mail and wire fraud statutes and the cases interpreting those statutes, in a mail or wire fraud case, the government must prove that:

(1) The defendant engaged in a scheme to defraud;

(2) The defendant acted with the specific intent (or purpose) to defraud;

(3) The scheme resulted, or would result upon completion, in the loss of money, property, or honest services; and

(4) The United States mail, a private courier, or interstate or international wires (a) were used in furtherance of the scheme to defraud, and (b) the defendant used, or caused the use, of the mail, courier, or wires.

The substantive elements of the mail fraud statute and the wire fraud statute are the same, and judicial interpretations of each statute apply to the other. Note that mail/wire fraud is an inchoate crime. Thus, the crime is complete if the above elements are met regardless of whether the scheme comes to fruition.

Each instance of the use of the mail or wire gives rise to a separate count under the statutes. A single fraudulent scheme that uses multiple mailings could, for example, lead to a huge number of criminal charges. The Sarbanes-Oxley Act of 2002 increased the penalty for each count from five to 20 years' imprisonment. The Federal Sentencing Guidelines do place some limits on consecutive sentences for convictions of multiple counts.[b] Nevertheless, a mail or wire fraud conviction will likely give rise to a substantial sentence.

[3]   Jurisdiction

There are two possible bases for federal jurisdiction under the mail fraud statute. First, any use of the federal mails provides jurisdiction pursuant to the federal government's postal power under the United States Constitution. Second, the use of "any private or commercial interstate carrier" qualifies under the statute. Under the Commerce Clause, *interstate* use of a courier will plainly provide federal jurisdiction. In addition, *intrastate* use of a private courier will suffice under the Commerce Clause when, as is generally the case, the courier's business affects interstate commerce. *See, e.g., United States v. Photogrammetric Data Serv., Inc.*, 259 F.3d 229, 247 (4th Cir. 2001).

Under the plain language of the wire fraud statute, wires used in *interstate* or foreign commerce provide federal jurisdiction under the Commerce Clause. The general rule under federal law is that the government need not prove that the defendant possessed any particular mens rea in connection with a purely jurisdictional element of a crime. *See, e.g., United States v. Feola*, 420 U.S. 671, 684 (1975) (the government is not required to show that the defendant had knowledge of a fact — in this case, that the intended victim was a federal officer — that provides the basis for federal jurisdiction). Courts have applied this principle to the wire fraud statute, holding that jurisdiction is present even if the defendant did not

---

[b] *See* Chapter 19, Sentencing, *infra.*

know, and could not reasonably have known, that the wire transmission would travel interstate. *See, e.g., United States v. Lindemann*, 85 F.3d 1232, 1241–1242 (7th Cir. 1996).

Does federal jurisdiction exist even when the government initiated the interstate use of the wires? In one early case, *United States v. Archer*, 486 F.2d 670 (2d Cir. 1973), the court dismissed a Travel Act prosecution under 18 U.S.C. § 1952. That section punishes whoever "travels in interstate or foreign commerce or uses the mail or any facility in interstate or foreign commerce, with intent to (1) distribute the proceeds of any unlawful activity; or (2) commit any crime of violence to further any unlawful activity; or (3) otherwise promote, manage, establish, carry on, or facilitate the promotion, management, establishment, or carrying on, of any unlawful activity." In *Archer*, the court found that the federal agents had induced the targets of a sting operation to place the interstate calls at issue, and thus had improperly "manufactured" federal jurisdiction. Later cases have severely limited *Archer's* importance, however. Courts in these cases have found that jurisdiction exists even where the government essentially created the circumstances providing jurisdiction. *See, e.g., United States v. Peters*, 952 F.2d 960, 963–964 (7th Cir. 1992).

[B]   INTENT TO DEFRAUD

The mail and wire fraud statutes punish one who has used the mail or wires in "any scheme or artifice *to defraud*, or for obtaining money or property by means of *false or fraudulent* pretenses, representations, or promises." The statutes, however, do not define the fraudulent schemes that fall within their ambit. In the cases in this section, the courts attempt to define the "fraud" that is at the heart of these statutes.

Many white collar crimes require prosecutors and courts to draw the line between merely aggressive business practices and those practices that are properly deemed criminal. The following case addresses this issue in the mail and wire fraud context. In this case, the defendants clearly made false representations, and did so for the purpose of obtaining money from the alleged victims. Is that all that is required under the statute?

UNITED STATES v. REGENT OFFICE SUPPLY CO.
421 F.2d 1174 (2d Cir. 1970)

MOORE, CIRCUIT JUDGE.

The appellants are in the business of selling stationery supplies through salesmen (called "agents") who solicit orders for their merchandise by telephone. [Defendants] stipulated in writing that their agents "secured sales" by making false representations to potential customers that:

> (a) the agent had been referred to the customer by a friend of the customer.

> (b) the agent had been referred to customer firms by officers of such firms.

> (c) the agent was a doctor, or other professional person, who had stationery to be disposed of.

(d) stationery of friends of the agent had to be disposed of because of a death and that the customer would help to relieve this difficult situation by purchasing it.

The government's case consisted entirely of the defendants' stipulation. For [their] defense, the accused corporations called the president of Regent, Harold Hartwig, who testified that the firms sell well-known, nationally advertised brands of stationery and some paper to large users among which are corporations; that many of these customers provide a large volume of reorder business; that the Regent-Oxford enterprise has over 20,000 customers; that sales are made exclusively through their customers' purchasing agents; that the false representations listed in the stipulation were made as a preliminary part of the salesmen's solicitation; that price and quality of the merchandise are always discussed honestly; that the price offered has been lower than the purchasing agent is or was paying at the time of the solicitation; that the goods could be returned if found to be unsatisfactory; and that when a complaint is made an additional discount is offered to induce the customer to keep the goods.

Cross-examination elicited that visits to the Regent-Oxford offices had been made by the Better Business Bureau and by a Post Office Inspector; that the "lies" were to "get by" secretaries on the telephone and to get "the purchasing agent to listen to our agent;" and that for business reasons various fictitious names were used both for their companies in different localities and for individuals.

The important substantive question on this appeal is: Does solicitation of a purchase by means of false representations not directed to the quality, adequacy or price of goods to be sold, or otherwise to the nature of the bargain, constitute a "scheme to defraud" or "obtaining money by false pretenses" within the prohibition of 18 U.S.C. § 1341? We hold that, as here presented, it does not and the convictions should be reversed. We do not, however, condone the deceitfulness such business practices represent. On the contrary, we find these "white lies" repugnant to "standards of business morality." Nevertheless, the facts as stipulated in the case before us do not, in our view, constitute a scheme to defraud or to obtain money by false pretenses punishable under § 1341. But this is not to say that we could not, on different facts or more specific proof, arrive at a different conclusion.

The case presented by the Regent-Oxford operation is unique (as the government, in effect, concedes) among prosecutions for violation of § 1341. The most nearly analogous cases sustaining convictions for mail fraud have involved sales tactics and representations which have tended to mislead the purchaser, or prospective purchaser, as to the quality or effectiveness of the thing being sold, or to mislead him with regard to the advantages of the bargain which should accrue to him. Thus claims or statements in advertising may go beyond mere puffing and enter the realm of fraud where the product must inherently fail to do what is claimed for it. *United States v. Andreadis*, 366 F.2d 423 (2d Cir. 1966) (claim that "Regimen Tablets" could reduce weight without dieting contradicted scientific evidence); *United States v. New South Farm and Home Company*, 241 U.S. 64 (1916) (false representations regarding climate, ability to grow crops, and expected future improvements in promotion of land sales); *Wilson v. United States*, 190 F. 427 (2d Cir. 1911) (sale of intrinsically worthless stock). And promotion of an inherently useful item may also be fraud when the scheme of promotion is based on claims of additional benefits to accrue to the customer, if the benefits as represented are not realistically attainable by the customer. *United States v. Armantrout*, 411

F.2d 60, 64 (2d Cir. 1969) (carpet sold at inflated price on customer's expectation that defendant's "chain referral" scheme would return purchase price and produce profit for him); *United States v. Baren*, 305 F.2d 527 (2d Cir. 1962) (promotion of knitting machines on representation that women customers could easily make complicated knitted garments for profitable resale, after it became known that average prospects could not so operate them).

The government does not contend that the Regent-Oxford agents made any false representations regarding the quality or price of their nationally advertised merchandise. Nor is there any suggestion of material benefits which the customer might expect from the transaction beyond the inherent utility of the goods purchased and the discount price at which they were offered. Thus the present case cannot fall within either of the classes of commercial fraud cases we have previously considered. We must, therefore, examine the government's theory that fraud may exist in a commercial transaction even when the customer gets exactly what he expected and at the price he expected to pay.

It is generally stated that there are two elements to the offense of mail fraud: use of the mails and a scheme to defraud. Since only a "scheme to defraud" and not actual fraud is required for conviction, we have said that "it is not essential that the government allege or prove that purchasers were in fact defrauded." *United States v. Andreadis*, 366 F.2d 423, 431 (2d Cir. 1966). But this does not mean that the government can escape the burden of showing that some actual harm or injury was *contemplated* by the schemer. Of course proof that someone was actually victimized by the fraud is good evidence of the schemer's intent.

[W]e have found no case in which an intent to deceive has been equated with an "intent to defraud" where the deceit did not go to the nature of the bargain itself. Where the false representations are directed to the quality, adequacy or price of the goods themselves, the fraudulent intent is apparent because the victim is made to bargain without facts obviously essential in deciding whether to enter the bargain. In closer cases, where the representations do not mislead as to the quality, adequacy or inherent worth of the goods themselves, fraud in the bargaining may be inferable from facts indicating a discrepancy between benefits reasonably anticipated because of the misleading representations and the actual benefits which the defendant delivered, or intended to deliver. In either instance, the intent of the schemer is to injure another to his own advantage by withholding or misrepresenting material facts. Although proof that the injury was accomplished is not required to convict under 1341, we believe the statute does require evidence from which it may be inferred that some actual injury to the victim, however slight, is a reasonably probable result of the deceitful representations if they are successful.

The Regent-Oxford agents did not attempt to deceive their prospective customers with respect to the bargain they were offering; rather, they gave a false reason for being able to offer the bargain. There was no substitution of merchandise contrary to the customer's understanding of the offer, and no "quid pro quo of equal value" exchanged for the customer's money which did not meet his reasonable expectations. No customer testified that he felt he had been cheated. The government asks us to infer some injury from the mere fact of the falseness of the representations and their connection with a commercial transaction. On the evidence before us, we conclude that the defendants intended to deceive their customers but they did not intend to defraud them, because the falsity of their representations was not shown to be capable of affecting the customer's understanding of the bargain nor of influencing his assessment of the value of the bargain to him, and thus no injury was shown to flow from the deception.

[T]he convictions are reversed.

NOTES AND QUESTIONS

1. *Fraudulent intent.* As the *Regent Office Supply* opinion makes clear, the "intent to defraud" is an essential part of the "scheme to defraud" that is at the core of a mail or wire fraud charge. In its opinion, the Second Circuit characterized the defendants' conduct as "despicable," and found that the defendants undoubtedly intended to deceive their customers. Given these conclusions, why did the court find that there was no scheme to defraud? The court provided a number of examples where a scheme to defraud *was* proven. Are you convinced that those cases are substantially different from the *Regent Office Supply* case? Why or why not?

2. *Literally true and misleading statements.* Can a defendant who has not made a false statement be convicted of mail or wire fraud? For example, assume that an enterprising salesperson marketed plots of land, stating in mailings to prospective customers that a lake would be available for recreational use only five miles from the property. The statement was literally true. The driving distance to the lake, however, was 15 to 40 miles on roads not suitable for passenger vehicles. Have property purchasers been defrauded under the mail fraud statute? *See Lustiger v. United States*, 386 F.2d 132 (9th Cir. 1967).

As we will see in Chapter 10, Perjury, *infra*, a literally true but misleading statement will *not* support a perjury charge under federal law. Should the result be different in a fraud case? Why or why not?

3. *Materiality.* In *Neder v. United States*, 527 U.S. 1 (1999), the Supreme Court held that a scheme to defraud under the mail and wire fraud statutes must include a *material* deception. Neder was convicted of mail and wire fraud based upon fraudulent bank loan applications. On appeal, the Court unanimously held that the trial judge erred in failing to require that the jury find that the defendant's misstatements were material to the transactions. Although the statutory language does not contain such a requirement, the Court reasoned that Congress incorporated the common law definition of "defraud" in the statutes. That definition includes a "misrepresentation or concealment of material fact." *Id.* at 3.

Although the Court did not define "material" in its opinion, the Court did cite the definition provided by the Restatement (Second) of Torts § 538. The Restatement provides that a matter is material when:

> (a) a reasonable man would attach importance to its existence or nonexistence in determining his choice of action in the transaction in question; or

> (b) the maker of the representation knows or has reason to know that its recipient regards or is likely to regard the matter as important in determining his choice of action, although a reasonable man would not so regard it.

Id. at 22 n.5.

4. *Reasonable reliance?* Does a defendant commit mail or wire fraud by making misleading statements that would not fool a reasonable person? In *United States v. Brown*, 79 F.3d 1550 (11th Cir. 1996), the court said not. The court found that the misstatements in the case — relating to the market and rental values of houses that the defendants were selling — would not have fooled a reasonable customer because a reasonable home buyer would conduct independent research into the home's market value. The court thus reversed the convictions, stating:

> A 'scheme to defraud' under the pertinent criminal statutes has not been proved where a reasonable juror would have to conclude that the representation is about something which the customer should, and could, easily confirm — if they wished to do so — from readily available external sources. In this case, the relevant market prices are not difficult to investigate.
>
> The exercise of federal government power to criminalize conduct and thereby to coerce and to deprive persons, by government action, of their liberty, reputation and property must be watched carefully in a country that values the liberties of its private citizens. Never can we allow federal prosecutors to make up the law as they go along.
>
> Looking at the evidence in this case, our worry is that the criminal fraud statutes were used to convict four people simply for charging high prices — all allegations of misconduct in this case involved the price customers paid for their homes, not the physical qualities of these homes.
>
> Although the line between unethical behavior and unlawful behavior is sometimes blurred — especially under the federal fraud statutes — we, in the absence of clear direction from Congress, conclude that the behavior established by the government's evidence in this case is not the kind that a reasonable jury could find, in fact, violated the federal fraud statutes.

In a later en banc decision, however, the Eleventh Circuit overturned its decision in *Brown. United States v. Svete*, 556 F.3d 1157, 1166 (11th Cir. 2009) (en banc). The court agreed with the other circuits that had considered the issue, and held that mail fraud and wire fraud occur even if the misrepresentations would not fool a reasonable person. Is this the correct result? Even without the reasonable person rule, was there sufficient evidence of intent to defraud in *Brown* under the *Regent Office Supply* standard? Why or why not?

PROBLEM

4-1. James Goodall was the president of Direct Mail, Inc., a direct mail marketing company. Goodall created a "mailgram" that was mailed to over one million people. The mailgram stated:

CONGRATULATIONS! YOU ARE DEFINITELY TO RECEIVE ONE OR MORE OF THE GIFTS LISTED BELOW:

GIFT(S): (1) $5,000 CASH; (2) $2,500.00 CASH; (3) $1,000.00 DISCOUNT SHOPPING SPREE.

SEE REVERSE SIDE FOR DETAILS.

On the reverse, the mailgram stated:

> Odds of receiving each gift: for $5,000, 1 in 300,000; for $2,500, 5 in 300,000; and for the discount shopping spree coupons, 1 in 1.

Below these odds, the mailgram indicated that the coupons could be used only toward the purchase of merchandise out of a catalog. The mailgram stated that the offer would expire 48 hours from receipt and told the recipients to call immediately "to see which gift(s) you will receive." It listed a "900" telephone number and indicated that a call would cost $3.98 plus 97 cents per minute, with a minimum three minute charge.

Of the one million mailgrams sent, 25,000 people called in response, and 22,000 discount shopping spree coupons were mailed out. Recipients of the coupons could use them to purchase one of 14 items contained in the catalog, items ranging from autographed basketballs and photographs to game-worn boxer shorts. After applying the coupons to the total prices, the price of these items still exceeded Direct Mail's cost in obtaining the items. A defense expert testified that the mark-ups were nonetheless, "very fair, even on the low side."

The government charged Goodall with mail fraud based on the theory that the mailgrams induced recipients to call the "900" number and to incur telephone charges in the belief that the callers would thereby receive money and things of value. In fact, the callers merely received an opportunity to purchase one of 14 items, the stated value of which was far in excess of their wholesale cost to Direct Mail.

Goodall was convicted, and appeals. What arguments should Goodall make on appeal? What are the government's best responses? How should the court rule? Why?

[C]   DEPRIVATION OF MONEY, PROPERTY, OR HONEST SERVICES

As seen in the materials below, when proving the existence of a scheme to defraud, the government must show that the defendant intended to deprive a victim of money, property, or "honest services." This section traces the evolution of this requirement and the difficulties that courts have had in defining the terms "property" and "honest services."

[1]   The *McNally* Decision

In *McNally v. United States*, the United States Supreme Court found that mail or wire fraud must be based upon an intended loss of money or property. In so holding, the Court overturned every court of appeals decision on this issue. Why did the Court take this unusual step?

McNALLY v. UNITED STATES
483 U.S. 350 (1987)

JUSTICE WHITE delivered the opinion of the Court.

This action involves the prosecution of petitioner Gray, a former public official of the Commonwealth of Kentucky, and petitioner McNally, a private individual, for alleged violation of the federal mail fraud statute, 18 U.S.C. § 1341. The prosecution's principal theory of the case, which was accepted by the courts below, was that petitioners' participation in a self-dealing patronage scheme defrauded the citizens and government of Kentucky of certain "intangible rights," such as the right to have the Commonwealth's affairs conducted honestly. We must consider whether the jury charge permitted a conviction for conduct not within the scope of the mail fraud statute.

We accept for the sake of argument the government's view of the evidence, as follows. Petitioners and a third individual, Howard P. "Sonny" Hunt, were politically active in the Democratic Party in the Commonwealth of Kentucky during the 1970's. After Democrat Julian Carroll was elected Governor of Kentucky in 1974, Hunt was made chairman of the state Democratic Party and given *de facto* control over selecting the insurance agencies from which the Commonwealth would purchase its policies. In 1975, the Wombwell Insurance Company of Lexington, Kentucky (Wombwell), which since 1971 had acted as the Commonwealth's agent for securing a workmen's compensation policy, agreed with Hunt that in exchange for a continued agency relationship it would share any resulting commissions in excess of $50,000 a year with other insurance agencies specified by him. The commissions in question were paid to Wombwell by the large insurance companies from which it secured coverage for the Commonwealth.

From 1975 to 1979, Wombwell funneled $851,000 in commissions to 21 separate insurance agencies designated by Hunt. Among the recipients of these payments was Seton Investments, Inc. (Seton), a company controlled by Hunt and petitioner Gray and nominally owned and operated by petitioner McNally.

Gray served as Secretary of Public Protection and Regulation from 1976 to 1978 and also as Secretary of the Governor's Cabinet from 1977 to 1979. Prior to his 1976 appointment, he and Hunt established Seton for the sole purpose of sharing in the commissions distributed by Wombwell. Wombwell paid some $200,000 to Seton between 1975 and 1979, and the money was used to benefit Gray and Hunt. Pursuant to Hunt's direction, Wombwell also made excess commission payments to the Snodgrass Insurance Agency, which in turn gave the money to McNally.

On account of the foregoing activities, Hunt was charged with and pleaded guilty to mail and tax fraud and was sentenced to three years' imprisonment. Petitioners were charged with one count of conspiracy and seven counts of mail fraud, six of which were dismissed before trial. The remaining mail fraud count was based on the mailing of a commission check to Wombwell by the insurance company from which it had secured coverage for the State. This count alleged that petitioners had devised a scheme (1) to defraud the citizens and government of Kentucky of their right to have the Commonwealth's affairs conducted honestly, and (2) to obtain, directly and indirectly, money and other things of value by means of false pretenses and the concealment of material facts. The conspiracy count alleged that petitioners had (1) conspired to violate the mail fraud statute through the scheme just described and (2) conspired to defraud the United States by obstructing the collection of federal taxes.

The jury convicted petitioners on both the mail fraud and conspiracy counts, and the Court of Appeals affirmed the convictions. In affirming the substantive mail fraud conviction, the court relied on a line of decisions from the Courts of Appeals holding that the mail fraud statute proscribes schemes to defraud citizens of their intangible rights to honest and impartial government. Under these cases, a public official owes a fiduciary duty to the public, and misuse of his office for private gain is a fraud.

We granted certiorari, and now reverse.

The mail fraud statute clearly protects property rights, but does not refer to the intangible right of the citizenry to good government. As first enacted in 1872, as part of a recodification of the postal laws, the statute contained a general proscription against using the mails to initiate correspondence in furtherance of "any scheme or artifice to defraud." The sponsor of the recodification stated, in apparent reference to the antifraud provision, that measures were needed "to prevent the frauds which are mostly gotten up in the large cities by thieves, forgers, and rapscallions generally, for the purpose of deceiving and fleecing the innocent people in the country." Insofar as the sparse legislative history reveals anything, it indicates that the original impetus behind the mail fraud statute was to protect the people from schemes to deprive them of their money or property.

Durland v. United States, 161 U.S. 306 (1896), the first case in which this Court construed the meaning of the phrase "any scheme or artifice to defraud," held that the phrase is to be interpreted broadly insofar as property rights are concerned, but did not indicate that the statute had a more extensive reach. The Court rejected the argument that "the statute reaches only such cases as, at common law, would come within the definition of 'false pretenses,' in order to make out which there must be a misrepresentation as to some existing fact and not a mere promise as to the future." *Id.* at 312. Instead, it construed the statute to "includ[e] everything designed to defraud by representations as to the past or present, or suggestions and promises as to the future." *Id.* at 313. Accordingly, the defendant's use of the mails to sell bonds which he did not intend to honor was within the statute. The Court explained that "it was with the purpose of protecting the public against all such intentional efforts to despoil, and to prevent the post office from being used to carry them into effect, that this statute was passed." *Id.* at 314.

Congress codified the holding of *Durland* in 1909, and in doing so gave further indication that the statute's purpose is protecting property rights. The amendment added the words "or for obtaining money or property by means of false or fraudulent pretenses, representations, or promises" after the original phrase "any scheme or artifice to defraud." The new language is based on the statement in *Durland* that the statute reaches "everything designed to defraud by representations as to the past or present, or suggestions and promises as to the future." 161 U.S. at 313. However, instead of the phrase "everything designed to defraud" Congress used the words "[any scheme or artifice] for obtaining money or property."

After 1909, therefore, the mail fraud statute criminalized schemes or artifices "to defraud" or "for obtaining money or property by means of false or fraudulent pretenses, representation, or promises." Because the two phrases identifying the proscribed schemes appear in the disjunctive, it is arguable that they are to be construed independently and that the money-or-property requirement of the latter phrase does not limit schemes to defraud to those aimed at causing deprivation of money or property. This is the approach that has been taken by each of the Courts of Appeals that has addressed the issue: schemes to defraud include those designed to deprive individuals, the people, or the government of intangible rights, such as the right to have public officials perform their duties honestly.

As the Court long ago stated, however, the words "to defraud" commonly refer "to wronging one in his property rights by dishonest methods or schemes," and "usually signify the deprivation of something of value by trick, deceit, chicane or overreaching." *Hammerschmidt v. United States*, 265 U.S. 182, 188 (1924). The codification of the holding in *Durland* in 1909 does not indicate that Congress was departing from this common understanding. As we see it, adding the second phrase simply made it unmistakable that the statute reached false promises and misrepresentations as to the future as well as other frauds involving money or property.

We believe that Congress' intent in passing the mail fraud statute was to prevent the use of the mails in furtherance of such schemes. The Court has often stated that when there are two rational readings of a criminal statute, one harsher than the other, we are to choose the harsher only when Congress has spoken in clear and definite language. As the Court said in a mail fraud case years ago: "There are no constructive offenses; and before one can be punished, it must be shown that his case is plainly within the statute." *Fasulo v. United States*, 272 U.S. 620, 629 (1926). Rather than construe the statute in a manner that leaves its outer boundaries ambiguous and involves the federal government in setting standards of disclosure and good government for local and state officials, we read § 1341 as limited in scope to the protection of property rights. If Congress desires to go further, it must speak more clearly than it has.

For purposes of this action, we assume that Hunt, as well as Gray, was a state officer. The issue is thus whether a state officer violates the mail fraud statute if he chooses an insurance agent to provide insurance for the State but specifies that the agent must share its commissions with other named insurance agencies, in one of which the officer has an ownership interest and hence profits when his agency receives part of the commissions. We note that as the action comes to us, there was no charge and the jury was not required to find that the Commonwealth itself was defrauded of any money or property. It was not charged that in the absence of the alleged scheme the Commonwealth would have paid a lower premium or secured better insurance. Hunt and Gray received part of the commissions but those commissions were not the Commonwealth's money. Nor was the jury charged that to convict it must find that the Commonwealth was deprived of control over how its money was spent. Indeed, the premium for insurance would have been paid to some agency, and what Hunt and Gray did was to assert control that the Commonwealth might not otherwise have made over the commissions paid by the insurance company to its agent.[9] Although the government now relies in part on

---

[9] JUSTICE STEVENS would affirm the convictions even though it was not charged that requiring the Wombwell agency to share commissions violated state law. We should assume that it did not. For the same reason we should assume that it was not illegal under state law for Hunt and Gray to own one of the agencies sharing in the commissions and hence to profit from the arrangement, whether or not they disclosed it to others in the state government. It is worth observing as well that it was not alleged that the mail fraud statute would have been violated, had Hunt and Gray reported to state officials the fact of their financial gain. The violation asserted is the failure to disclose their financial interest, even if state law did not require it, to other persons in the state government whose actions could have been affected by the disclosure. It was in this way that the indictment charged that the people of Kentucky had been deprived of their right to have the Commonwealth's affairs conducted honestly.

It may well be that Congress could criminalize using the mails to further a state officer's efforts to profit from governmental decisions he is empowered to make or over which he has some supervisory authority, even if there is no state law proscribing his profiteering or even if state law expressly

the assertion that petitioners obtained property by means of false representations to Wombwell, there was nothing in the jury charge that required such a finding. We hold, therefore, that the jury instruction on the substantive mail fraud count permitted a conviction for conduct not within the reach of § 1341.

The government concedes that if petitioners' substantive mail fraud convictions are reversed their conspiracy convictions should also be reversed.

The judgment of the Court of Appeals is reversed, and the case is remanded for proceedings consistent with this opinion.

It is so ordered.

JUSTICE STEVENS, with whom JUSTICE O'CONNOR joins as to Parts I, II, and III, dissenting.

Congress has broadly prohibited the use of the United States mails to carry out "any scheme or artifice to defraud." 18 U.S.C. § 1341.

In the public sector, judges, state governors, chairmen of state political parties, state cabinet officers, city aldermen, Congressmen and many other state and federal officials have been convicted of defrauding citizens of their right to the honest services of their governmental officials. In most of these cases, the officials have secretly made governmental decisions with the objective of benefitting themselves or promoting their own interests, instead of fulfilling their legal commitment to provide the citizens of the state or local government with their loyal service and honest government. Similarly, many elected officials and their campaign workers have been convicted of mail fraud when they have used the mails to falsify votes, thus defrauding the citizenry of its right to an honest election. In the private sector, purchasing agents, brokers, union leaders, and others with clear fiduciary duties to their employers or unions have been found guilty of defrauding their employers or unions by accepting kickbacks or selling confidential information. In other cases, defendants have been found guilty of using the mails to defraud individuals of their rights to privacy and other non-monetary rights. All of these cases have something in common — they involved what the Court now refers to as "intangible rights." They also share something else in common. The many federal courts that have confronted the question whether these sorts of schemes constitute a "scheme or artifice to defraud" have uniformly and consistently read the statute in the same, sensible way. They have realized that nothing in the words "any scheme or artifice to defraud," or in the purpose of the statute, justifies limiting its application to schemes intended to deprive victims of money or property.

I.

The mail fraud statute sets forth three separate prohibitions. It prohibits the use of the United States mails for the purpose of executing "[1] *any* scheme or artifice to defraud, [2] *or* for obtaining money or property by means of false or fraudulent pretenses, representations, or promises, [3] *or* to sell, dispose of, loan,

---

authorized it. But if state law expressly permitted or did not forbid a state officer such as Gray to have an ownership interest in an insurance agency handling the State's insurance, it would take a much clearer indication than the mail fraud statute evidences to convince us that having and concealing such an interest defrauds the State and is forbidden under federal law.

exchange, alter, give away, distribute, supply, or furnish or procure for unlawful use any counterfeit or spurious coin, obligation, security, or other article, or anything represented to be or intimated or held out to be such counterfeit or spurious article. " 18 U.S.C. § 1341 (emphasis and brackets added).

As the language makes clear, each of these restrictions is independent. One can violate the second clause — obtaining money or property by false pretenses — even though one does not violate the third clause — counterfeiting. Similarly, one can violate the first clause — devising a scheme or artifice to defraud — without violating the counterfeiting provision. Until today it was also obvious that one could violate the first clause by devising a scheme or artifice to defraud, even though one did not violate the second clause by seeking to obtain money or property from his victim through false pretenses. Every court to consider the matter had so held.

In considering the scope of the mail fraud statute it is essential to remember Congress' purpose in enacting it. Congress sought to protect the integrity of the United States mails by not allowing them to be used as "instruments of crime." *United States v. Brewer*, 528 F.2d 492, 498 (4th Cir. 1975). Once this purpose is considered, it becomes clear that the construction the Court adopts today is senseless. Can it be that Congress sought to purge the mails of schemes to defraud citizens of money but was willing to tolerate schemes to defraud citizens of their right to an honest government, or to unbiased public officials? Is it at all rational to assume that Congress wanted to ensure that the mails not be used for petty crimes, but did not prohibit election fraud accomplished through mailing fictitious ballots?

II.

Examination of the way the term "defraud" has long been defined, and was defined at the time of the statute's enactment, makes it clear that Congress' use of the term showed no intent to limit the statute to property loss. Similarly, the law dictionaries of the era broadly defined the type of interests subject to deprivation by fraudulent action. One leading dictionary stated that "to defraud is to withhold from another that which is justly due to him, or to deprive him of a right by deception or artifice." Another dictionary defined "defraud" as "to cheat; to deceive; to deprive of a right by an act of fraud to withhold from another what is justly due him, or to deprive him of a right, by deception or artifice."

It is, in fact, apparent that the common law criminalized frauds beyond those involving "tangible rights".

III.

To support its crabbed construction of the Act, the Court makes a straightforward but unpersuasive argument. Since there is no explicit, unambiguous evidence that Congress actually contemplated "intangible rights" when it enacted the mail fraud statute in 1872, the Court explains, any ambiguity in the meaning of the criminal statute should be resolved in favor of lenity. The doctrine of lenity is, of course, sound, for the citizen is entitled to fair notice of what sort of conduct may give rise to punishment. But the Court's reliance on that doctrine in this case is misplaced.

Especially in light of the statutory purpose, I believe that § 1341 unambiguously prohibits all schemes to defraud that use the United States mails — whether or not they involve money or property.

I recognize that there may have been some overly expansive applications of § 1341 in the past. With no guidance from this Court, the Courts of Appeals have struggled to define just when conduct which is clearly unethical is also criminal. In some instances, however, such as voting fraud cases, the criminality of the scheme and the fraudulent use of the mails could not be clearer. It is sometimes difficult to define when there has been a scheme to defraud someone of intangible rights. But it is also sometimes difficult to decide when a tangible loss was caused by fraud. The fact that the exercise of judgment is sometimes difficult is no excuse for rejecting an entire doctrine that is both sound and faithful to the intent of Congress.

IV.

Perhaps the most distressing aspect of the Court's action today is its casual — almost summary — rejection of the accumulated wisdom of the many distinguished federal judges who have thoughtfully considered and correctly answered the question these cases present. The quality of this Court's work is most suspect when it stands alone, or virtually so, against a tide of well-considered opinions issued by state or federal courts. In these cases I am convinced that those judges correctly understood the intent of the Congress that enacted this statute. Even if I were not so persuaded, I could not join a rejection of such a longstanding, consistent interpretation of a federal statute.

In the long run, it is not clear how grave the ramifications of today's decision will be. Congress can, of course, negate it by amending the statute. The possibilities that the decision's impact will be mitigated do not moderate my conviction that the Court has made a serious mistake. Nor do they erase my lingering questions about why a Court that has not been particularly receptive to the rights of criminal defendants in recent years has acted so dramatically to protect the elite class of powerful individuals who will benefit from this decision.

I respectfully dissent.

NOTES AND QUESTIONS

1. *A surprise decision.* As Justice Stevens noted in his dissent, the majority opinion rejected "the accumulated wisdom of the many distinguished federal judges who have thoughtfully considered and correctly answered the question these cases present." What concerns led the majority to reach its conclusion? What is the essential disagreement between the majority and the dissent?

2. *The rule of lenity.* The majority relied in part upon the rule of lenity in reaching its conclusion. Perhaps because of the vagueness of many white collar statutes, defendants in white collar cases often argue that the statutory language is ambiguous and should be read in their favor. Sometimes the Court accepts the argument, sometimes not. What precisely was the statutory language at issue in *McNally*? Why did the members of the majority find the language ambiguous? Were they correct?

3. *The* Durland *decision.* The Court in *McNally* discussed its earlier decision in *Durland v. United States*, 161 U.S. 306 (1896). That case was the United States Supreme Court's most important early decision interpreting a predecessor to the modern mail and wire fraud statutes. In *Durland*, the Court found that the mail fraud statute reached more broadly than the then-existing version of the common law crime of false pretenses. The Court thus found that the statute covered false promises of future actions. The Court's approach foretold subsequent, expansive readings of the mail and wire fraud statutes.

4. *Are white collar cases different?* As seen throughout this text, Supreme Court justices who are usually perceived to be "conservative" in criminal cases often vote for the defendant in white collar cases, while "liberal" justices often vote for the government. In his dissent, Justice Stevens emphasized "lingering questions about why a Court that has not been particularly receptive to the rights of criminal defendants in recent years has acted so dramatically to protect the elite class of powerful individuals who will benefit from this decision." Do you agree that the *McNally* decision is class-based?

[2]   Intangible Property Rights

In the next case, the Court applied *McNally* to what it termed "intangible" property rights. What exactly were the rights at issue in this case? How were they different from the "intangible" rights at issue in *McNally*?

CARPENTER v. UNITED STATES
484 U.S. 19 (1987)

Justice White delivered the opinion of the Court.

Petitioners Kenneth Felis and R. Foster Winans were convicted of violating section 10(b) of the Securities Exchange Act of 1934 and Rule 10b-5. They were also found guilty of violating the federal mail and wire fraud statutes, 18 U.S.C. §§ 1341, 1343, and were convicted for conspiracy under 18 U.S.C. § 371. Petitioner David Carpenter, Winans' roommate, was convicted for aiding and abetting. With a minor exception, the Court of Appeals for the Second Circuit affirmed; we granted certiorari.

I.

In 1981, Winans became a reporter for the *Wall Street Journal* (the Journal) and in the summer of 1982 became one of the two writers of a daily column, "Heard on the Street." That column discussed selected stocks or groups of stocks, giving positive and negative information about those stocks and taking "a point of view with respect to investment in the stocks that it reviews." Winans regularly interviewed corporate executives to put together interesting perspectives on the stocks that would be highlighted in upcoming columns, but, at least for the columns at issue here, none contained corporate inside information or any "hold for release" information. Because of the "Heard" column's perceived quality and integrity, it had the potential of affecting the price of the stocks which it examined. The District Court concluded on the basis of testimony presented at trial that the "Heard" column "does have an impact on the market, difficult though it may be to quantify in any particular case."

The official policy and practice at the Journal was that prior to publication, the contents of the column were the Journal's confidential information. Despite the rule, with which Winans was familiar, he entered into a scheme in October 1983 with Peter Brant and petitioner Felis, both connected with the Kidder Peabody brokerage firm in New York City, to give them advance information as to the timing and contents of the "Heard" column. This permitted Brant and Felis and another conspirator, David Clark, a client of Brant, to buy or sell based on the probable impact of the column on the market. Profits were to be shared. The conspirators agreed that the scheme would not affect the journalistic purity of the "Heard" column, and the District Court did not find that the contents of any of the articles were altered to further the profit potential of petitioners' stock-trading scheme. Over a four-month period, the brokers made prepublication trades on the basis of information given them by Winans about the contents of some 27 "Heard" columns. The net profits from these trades were about $690,000.

In November 1983, correlations between the "Heard" articles and trading in the Clark and Felis accounts were noted at Kidder Peabody and inquiries began. Brant and Felis denied knowing anyone at the Journal and took steps to conceal the trades. Later, the Securities and Exchange Commission ("SEC") began an investigation. Questions were met by denials both by the brokers at Kidder Peabody and by Winans at the Journal. As the investigation progressed, the conspirators quarreled, and on March 29, 1984, Winans and Carpenter went to the SEC and revealed the entire scheme. This indictment and a bench trial followed. Brant, who had pleaded guilty under a plea agreement, was a witness for the government.

The District Court found, and the Court of Appeals agreed, that Winans had knowingly breached a duty of confidentiality by misappropriating prepublication information regarding the timing and contents of the "Heard" column, information that had been gained in the course of his employment under the understanding that it would not be revealed in advance of publication and that if it were, he would report it to his employer. It was this appropriation of confidential information that underlay both the securities laws and mail and wire fraud counts.

In affirming the mail and wire fraud convictions, the Court of Appeals ruled that Winans had fraudulently misappropriated "property" within the meaning of the mail and wire fraud statutes and that its revelation had harmed the Journal. It was held as well that the use of the mail and wire services had a sufficient nexus with the scheme to satisfy §§ 1341 and 1343. The petition for certiorari challenged these conclusions.

The Court is evenly divided with respect to the convictions under the securities laws and for that reason affirms the judgment below on those counts. For the reasons that follow, we also affirm the judgment with respect to the mail and wire fraud convictions.

II.

Petitioners assert that their activities were not a scheme to defraud the Journal within the meaning of the mail and wire fraud statutes; and that in any event, they did not obtain any "money or property" from the Journal, which is a necessary element of the crime under our decision last Term in *McNally v. United States*,

483 U.S. 350 (1987). We are unpersuaded by either submission and address the latter first.

We held in *McNally* that the mail fraud statute does not reach "schemes to defraud citizens of their intangible rights to honest and impartial government," and that the statute is "limited in scope to the protection of property rights." Petitioners argue that the Journal's interest in prepublication confidentiality for the "Heard" columns is no more than an intangible consideration outside the reach of § 1341; nor does that law, it is urged, protect against mere injury to reputation. This is not a case like *McNally*, however. The Journal, as Winans' employer, was defrauded of much more than its contractual right to his honest and faithful service, an interest too ethereal in itself to fall within the protection of the mail fraud statute, which "had its origin in the desire to protect individual property rights." *McNally*, 483 U.S. at 359 n.8. Here, the object of the scheme was to take the Journal's confidential business information — the publication schedule and contents of the "Heard" column — and its intangible nature does not make it any less "property" protected by the mail and wire fraud statutes. *McNally* did not limit the scope of § 1341 to tangible as distinguished from intangible property rights.

Confidential business information has long been recognized as property. "Confidential information acquired or compiled by a corporation in the course and conduct of its business is a species of property to which the corporation has the exclusive right and benefit, and which a court of equity will protect through the injunctive process or other appropriate remedy." 3 W. Fletcher, Cyclopedia of Law of Private Corporations § 857.1 at 260 (1986). The Journal had a property right in keeping confidential and making exclusive use, prior to publication, of the schedule and contents of the "Heard" column. As the Court has observed before:

> [N]ews matter, however little susceptible of ownership or dominion in the absolute sense, is stock in trade, to be gathered at the cost of enterprise, organization, skill, labor, and money, and to be distributed and sold to those who will pay money for it, as for any other merchandise.

International News Service v. Associated Press, 248 U.S. 215, 236 (1918).

Petitioners' arguments that they did not interfere with the Journal's use of the information, or did not publicize it and deprive the Journal of the first public use of it, miss the point. The confidential information was generated from the business, and the business had a right to decide how to use it prior to disclosing it to the public. Petitioners cannot successfully contend that a scheme to defraud requires a monetary loss, such as giving the information to a competitor; it is sufficient that the Journal has been deprived of its right to exclusive use of the information, for exclusivity is an important aspect of confidential business information and most private property for that matter.

We cannot accept petitioners' further argument that Winans' conduct in revealing prepublication information was no more than a violation of workplace rules and did not amount to fraudulent activity that is proscribed by the mail fraud statute. Sections 1341 and 1343 reach any scheme to deprive another of money or property by means of false or fraudulent pretenses, representations, or promises.

The District Court found that Winans' undertaking at the Journal was not to reveal prepublication information about his column, a promise that became a sham when in violation of his duty he passed along to his co-conspirators confidential information belonging to the Journal, pursuant to an ongoing scheme to share profits from trading in anticipation of the "Heard" column's impact on the stock market. As the New York courts have recognized: "It is well established, as a general proposition, that a person who acquires special knowledge or information by virtue of a confidential or fiduciary relationship with another is not free to exploit that knowledge or information for his own personal benefit but must account to his principal for any profits derived therefrom." *Diamond v. Oreamuno*, 24 N.Y.2d 494, 497 (1969); *see also* Restatement (Second) of Agency §§ 388, Comment *c*, 396(c) (1958).

We have little trouble in holding that the conspiracy here to trade on the Journal's confidential information is not outside the reach of the mail and wire fraud statutes, provided the other elements of the offenses are satisfied. The Journal's business information that it intended to be kept confidential was its property; the declaration to that effect in the employee manual merely removed any doubts on that score and made the finding of specific intent to defraud that much easier. Winans continued in the employ of the Journal, appropriating its confidential business information for his own use, all the while pretending to perform his duty of safeguarding it. In fact, he told his editors twice about leaks of confidential information not related to the stock-trading scheme, demonstrating both his knowledge that the Journal viewed information concerning the "Heard" column as confidential and his deceit as he played the role of a loyal employee. Furthermore, the District Court's conclusion that each of the petitioners acted with the required specific intent to defraud is strongly supported by the evidence.

Lastly, we reject the submission that using the wires and the mail to print and send the Journal to its customers did not satisfy the requirement that those mediums be used to execute the scheme at issue. The courts below were quite right in observing that circulation of the "Heard" column was not only anticipated but an essential part of the scheme. Had the column not been made available to Journal customers, there would have been no effect on stock prices and no likelihood of profiting from the information leaked by Winans.

The judgment below is *affirmed.*

NOTES AND QUESTIONS

1. *Intangible property rights.* What exactly was the property right at stake in *Carpenter*? How was the victim harmed in *Carpenter*, if at all? Why did the Court reach a different result than the one it reached in *McNally*? Does *Carpenter* limit *McNally*'s significance?

2. *The "right to control" theory.* Is the right to control how property is used a "property" interest? In *United States v. Catalfo*, 64 F.3d 1070, 1076–1077 (7th Cir. 1995), *cert. denied*, 517 U.S. 1192 (1996), for example, the defendant engaged in a scheme to prevent the victim, a commodities firm, from controlling its *risk* of loss. The court found that this satisfied the property requirement. *See also United States v. Gray*, 405 F.3d 227, 234 (4th Cir. 2005) (insurance company's right to control to whom the benefits of an insurance policy would be paid amounted to property interest). Other courts, however, have rejected this theory on the ground that the right to control how property is used does not amount to a common law property interest. *See United States v. Evans*, 844 F.2d 36 (2d Cir. 1988).

3. *Criticisms of Carpenter.* Scholars have criticized the *Carpenter* decision's expansive reading of the mail and wire fraud statutes. As Professor Coffee has written,

> The current insider trading revelations have produced a Supreme Court decision, *Carpenter v. United States*, that exhibits all the characteristics of an overbroad, moralistic legislative response. In *Carpenter*, the Court held unanimously that an employee who leaks to third parties confidential business information belonging to his employer embezzles property in violation of the federal mail and wire fraud statutes, even though the employer suffers no apparent economic injury as a result. At bottom, *Carpenter* rests on an analogy that broadly characterizes the unauthorized communication of trade secrets as equivalent to the crime of embezzlement.

> [T]his view of "confidential information" as a form of property covered by the laws against larceny is (a) historically unsound, (b) inconsistent with most statutory law dealing with the subject of trade secrets, and (c) capable of trivializing the Court's decision only months earlier in *McNally v. United States*, which clearly sought to cut back on the amoebalike growth of the mail and wire fraud statutes. More important than all these considerations, however, is the fact that *Carpenter*'s logic has the potential to alter significantly the relationship between employers and employees across the landscape of American business life.

> More than any other theory that the Court could have chosen to address the evil of insider trading, *Carpenter*'s doctrinal invention — the idea that divulging confidential information of one's employer amounts to embezzlement — has the ability to chill employee mobility and increase the social control that employers have over employees.

John C. Coffee, Jr., *Hush!: The Criminal Status of Confidential Information after* McNally *and* Carpenter *and the Enduring Problem of Overcriminalization*, 26 Am. Crim. L. Rev. 121, 122–123 (1988). Are Professor Coffee's criticisms sound? Why or why not?

*   *   *

Following *McNally* and *Carpenter*, courts struggled to define the term "property," particularly in cases where the government alleged that the "property" at issue was a license or permit. In the next case, the Supreme Court addressed the question whether a license is "property."

CLEVELAND v. UNITED STATES
531 U.S. 12 (2000)

JUSTICE GINSBURG delivered the opinion of the Court.

This case presents the question whether the federal mail fraud statute, 18 U.S.C. § 1341, reaches false statements made in an application for a state license. Section 1341 proscribes use of the mails in furtherance of "any scheme or artifice to defraud, or for obtaining money or property by means of false or fraudulent pretenses, representations, or promises." Petitioner Carl W. Cleveland and others were prosecuted under this federal measure for making false statements in applying to the Louisiana State Police for permission to operate video poker machines. We conclude that permits or licenses of this order do not qualify as "property" within § 1341's compass. It does not suffice, we clarify, that the object of the fraud may become property in the recipient's hands; for purposes of the mail fraud statute, the thing obtained must be property in the hands of the victim. State and municipal licenses in general, and Louisiana's video poker licenses in particular, we hold, do not rank as "property," for purposes of § 1341, in the hands of the official licensor.

I.

Louisiana law allows certain businesses to operate video poker machines. The state itself, however, does not run such machinery. The law requires prospective owners of video poker machines to apply for a license from the State. The licenses are not transferable, and must be renewed annually. To qualify for a license, an applicant must meet suitability requirements designed to ensure that licensees have good character and fiscal integrity.

In 1992, Fred Goodson and his family formed a limited partnership, Truck Stop Gaming, Ltd. (TSG), in order to participate in the video poker business at their truck stop in Slidell, Louisiana. Cleveland, a New Orleans lawyer, assisted Goodson in preparing TSG's application for a video poker license. The application required TSG to identify its partners and to submit personal financial statements for all partners. It also required TSG to affirm that the listed partners were the sole beneficial owners of the business and that no partner held an interest in the partnership merely as an agent or nominee, or intended to transfer the interest in the future.

TSG's application identified Goodson's adult children, Alex and Maria, as the sole beneficial owners of the partnership. It also showed that Goodson and Cleveland's law firm had loaned Alex and Maria all initial capital for the partnership and that Goodson was TSG's general manager. In May 1992, the state approved the application and issued a license. TSG successfully renewed the license in 1993, 1994, and 1995. Each renewal application identified no ownership interests other than those of Alex and Maria.

In 1996, the Federal Bureau of Investigation (FBI) discovered evidence that Cleveland and Goodson had participated in a scheme to bribe state legislators to vote in a manner favorable to the video poker industry. The government charged Cleveland and Goodson with multiple counts of money laundering under 18 U.S.C. § 1957, as well as racketeering and conspiracy under § 1962. Among the predicate acts supporting these charges were four counts of mail fraud under § 1341. The indictment alleged that Cleveland and Goodson had violated § 1341 by fraudulently concealing that they were the true owners of TSG in the initial license application and three renewal applications mailed to the state. They concealed their ownership interests, according to the government, because they had tax and financial problems that could have undermined their suitability to receive a video poker license.

Before trial, Cleveland moved to dismiss the mail fraud counts on the ground that the alleged fraud did not deprive the State of "property" under § 1341. The District Court denied the motion, concluding that "licenses constitute property even before they are issued." A jury found Cleveland guilty on two counts of mail fraud (based on the 1994 and 1995 license renewals) and on money laundering,[c] racketeering,[d] and conspiracy counts predicated on the mail fraud. The District Court sentenced Cleveland to 121 months in prison.

On appeal, Cleveland again argued that Louisiana had no property interest in video poker licenses, relying on several Court of Appeals decisions holding that the government does not relinquish "property" for purposes of § 1341 when it issues a permit or license. *See United States v. Shotts*, 145 F.3d 1289, 1296 (11th Cir. 1998) (license to operate a bail bonds business); *United States v. Schwartz*, 924 F.2d 410, 418 (2d Cir. 1991) (arms export license); *United States v. Granberry*, 908 F.2d 278, 280 (8th Cir. 1990) (school bus operator's permit); *Toulabi v. United States*, 875 F.2d 122, 125 (7th Cir. 1989) (chauffeur's license); *United States v. Dadanian*, 856 F.2d 1391, 1392 (9th Cir. 1988) (gambling license); *United States v. Murphy*, 836 F.2d 248, 254 (6th Cir. 1988) (license to conduct charitable bingo games).

The Court of Appeals for the Fifth Circuit nevertheless affirmed Cleveland's conviction and sentence, considering itself bound by its holding in *United States v. Salvatore*, 110 F.3d 1131, 1138 (5th Cir. 1997), that Louisiana video poker licenses constitute "property" in the hands of the state. Two other circuits have concluded that the issuing authority has a property interest in unissued licenses under § 1341. *United States v. Bucuvalas*, 970 F.2d 937, 945 (1st Cir. 1992) (entertainment and liquor license); *United States v. Martinez*, 905 F.2d 709, 715 (3d Cir. 1990) (medical license).

We granted certiorari to resolve the conflict among the Courts of Appeals, and now reverse the Fifth Circuit's judgment.

II.

In *McNally v. United States*, 483 U.S. 350, 360 (1987), this Court held that the federal mail fraud statute is "limited in scope to the protection of property rights." At the time *McNally* was decided, federal prosecutors had been using § 1341 to attack various forms of corruption that deprived victims of "intangible rights" unrelated to money or property. Reviewing the history of § 1341, we concluded that "the original impetus behind the mail fraud statute was to protect the people from schemes to deprive them of their money or property." *Id.* at 356.

Soon after *McNally*, in *Carpenter v. United States*, 484 U.S. 19, 25 (1987), we again stated that § 1341 protects property rights only. *Carpenter* upheld convictions under § 1341 and the federal wire fraud statute, 18 U.S.C. § 1343, of defendants who had defrauded the *Wall Street Journal* of confidential business information. Citing decisions of this Court as well as a corporate law treatise, we observed that "confidential business information has long been recognized as property." 484 U.S. at 26.

---

[c] As discussed in Chapter 13, Money Laundering, *infra*, mail fraud is an "unlawful activity" that may give rise to money laundering charges under 18 U.S.C. § 1956.

[d] As discussed in Chapter 14, RICO, *infra*, mail fraud is a type of "racketeering activity" that may give rise to charges under the RICO statute, 18 U.S.C. § 1961.

III.

The question presented is whether, for purposes of the federal mail fraud statute, a government regulator parts with "property" when it issues a license. For the reasons we now set out, we hold that § 1341 does not reach fraud in obtaining a state or municipal license of the kind here involved, for such a license is not "property" in the government regulator's hands. Again, as we said in *McNally,* "if Congress desires to go further, it must speak more clearly than it has." 483 U.S. at 360.

To begin with, we think it beyond genuine dispute that whatever interests Louisiana might be said to have in its video poker licenses, the State's core concern is *regulatory.* Louisiana recognizes the importance of "public confidence and trust that gaming activities are conducted honestly and are free from criminal and corruptive elements." La. Rev. Stat. Ann. § 27:306(A)(1). The video poker licensing statute accordingly asserts the State's "legitimate interest in providing strict regulation of all persons, practices, associations, and activities related to the operation of establishments licensed to offer video draw poker devices." *Id.* The statute assigns the Office of State Police, a part of the Department of Public Safety and Corrections, the responsibility to promulgate rules and regulations concerning the licensing process. It also authorizes the state police to deny, condition, suspend, or revoke licenses, to levy fines of up to $1,000 per violation of any rule, and to inspect all premises where video poker devices are offered for play. In addition, the statute defines criminal penalties for unauthorized use of video poker devices, and prescribes detailed suitability requirements for licensees.

In short, the statute establishes a typical regulatory program. It licenses, subject to certain conditions, engagement in pursuits that private actors may not undertake without official authorization. In this regard, it resembles other licensing schemes long characterized by this Court as exercises of state police powers. *E.g., Ziffrin, Inc. v. Reeves,* 308 U.S. 132, 138 (1939) (license to transport alcoholic beverages); *Hall v. Geiger-Jones Co.,* 242 U.S. 539, 558 (1917) (license to sell corporate stock); *Fanning v. Gregoire,* 16 How. 524, 534 (1854) (ferry license); *License Cases,* 5 How. 504, 589 (1847) (license to sell liquor) (opinion of McLean, J.), *overruled on other grounds, Leisy v. Hardin,* 135 U.S. 100 (1890).

Acknowledging Louisiana's regulatory interests, the government offers two reasons why the state also has a property interest in its video poker licenses. First, the state receives a substantial sum of money in exchange for each license and continues to receive payments from the licensee as long as the license remains in effect. Second, the state has significant control over the issuance, renewal, suspension, and revocation of licenses.

Without doubt, Louisiana has a substantial economic stake in the video poker industry. The State collects an upfront "processing fee" for each new license application ($10,000 for truck stops), a separate "processing fee" for each renewal application ($1,000 for truck stops), an "annual fee" from each device owner ($2,000), an additional "device operation" fee, ($1,000 for truck stops), and, most importantly, a fixed percentage of net revenue from each video poker device (32.5% for truck stops). It is hardly evident, however, why these tolls should make video poker licenses "property" in the hands of the State. The State receives the lion's share of its expected revenue not while the licenses remain in its own hands, but only *after* they have been issued to licensees. Licenses pre-issuance do not generate an ongoing stream of revenue. At most, they entitle the State to collect a processing fee from applicants for new licenses. Were an entitlement of this order sufficient to establish a state property right, one could scarcely avoid the conclusion that States have property rights in any license or permit requiring an upfront fee, including drivers' licenses, medical licenses, and fishing and hunting licenses. Such licenses, as the government itself concedes, are "purely regulatory."

Tellingly, as to the character of Louisiana's stake in its video poker licenses, the government nowhere alleges that Cleveland defrauded the State of any money to which the State was entitled by law. Indeed, there is no dispute that TSG paid the State of Louisiana its proper share of revenue, which totaled more than $1.2 million, between 1993 and 1995. If Cleveland defrauded the State of "property," the nature of that property cannot be economic.

Addressing this concern, the government argues that Cleveland frustrated the State's right to control the issuance, renewal, and revocation of video poker licenses under La.Rev.Stat. Ann. §§ 27:306, 27:308. The Fifth Circuit has characterized the protected interest as "Louisiana's right to choose the persons to whom it issues video poker licenses." *Salvatore*, 110 F.3d at 1140. But far from composing an interest that "has long been recognized as property," *Carpenter*, 484 U.S. at 26, these intangible rights of allocation, exclusion, and control amount to no more and no less than Louisiana's sovereign power to regulate. Notably, the government overlooks the fact that these rights include the distinctively sovereign authority to impose criminal penalties for violations of the licensing scheme, La. Rev. Stat. Ann. § 27:309, including making false statements in a license application, § 27:309(A). Even when tied to an expected stream of revenue, the State's right of control does not create a property interest any more than a law licensing liquor sales in a State that levies a sales tax on liquor. Such regulations are paradigmatic exercises of the States' traditional police powers.

The government compares the State's interest in video poker licenses to a patent holder's interest in a patent that she has not yet licensed. Although it is true that both involve the right to exclude, we think the congruence ends there. Louisiana does not conduct gaming operations itself, it does not hold video poker licenses to reserve that prerogative, and it does not "sell" video poker licenses in the ordinary commercial sense. Furthermore, while a patent holder may sell her patent, *see* 35 U.S.C. § 261 ("patents shall have the attributes of personal property"), the State may not sell its licensing authority. Instead of a patent holder's interest in an unlicensed patent, the better analogy is to the federal government's interest in an unissued patent. That interest, like the State's interest in licensing video poker operations, surely implicates the government's role as sovereign, not as property holder.

The government also compares the State's licensing power to a franchisor's right to select its franchisees. On this view, Louisiana's video poker licensing scheme represents the State's venture into the video poker business. Although the State could have chosen to run the business itself, the government says, it decided to franchise private entities to carry out the operations instead. However, a franchisor's right to select its franchisees typically derives from its ownership of a trademark, brand name, business strategy, or other product that it may trade or sell in the open market. Louisiana's authority to select video poker licensees rests on no similar asset. It rests instead upon the State's sovereign right to exclude applicants deemed unsuitable to run video poker operations. A right to exclude in that governing capacity is not one appropriately labeled "property." Moreover, unlike an entrepreneur or business partner who shares both losses and gains arising from a business venture, Louisiana cannot be said to have put its labor or capital at risk through its fee-laden licensing scheme. In short, the State did not decide to venture into the video poker business; it decided typically to permit, regulate, and tax private operators of the games.

We reject the government's theories of property rights not simply because they stray from traditional concepts of property. We resist the government's reading of § 1341 as well because it invites us to approve a sweeping expansion of federal criminal jurisdiction in the absence of a clear statement by Congress. Equating issuance of licenses or permits with deprivation of property would subject to federal mail fraud prosecution a wide range of conduct traditionally regulated by state and local authorities. We note in this regard that Louisiana's video poker statute typically and unambiguously imposes criminal penalties for making false statements on license applications. La.Rev.Stat. Ann. § 27:309(A). As we reiterated last Term, " 'unless Congress conveys its purpose clearly, it will not be deemed to have significantly changed the federal-state balance' in the prosecution of crimes." *Jones v. United States*, 529 U.S. 848, 858 (2000) (quoting *United States v. Bass*, 404 U.S. 336, 349 (1971)).

Moreover, to the extent that the word "property" is ambiguous as placed in § 1341, we have instructed that "ambiguity concerning the ambit of criminal statutes should be resolved in favor of lenity." *Rewis v. United States*, 401 U.S. 808, 812 (1971). This interpretive guide is especially appropriate in construing § 1341 because, as this case demonstrates, mail fraud is a predicate offense under RICO, 18 U.S.C. § 1961(1), and the money laundering statute, § 1956(c)(7)(A). In deciding what is "property" under § 1341, we think "it is appropriate, before we choose the harsher alternative, to require that Congress should have spoken in language that is clear and definite." *United States v. Universal C.I.T. Credit Corp.*, 344 U.S. 218, 222 (1952).

IV.

We conclude that § 1341 requires the object of the fraud to be "property" in the victim's hands and that a Louisiana video poker license in the State's hands is not "property" under § 1341. Absent clear statement by Congress, we will not read the mail fraud statute to place under federal superintendence a vast array of conduct traditionally policed by the States. Our holding means that Cleveland's § 1341 conviction must be vacated. Accordingly, the judgment of the United States Court of Appeals for the Fifth Circuit is reversed, and the case is remanded for further proceedings consistent with this opinion.

NOTES AND QUESTIONS

1. *Varying interpretations of the mail and wire fraud statutes.* In *Carpenter*, the Court broadly interpreted the concept of "property" under the statutes. In *Cleveland*, the Court reverted to a narrow construction of the statutes. Can you explain the varying outcomes? Under these cases, what is the current definition of "property" for mail and wire fraud purposes?

2. *The right to collect taxes as a property interest.* By a five-to-four vote, the Supreme Court, in *Pasquantino v. United States,* 544 U.S. 349 (2005), held that Canada's right to collect taxes on imported liquor constitutes "property" under the wire fraud statute. The defendants had smuggled liquor from the United States into Canada, depriving Canada of importation and sales taxes on the liquor. The Court found that Canada's right to collect these taxes is a "straightforward 'economic' interest" that is distinguishable from the alleged property interest at issue in *Cleveland. Pasquantino,* 544 U.S. at 357. The case also extended the mail and wire fraud statutes to cases where the alleged victim was a foreign government. In her dissent, Justice Ginsburg concluded that "the Court has ascribed an exorbitant scope to the wire fraud statute." *Id.* at 373 (Ginsburg, J., dissenting).

3. *The charging decision.* As discussed in the introductory notes to this chapter, the mail and wire fraud statutes may give rise to charges under RICO and the money laundering statute — charges that carry substantial penalties, including forfeiture of the defendant's property. Can you speculate why the prosecutor in this case decided to include those charges?

PROBLEMS

4-2. Terry Howard was the Comptroller of the State Bridge Commission (the "Commission"). The Commission operates and maintains bridges within the state. Among these bridges are seven toll bridges that generate more than ten million dollars in revenue annually. Mike Moose was the state's executive auditor and was Howard's close personal friend. Ten people are members of the Commission.

The Commission invested toll bridge revenues in short-term certificates of deposit at banks selected through competitive bidding. As the Commission's Comptroller, Howard was responsible for this process. Howard would notify interested banks that the Commission had money it wished to deposit and would advise banks that they could submit confidential bids to him in writing or by telephone by a certain deadline. Commission guidelines required that, after the bidding deadline passed, the funds be deposited with the bank that had offered the highest interest rate on the certificates of deposit.

On 10 occasions, Howard disclosed bidding information to Moose, who in turn disclosed the information to a representative of Acme Bank. Acme Bank was thus able to outbid the other banks by offering a slightly higher rate of interest and, as a result, received deposits of $40,000,000 in Commission funds. Howard and Moose were both investors in Acme bank.

The government indicted Howard and Moose on the theory that they engaged in a scheme to defraud banks who submitted failed bids in the bidding process. According to the government, the victim banks were deprived of their intangible property interest in the chance to compete in a fair bidding process.

The defendants have moved to dismiss the indictment. How should the court rule? Why?

4-3. The defendants have been charged with defrauding the United States government by arranging sales of privately owned, U.S.-made weapons to Iran. United States law prohibits such sales. As part of the scheme, the defendants allegedly used the mail to deceive the United States into believing that the true destination of the arms was Israel, not Iran. The United States government has a right to veto the sale of U.S.-made weapons from one government to another, and thus would have had the right to veto a sale of the weapons by Israel to Iran. The weapons actually were sold directly to Iran. The government's theory is that its right to veto sales of U.S.-made or licensed weapons by one foreign government to another is a property right for wire and mail fraud purposes.

Defendants have moved to dismiss the indictment. Should they succeed? Why or why not?

4-4. The government has indicted the law firm of Milton & Wise, LLP, along with the two name partners. Milton & Wise is known as one of the country's leading plaintiffs' securities fraud class action law firms. The indictment alleges that defendants arranged for kickbacks to be paid to the named plaintiffs in law suits in which the firm represented the class members. Many of the kickbacks were in the form of checks sent through the U.S. mail. According to the indictment, the defendants paid the kickbacks so that they would have a "stable" of named plaintiffs and could be the "first lawyers to get to court" to file a class action law suit and thus could represent the class members and eventually obtain attorneys' fees resulting from the suit.

Among the charges is mail fraud based on the theory that the class members were defrauded of money in the form of "the amount of any kickback that Milberg Weiss paid using attorneys' fees obtained in the lawsuit." According to the indictment, the kickbacks came from court-approved attorneys' fees, not from the amount recovered by the plaintiff class members.

In addition to the deprivation of money, the indictment also alleges that class members were deprived of the intangible property interest in "material economic information that affected their right and ability to influence and control" their cases. Because the named plaintiffs were receiving kickbacks, according to this theory, the named plaintiffs had an interest in maximizing attorneys' fees rather than in maximizing the class members' recovery. The defendants have uncontroverted expert testimony, however, that "in the vast majority of securities class action cases, the plaintiffs' attorneys actually conduct the litigation without any oversight by the named plaintiffs."

Defendants seek your advice with respect to a possible motion to dismiss the indictment. Are there grounds for seeking dismissal? If so, what are the chances for success? Why?

[3]   Honest Services

Recall that *McNally* held that, in a mail or wire fraud prosecution, the government must prove an intended deprivation of money or property. The Court therefore reversed a conviction where the alleged loss was of "honest services." Congress, however, responded to *McNally*, and reinstated the deprivation of "honest services" as a viable mail or wire fraud theory. Specifically, Congress adopted the following provision, enacted at 18 U.S.C. § 1346, as part of the Drug-Abuse Act of 1988:

Definition of "scheme or artifice to defraud"

> For the purpose of this chapter, the term "scheme or artifice to defraud" includes a scheme or artifice to deprive another of the intangible right of honest services.

As is apparent from the text of § 1346, the statute does not define the term "honest services." As one appellate court noted, "[t]he central problem is that the concept of 'honest services' is vague and undefined by the statute." *United States v. Urciuoli*, 513 F.3d 290, 294 (1st Cir. 2008). The circuit courts have adopted widely divergent approaches to this issue, as the following decisions indicate. The first case below deals with a public sector employee; the case that follows concerns a private employee. As you read the cases, attempt to delineate as best you can the scope of potential liability for public and private sector defendants.

[a]   Public sector defendants

UNITED STATES v. CZUBINSKI
106 F.3d 1069 (1st Cir. 1997)

TORRUELLA, CHIEF JUDGE.

Defendant-appellant Richard Czubinski ("Czubinski") appeals his jury conviction on nine counts of wire fraud, 18 U.S.C. §§ 1343, 1346, and four counts of computer fraud, 18 U.S.C. § 1030(a)(4).[c]

BACKGROUND

I. Pertinent Facts

For all periods relevant to the acts giving rise to his conviction, the defendant Czubinski was employed as a Contact Representative in the Boston office of the Taxpayer Services Division of the Internal Revenue Service ("IRS"). To perform his official duties, which mainly involved answering questions from taxpayers regarding their returns, Czubinski routinely accessed information from one of the IRS's computer systems known as the Integrated Data Retrieval System ("IDRS"). Using a valid password given to Contact Representatives, certain search codes, and taxpayer social security numbers, Czubinski was able to retrieve, to his terminal screen in Boston, income tax return information regarding virtually any taxpayer — information that is permanently stored in the IDRS "master file" located in Martinsburg, West Virginia. In the period of Czubinski's employ, IRS rules plainly stated that employees with passwords and access codes were not permitted to access files on IDRS outside of the course of their official duties.

In 1992, Czubinski carried out numerous unauthorized searches of IDRS files. He knowingly disregarded IRS rules by looking at confidential information obtained by performing computer searches that were outside of the scope of his duties as a Contact Representative, including, but not limited to, the searches listed in the indictment. Audit trails performed by internal IRS auditors establish that Czubinski frequently made unauthorized accesses on IDRS in 1992.

---

[c] The computer fraud aspect of this case is discussed in Chapter 6, Computer Crimes, *infra.*

Nothing in the record indicates that Czubinski did anything more than knowingly disregard IRS rules by observing the confidential information he accessed. No evidence suggests, nor does the government contend, that Czubinski disclosed the confidential information he accessed to any third parties. The government's only evidence demonstrating any intent to use the confidential information for nefarious ends was the trial testimony of William A. Murray, an acquaintance of Czubinski who briefly participated in Czubinski's local Invisible Knights of the Ku Klux Klan ("KKK") chapter and worked with him on the David Duke campaign. Murray testified that Czubinski had once stated at a social gathering in "early 1992" that "he intended to use some of that information to build dossiers on people" involved in "the white supremacist movement." There is, however, no evidence that Czubinski created dossiers, took steps toward making dossiers (such as by printing out or recording the information he browsed), or shared any of the information he accessed in the years following the single comment to Murray. No other witness testified to having any knowledge of Czubinski's alleged intent to create "dossiers" on KKK members.

The portion of the indictment alleging wire fraud states that Czubinski defrauded the IRS of confidential property and defrauded the IRS and the public of his honest services by using his valid password to acquire confidential taxpayer information as part of a scheme to: (1) build "dossiers" on associates in the KKK; (2) seek information regarding an assistant district attorney who was then prosecuting Czubinski's father on an unrelated criminal charge; and (3) perform opposition research by inspecting the records of a political opponent in the race for a Boston City Councilor seat. The wire fraud indictment, therefore, articulated particular personal ends to which the unauthorized access to confidential information through interstate wires was allegedly a means.

DISCUSSION

*   *   *

The government pursued two theories of wire fraud in this prosecution: first, that Czubinski defrauded the IRS of its property, under § 1343, by acquiring confidential information for certain intended personal uses; second, that he defrauded the IRS and the public of their intangible right to his honest services, under §§ 1343 and 1346. We consider the evidence with regard to each theory, in turn.

A. Scheme to Defraud IRS of Property

The government correctly notes that confidential information may constitute intangible "property" and that its unauthorized dissemination or other use may deprive the owner of its property rights. *See Carpenter v. United States*, 484 U.S. 19, 26 (1987).

The government, however, provides no case in support of its contention here that merely accessing confidential information, without doing, or clearly intending to do, more, is tantamount to a deprivation of IRS property under the wire fraud statute. We do not think that Czubinski's unauthorized browsing, even if done with the intent to deceive the IRS into thinking he was performing only authorized searches, constitutes a "deprivation" within the meaning of the federal fraud statutes.

Binding precedents, and good sense, support the conclusion that to "deprive" a person of their intangible property interest in confidential information under § 1343, either some articulable harm must befall the holder of the information as a result of the defendant's activities, or some gainful use must be intended by the person accessing the information, whether or not this use is profitable in the economic sense. Here, neither the taking of the IRS' right to "exclusive use" of the confidential information, nor Czubinski's gain from access to the information, can be shown absent evidence of his "use" of the information. Accordingly, without evidence that Czubinski used or intended to use the taxpayer information (beyond mere browsing), an intent to deprive cannot be proven, and, *a fortiori*, a scheme to defraud is not shown.

All of the cases cited by the government in support of their contention that the confidentiality breached by Czubinski's search in itself constitutes a deprivation of property in fact support our holding today, for they all involve, at a minimum, a finding of a further intended use of the confidential information accessed by the defendants. The government's best support comes from *United States v. Seidlitz*, 589 F.2d 152, 160 (4th Cir.1978), in which a former employee of a computer systems firm secretly accessed its files, but never was shown to have sold or used the data he accessed, and was nevertheless convicted of wire fraud. The affirming Fourth Circuit held, however, that a jury could have reasonably found that, at the time the defendant raided a competitor's computer system, he intended to retrieve information that would be helpful for his own start-up, competing computer firm. In the instant case, Czubinski did indeed access confidential information through fraudulent pretenses — he appeared to be performing his duties when in fact he used IRS passwords to perform unauthorized searches. Nevertheless, it was not proven that he intended to deprive the IRS of their property interest through either disclosure or use of that information.

The resolution of the instant case is complex because it is well-established that to be convicted of mail or wire fraud, the defendant need not successfully carry out an intended scheme to defraud. The government does not contend either that Czubinski actually created dossiers or that he accomplished some other end through use of the information. It need not do so. All that the government was required to prove was the *intent* to follow through with a deprivation of the IRS's property and the use or foreseeable use of interstate wire transmissions pursuant to the accomplishment of the scheme to defraud. In the case at bar, the government failed to make even this showing

Mere browsing of the records of people about whom one might have a particular interest, although reprehensible, is not enough to sustain a wire fraud conviction on a "deprivation of intangible property" theory. Curiosity on the part of an IRS officer may lead to dismissal, but curiosity alone will not sustain a finding of participation in a felonious criminal scheme to deprive the IRS of its property.

B. Honest Services Fraud (§ 1346)

In *McNally v. United States*, 483 U.S. 350 (1987), the Supreme Court held that the mail and wire fraud statutes do not prohibit schemes to defraud individuals of their intangible, nonproperty right to honest government services. Congress responded to *McNally* in 1988 by enacting § 1346, the honest services amendment, which provides:

> For the purposes of this chapter, the term "scheme or artifice to defraud" includes a scheme or artifice to deprive another of the intangible right of honest services.

18 U.S.C. § 1346. We have held, after considering the relevant legislative history, that § 1346 effectively restores to the scope of the mail and wire fraud statutes their pre-*McNally* applications to government officials' schemes to defraud individuals of their intangible right to honest services.

We recently had the opportunity to discuss, at some length, the proper application of the § 1346 honest services amendment to the wrongful acts of public officials. *See United States v. Sawyer*, 85 F.3d 713, 723 (1st Cir. 1996). The discussion and holding in *Sawyer* directly guide our disposition of the instant appeal.[12] First, as a general matter, we noted in *Sawyer* that although the right to honest services "eludes easy definition," honest services convictions of public officials typically involve serious corruption, such as embezzlement of public funds, bribery of public officials, or the failure of public decision-makers to disclose certain conflicts of interest. Second, we cautioned that "[t]he broad scope of the mail fraud statute, however, does not encompass every instance of official misconduct that results in the official's personal gain." Third, and most importantly, *Sawyer* holds that the government must not merely indicate wrongdoing by a public official, but must also demonstrate that the wrongdoing at issue is intended to prevent or call into question the proper or impartial performance of that public servant's official duties. *Id.* at 725 (citing pre-*McNally* precedent to demonstrate that even where public officials violated state laws, their actions were not found to defraud citizens of their right to honest services, because the officials did not actually fail to perform their official duties properly). In other words, "although a public official might engage in reprehensible misconduct related to an official position, the conviction of that official cannot stand where the conduct does not actually deprive the public of its right to her honest services, and it is not shown to intend that result." *Id.*

Applying these principles to Czubinski's acts, it is clear that his conviction cannot stand. First, this case falls outside of the core of honest services fraud precedents. Czubinski was not bribed or otherwise influenced in any public decision-making capacity. Nor did he embezzle funds. He did not receive, nor can it be found that he intended to receive, any tangible benefit. His official duty was to respond to informational requests from taxpayers regarding their returns, a relatively straightforward task that simply does not raise the specter of secretive, self-interested action, as does a discretionary, decision-making role.

Second, we believe that the cautionary language of *Sawyer* is particularly appropriate here, given the evidence amassed by the defendant at trial indicating that during his span of employment at IRS, he received no indication from his employer that this workplace violation — the performance of unauthorized searches — would be punishable by anything more than dismissal. "To allow every transgression of state governmental obligations to amount to mail fraud would effectively turn every such violation into a federal felony; this cannot be countenanced." Here, the threat is one of transforming governmental workplace violations

---

[12] In *Sawyer*, we vacated and remanded for further fact-finding the mail and wire fraud conviction of a private lobbyist who was found to have violated Massachusetts' gift and gratuity statutes in the course of his lobbying activities. The conviction was vacated because the violation of the gift statute, in itself, was held insufficient to establish a scheme to defraud the public of its intangible right to honest services.

into felonies. We find no evidence that Congress intended to create what amounts to a draconian personnel regulation. We hesitate to imply such an unusual result in the absence of the clearest legislative mandate.

These general considerations, although serious, are not conclusive: they raise doubts as to the propriety of this conviction that can be outweighed by sufficient evidence of a scheme to defraud. The third principle identified in *Sawyer*, instructing us as to the basic requirements of a scheme to defraud in this context, settles any remaining doubts. The conclusive consideration is that the government simply did not prove that Czubinski deprived, or intended to deprive, the public or his employer of their right to his honest services. Although he clearly committed wrongdoing in searching confidential information, there is no suggestion that he failed to carry out his official tasks adequately, or intended to do so.

The government alleges that, in addition to defrauding the public of his honest services, Czubinski has defrauded the IRS as well. The IRS is a public entity, rendering this contention sufficiently answered by our holding above that Czubinski did not defraud the public of his honest services. Even if the IRS were a private employer, however, the pre-*McNally* honest services convictions involving private fraud victims indicate that there must be a breach of a fiduciary duty to an employer that involves self-dealing of an order significantly more serious than the misconduct at issue here. Once again, the government has failed to prove that Czubinski intended to use the IRS files he browsed for any private purposes, and hence his actions, however reprehensible, do not rise to the level of a scheme to defraud his employer of his honest services.

CONCLUSION

We add a cautionary note. The broad language of the mail and wire fraud statutes are both their blessing and their curse. They can address new forms of serious crime that fail to fall within more specific legislation. *See United States v. Maze*, 414 U.S. 395, 405–06 (1974) (observing that the mail fraud statute serves "as a first line of defense" or "stopgap device" to tackle new types of frauds before particularized legislation is developed) (Burger, C.J., dissenting). On the other hand, they might be used to prosecute kinds of behavior that, albeit offensive to the morals or aesthetics of federal prosecutors, cannot reasonably be expected by the instigators to form the basis of a federal felony. The case at bar falls within the latter category. Also discomforting is the prosecution's insistence, before trial, on the admission of inflammatory evidence regarding the defendant's membership in white supremacist groups purportedly as a means to prove a scheme to defraud, when, on appeal, it argues that unauthorized access in itself is a sufficient ground for conviction on all counts. Finally, we caution that the wire fraud statute must not serve as a vehicle for prosecuting only those citizens whose views run against the tide, no matter how incorrect or uncivilized such views are.

For the reasons stated in this opinion, the defendant's conviction is thus reversed on all counts.

NOTES AND QUESTIONS

1. *Public official "honest services" cases.* During the 1970s, prosecutors increasingly began to use the mail and wire fraud statutes in cases brought against federal, state, and local political officials for failure to provide "honest services." As Justice Stevens noted in his *McNally* dissent, "In the public sector, judges, state governors, chairmen of state political parties, state cabinet officers, city aldermen, Congressmen and many other state and federal officials have been convicted of defrauding citizens of their right to the honest services of their governmental officials." Are the mail and wire fraud statutes properly used as political corruption statutes?

2. *The meaning of "honest services" fraud.* The courts have adopted varying approaches to defining honest services fraud by public officials. If you were advising a public official client, how would you define such fraud?

a. *The* Czubinski *rule.* Why did the court in *Czubinski* find that the defendant had not committed honest services fraud? What standard did the court adopt in that case?

b. *Personal gain?* Some courts limit honest services fraud cases to instances where the defendant was misusing a public position for personal gain. For example, the Seventh Circuit limits honest services fraud cases against public officials to instances where the defendant was misusing a public position for personal gain. *See United States v. Thompson*, 484 F.3d 877, 883–884 (7th Cir. 2007) (reversing conviction of state official who arranged to have a state contract awarded to a politically favored travel agency); *United States v. Bloom*, 149 F.3d 649, 656–657 (7th Cir. 1998) (reversing conviction of city official, and holding that an employee deprives his employer of his honest services only if he misuses his position (or the information he obtained in it) for personal gain). That same court has held that the personal gain requirement is met where the defendant schemed to benefit a third party. *See United States v. Sorich*, 523 F.3d 702, 710–711 (7th Cir. 2008) (defendants were city employees who violated city hiring rules so that political allies would get city jobs, satisfying the private gain requirement). Other circuits have rejected the private gain requirement. *See, e.g., United States v. Welch*, 327 F.3d 1081, 1106 (10th Cir. 2003).

c. *State law violation?* Courts are split as to the role of state law in defining honest services fraud. As one court stated when attempting to discern the limits of honest services fraud:

> The relationship between state law and the federal honest services statute is unsettled. The Fifth Circuit has held that § 1346 extends only to conduct that independently violates state law. *United States v. Brumley*, 116 F.3d 728 (5th Cir.) (en banc). Other circuits have denied that state law plays any necessary role. *E.g., United States v. Margiotta*, 688 F.2d 108, 124 (2d Cir.1982); *United States v. Keane*, 522 F.2d 534, 545 (7th Cir.1975). It is plain that §§ 1341 and 1346 enact a federal crime — but beyond that, broad generalizations may be unsafe.

United States v. Urciuoli, 513 F.3d 290, 298 (1st Cir. 2008).

Do these varying approaches have anything common? What are the courts attempting to do in setting forth these rules?

3. *The deprivation of property theory.* The government's alternative theory was that *Czubinski* intended to deprive the IRS of its property. Given that *Carpenter* held that confidential business information constitutes "property," why did the court reject this theory?

4. *Legislative history.* The legislative history behind § 1346 provides scant guidance in defining "honest services." One opinion summarized the history as follows:

> The specific text of what has become 18 U.S.C. § 1346 was inserted in the Omnibus Drug Bill for the first time on the very day that the Omnibus Drug Bill was finally passed by both the House and the Senate. The text of what is now § 1346 was never included in any bill as filed in either the House of Representatives or the Senate. As a result, the text of § 1346 was never referred to any committee of either the House or the Senate, was never the subject of any committee report from either the House or the Senate, and was never the subject of any floor debate reported in the Congressional Record.

Brumley, 116 F.3d at 742 (Jolly, J., dissenting).

Thus, courts have little to go on when attempting to define "honest services" in public official cases. As seen in the next section, the situation is even more complicated in prosecutions of private sector defendants. Does this uncertainty raise constitutional concerns? That is one issue in the next case.

[b]   Private sector defendants

UNITED STATES v. RYBICKI
354 F.3d 124 (2d Cir. 2003) (en banc)

SACK, CIRCUIT JUDGE:

We agreed to rehear this case in banc in order to consider whether 18 U.S.C. § 1346, which provides that "for the purposes of the chapter [of the United States Code that prohibits, inter alia, mail fraud, 18 U.S.C. § 1341, and wire fraud, 18 U.S.C. § 1343], the term 'scheme or artifice to defraud' includes a scheme or artifice to deprive another of the intangible right of honest services," is unconstitutionally vague. Our analysis reveals that the statute's clear prohibition applies to a wide swath of behavior. We conclude that the statute is not unconstitutional on its face.

BACKGROUND

Thomas Rybicki and Fredric Grae, two of the three Defendants-Appellants, are lawyers with offices in New York City's Borough of Richmond. Specializing in personal injury cases, they are members of the third Defendant-Appellant, the law firm of Grae, Rybicki & Partners, P.C. The defendants, acting through intermediaries, arranged for payments to be made to claims adjusters employed by insurance companies that had insured against injuries sustained by the defendants' clients. The payments, designed to induce the adjusters to expedite the settlement of the clients' claims, were typically computed as a percentage of the total settlement amount. Each of the insurance companies maintained a written policy that prohibited the adjusters from accepting any gifts or fees and required them to report the offer of any such gratuities. The payments were nonetheless accepted by the adjusters and, not surprisingly, not reported to their employers. Between 1991 and 1994, the defendants caused such payments to be made to adjusters in at least twenty cases that settled for an aggregate of $3 million. The participants in the scheme, including Grae and Rybicki, took considerable steps to disguise and conceal the payments.

On June 3, 1998, the defendants were indicted for these actions. The superseding indictment charged the defendants with scheming to deprive the insurance companies of their intangible right of the honest services of their employees — the insurance adjusters — by the use of the mails and the wires, in violation of 18 U.S.C. § 1341 (mail fraud), 18 U.S.C. § 1343 (wire fraud), and 18 U.S.C. § 371 (conspiracy).

The jury returned a verdict of guilty against each defendant on twenty counts of mail fraud, two counts of wire fraud, and one count of conspiracy to commit mail fraud.

DISCUSSION

* * *

"Vagueness may invalidate a criminal law for either of two independent reasons. First, it may fail to provide the kind of notice that will enable ordinary people to understand what conduct it prohibits; second, it may authorize and even encourage arbitrary and discriminatory enforcement." *City of Chicago v. Morales*, 527 U.S. 41, 56 (1999) (plurality opinion).

We would, we think, labor long and with difficulty in seeking a clear and properly limited meaning of "scheme or artifice to deprive another of the intangible right of honest services" simply by consulting a dictionary for the literal, "plain" meaning of the phrase. But even if such a "clinical lexical dissection," would not yield a precise meaning to the statutes, that is not the end of our inquiry. *Immediato v. Rye Neck School Dist.*, 73 F.3d 454, 460 (2d Cir. 1996). Our task, then, is to determine whether, even if the meaning of the statute is not plain enough on its face, there was a "well-settled meaning" of "scheme or artifice to deprive another of the intangible right of honest services" at the time that Congress enacted § 1346 in 1988.

The sparse legislative history of § 1346 makes clear, if little else, that the statutory provision was designed to "overrule" *McNally* at least in part, *i.e.*, to place within the statutory proscription certain frauds that *McNally* had held were not covered by the mail- and wire-fraud statutes. Particularly in light of the strong presumption that § 1346, having been duly enacted by Congress and signed into law by the President, is valid, we must therefore look to the case law from the various circuits that *McNally* overruled in order to determine whether there was a clear meaning of "scheme or artifice to deprive another of the intangible right of honest services" at the time that Congress enacted § 1346, and then determine whether that meaning is sufficiently clear.

[T]he particular wording of § 1346 leads us to regard this approach as likely to be fruitful. The statute refers to "a scheme or artifice to deprive another of the intangible right of honest services." The definite article "the" suggests that "intangible right of honest services" had a specific meaning to Congress when it enacted the statute — Congress was recriminalizing mail- and wire-fraud schemes to deprive others of that "intangible right of honest services," which had been protected before *McNally*, not all intangible rights of honest services whatever they might be thought to be. There is no reason to think that Congress sought to grant carte blanche to federal prosecutors, judges and juries to define "honest services" from case to case for themselves.

A. The Pre-*McNally* Cases — Generally

To determine what Congress intended when it recriminalized "honest services" fraud, we have reviewed the principal pre-*McNally* decisions involving or purportedly involving "honest services" fraud in the private sector. The meaning of the phrase "scheme or artifice to defraud" with respect to public corruption cases is not at issue in the matter before us, and, although we have been given no reason to doubt that it is susceptible to a similar mode of analysis, we do not consider it.

The private-sector honest services cases fall into two general groups, cases involving bribes or kickbacks, and cases involving self-dealing.

B. The Bribery or Kickback Cases

In the bribery or kickback cases, a defendant who has or seeks some sort of business relationship or transaction with the victim secretly pays the victim's employee (or causes such a payment to be made) in exchange for favored treatment. In *United States v. George*, 477 F.2d 508 (7th Cir.), *cert. denied*, 414 U.S. 827 (1973), an employee and two of his employer's suppliers were convicted of mail fraud for taking part in a scheme in which the suppliers secretly paid kickbacks to the employee in exchange for the employer's business.

C. The Self-Dealing Cases

In the self-dealing cases, the defendant typically causes his or her employer to do business with a corporation or other enterprise in which the defendant has a secret interest, undisclosed to the employer. In *United States v. Ballard*, 663 F.2d 534 (5th Cir. 1981), *modified in part*, 680 F.2d 352 (5th Cir. 1982), the Fifth Circuit held, with respect to a scheme among employees to make secret profits trading fuel oil, that mail fraud could be established only if there was some detriment to the employer. Where the profit made by the employer was, in any event, the maximum fixed by law, there could be no such detriment and there was therefore no "honest services" fraud.

The self-dealing cases are thus of the same general import as the bribery cases, with this apparent difference: In bribery or kickback cases, the undisclosed bribery itself is sufficient to make out the crime, but in self-dealing cases, the existence of a conflict of interest alone is not sufficient to do so. In the self-dealing context, though not in the bribery context, the defendant's behavior must thus cause, or at least be capable of causing, some detriment — perhaps some economic or pecuniary detriment — to the employer.

D. The Meaning of § 1346 in Private-Sector Cases

In sum, we conclude from the cases in the various circuits that had employed an "honest services" theory prior to Congress's enactment of § 1346 that the term "scheme or artifice to deprive another of the intangible right to honest services" in § 1346, when applied to private actors, means a scheme or artifice to use the mails or wires to enable an officer or employee of a private entity (or a person in a relationship that gives rise to a duty of loyalty comparable to that owed by employees to employers)[17] purporting to act for and in the interests of his or her employer (or of the other person to whom the duty of loyalty is owed) secretly to act in his or her or the defendant's own interests instead, accompanied by a material misrepresentation made or omission of information disclosed to the employer or other person. As noted, in self-dealing cases, unlike bribery or kickback cases, there may also be a requirement of proof that the conflict caused, or at least was capable of causing, some detriment — but that is of no moment with respect to the case at bar, which involves secret payments, not conflicts of interest.

In the case before us, the defendants used the mails and wires to induce insurance adjusters, who were purporting to act for and in the interests of their employer insurance companies, secretly to expedite insurance claims in order to advance their own interest in receiving payments from the defendants. These actions were not disclosed to the employer insurance companies, and hence were accompanied by a material omission. They fall squarely within the meaning of "scheme or artifice to deprive another of the intangible right of honest services" as distilled from the pre-*McNally* private sector cases.

At the end of the day, we simply cannot believe that Messrs. Rybicki and Grae did not know that they were courting prosecution and conviction for mail and wire fraud when they undertook to use the wires and the mails, in effect, to pay off insurance adjustors, while assiduously covering their tracks.

Because we find that the phrase "scheme or artifice to deprive another of the intangible right of honest services" has the meaning it had in the pre-*McNally* case law, we think that the potential reach of § 1346 is not "virtually limitless," *Rybicki*, 287 F.3d at 264. We conclude that the statute, as applied to the defendants' intentionally fraudulent behavior, "define[s] the criminal offense with sufficient definiteness that ordinary people [such as the defendants] can understand what conduct is prohibited and in a manner that does not encourage arbitrary and discriminatory enforcement." *Kolender*, 461 U.S. at 357. It will also "channel the discretion of the prosecution," *Handakas*, 286 F.3d at 101; "it will provide[] explicit standards for those who apply it," *id.* (citation and internal quotation marks omitted). The statute as applied to the facts of this case is therefore not unconstitutionally vague.

The dissent makes much of the differing views among the various circuit courts of appeals in interpreting section 1346, suggesting the hopeless vagueness of the statute. In doing so, it studiously ignores one striking unanimous aspect of the case law: No circuit has ever held, as the dissent would, that section 1346 is unconstitutionally vague.

More important, divergence in panel or circuit views of a statute, criminal or otherwise, is inherent — and common — in our multi-circuit system. Disparity does not establish vagueness.

---

[17] Although the bulk of the pre-*McNally* honest-services cases involved employees, we see no reason the principle they establish would not apply to other persons who assume a legal duty of loyalty comparable to that owed by an officer or employee to a private entity.

[W]e think that a conclusion of facial invalidity would be inconsistent with the foregoing analysis. Our analysis reveals that the statute's clear prohibition applies to a wide swath of behavior. We conclude that the statute is not unconstitutional on its face.

* * *

The Intent Required for a § 1346 Violation

With respect to the intent necessary to make out a violation, we agree with the *Rybicki* panel's observation that, in accordance with our post-1988 case law, actual or intended economic or pecuniary harm to the victim need not be established. *Rybicki*, 287 F.3d at 261. "The only intent that need be proven in an honest services fraud is the intent to deprive another of the intangible right of honest services." *Id.* at 262 (citing *United States v. Sancho*, 157 F.3d 918, 921 (2d Cir. 1998)).

"Reasonably Foreseeable Harm" or "Materiality"?

The *Rybicki* panel also "held that the elements necessary to establish the offense of honest services fraud pursuant to 18 U.S.C. § 1346 are: (1) a scheme or artifice to defraud; (2) for the purpose of depriving another of the intangible right of honest services; (3) where it is reasonably foreseeable that the scheme could cause some economic or pecuniary harm to the victim that is more than de minimis; and (4) use of the mails or wires in furtherance of the scheme." *Rybicki*, 287 F.3d at 266. We agree as to the first, second and fourth elements of the crime, but disagree as to the third.

Courts defining the elements of "honest services" fraud have chosen between two tests, "reasonably foreseeable harm" and "materiality." *See United States v. Vinyard*, 266 F.3d 320, 327–28 (4th Cir. 2001). The "reasonably foreseeable harm" standard has had, as the *Rybicki* panel noted, several incarnations. In the version that the *Rybicki* panel adopted, it must have been "reasonably foreseeable that the scheme could cause some economic or pecuniary harm to the victim that [was] more than de minimis." 287 F.3d at 266.

In *Vinyard*, the Fourth Circuit explained that under the competing "materiality" test, the trier of fact determines whether the misrepresentation "has the natural tendency to influence or is capable of influencing the employer to change his behavior." 266 F.3d at 328. The *Rybicki* panel identified three Circuits that have taken an approach similar to the Fourth Circuit's. We agree with these Circuits, and adopt the materiality test, holding that the misrepresentation or omission at issue for an "honest services" fraud conviction must be "material," such that the misinformation or omission would naturally tend to lead or is capable of leading a reasonable employer to change its conduct. The question whether it is the business conduct of the defrauded victim that must always be at issue is not before us and we therefore do not decide it.

We prefer the "materiality" test because it has the virtue of arising out of fundamental principles of the law of fraud: A material misrepresentation is an element of the crime. The "non-de minimis reasonably foreseeable harm" test, by contrast, seems to be something of an *ipse dixit* designed simply to limit the scope of § 1346. As such, its foundation appears less secure.

The reasonably foreseeable harm test of the *Rybicki* panel opinion is limited to "economic or pecuniary harm." In this respect "materiality" may be a somewhat broader test: It may capture some cases of non-economic, yet serious, harm in the private sphere.

We expect the materiality requirement also to perform the function for which the panel opinion's "de minimis" requirement was designed. We doubt that the failure to disclose to an employer a de minimis "bribe" — the free telephone call, luncheon invitation, or modest Christmas present — is a material misrepresentation in the sense in which we and other Circuits use the term.

The district court instructed the jury not only, as the district court noted, as to reasonable forseeability, but also that to convict, the jury was required to find that the scheme or artifice of the defendants employed to its ends material omissions in the information given to the insurance companies by their employees. We think that based on the evidence presented at trial with respect to such omissions, the jury could reasonably have concluded that they occurred and that they were material.

CONCLUSION

We conclude that the behavior of the defendants falls squarely within the meaning of a "scheme or artifice to deprive another of the intangible right of honest services," measuring it against the use of the term in the case law at the time § 1346 was adopted. The phrase "scheme or artifice [to defraud] by depriving another of the intangible right of honest services," in the private sector context, means a scheme or artifice to use the mails or wires to enable an officer or employee of a private entity (or a person in a relationship that gives rise to a duty of loyalty comparable to that owed by employees to employers) purporting to act for and in the interests of his or her employer (or of the other person to whom the duty of loyalty is owed) secretly to act in his or her or the defendant's own interests instead, accompanied by a material misrepresentation made or omission of information disclosed to the employer or other person. The defendants in this case, using the mails and the wires with specific intent to defraud, caused the insurance-adjuster employees of the insurance companies to be bribed so that the insurance companies would pay claims in a manner that was not in the interests of the insurance companies but was, instead, secretly in the interests of the defendants. There were material omissions in the employees' communications with their employers that were necessary to the success of the scheme. The defendants' behavior therefore fell within the statutes' clear proscription.

There was sufficient evidence at trial to establish the four elements of the crime: (1) a scheme or artifice to defraud; (2) for the purpose of knowingly and intentionally depriving another of the intangible right of honest services as thus defined; (3) where the misrepresentations (or omissions) made by the defendants are material in that they have the natural tendency to influence or are capable of influencing the employer to change its behavior; and (4) use of the mails or wires in furtherance of the scheme.

The judgments of conviction and sentence of the district court are therefore affirmed.

DENNIS JACOBS, CIRCUIT JUDGE, joined by WALKER, CHIEF JUDGE, CABRANES and PARKER, CIRCUIT JUDGES, dissenting:

* * *

The first question that bears on the vagueness inquiry is whether "a penal statute define[s] the criminal offense with sufficient definiteness that ordinary people can understand what conduct is prohibited." *Kolender*, 461 U.S. at 357. "The plain meaning of 'honest services' in the text of § 1346 simply provides no clue to the public or the courts as to what conduct is prohibited under the statute." *Handakas*, 286 F.3d at 104. The majority opinion is a prolonged and sustained search for some prior settled meaning for an opaque statutory phrase — "the intangible right of honest services" — so that it can be construed as a term of art. That effort to infuse the putative term of art with meaning is conducted in a painstaking way, and considers an abundant variety of alternative meanings. However, a term of art has one single and apparent meaning, in the same way that a pun has two; it is as odd to conduct a scholarly search for the meaning of a term of art as it would be to hear a pun, conduct research in semantics, etymology and philology for a month, and then laugh.

It may be (as the majority holds) that, in enacting § 1346, Congress intended to reinstate a body of case law that had been overruled by the Supreme Court in *McNally*. But that insight gets us nowhere in terms of limits on prosecutorial power and notice to the public. A statute is unconstitutionally vague unless it provides a "person of ordinary intelligence a reasonable opportunity to know what is prohibited." *United States v. Strauss*, 999 F.2d 692, 697 (2d Cir. 1993). We have held that notice is insufficient if lay persons are required to "perform[] the lawyer-like task of statutory interpretation by reconciling the text of [] separate documents." *Chatin v. Coombe*, 186 F.3d 82, 89 (2d Cir. 1999). Construing a statute (as the majority does here) to say that scores of overruled cases are hereby revived, requires lay persons to do lawyer-like tasks that few lawyers would have the skills to perform:

> No one can know what is forbidden by § 1346 without undertaking the "lawyer-like task" of answering the following questions: [1] Can pre-*McNally* case law be consulted to illuminate the wording of § 1346? [2] Can any meaning be drawn from the case law, either the uneven pre-*McNally* cases or the few cases decided post- § 1346? [3] Is one to be guided only by case law within one's own circuit, or by the law of the circuits taken together (if that is possible)?

Handakas, 28 F.3d at 105.

It is only too obvious that there is no settled meaning to the phrase "the intangible right of honest services" that is capable of providing constitutionally adequate notice. How can the public be expected to know what the statute means when the judges and prosecutors themselves do not know, or must make it up as they go along?

The second question that bears on facial vagueness is whether the "legislature [has] established minimal guidelines to govern law enforcement." *Kolender*, 461 U.S. at 358. This second inquiry is "the more important" of the two, and is alone sufficient to decide constitutional infirmity. *Id.* at 358, 361 & n.10. The governing test is whether the statute "permit[s] 'a standardless sweep [that] allows policemen, prosecutors, and juries to pursue their personal predilections.'" *Id.* at 358 (second alteration in original). "An enactment fails to provide sufficiently explicit standards for those who apply it when it impermissibly delegates basic policy matters to policemen, judges and juries for resolution on an ad hoc and subjective basis."

Handakas, 286 F.3d at 107 (internal quotation marks and citations omitted). Thus, a statute is facially vague if it "necessarily entrusts lawmaking to the moment-to-moment judgment of law enforcement. *Morales*, 527 U.S. at 60.

The majority opinion's search for a meaning of art leans heavily on the overruled-pre-*McNally* case law of other circuits. But "even the circuits that have reinstated pre-*McNally* law recognize that ad hoc parameters are needed to give the statute shape." *Handakas*, 286 F.3d at 109 (collecting cases). Although a number of circuits have upheld § 1346 against a claim of facial vagueness, there is now wide disagreement among the circuits as to the elements of the "honest services" offense. These opinions, taken together, refute rather than support the idea that § 1346 has any settled or ascertainable meaning or that the offense it describes has known contours:

- What mens rea must be proved by the government? The majority follows Second Circuit precedent in holding that an intent to cause economic harm is not required — a defendant need only have intended to deprive another of the "intangible right of honest services." However, in the Seventh Circuit, an intent to achieve personal gain is an element of the offense. The Eight Circuit describes the mens rea element as "causing or intending to cause actual harm or injury, and in most business contexts, that means financial or economic harm." *See United States v. Pennington*, 168 F.3d 1060, 1065 (8th Cir. 1999). One circuit has held that, to secure an honest services conviction, "the prosecution must prove that the employee intended to breach a fiduciary duty." *United States v. Frost*, 125 F.3d 346, 368 (6th Cir. 1997). Other circuits merely require a showing of "fraudulent intent." *See United States v. Cochran*, 109 F.3d 660, 667 (10th Cir. 1997).

- Must the defendant have caused actual tangible harm? Some circuits have required that the misrepresentation be material, i.e., that the employee have reason to believe that the information would lead a reasonable employer to change its business conduct. Other circuits only require a showing that it was reasonably foreseeable for the victim to suffer economic harm. We adopted this last requirement in the *Rybicki* panel opinion, and now abandon it. *See Rybicki*, 287 F.3d at 265.

- What is the *duty* that must be breached to violate § 1346? The majority holds that it is the duty owed by an employee to an employer, or by "a person in a relationship that gives rise to a duty of loyalty comparable to that owed by employees to employers" (whatever that means). Some circuits only allow prosecutions for breach of an employee's duty to an employer. Other circuits require the breach of a fiduciary duty.

- Is the source of that duty state or federal law? The majority does not say, and other circuits are split.

- Did § 1346 revive pre-*McNally* case law; if so must each circuit look to its own governing precedent or to some set of rules distilled from the whole body of pre-*McNally* cases? In *Sancho*, we held that pre-*McNally* cases could not be considered in determining the meaning of the statute. *See* 157 F.3d at 921–22. We now overrule *Sancho* and adopt an approach divining statutory meaning by analyzing cases overruled by *McNally* as a whole.

In sum, the circuits are fractured on the basic issues: (1) the requisite mens rea to commit the crime, (2) whether the defendant must cause actual tangible harm, (3) the duty that must be breached, (4) the source of that duty, and (5) which body of law informs us of the statute's meaning. This lack of coherence has created "a truly extraordinary statute, in which the substantive force of the statute varies in each judicial circuit." *Brumley*, 116 F.3d at 743 n.7 (Jolly, J., dissenting).

[T]he vagueness of the statute has induced court after court to undertake a rescue operation by fashioning something that (if enacted) would withstand a vagueness challenge. The felt need to do that attests to the constitutional weakness of § 1346 as written. And the result of all these efforts — which has been to create different prohibitions and offenses in different circuits — confirms that the weakness is fatal. Judicial invention cannot save a statute from unconstitutional vagueness; courts should not try to fill out a statute that makes it an offense to "intentionally cause harm to another," or to "stray from the straight and narrow," or to fail to render "honest services."

I believe that Congress has not heeded the Supreme Court's admonition to "speak more clearly than it has." We should not "approve a sweeping expansion of federal criminal jurisdiction in the absence of a clear statement by Congress." *Cleveland v. United States*, 531 U.S. 12, 24 (2000).

The majority opinion exhibits deference to Congress by conscientiously seeking to understand congressional intent, and the effort and product are scholarly and scrupulous. But the work accomplished by the majority opinion, which is admirable in its way, is properly the work of legislators in statutory drafting and the work of the executive in framing prosecutorial standards. "If the words of a criminal statute insufficiently define the offense, it is no part of deference to Congress for us to intuit or invent the crime." *Handakas*, 286 F.3d at 109–10. I respectfully dissent.

NOTES AND QUESTIONS

1. *Due process and fair notice.* The majority and dissent plainly disagree as to whether § 1346 is void for vagueness. Who has the better of the argument? Why?

2. *Prosecutorial abuse.* The dissent indicates that one of the dangers of a vague statute is that prosecutors will be unguided in deciding when to bring a mail or wire fraud charge. Recall the court's concluding words in the *Czubinski* case. Is there a real danger in statutes that provide for such wide application?

3. *Private sector defendants.* The dissent lists five ways in which the application of § 1346 is unclear in the context of private sector defendants. How would you advise a client about the scope of potential liability in this context?

4. *The materiality test.* The court above stated that "[w]e adopt the materiality test, holding that the misrepresentation or omission at issue for an 'honest services' fraud conviction must be 'material,' such that the misinformation or omission would naturally tend to lead or is capable of leading a reasonable employer to change its conduct." How does this test differ from the "reasonably foreseeable harm" test? Why did the court reject the latter standard?

5. *The courts' role in statutory interpretation.* Just how far should a court go to fill in the blanks of an ambiguous statute? Is the dissent correct to say that "the majority opinion is properly the work of legislators in statutory drafting and the work of the executive in framing prosecutorial standards"? Why or why not?

6. *Participants in a scheme to defraud.* In *Rybicki*, the government's theory was that the adjusters omitted to advise their employers that the adjusters were

receiving kickbacks. In a case based on an omission, the government must show that the person engaging in the deception had a duty to disclose the omitted information. Because the adjusters had fiduciary duties to their employers, the adjusters had a duty to reveal the scheme. Their omission to do so was fraudulent.

The individual defendants in the case, however, were two attorneys who themselves had no duties to the insurance companies; the attorneys thus had no duty to reveal the kickback scheme. On these facts, why were the attorneys guilty of defrauding the companies?

The answer is that a defendant in a mail or wire fraud case need not be the person making the misrepresentation or engaging in the omission. Nor need the defendant have a personal duty to the victim in an omission case. All that the statutes require is proof that the defendant *participated in a scheme* to deprive the victim of money, property, or honest services. Because the defendants participated in a scheme to deprive the insurance companies of their employees' honest services, they engaged in a scheme to defraud the companies.

7. *The boundaries of fiduciary breaches.* Where the fiduciary clearly has acted contrary to the principal's economic interests, courts are likely to affirm private sector honest services convictions. In *United States v. Williams*, 441 F.3d 716 (9th Cir. 2006), for example, the Ninth Circuit upheld the mail and wire fraud conviction of a financial planner who breached fiduciary duties by stealing $400,000 of a client's funds. The court rejected the defendant's contention that § 1346 only applies to public officials.

In a high-profile Enron-related prosecution, however, the court reversed the private sector honest services conviction where the defendants acted to benefit the employer. *United States v. Brown*, 459 F.3d 509 (5th Cir. 2006), *cert. denied*, 127 S. Ct. 2249 (2007). In that case, known as the "Enron barge case," the government alleged that the defendants, former *Enron* and *Merrill Lynch* executives, participated in a sham transaction designed to create artificial revenues to help *Enron* meet its earnings goals. The court held that the defendants were acting in *Enron's* economic interests, and therefore did not deprive *Enron* of their "honest services." The court stated:

> What makes this case exceptional is that, in typical bribery and self-dealing cases, there is usually no question that the defendant understood the benefit to him resulting from his misconduct to be at odds with the employer's expectations. This case, in which Enron employees breached a fiduciary duty in pursuit of what they understood to be a corporate goal, presents a situation in which the dishonest conduct is disassociated from bribery or self-dealing and indeed associated with and concomitant to the employer's own immediate interest.

Brown, 459 F.3d at 522. Do *Williams* and *Brown* provide a clear distinction for courts to follow? Why or why not?

8. *The* Carpenter *case.* Reconsider the *Carpenter* decision. In that case, the government did not assert a deprivation of honest services theory because Congress had not yet enacted § 1346. Would this theory have succeeded? Why or why not?

PROBLEMS

4-5. The Metropolitan Community Association (MCA) is an agency of the city of Metropolis in the state of Pacifica. The agency oversees construction projects performed on Metropolis schools. Defendant, the president, and sole shareholder of Astro Restoration Company ("Astro"), submitted three successful general contracting bids to the MCA.

In awarding its contracts, the MCA is required to follow Pacifica state law mandating that contractors hired for MCA projects retain only union workers, pay those workers a specified "prevailing rate of wages," and submit payroll records that so certify as a condition of receiving payment. Pacifica state law provides that "any person or corporation that willfully hires non-union workers or pays less than the stipulated wage scale shall be guilty of a misdemeanor and shall be punished for such offense by a fine of five hundred dollars or by imprisonment for not more than thirty days." Defendant was aware of these provisions of Pacifica state law.

In the course of the MCA projects, Defendant submitted, via United States, certified mail payroll records reflecting compliance with the union and prevailing rate of wage requirements. Defendant, in fact, paid the workers substantially less than half the prevailing rate of wage. Additionally, on these records Defendant left certain non-union workers' names off the payroll and fraudulently substituted union workers' names. Defendant received payment from MCA based upon the false submissions. The evidence shows that Astro provided the services for which MCA contracted according to the terms of the contracts, and that Astro timely completed the work within the budget set by MCA.

Defendant has been convicted of mail fraud, and appeals. Should defendant prevail? Why or why not?

4-6. Defendants Bob Urchin and Frank Dresser served respectively as CEO and Senior Vice President of City Medical Center ("CMC"). CMC's subsidiaries included a local hospital, a local nursing home, and an assisted living facility called "The Village." The two executives were friends of state senator Joan Carona. State legislators worked part-time in the state legislature, and typically held outside jobs. Carona was having financial difficulties, and approached Urchin about obtaining employment with CMC. Ultimately, Carona signed a contract that purported to employ her as a part-time consultant to The Village at a salary of $1,000 per week.

Thereafter, Carona did engage in some minimal work on behalf of The Village, including referring several prospective residents to The Village. In addition, Carona engaged in three kinds of activities while employed by The Village:

> 1. Carona communicated with Urchin and Dresser about various pieces of legislation; defendants allegedly asked Carona to try to "kill" certain bills and otherwise to promote CMC's interests with respect to pending legislative matters.

> 2. Carona lobbied a number of municipal officials (mayors and fire chiefs) in order to increase the number of patients brought to the CMC hospital by ambulance service ("rescue runs"). Specifically, Carona correctly told the officials that state law required that patients be taken to the hospital of their choosing. State law permitted this kind of lobbying activity.

3. Carona facilitated meetings at her government office between Urchin and representatives of two major insurance companies, pressing the companies to pay outstanding reimbursements owed to CMC. Carona told the companies that if they did not make the reimbursements they would be treated unfavorably during the legislative process.

Carona did not publicly disclose in any of these instances that she was acting on behalf of CMC or its hospital.

Urchin and Dresser were indicted on counts of conspiracy to commit "honest services" mail fraud and various counts of such mail fraud; 18 U.S.C. §§ 371, 1341, 1346. In substance, the government asserted that the defendants had devised a scheme to offer Carona a disguised bribe in the form of a sham or largely sham job at The Village; in exchange, the government asserted, Carona advanced CMC's financial interests by exploiting her public office in the three ways described above. Carona entered into a plea agreement and cooperated with the government.

At the trial, the judge instructed the jury that any of the three types of Carona's activities could be covered by the honest services statutes. The judge instructed the jury:

> The honest services that an elected official owes to citizens is not limited to the official's formal votes on legislation. It includes the official's behind-the-scenes activities and influence in the legislation, and it also includes other actions that the official takes in an official capacity, not what he does as a private individual but what he does under the cloak of his office.

During the trial, the government strongly relied on all three types of activities.

Both defendants were convicted and appeal. How should the court rule? Why?

4-7. Davis was a member of the City of Metropolis City Council, having been elected last year to a four-year term. Davis's friend, Terry Thompson, owned a construction company, Terry's Construction, that specialized in city building construction projects. Davis owns a five percent interest in Terry's Construction.

Last March 1, the City Council began considering a major construction project to provide new office space for city agencies. The Council decided to acquire land with the assistance of a real-estate broker, and to hire a contractor to construct a new building on the site once it was purchased. The Council agreed to meet on March 18 to continue the discussions.

On March 12, Davis met with Thompson, and another acquaintance, real-estate broker Pat Parsons, over coffee at Davis's home. Parsons specialized in purchases of land for commercial and municipal building projects. During the meeting, Davis said to Parsons, "We have this big city project coming up. I sure would like for you to be our broker. Would you like a shot?" Parsons responded, "Of course." Davis then said, "Well, I can assure you that you will be considered, with a substantial brokerage fee. You know, it's a competitive business. But the only way I can assure that you will be considered would be for me to have a, you know, stake in the venture." Parsons said, "How does a half percent sound?" Davis nodded in response.

Davis next told Parsons that the City Council had already reached a confidential decision that it would only hire an agent who agreed to accept a real-estate commission of lower than the standard six percent of the purchase price. Davis also told Thompson and Parsons that, in required forms to be sent to the city, Davis would have to reveal Davis's interest in Terry's Construction but that Davis hoped to keep the arrangement with Parsons secret.

On March 18, prior to the continuation of City Council discussions of the construction project, Davis completed a conflict-of-interest form. The form quoted Metropolis City Ordinance § 100.10, which provides:

> No city officer, employee, or agent shall acquire any interest, direct or indirect, in any city construction project or in any property included or planned to be included in such a project, nor shall such person have any interest, direct or indirect, in any contract or proposed contract for materials or services to be furnished or used in connection with any project. If any such person owns or controls an interest, direct or indirect, in any property included or planned to be included in any such project, the member or employee shall immediately disclose the same in writing to the city. Nor shall any officer, employee, or agent of the city disclose confidential information relating to such projects.
>
> Violation of § 100.10 subjects the violator to a civil fine of up to $10,000.

In response to a question on the form asking for disclosure of all potential conflicts, Davis revealed his ownership interest in Terry's construction, but not his arrangement with Parsons. Davis then sent the form from the City Council office to the City's Attorney's office via Federal Express.

Davis refrained from participating in all City Council debates relating to the construction project. Davis also refrained from voting on all matters relating to the project. The City Council subsequently retained both Parsons and Terry's Construction for the project. The Council chose Parsons because Parsons' proposal to the Council indicated Parsons' willingness to accept less than the usual six percent real estate commission.

On July 1, the city purchased the property at a fair market value of $25 million. That day, Parsons gave Davis $125,000 in cash, Davis's share of Parsons' commission.

Davis has been convicted of mail fraud based upon the foregoing. What viable arguments does Davis have on appeal? What is the likely outcome? Why?

4-8. Please incorporate the facts from Problem 4-4 above, and add the following facts:

Finally, in support of the mail fraud charges, the government also alleges that "the kickback arrangements created a conflict of interest between the paid plaintiffs and the class members to whom they owed fiduciary duties because, as a result of the kickback arrangements, the paid plaintiffs had a greater interest in maximizing the amount of attorneys' fees awarded to Milton and Wise than in maximizing the net recovery to the absent class members." This arrangement, according to the indictment, thus violated the defendants' fiduciary duties to the class members.

Defendants seek your advice with respect to a possible motion to dismiss the indictment. Are there grounds for seeking dismissal? If so, what are the chances for success? Why?

[D] THE USE OF THE MAILS AND WIRES

[1] The "In Furtherance" Requirement

In a number of mail and wire fraud cases, the Supreme Court has stated that the government must show that the use of the mail or wires was "in furtherance" of the fraudulent scheme. Defining this element has not proven easy, as the cases that follow show.

SCHMUCK v. UNITED STATES
489 U.S. 705 (1989)

Justice Blackmun delivered the opinion of the Court.

In August 1983, petitioner Wayne T. Schmuck, a used-car distributor, was indicted in the United States District Court for the Western District of Wisconsin on 12 counts of mail fraud, in violation of 18 U.S.C. §§ 1341 and 1342.

The alleged fraud was a common and straightforward one. Schmuck purchased used cars, rolled back their odometers, and then sold the automobiles to Wisconsin retail dealers for prices artificially inflated because of the low-mileage readings. These unwitting car dealers, relying on the altered odometer figures, then resold the cars to customers, who in turn paid prices reflecting Schmuck's fraud. To complete the resale of each automobile, the dealer who purchased it from Schmuck would submit a title-application form to the Wisconsin Department of Transportation on behalf of his retail customer. The receipt of a Wisconsin title was a prerequisite for completing the resale; without it, the dealer could not transfer title to the customer and the customer could not obtain Wisconsin tags. The submission of the title application form supplied the mailing element of each of the alleged mail frauds.

Before trial, Schmuck moved to dismiss the indictment on the ground that the mailings at issue — the submissions of the title-application forms by the automobile dealers — were not in furtherance of the fraudulent scheme and, thus, did not satisfy the mailing element of the crime of mail fraud. The District Court denied the motion. After trial, the jury returned guilty verdicts on all 12 counts.

"The federal mail fraud statute does not purport to reach all frauds, but only those limited instances in which the use of the mails is a part of the execution of the fraud, leaving all other cases to be dealt with by appropriate state law." *Kann v. United States*, 323 U.S. 88, 95 (1944). To be part of the execution of the fraud, however, the use of the mails need not be an essential element of the scheme. *Pereira v. United States*, 347 U.S. 1, 8 (1954). It is sufficient for the mailing to be "incident to an essential part of the scheme," *id.*, or "a step in [the] plot," *Badders v. United States*, 240 U.S. 391, 394 (1916).

Schmuck, relying principally on this Court's decisions in *Kann, supra, Parr v. United States*, 363 U.S. 370 (1960), and *United States v. Maze*, 414 U.S. 395 (1974), argues that mail fraud can be predicated only on a mailing that affirmatively assists the perpetrator in carrying out his fraudulent scheme. The mailing element of the offense, he contends, cannot be satisfied by a mailing, such as those at issue here, that is routine and innocent in and of itself, and that, far from furthering the execution of the fraud, occurs after the fraud has come to fruition, is merely tangentially related to the fraud, and is counterproductive in that it creates a "paper trail" from which the fraud may be discovered. We disagree both with this characterization of the mailings in the present case and with this description of the applicable law.

We begin by considering the scope of Schmuck's fraudulent scheme. Schmuck was charged with devising and executing a scheme to defraud Wisconsin retail automobile customers who based their decisions to purchase certain automobiles at least in part on the low-mileage readings provided by the tampered odometers. This was a fairly large-scale operation. Evidence at trial indicated that Schmuck had employed a man known only as "Fred" to turn back the odometers on about 150 different cars. Schmuck then marketed these cars to a number of dealers, several of whom he dealt with on a consistent basis over a period of about 15 years. Indeed, of the 12 automobiles that are the subject of the counts of the indictment, five were sold to "P and A Sales," and 4 to "Southside Auto." Thus, Schmuck's was not a "one-shot" operation in which he sold a single car to an isolated dealer. His was an ongoing fraudulent venture. A rational jury could have concluded that the success of Schmuck's venture depended upon his continued harmonious relations with, and good reputation among, retail dealers, which in turn required the smooth flow of cars from the dealers to their Wisconsin customers.

Under these circumstances, we believe that a rational jury could have found that the title-registration mailings were part of the execution of the fraudulent scheme, a scheme which did not reach fruition until the retail dealers resold the cars and effected transfers of title. Schmuck's scheme would have come to an abrupt halt if the dealers either had lost faith in Schmuck or had not been able to resell the cars obtained from him. These resales and Schmuck's relationships with the retail dealers naturally depended on the successful passage of title among the various parties. Thus, although the registration-form mailings may not have contributed directly to the duping of either the retail dealers or the customers, they were necessary to the passage of title, which in turn was essential to the perpetuation of Schmuck's scheme. As noted earlier, a mailing that is "incident to an essential part of the scheme," *Pereira*, 347 U.S. at 8, satisfies the mailing element of the mail fraud offense. The mailings here fit this description.

Once the full flavor of Schmuck's scheme is appreciated, the critical distinctions between this case and the three cases in which this Court has delimited the reach of the mail fraud statute — *Kann, Parr,* and *Maze* — are readily apparent. The defendants in *Kann* were corporate officers and directors accused of setting up a dummy corporation through which to divert profits into their own pockets. As part of this fraudulent scheme, the defendants caused the corporation to issue two checks payable to them. The defendants cashed these checks at local banks, which then mailed the checks to the drawee banks for collection. This Court held that the mailing of the cashed checks to the drawee banks could not supply the mailing element of the mail fraud charges. The defendants' fraudulent scheme had reached fruition. "It was immaterial to them, or to any consummation of the scheme, how the bank which paid or credited the check would collect from the drawee bank." 323 U.S. at 94.

In *Parr*, several defendants were charged, *inter alia*, with having fraudulently obtained gasoline and a variety of other products and services through the unauthorized use of a credit card issued to the school district which employed them. The mailing element of the mail fraud charges in *Parr* was purportedly satisfied when the oil company which issued the credit card mailed invoices to the school district for payment, and when the district mailed payment in the form of a check. Relying on *Kann*, this Court held that these mailings were not in execution of the scheme as required by the statute because it was immaterial to the defendants how the oil company went about collecting its payment. 363 U.S. at 393.

Later, in *Maze*, the defendant allegedly stole his roommate's credit card, headed south on a winter jaunt, and obtained food and lodging at motels along the route by placing the charges on the stolen card. The mailing element of the mail fraud charge was supplied by the fact that the defendant knew that each motel proprietor would mail an invoice to the bank that had issued the credit card, which in turn would mail a bill to the card owner for payment. The Court found that these mailings could not support mail fraud charges because the defendant's scheme had reached fruition when he checked out of each motel. The success of his scheme in no way depended on the mailings; they merely determined which of his victims would ultimately bear the loss. 414 U.S. at 402.

The title-registration mailings at issue here served a function different from the mailings in *Kann, Parr,* and *Maze.* The intrabank mailings in *Kann* and the credit card invoice mailings in *Parr* and *Maze* involved little more than post-fraud accounting among the potential victims of the various schemes, and the long-term success of the fraud did not turn on which of the potential victims bore the ultimate loss. Here, in contrast, a jury rationally could have found that Schmuck by no means was indifferent to the fact of who bore the loss. The mailing of the title-registration forms was an essential step in the successful passage of title to the retail purchasers. Moreover, a failure of this passage of title would have jeopardized Schmuck's relationship of trust and goodwill with the retail dealers upon whose unwitting cooperation his scheme depended. Schmuck's reliance on our prior cases limiting the reach of the mail fraud statute is simply misplaced.

To the extent that Schmuck would draw from these previous cases a general rule that routine mailings that are innocent in themselves cannot supply the mailing element of the mail fraud offense, he misapprehends this Court's precedents. In *Parr* the Court specifically acknowledged that "innocent" mailings — ones that contain no false information — may supply the mailing element. 363 U.S. at 390. In other cases, the Court has found the elements of mail fraud to be satisfied where the mailings have been routine. *See, e.g., Carpenter v. United States,* 484 U.S. 19, 28 (1987) (mailing newspapers).

We also reject Schmuck's contention that mailings that someday may contribute to the uncovering of a fraudulent scheme cannot supply the mailing element of the mail fraud offense. The relevant question at all times is whether the mailing is part of the execution of the scheme as conceived by the perpetrator at the time, regardless of whether the mailing later, through hindsight, may prove to have been counterproductive and return to haunt the perpetrator of the fraud. The mail fraud statute includes no guarantee that the use of the mails for the purpose of executing a fraudulent scheme will be risk free. Those who use the mails to defraud proceed at their peril.

For these reasons, we agree with the Court of Appeals that the mailings in this case satisfy the mailing element of the mail fraud offenses.

* * *

We conclude that Schmuck's conviction was consistent with the statutory definition of mail fraud. The judgment of the Court of Appeals, accordingly, is affirmed.

It is so ordered.

JUSTICE SCALIA, with whom JUSTICE BRENNAN, JUSTICE MARSHALL, and JUSTICE O'CONNOR join, dissenting.

*   *   *

The purpose of the mail fraud statute is "to prevent the post office from being used to carry [fraudulent schemes] into effect." *Durland v. United States*, 161 U.S. 306, 314 (1896); *Parr v. United States*, 363 U.S. 370, 389 (1960). The law does not establish a general federal remedy against fraudulent conduct, with use of the mails as the jurisdictional hook, but reaches only "those limited instances in which the use of the mails is *a part of the execution of the fraud*, leaving all other cases to be dealt with by appropriate state law." *Kann v. United States*, 323 U.S. 88, 95 (1944) (emphasis added). In other words, it is mail fraud, not mail and fraud, that incurs liability. This federal statute is not violated by a fraudulent scheme in which, at some point, a mailing happens to occur — nor even by one in which a mailing predictably and necessarily occurs. The mailing must be in furtherance of the fraud.

In *Kann v. United States*, we concluded that even though defendants who cashed checks obtained as part of a fraudulent scheme knew that the bank cashing the checks would send them by mail to a drawee bank for collection, they did not thereby violate the mail fraud statute, because upon their receipt of the cash "[t]he scheme had reached fruition," and the mailing was "immaterial to any consummation of the scheme." *Id.* at 94. We held to the same effect in *United States v. Maze*, 414 U.S. 395, 400–402 (1974), declining to find that credit card fraud was converted into mail fraud by the certainty that, after the wrongdoer had fraudulently received his goods and services from the merchants, they would forward the credit charges by mail for payment. These cases are squarely on point here. For though the government chose to charge a defrauding of retail customers (to whom the innocent dealers resold the cars), it is obvious that, regardless of who the ultimate victim of the fraud may have been, the fraud was complete with respect to each car when petitioner pocketed the dealer's money. As far as each particular transaction was concerned, it was as inconsequential to him whether the dealer resold the car as it was inconsequential to the defendant in *Maze* whether the defrauded merchant ever forwarded the charges to the credit card company.

Nor can the force of our cases be avoided by combining all of the individual transactions into a single scheme, and saying, as the Court does, that if the dealers' mailings obtaining title for each retail purchaser had not occurred then the dealers would have stopped trusting petitioner for future transactions. (That conclusion seems to me a non sequitur, but I accept it for the sake of argument.) This establishes, at most, that the scheme could not technically have been consummated if the mechanical step of the mailings to obtain conveyance of title had not occurred. But we have held that the indispensability of such mechanical mailings, not strictly in furtherance of the fraud, is not enough to invoke the statute. For example, when officials of a school district embezzled tax funds over the course of several years, we held that no mail fraud had occurred even though the success of the scheme plainly depended on the officials' causing tax bills to be sent by mail (and thus tax payments to be received) every year. *Parr v. United States*, 363 U.S. at 388–392. Similarly, when those officials caused the school district to pay by mail credit card bills — a step plainly necessary to enable their continued fraudulent use of the credit card — we concluded that no mail fraud had occurred.

I find it impossible to escape these precedents in the present case. Assuming the Court to be correct in concluding that failure to pass title to the cars would have threatened the success of the scheme, the same could have been said of failure to collect taxes or to pay the credit card bills in *Parr*. And I think it particularly significant that in *Kann* the government proposed a theory *identical* to that which the Court today uses. Since the scheme was ongoing, the government urged, the fact that the mailing of the two checks had occurred after the defendants had pocketed the fraudulently obtained cash made no difference. The Court rejected this argument, concluding that "the subsequent banking transactions between the banks concerned were merely incidental and collateral to the scheme and not a part of it." I think the mailing of the title application forms equivalently incidental here.

What Justice Frankfurter observed almost three decades ago remains true: "The adequate degree of relationship between a mailing which occurs during the life of a scheme and the scheme is not a matter susceptible of geometric determination." *Parr v. United States, supra*, 363 U.S. at 397 (dissenting opinion). All the more reason to adhere as closely as possible to past cases. I think we have not done that today, and thus create problems for tomorrow.

NOTES AND QUESTIONS

1. *The "in furtherance" rule.* After reading *Schmuck*, what "rule" can you divine from the case? In particular, if you were advising a client, could you distinguish between the outcomes in *Kann, Parr*, and *Maze*, on the one hand, and *Schmuck* on the other? The four-member dissent in *Schmuck* argued that *Kann, Parr*, and *Maze* in fact cannot be distinguished from *Schmuck*. Is the dissent right?

2. *A federal case?* As noted elsewhere in this text, the vast majority of criminal cases, including fraud cases, are brought at the state and local level. Can you think of possible reasons why *Schmuck* was prosecuted at the federal level?

3. *Identity of the deceived party.* Suppose that an insurance company officer schemes to steal money from the company. As part of the scheme, the officer mails forms to the state insurance commissioner that contain material false statements. Has the officer committed mail fraud? *See Corcoran v. American Plan Corp*, 886 F.2d 16 (2d Cir. 1989).

Courts have been split as to whether there must be a "convergence" between the party the defendant intended to deceive and the party the defendant intended to be the victim of the fraud. *Compare United States v. Christopher*, 142 F.3d 46, 54 (1st Cir. 1998) (the *McNally* holding does not contain a convergence requirement), *with United States v. Lew*, 875 F.2d 219, 221–222 (9th Cir. 1989) (*McNally* implicitly requires that "the intent must be to obtain money or property from the one who is deceived").

In a civil RICO case based on mail fraud predicate acts, however, the United States Supreme Court seemed to assume — without explicitly holding — that convergence is not required. In *Bridge v. Phoenix Bond & Indemnity Co.*, 128 S. Ct. 2131, 2138 (2008), the defendants made false statements in mailings to local governments in a bid-rigging scheme. The victims in the scheme were other bidders who were deprived of the right to compete fairly in the bidding process and of the financial benefits of potentially successful bids. The Court found that this amounted to mail fraud.

In this light, the correct question may not be whether the deceived party (the government in *Phoenix Bond*) was the victim (the other bidders in *Phoenix Bond*). Instead of focusing on "convergence," it may be better to focus on the "in furtherance" requirement. Take a material, false statements made to a third party who is not the intended victim of the scheme and who therefore would not be deprived of money, property, or honest services if the scheme succeeded. A statement to the third party would not be "in furtherance" of the scheme to defraud unless it is directly related to the intended injury to the scheme's victim. Thus, in *Phoenix Bond*, the statements to the local government led directly to the intended injury to the victims and satisfied the requirement from *Schmuck, Parr,* and *Maze* that the use of the mails or wires be sufficiently tied to the scheme to be considered "in furtherance" of the scheme. What in your view is the correct result? Why?

4. *The "lulling" rule.* Can a use of the mails or wires be "in furtherance" of a fraudulent scheme where such use occurs *after* the scheme has reached fruition and the deceived party has already lost the money or property? The Supreme Court has answered in the affirmative in situations in which the use of the mail or wires was designed to "lull" the victim into a false sense of security. For example, in *United States v. Sampson*, 371 U.S. 75 (1962), the defendants offered services to potential customers that the defendants never intended to provide. After the customers paid for the services, the defendants mailed the customers letters assuring them that the defendants indeed would perform the promised services. Similarly, in *United States v. Lane*, 474 U.S. 438 (1986), the defendant defrauded an insurance company; after he received the payment for the fraudulent claim, he sent the company documentation supporting the claim. The Supreme Court affirmed both convictions. As the Court stated in *Lane*, "Mailings occurring after receipt of the goods obtained by fraud are within the statute if they 'were designed to lull the victims into a false sense of security, postpone their ultimate complaint to the authorities, and therefore, make the apprehension of the defendants less likely than if no mailings had taken place.'" *Id.* at 451–452, *quoting United States v. Maze*, 414 U.S. at 403.

[2]   The Causation Requirement

Under the terms of the mail and wire fraud statutes, a defendant must either use, or "cause[]" the use, of the mail, a private courier, or the wires. In some cases, even when a mailing may arguably have been "in furtherance" of the fraud, the defendant may not have "caused" the mailing. The meaning of the causation requirement is explored in the next case.

UNITED STATES v. WALTERS
997 F.2d 1219 (7th Cir. 1993)

EASTERBROOK, CIRCUIT JUDGE.

Norby Walters, who represents entertainers, tried to move into the sports business. He signed 58 college football players to contracts while they were still playing. Walters offered cars and money to those who would agree to use him as their representative in dealing with professional teams. Sports agents receive a percentage of the players' income, so Walters would profit only to the extent he could negotiate contracts for his clients. The athletes' pro prospects depended on successful completion of their collegiate careers. To the National Collegiate Athletic Association (NCAA), however, a student who signs a contract with an agent is a professional, ineligible to play on collegiate teams. To avoid jeopardizing his clients' careers, Walters dated the contracts after the end of their eligibility and locked them in a safe. He promised to lie to the universities in response to any inquiries. Walters inquired of sports lawyers at Shea & Gould whether this plan of operation would be lawful. The firm rendered an opinion that it would violate the NCAA's rules but not any statute.

Having recruited players willing to fool their universities and the NCAA, Walters discovered that they were equally willing to play false with him. Only 2 of the 58 players fulfilled their end of the bargain; the other 56 kept the cars and money, then signed with other agents. They relied on the fact that the contracts were locked away and dated in the future, and that Walters' business depended on continued secrecy, so he could not very well sue to enforce their promises. When the 56 would neither accept him as their representative nor return the payments, Walters resorted to threats. One player, Maurice Douglass, was told that his legs would be broken before the pro draft unless he repaid Walters' firm. A 75-page indictment charged Walters and his partner Lloyd Bloom with conspiracy, RICO violations (the predicate felony was extortion), and mail fraud. The fraud: causing the universities to pay scholarship funds to athletes who had become ineligible as a result of the agency contracts. The mail: each university required its athletes to verify their eligibility to play, then sent copies by mail to conferences such as the Big Ten.

After a month-long trial and a week of deliberations, the jury convicted Walters and Bloom. We reversed, holding that the district judge had erred in declining to instruct the jury that reliance on Shea & Gould's advice could prevent the formation of intent to defraud the universities. Any dispute about the adequacy of Walters' disclosure to his lawyers and the bona fides of his reliance was for the jury, we concluded. On remand, Walters asked the district court to dismiss the indictment, arguing that the evidence presented at trial is insufficient to support the convictions. After the judge denied this motion, Walters agreed to enter a conditional *Alford* plea: he would plead guilty to mail fraud, conceding that the record of the first trial supplies a factual basis for a conviction while reserving his right to contest the sufficiency of that evidence.

"Whoever, having devised any scheme or artifice to defraud, or for obtaining money or property by means of false or fraudulent pretenses, representations, or promises places in any post office or authorized depository for mail matter, any matter or thing whatever to be sent or delivered by the Postal Service or knowingly causes [such matter or thing] to be delivered by mail" commits the crime of mail fraud. 18 U.S.C. § 1341. Norby Walters did not mail anything or cause anyone else to do so (the universities were going to collect and mail the forms no matter what Walters did), but the Supreme Court has expanded the statute beyond its literal terms, holding that a mailing by a third party suffices if it is "incident to an essential part of the scheme," *Pereira v. United States*, 347 U.S. 1, 8 (1954). While stating that such mailings can turn ordinary fraud into mail fraud, the Court has cautioned that the statute "does not purport to reach all frauds, but only those limited instances in which the use of the mails is a part of the execution of the fraud." *Kann v. United States*, 323 U.S. 88, 95 (1944). Everything thus turns on matters of degree. Did the schemers foresee that the mails would be used? Did the mailing advance the success of the scheme? Which parts of a scheme are "essential"? Such questions lack obviously right answers, so it is no surprise that each side to this case can cite several of our decisions in support.

"The relevant question is whether the mailing is part of the execution of the scheme as conceived by the perpetrator at the time." *Schmuck v. United States*, 489 U.S. 705, 715 (1989). Did the evidence establish that Walters conceived a scheme in which mailings played a role? We think not — indeed, that no reasonable juror could give an affirmative answer to this question. For all Walters cared, the forms could sit forever in cartons. Movement to someplace else was irrelevant. In *Schmuck*, where the fraud was selling cars with rolled-back odometers, the mailing was essential to obtain a new and apparently "clean" certificate of title; no certificates of title, no marketable cars, no hope for success. Even so, the Court divided five to four on the question whether the mailing was sufficiently integral to the scheme. A college's mailing to its conference has less to do with the plot's success than the mailings that transferred title in *Schmuck*.

To this the United States responds that the mailings were essential because, if a college had neglected to send the athletes' forms to the conference, the NCAA would have barred that college's team from competing. Lack of competition would spoil the athletes' pro prospects. Thus the use of the mails was integral to the profits Walters hoped to reap, even though Walters would have been delighted had the colleges neither asked any questions of the athletes nor put the answers in the mail. Let us take this as sufficient under *Schmuck* (although we have our doubts). The question remains whether Walters caused the universities to use the mails. A person "knowingly causes" the use of the mails when he "acts with the knowledge that the use of the mails will follow in the ordinary course of business, or where such use can reasonably be foreseen." *United States v. Kuzniar*, 881 F.2d 466, 472 (7th Cir.1989), *quoting Pereira*, 347 U.S. at 8–9. The paradigm is insurance fraud. Perkins tells his auto insurer that his car has been stolen, when in fact it has been sold. The local employee mails the claim to the home office, which mails a check to Perkins. Such mailings in the ordinary course of business are foreseeable. Similarly, a judge who takes a bribe derived from the litigant's bail money causes the use of the mails when the ordinary course is to refund the bond by mail. The prosecutor contends that the same approach covers Walters.

No evidence demonstrates that Walters *actually* knew that the colleges would mail the athletes' forms. The record is barely sufficient to establish that Walters knew of the forms' existence; it is silent about Walters' knowledge of the forms' disposition. So the prosecutor is reduced to the argument that mailings could "reasonably be foreseen." Yet why should this be so? Universities frequently collect information that is stashed in file drawers. Perhaps the NCAA just wants answers available for inspection in the event a question arises, or the university wants the information for its own purposes (to show that it did not know about any improprieties that later come to light). What was it about these forms that should have led a reasonable person to foresee their mailing? Recall that Walters was trying to break into the sports business. Counsel specializing in sports law told him that his plan would not violate any statute. These lawyers were unaware of the forms (or, if they knew about the forms, were unaware that they would be mailed).

The prosecutor contends that Walters neglected to tell his lawyers about the eligibility forms, spoiling their opinion; yet why would Walters have to brief an expert in sports law if mailings were foreseeable even to a novice?

In the end, the prosecutor insists that the large size and interstate nature of the NCAA demonstrate that something would be dropped into the mails. To put this only slightly differently, the prosecutor submits that all frauds involving big organizations necessarily are mail frauds, because big organizations habitually mail things. No evidence put before the jury supports such a claim, and it is hardly appropriate for judicial notice in a criminal case. Moreover, adopting this perspective would contradict the assurance of *Kann*, 323 U.S. at 95, and many later cases that most frauds are covered by state law rather than § 1341. That statute has been expanded considerably by judicial interpretation, but it does not make a federal crime of every deceit. The prosecutor must prove that the use of the mails was foreseeable, rather than calling on judicial intuition to repair a rickety case.

There is a deeper problem with the theory of this prosecution. The United States tells us that the universities lost their scholarship money. Money is property; this aspect of the prosecution does not encounter a problem under *McNally v. United States*, 483 U.S. 350 (1987). Walters emphasizes that the universities put his 58 athletes on scholarship long before he met them and did not pay a penny more than they planned to do. But a jury could conclude that had Walters' clients told the truth, the colleges would have stopped their scholarships, thus saving money. So we must assume that the universities lost property by reason of Walters' deeds. Still, they were not out of pocket *to Walters*; he planned to profit by taking a percentage of the players' professional incomes, not of their scholarships. Section 1341 condemns "any scheme or artifice to defraud, or *for obtaining* money or property" (emphasis added). If the universities were the victims, how did he "obtain" their property?, Walters asks.

According to the United States, neither an actual nor a potential transfer of property from the victim to the defendant is essential. It is enough that the victim lose; what (if anything) the schemer hopes to gain plays no role in the definition of the offense. We asked the prosecutor at oral argument whether on this rationale practical jokes violate § 1341. *A* mails *B* an invitation to a surprise party for their mutual friend *C*. *B* drives his car to the place named in the invitation. But there is no party; the address is a vacant lot; *B* is the butt of a joke. The invitation came by post; the cost of gasoline means that *B* is out of pocket. The prosecutor said that this indeed violates § 1341, but that his office pledges to use prosecutorial discretion wisely. Many people will find this position unnerving (what if the prosecutor's policy changes, or *A* is politically unpopular and the prosecutor is looking for a way to nail him?). Others, who obey the law out of a sense of civic obligation rather than the fear of sanctions, will alter their conduct no matter what policy the prosecutor follows. Either way, the idea that practical jokes are federal felonies would make a joke of the Supreme Court's assurance that § 1341 does not cover the waterfront of deceit.

None of the Supreme Court's mail fraud cases deals with a scheme in which the defendant neither obtained nor tried to obtain the victim's property. We have been unable to find any appellate cases squarely resolving the question whether the victim's loss must be an objective of the scheme rather than a byproduct of it, perhaps because prosecutions of the kind this case represents are so rare.

[W]e hold that only a scheme to obtain money or other property from the victim by fraud violates § 1341. A deprivation is a necessary but not a sufficient condition of mail fraud. Losses that occur as byproducts of a deceitful scheme do not satisfy the statutory requirement.

Anticipating that we might come to this conclusion, the prosecutor contends that Walters is nonetheless guilty as an aider and abettor. If Walters did not defraud the universities, the argument goes, then the athletes did. Walters put them up to it and so is guilty under 18 U.S.C. § 2, the argument concludes. But the indictment charged a scheme by Walters to defraud; it did not depict Walters as an aide de camp in the students' scheme. The jury received a boilerplate § 2 instruction; this theory was not argued to the jury, or for that matter to the district court either before or after the remand. Independent problems dog this recasting of the scheme — not least the difficulty of believing that the students hatched a plot to employ fraud to receive scholarships that the universities had awarded them long before Walters arrived on the scene, and the lack of evidence that the students knew about or could foresee any mailings. Walters is by all accounts a nasty and untrustworthy fellow, but the prosecutor did not prove that his efforts to circumvent the NCAA's rules amounted to mail fraud.

Reversed.

NOTES AND QUESTIONS

1. *The "causation" and "in furtherance" requirements.* Did the *Walters* court find that the mailings were not in furtherance of the scheme? Did it find that Walters had not caused the mailings? What is the difference between the two requirements?

2. *The* Schmuck *decision revisited.* The Supreme Court found that the mailings in *Schmuck* were sufficient, in large part because the mailings were part of an ongoing scheme that would collapse if the mailings never occurred. Cannot the same be said for *Walters*? Then why the different outcome? In light of *Schmuck*, was *Walters* correctly decided?

3. *Must the defendant intend to gain property from the victim?* The *Walters* court also held that the mail fraud theory was faulty because Walters never intended to obtain money or property from the victims, the universities. The universities lost scholarship funds, but the scheme never envisioned that those funds would benefit Walters. Do you agree with this holding? Why or why not?

4. *Reliance on counsel.* The court in *Walters* noted that it had reversed the defendants' original conviction, "holding that the district judge had erred in declining to instruct the jury that reliance on [a law firm's] advice could prevent the formation of intent to defraud the universities." Recall the maxim that "ignorance of the law is no excuse." In that light, why is reliance on counsel a defense to a mail fraud charge?

PROBLEMS

4-9. The government has indicted Defendant for mail and wire fraud based upon the following evidence. Defendant was the Chief Executive Officer of Energy Corp., based in New York City. During the last four years, Defendant conspired with Energy Corp's accountant, Dern, artificially to inflate Energy Corp's earnings and stock prices. Many investors bought stock in the company, which is now worthless. Approximately 1,000 investors have lost a total of tens of millions of dollars. Many of these investors received copies of Energy Corp's annual reports in the mail, and relied on the reports when making their investment decisions. The annual reports contained the inflated earnings statements, along with a proviso that said, "These statements are preliminary and subject to change upon final review by our auditors."

Last July, Dern and Defendant had lunch. During the lunch, they discussed ways to hide the ongoing fraud. Dern made notes on a legal pad during this lunch. In August, Defendant learned that Energy Corp. was being investigated by the Securities and Exchange Commission for alleged securities fraud. From the Energy Corp. offices, Defendant called Dern, who was on vacation in Vermont, and asked Dern to throw away the notes. Dern complied. Dern is now cooperating with the government.

The government has charged Defendant with mail fraud based upon the mailings of the annual reports, and with wire fraud based upon the phone call. Defendant has moved to dismiss the charges. What is the likely outcome? Why?

4-10. Defendant is an immigration attorney who was retained by a number of clients. The clients paid Defendant to obtain labor certification that would allow them to work legally in the country. Defendant performed the services for which Defendant was retained. During the course of representing the clients, Defendant mailed documents to the federal government that made false, material misrepresentations concerning the clients' eligibility for labor certification.

Defendant has been indicted for mail fraud based upon the foregoing facts, and has filed a motion to dismiss. Should the motion be granted? Why or why not?

Chapter 5

SECURITIES FRAUD

[A] INTRODUCTORY NOTES

[1] The Quintessential White Collar Crime?

Securities fraud encompasses a wide range of crimes. For example, if a company makes material misstatements or omissions about the company in public documents, then the company and its agents may be liable for defrauding investors in that company. Such fraud has been alleged in a number of high-profile corporate scandals in recent decades.[a] In addition, securities fraud encompasses fraud committed by individual investors. The latter type of securities fraud includes what is perhaps the quintessential white collar crime — insider trading. The government has pursued a number of high profile insider trading investigations and prosecutions of public figures.[b]

This chapter provides an overview of the principal securities fraud statutes and examines common issues in securities fraud cases. Focusing primarily upon insider trading, the chapter also touches on a number of other kinds of securities fraud. Securities fraud is just one specific type of fraud covered in the federal criminal code.[c] It will be important during the course of this chapter to observe the interplay between specific securities fraud statutes on the one hand, and the more generally applicable crimes covered in the previous two chapters (conspiracy and mail and wire fraud) on the other. In addition, charges may also arise in specific fraud cases under the "cover-up" statutes involving false statements, perjury, and obstruction of justice covered later in this text. Readers may ask themselves, as

---

[a] For example, securities fraud was the principal allegation in the criminal cases arising out of the massive collapses of both Enron and WorldCom. *See* John R. Emshwiller, *Executives on Trial; Enron Ex-Official Pleads Not Guilty to Fraud, Agrees to Aid Probe*, Wall St. J., Aug. 2, 2004, at C3; Ken Belson, *Ex-Chief of WorldCom Is Found Guilty in $11 Billion Fraud*, Wall St. J., Mar. 16, 2005, at A1.

[b] As commentators have noted, "insider trading prosecutions have drawn more public attention to the securities markets than virtually any other event since the passage of the federal securities laws." Charles A. Stillman et al., *Securities Fraud, in* White Collar Crime: Business and Regulatory Offenses § 12.03 (Law Journal Press, Otto G. Obermaier & Robert G. Morvillo eds., 2009). Among the high profile public figures investigated for insider trading are Ivan Boesky, Michael Milken, and Martha Stewart. Boesky, perhaps the highest profile Wall Street entrepreneur during the 1980s, famously advised a group of business students, "[g]reed is all right, by the way. I want you to know that. I think greed is healthy. You can be greedy and still feel good about yourself." James B. Stewart, Den of Thieves 223 (1991). Milken, who was known for financing corporate deals through "junk bonds," was the highest paid investment banker in the United States during the 1980s. Milken ultimately pleaded guilty to securities fraud and other charges. United States v. Milken, 759 F. Supp. 109 (S.D.N.Y. 1990). Lifestyle guru Martha Stewart went to trial on a number of charges, including securities fraud, although the judge in the case ultimately dismissed that charge. United States v. Stewart, 305 F. Supp. 2d 368 (S.D.N.Y. 2004). Stewart also was named in a Securities and Exchange Commission civil suit charging her with insider trading.

[c] *See, e.g.,* 18 U.S.C. § 1344 (bank fraud), and 18 U.S.C. § 1347 (health care fraud).

they review the securities fraud materials below, why the defendants in these cases are so often charged with attempting to cover up their acts.[d]

The interplay among these various criminal laws also raises important questions that appear throughout this book concerning enforcement obstacles, prosecutorial discretion, and statutory vagueness. In particular, the relationships among these crimes provide some sense of the choices prosecutors must make in deciding whether and how to charge a criminal case. This is particularly true in the securities fraud context because, as noted below, the government in many cases will be able to choose among pursuing administrative and/or civil remedies in addition to, or instead of, criminal sanctions.

[2]   Civil and Criminal Enforcement

Securities fraud may be alleged in a number of different contexts. First, the government, through the Securities and Exchange Commission (the "SEC" or the "Commission"), may initiate an administrative proceeding or civil lawsuit alleging a violation of the federal securities laws. Second, private parties may bring causes of action and seek damages for alleged violations of those laws. Third, the United States Department of Justice may bring a criminal case in addition to, or instead of, any civil action brought by the SEC and/or a private party. Note that the legal issues decided in civil cases may also apply to criminal cases; many of the cases discussed in this chapter were civil cases brought by the SEC or by private parties.

[3]   The Federal Securities Regulation Scheme[e]

Congress enacted the two principal securities laws in the aftermath of the stock market crash of 1929. The Securities Act of 1933 (the "Securities Act" or the "1933 Act"), 15 U.S.C. §§ 77a–77aa, generally regulates a company's original *registration* and *issuance* of securities, known as the "primary" or "new-issue" securities market. This statute, and the regulations adopted pursuant to the statute, govern the disclosure of information to potential purchasers of those securities. The Securities Exchange Act of 1934 (the "Exchange Act" or the "1934 Act"), 15 U.S.C. §§ 78a–78ll, on the other hand, generally governs what is known as the "secondary" or "trading" market. Thus, this statute and the regulations adopted under the statute apply to *trading* in the securities markets.

The civil and criminal fraud provisions of these statutes only apply when there has been a purchase or sale of a "security." For present purposes, the most important securities include stocks (equity interests which give a stockholder an ownership interest in the issuing company) and bonds (debt instruments that essentially are loans that the bond holder makes to the company).

---

[d] Martha Stewart was convicted of conspiracy, obstruction of justice, and making false statements in connection with the sale of her ImClone Systems stock. *See* United States v. Stewart, 323 F. Supp. 2d 606 (S.D.N.Y. 2004). Enron's accounting firm, Arthur Anderson, L.L.P., was convicted of obstructing a Securities and Exchange Commission investigation into the company's accounting practices. *See* United States v. Arthur Andersen, 374 F.3d 281 (5th Cir. 2004), *rev'd*, 544 U.S. 696 (2005).

[e] The states have their own securities laws and regulations, which are referred to as "blue sky laws." Most of the important securities cases are brought at the federal level, although states have been increasingly active in enforcing their own securities statutes.

Section 24 of the 1933 Act, 15 U.S.C. § 77x, and Section 32(a) of the 1934 Act, 15 U.S.C. § 78ff, make it a crime to commit a "willful" violation of the statutes or of the rules and regulations adopted under the statutes. Most criminal securities fraud cases are brought for willful violations of the statutes' "catch-all" anti-fraud provisions, set forth at Section 17(a) of the 1933 Act, 15 U.S.C. § 77q(a), Section 10b of the 1934 Act, 15 U.S.C. § 78j, and Rule 10(b)(5) thereunder, 17 C.F.R. § 240.10b-5.[f]

In addition, the corporate accounting scandals of the early 21st century led to the passage of the Sarbanes-Oxley Act of 2002.[g] This broad-ranging legislation imposed new corporate compliance and corporate audit procedures on publicly traded companies and created new crimes relating to securities fraud. The latter are codified at 18 U.S.C. § 1348.[h] Some commentators have questioned whether the new crimes truly differ from the existing securities fraud statutes, or whether they will make prosecutions for securities fraud any easier.[i] To date, case law involving prosecutions under § 1348 is limited.[j]

[4]   Elements of Securities Fraud

Most of the cases discussed in this chapter were brought under Section 10b of the 1934 Act and Rule 10b-5 thereunder. To obtain a conviction under these provisions, the government must prove that:

(1) (a) the defendant engaged in a fraudulent scheme, or

(b) made a material misstatement, or

(c) omitted material information to one to whom the defendant owed a duty;

(2) the scheme, misstatement, or omission occurred in connection with the purchase or sale of a security; and

---

[f] The 1933 and 1934 Acts grant the SEC the power to issue regulations under the securities statutes. Rule 10b-5 is one such regulation and renders it unlawful "[t]o make any untrue statement of a material fact or to omit to state a material fact necessary in order to make the statements made . . . not misleading . . . in connection with the purchase or sale of a security."

[g] Pub. L. No. 107-204, 116 Stat. 745 (2002). The Act touches on many areas of securities regulation, and has been aptly termed "a securities regulation smorgasbord." Harold S. Bloomenthal, *Sarbanes-Oxley Act in Perspective*, SEC-SOAP § 1:10 (2007).

[h] This new securities fraud statute (set forth in the statutory supplement) was intended to "supplement the patchwork of existing technical securities law violations with a more general and less technical provision, with elements and intent requirements comparable to current bank fraud and health care fraud statutes." 148 Cong. Rec. S7418-01, S7418 (2002) (statement of Sen. Leahy).

[i] *See, e.g.*, Phillip Lambert, *Worlds are Colliding: A Critique of the Need for the Additional Criminal Securities Fraud Section in Sarbanes-Oxley*, 53 Case W. Res. L. Rev. 839, 851 (Spring 2003) ("[T]he language contained in section 807 of Sarbanes-Oxley . . . covers virtually identical transactions and conduct as the language in the Securities Act and Exchange Act.").

[j] One district court did opine that the statute should be broadly interpreted under principles applicable to the mail and wire fraud statutes. *See* United States v. Mahaffy, No. 05-CR-613, 2006 U.S. Dist. LEXIS 53577, at *33-*34 (E.D.N.Y. Aug. 2, 2006) ("The Court has identified no previous convictions under 18 U.S.C. § 1348. However, because the text and legislative history of 18 U.S.C. § 1348 clearly establish that it was modeled on the mail and wire fraud statutes, it is useful to be guided by the numerous and well-established precedents on those statutes in construing this statute. . . . A violation of section 1348(1) requires proof of three elements: (1) fraudulent intent (2) a scheme or artifice to defraud and (3) a nexus with a security.").

(3) the defendant acted "willfully."

The meanings of such key terms as "material" and "willfully" are discussed in the sections that follow. First, however, the chapter provides the doctrinal basis for the principal type of securities fraud discussed in this chapter — insider trading.

[B] INSIDER TRADING

The "insider" trader provides a classic image of the white collar criminal — the wealthy corporate officer who steals company's secret information and profits at the expense of the average investor. But the reality, of course, is more complex. Initially, it is important to note that the term "insider" trading is a misnomer. The crime actually applies to a broad range of people who trade on secret information, including but not limited to corporate "insiders."

There are two different, albeit overlapping, definitions of insider trading. First, under the "traditional" or "classical" theory, a corporate employee or agent — the "insider" — takes information from the corporation and uses the information to trade in the corporation's stock in violation of a duty to that corporation and its shareholders. This theory applies to two distinct categories of defendants: (a) officers and employees of that corporation ("insiders"); and (b) outside lawyers, accountants, and others who work for that corporation on a temporary basis ("quasi-" or "temporary-" insiders). Second, the broader "misappropriation" theory applies to anyone who steals confidential information in violation of a duty and uses the information to buy or sell securities. This theory would apply, for example, to a reporter who stole confidential information from a financial magazine prior to publication and then traded on that information.

This section highlights the historical development of insider trading law. Criminal liability under the traditional theory — trading on nonpublic information by corporate "insiders" for their own benefit — has long been criminalized and is not controversial. The first case in this section, *United States v. Chiarella*, was brought under the traditional theory, but the defendant's conviction was reversed by the Supreme Court because an essential element of that theory was not met. In the second case, *United States v. O'Hagan*, the Supreme Court approved of the misappropriation theory of insider trading. This theory dramatically expands the potential scope of insider trading liability, far beyond corporate insiders, and has been the subject of substantial criticism because of its expansive and somewhat uncertain scope. The third case is *Dirks v. Securities and Exchange Commission*, which examines the liability of "tippers" and "tippees," that is, people who give and receive confidential information used in connection with securities trading. The *Dirks* rule sets forth the specific requirements for the liability of those parties.

[1] The Elements of Insider Trading

Violations of laws prohibiting insider trading essentially constitute a subset of the general category of securities fraud. For this reason, it is helpful to identify the specific elements of a criminal insider trading case. Based upon the applicable statutes, regulations, and Supreme Court decisions, in a case brought against the principal[k] under Section 10b and Rule 10b-5, the government must prove that:

---

[k] Accessory liability is discussed in connection with the *Dirks* decision, *infra.*

1. The defendant bought or sold securities;
2. The defendant —

   (a) Was an insider of the company the securities of which were traded;
   (b) Was a temporary insider of the company the securities of which were traded; and/or
   (c) Was a misappropriator of information from a person or entity to whom the defendant owed a fiduciary duty;

3. The defendant knowingly possessed material, nonpublic information; and
4. The defendant acted willfully.

The law of insider trading is notoriously complex, largely because of the overlap between the traditional and misappropriation theories and the uncertain boundaries of the latter. In each case in this section, it is therefore critical to identify precisely: (a) to whom the defendant owed a duty; (b) the theoretical — "traditional" and/or "misappropriation" theory — basis for that duty; (c) the company the stock of which was traded; and (d) the harm that flowed from the trading.

[2]   The Traditional Theory

In the case that follows, a printing company employee uncovered secret information during his employment and traded on that information. A majority of the Supreme Court determined that the traditional insider trading theory did not apply to the defendant. Why did the Court reach this conclusion?

CHIARELLA v. UNITED STATES
445 U.S. 222 (1980)

Mr. JUSTICE POWELL delivered the opinion of the Court.

*   *   *

I.

Petitioner is a printer by trade. In 1975 and 1976, he worked as a "markup man" in the New York composing room of Pandick Press, a financial printer. Among documents that petitioner handled were five announcements of corporate takeover bids. When these documents were delivered to the printer, the identities of the acquiring and target corporations were concealed by blank spaces or false names. The true names were sent to the printer on the night of the final printing.

The petitioner, however, was able to deduce the names of the target companies before the final printing from other information contained in the documents. Without disclosing his knowledge, petitioner purchased stock in the target companies and sold the shares immediately after the takeover attempts were made public. By this method, petitioner realized a gain of slightly more than $30,000 in the course of 14 months. Subsequently, the Securities and Exchange Commission (Commission or SEC) began an investigation of his trading activities. In May 1977, petitioner entered into a consent decree with the Commission in which he agreed to return his profits to the sellers of the shares. On the same day, he was discharged by Pandick Press.

In January 1978, petitioner was indicted on 17 counts of violating Section 10(b) of the Securities Exchange Act of 1934 (1934 Act) and SEC Rule 10b-5. After petitioner unsuccessfully moved to dismiss the indictment, he was brought to trial and convicted on all counts.

The Court of Appeals for the Second Circuit affirmed petitioner's conviction. 588 F.2d 1358 (1978). We granted certiorari, and we now reverse.

II.

Section 10(b) of the 1934 Act, 15 U.S.C. § 78j, prohibits the use "in connection with the purchase or sale of any security . . . [of] any manipulative or deceptive device or contrivance in contravention of such rules and regulations as the Commission may prescribe." Pursuant to this section, the SEC promulgated Rule 10b-5 which provides in pertinent part:

> It shall be unlawful for any person, directly or indirectly, by the use of any means or instrumentality of interstate commerce, or of the mails or of any facility of any national securities exchange,
>
> (a) To employ any device, scheme, or artifice to defraud, [or] . . .
>
> (b) To engage in any act, practice, or course of business which operates or would operate as a fraud or deceit upon any person, in connection with the purchase or sale of any security.

17 CFR § 240.10b-5 (1979).

This case concerns the legal effect of the petitioner's silence. The District Court's charge permitted the jury to convict the petitioner if it found that he willfully failed to inform sellers of target company securities that he knew of a forthcoming takeover bid that would make their shares more valuable. In order to decide whether silence in such circumstances violates Section 10(b), it is necessary to review the language and legislative history of that statute as well as its interpretation by the Commission and the federal courts.

Although the starting point of our inquiry is the language of the statute, Section 10(b) does not state whether silence may constitute a manipulative or deceptive device. Section 10(b) was designed as a catch-all clause to prevent fraudulent practices. But neither the legislative history nor the statute itself affords specific guidance for the resolution of this case. When Rule 10b-5 was promulgated in 1942, the SEC did not discuss the possibility that failure to provide information might run afoul of Section 10(b).

The SEC took an important step in the development of Section 10(b) when it held that a broker-dealer and his firm violated that section by selling securities on the basis of undisclosed information obtained from a director of the issuer corporation who was also a registered representative of the brokerage firm. In *Cady, Roberts & Co.*, 40 S.E.C. 907 (1961), the Commission decided that a corporate insider must abstain from trading in the shares of his corporation unless he has first disclosed all material inside information known to him. The obligation to disclose or abstain derives from

> [a]n affirmative duty to disclose material information[, which] has been traditionally imposed on corporate "insiders," particular officers, directors,

or controlling stockholders. We, and the courts have consistently held that insiders must disclose material facts which are known to them by virtue of their position but which are not known to persons with whom they deal and which, if known, would affect their investment judgment.

Id. at 911.

The Commission emphasized that the duty arose from (i) the existence of a relationship affording access to inside information intended to be available only for a corporate purpose, and (ii) the unfairness of allowing a corporate insider to take advantage of that information by trading without disclosure. *Id.* at 912, and n.15.[8]

That the relationship between a corporate insider and the stockholders of his corporation gives rise to a disclosure obligation is not a novel twist of the law. At common law, misrepresentation made for the purpose of inducing reliance upon the false statement is fraudulent. But one who fails to disclose material information prior to the consummation of a transaction commits fraud only when he is under a duty to do so. And the duty to disclose arises when one party has information "that the other [party] is entitled to know because of a fiduciary or other similar relation of trust and confidence between them." In its *Cady, Roberts* decision, the Commission recognized a relationship of trust and confidence between the shareholders of a corporation and those insiders who have obtained confidential information by reason of their position with that corporation. This relationship gives rise to a duty to disclose because of the "necessity of preventing a corporate insider from . . . [taking] unfair advantage of the uninformed minority stockholders." *Speed v. Transamerica Corp.*, 99 F. Supp. 808, 829.

The federal courts have found violations of Section 10(b) where corporate insiders used undisclosed information for their own benefit. The cases also have emphasized, in accordance with the common-law rule, that "[t]he party charged with failing to disclose market information must be under a duty to disclose it." *Frigitemp Corp. v. Financial Dynamics Fund, Inc.*, 524 F.2d 275, 282 (2d Cir. 1975). Accordingly, a purchaser of stock who has no duty to a prospective seller because he is neither an insider nor a fiduciary has been held to have no obligation to reveal material facts. . . .

Thus, administrative and judicial interpretations have established that silence in connection with the purchase or sale of securities may operate as a fraud actionable under Section 10(b) despite the absence of statutory language or legislative history specifically addressing the legality of nondisclosure. But such liability is premised upon a duty to disclose arising from a relationship of trust and confidence between parties to a transaction. Application of a duty to disclose prior to trading guarantees that corporate insiders, who have an obligation to place the shareholder's welfare before their own, will not benefit personally through fraudulent use of material, nonpublic information.

---

[8] The transaction in *Cady, Roberts* involved sale of stock to persons who previously may not have been shareholders in the corporation. 40 S.E.C., at 913 and n.21. The Commission embraced the reasoning of Judge Learned Hand that "the director or officer assumed a fiduciary relation to the buyer by the very sale; for it would be a sorry distinction to allow him to use the advantage of his position to induce the buyer into the position of a beneficiary although he was forbidden to do so once the buyer had become one." *Id.* at 914, n.23.

III.

In this case, the petitioner was convicted of violating Section 10(b) although he was not a corporate insider and he received no confidential information from the target company. Moreover, the "market information" upon which he relied did not concern the earning power or operations of the target company, but only the plans of the acquiring company. Petitioner's use of that information was not a fraud under Section 10(b) unless he was subject to an affirmative duty to disclose it before trading. In this case, the jury instructions failed to specify any such duty. In effect, the trial court instructed the jury that petitioner owed a duty to everyone; to all sellers, indeed, to the market as a whole. The jury simply was told to decide whether petitioner used material, nonpublic information at a time when "he knew other people trading in the securities market did not have access to the same information."

The Court of Appeals affirmed the conviction by holding that "[a]nyone — corporate insider or not — who regularly receives material nonpublic information may not use that information to trade in securities without incurring an affirmative duty to disclose." 588 F.2d at 1365 (emphasis in original). Although the court said that its test would include only persons who regularly receive material, nonpublic information, its rationale for that limitation is unrelated to the existence of a duty to disclose. The Court of Appeals, like the trial court, failed to identify a relationship between petitioner and the sellers that could give rise to a duty. Its decision thus rested solely upon its belief that the federal securities laws have "created a system providing equal access to information necessary for reasoned and intelligent investment decisions." *Id.* at 1362. The use by anyone of material information not generally available is fraudulent, this theory suggests, because such information gives certain buyers or sellers an unfair advantage over less informed buyers and sellers.

This reasoning suffers from two defects. First, not every instance of financial unfairness constitutes fraudulent activity under Section 10(b). Second, the element required to make silence fraudulent — a duty to disclose — is absent in this case. No duty could arise from petitioner's relationship with the sellers of the target company's securities, for petitioner had no prior dealings with them. He was not their agent, he was not a fiduciary, he was not a person in whom the sellers had placed their trust and confidence. He was, in fact, a complete stranger who dealt with the sellers only through impersonal market transactions.

We cannot affirm petitioner's conviction without recognizing a general duty between all participants in market transactions to forgo actions based on material, nonpublic information. Formulation of such a broad duty, which departs radically from the established doctrine that duty arises from a specific relationship between two parties, should not be undertaken absent some explicit evidence of congressional intent.

As we have seen, no such evidence emerges from the language or legislative history of Section 10(b). Moreover, neither the Congress nor the Commission ever has adopted a parity-of-information rule. . . .

We see no basis for applying such a new and different theory of liability in this case. . . . Section 10(b) is aptly described as a catchall provision, but what it catches must be fraud. When an allegation of fraud is based upon nondisclosure, there can be no fraud absent a duty to speak. We hold that a duty to disclose under

Section 10(b) does not arise from the mere possession of nonpublic market information. The contrary result is without support in the legislative history of Section 10(b) and would be inconsistent with the careful plan that Congress has enacted for regulation of the securities markets.[20]

IV.

[T]he United States offers an alternative theory to support petitioner's conviction. It argues that petitioner breached a duty to the acquiring corporation when he acted upon information that he obtained by virtue of his position as an employee of a printer employed by the corporation. The breach of this duty is said to support a conviction under Section 10(b) for fraud perpetrated upon both the acquiring corporation and the sellers.

We need not decide whether this theory has merit for it was not submitted to the jury. . . .

The jury instructions demonstrate that petitioner was convicted merely because of his failure to disclose material, nonpublic information to sellers from whom he bought the stock of target corporations. The jury was not instructed on the nature or elements of a duty owed by petitioner to anyone other than the sellers. Because we cannot affirm a criminal conviction on the basis of a theory not presented to the jury, we will not speculate upon whether such a duty exists, whether it has been breached, or whether such a breach constitutes a violation of Section 10(b).

The judgment of the Court of Appeals is *reversed.*

Mr. CHIEF JUSTICE BURGER, dissenting.

I believe that the jury instructions in this case properly charged a violation of Section 10(b) and Rule 10b-5, and I would affirm the conviction.

I.

As a general rule, neither party to an arm's-length business transaction has an obligation to disclose information to the other unless the parties stand in some confidential or fiduciary relation. This rule permits a businessman to capitalize on his experience and skill in securing and evaluating relevant information; it provides incentive for hard work, careful analysis, and astute forecasting. But the policies that underlie the rule also should limit its scope. In particular, the rule should give way when an informational advantage is obtained, not by superior experience, foresight, or industry, but by some unlawful means. . . . I would read Section 10(b) and Rule 10b-5 to encompass and build on this principle: to mean that a person who has misappropriated nonpublic information has an absolute duty to disclose that information or to refrain from trading.

The language of Section 10(b) and of Rule 10b-5 plainly supports such a reading. By their terms, these provisions reach *any* person engaged in *any* fraudulent scheme. This broad language negates the suggestion that congressional concern was limited to trading by "corporate insiders" or to deceptive practices related to

---

[20] It is worth noting that this is apparently the first case in which criminal liability has been imposed upon a purchaser for Section 10(b) nondisclosure. Petitioner was sentenced to a year in prison, suspended except for one month, and a 5-year term of probation.

"corporate information." Just as surely Congress cannot have intended one standard of fair dealing for "white collar" insiders and another for the "blue collar" level.

The history of the statute and of the Rule also supports this reading. The antifraud provisions were designed in large measure "to assure that dealing in securities is fair and without undue preferences or advantages among investors." H.R. Conf. Rep. No. 94-229, p. 91 (1975), U.S. Code Cong. & Admin. News 1975, p. 323. An investor who purchases securities on the basis of misappropriated nonpublic information possesses just such an "undue" trading advantage; his conduct quite clearly serves no useful function except his own enrichment at the expense of others.

This interpretation of Section 10(b) and Rule 10b-5 is in no sense novel. It follows naturally from legal principles enunciated by the Securities and Exchange Commission in its seminal *Cady, Roberts* decision. 40 S.E.C. 907 (1961). There, the Commission relied upon two factors to impose a duty to disclose on corporate insiders: (1) " . . . access . . . to information intended to be available only for a corporate purpose *and not for the personal benefit of anyone*" (emphasis added); and (2) the unfairness inherent in trading on such information when it is inaccessible to those with whom one is dealing. Both of these factors are present whenever a party gains an informational advantage by unlawful means. . . .

II.

* * *

In sum, the evidence shows beyond all doubt that Chiarella, working literally in the shadows of the warning signs in the printshop misappropriated — stole to put it bluntly — valuable nonpublic information entrusted to him in the utmost confidence. He then exploited his ill-gotten informational advantage by purchasing securities in the market. In my view, such conduct plainly violates Section 10(b) and Rule 10b-5. Accordingly, I would affirm the judgment of the Court of Appeals.

Mr. JUSTICE BLACKMUN, with whom Mr. JUSTICE MARSHALL joins, dissenting.

Although I agree with much of what is said in Part I of the dissenting opinion of THE CHIEF JUSTICE, *ante*, I write separately because, in my view, it is unnecessary to rest petitioner's conviction on a "misappropriation" theory. . . . I also would find petitioner's conduct fraudulent within the meaning of Section § 10(b) of the Securities Exchange Act of 1934, 15 U.S.C. § 78j(b), and the Securities and Exchange Commission's Rule 10b-5, 17 CFR § 240.10b-5, even if he had obtained the blessing of his employer's principals before embarking on his profiteering scheme. Indeed, I think petitioner's brand of manipulative trading, with or without such approval, lies close to the heart of what the securities laws are intended to prohibit.

The Court continues to pursue a course, charted in certain recent decisions, designed to transform Section 10(b) from an intentionally elastic "catchall" provision to one that catches relatively little of the misbehavior that all too often makes investment in securities a needlessly risky business for the uninitiated investor. Such confinement in this case is now achieved by imposition of a requirement of a "special relationship" akin to fiduciary duty before the statute gives rise to a duty to disclose or to abstain from trading upon material, nonpublic information. The

Court admits that this conclusion finds no mandate in the language of the statute or its legislative history. Yet the Court fails even to attempt a justification of its ruling in terms of the purposes of the securities laws, or to square that ruling with the long-standing but now much abused principle that the federal securities laws are to be construed flexibly rather than with narrow technicality.

I, of course, agree with the Court that a relationship of trust can establish a duty to disclose under § 10(b) and Rule 10b-5. But I do not agree that a failure to disclose violates the Rule only when the responsibilities of a relationship of that kind have been breached. As applied to this case, the Court's approach unduly minimizes the importance of petitioner's *access* to confidential information that the honest investor no matter how diligently he tried, could not legally obtain. In doing so, it further advances an interpretation of Section 10(b) and Rule 10b-5 that stops short of their full implications. Although the Court draws support for its position from certain precedent, I find its decision neither fully consistent with developments in the common law of fraud, nor fully in step with administrative and judicial application of Rule 10b-5 to "insider" trading.

* * *

Whatever the outer limits of the Rule, petitioner Chiarella's case fits neatly near the center of its analytical framework. He occupied a relationship to the takeover companies giving him intimate access to concededly material information that was sedulously guarded from public access. Petitioner, moreover, knew that the information was unavailable to those with whom he dealt. And he took full, virtually riskless advantage of this artificial information gap by selling the stocks shortly after each takeover bid was announced. This misuse of confidential information was clearly placed before the jury. Petitioner's conviction, therefore, should be upheld, and I dissent from the Court's upsetting that conviction.

NOTES AND QUESTIONS

1. *Theories of "insider trading."* Why, precisely, did the majority reverse the conviction? Is it not clear that Chiarella did something wrong? In their dissents, what theories did Chief Justice Burger and Justice Blackmun cite in support of their arguments that the conviction should have been affirmed? In each case, how did the majority respond?

2. *"Inside" information.* There are many different types of "inside" information. Most insider trading cases, including *Chiarella*, arise in the context of "extraordinary corporate transactions." Such transactions include mergers, tender offers, and proxy contests.[l] In these situations, rapid fluctuations in stock prices make it possible to make (or lose) a lot of money very quickly. In other cases, such as the case relating to Sam Waksal, Martha Stewart, and ImClone stock — where the stock was sold shortly before an unfavorable United States Food and Drug Administration ruling was announced[m] — the defendants allegedly traded based

---

[l] In a tender offer, the offering company offers to buy all of a "target" company's stock at a specified price over the then-current market price for the stock. In a proxy contest, the shareholders vote, by giving their votes to "proxies," on corporate decisions such as the election of a board of directors or a merger.

[m] Waksal pleaded guilty to insider trading and was sentenced to more than seven years in prison. Kara Scannell, *Waksal's Sentence in Trading Case Tops Seven Years*, Wall St. J., June 11, 2003, at A2.

upon secret, un-released information that would likely affect the stock price. Other kinds of secret information include financial projections, earnings statements, and similar information that reflect the company's strengths and weaknesses.

3. *What is the harm?* In *Cady, Roberts & Co.*, 40 S.E.C. 907 (1961), the SEC stated that it is unfair for an insider to profit from secret information belonging to the company and its shareholders. And as the United States Supreme Court stated in *United States v. O'Hagan*, 521 U.S. 642, 658 (1997), "an animating purpose of the Exchange Act [is] to insure honest securities markets and thereby promote investor confidence." Some scholars have argued, however, that insider trading actually benefits the securities markets; the more information available, the more efficiently the securities markets will behave. Thus, when a trader buys or sells based on inside information, the price of the stock will react accordingly, and the price will more accurately reflect the true value of the stock. One author has written that "[t]oday, most commentators conclude that insider trading prohibitions are probably not worth the heavy regulatory cost and that the underlying efficiencies, rather than more amorphous 'fairness' concepts, should rule the day." Carol B. Swanson, *Insider Trading Madness: Rule 10b5-1 and the Death of Scienter*, 52 U. Kan. L. Rev. 147, 160–161 (2003). Which view do you believe is correct? Why? *See also* Eric Engle, *Insider Trading: Incoherent in Theory, Inefficient in Practice*, 32 Okla. City L. Rev. 37, 60 (2007) ("Insider trading is not harmful").

[3]   The Misappropriation Theory

In *Chiarella*, the Supreme Court declined to consider whether an insider trading conviction could be based upon the "misappropriation" theory. Seven years later, in *Carpenter v. United States*, 484 U.S. 19 (1987), the Court divided four-to-four on this issue. Finally, in the case that follows, a split court resolved the question. As you read the decision, consider whether the majority made a persuasive case for the rule it adopted.

UNITED STATES v. O'HAGAN
521 U.S. 642 (1997)

JUSTICE GINSBURG delivered the opinion of the Court.

Respondent James Herman O'Hagan was a partner in the law firm of Dorsey & Whitney in Minneapolis, Minnesota. In July 1988, Grand Metropolitan PLC (Grand Met), a company based in London, England, retained Dorsey & Whitney as local counsel to represent Grand Met regarding a potential tender offer for the common stock of the Pillsbury Company, headquartered in Minneapolis. Both Grand Met and Dorsey & Whitney took precautions to protect the confidentiality of Grand Met's tender offer plans. O'Hagan did no work on the Grand Met representation. Dorsey & Whitney withdrew from representing Grand Met on September 9, 1988. Less than a month later, on October 4, 1988, Grand Met publicly announced its tender offer for Pillsbury stock.

Stewart was not criminally charged with insider trading, but was named in a SEC civil suit based on that theory. Kara Scannell & Laurie P. Cohen, *Homemaking Maven Pleads Not Guilty to Criminal Counts; SEC Files Civil Insider Charges*, Wall St. J., June 5, 2003, at C1.

On August 18, 1988, while Dorsey & Whitney was still representing Grand Met, O'Hagan began purchasing call options for Pillsbury stock. Each option gave him the right to purchase 100 shares of Pillsbury stock by a specified date in September 1988. Later in August and in September, O'Hagan made additional purchases of Pillsbury call options. By the end of September, he owned 2,500 unexpired Pillsbury options, apparently more than any other individual investor. O'Hagan also purchased, in September 1988, some 5,000 shares of Pillsbury common stock, at a price just under $39 per share. When Grand Met announced its tender offer in October, the price of Pillsbury stock rose to nearly $60 per share. O'Hagan then sold his Pillsbury call options and common stock, making a profit of more than $4.3 million.

The Securities and Exchange Commission (SEC or Commission) initiated an investigation into O'Hagan's transactions, culminating in a 57-count indictment. The indictment alleged that O'Hagan defrauded his law firm and its client, Grand Met, by using for his own trading purposes material, nonpublic information regarding Grand Met's planned tender offer. According to the indictment, O'Hagan used the profits he gained through this trading to conceal his previous embezzlement and conversion of unrelated client trust funds. O'Hagan was charged with 20 counts of mail fraud, in violation of 18 U.S.C. § 1341; 17 counts of securities fraud, in violation of Section 10(b) of the Securities Exchange Act of 1934 (Exchange Act), 15 U.S.C. § 78j(b), and SEC Rule 10b-5, 17 CFR § 240.10b-5 (1996); 17 counts of fraudulent trading in connection with a tender offer, in violation of § 14(e) of the Exchange Act, 15 U.S.C. § 78n(e), and SEC Rule 14e-3(a), 17 CFR § 240.14e-3(a) (1996); and 3 counts of violating federal money laundering statutes, 18 U.S.C. §§ 1956(a)(1)(B)(I), 1957. A jury convicted O'Hagan on all 57 counts, and he was sentenced to a 41-month term of imprisonment.

A divided panel of the Court of Appeals for the Eighth Circuit reversed all of O'Hagan's convictions. Liability under Section 10(b) and Rule 10b-5, the Eighth Circuit held, may not be grounded on the "misappropriation theory" of securities fraud on which the prosecution relied. . . . The Eighth Circuit further concluded that O'Hagan's mail fraud and money laundering convictions rested on violations of the securities laws, and therefore could not stand once the securities fraud convictions were reversed. . . .

We address first the Court of Appeals' reversal of O'Hagan's convictions under Section 10(b) and Rule 10b-5. Following the Fourth Circuit's lead, the Eighth Circuit rejected the misappropriation theory as a basis for Section 10(b) liability. We hold, in accord with several other Courts of Appeals, that criminal liability under Section 10(b) may be predicated on the misappropriation theory.

The statute proscribes (1) using any deceptive device (2) in connection with the purchase or sale of securities, in contravention of rules prescribed by the Commission. The provision, as written, does not confine its coverage to deception of a purchaser or seller of securities; rather, the statute reaches any deceptive device used "in connection with the purchase or sale of any security." . . .

Under the "traditional" or "classical theory" of insider trading liability, Section 10(b) and Rule 10b-5 are violated when a corporate insider trades in the securities of his corporation on the basis of material, nonpublic information. Trading on such information qualifies as a "deceptive device" under Section 10(b), we have affirmed, because "a relationship of trust and confidence [exists] between the shareholders of a corporation and those insiders who have obtained confidential information by reason of their position with that corporation." *Chiarella v. United States*, 445 U.S. 222, 228 (1980). That relationship, we recognized, "gives rise to a duty to disclose [or to abstain from trading] because of the 'necessity of preventing a corporate insider   from . . . tak[ing]   unfair   advantage   of . . . uninformed . . . stockholders.'" *Id.* at 228–229 (citation omitted). The classical theory applies not only to officers, directors, and other permanent insiders of a corporation, but also to attorneys, accountants, consultants, and others who temporarily become fiduciaries of a corporation.

The "misappropriation theory" holds that a person commits fraud "in connection with" a securities transaction, and thereby violates Section 10(b) and Rule 10b-5, when he misappropriates confidential information for securities trading purposes, in breach of a duty owed to the source of the information. Under this theory, a fiduciary's undisclosed, self-serving use of a principal's information to purchase or sell securities, in breach of a duty of loyalty and confidentiality, defrauds the principal of the exclusive use of that information. In lieu of premising liability on a fiduciary relationship between company insider and purchaser or seller of the company's stock, the misappropriation theory premises liability on a fiduciary-turned-trader's deception of those who entrusted him with access to confidential information.

The two theories are complementary, each addressing efforts to capitalize on nonpublic information through the purchase or sale of securities. The classical theory targets a corporate insider's breach of duty to shareholders with whom the insider transacts; the misappropriation theory outlaws trading on the basis of nonpublic information by a corporate "outsider" in breach of a duty owed not to a trading party, but to the source of the information. The misappropriation theory is thus designed to "protec[t] the integrity of the securities markets against abuses by 'outsiders' to a corporation who have access to confidential information that will affect th[e] corporation's security price when revealed, but who owe no fiduciary or other duty to that corporation's shareholders." *Id.*

In this case, the indictment alleged that O'Hagan, in breach of a duty of trust and confidence he owed to his law firm, Dorsey & Whitney, and to its client, Grand Met, traded on the basis of nonpublic information regarding Grand Met's planned tender offer for Pillsbury common stock. This conduct, the government charged, constituted a fraudulent device in connection with the purchase and sale of securities.[5]

We agree with the government that misappropriation, as just defined, satisfies Section 10(b)'s requirement that chargeable conduct involve a "deceptive device or contrivance" used "in connection with" the purchase or sale of securities. We observe, first, that misappropriators, as the government describes them, deal in deception. A fiduciary who "[pretends] loyalty to the principal while secretly

---

[5] The government could not have prosecuted O'Hagan under the classical theory, for O'Hagan was not an "insider" of Pillsbury, the corporation in whose stock he traded. Although an "outsider" with respect to Pillsbury, O'Hagan had an intimate association with, and was found to have traded on confidential information from, Dorsey & Whitney, counsel to tender offeror Grand Met. Under the misappropriation theory, O'Hagan's securities trading does not escape Exchange Act sanction, as it would under Justice THOMAS' dissenting view, simply because he was associated with, and gained nonpublic information from, the bidder, rather than the target.

converting the principal's information for personal gain," Brief for United States 17, "dupes" or defrauds the principal.

We addressed fraud of the same species in *Carpenter v. United States*, 484 U.S. 19 (1987), which involved the mail fraud statute's proscription of "any scheme or artifice to defraud," 18 U.S.C. § 1341. Affirming convictions under that statute, we said in *Carpenter* that an employee's undertaking not to reveal his employer's confidential information "became a sham" when the employee provided the information to his co-conspirators in a scheme to obtain trading profits. 484 U.S. at 27. A company's confidential information, we recognized in *Carpenter*, qualifies as property to which the company has a right of exclusive use. The undisclosed misappropriation of such information, in violation of a fiduciary duty, the Court said in *Carpenter*, constitutes fraud akin to embezzlement — " 'the fraudulent appropriation to one's own use of the money or goods entrusted to one's care by another.' " *Id.* at 27. *Carpenter*'s discussion of the fraudulent misuse of confidential information, the government notes, "is a particularly apt source of guidance here, because [the mail fraud statute] (like Section 10(b)) has long been held to require deception, not merely the breach of a fiduciary duty." Brief for United States 18 n.9.

Deception through nondisclosure is central to the theory of liability for which the government seeks recognition. As counsel for the government stated in explanation of the theory at oral argument: "To satisfy the common law rule that a trustee may not use the property that [has] been entrusted [to] him, there would have to be consent. To satisfy the requirement of the Securities Act that there be no deception, there would only have to be disclosure." Tr. of Oral Arg. 12.[6]

The misappropriation theory advanced by the government is consistent with *Santa Fe Industries, Inc. v. Green*, 430 U.S. 462 (1977), a decision underscoring that Section 10(b) is not an all-purpose breach of fiduciary duty ban; rather, it trains on conduct involving manipulation or deception. In contrast to the government's allegations in this case, in *Santa Fe Industries*, all pertinent facts were disclosed by the persons charged with violating Section 10(b) and Rule 10b-5, therefore, there was no deception through nondisclosure to which liability under those provisions could attach. Similarly, full disclosure forecloses liability under the misappropriation theory: Because the deception essential to the misappropriation theory involves feigning fidelity to the source of information, if the fiduciary discloses to the source that he plans to trade on the nonpublic information, there is no "deceptive device" and thus no Section 10(b) violation — although the fiduciary-turned-trader may remain liable under state law for breach of a duty of loyalty.[7]

We turn next to the Section 10(b) requirement that the misappropriator's deceptive use of information be "in connection with the purchase or sale of [a] security." This element is satisfied because the fiduciary's fraud is consummated, not when the fiduciary gains the confidential information, but when, without

---

[6] Under the misappropriation theory urged in this case, the disclosure obligation runs to the source of the information, here, Dorsey & Whitney and Grand Met. Chief Justice Burger, dissenting in *Chiarella*, advanced a broader reading of § 10(b) and Rule 10b-5; the disclosure obligation, as he envisioned it, ran to those with whom the misappropriator trades. The government does not propose that we adopt a misappropriation theory of that breadth.

[7] Where, however, a person trading on the basis of material, nonpublic information owes a duty of loyalty and confidentiality to two entities or persons — for example, a law firm and its client — but makes disclosure to only one, the trader may still be liable under the misappropriation theory.

disclosure to his principal, he uses the information to purchase or sell securities. The securities transaction and the breach of duty thus coincide. This is so even though the person or entity defrauded is not the other party to the trade, but is, instead, the source of the nonpublic information. A misappropriator who trades on the basis of material, nonpublic information, in short, gains his advantageous market position through deception; he deceives the source of the information and simultaneously harms members of the investing public.

The misappropriation theory targets information of a sort that misappropriators ordinarily capitalize upon to gain no-risk profits through the purchase or sale of securities. Should a misappropriator put such information to other use, the statute's prohibition would not be implicated. The theory does not catch all conceivable forms of fraud involving confidential information; rather, it catches fraudulent means of capitalizing on such information through securities transactions.

The Government notes another limitation on the forms of fraud § 10(b) reaches: "The misappropriation theory would not . . . apply to a case in which a person defrauded a bank into giving him a loan or embezzled cash from another, and then used the proceeds of the misdeed to purchase securities." In such a case, the Government states, "the proceeds would have value to the malefactor apart from their use in a securities transaction, and the fraud would be complete as soon as the money was obtained." In other words, money can buy, if not anything, then at least many things; its misappropriation may thus be viewed as sufficiently detached from a subsequent securities transaction that § 10(b)'s "in connection with" requirement would not be met.

JUSTICE THOMAS' charge that the misappropriation theory is incoherent because information, like funds, can be put to multiple uses misses the point. The Exchange Act was enacted in part "to insure the maintenance of fair and honest markets,"15 U.S.C. § 78b, and there is no question that fraudulent uses of confidential information fall within § 10(b)'s prohibition if the fraud is "in connection with" a securities transaction. It is hardly remarkable that a rule suitably applied to the fraudulent uses of certain kinds of information would be stretched beyond reason were it applied to the fraudulent use of money. . . .

The misappropriation theory comports with Section 10(b)'s language, which requires deception "in connection with the purchase or sale of any security," not deception of an identifiable purchaser or seller. The theory is also well tuned to an animating purpose of the Exchange Act: to insure honest securities markets and thereby promote investor confidence. Although informational disparity is inevitable in the securities markets, investors likely would hesitate to venture their capital in a market where trading based on misappropriated nonpublic information is unchecked by law. An investor's informational disadvantage vis-à-vis a misappropriator with material, nonpublic information stems from contrivance, not luck; it is a disadvantage that cannot be overcome with research or skill.

[C]onsidering the inhibiting impact on market participation of trading on misappropriated information, and the congressional purposes underlying Section 10(b), it makes scant sense to hold a lawyer like O'Hagan a Section 10(b) violator if he works for a law firm representing the target of a tender offer, but not if he works for a law firm representing the bidder. The text of the statute requires no such result. The misappropriation at issue here was properly made the subject of a

Section 10(b) charge because it meets the statutory requirement that there be "deceptive" conduct "in connection with" securities transactions.

*   *   *

In sum, the misappropriation theory, as we have examined and explained it in this opinion, is both consistent with the statute and with our precedent. Vital to our decision that criminal liability may be sustained under the misappropriation theory, we emphasize, are two sturdy safeguards Congress has provided regarding scienter. To establish a criminal violation of Rule 10b-5, the government must prove that a person "willfully" violated the provision.[12] Furthermore, a defendant may not be imprisoned for violating Rule 10b-5 if he proves that he had no knowledge of the Rule. O'Hagan's charge that the misappropriation theory is too indefinite to permit the imposition of criminal liability, thus fails not only because the theory is limited to those who breach a recognized duty. In addition, the statute's "requirement of the presence of culpable intent as a necessary element of the offense does much to destroy any force in the argument that application of the [statute]" in circumstances such as O'Hagan's is unjust. *Boyce Motor Lines, Inc. v. United States*, 342 U.S. 337, 342 (1952).

The Eighth Circuit erred in holding that the misappropriation theory is inconsistent with Section 10(b). The Court of Appeals may address on remand O'Hagan's other challenges to his convictions under § 10(b) and Rule 10b-5. . . .

Justice Scalia, concurring in part and dissenting in part. (Omitted.)

Justice Thomas, with whom The Chief Justice joins, concurring in the judgment in part and dissenting in part.

Today the majority upholds respondent's convictions for violating Section 10(b) of the Securities Exchange Act of 1934, and Rule 10b-5 promulgated thereunder, based upon the Securities and Exchange Commission's "misappropriation theory." Central to the majority's holding is the need to interpret Section 10(b)'s requirement that a deceptive device be "use[d] or employ[ed], in connection with the purchase or sale of any security." 15 U.S.C. § 78j(b). Because the Commission's misappropriation theory fails to provide a coherent and consistent interpretation of this essential requirement for liability under Section 10(b), I dissent.

I do not take issue with the majority's determination that the undisclosed misappropriation of confidential information by a fiduciary can constitute a "deceptive device" within the meaning of Section 10(b). Nondisclosure where there is a pre-existing duty to disclose satisfies our definitions of fraud and deceit for purposes of the securities laws.

Unlike the majority, however, I cannot accept the Commission's interpretation of when a deceptive device is "use[d] . . . in connection with" a securities transaction. . . .

[The misappropriation theory should not] cover cases, such as this one, involving fraud on the source of information where the source has no connection with the

---

[12] In relevant part, Section 32 of the Exchange Act, as set forth in 15 U.S.C. § 78ff(a), provides: "Any person who willfully violates any provision of this chapter . . . shall upon conviction be fined not more than $1,000,000, or imprisoned not more than 10 years, or both . . . ; but no person shall be subject to imprisonment under this section for the violation of any rule or regulation if he proves that he had no knowledge of such rule or regulation."

other participant in a securities transaction. It seems obvious that the undisclosed misappropriation of confidential information is not necessarily consummated by a securities transaction. In this case, for example, upon learning of Grand Met's confidential takeover plans, O'Hagan could have done any number of things with the information: He could have sold it to a newspaper for publication; he could have given or sold the information to Pillsbury itself; or he could even have kept the information and used it solely for his personal amusement, perhaps in a fantasy stock trading game.

Any of these activities would have deprived Grand Met of its right to "exclusive use" of the information and, if undisclosed, would constitute "embezzlement" of Grand Met's informational property. Under *any* theory of liability, however, these activities would not violate § 10(b) and, according to the Commission's monetary embezzlement analogy, these possibilities are sufficient to preclude a violation under the misappropriation theory even where the informational property *was* used for securities trading. That O'Hagan actually did use the information to purchase securities is thus no more significant here than it is in the case of embezzling money used to purchase securities. In both cases the embezzler *could have* done something else with the property, and hence the Commission's necessary "connection" under the securities laws would not be met. If the relevant test under the "in connection with" language is whether the fraudulent act is *necessarily* tied to a securities transaction, then the misappropriation of confidential information used to trade no more violates § 10(b) than does the misappropriation of funds used to trade. As the Commission concedes that the latter is not covered under its theory, I am at a loss to see how the same theory can coherently be applied to the former.

*   *   *

In upholding respondent's convictions under the new and improved misappropriation theory, the majority also points to various policy considerations underlying the securities laws, such as maintaining fair and honest markets, promoting investor confidence, and protecting the integrity of the securities markets. But the repeated reliance on such broad-sweeping legislative purposes reaches too far and is misleading in the context of the misappropriation theory. It reaches too far in that, regardless of the overarching purpose of the securities laws, it is not illegal to run afoul of the "purpose" of a statute, only its letter. . . .

[A]s we have repeatedly held, use of nonpublic information to trade is not itself a violation of Section 10(b). Rather, it is the use of fraud "in connection with" a securities transaction that is forbidden. Where the relevant element of fraud has no impact on the integrity of the subsequent transactions as distinct from the nonfraudulent element of using nonpublic information, one can reasonably question whether the fraud was used in connection with a securities transaction. And one can likewise question whether removing that aspect of fraud, though perhaps laudable, has anything to do with the confidence or integrity of the market.

The absence of a coherent and consistent misappropriation theory and, by necessary implication, a coherent and consistent application of the statutory "use or employ, in connection with" language, is particularly problematic in the context of this case. The government claims a remarkable breadth to the delegation of authority in Section 10(b), arguing that "the very aim of this section was to pick up unforeseen, cunning, deceptive devices that people might cleverly use in the securities markets." Tr. of Oral Arg. 7. As the Court aptly queried, "[t]hat's rather unusual, for a criminal statute to be that open-ended, isn't it?" *Id.* Unusual indeed. Putting aside the dubious validity of an open-ended delegation to an independent agency to go forth and create regulations criminalizing "fraud," in this case we do not even have a formal regulation embodying the agency's misappropriation theory. . . . [17]

NOTES AND QUESTIONS

1. *The misappropriation theory.* Neither Section 10b nor Rule 10b-5 sets forth a "misappropriation" theory. Why did the majority affirm the use of that theory? Is the decision consistent with *Chiarella*? What is the dissent's complaint? Is the dissent correct?

What sorts of duties will support a misappropriation case? For example, assume that a patient discusses material nonpublic information during a session with a psychiatrist, and that the psychiatrist and the psychiatrist's broker then trade on the information. Does that suffice? *See, e.g., United States v. Willis*, 737 F. Supp. 269 (S.D.N.Y. 1990); *SEC v. Willis*, 825 F. Supp. 617 (S.D.N.Y. 1993) (upholding misappropriation theory based upon the psychiatrist's breach of duty to his patient).

2. *The "in connection with" requirement.* What is the dissent's argument concerning whether O'Hagan's deception was "in connection with" his securities trading? The majority concludes that one who embezzles an employer's money to use in trading securities has not committed insider trading, while one who steals an employer's confidential information for such use *has* committed insider trading. Does this distinction make sense? Why or why not?

3. *The Carpenter case.* In *Carpenter* (discussed in Chapter 4, Mail and Wire Fraud, *supra*), a Wall Street Journal reporter traded on information from a column he wrote for the Journal. Under newspaper policy, the information was confidential and was not to be disclosed prior to publication. The column often affected stock prices, and the reporter and his cohorts traded in advance of publication and made handsome profits. But note that the Wall Street Journal reporter had no duty to any of the participants in the transactions involved in the trading in *Carpenter*. In contrast, O'Hagan did have a duty to his firm's client, which was the offering party in the Pillsbury transaction. What was the potential harm from O'Hagan's actions? From the Wall Street Journal reporter's actions? Was the former more serious than the latter? Why or why not?

4. *Tender offer rules.*

a. *Rule 14e-3(a).* Insider trading can be prosecuted under laws other than Section 10b and Rule 10b-5. Section 14 of the Exchange Act and Rule 14e-3(a) thereunder, for example, prohibit trading while in possession of material nonpublic information relating to a tender offer. Rule 14e-3(a), 17 C.F.R. 240.14e-3(a), provides:

> If any person has taken a substantial step or steps to commence, or has commenced, a tender offer (the "offering person"), it shall constitute a

---

[17] The SEC subsequently adopted Rule 10b5-2, which attempts to define the fiduciary duties that may give rise to liability under the misappropriation theory. This Rule is discussed after the notes and questions following *O'Hagan*.

fraudulent, deceptive or manipulative act or practice within the meaning of section 14(e) of the [Exchange] Act for any other person who is in possession of material information relating to such tender offer which information he knows or has reason to know is nonpublic and which he knows or has reason to know has been acquired directly or indirectly from:

(1) The offering person,

(2) The issuer of the securities sought or to be sought by such tender offer, or

(3) Any officer, director, partner or employee or any other person acting on behalf of the offering person or such issuer, to purchase or sell or cause to be purchased or sold any of such securities . . . , unless within a reasonable time prior to any purchase or sale such information and its source are publicly disclosed by press release or otherwise.

O'Hagan was also convicted under this provision. On appeal, he argued that the SEC exceeded its rulemaking authority when it adopted Rule 14e-3(a). Because that Rule imposes liability even where the defendant has not obtained the information in breach of a fiduciary duty, O'Hagan argued, the Rule violates the *Chiarella* holding. The Court rejected O'Hagan's argument. The Court noted that O'Hagan had indeed breached a fiduciary duty and stated that the SEC, "to the extent relevant to this case, did not exceed its authority."

b. *Warehousing.* By the language quoted above, the Court implied that Rule 14e-3(a) might *not* be valid where there has been no breach of duty. What if, for example, the owner of the information specifically approved of the trading? In *O'Hagan*, the Court stated that "[w]e leave for another day, when the issue requires decision, the legitimacy of Rule 14e-3(a) as applied to 'warehousing,' which the government describes as 'the practice by which bidders leak advance information of a tender offer to allies and encourage them to purchase the target company's stock before the bid is announced.' " Should such trading be forbidden? Why or why not?

c. *Mens rea.* There is also some uncertainty as to the mens rea requirement under Section 14 and Rule 14e-3(a). What if a defendant obtained material, nonpublic information relating to a tender offer, but (a) did not breach a duty in obtaining the information and (b) did not *know* the information involved a tender offer? Could that defendant be liable under those provisions? Courts have not resolved this question. In one case, the court did hold that a defendant who traded on material, nonpublic information, but who did not breach a duty in obtaining the information and did not know that the information involved a tender offer, was not guilty under Section 14. *United States v. Cassese*, 290 F. Supp. 2d 443 (S.D.N.Y. 2003), *aff'd*, 428 F.3d 92 (2d Cir. 2005).

NOTE ON *UNITED STATES v. CHESTMAN* AND RULE 10B5-2

The Court in *O'Hagan* did not define the sorts of fiduciary duties that may give rise to a misappropriation case. In a pre-*O'Hagan* case, *United States v. Chestman*, 947 F.2d 551 (2d Cir. 1991) (*en banc*), the Second Circuit attempted to draw the boundaries of fiduciary duties among family members. In that case, Ira Waldbaum gave inside information concerning the sale of his company to his sister so that she could make the financial arrangements attendant to the sale. In turn, the sister gave the information to her daughter, who gave it to her husband. The husband,

Keith Loeb, and Chestman, the husband's stockbroker, then traded on the information. Each of these persons knew that the information was material and nonpublic information relating to a tender offer.

Loeb pleaded guilty and testified against Chestman, who was convicted under Section 10b. The Second Circuit reversed. As will be seen below in the discussion of tippee liability, for Chestman to be guilty under Section 10b, the government was required to show that Loeb breached a fiduciary duty when giving Chestman the information. The Second Circuit found that there was no such breach because the husband owed no duty to the company, to his wife, or to his wife's family to keep the information secret. The husband was not employed by the company, and had no history of maintaining the business confidences of his wife or his wife's family. (Because no such breach of duty is required under Section 14, however, the court affirmed the husband's conviction for illegal trading in connection with the tender offer.)

In the wake of *Chestman* and *O'Hagan*, the SEC, in 2000, adopted Rule 10b5-2. Entitled "Duties of trust or confidence in misappropriation insider trading cases," the rule attempts to define the fiduciary duties that may give rise to misappropriation liability:

> For purposes of this section, a "duty of trust or confidence" exists in the following circumstances, among others:
>
> (1) Whenever a person *agrees* to maintain information in confidence;
>
> (2) Whenever the person communicating the material nonpublic information and the person to whom it is communicated have a *history, pattern, or practice of sharing confidences*, such that the *recipient of the information knows or reasonably should know* that the person communicating the material nonpublic information expects that the recipient will maintain its confidentiality; or
>
> (3) Whenever a person receives or obtains material nonpublic information from his or her *spouse, parent, child, or sibling*; provided, however, that the person receiving or obtaining the information may demonstrate that no duty of trust or confidence existed with respect to the information, by establishing that he or she *neither knew nor reasonably should have known* that the person who was the source of the information expected that the person would keep the information confidential, because of the parties' history, pattern, or practice of sharing and maintaining confidences, and because there was no agreement or understanding to maintain the confidentiality of the information.

17 C.F.R. § 240.14e-(3)(a) (emphasis added).

Does this section provide clarity to the misappropriation theory? Does it overturn the result in *Chestman*?

PROBLEMS

5-1. Keith Joon was Chief Executive Officer ("CEO") of Goose Foods, Inc. He had also been a member, for 10 years, of the National Leaders Organization ("NLO"), a national organization of company executives under 50 years old. The NLO is organized into regional chapters, and further divided into small forums.

Joon was a member of the Northern California Forum.

The "Forum Principles" of the Northern California Forum stated that: "We operate in an atmosphere of absolute confidentiality. Nothing discussed in forum will be discussed with outsiders. Confidentiality, in all ways and for always." Members were also required to comply with a written "Confidentiality Commitment" as a condition of membership. That agreement provided: "I understand that to achieve the level of trust necessary to ensure the interchange we all seek in the Forum, all information shared by the membership must be held in absolute confidence." Joon knew of the Confidentiality Commitment, but did not sign an agreement to that effect or otherwise promise to adhere to the commitment. During his time as a member of NLO, Joon occasionally discussed confidential business information with other members. At no time during those conversations did Joon or the other members promise to maintain each others' confidences.

The CEO of Data, Inc. was also a member of the Northern California Forum. Data is a publicly traded corporation that manufactures computer storage devices. On March 1, the Northern California Forum members departed in a private plane for their annual retreat. Prior to departure, the CEO of Data informed the Forum Moderator that he could not attend because Data was involved in merger discussions with another company — Quantum Corporation. He authorized the Forum Moderator to tell the other members why he would be absent but asked the Moderator to emphasize the confidential nature of the information. The Forum Moderator relayed the information to Joon and other members of the Northern California Forum.

Based on this confidential information, between March 1 and March 4 last year, Joon purchased 187,300 shares of Data stock for between $2.00 and $4.12 per share. On May 11, Data publicly announced that it had agreed to be acquired by Quantum. Data's share price jumped to $7.56. Joon, thereby, realized a profit of $832,627 on an investment of $583,360.

The government is investigating whether Joon violated the federal securities laws. Does the government have a viable case against Joon? If so, what theory or theories should the government use? What are the likely defenses?

5-2. Alexandra Gogol owned an Internet-based stock brokerage firm. Last October 17, Gogol hacked into the computer network of Thomas Financial Advisers, Inc., and gained access to ONC Health's soon-to-be-released negative earnings announcement for the third quarter. There had been no media or analyst reports anticipating negative earnings for ONC Health, which was a client of Thomas Financial. Approximately 35 minutes after hacking into Thomas Financial's computer network, and two hours before the earnings announcement was to be made public, Gogol sold $300,000 worth of ONC Health stock that she owned. This purchase represented 90 percent of all sales of ONC stock that day. When the stock market opened at 9:30 the next morning, ONC Health stock immediately dropped 50 percent on news of the negative earnings.

The SEC has alleged that Gogol, by "hacking and trading," has violated Section 10(b) and Rule 10b-5. Gogol has moved to dismiss the charge. How should the court rule? Why?

5-3. Samantha Jones, a letter carrier, was serving on a federal grand jury investigating accounting fraud at ABC Pharmaceuticals. Jones was aware that matters occurring before a grand jury are confidential under federal law, and that only witnesses appearing before a grand jury may reveal their testimony. The Assistant United States Attorney in charge of the investigation, in accordance with the law concerning grand jury secrecy, publicly revealed that the grand jury was investigating ABC for accounting fraud, but did not reveal any information relating to the investigation. ABC's stock price fell sharply after the announcement. Jones later learned during a grand jury session that the government had decided not to seek an indictment. Before prosecutors publicly announced their decision not to seek an indictment, Jones bought stock in ABC. After the announcement, ABC's stock price rose sharply. Jones then sold her stock, netting a $100,000 profit.

Has Jones committed securities fraud? Why or why not?

[4]   Tipper/Tippee Liability

The cases above show that a corporate insider, temporary insider, or misappropriator may be liable for insider trading. However, what about a "tippee," that is, one who is not an insider, a quasi-insider, or a misappropriator but who has been "tipped" with secret information? The United States Supreme Court addressed this issue in the case that follows. As you read the case, be sure to identify precisely what the government must prove in a case against a tippee, particularly with respect to mens rea.

DIRKS v. SECURITIES AND EXCHANGE COMMISSION
463 U.S. 646 (1983)

JUSTICE POWELL delivered the opinion of the Court.

Petitioner Raymond Dirks received material nonpublic information from "insiders" of a corporation with which he had no connection. He disclosed this information to investors who relied on it in trading in the shares of the corporation. The question is whether Dirks violated the antifraud provisions of the federal securities laws by this disclosure.

In 1973, Dirks was an officer of a New York broker-dealer firm who specialized in providing investment analysis of insurance company securities to institutional investors. On March 6, Dirks received information from Ronald Secrist, a former officer of Equity Funding of America. Secrist alleged that the assets of Equity Funding, a diversified corporation primarily engaged in selling life insurance and mutual funds, were vastly overstated as the result of fraudulent corporate practices. Secrist also stated that various regulatory agencies had failed to act on similar charges made by Equity Funding employees. He urged Dirks to verify the fraud and disclose it publicly.

Dirks decided to investigate the allegations. He visited Equity Funding's headquarters in Los Angeles and interviewed several officers and employees of the corporation. The senior management denied any wrongdoing, but certain corporation employees corroborated the charges of fraud. Neither Dirks nor his firm owned or traded any Equity Funding stock, but throughout his investigation he openly discussed the information he had obtained with a number of clients and investors. Some of these persons sold their holdings of Equity Funding securities, including five investment advisers who liquidated holdings of more than $16 million.

While Dirks was in Los Angeles, he was in touch regularly with William Blundell, *The Wall Street Journal*'s Los Angeles bureau chief. Dirks urged Blundell to write a story on the fraud allegations. Blundell did not believe, however, that such a massive fraud could go undetected and declined to write the story. He feared that publishing such damaging hearsay might be libelous.

During the two-week period in which Dirks pursued his investigation and spread word of Secrist's charges, the price of Equity Funding stock fell from $26 per share to less than $15 per share. This led the New York Stock Exchange to halt trading on March 27. Shortly thereafter California insurance authorities impounded Equity Funding's records and uncovered evidence of the fraud. Only then did the Securities and Exchange Commission (SEC) file a complaint against Equity Funding and only then, on April 2, did *The Wall Street Journal* publish a front-page story based largely on information assembled by Dirks. Equity Funding immediately went into receivership.

The SEC began an investigation into Dirks' role in the exposure of the fraud. After a hearing by an administrative law judge, the SEC found that Dirks had aided and abetted violations of Section 17(a) of the Securities Act of 1933, Section 10(b) of the Securities Exchange Act of 1934, and SEC Rule 10b-5 by repeating the allegations of fraud to members of the investment community who later sold their Equity Funding stock. The SEC concluded: "Where 'tippees' — regardless of their motivation or occupation — come into possession of material 'information that they know is confidential and know or should know came from a corporate insider,' they must either publicly disclose that information or refrain from trading." 21 S.E.C. Docket 1401, 1407 (1981) (quoting *Chiarella v. United States*, 445 U.S. 222, 230 n. 12 (1980)). Recognizing, however, that Dirks "played an important role in bringing [Equity Funding's] massive fraud to light," 21 S.E.C. Docket at 1412, the SEC only censured him.

Dirks sought review in the Court of Appeals for the District of Columbia Circuit. The court entered judgment against Dirks "for the reasons stated by the Commission in its opinion." In view of the importance to the SEC and to the securities industry of the question presented by this case, we granted a writ of certiorari. We now reverse.

In the seminal case of *In re Cady, Roberts & Co.*, 40 S.E.C. 907 (1961), the SEC recognized that the common law in some jurisdictions imposes on "corporate 'insiders,' particularly officers, directors, or controlling stockholders" an "affirmative duty of disclosure . . . when dealing in securities." *Id.* at 911, and n.13.[10] The SEC found that not only did breach of this common-law duty also establish the elements of a Rule 10b-5 violation, but that individuals other than corporate insiders could be obligated either to disclose material nonpublic

---

[10] The duty that insiders owe to the corporation's shareholders not to trade on inside information differs from the common-law duty that officers and directors also have to the corporation itself not to mismanage corporate assets, of which confidential information is one. In holding that breaches of this duty to shareholders violated the Securities Exchange Act, the *Cady, Roberts* Commission recognized, and we agree, that "[a] significant purpose of the Exchange Act was to eliminate the idea that use of inside information for personal advantage was a normal emolument of corporate office."

information[11] before trading or to abstain from trading altogether. In *Chiarella*, we held that "a duty to disclose under Section 10(b) does not arise from the mere possession of nonpublic market information." 445 U.S. at 235. Such a duty arises rather from the existence of a fiduciary relationship.

Not "all breaches of fiduciary duty in connection with a securities transaction," however, come within the ambit of Rule 10b-5. *Santa Fe Industries, Inc. Green*, 430 U.S. 462, 472 (1977). There must also be "manipulation or deception." *Id.* at 473. In an inside-trading case this fraud derives from the "inherent unfairness involved where one takes advantage" of "information intended to be available only for a corporate purpose and not for the personal benefit of anyone." *In re Merrill Lynch, Pierce, Fenner & Smith, Inc.*, 43 S.E.C. 933, 936 (1968). Thus, an insider will be liable under Rule 10b-5 for inside trading only where he fails to disclose material nonpublic information before trading on it and thus makes "secret profits." *Cady, Roberts*, 40 S.E.C. at 916 n.31.

We were explicit in *Chiarella* in saying that there can be no duty to disclose where the person who has traded on inside information "was not [the corporation's] agent, . . . was not a fiduciary, [or] was not a person in whom the sellers [of the securities] had placed their trust and confidence." 445 U.S. at 232. Not to require such a fiduciary relationship, we recognized, would "depar[t] radically from the established doctrine that duty arises from a specific relationship between two parties" and would amount to "recognizing a general duty between all participants in market transactions to forgo actions based on material, nonpublic information." *Id.* at 232, 233. This requirement of a specific relationship between the shareholders and the individual trading on inside information has created analytical difficulties for the SEC and courts in policing tippees who trade on inside information. Unlike insiders who have independent fiduciary duties to both the corporation and its shareholders, the typical tippee has no such relationships.[14] In view of this absence, it has been unclear how a tippee acquires the *Cady, Roberts* duty to refrain from trading on inside information.

The SEC's position, as stated in its opinion in this case, is that a tippee "inherits" the *Cady, Roberts* obligation to shareholders whenever he receives inside information from an insider.

This view differs little from the view that we rejected as inconsistent with congressional intent in *Chiarella*. Here, the SEC maintains that anyone who knowingly receives nonpublic material information from an insider has a fiduciary duty to disclose before trading.

---

[11] The SEC views the disclosure duty as requiring more than disclosure to purchasers or sellers: "Proper and adequate disclosure of significant corporate developments can only be effected by a public release through the appropriate public media, designed to achieve a broad dissemination to the investing public generally and without favoring any special person or group." *In re* Faberge, Inc., 45 S.E.C. 249, 256 (1973).

[14] Under certain circumstances, such as where corporate information is revealed legitimately to an underwriter, accountant, lawyer, or consultant working for the corporation, these outsiders may become fiduciaries of the shareholders. The basis for recognizing this fiduciary duty is not simply that such persons acquired nonpublic corporate information, but rather that they have entered into a special confidential relationship in the conduct of the business of the enterprise and are given access to information solely for corporate purposes. When such a person breaches his fiduciary relationship, he may be treated more properly as a tipper than a tippee. For such a duty to be imposed, however, the corporation must expect the outsider to keep the disclosed nonpublic information confidential, and the relationship at least must imply such a duty.

In effect, the SEC's theory of tippee liability in both cases appears rooted in the idea that the antifraud provisions require equal information among all traders. This conflicts with the principle set forth in *Chiarella* that only some persons, under some circumstances, will be barred from trading while in possession of material nonpublic information. . . . We reaffirm today that "[a] duty [to disclose] arises from the relationship between parties . . . and not merely from one's ability to acquire information because of his position in the market." 445 U.S. at 231–32, n.14.

Imposing a duty to disclose or abstain solely because a person knowingly receives material nonpublic information from an insider and trades on it could have an inhibiting influence on the role of market analysts, which the SEC itself recognizes is necessary to the preservation of a healthy market. It is commonplace for analysts to "ferret out and analyze information," 21 S.E.C. at 1406, and this often is done by meeting with and questioning corporate officers and others who are insiders. And information that the analysts obtain normally may be the basis for judgments as to the market worth of a corporation's securities. The analyst's judgment in this respect is made available in market letters or otherwise to clients of the firm. It is the nature of this type of information, and indeed of the markets themselves, that such information cannot be made simultaneously available to all of the corporation's stockholders or the public generally.

The conclusion that recipients of inside information do not invariably acquire a duty to disclose or abstain does not mean that such tippees always are free to trade on the information. The need for a ban on some tippee trading is clear. Not only are insiders forbidden by their fiduciary relationship from personally using undisclosed corporate information to their advantage, but they may not give such information to an outsider for the same improper purpose of exploiting the information for their personal gain. Thus, the tippee's duty to disclose or abstain is derivative from that of the insider's duty. As we noted in *Chiarella*, "[t]he tippee's obligation has been viewed as arising from his role as a participant after the fact in the insider's breach of a fiduciary duty." 445 U.S. at 230 n.12.

Thus, some tippees must assume an insider's duty to the shareholders not because they receive inside information, but rather because it has been made available to them *improperly*.[19] And for Rule 10b-5 purposes, the insider's disclosure is improper only where it would violate his *Cady, Roberts* duty. Thus, a tippee assumes a fiduciary duty to the shareholders of a corporation not to trade on material nonpublic information only when the insider has breached his fiduciary duty to the shareholders by disclosing the information to the tippee and the tippee knows or should know that there has been a breach. . . . Tipping thus properly is viewed only as a means of indirectly violating the *Cady, Roberts* disclose-or-abstain rule.

*   *   *

Under the inside-trading and tipping rules set forth above, we find that there was no actionable violation by Dirks. It is undisputed that Dirks himself was a stranger to Equity Funding, with no pre-existing fiduciary duty to its shareholders. He took

---

[19] The SEC itself has recognized that tippee liability properly is imposed only in circumstances where the tippee knows, or has reason to know, that the insider has disclosed improperly inside corporate information.

no action, directly or indirectly, that induced the shareholders or officers of Equity Funding to repose trust or confidence in him. There was no expectation by Dirks' sources that he would keep their information in confidence. Nor did Dirks misappropriate or illegally obtain the information about Equity Funding. Unless the insiders breached their *Cady, Roberts* duty to shareholders in disclosing the nonpublic information to Dirks, he breached no duty when he passed it on to investors as well as to *The Wall Street Journal.*

It is clear that neither Secrist nor the other Equity Funding employees violated their *Cady, Roberts* duty to the corporation's shareholders by providing information to Dirks. The tippers received no monetary or personal benefit for revealing Equity Funding's secrets, nor was their purpose to make a gift of valuable information to Dirks. As the facts of this case clearly indicate, the tippers were motivated by a desire to expose the fraud. In the absence of a breach of duty to shareholders by the insiders, there was no derivative breach by Dirks. Dirks therefore could not have been "a participant after the fact in [an] insider's breach of a fiduciary duty." *Chiarella*, 445 U.S. at 230 n.12.

We conclude that Dirks, in the circumstances of this case, had no duty to abstain from use of the inside information that he obtained. The judgment of the Court of Appeals therefore is

Reversed.

JUSTICE BLACKMUN, with whom JUSTICE BRENNAN and JUSTICE MARSHALL join, dissenting.

The Court today takes still another step to limit the protections provided investors by Section 10(b) of the Securities Exchange Act of 1934. The device employed in this case engrafts a special motivational requirement on the fiduciary duty doctrine. This innovation excuses a knowing and intentional violation of an insider's duty to shareholders if the insider does not act from a motive of personal gain. Even on the extraordinary facts of this case, such an innovation is not justified. . . .

No one questions that Secrist himself could not trade on his inside information to the disadvantage of uninformed shareholders and purchasers of Equity Funding securities. Unlike the printer in *Chiarella*, Secrist stood in a fiduciary relationship with these shareholders.

The Court also acknowledges that Secrist could not do by proxy what he was prohibited from doing personally. But this is precisely what Secrist did. Secrist used Dirks to disseminate information to Dirks' clients, who in turn dumped stock on unknowing purchasers. Secrist thus intended Dirks to injure the purchasers of Equity Funding securities to whom Secrist had a duty to disclose. Accepting the Court's view of tippee liability, it appears that Dirks' knowledge of this breach makes him liable as a participant in the breach after the fact. . . .

The fact that the insider himself does not benefit from the breach does not eradicate the shareholder's injury. It makes no difference to the shareholder whether the corporate insider gained or intended to gain personally from the transaction; the shareholder still has lost because of the insider's misuse of nonpublic information. The duty is addressed not to the insider's motives, but to his actions and their consequences on the shareholder. Personal gain is not an element of the breach of this duty. . . .

The improper purpose requirement not only has no basis in law, but it rests implicitly on a policy that I cannot accept. The Court justifies Secrist's and Dirks' action because the general benefit derived from the violation of Secrist's duty to shareholders outweighed the harm caused to those shareholders, — in other words, because the end justified the means. Under this view, the benefit conferred on society by Secrist's and Dirks' activities may be paid for with the losses caused to shareholders trading with Dirks' clients.

Although Secrist's general motive to expose the Equity Funding fraud was laudable, the means he chose were not. Moreover, even assuming that Dirks played a substantial role in exposing the fraud, he and his clients should not profit from the information they obtained from Secrist. . . .

In my view, Secrist violated his duty to Equity Funding shareholders by transmitting material nonpublic information to Dirks with the intention that Dirks would cause his clients to trade on that information. Dirks, therefore, was under a duty to make the information publicly available or to refrain from actions that he knew would lead to trading. Because Dirks caused his clients to trade, he violated Section 10(b) and Rule 10b-5. Any other result is a disservice to this country's attempt to provide fair and efficient capital markets. I dissent.

NOTES AND QUESTIONS

1. *The* Dirks *rule.* What precisely must the government prove in order to gain a conviction of a "tippee?" What element was missing in the case against Dirks?

2. *The role of market analysts.* The Court was apparently concerned about imposing broad liability on "tippees." What exactly was the Court's concern? According to the dissent, what are the negative consequences of *not* imposing liability on tippees like Dirks? Who has the better of the argument? Why?

According to the dissent, what actions should Dirks have taken? Was it appropriate for Dirks to investigate Equity Funding's finances on behalf of his clients? If so, once Dirks had the information, what would have been the effect on Dirks' clients if Dirks had publicly disclosed the information before revealing it to his clients? How would his clients have likely reacted? Also, how would Dirks have made the disclosure? Why did the Wall Street Journal decline to make the information public? Finally, what was the effect of Dirks' disclosure on the market's valuation of Equity Funding's stock? Did the disclosure provide a market benefit? Why or why not?

3. *Intent to benefit.* The *Dirks* case arose under the traditional theory of insider trading — Secrist was an insider of Equity Funding. Does the "intent to benefit" prong of the *Dirks* rule also apply when the tipper is a misappropriator rather than insider? That is, when the tipper is a mere misappropriator, must the government prove that the tipper intended to benefit by giving the tip to the tippee? Most courts say that the government must prove, under either theory, that the tipper intended to benefit personally by giving the information to the tippee. *See SEC v. Yun,* 327 F.3d 1263, 1274–1281 (11th Cir. 2003).

4. *The willfulness requirement.* The Court said that, if a tippee knows or "should know" of the breach of fiduciary duty, then the tippee can be held liable. This language, which sounds like a negligence standard, has produced confusion because a mens rea standard of "willfulness" generally requires a higher level of

proof than negligence. As discussed *infra*, § 5[C], some courts require proof of knowledge, while others require proof only of recklessness. *See* J. Kelly Strader, Understanding White Collar Crime § 5[E][2][a] (2d ed. LexisNexis 2006); Julian W. Friedman & Charles A. Stillman, *Securities Fraud, in* White Collar Crime: Business and Regulatory Offenses Volume 2, § 12.01[1] (Otto Obermaier & Robert Morvillo eds., 2009).

5. *Remote tippees.* What if A tips B, who then tips C. Can C be liable? So long as the *Dirks* elements are met for both A and B as tippers, and for C as the tippee, then C can be liable.

6. *Does tippee liability apply to criminal misappropriation cases?* Some commentators have questioned whether tippees can be held criminally liable when the tipper was a misappropriator rather than an insider or quasi-insider. Given the animating purpose behind the misappropriation theory that the Court articulated in *O'Hagan*, there is no principled reason why tipper/tippee liability should not apply in this context. Indeed, tipper/tippee liability has been employed in a number of cases, including the *Carpenter* (Wall Street Journal) case discussed above, where the tipper was a misappropriator and the tippees were found guilty of securities fraud. *See* J. Kelly Strader, *White Collar Crime and Punishment — Reflections on Michael, Martha, and Milberg Weiss*, 15 Geo. Mason L. Rev. 45 (2007).

NOTE ON RULE 10B5-1

In an insider trading case, the government must show that the defendant acted "*on the basis of*" material nonpublic information. But what does this mean? For example, assume that before Dirks spoke with Secrist, Dirks had done independent research into the value of Equity Funding securities and had decided to recommend that his clients sell the stock. If Dirks had then recommended the sale to his clients after speaking with Secrist, would the trading have been "on the basis" of the secret information? In other words, is the element met when a person who possesses inside information has another, independent reason for trading?

The circuit courts split on this issue. In *United States v. Teicher*, 987 F.2d 112 (2d Cir. 1993), for example, the defendants appealed their insider trading convictions, arguing that the trial court erred by charging the jury that the defendants could be convicted if they traded while merely in *knowing possession* of the inside information. The Second Circuit found that the instruction was not erroneous. The court reasoned that requiring proof that the defendants actually used the information would place too great an evidentiary burden on the government. The Ninth and Eleventh circuits held to the contrary, reasoning that proof that the defendant knowingly *used* the information is an essential element of the crime. *See United States v. Smith*, 155 F.3d 1051, 1067 (9th Cir. 1998); *SEC v. Adler*, 137 F.3d 1325, 1334–1336 (11th Cir. 1998).

In 2000, the SEC issued Rule 10b5-1, which rejects the use standard and adopts the knowing possession standard. The rule provides that, in the insider trading context, a person has traded "on the basis" of inside information when the person was "aware" of the information when making the purchase or sale. The rule does provide an affirmative defense where the person making the purchase or sale demonstrates that, before becoming aware of the information, the person had (a) entered into a binding contract to purchase or sell the security, (b) instructed another person to purchase or sell the security for the instructing person's account, or (c) adopted a written plan for trading securities. The rule further requires that the contract, instruction, or plan meets specific conditions before the defense will be allowed.

Is this rule fair? For example, in the hypothetical above, assume that Dirks had done his research and made his decision to disclose the information to his clients before he learned of the inside information but that he could not meet the affirmative defense requirements of Rule 10b5-1. Also assume that Secrist breached a duty in giving Dirks the information. Would insider trading liability be appropriate in such circumstances? Why or why not? Would such a result improperly remove the "willfulness" element? For an argument that it would, see Carol B. Swanson, *Insider Trading Madness: Rule 10b5-1 and the Death of Scienter*, 52 U. Kan. L. Rev. 147 (2003).

PROBLEMS

5-4. A grand jury has investigated Deana for securities fraud, and has found the following facts. Deana is a self-employed businessperson who bought an independent sidewalk newsstand in New York City last January 3. She sells a wide variety of news and financial magazines, including "Business News." Business News magazine imposes a strict confidentiality policy on all employees who work for and are paid by the magazine. The policy forbids the employees to use nonpublic information contained in the magazine. Business News employees are required to sign a copy of this policy when first hired.

In addition, on March 1 every year, a copy of the confidentiality policy is sent by U.S. mail to all sellers of the magazine. A magazine representative testified that a copy of the policy was sent last year to Deana's business address, but there is no direct proof that Deana received, read, or knew of the policy.

In its confidentiality policy and notice sent to sellers, the magazine states that material, nonpublic information must be kept secret until the magazine appears on the newsstands. In particular, the magazine knows that its "Wall Street Week" column tends to affect the amount of trading and the prices of the stocks discussed in the column. The magazine arrives at stores each Wednesday before 5:00 p.m. Attached to each magazine are instructions that the magazine is not to be placed on shelves before 5:00 p.m. the following day. Individual subscribers generally receive the magazine in the mail on Fridays.

The evening of Wednesday, June 6, Deana attended a movie. Accompanying Deana was her brother Miles, a stockbroker in New York City. Miles and Deana regularly discuss the stock market. Waiting for the movie to begin, Deana told her brother that she had read the latest issue of Business News magazine and told him that the magazine would appear on newsstands late the next day. Deana also said that this issue's Wall Street Week column repeated a rumor, said to be based on inside sources, that Stealth Corp. was planning to announce a tender offer for the stock of X-Ray Corp. within two weeks. Deana also said that she thought the information was "probably hush-hush" and that Miles should not repeat or use the information in any way.

Miles responded that the story sounded "interesting" and, based on his knowledge of the market, was "probably true." Miles had been following X-Ray stock for a number of months and the previous week, he had sent his broker an e-mail instructing the broker to buy 1,000 shares no later than June 8.

That night, Miles went home and logged on to a financial website where he researched the financial conditions of the two companies involved in the rumored merger. At 9:00 a.m. the next day, he called his broker and instructed the broker to execute the purchase immediately.

The following Wednesday, June 13, Stealth Corp. announced its tender offer bid for X-Ray Corp. Miles later sold his stock at a large profit.

The government is preparing to indict Deana and Miles for insider trading. What theory or theories will the government likely use? What defenses are Deana and Miles likely to raise?

5-5. Albert Penn has owned and operated a barbershop for the past 45 years. Penn enjoys investing in the stock market, and often asks his clients about the corporations for which they work. Max Davis, a district manager at Wooster Foods, a wholesale food distribution company, has been getting his haircut by Penn for the past 15 years. During the barber appointments, Penn and Davis discussed family and personal matters, but they were not close personal friends and did not socialize with each other.

Penn knew that Davis worked for Wooster Foods in some capacity, and had asked Davis on several occasions if Wooster Foods was going to be sold. On one of those occasions, Davis recommended that Penn buy stock in Wooster Foods because it was a good company and would probably be acquired at some point.

Two weeks later, Davis told Penn, during a barber appointment, of a rumor that there were one or two buyers interested in Wooster, that he was confident a deal was going to happen, and that it was very likely Wooster's stock price would double as a result. In fact, Davis knew of negotiations between Wooster and Best Foods, and had been actively participating in preparations for the sale of Wooster to Best Foods. Davis also knew that Wooster had a policy prohibiting insider trading, that he was prohibited from trading in Wooster stock based on his knowledge of material, non-public information, and that he was also prohibited from tipping any others about the information.

Based on his conversation with Davis, Penn began buying Wooster stock. He first bought $14,000 worth of common stock, then another $18,000 in common stock. Penn sold all his Wooster stock on the day Wooster's sale to Best Foods was announced to the public. Penn's total profit from the sales was over $190,000.

Is David guilty of securities fraud? Is Penn guilty of securities fraud? Why or why not?

5-6. A federal grand jury has gathered the following evidence:

Sam Sherman and Andrea Adler ran a consulting company out of a small, one-room office in Sherman's basement. Their company operated with a single phone line for faxes, voicemail, and phone conversations. Sherman, on occasion, would retrieve voicemail and faxes for Adler, and, due to the small office, could overhear Adler's phone conversations.

In addition to her work as a consultant, Adler was on the board of directors of Pulse Instruments, a medical supply company. On July 13, Medilab offered to purchase all outstanding shares of Pulse for $22 a share. Negotiations ensued, and on October 3, the companies publically announced Pulse's acceptance of Medilab's tender offer of $25 a share. Knowing that Sherman would inevitably overhear Adler talking about the impending tender offer in their small office, Adler told Sherman in July that Pulse was being purchased. Adler also told Sherman the information was confidential, and Sherman agreed not to disclose the information.

On September 10, Sherman had dinner with Jeffrey Major. Major had been Sherman's dentist for over 10 years, and the two were friends. Sherman had referred over 75 people to Major for dental work. Sherman was also active with the local chamber of commerce, and periodically asked Major to help arrange networking events for that organization.

Recently, however, problems had developed between the two men. One of Sherman's sisters had been hired to decorate Major's home, but did not complete the work before filing for bankruptcy and keeping a $1000 retainer. Another of Sherman's sisters had missed several dental appointments without notifying Major. When Major said he would have to charge her next time that happened, she threatened to use Sherman's influence in the community to damage Major's business.

On September 11, Major contacted his broker and inquired about Pulse stock. Although his broker told him the stock was "a piece of crap" and was not the type of stock Major usually purchased, Major proceeded to buy over 20,000 shares prior to the tender offer announcement. To do so, he bought on margin and took out a $50,000 bank loan. This was the first time he ever took out a loan to buy stock. In the days following the tender offer announcement, Major sold his Pulse stock for a profit of over $140,000.

You are the Assistant United States Attorney leading the grand jury's investigation into trading in Pulse stock. You are considering charging Sherman and Major with violating Section 10b and Rule 10b-5. Both have asserted their Fifth Amendment right not to testify before the grand jury. Would you bring the case against either or both of the potential defendants? If so, what viable theory or theories would you use?

If you represented Sherman or Major, what arguments would you use in an attempt to persuade the Assistant United States Attorney not to seek criminal charges?

[C] PROOF OF WILLFULNESS

Although it is a crime willfully to violate the antifraud provisions of the federal securities laws, the statutes do not define "willfulness." The cases that follow attempt to provide some guidance on this issue.

UNITED STATES v. TARALLO
380 F.3d 1174 (9th Cir. 2004)

GRABER, CIRCUIT JUDGE.

Defendant Aldo Tarallo appeals his convictions on six counts of securities fraud, in violation of 15 U.S.C. §§ 78j(b) and 78ff and 17 C.F.R. § 240.10b-5; and four counts of mail fraud, in violation of 18 U.S.C. § 1341. [W]e hold that a defendant may commit securities fraud "willfully" in violation of 15 U.S.C. § 78ff and 17 C.F.R. § 240.10b-5 even if the defendant did not know at the time of the acts that the conduct violated the law. We further hold that a defendant may commit securities fraud "willfully" by intentionally acting with reckless disregard for the truth of material misleading statements. . . .

Defendant and two co-defendants, David Colvin and John Larson, together participated in a fraudulent telemarketing scheme. Colvin owned several companies used in the scheme, including Intellinet, Inc., and Larson was Intellinet's sales manager. Defendant was hired by Intellinet as a telemarketer, and he participated in the fraud from April 1997 until February 20, 1998. Defendant and others solicited those called to invest in various businesses whose value and operations were fictitious. These purported businesses included Medical Advantage, Inc. ("Medical Advantage"), Lamelli Medical Technology, Inc. ("Lamelli"), and R.A.C. International, Inc. ("R.A.C.").

Defendant and his co-defendants falsely represented to potential investors that Medical Advantage operated independent weight loss clinics around the country and had a projected 1997 revenue total of $8.2 million, and that C. Everett Koop and Tom Brokaw supported or were affiliated with the company. Defendant and his co-defendants falsely represented to potential investors that Lamelli had developed a detoxification system that could detoxify a person of all alcohol or drugs in 15 minutes, that the system had won FDA approval, and that $187 million in revenue was expected to be generated by this alleged invention in 1998. Defendant and his co-defendants falsely represented to potential investors that R.A.C. had generated $2.3 million in revenue in 1997 from sales of motor oil, car batteries, and tools, and that the company projected for 1998 revenues of approximately $3.5 million.

Defendant and his co-defendants told potential investors that they would be investing by means of promissory notes, which would be held in a "trust" for a fixed term of between 90 and 180 days. In return, the investors would receive 12 percent interest per annum and shares of "restricted stock" in the company. Defendant told investors that the company's Initial Public Offering ("IPO") would occur on or before the date on which the promissory note was to mature, at which point investors could (at their option) either receive back their invested principal or use it to purchase shares offered in the IPO. Instead of holding the invested funds in trust as promised, however, Colvin and others used those funds for the benefit of Colvin, Larson, Defendant, and their associates, and the investors never saw their money again.

After a nine-day trial, a jury convicted Defendant on six counts of securities fraud and four counts of mail fraud. The district court sentenced him to 37 months' imprisonment on each count, with the sentences to run concurrently. Defendant timely appealed.

Discussion

A. Evidence Supporting the Fraud Convictions

1. Standard of Review.

We review de novo the question whether sufficient evidence was adduced at trial to support a conviction. We view the evidence in the light most favorable to the government, and it is sufficient if any rational trier of fact could have found the essential elements of the crime beyond a reasonable doubt.

2. Defendant knowingly made false statements.

A defendant may be convicted of committing mail fraud in violation of 18 U.S.C. § 1341 only if the government proves beyond a reasonable doubt that the defendant had the specific intent to defraud. Likewise, a defendant may be convicted of committing securities fraud only if the government proves specific intent to defraud, mislead, or deceive.

Defendant argues that there was insufficient evidence that he knew that the statements he made to potential investors were false. If he did not even know that the statements were false, of course, he could not have had the specific intent to defraud. He points out that Colvin and Larson distributed typewritten scripts for salespeople to use during sales calls, and he asserts that the investment materials they provided to Defendant (and passed along to investors) were sophisticated and were not recognizably false. In essence, Defendant claims that no evidence at trial established that he was anything other than an innocent who was duped right along with the investors.

The record does not support Defendant's claim. A reasonable factfinder could have found beyond a reasonable doubt that Defendant knew of the fraudulent nature of the scheme in which he was participating.

For example, the jury was presented with evidence that Defendant knew that it was a lie to assure investors that their money was guaranteed and risk-free because it was held in a "trust" until the IPO occurred. For example, investor-victim Keith Crew testified that Defendant told him that his investment would be held in a trust and that, after the IPO, he could receive his principal back with interest, or else receive shares in the company. However, Defendant received paychecks from Sierra Ridge Management Trust, which was one of the trusts for which Defendant solicited investors. Agent Steven Goldman of the FBI testified that, after being arrested and Mirandized, Defendant admitted that he knew he was being paid out of the same "trust" companies that investors' money was being deposited. Paul Coynes, who worked with Defendant as a telemarketer, also testified for the prosecution. Coynes explained that he realized after a time that it was impossible for the money he was soliciting to be held safely in a trust:

> [W]e told people that all the money went into the trust company. And at some point it became clear to me how ridiculous that was because we were getting paid a commission, the sales manager was getting paid a commission, and the owner of the company was obviously living a decent life-style and that money had to come from somewhere.

A juror could reasonably conclude from this evidence that Defendant knew that the "trusts" were not actually safe, but were being raided for payroll. . . .

*   *   *

C. Jury Instructions

Defendant claims several errors in the jury instructions relating to the fraud counts as to which there was sufficient evidence. . . .

2. Instructions equating "willfully" and "knowingly."

Defendant was charged with, and convicted of, securities fraud under 15 U.S.C. § 78ff and under 17 C.F.R. § 240.10b-5, which was promulgated under the authority of 15 U.S.C. § 78j. Section 78ff(a) states:

> (a) Willful violations; false and misleading statements
>
> Any person who *willfully* violates any provision of this chapter . . . , or any rule or regulation thereunder the violation of which is made unlawful or the observance of which is required under the terms of this chapter, or any person who *willfully and knowingly* makes, or causes to be made, any statement in any application, report, or document required to be filed under this chapter or any rule or regulation thereunder or any undertaking contained in a registration statement as provided in subsection (d) of section 78o of this title, or by any self-regulatory organization in connection with an application for membership or participation therein or to become associated with a member thereof, which statement was false or misleading with respect to any material fact, shall upon conviction be fined not more than $5,000,000, or imprisoned not more than 20 years, or both . . . ; but no person shall be subject to imprisonment under this section for the violation of any rule or regulation if he proves that he had no knowledge of such rule or regulation.

15 U.S.C. § 78ff(a)(emphases added).

The district court instructed the jury on "knowingly" and "willfully" as follows:

> Each of the crimes charged in the indictment requires proof beyond a reasonable doubt that the defendant acted knowingly. An act is done knowingly if the defendant is aware of the act and does not act or fail to act through ignorance, mistake, or accident.
>
> The government is not required to prove that the defendant knew that his acts or omissions were unlawful. Thus, for example, to prove a defendant guilty of securities fraud or mail fraud based on making a false or misleading representation, the government must prove beyond a reasonable doubt that the defendant knew the representation was false or was made with reckless indifference to its truth or falsity, but it need not prove that in making the representation the defendant knew he was committing securities fraud, mail fraud, or any other criminal offense.
>
> In these statutes, willfully has the same meaning as knowingly.

Defendant argues that the court erred by instructing that "willfully" and "knowingly" mean the same thing, and by instructing that the government did not have to prove that defendant knew that his conduct was unlawful. He argues that the "willful" instruction runs afoul of *Bryan v. United States*, 524 U.S. 184, 191–92 (1998), in which the Supreme Court stated:

> As a general matter, when used in the criminal context, a "willful" act is one undertaken with a "bad purpose." In other words, in order to establish a "willful" violation of a statute, "the Government must prove that the defendant acted with knowledge that his conduct was unlawful." *Ratzlaf v. United States*, 510 U.S. 135, 137 (1994).

Because 15 U.S.C. § 78ff requires a showing of "willfulness," Defendant argues, it was error to instruct the jury that Defendant could be convicted even if the jury found that he did not know that his conduct was unlawful.

As an initial matter, we note that the district court did err in this instruction, although not in the way that Defendant claims.[2]

As quoted above, the district court instructed that "[e]ach of the crimes charged in the indictment requires proof beyond a reasonable doubt that the defendant acted *knowingly*." (Emphasis added.) However, § 78ff(a) states that a person who "willfully" violates any provision of the chapter or any rule or regulation promulgated thereunder is subject to criminal penalty. 15 U.S.C. § 78ff. "Knowingly" is not a required element. "Knowingly" is an element for the conviction of any individual who "makes, or causes to be made, any statement in any application, report, or document required to be filed under this chapter or any rule or regulation thereunder or any undertaking contained in a registration statement as provided in subsection (d) of section 78o of this title." As § 78ff makes clear, such a person must be found to have engaged in the proscribed conduct "willfully and knowingly."

The conduct for which Defendant was indicted, tried, and convicted did not involve the filing of an application, report, or document required by the securities laws. Instead, his conduct was covered by 17 C.F.R. § 240.10b-5. That conduct clearly falls under the first provision of § 78ff, which requires only that the act be done "willfully," but does not require that the act be done "knowingly." Therefore, the district court's instruction that "[e]ach of the crimes charged in the indictment requires proof beyond a reasonable doubt that the defendant acted knowingly" was erroneous.

However, the district court then went on to equate "willfully" with "knowingly." The district court's error in including "knowingly" in the instructions is therefore harmless so long as the definition the court provided for knowingly and willfully satisfies the statutory definition of "willfully." We turn now to that question.

The Supreme Court has taken pains to observe that the word "willful" "is a word of many meanings" and that "its construction is often influenced by its context." *Ratzlaf*, 510 U.S. at 141; *see also Bryan*, 524 U.S. at 191. We must consider, then, the context in which "willfully" is found in the securities fraud statutes. The question is whether the securities fraud statutes' use of the term "willfully" means that a defendant can be convicted of securities fraud only if he or she knows that the

---

[2] Although Defendant did not point to the error we are about to discuss, we mention it to put into context our discussion of the claim he does raise.

charged conduct is unlawful, or whether "willfully" simply means what the district court instructed it means: "knowingly" in the sense that the defendant intends those actions and that they are not the product of accident or mistake.

Defendant's argument — that willfulness requires that he knew that he was breaking the law at the time he made his false statements — has been previously rejected by this and other courts. In *United States v. Charnay*, 537 F.2d 341, 351–52 (9th Cir.1976), we cited with approval the Second Circuit's interpretation of § 78ff in *United States v. Peltz*, 433 F.2d 48, 54 (2d Cir.1970). The Second Circuit explained there that "[t]he language makes one point entirely clear. A person can willfully violate an SEC rule even if he does not know of its existence. This conclusion follows from the difference between the standard for violation of the statute or a rule or regulation, to wit, 'willfully,' and that for false or misleading statements, namely 'willfully and knowingly.' " *Id.* at 54. . . .

Even were we not bound by our existing precedent, we would reach the same result. The final clause of § 78ff(a) provides that "no person shall be subject to imprisonment under this section for the violation of any rule or regulation if he proves that he had no knowledge of such rule or regulation." 15 U.S.C. § 78ff(a). The opening sentence of subsection (a) explains that "[a]ny person who *willfully* violates any provision of this chapter . . . or any rule or regulation thereunder the violation of which is made unlawful or the observance of which is required under the terms of this chapter" commits a crime. *Id.* (emphasis added). If "willfully" meant "with knowledge that one's conduct violates a rule or regulation," the last clause proscribing imprisonment — but not a fine — in cases where a defendant did not know of the rule or regulation would be nonsensical: If willfully meant "with knowledge that one is breaking the law," there would be no need to proscribe imprisonment (but permit imposition of a fine) for someone who acted without knowing that he or she was violating a rule or regulation. Such a person could not have been convicted in the first place.

Under our jurisprudence, then, "willfully" as it is used in § 78ff(a) means intentionally undertaking an act that one knows to be wrongful; "willfully" in this context does not require that the actor know specifically that the conduct was unlawful. The district court's instructions correctly informed the jury that it had to find that defendant intentionally undertook such an act:

> [T]o prove a defendant guilty of securities fraud or mail fraud based on making a false or misleading representation, the government must prove beyond a reasonable doubt that the defendant knew the representation was false or was made with reckless indifference to its truth or falsity, but it need not prove that in making the representation the defendant knew he was committing securities fraud, mail fraud, or any other criminal offense.

The district court's instructions thus required the jury to find that Defendant had made statements that he knew at the time were false, or else made them with a reckless disregard for whether they were false. The district court therefore required the jury to find that Defendant undertook acts that he knew at the time to be wrongful, meeting the standard for defining "willfully" in this circuit. The district court's importation of the term "knowingly" into the jury instructions was harmless beyond a reasonable doubt, because the court equated "knowingly" with "willfully," and the court's definition properly explained "willfully."

3. *Recklessness standard for securities fraud.*

As discussed above, the district court instructed the jury that it could convict Defendant of both mail fraud and securities fraud if it found that he had made a false statement, which was a representation that either "(a) was then known to be untrue by the person making or causing it to be made or (b) was made or caused to be made with reckless indifference as to its truth or falsity." Defendant argues that the recklessness portion of the instruction was error as to the securities fraud counts.

The comment to Ninth Circuit Model Jury Instruction 9.7 (2000) states that reckless disregard for truth or falsity is sufficient to sustain a conviction for securities fraud. . . . Defendant argues that the comment incorrectly describes the law to be applied in this case, because [*inter alia*] the Supreme Court's decision in *United States v. O'Hagan*, 521 U.S. 642, 665–66 (1997), stands for the proposition that recklessness is insufficient to sustain a criminal conviction for securities fraud. In *O'Hagan*, 521 U.S. 642, 665–66, the Supreme Court said that, in order to convict a defendant of securities fraud, the government must prove that the defendant "willfully" violated Rule 10b-5. Defendant again cites *Bryan*, 524 U.S. at 191–93, for the proposition that willfulness requires actual knowledge and argues that recklessness cannot satisfy this requirement.

Defendant's argument fails. As we explained above, "willfully" in the context of § 78ff is best understood to mean "voluntarily and knowingly wrongful," not "with the intent to violate the law." We find no error in the recklessness instruction.

* * *

NOTES AND QUESTIONS

1. *Intent to violate the law.* The court concluded that proof that the defendant knew of and intended to violate the law is not required under Section 10b and Rule 10b-5. What was the statutory construction analysis that the court used to reach this conclusion? Should proof of an intent to violate the law be required? Why or why not?

2. *Knowledge and reckless disregard.* In holding that knowledge of the wrongful acts is sufficient, the court also held that proof of reckless disregard of the truth suffices. What level of mens rea was the court employing? Generally, a person acts recklessly when that person "consciously disregards" a risk that an element of a crime exists or will result from the person's conduct. *See* Model Penal Code § 2.02(2)(c). Such ordinary recklessness typically would not suffice for fraud, which, as the court noted above, requires proof of "specific intent to defraud." Is proof of ordinary recklessness sufficient for a securities fraud conviction? Or, did the court in effect hold that proof of "constructive knowledge" or "willful blindness" will suffice? The latter generally suffices for proof of *knowledge*, as opposed to mere recklessness. *See* Model Penal Code § 2.02(2)(b)(ii). The line between recklessness and constructive knowledge is far from clear, and courts are notoriously imprecise when employing such mens rea terminology.

Should proof of recklessness or constructive knowledge be sufficient to show specific intent to defraud? Why or why not? On the facts of this case, was there sufficient proof of specific intent? How could proof of recklessness or constructive knowledge equate to proof of specific intent to defraud?

3. *Good faith.* In a securities fraud case, the government has the burden of showing that the defendant acted with willful intent to defraud. If there is evidence that the defendant honestly believed the alleged fraudulent statements or omissions were true, the jury may weigh this evidence against the government's evidence to determine if the defendant acted in good faith. An honest, good faith belief in the ultimate success of a venture, however, is not a legitimate defense if the defendant knew the initial statements to investors were false. *See, e.g., United States v. Mabrook,* 301 F.3d 503, 509 (7th Cir. 2002).

4. *Reliance on professional advice.* Recall the general criminal law maxim that "ignorance of the law is no excuse." Yet, in a securities fraud case — as in a mail fraud case (*see United States v. Walters,* 997 F.2d 1219 (7th Cir. 1993), discussed in the Mail and Wire Fraud Chapter, *supra*) — good faith reliance on professional advice is a complete defense. *See, e.g., United States v. Bilzerian,* 926 F.2d 1285 (2d Cir. 1991). Why should this be so?

*   *   *

In the next case, the government did not allege that the defendant committed insider trading. Instead, the government's theory was that the defendant "willfully" misled her investors by making statements that artificially inflated her company's stock. In its opinion, the court addressed the sufficiency of the evidence on a motion for a judgment of acquittal at the end of the government's case. Judges rarely dismiss criminal charges at that point. Why did the court do so in this case?

UNITED STATES v. STEWART
305 F. Supp. 2d 368 (S.D.N.Y. 2004)

CEDARBAUM, DISTRICT JUDGE.

Defendant Martha Stewart has moved for a judgment of acquittal pursuant to Fed. R. Crim. P. 29.[1] The motion is granted with respect to Count Nine only. . . .

Count Nine of the Indictment charges that defendant Stewart made materially false statements of fact regarding her sale of ImClone securities with the intention of defrauding and deceiving investors by slowing or stopping the erosion of the value of the securities issued by her own company, Martha Stewart Living Omnimedia ("MSLO"). In assessing the sufficiency of the evidence, I have concluded that no reasonable juror can find beyond a reasonable doubt that the defendant lied for the purpose of influencing the market for the securities of her company. Another way of putting it would be that in order to find the essential element of criminal intent beyond a reasonable doubt, a rational juror would have to speculate.

---

[1] Rule 29(a) provides:

(a) Before Submission to the Jury. After the government closes its evidence or after the close of all the evidence, the court on the defendant's motion must enter a judgment of acquittal of any offense for which the evidence is insufficient to sustain a conviction. . . .

BACKGROUND

The criminal charges against Stewart and Bacanovic arose from Stewart's December 27, 2001 sale of 3,928 shares of stock in ImClone Systems, Inc. ("ImClone"). ImClone is a biotechnology company whose then-chief executive officer, Samuel Waksal, was a friend of Stewart's and a client of Stewart's stockbroker at Merrill Lynch, defendant Bacanovic. On December 28, 2001, the day after Stewart sold her shares, ImClone announced that the Food and Drug Administration had rejected the company's application for approval of Erbitux, a cancer-fighting drug that ImClone had previously described as its lead product.

The Indictment alleges that on the morning of December 27, 2001, defendant Bacanovic learned that Waksal and several of his family members were selling or attempting to sell their ImClone shares. Bacanovic allegedly instructed his assistant, Douglas Faneuil, to inform Stewart of the Waksals' trading activity, and she sold her shares in response to that information.

According to the Indictment, the defendants then lied about the real reason for Stewart's sale in order to cover up what was possibly an illegal trade and to deflect attention from Stewart in the ensuing investigations into suspicious ImClone trading in advance of the Erbitux announcement. The defendants claimed that they had a standing agreement that Stewart would sell her position in ImClone if the stock fell to $60 per share.

The Indictment charges the defendants with conspiracy, obstruction of an agency proceeding, and making false statements to government officials. Bacanovic is also charged with perjury and making and using false documents.

Count Nine of the Indictment charges Stewart, the CEO of MSLO, with fraud in connection with the purchase and sale of MSLO securities in violation of 15 U.S.C. §§ 78b and 78ff. The count is based on three repetitive public statements she made in June of 2002 after the media began reporting investigations of her ImClone trades by the Securities and Exchange Commission ("SEC"), the United States Attorney's Office, and a congressional subcommittee. In the critical statements, Stewart described the agreement to sell ImClone at a predetermined price, stated that her trade was proper and denied trading on nonpublic information.

DISCUSSION

The Supreme Court has held that "scienter," or intent, in the civil securities fraud context, indicates a "mental state embracing intent to deceive, manipulate, or defraud," and is a required element of any claim of securities fraud. *Ernst & Ernst v. Hochfelder*, 425 U.S. 185, 193 (1976). In a criminal prosecution, the Government must also prove that the defendant acted "willfully," that is, with a realization that she was acting wrongfully.

Taken in the light most favorable to the Government, the evidence presented at trial permits the jury to find the following facts relevant to the securities fraud charge.

Gregory Blatt, MSLO's former general counsel, testified that Stewart held approximately sixty percent of the shares of common stock in MSLO and over ninety percent of the voting shares. The jury could reasonably infer from this evidence that Stewart had a significant financial stake in MSLO.

Other evidence indicated that Stewart, like most if not all CEOs of public companies, kept abreast of the market price of MSLO securities and was aware that certain activities could send a negative message to the market. A reasonable jury could infer from this evidence that Stewart was aware of the market price of her company's stock and of matters that could affect the price of that stock.

The Government introduced into evidence MSLO's prospectus, written and disseminated at the time of the [initial public offering ("IPO") of the company's stock] in 1999, which detailed the importance of Stewart to the company's revenues and the value of its brands. Under the heading "Risk Factors," the prospectus notes:

*   *   *

Our success depends on our brands and their value. Our business would be adversely affected if: Martha Stewart's public image or reputation were to be tarnished. . . . Martha Stewart as well as her name, her image and the trademarks and other intellectual property rights relating to these, are integral to our marketing efforts and form the core of our brand name. Our continued success and the value of our brand name therefore depends, to a large degree, on the reputation of Martha Stewart.

A reasonable jury could infer from this evidence that Stewart was aware of the importance of her reputation to the continued health of MSLO.

The Government presented evidence that the share price of MSLO stock began to fall on June 7, 2002, the day that the investigations of Stewart's ImClone trade were first reported publicly, and continued falling throughout June of 2002. On June 13 and June 19 the share price experienced brief resurgences, only to continue to fall. The price of MSLO stock, which had closed at $19.01 on June 6, closed at $12.55 on June 24. The Government also presented evidence that throughout this period news coverage of Stewart's ImClone trade and the related investigations was widespread and intense. With respect to Stewart's state of mind, a reasonable jury could infer, based on the falling stock price and the ubiquitous news reports, that Stewart believed that the price of MSLO was falling in response to the negative publicity about the investigations.

The Government presented no evidence that Stewart expressed concerns to anyone about the response of MSLO stock to that negative publicity. . . .

The Government also introduced evidence of the timing, context, and substance of the three allegedly false public statements. The first statement appeared in *The Wall Street Journal* on June 7, 2002. Included in an article entitled "Martha Stewart Sold ImClone Stock," is the following paragraph:

According to her attorney, John Savarese, Ms. Stewart's sale, involving about 3,000 shares of ImClone, occurred on December 26 or 27. The sale was executed, he said, because Ms. Stewart had a predetermined price at which she planned to sell the stock. That determination, made more than a month before that trade, was to sell if the stock ever went below $60, he said. At the time, the stock was trading at about $60.

The second statement appeared in a press release issued after the close of business on June 12, 2002. Attributed to Stewart, the release read as follows:

In response to media inquiries, I want to reiterate the facts surrounding my sale of ImClone stock. . . . I agreed with my broker several weeks after the tender offer, at a time when the ImClone shares were trading at about $70, that, if the ImClone stock price were to fall below $60, we would sell my holdings. On December 27, I returned a call from my broker advising me that ImClone had fallen below $60. I reiterated my instructions to sell the shares. The trade was promptly executed, at $58 per share. I did not speak to Dr. Samuel Waksal regarding my sale, and did not have any nonpublic information regarding ImClone when I sold my ImClone shares. After directing my broker to sell, I placed a call to Dr. Waksal's office to inquire about ImClone. I did not reach Dr. Waksal and he did not return my call.

In placing my trade I had no improper information. My transaction was entirely lawful.[2]

After the close of business on June 18, 2002, Stewart issued a third statement that essentially repeated the June 12 statement, only adding that she was cooperating fully with the investigations. The following day, she read the June 18 statement, with no substantive alterations, at a "Mid-Year Media Review" conference held in midtown Manhattan. . . . [T]he conference . . . was attended primarily by securities analysts and portfolio managers. Investors were also present. The purpose of the conference was to provide a forum for the executives of media corporations to update the investment community about their companies' outlook and financial health. In addition to MSLO, executives from Gannet, Knight Ridder, and other organizations spoke at the conference. Stewart was one of four senior MSLO executives who participated in the presentation. Gruneich testified that MSLO's presentation lasted forty to forty-five minutes. The statement regarding her ImClone trade constitutes approximately one-half of one page of the eighteen-page transcript of MSLO's presentation at the conference. . . .

The pertinent section of the transcript of Stewart's presentation on June 19 reads as follows:

I'll be detailing our television and merchandising business efforts, and growth strategies. First, however, I would like to address an issue in which all of you are probably interested. And this is a statement that I prepared just a little while ago. I know that you, as media analysts, members of the investment community, and members of the press are aware that the media focus surrounding ImClone has generated an enormous amount of misinformation and confusion. Many have speculated about what might have happened. In my June 12th statement, I explained what did happen, at least as pertains to me. I had no insider information. My sale of ImClone stock was entirely proper and lawful. The sale was based on information that was available to the public that day. The stock price had dropped substantially, to below $60. Since the stock had fallen below $60, I sold my shares, as I had previously agreed with my broker.

---

[2] The Government alleges that within this statement, the following constitute materially false statements: Stewart's explanation that she had agreed with her broker to sell if ImClone's share price fell below $60; her claim that she reiterated her instructions to sell upon learning on December 27 that the price had fallen below $60; and her statement that she had no nonpublic information when she sold her shares.

These are the essential facts. I am confident that time will bear them out. Earlier this year I spoke with the S.E.C. and the U.S. Attorney's Office. I cooperated with them fully and to the best of my ability. . . . And I'm here to talk about our terrific company, Martha Stewart Living Omnimedia, which I'd like to start doing right now.[3]

A defendant seeking a judgment of acquittal pursuant to Fed. R. Crim. P. 29 faces a heavy burden. "Not only must the evidence be viewed in the light most favorable to the government and all permissible inferences drawn in its favor, but if the evidence, thus construed, suffices to convince any rational trier of fact of the defendant's guilt beyond a reasonable doubt," then the case must be presented to a jury. *United States v. Martinez*, 54 F.3d 1040, 1042 (2d Cir. 1995) (analyzing a post-conviction challenge to the sufficiency of the evidence). Moreover, "pieces of evidence must be viewed not in isolation but in conjunction," *United States v. Brown*, 776 F.2d 397, 403 (2d Cir. 1985). . . .

The Government contends that a reasonable jury could draw inferences from the evidence outlined above that would permit it to find beyond a reasonable doubt that Stewart intended to deceive investors with her statements. Specifically, the Government argues that the evidence supports the inferences that Stewart was aware of the impact of the negative publicity about her ImClone trade on the market value of MSLO securities and on her personal wealth, and that Stewart deliberately directed her statements to investors in MSLO securities. . . .

Mindful of the standards outlined above, and viewing the evidence in its totality and in the light most favorable to the Government's case, I hold that a reasonable juror could not, without resorting to speculation and surmise, find beyond a reasonable doubt that Stewart's purpose was to influence the market in MSLO securities.

While the Government has presented evidence about Stewart's financial stake in MSLO and her awareness that her own reputation was crucial to the company, the Government has offered no evidence that Stewart evinced a concern for the price of MSLO stock at any time during the relevant period. . . .

As for the first statement, the Government contends that an inference of intent can be drawn from the fact that *The Wall Street Journal* is "the most widely read financial publication in the nation." Specifically, by making the statement to that newspaper, Stewart intended to influence investors with her statement. The Government presented no evidence that Stewart or her lawyer reached out to *The Wall Street Journal* as opposed to other publications. Thus, there is no evidence that Stewart chose the forum for the statement. The fact that *The Wall Street Journal*, as a financial publication, had an interest in an investigation into a stock trade by the well-known CEO of a public company does not evidence Stewart's intent.

The Government argues that Stewart's intent with respect to the second statement can be inferred from the fact that she released it knowing that it would be widely disseminated in financial publications. This argument, which can be made

---

[3] Within this statement, the Government charges as materially false Stewart's statement that in her June 12, statement, she explained what happened; her statement that the sale on December 27, was based on publicly available information; her reiteration that her sale was pursuant to the $60 agreement; and her statement that she was cooperating with the authorities fully and to the best of her ability.

with respect to any public statement, adds nothing to the evidence of criminal intent.

With respect to the June 18 statement, the Government contends that Stewart's awareness that she was speaking to analysts and investors, her prefatory statement that she was embarking upon a topic about which her audience was "probably interested," and the timing of the statement, which occurred as the stock continued to fall, are sufficient, in conjunction with the evidence previously outlined, to permit the jury to infer that she intended to deceive investors in MSLO securities when she made the statement.

This statement presents a closer question than the previous two. But just as individual pieces of evidence about intent must be viewed in conjunction when assessing the sufficiency of the whole, the fact that the June 18 statement was read to an audience of analysts and investors on June 19 cannot be viewed in isolation — the entire context of the statement must be considered. Thus, any inference to be drawn from the makeup of the audience must also take into account the fact that Stewart was only one of several representatives of MSLO, and that MSLO was only one of several corporations making presentations at the conference. The evidence does not show that the conference was organized by Stewart or her company. There is no evidence that the negative publicity about ImClone influenced Stewart's decision to attend and take advantage of a platform from which to reach investors directly. To the contrary, her statement — a very brief portion of a much longer presentation — indicates otherwise. The Government argues that her statement indicating an awareness that the audience was "probably interested" in what she had to say about the ImClone trade is meaningful. Yet her remarks at the close of the statement — "I have nothing to add on this matter today. And I'm here to talk about our terrific company, Martha Stewart Living Omnimedia, which I'd like to start doing right now" — support an inference that she wanted to dispose of the issue and begin to address the subjects of the conference. . . .

Insofar as the text of the statement is concerned, the competing intentions appear to be nearly in equipoise. The Government has not offered any evidence that tips the balance in favor of a rational finding of criminal intent beyond a reasonable doubt. . . .

In sum, when the nature of the audience is viewed within the overall context of the statement, this is too slight an addition to the total mix of evidence of intent to carry the burden of proving criminal intent beyond a reasonable doubt. . . .

*   *   *

For the foregoing reasons, defendant Stewart's motion for a judgment of acquittal on Count Nine of the Indictment is granted.

NOTES AND QUESTIONS

1. *Judgments for the defendant.* There are three points under the Federal Rules of Criminal Procedure at which a trial judge may rule for the defendant: before trial on a motion to dismiss under Rule 12b; at the end of the government's case or after all the evidence has been presented under Rule 29; and after a jury verdict under Rule 33. What is the standard for dismissing a count under Rule 29? Why did the court rule in Stewart's favor? Do you agree with the outcome? Why or why not?

2. *The* Martha Stewart *case.* Martha Stewart was convicted of all the remaining charges against her — conspiracy, obstruction of justice, and false statements. She was sentenced to five months in prison and five months of home detention. *See* Kara Scannell & James Bandler, *Stewart Sentence Boosts Prospects of Her Company*, Wall St. J., July 19, 2004, at C1. Her co-defendant, Bacanovic, was convicted of conspiracy, lying to investigators, and perjury, but was acquitted of making false documents. He was also sentenced to 10 months split between prison and home detention.

ETHICAL EXERCISE

Reconsider the criminal securities fraud case brought against Martha Stewart. As noted above, the criminal investigation of Stewart originally focused on whether she was liable as a "tippee." The government believed that she sold her ImClone stock based upon material nonpublic information, that is, that ImClone insiders were selling their stock, indicating that the Food and Drug Administration would not approve the sale of ImClone's product Erbitux. Yet, the government did not charge Stewart on that theory in its criminal case. (The SEC's civil case against Stewart, however, did charge her as a tippee in connection with her ImClone stock sale.)

Instead, in the criminal case, the government alleged that Stewart defrauded stockholders of her company, Martha Stewart Living Omnimedia, when she publicly denied having committed insider trading in ImClone. According to the government's theory, her intent was artificially to inflate Omnimedia's stock price, harming investors who otherwise would have sold their stock before it later plummeted in value and investors who bought the stock at artificially inflated prices. Commentators noted that this was a novel — indeed, possibly unprecedented — theory upon which to base a criminal securities fraud case. *See, e.g.*, Geraldine Szott Moohr, *What the Martha Stewart Case Tells Us About White Collar Criminal Law*, 43 Hous. L. Rev. 591, 604–605 (2006) ("By rejecting Stewarts' motion to dismiss, the trial judge accepted the government theory — a defensive statement about a personal transaction can operate as a fraud on investors. Thus, a new application of the statute, a new theory of criminality, a new form of fraud, was established.").

Now consider the American Bar Association's Standards Relating to the Administration of Criminal Justice. Standard 3-1.2(b), entitled "The Function of the Prosecutor," provides that "[t]he prosecutor is an administrator of justice, an advocate, and an officer of the court; the prosecutor must exercise sound discretion in the performance of his or her functions." Standard 3-1.2(c) further provides that "[t]he duty of the prosecutor is to seek justice, not merely to convict." The comment to Standard 3-1.2 further explains:

> Although the prosecutor operates within the adversary system, it is fundamental that the prosecutor's obligation is to protect the innocent as well as to convict the guilty, to guard the rights of the accused as well as to enforce the rights of the public. Thus, the prosecutor has sometimes been described as a "minister of justice" or as occupying a quasi-judicial position.

> The prosecutor may also be characterized as an administrator of justice, since the prosecutor acts as a decision maker on a broad policy level and presides over a wide range of cases as director of public prosecutions. The

prosecutor also has responsibility for deciding whether to bring charges and, if so, what charges to bring against the accused, as well as deciding whether to prosecute or dismiss charges or to take other appropriate actions in the interest of justice. Since the prosecutor bears a large share of the responsibility for determining which cases are taken into the courts, the character, quality, and efficiency of the whole system is shaped in great measure by the manner in which the prosecutor exercises his or her broad discretionary powers.

Had you been the prosecutor in the *Stewart* case, would you have sought a criminal securities fraud charge? Why or why not? If so, what theory would you have used? Do you need additional information before you feel comfortable making this decision? If so, what information do you need?

[D] MATERIALITY

As noted throughout the materials above, the securities laws and regulations prohibit trading on the basis of "material" nonpublic information in certain circumstances. In addition, the law prohibits "material" omissions and misstatements in a number of contexts. For example, during a "proxy contest," shareholders vote via ballots called "proxies" on major corporate decisions. Companies solicit the votes with "proxy statements." If these statements contain misstatements or omissions, then they may provide the basis for securities fraud claims. Similar laws and regulations govern documents generated during tender offers and other "extraordinary corporate transactions," such as mergers. As you read the cases that follow, consider why the law requires that an actionable misstatement or omission be material.

TSC INDUSTRIES v. NORTHWAY, INC.
426 U.S. 438 (1976)

Mr. JUSTICE MARSHALL delivered the opinion of the Court.

The proxy rules promulgated by the Securities and Exchange Commission under the Securities Exchange Act of 1934 bar the use of proxy statements that are false or misleading with respect to the presentation or omission of material facts. We are called upon to consider the definition of a material fact under those rules, and the appropriateness of resolving the question of materiality by summary judgment in this case.

I.

[TSC Industries Inc., and another company, National Industries, Inc., agreed to merge their companies, and agreed that their shareholders would vote on the merger through a proxy contest. Northway, a TSC shareholder, sued TSC and National, alleging that TSC and National violated the proxy rules. Specifically, the plaintiff alleged that the defendants (1) failed to disclose in the proxy materials that National had already established a significant degree of control over TSC prior to the proxy contest, and (2) misstated the favorability of the terms of the proposed transaction to TSC shareholders. The plaintiff alleged, inter alia, that the defendants violated] Section 14(a) of the Securities Exchange Act of 1934,[2] and . . . Rule[] . . . 14a-9[6] [thereunder.]

Plaintiff [Northway] moved for summary judgment on the issue of TSC's and National's liability. The District Court denied the motion, but granted leave to appeal. . . . [T]he Court of Appeals reversed the District Court's denial of summary judgment to Northway on its Rule 14a-9 claims, holding that certain omissions of fact were material as a matter of law.

We granted certiorari because the standard applied by the Court of Appeals in resolving the question of materiality appeared to conflict with the standard applied by other Courts of Appeals. We now hold that the Court of Appeals erred in ordering that partial summary judgment be granted to Northway. . . .

The question of materiality, it is universally agreed, is an objective one, involving the significance of an omitted or misrepresented fact to a reasonable investor. Variations in the formulation of a general test of materiality occur in the articulation of just how significant a fact must be or, put another way, how certain it must be that the fact would affect a reasonable investor's judgment.

The Court of Appeals in this case concluded that material facts include "all facts which a reasonable shareholder *might* consider important." 512 F.2d at 330 (emphasis added). . . .

In formulating a standard of materiality under Rule 14a-9, we are guided, of course, by . . . the Rule's broad remedial purpose. That purpose is not merely to ensure by judicial means that the transaction, when judged by its real terms, is fair and otherwise adequate, but to ensure disclosures by corporate management in order to enable the shareholders to make an informed choice. As an abstract proposition, the most desirable role for a court in a suit of this sort, coming after the consummation of the proposed transaction, would perhaps be to determine whether in fact the proposal would have been favored by the shareholders and consummated in the absence of any misstatement or omission. But such matters are not subject to determination with certainty. Doubts as to the critical nature of information misstated or omitted will be commonplace. And particularly in view of the prophylactic purpose of the Rule and the fact that the content of the proxy statement is within management's control, it is appropriate that these doubts be resolved in favor of those the statute is designed to protect.

We are aware, however, that the disclosure policy embodied in the proxy regulations is not without limit. Some information is of such dubious significance that insistence on its disclosure may accomplish more harm than good. The potential liability for a Rule 14a-9 violation can be great indeed, and if the standard

---

[2] Section 14(a), 15 U.S.C. § 78n(a), provides:

     It shall be unlawful for any person . . . in contravention of such rules and regulations as the Commission may prescribe as necessary or appropriate in the public interest or for the protection of investors, to solicit or to permit the use of his name to solicit any proxy or consent or authorization in respect of any security. . . .

[6] Rule 14a-9(a), 17 C.F.R. § 240.14a-9 provides:

     No solicitation subject to this regulation shall be made by means of any proxy statement, form of proxy . . . containing any statement which, at the time and in the light of the circumstances under which it is made, is false or misleading with respect to any material fact, or which omits to state any material fact necessary in order to make the statements therein not false or misleading. . . .

of materiality is unnecessarily low, not only may the corporation and its management be subjected to liability for insignificant omissions or misstatements, but also management's fear of exposing itself to substantial liability may cause it simply to bury the shareholders in an avalanche of trivial information a result that is hardly conducive to informed decision making. Precisely these dangers are presented, we think, by the definition of a material fact adopted by the Court of Appeals in this case a fact which a reasonable shareholder *might* consider important. . . .

The general standard of materiality that we think best comports with the policies of Rule 14a-9 is as follows: An omitted fact is material if there is a substantial likelihood that a reasonable shareholder would consider it important in deciding how to vote. This standard does not require proof of a substantial likelihood that disclosure of the omitted fact would have caused the reasonable investor to change his vote. What the standard does contemplate is a showing of a substantial likelihood that, under all the circumstances, the omitted fact would have assumed actual significance in the deliberations of the reasonable shareholder. Put another way, there must be a substantial likelihood that the disclosure of the omitted fact would have been viewed by the reasonable investor as having significantly altered the "total mix" of information made available.

The issue of materiality may be characterized as a mixed question of law and fact, involving as it does the application of a legal standard to a particular set of facts. In considering whether summary judgment on the issue is appropriate, we must bear in mind that the underlying objective facts, which will often be free from dispute, are merely the starting point for the ultimate determination of materiality. The determination requires delicate assessments of the inferences a "reasonable shareholder" would draw from a given set of facts and the significance of those inferences to him, and these assessments are peculiarly ones for the trier of fact. Only if the established omissions are "so obviously important to an investor, that reasonable minds cannot differ on the question of materiality" is the ultimate issue of materiality appropriately resolved "as a matter of law" by summary judgment. *Johns Hopkins University v. Hutton*, 422 F.2d 1124, 1129 (4th Cir. 1970).

The omissions found by the Court of Appeals to have been materially misleading as a matter of law involved two general issues — the degree of National's control over TSC at the time of the proxy solicitation, and the favorability of the terms of the proposed transaction to TSC shareholders.

The Court of Appeals concluded that two omitted facts relating to National's potential influence, or control, over the management of TSC were material as a matter of law. . . .

We do not agree that the omission of these facts, when viewed against the disclosures contained in the proxy statement, warrants the entry of summary judgment against TSC and National on this record. Our conclusion is the same whether the omissions are considered separately or together. . . .

*   *   *

In summary, none of the omissions claimed to have been in violation of Rule 14a-9 were, so far as the record reveals, materially misleading as a matter of law, and Northway was not entitled to partial summary judgment. The judgment of the

Court of Appeals is reversed, and the case is remanded for further proceedings consistent with this opinion.

It is so ordered.

NOTES AND QUESTIONS

1. *The appropriate standard.* Why did the Supreme Court reject the materiality standard that the court of appeals adopted? Were the Court's concerns justified?

2. *Mixed question of law and fact.* The Court noted that the materiality issue is a mixed question of law and fact. In a civil case such as *TSC Industries*, this means that the court can decide the issue as a matter of law if reasonable jurors would necessarily determine that the information was, or was not, material by a preponderance of the evidence. In a criminal case, if the judge finds that no reasonable juror could find the information material beyond a reasonable doubt, the judge must dismiss the case; otherwise, the issue goes to the jury.

The Court in *TSC Industries* provided the general definition of materiality. But how does this definition apply to information concerning a transaction — such as a proposed merger — that might, or might not, come to pass? That is the issue in the next case.

BASIC INC. v. LEVINSON
485 U.S. 224 (1988)

JUSTICE BLACKMUN delivered the opinion of the Court.

This case requires us to apply the materiality requirement of Section 10(b) of the Securities Exchange Act of 1934 and the Securities and Exchange Commission's Rule 10b-5, in the context of preliminary corporate merger discussions. . . .

Prior to December 20, 1978, Basic Incorporated was a publicly traded company primarily engaged in the business of manufacturing chemical refractories for the steel industry. As early as 1965 or 1966, Combustion Engineering, Inc., a company producing mostly alumina-based refractories, expressed some interest in acquiring Basic, but was deterred from pursuing this inclination seriously because of antitrust concerns it then entertained. In 1976, however, regulatory action opened the way to a renewal of Combustion's interest. The "Strategic Plan," dated October 25, 1976, for Combustion's Industrial Products Group included the objective: "Acquire Basic Inc. $30 million."

Beginning in September 1976, Combustion representatives had meetings and telephone conversations with Basic officers and directors, including petitioners here, concerning the possibility of a merger. During 1977 and 1978, Basic made three public statements denying that it was engaged in merger negotiations. On December 18, 1978, Basic asked the New York Stock Exchange to suspend trading in its shares and issued a release stating that it had been "approached" by another company concerning a merger. On December 19, Basic's board endorsed Combustion's offer of $46 per share for its common stock, and on the following day publicly announced its approval of Combustion's tender offer for all outstanding shares.

Respondents are former Basic shareholders who sold their stock after Basic's first public statement of October 21, 1977, and before the suspension of trading in December 1978. Respondents brought a class action against Basic and its directors, asserting that the defendants issued three false or misleading public statements and thereby were in violation of Section 10(b) of the 1934 Act and of Rule 10b-5. Respondents alleged that they were injured by selling Basic shares at artificially depressed prices in a market affected by petitioners' misleading statements and in reliance thereon.

[T]he District Court granted summary judgment for the defendants. It held that, as a matter of law, any misstatements were immaterial: There were no negotiations ongoing at the time of the first statement, and although negotiations were taking place when the second and third statements were issued, those negotiations were not "destined, with reasonable certainty, to become a merger agreement in principle."

The United States Court of Appeals for the Sixth Circuit reversed the District Court's summary judgment, and remanded the case. The court reasoned that while petitioners were under no general duty to disclose their discussions with Combustion, any statement the company voluntarily released could not be "so incomplete as to mislead." In the Court of Appeals' view, Basic's statements that no negotiations were taking place, and that it knew of no corporate developments to account for the heavy trading activity, were misleading. With respect to materiality, the court rejected the argument that preliminary merger discussions are immaterial as a matter of law, and held that "once a statement is made denying the existence of any discussions, even discussions that might not have been material in absence of the denial are material because they make the statement made untrue."

We granted certiorari to resolve the split among the Courts of Appeals as to the standard of materiality applicable to preliminary merger discussions. . . .

The 1934 Act was designed to protect investors against manipulation of stock prices. Underlying the adoption of extensive disclosure requirements was a legislative philosophy: "There cannot be honest markets without honest publicity. Manipulation and dishonest practices of the market place thrive upon mystery and secrecy." H.R. Rep. No. 1383, 73d Cong., 2d Sess., 11 (1934). This Court "repeatedly has described the 'fundamental purpose' of the Act as implementing a 'philosophy of full disclosure.'" *Santa Fe Industries, Inc. v. Green*, 430 U.S. 462, 477–78 (1977). . . .

The Court previously has addressed various positive and common-law requirements for a violation of Section 10(b) or of Rule 10b-5. The Court also explicitly has defined a standard of materiality under the securities laws, concluding in the proxy-solicitation context that "[a]n omitted fact is material if there is a substantial likelihood that a reasonable shareholder would consider it important in deciding how to vote." . . . We now expressly adopt the *TSC Industries* standard of materiality for the Section 10(b) and Rule 10b-5 context.

The application of this materiality standard to preliminary merger discussions is not self-evident. Where the impact of the corporate development on the target's fortune is certain and clear, the *TSC Industries* materiality definition admits straightforward application. Where, on the other hand, the event is contingent or speculative in nature, it is difficult to ascertain whether the "reasonable investor" would have considered the omitted information significant at the time. Merger negotiations, because of the ever-present possibility that the contemplated transaction will not be effectuated, fall into the latter category.

Petitioners urge upon us a Third Circuit test for resolving this difficulty. Under this approach, preliminary merger discussions do not become material until "agreement-in-principle" as to the price and structure of the transaction has been reached between the would-be merger partners. By definition, then, information concerning any negotiations not yet at the agreement-in-principle stage could be withheld or even misrepresented without a violation of Rule 10b-5.

Three rationales have been offered in support of the 'agreement-in-principle" test. The first derives from the concern expressed in *TSC Industries* that an investor not be overwhelmed by excessively detailed and trivial information, and focuses on the substantial risk that preliminary merger discussions may collapse: because such discussions are inherently tentative, disclosure of their existence itself could mislead investors and foster false optimism. The other two justifications for the agreement-in-principle standard are based on management concerns: because the requirement of "agreement-in-principle" limits the scope of disclosure obligations, it helps preserve the confidentiality of merger discussions where earlier disclosure might prejudice the negotiations; and the test also provides a usable, bright-line rule for determining when disclosure must be made.

None of these policy-based rationales, however, purports to explain why drawing the line at agreement-in-principle reflects the significance of the information upon the investor's decision. . . .

We therefore find no valid justification for artificially excluding from the definition of materiality information concerning merger discussions, which would otherwise be considered significant to the trading decision of a reasonable investor, merely because agreement-in-principle as to price and structure has not yet been reached by the parties or their representatives.

The Sixth Circuit explicitly rejected the agreement-in-principle test, as we do today, but in its place adopted a rule that, if taken literally, would be equally insensitive, in our view, to the distinction between materiality and the other elements of an action under Rule 10b-5:

> When a company whose stock is publicly traded makes a statement, as Basic did, that "no negotiations" are underway, and that the corporation knows of "no reason for the stock's activity," and that "management is unaware of any present or pending corporate development that would result in the abnormally heavy trading activity," information concerning ongoing acquisition discussions becomes material *by virtue of the statement denying their existence.* . . .
>
> In analyzing whether information regarding merger discussions is material such that it must be affirmatively disclosed to avoid a violation of Rule 10b-5, the discussions and their progress are the primary considerations. However, once a statement is made denying the existence of any discussions, even discussions that might not have been material in absence of the denial are material because they make the statement made untrue.

786 F.2d at 748–749 (emphasis in original).

This approach, however, fails to recognize that, in order to prevail on a Rule 10b-5 claim, a plaintiff must show that the statements were *misleading* as to a *material* fact. It is not enough that a statement is false or incomplete, if the misrepresented fact is otherwise insignificant.

Even before this Court's decision in *TSC Industries*, the Second Circuit had explained the role of the materiality requirement of Rule 10b-5, with respect to contingent or speculative information or events, in a manner that gave that term meaning that is independent of the other provisions of the Rule. Under such circumstances, materiality "will depend at any given time upon a balancing of both the indicated probability that the event will occur and the anticipated magnitude of the event in light of the totality of the company activity." *SEC v. Texas Gulf Sulphur Co.*, 401 F.2d at 849.

In a subsequent decision, the late Judge Friendly, writing for a Second Circuit panel, applied the *Texas Gulf Sulphur* probability/magnitude approach in the specific context of preliminary merger negotiations. After acknowledging that materiality is something to be determined on the basis of the particular facts of each case, he stated:

> Since a merger in which it is bought out is the most important event that can occur in a small corporation's life, to wit, its death, we think that inside information, as regards a merger of this sort, can become material at an earlier stage than would be the case as regards lesser transactions — and this even though the mortality rate of mergers in such formative stages is doubtless high.

SEC v. Geon Industries, Inc., 531 F.2d 39, 47–48 (1976). We agree with that analysis.

Whether merger discussions in any particular case are material therefore depends on the facts. Generally, in order to assess the probability that the event will occur, a factfinder will need to look to indicia of interest in the transaction at the highest corporate levels. Without attempting to catalog all such possible factors, we note by way of example that board resolutions, instructions to investment bankers, and actual negotiations between principals or their intermediaries may serve as indicia of interest. To assess the magnitude of the transaction to the issuer of the securities allegedly manipulated, a factfinder will need to consider such facts as the size of the two corporate entities and of the potential premiums over market value. No particular event or factor short of closing the transaction need be either necessary or sufficient by itself to render merger discussions material.[17]

As we clarify today, materiality depends on the significance the reasonable investor would place on the withheld or misrepresented information. The fact-specific inquiry we endorse here is consistent with the approach a number of courts have taken in assessing the materiality of merger negotiations. Because the standard of materiality we have adopted differs from that used by both courts below, we remand the case for reconsideration of the question whether a grant of summary judgment is appropriate on this record. . . .

In summary:

---

[17] To be actionable, of course, a statement must also be misleading. Silence, absent a duty to disclose, is not misleading under Rule 10b-5. "No comment" statements are generally the functional equivalent of silence. . . .

1. We specifically adopt, for the Section 10(b) and Rule 10b-5 context, the standard of materiality set forth in *TSC Industries, Inc. v. Northway, Inc.*, 426 U.S. at 449.

2. We reject "agreement-in-principle as to price and structure" as the bright-line rule for materiality.

3. We also reject the proposition that "information becomes material by virtue of a public statement denying it."

4. Materiality in the merger context depends on the probability that the transaction will be consummated, and its significance to the issuer of the securities. Materiality depends on the facts and thus is to be determined on a case-by-case basis. . . .

The judgment of the Court of Appeals is vacated, and the case is remanded to that court for further proceedings consistent with this opinion.

JUSTICE WHITE, with whom JUSTICE O'CONNOR joins, concurring in part and dissenting in part [omitted].

NOTES AND QUESTIONS

Corporate mergers and acquisitions. What are the particular difficulties in assessing materiality in the context of extraordinary corporate transactions such as mergers and tender offers? How does the Court's approach take those difficulties into account? Among the alternatives presented in the opinion, is the Court's approach the best? Why or why not?

PROBLEMS

5-7. NVF Capital Management is a publically traded venture capital firm that invests in small and mid-sized businesses. One of the founders of NVF Capital, Steven Michael, had worked for two banks for a decade before becoming CEO and Chairman of the Board at NVF. Michael's biographical information stated he had received a B.A. in Economics from Smithford University. In fact, he had spent three years at Smithford studying economics, but left before receiving his degree. This statement was repeated in several NVF Capital documents, including the prospectus filed with the SEC in connection with NVF's initial offering of its stock for public sale.

About one year after NVF's initial public offering, word of Michael's biographical discrepancy reached a media outlet, and Michael subsequently revealed the truth to NVF's Board. Later that day, the Board issued a statement correcting Michael's misrepresentation. As a result of the Board's statement, several pundits in print and on television queried whether Michael's misrepresentation raised larger credibility issues concerning NVF.

The day of the Board's statement, NVF's stock price dropped from $11.85 to $8.40 per share. The next day it regained half of the previous day's loss, and within a month the price had risen back to $11.85 per share.

A group of NVF investors has sued Michael and NVF Capital for securities fraud under Section 10b and Rule 10(b)-5 for alleged material misstatements in the SEC filing. The defendants have moved to dismiss the charge. How should the court rule? Why?

5-8. Dom Dornan was the Chairman and President of Horizons Corporation ("Horizons"), a company located in Newark, New Jersey. Horizons engaged in the business of providing temporary staffing of computer and information technology personnel. The common stock of Horizons was registered with the United States Securities and Exchange Commission (the "SEC") and publicly traded on the New York Stock Exchange. As Chairman and President of Horizons, Dornan participated in negotiating mergers and acquisitions involving Horizons and other companies, including other publicly traded companies.

Dornan socialized from time to time with other executives in the same field. One of Dornan's social acquaintances was Kris Karman ("Karman"), Chief Executive Officer of Compuware Corporation ("Compuware"). Compuware was also engaged in the business of providing temporary staffing of computer and information technology personnel. Dornan and Karman were casual acquaintances, having met at business conferences four different times over the last 10 years. During conference meetings, they discussed their businesses, mentioning at times financial projections and other business information that was only available to those persons within their respective businesses. Neither Karman nor Dornan ever revealed this information for an improper purpose, and neither ever explicitly said that the information they discussed should not be repeated.

Last April 12, Dornan met with Karman at Karman's office. Karman told Dornan that Compuware was interested in acquiring Horizons through a merger by means of a friendly tender offer. Dornan responded positively, and the two engaged in an initial negotiation of the terms of the acquisition. After the meeting, negotiations regarding the proposed acquisition continued. On May 4, Compuware sent Horizons a letter of intent setting forth the proposed terms of Compuware's acquisition of Horizons through a tender offer.

In April and May, while the negotiations between Compuware and Horizons were ongoing, representatives of Compuware met with executives from Millennium Corp. to discuss a potential merger of those two companies. On May 26, Compuware advised Millennium Corp. that it was interested in acquiring all of the shares of Millennium Corp. through a tender offer of $25 per share, a price substantially above the then-prevailing market price of Millennium Corp. On June 2, Millennium Corp. privately advised Compuware that it would accept its $25 offer.

On June 21, Karman telephoned Dornan and advised Dornan that Compuware would not acquire Horizons, and told Dornan that "we have had initiated very preliminary merger negotiations with Millennium Corp. instead. We don't have clear idea whether this deal will materialize, but I didn't want to leave you in the lurch." At the time of this conversation, as Dornan knew, Compuware had not yet publicly announced its discussions with Millennium Corp.

The following day, Dornan placed two orders to purchase a total of 15,000 shares of Millennium Corp. Shortly thereafter, Dornan's orders were executed at prices of approximately $13.25 per share. Dornan did not disclose to the sellers of the shares the information Dornan had gotten from Compuware's Chief Executive Officer concerning Millennium Corp.

On June 23, the Board of Directors of Millennium Corp. and Compuware voted to approve Compuware's acquisition of Millennium Corp. by tender offer for $24 per share. On June 24, prior to the opening of trading on the New York Stock Exchange, Compuware and Millennium Corp. issued a press release publicly announcing that Compuware would acquire Millennium Corp. at approximately $24 per share. When trading began, the price of Millennium Corp.'s stock opened at approximately $23.50 per share, representing an increase of approximately $11.25 per share from the previous day's closing price.

On June 24, following the public announcements of the tender offer for Millennium Corp., Dornan sold the 15,000 shares of Millennium Corp. stock that Dornan had purchased on June 22. The securities were sold at an average price of $23.31, yielding profits for Dornan of approximately $150,937.50.

Is Dornan guilty of securities fraud? Why or why not?

Chapter 6

COMPUTER CRIMES

[A] INTRODUCTORY NOTES

[1] Scope of Computer Crimes

Computer-related crimes present tremendous challenges for law enforcement, the public, and defense counsel. Today's technological explosion provides unlimited ways for criminals to prey upon businesses and individuals via computers and the Internet. The scope of criminal activity that falls within the broad range of "computer crimes" is restricted only by the creative criminal mind. Computers can be used as tools to facilitate a wide range of criminal activity. Thus, computer crimes frequently overlap with other crimes, such as wire fraud, theft offenses, espionage, and privacy crimes. Computers have also been used in stalking cases, child pornography cases, and lottery fraud schemes, as well as many other types of fraud.

There is no universal definition of computer crime or cybercrime. It is impractical to formulate a comprehensive definition because most elements of modern life revolve around some use of computer systems. The United States Department of Justice ("DOJ") defines computer crimes as including "any violations of criminal law that involve a knowledge of computer technology for their perpetration, investigation, or prosecution." Nat'l Inst. of Justice, U.S. Dept. of Justice, Computer Crime: Criminal Justice Resource Manual 2 (1989).

One way to approach the study of computer crimes is to categorize the criminal activity depending on whether the computer is the (1) object, (2) subject, or (3) instrument of the criminal activity. An example of the first category occurs when computer hardware or software is stolen. Cases in this category involve the computer as a typical storage device, equivalent to a filing cabinet. The focus is on the computer itself because of what it contains. Crimes in the second category occur when the computer is the subject of the crimes. In today's technological environment, the computer is particularly vulnerable to infrastructure attacks including viruses and worms designed to create widespread disruption or even destruction. This type of criminal activity focuses on the integrity or confidentiality of the computer information. Crimes in the third category — where the computer is used as an instrument or tool of crime — involve more traditional crimes that are committed with the assistance of computers. Examples of such crimes include child pornography and identity theft. Within these three general types of offenses, most cybercrime centers around the unauthorized access to computer systems and the transmission of information stored on a computer for illegal purposes.

There has been a rapid emergence of legislation designed to address the vulnerability of this spawning technology. As much of our country's security system is computerized, recent terrorist activities have been promulgated on the

Internet in an effort to disarm United States security measures or to disrupt fundamental services. The USA PATRIOT Act of 2001 has intersected with the computer crime legislation to enhance punishment and widen the scope of the government's powers.[a]

Computer crimes are exceedingly difficult to investigate and prosecute partly because there is no single law enforcement organization that polices the use of computers and the Internet. Computer technology evolves at lightening speed. Ever increasing technical training thus is required to investigate these types of offenses. Juveniles, who typically have more up-to-date computer savvy than even law enforcement personnel, often commit technologically-based offenses with ease. The perpetrators of computer crimes have been called "hackers" and "crackers."[b]

The damage to computer systems caused by sabotage is often calculated in the billions of dollars. Nearly 80% of the losses come from three types of computer crime: virus attacks, unauthorized access, and information theft. Viruses and worms in particular are both fast moving and extremely destructive to businesses, governments, and individuals.[c] In addition, companies face data security attacks on a massive scale. One study showed that nearly half of U.S. companies suffered from data security breaches by the companies' own employees. *See Nearly Half of U.S. Companies Faced Insider Data Security Attacks in 2007, Survey Shows*, April 25, 2008, 3 White Collar Crime Report (BNA) d35.

[2]   National Information Infrastructure Protection Act of 1996 (NIIPA)

The computer crimes statutory scheme was initially entitled the "Counterfeit Access Device and Computer Fraud and Abuse Act" when it was passed in 1984. Some courts still refer to 18 U.S.C. § 1030 as the Computer Fraud and Abuse Act. The original act was narrowly tailored to protect only computers containing classified governmental defense and foreign relations information, financial institution and consumer reporting agency files, and access to computers operated for the government. Congress continued to expand the scope of the law through the 1980s and 1990s. The USA PATRIOT Act of 2001, Pub. L. No. 107-56, § 814, 115 (2001), amended sections of the computer crime laws, significantly extending the scope of the law to reach protected computers outside of the borders of the United States. Another key effort directed at computer-related offenses was the

---

[a] The Uniting and Strengthening America by Providing Appropriate Tools Required to Intercept and Obstruct Terrorist Act of 2001 (USA PATRIOT Act), Pub. L. No 107-56, 115 Stat. 272 (as amended by the Cyber Security Enhancement Act of 2002, Pub. L. No 107-298, § 225, 116 Stat. 2135, 2156).

[b] "Hackers" have been defined as individuals who "access [computer] systems, without any authorization, for their own interest and not for economic profit, and traditionally lack the criminal intent to damage systems." Cybercrime: The Investigation, Prosecution and Defense of a Computer-Related Crime 125 (Ralph D. Clifford, ed. 2001). "Crackers" are "hackers with criminal intent." *Id.*

[c] "A virus is a program that copies itself into other programs and becomes active when a program is run (e.g., clicked on); from there, a virus infects other files." Mark G. Milone, *Hactivism: Securing the National Infrastructure*, 20 Computer and Internet Law 2 n.18 (2003). "A worm is a self-replicating virus that does not alter files but resides in active memory and duplicates itself. Worms use parts of an operating system that are automatic and usually invisible to the user. It is common for worms to be noticed only when their uncontrolled replication consumes system resources, slowing or halting other tasks." *Id.* at 2 n.20.

Cyber Security Enhancement Act of 2002, enacted as part of the Homeland Security Act of 2002, Cyber Security Enhancement Act of 2001, Pub. L. No. 107-296, 116 Stat. 2135, 2156 (2002).[d]

Prior versions of the law covered crimes involving computers located in more than one state. The 1996 Act extended the definition of "protected computer" to include any computer attached to the Internet, in order to protect computers against attack from within their home state. The government has continued to update the existing statutes related to traditional crimes, such as wire fraud, to address computer abuse. In addition, the United States Sentencing Guidelines provide for the enhancement of criminal punishment if the offense was committed with the use of a computer.

[3]   Statutory Overview

The computer crimes statute, 18 U. S.C. § 1030, *et seq.*, contains seven different violations, each with its own specific elements and requisite mental states. As you review the statutory scheme, keep in mind that the elements of proof will differ depending on what subsection is used by the government and what relevant conduct is alleged:

- 1030(a)(1) criminalizes, *inter alia*, willfully attempting to or transmitting information to a person not entitled to receive it information that could injure the United States or advantage a foreign nation.
- 1030(a)(2) criminalizes the intentional theft of protected information from financial institutions, the United States, or other protected computers if they are connected to the Internet and used in interstate commerce.
- 1030(a)(3) criminalizes the intentional access of government information without authorization.
- 1030(a)(4) criminalizes accessing a protected computer with the intent to commit fraud.
- 1030(a)(5) criminalizes hacking by prohibiting intentionally, recklessly, or negligently causing damage to a protected computer.
- 1030(a)(6) criminalizes the fraudulent trafficking in passwords.
- 1030(a)(7) criminalizes certain extortionate threats transmitted in interstate or foreign commerce via the Internet.

(These summaries omit certain details from the statute. For the full text of the statute, please refer to the statutory supplement.)

Each of these different subsections grades the offense depending on the level of harm, and the mens rea. The government also utilizes a number of other laws to prosecute computer-related crimes, including mail and wire fraud, copyright infringement, espionage, interstate transportation of stolen property, and conspiracy.

---

[d] *Department of Justice prosecution manual.* A 2007 D.O.J. manual entitled *"Prosecuting Computer Crimes"* explores statutes, including the Computer Fraud and Abuse Act and the Wiretap Act, that may be used in computer crime prosecutions. *See* http://www.usdoj.gov/criminal/cybercrime/ccmaual/index.html.

[B]   PROVING THE ELEMENTS OF COMPUTER CRIMES

[1]   The "Thing of Value"

The following case was one of the first cases to test the application of § 1030(a)(4). The elements of this provision require the government to prove two levels of mens rea: the defendant must have (1) *knowingly* accessed a protected computer without authorization or by exceeding authorized access; and (2) acted with *intent* to defraud. The government must also show that the defendant committed three acts: (1) gained access to the computer without authorization or by exceeding authorized access; (2) used this conduct to further the fraud; and (3) obtained a thing of value. As you read the case, consider why the government failed to meet its burden of proof on the latter element.

UNITED STATES v. CZUBINSKI
106 F. 3d 1069 (1st Cir. 1997)

[Czubinski worked for the Internal Revenue Service. His primary duties were answering taxpayers' questions about their returns. Czubinski was authorized to use his Boston computer to retrieve information from the I.R.S. computer database in West Virginia. Acting outside the scope of official responsibilities, and in violation of I.R.S. policy, Czubinski retrieved information about various individuals. These individuals included two persons involved in a political campaign, a District Attorney who had prosecuted Czubinski's father in an unrelated case, a Boston Housing Authority Police Officer who was involved in an organization with Czubinski's brother, and others. The government alleged that Czubinski intended to use this information to build dossiers on people involved in the white supremacist movement and for other personal reasons. The government charged Czubinski with computer fraud and with wire fraud. At trial, the government did not prove that Czubinski actually used the information in any way, or that he disclosed the information to any third parties. (The full facts of this case are set forth in Chapter 4, Mail and Wire Fraud, *supra.*)]

* * *

Czubinski was convicted on all four of the computer fraud counts on which he was indicted; these counts arise out of unauthorized searches that also formed the basis of four of the ten wire fraud counts in the indictment. Specifically, he was convicted of violating 18 U.S.C. § 1030(a)(4), a provision enacted in the Computer Fraud and Abuse Act of 1986. Section 1030(a)(4) applies to:

> whoever . . . knowingly and with intent to defraud, accesses a Federal interest computer without authorization, or exceeds authorized access, and by means of such conduct furthers the intended fraud and obtains anything of value, unless the object of the fraud and the thing obtained consists only of the use of the computer.

We have never before addressed § 1030(a)(4). Czubinski unquestionably exceeded authorized access to a Federal interest computer.[14] On appeal he argues

---

[14] "[T]he term 'exceeds authorized access' means to access a computer with authorization and to use such access to obtain or alter information in the computer that the accessor is not entitled so to obtain or alter." 18 U.S.C. § 1030(e)(6).

that he did not obtain "anything of value." We agree, finding that his searches of taxpayer return information did not satisfy the statutory requirement that he obtain "anything of value." The value of information is relative to one's needs and objectives; here, the government had to show that the information was valuable to Czubinski in light of a fraudulent scheme. The government failed, however, to prove that Czubinski intended anything more than to satisfy idle curiosity.

The plain language of § 1030(a)(4) emphasizes that more than mere unauthorized use is required: the "thing obtained" may not merely be the unauthorized use. It is the showing of some additional end — to which the unauthorized access is a means — that is lacking here. The evidence did not show that Czubinski's end was anything more than to satisfy his curiosity by viewing information about friends, acquaintances, and political rivals. No evidence suggests that he printed out, recorded, or used the information he browsed. No rational jury could conclude beyond a reasonable doubt that Czubinski intended to use or disclose that information, and merely viewing information cannot be deemed the same as obtaining something of value for the purposes of this statute.

The legislative history further supports our reading of the term "anything of value." "In the game of statutory interpretation, statutory language is the ultimate trump card," and the remarks of sponsors of legislation are authoritative only to the extent that they are compatible with the plain language of § 1030(a)(4). *Rhode Island v. Narragansett Indian Tribe*, 19 F.3d 685, 699 (1st Cir. 1994). Here, a Senate co-sponsor's comments suggest that Congress intended § 1030(a)(4) to punish attempts to steal valuable data, and did not wish to punish mere unauthorized access:

> The acts of fraud we are addressing in proposed § 1030(a)(4) are essentially thefts in which someone uses a federal interest computer to wrongly obtain something of value from another. . . . Proposed § 1030(a)(4) is intended to reflect the distinction between the theft of information, a felony, and mere unauthorized access, a misdemeanor.

132 Cong. Rec. 7129, 99th Cong., 2d Sess. (1986).

The Senate Committee Report further underscores the fact that this section should apply to those who steal information through unauthorized access as part of an illegal scheme:

> The Committee remains convinced that there must be a clear distinction between computer theft, punishable as a felony [under § 1030(a)(4)], and computer trespass, punishable in the first instance as a misdemeanor [under a different provision]. The element in the new paragraph (a)(4), requiring a showing of an intent to defraud, is meant to preserve that distinction, as is the requirement that the property wrongfully obtained via computer furthers the intended fraud.

[W]e find that Czubinski has not obtained valuable information in furtherance of a fraudulent scheme for the purposes of § 1030(a)(4).

*   *   *

NOTES AND QUESTION

1. *Proving the "thing of value."* The district court denied a motion to dismiss the computer fraud counts in the indictment, finding that the indictment sufficiently alleged that the confidential taxpayer information was itself a "thing of value" to Czubinski, given his ends. The indictment, of course, alleged specific uses for the information that were not proven at trial, such as creating dossiers on KKK members. In light of the evidence admitted at trial, the circuit court said that because "there was no recording, disclosure or further use of the confidential information — we find that Czubinski did not obtain 'anything of value' through his unauthorized searches." 106 F.3d at 1078 n.15. Was this a case of failure of proof by the government? Should the determination of "value" be made from the perspective of the victim or the defendant? Does it matter?

2. *Quantifying value.* Given that the government spends considerable sums of money in order to protect confidential government information, is such information inherently valuable? If so, how should this value be quantified?

3. *Choosing a theory.* At the time Czubinski was prosecuted, § 1030(a)(4) punished one who "knowingly and with intent to defraud, accesse[d] a Federal interest computer without authorization, or exceed[ed] authorized access, and by means of such conduct further[ed] the intended fraud and obtain[ed] anything of value, unless the object of the fraud and the thing obtained consist[ed] only of the use of the computer." The current version of that statute states that the "thing of value" may be the computer time alone if that time is valued as more that $5,000 within one year. Could the case be successfully charged under § 1030(a)(4) today? Also note that the Taxpayer Browsing Protection Act, codified at 26 U.S.C. § 7213A, makes it misdemeanor for a federal employee to gain unauthorized access to tax return information. Also note that, under the current version of § 1030(a)(2), Czubinski arguably could be convicted for the misdemeanor of gaining access to the information in excess of his authorization.

[2]   Mens Rea

As in other areas of white collar crime, mens rea is often the key disputed element in computer crimes cases. In the next case, the court interpreted the mens rea provisions of an earlier version of § 1030(a)(5)(A). Be sure to identify precisely the statutory interpretation issue in the case.

UNITED STATES v. SABLAN
92 F.3d 865 (9th Cir. 1996)

HUG, CHIEF JUDGE:

In the early hours of August 15, 1992, Sablan, a former employee of the Bank of Hawaii's Agana, Guam branch, left a bar where she had been drinking with a friend. Sablan had recently been fired from the bank for circumventing security procedures in retrieving files. That morning, Sablan left the bar and entered the closed bank through an unlocked loading dock door. She went to her former work site (using a key she had kept) and used an old password to log into the bank's mainframe. Sablan contends that she then called up several computer files and logged off. The Government asserts that Sablan changed several of the files and deleted others. Under either version, Sablan's conduct severely damaged several bank files [resulting in losses to the bank of over $20,000].

Sablan was charged with computer fraud in violation of 18 U.S.C. § 1030(a)(5) (the "computer fraud statute"). In a pretrial motion to dismiss, Sablan attacked the statute for its failure to require a *mens rea* for each of the essential elements of the offense. In the alternative, Sablan requested a jury instruction that required the Government to prove intent as to all elements of the crime. In particular, Sablan wanted the jury to be instructed that the Government needed to prove that she had the intent to damage bank files. The district court denied the motion and ruled that, as used in the computer fraud statute, the word "intentionally" applied only to the access element of the crime. Sablan then entered into a conditional plea agreement that preserved her right to appellate review of the issue raised in her motion.

Sablan contends on appeal that the computer fraud statute must have a *mens rea* requirement for all elements of the crime. She asserts that the indictment was defective because it did not allege the appropriate *mens rea* required by the statute. In the alternative, Sablan asserts that a jury instruction was required to inform the jurors that the state had to prove intent for every element of the crime.

Sablan was convicted under the version of the computer fraud statute in effect from 1986 to 1994. That statute stated:

> (a) Whoever — . . .

> (5) intentionally accesses a Federal interest computer[*] without authorization, and by means of one or more instances of such conduct alters, damages, or destroys information in any such Federal interest computer- . . . and thereby —

> (A) causes loss to one or more others of a value aggregating $1,000 or more during any one year period; . . .

> shall be punished as provided. . . .

18 U.S.C. § 1030 (amended by Pub. L. No. 103–354). In order to have violated the statute, a defendant must have (1) accessed (2) a federal interest computer (3) without authorization and (4) have altered, damaged, or destroyed information (5) resulting in the loss to one or more others (6) of at least one thousand dollars. The district court held that the statute's *mens rea* requirement, "intentionally," applied only to the access element of the crime. We review questions of statutory interpretation *de novo*.

A.

We begin our analysis by noting that the statute is ambiguous as to its *mens rea* requirement. Although the statute explains that one must "intentionally access[ ] a Federal interest computer without authorization, and . . . destroy[ ] information

---

[*] Note that the new version of the statute replaces the term "federal interest computer" with the broader term "protected computer." The latter is defined as "a computer exclusively for the use of a financial institution or the United States Government, or, in the case of a computer not exclusively for such use, used by or for a financial institution or the United States Government and the conduct constituting the offense affects that use by or for the financial institution or the Government; or which is used in interstate or foreign commerce or communication." 18 U.S.C. § 1030(e).

in any such Federal interest computer," punctuation sets the "accesses" phrase off from the subsequent "damages" phrase. With some statutes punctuation has been used to indicate that a phrase set off by commas is independent of the language that followed. However, punctuation is not always decisive in construing statutes. In *Liparota v. United States*, 471 U.S. 419 (1985), and *United States v. X-Citement Video*, 115 S. Ct. 464 (1994), for example, the Supreme Court applied the mental state adjacent to initial words to later clauses without regard to intervening punctuation. In both cases, the Supreme Court resorted to legislative history to clarify the ambiguous language.

We conclude that the comma after "authorization" does not resolve the ambiguity. Allowing the *mens rea* requirement to reach subsequent elements of the crime would comport with general linguistic rules. Similarly, it is proper to read the statute without extending "intentionally" to the other clauses of the sentence. Therefore, we look to the statute's legislative history to clear up the textual ambiguity.

In *United States v. Morris*, 928 F.2d 504 (2d Cir.) (1991), the Second Circuit examined the legislative history of the computer fraud statute and concluded that the "intentionally" standard applied only to the "accesses" element of the crime. The court focused on the fact that original version of the statute, passed in 1984, punished anyone who,

> *knowingly* accesses a computer without authorization, or having accessed a computer with authorization, uses the opportunity such access provides for purposes to which such authorization does not extend, and by means of such conduct *knowingly* uses, modifies, destroys, or discloses information in, or prevents authorized use of, such computer, if such computer is operated for or on behalf of the Government of United States and such conduct affects such operation.

When the statute was amended in 1986, the scienter requirement was changed from knowingly to intentionally[2] and the second *mens rea* reference was eliminated. By contrast, other subsections of section 1030 retained the "dual-intent" language by placing the *mens rea* requirement at the beginning of both the "accesses" phrase and the "damages" phrase. *See, e.g.*,18 U.S.C. § 1030(a)(1). The court concluded that the decision of Congress not to repeat the scienter requirement within this statute evidenced an intent not to require the Government to prove a defendant's intent to cause damage. *Morris*, 928 F.2d at 509.

Sablan urges this court to reject the holding in *Morris*, contending that the 1986 bill was intended only to apply to those who intentionally damage computer data. She points to one line in a Senate report that evidenced a desire to retain the dual intent language: "The new subsection 1030(a)(5) to be created by the bill is designed to penalize those who intentionally alter, damage, or destroy certain computerized data belonging to another." 1986 U.S.C.C.A.N. at 2488. Thus, Sablan argues, the computer fraud statute has a *mens rea* requirement for the damages clause of the bill. We disagree.

---

[2] "The substitution of an 'intentional' standard [wa]s designed to focus Federal criminal prosecutions on those whose conduct evinces a clear intent to enter, without proper authorization, computer files or data belonging to another." S. Rep. No. 99-432, 99th Cong., 2d Sess. 6 (1986), *reprinted in* 1986 U.S.C.C.A.N. 2479, 2484.

As the *Morris* court concluded:

> gDespite some isolated language in the legislative history that arguably suggests a scienter component for the "damages" phrase of section 1030(a)(5)(A), the wording, structure, and purpose of the subsection, examined in comparison with its departure from the format of its predecessor provision persuade us that the "intentionally" standard applies only to the "accesses" phrase of section 1030(a)(5)(A), and not to its "damages" phrase.

Morris, 928 F.2d at 509. We adopt the reasoning of the *Morris* court and hold that the computer fraud statute does not require the government to prove that the defendant intentionally damaged computer files.

B.

Sablan contends that if the computer fraud statute does not have a *mens rea* requirement for the damages element of the offense, the statute is unconstitutional. Relying on the Supreme Court's decision in *X-Citement Video*, 115 S. Ct. at 464, Sablan states that a *mens rea* must be applied to all elements of an offense or due process standards are violated. We review *de novo* the district court's determination of federal constitutional law.

The Supreme Court has never ruled that *mens rea* is a constitutional requirement. However, in *X-Citement Video*, the Supreme Court stated that a statute without any scienter requirements "would raise serious constitutional doubts." *X-Citement Video*, 115 S. Ct. at 472. Sablan contends that lack of a scienter requirement for the damages element of the offense renders the statute constitutionally infirm. I n *X-Citement Video*, the Court construed the "knowingly" scienter requirement beyond the most proximate clause of 18 U.S.C. § 2252 to clarify that one charged with trafficking in child pornography must know that the material involves the use of a minor. *Id.* at 472.

After reviewing the cases interpreting criminal statutes to include broadly applicable scienter requirements the Court held that the "presumption in favor of a scienter requirement should apply to each of the statutory elements which criminalize otherwise innocent conduct." *X-Citement Video*, 115 S. Ct. at 469. However, the computer fraud statute does not criminalize otherwise innocent conduct. Under the statute, the Government must prove that the defendant intentionally accessed a federal interest computer without authorization. Thus, Sablan must have had a wrongful intent in accessing the computer in order to be convicted under the statute. This case does not present the prospect of a defendant being convicted without any wrongful intent as was the situation in *X-Citement Video*. Therefore, we hold that the computer fraud statute's *mens rea* requirement is sufficient to meet constitutional standards.

*   *   *

We therefore AFFIRM Sablan's conviction under 18 U.S.C. § 1030(a). . . .

Notes and Questions

1. *Unauthorized access.* Sablan had the password to the bank's computer system. Was her access unauthorized? Why? Would your answer be the same if the access had occurred while she was still employed by the bank? Why or why not?

2. *Statutory interpretation.* What was Sablan's statutory interpretation argument? Why did the court reject the argument? Do you agree with the court's conclusion?

3. *Constitutional challenge.* Review the court's conclusion as to Sablan's constitutional challenge. Does the court adequately distinguish *X-Citement Video*? Why or why not? Is accessing a computer without authorization inherently wrongful? Absent any damage, what is the nature of the wrong?

PROBLEMS

6-1. This problem is based on *United States v. Sablan.* Assume the following facts: While employed at the bank, Sablan was a bank officer in charge of customer relations for large accounts. Sablan's actions in accessing the computers after she left the bank's employ did not cause damage to the bank's computers. She merely gained access to the computers in order to retrieve files that she maintained that were related to her employment at the bank. Specifically, she copied and took files that contained personal information relating to other bank employees and information concerning customer accounts on which Sablan worked. When Sablan was arrested, the government found that she had copied these files to her personal computer at home. They also found letters that she had written applying for jobs at other banks.

Do these facts support a criminal case against Sablan? If so, under what theory or theories? If not, why not?

6-2. Marissa was an 18-year-old high school student who hoped to have a career in computer programming. She spent a lot of time in her school's computer science lab, and had explicit authorization to use the lab's computers. Her school's computer network was linked to other schools' networks across the country.

To bolster her college application credentials, Marissa began work on a computer program "worm" designed to deactivate spam filter programs. Marissa designed the program to spread from her school's network to the linked networks. Marissa intended that the program deactivate spam filters for only a short time. The program was supposed to occupy little computer operation time, and thus not to interfere with normal use of the computers or to damage the computers in any way. Marissa released the worm, which quickly spread to linked networks through the Internet.

Marissa soon discovered that the worm was not operating as intended. Instead, it permanently damaged spam filter programs on infected computers. The total estimated cost of repairing the damage to her school's computer network was over $2,000 and the cost of repairing the damage to linked networks was over $3 million.

You are the Assistant United States Attorney in charge of the investigation of Marissa. What theory or theories could you assert under 18 U.S.C. § 1030(a)? What defenses would you anticipate in response to each of those theories? Which charges would be the strongest? Why?

6-3. The following evidence was adduced at trial. Defendant Willy was employed by Collections, Inc., a debt collection agency. To obtain information on individuals for debt collection, the agency utilized a financial information services website called Accounts.com. The information available on Accounts.com includes the names, addresses, social security numbers, dates of birth, telephone numbers, and other property data of many individuals. In order to access the information on Accounts.com, customers must contract with the website and obtain a username and password. In his position as a small claims supervisor, Willy had significant responsibility for the computers in the agency. As part of his employment, Willy assigned to employees usernames and passwords to access Accounts.com. Employees were not authorized to obtain information from Accounts.com for personal use. Willy deactivated the usernames and passwords of employees who no longer worked for the company.

While investigating Mary for identity theft, police officers found pages printed out from Accounts.com with identifying information for many people. The information obtained from Accounts.com was used to make false identity documents, open instant store credit at various retailers, and use the store credit to purchase goods that were later sold for cash. A subpoena to Accounts.com revealed that the information had been obtained through the user name "Amanda Diaz," which was assigned to Collections, Inc. Federal agents interviewed Willy about the identity theft. Willy admitted that he had dated Mary, and that he began providing to her individuals' information he obtained through Accounts.com. After Mary continued to ask Willy for information, he gave her the Amanda Diaz username and password so that she could access Accounts.com herself. In exchange, Mary said that she would "take care of [Willy] later." She later gave him a silver watch. When Willy learned through a newspaper article that Mary had been arrested for identity theft, he deactivated the username and password.

The government has charged Willy with aiding and abetting Mary's violation of 18 U.S.C. § 1030(a)(2)(c). Willy has brought a motion under Fed. R. Crim. P. 29(a) to dismiss the government's case. That rule provides that "[a]fter the government closes its evidence or after the close of all the evidence, the court on the defendant's motion must enter a judgment of acquittal of any offense for which the evidence is insufficient to sustain a conviction."

Willy argues that there is insufficient evidence that (a) he intended to defraud and (b) he knew that Mary planned to obtain information of a certain value.

How should the court rule? Why?

[C]   CIVIL JURISDICTION

Computer-related offenses can be prosecuted both civilly and criminally. State crimes can cover some of the identical conduct addressed by the federal laws. As you read the next case, consider whether there was sufficient evidence to bring criminal charges, rather than or in addition to a civil action.

AMERICA ONLINE, INC. v. LCGM, INC.
46 F. Supp. 2d 444 (E.D. Va. 1998)

MEMORANDUM OPINION

LEE, DISTRICT JUDGE.

This matter is before the Court on plaintiff's Motion for Summary Judgment. . . . Plaintiff America Online, Inc. (AOL) complains that defendants sent large numbers of unauthorized and unsolicited bulk e-mail advertisements ("spam") to its members (AOL members). . . . Plaintiff seeks compensatory and punitive damages, attorney's fees, costs, and permanent injunctive relief. . . .

*   *   *

AOL, an Internet service provider located in the Eastern District of Virginia, provides a proprietary, content-based online service that provides its members (AOL members) access to the Internet and the capability to receive as well as send e-mail messages. AOL registered "AOL" as a trademark and service mark in 1996 and has registered its domain name "aol.com" with the InterNIC. At the time this cause of action arose, defendant LCGM, Inc. was a Michigan corporation which operated and transacted business from Internet domains offering pornographic web sites. Plaintiff alleges that defendant Web Promo is a d/b/a designation for FSJD, Inc., a Michigan corporation that operates Internet domains offering pornographic web sites. Defendant Francis Sharrak was the vice-president of Web Promo and the sole shareholder and president of LCGM. Defendant James Drakos was the president of Web Promo. Defendants Francis Sharrak and James Drakos have participated in the transmission of the bulk e-mails.

AOL alleges that defendants, in concert, sent unauthorized and unsolicited bulk e-mail advertisements ("spam") to AOL customers. AOL's Unsolicited Bulk E-mail Policy and its Terms of Service bar both members and nonmembers from sending bulk e-mail through AOL's computer systems. Plaintiff estimates that defendants, in concert with their "site partners," transmitted more than 92 million unsolicited and bulk e-mail messages advertising their pornographic Web sites to AOL members from approximately June 17, 1997 to January 21, 1998. Plaintiff bases this number on defendants' admissions that they sent approximately 300,000 e-mail messages a day at various intervals from their Michigan offices. Plaintiff asserts that defendants provided AOL with computer disks containing a list of the addresses of 820,296 AOL members to whom defendants admitted to transmitting bulk e-mail.

Plaintiff alleges that defendants harvested, or collected, the e-mail addresses of AOL members in violation of AOL's Terms of Service. Defendants have admitted to maintaining AOL memberships to harvest or collect the e-mail addresses of other AOL members. Defendants have admitted to maintaining AOL accounts and to using the AOL Collector and E-mail Pro/Stealth Mailer extractor programs to collect the e-mail addresses of AOL members, alleging that they did so in targeted adult AOL chat rooms. Defendants have admitted to using this software to evade AOL's filtering mechanisms.

Plaintiff alleges that defendants forged the domain information "aol.com" in the "from" line of e-mail messages sent to AOL members. Defendants have admitted to creating the domain information "aol.com" through an e-mail sending program, and to causing the AOL domain to appear in electronic header information of its commercial e-mails. Plaintiffs assert that as a result, many AOL members expressed confusion about whether AOL endorsed defendants' pornographic Web sites or their bulk e-mailing practices. Plaintiff also asserts that defendants' e-mail messages were sent through AOL's computer networks. Defendants have admitted to sending e-mail messages from their computers through defendants' network via e-mail software to AOL, which then relayed the messages to AOL members.

Plaintiff alleges that AOL sent defendants two cease and desist letters, dated respectively December 8, 1997 and December 30, 1997, but that defendants continued their e-mailing practices to AOL members after receiving those letters. Defendants have admitted to receiving those letters, contending that any e-mails sent after such receipt were "lawful."

Plaintiff alleges that defendants paid their "site partners" to transmit unsolicited bulk e-mail on their behalf and encouraged these site partners to advertise. Plaintiff further alleges that defendants conspired with CN Productions, another pornographic e-mailer, to transmit bulk e-mails to AOL members. Plaintiff alleges that many e-mails sent by defendants contained Hyper-Text Links both to defendants' web sites and CN Production's web sites.

Plaintiff alleges that defendants' actions injured AOL by consuming capacity on AOL's computers, causing AOL to incur technical costs, impairing the functioning of AOL's e-mail system, forcing AOL to upgrade its computer networks to process authorized e-mails in a timely manner, damaging AOL's goodwill with its members, and causing AOL to lose customers and revenue. Plaintiff asserts that between the months of December 1997 and April 1998, defendants' unsolicited bulk e-mails generated more than 450,000 complaints by AOL members.

*   *   *

Count III:

Exceeding Authorized Access in Violation of the Computer
Fraud and Abuse Act

The facts before the Court establish that defendants violated 18 U.S.C. § 1030(a)(2)(C) of the Computer Fraud and Abuse Act, which prohibits individuals from "intentionally access[ing] a computer without authorization or exceed[ing] authorized access, and thereby obtain[ing] information from any protected computer if the conduct involved an interstate or foreign communication." Defendants' own admissions satisfy the Act's requirements. Defendants have admitted to maintaining an AOL membership and using that membership to harvest the e-mail addresses of AOL members. Defendants have stated that they acquired these e-mail addresses by using extractor software programs. Defendants' actions violated AOL's Terms of Service, and as such was unauthorized. Plaintiff contends that the addresses of AOL members are "information" within the meaning of the Act because they are proprietary in nature. Plaintiff asserts that as a result of defendants' actions, it suffered damages exceeding $5,000, the statutory threshold requirement.

Count IV:

Impairing Computer Facilities In Violation of the Computer Fraud and Abuse Act

The undisputed facts establish that defendants violated 18 U.S.C. § 1030(a)(5)(C) of the Computer Fraud and Abuse Act, which prohibits anyone from "intentionally access[ing] a protected computer without authorization, and as a result of such conduct, causes damage." Another court found that spamming was an actionable claim under this Act. Defendants have admitted to utilizing software to collect AOL members' addresses. These actions were unauthorized because they violated AOL's Terms of Service. Defendants' intent to access a protected computer, in this case computers within AOL's network, is clear under the circumstances. Defendants' access of AOL's computer network enabled defendants to send large numbers of unsolicited bulk e-mail messages to AOL members.

In addition to defendants' admissions, plaintiff alleges that by using the domain information "aol.com" in their e-mails, defendants and their "site partners" camouflaged their identities, and evaded plaintiff's blocking filters and its members' mail controls. Defendants have admitted to using extractor software to evade AOL's filtering mechanisms. As a result of these actions, plaintiff asserts damages to its computer network, reputation and goodwill in excess of the minimum $5,000 statutory requirement.

* * *

Damages

AOL's claim for damages is unliquidated and therefore the Court must determine the issue at trial. Thus, the Court denies plaintiff's Motion for Summary Judgment on the issue of damages. However, the Court finds that AOL is entitled to injunctive relief preventing defendants from further distributing unsolicited bulk e-mail messages to AOL members. Defendants are further enjoined from using "aol.com" to send and distribute e-mail messages and from using the AOL network for the purpose of harvesting the addresses of AOL members. Defendants are to terminate any AOL membership. At trial, the Court can consider the parties' evidence and arguments regarding the appropriate terms of the injunction. . . .

NOTES AND QUESTIONS

1. *Civil actions.* As shown in this case, the computer crimes statutes create civil causes of action. Other criminal statutes, such as the securities fraud and RICO statute, also provide for civil causes of action. Why did Congress provide for civil liability under these statutes?

2. *Prosecutorial discretion.* If you were a federal prosecutor, would you have initiated a criminal action in this case? Why or why not?

3. *The plaintiff's theory.* Plaintiffs have many options when pursuing claims such as those presented in the AOL case. The case included allegations under the Lanham Act, 15 U.S.C. § 1125, making it unlawful to use a designation in interstate commerce designed to confuse or deceive people as to "origin, sponsorship, or

approval of his or her goods, services, or commercial activities." The plaintiff also asserted claims under the Virginia computer crimes act, common law trespass, and common law conspiracy.

4. *Trespass liability.* In *Sotelo v. DirectRevenue, LLC*, 384 F. Supp. 2d 1219 (N.D. Ill. 2005), the plaintiffs alleged that the defendants secretly installed "spyware" on personal computers in order to track consumers' behavior for direct marketing purposes. The plaintiffs asserted state law claims of trespass to personal property, consumer fraud, unjust enrichment, negligence, and computer tampering. On the defendant's motion for summary judgment, the trial court dismissed only the unjust enrichment claim.

In its decision, the court discussed the use of a "trespass" theory in computer invasion cases, citing *America Online* as support for the theory that computer invasion can be harmful. Even though spam may not directly damage a computer, it can overburden a user's electronic resources and diminish their function. Therefore, although the trespass cause of action has been largely unused for the last century, it seems to be resurfacing in response to Internet advertising and email cases. The *Direct Revenue* defendants later settled the case, agreeing to destroy the information they had harvested and to require future users to affirmatively consent to installation of the software.

5. *Civil liability for copyright infringement.* In *MGM v. Grokster, Ltd.*, 545 U.S. 913 (2005), a film studio sued a distributor of software that facilitated copyright infringement. The district court granted Grokster summary judgment on claims of contributory and vicarious infringement. The Supreme Court vacated and remanded. The Court held that contributory infringement occurs by "intentionally inducing or encouraging direct infringement," and that vicarious infringement occurs by "profiting from direct infringement while declining to exercise a right to stop or limit it." *Id.* at 929. Grokster thus could be liable if it knew its software could be used illegally and if it profited from that illegal use. A later case, *In re Napster, Inc. Copyright Litig. v. Hummer Windblad Venture Partners*, 2006 U.S. Dist. LEXIS 30338, 32 (D. Cal. 2006), explained that the "*Grokster* theory of liability . . . does not require actual or even reasonable knowledge of specific infringing files." . . . This means that the software distributor can be held liable without any knowledge of the illegal behavior.

PROBLEM

6-4. Plaintiff, PC Management (PCM), operates 15 retail stores selling discount party goods and related products. Defendant Huck worked as a consultant for PCM until the end of last November. Defendant Bail served as the company's executive vice president for merchandise and marketing also until the end of last November.

Unbeknownst to PCM, last August, Bail and Huck formed Superstore Corporation, also a defendant. Early last December, Superstore opened two retail party goods stores in the vicinity of two existing PCM Stores. PCM alleges that the stores opened "just in time to compete with plaintiff PCM stores during the December holiday selling season," and that sales during this time of year are critical to a successful business year.

The plaintiff claims that defendant Huck, "without authorization and on behalf of defendant Superstore Corporation and defendant Bail," accessed PCM's computer system from his home several times last November and December that year, thus violating 18 U.S.C. § 1030(a)(4). The November access lasted approximately twenty minutes and the December access approximately eight minutes.

With respect to the November access, Huck states that he had a home office during his years with PCM and had been authorized to use his computer from home; as proof, he offered emails demonstrating that he did so. Huck states that the December access appears to have been an automatic redial of the last call he had made to the PCM in November. There is no information as to precisely what could have been obtained from the PCM system in these incursions, although plaintiff PCM computer consultant states that "reports" could be ordered in a matter of seconds and then later downloaded and sent to a remote location.

The plaintiff alleges that the defendants used the information obtained from the November and December access to decide where to locate their stores, where to focus marketing efforts and budgets, and to obtain valuable information as to sales during the holiday season. The plaintiff asserts that, by using this valuable information, defendants obtained an unfair competitive advantage. The plaintiff specifically alleges that defendants' unauthorized access resulted in damage or loss to the PCM plaintiff of not less than $5,000 within the meaning of CFAA, 18 U.S.C. § 1030(a)(4).

The plaintiff seeks an injunction prohibiting defendants from operating the two stores and from using the plaintiff's trade secrets and confidential and proprietary information, and ordering the return of such information.

Based on the foregoing, how should the trial court rule? Why?

[D] INTERNATIONAL COMPUTER CRIME

As anyone who owns a computer is likely aware, a huge number of Internet fraud schemes targeting U.S. residents originate outside the United States. The next case deals with Congress' attempt to address this issue.

UNITED STATES v. IVANOV
175 F. Supp. 2d 367 (D. Conn. 2001)

THOMPSON, DISTRICT JUDGE.

Defendant Aleksey Vladimirovich Ivanov ("Ivanov") has been indicted, in a superseding indictment, on charges of conspiracy, computer fraud and related activity, extortion and possession of unauthorized access devices. Ivanov has moved to dismiss the indictment on the grounds that the court lacks subject matter jurisdiction. Ivanov argues that because it is alleged that he was physically located in Russia when the offenses were committed, he can not be charged with violations of United States law. For the reasons set forth below, the defendant's motion is being denied. . . .

I. BACKGROUND

Online Information Bureau, Inc. ("OIB"), the alleged victim in this case, is a Connecticut corporation based in Vernon, Connecticut. It is an "e-commerce" business which assists retail and Internet merchants by, among other things, hosting their websites and processing their credit card data and other financial transactions. In this capacity, OIB acts as a financial transaction "clearinghouse," by aggregating and assisting in the debiting or crediting of funds against each account for thousands of retail and Internet purchasers and vendors. In doing so, OIB collects and maintains customer credit card information, merchant account numbers, and related financial data from credit card companies and other financial institutions.

The government alleges that Ivanov "hacked" into OIB's computer system and obtained the key passwords to control OIB's entire network. The government contends that in late January and early February 2000, OIB received from Ivanov a series of unsolicited e-mails indicating that the defendant had obtained the "root" passwords for certain computer systems operated by OIB. A "root" password grants its user access to and control over an entire computer system, including the ability to manipulate, extract, and delete any and all data. Such passwords are generally reserved for use by the system administrator only.

The government claims that Ivanov then threatened OIB with the destruction of its computer systems (including its merchant account database) and demanded approximately $10,000 for his assistance in making those systems secure. It claims, for example, that on February 3, 2000, after his initial solicitations had been rebuffed, Ivanov sent the following e-mail to an employee of OIB:

> [name redacted], now imagine please Somebody hack you network (and not notify you about this), he download Atomic software with more than 300 merchants, transfer money, and after this did "rm-rf/" and after this you company be ruined. I don't want this, and because this I notify you about possible hack in you network, if you want you can hire me and im allways be check security in you network. What you think about this?[1]

The government contends that Ivanov's extortionate communications originated from an e-mail account at Lightrealm.com, an Internet Service Provider based in Kirkland, Washington. It contends that while he was in Russia, Ivanov gained access to the Lightrealm computer network and that he used that system to communicate with OIB, also while he was in Russia. Thus, each e-mail sent by Ivanov was allegedly transmitted from a Lightrealm.com computer in Kirkland, Washington through the Internet to an OIB computer in Vernon, Connecticut, where the e-mail was opened by an OIB employee.

The parties agree that the defendant was physically located in Russia (or one of the other former Soviet Bloc countries) when, it is alleged, he committed the offenses set forth in the superseding indictment.

The superseding indictment comprises eight counts. Count One charges that beginning in or about December 1999, or earlier, the defendant and others conspired to commit the substantive offenses charged in Counts Two through Eight

---

[1] An individual with "root access" who inputs the UNIX command "rm-rf/" will delete all files on the network server, including all operating system software.

of the indictment, in violation of 18 U.S.C. § 371. Count Two charges that the defendant, knowingly and with intent to defraud, accessed protected computers owned by OIB and by means of this conduct furthered a fraud and obtained something of value, in violation of 18 U.S.C. §§ 2, 1030(a)(4) and 1030(c)(3)(A). Count Three charges that the defendant intentionally accessed protected computers owned by OIB and thereby obtained information, which conduct involved interstate and foreign communications and was engaged in for purposes of financial gain and in furtherance of a criminal act, in violation of 18 U.S.C. §§ 2, 1030(a)(2)(C) and 1030(c)(2)(B). Counts Four and Five do not pertain to this defendant.

Count Six charges that the defendant transmitted in interstate and foreign commerce communications containing a threat to cause damage to protected computers owned by OIB, in violation of 18 U.S.C. §§ 1030(a)(7) and 1030(c)(3)(A). Count Seven charges that the defendant obstructed, delayed and affected commerce, and attempted to obstruct, delay and affect commerce, by means of extortion by attempting to obtain property from OIB with OIB's consent, inducing such consent by means of threats to damage OIB and its business unless OIB paid the defendant money and hired the defendant as a security consultant, in violation of 18 U.S.C. § 1951(a). Count Eight charges that the defendant, knowingly and with intent to defraud, possessed unauthorized access devices, which conduct affected interstate and foreign commerce, in violation of 18 U.S.C. §§ 1029(a)(3).

II. DISCUSSION

The defendant and the government agree that when Ivanov allegedly engaged in the conduct charged in the superseding indictment, he was physically present in Russia and using a computer there at all relevant times. Ivanov contends that for this reason, charging him under the Hobbs Act, 18 U.S.C. § 1951, under the Computer Fraud and Abuse Act, 18 U.S.C. § 1030, and under the access device statute, 18 U.S.C. § 1029, would in each case require extraterritorial application of that law and such application is impermissible. The court concludes that it has jurisdiction, first, because the intended and actual detrimental effects of Ivanov's actions in Russia occurred within the United States, and second, because each of the statutes under which Ivanov was charged with a substantive offense was intended by Congress to apply extraterritorially.

A. The Intended and Actual Detrimental Effects of the Charged Offenses Occurred Within the United States

As noted by the court in *United States v. Muench*, 694 F.2d 28 (2d Cir. 1982), "[t]he intent to cause effects within the United States . . . makes it reasonable to apply to persons outside United States territory a statute which is not expressly extraterritorial in scope." *Id.* at 33. "It has long been a commonplace of criminal liability that a person may be charged in the place where the evil results, though he is beyond the jurisdiction when he starts the train of events of which that evil is the fruit." *United States v. Steinberg*, 62 F.2d 77, 78 (2d Cir. 1932). "[T]he Government may punish a defendant in the same manner as if [he] were present in the jurisdiction when the detrimental effects occurred." *Marc Rich & Co., A.G. v. United States*, 707 F.2d 663, 666 (2d Cir. 1983).

*   *   *

Here, all of the intended and actual detrimental effects of the substantive offenses Ivanov is charged with in the indictment occurred within the United States. In Counts Two and Three, the defendant is charged with accessing OIB's computers. Those computers were located in Vernon, Connecticut. The fact that the computers were accessed by means of a complex process initiated and controlled from a remote location does not alter the fact that the accessing of the computers, i.e., part of the detrimental effect prohibited by the statute, occurred at the place where the computers were physically located, namely OIB's place of business in Vernon, Connecticut.

Count Two charges further that Ivanov obtained something of value when he accessed OIB's computers, that "something of value" being the data obtained from OIB's computers. In order for Ivanov to violate § 1030(a)(4), it was necessary that he do more than merely access OIB's computers and view the data. *See United States v. Czubinski*, 106 F.3d 1069, 1078 (1st Cir. 1997) ("[M]erely viewing information cannot be deemed the same as obtaining something of value for purposes of this statute." . . . "[T]his section should apply to those who steal information through unauthorized access." . . .). The indictment charges that Ivanov did more than merely gain unauthorized access and view the data. Ivanov allegedly obtained root access to the OIB computers located in Vernon, Connecticut. Once Ivanov had root access to the computers, he was able to control the data, e.g., credit card numbers and merchant account numbers, stored in the OIB computers; Ivanov could copy, sell, transfer, alter, or destroy that data. That data is intangible property of OIB. *See Carpenter v. United States*, 484 U.S. 19, 25 (1987) (noting that the "intangible nature [of confidential business information] does not make it any less 'property' protected by the mail and wire fraud statutes"). . . .

At the point Ivanov gained root access to OIB's computers, he had complete control over that data, and consequently, had possession of it. That data was in OIB's computers. Since Ivanov possessed that data while it was in OIB's computers in Vernon, Connecticut, the court concludes that he obtained it, for purposes of § 1030(a)(4), in Vernon, Connecticut. The fact that Ivanov is charged with obtaining OIB's valuable data by means of a complex process initiated and controlled from a remote location, and that he subsequently moved that data to a computer located in Russia, does not alter the fact that at the point when Ivanov first possessed that data, it was on OIB's computers in Vernon, Connecticut.

Count Three charges further that when he accessed OIB's computers, Ivanov obtained information from protected computers. The analysis as to the location at which Ivanov obtained the information referenced in this count is the same as the analysis as to the location at which he obtained the "something of value" referenced in Count Two. Thus, as to both Counts Two and Three, it is charged that the balance of the detrimental effect prohibited by the pertinent statute, i.e., Ivanov's obtaining something of value or obtaining information, also occurred within the United States.

Count Six charges that Ivanov transmitted a threat to cause damage to protected computers. The detrimental effect prohibited by § 1030(a)(7), namely the receipt by an individual or entity of a threat to cause damage to a protected computer, occurred in Vernon, Connecticut because that is where OIB was located, where it received the threat, and where the protected computers were located. The analysis is the same as to Count Seven, the charge under the Hobbs Act.

Count Eight charges that Ivanov knowingly and with intent to defraud possessed over ten thousand unauthorized access devices, i.e., credit card numbers and merchant account numbers. For the reasons discussed above, although it is charged that Ivanov later transferred this intangible property to Russia, he first possessed it while it was on OIB's computers in Vernon, Connecticut. Had he not possessed it here, he would not have been able to transfer it to his computer in Russia. Thus, the detrimental effect prohibited by the statute occurred within the United States.

Finally, Count One charges that Ivanov and others conspired to commit each of the substantive offenses charged in the indictment. . . . Federal jurisdiction over a conspiracy charge "is established by proof that the accused planned to commit a substantive offense which, if attainable, would have violated a federal statute, and that at least one overt act has been committed in furtherance of the conspiracy." *United States v. Giordano*, 693 F.2d 245, 249 (2d Cir. 1982). Here, Ivanov is charged with planning to commit substantive offenses in violation of federal statutes, and it is charged that at least one overt act was committed in furtherance of the conspiracy. As discussed above, the court has jurisdiction over the underlying substantive charges. Therefore, the court has jurisdiction over the conspiracy charge, at a minimum, to the extent it relates to Counts Two, Three, Six, Seven or Eight.

Accordingly, the court concludes that it has subject matter jurisdiction over each of the charges against Ivanov, whether or not the statutes under which the substantive offenses are charged are intended by Congress to apply extraterritorially, because the intended and actual detrimental effects of the substantive offenses Ivanov is charged with in the indictment occurred within the United States.

B. Intended Extraterritorial Application

The defendant's motion should also be denied because, as to each of the statutes under which the defendant has been indicted for a substantive offense, there is clear evidence that the statute was intended by Congress to apply extraterritorially. This fact is evidenced by both the plain language and the legislative history of each of these statutes.

There is a presumption that Congress intends its acts to apply only within the United States, and not extraterritorially. However, this "presumption against extraterritoriality" may be overcome by showing "clear evidence of congressional intent to apply a statute beyond our borders. . . . " *United States v. Gatlin*, 216 F.3d 207, 211 (2d Cir. 2000). "Congress has the authority to enforce its laws beyond the territorial boundaries of the United States. Whether Congress has in fact exercised that authority in [a particular case] is a matter of statutory construction." *Equal Employment Opportunity Comm. v. Arabian American Oil Co.*, 499 U.S. 244, 248 (1991).

1. 18 U.S.C. § 1951: The Hobbs Act

*   *   *

[T]his court concludes that the Hobbs Act encompasses not only all extortionate interference with interstate commerce by means of conduct occurring within the United States, but also all such conduct which, although it occurs outside the United

States, affects commerce within the borders of the United States. . . .

2. 18 U.S.C. § 1030: The Computer Fraud and Abuse Act

The Computer Fraud and Abuse Act ("CFAA") was amended in 1996 by Pub. L. No. 104-294, 110 Stat. 3491, 3508. The 1996 amendments made several changes that are relevant to the issue of extraterritoriality, including a change in the definition of "protected computer" so that it included any computer "which is used in interstate *or foreign* commerce or communication." 18 U.S.C. § 1030(e)(2)(B) (emphasis added). The 1996 amendments also added subsections (a)(2)(C) and (a)(7), which explicitly address "interstate or foreign commerce," and subsection (e)(9), which added to the definition of "government entity" the clause "any foreign country, and any state, province, municipality or other political subdivision of a foreign country."

The plain language of the statute, as amended, is clear. Congress intended the CFAA to apply to computers used "in interstate or foreign commerce or communication." The defendant argues that this language is ambiguous. The court disagrees. . . . In order for the word "foreign" to have meaning, and not be superfluous, it must mean something other than "interstate." In other words, "foreign" in this context must mean international. Thus, Congress has clearly manifested its intent to apply § 1030 to computers used either in interstate or in foreign commerce.

The legislative history of the CFAA supports this reading of the plain language of the statute. The Senate Judiciary Committee issued a report explaining its reasons for adopting the 1996 amendments. In that report, the Committee specifically noted its concern that the statute as it existed prior to the 1996 amendments did not cover "computers used in foreign communications or commerce, despite the fact that hackers are often foreign-based." *Id.* at 4. . . . Congress has the power to apply its statutes extraterritorially, and in the case of 18 U.S.C. § 1030 it has clearly manifested its intention to do so.

*   *   *

IV. CONCLUSION

For the reasons set forth above, the defendant's Motion to Dismiss for Lack of Subject Matter Jurisdiction is hereby DENIED.

NOTES AND QUESTIONS

1. *Constructing a criminal case.* Note that the government brought a number of charges in this case. Identify those charges precisely. Why did the government bring each of those charges? Was the government justified in seeking to assert so many counts of criminal wrongdoing in this case? Why or why not?

2. *The harm caused — § 1030(a)(4).* Note that, with respect to the charge under § 1030(a)(4), the court distinguished *Czubinski*. With respect to what the defendant did with the information, is this case really different from *Czubinski*? If so, how?

[E]   EVIDENCE GATHERING

[1]   Law Enforcement Challenges

Because criminal activity can be conducted with virtual anonymity, victims often do not discover their vulnerability until it is too late. Moreover, even when the government brings evidence to the victim, there can be a denial or fear of reporting because of negative publicity. This situation is most evident in corporate scandals.

The government is stepping up its efforts to meet these challenges. The United States Secret Service and the Federal Bureau of Investigation are the main agencies responsible for the investigation and enforcement of computer offenses. The Department of Justice handles the prosecution, and the USA PATRIOT Act places the federal crime of terrorism within the express jurisdiction of the Attorney General. The FBI has a cyber crime division, and an arm of the Criminal Investigative Division focuses on computer-related crimes against children. The Department of Justice has also coordinated its intellectual property section with the computer crimes division. Some United States Attorneys Offices have special task force units with primary responsibility for investigating and enforcing violations of law related to computer fraud and abuse.

[2]   Electronically-Stored Evidence

Much evidence in white collar and corporate criminal cases today is stored in desktop computers, laptop computers, CDs, DVDs, PDAs, floppy disks, and flash drives. Moreover, technology now allows information to be stored in cyberspace on the Internet and in various other technological locales beyond the visible eye.

To recognize the extent of the variety of evidence-gathering concerns presented by today's business climate, consider email, one of the most commonly used aspects of today's technology. Email can paint a vivid picture of the actors' mental thoughts during the planning of a crime. For example, email evidence was introduced in the case that produced the first conviction arising out of the Enron scandal. *See United States v. Arthur Andersen, LLP*, 374 F.3d 281, 287–288 (5th Cir. 2004), *rev'd*, 544 U.S. 696 (2005). In that case, the government charged the Arthur Andersen accounting firm with obstruction of justice, and emails provided key evidence of obstructive intent. (This case is set forth and discussed in Chapter 11, Obstruction of Justice, *infra.*)

[3]   Fourth Amendment Issues

Computer-related offenses raise novel Fourth Amendment issues. The Fourth Amendment requires that search warrants be based upon probable cause and particularly describe the places to be searched and the items to be seized. How is it possible to describe the various sorts of electronically-stored information in advance? The Supreme Court has held that the particularity requirement is to be applied under a sliding scale approach; the warrant need only be as particular as is reasonable under the circumstances. *See Andresen v. Maryland*, 427 U.S. 463 (1976) (finding a broad subpoena for business records to be sufficiently particular under a sliding scale test that allows the government flexibility according to the difficulty in describing in advance the items to be seized). Accordingly, courts have interpreted the Fourth Amendment's "particularity" requirement with flexibility in computer crimes cases. *See United States v. Sawyer*, 799 F.2d 1494 (11th Cir. 1986). The *Sawyer* court upheld a search warrant for "computer records or printouts relating to customer accounts, which are evidence and fruits of, and the means of commission of violations of [federal law]." *Id.* at 1508 n.15.

In addition, the Fourth Amendment only applies to "searches" and "seizures." Under *Katz v. United States*, 389 U.S. 347 (1967), there is no "search" unless the government action violates a person's actual and reasonable expectation of privacy. Thus, in instances where electronically-stored or -conveyed information has been revealed to others, governmental viewing of that information may not constitute a search. If that is so, then the requirements of the Fourth Amendment will not apply.

The United States Department of Justice has published a comprehensive manual outlining the legal issues pertaining to the gathering of evidence related to computer searches. In it, the DOJ states the following introductory information:

> In the last decade, computers and the Internet have entered the mainstream of American life. Millions of Americans spend several hours every day in front of computers, where they send and receive e-mail, surf the Web, maintain databases, and participate in countless other activities.
>
> Unfortunately, those who commit crime have not missed the computer revolution. An increasing number of criminals use pagers, cellular phones, laptop computers and network servers in the course of committing their crimes. In some cases, computers provide the means of committing crime. For example, the Internet can be used to deliver a death threat via e-mail; to launch hacker attacks against a vulnerable computer network; to disseminate computer viruses; or to transmit images of child pornography. In other cases, computers merely serve as convenient storage devices for evidence of crime. For example, a drug kingpin might keep a list of who owes him money in a file stored in his desktop computer at home, or a money laundering operation might retain false financial records in a file on a network server. . . .
>
> The dramatic increase in computer-related crime requires prosecutors and law enforcement agents to understand how to obtain electronic evidence stored in computers. Electronic records such as computer network logs, e-mails, word processing files, and ".jpg" picture files increasingly provide the government with important (and sometimes essential) evidence in criminal cases. The purpose of this publication is to provide Federal law enforcement agents and prosecutors with systematic guidance that can help them understand the legal issues that arise when they seek electronic evidence in criminal investigations. . . .
>
> To determine whether an individual has a reasonable expectation of privacy in information stored in a computer, it helps to treat the computer like a closed container such as a briefcase or file cabinet. The Fourth Amendment generally prohibits law enforcement from accessing and viewing information stored in a computer without a warrant if it would be prohibited from opening a closed container and examining its contents in the same situation.

The most basic Fourth Amendment question in computer cases asks whether an individual enjoys a reasonable expectation of privacy in electronic information stored within computers (or other electronic storage devices) under the individual's control. For example, do individuals have a reasonable expectation of privacy in the contents of their laptop computers, floppy disks or pagers? If the answer is "yes," then the government ordinarily must obtain a warrant before it accesses the information stored inside. . . .

Individuals who retain a reasonable expectation of privacy in stored electronic information under their control may lose Fourth Amendment protections when they relinquish that control to third parties. For example, an individual may offer a container of electronic information to a third party by bringing a malfunctioning computer to a repair shop, or by shipping a floppy diskette in the mail to a friend. Alternatively, a user may transmit information to third parties electronically, such as by sending data across the Internet. When law enforcement agents learn of information possessed by third parties that may provide evidence of a crime, they may wish to inspect it. Whether the Fourth Amendment requires them to obtain a warrant before examining the information depends first upon whether the third-party possession has eliminated the individual's reasonable expectation of privacy. . . .

U.S. Dept. of Justice, *Searching and Seizing Computers and Obtaining Electronic Evidence in Criminal Investigations* (2002) (available online at http://www.usdoj.gov/criminal/cybercrime/s&smanual2002.htm#_IA_ (last visited October 25, 2004)).

Congress has responded to the threats to individual privacy. Specifically, 18 U.S.C. § 2703, entitled "Required disclosure of customer communications or records," provides some protections by requiring search warrants, court orders, or consent in certain circumstances in order for the government to obtain wire and electronic communications.

What are the risks associated with searches of electronically-stored information? How much access should the government have to such information?

*   *   *

Several interesting applications of the *Katz* holding have emerged in the computer-related field:

Consent issues. In *United States v. Buckner,* 407 F. Supp. 2d 777 (W.D. Va. 2006), the defendant's wife allowed the police to search the couple's home, including the home computer. The police found evidence on the computer that was later used to convict her husband. The court held that the wife's consent was valid. The computer was rented in her name and she had access to it, so there was a reduced expectation of privacy consistent with *Katz* and other Fourth Amendment precedent. The holding was limited, however, because the court held that the wife could not consent to a search of the defendant's password-protected files.

Workplace materials. In *United States v. Ziegler,* 456 F. 3d 1138, 1145 (9th Cir. 2006), an employer acting in cooperation with the government provided the government with information stored on the computer in the defendant's personal office at the company. The defendant argued that the employer's action constituted an illegal search. In its original opinion, the Ninth Circuit found that, because the employee's computer use at work was subject to monitoring by the employer, the employee did not have a reasonable expectation of privacy in the computer's contents. The opinion, however, was withdrawn after rehearing, and was superseded by the opinion at 474 F.3d 1184 (9th Cir. 2007). In the later opinion, the court found that the employee did have a legitimate expectation of privacy in his work computer, but that the search was reasonable because the employee consented to the search. *Id.* at 1191–1193.

Intermingled records. Does it violate the Fourth Amendment to seize an entire file when there is probable cause only to seize a few individual files? In *United States v. Comprehensive Drug Testing Inc.*, 513 F.3d 1085 (9th Cir. 2006), federal agents executed a search warrant authorizing drug-testing records for 10 professional baseball players. The agents seized an entire computer directory containing the drug-testing records of all major league baseball players. The court held that the seizure of intermingled records was not unreasonable under the Fourth Amendment.

For an overview of certain Fourth Amendment issues relating to computer searches, see Elkan Abramowitz & Barry A. Bohrer, *The Fourth Amendment in the Age of Computers*, N.Y. L.J., Nov. 7, 2006, at p. 3, col. 1.

[4]   First Amendment Issues

Computer crimes prosecutions have raised significant First Amendment issues. For example, courts have invalidated Congressional attempts to criminalize internet pornography. In *Reno v. American Civil Liberties Union*, 521 U.S. 844 (1997), the Supreme Court found the Communications Decency Act of 1996 unconstitutional because it criminalized speech based on its content. Three years later, in *United States. v. Playboy Entertainment Group*, 529 U.S. 803 (2000), a cable television programmer argued that the Telecommunications Act's "signal bleed" provision, requiring cable operators either to scramble sexually explicit channels in full or limit programming on such channels to certain hours, was unconstitutional. The Court agreed, holding that the provision (1) was a content-based restriction subject to strict scrutiny and (2) violated the First Amendment. And in 2004, in *Ashcroft v. American Civil Liberties Union*, 542 U.S. 656 (2004), the plaintiffs alleged that the Child Online Protection Act (COPA) violated the First Amendment. The Court held that Internet content providers and civil liberties groups were likely to prevail on their claim that COPA violated the First Amendment by burdening adults' access to some protected speech. In *United States v. Williams*, 128 S. Ct. 1830 (2008), however, the Supreme Court upheld the PROTECT Act, which criminalizes offers to provide computer-generated images of child pornography.

First Amendment issues also arise under anti-spam statutes. In *Jaynes v. Commonwealth*, 666 S.E.2d 303 (Va. 2008), the defendant sent over 10,000 emails to America Online subscribers using false header information and sender domain names. Jaynes was convicted under Virginia's anti-spam statute, Va. Code Ann. § 18.2-152.3:1. On appeal, the Virginia Supreme Court held that the statute violated the First Amendment. The court found that the prohibition on false routing information in the dissemination of emails violates the First Amendment right to engage in anonymous speech. The court further held that the prohibition of the anonymous transmission of all unsolicited bulk emails, including those containing political, religious, or other protected speech, was substantially overbroad on its face.

Chapter 7

BRIBERY AND GRATUITIES

[A] INTRODUCTORY NOTES

The federal bribery and gratuity statutes, along with the federal extortion statute discussed in the next chapter, provide powerful tools in the effort to combat governmental corruption. Federal law broadly criminalizes both giving bribes and gratuities to federal public officials and receiving such bribes and gratuities. As seen in the cases below, the bribery and gratuity statutes have been interpreted to apply to a wide range of public officials and official acts.

The expanded federal power raises issues relating to matters traditionally reserved to state and local law enforcement. In addition, this power has given rise to questions as to whether some political bribery prosecutions have been politically motivated. Further, the expanded scope of the federal bribery statutes raises issues of fair notice to potential defendants.

Section 201 of the federal criminal code contains the principal federal bribery and gratuity statute. 18 U.S.C. § 201. Also, § 666 of the federal criminal code criminalizes giving and receiving bribes in connection with federal programs. 18 U.S.C. § 666. This chapter covers both of these statutes in detail.

[B] SECTION 201

[1] Section 201 — Statutory Elements

Section 201 sets forth the distinct crimes of bribery and gratuities, and defines the terms used in those offenses. Under § 201(b), in a case alleging that the defendant *gave, or offered to give*, a bribe, the government must prove that:

(1) The defendant gave or offered to give something of value;

(2) The recipient or offeree was a federal public official;

(3) The defendant acted with corrupt intent; and

(4) The defendant's scheme was designed to:

(a) influence the public official in an official act,

(b) influence the public official to commit a fraud on the United States, or

(c) induce the public official to act in violation of a lawful duty.

In a case alleging that the defendant *received, or agreed to receive*, a bribe, the government must prove that:

(1) The defendant received or agreed to receive something of value;

(2) The defendant was a federal public official;

(3) The defendant acted with corrupt intent; and

(4) The scheme was designed to

    (a) influence the defendant in an official act,

    (b) influence the defendant to commit a fraud on the United States, or

    (c) induce the defendant to act in violation of a lawful duty.

The statute provides that the defendant may be punished by a fine, by imprisonment of not more than 15 years, or both.

In a gratuities prosecution under § 201(c) for *giving or offering to give* an illegal gratuity, the government must prove that:

(1) The defendant gave or offered to give something of value;

(2) The recipient or offeree was a federal public official; and

(3) The defendant intended that the thing of value be given as compensation for an official act already performed or to be performed otherwise than as provided by law for the proper discharge of the defendant's official duty.

In a case alleging that the defendant *received or agreed to receive* an illegal gratuity, the government must show that:

(1) The defendant received or agreed to receive something of value;

(2) The defendant was a federal public official; and

(3) The defendant received or agreed to receive the thing of value as compensation for an official act already performed or to be performed, otherwise than as provided by law for the proper discharge of the defendant's official duty.

The statute provides that the defendant may be punished by a fine, by imprisonment of not more than two years, or both.

[2]   Public Official

Section 201(a) defines the term "public official" to include members of Congress and officers, employees, and other persons "acting for or on behalf of the United States, or any department, agency or branch of government thereof . . . in any official function." The statute, however, does not provide any guidance for determining when one is "acting for or on behalf of the United States." That task fell to the Supreme Court in the case that follows.

DIXSON v. UNITED STATES
465 U.S. 482 (1984)

JUSTICE MARSHALL delivered the opinion of the Court.

These consolidated cases present the question whether officers of a private, nonprofit corporation administering and expending federal community development block grants are "public officials" for purposes of the federal bribery statute. 18 U.S.C. § 201(a).

I.

In 1979, the City of Peoria received two federal block grants from the Department of Housing and Urban Development (HUD). The first was a $400,000 Community Development Block Grant; the second a $636,000 Metro Reallocation Grant. Both grants were funded through the Housing and Community Development Act of 1974. Under that Act, the Secretary of HUD is authorized to dispense federal block grants to state and local governments and nonprofit community organizations for urban renewal programs such as the rehabilitation of residential structures, code enforcement in deteriorating areas, and the construction of public works projects.

The City of Peoria subsequently designated United Neighborhoods, Inc. (UNI), a community-based, social-service organization, to be the City's subgrantee in charge of the administration of the federal block grant funds.[1] UNI in turn hired petitioner Dixson to serve as the corporation's Executive Director and petitioner Hinton as its Housing Rehabilitation Coordinator. Petitioner Dixson was responsible for the general supervision of UNI's programs, including fiscal control and execution of contracts. Petitioner Hinton's duties included contracting with persons applying for housing rehabilitation assistance, and contracting with demolition firms.

A federal grand jury named petitioners in an 11-count indictment filed on March 12, 1981. The indictment charged that petitioners, as "public officials" under 18 U.S.C. § 201(a), had sought a series of bribes in return for "being influenced in their performance of an official act in respect to the awarding of housing rehabilitation contracts" in violation of 18 U.S.C. § 201(c)(1), (2).

According to the Government's evidence at trial, petitioners used their positions to extract $42,604 in kick-backs from contractors seeking to work on UNI's housing rehabilitation projects. One contractor testified how he was approached by petitioner Hinton and persuaded to pay petitioners ten percent of each housing rehabilitation contract that petitioners awarded him. The contractor explained that on ten occasions, he received first draw checks from UNI for 20 percent of the contract price, deposited the check at his bank, and paid half the amount of the check in cash to petitioners. A second contractor testified as to substantially the same arrangement.

Before trial, petitioners moved to dismiss the indictment on the grounds that they were not "public officials" within the meaning of the federal statute. Their motions were denied, and following a jury trial in the United States District Court for the Central District of Illinois, petitioners were convicted as charged. The District Court sentenced each to 71/2 years imprisonment, to be followed by three years' probation. Petitioners appealed to the United States Court of Appeals for the Seventh Circuit, which affirmed. Both petitioners filed petitions for writs of certiorari, and we granted the writs. We now affirm.

---

[1] Local recipients of Housing and Community Development Act (HCDA) block grants have the option of distributing the funds directly or of subcontracting the administration of the funds to private, nonprofit organizations.

II.

Petitioners' sole claim is that they were not "public officials" within the meaning of 18 U.S.C. § 201(a) and therefore not subject to prosecution under the federal bribery statute. Since our disposition of this claim turns on the relationship between petitioners and the federal government, we begin our discussion with an analysis of the Housing and Community Development Act (HCDA) block grant program and petitioners' role in administering that program.

Congress passed the HCDA to meet the social, economic, and environmental problems facing cities. 42 U.S.C. § 5301(a). The primary objective of the Act is "the development of viable urban communities." § 5301(c). While the HCDA addressed a national problem, Congress enacted the legislation as a federal block grant statute, under which the day-to-day administration of the federal program, including the actual expenditure of federal funds, is delegated to State and local authorities.

The HCDA creates a "consistent system of Federal aid," § 5301(d), by distributing funds committed by Congress through organizations outside the federal government, while retaining federal control to assure compliance with statutory federal objectives and implementing regulations. Congress itself specified the 17 categories of community projects upon which HCDA grants can be spent. Within the federal constraints, grant recipients design programs addressing local needs. To obtain federal funds, local communities must submit to the Secretary a plan made in accordance with national urban growth policies, and supplement the plan with annual performance reports. The federal government retains the right to audit the records of HCDA programs, and to recover improperly expended funds.

HCDA grantees give assurances to HUD that they, and their subgrantees, will abide by specific financial accountability, equal opportunity, fair labor, environmental, and other requirements. By administering HCDA funds, private nonprofit organizations subject themselves to numerous federal restrictions beyond those imposed directly by HUD. Like other recipients of federal grant funds, HUD grantees and subgrantees are subject to a uniform audit procedure, adopted by the federal government as "an integral element" of "full accountability by those entrusted with responsibility for administering the programs."

UNI voluntarily assumed the status of CDA subgrantee when UNI and the City of Peoria signed five separate grant agreements in March and October 1979, pursuant to which UNI hired petitioners. . . .

*   *   *

III.

Petitioners contend now, as they have throughout this litigation, that, as executives of a private nonprofit corporation unaffiliated with the federal government, they were never "public officials" as Congress defined that term. . . .

Petitioners argue that they can not be considered to have acted "for or on behalf of the United States" because neither they nor their employer UNI ever entered into any agreement with the United States or any subdivision of the federal government. . . .

As is often the case in matters of statutory interpretation, the language of § 201(a) does not decide the dispute. The words can be interpreted to support either petitioners' or the Government's reading. We must turn, therefore, to the legislative history of the federal bribery statute to determine whether these materials clarify which of the proposed readings is consistent with Congress's intent. If the legislative history fails to clarify the statutory language, our rule of lenity would compel us to construe the statute in favor of petitioners, as criminal defendants in these cases.

A.

Congress passed the current federal bribery provision, including § 201(a), in 1962, as part of an effort to reformulate and rationalize all federal criminal statutes dealing with the integrity of government. At the time of the 1962 revisions, general federal bribery statutes had been in existence for more than a century. From the start, Congress drafted its bribery statutes with broad jurisdictional language, and periodically amended the provisions to ensure that the scope of federal criminal liability kept pace with the growth and diversification of the federal government. Prior to 1962, in recognition of Congress's apparent desire for the federal bribery statues to have wide application, the federal judiciary interpreted the statutes and, indeed, the phrase "person acting for or on behalf of the United States" to have a broad jurisdictional reach.

*   *   *

We find the legislative history of § 201(a) inconsistent with the view that the words "person acting for or on behalf of the United States" were added simply to bring within the jurisdiction of the federal bribery laws those individuals tied to the federal government by direct contractual obligations.

Of particular relevance to the instant case is the House Judiciary Committee's citation of the Second Circuit's decision in *United States v. Levine*, 129 F.2d 745 (2d Cir. 1942), as an example of how the judiciary had in the past properly construed the federal bribery laws. *See* H.R. Rep. No. 748 at 17. The *Levine* decision involved the application of the 1909 bribery statute to a low-level official in a decentralized federal assistance program. The defendant in *Levine* worked for a locally-administered price stabilization program, the Market Administrator of the New York Metropolitan Milk Marketing Area, and was responsible for receiving milk handlers' market surplus claims, and checking them for accuracy. Levine solicited a bribe from one of the handlers within his jurisdiction in return for his promise to prevent investigations of the claims.

Although hired by a Market Administrator who, in turn, had been appointed by the Secretary of Agriculture, Levine himself was neither employed by the United States nor paid with federal funds. Nevertheless, Levine's duties were critical to the proper administration of the federally assisted New York Milk Marketing Area. Because claims for payment were not rechecked by anyone else, his duties resulted in expenditures from the federal treasury. After reviewing these facts, the Second Circuit concluded that, notwithstanding the absence of a direct contractual bond between the defendant and the United States, Levine's responsible position made him a "public official" for purposes of the federal bribery laws. 129 F.2d at 747. By explicitly endorsing the Second Circuit's analysis in *Levine*, the House Judiciary Committee strongly intimated that the phrase "acting for or on behalf of the United

States" covers something more than a direct contractual bond.

Congress's long-standing commitment to a broadly-drafted federal bribery statute, its expressed desire to continue that tradition with the 1962 revisions, its affirmative adoption of the language at issue in this case, and the House Report's endorsement of the Second Circuit's reasoning in *Levine*, combine to persuade us that Congress never intended § 201(a)'s open-ended definition of "public official" to be given the cramped reading proposed by petitioners. We agree with the Government that § 201(a) has been accurately characterized as a "comprehensive statute applicable to all persons performing activities for or on behalf of the United States," whatever the form of delegation of authority. To determine whether any particular individual falls within this category, the proper inquiry is not simply whether the person had signed a contract with the United States or agreed to serve as the Government's agent, but rather whether the person occupies a position of public trust with official federal responsibilities. Persons who hold such positions are public officials within the meaning of § 201 and liable for prosecution under the federal bribery statute.

B.

Given the structure of the Housing and Community Development Act program and petitioners' responsible positions as administrators of the subgrant, we have little difficulty concluding that these persons served as public officials for purposes of § 201(a). As executives of UNI, petitioners had operational responsibility for the administration of the HCDA grant program within the City of Peoria. In allocating the federal resources made available to the City through the HCDA grant program, petitioners were charged with abiding by federal guidelines, which dictated both where and how the federal funds could be distributed. By accepting the responsibility for distributing these federal fiscal resources, petitioners assumed the quintessentially official role of administering a social service program established by the United States Congress.

Lest there be any doubt that Congress intended § 201(a) to cover local officials like petitioners, one need only compare petitioners to the defendant in *Levine*, whose conviction the House Judiciary Committee explicitly endorsed. Both Levine and petitioners worked in decentralized federal assistance programs. Both Levine and petitioners effectively determined who would be the beneficiary of federal dollars, and both solicited bribes to influence their official decisions. Levine held a position of public trust with official federal responsibilities: to collect and investigate the accuracy of data submitted by milk producers in support of their claims for federal subsidies. Petitioners held a position of public trust with official federal responsibilities: allocating federal resources, pursuant to complex statutory and regulatory guidelines, in the form of residential rehabilitation contracts. Indeed, in certain respects, petitioners performed duties that were more clearly "official" and more obviously undertaken "for or on behalf of the United States" than the responsibilities of the defendant in *Levine*. Where Levine was paid through a levy imposed on local businesses participating in the marketing order, petitioners' salaries were completely funded by the HCDA grant. Where Levine simply compiled data that was submitted to the Department of Agriculture for eventual disbursement, petitioners personally bestowed the benefits of the HCDA program to residents of Peoria.

IV.

*   *   *

B.

By finding petitioners to be public officials within the meaning of § 201(a), we do not mean to suggest that the mere presence of some federal assistance brings a local organization and its employees within the jurisdiction of the federal bribery statute or even that all employees of local organizations responsible for administering federal grant programs are public officials within the meaning of § 201(a). To be a public official under § 201(a), an individual must possess some degree of official responsibility for carrying out a federal program or policy. Our opinion today is, therefore, fully consistent with *Krichman v. United States*, 256 U.S. 363 (1921), in which this Court ruled that a baggage porter, although employed by a federally controlled railroad, could not be said to have "acted for or on behalf of the United States" because the porter lacked any duties of an official character. Similarly, individuals who work for block grant recipients and business people who provide recipients with goods and services can not be said to be public officials under § 201(a) unless they assume some duties of an official nature.

We recognize that the manner in which the HCDA block grant program combines local administration with federal funding initially creates some confusion as to whether local authorities administering HCDA grants should be considered public officials under the federal bribery statute. However, when one examines the structure of the program and sees that the HCDA vests in local administrators like petitioners Hinton and Dixson the power to allocate federal fiscal resources for the purpose of achieving congressionally-established goals, the confusion evaporates and it becomes clear that these local officials hold precisely the sort of positions of national public trust that Congress intended to cover with the "acting for or on behalf of" language in the bribery statute. The federal government has a strong and legitimate interest in prosecuting petitioners for their misuse of government funds. As this Court has said in another, closely related context, grant funds to state and local governments "are as much in need of protection from [fraud] as any other federal money, and the statute does not make the extent of [grant monies'] safeguard dependent upon the bookkeeping devices used for their distribution." *United States ex rel. Marcus v. Hess*, 317 U.S. 537, 544 (1943) (holding that one who contracts with a local governmental unit to work on federally-funded projects can "cheat the United States" through the state intermediary).

*   *   *

Because we agree with the Seventh Circuit that petitioners were public officials under § 201(a), the judgment of the Court of Appeals is affirmed.

It is so ordered.

JUSTICE O'CONNOR, with whom JUSTICE BRENNAN, JUSTICE REHNQUIST, and JUSTICE STEVENS join, dissenting.

The rule of lenity demands that "ambiguity concerning the ambit of criminal statutes should be resolved in favor of lenity." *Rewis v. United States*, 401 U.S. 808, 812 (1971). The Court concludes that congressional intent to include persons like petitioners within the coverage of 18 U.S.C. § 201 is clear enough to make the rule of lenity inapplicable. The statutory language admits of the Court's reading, and the case for that reading would be strong, though perhaps not persuasive, if § 201 were a civil statute. I differ with the Court in that I find the evidence of congressional intent too weak to meet the higher standard for resolving facial ambiguity against a defendant when interpreting a criminal statute. In my view, the evidence of intent offered by the Court's opinion cannot carry the weight the Court places on it, and there is good reason to reject the Court's interpretation of the statute.

The language of § 201 and of its predecessors, as the Court's opinion points out, is intentionally broad. But that fact merely creates the interpretive problem — it does not resolve it. Congress intended to carry forward the pre-1962 bribery statute when it enacted § 201, and it understood the coverage of the bribery law to be broad. Moreover, the purpose of the statute was undoubtedly to proscribe bribery of all those who carry out a federal trust. To say that the statute is broadly aimed at all persons bearing a federal trust, however, is not to resolve the ambiguity over what constitutes a federal trust. Indeed, the statutory language — "acting for or on behalf of the United States" — is merely a formulation of the public trust idea, and the Court concedes that the statutory language can accommodate both petitioners' and respondent's views. The breadth of the language accordingly offers little help in defining the ambiguous coverage of the statute.

The legislative history likewise provides no significant support for the Court's reading of the statute. The critical statutory language has been a part of the federal bribery statute for more than one hundred years. Yet, as the Court's opinion indicates, Congress apparently has never specifically considered the statute's coverage of federal grant recipients. The legislative history is simply silent on the question to be answered in these cases.

*   *   *

Moreover, the *Levine* case itself does not suggest inclusion of such individuals. The individual involved in *Levine* was an employee of a person appointed by the Federal Government to carry out a federally defined regulatory task. As an employee of an agent of the United States, he was obviously acting for the United States. An employee of a grantee or subgrantee of the United States is in a quite different position.

*   *   *

Finally, I think it especially inappropriate to construe an ambiguous criminal statute unfavorably to the defendant when the construction that is adopted leaves the statute as unclear in its coverage as the bare statutory language. The rule of lenity rests on the notion that people are entitled to know in advance whether an act they contemplate taking violates a particular criminal statute, even if the act is obviously condemnable and even if it violates other criminal statutes. The "public trust" standard adopted by the Court provides no more guidance to employees of a grant recipient or its subgrantee than does the statutory language, "acting for or on behalf of the United States." There are hundreds of federal grant programs. Yet it is impossible to tell from the Court's analysis just what sorts of federal regulation make a grant recipient subject to the bribery statute. A criminal statute, after if not before it is judicially construed, should have a discernible meaning. I do not think the Court offers one.

I respectfully dissent.

Notes and Questions

1. *The Dixson standard.* The dissent asserted that "it is impossible to tell from the Court's analysis just what sorts of federal regulation make a grant recipient subject to the bribery statute." Does the Court's test for determining whether a person is a federal public official provide clear notice to potential defendants? Can you devise a clearer rule? Lower courts have found that a wide range of defendants are encompassed within the *Dixson* definition of "federal public official." *See, e.g., United States v. Hang,* 75 F.3d 1275, 1279–1280 (8th Cir. 1996) (a low-level corporate employee responsible for determining eligibility for federally-subsidized housing); *United States v. Strissel,* 920 F.2d 1162, 1165–1166 (4th Cir. 1990) (a city housing authority director); *United States v. Velazquez,* 847 F.2d 140, 142 (4th Cir. 1988) (a state deputy sheriff with authority over federal and state prisoners).

2. *The vote.* The Court in *Dixson* split five-to-four along lines rarely seen in criminal cases. Why did Justice Marshall, typically a pro-defendants' rights justice, write an opinion adopting a broad rule of criminal liability in this case? Conversely, why did Justices Rehnquist and O'Connor favor the defense position? Are there policy issues at work in the case that may have produced these alliances?

3. *The "thing of value."* As noted above, an element in any § 201 case is that the defendant offered to give or receive something "of value." How broadly should this term be interpreted? Suppose that, as part of a government "sting" operation, an undercover agent offers to give a public official stock certificates that the official believes are valuable but are actually worthless. Is this element met? *See United States v. Williams,* 705 F.2d 603, 622–623 (2d Cir. 1983).

4. *The "official act."* As noted above, § 201 criminalizes offering to give or agreeing to receive something of value for any of three purposes: (a) to influence a public official in an official act; (b) to influence a public official to commit a fraud on the United States; or (c) to induce a public official to act in violation of a lawful duty. When the first theory is used, the government must prove the "official act" as an element of the offense.

Courts broadly interpret this term, finding acts to be "official acts" even when the acts were not formally within the public official's duties. For example, in *United States v. Parker,* 133 F.3d 322 (5th Cir. 1998), the defendant was a Social Security Administration employee who helped people fraudulently obtain benefits in exchange for money. The court affirmed the defendant's conviction, finding that the payments were made in connection with official acts even though the defendant's official duties did not encompass the authority to grant or deny the benefits. The court stated that "the term 'official act' encompasses use of governmental computer systems to fraudulently create documents for the benefit of the [public official] for compensation, even when the [public official's] scope of authority does not formally encompass the act." *Id.* at 326.

In *United States v. Muntain,* 610 F.2d 964 (D.C. 1979), on the other hand, the court found that the government had failed to prove the "official act" element. Muntain worked for the United States Department of Housing and Urban Development ("HUD"), and had labor relations duties. Using the contacts with labor unions that he developed through his duties at HUD, Muntain schemed with insurance companies to sell group automobile insurance policies to labor unions. As part of the scheme, Muntain received free trips and other things of value from the insurance companies. Based on these facts, Muntain was convicted of receiving illegal gratuities. The court of appeals reversed the conviction. The court found that "[t]he government did not contend, and produced no evidence at trial, to suggest that automobile insurance as a benefit for labor unions fell within HUD's jurisdiction." *Id.* at 966. Thus, Muntain's scheme did not involve "any question, matter, cause, suit, proceeding or controversy which by law might have been brought before Muntain in his official capacity." *Id.* at 967.

Are the results in *Parker* and *Muntain* consistent? Why or why not?

Also consider the decision in *Valdes v. United States*, 475 F.3d 1319 (D.C. Cir. 2007) (en banc). In that case, an undercover federal agent paid a police detective to search for publicly available information in the police department's database. Sitting en banc, the D.C. Circuit reversed the detective's gratuities conviction. The court relied on *Muntain* and *United States v. Sun-Diamond Growers*, 526 U.S. 398 (1999) (discussed below), reasoning that "the government failed to show that the payments received by Valdes were for any 'decision or action on any question, matter, cause, suit, proceeding or controversy, which may at any time be pending, or which may by law be brought before any public official,' as required by 18 U.S.C. § 201." The mere release of information, the court found, did not qualify as an official act. *Valdes*, 475 F.3d at 1330. The dissent argued that the detective's actions indeed qualified as "official acts." *Id.* at 1333 (Garland, J., dissenting). Which side has the better of the argument? Why?

The concurring opinion noted that Valdes had originally been charged with bribery under § 201(b)(2)(A) but was convicted instead of the lesser-included offense of gratuities under § 201(c)(1)(B). *Id.* at 1330–1331 (Kavanaugh, J., concurring). Because the scope of official acts covered under the gratuities statute is narrower than that under the bribery statute, Valdes could have been convicted of bribery but not of gratuities. Review the language of the relevant statutes. In what sense is the scope of acts encompassed by the bribery statute broader than the scope of acts encompassed by the gratuities statute? Upon what theory might the court have affirmed a bribery conviction against Valdes?

PROBLEM

7-1. FLY International, Inc. (FLY) is a large publicly traded company that, among other things, does extensive government engineering contract work with the United States Department of Defense. Ken is the manager of the Runway Repair Branch of FLY.

The Department of Defense awarded Moon Flight, Inc. (Moon) a contract to build a runway edge-marker system for an Air Force runway repair program. Susan is the president of Moon.

Ken was introduced to Susan. He told her that he was the primary contact on the project, and that if any problem arose, she should contact Ken. Ken also told Susan that Ken would be the "eyes and ears" of the Air Force during the project. As a result, Susan believed that Ken was the engineer on the project and had the decision making authority concerning the project.

In reality, Ken did not have final decision making authority and his decisions could not bind the government. He did, however, advise government decision makers with respect to certain technical issues involved in the edge-marker contract. Ken's salary was not paid by Air Force, but by FLY with funds it received from the government in payment for government services.

A week after Susan met Ken, Ken contacted her and suggested that Moon could cut costs by using a different brand of materials than that specified in Moon's contract. Ken offered to approve the change if Susan would pay him one-half of the cost savings. The contract was in fact modified to allow for a different brand of materials. Instead of paying Ken one-half of the cost savings, however, Susan reported Ken's suggestion to Air Force officials.

Ken has been charged with soliciting a bribe under 18 U.S.C. § 201. *Ken has moved to dismiss the charge on the ground that he is not a federal public official. How should the court rule? Why?*

[3]   Mens Rea

Prior to the United States Supreme Court's decision in the next case, lower courts had long disagreed about the intent that the government must show in order to obtain a conviction for the illegal receipt of a gratuity. In resolving that dispute, the Court endeavored clearly to delineate the difficult distinction between the crimes of bribery and gratuity. As you read this case, consider whether the Court succeeded in that effort.

UNITED STATES v. SUN-DIAMOND GROWERS OF CALIFORNIA
526 U.S. 398 (1999)

JUSTICE SCALIA delivered the opinion of the Court.

Talmudic sages believed that judges who accepted bribes would be punished by eventually losing all knowledge of the divine law. The Federal Government, dealing with many public officials who are not judges, and with at least some judges for whom this sanction holds no terror, has constructed a framework of human laws and regulations defining various sorts of impermissible gifts, and punishing those who give or receive them with administrative sanctions, fines, and incarceration. One element of that framework is 18 U.S.C. § 201(c)(1)(A), the "illegal gratuity statute," which prohibits giving "anything of value" to a present, past, or future public official "for or because of any official act performed or to be performed by such public official." In this case, we consider whether conviction under the illegal gratuity statute requires any showing beyond the fact that a gratuity was given because of the recipient's official position.

I.

Respondent is a trade association that engaged in marketing and lobbying activities on behalf of its member cooperatives, which were owned by approximately 5,000 individual growers of raisins, figs, walnuts, prunes, and hazelnuts. Petitioner United States is represented by Independent Counsel Donald Smaltz, who, as a consequence of his investigation of former Secretary of Agriculture Michael Espy, charged respondent with, *inter alia*, making illegal gifts to Espy in violation of § 201(c)(1)(A). . . .

Count One of the indictment charged Sun-Diamond with giving Espy approximately $5,900 in illegal gratuities: tickets to the 1993 U.S. Open Tennis

Tournament (worth $2,295), luggage ($2,427), meals ($665), and a framed print and crystal bowl ($524). The indictment alluded to two matters in which respondent had an interest in favorable treatment from the Secretary at the time it bestowed the gratuities. First, respondent's member cooperatives participated in the Market Promotion Plan (MPP), a grant program administered by the Department of Agriculture to promote the sale of U.S. farm commodities in foreign countries. The cooperatives belonged to trade organizations, such as the California Prune Board and the Raisin Administrative Committee, which submitted overseas marketing plans for their respective commodities. If their plans were approved by the Secretary of Agriculture, the trade organizations received funds to be used in defraying the foreign marketing expenses of their constituents. Each of respondent's member cooperatives was the largest member of its respective trade organization, and each received significant MPP funding. Respondent was understandably concerned, then, when Congress in 1993 instructed the Secretary to promulgate regulations giving small-sized entities preference in obtaining MPP funds. If the Secretary did not deem respondent's member cooperatives to be small-sized entities, there was a good chance they would no longer receive MPP grants. Thus, respondent had an interest in persuading the Secretary to adopt a regulatory definition of "small-sized entity" that would include its member cooperatives.

Second, respondent had an interest in the Federal Government's regulation of methyl bromide, a low-cost pesticide used by many individual growers in respondent's member cooperatives. In 1992, the Environmental Protection Agency announced plans to promulgate a rule to phase out the use of methyl bromide in the United States. The indictment alleged that respondent sought the Department of Agriculture's assistance in persuading the EPA to abandon its proposed rule altogether, or at least to mitigate its impact. In the latter event, respondent wanted the Department to fund research efforts to develop reliable alternatives to methyl bromide.

Although describing these two matters before the Secretary in which respondent had an interest, the indictment did not allege a specific connection between either of them — or between any other action of the Secretary — and the gratuities conferred. The District Court denied respondent's motion to dismiss Count One because of this omission. 941 F. Supp. 1262 (D.D.C. 1996). The court stated:

> [T]o sustain a charge under the gratuity statute, it is not necessary for the indictment to allege a direct nexus between the value conferred to Secretary Espy by Sun-Diamond and an official act performed or to be performed by Secretary Espy. It is sufficient for the indictment to allege that Sun-Diamond provided things of value to Secretary Espy because of his position.

Id. at 1265.

At trial, the District Court instructed the jury along these same lines. It read § 201(c)(1)(A) to the jury twice, but then placed an expansive gloss on that statutory language, saying, among other things, that "[i]t is sufficient if Sun-Diamond provided Espy with unauthorized compensation simply because he held public office," and that "[t]he government need not prove that the alleged gratuity was linked to a specific or identifiable official act or any act at all." The jury convicted respondent on, *inter alia*, Count One (the only subject of this appeal), and the District Court sentenced respondent on this count to pay a fine of $400,000. . . . [The Court of Appeals reversed, and the Supreme Court granted certiorari.]

II.

Initially, it will be helpful to place § 201(c)(1)(A) within the context of the statutory scheme. Subsection (a) of § 201 sets forth definitions applicable to the section — including a definition of "official act," § 201(a)(3). Subsections (b) and (c) then set forth, respectively, two separate crimes — or two pairs of crimes, if one counts the giving and receiving of unlawful gifts as separate crimes — with two different sets of elements and authorized punishments. The first crime, described in § 201(b)(1) as to the giver, and § 201(b)(2) as to the recipient, is bribery, which requires a showing that something of value was corruptly given, offered, or promised to a public official (as to the giver) or corruptly demanded, sought, received, accepted, or agreed to be received or accepted by a public official (as to the recipient) with intent, *inter alia*, "to influence any official act" (giver) or in return for "being influenced in the performance of any official act" (recipient). The second crime, defined in § 201(c)(1)(A) as to the giver, and in § 201(c)(1)(B) as to the recipient, is illegal gratuity, which requires a showing that something of value was given, offered, or promised to a public official (as to the giver), or demanded, sought, received, accepted, or agreed to be received or accepted by a public official (as to the recipient), "for or because of any official act performed or to be performed by such public official."

The distinguishing feature of each crime is its intent element. Bribery requires intent "to influence" an official act or "to be influenced" in an official act, while illegal gratuity requires only that the gratuity be given or accepted "for or because of" an official act. In other words, for bribery there must be a *quid pro quo* — a specific intent to give or receive something of value *in exchange* for an official act. An illegal gratuity, on the other hand, may constitute merely a reward for some future act that the public official will take (and may already have determined to take), or for a past act that he has already taken. The punishments prescribed for the two offenses reflect their relative seriousness: Bribery may be punished by up to 15 years' imprisonment, a fine of $250,000 ($500,000 for organizations) or triple the value of the bribe, whichever is greater, and disqualification from holding government office. Violation of the illegal gratuity statute, on the other hand, may be punished by up to two years' imprisonment and a fine of $250,000 ($500,000 for organizations).

The District Court's instructions in this case, in differentiating between a bribe and an illegal gratuity, correctly noted that only a bribe requires proof of a *quid pro quo*. The point in controversy here is that the instructions went on to suggest that § 201(c)(1)(A), unlike the bribery statute, did not require any connection between respondent's intent and a specific official act. It would be satisfied, according to the instructions, merely by a showing that respondent gave Secretary Espy a gratuity because of his official position — perhaps, for example, to build a reservoir of goodwill that might ultimately affect one or more of a multitude of unspecified acts, now and in the future. The United States, represented by the Independent Counsel, and the Solicitor General as *amicus curiae*, contend that this instruction was correct. The Independent Counsel asserts that "section 201(c)(1)(A) reaches any effort to buy favor or generalized goodwill from an official who either has been, is, or may at some unknown, unspecified later time, be *in a position to act* favorably to the giver's interests." The Solicitor General contends that § 201(c)(1)(A) requires only a showing that a "gift was motivated, at least in part, by the recipient's *capacity to exercise governmental power or influence* in the donor's favor" without necessarily showing that it was connected to a particular official act.

In our view, this interpretation does not fit comfortably with the statutory text, which prohibits only gratuities given or received "for or because of *any official act* performed or to be performed" (emphasis added). It seems to us that this means "for or because of some particular official act of whatever identity" — just as the question "Do you like any composer?" normally means "Do you like some particular composer?" It is linguistically possible, of course, for the phrase to mean "for or because of official acts in general, without specification as to which one" — just as the question "Do you like any composer?" could mean "Do you like all composers, no matter what their names or music?" But the former seems to us the more natural meaning, especially given the complex structure of the provision before us here. Why go through the trouble of requiring that the gift be made "for or because of any official act performed or to be performed by such public official," and then defining "official act" (in § 201(a)(3)) to mean "any decision or action on any question, matter, cause, suit, proceeding or controversy, which may at any time be pending, or which may by law be brought before any public official, in such official's official capacity," when, if the Government's interpretation were correct, it would have sufficed to say "for or because of such official's ability to favor the donor in executing the functions of his office"? The insistence upon an "official act," carefully defined, seems pregnant with the requirement that some particular official act be identified and proved.

Besides thinking that this is the more natural meaning of § 201(c)(1)(A), we are inclined to believe it correct because of the peculiar results that the Government's alternative reading would produce. It would criminalize, for example, token gifts to the President based on his official position and not linked to any identifiable act — such as the replica jerseys given by championship sports teams each year during ceremonial White House visits. Similarly, it would criminalize a high school principal's gift of a school baseball cap to the Secretary of Education, by reason of his office, on the occasion of the latter's visit to the school. That these examples are not fanciful is demonstrated by the fact that counsel for the United States maintained at oral argument that a group of farmers would violate § 201(c)(1)(A) by providing a complimentary lunch for the Secretary of Agriculture in conjunction with his speech to the farmers concerning various matters of USDA policy — so long as the Secretary had before him, or had in prospect, matters affecting the farmers. Of course the Secretary of Agriculture *always* has before him or in prospect matters that affect farmers, just as the President always has before him or in prospect matters that affect college and professional sports, and the Secretary of Education matters that affect high schools.

It might be said in reply to this that the more narrow interpretation of the statute can also produce some peculiar results. In fact, in the above-given examples, the gifts could easily be regarded as having been conferred, not only because of the official's position as President or Secretary, but also (and perhaps principally) "for or because of" the official acts of receiving the sports teams at the White House, visiting the high school, and speaking to the farmers about USDA policy, respectively. The answer to this objection is that those actions — while they are assuredly "official acts" in some sense — are not "official acts" within the meaning of the statute, which, as we have noted, defines "official act" to mean "any decision or action on any question, matter, cause, suit, proceeding or controversy, which may at any time be pending, or which may by law be brought before any public official, in such official's official capacity, or in such official's place of trust or profit." 18 U.S.C. § 201(a)(3). Thus, when the violation is linked to a particular "official act," it is possible to eliminate the absurdities *through the definition of that term.* When, however, no particular "official act" need be identified, and the giving of gifts by reason of the recipient's mere tenure in office constitutes a violation, nothing but the Government's discretion prevents the foregoing examples from being prosecuted.

The Government insists that its interpretation is the only one that gives effect to all of the statutory language. Specifically, it claims that the "official position" construction is the only way to give effect to § 201(c)(1)(A)'s forward-looking prohibition on gratuities to persons who have been selected to be public officials but have not yet taken office. Because, it contends, such individuals would not know of specific matters that would come before them, the only way to give this provision effect is to interpret "official act" to mean "official position." But we have no trouble envisioning the application of § 201(c)(1)(A) to a selectee for federal office under the more narrow interpretation. If, for instance, a large computer company that has planned to merge with another large computer company makes a gift to a person who has been chosen to be Assistant Attorney General for the Antitrust Division of the Department of Justice and who has publicly indicated his approval of the merger, it would be quite possible for a jury to find that the gift was made "for or because of" the person's anticipated decision, once he is in office, not to challenge the merger. The uncertainty of future action seems to us, in principle, no more an impediment to prosecution of a selectee with respect to some future official act than it is to prosecution of an officeholder with respect to some future official act.

Our refusal to read § 201(c)(1)(A) as a prohibition of gifts given by reason of the donee's office is supported by the fact that when Congress has wanted to adopt such a broadly prophylactic criminal prohibition upon gift giving, it has done so in a more precise and more administrable fashion. For example, another provision of Chapter 11 of Title 18, the chapter entitled "Bribery, Graft, and Conflicts of Interest," criminalizes the giving or receiving of any "supplementation" of an Executive official's salary, without regard to the purpose of the payment. Other provisions of the same chapter make it a crime for a bank employee to give a bank examiner, and for a bank examiner to receive from a bank employee, "any loan or gratuity," again without regard to the purpose for which it is given. A provision of the Labor Management Relations Act makes it a felony for an employer to give to a union representative, and for a union representative to receive from an employer, anything of value. With clearly framed and easily administrable provisions such as these on the books imposing gift-giving and gift-receiving prohibitions specifically based upon the holding of office, it seems to us most implausible that Congress intended the language of the gratuity statute — "for or because of any official act performed or to be performed" — to pertain to the office rather than (as the language more naturally suggests) to *particular* official acts.

* * *

More important for present purposes, however, this regulation, and the numerous other regulations and statutes littering this field, demonstrate that this is an area where precisely targeted prohibitions are commonplace, and where more general prohibitions have been qualified by numerous exceptions. Given that reality, a statute in this field that can linguistically be interpreted to be either a meat axe or a scalpel should reasonably be taken to be the latter. Absent a text that clearly requires it, we ought not expand this one piece of the regulatory puzzle so dramatically as to make many other pieces misfits. As discussed earlier, not only does the text here not require that result; its more natural reading forbids it.

III.

* * *

We hold that, in order to establish a violation of 18 U.S.C. § 201(c)(1)(A), the Government must prove a link between a thing of value conferred upon a public official and a specific "official act" for or because of which it was given. Our decision today casts doubt upon the lower courts' resolution of respondent's challenge to the sufficiency of the indictment on Count One — an issue on which certiorari was neither sought nor granted. We leave it to the District Court to determine whether that issue should be reopened on remand.

It is so ordered.

Notes and Questions

1. *The difference between bribery and gratuity.* In *Sun-Diamond*, the government argued that the gratuities statute "requires only a showing that a 'gift was motivated, at least in part, by the recipient's *capacity to exercise governmental power or influence* in the donor's favor' without necessarily showing that it was connected to a particular official act." Under this reading, the crime of offering or receiving a gratuity would be much broader than the crime of offering or receiving a bribe. The Court, however, rejected the government's approach and offered its own distinction between the crimes of bribery and gratuity. Is the distinction as clear as the Court indicates? If a client asked you for an explanation of the law, how would you explain the difference between the two crimes?

2. *Double jeopardy.* Could a defendant be charged, convicted, and punished under both the bribery and gratuity statutes? Some courts have concluded that gratuity is a lesser-included offense of bribery. *See, e.g., United States v. Alfisi*, 308 F.3d 144, 152 (2d Cir. 2002). Thus, if the government were to charge both bribery and gratuity, the jury would determine whether the defendant had committed a crime and, if so, whether it amounted to bribery or gratuity. How would the jury make this distinction?

3. *Corrupt intent.* Bribery under § 201(b)(1) requires proof that the defendant acted "corruptly." As the Court in *Sun-Diamond* made clear, proof of corrupt intent for the crime of bribery rests on the party's understanding that the payment was offered for a *quid pro quo*. In that light, has bribery been committed when the public official — unbeknownst to the bribing party — has *already* performed the official act at the time the bribe is offered or received? *See United States v. Arroyo*, 581 F.2d 649, 655 (7th Cir. 1978).

How far does the definition of corrupt intent extend? If one is threatened with harm, and makes a pay-off to a federal official to avoid the harm, has one acted corruptly? This issue arose in *Alfisi*, 308 F.3d 144. Alfisi was employed by a produce wholesaler, and made payments to a federal food inspector in exchange for favorable treatment by the inspector. At trial, the defendant argued that the inspector had extorted him, and that the defendant made the payments so that the inspector would perform the inspector's duties in a lawful manner. On appeal, the defendant asserted that the jury should have been required to find an intent to induce a *quid pro quo* beyond performance of the public official's lawful duties. The majority rejected the argument, and affirmed the conviction. The dissent argued that the bribery statute should not apply in such circumstances. Which result seems correct to you? Why?

4. *The harm.* The harm from offering or receiving a bribe seems clear enough; the act calls into question the integrity of the official's performance of public duties. But where is the harm from offering or receiving a gratuity? Note that, in the mail/wire fraud context, some courts have opined that the mere receipt of a gratuity — as opposed to a bribe — might not qualify as deprivation of "honest services" by a public official. *See United States v. Brumley*, 116 F.3d 728, 734–736 (1st Cir. 1997). And under the statutory scheme, gratuities are punished much less severely than bribery — two years as opposed to fifteen years in prison. Is offering or receiving a gratuity something that properly rises to the level of a criminal offense? Why or why not?

Problems

7-2. Neder is a case manager for the Internal Revenue Service (IRS). This position requires Neder to supervise a group of revenue agents assigned to audit certain corporate income tax returns filed by Gulf Coast Oil (Gulf). Neder's responsibilities include developing and giving final approval of the audit plan, which is a detailed outline of the specific procedures to be utilized during the course of a particular audit. During the development of an audit plan, Neder had the power to make all final decisions regarding the scope and depth of the areas of corporate taxation that were to be reviewed in the audit. Neder has been supervising the audits of Gulf's tax returns for more than 10 years.

Evidence presented to a federal grand jury demonstrates the following facts. In January of last year, Neder spent four days at a country club with the Manager of Federal Tax Compliance for Gulf. Neder's entire bill was paid for by the Manager. In August and September, Neder and his wife spent four days on vacation with Gulf's Vice-President of Tax Administration. All expenses were paid for by the Vice-President. In December, again Neder spent three days on vacation in the company of both the Manager and Vice-President. Once again, the Gulf employees paid all of Neder's expenses.

You are the Assistant United States Attorney in charge of the investigation of Neder. What charges, if any, would ask the grand jury to bring against Neder under 18 U.S.C. § 201? Why?

7-3. The City of Metropolis created the Metropolitan Housing Authority ("the Authority") to develop and operate public housing units for eligible families. The Authority received millions of dollars annually from the United States Department of Housing and Urban Development ("HUD") to assist it in providing housing. Among the HUD funds received by the Authority were "Section 8" funds, which were used by the Authority to pay the rent of qualified families who lived outside of Authority owned public housing. The Authority made rent payments for low income families who became clients of the Authority and resided in private housing.

The River Development Corp. ("RDC") is a non-profit corporation created at the direction of the Authority to provide and develop affordable housing opportunities for low income persons. RDC was created as an instrumentality of the Authority for the purpose of implementing the housing plans and programs of the Authority. RDC is an independent corporation that is not under city control.

RDC owned and operated several residential properties. RDC received Section 8 funds from the Authority for eligible families who resided in RDC properties. In each of the last two calendar years, RDC received more than $350,000 in HUD funds. All of these funds were paid by the Authority to RDC to offset the rent payments of eligible low income residents in RDC properties.

In January of last year, defendant Evers became the Executive Director of RDC. Evers was essentially the general manager of the RDC properties. Beginning in February, Evers awarded three RDC contracts to Construction Corp., Inc.; the first contract was awarded in February, the second in March, and the third in May. Construction Corp. was controlled by Evers' friend, Chadwick. In April, Chadwick had Construction Corp. post a $50,000 letter of credit as collateral to allow Evers to take out a loan. The letter was necessary because of Evers' low credit rating. Evers repaid the loan the following month, and the letter of credit was never used. In June, Chadwick had Construction Corp. pay $125,000 to one of Evers' creditors. Evers repaid the $125,000 two months later, with a market rate of interest.

The government later initiated a grand jury investigation. Chadwick agreed to testify against Evers in exchange for immunity. The government has charged Evers with (1) bribery under § 201(b)(2)(A) for the $50,000 letter of credit, (2) bribery under § 201(b)(2)(A) for the $125,000 payment, (3) gratuities under § 201(c)(1)(B) for the $50,000 letter of credit, and (4) gratuities under § 201(c)(1)(B) for the $125,000 payment. Evers has moved to dismiss all the charges.

Should the court grant the motion as to any or all of the charges? Why or why not?

[C]   FEDERAL PROGRAM BRIBERY — § 666

[1]   Statutory Elements

Section 666 criminalizes bribery in connection with federal programs. Unlike § 201, § 666 is not limited to cases involving federal public officials, and encompasses bribery involving a wide range of private and governmental entities. Prosecutors have become increasingly aggressive in using § 666, particularly in cases involved state and local corruption.

In a prosecution under § 666(a)(1)–(2) against the *bribed party*, the government must prove that:

(1) The defendant solicited or received a thing of value;

(2) The defendant was an agent of a private organization or of a state, local, or tribal government or agency that received more than $10,000 a year in federal benefits;

(3) The defendant solicited or received the thing of value in connection with business of the entity valued at $5,000 or more; and

(4) The defendant acted corruptly.

In a prosecution under § 666(a)(1)–(2) against the *bribing party*, the government must prove that:

(1) The defendant offered or gave a thing of value;

(2) The offeree was an agent of a private organization or of a state, local, or tribal government or agency that received more than $10,000 a year in federal benefits;

(3) The defendant offered or gave the thing of value in connection with business of the entity valued at $5,000 or more; and

(4) The defendant acted corruptly.

The statute provides that the defendant may be punished by a fine, by imprisonment of not more than 10 years, or both.

[2]   The Reach of the Statute

In a pair of decisions, the United States Supreme Court has rejected attempts to narrow the reach of § 666. In *Salinas v. United States*, 522 U.S. 52 (1997), the defendant argued that his conviction under § 666 could not stand because the bribes he received did not involve the misuse or misappropriation of federal funds. Salinas was a sheriff's deputy at a county prison that received over $10,000 a year in federal money in exchange for housing federal prisoners.[a] A prisoner paid bribes to Salinas, who in return arranged "contact visits" with the prisoner's girlfriend. The Court affirmed the conviction under § 666, holding that the government is not required to prove that the bribes led to the misappropriation or misuse of federal funds. In *Salinas*, the Court did not answer the question whether § 666 "requires some other kind of connection between a bribe and the expenditure of federal funds." The circuit courts split on this issue, and the Supreme Court resolved the split in the case that follows.

SABRI v. UNITED STATES
541 U.S. 600 (2004)

JUSTICE SOUTER delivered the opinion of the Court.

The question is whether 18 U.S.C. § 666(a)(2), proscribing bribery of state, local, and tribal officials of entities that receive at least $10,000 in federal funds, is a valid exercise of congressional authority under Article I of the Constitution. We hold that it is.

---

[a] Another aspect of this case is discussed in Chapter 14, RICO, *infra*.

I.

Petitioner Basim Omar Sabri is a real estate developer who proposed to build a hotel and retail structure in the city of Minneapolis. Sabri lacked confidence, however, in his ability to adapt to the lawful administration of licensing and zoning laws, and offered three separate bribes to a city councilman, Brian Herron, according to the grand jury indictment that gave rise to this case. At the time the bribes were allegedly offered (between July 2, 2001, and July 17, 2001), Herron served as a member of the Board of Commissioners of the Minneapolis Community Development Agency (MCDA), a public body created by the city council to fund housing and economic development within the city.

Count 1 of the indictment charged Sabri with offering a $5,000 kickback for obtaining various regulatory approvals, and according to Count 2, Sabri offered Herron a $10,000 bribe to set up and attend a meeting with owners of land near the site Sabri had in mind, at which Herron would threaten to use the city's eminent domain authority to seize their property if they were troublesome to Sabri. Count 3 alleged that Sabri offered Herron a commission of 10% on some $800,000 in community economic development grants that Sabri sought from the city, the MCDA, and other sources. . . .

Before trial, Sabri moved to dismiss the indictment on the ground that § 666(a)(2) is unconstitutional on its face for failure to require proof of a connection between the federal funds and the alleged bribe, as an element of liability. The Government responded that "even if an additional nexus between the bribery conduct and the federal funds is required, the evidence in this case will easily meet such a standard" because Sabri's alleged actions related to federal dollars. Although Sabri did not contradict this factual claim, the District Court agreed with him that the law was facially invalid. A divided panel of the Eighth Circuit reversed, holding that there was nothing fatal in the absence of an express requirement to prove some connection between a given bribe and federally pedigreed dollars, and that the statute was constitutional under the Necessary and Proper Clause in serving the objects of the congressional spending power. Judge Bye dissented out of concern about the implications of the law for dual sovereignty. We granted certiorari to resolve a split among the Courts of Appeals over the need to require connection between forbidden conduct and federal funds. We now affirm.

II.

Sabri raises what he calls a facial challenge to § 666(a)(2): the law can never be applied constitutionally because it fails to require proof of any connection between a bribe or kickback and some federal money. It is fatal, as he sees it, that the statute does not make the link an element of the crime, to be charged in the indictment and demonstrated beyond a reasonable doubt. Thus, Sabri claims his attack meets the demanding standard set out in *United States v. Salerno*, 481 U.S. 739, 745 (1987), since he says no prosecution can satisfy the Constitution under this statute, owing to its failure to require proof that its particular application falls within Congress's jurisdiction to legislate.

We can readily dispose of this position that, to qualify as a valid exercise of Article I power, the statute must require proof of connection with federal money as an element of the offense. We simply do not presume the unconstitutionality of federal criminal statutes lacking explicit provision of a jurisdictional hook, and there is no occasion even to consider the need for such a requirement where there is no reason to suspect that enforcement of a criminal statute would extend beyond a legitimate interest cognizable under Article I, § 8.

Congress has authority under the Spending Clause to appropriate federal monies to promote the general welfare, Art. I, § 8, cl. 1, and it has corresponding authority under the Necessary and Proper Clause, Art. I, § 8, cl. 18, to see to it that taxpayer dollars appropriated under that power are in fact spent for the general welfare, and not frittered away in graft or on projects undermined when funds are siphoned off or corrupt public officers are derelict about demanding value for dollars. Congress does not have to sit by and accept the risk of operations thwarted by local and state improbity. Section 666(a)(2) addresses the problem at the sources of bribes, by rational means, to safeguard the integrity of the state, local, and tribal recipients of federal dollars.

It is true, just as Sabri says, that not every bribe or kickback offered or paid to agents of governments covered by § 666(b) will be traceably skimmed from specific federal payments, or show up in the guise of a *quid pro quo* for some dereliction in spending a federal grant. *Cf. Salinas v. United States*, 522 U.S. 52, 56–57 (1997) (the "expansive, unqualified" language of the statute "does not support the interpretation that federal funds must be affected to violate § 666(a)(1)(B)"). But this possibility portends no enforcement beyond the scope of federal interest, for the reason that corruption does not have to be that limited to affect the federal interest. Money is fungible, bribed officials are untrustworthy stewards of federal funds, and corrupt contractors do not deliver dollar-for-dollar value. Liquidity is not a financial term for nothing; money can be drained off here because a federal grant is pouring in there. And officials are not any the less threatening to the objects behind federal spending just because they may accept general retainers. It is certainly enough that the statutes condition the offense on a threshold amount of federal dollars defining the federal interest, such as that provided here, and on a bribe that goes well beyond liquor and cigars.

For those of us who accept help from legislative history, it is worth noting that the legislative record confirms that § 666(a)(2) is an instance of necessary and proper legislation. The design was generally to "protect the integrity of the vast sums of money distributed through Federal programs from theft, fraud, and undue influence by bribery," *see* S. Rep. No. 98-225, p. 370 (1983), in contrast to prior federal law affording only two limited opportunities to prosecute such threats to the federal interest: 18 U.S.C. § 641, the federal theft statute, and § 201, the federal bribery law. Those laws had proven inadequate to the task. The former went only to outright theft of unadulterated federal funds, and prior to this Court's opinion in *Dixson v. United States*, 465 U.S. 482 (1984), which came after passage of § 666, the bribery statute had been interpreted by lower courts to bar prosecution of bribes directed at state and local officials. Thus we said that § 666 "was designed to extend federal bribery prohibitions to bribes offered to state and local officials employed by agencies receiving federal funds," *Salina*, 522 U.S. at 58, thereby filling the regulatory gaps. Congress's decision to enact § 666 only after other legislation had failed to protect federal interests is further indication that it was acting within the ambit of the Necessary and Proper Clause.

Petitioner presses two more particular arguments against the constitutionality of § 666(a)(2), neither of which helps him. First, he says that § 666 is all of a piece with the legislation that a majority of this Court held to exceed Congress's authority under the Commerce Clause in *United States v. Lopez*, 514 U.S. 549 (1995), and *United States v. Morrison*, 529 U.S. 598 (2000). But these precedents do not control here. In *Lopez* and *Morrison*, the Court struck down federal statutes regulating gun possession near schools and gender-motivated violence, respectively, because it found the effects of those activities on interstate commerce insufficiently robust. The Court emphasized the noneconomic nature of the regulated conduct, commenting on the law at issue in *Lopez*, for example, "that by its terms [it] has nothing to do with 'commerce' or any sort of economic enterprise, however broadly one might define those terms." 514 U.S. at 561. The Court rejected the Government's contentions that the gun law was valid Commerce Clause legislation because guns near schools ultimately bore on social prosperity and productivity, reasoning that on that logic, Commerce Clause authority would effectively know no limit. *Cf. Morrison*, 529 U.S. at 615–616 (rejecting comparable congressional justification for Violence Against Women Act of 1994). In order to uphold the legislation, the Court concluded, it would be necessary "to pile inference upon inference in a manner that would bid fair to convert congressional authority under the Commerce Clause to a general police power of the sort retained by the States." *Lopez*, 514 U.S. at 567.

No piling is needed here to show that Congress was within its prerogative to protect spending objects from the menace of local administrators on the take. The power to keep a watchful eye on expenditures and on the reliability of those who use public money is bound up with congressional authority to spend in the first place, and Sabri would be hard pressed to claim, in the words of the *Lopez* Court, that § 666(a)(2) "has nothing to do with" the congressional spending power. *Id.* at 561.

Sabri next argues that § 666(a)(2) amounts to an unduly coercive, and impermissibly sweeping, condition on the grant of federal funds as judged under the criterion applied in *South Dakota v. Dole*, 483 U.S. 203 (1987). This is not so. Section 666(a)(2) is authority to bring federal power to bear directly on individuals who convert public spending into unearned private gain, not a means for bringing federal economic might to bear on a State's own choices of public policy.[*]

* * *

IV.

We remand for proceedings consistent with this opinion. The judgment of the Court of Appeals for the Eighth Circuit is

Affirmed.

JUSTICE KENNEDY, with whom JUSTICE SCALIA joins, concurring in part. (Omitted.)

JUSTICE THOMAS, concurring in the judgment (Omitted).

---

[*] In enacting § 666, Congress addressed a legitimate federal concern by licensing federal prosecution in an area historically of state concern. In upholding the constitutionality of the law, we mean to express no view as to its soundness as a policy matter.

NOTES AND QUESTIONS

1. *Scope of § 666.* What exactly is the scope of § 666? In light of the Court's holding in *Dixson*, does § 666 give the government any power that it does not have under § 201? If so, what?

2. *Federalism.* Many commentators believed that, after *Lopez*, 514 U.S. 549, the Court would strike down federal criminal statutes that intruded into matters historically reserved to the states. Why did the reasoning in *Lopez* fail to control the outcome in *Sabri*? In a footnote in *Sabri*, the Court stated, "[i]n enacting § 666, Congress addressed a legitimate federal concern by licensing federal prosecution in an area historically of state concern. In upholding the constitutionality of the law, we mean to express no view as to its soundness as a policy matter." Does § 666 rest on sound policy? Why or why not?

3. *The meaning of "benefits."* Section 666 requires that the "organization, government, or agency receive, in any one year period, benefits in excess of $10,000 under a Federal program involving a grant, contract, subsidy, loan, guarantee, insurance, or other form of Federal assistance." In *Fischer v. United States*, 529 U.S. 667 (2000), the Supreme Court considered whether a health care provider participating in the Medicare program receives "benefits" under § 666. The defendant in that case was convicted of paying bribes to an agent of a local hospital authority. Although the authority received Medicare payments of more than $10,000 a year, the defense asserted that these payments did not constitute "benefits." According to this argument, the only "benefits" were received by the covered patients.

The Court rejected the defendant's argument, concluding that "the payments are made not simply to reimburse for treatment of qualifying patients but to assist the hospital in making available and maintaining a certain level and quality of medical care, all in the interest of both the hospital and the greater community." *Id.* at 679–680. The Court continued:

> To determine whether an organization participating in a federal assistance program receives "benefits," an examination must be undertaken of the program's structure, operation, and purpose. The inquiry should examine the conditions under which the organization receives the federal payments. The answer could depend, as it does here, on whether the recipient's own operations are one of the reasons for maintaining the program. Health care organizations participating in the Medicare program satisfy this standard.

Id. at 681.

Justices Thomas and Scalia dissented, concluding that "the only persons who receive 'benefits' under Medicare are the individual elderly and disabled Medicare patients, not the medical providers who serve them." *Id.* at 68 (Thomas, J., dissenting). The dissent characterized the majority's approach to defining "benefits" as "unpersuasive and boundless," and as violating the rule of lenity. *Id.* at 686, 691.

Which side has the better of the argument? Under the majority's approach, what are the limits of the definition of "benefits"? Take a corner grocery store that receives food stamp payments of more than $10,000 a year. To receive the payments, the store is subject to federal regulations concerning the store's inventory and business integrity. Would these payments qualify as "benefits" under the statute? *See id.* at 691–692.

4. *Does § 666 encompass gratuities?* Section 666 requires proof that the defendant acted "corruptly." Some courts have interpreted this language to require proof of a *quid pro quo. See United States v. Jennings*, 160 F.3d 1006, 1015 n.4 (4th Cir. 1998) (concluding that gratuities are not prohibited by § 666, but declining to decide the issue). One federal circuit court has held, however, that § 666 does encompass gratuities. *United States v. Bonito*, 57 F.3d 167, 171 (2d Cir. 1995). Which is the correct result? Why?

5. *Connection with an official act.* In *Sun-Diamond Growers*, the Supreme Court held that the benefit to the public official must be in connection with a specific official act. 526 U.S. 398. Does the same requirement apply to cases brought under § 666 based on a bribery theory? The court in *United States v. Ganim*, 510 F.3d 134, 134 (2d Cir. 2007), held not. The court reasoned that the language in the gratuities statute — referring to giving benefits to a public official "for or because of *any official act* performed or to be performed," — compelled the outcome in *Sun-Diamond*. By contrast, the court reasoned, the elements of § 666 bribery are met so long as the official accepted the benefit in exchange for a promise to perform official acts for the giver; the government need not specify the official acts.

6. *The meaning of "misapplies."* Section 666 criminalizes, among other acts, "intentionally misapply[ing]" property valued at $5,000 or more. In *United States v. Thompson*, 484 F.3d 877 (7th Cir. 2007), a state official arranged to have a state contract awarded to a politically favored travel agency. The defendant was charged under § 666 under the theory that she misapplied the property by steering the contract away from another bidder, who would have been awarded the contract had the defendant not interfered in the process. The benefit to the defendant, according to the government, was the raise she received that reflected, in part, her actions concerning the contract. In a decision written by Judge Easterbrook, the Seventh Circuit reversed the conviction. The court reasoned:

> Section 666 is captioned "Theft or bribery concerning programs receiving Federal funds," and the Supreme Court refers to it as an anti-bribery rule. Neither Thompson nor anyone else in state government was accused of taking a bribe or receiving a kickback. A statute's caption does not override its text, but the word "misapplies" is not a defined term. We could read that word broadly, so that it means any disbursement that would not have occurred had all state laws been enforced without any political considerations. Or we could read it narrowly, so that it means a disbursement in exchange for services not rendered (as with ghost workers), or to suppliers that would not have received any contract but for bribes, or for services that were overpriced (to cover the cost of baksheesh), or for shoddy goods at the price prevailing for high-quality goods. All of these conditions were satisfied in [earlier] cases. . . . None is satisfied here.

> Faced with a choice between a broad reading that turns all (or a goodly fraction of) state-law errors or political considerations in state procurement into federal crimes, and a narrow reading that limits § 666 to theft, extortion, bribery, and similarly corrupt acts, a court properly uses the statute's caption for guidance. That plus the Rule of Lenity, which insists that ambiguity in criminal legislation be read against the prosecutor, lest

the judiciary create, in common-law fashion, offenses that have never received legislative approbation, and about which adequate notice has not been given to those who might be ensnared.

Id. at 881. Do you agree that the government's theory in this case was flawed? Why or why not?

7. *Potential for abuse*? As the materials in this chapter show, the federal bribery statues have been broadly interpreted by both courts and prosecutors. Are there dangers in such interpretations? Do the broad readings open the door for politically motivated prosecutions? In one high profile case, the government prosecuted former Alabama governor Don Siegelman on various political corruption charges, including bribery. Many observers, including members of both political parties, questioned whether the case may have been politically motivated. *See* Editorial, *A Case of Politics*, N.Y. Times, June 16, 2008, at A18. Commentators have suggested that "the conversion of traditionally accepted political practices into aggressively interpreted criminal law violations by 'good government' prosecutors flirts with the danger of unfairness, or worse, revenge politics." Robert G. Morvillo & Robert J. Anello, *Criminalization of Political Processes*, N.Y.L.J., Oct. 3, 2006, at 3, col. 1. Do you agree? Why or why not?

PROBLEM

7-4 Defendant was a manager of Aerospace, Inc. ("Aerospace"), and was responsible for acquiring property for Aerospace. Acting in that capacity, defendant retained Broker in connection with the acquisition of property, and agreed to pay Broker an above-market rate of commission. In return, Broker paid Defendant $20,000 in kick-backs. During the year in question, Aerospace received more than one million dollars under contracts to produce weapons systems for the United States Department of Defense.

A grand jury targeted Defendant and Broker in connection with this arrangement. Broker entered into a cooperation agreement with the government, and testified against Defendant. Defendant was convicted of federal program bribery under § 666. Defendant appeals the conviction.

What is the likely outcome? Why?

Chapter 8

EXTORTION

[A] INTRODUCTORY NOTES

[1] The Breadth of the Federal Extortion Statute

Extortion is a crime that is closely related to bribery. The Hobbs Act, codified at 18 U.S.C. § 1951, is the principal federal extortion statute and is often used to prosecute political corruption. Congress passed the Hobbs Act in 1946 in an effort to deter and punish robbery and extortion in interstate commerce. Section (a) of the Hobbs Act provides that "[w]hoever in any way obstructs, delays, or affects commerce . . . by robbery or extortion or attempts or conspires so to do" shall be punished under the Act. Section (b) defines extortion as "the obtaining of property from another, with his consent, induced by wrongful use of actual or threatened force, violence, or fear, *or* under color of official right."

Thus, there are two types of extortion under the Hobbs Act   (1) extortion by force, violence, or fear, and (2) extortion "under color of official right." The latter theory is used in political corruption cases against federal, state, and local officials. In addition, extortion by the use of fear includes cases where the defendant has allegedly induced a fear of economic harm in the victim. This theory properly falls within the "white collar" rubric, and is discussed in this chapter in cases involving public official defendants and private defendants. As these definitions show, the federal extortion statute applies more broadly than the federal bribery and gratuities statutes, 18 U.S.C. § 201, or the federal program bribery statute, 18 U.S.C. § 666.

[2] Statutory Elements and Definitions

In an extortion case brought in the white collar context, the government must prove that:

(1) The defendant's acts affected interstate commerce;

(2) The defendant obtained, or attempted or conspired to obtain, property of another;

(3) The property was obtained, or would have been obtained, with the other person's consent;

(4) The defendant acted with the required mens rea; *and*

(5) The property was obtained, or would have been obtained, either:

(a) by the wrongful use of fear of economic harm; *and/or*

(b) under color of official right.

The mens rea required for an extortion conviction depends upon the theory — use of fear or color of official right — that the government has asserted. *See* §§ 8[C]–[D], *infra.* Under the terms of the statute, extortion includes the inchoate conduct of conspiring or attempting to commit extortion. Note that the consent element of extortion distinguishes this crime from the crime of robbery, during which the victim's will is overborne by the defendant's immediate use of physical force, violence, or fear of force or violence. Extortion is punished by a fine and imprisonment of not more than 20 years.

[3]   Jurisdiction

As noted above, extortion under color of official right under the Hobbs Act is not limited to extortion by federal public officials or to extortion relating to federal programs. The crime thus relies upon the Interstate Commerce Clause to confer federal jurisdiction. The statute provides that jurisdiction is present where the defendant has obstructed, delayed, or affected commerce "in any way or degree." Applying this language, courts have held that even minor effects on interstate commerce will provide federal jurisdiction. *See, e.g., United States v. Stillo,* 57 F.3d 553 (7th Cir. 1995) (where a judge took money from a lawyer in return for fixing cases, interstate commerce was affected because the payment would have depleted the lawyer's firm's assets, and the firm purchased supplies in interstate commerce).

[B]   THE PROPERTY REQUIREMENT

In the following case, the Supreme Court interpreted the property element of extortion. As you read the case, carefully consider the policy implications upon which the majority, concurring, and dissenting opinions focus.

SCHEIDLER v. NATIONAL ORGANIZATION FOR WOMEN
537 U.S. 393 (2003)

CHIEF JUSTICE REHNQUIST delivered the opinion of the Court.

We once again address questions arising from litigation between petitioners, a coalition of antiabortion groups called the Pro-Life Action Network (PLAN), Joseph Scheidler, and other individuals and organizations that oppose legal abortion, and respondents, the National Organization for Women, Inc. (NOW), a national nonprofit organization that supports the legal availability of abortion, and two health care centers that perform abortions.[a]

In 1986, respondents sued in the United States District Court for the Northern District of Illinois alleging, *inter alia,* that petitioners violated RICO's §§ 1962(a), (c), and (d). They claimed that petitioners, all of whom were associated with PLAN, the alleged racketeering enterprise, were members of a nationwide conspiracy to "shut down" abortion clinics through a pattern of racketeering activity that included acts of extortion in violation of the Hobbs Act.

After a seven-week trial, a six-member jury concluded that petitioners violated the civil provisions of RICO. By answering a series of special interrogatory questions, the jury found, *inter alia,* that petitioners' alleged "pattern of

---

[a] An earlier United States Supreme Court decision in this litigation is set forth in Chapter 14, RICO, *infra.* — Eds.

racketeering activity" included 21 violations of the Hobbs Act, 18 U.S.C. § 1951. . . . The jury awarded $31,455.64 to respondent, the National Women's Health Organization of Delaware, Inc., and $54,471.28 to the National Women's Health Organization of Summit, Inc. These damages were trebled pursuant to § 1964(c). Additionally, the District Court entered a permanent nationwide injunction prohibiting petitioners from obstructing access to the clinics, trespassing on clinic property, damaging clinic property, or using violence or threats of violence against the clinics, their employees, or their patients.

The Court of Appeals for the Seventh Circuit affirmed in relevant part. The Court of Appeals rejected petitioners' contention that the things respondents claimed were "obtained" — the class women's right to seek medical services from the clinics, the clinic doctors' rights to perform their jobs, and the clinics' rights to provide medical services and otherwise conduct their business — were not "property" for purposes of the Hobbs Act. The court explained that it had "repeatedly held that intangible property such as the right to conduct a business can be considered 'property' under the Hobbs Act." Likewise, the Court of Appeals dismissed petitioners' claim that even if "property" was involved, petitioners did not "obtain" that property; they merely forced respondents to part with it. Again relying on Circuit precedent, the court held that " 'as a legal matter, an extortionist can violate the Hobbs Act without either seeking or receiving money or anything else. A loss to, or interference with the rights of, the victim is all that is required.' " We granted certiorari, and now reverse.

We first address the question whether petitioners' actions constituted extortion in violation of the Hobbs Act. That Act defines extortion as "the obtaining of property from another, with his consent, induced by wrongful use of actual or threatened force, violence, or fear, or under color of official right." 18 U.S.C. § 1951(b)(2). Petitioners allege that the jury's verdict and the Court of Appeals' decision upholding the verdict represent a vast and unwarranted expansion of extortion under the Hobbs Act. They say that the decisions below "rea[d] the requirement of 'obtaining' completely out of the statute" and conflict with the proper understanding of property for purposes of the Hobbs Act.

Respondents, throughout the course of this litigation, have asserted, as the jury instructions at the trial reflected, that petitioners committed extortion under the Hobbs Act by using or threatening to use force, violence, or fear to cause respondents "to give up" property rights, namely, "a woman's right to seek medical services from a clinic, the right of the doctors, nurses or other clinic staff to perform their jobs, and the right of the clinics to provide medical services free from wrongful threats, violence, coercion and fear." Perhaps recognizing the apparent difficulty in reconciling either its position (that "giv[ing] up" these alleged property rights is sufficient) or the Court of Appeals' holding (that "interfer[ing] with such rights" is sufficient) with the requirement that petitioners "obtain[ed] . . . property from" them, respondents have shifted the thrust of their theory. Respondents now assert that petitioners violated the Hobbs Act by "seeking to get control of the use and disposition of respondents' property." They argue that because the right to control the use and disposition of an asset is property, petitioners, who interfered with, and in some instances completely disrupted, the ability of the clinics to function, obtained or attempted to obtain respondents' property.

The United States offers a view similar to that of respondents, asserting that "where the property at issue is a business's *intangible* right to exercise exclusive control over the use of its assets, [a] defendant obtains that property by obtaining control over the use of those assets." Brief for United States as *Amicus Curiae* 22. Although the Government acknowledges that the jury's finding of extortion may have been improperly based on the conclusion that petitioners deprived respondents of a liberty interest, it maintains that under its theory of liability, petitioners committed extortion.

We need not now trace what are the outer boundaries of extortion liability under the Hobbs Act, so that liability might be based on obtaining something as intangible as another's right to exercise exclusive control over the use of a party's business assets. Whatever the outer boundaries may be, the effort to characterize petitioners' actions here as an "obtaining of property from" respondents is well beyond them. Such a result would be an unwarranted expansion of the meaning of that phrase.

Absent contrary direction from Congress, we begin our interpretation of statutory language with the general presumption that a statutory term has its common-law meaning. At common law, extortion was a property offense committed by a public official who took "any money or thing of value" that was not due to him under the pretense that he was entitled to such property by virtue of his office. 4 W. Blackstone, Commentaries on the Laws of England 141 (1765). In 1946, Congress enacted the Hobbs Act, which explicitly "expanded the common-law definition of extortion to include acts by private individuals." *Evans v. United States*, 504 U.S. 255, 261 (1992). While the Hobbs Act expanded the scope of common-law extortion to include private individuals, the statutory language retained the requirement that property must be "obtained."

* * *

We have said that the words of the Hobbs Act "do not lend themselves to restrictive interpretation" because they " 'manifes[t] . . . a purpose to use all the constitutional power Congress has to punish interference with interstate commerce by extortion, robbery or physical violence.' " *United States v. Culbert*, 435 U.S. 371, 373 (1978). We have also said, construing the Hobbs Act in *United States v. Enmons*, 410 U.S. 396, 411 (1973): "Even if the language and history of the Act were less clear than we have found them to be, the Act could not properly be expanded as the Government suggests — for two related reasons. First, this being a criminal statute, it must be strictly construed, and any ambiguity must be resolved in favor of lenity."

We think that these two seemingly antithetical statements can be reconciled. *Culbert* refused to adopt the view that Congress had not exercised the full extent of its commerce power in prohibiting extortion which "affects commerce or the movement of any article or commodity in commerce." But there is no contention by petitioners here that their acts did not affect interstate commerce. Their argument is that their acts did not amount to the crime of extortion as set forth in the Act, so the rule of lenity referred to in *Enmons* may apply to their case quite consistently with the statement in *Culbert*. "[W]hen there are two rational readings of a criminal statute, one harsher than the other, we are to choose the harsher only when Congress has spoken in clear and definite language." *McNally v. United States*, 483 U.S. 350, 359–360 (1987). . . .

Because we find that petitioners did not obtain or attempt to obtain property from respondents, we conclude that there was no basis upon which to find that they committed extortion under the Hobbs Act. Because all of the predicate acts supporting the jury's finding of a RICO violation must be reversed, the judgment that petitioners violated RICO must also be reversed.

The judgment of the Court of Appeals is accordingly *reversed.*

JUSTICE GINSBURG, with whom JUSTICE BREYER joins, concurring.

I join the Court's opinion, persuaded that the Seventh Circuit's decision accords undue breadth to the Racketeer Influenced and Corrupt Organizations Act (RICO or Act). As Justice Stevens recognizes, "Congress has enacted specific legislation responsive to the concerns that gave rise to these cases." In the Freedom of Access to Clinic Entrances Act of 1994, 18 U.S.C. § 248, Congress crafted a statutory response that homes in on the problem of criminal activity at health care facilities. Thus, the principal effect of a decision against petitioners here would have been on other cases pursued under RICO.

RICO, which empowers both prosecutors and private enforcers, imposes severe criminal penalties and hefty civil liability on those engaged in conduct within the Act's compass. *See, e.g.,* § 1963(a) (up to 20 years' imprisonment and wide-ranging forfeiture for a single criminal violation); § 1964(a) (broad civil injunctive relief); § 1964(c) (treble damages and attorneys' fees for private plaintiffs). The Court is rightly reluctant, as I see it, to extend RICO's domain further by endorsing the expansive definition of "extortion" adopted by the Seventh Circuit.

JUSTICE STEVENS, dissenting.

The term "extortion" as defined in the Hobbs Act refers to "the obtaining of property from another." 18 U.S.C. § 1951(b)(2). The Court's murky opinion seems to hold that this phrase covers nothing more than the acquisition of tangible property. No other federal court has ever construed this statute so narrowly.

For decades federal judges have uniformly given the term "property" an expansive construction that encompasses the intangible right to exercise exclusive control over the lawful use of business assets. The right to serve customers or to solicit new business is thus a protected property right. The use of violence or threats of violence to persuade the owner of a business to surrender control of such an intangible right is an appropriation of control embraced by the term "obtaining." That is the commonsense reading of the statute that other federal judges have consistently and wisely embraced in numerous cases that the Court does not discuss or even cite. Recognizing this settled definition of property, as I believe one must, the conclusion that petitioners obtained this property from respondents is amply supported by the evidence in the record.

* * *

I respectfully dissent.

NOTES AND QUESTIONS

1. *The* Scheidler *litigation.* As the above opinion notes, the Supreme Court's decision in this case was just one of a number of judicial decisions in litigation that stretched over nearly two decades. Yet the Court in this case concluded that the

theory of the plaintiff's case was fundamentally flawed. Do you agree? If so, why did this case consume so much of the federal judiciary's resources?

2. *The dissent.* Justice Stevens' interpretation of the Hobbs Act is fundamentally different from the majority's interpretation. Do you agree with Justice Stevens? Why or why not?

3. *Intangible rights.* Under *Scheidler*, does the extortion statute apply when the defendant attempted to deprive the alleged victim of intangible rights? Suppose that the government shows that the defendant fixed labor union elections and controlled how the elected officials performed their union duties, depriving union members of their statutory right to participate in union governance. In *United States v. Gotti*, 459 F.3d 296, 326 (2d Cir. 2006), the court held that this conduct amounted to extortion. Because the defendant obtained the benefits of which the victims were deprived, the *Scheidler* requirement was met. According to this reasoning, it did not matter that the right obtained was an intangible right.

Was the Court correct that the rights at issue were intangible "property rights?" Would these rights qualify as property under the mail and wire fraud statutes? Why or why not?

4. *The government as beneficiary.* Does the Hobbs Act apply when the federal government is the intended beneficiary of the extortion? In *Wilkie v. Robbins*, 127 S. Ct. 2588, 2607 (2007), the Court held not. In that case, the plaintiff alleged that the government attempted to extort him to force him to grant the government an easement over his property. The Court found that neither the text of the statute nor the common law of extortion supported this theory. The Court also opined that a contrary holding would subject federal employees to possible extortion charges in a wide range of circumstances.

5. *RICO.* This case provides a preview of the RICO statute, discussed in detail in Chapter 14, RICO, *infra.* According to Justice Ginsburg's concurring opinion, what is the danger of allowing a case like this to go forward under the RICO statute?

[C] THE COLOR OF OFFICIAL RIGHT THEORY

In the next two cases, the Supreme Court attempted to delineate the reach of the color of official right theory in the context of campaign contributions. Are the outcomes consistent? Can you divine a clear rule from the cases? As you read the opinions, consider whether the individual Justices' votes help to answer these questions.

McCORMICK v. UNITED STATES
500 U.S. 257 (1991)

JUSTICE WHITE delivered the opinion of the Court.

This case requires us to consider whether the Court of Appeals properly affirmed the conviction of petitioner, an elected public official, for extorting property under color of official right in violation of the Hobbs Act, 18 U.S.C. § 1951.

I.

Petitioner Robert L. McCormick was a member of the West Virginia House of Delegates in 1984. He represented a district that had long suffered from a shortage of medical doctors. For several years, West Virginia had allowed foreign medical school graduates to practice under temporary permits while studying for the state licensing exams. Under this program, some doctors were allowed to practice under temporary permits for years even though they repeatedly failed the state exams. McCormick was a leading advocate and supporter of this program.

In the early 1980's, following a move in the House of Delegates to end the temporary permit program, several of the temporarily licensed doctors formed an organization to press their interests in Charleston. The organization hired a lobbyist, John Vandergrift, who in 1984 worked for legislation that would extend the expiration date of the temporary permit program. McCormick sponsored the House version of the proposed legislation and a bill was passed extending the program for another year. Shortly thereafter, Vandergrift and McCormick discussed the possibility of introducing legislation during the 1985 session that would grant the doctors a permanent medical license by virtue of their years of experience. McCormick agreed to sponsor such legislation.

During his 1984 reelection campaign, McCormick informed Vandergrift that his campaign was expensive, that he had paid considerable sums out of his own pocket, and that he had not heard anything from the foreign doctors. Vandergrift told McCormick that he would contact the doctors and see what he could do. Vandergrift contacted one of the foreign doctors and later received from the doctors $1,200 in cash. Vandergrift delivered an envelope containing nine $100 bills to McCormick. Later the same day, a second delivery of $2,000 in cash was made to McCormick. During the fall of 1984, McCormick received two more cash payments from the doctors. McCormick did not list any of these payments as campaign contributions[1] nor did he report the money as income on his 1984 federal income tax return. And although the doctors' organization kept detailed books of its expenditures, the cash payments were not listed as campaign contributions. Rather, the entries for the payments were accompanied only by initials or other codes signifying that the money was for McCormick.

In the spring of 1985, McCormick sponsored legislation permitting experienced doctors to be permanently licensed without passing the state licensing exams. McCormick spoke at length in favor of the bill during floor debate and the bill ultimately was enacted into law. Two weeks after the legislation was enacted, McCormick received another cash payment from the foreign doctors.

Following an investigation, a federal grand jury returned an indictment charging McCormick with five counts of violating the Hobbs Act,[2] by extorting payments under color of official right, and with one count of filing a false income

---

[1] West Virginia law prohibits cash campaign contributions in excess of $50 per person. W. Va. Code § 3-8-5d (1990).

[2] The Hobbs Act, 18 U.S.C. § 1951, provides in relevant part as follows:

(a) Whoever in any way or degree obstructs, delays, or affects commerce . . . by robbery or extortion . . . in violation of this section shall be fined not more than $10,000 or imprisoned not more than twenty years, or both.

(b) As used in this section —

. . . .

tax return in violation of 26 U.S.C. § 7206(1), by failing to report as income the cash payments he received from the foreign doctors. At the close of a 6-day trial, the jury was instructed that to establish a Hobbs Act violation the Government had to prove that McCormick induced a cash payment and that he did so knowingly and willfully by extortion.

The next day the jury informed the court that it "would like to hear the instructions again with particular emphasis on the definition of extortion under the color of official right and on the law as regards the portion of moneys received that does not have to be reported as income." The court then reread most of the extortion instructions to the jury, but reordered some of the paragraphs and made the following significant addition:

> Extortion under color of official right means the obtaining of money by a public official when the money obtained was not lawfully due and owing to him or to his office. Of course, extortion does not occur where one who is a public official receives a legitimate gift or a voluntary political contribution even though the political contribution may have been made in cash in violation of local law. Voluntary is that which is freely given without expectation of benefit.

It is also worth noting that with respect to political contributions, the last two paragraphs of the supplemental instructions on the extortion counts were as follows:

> It would not be illegal, in and of itself, for Mr. McCormick to solicit or accept political contributions from foreign doctors who would benefit from this legislation.

> In order to find Mr. McCormick guilty of extortion, you must be convinced beyond a reasonable doubt that the payment alleged in a given count of the indictment was made by or on behalf of the doctors with the expectation that such payment would influence Mr. McCormick's official conduct, and with knowledge on the part of Mr. McCormick that they were paid to him with that expectation by virtue of the office he held.

The jury convicted McCormick of the first Hobbs Act count (charging him with receiving the initial $900 cash payment) . . . but could not reach verdicts on the remaining four Hobbs Act counts. The District Court declared a mistrial on those four counts.

The Court of Appeals affirmed.

* * *

Because of disagreement in the Courts of Appeals regarding the meaning of the phrase "under color of official right" as it is used in the Hobbs Act, we granted certiorari. We reverse and remand for further proceedings.

---

(2) The term "extortion" means the obtaining of property from another, with his consent, induced by wrongful use of actual or threatened force, violence, or fear, or under color of official right.

II.

McCormick's challenge to the judgment below affirming his conviction is limited to the Court of Appeals' rejection of his claim that the payments made to him by or on behalf of the doctors were campaign contributions, the receipt of which did not violate the Hobbs Act.

*   *   *

We agree with the Court of Appeals that in a case like this it is proper to inquire whether payments made to an elected official are in fact campaign contributions, and we agree that the intention of the parties is a relevant consideration in pursuing this inquiry. But we cannot accept the Court of Appeals' approach to distinguishing between legal and illegal campaign contributions. The Court of Appeals stated that payments to elected officials could violate the Hobbs Act without proof of an explicit quid pro quo by proving that the payments "were never intended to be *legitimate* campaign contributions."

Serving constituents and supporting legislation that will benefit the district and individuals and groups therein is the everyday business of a legislator. It is also true that campaigns must be run and financed. Money is constantly being solicited on behalf of candidates, who run on platforms and who claim support on the basis of their views and what they intend to do or have done. Whatever ethical considerations and appearances may indicate, to hold that legislators commit the federal crime of extortion when they act for the benefit of constituents or support legislation furthering the interests of some of their constituents, shortly before or after campaign contributions are solicited and received from those beneficiaries, is an unrealistic assessment of what Congress could have meant by making it a crime to obtain property from another, with his consent, "under color of official right." To hold otherwise would open to prosecution not only conduct that has long been thought to be well within the law but also conduct that in a very real sense is unavoidable so long as election campaigns are financed by private contributions or expenditures, as they have been from the beginning of the Nation. It would require statutory language more explicit than the Hobbs Act contains to justify a contrary conclusion.

This is not to say that it is impossible for an elected official to commit extortion in the course of financing an election campaign. Political contributions are of course vulnerable if induced by the use of force, violence, or fear. The receipt of such contributions is also vulnerable under the Act as having been taken under color of official right, but only if the payments are made in return for an explicit promise or undertaking by the official to perform or not to perform an official act. In such situations the official asserts that his official conduct will be controlled by the terms of the promise or undertaking. This is the receipt of money by an elected official under color of official right within the meaning of the Hobbs Act.

This formulation defines the forbidden zone of conduct with sufficient clarity. As the Court of Appeals for the Fifth Circuit observed in *United States v. Dozier*, 672 F.2d 531, 537 (5th Cir. 1982):

> "A moment's reflection should enable one to distinguish, at least in the abstract, a legitimate solicitation from the exaction of a fee for a benefit conferred or an injury withheld. Whether described familiarly as a payoff or with the Latinate precision of *quid pro quo*, the prohibited exchange is

the same: a public official may not demand payment as inducement for the promise to perform (or not to perform) an official act."

The United States agrees that if the payments to McCormick were campaign contributions, proof of a quid pro quo would be essential for an extortion conviction, and quotes the instruction given on this subject in 9 Department of Justice Manual § 9-85A.306, p. 9-1938.134: "campaign contributions will not be authorized as the subject of a Hobbs Act prosecution unless they can be proven to have been given in return for the performance of or abstaining from an official act; otherwise any campaign contribution might constitute a violation."

We thus disagree with the Court of Appeals' holding in this case that a quid pro quo is not necessary for conviction under the Hobbs Act when an official receives a campaign contribution.[4] By the same token, we hold, as McCormick urges, that the District Court's instruction to the same effect was error.

* * *

Accordingly we reverse the judgment of the Court of Appeals and remand for further proceedings consistent with this opinion.

So ordered.

JUSTICE SCALIA, concurring (omitted).

JUSTICE STEVENS, with whom JUSTICE BLACKMUN and JUSTICE O'CONNOR join, dissenting.

As I understand its opinion, the Court would agree that these facts would constitute a violation of the Hobbs Act if the understanding that the money was a personal payment rather than a campaign contribution had been explicit rather than implicit and if the understanding that, in response to the payment, petitioner would endeavor to provide the payers with the specific benefit they sought had also been explicit rather than implicit. In my opinion there is no statutory requirement that illegal agreements, threats, or promises be in writing, or in any particular form. Subtle extortion is just as wrongful — and probably much more common — than the kind of express understanding that the Court's opinion seems to require.

Nevertheless, to prove a violation of the Hobbs Act, I agree with the Court that it is essential that the payment in question be contingent on a mutual understanding that the motivation for the payment is the payer's desire to avoid a specific threatened harm or to obtain a promised benefit that the defendant has the apparent power to deliver, either through the use of force or the use of public office. In this sense, the crime does require a *"quid pro quo."* Because the use of the Latin term *"quid pro quo"* tends to confuse the analysis, however, it is important to clarify the sense in which the term was used in the District Court's instructions.

The crime of extortion was complete when petitioner accepted the cash pursuant to an understanding that he would not carry out his earlier threat to withhold official action and instead would go forward with his contingent promise to take favorable action on behalf of the unlicensed physicians. What he did thereafter

---

[4] As noted previously, McCormick's sole contention in this case is that the payments made to him were campaign contributions. Therefore, we do not decide whether a quid pro quo requirement exists in other contexts, such as when an elected official receives gifts, meals, travel expenses, or other items of value.

might have evidentiary significance, but could neither undo a completed crime nor complete an uncommitted offense. When petitioner took the money, he was either guilty or not guilty. For that reason, proof of a subsequent *quid pro quo* — his actual support of the legislation — was not necessary for the Government's case. And conversely, evidence that petitioner would have supported the legislation anyway is not a defense to the already completed crime. The thug who extorts protection money cannot defend on the ground that his threat was only a bluff because he would not have smashed the shopkeeper's windows even if the extortion had been unsuccessful. It was in this sense that the District Court correctly advised the jury that the Government did not have to prove the delivery of a postpayment *quid pro quo*.

*   *   *

I respectfully dissent.

NOTES AND QUESTIONS

1. *Bribery v. extortion.* Re-consider the trial judge's instruction to the jury. Under this instruction, is there a distinction between bribery and extortion? Next consider Justice Scalia's concurring opinion. According to Justice Scalia, is it clear that the courts have correctly interpreted the crime of extortion "under color of official right"? What is an alternate interpretation of that crime?

2. *The policy debate.* What was the primary policy concern of the majority? Of the dissent? Which side has the better of the argument? Why?

3. *The Travel Act.* In a concurring opinion, Justice Scalia concluded that the crime that McCormick committed was bribery, not extortion. Justice Scalia also concluded that McCormick, although not a federal official for purposes of the federal bribery statute, could be guilty under the Travel Act, 18 U.S.C. § 1952, which criminalizes the use of interstate commerce for bribery.

*   *   *

In the next case, the Court addressed the issue whether extortion under color of official right occurs when the public official does not initiate the transaction. In the course of resolving this issue, the Court attempted to reconcile its holding with the *McCormick* decision. Pay particular attention to Justice Kennedy's concurring opinion in this regard.

EVANS v. UNITED STATES
504 U.S. 255 (1992)

JUSTICE STEVENS delivered the opinion of the Court.

We granted certiorari to resolve a conflict in the Circuits over the question whether an affirmative act of inducement by a public official, such as a demand, is an element of the offense of extortion "under color of official right" prohibited by the Hobbs Act, 18 U.S.C. § 1951. We agree with the Court of Appeals for the Eleventh Circuit that it is not, and therefore affirm the judgment of the court below.

I.

Petitioner was an elected member of the Board of Commissioners of DeKalb County, Georgia. During the period between March 1985 and October 1986, as part of an effort by the Federal Bureau of Investigation (FBI) to investigate allegations of public corruption in the Atlanta area, particularly in the area of rezonings of property, an FBI agent posing as a real estate developer talked on the telephone and met with petitioner on a number of occasions. Virtually all, if not all, of those conversations were initiated by the agent and most were recorded on tape or video. In those conversations, the agent sought petitioner's assistance in an effort to rezone a 25-acre tract of land for high-density residential use. On July 25, 1986, the agent handed petitioner cash totaling $7,000 and a check, payable to petitioner's campaign, for $1,000. Petitioner reported the check, but not the cash, on his state campaign-financing disclosure form; he also did not report the $7,000 on his 1986 federal income tax return. Viewing the evidence in the light most favorable to the Government, as we must in light of the verdict, we assume that the jury found that petitioner accepted the cash knowing that it was intended to ensure that he would vote in favor of the rezoning application and that he would try to persuade his fellow commissioners to do likewise. Thus, although petitioner did not initiate the transaction, his acceptance of the bribe constituted an implicit promise to use his official position to serve the interests of the bribe-giver.

In a two-count indictment, petitioner was charged with extortion in violation of 18 U.S.C. § 1951 and with failure to report income in violation of 26 U.S.C. § 7206(1). He was convicted by a jury on both counts. With respect to the extortion count, the trial judge gave the following instruction:

> The defendant contends that the $8,000 he received from agent Cormany was a campaign contribution. The solicitation of campaign contributions from any person is a necessary and permissible form of political activity on the part of persons who seek political office and persons who have been elected to political office. Thus, the acceptance by an elected official of a campaign contribution does not, in itself, constitute a violation of the Hobbs Act even though the donor has business pending before the official.

> However, if a public official demands or accepts money in exchange for [a] specific requested exercise of his or her official power, such a demand or acceptance does constitute a violation of the Hobbs Act regardless of whether the payment is made in the form of a campaign contribution.

In affirming petitioner's conviction, the Court of Appeals noted that the instruction did not require the jury to find that petitioner had demanded or requested the money, or that he had conditioned the performance of any official act upon its receipt. The Court of Appeals held, however, that "passive acceptance of a benefit by a public official *is* sufficient to form the basis of a Hobbs Act violation if the official knows that he is being offered the payment in exchange for a specific requested exercise of his official power. The official need not take any specific action to induce the offering of the benefit." (emphasis in original).

This statement of the law by the Court of Appeals for the Eleventh Circuit is consistent with holdings in eight other Circuits. Two Circuits, however, have held that an affirmative act of inducement by the public official is required to support a conviction of extortion under color of official right. Because the majority view is consistent with the common-law definition of extortion, which we believe Congress intended to adopt, we endorse that position.

II.

It is a familiar "maxim that a statutory term is generally presumed to have its common-law meaning." *Taylor v. United States*, 495 U.S. 575, 592 (1990). As we have explained, "where Congress borrows terms of art in which are accumulated the legal tradition and meaning of centuries of practice, it presumably knows and adopts the cluster of ideas that were attached to each borrowed word in the body of learning from which it was taken and the meaning its use will convey to the judicial mind unless otherwise instructed. In such case, absence of contrary direction may be taken as satisfaction with widely accepted definitions, not as a departure from them." *Morissette v. United States*, 342 U.S. 246, 263 (1952).

At common law, extortion was an offense committed by a public official who took "by colour of his office" money that was not due to him for the performance of his official duties. A demand, or request, by the public official was not an element of the offense. Extortion by the public official was the rough equivalent of what we would now describe as "taking a bribe." It is clear that petitioner committed that offense. The question is whether the federal statute, insofar as it applies to official extortion, has narrowed the common-law definition.

Congress has unquestionably expanded the common-law definition of extortion to include acts by private individuals pursuant to which property is obtained by means of force, fear, or threats. It did so by implication in the Travel Act, 18 U.S.C. § 1952, and expressly in the Hobbs Act.

Although the present statutory text is much broader than the common-law definition of extortion because it encompasses conduct by a private individual as well as conduct by a public official, the portion of the statute that refers to official misconduct continues to mirror the common-law definition. There is nothing in either the statutory text or the legislative history that could fairly be described as a "contrary direction," *Morissette v. United States*, 342 U.S. at 263, from Congress to narrow the scope of the offense.

The two courts that have disagreed with the decision to apply the common-law definition have interpreted the word "induced" as requiring a wrongful use of official power that "begins with the public official, not with the gratuitous actions of another." If we had no common-law history to guide our interpretation of the statutory text, that reading would be plausible. For two reasons, however, we are convinced that it is incorrect.

First, we think the word "induced" is a part of the definition of the offense by the private individual, but not the offense by the public official. In the case of the private individual, the victim's consent must be "induced by wrongful use of actual or threatened force, violence or fear." In the case of the public official, however, there is no such requirement. The statute merely requires of the public official that he obtain "property from another, with his consent, . . . under color of official right." The use of the word "or" before "under color of official right" supports this reading.[15]

---

[15] This meaning would, of course, have been completely clear if Congress had inserted the word

Second, even if the statute were parsed so that the word "induced" applied to the public officeholder, we do not believe the word "induced" necessarily indicates that the transaction must be initiated by the recipient of the bribe. Many of the cases applying the majority rule have concluded that the wrongful acceptance of a bribe establishes all the inducement that the statute requires. They conclude that the coercive element is provided by the public office itself. And even the two courts that have adopted an inducement requirement for extortion under color of official right do not require proof that the inducement took the form of a threat or demand.

Petitioner argues that the jury charge with respect to extortion allowed the jury to convict him on the basis of the "passive acceptance of a contribution."[18] He contends that the instruction did not require the jury to find "an element of duress such as a demand," and it did not properly describe the quid pro quo requirement for conviction if the jury found that the payment was a campaign contribution.

We reject petitioner's criticism of the instruction, and conclude that it satisfies the quid pro quo requirement of *McCormick v. United States*, 500 U.S. 257 (1991), because the offense is completed at the time when the public official receives a payment in return for his agreement to perform specific official acts; fulfillment of the quid pro quo is not an element of the offense. We also reject petitioner's contention that an affirmative step is an element of the offense of extortion "under color of official right" and need be included in the instruction. As we explained above, our construction of the statute is informed by the common-law tradition from which the term of art was drawn and understood. We hold today that the Government need only show that a public official has obtained a payment to which he was not entitled, knowing that the payment was made in return for official acts.

The judgment is affirmed.

It is so ordered.

Justice Kennedy, concurring in part and concurring in the judgment.

The Court gives a summary of its decision in these words: "We hold today that the Government need only show that a public official has obtained a payment to which he was not entitled, knowing that the payment was made in return for official acts." In my view the dissent is correct to conclude that this language requires a *quid pro quo* as an element of the Government's case in a prosecution under 18 U.S.C. § 1951, and the Court's opinion can be interpreted in a way that is consistent with this rule. Although the Court appears to accept the requirement of a *quid pro quo* as an alternative rationale, in my view this element of the offense is essential to a determination of those acts which are criminal and those which are not in a case in which the official does not pretend that he is entitled by law to the property in

---

"either" before its description of the private offense because the word "or" already precedes the description of the public offense. The definition would then read: "The term 'extortion' means the obtaining of property from another, with his consent, either induced by wrongful use of actual or threatened force, violence, or fear, or under color of official right."

[18] Petitioner also makes the point that "[t]he evidence at trial against [petitioner] is more conducive to a charge of bribery than one of extortion." Although the evidence in this case may have supported a charge of bribery, it is not a defense to a charge of extortion under color of official right that the defendant could also have been convicted of bribery. Courts addressing extortion by force or fear have occasionally said that extortion and bribery are mutually exclusive, while that may be correct when the victim was intimidated into making a payment (extortion by force or fear), and did not offer it voluntarily (bribery), that does not lead to the conclusion that extortion under color of official right and bribery are mutually exclusive under either common law or the Hobbs Act.

question. Here the prosecution did establish a *quid pro quo* that embodied the necessary elements of a statutory violation.

With regard to the question whether the word "induced" in the statutory definition of extortion applies to the phrase "under color of official right," 18 U.S.C. § 1951(b)(2), I find myself in substantial agreement with the dissent. Scrutiny of the placement of commas will not, in the final analysis, yield a convincing answer, and we are left with two quite plausible interpretations. Under these circumstances, I agree with the dissent that the rule of lenity requires that we avoid the harsher one. We must take as our starting point the assumption that the portion of the statute at issue here defines extortion as "the obtaining of property from another, with his consent, induced . . . under color of official right."

I agree with the Court, on the other hand, that the word "induced" does not "necessarily indicat[e] that the transaction must be *initiated* by the" public official. Something beyond the mere acceptance of property from another is required, however, or else the word "induced" would be superfluous. That something, I submit, is the *quid pro quo.* The ability of the official to use or refrain from using authority is the "color of official right" which can be invoked in a corrupt way to induce payment of money or to otherwise obtain property. The inducement generates a *quid pro quo,* under color of official right, that the statute prohibits. The term "under color of" is used, as I think both the Court and the dissent agree, to sweep within the statute those corrupt exercises of authority that the law forbids but that nevertheless cause damage because the exercise is by a governmental official.

The requirement of a *quid pro quo* means that without pretense of any entitlement to the payment, a public official violates § 1951 if he intends the payor to believe that absent payment the official is likely to abuse his office and his trust to the detriment and injury of the prospective payor or to give the prospective payor less favorable treatment if the *quid pro quo* is not satisfied. The official and the payor need not state the *quid pro quo* in express terms, for otherwise the law's effect could be frustrated by knowing winks and nods. The inducement from the official is criminal if it is express or if it is implied from his words and actions, so long as he intends it to be so and the payor so interprets it.

The criminal law in the usual course concerns itself with motives and consequences, not formalities. And the trier of fact is quite capable of deciding the intent with which words were spoken or actions taken as well as the reasonable construction given to them by the official and the payor. [F]or a public official to commit extortion under color of official right, his course of dealings must establish a real understanding that failure to make a payment will result in the victimization of the prospective payor or the withholding of more favorable treatment, a victimization or withholding accomplished by taking or refraining from taking official action, all in breach of the official's trust.

Moreover, the mechanism which controls and limits the scope of official right extortion is a familiar one: a state of mind requirement. Hence, even if the *quid pro quo* requirement did not have firm roots in the statutory language, it would constitute no abuse of judicial power for us to find it by implication.

The requirement of a *quid pro quo* in a § 1951 prosecution such as the one before us, in which it is alleged that money was given to the public official in the form of a campaign contribution, was established by our decision last Term in *McCormick v. United States*, 500 U.S. 257 (1991). Readers of today's opinion should have little difficulty in understanding that the rationale underlying the Court's holding applies not only in campaign contribution cases, but in all § 1951 prosecutions. That is as it should be, for, given a corrupt motive, the *quid pro quo*, as I have said, is the essence of the offense.

Because I agree that the jury instruction in this case complied with the *quid pro quo* requirement, I concur in the judgment of the Court.

Justice Thomas, with whom The Chief Justice and Justice Scalia join, dissenting.

* * *

The "under color of office" element of extortion had a definite and well-established meaning at common law. "At common law it was essential that the money or property be obtained under color of office, *that is, under the pretense that the officer was entitled thereto by virtue of his office.* The money or thing received must have been claimed or accepted in right of office, and the person paying must have yielded to official authority." 3 R. Anderson, Wharton's Criminal Law and Procedure § 1393, pp. 790–791 (1957) (emphasis added). Thus, although the Court purports to define official extortion under the Hobbs Act by reference to the common law, its definition bears scant resemblance to the common-law crime Congress presumably codified in 1946.

The Court errs in asserting that common-law extortion is the "rough equivalent of what we would now describe as 'taking a bribe.'" Regardless of whether extortion contains an "inducement" requirement, bribery and extortion are different crimes. An official who solicits or takes a bribe does *not* do so "under color of office;" i.e., under any pretense of official entitlement. "The distinction between bribery and extortion seems to be that the former offense consists in offering a present or receiving one, the latter in demanding a fee or present by color of office." *State v. Pritchard*, 12 S.E. 50, 52 (1890). Where extortion is at issue, the public official is the sole wrongdoer; because he acts "under color of office," the law regards the payor as an innocent victim and not an accomplice. With bribery, in contrast, the payor knows the recipient official is not entitled to the payment; he, as well as the official, may be punished for the offense. Congress is well aware of the distinction between the crimes; it has always treated them separately. By stretching the bounds of extortion to make it encompass bribery, the Court today blurs the traditional distinction between the crimes.

Perhaps because the common-law crime — as the Court defines it — is so expansive, the Court, at the very end of its opinion, appends a qualification: "We hold today that the Government need only show that a public official has obtained a payment to which he was not entitled, *knowing that the payment was made in return for official acts.*" (emphasis added). This *quid pro quo* requirement is simply made up. The Court does not suggest that it has any basis in the common law or the language of the Hobbs Act, and I have found no treatise or dictionary that refers to any such requirement in defining "extortion."

Its only conceivable source, in fact, is our opinion last Term in *McCormick v. United States*, 500 U.S. 257 (1991). Quite sensibly, we insisted in that case that, unless the Government established the existence of a *quid pro quo*, a public official could not be convicted of extortion under the Hobbs Act for accepting a campaign contribution.

Because the common-law history of extortion was neither properly briefed nor argued in *McCormick*, the *quid pro quo* limitation imposed there represented a reasonable first step in the right direction. Now that we squarely consider that history, however, it is apparent that that limitation was in fact overly modest: at common law, McCormick was innocent of extortion *not* because he failed to offer a *quid pro quo* in return for campaign contributions, but because he did not take the contributions under color of official right. Today's extension of *McCormick's* reasonable (but textually and historically artificial) *quid pro quo* limitation to *all* cases of official extortion is both unexplained and inexplicable — except insofar as it may serve to rescue the Court's definition of extortion from substantial overbreadth.

As serious as the Court's disregard for history is its disregard for well-established principles of statutory construction. The Court chooses not only the harshest interpretation of a criminal statute, but also the interpretation that maximizes federal criminal jurisdiction over state and local officials. I would reject both choices.

*   *   *

Our duty in construing this criminal statute, then, is clear: "The Court has often stated that when there are two rational readings of a criminal statute, one harsher than the other, we are to choose the harsher only when Congress has spoken in clear and definite language." *McNally v. United States*, 483 U.S. 350, 359–360 (1987). Because the Court's expansive interpretation of the statute is not the only plausible one, the rule of lenity compels adoption of the narrower interpretation.

The Court's construction of the Hobbs Act is repugnant not only to the basic tenets of criminal justice reflected in the rule of lenity, but also to basic tenets of federalism. Over the past 20 years, the Hobbs Act has served as the engine for a stunning expansion of federal criminal jurisdiction into a field traditionally policed by state and local laws — acts of public corruption by state and local officials.

I have no doubt that today's opinion is motivated by noble aims. Political corruption at any level of government is a serious evil, and, from a policy perspective, perhaps one well suited for federal law enforcement. But federal judges are not free to devise new crimes to meet the occasion. Chief Justice Marshall's warning is as timely today as ever: "It would be dangerous, indeed, to carry the principle that a case which is within the reason or mischief of a statute, is within its provisions, so far as to punish a crime not enumerated in the statute, because it is of equal atrocity, or of kindred character, with those which are enumerated." *United States v. Wiltberger*, 5 Wheat. 76, 96 (1820).

Our criminal-justice system runs on the premise that prosecutors will respect and courts will enforce the boundaries on criminal conduct set by the legislature. Where, as here, those boundaries are breached, it becomes impossible to tell where prosecutorial discretion ends and prosecutorial abuse, or even discrimination, begins. The potential for abuse, of course, is particularly grave in the inherently political context of public-corruption prosecutions.

In my view, Evans is plainly innocent of extortion. With all due respect, I am compelled to dissent.

NOTES AND QUESTIONS

1. *The quid pro quo requirement.*

a. *Non-campaign contribution cases?* In *McCormick*, the Court explicitly declined to decide whether the quid pro quo requirement applies in all color of official right extortion cases, or only in campaign contribution cases. 500 U.S. at 274 n.10. The majority in *Evans* did not address the question, although Justice Kennedy in concurrence opined that a quid pro quo must be proven in all color of official right extortion prosecutions. 504 U.S. at 278 (Kennedy, J., concurring). Lower courts have generally concluded that the government must prove a quid pro quo in all color of official right cases. *See, e.g., United States v. Giles*, 246 F.3d 966, 970–972 (7th Cir. 2001).

b. *Explicit vs. implicit?* Assuming that the quid pro quo requirement applies, what is the standard for determining whether the government has met its burden of proof? In *McCormick*, the Court stated that the government must prove that the defendant made "an explicit" promise to engage in an official act in return for the payment. 500 U.S. at 273. In *Evans*, however, the Court stated that the evidence was sufficient because the defendant's "acceptance of the bribe constituted an implicit promise to use his official position to serve the interests of the bribe-giver." 504 U.S. at 257. One commentator has described the *Evans* approach as a "watered-down version of the [*McCormick*] quid pro quo requirement." James Lindgren, *The Theory, History, and Practice of the Bribery-Extortion Distinction*, 141 U. Pa. L. Rev. 1695, 1733 (1993).

What is the correct approach? Some lower federal courts require proof of an explicit quid pro quo in campaign contribution cases, but require proof of only an implicit quid pro quo in non-campaign contribution cases. Other courts require only an implicit quid pro quo in all cases. Given the underlying policy rationales of *McCormick* and *Evans*, which approach makes the most sense?

Needless to say, the law as it now stands has produced a fair amount of confusion. *See generally* David Mills, *Corrupting the Harm Requirement in White Collar Crime*, 60 Stan. L. Rev. 1371 (2008); Jeremy N. Gayed, *"Corruptly": Why Corrupt State of Mind is an Essential Element for Hobbs Act Extortion Under Color of Official Right*, 78 Notre Dame L. Rev. 1731 (2003); Steven C. Yarbrough, *The Hobbs Act in the Nineties: Confusion or Clarification of the Quid Pro Quo Standard in Extortion Cases Involving Public Officials*, 31 Tulsa L.J. 781 (1996).

2. *Role of the courts in interpreting statutes.* The majority and dissent in *Evans* plainly disagree over whether the court should undertake to interpret the Hobbs Act in an expansive way. What considerations underlie this debate? Which side has the better of the argument?

3. *Bribery vs. extortion.* After *Evans*, what is the difference between bribery and extortion under color of official right? Does your answer to this question affect your view as to whether *Evans* was correctly decided?

4. *Lenity.* The dissent in *Evans* relies upon the rule of lenity in reaching its conclusion. This rule is cited by majority and dissenting opinions in many of the cases in this text. Can you discern when the rule should, and should not, be applied?

5. *Potential for abuse?* Revisit the concluding note in the previous chapter, raising the question of whether the expansive reading of the federal bribery statutes creates the potential for abuse. Also recall Justice Thomas's dissent in *Evans*, concluding that because of the Court's broad reading of the extortion statute it will "become[] impossible to tell where prosecutorial discretion ends and prosecutorial abuse, or even discrimination, begins. The potential for abuse, of course, is particularly grave in the inherently political context of public corruption prosecutions." Is Justice Thomas correct? If so, what is the solution?

Problems

8-1. Pat Oaks is a newly elected state senator. During Oaks's campaign, Oaks did not take a position on the troublesome issue of logging in state forest land in Oaks's state. Such logging occurs in Oaks's state under temporary permits. Last year, as the expiration date for the temporary permit program approached, Oaks unsuccessfully opposed legislation granting a temporary permit for an additional year. Thereafter, Oaks discussed the logging issue with the logger's lobbyist.

At one point, Oaks personally advised the loggers' lobbyist, Larry Larsons, that Oaks was "surprised that the loggers had not been more supportive of me." Larsons responded, "We certainly need your support." Over the next two months, Oaks received the first of several cash payments from the loggers. When Oaks's campaign manager thereafter called the lobbyist to ask for more money, the lobbyist assured Oaks that more would be forthcoming. The payments were made directly to Oaks, and Oaks did not inform the staff accountant or campaign finance director of the payments. The money was not reported as income on Oaks's personal income tax returns, and was not reported on Oaks's campaign finance disclosure forms.

During the next legislative session, Oaks sponsored and secured the passage of legislation permitting permanent logging permits to be issued to the loggers. Over the succeeding two months, Oaks received three more cash payments from the loggers. Again, Oaks did not reveal the payments to Oaks's staff, and the money was not reported as personal income for Oaks or on Oaks's campaign finance disclosure forms. All the payments together totaled $127,000.

Oaks is charged with extortion under color of official right under 18 U.S.C. § 1951. The defense position at trial is that the payments were campaign contributions, and that they were not reported as such because Oaks assumed that Oaks's accountant and campaign finance manager would discover the deposits from bank records Oaks provided them. The staffers have substantiated that the bank records revealed the deposits, which they failed to notice. The lobbyist has declined to testify, citing the Fifth Amendment privilege against compelled testimony.

Prepare closing arguments to the jury for the government and the defense.

8-2. Antonio held various positions at the Department of Licenses and Inspections ("L & I") for the City. L & I's function is to administer and enforce the City's code requirements, including building, electrical, fire, health, housing, business, and zoning regulations. Officials of L & I are empowered to issue zoning and use permits and licenses according to a first-come-first-served policy, conduct inspections, and enforce applicable codes and regulations. In his positions, Antonio had the discretionary authority to approve zoning and use permits and licenses, and to cite and close businesses for violations.

On December 20 last year, L & I closed for zoning violations one of Westside Check Cashing's stores. The controller of the check cashing business met with Antonio to discuss reopening the business. Antonio explained that Westside had to file a new application for a zoning and/or use registration permit and make other changes. Several days later, Antonio called the controller and told her that he wanted a piece of jewelry to give his wife for their anniversary. The controller selected a diamond pendant appraised at $4,275 and sent it to Antonio's office by courier. The controller decided not bill Antonio for the pendant because of Antonio's position with L & I. The zoning issue that led to the store closing on December 20 was still pending and the controller was concerned that Antonio would use his position to keep the business closed. Shortly after the exchange of the jewelry, Antonio permitted the store to reopen.

A federal grand jury indicted Antonio for extortion under color of official right under the Hobbs Act. At the trial, the judge instructed the jury that one of the elements of the offense was proof beyond a reasonable doubt of an implicit quid pro quo. Antonio was convicted, and appeals.

What arguments should Antonio assert? How should the government respond? How should the court rule? Why?

[D] THE USE OF FEAR THEORY

In the next case, the government employed both the "use of fear" theory and the "color of official right" theory in a political corruption prosecution. As you read the case, consider which theory better fits the facts. Given that the court found one of the theories sufficient, why did the court feel compelled to reverse the conviction?

UNITED STATES v. GARCIA
907 F.2d 380 (2d Cir. 1990)

GEORGE C. PRATT, CIRCUIT JUDGE:

Defendants Robert and Jane Garcia appeal from judgments of conviction on two counts of extortion (18 U.S.C. § 1951) and one count of conspiracy to commit extortion (18 U.S.C. § 371) entered against them in the United States District Court for the Southern District of New York. For the reasons that follow, we reverse the Garcias' convictions and remand to the district court for further proceedings.

BACKGROUND

Robert and Jane Garcia were charged with conspiracy, extortion, bribery, and receiving gratuities in connection with Robert Garcia's congressional activities on behalf of the now infamous Wedtech Corporation. The extortion and conspiracy charges were premised on two theories: (1) extortion by wrongful use of fear and (2) extortion under color of official right. At the close of the government's case, the Garcias moved for dismissal of the first theory. The district judge denied this request, concluding — erroneously, as we establish below — that the government had adequately demonstrated that the Garcias intended to exploit Wedtech's fear of economic loss.

The Garcias were acquitted by the jury of the bribery and gratuity charges, but were convicted of the substantive and conspiracy charges of extortion. Following the jury's verdicts, the Garcias moved for a new trial, claiming that the jury's acquittal of them on the bribery and gratuity counts suggested that the guilty verdicts on the extortion counts were based not on the second theory — under color of official right — but instead on the first theory of extortion — wrongful use of fear — and that the evidence could not support that conclusion. Neither the government nor the Garcias had requested that special interrogatories be given to the jury in order to learn the actual basis for their decision. The district judge denied the new trial motion, and the Garcias appeal their convictions.

Since the jury was not given special interrogatories we cannot determine on this record the precise basis for the guilty verdicts. Therefore, for our purposes, we must assume the jury could have found the Garcias guilty of extortion under either theory presented by the government. Consequently, if there was insufficient evidence for one of the theories, then the verdict is ambiguous and a new trial must be granted. By their Rule 29 motion to withhold from the jury the theory of extortion by fear of economic loss, the Garcias preserved their right to argue here that if the evidence was insufficient to support their extortion convictions on that theory, we should reverse and order a new trial on the remaining theory — extortion under color of official right. We turn, then, to the sufficiency of the evidence to prove extortion by fear of economic loss.

Extortion is defined in the Hobbs Act as "the obtaining of property from another, with his consent, induced by wrongful use of actual or threatened force, violence, or fear, or under color of official right." 18 U.S.C. § 1951(b)(2). Over the years, our cases have concluded that the fear required in extortion cases "can be satisfied by putting the victim in fear of economic loss." *United States v. Brecht*, 540 F.2d 45, 52 (2d Cir.1976).

In *United States v. Capo*, 817 F.2d 947 (2d Cir.1987), our court, sitting in banc, focused specifically on what factors are necessary to establish fear of economic loss. The present appeal requires us to apply the standards that we developed in *Capo* to a factual setting involving an elected official who sold his influence and power. *Capo* involved a job-selling scheme that took place at a plant of the Eastman Kodak Company. In 1982 Kodak announced that production of its new "disc camera" created the need for approximately 2,300 new employees. In the rush to fill these jobs, standard hiring procedures were ignored. Exploiting this situation, the defendants used their influence with an employment counselor at Kodak to see that individuals who paid them were hired as Kodak employees. This job-selling network formed the basis of an indictment for extortion based on a fear of economic loss, and the jury convicted.

On appeal, a panel of this court affirmed, but after an in banc rehearing we reversed, holding that a fear of economic loss must be viewed from the victim's perspective and that the victim must have reasonably believed "first, that the defendant had the power to harm the victim, and second, that the defendant would exploit that power to the victim's detriment." *Capo*, 817 F.2d at 951. Concluding that the Kodak job-selling scheme was not extortion, we emphasized that the "victims" had paid the defendants in an attempt to obtain influence. The "victims" in *Capo* thus did not act out of fear of the defendants or of what the defendants might do to them; rather, they were willing participants who were seeking to secure the defendants' assistance in order to improve their chances of obtaining a job.

The Garcias claim that their situation is similar to the one in *Capo*. They argue, in effect, that the payments that they received, like the payments in *Capo*, were not made out of fear but as a way of obtaining influence. For this reason, they claim, there was insufficient evidence to convict them of extortion based on a fear of economic loss. While a defendant challenging the sufficiency of the evidence "bears a very heavy burden," *United States v. Chang An-Lo*, 851 F.2d 547, 553 (2d Cir.1988), we nevertheless agree with the Garcias and conclude that the evidence in this case was insufficient to support an extortion conviction based on a fear of economic loss.

DISCUSSION

At trial the government relied on two claimed extortionate events: (1) a dinner meeting at a Manhattan restaurant and (2) a $20,000 loan by Wedtech to the Garcias.

A. The Alleged Dinner Extortion.

In 1978 Robert Garcia was elected to the United States Congress as a representative of the South Bronx, where the Wedtech Corporation was located. During his first years in office, Garcia extended normal congressional assistance to Wedtech in connection with a $550,000 loan from the Small Business Administration, $4 million in loans from the Economic Development Administration, and a bid for an army contract.

In April of 1984, Wedtech received a $24 million dollar contract to build pontoons for the navy. A few weeks after Garcia, along with other congressional figures, had attended a press conference announcing the award of this contract, Garcia called Mario Moreno, a Wedtech officer, and told him that it was important that the two of them meet. They agreed to have dinner the next evening at a midtown Manhattan restaurant.

Garcia and his wife, Jane, met Moreno. The congressman complained that Moreno had not kept him properly informed about Wedtech's activities. Moreno first described Wedtech's success and rapid growth in recent months. Then, when Moreno told the Garcias that Wedtech was having difficulties with the navy pontoon contract, Jane Garcia interjected that she and her husband were friendly with a classmate of then Secretary of the Navy John Lehman and that they could arrange a meeting with Lehman to resolve some of the problems with the contract. Robert Garcia boasted of his increasing influence in congress, and then proposed that Wedtech hire Jane Garcia as a public relations consultant.

Moreno told the Garcias that Wedtech, which was dealing primarily with government contracts, had no need for a public relations consultant and even if it did, it would be "crazy" to hire the wife of a congressman for the position. Garcia persisted, commenting that perhaps the payments to his wife could be made in another way. Jane Garcia then suggested that she be paid through an intermediary, Ralph Vallone, Jr., a lawyer in Puerto Rico who was a good friend of the Garcias.

As the dinner came to an end, the Garcias emphasized their influence with top officials at the navy and at the United States Postal Service. They did this knowing that Wedtech was attempting not only to resolve its problems with the navy pontoon contract, but also that the company was attempting to obtain postal contracts. At this point, Moreno told the Garcias that he personally supported their proposal and would seek approval for it from other Wedtech officials.

Fearing that a denial of payments to Jane Garcia would induce Garcia to withhold his support for the postal contracts Wedtech sought, the Wedtech officers approved the payments.

Wedtech began to send monthly checks to Vallone, who then deposited them and sent Jane Garcia's consulting company, Leesonia Enterprises, checks of comparable amounts. During the period that these payments were made, Jane Garcia received $76,000.

In support of its claim that Wedtech made these payments out of economic fear, the government points primarily to Robert Garcia's statement at the beginning of the dinner conversation. Moreno testified that Garcia had said:

> We have been apart for a long period of time. We don't communicate as much as we used to before, several years before, two or three years before. We had to find out from somebody else that the company had gone public, and that other people had benefitted from the company. . . . Can you explain to me what has happened there at the company in reality in the last year or so?

The government claims that Garcia made this statement knowing that Wedtech's economic life depended on continued political influence. This statement, it argues, was therefore an implicit threat: Garcia was warning Wedtech that unless he and his wife were paid, the company could no longer count on Garcia as a congressional advocate. This could in turn lead to a failure to obtain any more government contracts. But did Moreno perceive this statement as such a threat? There is no evidence that he did; on the contrary, the evidence shows that he did not.

During the dinner, the Garcias mentioned their contacts in the Postal Service, from which Wedtech was attempting to obtain a contract. Moreno stated that during the dinner he was thinking "that the Congressman [Garcia] could be a tremendous ally in . . . trying to get [the] contracts from the Postal Service."

When asked at trial why he approved the payment of money to Jane Garcia, Moreno answered:

> Because I felt that if we were not going to make those payments, the Congressman was not going to do the kind of activity that we would need to have done to convince Postmaster General Bolger to set aside those contracts for Wedtech.

Later, Moreno testified: "I felt that if we were not to satisfy those payments, we were not going to receive any activity beneficial to us regarding those postal contracts."

This is not the mindset of a victim of economic extortion; rather, it is the thinking of a shrewd, unethical businessman who senses and seeks to capitalize on a money-making opportunity.

The central fact is clear: even in the face of Garcia's disgraceful request for money, Wedtech was not risking the loss of anything to which it was legally entitled. Wedtech would still be permitted to bid on government contracts. But without Garcia's favorable attitude, the company might not be able to count on continued preferential treatment, nor could it secure Garcia's favorable intervention in the future. Garcia, in turn, was in effect offering to sell his congressional power, but he was not using that power as a way to intimidate Wedtech. By paying the Garcias, Wedtech was purchasing an advocate, not buying off a thug.

On redirect examination of Moreno, the prosecutor crystallized the motivating reason behind Moreno's decision to make the payments:

Q.   Now, sir, you were asked questions about — by both lawyers about the meeting at Lelo's [the Manhattan restaurant]. Did you consider it legal or illegal to agree to Congressman Garcia's request that you pay his wife through Vallone?

A.   Illegal.

Q.   Why did you consider it illegal?

A.   Because we were the constituents in Congressman Garcia's district. And to my knowledge, he is not supposed to be receiving any payments for any services he may perform for the company with the government. And I always viewed him and his wife as one unit.

Q.   When you made that agreement in Lelo's in May of 1984, did you agree to pay the money for services from Jane Garcia or Congressman Robert Garcia?

A.   For Congressman Garcia's services.

In short, the dinner meeting did not generate in Moreno or Wedtech any fear of economic loss within the meaning of the federal extortion statute as we have interpreted it in *Capo.*

B. The Alleged $20,000 Loan Extortion.

The Garcias were also convicted of extorting a $20,000 loan from Wedtech. On August 2, 1985, Robert Garcia told Moreno it was urgent that they meet and discuss a matter that was too sensitive to discuss over the phone. Moreno agreed and met Garcia at his Bronx congressional office. When Moreno arrived, Garcia asked to borrow $20,000 immediately, since he was leaving shortly for the Middle East. Moreno, who was $12,000 overdrawn at the bank himself, told Garcia that this loan could probably be arranged, but that he would have to check with other Wedtech officials. After getting the necessary funds from Wedtech's "slush fund," Moreno returned the same day to Garcia's office where Garcia suggested that the check be made payable to his sister, the Reverend Aimee Cortese, who would in turn forward the money to the Garcias. Garcia then directed a congressional aide to prepare documentation showing a loan between Moreno and Cortese. In Garcia's office, Moreno gave a check for $20,000 to Cortese, who deposited it and wrote another check to Jane Garcia for the same amount. Moreno testified that he believed that if he did not lend Garcia the money, Garcia would no longer help Wedtech.

Although the loan was supposed to be repaid in October of 1985, the Garcias did not repay it until March of 1986. Before finally repaying the loan, Robert Garcia asked Moreno to donate the $20,000 to the Reverend Cortese's church. Moreno declined, telling Garcia that he needed the money himself but that perhaps he would make a donation to the church in the future.

Recognizing that it has presented no evidence to demonstrate that even an implicit threat accompanied Robert Garcia's request that Wedtech lend him $20,000, the government argues that the Garcias' original "threat" created a "climate of fear" that colored all their future dealings with the company. While Moreno testified that he had agreed to the loan because without it Garcia "would not continue to do things in the same way that [Moreno] felt he could do," this does not demonstrate the kind of fear that is required by our decision in *Capo*. Had Garcia actually established a climate of fear, as the government contends, Wedtech would not have refused Robert Garcia's request that Wedtech convert its loan into a "donation" to his sister's church. But this is precisely what Wedtech did, and its refusal powerfully illustrates Wedtech's lack of fear.

The government does not have to prove that a climate of fear was created by a direct threat; nevertheless, the government must at least prove the existence of the victim's belief that the defendant had the power to harm it and the victim's fear that the defendant would exploit that power. However, there was no evidence that in making these payments Wedtech acted out of fear. At the time the alleged initial "threat" was made, Moreno viewed Garcia as an "ally." Moreover, the Garcias did not threaten Wedtech with harm, but instead underscored the mutual benefits that would flow from Wedtech's payments: the Garcias would obtain badly needed cash, and Wedtech would receive more government contracts than was likely without Garcia's help.

While the evidence readily proved that Wedtech paid the Garcias in the hope of receiving future favors, it did not establish that the company acted out of fear that without these payments it would lose existing contracts or even opportunities to which it was legally entitled. As in *Capo*, there was an "absence of any evidence of detrimental action for nonpayment. . . . " 817 F.2d at 953. Garcia never even hinted that he was prepared to use his power to harm Wedtech.

Without expressing — however implicitly — such a threat, the Garcias did not create in Moreno or Wedtech any feeling of fear; there is no evidence of any other cause of fear; and without the victim feeling some fear, extortion through fear of economic loss cannot exist. Wedtech paid the Garcias to ensure that it would receive special, preferential treatment; in making the payments, the company was motivated by desire, not fear; by opportunity, not by concern with retribution. As we sought to make clear in *Capo*, that is not the stuff of which extortion is made.

SUMMARY AND CONCLUSION

Because there were no special jury interrogatories, we have no way of knowing on which theory of extortion the Garcias were convicted. The district court, over objection, permitted the jury to consider the theory of economic loss, but we have concluded that the evidence presented was insufficient to support that conviction. Accordingly, we must reverse the judgments of conviction and remand to the district court for further proceedings.

NOTES AND QUESTIONS

1. *Inconsistent verdicts?* Consider the specific charges against the defendants, and the outcome at the trial. On its face, the jury's verdict may seem inconsistent. Was it? Can you explain the trial outcome?

2. *The* Garcia *result.* Isn't it clear that Congressman Garcia behaved in a blatantly corrupt way? Why did the appeals court reverse his conviction? Are you persuaded that the result was compelled by the holding in *Capo*? Why or why not?

3. *The retrial.* Following the reversal, the government retried the defendants on the color of official right theory, and obtained partial convictions. In instructing the jury, the trial judge declined to require proof of a quid pro quo, holding that such proof is only required in campaign contribution cases. *See United States v. Garcia,* 774 F. Supp. 848, 848–849 (S.D.N.Y. 1991). On appeal, the Second Circuit reversed, holding that *Evans* requires that the jury find a quid pro quo in all color of official right extortion cases. *United States v. Garcia,* 992 F.2d 409, 414–415 (2d Cir. 1993). The government chose not to retry the defendants for a third time. Were the government's resources wisely spend in this case? Why or why not?

4. *The line between ally and enemy.* In *Garcia,* the court concluded that, "[b]y paying the Garcias, Wedtech was purchasing an advocate, not buying off a thug." Because the purported victim viewed the defendants as allies rather than adversaries, the facts did not show extortion by threat of economic harm. But suppose the Congressman had said, "I only allow bills supporting my friends to come before Congress when my friends have helped me out." Would that amount to the use of fear? Take the case where state officials solicit financial benefits from out-of-state banks, and thereafter arrange for those banks to obtain state business that they otherwise would not have obtained. Would this amount to extortion by use of fear? *See United States v. Collins,* 78 F.3d 1021, 1030 (6th Cir. 1996) (because failure to provide the benefits would have deprived the banks of an opportunity to compete on a fair basis for the state business, facts supported conviction for extortion by use of fear).

PROBLEMS

8-3. Dern is a member of the City of Metropolis City Council, having been elected last year to a four-year term. Last March 1, the City Council began considering a major construction project to provide new office space for city agencies. The Council decided to acquire land with the assistance of a real estate broker, and to hire a contractor to construct a new building on the site once it was purchased. The Council agreed to meet on March 18 to continue the discussions.

On March 12, Dern met with real estate broker Pat Parsons over coffee at Dern's home. Parsons specialized in purchases of land for commercial and municipal building projects. During the meeting, Dern said to Parsons, "We have this big city project coming up. I sure would like for you to be our broker. Would you like a shot?" Parsons responded, "Of course." Dern then said, "Well, I can assure you that you will be considered, with a substantial brokerage fee. You know, it's a competitive business. But the only way I can assure that you will be considered would be for me to have a, you know, stake in the venture." Parsons said, "How does a half percent sound?" Dern nodded in response. Parsons then said, "I think it would also be a good idea to contribute to your campaign, don't you think?" Dern responded, "I never turn down an offer for a contribution." The next day, Parsons sent a $5,000 check to Dern for Dern's reelection campaign. Dern reported the contribution in accordance with local election regulations.

Dern next told Parsons that the City Council had already reached a confidential decision that it would only hire an agent who agreed to accept a real estate commission of lower than the standard six percent of the purchase price.

The City Council subsequently retained Parsons for the project. The Council chose Parsons because Parsons' proposal to the Council indicated Parsons' willingness to accept less than the usual six percent real estate commission.

On July 1, the city purchased the property at a fair market value of $25 million. That day, Parsons gave Dern $125,000 in cash, Dern's share of Parsons' commission.

In a jurisdiction that follows the *Capo* rule, a jury convicted Dern of extortion, 18 U.S.C. § 1951, based upon the foregoing. In the indictment and at trial, the government asserted that Dern was guilty under (a) the use of force theory, and (b) the color of official right theory. By means of a general verdict form, the jury convicted Dern.

What viable arguments does Dern have on appeal? What is the likely outcome? Why?

8-4. Defendant Felicia Suarez has had a career as attorney, judge, and politician. After practicing law, she served as a Central City Court Judge. Subsequently, Suarez was elected to the County Board of Commissioners. She served alongside her friends and co-commissioners Larry Kim and Noelle Spam. This elected three-member Board of Commissioners has exclusive authority to transact county business, including entering into contracts on behalf of the County. By law, contracts with the county are awarded through sealed bidding to the lowest responsible and responsive bidder.

The Commissioners, however, decided not to award contracts by following the law, but instead, awarded contracts to their "friends." Among the contracts that the Commissioners controlled was the contract to clean the County Government Complex. The cleaning contract was for about $200,000 annually. After Suarez was elected, she and the other commissioners had a meeting with the owner of Professional Building Maintenance (PBM), Harold Mitchell, to inform him that he would have to pay the Commissioners kickback money in order to keep the cleaning contract. The commissioners devised the following plan: PBM would submit invoices to the County for additional work — for example, carpet cleaning, wall washing, and other services not included in the general cleaning contract — and inflate the price for the work. The Commissioners would approve the invoices for the extra work, and PBM would receive a check from the County for the inflated amount. After receiving the check from the County, PBM would give the Commissioners the difference between the actual price of the extra work and the amount paid by the County. (Mitchell agreed to plead guilty and cooperate with the government. At defendant's trial, Mitchell testified that he believed PBM would lose the cleaning contract if he did not give kickbacks to the Commissioners.)

A few years later, PBM stopped paying kickbacks and lost the cleaning contract. Suarez suggested to Kim that they give the cleaning contract to Global Management Services ("GMS"), owned by her friends Larry Crowel and Randy

Norris. Suarez told Kim that Crowel "knows how to play the game" and "could do a better job" for them. Crowel had known Suarez for approximately 20 years and had worked on Suarez's campaign for County Commissioner. Crowel had several conversations with Suarez and Kim about getting the cleaning contract. Kim told Crowel that PBM was paying him $600 to $700 a month. Crowel offered Kim $900 to $1000. In a similar meeting with Commissioner Spam, Crowel offered Spam $1000 to $1100 a month. Shortly thereafter, Suarez, Spam, and Kim had a secret meeting and awarded the cleaning contract to GMS.

For the next two years, GMS made monthly payments to the Commissioners. GMS financed the bribes by inflating the annual contract price. Then, after GMS received its monthly check from the County, Crowel would cash the check for the inflated amount and meet with each Commissioner to give the kickback money.

A federal grand jury returned an indictment against Suarez. Count 1, which related to the payments obtained from PBM and GMS, charged Suarez with conspiracy to affect commerce by extortion through the use of fear of economic harm, in violation of the Hobbs Act, 18 U.S.C. § 1951. Suarez appeals her conviction on Count 1, contending there was insufficient evidence to prove extortion under the Hobbs Act.

How should the court rule? Why?

Chapter 9

FALSE STATEMENTS

[A] INTRODUCTORY NOTES

The principal federal false statements statute, 18 U.S.C. § 1001, criminalizes the making of a wide range of both sworn and unsworn statements to the federal government. A false statements charge typically arises in one of two ways. First, prosecutors may employ this statute to charge those who have lied to cover up other illegal activities.[a] In this context, the charge is a "cover-up" crime akin to the perjury and obstruction of justice statutes discussed in the next two chapters. Second, the government may also use § 1001 to prosecute those who have lied in efforts to defraud the government or to disrupt government functions in such matters as federal employment, government benefits, and federal regulations. Here, the statute acts as a fraud statute in much the same way as the mail and wire fraud statutes discussed in Chapter 4. Because of its breadth, § 1001 is one of the most frequently charged crimes in white collar cases.[b]

[B] ELEMENTS OF FALSE STATEMENTS STATUTE

Section 1001 makes it a crime "knowingly and willfully" to engage in one of three types of conduct:

(1) Falsifying, concealing, or covering up a material fact by any trick, scheme, or device;

(2) Making any materially false, fictitious, or fraudulent statement, or representation; or

(3) Making or using any false writing or document knowing it to contain any materially false, fictitious, or fraudulent statement or entry.

The first theory requires proof that the defendant engaged in an affirmative act of non-disclosure by means of a trick, scheme, or device. As discussed in § [E] below, courts also generally require, when the charge is based on an omission, that the government prove that the defendant had legal duty to disclose the omitted facts.

---

[a] For example, I. Lewis "Scooter" Libby, former Vice-President Cheney's Chief of Staff, was convicted under § 1001 in connection with the CIA leak case. United States v. Libby, 498 F. Supp. 2d 1(D.D.C. 2007). And in her securities fraud prosecution, media personality Martha Stewart was convicted of, among other cover-up crimes, making false statements in connection with her 2001 sale of ImClone Systems stock. *See* United States v. Stewart, 323 F. Supp. 2d 606 (S.D.N.Y. 2004) *aff'd* 433 F.3d 273 (2d. Cir. 2006)..

[b] For an analysis of the false statements statute, see Stuart P. Green, *False Statements, in* Lying, Cheating, and Stealing: A Moral Theory of White Collar Crime 161–170 (2006). In addition to § 1001, there are dozens of statutes that criminalize false statements to the government in specific contexts. *See, e.g.,* 18 U.S.C. § 1014 (false statements for the purpose of influencing certain financial institutions). Another important and related statute is the False Claims Act, 18 U.S.C. § 287, which criminalizes knowing submission of a false or fraudulent claim to the federal government.

The second and third theories require proof that the defendant verbally or in writing made a false or fraudulent statement.

Courts generally interpret § 1001 to require proof of the following elements:

(1) The defendant (a) made or used an oral or written statement, or (b) concealed information that the defendant had a legal duty to disclose;

(2) The statement or information was false or fraudulent;

(3) The statement or information was material;

(4) The defendant acted knowingly and willfully; and

(5) The defendant made the statement or concealed the information within the jurisdiction of the executive, legislative, or judicial branch of the federal government.

As discussed below, the statute explicitly excludes from its coverage (a) certain statements made by parties or attorneys in court proceedings, and (b) certain statements made in connection with Congressional proceedings. The statutory maximum sentence under § 1001 is five years imprisonment.

[C] JURISDICTION

Defendants in false statements cases have frequently argued that the particular statements at issue did not qualify under the statute. The following case is the principal United States Supreme Court case delineating the jurisdictional scope of the statute.

UNITED STATES v. RODGERS
466 U.S. 475 (1984)

JUSTICE REHNQUIST delivered the opinion of the Court.

Respondent Larry Rodgers was charged in a two-count indictment with making "false, fictitious or fraudulent statements" to the Federal Bureau of Investigation (FBI) and the United States Secret Service, in violation of 18 U.S.C. § 1001. Rodgers allegedly lied in telling the FBI that his wife had been kidnaped and in telling the Secret Service that his wife was involved in a plot to kill the President. Rodgers moved to dismiss the indictment for failure to state an offense on the grounds that the investigation of kidnapings and the protection of the President are not matters "within the jurisdiction" of the respective agencies, as that phrase is used in § 1001. The District Court for the Western District of Missouri granted the motion, and the United States Court of Appeals for the Eighth Circuit affirmed. We now reverse. The statutory language clearly encompasses criminal investigations conducted by the FBI and the Secret Service, and nothing in the legislative history indicates that Congress intended a more restricted reach for the statute.

On June 2, 1982, Larry Rodgers telephoned the Kansas City, Missouri, office of the FBI and reported that his wife had been kidnaped. The FBI spent over 100 agent hours investigating the alleged kidnaping only to determine that Rodgers' wife had left him voluntarily. Two weeks later, Rodgers contacted the Kansas City office of the Secret Service and reported that his "estranged girlfriend" (actually his wife) was involved in a plot to assassinate the President. The Secret Service spent over 150 hours of agent and clerical time investigating this threat and eventually located Rodgers' wife in Arizona. She stated that she left Kansas City to get away from her husband. Rodgers later confessed that he made the false reports to induce the federal agencies to locate his wife.

In granting Rodgers' motion to dismiss the indictment, the District Court considered itself bound by a prior decision of the Eighth Circuit in *Friedman v. United States*, 374 F.2d 363 (1967). *Friedman* also involved false statements made to the FBI to initiate a criminal investigation. In that case, the Court of Appeals reversed the defendant's conviction under § 1001, holding that the phrase "within the jurisdiction," as used in that provision, referred only to "the power to make final or binding determinations." . . .

Reading the term "jurisdiction" in this restrictive light, the Court of Appeals included within its scope the "power to make monetary awards, grant governmental privileges, or promulgate binding administrative and regulative determinations," while excluding "the mere authority to conduct an investigation in a given area without the power to dispose of the problems or compel action." *Id.* at 367. The court concluded that false statements made to the FBI were not covered by § 1001 because the FBI "had no power to adjudicate rights, establish binding regulations, compel the action or finally dispose of the problem giving rise to the inquiry." *Id.* at 368.

In the present case, the Court of Appeals adhered to its decision in *Friedman* and affirmed the dismissal of the indictment. The court acknowledged that two other Courts of Appeals had expressly rejected the reasoning of *Friedman*. But the Eighth Circuit found its own analysis more persuasive. We granted certiorari to resolve this conflict.

It seems to us that the interpretation of § 1001 adopted by the Court of Appeals for the Eighth Circuit is unduly strained. Section 1001 expressly embraces false statements made "in any matter within the jurisdiction of any department or agency of the United States." A criminal investigation surely falls within the meaning of "any matter," and the FBI and the Secret Service equally surely qualify as "department[s] or agenc[ies] of the United States." The only possible verbal vehicle for narrowing the sweeping language Congress enacted is the word "jurisdiction." But we do not think that that term, as used in this statute, admits of the constricted construction given it by the Court of Appeals.

"Jurisdiction" is not defined in the statute. We therefore "start with the assumption that the legislative purpose is expressed by the ordinary meaning of the words used." *Richards v. United States*, 369 U.S. 1, 9 (1962). The most natural, nontechnical reading of the statutory language is that it covers all matters confided to the authority of an agency or department. Thus, Webster's Third New International Dictionary 1227 (1976) broadly defines "jurisdiction" as, among other things, "the limits or territory within which any particular power may be exercised: sphere of authority." A department or agency has jurisdiction, in this sense, when it has the power to exercise authority in a particular situation. Understood in this way, the phrase "within the jurisdiction" merely differentiates the official, authorized functions of an agency or department from matters peripheral to the business of that body.

There are of course narrower, more technical meanings of the term "jurisdiction." For example, an alternative definition provided by Webster's is the "legal power to interpret and administer the law." But a narrow, technical definition of this sort, limiting the statute's protections to judicial or quasi-judicial activities, clashes strongly with the sweeping, everyday language on either side of the term. It is also far too restricted to embrace some of the myriad governmental activities that we have previously concluded § 1001 was designed to protect.

* * *

There is no doubt that there exists a "statutory basis" for the authority of the FBI and the Secret Service over the investigations sparked by respondent Rodgers' false reports. The FBI is authorized "to detect and prosecute crimes against the United States," including kidnaping. 28 U.S.C. § 533(1). And the Secret Service is authorized "to protect the person of the President." 18 U.S.C. § 3056. It is a perversion of these authorized functions to turn either agency into a Missing Person's Bureau for domestic squabbles. The knowing filing of a false crime report, leading to an investigation and possible prosecution, can also have grave consequences for the individuals accused of crime. There is, therefore, a "valid legislative interest in protecting the integrity of [such] official inquiries," an interest clearly embraced in, and furthered by, the broad language of § 1001.

Limiting the term "jurisdiction" as used in this statute to "the power to make final or binding determinations," as the Court of Appeals thought it should be limited, would exclude from the coverage of the statute most, if not all, of the authorized activities of many "departments" and "agencies" of the federal government, and thereby defeat the purpose of Congress in using the broad inclusive language which it did. If the statute referred only to courts, a narrower construction of the word "jurisdiction" might well be indicated; but referring as it does to "any department or agency" we think that such a narrow construction is simply inconsistent with the rest of the statutory language.

The Court of Appeals supported its failure to give the statute a "literal interpretation" by offering several policy arguments in favor of a more limited construction. For example, the court noted that § 1001 carries a penalty exceeding the penalty for perjury and argued that Congress could not have "considered it more serious for one to informally volunteer an untrue statement to an F.B.I. agent than to relate the same story under oath before a court of law." *Friedman v. United States, supra,* at 366. A similar argument was made and rejected in *United States v. Gilliland,* 312 U.S. at 95. The fact that the maximum possible penalty under § 1001 marginally exceeds that for perjury provides no indication of the particular penalties, within the permitted range, that Congress thought appropriate for each of the myriad violations covered by the statute. Section 1001 covers "a variety of offenses and the penalties prescribed were maximum penalties which gave a range for judicial sentences according to the circumstances and gravity of particular violations." *Id.*

Perhaps most influential in the reasoning of the court below was its perception that "the specter of criminal prosecution" would make citizens hesitant to report suspected crimes and thereby thwart "the important social policy that is served by an open line of communication between the general public and law enforcement agencies." *Friedman v. United States, supra,* at 369. But the justification for this concern is debatable. Section 1001 only applies to those who "knowingly and willfully" lie to the government. It seems likely that "individuals acting innocently and in good faith, will not be deterred from voluntarily giving information or making complaints to the F.B.I." *United States v. Adler,* 380 F.2d 917, 922 (2d Cir. 1967).

Even if we were more persuaded than we are by these policy arguments, the result in this case would be unchanged. Resolution of the pros and cons of whether a statute should sweep broadly or narrowly is for Congress. Its decision that the perversion of agency resources and the potential harm to those implicated by false reports of crime justifies punishing those who "knowingly and willfully" make such reports is not so "absurd or glaringly unjust," *Sorrells v. United States*, 287 U.S. 435, 450 (1932), as to lead us to question whether Congress actually intended what the plain language of § 1001 so clearly imports.

Finally, respondent urges that the rule of lenity in construing criminal statutes should be applied to § 1001, and that because the *Friedman* case has been on the books in the Eighth Circuit for a number of years a contrary decision by this Court should not be applied retroactively to him. The rule of lenity is of course a well-recognized principle of statutory construction, but the critical statutory language of § 1001 is not sufficiently ambiguous, in our view, to permit the rule to be controlling here. And any argument by respondent against retroactive application to him of our present decision, even if he could establish reliance upon the earlier *Friedman* decision, would be unavailing since the existence of conflicting cases from other Courts of Appeals made review of that issue by this Court and decision against the position of the respondent reasonably foreseeable.

The judgment of the Court of Appeals is reversed, and the case is remanded for further proceedings consistent with this opinion.

NOTES AND QUESTIONS

1. *The policy debate.* In *Rodgers*, the Supreme Court quickly rejected the Eighth Circuit's interpretation of § 1001's statutory history and language. The Court seemed to take more seriously, however, the lower court's concerns that a broad application of the statute might have negative consequences. What were the Eighth's Circuit's concerns? Why did the Supreme Court fail to find those concerns compelling?

2. *Statutory coverage.*

a. *Judicial proceedings.* As *Rodgers* indicates, material false statements made to federal agents run afoul of § 1001 in a broad range of circumstances. In *Hubbard v. United States*, 514 U.S. 695 (1995), however, the Supreme Court held that § 1001 — then limited to "any matter within the jurisdiction of any department or agency of the United States" — did not encompass statements made in judicial settings. The following year, Congress responded by amending the statute to cover statements made "in any matter within the jurisdiction of the executive, legislative, or judicial branch of the Government of the United States." At the same time, however, Congress explicitly excluded from § 1001's reach all "statements, representations, writings or documents submitted by [a party to a judicial proceeding, or that party's counsel] to a judge or a magistrate in that proceeding." Courts have not read the "judicial proceeding" exception literally, and have applied the exception to statements made to agents, such as court clerks, acting on a judge's behalf. *See United States v. Manning*, 526 F.3d 611, 615 (10th Cir. 2008).

Congress added the judicial proceeding exception in response to concerns that the use of § 1001 "chill advocacy in judicial proceedings." *Id.* at 617. In this light, would a false statement made by a defendant to a probation officer preparing a report in advance of the defendant's sentencing fall within § 1001? *Compare Manning*, 526 F.3d at 619–621 (because probation officer did not act as mere conduit to the judge but performed an independent function, defendant's false statements fell within § 1001), *with United States v. Horvath*, 492 F.3d 1075 (9th Cir. 2007), *reh'g en banc denied*, 522 F.3d 904 (9th Cir. 2008) (statement made to probation officer concerning a matter that the law required to be included in the presentence report fell within the judicial proceeding exception).

b. *Congressional matters.* Section 1001's application to Congressional matters is limited to specified administrative matters, such as personnel and employment practices, and to investigative proceedings. Constituents' statements made to members of Congress are therefore excluded from the statute's reach. Why should this be so? What policy concerns might have led Congress to adopt this exclusion?

c. *Contractors and subcontractors.* Private parties who enter into contracts and subcontracts with entities other than the federal government are sometimes paid with federal funds and/or are subject to certain federal regulations. When are statements made by such parties within § 1001's reach?

In *United States v. Blankenship*, 382 F.3d 1110 (11th Cir. 2004), a private construction company entered into a contract with the Florida Department of Transportation, which received federal funds and agreed with the United States Department of Transportation to adhere to federal requirements. In order to appear to meet the federal requirements, subcontractors of the construction company made false statements in their contracts with the construction company. Did the statements made in the contracts fall within federal jurisdiction under § 1001? The majority held not, explaining that "if § 1001 were interpreted to prohibit any false statement to any private entity whose funds, in whole or in part, happened to originate with the federal government, the results would be shocking. To start with a simple example, any employee of either [the construction company] or its subcontractors who may have padded his resume to obtain a job on the project would be guilty of a federal offense." *Id.* at 1137–1138. The dissent argued that jurisdiction was present because the state was obliged to follow federal requirements and, if it failed to do so, it would lose the federal funds. Which approach best comports with *Rodgers*? Why?

Compare*Blankenship* with *United States v. Lutz*, 154 F.3d 581, 587–588 (6th Cir. 1998), where the defendant made false statements to a mortgage brokerage company that was authorized by the U.S. government to originate home loans. Although the statements were not submitted to the U.S. government, the court found that they fell within § 1001 because the statements were material to the U.S. government's supervisory powers over the company.

Are these cases distinguishable? Why or why not?

d. *State and local government benefits.* State and local government programs, such as unemployment benefit programs, may be supported by federal funding. Does a recipient who makes a false statement in connection with the receipt of such a benefit fall within § 1001? *Compare United States v. Holmes*, 111 F.3d 463, 466 (6th Cir. 1997) (no federal jurisdiction because the state has control over the award of benefits, and the only federal funding is for administration of the state program, not for the actual benefits), *with United States v. Herring*, 916 F.2d 1543, 1547 (11th Cir. 1990) (federal administrative funding and control provided sufficient nexus for federal jurisdiction).

Problems

9-1. Nell was indicted on one count of possessing stolen property. She asserted that she did not have sufficient funds to retain an attorney, and requested that the United States District Court appoint counsel to represent her. In support of the request, Nell submitted a signed financial status form. The form required the defendant to list her assets to determine if she qualified for a court-appointed attorney. Nell completed the form, omitting references to real estate and other assets that she held at the time. The government has indicted Nell under § 1001, and Nell has filed a motion to dismiss the charge.

Should the court grant Nell's motion? Why or why not?

9-2. Larry owns a gas station, LJ's Auto. Energy Authority, an agency of the United States government, owns nearby land. Peaberry Coal Company uses the land to mine for coal under a contract between Peaberry and Energy Authority.

Energy Authority's contract with Peaberry requires that Peaberry's subcontractors agree to obey certain federal laws and requires advance approval from Energy Authority for any Peaberry subcontracts exceeding $100,000. The contract further requires that Peaberry submit all documents related to any transactions with subcontractors to Energy Authority upon request. Peaberry advised Larry of these requirements.

LJ's Auto sold tires and equipment to Peaberry for use on the trucks used in the mining project. An investigation uncovered that LJ's Auto overcharged Peaberry by nearly $120,000 over several years. A federal grand jury indicted Larry under 18 U.S.C. § 1001 based on the inflated prices and charges written on purchase orders that Larry submitted to Peaberry. A jury convicted Larry of the charges, and he appeals.

How should the court rule on Larry's appeal? Why?

9-3. Federal officers arrested Arnold for violating federal immigration laws and placed Arnold in the Gotham Detention Center (GDC). Federal law allows the United States Attorney General to contract with local officials to house federal prisoners. The U.S. Marshal and Gotham City Sheriff entered into such an agreement. GDC is completely supervised and operated by the Sheriff's office, and all employees are local officials. The federal government neither has supervision over the day-to-day operations of GDC nor does it have the authority to determine the security level in which the federal prisoners are housed.

Approximately one week after Arnold was arrested, his sister Susan went to the GDC to visit her brother. When the deputy sheriff in charge told her that Arnold could not have visitors, Susan falsely told the deputy sheriff that she was a "medical doctor summoned to render medical treatment to Arnold."

Susan was indicted for making a false statement in violation of 18 U.S.C. § 1001. She has now hired you to seek dismissal of the false statement charge, arguing that the alleged false statement was not within federal jurisdiction.

How do you advise her as to the likelihood of success?

[D] THE "FALSE STATEMENT"

When proceeding under the theory that the defendant made or used a false statement or writing, courts have broadly interpreted the term "false statement" so as to include, for example, false invoices, false marriage vows to obtain citizenship, and false information given to federal investigators. *See* Jeremy Baker & Rebecca Young, *False Statements and False Claims*, 42 Am. Crim. L. Rev. 427, 432–433 (2005). As the cases in this section illustrate, however, the boundaries of the term "false statement" are not always immediately apparent.

[1] The "Exculpatory 'No' " Doctrine

One issue under § 1001 that had produced a distinct split among the courts of appeal involved prosecutions based upon statements that merely denied wrongdoing. Some lower courts had held that such statements — termed "exculpatory 'nos' " — could not be the basis for false statements prosecutions. The Supreme Court resolved this issue in the case that follows. Seven members of the Court agreed with the result in the case. In her concurring opinion, however, Justice Ginsburg expressed an unusual degree of concern over the outcome. Consider why she did so as you read her opinion.

BROGAN v. UNITED STATES
522 U.S. 398 (1998)

JUSTICE SCALIA delivered the opinion of the Court.

This case presents the question whether there is an exception to criminal liability under 18 U.S.C. § 1001 for a false statement that consists of the mere denial of wrongdoing, the so-called "exculpatory no."

I.

While acting as a union officer during 1987 and 1988, petitioner James Brogan accepted cash payments from JRD Management Corporation, a real estate company whose employees were represented by the union. On October 4, 1993, federal agents from the Department of Labor and the Internal Revenue Service visited petitioner at his home. The agents identified themselves and explained that they were seeking petitioner's cooperation in an investigation of JRD and various individuals. They told petitioner that if he wished to cooperate, he should have an attorney contact the United States Attorney's Office, and that if he could not afford an attorney, one could be appointed for him.

The agents then asked petitioner if he would answer some questions, and he agreed. One question was whether he had received any cash or gifts from JRD when he was a union officer. Petitioner's response was "no." At that point, the agents disclosed that a search of JRD headquarters had produced company records showing the contrary. They also told petitioner that lying to federal agents in the course of an investigation was a crime. Petitioner did not modify his answers, and the interview ended shortly thereafter. . . .

II.

At the time petitioner falsely replied "no" to the government investigators' question, 18 U.S.C. § 1001 provided:

> Whoever, in any matter within the jurisdiction of any department or agency of the United States knowingly and willfully falsifies, conceals or covers up by any trick, scheme, or device a material fact, or makes any false, fictitious or fraudulent statements or representations, or makes or uses any false writing or document knowing the same to contain any false, fictitious or fraudulent statement or entry, shall be fined not more than $10,000 or imprisoned not more than five years, or both.

By its terms, 18 U.S.C. § 1001 covers "any" false statement — that is, a false statement "of whatever kind," *United States v. Gonzales*, 520 U.S. 1, 5 (1997). The word "no" in response to a question assuredly makes a "statement," *see, e.g.,* Webster's New International Dictionary 2461 (2d ed.1950) (def. 2: "That which is stated; an embodiment in words of facts or opinions"), and petitioner does not contest that his utterance was false or that it was made "knowingly and willfully." In fact, petitioner concedes that under a "literal reading" of the statute he loses.

Petitioner asks us, however, to depart from the literal text that Congress has enacted, and to approve the doctrine adopted by many Circuits which excludes from the scope of § 1001 the "exculpatory no." The central feature of this doctrine is that a simple denial of guilt does not come within the statute. There is considerable variation among the Circuits concerning, among other things, what degree of elaborated tale-telling carries a statement beyond simple denial. In the present case, however, the Second Circuit agreed with petitioner that his statement would constitute a "true 'exculpatory n[o]' as recognized in other circuits," but aligned itself with the Fifth Circuit in categorically rejecting the doctrine.

Petitioner's argument in support of the "exculpatory no" doctrine proceeds from the major premise that § 1001 criminalizes only those statements to government investigators that "pervert governmental functions;" to the minor premise that simple denials of guilt to government investigators do not pervert governmental functions; to the conclusion that § 1001 does not criminalize simple denials of guilt to government investigators. Both premises seem to us mistaken. As to the minor: We cannot imagine how it could be true that falsely denying guilt in a government investigation does not pervert a governmental function. Certainly the investigation of wrongdoing is a proper governmental function; and since it is the very *purpose* of an investigation to uncover the truth, any falsehood relating to the subject of the investigation perverts that function. It could be argued, perhaps, that a *disbelieved* falsehood does not pervert an investigation. But making the existence of this crime turn upon the credulousness of the federal investigator (or the persuasiveness of the liar) would be exceedingly strange; such a defense to the analogous crime of perjury is certainly unheard of. Moreover, as we shall see, the only support for the "perversion of governmental functions" limitation is a statement of this Court referring to the *possibility* (as opposed to the certainty) of perversion of function — a possibility that exists whenever investigators are told a falsehood relevant to their task.

In any event, we find no basis for the major premise that only those falsehoods that pervert governmental functions are covered by § 1001. . . .

[Petitioner] argues that a literal reading of § 1001 violates the "spirit" of the Fifth Amendment because it places a "cornered suspect" in the "cruel trilemma" of admitting guilt, remaining silent, or falsely denying guilt. This "trilemma" is wholly of the guilty suspect's own making, of course. An innocent person will not find himself in a similar quandary. And even the honest and contrite guilty person will not regard the third prong of the "trilemma" (the blatant lie) as an available option. . . .

Whether or not the predicament of the wrongdoer run to ground tugs at the heartstrings, neither the text nor the spirit of the Fifth Amendment confers a privilege to lie. "[P]roper invocation of the Fifth Amendment privilege against compulsory self-incrimination allows a witness to remain silent, but not to swear falsely." *United States v. Apfelbaum*, 445 U.S. 115, 117 (1980). Petitioner contends that silence is an "illusory" option because a suspect may fear that his silence will be used against him later, or may not even know that silence is an available option. As to the former: It is well established that the fact that a person's silence can be used against him — either as substantive evidence of guilt or to impeach him if he takes the stand — does not exert a form of pressure that exonerates an otherwise unlawful lie. And as for the possibility that the person under investigation may be unaware of his right to remain silent: In the modern age of frequently dramatized "Miranda" warnings, that is implausible. Indeed, we found it implausible (or irrelevant) 30 years ago, unless the suspect was "in custody or otherwise deprived of his freedom of action in any significant way," *Miranda v. Arizona*, 384 U.S. 436, 445 (1966).

Petitioner repeats the argument made by many supporters of the "exculpatory no," that the doctrine is necessary to eliminate the grave risk that § 1001 will become an instrument of prosecutorial abuse. The supposed danger is that overzealous prosecutors will use this provision as a means of "piling on" offenses — sometimes punishing the denial of wrongdoing more severely than the wrongdoing itself. The objectors' principal grievance on this score, however, lies not with the hypothetical prosecutors but with Congress itself, which has decreed the obstruction of a legitimate investigation to be a separate offense, and a serious one. It is not for us to revise that judgment. Petitioner has been unable to demonstrate, moreover, any history of prosecutorial excess, either before or after widespread judicial acceptance of the "exculpatory no." And finally, if there is a problem of supposed "overreaching" it is hard to see how the doctrine of the "exculpatory no" could solve it. It is easy enough for an interrogator to press the liar from the initial simple denial to a more detailed fabrication that would not qualify for the exemption.

*   *   *

In sum, we find nothing to support the "exculpatory no" doctrine except the many Court of Appeals decisions that have embraced it. Courts may not create their own limitations on legislation, no matter how alluring the policy arguments for doing so, and no matter how widely the blame may be spread. Because the plain language of § 1001 admits of no exception for an "exculpatory no," we affirm the judgment of the Court of Appeals.

JUSTICE GINSBURG, with whom JUSTICE SOUTER joins, concurring in the judgment.

Because a false denial fits the unqualified language of 18 U.S.C. § 1001, I concur in the affirmance of Brogan's conviction. I write separately, however, to call attention to the extraordinary authority Congress, perhaps unwittingly, has conferred on prosecutors to manufacture crimes. I note, at the same time, how far removed the "exculpatory no" is from the problems Congress initially sought to address when it proscribed falsehoods designed to elicit a benefit from the government or to hinder government operations.

At the time of Brogan's offense, § 1001 made it a felony "knowingly and willfully" to make "any false, fictitious or fraudulent statements or representations" in "any matter within the jurisdiction of any department or agency of the United States." That encompassing formulation arms government agents with authority not simply to apprehend lawbreakers, but to generate felonies, crimes of a kind that only a government officer could prompt.

This case is illustrative. Two federal investigators paid an unannounced visit one evening to James Brogan's home. The investigators already possessed records indicating that Brogan, a union officer, had received cash from a company that employed members of the union Brogan served. (The agents gave no advance warning, one later testified, because they wanted to retain the element of surprise.) When the agents asked Brogan whether he had received any money or gifts from the company, Brogan responded "No." The agents asked no further questions. *After* Brogan just said "No," however, the agents told him: (1) the government had in hand the records indicating that his answer was false; and (2) lying to federal agents in the course of an investigation is a crime. Had counsel appeared on the spot, Brogan likely would have received and followed advice to amend his answer, to say immediately: "Strike that; I plead not guilty." But no counsel attended the unannounced interview, and Brogan divulged nothing more. Thus, when the interview ended, a federal offense had been completed — even though, for all we can tell, Brogan's unadorned denial misled no one.

A further illustration. In *United States v. Tabor*, 788 F.2d 714 (11th Cir.1986), an Internal Revenue Service (IRS) agent discovered that Tabor, a notary public, had violated Florida law by notarizing a deed even though two signatories had not personally appeared before her (one had died five weeks before the document was signed). With this knowledge in hand, and without "warn[ing] Tabor of the possible consequences of her statements," the agent went to her home with a deputy sheriff and questioned her about the transaction. When Tabor, regrettably but humanly, denied wrongdoing, the government prosecuted her under § 1001. An IRS agent thus turned a violation of state law into a federal felony by eliciting a lie that misled no one. (The Eleventh Circuit reversed the § 1001 conviction, relying on the "exculpatory no" doctrine.)

As these not altogether uncommon episodes show, § 1001 may apply to encounters between agents and their targets "under extremely informal circumstances which do not sufficiently alert the person interviewed to the danger that false statements may lead to a felony conviction." *United States v. Ehrlichman*, 379 F. Supp. 291, 292 (D.D.C. 1974). Because the questioning occurs in a noncustodial setting, the suspect is not informed of the right to remain silent. Unlike proceedings in which a false statement can be prosecuted as perjury, there may be no oath, no pause to concentrate the speaker's mind on the importance of his or her answers. As in Brogan's case, the target may not be informed that a false "No" is a criminal offense until *after* he speaks.

At oral argument, the Solicitor General forthrightly observed that § 1001 could even be used to "escalate completely innocent conduct into a felony." More likely to occur, "if an investigator finds it difficult to prove some elements of a crime, she can ask questions about other elements to which she already knows the answers. . . . If the suspect lies, she can then use the crime she has prompted as leverage or can seek prosecution for the lie as a substitute for the crime she cannot prove." Comment, *False Statements to Federal Agents: Induced Lies and the Exculpatory No*, 57 U. Chi. L. Rev. 1273, 1278 (1990). If the statute of limitations has run on an offense — as it had on four of the five payments Brogan was accused of accepting — the prosecutor can endeavor to revive the case by instructing an investigator to elicit a fresh denial of guilt. Prosecution in these circumstances is not an instance of government "punishing the denial of wrongdoing more severely than the wrongdoing itself;" it is, instead, government generation of a crime when the underlying suspected wrongdoing is or has become nonpunishable.

*   *   *

Since *Nunley v. United States*, 434 U.S. 962 (1977), the Department of Justice has maintained a policy against bringing § 1001 prosecutions for statements amounting to an "exculpatory no." At the time the charges against Brogan were filed, the United States Attorneys' Manual firmly declared: "Where the statement takes the form of an 'exculpatory no,' 18 U.S.C. § 1001 does not apply regardless who asks the question." United States Attorneys' Manual (Oct. 1, 1988). After the Fifth Circuit abandoned the "exculpatory no" doctrine in *United States v. Rodriguez-Rios*, 14 F.3d 1040 (1994) (en banc), the manual was amended to read: "It is the Department's policy that it is not appropriate to charge a § 1001 violation where a suspect, during an investigation, merely denies his guilt in response to questioning by the government." United States Attorneys' Manual (Feb. 12, 1996).[3]

These pronouncements indicate, at the least, the dubious propriety of bringing felony prosecutions for bare exculpatory denials informally made to government agents. Although today's decision holds that such prosecutions can be sustained under the broad language of § 1001, the Department of Justice's prosecutorial guide continues to caution restraint in each exercise of this large authority. . . .

The prospect remains that an overzealous prosecutor or investigator — aware that a person has committed some suspicious acts, but unable to make a criminal case — will create a crime by surprising the suspect, asking about those acts, and receiving a false denial. Congress alone can provide the appropriate instruction.

*   *   *

JUSTICE STEVENS, with whom JUSTICE BREYER joins, dissenting.

The mere fact that a false denial fits within the unqualified language of 18 U.S.C. § 1001 is not, in my opinion, a sufficient reason for rejecting a well-settled interpretation of that statute. It is not at all unusual for this Court to conclude that the literal text of a criminal statute is broader than the coverage intended by Congress. Although the text of § 1001, read literally, makes it a crime for an

---

[3] While this case was pending before us, the Department of Justice issued yet another version of the manual, which deleted the words "that it is" and "appropriate" from the sentence just quoted. The new version reads: "It is the Department's policy not to charge a § 1001 violation in situations in which a suspect, during an investigation, merely denies guilt in response to questioning by the government." United States Attorneys' Manual 9-42.160 (Sept. 1997).

undercover narcotics agent to make a false statement to a drug peddler, I am confident that Congress did not intend any such result. It seems equally clear that Congress did not intend to make every "exculpatory no" a felony. . . .

Accordingly, I respectfully dissent.

NOTES AND QUESTIONS

1. *The purpose of § 1001.* The majority rejected the defendant's argument that "only those falsehoods that pervert governmental functions are covered by § 1001." Why? If that is not the purpose of § 1001, what is?

2. *The Fifth Amendment.* What exactly was the defendant's Fifth Amendment argument? Does the Fifth Amendment provide a right to lie to the government? If not, why had lower courts relied upon that amendment in adopting an "exculpatory 'no'" exception for § 1001 prosecutions?

How does the majority respond to the defendant's argument? Upon what precise assumptions does the majority rely? Do you agree with those assumptions?

3. *Prosecutorial guidelines.* In *Brogan,* the Supreme Court sanctioned the use of "exculpatory 'nos'" as the basis for false statements prosecutions. As Justice Ginsburg noted in her concurring opinion, however, the Department of Justice has adopted various versions of a guideline that disapproves of prosecutions based upon "exculpatory 'nos.'" The current guidelines provide that "[i]t is the Department's policy not to charge a § 1001 violation in situations in which a suspect, during an investigation, merely denies guilt in response to questioning by the government." United States Attorneys' Manual ¶ 9-42.160. In your opinion, why did the DOJ adopt this guideline? The guideline, of course, is just that; it does not have the force of law. Can you ascertain why the government decided to violate its own guideline in Brogan's case?

4. *Potential for abuse?* Four Justices, two in concurrence and two in dissent, expressed concern that the *Brogan* decision leaves the door open for prosecutorial abuse. What exactly is the possible abuse that concerned those Justices? Why did those concerns appear not to trouble the remaining members of the Court?

5. *Promises concerning future actions.* Can a promise to undertake, or not undertake, a future action be the basis for a false statements charge? Can such a promise be literally false? Courts have upheld such charges. *See, e.g., United States v. Sattar,* 272 F. Supp. 2d 348, 377 (S.D.N.Y. 2003) (in prosecution of criminal defense attorney Lynne Stewart, the government charged that Stewart made a false statement when she agreed to adhere to government regulations regarding her representation of an alleged terrorist). *Accord United States v. Shah,* 44 F.3d 285, 293 (5th Cir. 1995) ("[A] promise to perform is not only a prediction, but is generally also a representation of present intent. Promises and representations are simply not mutually exclusive categories. The plain terms of the statute can therefore be said to cover representations of present intent.")

[2]   Implied False Statements —*United States v. Williams*

The Court in *Brogan* held that an "exculpatory 'no'" is a "false statement" covered by § 1001. But how do we define the boundaries of a "false statement" under the statute? Suppose, for example, that a person intentionally writes checks on an account with insufficient funds to cover the checks, and cashes the checks at a federally insured bank. Under 18 U.S.C. § 1014, it is a crime knowingly to make a false statement for the purpose of influencing a federally insured bank. Is the bad check a "false statement" under this statute because it implies that there are sufficient funds in the account to cover the check? In *Williams v. United States*, 458 U.S. 279 (1982), the Supreme Court held five-to-four that it is not. The Court stated:

> Although [the defendant] deposited several checks that were not supported by sufficient funds, that course of conduct did not involve the making of a "false statement," for a simple reason: technically speaking, a check is not a factual assertion at all, and therefore cannot be characterized as "true" or "false." Petitioner's bank checks served only to direct the drawee banks to pay the face value to the bearer, while committing petitioner to make good on the obligations if the bank dishonored the drafts. Each check did not, in terms, make any representations as to the state of petitioner's bank balance.

Id. at 284–285. The dissent countered that "[i]t defies common sense and everyday practice to maintain, as the majority does, that a check carries with it no representation as to the drawer's account balance." *Id.* at 291 (White, J., dissenting).

What is the reach of the *Williams* decision? Assume, for example, that a state department of transportation received grants from the federal government to subsidize highway construction. As a condition of receiving the grants, the state was contractually obligated to ensure that a portion of the funds went to businesses owned by women and minorities. Company A qualified for the program and was awarded a construction contract. Company A, however, did not have sufficient equipment to actually perform the contract. Company A therefore arranged with Company B — which did *not* qualify for the program — to do the work. Companies A and B then entered into sham contracts that obligated Company A to do the construction, although both companies intended that Company B do the work. The contracts were then forwarded to the federal government.

Are the companies guilty of making false statements to the government? In *United States v. Blankenship*, 382 F.3d 1110, 1135 (11th Cir. 2004), the Eleventh Circuit relied upon *Williams* in reversing the § 1001 conviction on these facts. The court stated: "Like a check, a contract is not a factual assertion, and therefore cannot be characterized as 'true' or 'false.' Just as a check is not 'false' simply because neither the drawer nor the drawee intends that the drawee cash it, a contract is not false simply because neither party intends to enforce it."

The *Williams* and *Blankenship* decisions raise two distinct but related issues. First, can an implied false statement be the basis for a false statement conviction? The *Williams* dissent clearly answered this question in the affirmative. Second, if an implied false statement is actionable under § 1001, did the check in *Williams* and the contact in *Blankenship* impliedly assert facts — that is, that the drawer had sufficient funds to cover the check in *Williams*, and that Companies A and B in *Blankenship* intended to perform their contractual obligations?

PROBLEM

9-4. Concerned about protecting their elderly father's assets, Ellen and her brother William opened a three-party account at a federally insured bank into which they placed the father's funds. The account provided that Ellen, William, and their father would each be a principal. A check drawn on the account would be negotiable only if it carried the endorsement of each of the three principals. Ellen held her father's power-of-attorney. Over a four-year period before the father's death, Ellen deposited 10 checks from the three-party account into her personal account. Although the checks bore the signatures purporting to be the signatures of all three account holders, William did not sign the checks or otherwise agree to the transfer of the funds. On each of the checks, Ellen had forged William's signature.

Based on the forged endorsements, Ellen was indicted on 10 counts under 18 U.S.C. § 1014, which criminalizes knowingly making any false statement for the purpose of influencing in any way the action of any federally-insured financial institution.

Ellen was convicted, and appeals. What arguments should she make on appeal? How should the government respond? How should the court rule? Why?

[E] CONCEALMENT

A charge under § 1001 may be based upon the theory that the defendant had a duty to disclose facts but failed to do so. The following case arose from a high-profile political corruption scandal. In the case, the court addressed whether the defendant had a duty to disclose facts to the government. As you read the decision, consider whether prosecutors exercised their discretion wisely when bringing the § 1001 charges.

UNITED STATES v. SAFAVIAN
528 F.3d 957 (D.C. Cir. 2008)

RANDOLPH, CIRCUIT JUDGE.

A jury convicted David H. Safavian of three counts of concealing material facts and making false statements in violation of 18 U.S.C. § 1001(a)(1). . . . The prosecution arose from investigations into a golfing trip he took with lobbyist Jack Abramoff in August 2002 while Safavian was chief of staff of the General Services Administration. We reverse on all counts.

The evidence, viewed most favorably to the government, showed as follows. Safavian and Abramoff met in 1994 when Safavian joined a law firm in which Abramoff was a partner. Abramoff became a mentor to Safavian there, and the two remained close friends after Safavian left the firm. They continued to play golf and racquetball together and saw each other socially for drinks and dinner. And when Safavian was looking to leave the congressman for whom he was working in 2002, Abramoff arranged for Safavian to interview at his new firm, though he did not receive an offer.

Safavian instead became the General Services Administration's (GSA) deputy chief of staff in May 2002 and was named chief of staff two months later. GSA is responsible for procurement and property management on behalf of federal agencies. Shortly after Safavian arrived at GSA, Abramoff asked him for information about two GSA-controlled properties: the White Oak property in Silver Spring, Maryland, a 600-acre former Naval facility; and the Old Post Office in Washington, D.C.

Abramoff was interested in having a portion of the White Oak property serve as a new location for the religious school his children attended. As to the Old Post Office building, GSA was considering redeveloping it and had been asking private parties about that possibility. Abramoff thought opportunities for one of his clients might develop.

Safavian and Abramoff exchanged e-mails about these properties between May and August 2002. Abramoff sent messages to both Safavian's work and home accounts, sometimes e-mailing his work account only to inform him a message was waiting on his home account. Safavian's assistance ranged from simply obtaining information that GSA had already compiled for distribution to other parties, to more involved support that Safavian could provide as a GSA insider. For example, he supplied Abramoff with internal GSA information, told Abramoff that he had "overruled" a GSA employee who had "reservations," reviewed and edited Abramoff's letters to GSA, and set up a meeting to discuss the White Oak property. Nothing ever came of any of this and both properties remained with GSA through Safavian's tenure.

While these discussions were ongoing, Abramoff invited Safavian to join him on a five-day golfing trip to Scotland in August 2002, to which Abramoff later added a weekend in London. In addition to Abramoff and Safavian, the group included Abramoff's son and colleagues, a congressman and his chief of staff, and the staff director for the House Administration Committee. Abramoff arranged the schedule and accommodations and chartered a plane for the group.

On July 25, 2002, Safavian requested an ethics opinion from GSA's general counsel about whether he could accept the air transportation as a gift. His e-mail stated:

> I am in need of an ethics opinion. I (along with wto [sic] members of Congress and a few Congressional staff) have been invited by a friend and former colleague on a trip to Scotland to play golf for four days. I will be paying for all of my hotels, meals, and greens fees. The issue is airfare.

> The host of the trip is chartering a private jet to take the eight of us from BWI to Scottland [sic] and back. He is paying the cost for the aircraft regardless of whether I go or not. In fact, none of the other guest [sic] will be paying a proportional share of the aircraft costs. I need to know how to treat this activity.

> One other point of relevance: the host is a lawyer and lobbyist, but one that has no business before GSA (he does all of his work on Capitol Hill).

The GSA ethics officer responded in part:

> This is in response to your inquiry on whether you can accept a gift of free air transportation from a friend to attend an [sic] golf trip. You stated that a friend and former colleague, Jack Abramhoff [sic], invited you, along with several members of Congress and a few Congressional staff, to Scotland to play golf for four days. You stated that you will be paying for

all of your hotel expenses, meals and greens fees. You noted, however, that your friend would be providing the air transportation at no cost to you and the other guests attending the event. You stated that your friend, who is a lawyer and lobbyist with Greenberg and Traurig, is chartering a private jet to take you and the other participants from BWI Scotland and back. You stated that neither Mr. Abramhoff [sic] nor his firm does business with or is seeking to do business with GSA. Based upon the information you have provided, you may accept the gift of free transportation from your friend.

The ethics opinion recited information not provided in Safavian's e-mail request, such as Abramoff's name and firm, so it appears that further communications must have occurred. Notably, the response also suggests that Safavian said Abramoff is not "seeking to do business with GSA." At trial the government presented no evidence that Safavian had ever told this to an ethics officer and the district judge therefore struck the "seeking to do business" language from the indictment.

After receiving the ethics advice, Safavian forwarded a copy to Abramoff, indicating that he would go on the trip. Abramoff sent Safavian an itinerary showing the travel schedule, hotels, golfing times, a dinner and a lunch with the notation "included in package," and several other scheduled meals. Safavian told Abramoff he wanted to pay for his share of the trip. On the evening of the departure date — August 3, 2002 — Safavian gave Abramoff a check for $3,100, the amount Abramoff said would cover the costs.

The chartered plane landed the morning of August 4th at a small airport adjacent to the St. Andrews Links Old Course, where the group's hotel also was located. Most of their five days in Scotland were spent golfing. They played at several different courses and smoked cigars and drank while playing. Some, including Safavian, played golf more than once per day at various courses. At the Old Course, greens fees and caddy tips for one person totaled $400. The group also ate and had drinks together. Meals — some at the hotel, some elsewhere — ranged from $20–$100 a person, and sometimes a round of drinks reached $100. . . .

The group flew from Scotland to London on Thursday the 9th, using the same chartered plane. Upon landing, they were driven to their hotel, the Mandarin Oriental. . . . On Sunday, Safavian and Abramoff flew back to the United States on the chartered jet.

Both Safavian and another participant testified that they believed the trip was prepaid. Safavian also paid for some costs himself. He withdrew $500 from his bank account before leaving and $150 on the trip's second day. He tipped the caddies once for two people and bought a few rounds of drinks. Safavian also used his credit card to buy some gifts, a few meals, and some other goods.

In March 2003, acting on an anonymous tip, the GSA Office of Inspector General (GSA-OIG) began investigating the trip. GSA agent Gregory Rowe interviewed Safavian twice. Rowe testified that Safavian told him that he "paid for the trip," including airfare, and that Abramoff did not have any business with GSA. Safavian also provided Rowe with a copy of the $3,100 check he had given to Abramoff on the day they had left and a work attendance sheet showing that he took five days of leave. Safavian did not mention the weekend in London or Abramoff's interest in the two GSA properties. Rowe closed the investigation. Rowe did not review the ethics opinion Safavian had received about the trip.

A year later, in March 2004, the Senate Committee on Indian Affairs began investigating Abramoff. The Committee asked Safavian to produce "all records reflecting, referring, or relating to the 2002 Scotland golf trip." Safavian's letter responded in part:

> When the invitation was made, I was the chief of staff to the U.S. General Services Administration ("GSA"). Mr. Abramoff did not have any business before the agency at that time. Prior to departure, I consulted the GSA Office of General Counsel to obtain guidance on the propriety of this trip. Counsel determined that I could accept the value of the trip gratis; it did not meet the definition of a 'gift from a prohibited source' under the applicable regulations, nor was it considered a gift because of my official position. Nevertheless, in the exercise of discretion, I gave Mr. Abramoff a check for the value of the trip prior to departure. In addition, I took leave without pay to travel.

Safavian also provided, among other things, his July 25 request for the ethics opinion, the opinion, and a copy of the $3,100 check.

A grand jury indicted Safavian on October 5, 2005, on three counts of "falsify-[ing], conceal[ing] and cover[ing] up by a trick, scheme, and device material facts" in violation of 18 U.S.C. § 1001(a)(1) (Counts 2, 3, and 5) . . . .c [Count 3 was] based on Safavian's interviews with GSA inspector Rowe. Count 2 was based on Safavian's request for the ethics opinion. And Count[] . . . 5 related to his letter to the Senate Committee.

The trial began May 22, 2006, and included testimony from Rowe, the ethics officer, the investigative counsel for the Committee, and one of Abramoff's colleagues who went on the Scotland trip, among others. Safavian, testifying in his defense, discussed the golf trip, his work at GSA, and his interactions with Abramoff. Safavian testified that in his view, Abramoff was "not doing business with GSA" because Abramoff "is not a contractor, he is not exchanging property or services for money, he does not have a business relationship with GSA." As to the golf trip, Safavian claimed that he thought it was a prepaid package and that he was reimbursing Abramoff fully with the $3,100 check . . . .

On June 20, the jury convicted Safavian [of Counts 2, 3, and 5, the false statements charges]. Count 2 was based on the exchange with the ethics officer. On a special verdict form, the jury found that Safavian "concealed his assistance to Mr. Abramoff in GSA-related activities" (Specification A) and "falsely stated to the GSA ethics officer that Mr. Abramoff did all his work on Capitol Hill" (Specification C). Count 3 was based on Safavian's statements and omissions during his interviews with GSA-OIG agent Rowe. The jury found that Safavian "concealed his assistance to Mr. Abramoff in GSA-related activities" (Specification A). Count 5 was based on Safavian's letter to the Committee. The jury found that he "falsely stated in a letter to the Committee that Mr. Abramoff did not have any business with GSA at the time Mr. Safavian was invited on the trip to Scotland" (Specification C) . . . .

The court sentenced Safavian to concurrent terms of 18 months imprisonment on each count, followed by two years of supervised release.

---

c In Counts 1 and 4, the government charged Safavian with obstruction of justice, 18 U.S.C. § 1505, based upon his interview with the GSA inspector and his letter to the Senate Committee. The jury convicted Safavian on Count 1 and acquitted him on Count 4. — Ed.

We will begin with Safavian's convictions on Counts 2 and 3. Each of these counts, and Count 5, charged violations of 18 U.S.C. § 1001(a)(1): a person "in any matter within the jurisdiction of the executive, legislative, or judicial branch of the Government of the United States," commits an offense if he "knowingly and willfully falsifies, conceals, or covers up by any trick, scheme, or device a material fact." *Id.* On Count 2, which dealt with Safavian's request for a GSA ethics opinion, the jury found that he violated § 1001(a)(1) when he "concealed his assistance to [Abramoff] in official GSA-related activities." On Count 3, which dealt with the GSA Inspector General's investigation, the jury found that Safavian violated § 1001(a)(1) when he "concealed his assistance to [Abramoff] in official GSA-related activities," the same concealment allegation contained in Count 2.

Safavian raises several serious objections to his convictions on the concealment charges, though we only reach the question whether he had a duty to disclose his assistance. As to Count 2, he points out that officers and employees of the executive, judicial, and legislative branches regularly seek advice from their respective ethics committees. They are encouraged to do so. The value of the advice they receive depends upon the accuracy and fullness of the information they provide. At GSA, as elsewhere in the federal government, the officer or employee making the inquiry may or may not follow the advice of the ethics committee. That he did not follow that advice does not in itself constitute an ethical transgression. The prosecutors in this case are mistaken when they write that the GSA "ethics opinion   permitted [Safavian] to engage in behavior that would be prohibited if he had disclosed all relevant information." The ethics opinion did no such thing. It was not up to the GSA ethics officers to permit or forbid; their function was to offer advice. It is not apparent how this voluntary system, replicated throughout the government, imposes a duty on those seeking ethical advice to disclose — in the government's words — "all relevant information" upon pain of prosecution for violating § 1001(a)(1).[5] As Safavian argues and as the government agrees, there must be a legal duty to disclose in order for there to be a concealment offense in violation of § 1001(a)(1), yet the government failed to identify a legal disclosure duty except by reference to vague standards of conduct for government employees.

These standards are formulated as fourteen "general principles" that executive branch "employees shall apply . . . in determining whether their conduct is proper." 5 C.F.R. § 2635.101(b). They range from exceedingly vague — "Employees shall put forth honest effort in the performance of their duties,"§ 2635.101(b)(5) — to somewhat more descriptive — "Employees shall not use public office for private gain."§ 2635.101(b)(7). Only one has anything to do with disclosure. *See* § 2635.101(b)(11) ("Employees shall disclose waste, fraud, abuse, and corruption to appropriate authorities."). These strictures are of no more help to the government's argument than the regulation on seeking ethics advice. Their relationship to Safavian's duty under § 1001(a)(1) is tenuous at best. If an employee violates a standard of conduct, he may be subject to disciplinary action. § 2635.106(a). We cannot see how this translates into criminal liability under 18 U.S.C. § 1001(a)(1)

---

[5] Disclosing all relevant circumstances merely offers the employee protection from disciplinary action: "Disciplinary action for violating this part or any supplemental agency regulations will not be taken against an employee who has engaged in conduct in good faith reliance upon the advice of an agency ethics official, provided that the employee, in seeking such advice, has made full disclosure of all relevant circumstances." 5 C.F.R. § 2635.107(b).

whenever someone seeking ethical advice or being interviewed by a GSA investigator omits "relevant information."

Concealment cases in this circuit and others have found a duty to disclose material facts on the basis of specific requirements for disclosure of specific information. There is good reason for demanding such specificity: to comply with Fifth Amendment due process, the defendant must have "fair notice . . . of what conduct is forbidden. . . . [T]his 'fair warning' requirement prohibits application of a criminal statute to a defendant unless it was reasonably clear at the time of the alleged action that defendants' actions were criminal." *United States v. Kanchanalak*, 192 F.3d 1037, 1046 (D.C. Cir. 1999) (*citing United States v. Lanier*, 520 U.S. 259 (1997)). The ethical principles give no indication of the particular facts or information an executive employee must disclose. Nor do they suggest that they have any bearing on conduct during a GSA investigation or a request for an ethics opinion.

The government also invoked, in support of the verdict on the concealment charges in Count 2 and Count 3, "the principle that once one begins speaking when seeking government action or in response to questioning, one must disclose all relevant facts." The government cites no regulation, form, or statute to this effect and the defense maintains that no such general principle exists. Attorneys commonly advise their clients to answer questions truthfully but not to volunteer information. Are we to suppose that once the client starts answering a government agent's questions, in a deposition or during an investigation, the client must disregard his attorney's advice or risk prosecution under § 1001(a)(1)? The government essentially asks us to hold that once an individual starts talking, he cannot stop. We do not think § 1001 demands that individuals choose between saying everything and saying nothing. No case stands for that proposition.[7] We therefore conclude that Safavian had no legal duty to disclose and that his concealment convictions cannot stand.

The remaining charges are the alleged false statements Safavian made, as specified in Counts 2 and 5 (§ 1001(a)(1)).[9] Each of the statements was to the effect that Abramoff had no business with GSA at the time of the golf trip. In defense of these charges, Safavian maintained that when he made the statements he intended the meaning common to government contracts professionals — that is, someone who does not have a contract with GSA is not doing business or working with GSA. Safavian contended that his statements were truthful because Abramoff never secured any GSA contract. With respect to the White Oak property, the headmaster of the school never requested a lease and GSA never transferred the property to the school. As to the Old Post Office, GSA issued no proposal during the tenure of the

---

[7] The government cites United States v. Moore, 446 F.3d 671 (7th Cir. 2006), and United States v. Cisneros, 26 F. Supp. 2d 24 (D.D.C. 1998), as supporting its position. However, the jury instructions in *Moore* stated, "The duty to disclose a particular fact to the executive branch of the federal government or its agent arises from requirements in federal statutes, regulations, or government forms." 446 F.3d at 680. In *Cisneros*, the questions posed to the defendant by the FBI agent were rooted in a government form that the defendant had filled out. *See* 26 F. Supp. 2d at 32.

[9] Safavian argues that his statements should not have been submitted to the jury because they were fundamentally ambiguous and thus the jurors "could only guess what he may have meant." Assuming *arguendo* that the doctrine of fundamental ambiguity applies to false statements such as these, it was well within the province of the jury to determine what Safavian meant. Likewise, we reject Safavian's argument that there was insufficient evidence for the jury to conclude that the statements were false as Safavian intended them.

GSA Administrator for whom Safavian worked.

We agree with Safavian that the district court abused its discretion in excluding favorable expert testimony on how government contracting professionals view having business or working with GSA. Safavian's expert would have testified that an individual is not doing business with GSA until a contract is awarded and that getting information from GSA is simply that, getting information. Defense counsel offered this testimony to show that Safavian's definition "isn't made up out of whole cloth." The testimony would have bolstered Safavian's contention that, as a government contracts professional himself, he had this meaning in mind when he communicated with the GSA ethics official, Rowe, and with the Senate Committee.

In excluding this testimony, the district court reasoned that it would not help the jury and would be confusing. The court asserted that the meaning of "business" "is within the common parlance of the jury," and thus "the layman's definition of these terms are the best guide for the jury. There's no need for expert testimony." This ruling usurped the jury's role by deciding that the lay meaning of "business" is what Safavian meant to convey. The court at one point recognized that "[w]hat was in the defendant's mind is at issue in this case." But excluding the expert testimony effectively preempted the jury's conclusion on this issue. . . .

We do not find the exclusion of the expert's testimony harmless. With respect to Counts 2 and 5, which charged violations of § 1001(a)(1), literal truth would have been a complete defense. The jury's duty was to decide which meaning Safavian intended — the contracting meaning or the "lay" meaning — "by considering the term in context, taking into account the setting in which it appeared and the purpose for which it was used." Evidence showed that Safavian had substantial experience in the field of government contracts. The expert's testimony would have supplied crucial context and support for Safavian's proposed meaning. This testimony would have been especially important in light of the fact that two government witnesses, though not appearing as experts, testified regarding their own interpretations of the phrase "doing business." Excluding the expert's testimony thus was not harmless.

[The court thus reversed Safavian's conviction on the omission theory under Counts 2 and 3, and remanded for a new trial on Count 2 based on the alternative theory that Safavian made an affirmative material misstatement when he stated that the $3,100 payment covered the entire cost of the trip. The court also vacated and remanded Count 5 for a new trial.]

NOTES AND QUESTIONS

1. *Duty to disclose.* When does a duty to disclose arise under § 1001? Courts have found such duties in varying circumstances. *See, e.g., United States v. Moore,* 446 F.3d 671 (7th Cir. 2006) (finding a duty to disclose existed when a HUD form contract incorporated a conflict of interest regulation); *United States v. Kingston,* 971 F.2d 481, 489 (10th Cir. 1992) (holding that "a defendant's duty to disclose is established where a government form required a disclosure of concealed information.") *But see United States v. Curran,* 20 F.3d 560, 566 (3d Cir. 1994) (holding no duty to disclose existed where duty to disclose source of campaign contributions to Federal Election Commission was that of campaign treasurers, rather than defendant at whose behest contributions were purportedly made); *United States v. Crop Growers Corp.,* 954 F. Supp. 335, 348 (D.D.C. 1997) ("to the

extent that any duty to disclose is predicated on professional standards not codified in any statute or regulation, there can be no criminal liability").

Why did the court in *Safavian* find that no duty was present in his case?

2. *Literal truth.* Most courts agree with the Safavian court that a literally true statement, even if misleading, cannot be the basis for a false statement charge under § 1001. *See, e.g., United States v. Kosth*, 257 F.3d 712, 719–720 (7th Cir. 2001); *United States v. Hixon*, 987 F.2d 1261, 1265–1268 (6th Cir. 1993). The same rule holds under the federal perjury statutes examined in the next chapter. *See* Chapter 10, Perjury and False Declarations, *infra*, § C. How does a jury determine whether a defendant's statement, as the defendant intended the statement's meaning, was literally true? Why did the appeals court find that the trial court had erred on this issue?

3. *Ambiguous answers.* Reconsider footnote 9 in the *Safavian* opinion. Was the statement that "Abramoff had no business with GSA" ambiguous? Why or why not? The court stated that it is up to the jury to decide, in the event of an ambiguous statement, what meaning the defendant intended. This is also the general rule with respect to ambiguous statements made under oath that are the basis of perjury charges. *See* Chapter 10, Perjury and False Declarations, *infra*, § C.

[F] MENS REA

Section 1001 requires that the government prove that the defendant acted "knowingly and willfully." As seen in the *Safavian* opinion, *supra*, § [E], and as discussed more fully in the notes below, the government must show beyond a reasonable doubt that the defendant intended to make a false statement. Thus, Safavian's proffered expert testimony — regarding the commonly understood meaning of his statement that Abramoff did not do "business" with the GSA — was relevant to Safavian's intent when he made the alleged false statement.

Now assume for a moment that Safavian was not speaking to a person whom Safavian knew to be an agent of the United States government. Also assume that Safavian did not know that his statement would be relayed to the federal government. Even if Safavian acted with the intent to deceive the listener, did he act "knowingly and willfully" under the statute?

Section 1001 states that the statute applies to "whoever, in any matter within the jurisdiction of the executive, legislative, or judicial branch of the Government of the United States, *knowingly and willfully* . . . (2) makes any materially false, fictitious, or fraudulent statement or representation . . . " Thus, the question is whether the words "knowingly and willfully" modify not only the acts that follow those words but also the preceding requirement that the acts be "in any matter within the jurisdiction" of the U.S. government.

NOTE ON UNITED STATES v. YERMIAN

The Supreme Court addressed this issue in *United States v. Yermian*, 468 U.S. 63 (1984). Yermian was charged with three counts of violating § 1001 based upon material false statements that he made on a security clearance questionnaire that he completed for his employer. The employer was a private defense contracting firm that did business with the United States government. The employer forwarded Yermian's completed questionnaire to the United States Department of Defense.

On appeal from his conviction, Yermian admitted that he had known that his statements were false. He argued that his conviction should nonetheless be reversed because the jury instructions had not required the jury to find that he had "actual knowledge that his false statements would be transmitted to a federal agency." In a five-to-four decision, the Supreme Court affirmed Yermian's conviction. Interpreting the statutory language, the Court noted that "[t]he jurisdictional language appears in a phrase separate from the prohibited conduct modified by the terms 'knowingly and willfully.' " Thus, the terms "knowingly and willfully" naturally relate only to the making of "false, fictitious, or fraudulent statements . . . and not the predicate circumstance that those statements be made in a matter within the jurisdiction of a federal agency." The Court in *Yermian* held that the government need not prove that the defendant had actual knowledge of federal jurisdiction; it did not determine whether the statute requires that the government prove some lower level of mens rea, such as negligence.

Justice Rehnquist dissented in an opinion joined by Justices Brennan, Stevens, and O'Connor. The dissent concluded that both Congressional intent and the statutory language were ambiguous, and that under the doctrine of lenity, the issue should have been resolved in favor of the defendant.

NOTES AND QUESTIONS

1. *The jurisdictional element.*

a. *Statements within federal jurisdiction.* Why were Yermian's false statements within federal jurisdiction? Were they made directly to the United States government? Reconsider the *Blankenship* case, discussed in the notes following *United States v. Rodgers*, § C, *supra.* If the facts in *Yermian* arose today, could the defendant successfully argue that, under the *Blankenship* reasoning, the statements were not made within federal jurisdiction under § 1001? Why or why not?

b. *Mens rea as to jurisdiction.* In *Yermian*, the Court relied upon its earlier holding in *United States v. Feola*, 420 U.S. 671 (1975). In *Feola*, the defendants were convicted of conspiring to assault a federal officer, whom the defendants did not know was an undercover federal officer. The court of appeals reversed the conspiracy conviction, holding that the jury should have been required to find that the defendants *knew* that their intended victim was a federal officer. The Supreme Court reinstated the conviction. The Court found that knowledge of the victim's status is not required for the object crime of assault. The Court reasoned that such a requirement would frustrate the statute's intent to protect both federal officers and federal functions. The Court concluded that "[t]he concept of criminal intent does not extend so far as to require that the actor understand not only the nature of his act but also its consequence for the choice of a judicial forum." Consequently, the Court also found that the crime of conspiring to violate § 111 does not require proof that the defendant knew that the intended victim was a federal officer.

2. *The rule from* Yermian.

a. *The majority decision.* The Court in *Yermian* did not decide if the government must prove that the defendant acted negligently, that is, that the defendant should have known the statement was within federal jurisdiction. If you were a judge in a case with facts similar to those in *Yermian*, would you require the jury to find that the defendant possessed any particular mental state concerning jurisdiction? If so, what precise instruction would you give? Why?

b. *The lower courts' responses.* Those circuit courts that have considered the issue have held that the government need not prove any mental state with respect to facts giving rise to federal jurisdiction under § 1001. *See, e.g., United States v. Leo*, 941 F.2d 181, 190 (3d Cir. 1991) (agreeing with four other circuits that no mens rea as to jurisdiction is required under § 1001). *Cf. United States v. Gibson*, 881 F.2d 318, 323–324 (6th Cir. 1989) (Merritt, J., dissenting) (asserting that the *Yermian* decision is no longer good law and that mens rea as to jurisdiction is required under § 1001). The United States Supreme Court has yet to resolve the issue as to whether the government must prove that the defendant reasonably should have known that the false statement fell within federal jurisdiction.

c. *Effect of strict liability.* Are there dangers from imposing strict liability on the jurisdictional element? One circuit court judge has noted that "*Yermian* might be read to permit § 1001 to reach any material, knowing false statement that turns out to have a fortuitous federal involvement — for example, a statement that the IRS happens upon in the course of a tax audit, or a casual falsehood made in the unknown presence of a federal officer and somehow pertinent to his mission." *Unites States v. Oakar*, 111 F.3d 146, 161 (D.C. Cir. 1997) (Williams, J., dissenting in part). The court in *Blankenship*, discussed in the notes following *United States v. Rodgers*, § C, *supra*, voiced similar concerns. Are these courts' concerns legitimate? Why or why not?

d. *The rule of lenity.* As so often happens in white collar prosecutions, the defendant in *Yermian* — like the defendant in *Rodgers* — cited the rule of lenity in support of his interpretation of the statute. What precisely is the alleged ambiguity in *Yermian*? Do you agree with the dissent that the statute is indeed ambiguous? Why or why not?

e. *The votes.* The *Yermian* decision is just one of many important Supreme Court white collar cases decided by a bare majority. Why do these cases split the Court so narrowly? Further, once again we see an unusual alignment of justices. Rare indeed were the criminal cases in which the Court was closely divided and Justices Rehnquist and Brennan found themselves on the same side. Can you explain why the dissenters joined forces in this case?

3. *The general mens rea requirement under § 1001.* As noted above, § 1001 requires that the government prove that the defendant acted "knowingly and willfully." Several interpretive issues arise when considering proof of mens rea under § 1001.

a. *Constructive knowledge.* As in other areas of the criminal law, knowledge can be proven by actual or constructive knowledge. Knowledge is therefore shown where defendant "deliberately ignores a high probability that [a statement] contains material false information." *United States v. Arnous*, 122 F.3d 321, 323 (6th Cir. 1997).

b. *Willfulness.* Does willfulness under § 1001 require proof of an intent to violate a known legal duty, as the Supreme Court has required in some areas? *See, e.g., Cheek v. United States*, 498 U.S. 192 (1991) (willfulness in tax fraud statutes requires proof of an intentional violation of a known legal duty). Or, is the requirement met when a defendant knows that the statement is false and knows that making a false statement is generally unlawful? Courts have generally held that the latter is sufficient. *See, e.g., United States v. Whab*, 355 F.3d 155, 162 (2d Cir. 2004) (it was not plain error for the district court to instruct the jury that "willfully" under § 1001 requires only that the defendant have been aware of the generally unlawful nature of the conduct).

c. *Specific intent*. Many courts also require that the government show an intent to deceive — sometimes described as "specific intent" — under § 1001. *See, e.g., United States v. Brown*, 151 F.3d 476, 484 (6th Cir. 1998). Such intent can be proven by circumstantial evidence, including knowledge of falsity. As a practical matter, does the "specific intent" requirement impose a significant additional burden on the government?

Problem

9-5. Defendants Broom and Meade were employees of a city Public Housing Authority (PHA). The PHA administered a program that provided housing for low-income families with funding from the United States Department of Housing and Urban Development (HUD). The applicable federal statutes, regulations, and policies were designed to ensure that beneficiaries of the program received assistance through an impartial system based on (1) the degree of the family's need, and (2) the time of the family's application. Because the program did not have sufficient funding to assist all who would qualify, the program required an allocation system based on (a) the date of application, (b) the percentage of income currently spent on housing, and (c) the current housing situation. In addition, the program established a procedure for choosing qualified families in a particular order based upon a waiting list.

Broom was a PHA supervisor. Meade was a PHA staff member in charge of processing applications. Because of ongoing problems with the low-income housing program, the PHA provided employees with various training videotapes and with pamphlets and booklets. There is no evidence, however, that Meade ever saw this material or ever discussed the waiting list procedure with representatives of HUD or PHA. Broom did request and receive the relevant regulations, some of which referred to the use of waiting lists. Broom also discussed the waiting lists with an HUD representative.

In order to favor certain applicants, including friends and political allies, the defendants did not require that those applicants be placed on the waiting list. Rather, the defendants submitted applications for those people as soon as the applications were received. On these applications, the defendants stated that the applicants were "eligible" for the federal program. The evidence showed that the applicants met the program criteria listed above. The defendants were convicted of violating § 1001 based upon PHA applications that the agency forwarded to the federal government.

What theory or theories would support the convictions? What arguments do the defendants have on appeal? Are the arguments likely to succeed? Why or why not?

[G] MATERIALITY

In many white collar crime contexts, materiality is a potential issue for the finder of fact. For example, as discussed in other chapters in this text, materiality is an element in any securities fraud case and is also an element in perjury cases. In the False Statements Accountability Act of 1996, Congress amended § 1001 to make it clear that the government must prove materiality as an element in a case brought under that section.

In *United States v. Gaudin*, 515 U.S. 506 (1995), the Supreme Court described a material statement under § 1001 as a statement having " 'a natural tendency to influence, or [be] capable of influencing, the decision of the decisionmaking body to which it was addressed.' " *Id.* at 510, *quoting Kungys v. United States*, 485 U.S. 759, 770 (1988). The Court in *Gaudin* further stated:

> Deciding whether a statement is "material" requires the determination of at least two subsidiary questions of purely historical fact: (a) "what statement was made?" and (b) "what decision was the agency trying to make?" The ultimate question: (c) "whether the statement was material to the decision," requires applying the legal standard of materiality . . . to these historical facts.

Id. at 512. Finally, the Court in *Gaudin* held that materiality is a mixed question of law and fact that must be decided by the trier of fact.

PROBLEM

9-6. Defendant was a federal agent ("Agent") who drove a government-issued car. Agent's car was parked illegally and was towed by local parking enforcement officials. Angry that the car had been towed, Agent went to the lot where the car was being kept and removed the car from the tow lot without paying the towing fee, damaging a fence in the process. Agent later paid $500 for the towing fee and damage to the property. Agent received an invoice for $500 from the towing company, and submitted the invoice to the federal government for reimbursement. Embarrassed by the property damage, Agent altered the invoice to remove the reference to the damage. Under applicable federal regulations, Agent would have been entitled to be reimbursed for the $500 regardless of whether the invoice was altered.

Was the altered invoice a material false statement? If so, under what theory?

[H] DOUBLE JEOPARDY AND RELATED ISSUES

In many white collar contexts, multiple charges or successive prosecutions based upon the same incident may give rise to a challenge under the Fifth Amendment's Double Jeopardy Clause, which provides that a defendant may not be "subject for the same offense to be twice put in jeopardy of life or limb." The next case is a leading Supreme Court decision dealing with the application of the Double Jeopardy Clause to multiple criminal charges arising out of the same event.

UNITED STATES v. WOODWARD
469 U.S. 105 (1985)

PER CURIAM.

On March 1, 1980, respondent Charles Woodward and his wife arrived at Los Angeles International Airport on a flight from Brazil. In passing through Customs, respondent was handed the usual form that included the following question: "Are you or any family member carrying over $5,000 (or the equivalent value in any currency) in monetary instruments such as coin, currency, traveler's checks, money orders, or negotiable instruments in bearer form?"[d] Respondent checked the "no" box.

After questioning respondent for a brief period, customs officials decided to search respondent and his wife. As he was being escorted to a search room, respondent told an official that he and his wife were carrying over $20,000 in cash. Woodward removed approximately $12,000 from his boot; another $10,000 was found in a makeshift money belt concealed under his wife's clothing.

Woodward was indicted on charges of making a false statement to an agency of the United States, 18 U.S.C. § 1001, and willfully failing to report that he was carrying in excess of $5,000 into the United States, 31 U.S.C. §§ 1058, 1101. The same conduct — answering "no" to the question whether he was carrying more than $5,000 into the country — formed the basis of each count. A jury convicted Woodward on both charges; he received a sentence of six months in prison on the false statement count, and a consecutive three-year term of probation on the currency reporting count. During the proceedings in the district court, the respondent never asserted that Congress did not intend to permit cumulative punishment for conduct violating the false statement and the currency reporting statutes.

The United States Court of Appeals for the Ninth Circuit held that respondent's conduct could not be punished under both 18 U.S.C. § 1001 and 31 U.S.C. §§ 1058, 1101. The court applied the rule of statutory construction contained in *Blockburger v. United States*, 284 U.S. 299, 304 (1932) — "whether each provision requires proof of a fact which the other does not" — and held that the false statement felony was a lesser included offense of the currency reporting misdemeanor. In other words, every violation of the currency reporting statute necessarily entails a violation of the false statement law.[3] The court reasoned that a willful failure to file a required report is a form of concealment prohibited by 18 U.S.C. § 1001. Concluding that Congress presumably intended someone in respondent's position to be punished only under the currency reporting misdemeanor, the Court of Appeals reversed respondent's felony conviction for making a false statement.

The Court of Appeals plainly misapplied the *Blockburger* rule for determining whether Congress intended to permit cumulative punishment; proof of a currency reporting violation does *not* necessarily include proof of a false statement offense. Section 1001 proscribes the nondisclosure of a material fact only if the fact is "conceal[ed] . . . by any *trick, scheme, or device*" (emphasis added). A person

---

[d] After Woodward was decided, Congress increased the triggering amount to cash in excess of $10,000. — Eds.

[3] The converse is clearly not true; 31 U.S.C. §§ 1058, 1101, but not 18 U.S.C. § 1001, involve the failure to file a currency disclosure report.

could, without employing a "trick, scheme, or device," simply and willfully fail to file a currency disclosure report. A traveler who enters the country and passes through Customs prepared to answer questions truthfully, but is never asked whether he is carrying over $5,000 in currency, might nonetheless be subject to conviction under 31 U.S.C. § 1058 for willfully transporting money without filing the required currency report. However, because he did not conceal a material fact by means of a "trick, scheme, or device" (and did not make any false statement) his conduct would not fall within 18 U.S.C. § 1001.[4]

There is no evidence in 18 U.S.C. § 1001 and 31 U.S.C. §§ 1058, 1101 that Congress did not intend to allow separate punishment for the two different offenses. Sections 1058 and 1101 were enacted by Congress in 1970 as part of the Currency and Foreign Transactions Reporting Act. Section 203(k) of that Act expressly provided: "For the purposes of § 1001 of title 18, United States Code, the contents of reports required under any provision of this title are statements and representations in matters within the jurisdiction of an agency of the United States." 31 U.S.C. § 1052(k).[5]

It is clear that in passing the currency reporting law, Congress' attention was drawn to 18 U.S.C. § 1001, but at no time did it suggest that the two statutes could not be applied together. We cannot assume, therefore, that Congress was unaware that it had created two different offenses permitting multiple punishment for the same conduct.

Finally, Congress' intent to allow punishment under both 18 U.S.C. § 1001 and 31 U.S.C. §§ 1058, 1101 is shown by the fact that the statutes "are directed to separate evils." The currency reporting statute was enacted to develop records that would "have a high degree of usefulness in criminal, tax, or regulatory investigations." 31 U.S.C. § 1051. The false statement statute, on the other hand, was designed "to protect the authorized functions of governmental departments and agencies from the perversion which might result from the deceptive practices described." *United States v. Gilliland*, 312 U.S. 86, 93 (1941).

All guides to legislative intent reveal that Congress intended respondent's conduct to be punishable under both 18 U.S.C. § 1001, and 31 U.S.C. §§ 1058, 1101. Accordingly, the petition for a writ of certiorari is granted, and that part of the Court of Appeals' judgment reversing respondent's 18 U.S.C. § 1001 conviction is reversed.

NOTES AND QUESTIONS

1. *The* Blockburger *test.* On its face, the *Blockburger* test is easy to apply: a defendant generally may not be punished for multiple crimes for the same act if: (1) (a) the crimes have the same elements, or (b) one of the crimes is a lesser included offense of the other; or (2) Congress did not intend that a defendant be punished for both crimes.

---

[4] In Woodward's case, the government did not have to prove the existence of a trick, scheme, or device. Woodward was charged with violating § 1001 because he made a false statement on the customs form. This type of affirmative misrepresentation is proscribed under the statute even if not accompanied by a trick, scheme, or device.

[5] When Title 31 was recodified in 1982, this provision was eliminated as "[u]nnecessary" because "§ 1001 applies unless otherwise provided." H.R. Rep. No. 97-651, p. 301 (1982).

It is not always easy to determine whether one crime is a lesser included offense of another. In simple terms, under federal law, Crime A is a lesser included offense of Crime B when proof of Crime B always requires proof of Crime A. Thus, if Crime A requires proof of elements 1 & 2, and Crime B requires proof of elements 1, 2, & 3, then Crime A is a lesser included offense of Crime B and the defendant generally cannot be punished for both crimes.[e] For example, as discussed in Chapter 7, Bribery and Gratuities, *supra*, the crime of receiving an illegal gratuity requires proof that a federal public official received something of value as compensation for an official act other than as provided by law. The crime of bribery essentially requires proof of these elements, plus the public official's "corrupt" intent — receiving the payment knowing that it is being given specifically to influence how the public official carries out the official act. For this reason, gratuity is generally considered to be a lesser included offense of bribery. *See* Chapter 7, Bribery and Gratuities, *supra*, § B[3].

Thus, if a defendant is charged with the separate crimes of receiving a bribe and of receiving a gratuity, the defendant may be convicted of and punished for either crime, but not both. A prosecutor may make a tactical decision to include the lesser offense in the hope of gaining some conviction if the jury rejects the more serious charge, or may decide to omit the lesser charge in an attempt to avoid jury compromise.

What were the elements of the crimes in *Woodward*? Why did the Court conclude that they are separate crimes?

2. *Multiple charges in a single trial.* The issue in *Woodward* involved multiple charges in a single trial. Note that the Court assumed that, even if the crimes have different elements, multiple punishments would not be appropriate if Congress had expressed an intent not to allow multiple punishments. Conversely, the Supreme Court has held that *Blockburger* does not bar multiple punishments for the same act at one trial where the legislature intended to permit such punishment. *See Missouri v. Hunter*, 459 U.S. 359 (1983). Thus, if Congressional intent were clear, then the government could obtain multiple convictions at a single prosecution for the same act for crimes that have the same elements, or for crimes where one is a lesser included offense of the other.

3. *Successive prosecutions.* Issues under *Blockburger* arise in many contexts, including both multiple charges at the same trial, and successive prosecutions arising out of the same facts. Successive prosecutions are prohibited by the Double Jeopardy Clause if the charges violate the *Blockburger* test.[f]

PROBLEMS

9-7. Defendant was convicted under 18 U.S.C. § 542, which provides:

---

[e] Some states use different tests for determining whether one crime is a lesser included offense of another. For an overview of legal and strategic issues concerning lesser included offenses, see Catherine L. Carpenter, *The All-or-Nothing Doctrine in Criminal Cases: Independent Trial Strategy or Gamesmanship Gone Awry?* 26 Am. J. Crim. L. 257 (1999).

[f] For an excellent overview of these and other issues relating to the *Blockburger* rule, see Joshua Dressler & Alan C. Michaels, *Understanding Criminal Procedure, Vol. 2: Adjudication* §§ 14.07-08 (4th ed. 2006).

Whoever enters or introduces, or attempts to enter or introduce, into the commerce of the United States any imported merchandise by means of any fraudulent or false invoice, declaration, affidavit, letter, paper, or by means of any false statement, written or verbal, or by means of any false or fraudulent practice or appliance, or makes any false statement in any declaration without reasonable cause to believe the truth of such statement, or procures the making of any such false statement as to any matter material thereto without reasonable cause to believe the truth of such statement, whether or not the United States shall or may be deprived of any lawful duties . . . shall be fined for each offense under this title or imprisoned not more than two years, or both.

Defendant was also convicted under § 1001 for the same statement.

Can defendant be punished under both statutes? Why or why not?

9-8. Defendant has been convicted under both 18 U.S.C. § 1035 and 18 U.S.C. § 1001. Section 1035 provides:

(a) Whoever, in any matter involving a health care benefit program, knowingly and willfully —

(1) falsifies, conceals, or covers up by any trick, scheme, or device a material fact; or

(2) makes any materially false, fictitious, or fraudulent statements or representations, or makes or uses any materially false writing or document knowing the same to contain any materially false, fictitious, or fraudulent statement or entry, in connection with the delivery of or payment for health care benefits, items, or services, shall be fined under this title or imprisoned not more than 5 years, or both.

Assuming that both charges arose out of the same false statement, assess whether defendant can be convicted and punished under both statutes.

Chapter 10

PERJURY AND FALSE DECLARATIONS

[A] INTRODUCTORY NOTES

[1]   The Federal Perjury Statutes

The federal criminal code contains a number of perjury statutes. The most significant of these are the general perjury statute, 18 U.S.C. § 1621, which applies to various types of federal proceedings, and the false declarations statute, 18 U.S.C. § 1623, which applies only to federal judicial and grand jury proceedings. In addition, there are federal statutes that make it a crime to lie under oath in connection with particular matters. For example, the federal tax code, 26 U.S.C. § 7206, criminalizes perjury in connection with the filing of a tax return. Because perjury potentially affects the functioning of the body to which it is directed, it is a serious crime that carries significant penalties.

Perjury charges may arise in one of two ways. First, the government may believe that the defendant has lied under oath, and may initiate an investigation and bring an indictment focused solely on the alleged perjury. The investigation and subsequent impeachment of former President Bill Clinton regarding his sworn testimony in a civil lawsuit is perhaps the most famous example of a perjury-focused investigation.[a]

Second, the government may bring a perjury charge in addition to or instead of the primary subject of the criminal investigation. For example, assume that the SEC subpoenas the testimony of one suspected of securities fraud, and that the witness denies the fraud during an SEC deposition. If the defendant is later charged in a criminal securities fraud case, the government may decide to include in that case a perjury charge in addition to the substantive securities fraud charges. High-profile defendants in perjury cases that resulted from investigations into other types of wrongdoing include baseball player Barry Bonds, media personality Martha Stewart, and vice-presidential aid Scooter Libby.[b]

---

[a] For an insightful analysis of the Clinton matter, see Stuart P. Green, *Perjury*, *in* Lying, Cheating, and Stealing: A Moral Theory of White Collar Crime 140–147 (2006).

[b] Initially, under investigation for the use of illegal performance-enhancing substances, Bonds was ultimately charged only with perjury and obstruction of justice based upon his grand jury testimony denying such use. *See* Michael S. Schmidt, *Prosecutors Rework Indictment of Bonds*, N.Y. Times, May 14, 2008, at D4. Martha Stewart was under investigation for insider trading, but ultimately was found guilty only of cover-up crimes, including conspiracy to commit perjury. Peter Bacanovic, her broker and co-defendant, was found guilty of perjury. *See* United States v. Stewart, 323 F. Supp. 2d 606 (S.D.N.Y. 2004). Libby was under investigation for violating national security laws in connection with the CIA leak case, but was charged and convicted only of cover-up crimes, including perjury. United States v. Libby, 498 F. Supp. 2d 1 (D.D.C. 2007).

[2]   Overview and Elements of §§ 1621 and 1623

[a]   Coverage

Initially, it is important to note the differences in the proceedings covered by § 1621 and § 1623. Section 1621 applies to court proceedings, grand jury proceedings, and all other federal proceedings in which an oath is authorized by law. The latter include Congressional and administrative agency proceedings. By way of contrast, § 1623 *only* applies to proceedings "before or ancillary to any court or grand jury." Thus, the two statutes overlap. Perjury committed in a judicial or grand jury proceeding can be charged under either statute. Perjury not committed before a court or grand jury, but rather during an administrative agency or Congressional proceeding, for example, can only be charged under § 1621. In instances where both statutes apply, courts have generally allowed prosecutors discretion in choosing which statute to employ. The maximum statutory prison sentence under both statutes is five years.[c]

[b]   The elements

Under § 1621, the government must prove the following elements:

(1) The defendant undertook an oath administered by one authorized by federal law to do so;

(2) The defendant undertook the oath before a competent tribunal, officer, or person;

(3) The oath was administered in a case in which federal law allowed an oath to be administered;

(4) The defendant made a false statement;

(5) The statement was material to the proceedings; and

(6) The defendant acted willfully and with knowledge of the statement's falsity.

Under § 1623, the government must prove the following elements:

(1) The defendant undertook an oath;

(2) The oath was administered before or ancillary to a court or grand jury proceeding;

(3) The defendant made a false statement or used false information;

(4) The false statement or information was material to the proceeding; and

(5) The defendant knew the statement or information was false.

---

[c] For an analysis of the principal federal perjury statutes, see Green, *supra* note a, at 133–147; James Nesland, *Perjury and False Declarations, in* White Collar Crime: Business and Regulatory Offenses § 10.01[1]–[3] (Otto Obermaier & Robert Morvillo, eds. 2009).

[c]   Differences between §§ 1621 and 1623

Congress enacted § 1623, the false declarations statute, as a supplement to § 1621, the general perjury statute. Congress intended that the new statute promote truthfulness in court and grand jury proceedings. Thus, Congress made it easier in several respects for the government to prove a case under § 1623 than under § 1621:

1. *Inconsistent statements.* Section 1623 contains an "inconsistent statements" provision. Under this provision, the government may prove a false declaration by showing that the defendant made "two or more declarations, which are inconsistent to the degree that one of them is necessarily false." Section 1621 contains no such provision.

2. *Two-witness rule.* Section 1623 does away with the "two-witness" rule that courts have applied to cases brought under § 1621. The two-witness rule requires that a perjury charge be proven by one witness *plus* corroborating evidence. That requirement still applies under § 1621.

3. *False information.* Under § 1623, the prosecution may be based not only on a false statement but also on the use of false information.

4. *Mens rea.* Section 1621 requires proof of willfulness and knowledge of falsity, while § 1623 only requires proof of the latter. In practice, however, the willfulness requirement is usually met whenever the government is able to prove knowledge of falsity.

Although § 1623 does provide these advantages to prosecutors, Congress apparently did intend to mollify those advantages to prosecutors in one respect. Thus, § 1623 provides a defense for a witness who takes back, or "recants," earlier sworn testimony. Section § 1621 does not provide for this defense. In practice, however, and as discussed more fully in § [E] below, the recantation defense is seldom successful.

[B]   TRIBUNALS AND PROCEEDINGS

Prosecutions under § 1623 may raise the issue whether the alleged falsity occurred "before or ancillary to any court or grand jury." The statute itself does not define or describe ancillary proceedings. That task fell to the United States Supreme Court in the case that follows. In addition, the case illustrates the use of the inconsistent statements provision of § 1623. Finally, the Court discusses an alleged "variance," a due process issue that often arises in white collar cases.

DUNN v. UNITED STATES
442 U.S. 100 (1979)

Mr. JUSTICE MARSHALL delivered the opinion of the Court.

Title IV of the Organized Crime Control Act of 1970, 18 U.S.C. § 1623, prohibits false declarations made under oath "in any proceeding before or ancillary to any court or grand jury of the United States." This case turns on the scope of the term ancillary proceeding in § 1623, a phrase not defined in that provision or elsewhere in the Criminal Code. More specifically, we must determine whether an interview in a private attorney's office at which a sworn statement is given constitutes a proceeding ancillary to a court or grand jury within the meaning of the statute.

I.

On June 16, 1976, petitioner Robert Dunn testified before a federal grand jury under a grant of immunity pursuant to 18 U.S.C. § 6002. The grand jury was investigating illicit drug activity at the Colorado State Penitentiary where petitioner had been incarcerated. Dunn's testimony implicated a fellow inmate, Phillip Musgrave, in various drug-related offenses. Following petitioner's appearance, the grand jury indicted Musgrave for conspiracy to manufacture and distribute methamphetamine.

Several months later, on September 30, 1976, Dunn arrived without counsel in the office of Musgrave's attorney, Michael Canges. In the presence of Canges and a notary public, petitioner made an oral statement under oath in which he recanted his grand jury testimony implicating Musgrave. Canges subsequently moved to dismiss the indictment against Musgrave, alleging that it was based on perjured testimony. In support of this motion, the attorney submitted a transcript of Dunn's September 30 statement.

The District Court held an evidentiary hearing on Musgrave's motion to dismiss on October 21, 1976. At that hearing, petitioner, who was then represented by counsel, adopted the statement he had given in Canges' office and testified that only a small part of what he had told the grand jury was in fact true. As a result of petitioner's testimony, the government reduced the charges against Musgrave to misdemeanor possession of methamphetamine.

Petitioner was subsequently indicted on five counts of making false declarations in violation of 18 U.S.C. § 1623. The indictment charged that Dunn's testimony before the grand jury was inconsistent with statements made "on September 30, 1976, while under oath as a witness in a proceeding ancillary to *United States v. Musgrave*, . . . to the degree that one of said declarations was false. . . . " In response to petitioner's motion for a bill of particulars, the government indicated that it would rely on the "inconsistent declarations" method of proof authorized by § 1623(c). Under that subsection, the government must establish the materiality and inconsistency of declarations made in proceedings before or ancillary to a court or grand jury, but need not prove which of the declarations is false.

At trial, the government introduced over objection pertinent parts of Dunn's grand jury testimony, his testimony at the October 21 evidentiary hearing, and his sworn statement to Musgrave's attorney. After the government rested its case, petitioner renewed his objections in a motion for acquittal. He contended that the September 30 statement was not made in a proceeding ancillary to a federal court or grand jury as required by § 1623(c). The court denied the motion and submitted the case to the jury. Petitioner was convicted on three of the five counts of the indictment and sentenced to concurrent five-year terms on each count.

The Court of Appeals for the Tenth Circuit affirmed. Although it agreed with petitioner that the interview in Canges' office was not an ancillary proceeding under § 1623, the court determined that the October 21 hearing at which petitioner adopted his September statement was a proceeding ancillary to a grand jury investigation. Acknowledging that the indictment specified the September 30 interview rather than the October 21 hearing as the ancillary proceeding, the Court of Appeals construed this discrepancy as a nonprejudicial variance between the indictment and proof at trial. . . .

We granted certiorari. Because we disagree with the Court of Appeals' ultimate disposition of the ancillary-proceeding issue, we reverse.

II.

A variance arises when the evidence adduced at trial establishes facts different from those alleged in an indictment. In the instant case, since the indictment specified the September 30 interview rather than the October 21 hearing as the ancillary proceeding, the Court of Appeals identified a variance between the pleadings and the government's proof at trial. However, reasoning that petitioner's October 21 testimony was "inextricably related" to his September 30 declaration, the court concluded that petitioner could have anticipated that the prosecution would introduce the October testimony. The court therefore determined that the variance was not fatal to the government's case.

In our view, it is unnecessary to inquire, as did the Court of Appeals, whether petitioner was prejudiced by a variance between what was alleged in the indictment and what was proved at trial. For we discern no such variance. The indictment charged inconsistency between petitioner's statements in the September 30 interview and his grand jury testimony. That was also the theory on which the case was tried and submitted to the jury. But while there was no variance between the indictment and proof at trial, there was a discrepancy between the basis on which the jury rendered its verdict and that on which the Court of Appeals sustained petitioner's conviction. Whereas the jury was instructed to rest its decision on Dunn's September statement, the Tenth Circuit predicated its affirmance on petitioner's October testimony. The government concedes that this ruling was erroneous. We agree.

To uphold a conviction on a charge that was neither alleged in an indictment nor presented to a jury at trial offends the most basic notions of due process. Few constitutional principles are more firmly established than a defendant's right to be heard on the specific charges of which he is accused. There is, to be sure, no glaring distinction between the government's theory at trial and the Tenth Circuit's analysis on appeal. The jury might well have reached the same verdict had the prosecution built its case on petitioner's October 21 testimony adopting his September 30 statement rather than on the September statement itself. But the offense was not so defined, and appellate courts are not free to revise the basis on which a defendant is convicted simply because the same result would likely obtain on retrial. As we recognized in *Cole v. Arkansas*, 333 U.S. 196, 201 (1948) "[i]t is as much a violation of due process to send an accused to prison following conviction of a charge on which he was never tried as it would be to convict him upon a charge that was never made." Thus, unless the September 30 interview constituted an ancillary proceeding, petitioner's conviction cannot stand.

III.

Congress enacted § 1623 as part of the 1970 Organized Crime Control Act to facilitate perjury prosecutions and thereby enhance the reliability of testimony before federal courts and grand juries. Invoking this broad congressional purpose, the government argues for an expansive construction of the term ancillary proceeding. Under the government's analysis, false swearing in an affidavit poses the same threat to the fact-finding process as false testimony in open court. Thus, the government contends that any statements made under oath for submission to a court, whether given in an attorney's office or in a local bar and grill, fall within the ambit of § 1623. In our judgment, the term "proceeding," which carries a somewhat more formal connotation, suggests that Congress had a narrower end in view when enacting § 1623. And the legislative history of the Organized Crime Control Act confirms that conclusion.

Section 1623 was a response to perceived evidentiary problems in demonstrating perjury under the existing federal statute, 18 U.S.C. § 1621. As Congress noted, the strict common-law requirements for establishing falsity which had been engrafted onto the federal perjury statute often made prosecution for false statements exceptionally difficult. By relieving the government of the burden of proving which of two or more inconsistent declarations was false, *see* § 1623(c), Congress sought to afford "greater assurance that testimony obtained in grand jury and court proceedings will aid the cause of truth." S. Rep. No. 91–617, p. 59 (1969). But nothing in the language or legislative history of the statute suggests that Congress contemplated a relaxation of the government's burden of proof with respect to all inconsistent statements given under oath. Had Congress intended such a result, it presumably would have drafted § 1623 to encompass all sworn declarations irrespective of whether they were made in proceedings before or ancillary to a court or grand jury. Particularly since Congress was aware that statements under oath were embraced by the federal perjury statute without regard to where they were given, the choice of less comprehensive language in § 1623 does not appear inadvertent.

That Congress intended § 1623 to sweep less broadly than the perjury statute is also apparent from the origin of the term ancillary proceeding. As initially introduced in Congress, the Organized Crime Control Act contained a version of § 1623 which encompassed only inconsistent statements made in any "trial, hearing, or proceeding before any court or grand jury." When asked to comment on the proposed statute, the Department of Justice noted that the scope of the inconsistent declarations provision was "not as inclusive" as the perjury statute. *See* Hearings on S. 30 *et al.* before the Subcommittee on Criminal Laws and Procedures of the Senate Committee on the Judiciary, 91st Cong., 1st Sess., 372 (1969) (hereinafter S. 30 Hearings). Significantly, the Justice Department did not suggest that the provision be made coextensive with the perjury statute. However, in subsequent Senate Subcommittee hearings, Assistant Attorney General Wilson indicated, without elaboration, that the Department advocated "including [under § 1623] other testimony, preliminary testimony and other statements, in the perjury field." *Id.* at 389.

In response to that general suggestion, Senator McClellan, on behalf of the Subcommittee, sent a letter to the Assistant Attorney General clarifying its purpose:

> You also read Title IV not to cover "pre-trial depositions, affidavits and certifications." This was not our intent in drafting the bill. We had hoped that it would be applicable, for example, to situations such as [the] kind of pre-trial depositions that the enforcement of S. 1861 would present. If we included in the statute the phrase "proceedings before or ancillary to any court or grand jury," do you feel that this intent would be adequately expressed?

Id. at 409.

The government attaches great significance to the qualification, "for example," in Senator McClellan's letter. Because pretrial depositions were mentioned as illustrative, the government interprets the term ancillary proceeding to subsume affidavits and certifications as well. But that is not the inference the Department of Justice originally drew from the Senator's letter. Responding to the proposed modification of § 1623, Assistant Attorney General Wilson did not advert to affidavits or certifications but stated only that

> [i]nclusion of the phrase "proceedings before or ancillary to any court or grand jury" in the false statement provision would in our opinion adequately bring within the coverage of the provision pre-trial depositions such as that contained in S. 1861.

S. 30 Hearings 411.

In our view, the Justice Department's contemporaneous rather than its current interpretation offers the more plausible reading of the Subcommittee's intent. Its attention having been drawn to the issue, had the Subcommittee wished to bring *all* affidavits and certifications within the statutory prohibition, Senator McClellan presumably would have so stated. . . .

Thus, both the language and history of the Act support the Court of Appeals' conclusion that petitioner's September 30 interview "lack[ed] the degree of formality" required by § 1623. 577 F.2d at 123. For the government does not and could not seriously maintain that the interview in Canges' office constituted a deposition. Musgrave's counsel made no attempt to comply with the procedural safeguards for depositions set forth in Fed. Rule Crim. Proc. 15 and 18 U.S.C. § 3503. A court order authorizing the deposition was never obtained. Nor did petitioner receive formal notice of the proceeding or of his right to have counsel present. Indeed, petitioner did not even certify the transcript of the interview as accurate.

To characterize such an interview as an ancillary proceeding would not only take liberties with the language and legislative history of § 1623, it would also contravene this Court's long-established practice of resolving questions concerning the ambit of a criminal statute in favor of lenity. This practice reflects not merely a convenient maxim of statutory construction. Rather, it is rooted in fundamental principles of due process which mandate that no individual be forced to speculate, at peril of indictment, whether his conduct is prohibited. Thus, to ensure that a legislature speaks with special clarity when marking the boundaries of criminal conduct, courts must decline to impose punishment for actions that are not " 'plainly and unmistakably' " proscribed. *United States v. Gradwell*, 243 U.S. 476, 485 (1917).

We cannot conclude here that Congress in fact intended or clearly expressed an intent that § 1623 should encompass statements made in contexts less formal than a deposition. Accordingly, we hold that petitioner's September 30 declarations were not given in a proceeding ancillary to a court or grand jury within the meaning of the statute.

The judgment of the Court of Appeals is reversed.

Notes and Questions

1. *Inconsistent declarations.*

a. According to the Court, why did Congress include the inconsistent declarations provision when it enacted § 1623? Does this provision appear to accomplish Congress' objective? Why or why not?

b. What declarations did the defendant make? Which of those declarations, according to the government's argument before the Court, were inconsistent? Which declarations did the Court of Appeals find to be inconsistent?

2. *Variance.*

a. What was the "variance" issue discussed by the court? Why does it matter to a defendant whether there is such a variance?

b. The Court found that there was no variance. Why?

c. Given that the Court did not find a variance, why did it reverse?

3. *Ancillary proceedings.*

a. In determining that Dunn's statement did not constitute a declaration in a proceeding ancillary to a court or grand jury, the Court relied heavily on § 1623's legislative history. The defense argued that the legislative history of the statute supported its proposed interpretation. Precisely what language in the legislative history supported the defendant's argument? Absent an effective defense argument on this point, would the result likely have been different? Why or why not?

b. The Court in *Dunn* did not establish precise boundaries for determining which proceedings qualify under § 1623. This issue thus continues to arise in prosecutions under that section. For example, in *United States v. Lamplugh*, 17 F. Supp. 2d 354 (M.D. Pa. 1998), the court held that a declaration signed under penalty of perjury in support of a motion in a civil law suit does not qualify under § 1623.

Problem

10-1. Federal agents asked Witness to assist them in an investigation of Target's drug trafficking activities. Witness submitted a written statement. Witness read the statement, made corrections, and reviewed numerous drafts. At the United States Attorney's Office, an Assistant U.S. Attorney told Witness that a lie in the statement would constitute perjury and he would be criminally punished. Witness signed the statement and a notary public acknowledged the signature. Under the signature, the statement provided that Witness affirmed the truth of the statement under "penalty of perjury." In the statement, Witness said:

> I saw a huge stack of money on top of a table in Target's kitchen. It was about two feet high and in the shape of a volcano. It was in stacks of 100 dollar bills, separated by rubber bands. I went to Target's house and he was in the garage. He had a huge cardboard box that was stuffed with newspaper. He was taking out brown packages wrapped in shiny brown tape and marked with a black squiggly line. I realized it was cocaine.

Witness was called as a witness at Target's trial, and testified under oath as follows:

Q: "Did you ever see a large amount of money on the table in Target's house?"

A: "No."

Q: "Have you ever seen Target with any cocaine?"

A: "No."

The government has charged Witness with perjury, using the inconsistent statements provision of § 1623.

Witness has moved to dismiss the charge. How should the court rule? Why?

[C]   FALSITY

Under § 1621, the government must show that the defendant *willfully* committed perjury. Under § 1623, the government must prove that the defendant *knowingly* made a false statement or declaration. Either level of mens rea is likely met if the defendant is shown to have knowingly given false testimony.

Assume that a witness, deliberately intending to produce a false impression, gives a misleading but literally true answer during sworn testimony. Would this suffice for a perjury conviction? The Supreme Court addressed this question in the following § 1621 case. Note that the Court's analysis also applies to § 1623 prosecutions.

BRONSTON v. UNITED STATES
409 U.S. 352 (1973)

Mr. CHIEF JUSTICE BURGER delivered the opinion of the Court.

We granted the writ in this case to consider a narrow but important question in the application of the federal perjury statute, 18 U.S.C. § 1621: whether a witness may be convicted of perjury for an answer, under oath, that is literally true but not responsive to the question asked and arguably misleading by negative implication.

Petitioner is the sole owner of Samuel Bronston Productions, Inc., a company that between 1958 and 1964, produced motion pictures in various European locations. For these enterprises, Bronston Productions opened bank accounts in a number of foreign countries; in 1962, for example, it had 37 accounts in five countries. As president of Bronston Productions, petitioner supervised transactions involving the foreign bank accounts.

In June 1964, Bronston Productions petitioned for an arrangement with creditors under Chapter XI of the Bankruptcy Act. On June 10, 1966, a referee in bankruptcy held a hearing to determine, for the benefit of creditors, the extent and location of the company's assets. Petitioner's perjury conviction was founded on the answers given by him as a witness at that bankruptcy hearing, and in particular on the following colloquy with a lawyer for a creditor of Bronston Productions:

Q.   Do you have any bank accounts in Swiss banks, Mr. Bronston?

A.   No, sir.

Q.   Have you ever?

A.   The company had an account there for about six months, in Zurich.

Q.   Have you any nominees who have bank accounts in Swiss banks?

A.   No, sir.

Q.   Have you ever?

A.   No, sir.

It is undisputed that for a period of nearly five years, between October 1959 and June 1964, petitioner had a personal bank account at the International Credit Bank in Geneva, Switzerland, into which he made deposits and upon which he drew checks totaling more than $180,000. It is likewise undisputed that petitioner's answers were literally truthful. (a) Petitioner did not at the time of questioning have a Swiss bank account. (b) Bronston Productions, Inc., did have the account in Zurich described by petitioner. (c) Neither at the time of questioning nor before did petitioner have nominees who had Swiss accounts. The government's prosecution for perjury went forward on the theory that in order to mislead his questioner, petitioner answered the second question with literal truthfulness but unresponsively addressed his answer to the company's assets and not to his own — thereby implying that he had no personal Swiss bank account at the relevant time.

At petitioner's trial, the District Court instructed the jury that the "basic issue" was whether petitioner "spoke his true belief." Perjury, the court stated, "necessarily involves the state of mind of the accused" and "essentially consists of wilfully testifying to the truth of a fact which the defendant does not believe to be true;" petitioner's testimony could not be found "wilfully" false unless at the time his testimony was given petitioner "fully understood the questions put to him but nevertheless gave false answers knowing the same to be false." The court further instructed the jury that if petitioner did not understand the question put to him and for that reason gave an unresponsive answer, he could not be convicted of perjury. Petitioner could, however, be convicted if he gave an answer "not literally false but when considered in the context in which it was given, nevertheless constitute[d] a false statement."[3]

The jury began its deliberations at 11:30 a.m. Several times it requested exhibits or additional instructions from the court, and at one point, at the request of the jury, the District Court repeated its instructions in full. At 6:10 p.m., the jury returned its verdict, finding petitioner guilty on the count of perjury before us today.

In the Court of Appeals, petitioner contended, as he had in post-trial motions before the District Court, that the key question was imprecise and suggestive of

---

[3] The District Court gave the following example "as an illustration only:"

> [I]f it is material to ascertain how many times a person has entered a store on a given day and that person responds to such a question by saying five times when in fact he knows that he entered the store 50 times that day, that person may be guilty of perjury even though it is technically true that he entered the store five times.

The illustration given by the District Court is hardly comparable to petitioner's answer; the answer "five times" is responsive to the hypothetical question and contains nothing to alert the questioner that he may be sidetracked. Moreover, it is very doubtful that an answer which, in response to a specific quantitative inquiry, baldly understates a numerical fact can be described as even "technically true." Whether an answer is true must be determined with reference to the question it purports to answer, not in isolation. An unresponsive answer is unique in this respect because its unresponsiveness by definition prevents its truthfulness from being tested in the context of the question — unless there is to be speculation as to what the unresponsive answer "implies."

various interpretations. In addition, petitioner contended that he could not be convicted of perjury on the basis of testimony that was concededly truthful, however unresponsive. A divided Court of Appeals held that the question was readily susceptible of a responsive reply and that it adequately tested the defendant's belief in the veracity of his answer. The Court of Appeals further held that, "[f]or the purposes of 18 U.S.C. § 1621, an answer containing half of the truth which also constitutes a lie by negative implication, when the answer is intentionally given in place of the responsive answer called for by a proper question, is perjury." In this Court, petitioner renews his attack on the specificity of the question asked him and the legal sufficiency of his answer to support a conviction for perjury. The problem of the ambiguity of the question is not free from doubt, but we need not reach that issue. Even assuming, as we do, that the question asked petitioner specifically focused on petitioner's personal bank accounts, we conclude that the federal perjury statute cannot be construed to sustain a conviction based on petitioner's answer.

The statute, 18 U.S.C. § 1621, substantially identical in its relevant language to its predecessors for nearly a century, is "a federal statute enacted in an effort to keep the course of justice free from the pollution of perjury." *United States v. Williams*, 341 U.S. 58, 68 (1951). We have held that the general federal perjury provision is applicable to federal bankruptcy proceedings. The need for truthful testimony in a bankruptcy proceeding is great, since the proceeding is "a searching inquiry into the condition of the estate of the bankrupt, to assist in discovering and collecting the assets, and to develop facts and circumstances which bear upon the question of discharge." *Travis v. United States*, 123 F.2d 268, 271 (10th Cir.1941). Here, as elsewhere, the perpetration of perjury "well may affect the dearest concerns of the parties before a tribunal. . . . " *United States v. Norris*, 300 U.S. 564, 574 (1937).

There is, at the outset, a serious literal problem in applying § 1621 to petitioner's answer. The words of the statute confine the offense to the witness who "willfully . . . states . . . any material matter which he does not believe to be true." Beyond question, petitioner's answer to the crucial question was not responsive if we assume, as we do, that the first question was directed at personal bank accounts. There is, indeed, an implication in the answer to the second question that there was never a personal bank account; in casual conversation this interpretation might reasonably be drawn. But we are not dealing with casual conversation and the statute does not make it a criminal act for a witness to willfully state any material matter that *implies* any material matter that he does not believe to be true.[4]

The government urges that the perjury statute be construed broadly to reach petitioner's answer and thereby fulfill its historic purpose of reinforcing our adversary factfinding process. We might go beyond the precise words of the statute if we thought they did not adequately express the intention of Congress, but we perceive no reason why Congress would intend the drastic sanction of a perjury prosecution to cure a testimonial mishap that could readily have been reached with

---

[4] Petitioner's answer is not to be measured by the same standards applicable to criminally fraudulent or extortionate statements. In that context, the law goes "rather far in punishing intentional creation of false impressions by a selection of literally true representations, because the actor himself generally selects and arranges the representations." In contrast, "under our system of adversary questioning and cross-examination the scope of disclosure is largely in the hands of counsel and presiding officer." A.L.I. Model Penal Code § 208.20, Comment (Tent. Draft No. 6, 1957, p. 124).

a single additional question by counsel alert — as every examiner ought to be — to the incongruity of petitioner's unresponsive answer. Under the pressures and tensions of interrogation, it is not uncommon for the most earnest witnesses to give answers that are not entirely responsive. Sometimes the witness does not understand the question, or may in an excess of caution or apprehension read too much or too little into it. It should come as no surprise that a participant in a bankruptcy proceeding may have something to conceal and consciously tries to do so, or that a debtor may be embarrassed at his plight and yield information reluctantly. It is the responsibility of the lawyer to probe; testimonial interrogation, and cross-examination in particular, is a probing, prying, pressing form of inquiry. If a witness evades, it is the lawyer's responsibility to recognize the evasion and to bring the witness back to the mark, to flush out the whole truth with the tools of adversary examination.

It is no answer to say that here the jury found that petitioner intended to mislead his examiner. A jury should not be permitted to engage in conjecture whether an unresponsive answer, true and complete on its face, was intended to mislead or divert the examiner; the state of mind of the witness is relevant only to the extent that it bears on whether "he does not believe (his answer) to be true." To hold otherwise would be to inject a new and confusing element into the adversary testimonial system we know. Witnesses would be unsure of the extent of their responsibility for the misunderstandings and inadequacies of examiners, and might well fear having that responsibility tested by a jury under the vague rubric of "intent to mislead" or "perjury by implication." The seminal modern treatment of the history of the offense concludes that one consideration of policy overshadowed all others during the years when perjury first emerged as a common-law offense: "that the measures taken against the offense must not be so severe as to discourage witnesses from appearing or testifying." Study of Perjury, reprinted in Report of New York Law Revision Commission, Legis. Doc. No. 60, p. 249 (1935). . . .

Thus, we must read § 1621 in light of our own and the traditional Anglo-American judgment that a prosecution for perjury is not the sole, or even the primary, safeguard against errant testimony. . . . The cases support petitioner's position that the perjury statute is not to be loosely construed, nor the statute invoked simply because a wily witness succeeds in derailing the questioner — so long as the witness speaks the literal truth. The burden is on the questioner to pin the witness down to the specific object to the questioner's inquiry.

The government does not contend that any misleading or incomplete response must be sent to the jury to determine whether a witness committed perjury because he intended to sidetrack his questioner. As the government recognizes, the effect of so unlimited an interpretation of § 1621 would be broadly unsettling. It is said, rather, that petitioner's testimony falls within a more limited category of intentionally misleading responses with an especially strong tendency to mislead the questioner. Thus the government isolates two factors which are said to require application of the perjury statute in the circumstances of this case; the unresponsiveness of petitioner's answer and the affirmative cast of that answer, with its accompanying negative implication.

This analysis succeeds in confining the government's position, but it does not persuade us that Congress intended to extend the coverage of § 1621 to answers unresponsive on their face but untrue only by "negative implication." Though perhaps a plausible argument can be made that unresponsive answers are especially likely to mislead,[5] any such argument must, we think, be predicated upon the questioner's being aware of the unresponsiveness of the relevant answer. Yet, if the questioner is aware of the unresponsiveness of the answer, with equal force it can be argued that the very unresponsiveness of the answer should alert counsel to press on for the information he desires. It does not matter that the unresponsive answer is stated in the affirmative, thereby implying the negative of the question actually posed; for again, by hypothesis, the examiner's awareness of unresponsiveness should lead him to press another question or reframe his initial question with greater precision. Precise questioning is imperative as a predicate for the offense of perjury.

It may well be that petitioner's answers were not guileless but were shrewdly calculated to evade. Nevertheless, we are constrained to agree that any special problems arising from the literally true but unresponsive answer are to be remedied through the "questioner's acuity" and not by a federal perjury prosecution.

Reversed.

NOTES AND QUESTIONS

1. *A prescription for evasion?*

a. The jury in *Bronston* presumably found beyond a reasonable doubt that Bronston intended that his testimony produce a false impression. Would it not serve the purposes of the perjury statute to sustain a conviction in such a circumstance? Does the result in *Bronston* actually encourage witnesses to provide evasive and misleading answers?

The Court was concerned that allowing literally true answers to suffice would result in an overly broad application of the statute. The government responded by proposing a rule limiting convictions based upon literally true answers to the "category of intentionally misleading responses with an especially strong tendency to mislead the questioner." Is this a sufficient response to the Court's concerns? Why or why not?

b. As seen elsewhere in this text, and as the Court acknowledged, a literally true but misleading statement may well be sufficient for a fraud charge. Is perjury so different from fraud as to warrant the result in *Bronston*? Why or why not?

2. *Perjury as a disfavored crime.*

a. Perjury cases are often considered difficult to prove. *See* Robert G. Morvillo & Christopher J. Morvillo, *Untangling the Web: Defending a Perjury Case*, 33 Litigation, Winter 2007, at 8 ("[t]he lack of perjury prosecutions is due . . . to the fact that perjury statutes are deliberately (and notoriously) difficult to enforce"). Why should that be so? When enacting § 1623, Congress attempted to overcome

---

[5] Arguably, the questioner will assume there is some logical justification for the unresponsive answer, since competent witnesses do not usually answer in irrelevancies. Thus the questioner may conclude that the unresponsive answer is given only because it is intended to make a statement — a negative statement — relevant to the question asked. In this case, petitioner's questioner may have assumed that petitioner denied having a personal account in Switzerland; only this unspoken denial would provide a logical nexus between inquiry directed to petitioner's personal account and petitioner's adverting, in response, to the company account in Zurich.

this perceived difficulty by (i) allowing convictions based upon inconsistent declarations, and (ii) abolishing the common law "two-witness" rule (discussed in the section below).

b. The Court cited one study for the proposition that "the measures taken against the offense must not be so severe as to discourage witnesses from appearing or testifying." What did the Court mean when it said this? Why did the Court emphasize the risks from perjury charges?

3. *Literal truth and the Clinton case.*

a. *Numerical answers.* Is it always clear when a numerical answer is "literally true?" Revisit footnote 3 in the *Bronston* opinion. If you entered a store 50 times in a day, it is literally true to say that you entered five times that day? Would such an answer obviously be false? In his sworn deposition in the Paula Jones case, the questioner asked then-President Bill Clinton, "[h]as Monica Lewinsky ever given you any gifts?" His answer: "[O]nce or twice. I think she's given me a book or two." In fact, Lewinsky stated, she gave Clinton as many as 38 gifts. Was Clinton's answer literally true? *See* Stuart P. Green, *Perjury*, in Lying, Cheating, and Stealing: A Moral Theory of White Collar Crime 145–146 (2006).

b. *Responsive but misleading answers.* Bronston was asked, "Have you ever [had any Swiss bank accounts]?" The logical reading of the question was that the "you" referred to Bronston personally. Therefore, Bronston's answer, "The Company had an account there for about six months, in Zurich," was nonresponsive. The questioner could easily have realized that the answer was nonresponsive, and could have followed up, "OK, did you personally ever have any bank accounts in Swiss banks?"

But what about a responsive but misleading answer? In the Clinton investigation, Clinton was asked, "[H]ave you ever had sexual relations with Monica Lewinsky, as that term is defined in Deposition Exhibit 1, as modified by the court?" He responded, "I have never had sexual relations with Monica Lewinsky." Exhibit 1 stated that "a person engages in 'sexual relations' when the person knowingly engages or causes contact with the genitalia, anus, groin, breast, inner thigh, or buttocks of any person with an intent to arouse or gratify the sexual desire of any person." Assuming that the contact was limited to Lewinsky performing oral sex on Clinton, was Clinton's answer literally true? *See id.* at 142–144.

4. *Ambiguous questions and answers.*

The Court in *Bronston* did not reach the issue whether a perjury conviction can be sustained when the question is ambiguous. Was there an ambiguous question in *Bronston*? If a question is genuinely ambiguous, does the issue of a literally truthful answer arise?

Bronston was charged with perjury based upon an answer that was literally true. Take instead the circumstance in which an answer is subject to two different interpretations, one of which is false. Could such an answer provide the basis for a perjury conviction?

The answers to these questions tend to be very case- and fact-specific. For example, in *United States v. Long*, 534 F.2d 1097 (3d Cir. 1976), the district court dismissed perjury charges, finding that the terms used in the questions —

including "bribe," "kickback," and "payoff" — were legal terms that would be ambiguous to a layperson. The court of appeals reversed and reinstated the charges. Finding that the terms used were not technical legal terms, the court concluded that "we may not dismiss a charge of perjury when it is entirely reasonable to expect a defendant to have understood the terms used in the questions." *Id.* at 1101. Therefore, even if a question is confusing or ambiguous, the jury must ultimately determine whether the defendant understood the intended meaning of the question.

5. *Materiality.*

As in a false statements prosecution, materiality is an element in a perjury case that must be submitted to the jury. *See United States v. Johnson*, 520 U.S. 461, 464 (1997). The courts of appeal vary in their precise wording of the test for materiality, but it is generally broadly interpreted. For example, some courts state that, to be material, a statement must be capable of having an effect on the tribunal or proceeding. For a further discussion of the tests for materiality, see Richard H. Underwood, *Perjury! The Charges and the Defenses*, 36 Duq. L. Rev. 715, 727–732 (1998). Although defendants frequently raise the materiality defense, it is rarely successful.

PROBLEMS

10-2. In April, a group of individuals, including defendant Zarn, met at Wells' home to discuss raising funds for Smith's gubernatorial campaign. At that meeting, the individuals discussed raising money for Smith. The funds were to be collected at a Memorial Day Party being held at Wells' home.

As indicated, the Memorial Day Party was held that May. Invitations were sent out, inviting guests to a "Memorial Day Party . . . for an evening of fun on the farm." Sixty guests attended and gubernatorial candidate Smith made a short speech. Zarn collected contributions to Smith's campaign at that event. After he was elected governor, Smith appointed Zarn and other contributors to various government positions, allegedly based upon an agreement made at the time the contributions were given.

Later that summer, Wells held a Labor Day dinner that Zarn also attended. This was a small dinner party, attended only by six people. Governor Smith neither attended nor was invited to that party.

Zarn was subpoenaed to appear before a grand jury investigating bribery in connection with the Smith campaign. Under oath, the prosecutor asked Zarn approximately 60 questions about the Memorial Day Party, but had not questioned Zarn about the Labor Day dinner. Towards the end of his testimony, Zarn stated as follows:

Q: Okay, sir. My question is going to deal with Mr. Wells. Did you attend the Memorial Day Party at issue here?

A: Yes.

Q: How many people were present?

A: About 60 people.

Q: Okay. Sir, was that Labor Day Party a political fundraising activity?

A: *Absolutely not.*

Q: All right, sir. You said it was not a political fundraising activity. Were there any contributions to Governor Smith's campaign made at that party?

A: *I don't know.*

Q: Okay. You did not see any, though?

A: *No.*

Q: And you were not aware of any?

A: *No.*

No questions other than that set forth above referred to the "Labor Day Party." A number of witnesses testified that Zarn attended the Memorial Day Party and actively solicited funds for Smith's campaign during the party. Zarn was later indicted for perjury under § 1621 based upon the italicized answers above.

Assume that Zarn has moved to dismiss the indictment. What are his likely arguments? What are the likely government responses? What is the likely outcome? Why?

10-3. In Mary Mann's criminal case, the defense called Fred Farder as a witness at a pre-trial hearing. Cross-examining Farder at the hearing, the prosecutor asked, "Have you talked to Ms. Mann about your testimony here today?" Farder responded, "No." The government charged Farder with perjury under § 1623 based upon this answer.

In order to prove falsity of Farder's answer, the government introduced at Farder's trial a statement that Farder made and signed on the day of his arraignment. The relevant portion of the statement read: "Mary Mann did call me before I got the subpoena to appear at the pre-trial hearing. She called me and she was telling me about her arrest. She told me that she could not have sold drugs to a confidential informant because she was at my house the day of the drug sale, but she kept asking me to pinpoint a date. Just before she hung up the phone she told me that I was going to get a subpoena. Mary never told me to lie for her, but she did want me to mention a date she was at my house but I couldn't remember the date she was there."

Farder was convicted and appeals. How should the court rule? Why?

[D]   THE TWO-WITNESS RULE

In perjury cases, courts have historically required that the government's case rely upon two witnesses or, more accurately, upon one witness plus corroborating evidence. Although Congress removed this burden in prosecutions under § 1623, the government still must satisfy the rule in § 1621 cases.

Courts generally find that the two-witness rule is necessary for two reasons. First, the requirement encourages a witness to testify without the fear of later being charged with perjury simply because the witness has contradicted another witness. Second, the rule prevents prosecutions based solely on a "swearing contest" between two witnesses. Are those purposes served in the following case?

UNITED STATES v. CHESTMAN
903 F.2d 75 (2d Cir. 1990), *rev'd in part on other grounds*
, 947 F.2d 551 (2d Cir. 1991) (*en banc*)

Before MINER and MAHONEY, CIRCUIT JUDGES, and CARMAN, JUDGE.

MINER, CIRCUIT JUDGE:

[The Securities and Exchange Commission ("SEC") investigated whether Chestman, a stock broker, had committed insider trading in the stock of Waldbaum, Inc. The SEC believed that Chestman had obtained the inside information from Keith Loeb. In an SEC deposition, Chestman testified that he did not speak with Loeb prior to purchasing Waldbaum stock at 10:30 a.m. on November 26. Based upon this testimony, Chestman was charged with perjury under § 1621.]

[Loeb, the government's sole witness on the perjury charge, testified that he gave Chestman inside information concerning an impending tender offer for Waldbaum, and that this conversation occurred before 10:30 a.m. on November 26, when Chestman purchased the securities. As additional evidence, the government offered (1) an 8:50 a.m. phone message indicating that Loeb had called Chestman prior to the trading, (2) Chestman's failure to record the trade in his personal blotter notes on the day of the trade, and (3) the timing of the trade. The jury convicted Chestman of perjury under § 1621, and he appealed.]

* * *

The undisputed "rule in prosecutions for perjury is that the uncorroborated oath of one witness is not enough to establish the falsity of the testimony of the accused set forth in the indictment. . . . " *Hammer v. United States*, 271 U.S. 620, 626 (1926). The "two-witness" rule requires that the alleged perjurious statement be established either by the testimony of two independent witnesses or by one witness and corroborating evidence that is "inconsistent with the innocence of the [defendant]." *United States v. Weiner*, 479 F.2d 923, 926 (2d Cir.1973). . . .

Loeb's testimony that he spoke to Chestman prior to [Chestman's trade at] 10:30 a.m. would be sufficient, if supported by corroborative evidence, to sustain a perjury conviction. We therefore examine the sufficiency of the corroborative evidence proffered by the government in support of Loeb's testimony.

In assessing the sufficiency of the corroborative evidence, two elements are considered: "(1) that the evidence, if true, substantiates the testimony of a single witness who has sworn to the falsity of the alleged perjurious statement; (2) that the corroborative evidence is trustworthy." *Weiler v. United States*, 323 U.S. 606, 610 (1945). While the independent evidence must be inconsistent with the innocence of the accused, it need only "tend to substantiate that part of the testimony of the principal prosecution witness which is material in showing" the accused's statement is false. *Weiner*, 479 F.2d at 927–28.

The corroborative evidence relied on by the government is wholly insufficient to satisfy the two-witness rule. For instance, the phone message at 8:58 a.m. merely establishes that Loeb attempted to contact Chestman and that Chestman was not in his office. Thus, it is equally supportive of Chestman's contention that he did not speak to Loeb on the morning of November 26. It does not establish that Chestman returned Loeb's call prior to 10:30 a.m. Chestman's position is buttressed further by the testimony of his administrative assistant. She testified that Loeb called between 9 and 10 a.m. and then again in the late morning or early afternoon. She noted that as of the time of the second phone call Loeb had not yet spoken to Chestman. The theory put forth by the government that stockbrokers always return calls by virtue of the nature of their business requires a presumption we do not care to adopt in the context of a perjury charge.

While the government also highlights the fact that Chestman's blotter notes omitted reference to the Loeb trade, we are unconvinced that this provides adequate proof that Chestman spoke to Loeb prior to execution of the trades. These notations were made solely for Chestman's personal use. As an experienced stockbroker, he certainly realized that the Loeb trade could not be concealed because it would be memorialized by the order and subsequent confirmation slip. Under these circumstances, the blotter omissions cannot serve as corroboration.

The government also would have this Court rely on the propitious timing of the trade as sufficient support for Loeb's testimony. Sole reliance on the timing of the trade would nullify the purpose of the two-witness rule. We recognize that the circumstances surrounding an alleged perjurious statement may constitute better corroborative evidence than oral testimony. When a jury relies on circumstantial evidence, however, it must be demonstrated that this evidence has "independent probative value" if "standing alone." *United States v. Freedman*, 445 F.2d 1220, 1226 (2d Cir.1971). The timing of the trade here does not meet the standard. The fact that Chestman bought Waldbaum stock prior to the announcement of the tender offer is consistent with Chestman's position that he researched the company, assumed it was a takeover target, and invested accordingly. Standing alone, the timing of the trade does not have sufficient independent probative value to support the Loeb testimony at odds with that position.

*   *   *

After careful review, we find the evidence insufficient to sustain the conviction. Accordingly, we reverse Chestman's conviction for perjury.

NOTES AND QUESTIONS

1. *Sufficiency of the evidence.* A defendant bears a heavy burden when arguing that a conviction should be overturned because of insufficient evidence. In such a circumstance, the appellate court must draw all factual inferences in favor of the government. Was the court correct in concluding that the inferences from the corroborative evidence were insufficient, as a matter of law, to sustain Chestman's conviction?

2. *The two-witness rule.* Are there dangers from allowing a perjury conviction based upon a single witness' testimony? What would be the dangers, if any, of allowing Chestman's conviction to stand based solely on Loeb's testimony?

3. *What counts as corroboration?* The two-witness rule was implicated in the criminal case against Martha Stewart's co-defendant, her broker, Peter Bacanovic. (This case is discussed in Chapter 5, Securities Fraud, *supra*, at § 5[C]). Bacanovic was charged with perjury based on testimony he gave before the SEC during its investigation into the trading of ImClone stock. During his testimony, Bacanovic recalled leaving a phone message for Stewart with Stewart's assistant, but denied remembering telling the assistant that the price of ImClone stock was falling. The

government alleged that his denial of recollection was a false statement. The government's proof of falsity was (1) the assistant's testimony, and (2) an electronic message that the assistant wrote for Stewart stating that "Peter Bacanovic thinks ImClone is going to start trading downward." On appeal, Bacanovic argued that corroborating evidence consisting solely of a document created by the only witness did not satisfy the two-witness rule. The Second Circuit rejected the argument and affirmed the perjury conviction. *United States v. Stewart*, 433 F.3d 273, 315–317 (2d Cir. 2006). How do you explain this result?

PROBLEMS

10-4. Chapman filed for bankruptcy. As part of the bankruptcy proceeding, Chapman gave deposition testimony under oath to determine the extent of the bankruptcy estate's assets. During the deposition, the following exchange took place:

Q: "Did you give Moss $80,000 in currency on October 23 last year?"

A: "I don't recall doing that, no."

Based upon this answer, the government charged Chapman with perjury under § 1621. At Chapman's trial, the government called Moss to testify in the trial. Moss testified as follows:

Q: "Did Chapman give you $80,000 on October 23 last year?"

A: "Yes. Chapman asked me to purchase some real estate to put in Chapman's name. He gave me the money probably about October of last year."

As corroborating evidence, the government introduced Moss's banking records. The records showed that that Moss deposited $80,000 into his bank account on October 23 last year.

At the end of the government's case, Chapman filed a motion to dismiss the perjury charge. How should the court rule? Why?

10-5. In a deposition in a divorce proceeding, Fred Farmer testified concerning the assets that he held with his wife Maria. Fred testified as follows:

Q: "Did you call Ralph on Monday morning, June 19, and tell him that you had a large screen television that you wanted to sell?"

A: "No, sir, I did not. I mean, I might have called him that morning, but I have not called him about any television."

Fred was charged with perjury based under § 1621 based upon the above answer. At Fred's trial, Ralph testified as follows:

Q: "Did you have a telephone conversation with Fred on June 19?"

A: "Well, Maria called, then I called back three times that day and each time spoke with Fred."

Q: "What was discussed in those telephone conversations?"

A: "I told Fred that I would buy the TV and give him cash."

The government next called two neighbors of Fred and Maria. They both testified that on June 20, they had helped Fred load a large screen television onto Fred's pick-up truck and drove with Fred to Ralph's house, where they unloaded the TV and saw Ralph give Fred a large quantity of cash.

Is the two-witness rule met on these facts? Why or why not?

[E] THE RECANTATION DEFENSE

As noted above, perjury prosecutions are easier under § 1623 than under § 1621 because of § 1623's inconsistent declarations provision and because § 1623 abolishes the two-witness rule. On the other hand, § 1623 alone provides a "recantation" defense if the witness takes back, or "recants," the allegedly false testimony. Recantation, however, is rarely a successful defense; as the court notes in the decision that follows, the broad reading of the recantation defense that the court adopts is clearly the minority rule. As you read the case, consider why the majority of courts have read the defense narrowly.

UNITED STATES v. SMITH
35 F.3d 344 (8th Cir. 1994)

BOWMAN, CIRCUIT JUDGE.

Sherry Lynn Smith timely appeals her conviction following her conditional guilty plea to one count of perjury. We vacate and remand for further proceedings.

I.

On May 18, 1993, a grand jury indicted Smith, charging her with three offenses: conspiracy to structure a cash transaction in violation of 18 U.S.C. § 371; structuring a cash transaction with a trade or business in violation of 26 U.S.C. § 6050I(f)(1)(C) and 18 U.S.C. § 2; and perjury in violation of 18 U.S.C. § 1623(a). In exchange for her conditional guilty plea to the perjury charge, the other charges were dismissed.

The perjury charge arose out of Smith's testimony before a grand jury investigating several individuals, including Smith's boyfriend Craig Keltner, and their involvement in a series of crimes including car theft, kidnaping, mail fraud, burglaries, robberies, and money laundering. The grand jury questioned Smith about the source of funds with which Keltner had purchased a Chevrolet Corvette. Keltner first attempted to make the purchase from a dealership with $12,200 in cash. When the dealership informed him that it would have to file a report with the Internal Revenue Service on any cash transaction in excess of $10,000, Keltner arranged to pay with $9,800 in cash and $2,400 in the form of a check from Smith. The dealership held the $12,200 until Keltner returned with Smith's check, then the dealership returned $2,400 in cash to Keltner. Smith deposited $2,400 in cash into her bank account the same day.

Before the grand jury, Smith initially testified that she had invested $3,000 from her savings toward the purchase of the car. She denied that the $2,400 deposited into her bank account after the purchase came from Keltner. After a thirty-eight-minute break in the proceeding, during which Smith reviewed her bank records, she resumed her testimony and recanted her previous statements. Smith admitted that the $2,400 belonged to Keltner and was given to her to deposit as part of the transaction to purchase the Corvette.

II.

Prior to her conditional guilty plea to the perjury charge, Smith moved for dismissal of that charge on the ground that 18 U.S.C. § 1623(d) bars prosecution for perjury on the facts of her case. The District Court disagreed with Smith's interpretation of the statute and denied her motion. Her conditional plea preserved the issue for appellate review, and she now asks this court to address it.

We review questions of statutory interpretation de novo. Our analysis begins with the statutory language. Section 1623(d) states:

> Where, in the same continuous court or grand jury proceeding in which a declaration is made, the person making the declaration admits such declaration to be false, such admission shall bar prosecution under this section if, at the time the admission is made, the declaration has not substantially affected the proceeding, or it has not become manifest that such falsity has been or will be exposed.

18 U.S.C. § 1623(d).

The District Court denied Smith's motion on the ground that § 1623(d) "bars prosecution only if the false statement has not substantially affected the proceeding and if it has not become manifest that the falsity has been or will be exposed." The District Court construed the two conditions as conjunctive, reading "or" to mean "and," and found that Smith did not satisfy the latter condition. Smith contends that the two conditions are disjunctive and thus satisfaction of either bars her prosecution for perjury.

In interpreting § 1623(d), we adhere to the general principle that "when the plain language of a statute is clear in its context, it is controlling." The plain language of the statute indicates that after recantation, a perjury charge is barred if (1) the proceeding has not been substantially affected by the false testimony, or (2) it has not become manifest that the false nature of the testimony has been or will be exposed. Because the wording of § 1623(d) "is plain, simple, and straightforward, the words must be accorded their normal meanings." *United States v. Jones*, 811 F.2d 444, 447 (8th Cir.1987). The ordinary usage of the word "or" is disjunctive, indicating an alternative. Construing the word "or" to mean "and" is conjunctive, and is clearly in contravention of its ordinary usage. Thus, we find the plain language of § 1623(d) controlling and accord the word "or" its ordinary, disjunctive meaning.

According the word "or" its ordinary meaning does not defeat the intent of Congress in enacting the statute and creating the § 1623(d) recantation defense. In *United States v. Del Toro*, the Second Circuit looked to the legislative history and found that the purpose of the statute "was obviously to induce the witness to give truthful testimony by permitting him voluntarily to correct a false statement without incurring the risk of prosecution for doing so." 513 F.2d 656, 665 (2d Cir.1975). "Section 1623(d) balances the need to encourage a witness to correct [false] testimony against the need to prevent perjury at the outset." *United States v. Denison*, 663 F.2d 611, 617 (5th Cir.1981). To meet the congressional goal of encouraging truthful testimony, we need only apply the plain language of the statute in its ordinary usage. Reading the two conditions in the alternative, as the word "or" demands, the statute creates an incentive for witnesses to correct false testimony early in the proceeding. Arguably, construing the word "or" to mean "and" creates a statutory scheme providing a stronger incentive for witnesses to testify truthfully at the outset; however, we defer to Congress's chosen scheme as manifested by its language which balances encouragement of truthful testimony and penalties for perjury.

Additionally, because § 1623(d) is a penal statute, we must apply the rule of lenity. We conclude that to read "or" as "and" in the context of § 1623(d) would "contravene [the Supreme] Court's long-established practice of resolving questions concerning the ambit of a criminal statute in favor of lenity." *Dunn v. United States*, 442 U.S. 100, 112 (1979). Thus, we accord the word "or" its ordinary meaning, reading the statute as setting forth two alternative conditions, satisfaction of either of which will allow a declarant to employ the recantation defense to bar prosecution for perjury.

III.

We recognize that the District Court followed existing authority in construing § 1623(d) against its plain meaning. Each of the other circuits addressing the language of § 1623(d) has construed "or" to mean "and."

Explaining its rationale for this construction, the District of Columbia Circuit stated in *Moore* that "Congress did not countenance in § 1623(d) the flagrant injustice that would result if a witness is permitted to lie to a judicial tribunal and then, upon only learning that he had been discovered, grudgingly to recant in order to bar prosecution." *United States v. Moore*, 613 F.2d 1029, 1043 (D.C. Cir.1979). The court also discussed the legislative history of § 1623(d), noting that it was modeled after the New York recantation defense statute. The New York statute is similar but employs "and" rather than "or," clearly making the two conditions conjunctive. *Id.* at 1042.

While this observation may raise some uncertainty about the language Congress intended to enact, it does not create an ambiguity in an otherwise plainly worded statute nor does it militate against according the enacted language its ordinary meaning. "[I]t is appropriate to assume that the ordinary meaning of [the statutory language] accurately expresses the legislative purpose." *Jones*, 811 F.2d at 447. In this case, where the statute is unambiguous on its face, the language of the statute is conclusive as to legislative intent, and we thus decline to abandon the ordinary disjunctive meaning accorded to "or" in favor of a conjunctive "and," as such a construction would defeat the plain language of the statute and would not foster any clearly articulated legislative intent to the contrary.

In order to employ § 1623(d) to claim protection from prosecution for perjury, a party is not required to recant before it has become manifest that the falsehoods have been or will be exposed; rather, this is but one of two circumstances in which the defense applies. The declarant may also use the defense if she explicitly recants before the false testimony has substantially affected the proceeding.

IV.

On remand, Smith may defeat the perjury charge if she can show that she satisfies either of § 1623(d)'s conditions. As to the condition that she recant before her false testimony has substantially affected the proceedings, the District Court did not address the issue at length, but appears to have found that her false statements may not have affected the proceedings. It is not clear to us that the District Court intended to make a definitive finding on this point, and we do not think the court should be precluded from revisiting this issue on remand.

We turn now to the alternative statutory condition, that the declarant recant before it becomes manifest that the falsity of her statement has been or will be exposed, because the District Court relied upon Smith's failure to fulfill this condition in denying her motion to dismiss.

We believe the District Court misapplied the "manifest" test. The court reasoned that because the government had the bank records with which to confront Smith, the falsity of her statements was manifest to the government before she recanted, and the court stopped its analysis at that point. The proper test to apply, however, when determining whether recantation occurred before imminent exposure was manifest, is whether the fact that the statements have been or will be exposed as false is objectively manifest to the declarant. On remand, if the District Court reaches consideration of this condition, it must determine whether it had become objectively manifest to Smith, before she recanted, that the falsity of her statements had been or would be exposed.

V.

For the reasons stated, we hold that the District Court erred in its interpretation of 18 U.S.C. § 1623(d). The judgment of the District Court is vacated and the case is remanded for further consideration of Smith's § 1623(d) recantation defense in a manner consistent with this opinion.

NOTES AND QUESTIONS

1. *The majority rule.* As the court in *Smith* noted, its holding is the minority position; the other circuits that have considered the issue have interpreted "or" to mean "and." Why precisely did the court in *Moore*, discussed in *Smith*, read "or" to mean "and"? Why did the court in *Smith* reject *Moore*'s reasoning? How do the incentives differ for a witness under a conjunction and a disjunctive reading? See *United States v. Fornaro*, 894 F.2d 508 (2d Cir. 1990), for an extended discussion of this issue.

2. *When is a proceeding "substantially affected"?* In what circumstances has a proceeding been "substantially affected"? Courts have not established clear standards for this element of the defense. Was it likely that the proceeding had been substantially affected in *Smith*? Why or why not?

3. *When has the falsity become manifest?* Had the falsity become manifest at the time Smith attempted to recant? Why or why not? Do you need additional facts to answer this question?

4. *What constitutes a "recantation"?* Courts have held that, for a change in testimony to constitute a recantation, the defendant must unequivocally retract the earlier testimony. A mere attempt to explain earlier testimony, or to later claim faulty memory, will not constitute recantation. *See, e.g., United States v. D'Auria*, 672 F.2d 1085, 1085 (2d Cir. 1982) (ineffective attempt to recant where defendant offered to "clarify" his testimony, but did not use the word "recant" and did not admit that his previous testimony was false).

5. *Procedural rules.* Courts agree that, if the defendant fails to raise the recantation defense prior to trial, the defense is waived. Courts are split, however, as to whether the government or the defense has the burden of proof once the issue is raised.

6. *Prosecutorial discretion.* As noted above, perjury during a court or grand jury proceeding may be prosecuted under either § 1621 or § 1623. Because § 1623 is specifically directed to such proceedings, and because the required proof under that section is less burdensome than under § 1621, prosecutors will generally use § 1623 when the testimony was given before a court or grand jury. But what if the defendant has a recantation defense? May the government then choose to use § 1621, which does not recognize the defense? The issue was raised, but not decided, in *United States v. Kahn*, 472 F.2d 272, 283 (2d Cir. 1973). In that case, the Second Circuit commented, "we find not a little disturbing the prospect of the government employing § 1621 whenever a recantation exists, and § 1623 when one does not, simply to place perjury defendants in the most disadvantageous trial position."

[F] ETHICAL CONSIDERATIONS

Perjury often raises competing ethical concerns. What if a client has committed or is about to commit perjury? The Preamble to the American Bar Association's Model Rules of Professional Conduct affirms the basic principle that it is the "lawyer's obligation zealously to protect and pursue a client's legitimate interests, within the bounds of the law. . . . " Rule 1.6(a) generally provides that "[a] lawyer shall not reveal information relating to the representation of a client unless the client gives informed consent. . . . " This requirement is subject to exceptions, as the following rule demonstrates. How do the attorney's obligations to the client square with the attorney's obligations under Rule 3.3?

AMERICAN BAR ASSOCIATION
Model Rules of Professional Conduct

Rule 3.3. Candor Toward the Tribunal

(a) A lawyer shall not knowingly:

*   *   *

(3) offer evidence that the lawyer knows to be false. If a lawyer, the lawyer's client, or a witness called by the lawyer, has offered material evidence and the lawyer comes to know of its falsity, the lawyer shall take reasonable remedial measures, including, if necessary, disclosure to the tribunal. A lawyer may refuse to offer evidence, other than the testimony of a defendant in a criminal matter, that the lawyer reasonably believes is false.

Comment

*   *   *

[6] If a lawyer knows that the client intends to testify falsely or wants the lawyer to introduce false evidence, the lawyer should seek to persuade the client that the evidence should not be offered. If the persuasion is ineffective and the lawyer continues to represent the client, the lawyer must refuse to offer the false evidence. If only a portion of a witness's testimony will be false, the lawyer may call the witness to testify but may not elicit or otherwise permit the witness to present the testimony that the lawyer knows is false.

[7] The duties stated [above] apply to all lawyers, including defense counsel in criminal cases. In some jurisdictions, however, courts have required counsel to present the accused as a witness or to give a narrative statement if the accused so desires, even if counsel knows that the testimony or statement will be false. The obligation of the advocate under the Rules of Professional Conduct is subordinate to such requirements.

[8] The prohibition against offering false evidence only applies if the lawyer knows that the evidence is false. A lawyer's reasonable belief that evidence is false does not preclude its presentation to the trier of fact. A lawyer's knowledge that evidence is false, however, can be inferred from the circumstances. Thus, although a lawyer should resolve doubts about the veracity of testimony or other evidence in favor of the client, the lawyer cannot ignore an obvious falsehood.

[9] Although paragraph (a)(3) only prohibits a lawyer from offering evidence the lawyer knows to be false, it permits the lawyer to refuse to offer testimony or other proof that the lawyer reasonably believes is false. Offering such proof may reflect adversely on the lawyer's ability to discriminate in the quality of evidence and thus impair the lawyer's effectiveness as an advocate. Because of the special protections historically provided criminal defendants, however, this Rule does not permit a lawyer to refuse to offer the testimony of such a client where the lawyer reasonably believes but does not know that the testimony will be false. Unless the lawyer knows the testimony will be false, the lawyer must honor the client's decision to testify.

[10] Having offered material evidence in the belief that it was true, a lawyer may subsequently come to know that the evidence is false. Or, a lawyer may be surprised when the lawyer's client, or another witness called by the lawyer, offers testimony the lawyer knows to be false, either during the lawyer's direct examination or in response to cross-examination by the opposing lawyer. In such situations, or if the lawyer knows of the falsity of testimony elicited from the client during a deposition, the lawyer must take reasonable remedial measures. In such situations, the advocate's proper course is to remonstrate with the client confidentially, advise the client of the lawyer's duty of candor to the tribunal and seek the client's cooperation with respect to the withdrawal or correction of the false statements or evidence. If that fails, the advocate must take further remedial action. If withdrawal from the representation is not permitted or will not undo the effect of the false evidence, the advocate must make such disclosure to the tribunal as is reasonably necessary to remedy the situation, even if doing so requires the lawyer to reveal information that otherwise would be protected by Rule 1.6. It is for the tribunal then to determine what should be done — making a statement about the matter to the trier of fact, ordering a mistrial or perhaps nothing.

* * *

[12] The general rule that an advocate must reveal the existence of perjury with respect to a material fact — even that of a client — applies to defense counsel in

criminal cases, as well as in other instances. However, the definition of the lawyer's ethical duty in such a situation may be qualified by constitutional provisions for due process and the right to counsel in criminal cases. In some jurisdictions these provisions have been construed to require that counsel present an accused as a witness if the accused wishes to testify, even if counsel knows the testimony will be false. The obligation of the advocate under these Rules is subordinate to such a constitutional requirement.

* * *

[15] Normally, a lawyer's compliance with the duty of candor imposed by this Rule does not require that the lawyer withdraw from the representation of a client whose interests will be or have been adversely affected by the lawyer's disclosure. The lawyer may, however, be required to seek permission of the tribunal to withdraw if the lawyer's compliance with this Rule's duty of candor results in such an extreme deterioration of the client-lawyer relationship that the lawyer can no longer competently represent the client. In connection with a request for permission to withdraw that is premised on a client's misconduct, a lawyer may reveal information relating to the representation only to the extent reasonably necessary to comply with this Rule or as otherwise permitted by Rule 1.6.

NOTES AND QUESTIONS

1. *Future testimony.* Any criminal defense attorney or prosecutor may well, at some point, face ethical issues involving perjurious testimony. The issue can arise in a number of ways. For example, an attorney may believe that a client or witness plans to commit perjury. The belief may be based upon a suspicion. Or, less often, the attorney may have actual or constructive knowledge that a witness intends to commit perjury. A prosecutor, of course, can simply decline to present the witness. But what if the witness is a criminal defendant who insists on testifying? May the defendant's attorney elicit the testimony during direct examination?

2. *Past testimony.* Another tricky circumstance arises when a witness or criminal defendant commits perjury, and the attorney who offered the testimony later becomes aware that the testimony was perjurious. A prosecutor does not have a duty to the witness as a client. As an officer of the court, must the prosecutor reveal the perjury? Or what about a defense attorney? How does the attorney square the obligation of candor to the court with the obligation to zealously represent the client?

3. *Government witness perjury at trial.* Assume that a government witness commits perjury at a criminal trial, and that the defendant is convicted. Must the conviction be overturned when the perjury comes to light? This issue arose in the case against Martha Stewart and her broker Peter Bacanovic, during which a government expert witness committed perjury during trial. *United States v. Stewart*, 323 F. Supp. 2d 606 (S.D.N.Y. 2004). The defendants moved under Fed. R. Crim. P. 33 to vacate the judgment and for a new trial. In denying the motion, the court wrote:

> [T]he mere fact that a witness committed perjury is insufficient, standing alone, to warrant relief under Rule 33. "Whether the introduction of perjured testimony requires a new trial initially depends on the extent to which the prosecution was aware of the alleged perjury. To prevent

prosecutorial misconduct, a conviction obtained when the prosecution's case includes testimony that was known or should have been known to be perjured must be reversed if there is any reasonable likelihood that the perjured testimony influenced the jury." When the government is unaware of the perjury at the time of trial, "a new trial is warranted only if the testimony was material and the court [is left] with a firm belief that but for the perjured testimony, the defendant would most likely not have been convicted."

Id. at 615. (citations omitted).

Analyzing the facts, the court concluded:

> Defendants have failed to demonstrate that the prosecution knew or should have known of [the] perjury. However, even under the stricter prejudice standard applicable when the government is aware of a witness's perjury, defendants' motions fail. There is no reasonable likelihood that knowledge by the jury that [the witness] lied . . . could have affected the verdict.

Id. at 619.

How likely is it that a defendant will be able to prove that the government knew or should have known of a witness's perjury? How likely is it that a defendant will be able to prove that perjured testimony was prejudicial? As the court noted in *Stewart*, few cases in the circuit in which the case was decided have ever ordered a new trial because of witness perjury. *Id.* at 615. Why is this so?

PROBLEM

10-6. The federal government charged a pharmaceutical company officer, Manny, with knowingly causing 40 barrels of toxic waste to be illegally dumped on August 30 of last year. Manny's trial is now taking place before a jury.

The government believes that David, a truck driver, had hauled the waste. In addition, the government has evidence that, during a telephone conversation on August 29 last year, Manny had instructed David to haul the waste. For tactical reasons, however, the government decided not to call David as a witness in its case-in-chief.

The defense, however, has called David as a witness. Following the direct examination by Manny's attorney, the government cross-examined David. David gave the following testimony during the cross-examination:

Q: Do you know a person by the name of Manny?

A: *No.*

Q: On August 30 last year, how many barrels of waste did you carry?

A: *Somewhere between ten and fifteen.*

At that point, the trial adjourned for the day.

*   *   *

Question (a): Assume that you are the attorney for David. Prior to testifying, David had told you that a person who identified himself to David to be Manny had telephoned David on August 29. During the conversation, Manny had instructed David to haul the waste the next day. David also tells you that he had never met Manny before the trial, and does not believe, in the common meaning of the word, that he "knows" Manny. You have listened to the above testimony.

Should you take any action? If so, what?

*   *   *

Question (b): Now assume that David continued the testimony the next day without having discussed the testimony with his attorney. The government played a recording of a telephone conversation between David and Manny. David's testimony continued:

Q: Having had that opportunity to listen to yourself talking to Manny on the telephone, does that refresh your recollection concerning whether you know Manny?

A: I don't know Manny personally.

Q: What do you mean by that?

A: I mean I've never had personal contact with Manny other than the one phone call. I don't know him.

Q: That is your voice on the tape, isn't it, talking to Manny?

A: I do recall that phone call I received, yes.

Q: And that is your voice.

A: Yes.

Q: Yesterday, Mr. David, you were asked, "Do you know a person by the name of Manny?" Your answer was, "No." Was that answer truthful?

A: I do not know the individual in the sense that I've never met him. If you mean do I know who he is, the answer is yes. If I gave another impression yesterday, I'd like to withdraw my testimony of yesterday.

Other witnesses testified that David carried 40 barrels of toxic waste on the date in question. Although Manny was charged with causing the illegal dumping of 40 barrels of waste, the charges and penalties would have been the same for the dumping of 10, 15, or 40 barrels.

Based upon the italicized answers given during his first day of testimony, David is charged with two counts of perjury under § 1623. David seeks to dismiss the charges.

What possible argument or arguments could David make? Will David succeed as to any of the arguments? Why or why not?

Chapter 11

OBSTRUCTION OF JUSTICE

[A] INTRODUCTORY NOTES

[1] Statutory Scheme

Federal obstruction of justice statutes broadly criminalize efforts to interfere with federal judicial, administrative, and legislative proceedings. Examples of obstructive efforts include destroying or altering physical evidence, procuring false testimony, and threatening witnesses, jurors, and others involving in official proceedings. As with other "cover-up" crimes, an obstruction case may stand on its own, or may arise out of attempts to cover up earlier, illegal activity. It is noteworthy, for example, that the first criminal trial arising out of the Enron scandal was of the Arthur Andersen accounting firm for obstruction of justice. As discussed more fully below, the Supreme Court later reversed the conviction, finding that the trial judge erred when instructing the jury on the element of the offense. *See Arthur Andersen LLP v. United States*, 544 U.S. 696 (2005).

The federal criminal code contains a myriad of obstruction statutes, many of them overlapping. The principal statutes are set forth in §§ 1501–1520. These include § 1503 (obstruction of judicial proceedings), § 1505 (obstruction of administrative and Congressional proceedings), § 1510 (bribery of witnesses), § 1512 (tampering with witnesses and documents), § 1513 (tampering with a witness), § 1519 (destruction, alteration, or falsification of records in federal investigations and bankruptcy), and § 1520 (destruction of corporate audit records). The Sarbanes-Oxley Act of 2002, which Congress enacted in response to the corporate accounting scandals, expanded § 1512 to include document tampering and added §§ 1519 and 1520 to the federal criminal code.

Most obstruction cases are brought under §§ 1503, 1505, and 1512, and it is upon those sections that this chapter largely focuses. The most wide-ranging provisions are contained in the "omnibus" clauses of §§ 1503 and 1505. The statutes do not overlap; § 1503 applies to federal judicial proceedings, while § 1505 applies only to federal administrative and legislative proceedings. In addition, the chapter covers those portions of § 1512 most applicable to white collar cases, including attempts to influence testimony and destroy or alter documents.

[2] Statutory Overview and Elements

[a] Sections 1503 and 1505

Section 1503(a) encompasses three distinct activities in connection with judicial proceedings. First, the statute criminalizes an endeavor to influence, intimidate, or impede a grand juror or trial juror, or any court officer. The term "court officer" generally applies to judges and other court officials, such as clerks, as well as to attorneys appearing before the court. Second, the statute criminalizes injuring a juror or court officer. Third, the statute criminalizes acting "corruptly" or by threats to influence, obstruct, or impede a judicial proceeding, or to endeavor to influence, obstruct, or impede, a judicial proceeding. The latter is referred to as the catch-all or "omnibus" clause. Note that the omnibus clause, on its face, both subsumes and expands upon the more specific preceding clauses. Section 1505 contains a parallel omnibus provision applicable to legislative and administrative proceedings.

Most obstruction charges under § 1503 and § 1505 are brought under the omnibus clauses of those statutes. Under the omnibus clause of either section, most circuit courts require the government to prove that:

(1) The defendant acted with "corrupt" intent;

(2) The defendant endeavored to interfere with a judicial, administrative, or congressional proceeding;

(3) There was a "nexus" between the endeavor and the proceeding;

(4) The proceeding was actually pending at the time of the endeavor; and

(5) The defendant knew that the proceeding was pending.

Obstruction under the omnibus clauses is an inchoate offense; the defendant's "endeavor" need not succeed for the crime to be complete. Also, note that the obstruction statutes enacted as part of the Sarbanes-Oxley Act eliminate the pending proceeding element.[1]

[b]   Section 1512

Under the portion of § 1512(b) most applicable to white collar cases, the government must prove that:

(1)   The defendant acted corruptly;

(2)   The defendant persuaded, or attempted to persuade, or misled another person; *and*

(3)   The defendant acted with intent to:

    (a)   influence, delay, or prevent the testimony of any person in an official proceeding (18 U.S.C. § 1512(b)(1)); *or*

    (b)   cause or induce any person to —

        (i)   withhold testimony, or withhold a record, document, or other object, from an official proceeding (18 U.S.C. § 1512(b)(2)(A)); *or*

        (ii)   alter, destroy, mutilate, or conceal an object with intent to impair the object's integrity or availability for use in an official proceeding (18 U.S.C. § 1512(b)(2)(B)).

---

[1] Section 1519 is entitled "Destruction, alteration, or falsification of records in Federal investigations and bankruptcy." That section applies to "*any matter* within the jurisdiction of any department or agency of the United States or any case filed under title 11, or in relation to or contemplation of any such matter or case." Section 1520, "Destruction of corporate audit records," applies to destruction of records relating to audits of issuers of registered securities.

Under § 1512(c), added by the Sarbanes-Oxley Act, the government must show that:

(1) The defendant acted corruptly; *and*

(2)(a)(i) The defendant altered, destroyed, mutilated, or concealed a record, document, or other object, or attempted to do so; *and*

(ii) The defendant acted with the intent to impair the object's integrity or availability for use in an official proceeding; *or*

(b) The defendant otherwise obstructed, influenced, or impeded any official proceeding, or attempted to do so.

Section 1512(f)(1) further provides that "an official proceeding need not be pending or about to be instituted at the time of the offense." As is apparent from the foregoing, § 1512 largely duplicates the omnibus clauses, though it reaches farther in some cases by not requiring that a proceeding be pending at the time of the obstructive acts. Nonetheless, as discussed in § [D] below, the government must show that the defendant at least contemplated an official proceeding in order to prove corrupt intent.

[B]   THE ENDEAVOR

The omnibus clauses of §§ 1503 and 1505 criminalize "*endeavor*[*ing*] to influence, obstruct, or impede" a pending judicial, legislative, or administrative proceeding. The inchoate crime of endeavoring to obstruct justice may give rise to liability in circumstances even broader than those that would qualify for the common law of attempt. In the case that follows, the Supreme Court provides a definition of the "endeavor" element. Note that, under the Court's approach, the actus reus of the "endeavor" also implicates the mens rea of the crime.

UNITED STATES v. AGUILAR
515 U.S. 593 (1995)

CHIEF JUSTICE REHNQUIST delivered the opinion of the Court.

A jury convicted United States District Judge Robert Aguilar of one count of endeavoring to obstruct the due administration of justice in violation of § 1503. A panel of the Court of Appeals for the Ninth Circuit reversed the conviction under § 1503. We granted certiorari to resolve a conflict among the federal circuits over whether § 1503 punishes false statements made to potential grand jury witnesses.

Many facts remain disputed by the parties. Both parties appear to agree, however, that a motion for postconviction relief filed by one Michael Rudy Tham represents the starting point from which events bearing on this case unfolded. Tham was an officer of the International Brotherhood of Teamsters, and was convicted of embezzling funds from the local affiliate of that organization. In July 1987, he filed a motion to have his conviction set aside. The motion was assigned to Judge Stanley Weigel. Tham, seeking to enhance the odds that his petition would be granted, asked Edward Solomon and Abraham Chalupowitz, a.k.a. Abe Chapman, to assist him by capitalizing on their respective acquaintances with another judge in the Northern District of California, respondent Aguilar. Respondent knew Chapman as a distant relation by marriage and knew Solomon from law school. Solomon and Chapman met with respondent to discuss Tham's case, as a result of which respondent spoke with Judge Weigel about the matter.

Independent of the embezzlement conviction, the Federal Bureau of Investigation (FBI) identified Tham as a suspect in an investigation of labor racketeering. On April 20, 1987, the FBI applied for authorization to install a wiretap on Tham's business phones. Chapman appeared on the application as a potential interceptee. Chief District Judge Robert Peckham authorized the wiretap. During the course of the racketeering investigation, the FBI learned of the meetings between Chapman and respondent. The FBI informed Chief Judge Peckham, who, concerned with appearances of impropriety, advised respondent in August 1987 that Chapman might be connected with criminal elements because Chapman's name had appeared on a wiretap authorization.

Five months after respondent learned that Chapman had been named in a wiretap authorization, he noticed a man observing his home during a visit by Chapman. He alerted his nephew to this fact and conveyed the message (with an intent that his nephew relay the information to Chapman) that Chapman's phone was being wiretapped. . . .

At this point, respondent's involvement in the two separate Tham matters converged. Two months after the disclosure to his nephew, a grand jury began to investigate an alleged conspiracy to influence the outcome of Tham's habeas case. Two FBI agents questioned respondent. During the interview, respondent lied about his participation in the Tham case and his knowledge of the wiretap. The grand jury returned an indictment; a jury convicted Aguilar of one count of endeavoring to obstruct the due administration of justice, § 1503. The Court of Appeals reversed the conviction for the reason that the conduct was not covered by the statutory language. . . . [2]

Section 1503 is structured as follows: first it proscribes persons from endeavoring to influence, intimidate, or impede grand or petit jurors or court officers in the discharge of their duties; it then prohibits injuring grand or petit jurors in their person or property because of any verdict or indictment rendered by them; it then prohibits injury of any court officer, commissioner, or similar officer on account of the performance of his official duties; finally, the "Omnibus Clause" serves as a catchall, prohibiting persons from endeavoring to influence, obstruct, or impede the due administration of justice. The latter clause, it can be seen, is far more general in scope than the earlier clauses of the statute. Respondent was charged with a violation of the Omnibus Clause, to wit: with "corruptly endeavor[ing] to influence, obstruct, and impede the . . . grand jury investigation."

The first case from this Court construing the predecessor statute to § 1503 was *Pettibone v. United States*, 148 U.S. 197 (1893). There we held that "a person is not sufficiently charged with obstructing or impeding the due administration of justice in a court unless it appears that he knew or had notice that justice was being administered in such court." *Id.* at 206. The Court reasoned that a person lacking knowledge of a pending proceeding necessarily lacked the evil intent to obstruct. Recent decisions of Courts of Appeals have likewise tended to place metes and bounds on the very broad language of the catchall provision. The action taken by

---

[2] The Court of Appeals sitting en banc also reversed the defendant's conviction for unauthorized disclosure of a wiretap. 21 F.3d 1475 (1994). In a portion of the opinion not reproduced here, the Supreme Court reinstated that conviction. — Eds.

the accused must be with an intent to influence judicial or grand jury proceedings; it is not enough that there be an intent to influence some ancillary proceeding, such as an investigation independent of the court's or grand jury's authority. Some courts have phrased this showing as a "nexus" requirement — that the act must have a relationship in time, causation, or logic with the judicial proceedings. In other words, the endeavor must have the "'natural and probable effect'" of interfering with the due administration of justice. This is not to say that the defendant's actions need be successful; an "endeavor" suffices. But as in *Pettibone*, if the defendant lacks knowledge that his actions are likely to affect the judicial proceeding, he lacks the requisite intent to obstruct.

Although respondent urges various broader grounds for affirmance, we find it unnecessary to address them because we think the "nexus" requirement developed in the decisions of the Courts of Appeals is a correct construction of § 1503. We have traditionally exercised restraint in assessing the reach of a federal criminal statute, both out of deference to the prerogatives of Congress, and out of concern that "a fair warning should be given to the world in language that the common world will understand, of what the law intends to do if a certain line is passed," *McBoyle v. United States*, 283 U.S. 25, 27 (1931). We do not believe that uttering false statements to an investigating agent — and that seems to be all that was proved here — who might or might not testify before a grand jury is sufficient to make out a violation of the catchall provision of § 1503.

The government did not show here that the agents acted as an arm of the grand jury, or indeed that the grand jury had even summoned the testimony of these particular agents. The government argues that respondent "understood that his false statements would be provided to the grand jury" and that he made the statements with the intent to thwart the grand jury investigation and not just the FBI investigation. The government supports its argument with a citation to the transcript of the recorded conversation between Aguilar and the FBI agent at the point where Aguilar asks whether he is a target of a grand jury investigation. The agent responded to the question by stating:

> [T]here is a Grand Jury meeting. Convening I guess that's the correct word. Um some evidence will be heard I'm . . . I'm sure on this issue.

Because respondent knew of the pending proceeding, the government therefore contends that Aguilar's statements are analogous to those made directly to the grand jury itself, in the form of false testimony or false documents.

We think the transcript citation relied upon by the government would not enable a rational trier of fact to conclude that respondent knew that his false statement would be provided to the grand jury, and that the evidence goes no further than showing that respondent testified falsely to an investigating agent. Such conduct, we believe, falls on the other side of the statutory line from that of one who delivers false documents or testimony to the grand jury itself. Conduct of the latter sort all but assures that the grand jury will consider the material in its deliberations. But what use will be made of false testimony given to an investigating agent who has not been subpoenaed or otherwise directed to appear before the grand jury is far more speculative. We think it cannot be said to have the "natural and probable effect" of interfering with the due administration of justice.

JUSTICE SCALIA criticizes our treatment of the statutory language for reading the word "endeavor" out of it, inasmuch as it excludes defendants who have an evil purpose but use means that would "only unnaturally and improbably be successful." This criticism is unwarranted. Our reading of the statute gives the term "endeavor" a useful function to fulfill: It makes conduct punishable where the defendant acts with an intent to obstruct justice, and in a manner that is likely to obstruct justice, but is foiled in some way. Were a defendant with the requisite intent to lie to a subpoenaed witness who is ultimately not called to testify, or who testifies but does not transmit the defendant's version of the story, the defendant has endeavored to obstruct, but has not actually obstructed, justice. Under our approach, a jury could find such defendant guilty.

JUSTICE SCALIA's dissent also apparently believes that *any* act, done with the intent to "obstruct . . . the due administration of justice," is sufficient to impose criminal liability. Under the dissent's theory, a man could be found guilty under § 1503 if he knew of a pending investigation and lied to his wife about his whereabouts at the time of the crime, thinking that an FBI agent might decide to interview her and that she might in turn be influenced in her statement to the agent by her husband's false account of his whereabouts. The intent to obstruct justice is indeed present, but the man's culpability is a good deal less clear from the statute than we usually require in order to impose criminal liability.

* * *

We affirm the decision of the Court of Appeals with respect to respondent's conviction under § 1503.

JUSTICE SCALIA, with whom JUSTICE KENNEDY and JUSTICE THOMAS join, concurring in part and dissenting in part.

I would reverse the Court of Appeals, and would uphold respondent's conviction, on the count charging violation of 18 U.S.C. § 1503.

The "omnibus clause" of § 1503 . . . makes criminal not just success in corruptly influencing the due administration of justice, but also the "endeavor" to do so. We have given this latter proscription, which respondent was specifically charged with violating, a generous reading: "The word of the section is 'endeavor,' and by using it the section got rid of the technicalities which might be urged as besetting the word 'attempt,' and it describes *any effort or essay* to accomplish the evil purpose that the section was enacted to prevent." *United States v. Russell*, 255 U.S. 138, 143 (1921) (emphasis added) (interpreting substantially identical predecessor statute). Under this reading of the statute, it is even immaterial whether the endeavor to obstruct pending proceedings is possible of accomplishment. In *Osborn v. United States*, 385 U.S. 323, 333 (1966), we dismissed out of hand the "impossibility" defense of a defendant who had sought to convey a bribe to a prospective juror through an intermediary who was secretly working for the government. "Whatever continuing validity," we said, "the doctrine of 'impossibility' . . . may continue to have in the law of criminal attempt, that body of law is inapplicable here." *Id.*[3]

Even read at its broadest, however, § 1503's prohibition of "endeavors" to impede justice is not without limits. To "endeavor" means to strive or work for a

---

[3] This complete disavowal of the impossibility defense may be excessive. As Pettibone v. United States, 148 U.S. 197 (1893), acknowledged, an endeavor to obstruct proceedings that did not exist would not violate the statute. "[O]bstruction can only arise when justice is being administered." *Id.* at 207.

certain end. Webster's New International Dictionary 844 (2d ed. 1950); 1 New Shorter Oxford English Dictionary 816 (1993). Thus, § 1503 reaches only *purposeful* efforts to obstruct the due administration of justice, *i.e.*, acts performed with that very object in mind. This limitation was clearly set forth in our first decision construing § 1503's predecessor statute, *Pettibone v. United States*, 148 U.S. 197 (1893), which held an indictment insufficient because it had failed to allege the intent to obstruct justice. That opinion rejected the government's contention that the intent required to violate the statute could be found in "the intent to commit an unlawful act, in the doing of which justice was in fact obstructed"; to justify a conviction, it said, "the specific intent to violate the statute must exist." *Id.* at 207. *Pettibone* did acknowledge, however — and here is the point that is distorted to produce today's opinion — that the specific intent to obstruct justice could be found where the defendant intentionally committed a wrongful act that had obstruction of justice as its "natural and probable consequence." *Id.*

Today's "nexus" requirement sounds like this, but is in reality quite different. Instead of reaffirming that "natural and probable consequence" is one way of establishing intent, it *substitutes* "natural and probable effect" *for* intent, requiring that factor even when intent to obstruct justice is otherwise clear. But while it is quite proper to derive an *intent* requirement from § 1503's use of the word "endeavor," it is quite impossible to derive a *"natural and probable consequence"* requirement. One would be "endeavoring" to obstruct justice if he intentionally set out to do it by means that would only unnaturally and improbably be successful. . . .

The Court does not indicate where its "nexus" requirement is to be found in the words of the statute. Instead, it justifies its holding with the assertion that "[w]e have traditionally exercised restraint in assessing the reach of a federal criminal statute, both out of deference to the prerogatives of Congress and out of concern that a fair warning should be given . . . of what the law intends to do if a certain line is passed." But "exercising restraint *in assessing the reach* of a federal criminal statute" (which is what the rule of lenity requires) is quite different from importing extratextual requirements *in order to limit the reach* of a federal criminal statute, which is what the Court has done here. By limiting § 1503 to acts having the "natural and probable effect" of interfering with the due administration of justice, the Court effectively reads the word "endeavor," which we said in *Russell* embraced "any effort or essay" to obstruct justice, 255 U.S. at 143, out of the omnibus clause, leaving a prohibition of only actual obstruction and competent attempts.

The Court apparently adds to its "natural and probable effect" requirement the requirement that the defendant *know* of that natural and probable effect. ("[I]f the defendant lacks knowledge that his actions are likely to affect the judicial proceeding, he lacks the requisite intent to obstruct"). Separate proof of such knowledge is not, I think, required for the orthodox use of the "natural and probable effect" rule discussed in *Pettibone:* Where the defendant intentionally commits a wrongful act that *in fact* has the "natural and probable consequence" of obstructing justice, "the unintended wrong may derive its character from the wrong that was intended." 148 U.S., at 207. Or, as we would put the point in modern times, the jury is entitled to presume that a person intends the natural and probable consequences of his acts.

While inquiry into the state of the defendant's knowledge seems quite superfluous to the Court's opinion (since the act performed did not have the requisite "natural and probable effect" anyway), it is necessary to my disposition of the case. As I have said, I think an act committed *with intent to obstruct* is all that matters; and what one can fairly be thought to have intended depends in part upon what one can fairly be thought to have known. The critical point of knowledge at issue, in my view, is not whether "respondent knew that his false statement *would be provided* to the grand jury," but rather whether respondent knew — or indeed, even erroneously *believed* — that his false statement *might* be provided to the grand jury (which is all the knowledge needed to support the conclusion that the purpose of his lie was to mislead the jury). I find that a rational juror could readily have concluded beyond a reasonable doubt that respondent had corruptly endeavored to impede the due administration of justice, *i.e.*, that he lied to the FBI agents intending to interfere with a grand jury investigation into his misdeeds.

Recorded conversations established that respondent knew a grand jury had been convened; that he had been told he was a target of its investigation; and that he feared he would be unable to explain his actions if he were subpoenaed to testify. Respondent himself testified that, at least at the conclusion of the interview, it was his "impression" that his statements to the FBI agents would be reported to the grand jury. The evidence further established that respondent made false statements to the FBI agents that minimized his involvement in the matters the grand jury was investigating. Viewing this evidence in the light most favorable to the government, I am simply unable to conclude that no rational trier of fact could have found beyond a reasonable doubt that respondent lied specifically because he thought the agents *might* convey what he said to the grand jury — which suffices to constitute a corrupt endeavor to impede the due administration of justice. In fact, I think it would be hard for a juror to conclude otherwise. . . .

*   *   *

The "nexus" requirement that the Court today engrafts into § 1503 has no basis in the words Congress enacted. I would reverse that part of the Court of Appeals' judgment which set aside respondent's conviction under that statute.

[Opinion of JUSTICE STEVENS, concurring in part and dissenting in part, omitted.]

NOTES AND QUESTIONS

1. *The "endeavor."*

a. *The role of federal investigators.* The Court held that the government had not proven that the defendant's false statement to the FBI agent would "have the 'natural and probable effect' of interfering with the due administration of justice." Why not? Note that federal grand juries typically rely upon federal investigators — principally FBI agents — to gather evidence. Such agents often present the evidence they have gathered both at the grand jury and at the defendant's trial. *See* United States Attorneys' Manual § 1.2.303; Grand Jury Practice Manual § 3.04. What additional proof would have satisfied the majority?

b. *Subpoenas for documents.* Obstruction charges often arise out of defendants' efforts to destroy, conceal, or hide documents. For example, in *United States v. Lench*, 806 F.2d 1443 (9th Cir. 1986), the defendant was convicted of obstruction for concealing documents responsive to a grand jury subpoena. *See also United States v. Arthur Andersen, infra.*

c. *False testimony.* Under the *Blockburger* test, discussed in Chapter 9, § G, *supra,* could a defendant be punished for both perjury and obstruction based upon the same false testimony? Most courts have answered in the affirmative where all the elements of obstruction are met. If, however, the government has failed to prove an element of obstruction — such as the defendant's intent to obstruct, or the "nexus" between the testimony and the pending proceeding — then perjury alone will not support an obstruction conviction. *See, e.g., United States v. Littleton,* 76 F.3d 614, 619 (4th Cir. 1996) (perjury can constitute the actus reus of obstruction, but an obstruction charge cannot rest solely on the allegation of perjury; there must also be proof that the false statement either obstructed or was intended to obstruct justice). Can you imagine a circumstance in which proof of perjury would not also qualify for proof of obstruction?

2. *Obstructive intent.* Even though the FBI agent told Aguilar that a grand jury had been convened, the Court found insufficient proof that Aguilar "made the statements with the intent to thwart the grand jury investigation and not just the FBI investigation." The Court concluded that, to hold otherwise, "a man could be found guilty under § 1503 if he knew of a pending investigation and lied to his wife about his whereabouts at the time of the crime, thinking that an FBI agent might decide to interview her and that she might in turn be influenced in her statement to the agent by her husband's false account of his whereabouts." Is this a correct reading of the dissent's position?

3. *False statement.* Why did not the government simply charge the defendant with making a false statement under § 1001? Note that *Aguilar* was decided in 1995; it was not until *Brogan v. United States,* 522 U.S. 398 (1998), that the Supreme Court disallowed the "exculpatory 'no' " defense to a § 1001 prosecution.

[C]   THE PENDING PROCEEDING

The essence of an obstruction case under the omnibus clauses of §§ 1503 and 1505 is that the defendant endeavored to interfere with a governmental proceeding. Most courts hold that the government must show both that a proceeding was pending at the time of the endeavor and that the defendant knew of the proceeding. It may be difficult to determine, however, exactly when a court case or other "proceeding" begins or when it ends. In the next case, the court attempted to define both the "proceeding" element of the omnibus clause and the "court officer" element of the second clause of § 1503. As you read the case, consider both the evils at which the obstruction statutes are directed and the court's apparent concern about the potential for prosecutorial overreaching in obstruction cases.

UNITED STATES v. FULBRIGHT
105 F.3d 443 (9th Cir. 1997)

MICHAEL DALY HAWKINS, CIRCUIT JUDGE:

This appeal deals with a dangerous intersection in a free society, one at which the expression of discontent or disagreement with the actions of government can collide with legitimate efforts to deal with actions intended to threaten or impede federal officials in the carrying out of their duties.

Defendant-appellant Ronald Fulbright ("Fulbright") is a Montana farmer who experienced some financial reverses. When his creditors sought foreclosure, he sought bankruptcy protection. When these efforts failed, Fulbright mailed a series of documents to United States Bankruptcy Judge John Peterson. Among the documents mailed by Fulbright was a "Notice and Demand for Declaration of Judge's Impartiality" and a "Citizens' Arrest Warrant for Citizens' Arrest." The notice "charged" Judge Peterson with numerous "crimes," including sedition, high treason, bank fraud, and armed robbery. The "warrant" purportedly authorized peace officers to somehow arrest Judge Peterson. Before Fulbright mailed either of these documents, Judge Peterson recused himself from further participation in Fulbright's bankruptcy matters. On April 16, 1993, shortly after the recusal, Fulbright mailed the "Notice" to Judge Peterson. Several weeks later, on June 2, 1993, Fulbright filed the "Warrant" in bankruptcy court. On May 10, 1993, after the "Notice" was mailed but before the "Warrant" was filed, Fulbright's bankruptcy case was dismissed.

Fulbright was indicted for conspiracy to impede or injure federal officers under 18 U.S.C. § 372 (Count I) and for obstruction of justice by intimidating or injuring federal officers (Count II), and aiding and abetting the obstruction of justice (Count III), in violation of 18 U.S.C. § 1503. At his jury trial, Fulbright took the stand in his own defense, admitted the mailings, but claimed that he had not intended to intimidate or harass Judge Peterson: "I was just trying to get a farm foreclosure action hopefully remedied." Fulbright was convicted and later sentenced to a 27-month prison term, and a three-year period of supervised release.

Fulbright appeals, claiming a series of errors. We affirm in part, reverse in part and remand.

In his petition for rehearing, Fulbright advances two arguments why the timing of his mailings to Judge Peterson precludes his conviction, under Count II, for obstruction of justice in violation of 18 U.S.C. § 1503. First, he contends that because Judge Peterson had recused himself before Fulbright sent either the "Notice" or the "Warrant," Judge Peterson was not acting "in the discharge of his duties" at that time. Second, he argues that there was no "proceeding" pending at the time Fulbright filed the "Warrant," since his bankruptcy case had already been dismissed.

* * *

1. The "discharge of duty" element

Count II contained three separate allegations: Fulbright and others (1) endeavored to influence and intimidate Judge Peterson "in the discharge of his duties;" (2) knowingly injured Judge Peterson on account of his performance of his official duties; and (3) tried to obstruct the due administration of justice in connection with his "bankruptcy proceeding . . . then pending." These three allegations correspond to the three types of conduct 18 U.S.C. § 1503 prohibits. Where a statute enumerates several means of committing an offense, an indictment may contain several allegations in the conjunctive.

One of the government's three alternative theories under Count II was that Fulbright violated 18 U.S.C. § 1503 by endeavoring to influence or impede Judge Peterson "in the discharge of his duties." Conviction under that theory required the government to prove that Judge Peterson was engaged in the "discharge of his duties." 18 U.S.C. § 1503.

Although few courts have construed how § 1503 defines a judge's duties,[4] cases construing the duties of analogous officials suggest that Judge Peterson was engaged in the discharge of his duties when Fulbright sent the "Notice" and "Warrant," even though Judge Peterson had already recused himself from Fulbright's bankruptcy case. In *Hodgdon v. United States*, 365 F.2d 679 (8th Cir. 1966), for example, the Eighth Circuit affirmed a conviction for obstruction of justice where a defendant, displeased with a United States Commissioner's past handling of a tax case in which the defendant was not involved, appeared in the Commissioner's office, complained about his handling of the tax case, then placed a pistol on the Commissioner's desk. Although *Hodgdon* did not address the meaning of "discharge of duty," another court discussing that case noted that, while the Commissioner in *Hodgdon* "had no further duties or responsibilities" in regard to the tax matter, he nevertheless could be said to be engaged in the discharge of his official duties. *United States v. Knife*, 371 F. Supp. 1345, 1348 (D.S.D. 1974) (discussing *Hodgdon*). The court in *Knife* explained that "a federal court officer in his daily work would always be assumed to be in the discharge of his federal duty. . . . " *Id.* at 1348.

Although Judge Peterson had recused himself from Fulbright's case before Fulbright sent the "Notice" and "Warrant," we conclude that the judge was nevertheless engaged in the discharge of his duties. Although he was no longer involved in the adjudication of Fulbright's case, Judge Peterson was still involved in adjudicating other cases, and was therefore discharging his official duties as a United States bankruptcy judge. The danger of Fulbright's "Notice" and "Warrant" lay in their potential to intimidate Judge Peterson and to dissuade him from the zealous execution of his ongoing official duties. We therefore reject Fulbright's first challenge to his conviction under Count II.

2. The "judicial proceeding" element

It is well-settled that conviction under *any* portion of 18 U.S.C. § 1503 requires the government to prove the existence of a judicial "proceeding." *Pettibone v. United States*, 148 U.S. 197, 205–06 (1893) (interpreting predecessor statute to 18 U.S.C. § 1503). The trial court in this case properly instructed the jury that to convict under any of the government's three theories, it must find that "there existed a proceeding before a Federal District Court or a Federal Bankruptcy Court," although it nowhere defined the term "proceeding."

Courts have construed the "proceeding" element fairly strictly. Although most cases interpret the term "proceeding" in the context of a defendant's pre-trial conduct,[5] a few cases address post-trial conduct. In one such case, a criminal action was deemed "pending" until "disposition is made of any direct appeal taken by the

---

[4] Most cases construing the phrase "discharge of duty" involve the "duties" of witnesses or jurors. In such contexts, "discharge of duty" is fairly broadly construed. *See, e.g.*, United States v. Jackson, 513 F.2d 456 (D.C. Cir. 1975) (although both prosecution and defense had rested, witness threatened by criminal defendant was still considered to be a witness engaged in the discharge of his duties because the trial was not yet over and the court retained the power to re-call witness to testify).

[5] These cases hold that a proceeding exists only where there is a "judicial or grand jury proceeding." United States v. Aguilar, 515 U.S. 593 (1995). "Ancillary" proceedings, such as an FBI investigation,

defendant assigning error that could result in a new trial." *United States v. Johnson*, 605 F.2d 729, 731 (4th Cir. 1979) (affirming conviction of defendant who, after he was convicted at trial but while his appeal was still pending, tried to induce the key witness who had testified against him to recant his testimony).

In this case, the "proceeding" in question was Fulbright's bankruptcy case. The order dismissing that case was filed May 10, 1993. Although Fulbright could have appealed that dismissal order, under Federal Rule of Bankruptcy Procedure 8002, he had only ten days from the date of that order to do so. We have construed the ten-day bankruptcy appeal period as a strict jurisdictional limit. We conclude that Fulbright's bankruptcy "proceeding" terminated with the lapse of the ten-day appeal period following the May 10, 1993 order dismissing his bankruptcy case.

Because Fulbright's bankruptcy proceeding ended around May 20, 1993, we conclude that the jury could not, as a matter of law, have convicted Fulbright for obstruction of justice on the basis of the "Arrest Warrant," since Fulbright sent the "Warrant" to Judge Peterson in early June, *after* the "proceeding" element had been eliminated. Although the jury could have convicted Fulbright on the basis of the "Notice," which he sent before his bankruptcy case was dismissed, the dilemma in this case is that the jury instructions permitted the jury to convict Fulbright on the basis of *either* the "Warrant" *or* the "Notice." As noted above, Count II contained three separate allegations: Fulbright and others (1) endeavored, "by threatening letters and communications," to influence and intimidate Judge Peterson "in the discharge of his duties;" (2) knowingly injured Judge Peterson on account of his performance of his official duties; and (3) by "a threatening letter and communication," tried to obstruct the due administration of justice in connection with his "bankruptcy proceeding . . . then pending." The district court instructed the jury that it could convict under *any one* of the three allegations, provided the jurors agreed unanimously.

Where a jury returns a general verdict that is potentially based on a theory that was *legally impermissible* or *unconstitutional*, the conviction cannot be sustained. The rationale for this principle is that jurors, as non-lawyers, cannot be expected to eliminate the legally impermissible option.[6] . . .

In Fulbright's case, the court never defined the term "proceeding" for the jury, but simply required that to convict under any one of the government's three theories, the jury must find that there was a "proceeding" pending in the bankruptcy court or district court. Because the instructions allowed the jury to convict on the basis of a piece of evidence (the "Warrant") that precluded, as a matter of law, the existence of the "proceeding" element, we conclude that the jury instructions permitted the jury to choose a basis for conviction that was legally impermissible. Although the evidence would support a conviction on the basis of the "Notice," the jury may have convicted on the basis of the "Warrant" rather than the "Notice." Because we have no way to ascertain the factual basis on which the jury convicted Fulbright, his conviction under Count II cannot stand. We therefore vacate Fulbright's conviction under Count II.

---

independent of a court's or a grand jury's authority, do not satisfy § 1503's "proceeding" requirement. *Id.*

[6] In contrast, a reviewing court may uphold a general verdict if there was sufficient evidence on at least one of the submitted grounds for conviction, even if there was insufficient evidence to sustain the other theories of the case. In such instances, the court presumes that the jury, as fact-finder, reached its verdict on the basis of the correct evidence.

[The court also reversed Fulbright's conviction under Count III for aiding and abetting another person's endeavor to obstruct justice. The court found that there was insufficient evidence that an offense had been committed by the principal actor, thus precluding the defendant's liability as an aider and abettor.]

*   *   *

CONCLUSION

Fulbright's conviction on Count I is affirmed, on Count II is vacated, and on Count III is reversed.

NOTES AND QUESTIONS

1. *The pending proceeding.* Determining exactly when a "proceeding" begins and ends is a potentially problematic issue under both § 1503 and § 1505.

a. *Court proceedings.* With respect to court proceedings, courts generally agree that a proceeding begins when a complaint or indictment initiating the case is filed. Courts also generally hold that a court case is over when the time for appeal has lapsed or been exhausted. *See generally* Andrea Kendall & Kimberly Cuff, *Obstruction of Justice*, 45 Am. Crim. L. Rev. 765, 769–770 (2008).

b. *Grand jury proceedings.* The circuits are split as to whether a grand jury proceeding commences with the gathering of evidence to be presented to a grand jury, or whether the proceeding commences only when the grand jury itself initiates the investigation. *See id.* at 726. The fact that a grand jury is sitting in a particular district will not be sufficient. As the court held in United *States v. Davis*, 183 F.3d 231, 241 (3d Cir. 1999), *as amended*, 197 F.3d 662 (3d Cir. 1999), because most federal judicial districts grand jury sitting at any given time, "the mere existence of a grand jury in a district does not trigger § 1503; the grand jury must have some relationship to the investigation that is obstructed." And as the court noted in *Fulbright*, " 'ancillary' proceedings, such as an FBI investigation, independent of a court's or a grand jury's authority, do not satisfy § 1503's 'proceeding' requirement") 105 F.3d at 450 n.4 (quoting *Aguilar*).

c. *Congressional and executive agency proceedings.* Courts seem to agree that informal investigations pursuant to statutory authority qualify as proceedings under § 1505. Thus, any authorized investigation, even without the filing of a former order of investigation, should qualify under the statute. *See, e.g., United States v. Hopper*, 177 F.3d 824, 830–831 (9th Cir. 1999); *United States v. Cisneros*, 26 F. Supp. 2d 24, 39 (D.D.C. 1998). *See generally* Kendall & Cuff, *supra*, 45 Am. Crim. L. Rev. at 780–781.

2. *Discharge of duties.*

a. *Judges.* Fulbright argued that, because the judge had recused himself, the judge was not acting in the discharge of his duties at the time the "notice" and "warrant" were mailed. Given that the court found that the bankruptcy case was over at the time the warrant was sent, why did the court reject Fulbright's argument?

b. *Prosecutors.* In *United States v. Fernandez*, 837 F.2d 1031 (11th Cir. 1988), a defendant's brother threatened a prosecutor immediately after the defendant's sentencing. The Eleventh Circuit affirmed the brother's conviction under § 1503, finding that the prosecutor was still on the case for purposes of an appeal or a motion to reduce the sentence of the defendant.

c. *Jurors.* Both prospective jurors and sworn jurors appear to fall within the scope of § 1503. *See United States v. Osborn*, 415 F.2d 1021, 1024 (6th Cir. 1969) (affirming conviction of defendant who attempted to bribe a juror on a jury panel that the defendant expected would hear the case, even though that panel ultimately did not hear the case).

d. *Witnesses.* In *United States v. Jackson*, 513 F.2d 456, 458 (D.C. Cir. 1975), the defendant threatened a witness after all the evidence in the case had been presented but before the closing arguments. The court affirmed the defendant's conviction for threatening and injuring the witness, reasoning that the victim was a witness under § 1503 because the proceeding was still pending.

3. *Alternative theories and reversible error.* The government charged Fulbright under alternative theories — the April "Notice" and the June "Warrant" — not an uncommon practice in criminal cases. If a jury convicts without using a special verdict form, and one of the alternative theories will not support a conviction, can the conviction rest on the remaining theory or theories? The court in *Fulbright* distinguished charges that are legally deficient from charges that are based upon insufficient evidence. An alternative theory that is legally deficient, the court held, requires reversal, while an alternative theory that is factually deficient does not. Why does the court draw this distinction? Does it make sense? Note that the United States Supreme Court has held that an error in submitting an invalid theory to the jury does not require reversal but is subject to harmless error analysis. *See Hedgpeth v. Pulido*, 129 S. Ct. 530 (2008).

PROBLEMS

11-1. The United States Department of Justice was investigating insider trading of Clover Industries Inc. ("Clover Industries") stock. The government believed that a number of Clover Industries stockholders traded in Clover Industries stock based upon secret information that Clover Industries was engaged in merger negotiations. In addition, the Securities and Exchange Commission ("SEC") had begun a preliminary investigation of the same matter. Lawyer represented Client, a former Clover Industries investor. An Assistant United States Attorney ("AUSA") called Lawyer to see if Client would submit to an informal interview at the AUSA's office. After consulting with Client, Lawyer informed the AUSA that Client had agreed to be interviewed.

Client and lawyer subsequently appeared for the interview in the AUSA's office. Also present was another person whom the AUSA introduced as "an SEC staff member." The press had widely reported that the SEC was investigating trading in Clover Industries stock. Although the SEC representative was present for the entire interview, only the AUSA asked questions of Client.

During the meeting, the following exchange took place:

AUSA: As you know, we are investigating trading of Clover Industries stock prior to the announcement of the merger negotiations. Prior to the time you traded in Clover Industries stock, were you aware that the company was engaged in merger talks?

Client:　　　　No one told me that specifically.

AUSA:　　　　So, when you bought the stock, you did not know that a merger announcement might be forthcoming?

Client:　　　　No.

Two weeks later, a federal grand jury was convened to investigate the alleged insider trading, and the SEC launched formal investigation into the same matter. The grand jury obtained substantial evidence that Client in fact had been aware of the merger negotiations prior to the trade. Based on the above exchange, the grand jury subsequently issued a two-count indictment. Count I alleged that Client had violated 18 U.S.C. § 1503 and Count II alleged that Client had violated 18 U.S.C. § 1505.

Client has filed a motion to dismiss both counts of the indictment. Will Client succeed? Why or why not?

11-2. Moore was the head of a not-for-profit, tax-exempt organization. Three years ago, Moore deposited $1.5 million of his personal funds into his personal bank account. Moore's attorney advised him to keep his personal assets separate from the organization's assets, and to file an individual return for the year in question. Moore thereafter hired Accountant to assist in preparing Moore's personal tax return for that year. Moore told Accountant that Accountant should make it appear as though Moore was holding the $1.5 million as a fiduciary for Moore's organization, although Accountant was aware that the funds actually belonged to Moore. Accountant then created and backdated two fraudulent ledgers showing that the money originated from Moore's organization.

The year after Moore filed the return, a grand jury was convened to investigate whether Moore and Accountant conspired to file a false tax return. The grand jury subpoenaed various documents from Accountant. Among the responsive documents that Accountant produced were the fraudulent ledgers. Accountant did not vouch for the ledgers' accuracy. Accountant also was unaware that production of the documents might have been protected under the Fifth Amendment's Self-Incrimination Clause.

The grand jury has issued an indictment of Accountant for endeavoring to obstruct justice under § 1503 based upon Accountant's submission of the fraudulent ledgers. Accountant has filed a motion to dismiss the charges.

How should the court rule on Accountant's motion? Why?

[D]　MENS REA

Sections 1512(b) and (c), like the omnibus clauses of §§ 1503 and 1505, require proof that the defendant acted "corruptly." In addition, § 1512(b) and (c) require proof of a second level of mens rea — an intent to engage in further, specified activity, such as witness tampering or document destruction. Section 1512(b) also requires proof that the defendant acted knowingly.

In the next case, the Supreme Court interpreted the mens rea requirement of § 1512(b). This was a high-profile prosecution that resulted in the first criminal conviction arising from the notorious Enron scandal. The defendant was Arthur Andersen, LLP, then one of the "big five" accounting firms. The facts are unusually complicated. As you read the case, you may find it helpful to (a) diagram the entities and parties involved and (b) develop a time-line of the key events.

ARTHUR ANDERSEN, LLP v. UNITED STATES
544 U.S. 696 (2005)

CHIEF JUSTICE REHNQUIST delivered the opinion of the Court.

As Enron Corporation's financial difficulties became public in 2001, petitioner Arthur Andersen LLP, Enron's auditor, instructed its employees to destroy documents pursuant to its document retention policy. A jury found that this action made petitioner guilty of violating 18 U.S.C. §§ 1512(b)(2)(A) and (B). These sections make it a crime to "knowingly us[e] intimidation or physical force, threate[n], or corruptly persuad[e] another person . . . with intent to . . . cause" that person to "withhold" documents from, or "alter" documents for use in, an "official proceeding."[7] The Court of Appeals for the Fifth Circuit affirmed. We hold that the jury instructions failed to convey properly the elements of a "corrup[t] persuas[ion]" conviction under § 1512(b), and therefore reverse.

Enron Corporation, during the 1990's, switched its business from operation of natural gas pipelines to an energy conglomerate, a move that was accompanied by aggressive accounting practices and rapid growth. Petitioner audited Enron's publicly filed financial statements and provided internal audit and consulting services to it. Petitioner's "engagement team" for Enron was headed by David Duncan. Beginning in 2000, Enron's financial performance began to suffer, and, as 2001 wore on, worsened.[8] On August 14, 2001, Jeffrey Skilling, Enron's Chief Executive Officer (CEO), unexpectedly resigned. Within days, Sherron Watkins, a senior accountant at Enron, warned Kenneth Lay, Enron's newly reappointed CEO, that Enron could "implode in a wave of accounting scandals." She likewise informed Duncan and Michael Odom, one of petitioner's partners who had supervisory responsibility over Duncan, of the looming problems.

On August 28, an article in the Wall Street Journal suggested improprieties at Enron, and the SEC opened an informal investigation. By early September, petitioner had formed an Enron "crisis-response" team, which included Nancy Temple, an in-house counsel.[9] On October 8, petitioner retained outside counsel to represent it in any litigation that might arise from the Enron matter. The next day, Temple discussed Enron with other in-house counsel. Her notes from that meeting reflect that "some SEC investigation" is "highly probable."

On October 10, Odom spoke at a general training meeting attended by 89 employees, including 10 from the Enron engagement team. Odom urged everyone

---

[7] We refer to the 2000 version of the statute, which has since been amended by Congress.

[8] During this time, petitioner faced problems of its own. In June 2001, petitioner entered into a settlement agreement with the Securities and Exchange Commission (SEC) related to its audit work of Waste Management, Inc. As part of the settlement, petitioner paid a massive fine. It also was censured and enjoined from committing further violations of the securities laws. In July 2001, the SEC filed an amended complaint alleging improprieties by Sunbeam Corporation, and petitioner's lead partner on the Sunbeam audit was named.

[9] A key accounting problem involved Enron's use of "Raptors," which were special purpose entities used to engage in "off-balance-sheet" activities. Petitioner's engagement team had allowed Enron to "aggregate" the Raptors for accounting purposes so that they reflected a positive return. This was, in the words of petitioner's experts, a "black-and-white" violation of Generally Accepted Accounting Principles.

to comply with the firm's document retention policy.[10] He added: " '[I]f it's destroyed in the course of [the] normal policy and litigation is filed the next day, that's great. . . . [W]e've followed our own policy, and whatever there was that might have been of interest to somebody is gone and irretrievable.' " 374 F.3d 281, 286 (5th Cir. 2004). On October 12, Temple entered the Enron matter into her computer, designating the "Type of Potential Claim" as "Professional Practice — Government/Regulatory Inv[estigation]." App. JA-127. Temple also e-mailed Odom, suggesting that he " 'remin[d] the engagement team of our documentation and retention policy.' "

On October 16, Enron announced its third quarter results. That release disclosed a $1.01 billion charge to earnings.[11] The following day, the SEC notified Enron by letter that it had opened an investigation in August and requested certain information and documents. On October 19, Enron forwarded a copy of that letter to petitioner.

On the same day, Temple also sent an e-mail to a member of petitioner's internal team of accounting experts and attached a copy of the document policy. On October 20, the Enron crisis-response team held a conference call, during which Temple instructed everyone to "[m]ake sure to follow the [document] policy." On October 23, Enron CEO Lay declined to answer questions during a call with analysts because of "potential lawsuits, as well as the SEC inquiry." After the call, Duncan met with other Andersen partners on the Enron engagement team and told them that they should ensure team members were complying with the document policy. Another meeting for all team members followed, during which Duncan distributed the policy and told everyone to comply. These, and other smaller meetings, were followed by substantial destruction of paper and electronic documents.

On October 26, one of petitioner's senior partners circulated a New York Times article discussing the SEC's response to Enron. His e-mail commented that "the problems are just beginning and we will be in the cross hairs. The marketplace is going to keep the pressure on this and is going to force the SEC to be tough." On October 30, the SEC opened a formal investigation and sent Enron a letter that requested accounting documents.

Throughout this time period, the document destruction continued, despite reservations by some of petitioner's managers.[12] On November 8, Enron

---

[10] The firm's policy called for a single central engagement file, which "should contain only that information which is relevant to supporting our work." The policy stated that, "in cases of threatened litigation, . . . no related information will be destroyed." It also separately provided that, if petitioner is "advised of litigation or subpoenas regarding a particular engagement, the related information should not be destroyed. See Policy Statement No. 780 — Notification of Litigation." Policy Statement No. 780 set forth "notification" procedures for whenever "professional practice litigation against [petitioner] or any of its personnel has been commenced, has been threatened or is judged likely to occur, or when governmental or professional investigations that may involve [petitioner] or any of its personnel have been commenced or are judged likely."

[11] The release characterized the charge to earnings as "non-recurring." Petitioner had expressed doubts about this characterization to Enron, but Enron refused to alter the release. Temple wrote an e-mail to Duncan that "suggested deleting some language that might suggest we have concluded the release is misleading."

[12] For example, on October 26, John Riley, another partner with petitioner, saw Duncan shredding documents and told him "this wouldn't be the best time in the world for you guys to be shredding a bunch of stuff." On October 31, David Stulb, a forensics investigator for petitioner, met with Duncan. During

announced that it would issue a comprehensive restatement of its earnings and assets. Also on November 8, the SEC served Enron and petitioner with subpoenas for records. On November 9, Duncan's secretary sent an e-mail that stated: "Per Dave — No more shredding. . . . We have been officially served for our documents." Enron filed for bankruptcy less than a month later. Duncan was fired and later pleaded guilty to witness tampering.

In March 2002, petitioner was indicted in the Southern District of Texas on one count of violating §§ 1512(b)(2)(A) and (B). The indictment alleged that, between October 10 and November 9, 2001, petitioner "did knowingly, intentionally and corruptly persuade . . . other persons, to wit: [petitioner's] employees, with intent to cause" them to withhold documents from, and alter documents for use in, "official proceedings, namely: regulatory and criminal proceedings and investigations." A jury trial followed. When the case went to the jury, that body deliberated for seven days and then declared that it was deadlocked. The District Court delivered an "*Allen* charge" [strongly encouraging the jury to reach a verdict], *Allen v. United States*, 164 U.S. 492 (1896), and, after three more days of deliberation, the jury returned a guilty verdict. The District Court denied petitioner's motion for a judgment of acquittal.

The Court of Appeals for the Fifth Circuit affirmed. It held that the jury instructions properly conveyed the meaning of "corruptly persuades" and "official proceeding"; that the jury need not find any consciousness of wrongdoing; and that there was no reversible error. Because of a split of authority regarding the meaning of § 1512(b), we granted certiorari.

Chapter 73 of Title 18 of the United States Code provides criminal sanctions for those who obstruct justice. Sections 1512(b)(2)(A) and (B), part of the witness tampering provisions, provide in relevant part:

> Whoever knowingly uses intimidation or physical force, threatens, or corruptly persuades another person, or attempts to do so, or engages in misleading conduct toward another person, with intent to . . . cause or induce any person to . . . withhold testimony, or withhold a record, document, or other object, from an official proceeding [or] alter, destroy, mutilate, or conceal an object with intent to impair the object's integrity or availability for use in an official proceeding . . . shall be fined under this title or imprisoned not more than ten years, or both.

In this case, our attention is focused on what it means to "knowingly . . . corruptly persuad[e]" another person "with intent to . . . cause" that person to "withhold" documents from, or "alter" documents for use in, an "official proceeding."

"We have traditionally exercised restraint in assessing the reach of a federal criminal statute, both out of deference to the prerogatives of Congress, *Dowling v. United States*, 473 U.S. 207 (1985), and out of concern that 'a fair warning should be given to the world in language that the common world will understand, of what the law intends to do if a certain line is passed,' *McBoyle v. United States*, 283 U.S. 25, 27 (1931)." *United States v. Aguilar*, 515 U.S. 593, 600 (1995).

---

the meeting, Duncan picked up a document with the words "smoking gun" written on it and began to destroy it, adding "we don't need this." Stulb cautioned Duncan on the need to maintain documents and later informed Temple that Duncan needed advice on the document retention policy.

Such restraint is particularly appropriate here, where the act underlying the conviction — "persua[sion]" — is by itself innocuous. Indeed, "persuad[ing]" a person "with intent to . . . cause" that person to "withhold" testimony or documents from a Government proceeding or Government official is not inherently malign.[13] Consider, for instance, a mother who suggests to her son that he invoke his right against compelled self-incrimination, *see* U.S. Const., Amdt. 5, or a wife who persuades her husband not to disclose marital confidences.

Nor is it necessarily corrupt for an attorney to "persuad[e]" a client "with intent to . . . cause" that client to "withhold" documents from the Government. In *Upjohn Co. v. United States*, 449 U.S. 383 (1981), for example, we held that Upjohn was justified in withholding documents that were covered by the attorney-client privilege from the Internal Revenue Service (IRS). No one would suggest that an attorney who "persuade[d]" Upjohn to take that step acted wrongfully, even though he surely intended that his client keep those documents out of the IRS' hands.

"Document retention policies," which are created in part to keep certain information from getting into the hands of others, including the Government, are common in business. *See generally* Chase, *To Shred or Not to Shred: Document Retention Policies and Federal Obstruction of Justice Statutes*, 8 Ford. J. Corp. & Fin. L. 721 (2003). It is, of course, not wrongful for a manager to instruct his employees to comply with a valid document retention policy under ordinary circumstances.

Acknowledging this point, the parties have largely focused their attention on the word "corruptly" as the key to what may or may not lawfully be done in the situation presented here. Section 1512(b) punishes not just "corruptly persuad[ing]" another, but "*knowingly* . . . corruptly persuad[ing]" another. (Emphasis added.) The Government suggests that "knowingly" does not modify "corruptly persuades," but that is not how the statute most naturally reads. It provides the *mens rea* — "knowingly" — and then a list of acts — "uses intimidation or physical force, threatens, or corruptly persuades." We have recognized with regard to similar statutory language that the *mens rea* at least applies to the acts that immediately follow, if not to other elements down the statutory chain. The Government suggests that it is "questionable whether Congress would employ such an inelegant formulation as 'knowingly . . . corruptly persuades.'" Long experience has not taught us to share the Government's doubts on this score, and we must simply interpret the statute as written.

The parties have not pointed us to another interpretation of "knowingly . . . corruptly" to guide us here. In any event, the natural meaning of these terms provides a clear answer. *See* Black's Law Dictionary 888 (8th ed.2004) (hereinafter Black's); Webster's Third New International Dictionary 1252–1253 (1993) (hereinafter Webster's 3d); American Heritage Dictionary of the English Language 725 (1981) (hereinafter Am. Hert.). "Corrupt" and "corruptly" are normally associated with wrongful, immoral, depraved, or evil. *See* Black's 371; Webster's 3d 512; Am. Hert. 299–300. Joining these meanings together here makes sense both linguistically and in the statutory scheme. Only persons conscious of wrongdoing can be said to "knowingly . . . corruptly persuad[e]." And limiting criminality to persuaders

---

[13] Section 1512(b)(2) addresses testimony, as well as documents. Section 1512(b)(1) also addresses testimony. Section 1512(b)(3) addresses "persuade[rs]" who intend to prevent "the communication to a law enforcement officer or judge of the United States of information" relating to a federal crime.

conscious of their wrongdoing sensibly allows § 1512(b) to reach only those with the level of "culpability . . . we usually require in order to impose criminal liability." *United States v. Aguilar*, 515 U.S. at 602.

The outer limits of this element need not be explored here because the jury instructions at issue simply failed to convey the requisite consciousness of wrongdoing. Indeed, it is striking how little culpability the instructions required. For example, the jury was told that, "even if [petitioner] honestly and sincerely believed that its conduct was lawful, you may find [petitioner] guilty." The instructions also diluted the meaning of "corruptly" so that it covered innocent conduct.

The parties vigorously disputed how the jury would be instructed on "corruptly." The District Court based its instruction on the definition of that term found in the Fifth Circuit Pattern Jury Instruction for § 1503. This pattern instruction defined "corruptly" as " 'knowingly and dishonestly, with the specific intent to subvert or undermine the integrity' " of a proceeding. The Government, however, insisted on excluding "dishonestly" and adding the term "impede" to the phrase "subvert or undermine." The District Court agreed over petitioner's objections, and the jury was told to convict if it found petitioner intended to "subvert, undermine, or impede" governmental factfinding by suggesting to its employees that they enforce the document retention policy.

These changes were significant. No longer was any type of "dishonest[y]" necessary to a finding of guilt, and it was enough for petitioner to have simply "impede[d]" the Government's factfinding ability. As the Government conceded at oral argument, " 'impede' " has broader connotations than " 'subvert' " or even " 'undermine,' " and many of these connotations do not incorporate any "corrupt-[ness]" at all. The dictionary defines "impede" as "to interfere with or get in the way of the progress of" or "hold up" or "detract from." Webster's 3d 1132. By definition, anyone who innocently persuades another to withhold information from the Government "get[s] in the way of the progress of" the Government. With regard to such innocent conduct, the "corruptly" instructions did no limiting work whatsoever.

The instructions also were infirm for another reason. They led the jury to believe that it did not have to find *any* nexus between the "persua[sion]" to destroy documents and any particular proceeding. In resisting any type of nexus element, the Government relies heavily on § 1512(e)(1), which states that an official proceeding "need not be pending or about to be instituted at the time of the offense." It is, however, one thing to say that a proceeding "need not be pending or about to be instituted at the time of the offense," and quite another to say a proceeding need not even be foreseen. A "knowingly . . . corrup[t] persaude[r]" cannot be someone who persuades others to shred documents under a document retention policy when he does not have in contemplation any particular official proceeding in which those documents might be material.

We faced a similar situation in *Aguilar, supra.* Respondent Aguilar lied to a Federal Bureau of Investigation agent in the course of an investigation and was convicted of " 'corruptly endeavor[ing] to influence, obstruct, and impede [a] . . . grand jury investigation' " under § 1503. 515 U.S. at 599. All the Government had shown was that Aguilar had uttered false statements to an investigating agent "who might or might not testify before a grand jury." *Id.* at 600. We held that § 1503 required something more — specifically, a "nexus" between the obstructive act and the proceeding. *Id.* at 599–600. "[I]f the defendant lacks knowledge that his actions are likely to affect the judicial proceeding," we explained, "he lacks the requisite intent to obstruct." *Id.* at 599.

For these reasons, the jury instructions here were flawed in important respects. The judgment of the Court of Appeals is reversed, and the case is remanded for further proceedings consistent with this opinion.

NOTES AND QUESTIONS

1. *Mens rea under § 1512(b).* What was the essential disagreement between the Supreme Court and the lower courts over the proper interpretation of the statute? Which approach is better? Why?

2. *Document retention policies.* Large organizations routinely destroy documents, both as a matter of policy and necessity. Do such policies run the risk of providing the basis for an obstruction charge? Does the Supreme Court's approach provide some protection for such policies? If so, in what circumstances?

3. *Prosecutorial discretion.* Andersen argued strenuously that a criminal charge was not appropriate in its case, particularly because such a charge would likely imperil the organization's existence and cost a large number of jobs. *See* Elkan Abramowitz & Barry A. Bohrer, *White-Collar Crime: Principles of Federal Prosecution of Business Organizations*, N.Y. L.J. Mar. 4, 2003, at 3, col. 1 ("the government's decision to prosecute Arthur Andersen for its role in the Enron debacle amounted to the imposition of the corporate death penalty on that venerable accounting firm").

Was this a case of prosecutorial overkill? One prominent former federal prosecutor thought so. According to a newspaper report, Mary Jo White, former United States Attorney for the Southern District of New York, "called the decision to indict the accounting giant 'very wrongheaded,' and a sacrifice of the best interests of the public in order to 'message send.' White stated, 'To indict a corporation, as a legal matter, is like shooting fish in a barrel.'" David Ziemer, *Seventh Circuit Bar Association Meets in Milwaukee*, Wis. L.J., May 14, 2003. Indeed, does the Andersen prosecution require rethinking of the doctrine of corporate liability under respondeat superior?

PROBLEM

11-3. LeMont was a Central City police officer accused of using unjustified force on Grace, who had insulted LeMont after he arrested Grace for selling illegal narcotics. Grace later filed a complaint with the Central City Police Department, and the Department's Internal Affairs Division ("IAD") initiated an investigation into the incident. As a result of the investigation, LeMont was fired.

A federal grand jury was then convened to investigate whether LeMont had violated federal civil rights laws when inflicting physical abuse on Grace. LeMont approached Delores DeRota, who had witnessed the incident, and paid her $7,000 to leave town before the grand jury could subpoena her. The grand jury later indicted LeMont under the corrupt persuasion statute, 18 U.S.C. § 1512(b)(2)(A).

At LeMont's trial, the judge instructed the jury as follows: "In order to find that the defendant intended to corruptly persuade the witness to withhold testimony, you must find that he knowingly persuaded the witnesses, and that he did so with an improper purpose."

LeMont was convicted. On appeal, he argues that the trial judge committed reversible error when instructing the jury.

How should the court rule? Why?

[E] LEGAL AND ETHICAL CONSIDERATIONS FOR ATTORNEYS

All "cover-up" crimes provide potential pitfalls for attorneys, none perhaps more so than the obstruction statutes. *See, e.g., United States v. Cintolo*, 818 F.2d 980 (1st Cir. 1987), discussed below. The wide scope of an "endeavor" to obstruct justice can all too easily sweep an attorney's actions into its coverage. Note that 18 U.S.C. § 1515(c), adopted in 1986, provides that "[t]his chapter does not prohibit or punish the providing of lawful, bona fide, legal representation services in connection with or anticipation of an official proceeding."

One particular dilemma arises when the attorney's duties to perform as a zealous advocate on behalf of clients appears to conflict with the government's efforts to obtain facts in a civil or criminal investigation.

1. *Role of in-house counsel.* What are the particular difficulties facing in-house counsel when the government begins an investigation of corporate wrongdoing? Review the actions taken by the in-house counsel for Enron. Also, recall that in-house counsel represents the employer/entity, not individual employees. Does in-house counsel often confront conflicting loyalties? How did these conflicts appear to manifest themselves in the Enron investigation?

2. *Production of documents.* White collar investigations often gain evidence through grand jury subpoenas for the production of documents. A corporate client will likely have to gather and produce the documents largely on its own, under the general supervision of its attorneys. What if the attorney suspects that the client is altering or destroying documents? The attorney has duties to represent the client zealously and to maintain client confidences. If, however, it appears to the government that the attorney has assisted the obstructive efforts in some way, then the prosecutor may well turn the grand jury's attention to the attorney.

3. *Assertion of the Fifth Amendment privilege.* Assume that an attorney instructs a potential witness to assert the privilege against compelled self-incrimination and to refuse to testify in an official proceeding. Are there circumstances under which an attorney would commit obstruction in such a situation? In *United States v. Cintolo*, 818 F.2d 980 (1st Cir. 1987), the defendant was an attorney who advised a potential witness not to testify before the grand jury, even though the witness had been granted immunity and threatened with contempt for not testifying. The government charged Cintolo with obstruction, alleging that he had acted to protect the target of the investigation, not the interests of the potential witness. The court of appeals affirmed the conviction, finding sufficient evidence of obstructive intent.

4. *Assertion of the attorney-client privilege.* In the tax fraud prosecution of defendants associated with the KPMG accounting firm — a case the government labeled as the largest tax fraud case in U.S. history — the indictment charged that

the defendants conspired to commit tax fraud and obstruction of justice. *See United States v. Stein*, ___F.3d___ (2d Cir. 2008) (affirming dismissal of the case on Sixth Amendment grounds). One of the alleged means of the conspiracy was the phony assertion of the attorney-client privilege. According to the government, the assertion was designed to cover up the fraud. Does an obstruction charge based on such an allegation carry the potential for abuse? Consider the following observation with respect to the KPMG case:

> Charging privilege assertions as fraud or obstruction could turn a defense lawyer into a defendant or, at the very least, make the attorney's intent a discoverable issue. . . .   As the privilege belongs to the client, most lawyers are conditioned as an ethical matter to err on the side of protecting the privilege. Defense lawyers may find themselves torn between their duties to their client and the threat of prosecution.

Douglas M. Tween & James D. Bailey, *Over-Assertion of the Attorney-Client Privilege*, 13 No. 6, Bus. Crimes Bull. 3 (Feb. 2006). Are these concerns valid? Why or why not?

5. *Testimony.* When an attorney is preparing a witness, where is the line between zealous advocacy and obstruction of justice?

PROBLEM

11-4. You are the attorney for Witness, an employee of Acme Lending Corp. ("Acme"). Witness has been subpoenaed to give grand jury testimony in connection with alleged money laundering involving Acme. The grand jury believes that Dern, a target of its investigation, has evaded income tax by putting income into phony accounts and not reporting the income. The grand jury is investigating whether Acme assisted Dern in that endeavor. Witness has told you that Witness never knowingly assisted Dern in money laundering, and insists on testifying.

The grand jury is aware that Witness and Dern are acquainted. The grand jury wants to find out if Witness has information bearing on the investigation. You are now preparing Witness for the grand jury testimony.

Witness advises you that Dern is a family friend with whom Witness has discussed business from time to time. Witness also tells you that, as a favor, Witness allowed Dern to deposit $20,000 cash into Witness' bank account because Dern's bank had gone out of business and Dern needed somewhere to put the money. There appears to be no paper record that Witness did this favor for Dern.

You believe the grand jury is unaware that Witness allowed Dern to deposit money into Witness' bank account. You have concluded that if Dern's deposit in Witness' account comes to light, it would lead the government incorrectly to believe that Witness had knowingly participated in Dern' money laundering efforts.

Assume that Witness is your largest client, and that fees from representing Witness are paying your office rent and student loan bills. Witness insists on not revealing the deposit that Dern made into Witness' account.

Advise Witness as to how Witness should answer the expected line of grand jury questions concerning dealings with Dern:

1. *Do you know a person named Dern?*
2. *What is the nature of your relationship with Dern?*
3. *Have you ever discussed any business with Dern?*
4. *Have you had any business dealings with Dern?*
5. *Are you aware of any monetary transactions in which Dern has engaged?*

Chapter 12

TAX CRIMES

[A] INTRODUCTORY NOTES

[1] Types of Tax Prosecutions

Federal laws relating to tax offenses provide prosecutors with a great deal of flexibility in white collar cases. Proof of tax crimes tends to be fairly straightforward. Thus, in many white collar investigations, it may be easier to bring tax fraud charges rather than other offenses that were originally the focus of the investigation. Also, as in other areas of white collar crime, in tax cases the government has wide latitude in deciding to pursue civil charges in addition to or instead of criminal charges.

Criminal tax charges may arise in two contexts. First, the government may proceed with a pure tax fraud case. Pure tax cases typically arise when routine tax audits and other Internal Revenue Service investigations uncover evidence of tax offenses. Second, tax offenses may be charged in addition to or instead of other substantive offenses. Those engaging in crimes such as money laundering, securities fraud, bribery, and mail and wire fraud often either fail to report their income or mislabel the source of the income on their tax returns. In an investigation originally focused on one of these non-tax offenses, the government may uncover tax crimes and include them in the charges. Or, the government may determine that the tax offenses will be easier to prove than the other crimes and thus only bring the tax offenses. This was the approach in the criminal case against notorious racketeer Al Capone, who was convicted of tax fraud rather than murder and other crimes for which he was originally being investigated. Unlike such complex offenses as RICO and money laundering, juries generally have some familiarity with tax laws and may be more likely to convict for tax offenses.

The federal tax code provides what courts term a "hierarchy" of tax crimes. These range from tax evasion, which is a felony, to failure to file a return or pay taxes, which is a misdemeanor. This chapter focuses on three principal tax offenses — tax evasion, 26 U.S.C. § 7201, filing of false returns, 26 U.S.C. § 7206, and failing to file a return or pay taxes, 26 U.S.C. § 7203. It is critical to distinguish among these different tax crimes and the conduct at which they are directed.

[2] Voluntary Compliance and Deterrence

The United States government loses tens of billions of dollars annually because of tax evasion. Nonetheless, given the millions of tax returns filed every year, criminal tax cases are relatively rare.[a] Thus, the government has chosen in many instances to bring criminal cases against high-profile defendants in order to

---

[a] In 2006, for example, the IRS initiated only 3907 investigations; of those, 2020 resulted in

encourage voluntary compliance with the tax code and to deter tax fraud.[b] For example, the government has brought criminal tax cases against actor Wesley Snipes, hotelier Leona Helmsley, former Vice-President Spiro Agnew, baseball star Pete Rose, financier J.P. Morgan, "Hollywood Madam" Heidi Fleiss, organized crime figure John Gotti, former IRS Commissioner Joseph Nunan, and many others.

[3]   The Process of Tax Investigations

The process of federal criminal tax investigations differs from most other white collar crimes. Most criminal tax cases begin as civil investigations triggered by routine audits. If an audit produces evidence of crime, the matter is referred to the I.R.S.'s Criminal Investigation Division for investigation by a "Special Agent."

In addition, criminal tax prosecutions must be reviewed and approved at several points. The Special Agent may refer the matter to the I.R.S. Regional Counsel. If the Regional Counsel determines that the matter should proceed, the Counsel will refer the case to the Tax Division of the United States Department of Justice ("DOJ") in Washington for possible further investigation and prosecution. Unlike most other white collar crimes — RICO being a notable exception — all tax prosecutions must be approved by the DOJ in Washington. Can you imagine why this is so?

[4]   Statutory Overview

[a]   Elements of Tax Evasion — § 7201

Tax evasion, 26 U.S.C. § 7201, is the most serious tax violation and carries with it the harshest penalties. The defendant is subject to an evasion count for each year that the defendant evaded the payment of taxes. To establish tax evasion beyond a reasonable doubt, the government must prove that the defendant:

    (1) Underpaid taxes;

    (2) Engaged in an affirmative act of evasion or attempt to evade; and

    (3) Acted willfully.

With respect to the underpayment, some courts require proof that the defendant "substantially" underpaid the taxes due. A defendant convicted of tax evasion can be sentenced to imprisonment of not more than five years along with the costs of the prosecution and a $100,000 fine. For corporations, the penalties include a $500,000 fine.

---

convictions and 1657 led to prison sentences. *See* http://www.irs.gov/compliance/enforcement/article/0,,id=107484,00.html.

   [b] As one court stated, "selection for prosecution based in part upon the potential deterrent effect on others serves a legitimate interest in promoting more general compliance with the tax laws. Since the government lacks the means to investigate and prosecute every suspected violation of the tax laws, it makes good sense to prosecute those who will receive, or are likely to receive, the attention of the media." *United States v. Catlett*, 584 F.2d 864, 868 (8th Cir. 1978).

[b]   Elements of Filing False Tax Returns — § 7206

Individuals and entities, including the filer and/or preparer of the tax return, may also be investigated for filing a false tax return, 26 U.S.C. § 7206(1). This crime is punished as a felony. To establish this offense, the government must show that:

(1) The defendant signed the tax return or related document;

(2) The defendant signed under penalty of perjury;

(3) The return or related document was false;

(4) The falsity was material; and

(5) The defendant acted willfully.

This provision is sometimes called "tax perjury" because it focuses on the falsification of the documents. Under § 7206(2), anyone who assists in the filing of a false return is also subject to prosecution. Both of these sections subject the offender to a maximum prison term of three years, a maximum fine of $100,000 for individuals and $500,000 for organizations, plus costs of the prosecution. As with all tax offenses, each filing constitutes a separate crime.

[c]   Elements of Failure to File — § 7203

To prove a violation of § 7203, the government must show that the defendant:

(1) Acted willfully;

(2) Failed to (a) file a required return, (b) pay a required tax, (c) keep required records, or (d) supply required information; and

(3) Failed to act at the time the law specified.

Frequently, "tax protestors" — those who claim that the federal tax laws are illegal and/or unconstitutional, for example — are charged with failing to file returns. *See* § D[1], *infra.* Penalties for violations of § 7203, a misdemeanor, are not more than $25,000 and/or imprisonment of not more than one year, or both, together with the costs of prosecution. For organizations, the penalty is increased to $100,000.

Finally, with respect to sentencing, the actual sentence for any of the tax crimes discussed in this chapter will vary based upon the application of the United States Sentencing Guidelines, discussed in Chapter 19, Sentencing, *infra.*[c]

[B]   TAX EVASION AND FAILURE TO FILE — §§ 7201 & 7203

The next case illustrates the distinction between the felony of tax evasion (§ 145(b) in the opinion, now codified at 26 U.S.C. § 7201) and the misdemeanor of failing to file a return (§ 145(a) in the opinion, now codified at 26 U.S.C. § 7203). As you read the case, consider why evasion is considered to be a substantially more serious offense than failing to file a return.

---

[c] There is some indication that judges are issuing below-Guidelines range sentences fairly often in criminal tax cases. *See* John J. Tigue Jr. and Jeremy H. Temkin, *Tax Litigation Issues: Sentencing in Criminal Tax Cases Post-Booker*, 235 N.Y. L.J. 3, col. 1 (May 18, 2006).

SPIES v. UNITED STATES
317 U.S. 492 (1943)

Mr. JUSTICE JACKSON delivered the opinion of the Court.

Petitioner has been convicted of attempting to defeat and evade income tax. . . . Petitioner admitted at the opening of the trial that he had sufficient income during the year in question to place him under a statutory duty to file a return and to pay a tax, and that he failed to do either. The evidence during nearly two weeks of trial was directed principally toward establishing the exact amount of the tax and the manner of receiving and handling income and accounting, which the Government contends shows an intent to evade and defeat tax. Petitioner's testimony related to his good character, his physical illness at the time the return became due, and lack of willfulness in his defaults, chiefly because of a psychological disturbance, amounting to something more than worry but something less than insanity.

Section 145(a) makes, among other things, willful failure to pay a tax or make a return by one having petitioner's income at the time or times required by law a misdemeanor. Section 145(b) makes a willful attempt in any manner to evade or defeat any tax such as his a felony. Petitioner was not indicted for either misdemeanor. The indictment contained a single count setting forth the felony charge of willfully attempting to defeat and evade the tax, and recited willful failure to file a return and willful failure to pay the tax as the means to the felonious end.

The petitioner requested an instruction that "You may not find the defendant guilty of a willful attempt to defeat and evade the income tax, if you find only that he had willfully failed to make a return of taxable income and has willfully failed to pay the tax on that income." This was refused, and the Court charged that "If you find that the defendant had a net income for 1936 upon which some income tax was due, and I believe that is conceded, if you find that the defendant willfully failed to file an income tax return for that year, if you find that the defendant willfully failed to pay the tax due on his income for that year, you may, if you find that the facts and circumstances warrant it find that the defendant willfully attempted to evade or defeat the tax." The Court refused a request to instruct that an affirmative act was necessary to constitute a willful attempt and charged that "Attempt means to try to do or accomplish. In order to find an attempt it is not necessary to find affirmative steps to accomplish the prohibited purpose. An attempt may be found on the basis of inactivity or on refraining to act, as well."

It is the Government's contention that a willful failure to file a return together with a willful failure to pay the tax may, without more, constitute an attempt to defeat or evade a tax within § 145(b). Petitioner claims that such proof establishes only two misdemeanors under § 145(a) and that it takes more than the sum of two such misdemeanors to make the felony under § 145(b). The legislative history of the section contains nothing helpful on the question here at issue, and we must find the answer from the section itself and its context in the revenue laws.

The United States has relied for the collection of its income tax largely upon the taxpayer's own disclosures rather than upon a system of withholding the tax from him by those from whom income may be received. This system can function successfully only if those within and near taxable income keep and render true accounts. In many ways taxpayers' neglect or deceit may prejudice the orderly and punctual administration of the system as well as the revenues themselves. Congress has imposed a variety of sanctions for the protection of the system and the revenues. The relation of the offense of which this petitioner has been convicted to other and lesser revenue offenses appears more clearly from its position in this structure of sanctions.

The penalties imposed by Congress to enforce the tax laws embrace both civil and criminal sanctions. The former consist of additions to the tax upon determinations of fact made by an administrative agency and with no burden on the Government to prove its case beyond a reasonable doubt. The latter consist of penal offenses enforced by the criminal process in the familiar manner. Invocation of one does not exclude resort to the other.

The failure in a duty to make a timely return, unless it is shown that such failure is due to reasonable cause and not due to willful neglect, is punishable by an addition to the tax of 5 to 25 per cent thereof, depending on the duration of the default. But a duty may exist even when there is no tax liability to serve as a base for application of a percentage delinquency penalty; the default may relate to matters not identifiable with tax for a particular period; and the offense may be more grievous than a case for civil penalty. Hence the willful failure to make a return, keep records, or supply information when required, is made a misdemeanor, without regard to existence of a tax liability. § 145(a). Punctuality is important to the fiscal system, and these are sanctions to assure punctual as well as faithful performance of these duties.

Sanctions to insure payment of the tax are even more varied to meet the variety of causes of default. . . . Willful failure to pay the tax when due is punishable as a misdemeanor. § 145(a). The climax of this variety of sanctions is the serious and inclusive felony defined to consist of willful attempt in any manner to evade or defeat the tax. § 145(b). The question here is whether there is a distinction between the acts necessary to make out the felony and those which may make out the misdemeanor.

A felony may, and frequently does, include lesser offenses in combination either with each other or with other elements. We think it clear that this felony may include one or several of the other offenses against the revenue laws. But it would be unusual and we would not readily assume that Congress by the felony defined in § 145(b) meant no more than the same derelictions it had just defined in § 145(a) as a misdemeanor. Such an interpretation becomes even more difficult to accept when we consider this felony as the capstone of a system of sanctions which singly or in combination were calculated to induce prompt and forthright fulfillment of every duty under the income tax law and to provide a penalty suitable to every degree of delinquency.

The difference between willful failure to pay a tax when due, which is made a misdemeanor, and willful attempt to defeat and evade one, which is made a felony, is not easy to detect or define. Both must be willful, and willful, as we have said, is a word of many meanings, its construction often being influenced by its context. It may well mean something more as applied to nonpayment of a tax than when applied to failure to make a return. Mere voluntary and purposeful, as distinguished from accidental, omission to make a timely return might meet the test of willfulness. But in view of our traditional aversion to imprisonment for debt, we would not without the clearest manifestation of Congressional intent assume that mere knowing and intentional default in payment of a tax where there had been no willful failure to disclose the liability is intended to constitute a criminal offense of any degree. We would expect willfulness in such a case to include some element of evil motive and want of justification in view of all the financial circumstances of the taxpayer.

Had § 145(a) not included willful failure to pay a tax, it would have defined as misdemeanors generally a failure to observe statutory duties to make timely returns, keep records, or supply information — duties imposed to facilitate administration of the Act even if, because of insufficient net income, there were no duty to pay a tax. It would then be a permissible and perhaps an appropriate construction of § 145(b) that it made felonies of the same willful omissions when there was the added element of duty to pay a tax. The definition of such nonpayment as a misdemeanor we think argues strongly against such an interpretation.

The difference between the two offenses, it seems to us, is found in the affirmative action implied from the term "attempt," as used in the felony subsection. It is not necessary to involve this subject with the complexities of the common-law "attempt." The attempt made criminal by this statute does not consist of conduct that would culminate in a more serious crime but for some impossibility of completion or interruption or frustration. This is an independent crime, complete in its most serious form when the attempt is complete and nothing is added to its criminality by success or consummation, as would be the case, say, of attempted murder. Although the attempt succeed in evading tax, there is no criminal offense of that kind, and the prosecution can be only for the attempt. We think that in employing the terminology of attempt to embrace the gravest of offenses against the revenues Congress intended some willful commission in addition to the willful omissions that make up the list of misdemeanors. Willful but passive neglect of the statutory duty may constitute the lesser offense, but to combine with it a willful and positive attempt to evade tax in any manner or to defeat it by any means lifts the offense to the degree of felony.

Congress did not define or limit the methods by which a willful attempt to defeat and evade might be accomplished and perhaps did not define lest its effort to do so result in some unexpected limitation. Nor would we by definition constrict the scope of the Congressional provision that it may be accomplished "in any manner." By way of illustration, and not by way of limitation, we would think affirmative willful attempt may be inferred from conduct such as keeping a double set of books, making false entries of alterations, or false invoices or documents, destruction of books or records, concealment of assets or covering up sources of income, handling of one's affairs to avoid making the records usual in transactions of the kind, and any conduct, the likely effect of which would be to mislead or to conceal. If the tax-evasion motive plays any part in such conduct the offense may be made out even though the conduct may also serve other purposes such as concealment of other crime.

In this case there are several items of evidence apart from the default in filing the return and paying the tax which the Government claims will support an inference of willful attempt to evade or defeat the tax. These go to establish that petitioner insisted that certain income be paid to him in cash, transferred it to his own bank by armored car, deposited it, not in his own name but in the names of others of his family, and kept inadequate and misleading records. Petitioner claims other motives animated him in these matters. We intimate no opinion. Such inferences are for the jury. If on proper submission the jury found these acts, taken together with willful failure to file a return and willful failure to pay the tax, to constitute a willful attempt to defeat and evade tax, we would consider conviction of a felony sustainable. But we think a defendant is entitled to a charge which will point out the necessity for such an inference of willful attempt to defeat or evade tax from some proof in the case other than that necessary to make out the misdemeanors; and if the evidence fails to afford such an inference, the defendant should be acquitted.

The Government argues against this construction, contending that the milder punishment of a misdemeanor and the benefits of a short statute of limitation should not be extended to violators of the income tax laws such as political grafters, gamblers, racketeers, and gangsters. We doubt that this construction will handicap prosecution for felony of such flagrant violators. Few of them, we think, in their efforts to escape tax stop with mere omission of the duties put upon them by the statute, but if such there be, they are entitled to be convicted only of the offense which they have committed.

Reversed.

NOTES AND QUESTIONS

1. *Distinguishing the crimes.* According to the Court, what is the essential difference between the crimes of tax evasion and failure to file? Why is the former punished more harshly than the latter? What types of evidence, according to the Court, will support an evasion charge?

2. *The trial court's error.* What was the precise error committed by the trial judge? Was there evidence in the record to support an evasion conviction? If so, then why didn't the Court rule that the trial court's error was harmless and allow the conviction to stand?

3. *Psychological disturbance as a defense in tax cases.* The Court characterized the defense thus: "Petitioner's testimony related to his good character, his physical illness at the time the return became due, and lack of willfulness in his defaults, chiefly because of a psychological disturbance, amounting to something more than worry but something less than insanity." Claims of "psychological disturbance" abound in tax fraud cases. Consider the following cases. In *United States v. Cohen,* 510 F.3d 1114, 1124 (9th Cir. 2007), the court held that the jury should have been able to consider a defense psychiatrist's expert testimony to rebut proof of willfulness. The psychiatrist would have testified that the defendant suffered from narcissistic personality disorder and was dysfunctional to the point of being irrational. In *United States v. Ettorre,* 387 F. Supp. 582, 587 (E.D. Pa. 1975), the court held that the defendant, although under much stress and suffering from some mental abnormalities, did have the capacity to know that he should file his returns in a timely way based on evidence he was running his business and teaching school at the time of the offense.

How much leeway should courts provide defendants in allowing them to offer evidence of mental disturbance? How seriously should prosecutors and jurors take arguments based on such evidence?

PROBLEM

12-1. Last November, Roberto Rodriguez was driving from the United States to Canada. Upon reaching the Canadian border, a Canadian customs officer inspected Roberto's car and discovered two bags in the trunk. The customs officer found that one of the bags contained large sums of cash. When asked how much money was in the bag, Roberto said "several thousand dollars." The customs officer sent Roberto back to the United States side of the border to talk to U.S. customs officials.

When a U.S. customs agent asked if Roberto had anything in the car, he said there was money in the trunk. When asked how much, Roberto initially responded $30,000 or $35,000. The agent asked several more times, and each time the amount went up until Roberto finally said there was over $300,000 in the car. The agent had Roberto fill out a customs report of international transport of currency in excess of $10,000, then seized the money because Roberto had not filled out the customs report form before crossing the Canadian border. The bags contained $359,500 in $10 and $20 bills.

The IRS then served Roberto with a termination assessment for $169,973 as income tax due on the money. A termination notice serves to terminate the person's tax year as of a certain date. At that point, any tax liability becomes due immediately, and the IRS files a tax lien to secure payment of the tax debt. The termination assessment does not relieve the taxpayer from the obligation to file a tax return for the year. Upon his lawyer's advice, Roberto did not file a tax return for 1983 because of pending litigation concerning Roberto's failure to file the required customs report form.

Roberto was convicted of income tax evasion under § 7201 based on the foregoing facts. He now appeals. How should the court rule? Why?

[C]   FILING A FALSE RETURN — § 7206

The next case addresses the crime of "tax perjury." As you read the case, consider the potential scope of those who may be liable for this crime.

UNITED STATES v. SHORTT ACCOUNTANCY CORP.
785 F.2d 1448 (9th Cir. 1986)

DUNIWAY, CIRCUIT JUDGE:

Shortt Accountancy Corporation appeals from its conviction on seven counts of making and subscribing false tax returns in violation of § 7206(1) of the Internal Revenue Code of 1954. We affirm.

FACTS

Appellant Shortt Accountancy Corporation (SAC) is a CPA firm that performs accounting services, prepares tax returns and gives tax planning advice to its clients. Ronald Ashida was its chief operating officer and ran its day-to-day activities in 1981–82.

In the fall of 1981, Clifford Wilson contacted SAC for tax planning advice and services. In late December 1981, Ashida told Wilson that he could invest through SAC in a "straddle" position in government securities that would enable Wilson to claim a sizable deduction on his 1981 federal income tax return. A straddle is the simultaneous holding of a contract to purchase and a contract to sell a specific commodity at some time in the future. It is used to minimize risks by offsetting losses and gains. In order to claim the deduction, however, Wilson would have to backdate a promissory note so that the investment would appear to have been made in May, 1981, rather than December. The backdating was necessary, said Ashida, because Congress had changed the law to disallow deductions to taxpayers who purchased a straddle investment after June 23, 1981. Wilson agreed to consider the investment, but made no decision before the end of the year.

In early January 1982, Wilson told an Assistant U.S. Attorney about Ashida's investment advice. The Attorney put him in touch with the IRS, which proposed that Wilson cooperate with it in building a criminal case against SAC. He agreed upon the condition that the IRS reimburse him for the purchase price of the straddle position and for any fees charged him by SAC. He also understood that if SAC eventually prepared a tax return for him, the IRS would audit it and disallow any improper deductions claimed by SAC on his behalf. In that case, the IRS would assess Wilson for additional taxes owed, but would not require him to pay interest or penalties resulting from the improper deductions.

Wilson ultimately purchased a straddle position from SAC in April 1982. In addition to the purchase price of $3400, SAC charged Wilson interest calculated from May 1, 1981, so that it appeared that the transaction had occurred before the June 1981 cutoff date. No backdated documents were ultimately used in the transaction.

SAC completed preparation of Wilson's 1981 tax return in January 1983. In it, the firm claimed a $23,024 deduction for Wilson relating to his April 1982 straddle investment. Paul Whatley, who supervised the actual preparation of the return and subscribed to its correctness on behalf of SAC, based this figure on information provided to him by Ashida. Whatley did not know, when he signed the return, that the straddle investment was improperly claimed.

After receiving his 1981 return from SAC, Wilson delivered it to an IRS special agent who immediately filed it with the IRS District Director. He forwarded it to a processing center in October 1983 and Wilson has since received the tax refund claimed, plus applicable interest. He has not filed any other 1981 federal income tax return.

In the subsequent investigation of SAC's preparation of Wilson's 1981 return, the grand jury determined that SAC had prepared tax returns for at least six additional clients in which it improperly claimed deductions for straddle investments. In each case, the straddle position at issue was originally owned by other SAC clients who had purchased their interests from SAC before Congress' disallowance of the deduction in June 1981. Although these clients incurred straddle losses in May 1981 that properly could have been claimed on their 1981 tax returns, SAC determined that the original owners were oversheltered for the year and did not need the deductions. As a result, SAC, which was authorized to sell the client's interest in the straddle should it deem it to be in the client's best interest, sold their straddle positions and resulting losses to Wilson and the other new clients. Each sale occurred after the change in the law disallowing straddle deductions and each was structured to appear that it had occurred before the cutoff date.

In June 1984, the grand jury issued a fourteen count indictment charging [SAC] and Ashida with violations of 18 U.S.C. § 371, conspiracy to commit an offense against or to defraud the United States, and 26 U.S.C. §§ 7206(1), false declaration under penalty of perjury, and (2), aiding preparation or presentation of false documents, under the internal revenue laws. The indictment's basis was SAC's alleged sale of interests in straddle positions after Congress disallowed deductions from such investments and its knowing preparation of tax returns claiming improper straddle deductions. . . .

At trial, defendants moved for judgment of acquittal following the opening statement and again at the close of the government's case. They claimed that a preparer of tax returns cannot be charged under § 7206(1), which proscribes making and subscribing a false return, because it cannot "make" a return within the meaning of the statute. Defendants also argued that a corporation cannot be guilty of an offense under § 7206(1) when the person who actually subscribes the false return believes it to be true and correct. The district court denied the motions. . . .

The jury ultimately convicted SAC on seven counts of willfully making and subscribing as preparer false income tax returns in violation of 26 U.S.C. § 7206(1). SAC timely appeals.

*   *   *

III. *"Making" a Return Under § 7206(1).*

SAC claims that its convictions on seven counts of violating § 7206(1) should be reversed as a matter of law because a tax return preparer cannot "make" a return within the meaning of the statute. While SAC does not deny its participation in preparing the false returns, it claims that it could only be charged under § 7206(2) for *assisting* in the preparation of a false return. It bases its distinction on the fact that the taxpayer alone has the statutory duty to file a federal income tax return.

Nothing in the statute or case law indicates that a charge under § 7206(1) for making and subscribing a false return is based on the taxpayer's duty to file or "make" an income tax return. Instead, §§ 7206(1) and 7206(2) are "closely related companion provisions" that differ in emphasis more than in substance. *United States v. Haynes*, 5 Cir., 1978, 573 F.2d 236, 240. Section 7206(1) is a perjury statute, making any person who knowingly makes and subscribes a false statement on any return criminally liable. Section 7206(2) has a broader sweep, making all forms of willful assistance in preparing a false return an offense. Perjury in connection with the preparation of a federal tax return is chargeable under either section. *Haynes*, 573 F.2d at 240; *see United States v. Miller, 491 F.2d 638, 649* (5th Cir. 1974). The Fifth Circuit has considered the exact issue of whether a tax preparer can be charged under § 7206(1) rather than § 7206(2) and held that he could. *Miller*, 491 F.2d at 649; *see Haynes, 573 F.2d at 240*. We are persuaded to do the same.

SAC argues that our decision in *United States v. Miller*, 545 F.2d 1204 (9th Cir. 1976), recognizes the exclusivity of §§ 7206(1) and (2). We disagree. In *Miller*, we commented *sua sponte* in a footnote that the defendant, who had prepared a false return for his wife, should have been charged under § 7206(2) for assisting in the preparation of the return, rather than under § 7206(1) for subscribing the return. It is not clear from the opinion whether the defendant actually committed perjury by subscribing his wife's false return or whether he merely prepared it in advance of her subscription. In either case, we went on to hold that the possible error was not fatal because indictment under § 7206(1) contains the elements of the § 7206(2) offense sufficiently to apprise the defendant of what he has to be prepared to meet at trial and is detailed enough to assure against double jeopardy. This holding does not conflict with our conclusion here that a tax return preparer can properly be charged under § 7206(1) for willfully making and subscribing a false return.

IV. *Collective Intent in Subscribing the Returns.*

SAC also claims that six of its convictions under § 7206(1) should be reversed because Paul Whatley, the corporate agent who actually subscribed six of the seven contested returns on behalf of SAC, did not have the requisite intent of willfully making and subscribing a false return. While it acknowledges that Ashida, who supplied Whatley with all of his information regarding the straddle losses, did have the requisite intent, it contends that his intent is irrelevant to a § 7206(1) charge because he did not physically subscribe the return. SAC concludes that if the government wanted to charge SAC for Ashida's admittedly illegal conduct and intent, it should have drawn up the indictment under § 7206(2) or some other statute, and not under § 7206(1).

SAC's argument is completely meritless. If it were accepted by the courts, any tax return preparer could escape prosecution for perjury by arranging for an innocent employee to complete the proscribed act of subscribing a false return. This interpretation of § 7206(1) defies logic and has no support in the case law. A corporation will be held liable under § 7206(1) when its agent deliberately causes it to make and subscribe to a false income tax return.

*   *   *

AFFIRMED.

NOTES AND QUESTIONS

1. *Choosing the theory of prosecution.* Section 7206(2) criminalizes the actions of those who assist in the preparation of a false return and is usually directed to tax preparers. Section 7206(1) criminalizes actions of those who make or subscribe the return. Under *Shortt*, must the government charge the tax preparer under § 7206(2) instead of under § 7206(1)? Why or why not?

2. *Mens rea.* In the *Shortt* case, the corporation was convicted of the crime even though the employee who signed the return had no knowledge of the fraudulent scheme. What was the government's evidence of knowledge?

3. *Materiality.* In any prosecution under § 7206, the government must prove that the falsity was material. In *United States v. DiVarco*, 484 F.2d 670 (7th Cir. 1973), the defendants argued on appeal from their § 7206 conviction that their misstatements as to the source of their income were not material because there was no showing that they had underpaid their taxes. The court, in determining materiality, found that "the purpose behind the statute is to prosecute those who intentionally falsify their tax returns regardless of the precise ultimate effect that falsification may have." Does this mean that a false statement may be material even if the statement did not mislead the government and had no potential for

affecting the government's assessment of tax liability? Were the false statements material in *Shortt*? Why or why not?

Prior to the Supreme Court's 1995 decision in *United States v. Gaudin*, 515 U.S. 506 (1995), materiality was generally considered to be a question of law for the judge. In *Gaudin*, however, the Court held that, in a false statements prosecution under § 1001, materiality should be determined by the jury. In 1999, the Supreme Court determined that materiality is likewise a question for the jury in tax perjury cases. *See Neder v. United States*, 527 U.S. 1, 8 (1999) (holding that the District Court committed harmless error in a § 7206(1) prosecution by determining materiality element itself rather than submitting the issue to the jury).

4. *Tax deficiency.* There is no requirement that a tax deficiency be shown for a § 7206 charge to succeed. It is only necessary that the return be "materially false." Can a falsity be material if it did not produce a deficiency? Why or why not?

[D] MENS REA

[1] Defining "Willfulness" in Criminal Tax Cases

In any criminal tax fraud case, the government must prove beyond a reasonable doubt that the defendant acted willfully. Willfulness takes on a distinct meaning when used in the context of criminal tax offenses. The next case is a leading U.S. Supreme Court decision on the meaning of "willfulness" in criminal tax cases. As you read the case, consider whether the majority's approach to defining "willfulness" is justified.

CHEEK v. UNITED STATES
498 U.S. 192 (1991)

JUSTICE WHITE delivered the opinion of the Court.

Title 26, § 7201 of the United States Code provides that any person "who willfully attempts in any manner to evade or defeat any tax imposed by this title or the payment thereof" shall be guilty of a felony. Under 26 U.S.C. § 7203, "[a]ny person required under this title . . . or by regulations made under authority thereof to make a return . . . who willfully fails to . . . make such return" shall be guilty of a misdemeanor. This case turns on the meaning of the word "willfully" as used in §§ 7201 and 7203.

I.

Petitioner John L. Cheek has been a pilot for American Airlines since 1973. He filed federal income tax returns through 1979 but thereafter ceased to file returns. He also claimed an increasing number of withholding allowances — eventually claiming 60 allowances by mid-1980 — and for the years 1981 to 1984 indicated on his W-4 forms that he was exempt from federal income taxes. In 1983, petitioner unsuccessfully sought a refund of all tax withheld by his employer in 1982. Petitioner's income during this period at all times far exceeded the minimum necessary to trigger the statutory filing requirement.

As a result of his activities, petitioner was indicted for 10 violations of federal law. He was charged with six counts of willfully failing to file a federal income tax return for the years 1980, 1981, and 1983 through 1986, in violation of § 7203. He was further charged with three counts of willfully attempting to evade his income taxes for the years 1980, 1981, and 1983 in violation of 26 U.S.C. § 7201. In those years, American Airlines withheld substantially less than the amount of tax petitioner owed because of the numerous allowances and exempt status he claimed on his W-4 forms. The tax offenses with which petitioner was charged are specific intent crimes that require the defendant to have acted willfully.

At trial, the evidence established that between 1982 and 1986, petitioner was involved in at least four civil cases that challenged various aspects of the federal income tax system. In all four of those cases, the plaintiffs were informed by the courts that many of their arguments, including that they were not taxpayers within the meaning of the tax laws, that wages are not income, that the Sixteenth Amendment does not authorize the imposition of an income tax on individuals, and that the Sixteenth Amendment is unenforceable, were frivolous or had been repeatedly rejected by the courts. During this time period, petitioner also attended at least two criminal trials of persons charged with tax offenses. In addition, there was evidence that in 1980 or 1981 an attorney had advised Cheek that the courts had rejected as frivolous the claim that wages are not income.[4]

Cheek represented himself at trial and testified in his defense. He admitted that he had not filed personal income tax returns during the years in question. He testified that as early as 1978, he had begun attending seminars sponsored by, and following the advice of, a group that believes, among other things, that the federal tax system is unconstitutional. Some of the speakers at these meetings were lawyers who purported to give professional opinions about the invalidity of the federal income tax laws. Cheek produced a letter from an attorney stating that the Sixteenth Amendment did not authorize a tax on wages and salaries but only on gain or profit. Petitioner's defense was that, based on the indoctrination he received from this group and from his own study, he sincerely believed that the tax laws were being unconstitutionally enforced and that his actions during the 1980–1986 period were lawful. He therefore argued that he had acted without the willfulness required for conviction of the various offenses with which he was charged.

In the course of its instructions, the trial court advised the jury that to prove "willfulness" the Government must prove the voluntary and intentional violation of a known legal duty, a burden that could not be proved by showing mistake, ignorance, or negligence. The court further advised the jury that an objectively reasonable good-faith misunderstanding of the law would negate willfulness, but mere disagreement with the law would not. The court described Cheek's beliefs about the income tax system and instructed the jury that if it found that Cheek "honestly and reasonably believed that he was not required to pay income taxes or to file tax returns," a not guilty verdict should be returned.

After several hours of deliberation, the jury sent a note to the judge that stated in part:

---

[4] The attorney also advised that despite the Fifth Amendment, the filing of a tax return was required and that a person could challenge the constitutionality of the system by suing for a refund after the taxes had been withheld, or by putting himself "at risk of criminal prosecution."

" 'We have a basic disagreement between some of us as to if Mr. Cheek honestly and reasonably believed that he was not required to pay income taxes.

" '. . . .

" 'Page 32 [the relevant jury instruction] discusses good faith misunderstanding and disagreement. Is there any additional clarification you can give us on this point?' "

Id. at 85.

The District Judge responded with a supplemental instruction containing the following statements:

"[A] person's opinion that the tax laws violate his constitutional rights does not constitute a good faith misunderstanding of the law. Furthermore, a person's disagreement with the government's tax collection systems and policies does not constitute a good faith misunderstanding of the law."

Id. at 86.

At the end of the first day of deliberation, the jury sent out another note saying that it still could not reach a verdict because " '[w]e are divided on the issue as to if Mr. Cheek honestly & reasonably believed that he was not required to pay income tax.' " *Id.* at 87. When the jury resumed its deliberations, the District Judge gave the jury an additional instruction. This instruction stated in part that "[a]n honest but unreasonable belief is not a defense and does not negate willfulness," *id.* at 88, and that "[a]dvice or research resulting in the conclusion that wages of a privately employed person are not income or that the tax laws are unconstitutional is not objectively reasonable and cannot serve as the basis for a good faith misunderstanding of the law defense." *Id.* The court also instructed the jury that "[p]ersistent refusal to acknowledge the law does not constitute a good faith misunderstanding of the law." *Id.* Approximately two hours later, the jury returned a verdict finding petitioner guilty on all counts.[6]

Petitioner appealed his convictions, arguing that the District Court erred by instructing the jury that only an objectively reasonable misunderstanding of the law negates the statutory willfulness requirement. The United States Court of Appeals for the Seventh Circuit rejected that contention and affirmed the convictions. 882 F.2d 1263 (7th Cir. 1989). In prior cases, the Seventh Circuit had made clear that good-faith misunderstanding of the law negates willfulness only if the defendant's beliefs are objectively reasonable; in the Seventh Circuit, even actual ignorance is not a defense unless the defendant's ignorance was itself objectively reasonable. In its opinion in this case, the court noted that several specified beliefs, including the beliefs that the tax laws are unconstitutional and that wages are not income, would not be objectively reasonable. Because the Seventh Circuit's interpretation of "willfully" as used in these statutes conflicts with the decisions of several other Courts of Appeals, . . . we granted certiorari.

---

[6] A note signed by all 12 jurors also informed the judge that although the jury found petitioner guilty, several jurors wanted to express their personal opinions of the case and that notes from these individual jurors to the court were "a complaint against the narrow & hard expression under the constraints of the law." *Id.* at 90. At least two notes from individual jurors expressed the opinion that petitioner sincerely believed in his cause even though his beliefs might have been unreasonable.

II.

The general rule that ignorance of the law or a mistake of law is no defense to criminal prosecution is deeply rooted in the American legal system. Based on the notion that the law is definite and knowable, the common law presumed that every person knew the law. This common-law rule has been applied by the Court in numerous cases construing criminal statutes. . . .

The proliferation of statutes and regulations has sometimes made it difficult for the average citizen to know and comprehend the extent of the duties and obligations imposed by the tax laws. Congress has accordingly softened the impact of the common-law presumption by making specific intent to violate the law an element of certain federal criminal tax offenses. Thus, the Court almost 60 years ago interpreted the statutory term "willfully" as used in the federal criminal tax statutes as carving out an exception to the traditional rule. This special treatment of criminal tax offenses is largely due to the complexity of the tax laws. . . .

III.

[Cheek] . . . challenges the ruling that a good-faith misunderstanding of the law or a good-faith belief that one is not violating the law, if it is to negate willfulness, must be objectively reasonable. We agree that the Court of Appeals and the District Court erred in this respect.

A.

Willfulness, as construed by our prior decisions in criminal tax cases, requires the Government to prove that the law imposed a duty on the defendant, that the defendant knew of this duty, and that he voluntarily and intentionally violated that duty. We deal first with the case where the issue is whether the defendant knew of the duty purportedly imposed by the provision of the statute or regulation he is accused of violating, a case in which there is no claim that the provision at issue is invalid. In such a case, if the Government proves actual knowledge of the pertinent legal duty, the prosecution, without more, has satisfied the knowledge component of the willfulness requirement. But carrying this burden requires negating a defendant's claim of ignorance of the law or a claim that because of a misunderstanding of the law, he had a good-faith belief that he was not violating any of the provisions of the tax laws. This is so because one cannot be aware that the law imposes a duty upon him and yet be ignorant of it, misunderstand the law, or believe that the duty does not exist. In the end, the issue is whether, based on all the evidence, the Government has proved that the defendant was aware of the duty at issue, which cannot be true if the jury credits a good-faith misunderstanding and belief submission, whether or not the claimed belief or misunderstanding is objectively reasonable.

In this case, if Cheek asserted that he truly believed that the Internal Revenue Code did not purport to treat wages as income, and the jury believed him, the Government would not have carried its burden to prove willfulness, however unreasonable a court might deem such a belief. Of course, in deciding whether to credit Cheek's good-faith belief claim, the jury would be free to consider any admissible evidence from any source showing that Cheek was aware of his duty to file a return and to treat wages as income, including evidence showing his awareness of the relevant provisions of the Code or regulations, of court decisions rejecting his interpretation of the tax law, of authoritative rulings of the Internal Revenue Service, or of any contents of the personal income tax return forms and accompanying instructions that made it plain that wages should be returned as income.

We thus disagree with the Court of Appeals' requirement that a claimed good-faith belief must be objectively reasonable if it is to be considered as possibly negating the Government's evidence purporting to show a defendant's awareness of the legal duty at issue. Knowledge and belief are characteristically questions for the factfinder, in this case the jury. Characterizing a particular belief as not objectively reasonable transforms the inquiry into a legal one and would prevent the jury from considering it. It would of course be proper to exclude evidence having no relevance or probative value with respect to willfulness; but it is not contrary to common sense, let alone impossible, for a defendant to be ignorant of his duty based on an irrational belief that he has no duty, and forbidding the jury to consider evidence that might negate willfulness would raise a serious question under the Sixth Amendment's jury trial provision. . . .

It was therefore error to instruct the jury to disregard evidence of Cheek's understanding that, within the meaning of the tax laws, he was not a person required to file a return or to pay income taxes and that wages are not taxable income, as incredible as such misunderstandings of and beliefs about the law might be. Of course, the more unreasonable the asserted beliefs or misunderstandings are, the more likely the jury will consider them to be nothing more than simple disagreement with known legal duties imposed by the tax laws and will find that the Government has carried its burden of proving knowledge.

B.

Cheek asserted in the trial court that he should be acquitted because he believed in good faith that the income tax law is unconstitutional as applied to him and thus could not legally impose any duty upon him of which he should have been aware. Such a submission is unsound, not because Cheek's constitutional arguments are not objectively reasonable or frivolous, which they surely are, but because the *Murdock-Pomponio* [*United States v. Murdock*, 290 U.S. 389 (1933), and *United States v. Pomponio*, 429 U.S. 10 (1976),] line of cases does not support such a position. Those cases construed the willfulness requirement in the criminal provisions of the Internal Revenue Code to require proof of knowledge of the law. This was because in "our complex tax system, uncertainty often arises even among taxpayers who earnestly wish to follow the law," and "[i]t is not the purpose of the law to penalize frank difference of opinion or innocent errors made despite the exercise of reasonable care." *United States v. Bishop*, 412 U.S. 346, 360–361 (1973). . . .

Claims that some of the provisions of the tax code are unconstitutional are submissions of a different order. They do not arise from innocent mistakes caused by the complexity of the Internal Revenue Code. Rather, they reveal full knowledge of the provisions at issue and a studied conclusion, however wrong, that those provisions are invalid and unenforceable. Thus in this case, Cheek paid his taxes for years, but after attending various seminars and based on his own study, he concluded that the income tax laws could not constitutionally require him to pay a tax.

We do not believe that Congress contemplated that such a taxpayer, without risking criminal prosecution, could ignore the duties imposed upon him by the Internal Revenue Code and refuse to utilize the mechanisms provided by Congress to present his claims of invalidity to the courts and to abide by their decisions. There is no doubt that Cheek, from year to year, was free to pay the tax that the law purported to require, file for a refund and, if denied, present his claims of invalidity, constitutional or otherwise, to the courts. Also, without paying the tax, he could have challenged claims of tax deficiencies in the Tax Court, § 6213, with the right to appeal to a higher court if unsuccessful. Cheek took neither course in some years, and when he did was unwilling to accept the outcome. As we see it, he is in no position to claim that his good-faith belief about the validity of the Internal Revenue Code negates willfulness or provides a defense to criminal prosecution under §§ 7201 and 7203. Of course, Cheek was free in this very case to present his claims of invalidity and have them adjudicated, but like defendants in criminal cases in other contexts, who "willfully" refuse to comply with the duties placed upon them by the law, he must take the risk of being wrong.

We thus hold that in a case like this, a defendant's views about the validity of the tax statutes are irrelevant to the issue of willfulness and need not be heard by the jury, and, if they are, an instruction to disregard them would be proper. For this purpose, it makes no difference whether the claims of invalidity are frivolous or have substance. It was therefore not error in this case for the District Judge to instruct the jury not to consider Cheek's claims that the tax laws were unconstitutional. However, it was error for the court to instruct the jury that petitioner's asserted beliefs that wages are not income and that he was not a taxpayer within the meaning of the Internal Revenue Code should not be considered by the jury in determining whether Cheek had acted willfully.

IV.

For the reasons set forth in the opinion above, the judgment of the Court of Appeals is vacated, and the case is remanded for further proceedings consistent with this opinion.

It is so ordered.

JUSTICE SOUTER took no part in the consideration or decision of this case.

JUSTICE SCALIA, concurring in the judgment.

I concur in the judgment of the Court because our cases have consistently held that the failure to pay a tax in the good-faith belief that it is not legally owing is not "willful." I do not join the Court's opinion because I do not agree with the test for willfulness that it directs the Court of Appeals to apply on remand.

As the Court acknowledges, our opinions from the 1930s to the 1970s have interpreted the word "willfully" in the criminal tax statutes as requiring the "bad purpose" or "evil motive" of "intentional[ly] violat[ing] a known legal duty." It seems to me that today's opinion squarely reverses that long-established statutory construction when it says that a good-faith erroneous belief in the unconstitutionality of a tax law is no defense. It is quite impossible to say that a statute which one believes unconstitutional represents a "known legal duty." . . .

JUSTICE BLACKMUN, with whom JUSTICE MARSHALL joins, dissenting.

It seems to me that we are concerned in this case not with "the complexity of the tax laws," but with the income tax law in its most elementary and basic aspect: Is a wage earner a taxpayer and are wages income?

The Court acknowledges that the conclusively established standard for willfulness under the applicable statutes is the " 'voluntary, intentional violation of a known legal duty.' " *See United States v. Bishop*, 412 U.S. 346, 360 (1973), and *United States v. Pomponio*, 429 U.S. 10, 12 (1976). That being so, it is incomprehensible to me how, in this day, more than 70 years after the institution of our present federal income tax system with the passage of the Income Tax Act of 1913, any taxpayer of competent mentality can assert as his defense to charges of statutory willfulness the proposition that the wage he receives for his labor is not income, irrespective of a cult that says otherwise and advises the gullible to resist income tax collections. One might note in passing that this particular taxpayer, after all, was a licensed pilot for one of our major commercial airlines; he presumably was a person of at least minimum intellectual competence.

The District Court's instruction that an objectively reasonable and good-faith misunderstanding of the law negates willfulness lends further, rather than less, protection to this defendant, for it adds an additional hurdle for the prosecution to overcome. Petitioner should be grateful for this further protection, rather than be opposed to it.

This Court's opinion today, I fear, will encourage taxpayers to cling to frivolous views of the law in the hope of convincing a jury of their sincerity. If that ensues, I suspect we have gone beyond the limits of common sense.

While I may not agree with every word the Court of Appeals has enunciated in its opinion, I would affirm its judgment in this case. I therefore dissent.

NOTE AND QUESTIONS

1. *Intent to violate a known legal duty.* The *Cheek* decision is the principal case on the interpretation of mens rea in tax cases. In this decision, as in *Ratzlaf v. United States*, 510 U.S. 135 (1994), discussed in Chapter 13, Money Laundering, *infra*, the Court imposed proof of specific intent to violate the law as a requirement in cases involving complicated conduct that is not inherently evil, such as certain banking and tax offenses. (Congress subsequently amended the statute at issue in *Ratzlaf*, effectively overturning the decision, but has yet to enact a similar legislative response to the *Cheek* decision.)

The Court in *Cheek* reasoned that the common law notion that every person is presumed to know the law is not applicable in tax offenses because of the complexity and difficulty of the law in this area. Why did the Court find it necessary to establish a higher mens rea requirement in tax cases? Are there any policy justifications for such an imposition? As a practical matter, how often will this requirement substantially assist a defendant?

Some courts continue to express confusion over the precise application of the willfulness requirement in criminal tax cases. This confusion might be attributed to the Court's earlier decisions in which the Court spoke of willfulness as requiring "bad faith," "evil motive," or "evil intent." *See Spies v. United States*, 317 U.S. 492, 498 (1943); *United States v. Bishop*, 412 U.S. 346, 360 (1973); *United States v. Murdock*, 290 U.S. 389, 398 (1933). As the Court stated in *United States v. Pomponio*, 429 U.S. 10, 12 (1976), however, the standard is simply proof of a voluntary, intentional violation of a known legal duty. What, if anything, did *Cheek* add to the *Pomponio* standard?

2. *Mens rea as to constitutionality.* The *Cheek* decision drew a distinction between those who possess a good faith belief that they are not violating the tax laws and those who believe that the tax system itself is invalid. According to Justice Scalia's concurring opinion, is this a valid distinction? Why are people who believe that their conduct does not violate the law less culpable than those who have an honest disagreement with the taxing system itself? Courts continue to distinguish between a defendant's misinterpretation of the tax laws and a defendant's disagreement with the tax laws, holding that the latter is irrelevant to the issue of willfulness. *See United States v. Ambort*, 405 F.3d 1109, 1115 (10th Cir. 2005) (defendant's view that certain people could claim to be "non-resident" aliens not subject to the tax laws was irrelevant to the issue of willfulness because defendant knew this view had been repeatedly rejected).

3. *An honest but unreasonable belief.* The Court also held that the defendant's belief need not be an objectively reasonable one. This opens the door for even the unreasonable belief to be put forth as a defense to a tax prosecution. Why should an unreasonably held belief be a defense to a criminal tax prosecution?

4. *Tax protestors.* To what extent does the *Cheek* decision assist tax protestors and other defendants in criminal tax cases? As the majority stated, "*the more unreasonable* the asserted beliefs or misunderstandings are, the more likely the jury will consider them to be nothing more than *simple disagreement* with known legal duties imposed by the tax laws and will find that the government has carried its burden of proving knowledge." At his retrial, Cheek was convicted of the charges against him. *See United States v. Cheek*, 3 F.3d 1057 (7th Cir. 1993).

The defendant in *Cheek* was just one of many thousands of tax protestors in the United States. Such protestors have made an array of legal and constitutional arguments in order to avoid paying taxes. One recent high profile tax protestor case involved actor Wesley Snipes. Based on advice he received from Eddie Ray Kahn, a founder and organizer of two tax protestor organizations, Snipes did not file income tax returns for six consecutive years and sought tax refunds. Snipes, Kahn, and accountant Douglas Rosile were indicted on felony charges of conspiracy to defraud the United States and filing a false, fictitious, or fraudulent claim in violation of 18 U.S.C. § 287. Snipes was also indicted on six counts of failing to file a tax return. At trial, the defense asserted that Snipes was well-intentioned and was misled by Kahn's advice. In a split verdict, Snipes was acquitted of the felony charges but was convicted on three counts of failure to file. Snipes was sentenced to the maximum of three years in prison, and was required to pay back taxes, interest, and penalties of around $15 million. *See* John J. Tigue Jr. and Jeremy H. Temkin, *Tax Litigation Issues: The Wesley Snipes Trial*, 239 N.Y.L.J. 3, col. 1 (May 15, 2008). Both sides asserted that this outcome was a victory. Which side won? Why?

5. *Selective prosecution.* Prior to trial, Snipes moved to have the case against him dismissed on selective prosecution grounds. Selective prosecution is not a

defense specific to tax crimes, but rather is a general criminal law defense based upon the prosecutor's alleged violation of the Equal Protection Clause due to racial or other bias. Snipes, who is African-American, argued he had been treated differently than Kahn, who is white and was not charged with failure to file despite not filing his own returns for several years. The district court judge rejected this argument. The court stated that prosecuting Snipes on the additional charges served the goal of general deterrence because of the likely attention the media would pay to the case. *See* John J. Tigue Jr. and Jeremy H. Temkin, *Tax Litigation Issues: The Wesley Snipes Trial*, 239 N.Y.L.J. 3 (May 15, 2008). For a discussion of the selective prosecution defense, see *United States v. Armstrong*, 517 U.S. 456 (1996).

[2]   Defenses

There are a number of ways to defend against the government's proof of willfulness. Cheek asserted a good faith defense — that he honestly believed that he was acting within the law. Although the law was clear that wages are "income" under the Internal Revenue Code, Cheek asserted a good faith misunderstanding of the law.

A defendant may make a related argument when an aspect of the tax law is actually unclear. What happens if the defendant claims a good faith interpretation of a complicated, unsettled aspect of tax law, and the government disagrees with that interpretation? That was the issue in the next case, a high-profile prosecution that arose from the Wall Street insider trading scandals of the 1980s. Although the case involved a somewhat technical aspect of securities law, the tax law issue on appeal was a fairly simple one involving the jury instruction. As you read the case, consider (a) the nature of the legal uncertainty in the case, and (b) the essential disagreement between the majority and the dissent on the jury instruction issue.

UNITED STATES v. REGAN
937 F.2d 823 (2d Cir. 1991)

VAN GRAAFEILAND, CIRCUIT JUDGE:

[Regan and the other defendants were affiliated with a stock brokerage firm, Princeton-Newport Partners ("P.N."). Regan was a managing partner of P.N. and was its resident tax expert. The government alleged that the defendants committed tax fraud by arranging for P.N. to engage in "stock parking" transactions that produced phony tax losses.

[In the alleged stock parking transactions, P.N. temporarily sold stock to other brokerage firms at a loss. P.N. then deducted the losses on its tax returns. Later, P.N. bought the same stock back from the firms to which it had previously sold the stock.

[At trial, Regan asserted that he believed the tax deductions were proper. He said that he based his conclusion on (1) correspondence from P.N.'s accountants, (2) a report of the Tax Section of the Association of the Bar of the City of New York, and (3) Regan's own study of the relevant statute (IRC § 1078) and proposed regulation 1.1058-1.[d]

---

[d]   Section 1058 provides that no loss may be taken if the stock transaction agreement (1) provides for

[The government asserted that P.N.'s transactions, evaluated under § 1058, produced phony deductions. These deductions formed the basis for the tax perjury prosecution. Although essentially a tax fraud case, the government also charged the defendants with conspiracy, securities fraud, mail fraud based upon the mailing of the tax returns, and RICO based upon the mail fraud.]

* * *

From time to time in the period between 1984 and 1987, P.N. owned substantial quantities of stock that had depreciated in value and whose sale would provide P.N. with opportunities to take tax losses. Regan testified that, prompted by correspondence from his accountants, a report of the Tax Section of the Association of the Bar of the City of New York, and his own study of § 1058 and proposed regulation 1.1058-1, he concluded that P.N. could take those losses by means of sales and repurchase arrangements with other brokerage or investment houses so long as the arrangements between P.N. and the other houses did not satisfy the requirements of § 1058. Regan felt that this very lack of compliance would enable P.N. to take tax losses on the transactions. Based on this belief, P.N. entered into some fifty-nine transactions with other brokerage and investment houses, consisting of sales of stock by P.N. to those houses and agreements to resell to P.N. at fixed prices at later dates.

Appellants, following Regan's lead, believed that these transactions did not satisfy § 1058 requirements in that their terms were not reduced to writing, did not provide for termination upon short notice, and did not contain legally enforceable rights of repurchase. Moreover, the brokerage houses to whom the stock was sold had complete control of the stock in their possession while P.N. had none, thus depriving P.N. of the opportunity to avoid loss or capitalize on gain during that period. Also, the agreed-upon repurchase price might vary substantially from the then-existing market price.

The district court described this as a "sophistical" treatment of § 1058, and rejected it out of hand. Stating that he didn't think he had "to give a contention that was contrary to what [he] regarded] as being the law," he held that appellants' contention concerning § 1058 had no substance and the section had "no applicability to defendants' case." This was prejudicial error. The issue in the case was not whether appellants' construction of § 1058 was correct or even objectively reasonable but whether it was made in good faith. *Cheek v. United States*, 498 U.S. 192 (1991).

Although appellants were not charged with violating § 1058, that section became pivotal in the case because appellants believed that it authorized them to do just what they did, i.e., take tax losses. If this belief was held in good faith, they could not be held criminally liable for proceeding on that basis. Appellants offered substantial evidence of their good faith reliance on their interpretation of § 1058, some of which the court received and some of which it rejected. For example, the Tax Section of the Association of the Bar of the City of New York appears to have

---

the return of securities identical to those transferred; (2) requires that payments be made to the transferor in amounts equal to the interest, dividends, and other distributions paid on the transferred securities; (3) does not reduce the transferor's risk of loss or opportunity for gain on the transferred securities; and (4) meets such other requirements as may be prescribed by Treasury regulations. If these requirements are met, then the stock has been "parked" and no losses from that arrangement may be deducted.

interpreted § 1058 in somewhat the same manner as did Regan. The report of the Committee upon which Regan relied stated in substance that the distinguishing feature between a loan and a sale of securities was whether the risk of loss or opportunity for gain was retained by the person making the transfer. This, of course, was in accord with the generally accepted rule that "for Federal income tax purposes, the owner of property must possess meaningful burdens and benefits of ownership." Appellants also offered the testimony of two acknowledged tax experts to the effect that Regan's interpretation of § 1058 was not unreasonable, but the district court refused to permit these experts to testify.

Whether, as appellants contend, the district court erred in its evidentiary rulings concerning this evidence is a matter we need not decide. The issue of appellants' good faith reliance on § 1058 as appellants interpreted it was squarely raised and argued. The district court should have instructed the jury that, if it found the reliance was held in good faith, the defendants could not be held criminally liable for proceeding in accordance with that reliance.

The record is clear that appellants requested a charge specifically directed to their claim of good faith reliance on § 1058. . . .

In the instant case, where appellants were charged with sixty-four counts covering the waterfront of tax fraud, securities fraud, mail and wire fraud, conspiracy, and RICO, a generalized charge on good faith was insufficient to instruct the jury concerning appellants' specific good faith defense based on § 1058. Appellants were entitled to have the trial court clearly instruct the jury, relative to appellants' theory of defense to the tax charges, that the theory if believed justified acquittal on those charges.

One of the most esoteric areas of the law is that of federal taxation. It is replete with "full-grown intricacies," and it is rare that a "simple, direct statement of the law can be made without caveat." 1 Mertens Law of Federal Income Tax § 1.01. Justice White, writing for the Court majority in *Cheek, supra,* stated that, because of the proliferation of tax statutes and regulations, the common-law presumption that every person knows the law does not apply where violations of federal criminal tax laws are alleged. Instead, proof of guilt in such cases must be predicated upon a " 'voluntary, intentional violation of a known legal duty.' "

This rule applies to alleged violations of the "hierarchy of tax offenses set forth in §§ 7201–7207, inclusive." *United States v. Bishop,* 412 U.S. 346 (1973). It also applies to 18 U.S.C. § 371 conspiracies to violate one or more of the hierarchy of tax offenses.

The Government's burden in proving a mail or wire fraud offense, 18 U.S.C. §§ 1341 and 1343, is even more onerous. These are specific intent crimes. . . . Where, as here, there is little dispute concerning the making and filing of the allegedly fraudulent returns, the existence vel non of culpable intent or lack of good faith is a crucially important issue in the case.

Despite numerous requests by appellants to charge otherwise, the district court persisted in viewing § 1058 objectively, insisting that the court was the sole judge of the law. That, of course, was true. However, the issue for the jury was not how the district court interpreted § 1058; it was how the defendants in good faith interpreted it. "A jury is the ultimate discipline to a silly argument." *United States v. Burton,* 737 F.2d 439, 443 (5th Cir.1984). The district court's failure to squarely present this issue to the jury was a prejudicial error that tainted all of the tax hierarchy charges.

* * *

[The court affirmed the conspiracy and securities fraud convictions, but reversed and remanded the convictions for tax fraud, mail fraud, and RICO.]

MAHONEY, CIRCUIT JUDGE, concurring in part and dissenting in part:

* * *

My colleagues conclude:

> The district court should have instructed the jury that, if it found that the reliance [on § 1058 as appellants interpreted it] was held in good faith, the defendants could not be held criminally liable for proceeding in accordance with that reliance.

The district court in fact gave the following instructions with regard to good faith:

> If you find that the defendant acted in good faith in the honest belief that the representations he made were true, that he did not intend to defraud anyone, this constitutes a complete defense to the crime of mail or wire fraud. . . .

The defendants contend the government has failed to prove that they did not act in good faith. . . .

In connection with the false return counts, the court additionally instructed as follows:

> If the defendant signed the tax return in good faith and believed it to be true in all material matters, he has not committed a crime and must be acquitted on these counts, even if the return was incorrect. If you find that the tax return was not true as to a material matter, the central question is whether or not the defendant honestly believed that the return was true. The government has the burden of proving that the defendant did not have an honest belief in the truthfulness of the return.

Characterizing these rather extensive instructions as a "generalized charge on good faith," my colleagues find them "insufficient to instruct the jury concerning the appellants' specific good faith defense based on § 1058." In other words, the defendants were prejudiced by an instruction that their good faith defense was premised on Regan's "general knowledge of the tax laws," because defendants more specifically contended that Regan relied on § 1058. I am unpersuaded that a district court is required to present a defendant's contentions with this level of particularity. The fact is that the theory of defense — to wit, bona fide reliance on the tax code — was squarely presented to the jury. It is unlikely that the jurors were misled because the district court failed to remind them of Regan's contention that § 1058 was at the center of his tax analysis. . . .

* * *

Notes and Questions

1. *Prejudicial error?* Why did the Court reverse the defendants' tax fraud convictions? Did the trial judge err? Even if so, did the error prejudice the defense? Why or why not? And even if there was error in the jury charge on the tax offenses, why did the error taint the mail fraud and RICO charges?

2. *Charging tax cases.* As discussed in the introductory materials, criminal tax fraud cases often develop from investigations that originally focused on other sorts of wrongdoing. The *Regan* case, for example, arose out of a 1980s *securities fraud* investigation of major Wall Street figures including Ivan Boesky and Michael Milken. (*See* Introductory Notes to Chapter 5, Securities Fraud, *supra.*) Ultimately, however, the case was charged principally as a tax fraud case, with mail fraud and RICO charges based upon the tax fraud charges. And the racketeering investigation of organized crime figure Al Capone ultimately led to a tax fraud prosecution. Is it appropriate to charge tax fraud in such circumstances? *See* Harry Litman, *Pretextual Prosecution*, 92 Geo. L.J. 1135 (2004) (evaluating what the author terms the "Al Capone approach" to the exercise of prosecutorial discretion).

3. *Evidence of willfulness.* As in other areas of white collar crime, mens rea in tax cases is often based on circumstantial evidence. How far can the government go in relying on such evidence? Assume, for example, that the government has charged an attorney with tax evasion and tax perjury based upon the following evidence:

> (a) The defendant exhibited a pattern of understating his income on his tax returns over three years;

> (b) The defendant had a law degree;

> (c) The defendant had substantial professional experience, including the practice of law;

> (d) The defendant was able to bill clients and maintain expense records for his private practice; and

> (e) The defendant, when asked by an I.R.S. agent to disclose his bank accounts, failed to disclose one of the accounts.

Which of these pieces of evidence, if any, is probative of willfulness? Is this evidence sufficient to show willfulness beyond a reasonable doubt? *See United States v. Rischard*, 471 F.2d 105 (8th Cir. 1973).

4. *Reliance on professional advice.* As in other fraud prosecutions, such as mail fraud and securities fraud, good faith reliance on professional advice is a complete defense to a tax fraud charge. To prove such a defense, the defendant must adduce facts showing that (a) the defendant relied in good faith on a professional, and (b) the defendant made complete disclosure of all the relevant facts. *See United States v. Masat*, 948 F.2d 923 (5th Cir. 1991). If a defendant adduces the facts necessary to show reliance on counsel, is the defendant entitled to a specific jury instruction on this issue or is a general good faith charge sufficient? Under the *Regan* approach, what's the correct answer? *See Bursten v. United States*, 395 F.2d 976 (5th Cir. 1968).

PROBLEMS

12-2. Horace Kilborne became a United States district judge three years ago, and has presided over five criminal tax cases. Prior to becoming a judge, he had practiced law for over 30 years. His annual salary as a judge was approximately one tenth the income he received during his last years in private practice.

Judge Kilborne was charged with two counts of tax perjury, in violation of § 7206, for allegedly underreporting the amount of legal fees he received from his law firm for work he had performed before becoming a judge. At trial, the government introduced duplicates of checks sent to the defendant from attorneys at his prior firm representing fee income the defendant had earned before becoming a judge. The government also introduced bank records showing amounts that the defendant deposited in his personal account after receiving the checks from the law firm. Both sides agreed that he had not deposited all the checks, but had cashed several of them. The evidence showed that the defendant had reported all the deposited checks on his tax returns, but did not report any money from checks that he had cashed.

With respect to the first return, the government contends Kilborne received $141,000 in fee income, but only reported $72,000 as fee income. The government submitted correspondence from Kilborne to his long-time accountant, James White, which understated Kilborne's fee income for that year by $65,000. Kilborne, however, stated that he instructed his secretary to deliver another letter to White which fully disclosed his fee income. The secretary testified she delivered this letter, but White testified that he never received it and had used the figures from Kilborne's initial letter to complete the return.

Kilborne did not use White for the preparation of the second return, but instead hired Joseph Holmes. The government alleged that Kilborne received over $88,000 in fee income during that tax year, but that his tax return showed no fee income. Kilborne stated that he included this fee income as part of a $350,000 sale price of his interest in the law firm. This sale price appeared on Schedule D of his return, where he also claimed a $200,000 capital loss on the sale of his interest in the law firm. He later conceded that his fee income for that year was wrongly categorized as a capital gain. Kilborne stated that he had innocently relied on Holmes to prepare the return correctly, that he was generally ignorant about the details of tax law, and that he had no reason to doubt the return's accuracy. Kilborne perused the return for 10 or 15 minutes before signing it.

At trial, Kilborne asserts reliance on professional advice as a defense to each count of filing a false return. Is he likely to succeed? Why or why not?

12-3. William Fuller owns and operates a small accounting firm. He is a Certified Public Accountant, and has been filing income taxes for clients for the past 10 years. Despite the over 500 filings he has made over the past 10 years for other people, he failed to file his own income tax return for the past three years. He filed his returns for several years prior to this delinquency. William is a college graduate, and has routinely completed the yearly continuing education requirements for his accounting license. He is married, has raised three children, and occasionally finds the time to golf. The Department of Justice is seeking to indict William on three counts of willful failure to file under 26 U.S.C. § 7203.

Assume that William's attorney seeks a meeting with the prosecutor in an attempt to persuade the government not to indict William. The attorney asserts the following defenses on behalf of William:

a. Good faith misunderstanding of the law. William claims that he believed it was unnecessary for him to file his returns because he didn't have the money necessary to pay his taxes. He claims that he stopped filing returns when his accounting firm became significantly less profitable than it had been in previous years.

b. Chronic depression/sleeping disorder. William's attorney asserts that several medical experts will testify that William has severe depression and a related sleeping disorder. William claims that his failure to file was a result of his medical disorder and not a willful avoidance or omission.

c. Preoccupation with personal and business affairs. William claims that he is so overwhelmed with running his business, especially during tax season, that he is forced to choose between neglecting his clients and neglecting personal business obligations.

d. Habit. William claims that his failure to file was not willful but rather a result of a habit of procrastination established in college.

e. Alcoholism. William claims that his life outside of the office is clouded by severe alcoholism. He manages to fulfill his professional obligations before happy hour, but completely neglects any personal or social obligations.

f. Filing of delinquent returns. Assume William gets word from a college friend that the IRS has begun investigating him. In an attempt to avoid prosecution, William files all of his delinquent tax returns immediately.

g. Intent unrelated to tax consequences. William asserts that during a visit to Las Vegas for a CPA convention, he committed a state crime. He immediately fled back home but stopped filing his tax returns because of a fear that it would alert Las Vegas authorities to his whereabouts.

If you were the prosecutor, would any of these arguments be effective in persuading you not to seek charges against William? Why or why not?

12-4. At the trial of Pat Hayward for tax evasion and for filing false tax returns, the following facts have been proven:

Pat Hayward is a 50-year-old aircraft structural designer with a consulting business. Pat founded the business 15 years ago. Initially, Pat received payments from clients in two ways. First, Pat received set monthly retainer fees to assure that Pat would be available to work for each client. For the last three tax years, Pat received from $500 to $2,000 per month from various clients. Pat received this amount whether or not Pat performed work for the client during a given month. Second, if Pat's hourly billings for a particular client exceeded the retainer fee for a given month, Pat would bill the client for the hours above and beyond the retainer amount. For example, if a client paid Pat a $1,000 monthly retainer fee, and Pat worked 15 hours in a given month at $100 per hour, then Pat would bill the client an additional $500 for that month.

For the first five years, Pat maintained the company books and records and prepared its tax returns. The business began to boom, however, and Pat retained

Graphic Accountants ("Graphic") to keep the company books and to prepare both the company's tax returns and Pat's individual returns.

Upon being retained, Graphic set up an accounting system for Pat. Graphic advised Pat to report all consulting fees to Graphic's office, along with all business expenses. In doing so, Pat provided summaries of fees and expenses instead of original invoices. These summaries were prepared from the bank statements of the company's general operating account.

Beginning five years ago, Pat's main client, Boomerang Air, began to pay Pat regular bonuses apart from the retainer fees and hourly consulting fees. Pat deposited these bonuses in the business's petty cash account instead of in the company's general operating account. As a result, these bonuses were not reflected on the summaries Pat provided to the accountants. Pat has no training as a bookkeeper, and Pat states that any error in amounts provided to the accountants was unintentional. Pat also says that the accountants failed to follow professional standards by failing to ask for original information. The government has no direct evidence to contradict these assertions.

Five years ago, Pat joined the Economic Libertarian Party (ELP). During ELP meetings, the members discussed whether the federal income taxation system was legal. Pat asserts that labor constitutes property which, when exchanged for fees, produces no net gain subject to taxation as "income." Pat also came to disagree with the philosophy of the IRS concerning the definition of income.

As a result of Pat's new philosophy, beginning three years ago, Pat stopped placing on the summaries given to the accountants any fees that Pat earned above and beyond the regular monthly retainer fees that Pat received from clients.

Pat testified, "I genuinely believed that the ELP's interpretation of the law was the correct one." In support, Pat provided records of regular attendance at ELP meetings and copies of party literature with notes that Pat took during the meetings.

Graphic never requested underlying documentation for the summaries. Even though the documentation was readily available to the Graphic accountants, Graphic did not examine that documentation when conducting its routine audits of Pat's business. Whenever Graphic did request documentation, Pat provided complete and accurate records.

Based upon the company's tax returns, which Pat signed, the government indicted Pat for filing false income tax returns and for tax evasion for the past three tax years. The government relied on Pat's failure to report (1) the bonuses, and (2) the hourly fees Pat earned each month above the regular retainer fees. The understatements of income resulted in tax deficiencies of $33,000, $45,000, and $70,000 for the respective years in question.

In defense, Pat argues that (1) as to the bonuses, although Pat believed them to be taxable because they were not necessarily in return for actual labor, Pat relied on the accounting system set up by Graphic and assumed they would be reported, and (2) as to the hourly fees, Pat held a good faith belief that these monies were not taxable.

Assume that you are on the jury in Pat's case, and have heard the foregoing evidence. Also assume that Pat testified, and that you found Pat to be a generally credible witness. You have been instructed according to the decision in *Cheek*.

Evaluate the government's proof on the elements of filing false returns, 18 U.S.C. § 7206, and tax evasion, 18 U.S.C. § 7201. Would you vote to convict or acquit Pat? Why?

[E]   METHODS OF PROOF

In a tax evasion case, the government must prove beyond a reasonable doubt that the defendant underpaid taxes. *See Holland v. United States*, 348 U.S. 121, 126 (1954). In many instances, such proof may be hard to adduce. For example, underpayment may be difficult to prove when the defendant kept incomplete or inaccurate records. Courts have thus allowed various "methods of proof" concerning underpayment of taxes. First, the government may employ the "direct" method by showing, for example, that the taxpayer failed to report a specific item of income. Second, the government may use an "indirect" method of proof. The latter category includes proof of (a) net worth, (b) expenditures, and (c) bank deposits. In such cases, the government may show, for example, that a taxpayer's expenditures far exceeded reported income for the tax year. The following case examines the distinction between direct and indirect methods of proving underpayment.

UNITED STATES v. BLACK
843 F.2d 1456 (D.C. Cir. 1988)

SILBERMAN CIRCUIT JUDGE:

This is an appeal from a conviction of income tax evasion. Appellant, Fred Black, complains of insufficiency of the government's evidence. . . .

After a forty day trial, Black was convicted on three counts of tax evasion. The government charged that although Black received $65,827 of taxable income in 1978, $109,251 of taxable income in 1979, and $174,755 of taxable income in 1981, he failed to file a return for any of those years.

I.

The resolution of Black's claims concerning sufficiency of evidence and adequacy of the jury charge turns entirely upon the proper characterization of the actual method used by the government to prove Black's tax evasion. The government contends it employed the "specific items" method of proof, a direct method of demonstrating tax evasion in which the government "produce[s] evidence of the receipt of specific items of reportable income by the defendant that do not appear on his income tax return." Black claims, however, that the government used the "bank deposits/cash expenditures" method. When using that indirect method of proof, the government shows, either through increases in net worth, increases in bank deposits, or the presence of cash expenditures, that the taxpayer's wealth grew during a tax year beyond what could be attributed to the taxpayer's reported income, thereby raising the inference of unreported income.

In any indirect method case, the government must prove that the increased wealth did not come from nontaxable sources. Otherwise the evidence will be insufficient, for

> [t]here is always the possibility that the taxpayer deposited cash that he received from a non-taxable source or from income taxed in a prior year but kept on hand as cash or even from unreported income from a prior year kept on hand in cash. Such events are common human occurrences, and this possibility may of itself create reasonable doubt. Therefore, the government must establish in some fashion the amount of cash the taxpayer had on hand at the start of the period. This is part of the government's duty to negate the possibility that bank deposits or cash expenditures in the year under investigation originated from non-taxable sources.

On the other hand, where the government's case is based on evidence showing *specific items* of unreported income, the safeguards required for indirect methods of proof are not necessary, as the possibility that the defendant may be convicted because non-taxable income is mistakenly presumed to be taxable income, or because cash expenditures are mistakenly assumed to be made from taxable income, is not present.

Black claims that the government relied on a bank deposits/cash expenditures method of proof, but utterly failed to rebut the possibility that his expenditures originated from non-taxable sources, and therefore the evidence was insufficient to sustain a conviction. In particular, Black maintains that the government was obliged to negate the possibility that his bank deposits and cash expenditures were from non-income sources, and to establish his opening net worth for the years in question. In short, Black claims the government tried to convict him of tax evasion "by simply showing that he spent money and did not file a tax return during the tax years in question."

The government's response is that since it introduced evidence of *specific items* of *income* received by Black, it was not required to disprove the likelihood of a cash hoard or a non-taxable source of income. From approximately 1975 to the time of the trial, Black was subject to an IRS lien of approximately three million dollars. During this time, Black created two corporations, Dunbar and Machine-A-Rama, portrayed by the government as dummy corporations which had neither paid employees nor offices. At trial, Black disputed the bogus nature of these entities, claiming the corporations were involved in developing a casino in Atlantic City — a project which never materialized — and he also insisted that any money he took from these corporations was in the form of loans which he felt obligated to repay. Nevertheless, it was uncontroverted that during the period covered by the indictment Black had no personal bank accounts and that many of Black's personal expenses were paid by checks drawn on accounts of these two corporations. Black further conceded that he created Dunbar because he did not want to put property in his own name and because he wished to conceal from the IRS money he was spending.

In the government's view, Black received taxable income each time he wrote a check on the accounts of Dunbar and Machine-A-Rama to cover his personal expenses. Evidence that Black paid for personal expenses with checks drawn on corporate accounts and that Black never truly considered the checks to be loans would be sufficient for conviction, for "[a]ll the law requires is that there be proof sufficient to establish that there has been a receipt of taxable income by the accused and a willful evasion of the tax thereon." *United States v. Nunan*, 236 F.2d 576, 586 (2d Cir.1956).

Black, by focusing on isolated remarks at trial, argues that the government presented only a cash expenditures case against him. We disagree. If the statements by the prosecutor, the testimony of the government's tax witness, and the trial judge's instructions to the jury, are each considered in light of the evidence actually submitted, it is clear that the government presented direct proof that Black received specific items of taxable income and did not pay tax on that income. . . .

While there were several explicit references to the "personal expenditures method" by the prosecutor, the government's expert witness, and the trial judge in his instructions, at no point in the trial was it suggested to the jury that evidence of personal expenditures, without more, would be sufficient to convict Black of tax evasion. Evidence of personal expenditures was relevant only because the government contended that the very writing of the checks created income to Black. Thus, the danger encountered in a classic "cash expenditure" case — that the defendant could be convicted for spending non-taxable income — is not at all present here. In this case, the use of the phrase "personal expenditures method" was not associated at all with the "cash expenditures method" of proving tax evasion; the phrase was used solely to distinguish Black's business expenditures from his personal expenditures.

* * *

Appellant's conviction is therefore *affirmed*.

NOTES AND QUESTIONS

1. *Direct evidence*. Direct evidence is most simply established through the "specific items" method of proof as discussed in *Black*. Often there is direct evidence that the defendant received unreported income, or direct evidence that the defendant claimed an improper deduction. Under this approach, the taxpayer's books and records usually provide the basis for the direct evidence of underpayment.

2. *Indirect methods of proof*. Tax deficiency may also be proven indirectly, by circumstantial evidence. In such cases, the government must follow all reasonable leads, such as gifts and prior savings, that might explain unreported sources of income. Why is it appropriate to use such an "indirect" method of proof in a criminal case with substantial penalties?

a. *The bank deposits method*. In *United States v. Mounkes*, 204 F.3d 1024, 1028 (10th Cir. 2000), the government presented evidence that the defendants' bank deposits exceeded their reported income after adjustments, thus supporting an inference of unreported income. The court stated that, when using the bank deposits method, the government must establish the defendant's "pre-income cash on hand with reasonable certainty, while negating other sources of nontaxable income during the same period." *Id.* The cash on hand figure need not be proven precisely. When using the bank deposits method, the government must prove only a substantial difference between the bank deposits and reported income, and not an exact amount. *See United States v. Boulware*, 384 F.3d 794, 811 (9th Cir. 2004).

b. *The net worth method*. In *Holland v. United States*, 348 U.S. 121 (1954), the Supreme Court approved the use of the "net worth" method of proving a tax deficiency. After showing the total net value of the defendant's assets at the beginning of a tax period, this method requires the government to demonstrate the defendant's total net worth increased over a tax year by an amount substantially greater than the reported income for the year. The government must also investigate all reasonable leads that would tend to establish that any monies were not directly attributable to taxable income. The Supreme Court noted in *Holland* that the net worth method was originally used to corroborate direct proof of unreported income in cases such as *Capone v. United States*, 51 F.2d 609 (7th Cir. 1931), but was increasingly being used as a main tool in ordinary income-bracket investigations. *Holland*, 348 U.S. at 126–127. The Court also pointed out several pitfalls, as well as the need to exercise care and restraint, when using this method. *Id.* at 127–129. The net worth method is perhaps the most challenging indirect method to prove, and investigations using this method are often long and difficult.

c. *The cash expenditures method.* The "cash expenditures" method of proving a deficiency is similar to the net worth method. This method requires the government to prove that the defendant spent more money from taxable income than was reported to the government during a given tax year.

The court in *Black* stated that any indirect method of proof requires the government "to establish in some fashion the amount of cash the taxpayer had on hand at the start of the period." The Ninth Circuit Court of Appeals, however, did not require a determination of beginning cash on hand when using a "bank deposits plus cash expenditures" method in *United States v. Brickey*, 289 F.3d 1144, 1152 (9th Cir. 2002). There the court stated that a determination of opening net worth is only required when using the "net worth" method. *Id.*

3. *Amount of tax deficiency required.* The circuits are split as to whether, in an evasion case, the government must prove a "substantial" deficiency. *Compare United States v. Bencs*, 28 F.3d 555, 563 (6th Cir. 1994), *and United States v. Koskerides*, 877 F.2d 1129, 1137 (2d Cir. 1989) (requiring a substantial deficiency), *with United States v. Tanios*, 82 F.3d 98, 100 (5th Cir. 1996), *and United States v. McGill*, 964 F.2d 222, 230 (3d Cir. 1992) (requiring only that there be a deficiency).

4. *Civil tax collection.* While a precise assessment of tax due is relevant for civil tax collection, it is not critical for a successful criminal prosecution. In a criminal case, the government need only establish that there was an evasion, a false statement, or the failure to file, not the precise amount of taxes due. This question is left for the civil collection action that usually follows the criminal case. Frequently, however, the defendant's records are insufficient to make an accurate determination in a specific items case.

5. *Sentencing in tax fraud cases.* While proving the amount of tax due is not required for conviction in a criminal case, the amount of tax loss caused by the offense is relevant at sentencing. In general, the amount of tax loss caused by the offense affects the base offense level under the U.S. Sentencing Guidelines. *See* John J. Tigue Jr. and Jeremy H. Temkin, *Tax Litigation Issues: Sentencing in Criminal Tax Cases Post*-Booker, 235 N.Y.L.J. 3, col. 1 (May 18, 2006). Sentencing enhancements may apply if the offense involved, among others, "sophisticated means" or if the unreported income came as a result of criminal activity. *Id.*

The Supreme Court's ruling in *United States v. Booker*, 543 U.S. 220, 244 (2005), has had an impact on sentencing in tax cases. Prior to *Booker*, the sentencing guidelines were mandatory. Tax crime sentences tended to be longer than those "for other white-collar offenses involving comparable losses, resulting in a higher rate of incarceration for convicted tax defendants." Tigue & Temkin, *supra*, 235

N.Y.L.J. at 3. In *Booker*, however, the Supreme Court ruled the Guidelines should be advisory and not mandatory. 543 U.S. at 244. *See* Chapter 19, *infra*. Statistics show that, within the first year after *Booker*, courts were sentencing tax offenders outside the guidelines range with "the resulting sentences . . . significantly below the applicable guidelines." Tigue & Temkin, *supra*, 235 N.Y.L.J. at 3.

PROBLEM

12-5. Josephine Dickey worked for the Immigration and Naturalization Service ("INS") at a New Mexico port of entry. Her salary as an INS inspector for the tax year in question year was $45,414. Prior to working for the INS, she had had several low paying jobs. Her husband worked as a custodian and earned minimum wage.

Beginning in March for the tax year at issue, Dickey purchased a new truck, a digital camera, a laptop computer, a new car, and furniture. She paid for most of these items in cash. After overhearing a phone call between Dickey and her uncle, her husband asked her if she was doing any "dirty business." She responded, "I just had to close my eyes and I would get $15,000 per car. My uncle was the one arranging the cars that would go across the border." Later, Dickey's husband saw her in possession of large amounts of cash on several occasions.

Dickey had her annual tax return prepared by a professional tax preparer. Dickey told the preparer she had no other income other than her INS salary. Her return showed adjusted gross income of $45,414, taxable income of $34,315, and tax due of $6,013. An IRS investigation, however, found bank deposits of $32,245 and total cash expenditures of $140,264 for the tax year at issue.

You are an assistant U.S. Attorney in charge of a grand jury investigation into possible criminal tax offenses committed by Dickey. What charges would you likely seek? How would you seek to prove those charges?

Chapter 13

MONEY LAUNDERING AND RELATED FINANCIAL CRIMES

[A] INTRODUCTORY NOTES

During the 1970s and 1980s, Congress enacted a series of statutes designed to allow the government to track the flow of large sums of cash in the economy — the currency transaction reporting statutes — and to criminalize the flow of illegally-generated funds in the economy — the money laundering statutes. The latter are far-reaching, particularly in light of the increased scope of money laundering crimes effected by the USA PATRIOT Act of 2001. Because of their substantial breadth and substantial penalties, including forfeiture, the money laundering statutes have gained wide use in federal criminal cases, including white collar cases.

Tracking the flow of cash, and criminalizing efforts to hide "dirty" money or to use dirty money to carry out illegal activity, provide the government with a means both to uncover crimes such as tax evasion and to remove the incentive for drug dealers and others to engage in the criminal activity in the first place. In white collar cases, crimes such as bribery, mail and wire fraud, and securities fraud often generate proceeds that need to be hidden or disguised. When considering the materials in this chapter, it is critical to keep in mind the purposes of these financial crimes statutes.

First, this chapter discusses the currency transaction reporting ("CTR") laws that apply to financial institutions and to trades and businesses. Second, the chapter discusses the "structuring" statutes that criminalize efforts to avoid the CTR requirements. Third, the chapter discusses the money laundering statutes, which are broader than but work in tandem with the CTR laws. Finally, the chapter addresses important issues concerning the attorney-client relationship that arise under these statutes, which require attorneys to disclose information provided by clients in certain circumstances.

[B] THE CURRENCY TRANSACTION REPORTING, CASH REPORTING, AND STRUCTURING LAWS

[1]   Statutory Overview

The Bank Secrecy Act of 1970 and its companion statute, the Currency and Foreign Transactions Reporting Act, provide the government with mechanisms to track the flow of money both within the United States and to and from the United States. In addition, related provisions of the federal tax code require trades and businesses to report cash transactions to the government.[a] Congress stated that

---

[a] The Bank Secrecy Act is codified at 31 U.S.C. § 5311-22. The companion statute, the Currency and

the purpose of the currency transaction reporting laws is to "require certain reports or records where they have a high degree of usefulness in criminal, tax, or regulatory investigations or proceedings, or in the conduct of intelligence or counterintelligence activities, including analysis, to protect against international terrorism."It is important to note that the currency transaction reporting statutes criminalize simply failing to disclose the required information; the government need not prove that the transaction represented any underlying criminal activity.[b]

This chapter focuses on the principal currency transaction reporting provisions of the Bank Secrecy Act, and on related provisions of the federal tax code. This section also focuses on statutes that criminalize efforts to "structure" transactions so as to avoid the CTR filing requirements. Finally, this section addresses the laws and regulations that require financial institutions "to report any suspicious transaction relevant to a possible violation of law or regulation." These reports are known as "Suspicious Activity Reports," and generally must be filed for transactions of $5,000 or more that the bank suspects involve money laundering or CTR evasion, or that are otherwise unusual for the customer involved.

[a]   The Currency Transaction and Cash Reporting Laws

Section 5313(a) sets forth the CTR filing requirement, and provides for criminal penalties when the defendant acted willfully in violating the requirement.[c] To prove a violation of § 5313(a), the government must show that:

(1)   A "domestic financial institution" was involved in a transaction;
(2)   The transaction involved U.S. currency or specified monetary instruments;[d]
(3)   The transaction was for more than $10,000;
(4)   The domestic financial institution failed to file the required report; *and*
(5)   The defendant acted willfully.

Under § 5312(a)(2) of the Bank Secrecy Act and regulations promulgated thereunder, the term "financial institutions" is broadly defined to include, among

---

Foreign Transactions Reporting Act (CFTR), which deals with transactions that cross international borders, is codified at 31 U.S.C. § 5316. Related statutes include 31 U.S.C. § 5314 (record keeping and reporting concerning foreign financial agency transactions); 31 U.S.C. § 5315 (reports on foreign currency transactions). The CFTR allows the government to monitor large monetary transactions, including exports and imports of currency. The tax code reporting provision is codified at 26 U.S.C. § 6050I. In 2001 Congress passed the Uniting and Strengthening America By Providing Appropriate Tools Required to Intercept and Obstruct Terrorism Act of 2001 (the "Act"), Pub. L. 107-156. Under the Act, certain financial institutions are required to implement programs designed to prevent their institutions from being used to facilitate money laundering or the financing of terrorism. For an overview of these laws, see Helen Gredd, *Banking Crimes, in* White Collar Crime: Business and Regulatory Offenses § 2.01 (Otto Obermaier & Robert Morvillo, eds. 2009).

[b] The enforcement of the CTR statutes was given a boost by the decision in *United States v. Bank of New England*, 821 F.2d 844 (1st Cir. 1987), which increased the exposure of financial institutions to felony convictions for failure to file the required CTRs. As discussed in Chapter 2, *supra*, this case was noteworthy for its adoption of the collective knowledge theory of mens rea. The case involved the bank's failure to file CTRs for a pattern of cash transactions in excess of $100,000 over a twelve-month period. No individual within the bank knowingly violated the law, but the court found that the collective knowledge of all of the employees was sufficient to hold the bank accountable for the failure to file the reports.

[c]   31 U.S.C. § 5322.

[d]   31 U.S.C. § 5312(a)(3).

other entities, banks, stock brokers, insurance companies, pawn brokers, and car dealers. Courts have also held that individuals who engage in the types of financial matters listed in the statutes and regulations may constitute "financial institutions." Criminal punishment includes a maximum five-year prison term, a $250,000 fine, or both. § 5322(a).

In 1984, Congress applied the cash-reporting requirement to all persons "engaged in a trade or business." This requirement is contained in § 6050I of the Internal Revenue Code. 26 U.S.C. § 6050I. Under this provision, all cash transactions of over $10,000 must be reported to the IRS on Form 8300, which must provide (a) the name, address, and [tax identification number] of the person from whom the cash was received, (b) the amount of cash received, (c) the date and nature of the transaction, and (d) such other information as the Secretary may prescribe.

To prove that a person *failed to file* a required Form 8300 under Section 6050I, the government must prove all the elements of the crime of failing to file a tax return.[e] To prove *the filing of a false* Form 8300, the government must prove all the elements of the crime of filing a false tax return.[f] These violations are prosecuted as tax crimes, and therefore the government must prove that the defendant both intended to violate the reporting requirements and also that the defendant knew the conduct was illegal.[g] As discussed below, these laws raise important issues concerning the attorney-client relationship.

[b]   The Structuring Statutes

After passage of the CTR laws and regulations, individuals began to structure their transactions so as to avoid triggering the reporting requirements. This practice came to be known as "smurfing,"[h] that is, breaking transactions into amounts below the $10,000 threshold.[i] To address this structuring activity, Congress passed the anti-structuring laws to close this loophole in the statute. 31 U.S.C. § 5324(a).[j] In order for the government to prove a violation of § 5324(a), it must establish that the defendant:

(a)   Acted with the purpose of evading the CTR laws and regulations; *and*

(b)   One or more of the following:

     (1)   Caused or attempted to cause a domestic financial institution to fail to file a CTR;

---

[e] 26 U.S.C. § 7203. This section is discussed in the Tax Crimes Chapter, *supra*, §§ 12[A][4][c], 12[B].

[f] 26 U.S.C. § 7206. This section is discussed in the Tax Crimes Chapter, *supra*, §§ 12[A][4][b], 12[C].

[g] *See* Tax Crimes Chapter, *supra*, § 12[D][1].

[h] The term "smurfing" comes from the children's cartoon show "The Smurfs," which was wildly popular when the structuring statutes were adopted. The smurfs were blue little people who scattered from here to there to perform certain tasks and who were constantly chased by a cat and the big bad guy named Gargamel.

[i] In reality the information flowing from the daily processing of millions of CTRs seldom leads to actual criminal prosecutions. Rather, the CTRs themselves provide the necessary underlying information for the investigation and prosecution of any number of crimes involving money.

[j] The statute provides: "No person shall for the purpose of evading the reporting requirement of section 5313(a) or 5325 or any regulation prescribed under any such section. . . (3) structure or assist in structuring, or attempting to structure or assist in structuring, any transaction with one or more domestic financial institutions."

(2)   Caused or attempted to cause a domestic financial institution to file a CTR that contained a material false statement or omission; *and/or*

(3)   Structured or attempted to structure any transaction with one or more domestic financial institutions.[k]

All violations of § 5324 are punished criminally. *See* 31 U.S.C. § 5324(c). The penalty includes a prison term of not more than five years, a statutory fine, or both. The statute also specifies an "aggravated" sentence for "[w]hoever violates this section while violating another law of the United States or as part of a pattern of any illegal activity involving more than $100,000 in a 12-month period." 31 U.S.C. § 5324(d)(2). In such cases, the penalty is a prison term of no more than 10 years, twice the statutory fine, or both.

In addition, § 6050I(f) of the Internal Revenue Code prohibits the structuring of transactions to avoid the cash-reporting requirement of 26 U.S.C. § 6050I. As explained in the notes following the next case, an intent to violate the law is an element under § 6050I but not under § 5324. A "willful" *failure to file* a Form 8300 is punished under § 7203 of the Internal Revenue Code; the penalty includes a prison term of not more than one year, or a statutory fine, or both. A "willful" *submission of a false* Form 8300 is punished under § 7206 of the Internal Revenue Code with a prison term of not more than three years, or a statutory fine, or both.

[2]   Mens Rea — The Anti-Structuring Statute (§ 5324)

The currency transaction reporting statutes criminalize the failure to provide the government with the information required by the applicable statutes and regulations. These statutes do not require that the funds at issue have been derived from criminal activity. As you read the next case, consider the purpose of the CTR laws. Were the defendant's actions in this case sufficiently culpable to warrant a multi-count criminal conviction? Why or why not?

UNITED STATES v. MACPHERSON
424 F.3d 183 (2d Cir. 2005)

RAGGI, CIRCUIT JUDGE.

After trial, a jury found William MacPherson guilty of structuring a quarter-million dollars into thirty-two separate cash transactions, each less than $10,000, in violation of 31 U.S.C. § 5324(a)(3). Nevertheless, the United States District Court for the Eastern District of New York (Sterling Johnson, Jr., *Judge*) set aside the verdict and entered a judgment of acquittal, ruling that the trial evidence was insufficient to establish the requisite *mens rea* elements of the charged offense, specifically, MacPherson's knowledge of and intent to avoid federal currency reporting requirements for cash transactions exceeding $10,000. The United States appeals, arguing that the totality of the circumstantial evidence permitted the jury to infer MacPherson's guilty knowledge and intent. We agree and, accordingly, reverse the judgment of acquittal and remand the case to the district court with directions that it reinstate the jury verdict, proceed to sentencing, and enter a judgment of conviction.

---

[k] Section 5324(c) criminalizes structuring in connection with international monetary instrument transactions.

I. BACKGROUND

A. *The Structured Cash Deposits*

At times relevant to this case, William MacPherson was a New York City police officer who supplemented his salary with rental income from various real estate holdings. In a four-month period between September 26, 2000, and January 16, 2001, MacPherson deposited a total of $258,100 in cash into three Staten Island bank accounts by means of thirty-two transactions, structured so that no single transaction exceeded $10,000. [The Court detailed the chronology of these deposits.]. . . .

B. *The Background to the Structured Deposits*

1. *MacPherson's Attempt to Shield Assets from a Civil Judgment*

At trial, the government did not contend that the deposited funds derived from any criminal activity. Rather, it suggested that the deposits were made with monies that MacPherson had previously shielded against a possible civil judgment. To support this theory, the government adduced the following evidence.

In December 1997, MacPherson was sued for $2.5 million by an individual who was injured at one of his rental properties. MacPherson was uninsured against a possible damages award. Starting in January 1998 and continuing for some years thereafter while the tort suit was pending against him, MacPherson liquidated or transferred significant assets in an apparent effort to shield them from judgment. For example, between January 1998 and September 2000, MacPherson sold five real properties for just under $1 million, realizing a net profit of approximately $343,000. He also made four large cash withdrawals totaling $220,000 from a Citibank account held jointly with his wife. The first withdrawal, for $80,000, was on January 21, 1998, from a branch located at 577 Bay Street on Staten Island. The other three cash withdrawals were all made on August 31, 1999: $50,000 from the aforementioned Bay Street branch; another $50,000 from a branch at 1492 Hylan Boulevard on Staten Island; and $40,000 from a branch at 1910 Victory Boulevard, also on Staten Island.

In September 2000, MacPherson settled the pending tort suit for $27,000. That same month, he made the first three of the charged structured deposits.[2]

---

[2] MacPherson argues that, with the settlement of the tort case, any interest he may have had in sheltering his cash assets ended, leaving him without any motive to avoid federal reporting requirements. We will not speculate as to what may have prompted MacPherson to engage in the charged structuring. Motive is not an element of the crime, and, thus, the lack of evidence on this point does not, as a matter of law, preclude conviction. We recognize, of course, that evidence of motive, or the lack thereof, is a factor that a jury may weigh in considering whether the totality of the circumstances permits it to infer guilty knowledge and intent beyond a reasonable doubt. For the reasons discussed herein, however, we conclude that the evidence in this case was sufficient, even without proof of motive, to support a jury finding that MacPherson structured the charged cash transactions with the knowledge and intent required to support conviction.

2. *The CTR Filings with Respect to MacPherson's 1998–99 Cash Withdrawals*

Because MacPherson's large cash withdrawals in 1998 and 1999 each exceeded $10,000, Citibank was required by law to document them to the Internal Revenue Service, which it did by filing a Form 4789 Currency Transaction Report ("CTR"). The January 21, 1998 CTR reported the persons involved in the cash transaction as William J. MacPherson and his wife, Tracy A. MacPherson. The bank verified Mr. MacPherson's identity by reference to his New York State driver's license. Mrs. MacPherson's identity was verified by reference to her Citicard number. Edith Steuerman, a Citibank Manager, testified that she filled out most of the MacPhersons' January 21, 1998 CTR, with a teller filling out other parts. Although Steuerman had no specific recollection of the MacPherson transaction — for example, she could not recall if Mrs. MacPherson was actually present on the occasion — she testified that her uniform practice in preparing CTRs was to have the customer sit down across from her at a desk while she took down identifying data.

Steuerman did not prepare any of the August 31, 1999 CTRs, and no persons involved in their preparation were called to testify. Nevertheless, the CTR filed in connection with the $50,000 cash withdrawal from the Bay Street branch itself indicates that Mr. MacPherson was the sole person involved in that transaction and that his identity was verified on this occasion by reference to his Citicard number. The Hylan Boulevard CTR of the same date indicates that both MacPhersons were involved in that $50,000 cash withdrawal, with their identities verified by reference to their driver's licenses. The Victory Boulevard CTR similarly indicates the involvement of both MacPhersons in that $40,000 withdrawal, with their identities again verified by their driver's licenses.

II. DISCUSSION

A. *Standard of Review*

*   *   *

B. *The Totality of the Circumstantial Evidence Would Permit a Rational Jury to Find the Knowledge and Intent Elements of Structuring Proved Beyond a Reasonable Doubt*

1. *The Federal Law Prohibiting Structuring*

Preliminary to discussing the evidence from which a reasonable jury could have found the requisite knowledge and intent proved in this case, we briefly review the evolution of federal law prohibiting structuring.

In 1970, Congress enacted the Currency and Foreign Transactions Reporting Act ("CFTRA" or "the Act"), also referred to as the "Bank Secrecy Act," which requires, *inter alia*, that domestic financial institutions report to the Internal Revenue Service any cash transactions exceeding $10,000. Underlying this legislation was Congress's recognition of "the importance of reports of large and unusual currency transactions in ferreting out criminal activity." No criminal predicate as to the source of cash in excess of $10,000 was required to prosecute those who failed to comply with the specified reporting requirements.

Prior to 1986, the law did not explicitly prohibit persons from structuring cash transactions so that no one transaction exceeded $10,000 in an effort to avoid CTR filings. Although such structuring was sometimes prosecuted under 18 U.S.C. § 371 as a scheme to defraud the United States, in 1986, Congress decided to address the problem directly by specifically criminalizing structuring in the Money Laundering Control Act § 1354(a). Title 31 U.S.C. § 5324 states, in pertinent part:

> No person shall, for the purpose of evading the reporting requirements of section 5313(a) . . . or any regulation prescribed under any such section . . . (3) structure or assist in structuring, or attempt to structure or assist in structuring, any transaction with one or more domestic financial institutions.

31 U.S.C. § 5324(a). The applicable regulations define "structuring" by reference to both the *actus reus* and *mens rea* elements of § 5324(a):

> [A] person structures a transaction if that person, acting alone, or in conjunction with, or on behalf of, other persons, conducts or attempts to conduct one or more transactions in currency, in any amount, at one or more financial institutions, on one or more days, in any manner, for the purpose of evading the reporting requirements under section 103.22 of this Part. "In any manner" includes, but is not limited to, the breaking down of a single sum of currency exceeding $10,000 into smaller sums, including sums at or below $10,000, or the conduct of a transaction, or series of currency transactions, including transactions at or below $10,000. The transaction or transactions need not exceed the $10,000 reporting threshold at any single financial institution on any single day in order to constitute structuring within the meaning of this definition.

31 C.F.R. § 103.11(gg).

This court construed this willfulness element to require proof that a defendant, with knowledge of the reporting requirement imposed by law, structured a currency transaction "intend[ing] to deprive the government of information to which it is entitled." In *Ratzlaf v. United States*, the Supreme Court took a different view, ruling that structuring was "willful" only if the government further proved "that the defendant acted with knowledge that his conduct was unlawful." 510 U.S. 135, 137 (1994). Within the year, Congress responded by eliminating willfulness as an element necessary to convict a person of structuring in violation of § 5324. The net result, as this court has previously observed, was to conform federal anti-structuring law "to the *Scanio* interpretation." *United States v. Scanio*, 900 F.2d 485, 487 (2d Cir. 1990).

Because the conduct at issue in this case all occurred well after 1994, we look to *Scanio* to identify the three elements that the government was required to prove beyond a reasonable doubt to convict MacPherson of the charged § 5324 offense: (1) the defendant must, in fact, have engaged in acts of structuring; (2) he must have done so with knowledge that the financial institutions involved were legally obligated to report currency transactions in excess of $10,000; and (3) he must have acted with the intent to evade this reporting requirement.

2. *The Circumstantial Evidence Supported an Inference of MacPherson's Knowledge of and Intent to Evade Currency Reporting Requirements*

As noted in our discussion of the case's procedural history, MacPherson did not argue in the district court, nor does he assert in opposition to the government's appeal, that the trial evidence was insufficient to permit a reasonable jury to find the first element of a § 5324 offense — acts of structuring — proved beyond a reasonable doubt. Indeed, the evidence would not support such an argument. Instead, MacPherson argued, and it appears the district court concluded, that the government's proof failed at the second and third elements: knowledge and intent. Accordingly, we focus our sufficiency discussion on these two aspects of *mens rea.*

a. *Inferring Knowledge and Intent from Circumstantial Evidence*

The record is devoid of any direct evidence that MacPherson knew of or intended to evade the reporting requirements for cash transactions exceeding $10,000. The law, however, recognizes that the *mens rea* elements of knowledge and intent can often be proved through circumstantial evidence and the reasonable inferences drawn therefrom. Indeed, the law draws no distinction between direct and circumstantial evidence in requiring the government to carry its burden of proof. A verdict of guilty may be based entirely on circumstantial evidence as long as the inferences of culpability drawn from the circumstances are reasonable. The possibility that inferences consistent with innocence as well as with guilt might be drawn from circumstantial evidence is of no matter to sufficiency analysis because "it is the task of the jury, not the court, to choose among competing inferences.". . . .

Applying these principles to this case, we conclude that the totality of circumstantial evidence permitted a jury to find beyond a reasonable doubt that MacPherson engaged in the charged structuring with the requisite guilty knowledge and intent. Specifically, the jury could have reasonably inferred from the pattern of MacPherson's structuring, as well as from the record of his earlier cash withdrawals that did generate CTR filings, that MacPherson knew of and, in connection with the charged deposits, intended to evade currency reporting requirements.

b. *The Pattern of MacPherson's Cash Transactions Supported a Jury Inference of Knowledge and Intent*

(1) United States v. Nersesian *Recognizes that Knowledge of and Intent to Evade Reporting Requirements Can Be Inferred from a Pattern of Structured Transactions*

The government submits that the jury could have inferred MacPherson's guilty knowledge and intent from the pattern of his structured transactions. This argument finds support in our decision in *United States v. Nersesian*, 824 F.2d 1294 (2d Cir. 1987). In that case, a defendant and co-conspirators had used $117,000 in cash to purchase more than one hundred $1,000 money orders at numerous banks throughout New York City over a one-month period. In challenging the sufficiency of the evidence supporting his conviction for conspiring to defraud the government by engaging in cash transactions aimed at avoiding currency reporting requirements, the *Nersesian* defendant argued that the pattern of his transactions could not support an inference that he knew of and intended to evade CTR filing requirements. He specifically noted that his money order purchases did not fall "just short of" the $10,000 reporting trigger, no evidence indicated that he had ever been alerted to the CTR filing requirement, and certain evidence in the case was actually inconsistent with such knowledge. This court acknowledged that "the evidence does permit the inference that [the defendant] did not know of the reporting requirements." Nevertheless, given the pattern of transactions, the court could not conclude that the evidence was insufficient to permit "*any* rational trier of fact" to find knowledge and intent: "The jury could have inferred from the fact that [the defendant] chose to carry out his currency exchanges in a series of small transactions over a number of days, rather than in a single transaction or several larger transactions, that he knew of the reporting requirements and was attempting to avoid them." (emphasis in original).

(2) Nersesian's *Reasoning Supports the Jury Verdict in This Case*

Applying *Nersesian*'s reasoning to this case, we conclude that the jury that convicted MacPherson could have reasonably inferred from the fact that the defendant chose to deposit a quarter-million dollars through a series of thirty-two small transactions all under $10,000 that he knew of the reporting requirements applicable to cash transactions over $10,000 and was intent on avoiding them. The trial evidence indicated that the $258,100 at issue did not represent income earned during the four-month period so as to require multiple deposits. Rather, the evidence suggested that the cash was a long-held asset that MacPherson had shielded for some years from a possible tort judgment. Once the tort suit was settled in September 2000, MacPherson apparently concluded that there was no further risk in placing this cash in bank accounts traceable to him. Nevertheless, he deliberately decided not to deposit the money in one lump sum or even through several five-figure transactions. Instead, he employed the more burdensome technique of thirty-two separate transactions, no one of which exceeded $10,000. As the Seventh Circuit observed in a similar context, "it is unlikely, to the point of absurdity, that it was pure coincidence" that a defendant would engage in multiple transactions, all under $10,000, to achieve his purpose. *United States v. Cassano*, 372 F.3d 868, 879 (7th Cir. 2004).

That MacPherson's avoidance of five-figure transactions was calculated rather than coincidental is evidenced by the fact that twenty-three deposits were in amounts of $9,000-$9,200. Indeed, in six out of seven consecutive weeks, MacPherson traveled to three different banks on the same day to make identical deposits of $9,000, thereby providing even stronger circumstantial evidence than existed in *Nersesian* that the defendant knew of and was intent on avoiding the $10,000 trigger for CTR filings. *Cf. United States v. Nersesian*, 824 F.2d at 1314 (rejecting argument that knowledge and intent could not be inferred because monies were not structured in amounts "just short" of the reporting trigger). In sum, MacPherson's willingness to sacrifice efficiency and convenience in depositing a quarter-million dollars through multiple small transactions structured to ensure that no one exceeded $10,000 amply supported a reasonable inference that MacPherson knew of and was intent on avoiding CTR reporting requirements.

(3) *MacPherson's Arguments for Not Applying Nersesian's Reasoning to This Case Are Unconvincing*

In urging affirmance of the district court's judgment of acquittal, MacPherson submits that *Nersesian*'s reasoning is inapplicable to his case because the *Nersesian* defendant was convicted of violating 18 U.S.C. § 371, which did not require the government to prove the elements of structuring under 31 U.S.C. § 5324. We are not convinced. Although the first element of a § 5324 offense — acts of structuring as defined in 31 C.F.R. § 103.11(gg) — may not have been an element of the § 371 charge in *Nersesian*, as we have already noted, the sufficiency of the government's proof as to that § 5324 element is not here at issue. As to the remaining knowledge and intent elements of § 5324, they are, in fact, identical to the *mens rea* elements in *Nersesian*. . . . Precisely because *Nersesian* addressed the same *mens rea* elements as are here at issue, its recognition that knowledge and evasive intent could reasonably be inferred from the pattern of structured transactions is appropriately applied to sufficiency review in this case.

This conclusion is reinforced by the fact that, even when the government's *mens rea* burden in a § 5324 prosecution was heavier, requiring proof of willfulness as defined in *Ratzlaf*, this court ruled that a jury could infer the requisite knowledge of illegality from the pattern of structured transactions.

In a final attempt to avoid application of *Nersesian* to this case, MacPherson argues that, in *Nersesian*, the cash at issue was criminally derived, which is not a contention in his case. Certainly, the criminal origin of structured funds, to the extent it provides a motive for concealment from government authorities, may constitute an additional circumstance from which a jury can infer a defendant's knowledge of and intent to avoid CTR filings. But proof of criminal derivation was not necessary to secure a § 371 conviction in *Nersesian*, and this court did *not* reference this fact in concluding that the pattern of defendant's structured transactions was sufficient to support a jury inference of guilty knowledge and intent. . . . More to the point, whether or not a § 5324 prosecution relates to criminal proceeds, a jury may properly consider the pattern of structuring activities and draw reasonable inferences therefrom as to whether the defendant possessed the requisite *mens rea*.

c. *MacPherson's Prior Cash Transactions Prompting CTR Filings Further Supported the Jury Inference of Knowledge*

Although the pattern of MacPherson's structured deposits, by itself, provided evidence from which a reasonable jury could have inferred his knowledge of and intent to evade currency reporting requirements, that conclusion was reinforced by circumstantial evidence that MacPherson acquired knowledge of CTR filing requirements in 1998 and 1999 when his four cash withdrawals of sums ranging from $40,000 to $80,000 prompted Citibank to file CTRs. Although no bank employee specifically recalled dealing with MacPherson at the time of these withdrawals, bank manager Edith Steuerman, who filled out part of the CTR relating to the $80,000 withdrawal, testified that it was her practice to prepare the document sitting across the desk from the customer while she obtained necessary identifying information from him. Steuerman's testimony could support a jury inference that MacPherson thereby acquired knowledge of the reporting requirement for cash transactions exceeding $10,000. We conclude that this evidence strongly reinforces the inference that a jury could reasonably draw from MacPherson's careful structuring of his subsequent cash deposits: he was intent on avoiding any further CTR filings with respect to his money movements. . . .

When the circumstances of MacPherson's CTR-triggering withdrawals are reviewed together with the pattern of his charged structured deposits in the light most favorable to the government, we cannot conclude that this evidence was insufficient to permit any rational jury to find that MacPherson knew of and intended to evade currency reporting requirements when he engaged in the charged structuring.

III. CONCLUSION

To summarize, we conclude that a pattern of structured transactions, such as occurred in this case, may, by itself, permit a rational jury to infer that a defendant had knowledge of and the intent to evade currency reporting requirements. Further supporting a jury inference of knowledge in this case were the circumstances of MacPherson's past cash transactions triggering CTR filings. Because the totality of this circumstantial evidence was sufficient to establish the elements of knowledge and intent required to convict MacPherson of structuring in violation of 31 U.S.C. § 5324(a)(3), the jury verdict of guilty should not have been set aside nor a judgment of acquittal entered by the court. Accordingly, we REVERSE the judgment of acquittal and REMAND this case to the district court with directions that it reinstate the jury verdict, proceed to sentencing, and enter a judgment of conviction.

NOTES AND QUESTIONS

1. *Intent and motive.* Why did MacPherson engage in his elaborate pattern of depositing cash in amounts under $10,000? Was there evidence of motive? If not, why did the court find sufficient evidence of knowledge and intent? What *was* MacPherson's likely motive, if any?

2. *The mens rea requirement and the* Ratzlaf *decision.* As the court in *MacPherson* noted, in 1994, the United States Supreme Court interpreted § 5324's "willful violation" requirement to require proof that the defendant "acted with knowledge that the conduct was unlawful." *Ratzlaf v. United States*, 510 U.S. 135, 137 (1994). The Court had previously applied this heightened level of required mens rea — intent to violate the law — to tax crimes in *Cheek v. United States*, 498 U.S. 192 (1991). In *Ratzlaf* dissent, Justice Blackmun strongly objected to the majority's interpretation of the statute, saying it "is at odds with the statutory text, the intent of Congress, and the fundamental principle that knowledge of illegality is not required for a criminal act." *Id.* at 162. In the aftermath of that case, Congress quickly removed the willfulness requirement from the structuring statute, effectively overturning *Ratzlaf.* Pub. L. No. 103-325, § 411, 108 Stat. 2253 (1994).

3. *Structuring under the Internal Revenue Code.* As discussed in the preceding note, proof of specific intent to violate a known legal duty is an element in the prosecution of tax crimes. This is an exception to the general rule that "ignorance of the law . . . is no defense to criminal prosecution." *Cheek*, 498 U.S. at 199. The Internal Revenue Code prohibits structuring of cash transaction reports by

someone engaged in a trade or business. 26 U.S.C. § 6050. A violation of § 6050I is a tax crime, so, unlike a case brought under § 5324, the government must prove an intent to violate a known legal duty as required by *Cheek* in a structuring case brought under § 6050. *See, e.g., United States v. Loe*, 262 F.3d 427 (5th Cir. 2001); *United States v. McLamb*, 985 F.2d 1284 (4th Cir. 1993).

4. *Conspiracy to defraud.* The court noted above that, prior to the enactment of the anti-structuring statute, structuring activities were prosecuted as conspiracies to defraud the United States under 18 U.S.C. § 371. Recall that § 371 contains two distinct offenses — conspiracies to commit offenses against the United States and conspiracies to defraud the United States. *See* Chapter 3, Conspiracy, *supra*, at § 3[C]. In what way does structuring represent an effort to "defraud" the United States?

5. *The law enforcement challenge.* Tens of millions of CTRs are filed each year. For example, in 2004–2006, the federal government reported the filing of nearly 37.8 million CTRs pursuant to the Bank Secrecy Act. These CTRs were collected by banks and other financial institutions and forwarded to the government. Report to Congressional Committees, *Bank Secrecy Act: Increased Use of Exemption Provisions Could Reduce Currency Transaction Reporting While Maintaining Usefulness to Law Enforcement Efforts*, United States Government Accountability Office, p. 81 (Feb. 2008). The U.S. Treasury Department directed the Financial Crimes Enforcement Network, commonly called FinCEN, to maintain and control the CTR filings. Given the sheer volume of filings, how can the government identify "structured" transactions?

FinCEN has as one of its tasks the collection and analysis of the millions of CTRs filed yearly. *See* http://www.fincen.gov. The process of sorting through the paperwork is daunting. Surely, tracking the flow of criminally derived money is critically important to the government, but the reporting requirements encompass millions of transactions that are entirely legitimate. FinCEN uses sophisticated computerized technology to cross-reference these filings and to track and trace the domestic and international flow of currency. What are the policy implications of having third parties, such as securities brokers and even attorneys, collect and remit financial information on customers that is ultimately used for law enforcement purposes?

6. *The regulatory scheme.* The currency transaction and structuring statutes are not self-enforcing. The Code of Federal Regulations ("CFR") provides the specific regulations that govern the implementation of the statutes, including the monetary limits, which are, from time to time, adjusted. In addition, the CFR dictates the ways in which an institution can secure an exemption from the cumbersome reporting requirements. *See* 31 C.F.R. § 103 *et seq.*

7. *Suspicious activity reports.* Although the primary tool for identifying large cash transactions has been CTRs, since 1996, the government has been collecting data on suspicious financial activities. The Bank Secrecy Act, 31 U.S.C. § 5318(g), authorizes the U.S. Department of the Treasury to adopt suspicious activity reporting requirements for financial institutions. This information is contained on a Suspicious Activity Report (SAR) which has replaced CTRs as the primary tool of law enforcement for identifying suspicious activity. This report has a $5,000 reporting threshold. Many money laundering investigations are initiated with the suspicious activity report or the currency transaction report. *See The SAR Activity*

Review: Trends, Tips, and Issues, Bank Secrecy Act Advisory Group, Issue 13, May 2008, *at* www.fincen.gov. This review regularly reports on the types of cases that are prompted by the suspicious activity reports, including international money laundering, terrorist-related investigations, and domestic fraud cases.

PROBLEM

13-1. A federal grand jury has adduced the following evidence:

Victor Aiden made a living in the used auto parts business, purchasing parts from junkyards and reselling them to auto rebuilders. In running the unincorporated business, Aiden maintained several bank accounts, including an account at Archer Bank.

For a period of two years, Aiden wrote more than 3,000 checks to himself on the Archer account. All of the checks were cashed, mostly at a currency exchange which charged a processing fee. This business practice stemmed (or so Aiden claims) from the nature of the used auto parts business: Aiden's suppliers dealt exclusively in cash, and Aiden wrote checks that he expected to be sufficient to cover each day's purchase of parts. Aiden's customers also paid by cash.

For the two-year period in question, Aiden made 116 cash deposits at Archer Bank. He states that his practice was to collect cash from customers and then deposit the cash at points when he needed to visit the bank or when it was otherwise convenient for him. The deposits in question totaled $240,000, and ranged in amount from $54 to $9,462. The average amount was $2,000. Eight deposits were between $9,000 and $10,000, but none exceeded $10,000.

If you were the Assistant United States Attorney in charge of the investigation, would you ask the grand jury to bring criminal charges? If so, based on what theory or theories? If you were Aiden's defense attorney, what arguments would you make to try to persuade the government not to bring criminal charges?

[C]   MONEY LAUNDERING

[1]   Statutory Overview and Elements

In 1986 Congress enacted the principal money laundering statutes, 18 U.S.C. §§ 1956and 1957. These statutes criminalize financial and monetary transactions with proceeds of underlying criminal activity specified in the statutes. In that way, the money laundering statutes provide for penalties in addition to the penalties for the underlying offenses alone. As one member of the U.S. Supreme Court wrote in a money laundering case:

> Money laundering provisions serve two chief ends. First, they provide deterrence by preventing drug traffickers and other criminals who amass large quantities of cash from using these funds "to support a luxurious lifestyle" or otherwise to enjoy the fruits of their crimes. Second, they inhibit the growth of criminal enterprises by preventing the use of dirty money to promote the enterprise's growth.

United States v. Santos, 128 S. Ct. 2020, 2038 (2008) (citations omitted) (Alito, J., dissenting).

Over time, the money laundering statutes have joined with — and in some cases supplanted — the federal racketeering (RICO) statute as one of the government's principal weapons against large-scale criminal activity.[l] This has occurred because the money laundering statutes reach a broad range of criminal activities, including mail and wire fraud, and can be employed in a wide range of cases. Money laundering is sometimes easier to prove than RICO, and a money laundering case — unlike a RICO case — does not have to be approved by the Department of Justice in Washington. In addition, money laundering can lead to severe penalties, including substantial prison time and forfeitures.[m] Finally, note that money laundering charges can be brought in cases involving both domestic and international transactions.[n]

Although initially enacted principally as a means of countering narcotics trafficking activities, the money laundering statutes apply to many kinds of white collar offenses. There are several types of money laundering under the federal criminal code, but the classic form of money laundering is "concealment" money laundering that attempts to make "dirty" money look "clean" or that attempts to hide money from the government.[o] For example, money laundering may occur whenever a defendant has attempted to conceal income to avoid paying taxes. And in any fraud or bribery scheme, the defendant may have attempted to conceal the proceeds from the scheme. Further, those engaging in criminal activity often use the proceeds of the activity to further their activity, thus engaging in "promotion" money laundering. This section focuses on both concealment and promotion money laundering.

[a]   Section 1956

Section 1956(a)(1) covers domestic money laundering, and is at the heart of the statute. To establish a violation of § 1956, the government must show that:

> (1) The defendant conducted or attempted to conduct a *financial transaction*;
>
> (2) The defendant knew that the financial transaction involved the proceeds of some type of unlawful activity, which activity constitutes a felony under state, federal, or foreign law;
>
> (3) The funds in fact were proceeds from a *specified unlawful activity* ("SUA"); *and*

---

[l] The RICO statute, 18 U.S.C. §§ 1961–68, is discussed in Chapter 14, *infra*. For an analysis of the money laundering statutes' increasing role in prosecuting large scale criminal activity, see Helen Gredd & Karl D. Cooper, *Money Laundering*, *in* White Collar Crime: Business and Regulatory Offenses § 2A.01 (Otto Obermaier & Robert Morvillo, eds. 2009); Elkan Abramowitz, *Money Laundering: The New Rico?*, N.Y.L.J., Sept. 1, 1992, at 3.

[m] Money laundering offenses may lead to prison terms of up to 20 years. In 2001, however, the United States Sentencing Guidelines were changed so as to tie money laundering sentences to the sentences for the underlying offenses and to avoid overly-harsh money laundering sentences. *See White Collar Crime Institute Focuses on Recent Changes to Sentencing Guidelines*, Crim. L. Rep. 561, 561 (March 27, 2002). For a discussion of the Sentencing Guidelines, see Chapter 19, *infra*.

[n] Placement involves introducing the cash into the banking system or into legitimate commerce.

[o] Layering occurs by separating the money from its criminal origins in an effort to disguise its source. This is usually done by passing the money through several financial institutions and transferring the money into other negotiable instruments, such as cashier's checks and money orders.

(4) Any one or more of the following:

(a) The defendant engaged in the transaction done with the intent to further a specified unlawful activity ("promotion" money laundering);

(b) The defendant engaged in the transaction with the intent to commit tax fraud in violation of § 7201 (tax evasion) or § 7206 (false returns) of the Internal Revenue Code;

(c) The defendant engaged in the transaction knowing that the transaction is designed in whole or in part to disguise, conceal, or hide the source of the money ("concealment" money laundering); *or*

(d) The defendant engaged in the transaction knowing that the transaction is designed in whole or in part to avoid the currency transaction reporting laws.

The statute defines "financial transaction" to include a broad range of financial dealings that affect interstate or foreign commerce. The term thus encompasses bank transactions, gifts, and other transfers of money and property.

As noted in the introduction to this section, the money laundering offenses — like offenses under the RICO statute — are built upon underlying criminal activity. In the money laundering statutes, this activity is termed "specified unlawful activity." Section 1956(C)(7) defines this term to include dozens of crimes, including nearly all the RICO predicate crimes. Many prosecutions of money laundering in the white collar and corporate criminal arena involve mail and wire fraud, financial institution fraud, obstruction of justice, and securities fraud.

Penalties for money laundering include a fine of not more than $500,000 or twice the value of the property involved in the transaction, whichever is greater, or imprisonment for not more than 20 years, or both. In addition, the money laundering statutes contain powerful civil and criminal forfeiture provisions, which are discussed in Chapter 20, Forfeitures, *infra.*

[b]   Section 1957

Section 1957, known as the monetary transaction money laundering statute, is the companion statute to § 1956. Section 1957 is not focused upon attempts to hide the source of funds produced by illegal activities. Instead, the section focuses on the use of illegally derived funds within the financial system. Section 1957 is entitled "Engaging in Monetary Transactions in Property Derived from Specified Unlawful Activity." Under § 1957, the government must prove that:

(1)   The defendant engaged or attempted to engage in a monetary transaction;
(2)   The monetary transaction was of a value greater than $10,000;
(3)   The transaction was derived from specified unlawful activity ("SUA");
(4)   The transaction took place in the United States or the defendant is a "United States person"; *and*
(5)   The defendant knew that the property was criminally derived.

The statute defines the key terms:

- "Monetary transaction[s]" include "the deposit, withdrawal, transfer, or exchange, in or affecting interstate or foreign commerce, of funds or a monetary instrument by, through, or to a financial institution, including any transaction that would be a financial transaction under § 1956(c)(4)(B) of this title." Note that Congress amended this provision to exclude "any transaction necessary to preserve a person's right to representation as guaranteed by the Sixth Amendment to the Constitution."

- The term "specified unlawful activity" is defined as having "the meaning given that term in § 1956 [RICO] of this title."
- The term "criminally derived property" is defined as "any property constituting, or derived from, proceeds obtained from a criminal offense."

As is clear from the face of the statute, under § 1957, as under § 1956, the government must prove that the defendant knew that the funds were criminally derived, but does not have to prove that the defendant knew the specific type of criminal activity that generated the funds.

[c]   A Comparison of § 1956 and § 1957

Although the proliferation of drug proceeds was the impetus for the passage of the money laundering provisions, the wide range of "specified unlawful activity" encompasses many of the offenses that we traditionally think of as white collar crimes. Both 18 U.S.C. §§ 1956 and 1957 can often be added to most financial crime indictments. Although the statutes have similarities, there are some important differences.

"Financial transaction" (§ 1956) and "monetary transaction" (§ 1957) are terms of art that point out a key distinction between these two statutes. Section 1956 is principally concerned with the actual laundering of the money in an effort to hide its true source. There is no monetary threshold for the "financial transactions" that trigger the statute. The transaction could entail the purchase or sale of many items or services, such as artwork, travel, jewelry, precious metals, vehicles, or investments.

With § 1957 "monetary transactions," the activity must be "by, through, or to a financial institution," and it must exceed $10,000. Section 1957 could apply to almost any interaction that a criminal has with the financial system, typically with a bank. It prohibits the entry of any dirty money, in excess of $10,000, into the financial channels by deposit, withdrawal, transfer, or exchange.

[2]   Mens Rea — § 1956

As seen above, § 1956 provides the government with four possible theories of mens rea with respect to the financial transaction, that is, the transaction was undertaken with the (1) intent to promote the illegal activity (the "promotion" theory), (2) intent to commit tax fraud, (3) knowledge of a design to conceal the source of the money (the "concealment" theory), or (4) knowledge of a design to avoid the CTR laws.

[a]   Concealment Money Laundering

In the decision below, the defendant contested the sufficiency of the proof of mens rea in a concealment case. Be sure to identify the two levels of mens rea required, and the evidence offered as to each level.

UNITED STATES v. CORCHADO-PERALTA
318 F.3d 255 (1st Cir. 2003)

BOUDIN, CHIEF JUDGE.

Between 1987 and 1996, Ubaldo Rivera Colon ("Colon") smuggled over 150 kilograms of cocaine into Puerto Rico, yielding some $4 million in profits, which he then laundered through a variety of investments and purchases. Colon was indicted on drug, bank fraud, and conspiracy charges and, based on a plea agreement, was sentenced in June 2002 to over 20 years in prison.

Colon's wife, Elena Corchado Peralta ("Corchado"), and two associates, Basilio Rivera Rodriguez ("Rivera") and Oscar Trinidad Rodriguez ("Trinidad") were indicted and tried together on one count of conspiring with Colon to launder money. 18 U.S.C. §§ 1956(a)(1)(B) and (h). Corchado was also indicted on one count of bank fraud. 18 U.S.C. § 1344. During their eight-day trial, Colon provided extensive testimony about his money laundering methods, which included a variety of transactions (purchases, investments, and loans) involving the defendants.

All three defendants were convicted on the charges against them. Corchado received a 27-month sentence, Rivera, 57 months, and Trinidad, 63 months. Corchado appeals. . . . [I]t is helpful to begin by outlining the criminal offense that was the principal charge against all of them.

The money laundering statute, 18 U.S.C. § 1956, among other things makes it criminal for anyone, "knowing that the property involved in a financial transaction represents the proceeds of some form of unlawful activity" to "conduct . . . such a financial transaction which in fact involves the proceeds of specified unlawful activity" —

> (A) (i) with the intent to promote the carrying on of specified unlawful activity; or . . .

> (B) knowing that the transaction is designed in whole or in part —

> (i) to conceal or disguise the nature, the location, the source, the ownership or the control of the proceeds of specified unlawful activity;

> . . . .

The three defendants in this case were charged under subsection (B)(i), based on knowledge of "design[ ]", and not under (A)(i), based on an "intent to promote." In each instance, there is no doubt that the defendant did engage in one or more financial transactions involving Colon's drug proceeds. The issue turns, rather, on state of mind elements. Pertinently, as to Corchado, she disputes knowing either that the "property" represented proceeds of drug dealing or that "the transaction" was "designed . . . to conceal or disguise. . . . " The evidence, taken most favorably to the government, showed the following.

Elena Corchado Peralta met Colon sometime in the early 1990s and they were married in 1994. Corchado, then about 25 years old, was a student when they met and later worked part-time in her mother's jewelry store. She has a college degree in business administration and some training in accounting. Colon testified that he held himself out as a successful legitimate businessman throughout their relationship and that his wife knew about neither his drug smuggling nor his own money laundering activities.

Corchado performed many transactions involving Colon's drug proceeds. These transactions fell into two broad categories — expenditures and deposits. On the expenditure side, Colon directed Corchado to write and endorse checks to purchase a cornucopia of expensive cars, boats, real estate, and personal services. Colon maintained that his wife thought that the money was derived from legitimate businesses.

The purchases themselves were extensive and expensive, affording the couple a fancy lifestyle. For example, Corchado purchased a BMW, a Mercedes Benz, and a Porsche for the couple. At another time, she made a single monthly payment to American Express of $18,384 for interior decorating purchases. And on another day, she signed three checks totaling $350,000 that were used to purchase land for one of Colon's businesses. In total, Corchado signed the majority of 253 checks, representing many hundreds of thousands of dollars of purchases.

With respect to deposits, Corchado's main responsibility was to deposit $6,000 checks on a monthly basis into one of Colon's accounts. Colon testified that he had made a $700,000 loan to an associate using his drug profits with the understanding that the associate was to pay him back over the course of many months so as to dissociate Colon from the illegal proceeds. Under the terms of the arrangement, the checks came from legitimate businesses, and Colon testified that his wife was not aware of the circumstances underlying the monthly payments. At trial, the government also presented evidence showing that on one occasion Corchado wired $40,000 to a Florida company at Colon's request.

Tax records signed by Corchado showed that she knew that her husband's reported income from his legitimate businesses was far less than the money she was handling. For example, the joint tax return that Corchado signed for 1995 listed a total amount of claimed income of only $12,390. The government presented evidence showing that the couple's total reported income between 1992 and 1997 was only approximately $150,000. Corchado did not testify at trial.

We begin with the first knowledge requirement — namely, that Corchado was aware, at the time of the transactions she conducted, that the money she was handling, at least much of the time, was derived from drug dealings.[3] Corchado argues, correctly, that there is no direct evidence of her knowledge (say, by an admission by her or testimony from Colon that he told her about his business). Indeed, he testified repeatedly that she was unaware of his drug business; that in response to a question from her he had denied doing anything unlawful; that he never allowed her to attend meetings involving his drug business; and that he stopped distributing drugs when they were married.

Needless to say, the jury did not have to accept Colon's exculpatory testimony. It was clearly self-interested since Corchado was his wife and mother of their two children. But here, at least, the jury's disbelief could not count for much in the way of affirmative proof. Rather, whether there was knowledge of drug dealing, or so much awareness that ignorance was willful blindness, turns in this case on the same circumstantial evidence.

---

[3] Formally, the charge is "conspiracy," under subsection (h) to violate subsection (a)(1)(B)(i); but the "agreement" requirement is undisputed: many, if not all, of the transactions were performed at Colon's request or with his consent. Thus, the open issue is Corchado's state of mind.

What the evidence shows is that Corchado knew that the family expenditures were huge, that reported income was a fraction of what was being spent and that legitimate sources were not so obvious as to banish all thoughts of possible illegal origin — as demonstrated by Colon's testimony that Corchado once raised the issue. Interviewed by an FBI agent, Corchado told him that her husband had been involved in the cattle business and, more recently, in real estate development but that none of the businesses had employees and that Colon had worked mainly out of his house. And, as the government fairly points out, Corchado was herself well educated and involved in the family bookkeeping.

This might seem to some a modest basis for concluding — beyond a reasonable doubt — that Corchado knew that her husband's income was badly tainted. But the issue turns on judgments about relationships within families and about inferences that might be drawn in the community from certain patterns of working and spending. Further, it is enough to know that the proceeds came from "some form, though not necessarily which form," of felony under state or federal law. 18 U.S.C. § 1956(c)(1). The jury's judgment on this factual issue cannot be called irrational.

The other knowledge requirement is harder for the government. Here, the statute requires, somewhat confusingly, that Corchado have known that "the transaction" was "designed," at least in part, "to conceal or disguise the nature, the location, the source, the ownership or the control of the proceeds." 18 U.S.C. § 1956(a)(1)(B)(i). We will assume that it would be enough if Corchado herself undertook a transaction for her husband, knowing that her husband had such a design to conceal or disguise the proceeds, or if she undertook a transaction on her own having such a design herself. Other variations might exist, but these two seem the foremost possibilities.

It may help to treat separately the purchases on the one hand and the check deposits (and in one case a transfer) on the other. Any purchase of goods or services, whether by cash or by check, has a potential to conceal or disguise proceeds simply because it transforms them from money into objects or dissipates them in the performance of the services. But if this were enough, every expenditure of proceeds known to be tainted would itself be unlawful. Instead, the statute requires that someone — the instigator or spender — must have an intent to disguise or conceal and the spender must share or know of that intent.

Here, the government showed that from their marriage onward Corchado wrote most of the checks used by the couple to purchase expensive items (*e.g.*, several high-priced cars) and pay off credit card bills and that some of these payments were very large (one credit card bill exceeded $18,000). And, for reasons already given, it is assumed that the jury permissibly found that Corchado knew that some of the money she was spending was criminally derived. Finally, the government stresses that she must have known that Colon was bringing in and spending far more than he reported on his income tax returns. Is this enough for the jury to infer a specific intent to conceal or disguise and impute the intent itself, or knowledge of it, to Corchado?

In this case, nothing about the purchases, or their manner, points toward concealment or disguise beyond the fact that virtually *all expenditures* transform cash into something else. Here, the purchased assets were not readily concealable (*e.g.*, diamonds) nor peculiarly concealed (*e.g.*, buried in the garden) nor acquired in someone else's name nor spirited away to a foreign repository (*e.g.*, a Swiss bank deposit box). Indicia of this kind have been stressed in cases upholding money laundering charges and their absence noted in cases coming out the other way.

To hold that a jury may convict on this evidence — that Corchado spent her husband's money knowing that the money was tainted — is to make it unlawful wherever a wife spends any of her husband's money, knowing or believing him to be a criminal. That the purchases here were lavish or numerous hardly distinguishes this case from one in which a thief's wife buys a jar of baby food; if anything, Corchado's more flamboyant purchases were less likely than the baby food to disguise or conceal. Perhaps a hard-nosed Congress might be willing to adopt such a statute, *compare* 18 U.S.C. § 1957 (2000), but it did not do so here.

Less need be said about the deposit and transfer side. So far as we can tell, Corchado mostly did no more than make large regular deposits in an account given to her by her husband; there was no inference of concealment or disguise. As for the single transfer she made to another person at her husband's request, nothing suspicious about the circumstances is cited to us, let alone anything that would suggest knowledge on Corchado's part that the transfer was meant to conceal or disguise proceeds — as opposed to merely paying off a debt, making an investment, or conducting some other transaction incident to a business, lawful or otherwise.

*   *   *

Corchado's bank fraud conviction is *affirmed;* her money laundering conviction is *reversed;* the sentences are *vacated;* and the case is *remanded* for re-sentencing on the bank fraud conviction.

Notes and Questions

1. *The money laundering theory.* What was the money laundering theory in this case? Why did the court find insufficient evidence? What additional facts would likely have sufficed? As one court explained:

> The statute speaks in terms of transactions that are "designed" to conceal the proceeds of unlawful activity. Whenever a drug dealer uses his profits to acquire any asset — whether a house, a car, a horse, or a television — a jury could reasonably suspect that on some level he is motivated by a desire to convert his cash into a more legitimate form. The requirement that the transaction be "designed" to conceal, however, requires more than a trivial motivation to conceal. [For example:] [S]tatements by a defendant probative of intent to conceal; unusual secrecy surrounding the transaction; structuring the transaction in a way to avoid attention; depositing illegal profits in the bank account of a legitimate business; highly irregular features of the transaction; using third parties to conceal the real owner; a series of unusual financial moves cumulating in the transaction; or expert testimony on practices of criminals.

United States v. Garcia-Emanuel, 14 F.3d 1469, 1474–1476 (10th Cir. 1994).

2. *Section 1957.* The court noted that concealment money laundering under § 1956 is not as far reaching as offenses under § 1957. What was the basis for this conclusion? Could the government have successfully charged the defendant under § 1957 in this case? Why or why not?

3. *Willful blindness.* What amounts to knowledge that the proceeds were "dirty?" As the court stated above, "it is enough to know that the proceeds came from 'some form, though not necessarily which form,' of felony under state or federal law. 18 U.S.C. § 1956(c)(1)." As the court also noted, proof of willful blindness will suffice in proving such knowledge. Was there sufficient proof of willful blindness, also known as "constructive knowledge," in this case? Why or why not?

What facts are necessary to prove willful blindness? In *United States v. Flores*, 454 F.3d 149 (3d Cir. 2006), an attorney who asserted a defense of lack of knowledge as to the illegal source of the client's money was convicted of conspiring with the client to commit money laundering. The court found sufficient proof of willful blindness based upon the defendant's acts of opening bank accounts and conducting financial transactions for the client. The U.S. Department of Justice Manual provides specific examples of conduct that may support a finding of willful blindness in money laundering cases, such as "conducting business under odd circumstances, at irregular hours, or in unusual locations by industry standards." DOJ Manual § 9-105.400 at 9-21128.36.

Can financial institutions claim willful blindness? Note that the money laundering statutes and the Bank Secrecy Act reporting requirements are intended to ensure that financial institutions do not remain willfully blind about the money laundering activities, but instead investigate and report these transactions to the government. *See United States v. Rodriguez*, 53 F.3d 1439 (7th Cir. 1995).

NOTE ON TRANSPORTATION MONEY LAUNDERING AND THE *CUELLAR* DECISION

Section 1956(a)(1) defines money laundering offenses involving "financial transactions." A companion statute, § 1956(a)(2), criminalizes the international transport of money derived from unlawful activities. The elements of "financial transaction" and "transportation" money laundering are largely the same: both require knowledge that the proceeds derived from unlawful activity. Both statutes also allow conviction based upon proof of "promotion" or "concealment" money laundering, among other theories.

In *Cuellar v. United States*, 128 S. Ct. 1994, 1997–1998 (2008), the Supreme Court evaluated the required proof for transportation money laundering under a concealment theory, § 1956(a)(2)(B)(i). In that case, the defendant was discovered transporting approximately $81,000 in cash proceeds of narcotics trafficking. The cash was hidden in a secret compartment under the floorboard of a Volkswagen Beetle that the defendant was driving in Texas en route to Mexico. The money was bundled in plastic bags and duct tape. Animal hair was spread in the rear of the vehicle, apparently to mask the smell of marijuana that had been transported in the car.

The Court unanimously reversed the money laundering conviction, stating:

> The provision of the money laundering statute under which petitioner was convicted requires proof that the transportation was "designed in whole or in part to conceal or disguise the nature, the location, the source, the ownership, or the control" of the funds. § 1956(a)(2)(B)(i). Although this element does not require proof that the defendant attempted to create the appearance of legitimate wealth, neither can it be satisfied solely by

evidence that a defendant concealed the funds during their transport. In this case, the only evidence introduced to prove this element showed that petitioner engaged in extensive efforts to conceal the funds *en route* to Mexico, and thus his conviction cannot stand. We reverse the judgment of the Fifth Circuit.

Id. at 1998. As Justice Alito noted in his concurring opinion, the government did not present any evidence from which the trier of fact could have inferred that petitioner knew that taking the funds to Mexico would have had one of the required effects — that is, to make it more difficult for United States law enforcement officials to determine the nature, location, source, ownership, or control of the funds. *Id.* at 2006 (Alito, J., concurring).

Does this holding present a significant barrier to concealment prosecutions? What additional facts likely would have satisfied the Court? *Compare United States v. Warshak*, 562 F. Supp. 2d 986, 991–999 (S.D. Ohio 2008) (evidence of convoluted transactions was sufficient to show knowledge of a design to conceal).

PROBLEM

13-2. Nester ran an armored carrier business that transported valuables, such as artwork and jewelry, internationally. On five separate occasions over the past year, Nester placed cash inside containers that held jewelry, artwork, and other valuables. The cash was placed in paper packages that were commingled with the valuables inside the sealed and locked metal shipping containers. The containers were first transferred to Los Angeles International Airport in armored trucks and placed onto planes being loaded with cargo. In each case, the container was moved later that day to a different cargo plane, which then carried the container to a location outside the United States. A total of over $5 million was transported in this manner. As Nester knew, the cash represented the proceeds from sales of illegal narcotics.

Nester has been charged with transportation money laundering in violation of § 1956(a)(2)(B)(i), and moves to dismiss the charges based on Cuellar. *How should the court rule? Why?*

[b]   Promotion Money Laundering

In the next case, the government charged the defendant with promotion money laundering. As you read the decision, consider how the government might have proceeded differently in constructing its theory of the case.

UNITED STATES v. BROWN
186 F.3d 661 (5th Cir. 1999)

JERRY E. SMITH, CIRCUIT JUDGE:

Leonard Graves appeals his money laundering convictions, a number of his fraud convictions, and his sentence. We affirm Graves's fraud convictions, reverse his money laundering convictions, and vacate and remand his sentence.

The fraud and money laundering charges of which Graves was convicted relate to business dealings conducted at Steve Graves Chevrolet-Pontiac-Cadillac, Inc. ("SGC"), an auto dealership in Ruston, Louisiana. Graves was the dealer, president, and 41% owner of SGC, and [co-defendant Gregory] Brown managed its body shop.

The 120-count indictment against Graves alleged six distinct types of fraud, and for each fraud allegation there was a corresponding money laundering charge. Graves was convicted on counts stemming from three of the six types of fraud and was convicted of money laundering the funds derived from these frauds.

The first type of fraud involved SGC's charging car buyers more than the amount authorized by state law for document and license/title fees. SGC charged purchasers $59 in document fees, which is $9 more than Louisiana law permits; automobile dealerships are allowed to charge only $35 for processing paperwork and $15 for a notary fee. For the license and title fees, which varied from vehicle to vehicle, SGC overcharged an average of $50 per automobile listed in the indictment. The eighteen instances of overcharging were charged against Graves as mail frauds, because the Louisiana Department of Motor Vehicles mailed the automobile titles. Graves was also charged with money laundering the proceeds of the excessive fees. The jury found Graves guilty on some of the counts and not guilty on others.

Graves was convicted of fraud based on SGC's financing the purchases of used cars with "cash for gas." In seven instances, SGC advanced to the purchaser all or part of the down payment required by the financing institution — under the guise of giving the buyer some "cash for gas" — and increased the purchase price of the car by a corresponding amount. This conduct constituted fraud, because the lending institution would not have extended credit to the purchaser absent his having some genuine equity interest in the automobile. The counts of which Graves was convicted were charged as mail frauds, because SGC mailed loan documentation to General Motors Acceptance Corporation ("GMAC"), the financing institution. The jury also found Graves guilty of money laundering the funds derived from cash for gas frauds.

The final form of fraud of which Graves was convicted also involved the financing of used cars. For ten cars financed by Union Federal Credit Union, SGC, on behalf of the buyer, forwarded to the credit union 25% of the sale price, which the credit union maintained in a savings account in the purchaser's name until the loan was paid off. The dealership increased the sale price of the vehicle by a corresponding amount. As with "cash for gas," this scheme had the effect of fraudulently inducing advances of credit, for the credit union believed that the 25% down payment represented genuine purchaser equity in the purchased automobiles. These counts were charged as bank frauds, and the jury returned a guilty verdict. It also found Graves guilty of money laundering the proceeds derived from the bank frauds. Graves does not appeal these bank fraud convictions, but he does appeal the corresponding money laundering convictions.

*   *   *

Graves appeals his convictions on fraud counts stemming from excessive document and license/title fees and "cash for gas" frauds. He also appeals all his money laundering convictions and his sentence.

[The Court concluded that there was sufficient evidence to sustain Graves's fraud convictions stemming from the excessive fees and "cash for gas" schemes].

Each money laundering count on which Graves was indicted was charged under 18 U.S.C. § 1956(a)(1)(A)(i), which reads, in part:

> (A) Whoever, knowing that the property involved in a financial transaction represents the proceeds of some form of unlawful activity, conducts or attempts to conduct such a financial transaction which in fact involves the proceeds of specified unlawful activity.

> (i) with the intent to promote the carrying on of specified unlawful activity; . . .

To obtain a conviction under § 1956(a)(1)(A)(i), the government must prove beyond a reasonable doubt "[t]hat the defendant (1) conducted or attempted to conduct a financial transaction, (2) which the defendant knew involved the proceeds of unlawful activity, (3) with the intent to promote or further unlawful activity." *United States v. Cavalier*, 17 F.3d 90, 92 (5th Cir. 1994). Graves asserts that there was insufficient evidence to establish that the charged money laundering transactions were intended to promote any fraud committed at SGC. We agree.

The transactions the indictment charged as money laundering consisted of expenditures, paid by checks written by SGC, that allegedly promoted the fraud.[4] Graves contends that there was no evidence that the payment of those checks was intended to promote any fraud at SGC; the checks were simply legitimate business expenses of the dealership. Indeed, a review of the checks indicates that they were for "above board" expenses.[5] Graves argues that such expenditures are not the sort of crime-promoting transactions criminalized by § 1956(a)(1)(A)(i), for the promotion element requires some identifiable and affirmative advancement of the specified criminal activity. In support of this claim, he points to a number of cases involving "promotion" money laundering in which the court highlighted how the expenditures explicitly furthered specified unlawful activity. He then contrasts those cases to the case at hand, in which the nexus between the charged expenditures and any fraud activity is non-existent or weak.

---

[4] The government, in selecting financial transactions to fulfill the *actus reus* requirement of the money laundering charges, picked benign business expenditures — purchases of goods and services necessary to maintain SGC's legitimate business operations. It did not have to do so. Courts have held that a promotion money laundering offense may occur when a defendant receives and deposits criminally derived funds, in which case the *deposit* of the funds is the transaction intended to promote the specified unlawful activity. But the government chose not to indict Graves for depositing the proceeds of fraud. Instead, it made a strategic decision to focus on SGC's spending transactions (*i.e.*, the checks the dealership wrote), not on SGC's depositing of funds, perhaps because "receipt and deposit" money laundering prosecutions are disfavored. Such prosecutions have been criticized because the harm of the money laundering transaction (*i.e.*, the deposit) is not significantly greater than that of the underlying offense. Indeed, the Department of Justice issued a Blue Sheet to chapter 9-105.000 of the U.S. Attorney's Manual requiring consultation by a U.S. Attorney's Office with the Department before a receipt and deposit case may be prosecuted. Having chosen to prosecute Graves for spending (not merely depositing) dirty money, the government was required to show that the expenditures were conducted with an "intent to promote" SGC's fraudulent activity.

[5] The allegedly laundered funds paid for (1) parts, paints, and materials; (2) the floor plan, cars that had been traded in, floor plan interest, and a charge back; (3) software support and office supplies; (4) conversions; (5) used cars; (6) disposal of waste oil and used oil filters; (7) t-shirts, caps, coffee mugs; (8) yearbook advertisements; (9) a computer system lease; (10) advertising representation; (11) Graves's travel expenses; (12) extended warranties on used automobiles; (13) glass replacement; (14) automobile association membership fees; (15) photocopier supplies; and (16) a health plan.

Graves also points to *United States v. Jackson*, 935 F.2d 832 (7th Cir. 1991), in which the defendant, who was both a preacher and drug dealer, deposited drug proceeds into his church's checking account. From the church account, he wrote checks to pay for beepers, mobile phones, and rent; he also wrote some checks for cash. The defendant's drug runners used the beepers to communicate with each other, and the court therefore held that the beeper purchases were intended to promote the specified unlawful conduct. The checks for mobile phones, rent, and cash, however, did not promote the criminal activity and thus did not constitute money laundering. The court explained:

> The government did not prove that the cellular phones played the same role — or indeed any role — in Davis' drug operations as the beepers. Likewise the rental payments and the checks written to cash; certainly these expenditures maintained Davis' lifestyle, but more than this is needed to establish that they promoted his drug activities.

Id.

Graves argues that the expenditures charged in the money laundering counts of the indictment are analogous to the *Jackson* defendant's expenditures on mobile phones and rent: They were intended to support the dealership's legitimate business activities and evince no intent to promote fraud.

The government insists that the expenditures did promote fraud. Its theory, which the district court accepted, is that the transactions charged in the indictment promoted the ongoing and future criminal activity at SGC, despite the fact that they were expenditures on the basic operations of the car dealership, because the operation of the dealership was one grand scheme to defraud. In other words, any legitimate operating expense that permitted SGC to stay in business and maintain or increase its customer base would also be an expenditure intended to promote fraud, because it would ensure a steady supply of potential victims.

Despite the government's creative argument, we agree with Graves that there is insufficient evidence that the charged expenditures were financial transactions conducted "with the intent to promote the carrying on of specified unlawful activity." The problem with the government's position is that it ignores the *intent* aspect of the promotion element. Section 1956(a)(1)(A)(i) is not satisfied by a showing that a financial transaction involving the proceeds of specified unlawful activity merely promoted the carrying on of unlawful activity. The provision has a specific intent element: The government must show that the "dirty money" transaction was conducted *"with the intent* to promote the carrying on of specified unlawful activity.". . . .

This does not mean that there must always be direct evidence, such as a statement by the defendant, of an intent to promote specified unlawful activity. In many cases, the intent to promote criminal activity may be inferred from the particular type of transaction. For example, an intent to promote drug trafficking activities could be inferred from the *Jackson* defendant's purchase of beepers, because beepers were not necessary to the defendant's legitimate business operations and played an important role in his drug trafficking scheme.

In the case at hand, had the government produced evidence of, say, payments for postage for mailing fraudulent warranty claims, such payments might have provided evidence of an intent to promote fraud. Mere evidence of legitimate business expenditures that were necessary to support SGC's non-fraudulent operations, however, was not enough to establish an intent to promote fraud at SGC, even though the expenditures may in fact have promoted SGC's fraudulent activities by increasing the number of potential fraud victims.

We have previously stressed the importance of not turning the "money laundering statute into a 'money spending statute.'" Strictly adhering to the specific intent requirement of the promotion element of § 1956(a)(1)(A)(i) helps ensure that the money laundering statute will punish conduct that is really distinct from the underlying specified unlawful activity and will not simply provide overzealous prosecutors with a means of imposing additional criminal liability any time a defendant makes benign expenditures with funds derived from unlawful acts.

In a separate money laundering statute, 18 U.S.C. § 1957(a), Congress did criminalize the mere spending of "criminally derived property that is of a value greater than $10,000" with knowledge of the unlawful source. The fact that Congress established a $10,000 per transaction threshold for convictions for simply spending dirty money further supports our decision to read § 1956(a)(1)(A)(i) to require either direct proof that the charged transaction was intended to promote specified unlawful activity or proof of a type of transaction (such as the *Jackson* defendant's purchase of beepers) that, on its face, indicates an intent to promote such activity.

Absent such proof, § 1956(a)(1)(A)(i) does not permit conviction of a defendant who, like Graves, deposits proceeds of some relatively minor fraudulent transactions into the operating account of an otherwise legitimate business enterprise and then writes checks out of that account for general business purposes. Accordingly, we reverse Graves's money laundering convictions.

Notes and Questions

1. *Deposits and expenditures.* What were the transactions upon which the government based its case? Would a case built on deposits of funds derived from the fraud have succeeded? If so, why did the government decline to bring such a case?

2. *Sections 1956 and 1957.* What is the difference between a promotion case under § 1956 and a case under § 1957? Could the government have used § 1957 to prosecute the defendant in this case? Why or why not?

Problems

13-3. Rick Port was issued a MasterCard by Maryland National Bank ("MNB"). Marla Oaks impersonated Port in notifying MNB that Port's address had changed to a mailbox rented by Oaks in Baltimore, Maryland. MNB later mailed three convenience checks to Oaks's mailbox, one of which later was found at Oaks's residence in a town 30 miles from Baltimore.

One of the checks was used partially to pay off the balance of another credit card owned by Oaks, a Union Bank Visa card. The address for the Visa had also been changed by Oaks, and a requested replacement card had been sent to Oaks's mailbox. After the credit balance was partially paid by the MNB check, the Visa was used to purchase one computer at each of two different stores in Baltimore.

The computers were found in Oaks's residence and were for her personal use.

Based upon the purchase of the two computers. Oaks was convicted of bank fraud and of both concealment and promotion money laundering. Oaks appeals her money laundering convictions. How should the court rule? Why?

13-4. For a period of four years, the defendants defrauded banks of millions of dollars through real estate and mortgage transactions involving properties. The scheme consisted of a series of fraudulently executed land "flips:" the defendants bought cheap properties with fake identities and then sold them to each other for artificially high prices, using bank loans to fund the purchases. The defendants fabricated the identities of the buyers, providing the straw buyers with false employment histories, financial records, and addresses. At the defendants' behest, appraisers lied about the properties' values, inflating the listing prices.

The schemers submitted the fraudulent loan applications to banks, which relied on them in making lending decisions. On the issuance of loan checks to the straw buyers, the defendants endorsed the checks with the straw buyers' names, deposited the checks into their personal bank accounts, and then distributed the fraud proceeds by writing checks drawn on their accounts to the various participants in the scheme. The non-existent buyers failed to make mortgage payments, which eventually led the banks to foreclose.

Aden served as the real-estate broker and orchestrated many facets of the scheme. Aden owned Protech, a company which was listed as the employer of the straw buyers, and signed a variety of loan documents in the straw buyers' names. Bowen, a co-owner and officer of Protech, played various roles, helping to fabricate the straw buyers' financial and employment records and facilitating the purchase and sale of properties.

Bowen and Aden were convicted of bank fraud and of concealment and promotion money laundering based on the deposits of the straw buyers' checks, and appeal the money laundering convictions. How should the court rule? Why?

13-5. A mother and her 17-year-old son went to the Quick Auto Dealership one afternoon to buy a car for the son. After they took a car for a test drive, the mother asked the salesperson if she could pay for the car with cash. He agreed. The son contributed $6,000 that he had saved from "odd jobs," and his mother gave another $5,000 to complete the purchase. The son's "odd jobs" consisted of selling DVDs that he copied on his computer to his friends at the local high school. Surprised by how much money he had saved, the mother asked the son where the money came from. Before he could answer she said, "I don't want to know, let's just get the car." She thought that he was involved in drug activities with his friends.

The total price for the car was $11,000. The mother made an initial cash deposit of $1,500. Two days later, the mother and son returned to get the car and the son brought his $6,000 in cash for the purchase. The mother asked the dealer to title the car in her name "for insurance purposes." The mother added another $3,500 in cash. The son used the car to make timely deliveries of his counterfeit DVDs, and he began to expand his business to the high school in the neighboring county.

a. *You are the Assistant U.S. Attorney in charge of the investigation, and these facts have been presented to you. Would you ask a grand jury to return criminal charges in this case against the son and the mother? If so, based on what theory or theories?*

b. *You are private counsel and you represent the Quick Auto Dealership. What obligations does the dealership have, if any, in connection with this transaction?*

[3] Criminally-derived property

In a money laundering case, the government must prove that the financial or monetary transaction actually involved criminally derived property. This requirement raises several distinct issues. First, in a case involving "proceeds" of unlawful activity, does that term encompass all receipts from the activity, or only net profits? Second, in an ongoing scheme, at what point in time can property be considered criminally derived? Third, how does a fact-finder identify criminally-derived property when that property has been mixed together — "comingled" — with non criminally-derived property? This section considers each of these issues.

[a] Proceeds

NOTE ON THE DEFINITION OF "PROCEEDS"

Federal circuit courts split over whether the term "proceeds" in the money laundering statutes means gross proceeds or net profits. *Compare, e.g., United States v. Iacaboni*, 363 F.3d 1 (1st Cir. 2004) ("proceeds" means gross income) *with United States v. Scialabba*, 282 F.3d 475 (7th Cir. 2002) ("proceeds" means net profits).

In *United States v. Santos*, 128 S. Ct. 2020 (2008), the U.S. Supreme Court attempted to resolve this issue. In *Santos*, the defendant was convicted of money laundering in connection with an illegal lottery scheme. In a fractured decision, the four-member plurality found that the term "proceeds" is ambiguous. Because the rule of lenity applies when interpreting the term, it must be read in favor of the defendant to mean net profits. In addition, the plurality opinion based its conclusion on the "merger" issue that arises under the broader definition of proceeds:

> If 'proceeds' meant 'receipts,' nearly every violation of the illegal-lottery statute would also be a violation of the money-laundering statute, because paying a winning bettor is a transaction involving receipts that the defendant intends to promote the carrying on of the lottery. Since few lotteries, if any, will not pay their winners, the statute criminalizing illegal lotteries, 18 U.S.C. § 1955, would 'merge' with the money-laundering statute. Congress evidently decided that lottery operators ordinarily deserve up to 5 years of imprisonment, § 1955(a), but as a result of merger they would face an additional 20 years, § 1956(a)(1). Prosecutors, of course, would acquire the discretion to charge the lesser lottery offense, the greater money-laundering offense, or both — which would predictably be used to induce a plea bargain to the lesser charge.

> The merger problem is not limited to lottery operators. For a host of predicate crimes, merger would depend on the manner and timing of payment for the expenses associated with the commission of the crime. Few crimes are entirely free of cost, and costs are not always paid in advance. Anyone who pays for the costs of a crime with its proceeds — for example, the felon who uses the stolen money to pay for the rented getaway car — would violate the money-laundering statute. And any wealth-acquiring

crime with multiple participants would become money-laundering when the initial recipient of the wealth gives his confederates their shares. . . .

The Government suggests no explanation for why Congress would have wanted a transaction that is a normal part of a crime it had duly considered and appropriately punished elsewhere in the Criminal Code to radically increase the sentence for that crime. Interpreting 'proceeds' to mean 'profits' eliminates the merger problem. Transactions that normally occur during the course of running a lottery are not identifiable uses of profits and thus do not violate the money-laundering statute. More generally, a criminal who enters into a transaction paying the expenses of his illegal activity cannot possibly violate the money-laundering statute, because by definition profits consist of what remains after expenses are paid. Defraying an activity's costs with its receipts simply will not be covered.

Id. at 2026–27.

Concurring in the judgment, Justice Stevens wrote that "the legislative history of § 1956 makes it clear that Congress intended the term 'proceeds' to include gross revenues from the sale of contraband and the operation of organized crime syndicates involving such sales. But that history sheds no light on how to identify the proceeds of many other types of specified unlawful activities. . . . " Thus, according to Justice Stevens, whether "proceeds" means receipts or profits depends upon the legislative history of the specified unlawful activity. *Id.* at 2037 (Stevens, J., concurring in the judgment).

Writing for a four-member dissent, Justice Alito concluded that the term "proceeds" in state and federal money laundering statutes consistently refers to gross receipts. He stated:

There is a very good reason for this uniform pattern of usage. Money laundering provisions serve two chief ends. First, they provide deterrence by preventing drug traffickers and other criminals who amass large quantities of cash from using these funds "to support a luxurious lifestyle" or otherwise to enjoy the fruits of their crimes. Second, they inhibit the growth of criminal enterprises by preventing the use of dirty money to promote the enterprise's growth.

Both of these objectives are frustrated if a money laundering statute is limited to profits. Dirty money may be used to support "a luxurious lifestyle" and to grow an illegal enterprise whenever the enterprise possesses large amounts of illegally obtained cash. And illegal enterprises may acquire such cash while engaging in unlawful activity that is unprofitable.

Id. at 2038 (Alito, J., dissenting). The dissent also concluded that the plurality approach would create severe problems of proof both as to "profits" and the defendant's knowledge of such profits. Finally, the dissent noted that "the so-called merger problem is fundamentally a sentencing problem, and the proper remedy is a sentencing remedy. . . . " *Id.* at 2044.

NOTES AND QUESTIONS

1. *Difficulties of proof.*

a. *Profits*. How difficult would be it for the government to prove that the financial transaction involved the proceeds of criminal activity under the plurality's definition of "proceeds?" Is the dissent correct that this proof would pose a formidable barrier in money laundering prosecutions? Why or why not?

b. *Knowledge*. In a money laundering case, the government must prove that the defendant knew the "proceeds" were generated by unlawful activity. Would the plurality approach make this element more difficult to prove? Why or why not?

2. *The Congressional response*. After *Santos* was decided, Congress enacted the Fraud Enforcement and Enhancement Act of 2009 (FERA). Among other provisions, FERA amends the money laundering statutes and provides that "the term 'proceeds' means any property derived from or obtained or retained, directly or indirectly, through some form of unlawful activity, including the gross receipts of such activity." The bill also includes a provision entitled "Sense of the Congress and Report Concerning Required Approval for Merger Cases:"

> It is the sense of the Congress that no prosecution of an offense under section 1956 or 1957 of title 18, United States Code, should be undertaken in combination with the prosecution of any other offense, without prior approval of the Attorney General, the Deputy Attorney General, the Assistant Attorney General in charge of the Criminal Division, a Deputy Assistant Attorney General in the Criminal Division, or the relevant United States Attorney, if the conduct to be charged as "specified unlawful activity" in connection with the offense under section 1956 or 1957 is so closely connected with the conduct to be charged as the other offense that there is no clear delineation between the two offenses.

The bill also requires that the DOJ provide annual reports to Congress for four years as to whether the DOJ is adhering to the provisions of the Sense of the Congress statement.

Is FERA's amendment to the money laundering statutes an appropriate and effective responses to *Santos*? Does the Sense of the Congress provision adequately address the plurality's "merger" concerns? Why or why not?

[b]   Timing

NOTE ON TIMING

Under § 1956(a)(1), the financial transaction must involve the proceeds of specified unlawful activity. Under § 1957, the government must show that the defendant engaged in a "monetary transaction in criminally derived property." 18 U.S.C. § 1957(a). The term "criminally derived property" is defined as "any property constituting, or derived from, proceeds obtained from a criminal offense." 18 U.S.C. § 1957(f)(2). At what point can funds be considered to be the product of the unlawful activity?

This issue arose in *United States v. Kennedy*, 64 F.3d 1465 (10th Cir. 1995). The defendant used mail and wires to fraudulently obtain funds that he deposited into his bank account as part of a Ponzi scheme. Based on the deposits, he was convicted of promotion money laundering under 18 U.S.C. § 1956(a)(1)(A)(i). On appeal, he argued that the funds were not "proceeds" at the time of the deposits, and did not become proceeds until he used them in transactions subsequent to the deposits. The court disagreed, finding that the crimes of mail and wire fraud were complete upon the use of mail and wires, and that the funds therefore were proceeds of the fraud when the defendant received them.

In reaching that conclusion, the court distinguished a case brought under § 1957, *United States v. Johnson*, 971 F.2d 562 (10th Cir. 1992). In *Johnson*, the defendant defrauded investors, who wired money to his bank account. The defendant was convicted under § 1957 based upon these wire transfers. Reversing the conviction, the court of appeals held that "both the plain language of § 1957 and the legislative history behind it suggest that Congress targeted only those transactions occurring after proceeds have been obtained from the underlying unlawful activity." *Id.* at 568. The wiring of the money was itself the wire fraud, which was not complete until the funds were deposited into the defendant's account. Therefore, at the time of the wiring, the funds were not "criminally derived property." *Accord United States v. Piervinanzi*, 23 F.3d 670 (2d Cir. 1994).

Why was the outcome in *Kennedy* different from that in *Johnson*? As the *Kennedy* court explained:

> [T]he only use of the wires alleged in *Johnson* to prove the predicate wire fraud crimes were the very wire transfers that allegedly involved "criminally derived property" under the money laundering statute. In Kennedy's case, in contrast, the government alleged many *prior* mailings to prove the predicate mail fraud crimes, which occurred before the monetary transactions that formed the basis of his money laundering counts. Thus, unlike in *Johnson*, the illegal mailings in this case involved discrete, earlier mailings by Kennedy, rather than the receipt of funds by Kennedy from his victims. It was the subsequent and distinct transfers of funds that were alleged as the separate transactions involving "proceeds of specified unlawful activity" which constituted the alleged money laundering under § 1956.
>
> This factual difference is important because Congress clearly intended the money laundering statutes to punish new conduct that occurs after the completion of certain criminal activity, rather than simply to create an additional punishment for that criminal activity. The "completion" of both wire and mail fraud occurs when any wiring or mailing is used in execution of a scheme; there is no requirement that the scheme actually defraud a victim into investing money for the crime to be complete. Thus, because the money deposits in Kennedy's case occurred after other mailings had already completed the predicate mail fraud crime, those transfers properly could be construed as new transactions involving the proceeds of mail fraud. In contrast, because the specific wire fraud violations alleged in *Johnson* were not complete until the wires were used to transfer the funds, those transfers could not be construed as new transactions to support a money laundering offense. Accordingly, we reject Kennedy's contention that his money laundering convictions must be set aside for failure to allege the "proceeds" element of those crimes.

Is this distinction persuasive? Why or why not?

[c]   Commingling

Under § 1956, the government must prove that the financial transaction involved the "proceeds" of the specified unlawful activity. Under § 1957, the government must prove that the monetary transaction was "derived" from the unlawful activity. How does the government meet its burden of proof when "clean" money has been mixed or "commingled" with "dirty" money? Under § 1956, courts generally hold that, where clean and dirty money have been commingled, the government need not prove that the financial transaction specifically derived from the dirty money. Courts are split on this issue, however, under § 1957. As you read the next case, consider which approach should be followed on this issue under § 1957.

UNITED STATES v. RUTGARD
116 F.3d 1270 (9th Cir. 1997)

NOONAN, CIRCUIT JUDGE.

Jeffrey Jay Rutgard appeals his conviction of numerous counts of mail fraud on, and false claims to, Medicare, of counts of mail fraud on other insurers, and of transactions in money derived from the frauds. He appeals as well a judgment of forfeiture. . . .

This case . . . has required this court to determine whether proof of particular examples of fraud in billing insurers establishes that the [defendant's medical] practice is, as a whole, a scheme to defraud. It has required us to decide whether 18 U.S.C § 1957, the statute forbidding certain bank transfers, is violated if the transfers involve commingled criminal and innocent funds. . . .

Dr. Rutgard, the defendant, was born in Chicago, Illinois, in 1951. His father was a physician. He attended the College of Medicine of the University of Illinois. He also enrolled in the university's graduate school where he was a James Scholar. On the basis of his proficiency in these schools he skipped internship and moved directly to a three-year residency in ophthalmology at the Medical School of the University of Iowa. In 1981 he came from this residency to practice in San Diego, California. . . .

In 1982, he secured his own medical practice. . . . His practice flourished. He kept an extraordinary schedule of working 61/2 days per week, 16 hours a day, with trips to medical meetings but without vacations. He also made a great deal of money. From 1988 through May, 1992 he received from Medicare (80% of his practice) over $151/2 million. . . .

[At trial, the government argued that the defendant defrauded Medicare by (a) making false diagnoses, (b) performing unnecessary procedures, and (c) falsely describing the procedures that he performed. The jury found Rutgard guilty of 132 counts of fraud. The Ninth Circuit reversed 23 of the 132 counts of fraud on the grounds of insufficient evidence, and found sufficient evidence to support the remaining counts.]

[The court then turned to the issue whether there was sufficient evidence to show that Rutgard's entire medical practice was a fraud. The government attempted to prove this theory to support its argument that all the monetary transactions at issue were illegally-derived. Because a large part of Rutgard's practice did not involve defrauding insurers, the court rejected the government's argument that the entire medical practice was a fraud. The court then turned its attention to the specific charges under § 1957.]

*   *   *

The Monetary Transactions Count. In May, 1992, [defendant's wife] Linda, at his direction, made two wire transfers to the National Westminster Bank on the Isle of Man, one of $5,629,220.74 on May 5 and one of $1,935,220.48 on May 6. The transfers were made from the Rutgard Family Trust, whose accounts were at the Imperial Trust Company in San Diego.

The government's accounting expert noted $15.8 million paid by Medicare to Rutgard between the beginning of 1988 and April, 1992. He testified that Rutgard deposited $3,754,056 derived from these entities into the family trust account during this period and deposited $1.9 million in municipal bonds so that a total of $5,654,056 entered this account from October 29, 1990, when Rutgard opened the account with a personal check for $560,000, to May, 1992. He testified that the balance of the account came from municipal bonds delivered to the trust account at unspecified times. On appeal the government argues that the jury could take into account the first year, 1987, when insurance fraud began, and come to the conclusion that the entire amount transferred by wire transfers on May 5 and 6 was the proceeds of insurance fraud.

To prove this contention the government advanced the theory that all of Rutgard's practice was a fraud. If the government had succeeded in this proof, it would have properly convicted him of the monetary transaction counts. But we have just determined that the government's proof was deficient. The government, as we have also held, established Rutgard's guilt of particular counts of fraud. The proceeds of that fraud come to over $46,000. Can the convictions under § 1957 be sustained on the theory that at least $20,000 of fruits of fraud were incorporated in the wire transfers of May 6 and 7? To answer that question requires a consideration of the terms and purpose of § 1957 and a close look at the companion statute, § 1956.

These statutes govern monetary transactions in criminally derived property. The standard money laundering statute is 18 U.S.C. § 1956. The other statute, the one under which Rutgard was convicted, is 18 U.S.C. § 1957. In construing § 1956, we referred to § 1957 as "a companion money laundering statute," *United States v. Garcia*, 37 F.3d 1359, 1365 (9th Cir. 1994), without having occasion to mark the differences between the two. We now have occasion to mark those differences.

Section 1956, alone at issue in *Garcia*, bears the title "Laundering of monetary instruments." It punishes by imprisonment of up to 20 years and a fine a defendant who:

> knowing that the property involved in a financial transaction represents the proceeds of some form of unlawful activity, conducts or attempts to conduct such a financial transaction which in fact involves the proceeds of specified unlawful activity —

> (A) (i) with the intent to promote the carrying on of specified unlawful activity; or

> (ii) with intent to engage in conduct constituting a violation of section 7201 or 7206 of the Internal Revenue Code of 1986; or

> (B) knowing that the transaction is designed in whole or in part —

> (i) to conceal or disguise the nature, the location, the source, the ownership, or the control of the proceeds of specified unlawful activity; or

> (ii) to avoid a transaction reporting requirement under State or Federal law.

18 U.S.C. § 1956(a)(1). For present purposes, five elements of § 1956 differentiate it from § 1957, the statute at issue here — its title, its requirement of intent, its broad reference to "the property involved," its satisfaction by a transaction that "in part" accomplishes the design, and its requirement that the intent be to commit another crime or to hide the fruits of a crime already committed.

Section 1957 has a different heading: "Engaging in monetary transactions in property derived from specified unlawful activity." It punishes by up to ten years' imprisonment and a fine anyone who:

> knowingly engages or attempts to engage in a monetary transaction in criminally derived property that is of a value greater than $10,000 and is derived from specified unlawful activity.

18 U.S.C. § 1957(a). The description of the crime does not speak to the attempt to cleanse dirty money by putting it in a clean form and so disguising it. This statute applies to the most open, above-board transaction. *See* 18 U.S.C. § 1957(f)(1) (broadly defining "monetary transaction"). The intent to commit a crime or the design of concealing criminal fruits is eliminated. These differences make violation of § 1957 easier to prove. But also eliminated are references to "the property involved" and the satisfaction of the statute by a design that "in part" accomplishes the intended result. These differences indicate that proof of violation of § 1957 may be more difficult.

Section 1957 could apply to any transaction by a criminal with his bank. Two years after its enactment an amendment was necessary to provide that the term "monetary transaction" does not include "any transaction necessary to preserve a person's right to representation as guaranteed by the sixth amendment to the Constitution." Pub. L. 100-690, § 6182, 102 Stat. 4181, 4354 (1988). Without the amendment a drug dealer's check to his lawyer might have constituted a new federal felony.

Section 1957 was enacted as a tool in the war against drugs. It is a powerful tool because it makes any dealing with a bank potentially a trap for the drug dealer or any other defendant who has a hoard of criminal cash derived from the specified crimes. If he makes a "deposit, withdrawal, transfer or exchange" with this cash, he commits the crime; he's forced to commit another felony if he wants to use a bank. This draconian law, so powerful by its elimination of criminal intent, freezes the proceeds of specific crimes out of the banking system. As long as the underlying crime has been completed and the defendant "possesses" the funds at the time of deposit, the proceeds cannot enter the banking system without a new crime being committed. A type of regulatory crime has been created where criminal intent is not an element. *See Morissette v. United States*, 342 U.S. 246, 252–56 (1952). Such a powerful instrument of criminal justice should not be expanded by judicial invention or ingenuity. We "should not enlarge the reach of enacted crimes by constituting them from anything less than the incriminating components contemplated by the words used in the statute." *Id.* at 263.

For these reasons we do not find helpful in interpreting § 1957 the cases applying § 1956, which speaks of design "in whole or in part" and of "a financial transaction involving property." Other circuits, however, have used the § 1956 precedents to eliminate any tracing of funds in a § 1957 case. *See United States v. Moore*, 27 F.3d 969, 976–77 (4th Cir. 1994); *United States v. Johnson*, 971 F.2d 562 (10th Cir. 1992). They have reasoned that otherwise § 1957 could be defeated by a criminal mingling innocently-obtained funds with his ill-gotten moneys.

This reasoning rests on the fungibility of money in a bank. That fungibility, destroying the specific identity of any particular funds, makes the commingling of innocent funds with criminal funds an obvious way to hide the criminal funds. If § 1956 required tracing of specific funds, it could be wholly frustrated by commingling. For that reason, the statute not only proscribes any transaction whose purpose is to hide criminal funds but reaches any funds "involved" in the transaction. Neither the same reasoning nor the same language is present in § 1957, the statute here applied.

The monetary transaction statute cannot be made wholly ineffective by commingling. To prevail, the government need show only a single $10,000 deposit of criminally-derived proceeds. Any innocent money already in the account, or later deposited, cannot wipe out the crime committed by the deposit of criminally-derived proceeds. Commingling with innocent funds can defeat application of the statute to a withdrawal of less than the total funds in the account, but ordinarily that fact presents no problem to the government which, if it has proof of a deposit of $10,000 of criminally-derived funds, can succeed by charging the deposit as the crime; or the government may prevail by showing that all the funds in the account are the proceeds of crime. Commingling will frustrate the statute if criminal deposits have been kept under $10,000. But that is the way the statute is written, to catch only large transfers. Moreover, if the criminal intent was to hide criminal proceeds, as would presumably be the case any time criminally derived cash was deposited with innocently derived funds to hide its identity, § 1956 can kick in and the depositor of amounts under $10,000 will be guilty of a § 1956 crime.

The government did not take its possible course of charging Rutgard with deposits of over $10,000 of fraudulent proceeds. The government had the means of doing so because its accounting expert identified the large deposits Rutgard made. But as Rutgard was neither charged nor convicted of deposits in violation of § 1957, we cannot uphold his convictions on that basis.

Rutgard's convictions may be upheld if he transferred out of the account all the funds that were in it or if there was a rule or presumption that, once criminally-derived funds were deposited, any transfer from the account would be presumed to involve them for the purpose of applying § 1957. Rutgard did not transfer all the funds in the family trust account, however. The government showed that the account held $8.5 million on April 2, 1992 and $13,901 on July 2, 1992, the dates of the quarterly bank statements. But so far as evidence at trial goes, more than $46,000 remained in the account after the May 5 and 6 transfers. These transfers therefore did not necessarily transfer the $46,000 of fraudulent proceeds.

The alternative way of sustaining the convictions depends on a presumption, which the Fourth Circuit created in *Moore*, 27 F.3d at 976–77, but which we decline to create. The statute does not create a presumption that any transfer of cash in an account tainted by the presence of a small amount of fraudulent proceeds must be a transfer of these proceeds. Unlike § 1956, § 1957 does not cover any funds "involved." To create such a presumption in order to sustain a conviction under § 1957 would be to multiply many times the power of that draconian law. It would be an essay in judicial lawmaking, not an application of the statute. As the government did not prove that any fraudulently-derived proceeds left the account on May 5 or May 6, 1992, the monetary transfer counts, Counts 216 and 217, were not proved beyond a reasonable doubt.

* * *

NOTES AND QUESTIONS

1. *The circuit split.* A number of circuits have declined to require the government to prove that financial transactions under § 1957 involved illegally-derived funds. In *United States v. Johnson*, 971 F.2d 562 (10th Cir. 1992), for example, the defendant had commingled dirty and clean money in his bank account. Of the $5.5 million he had deposited into his account, only about half could be traced to the illegal activity. The defendant was charged under § 1957 based upon a $1.8 million withdrawal from the account, all of which was not necessarily from dirty money. The Tenth Circuit affirmed the conviction, holding that to require the government to trace the transaction to dirty money would defeat the purpose of § 1957. *Id.* at 570.

In rejecting the *Johnson* approach, the court in *Rutgard* relied heavily upon the differences between § 1956 and § 1957. Is the court's reasoning persuasive? Was the court's description of § 1957 as "draconian" fair? Why or why not?

2. *The government's theory.* The court in *Rutgard* also stated that the government used the wrong money laundering theory in this case. Would other, viable theories of money laundering have been available to the government in this case?

PROBLEM

13-6. The following evidence was adduced at Harris's trial for money laundering:

Three years ago, Harris offered to lend $160,000 to his friends Carey and Bourne, to buy a parcel of land. Carey and Bourne accepted Harris's offer and, after executing a mortgage to secure the loan, Harris gave them the loan proceeds in cash. There was testimony that, when later discussing the loan with a friend, Harris stated that the reason he wanted to lend the money was to "get some of his money more legal." Over the next several years, Harris deposited 46 repayment checks from Carey and Bourne into Harris's personal bank account.

When Carey and Bourne asked Harris where he got the money for the loans, Harris told them that he got most of it from an inheritance from his father. But there was evidence that Harris's father had intentionally omitted him from his will and that Harris did not receive anything from his father's estate. There is also evidence that Harris engaged in narcotics trafficking activities in the two months preceding the loan, generating approximately $180,000 in gross receipts that he placed in his personal bank account. Harris paid $50,000 cash for the narcotics. Harris used three dealers, to whom he paid 30% of the sale price in cash, to sell the narcotics. The money that Harris lent out was obtained from Harris's personal bank account. Immediately before Harris made the loan, his account had a balance of approximately $700,000, which consisted of the narcotics trafficking gross proceeds and income that Harris had legitimately earned over the years as a real-estate developer.

Harris was convicted of conspiracy to distribute narcotics and of 46 counts of concealment money laundering under § 1956(a)(1)(B)(i) based upon the deposits of the loan repayment checks.

On appeal, Harris argues that there was insufficient evidence that (a) he acted with knowledge of a design to conceal, and (b) the checks represented "proceeds" of specified unlawful activity. How should the court rule? Why?

[D]   THE USA PATRIOT ACT

The USA PATRIOT Act of 2001, Pub. L. No. 107-56, strengthened the government's ability to combat terrorism in several important ways, including the implementation of "more stringent anti-money laundering statutes and regulations." Michael Shapiro, *The USA PATRIOT ACT and Money Laundering*, 123 Banking L.J. 629, 629 (July/Aug. 2006). Title III of the PATRIOT Act, entitled the International Money Laundering Abatement and Anti-Terrorist Financing Act of 2001, amended the main laws used to combat money laundering: the Bank Secrecy Act (BSA) of 1970 and the Money Laundering Control Act of 1986 (codified as 18 U.S.C. § 1956 and 18 U.S.C. § 1957). *Id.* at 630.

Section 1956 was amended in the PATRIOT Act to include foreign corruption offenses, Pub. L. No. 107-56, § 315, long-arm jurisdiction over foreign money launderers, § 317, and offenses for laundering money through a foreign bank, § 318. In addition, the USA PATRIOT Improvement and Reauthorization Act of 2005 ("PATRIOT II"), Pub. L. No. 109-177, added the following to § 1956(a)(1): "For purposes of this paragraph, a financial transaction shall be considered to be one involving the proceeds of specified unlawful activity if it is part of a set of parallel or dependent transactions, any one of which involves the proceeds of specified unlawful activity, and all of which are part of a single plan or arrangement." Pub. L. No. 109-177, § 405.

The BSA's recordkeeping and reporting requirements, including Currency Transaction Reports (CTRs) and Suspicious Activity Reports (SARs), already put domestic banks at the forefront of anti-money laundering enforcement. Shapiro, 123 Banking L.J. at 631. The PATRIOT Act expanded those requirements by mandating that each bank, at the minimum, designate a compliance officer, develop internal anti-money laundering controls, provide periodic training, and go through independent audits of their controls. Pub. L. No. 107-56, § 352. The PATRIOT Act does allow individual banks some flexibility to adjust their anti-money laundering programs depending on the size, location, and overall nature of the bank's business. § 311. However, all banks must have a Customer Identification Program and periodically check their customer lists with the government's lists of known or suspected terrorists, as well as other Treasury Department lists. Shapiro, 123 Banking L.J. at 633. With increased responsibilities under the PATRIOT Act, banks now shoulder even more of the burden for tracking money laundering activities than in the past:

> With the events of 9/11 the personification of the money launderer changed from drug dealer to terrorist. Despite enormous additional costs necessitated by myriad new laws and regulations, U.S. banks have, for the most part, risen to the additional burdens placed on them. With the new and complex rules comes the need for better and increased compliance, supervision and advice, both internal and external if banks are to navigate successfully the legal and regulatory shoals and shallows created post-9/11.

Id. at 635–636. In addition, the National Commission on Terrorist Attacks (known as the "9/11 Commission") issued a report that focuses on the close connection between international terrorism and money laundering. Specifically, the Commission addressed the use of laundered money to finance international terrorist efforts. For a discussion of the Commission's findings, see Paul Fagyal, Comment, *The Anti-Money Laundering Provisions of the Patriot Act: Should They Be Allowed to Sunset?*, 50 St. Louis U.L.J. 1361 (2006).

[E]　ATTORNEY-CLIENT ISSUES

[1]　Cash Transaction Reporting by Attorneys

Although the criminal defense bar lobbied for an exemption to the currency transaction reporting requirements imposed on trades and businesses, Congress did not exempt attorneys from those requirements. Because attorneys are engaged in a trade or business as that term is contemplated by 26 U.S.C. § 6050I, they must complete a Form 8300 when accepting cash from their clients and prospective clients. Virtually any exchange of money between a client and attorney constitutes a financial transaction and is subject to the reporting requirements if it exceeds $10,000.

For the criminal defense bar, this law has obvious and serious implications. First, the transaction may subject the attorney to money laundering liability if the money is derived from specified unlawful activity. Second, as discussed above, there are criminal penalties for failing to file a Form 8300, for filing a false Form 8300, or for structuring transactions to avoid filing the form. Finally, the reporting requirements have the potential to affect the attorney-client relationship in profound ways. *See generally* Ellen Podgor, *Form 8300: The Demise of Law as a Profession*, Geo. J. Legal Ethics 485 (1992).

[2]　Attorney-Client Privilege Issues

The general rule is that information relating to client identity and fees is not covered by the attorney-client privilege. That privilege is designed to protect confidential information that a client conveys to the attorney in order to obtain legal advice. In most cases, information about client identity and fees does not relate to legal advice. Courts therefore hold that identity and fee information does not fall within the privilege's purpose.

Courts have identified three specific circumstances, however, in which the attorney-client privilege may protect against the disclosure of client fee and identity information. This may occur where the disclosure would:

1.　Implicate the client in the very matter for which the client retained counsel (the "legal advice" exception);

2. Incriminate the client by providing the last piece of evidence needed to convict the client (the "last linkage" exception); or

3. Reveal the nature of a confidential client-attorney communication (the "confidential communication" exception).

The "legal advice" exception is the broadest exception, and the one most favorable to defendants and potential defendants. The last two exceptions apply in relatively few circumstances. Also, these exceptions sometimes overlap and, as seen in the case and notes below, are not always clearly defined.

*   *   *

In the next case, the government and a law firm engaged in what has become an all-too-common battle over the disclosure of client information. The government issued a subpoena to the law firm and claimed that the subpoena really was directed at obtaining information from the law firm about the law firm — a claim the court labeled as a pretext for gaining information about the firm's client. Because the government did not follow the rules for subpoenaing information from the firm's client, this characterization was critical to the outcome of the case on appeal. As you read the case, focus upon the competing policy concerns underlying the ongoing battle between the government and the criminal defense bar.

UNITED STATES v. GERTNER
873 F. Supp. 729 (W.D. Mass. 1995), *aff'd on other grounds*, 65 F.3d 963 (1st Cir. 1995)

BRODY, DISTRICT JUDGE.

This case presents an issue of first impression in this Circuit, namely, whether the Internal Revenue Service may require an attorney to disclose the identity of a client from whom the attorney received more than $10,000 in cash without violating the client's constitutional rights, the attorney-client privilege, or the attorney's ethical duty to keep client secrets confidential. The Court concludes that, under the special circumstances presented in this case, the information demanded by the IRS is privileged and need not be disclosed.

In 1981, according to Congressional estimates, underreported income in the United States resulted in an estimated $55 billion in lost tax revenues. *United States v. Goldberger & Dubin, P.C.*, 935 F.2d 501, 505 (2d Cir. 1991). Congress also determined that an additional $9 billion in lost tax revenue resulted from unreported income connected with illegal activities. *Id.* In response, Congress enacted 26 U.S.C. § 6050I, which provided the Internal Revenue Service (IRS) with means to identify taxpayers with large cash incomes. Specifically, the legislation requires "any person . . . engaged in a trade or business" to report any cash transaction that exceeds $10,000. 26 U.S.C. § 6050I. The provision also requires the disclosure of information such as: the name, address, and tax identification number of the person from whom the cash was received; and the date and nature of the transaction. *Id.*

The disclosure required by § 6050I is made on a form prepared by the IRS known as "Form 8300." The IRS states, in the directions to Form 8300, that: "Often smugglers and drug dealers use large cash payments to launder money from illegal activities . . . [thus] compliance with the law provides valuable information that can stop those who evade taxes and those who profit from the drug trade and other illegal activities." Samuel J. Rabin, Jr., *A Survey of the Statute and Caselaw Pertaining to 26 U.S.C. § 6050I*, 68 Fla. Bar J. 26 (1994) (quoting Form 8300).

Nancy Gertner and Jody Newman, attorneys at the law firm of Dwyer, Collora & Gertner, represent an unidentified client, referred to in this proceeding as John Doe. Doe was charged in a narcotics case "relating to years prior to 1991 and 1992" and "there are still pending criminal charges against ⌊him⌋."

From June 1991 to April 1992, Doe paid Gertner and Newman in four cash transactions of $25,000, $17,260, $15,000, and $25,000. Gertner and Newman reported the transactions to the IRS on four separate Forms 8300 dated June 25, 1991; August 5, 1991; November 14, 1991; and April 30, 1992; respectively. Respondents refused, however, to include any identifying information about Doe or the nature of the transaction. Respondents included with the forms, a statement explaining that "the information requested violates the attorney client privilege, conflicts with the broader ethical obligation of an attorney[,] . . . and violates the First, Fifth, and Sixth Amendment rights of attorneys and their clients."

A series of letters between the IRS and Respondents ensued. Respondents informed the IRS, among other things, that there were criminal charges pending against Doe and that Respondents were currently representing him in those proceedings. Nevertheless, the IRS issued summonses demanding that Respondents appear on February 22 and 24, 1993 accompanied by certain records and other information. In part, the IRS sought the complete name, address, business or occupation, social security or taxpayer identification number, passport number, alien registration number and any other identifying data for the client involved in each of the transactions. Neither Respondent appeared as directed by the summonses.

On March 16, 1994, Respondents sought guidance from the Massachusetts Bar Association Committee on Professional Ethics. The Committee responded citing Disciplinary Rule 4–101 which provides that "a lawyer shall not knowingly . . . reveal a confidence or secret of his client" unless the client consents; the disclosure is permitted under the Disciplinary Rules; or the disclosure is "required by law or court order." The opinion concluded:

> Given your client's refusal to consent to disclosure, the Committee believes that, if you have any doubt about the lawfulness of Section 6050(I)'s disclosure obligations as they impinge on your obligations under DR 4–101, you should continue to resist disclosure of the client's identity, and require [the Government] to obtain a court order mandating disclosure.

(*Id.*) Both Respondents have continually refused to provide the information requested by the summonses.

The Government filed a Petition to Enforce the IRS Summonses in this Court on March 28, 1994. In support of its Petition, the Government provided the affidavit of Sophia Ameno, an Internal Revenue Agent. Ameno asserted that she was investigating "the compliance by the law firm with Section 6050I of the Code, and its potential liability under Section 6721 through 6723 of the Code." She also alleged that the information sought by the summonses was relevant and not already in the IRS's possession. Finally, she averred that the appropriate administrative procedures had been followed. This Court concluded that the Government, through the

Ameno affidavit, made the prima facie showing of good faith required by *United States v. Powell*, 379 U.S. 48, 57–58 (1964). Accordingly, the Court issued an Order directing Respondents to show cause why the summonses should not be enforced.

Subsequently, the Court granted a Motion on the part of the unidentified client, John Doe, to intervene in the proceeding. The matter has now been thoroughly briefed and argued, including *amici curiae* appearances by the Boston Bar Association, the Massachusetts Association of Criminal Defense Lawyers, and the Massachusetts Bar Association. . . .

Respondents and *amici* argue that § 6050I, when applied to attorneys, violates the First, Fifth, and Sixth Amendments of the United States Constitution. They also argue that the disclosures required by § 6050I are protected by the doctrine of attorney-client privilege and that compliance with § 6050I would violate their ethical obligations, pursuant to Massachusetts Disciplinary Rule 4–101, to keep client secrets confidential. Finally, they argue that the summonses are void and unenforceable because the Government failed to provide the procedural protections required for issuing a "John Doe" summons under § 7609 of the Code.

A. *Procedure Followed by Government*

The Court first addresses Respondents' argument that the Government failed to comply with the procedural requirements of § 7609(f) of the Internal Revenue Code. Section 7609 governs summonses served, not on the taxpayer personally, but rather on third-party recordkeepers, such as banks, accountants, brokers, and attorneys. A summons served on a third-party recordkeeper may or may not "identify the person with respect to whose liability the summons is issued." 26 U.S.C. § 7609(f). A summons that does not identify the taxpayer under investigation is referred to as a "John Doe" summons. Advance notice to the unnamed taxpayer, by the Government, is generally impossible in these situations. In order to protect the interests of the unnamed taxpayer, therefore, Congress requires prior judicial approval for the issuance of John Doe summonses. No such prior judicial approval was either sought or obtained in this case. . . .

The Government argues that it was not required to obtain prior approval because the summonses in this case were not John Doe summonses. Instead, the Government asserts that the summonses in this case identified the taxpayer under investigation — the law firm. Agent Ameno, in her Affidavit, alleged that her investigation was intended "to ascertain the correctness of Forms 8300" filed by Gertner and Newman, and to determine "the liability, if any, of the law firm for penalties imposed by Sections 6721 through 6723 of the Code." Respondents argue, however, that the Government's assertion, that the law firm is the subject of its investigation, is "clearly pretextual." Respondents contend that the omissions on the Forms 8300 they filed are apparent on their face and that the identity of the client is immaterial to the firm's tax liability. The Court agrees with Respondents. The claim by the Government, that it is investigating the law firm is simply not credible. . . . Accordingly, the Court concludes that the Government's contention that it was investigating the law firm is pretextual and that the summonses were, in fact, John Doe summonses. . . .

B. *Attorney-Client Privilege*

Respondents argue that the disclosures required by § 6050I violate the attorney-client privilege whenever applied to attorneys in general, or, in the alternative, at least when applied to the facts of this case.

The individual asserting the attorney-client privilege has the burden of proving the existence of the privilege. In an action involving questions of federal law, the federal common law of privilege applies.

"It is well recognized in every circuit, . . . that the identity of an attorney's client and the source of payment for legal fees are not normally protected by the attorney-client privilege." *In re Grand Jury Subpoenas (Anderson)*, 906 F.2d 1485, 1488 (10th Cir. 1990). The Court is in agreement with this general rule, and therefore holds that a blanket rule exempting attorneys from complying with § 6050I would be inappropriate.

Despite its rejection of a bright-line test, the Court must nevertheless consider the specific facts presented by this case because it is clear that the identity of a client and the source of legal fees are privileged in certain special circumstances. The *Anderson* court identified the "three major exceptions" to the general rule as "the legal advice exception, the last link exception, and the confidential communication exception." *Anderson*, 906 F.2d at 1488. The Court need consider only the first of these, the legal advice exception.

Several courts, including the First Circuit, have recognized the legal advice exception. Under this exception, a client's identity or fee arrangement may be privileged "where there is a strong probability that disclosure would implicate the client in the very criminal activity for which legal advice was sought." *Anderson*, 906 F.2d at 1488. The legal advice exception is obviously very narrow and strongly fact-driven. The leading case applying this exception is *Baird v. Koerner*, 279 F.2d 623 (9th Cir. 1960). In *Baird*, the Ninth Circuit held that an attorney was not required to disclose the identity of a client when that client consulted him regarding improperly paid taxes and the attorney subsequently forwarded an anonymous check to the IRS on the client's behalf.

The First Circuit also considered this exception in *United States v. Strahl*, 590 F.2d 10 (1st Cir. 1978). In that case, the Government charged *Strahl* with stealing Treasury notes and counterfeiting. At trial, the Government introduced the testimony of Strahl's former attorney, who testified that Strahl gave him a stolen treasury note in partial payment for legal services. The *Strahl* court concluded that the legal advice exception did not apply because "there is no indication, either in the briefs or the record, that appellant Strahl went to [his former attorney] for legal advice concerning his counterfeiting activities." *Id.* at 12.

In this case, John Doe "has been charged in a narcotics case" and "there are still pending criminal charges against [him]." Those charges prompted Doe to seek representation from Respondents. The Court is convinced that there is a "strong probability" that disclosure of a large unexplained cash income could certainly be incriminating evidence in the pending narcotics prosecution. Therefore, given the facts of this case, the information demanded by the Government is privileged under the legal advice exception as articulated by the First Circuit in *Strahl*. The Court emphasizes the narrow scope of this fact-based holding. The decision to find the disclosures required by § 6050I privileged must be made on a case-by-case basis.

The Court acknowledges that other courts have declined to hold that the disclosures required by § 6050I are privileged. *See United States v. Goldberger & Dubin, P.C.*, 935 F.2d 501, 505 (2d Cir. 1991); *United States v. Leventhal*, 961 F.2d 936, 940–41 (11th Cir. 1992); and *United States v. Ritchie*, 15 F.3d 592, 602 (6th Cir. 1994). Of these cases, a thorough analysis of this question can be found in the Second Circuit's decision in *United States v. Goldberger & Dubin, P.C.*, 935 F.2d 501, 505 (2d Cir. 1991). That court appears to have at least contemplated that the information required by § 6050I may be privileged under some circumstances. . . . [T]hat court suggested that a "direct linkage" between the disclosure and the incrimination of the client was required. This Court concludes that the disclosures required by the summonses in this case would provide such a "direct linkage." There is a strong probability that the disclosure would not only incriminate John Doe, but incriminate him in the very activity for which he sought legal advice. . . .

Determining that the information is privileged, however, does not end the inquiry. First, "[a] client, for whose benefit the attorney-client privilege exists, should not be permitted to claim the privilege, either directly or through his attorney, for the purpose of concealing his own ongoing or contemplated fraud." *Goldberger*, 935 F.2d at 506 (citations omitted). The Court does not find any evidence of an ongoing or contemplated fraud in this case. The fact that a large cash income may be incriminating on narcotics charges does not make that income an ongoing or contemplated fraud.

Next, a "privilege cannot stand in the face of countervailing law or strong public policy." *Goldberger*, 935 F.2d at 504 (citations omitted). The Second Circuit in *Goldberger* concluded that, even if the information were privileged, the privilege should not be applied because it "collides head on with a federal statute that implicitly precludes its application." *Id.* at 505. The *Goldberger* court reasoned that, because Congress did not exempt attorneys from the phrase "any person . . . engaged in a trade or business" in § 6050I, it intended the provision to override any applicable attorney-client privilege. *Id.* at 506.

This Court disagrees with the conclusion in *Goldberger*. As this Court has concluded above, the summonses in this case are "John Doe" summonses issued to a third-party recordkeeper, the law firm. Congress has specifically stated that, when attorneys are summoned to appear as third-party recordkeepers, they may raise the attorney-client privilege. *See* H.R. Rep. No. 658, 94th Cong., 2d Sess., at 666 (1976) ("where the summons is served on a person who is not the taxpayer (i.e., a third-party summons), the party summoned may challenge the summons for procedural defects . . . , on [the] ground[s] of the attorney-client privilege (where applicable) and on other grounds. . . . ").

The Court is also not persuaded that the application of the attorney-client privilege in this case would be contrary to public policy. Rather, there are competing public policy concerns, which in this instance, weigh in favor of applying the attorney-client privilege. First, the Court is mindful that this dilemma could have been avoided had Doe paid Respondents in some other manner. Unfortunately, he did not. Second, the Court recognizes that the IRS "has a legitimate interest in large or unusual financial transactions, especially those involving cash." *United States v. Ritchie*, 15 F.3d 592, 601 (6th Cir. 1994). Section 6050I may well be an important tool for the IRS to investigate cash transactions and to uncover tax evasion; and Congress undoubtedly has a legitimate interest in preventing revenue losses resulting from tax evasion. Third, some courts have further suggested that exempting attorneys from § 6050I's reporting requirements would "grant law firms a potential monopoly on money laundering simply because their services are personal and confidential." *Ritchie*, 15 F.3d at 601.

Notwithstanding these policy arguments, the Court is satisfied that the balance of policy concerns weigh in favor of applying the attorney-client privilege in this case. First, it is unlikely that applying the privilege in this case would give lawyers a "potential monopoly on money laundering." *Ritchie*, 15 F.3d at 601. Generally, lawyers would be required to report the identity of clients from whom they receive substantial cash payments. An attorney may only assert the attorney-client privilege when the IRS seeks disclosures regarding a client who is being repre- sented on currently pending criminal charges and the disclosures are likely to incriminate the client in that very proceeding.

Under these circumstances, the attorney-client relationship becomes more than just "personal and confidential." *Ritchie*, 15 F.3d at 601. More than just lost tax revenues or the method of paying one's attorney is at stake. The attorney-client relationship, during a pending criminal prosecution, implicates bedrock constitu- tional protections such as the right against self-incrimination and the right to be represented by counsel of one's choice. While the Court does not consider the constitutionality of § 6050I, these fundamental precepts must not be ignored when deciding how public policy impacts the application of the attorney-client privilege. Each factual scenario should be considered separately and the policy issues weighed by the Court on a case-by-case basis. Courts could require attorneys refusing to disclose information required by § 6050I to make an in camera showing that their clients are in fact the subject of pending charges which could be substantiated by the § 6050I disclosures. On balance, the Court is satisfied that, given the specific facts of this case, neither the plain language of § 6050I nor public policy weigh against the application of the attorney-client privilege. Accordingly, the Court finds that the disclosures requested by the IRS summonses are privileged. . . .

Notes and Questions

1. *The attorney-client privilege.* As noted above, there are three exceptions to the general rule that client fee and identity information is not protected by the attorney-client privilege. Which of these exceptions did the court adopt in *Gertner*? *Gertner* is the rare case in which the court found the information to be protected; in most cases, courts require that the attorney disclose client identity and fee information. In *Lefcourt v. United States*, 125 F.3d 79 (2d Cir. 1997), for example, a prominent criminal defense attorney declined to reveal his client's name on a Form 8300. Lefcourt argued that the "legal advice" exception should apply, and that the evidence that the client possessed the cash used to pay Lefcourt would incriminate the client in the matter for which the client sought legal advice from Lefcourt. The Second Circuit declined to adopt the legal advice exception, and held that Lefcourt should have revealed the information.

2. *The policy debate.* What is the policy tension underlying the decision in *Gertner*? What is the difference between the analysis in *Gertner* and that in *Goldberger*, 935 F.2d at 504–505, as discussed in *Gertner*? How did the policy tension inform the outcomes in those cases? Which decision is more persuasive? Is it fair or appropriate for the government to seek evidence in a criminal case from

the defendant's or potential defendant's attorney? Conversely, what dangers might arise if attorneys were exempted from the currency transaction reporting requirement?

3. *The John Doe summons.* The district court found that the summonses were not valid because the government had not followed the required procedures. What was the government's mistake? How did the government attempt to justify its approach? Was its justification plausible? On appeal, the First Circuit thought not, and affirmed the district court's decision on this ground alone; the court therefore did not reach the attorney-client privilege issue. *United States v. Gertner,* 65 F.3d 963 (1st Cir. 1995). A defendant in this case, Nancy Gertner, went on to become a federal judge for the United States District Court for Massachusetts.

4. *Challenges for defense attorneys.* If you were a criminal defense attorney in the position of the attorneys in these cases, how would you advise a client who wanted to pay you more than $10,000 in cash? If the client offered to make a number of payments in amounts under $10,000, how would you respond? Why?

PROBLEM

13-7. Over a two-year period, attorney Susan received four cash payments totaling over $100,000 from her client John Doe and two cash payments of $20,000 each from her client Jane Doe for legal services rendered. The clients had retained Susan in connection with a pending criminal investigation into tax evasion. Susan had reason to believe that revelation of the payments to the government might provide the government with evidence in that investigation.

Susan reported each of these transactions on IRS Form 8300, but omitted any identifying information regarding the payors or the persons on whose behalf payments were made. In an attachment to each form, Susan stated that disclosure would "violate ethical duties owed said client, and constitutional and/or attorney-client privileges that the reporting attorney is entitled or required to invoke," and that the client had not authorized release of the information. These forms ask the reporting party to check a box if the payment is a "suspicious transaction." The instructions accompanying the form defined a suspicious transaction as "[a] transaction in which it appears that a person is attempting to cause this report not to be filed or a false or incomplete report to be filed; or where there is an indication of possible illegal activity." Susan left the box blank. After filing these forms, Susan was served with an IRS summons requesting the missing information.

The government has brought an enforcement action before the district court. How should the court rule? Why?

Chapter 14

RICO

[A] INTRODUCTORY NOTES

[1] History and Scope of the RICO Statute

The Racketeer Influenced and Corrupt Organizations ("RICO") statute, 18 U.S.C. §§ 1961–1968, applies to a broad range of white collar and non-white collar criminal cases, and to an even broader range of civil cases. In basic terms, RICO is violated when: (1) a person commits repeated "predicate acts" constituting a "pattern of racketeering activity"; and (2) those acts involve an entity known as a RICO "enterprise" used in a manner the statute specifies. RICO is an unusual statute because it is based upon the commission of crimes — the "predicate acts" — defined elsewhere under federal and state law. Common predicate acts in white collar cases include the federal crimes of mail and wire fraud, securities fraud, obstruction of justice, bribery, extortion, and money laundering, as well as the state law crimes of bribery and extortion.

As applied in the white collar context, RICO is controversial. Although some have argued that Congress intended the statute primarily to apply to organized crime cases, others assert that a RICO charge is entirely appropriate in a white collar case. *Compare* Gerard E. Lynch, *A Reply to Michael Goldsmith*, 88 Colum. L. Rev. 802, 802 (1988) (arguing that RICO has been used in ways Congress never intended), *with* Michael Goldsmith, *RICO and Enterprise Criminality: A Response to Gerard E. Lynch*, 88 Colum. L. Rev. 774, 776 (1988) (arguing that RICO is appropriately applied in a broad range of cases). Despite the controversy, courts have sanctioned the use of RICO in both the white collar crime context and in a broad range of civil cases brought by both private parties and by the government.

RICO is also controversial because it is used in many civil and criminal matters that traditionally would be left to state courts. As Justice Marshall noted in his dissent in *Sedima, S.P.R.L. v. Imrex Co.*, 473 U.S. 479, 501 (1985), the wide-ranging application of RICO has "quite simply revolutionize[d] private litigation" and "validate[d] the federalization of broad areas of state common law of frauds." The latter observation applies equally to criminal RICO cases.

Although the United States Supreme Court has consistently interpreted RICO in a broad manner, federal district courts and courts of appeals are often hostile to private civil RICO suits. As a result, the appeals court decisions enforce technical pleading rules designed to limit civil RICO actions; these rules, however, apply in both criminal and civil cases. Thus, as in other areas such as securities fraud, this chapter includes civil case holdings that also apply in the criminal context.

While RICO has long provided a powerful tool for prosecutors, to some degree, the money laundering statutes have supplanted RICO as prosecutors' favored tool for fighting large-scale criminal activity.[a] This has occurred in part because of the technical pleading rules in RICO cases described above. RICO remains a potent weapon for prosecutors, however, particularly because a RICO defendant faces a lengthy sentence and asset forfeiture. Familiarity with the statute therefore remains essential for white collar criminal practice. In addition, RICO is widely used in complex civil litigation, and for that reason alone, the statute merits close examination.

[2]   Statutory Elements

Section 1962 sets forth the requirements for proving a RICO case. Under this statute, the government must prove that:

(1) A RICO enterprise existed;

(2) The defendant committed two or more predicate acts (the "racketeering activity");[b]

(3) The commission of the predicate acts constituted a "pattern" of racketeering activity;

(4) The defendant:

(a)   invested in or operated an enterprise with money obtained through a pattern of racketeering activity (18 U.S.C. § 1962(a));

(b)   acquired an interest in or maintained control over an enterprise through the pattern of racketeering activity (18 U.S.C. § 1962(b));

(c)   conducted the affairs of an enterprise through the pattern of racketeering activity (18 U.S.C. § 1962(c)); *or*

(d)   conspired to do any of (a)–(c) (18 U.S.C. § 1962(d)); and

(5) The racketeering activity affected interstate commerce, or the enterprise "engaged in . . . interstate or foreign commerce."

As shown above, § 1962 defines three different substantive crimes, as set forth in §§ 1962(a), 1962(b), and 1962(c), and criminalizes conspiring to commit any of those crimes under § 1962(d). Section 1962(c) is by far the most often-used substantive RICO section, and most of the cases discussed below were brought under that section. Note that Congress has mandated that RICO "be liberally construed to effectuate its remedial purposes."

[3]   Jurisdiction

The Supreme Court has broadly interpreted the statutory elements in a number of contexts, including the interstate commerce requirement. In *United States v. Robertson*, 514 U.S. 669 (1995), the Court held that the interstate commerce

---

[a] The Travel Act, 18 U.S.C. § 1952, is another statute that provides prosecutors with a tool for fighting large-scale criminal activity. Like RICO, the Travel Act is based on the intent to commit certain predicate acts. The Travel Act criminalizes the use of the mail or any facility in interstate or foreign commerce with the intent to promote such predicate acts. United States v. Welch, 327 F.3d 1081, 1092 (10th Cir. 2003) (explaining that the Travel Act does not make illegal the predicate act of bribery per se, but the "requisite intent to promote such unlawful activity").

[b] Note that the government may allege predicate acts that would be barred by the statutes of limitations for those crimes, so long as the last predicate fell within RICO's five year statute of limitations.

requirement was met under § 1962(a) where the defendant invested proceeds from narcotics offenses in the enterprise, an Alaskan gold mine. Applying the statutory language, the Court found that the mine produced, distributed, or acquired goods or services in interstate commerce.

[4]   Criminal and Civil Sanctions

Criminal or civil liability under RICO leads to very severe consequences. Initially, a defendant stands to be labeled as a "racketeer," even if — as is usually true — the case has nothing to do with organized crime. Further, each count of a RICO conviction may lead to up to 20 years' imprisonment, fines, and forfeiture of the defendant's property.[c] 18 U.S.C. §§ 1963(a)–(b). In a civil case, a private plaintiff is entitled to treble damages and attorneys' fees, 18 U.S.C. § 1964(c), providing a strong incentive for a private plaintiff to assert a RICO claim whenever possible. The government may also bring a civil RICO suit, and may obtain broad injunctive relief under the statute. 18 U.S.C. § 1964(b).

[B]   THE ENTERPRISE

[1]   The Nature of the Enterprise

Under § 1961(4), an "enterprise" includes "any individual, partnership, corporation, association, or other legal entity, and any union or group of individuals associated in fact although not a legal entity." A RICO enterprise thus may be a formal legal entity, such as a corporation, or an "association-in-fact." Considering that RICO was largely designed to ferret crime out of legitimate businesses, does an association that exists solely for criminal purposes qualify as a RICO "enterprise"? The Supreme Court addressed that issue in the case that follows.

UNITED STATES v. TURKETTE
452 U.S. 576 (1981)

JUSTICE WHITE delivered the opinion of the Court.

The question in this case is whether the term "enterprise" as used in RICO encompasses both legitimate and illegitimate enterprises or is limited in application to the former. The Court of Appeals for the First Circuit held that Congress did not intend to include within the definition of "enterprise" those organizations which are exclusively criminal. This position is contrary to that adopted by every other Circuit that has addressed the issue. We granted certiorari to resolve this conflict.

I.

Count Nine of a nine-count indictment charged respondent and 12 others with conspiracy to conduct and participate in the affairs of an enterprise engaged in interstate commerce through a pattern of racketeering activities, in violation of 18

---

[c] RICO's forfeiture provisions are discussed in Chapter 20, Forfeitures, *infra.* As always, the actual sentence imposed will depend upon the sentencing calculation under the U.S. Sentencing Guidelines. *See* Chapter 19, *infra.*

U.S.C. § 1962(d). The indictment described the enterprise as "a group of individuals associated in fact for the purpose of illegally trafficking in narcotics and other dangerous drugs, committing arsons, utilizing the United States mails to defraud insurance companies, bribing and attempting to bribe local police officers, and corruptly influencing and attempting to corruptly influence the outcome of state court proceedings . . . ." The other eight counts of the indictment charged the commission of various substantive criminal acts by those engaged in and associated with the criminal enterprise, including possession with intent to distribute and distribution of controlled substances, and several counts of insurance fraud by arson and other means. The common thread to all counts was respondent's alleged leadership of this criminal organization through which he orchestrated and participated in the commission of the various crimes delineated in the RICO count or charged in the eight preceding counts.

After a six-week jury trial, in which the evidence focused upon both the professional nature of this organization and the execution of a number of distinct criminal acts, respondent was convicted on all nine counts. He was sentenced to a term of 20 years on the substantive counts, as well as a two-year special parole term on the drug count. On the RICO conspiracy count he was sentenced to a 20-year concurrent term and fined $20,000.

On appeal, respondent argued that RICO was intended solely to protect legitimate business enterprises from infiltration by racketeers and that RICO does not make criminal the participation in an association which performs only illegal acts and which has not infiltrated or attempted to infiltrate a legitimate enterprise. The Court of Appeals agreed. We reverse.

II.

In determining the scope of a statute, we look first to its language . . . .

Section 1962(c) makes it unlawful "for any person employed by or associated with any enterprise engaged in, or the activities of which affect, interstate or foreign commerce, to conduct or participate, directly or indirectly, in the conduct of such enterprise's affairs through a pattern of racketeering activity or collection of unlawful debt." The term "enterprise" is defined as including "any individual, partnership, corporation, association, or other legal entity, and any union or group of individuals associated in fact although not a legal entity." There is no restriction upon the associations embraced by the definition: an enterprise includes any union or group of individuals associated in fact. On its face, the definition appears to include both legitimate and illegitimate enterprises within its scope; it no more excludes criminal enterprises than it does legitimate ones. Had Congress not intended to reach criminal associations, it could easily have narrowed the sweep of the definition by inserting a single word, "legitimate." But it did nothing to indicate that an enterprise consisting of a group of individuals was not covered by RICO if the purpose of the enterprise was exclusively criminal.

The Court of Appeals, however, clearly departed from and limited the statutory language. It gave several reasons for doing so, none of which is adequate. First, it relied in part on the rule of *ejusdem generis*, an aid to statutory construction problems suggesting that where general words follow a specific enumeration of persons or things the general words should be limited to persons or things similar to those specifically enumerated. The Court of Appeals ruled that because each of the specific enterprises enumerated in § 1961(4) is a "legitimate" one, the final catchall phrase — "any union or group of individuals associated in fact" — should also be limited to legitimate enterprises. There are at least two flaws in this reasoning. The rule of *ejusdem generis* is no more than an aid to construction and comes into play only when there is some uncertainty as to the meaning of a particular clause in a statute. Considering the language and structure of § 1961(4), however, we not only perceive no uncertainty in the meaning to be attributed to the phrase, "any union or group of individuals associated in fact" but we are convinced for another reason that *ejusdem generis* is wholly inapplicable in this context.

Section 1961(4) describes two categories of associations that come within the purview of the "enterprise" definition. The first encompasses organizations such as corporations and partnerships, and other "legal entities." The second covers "any union or group of individuals associated in fact although not a legal entity." The Court of Appeals assumed that the second category was merely a more general description of the first. Having made that assumption, the court concluded that the more generalized description in the second category should be limited by the specific examples enumerated in the first. But that assumption is untenable. Each category describes a separate type of enterprise to be covered by the statute — those that are recognized as legal entities and those that are not. The latter is not a more general description of the former. The second category itself not containing any specific enumeration that is followed by a general description, *ejusdem generis* has no bearing on the meaning to be attributed to that part of § 1961(4).

A second reason offered by the Court of Appeals in support of its judgment was that giving the definition of "enterprise" its ordinary meaning would create several internal inconsistencies in the Act. With respect to § 1962(c), it was said:

> If "a pattern of racketeering" can itself be an "enterprise" for purposes of section 1962(c), then the two phrases "employed by or associated with any enterprise" and "the conduct of such enterprise's affairs through [a pattern of racketeering activity]" add nothing to the meaning of the section. The words of the statute are coherent and logical only if they are read as applying to legitimate enterprises.

632 F.2d at 899.

This conclusion is based on a faulty premise. That a wholly criminal enterprise comes within the ambit of the statute does not mean that a "pattern of racketeering activity" is an "enterprise." In order to secure a conviction under RICO, the Government must prove both the existence of an "enterprise" and the connected "pattern of racketeering activity." The enterprise is an entity, for present purposes a group of persons associated together for a common purpose of engaging in a course of conduct. The pattern of racketeering activity is, on the other hand, a series of criminal acts as defined by the statute. The former is proved by evidence of an ongoing organization, formal or informal, and by evidence that the various associates function as a continuing unit. The latter is proved by evidence of the requisite number of acts of racketeering committed by the participants in the enterprise. While the proof used to establish these separate elements may in particular cases coalesce, proof of one does not necessarily establish the other. The "enterprise" is not the "pattern of racketeering activity"; it is an entity separate and apart from the pattern of activity in which it engages. The existence of an enterprise at all times remains a separate element which must be proved by the Government.

Apart from § 1962(c)'s proscription against participating in an enterprise through a pattern of racketeering activities, RICO also proscribes the investment of income derived from racketeering activity in an enterprise engaged in or which affects interstate commerce as well as the acquisition of an interest in or control of any such enterprise through a pattern of racketeering activity. 18 U.S.C. §§ 1962(a) and (b). The Court of Appeals concluded that these provisions of RICO should be interpreted so as to apply only to legitimate enterprises. If these two sections are so limited, the Court of Appeals held that the proscription in § 1962(c), at issue here, must be similarly limited. Again, we do not accept the premise from which the Court of Appeals derived its conclusion. It is obvious that § 1962(a) and (b) address the infiltration by organized crime of legitimate businesses, but we cannot agree that these sections were not also aimed at preventing racketeers from investing or reinvesting in wholly illegal enterprises and from acquiring through a pattern of racketeering activity wholly illegitimate enterprises such as an illegal gambling business or a loan-sharking operation. There is no inconsistency or anomaly in recognizing that § 1962 applies to both legitimate and illegitimate enterprises. Certainly the language of the statute does not warrant the Court of Appeals' conclusion to the contrary . . . .

Finally, it is urged that the interpretation of RICO to include both legitimate and illegitimate enterprises will substantially alter the balance between federal and state enforcement of criminal law. This is particularly true, so the argument goes, since included within the definition of racketeering activity are a significant number of acts made criminal under state law. But even assuming that the more inclusive definition of enterprise will have the effect suggested,[9] the language of the statute and its legislative history indicate that Congress was well aware that it was entering a new domain of federal involvement through the enactment of this measure. Indeed, the very purpose of the Organized Crime Control Act of 1970 was to enable the Federal Government to address a large and seemingly neglected problem. The view was that existing law, state and federal, was not adequate to address the problem, which was of national dimensions. That Congress included within the definition of racketeering activities a number of state crimes strongly indicates that RICO criminalized conduct that was also criminal under state law, at least when the requisite elements of a RICO offense are present. As the hearings and legislative debates reveal, Congress was well aware of the fear that RICO would "mov[e] large substantive areas formerly totally within the police power of the State into the Federal realm." 116 Cong. Rec. 35217 (1970) (remarks of Rep. Eckhardt). In the face of these objections, Congress nonetheless proceeded to enact the measure, knowing that it would alter somewhat the role of the Federal Government in the war against organized crime and that the alteration would entail prosecutions involving acts of racketeering that are also crimes under state law. There is no argument that Congress acted beyond its power in so doing. That being the case, the courts are without authority to restrict the application of the statute.

---

[9] RICO imposes no restrictions upon the criminal justice systems of the States. See 84 Stat. 947 ("Nothing in this title shall supersede any provision of Federal, State, or other law imposing criminal penalties or affording civil remedies in addition to those provided for in this title"). Thus, under RICO, the States, remain free to exercise their police powers to the fullest constitutional extent in defining and prosecuting crimes within their respective jurisdictions. That some of those crimes may also constitute predicate acts of racketeering under RICO, is no restriction on the separate administration of criminal justice by the States.

Contrary to the judgment below, neither the language nor structure of RICO limits its application to legitimate "enterprises." Applying it also to criminal organizations does not render any portion of the statute superfluous nor does it create any structural incongruities within the framework of the Act. The result is neither absurd nor surprising. On the contrary, insulating the wholly criminal enterprise from prosecution under RICO is the more incongruous position.

Section 904(a) of RICO, 84 Stat. 947, directs that "[t]he provisions of this Title shall be liberally construed to effectuate its remedial purposes." With or without this admonition, we could not agree with the Court of Appeals that illegitimate enterprises should be excluded from coverage. We are also quite sure that nothing in the legislative history of RICO requires a contrary conclusion.

III.

[T]he construction of RICO suggested by respondent and the court below is unacceptable. Whole areas of organized criminal activity would be placed beyond the substantive reach of the enactment. For example, associations of persons engaged solely in "loan sharking, the theft and fencing of property, the importation and distribution of narcotics and other dangerous drugs," would be immune from prosecution under RICO so long as the association did not deviate from the criminal path. Yet these are among the very crimes that Congress specifically found to be typical of the crimes committed by persons involved in organized crime, and as a major source of revenue and power for such organizations. In view of the purposes and goals of the Act, as well as the language of the statute, we are unpersuaded that Congress nevertheless confined the reach of the law to only narrow aspects of organized crime, and, in particular, under RICO, *only* the infiltration of legitimate business.

This is not to gainsay that the legislative history forcefully supports the view that the major purpose of Title IX is to address the infiltration of legitimate business by organized crime. The point is made time and again during the debates and in the hearings before the House and Senate. But none of these statements requires the negative inference that Title IX did not reach the activities of enterprises organized and existing for criminal purposes.

On the contrary, these statements are in full accord with the proposition that RICO is equally applicable to a criminal enterprise that has no legitimate dimension or has yet to acquire one. Accepting that the primary purpose of RICO is to cope with the infiltration of legitimate businesses, applying the statute in accordance with its terms, so as to reach criminal enterprises, would seek to deal with the problem at its very source. Supporters of the bill recognized that organized crime uses its primary sources of revenue and power — illegal gambling, loan sharking and illicit drug distribution — as a springboard into the sphere of legitimate enterprise. . . .

As a measure to deal with the infiltration of legitimate businesses by organized crime, RICO was both preventive and remedial. Respondent's view would ignore the preventive function of the statute. If Congress had intended the more circumscribed approach espoused by the Court of Appeals, there would have been some positive sign that the law was not to reach organized criminal activities that give rise to the concerns about infiltration. The language of the statute, however — the most reliable evidence of its intent — reveals that Congress opted for a far broader definition of the word "enterprise," and we are unconvinced by anything in the legislative history that this definition should be given less than its full effect.

The judgment of the Court of Appeals is accordingly reversed.

NOTES AND QUESTIONS

1. *Formal and informal enterprises.* Under RICO, the term "enterprise" includes "any individual, partnership, corporation, association, or other legal entity, and any union or group of individuals associated in fact although not a legal entity." Most issues arise in connection with "association-in-fact" enterprises, which consist of individual persons and/or legal entities, such as corporations. Does this statutory definition provide clear guidance to prosecutors and potential defendants? Why or why not? Does the *Turkette* decision offer guidelines?

2. *Federalism.* The Court noted the concerns over federalism that had influenced the Court of Appeals. What was the Supreme Court's response? Does RICO pose serious issues of federalism? Why or why not?

*   *   *

In the case that follows, the defendants argued that a RICO enterprise must have an economic motive. As you read the case, identify the meaning and purpose of the enterprise requirement.[d]

NATIONAL ORGANIZATION FOR WOMEN v. SCHEIDLER
510 U.S. 249 (1994)

REHNQUIST, C.J., delivered the opinion for a unanimous Court.

We are required once again to interpret the provisions of the Racketeer Influenced and Corrupt Organizations (RICO) chapter of the Organized Crime Control Act of 1970 (OCCA), 18 U.S.C. §§ 1961–1968. Section 1962(c) prohibits any person associated with an enterprise from conducting its affairs through a pattern of racketeering activity. We granted certiorari to determine whether RICO requires proof that either the racketeering enterprise or the predicate acts of racketeering were motivated by an economic purpose. We hold that RICO requires no such economic motive.

I.

Petitioner National Organization For Women, Inc. (NOW), is a national nonprofit organization that supports the legal availability of abortion; petitioners Delaware Women's Health Organization, Inc. (DWHO), and Summit Women's Health Organization, Inc. (SWHO), are health care centers that perform abortions and other medical procedures. Respondents are a coalition of antiabortion groups called the Pro-Life Action Network (PLAN), Joseph Scheidler and other individuals and organizations that oppose legal abortion, and a medical laboratory that formerly provided services to the two petitioner health care centers.

Petitioners sued respondents in the United States District Court for the Northern District of Illinois, alleging violations of RICO's §§ 1962(a), (c), and (d).

---

[d] A later decision in this litigation is discussed in Chapter 8, Extortion, *supra.*

According to respondent Scheidler's congressional testimony, these protesters aim to shut down the clinics and persuade women not to have abortions. Petitioners sought injunctive relief, along with treble damages, costs, and attorneys' fees. . . .

The amended complaint alleged that respondents were members of a nationwide conspiracy to shut down abortion clinics through a pattern of racketeering activity including extortion in violation of the Hobbs Act, 18 U.S.C. § 1951. Section 1951(b)(2) defines extortion as "the obtaining of property from another, with his consent, induced by wrongful use of actual or threatened force, violence, or fear, or under color of official right." Petitioners alleged that respondents conspired to use threatened or actual force, violence or fear to induce clinic employees, doctors, and patients to give up their jobs, give up their economic right to practice medicine, and give up their right to obtain medical services at the clinics. Petitioners claimed that this conspiracy "has injured the business and/or property interests of the [petitioners]." According to the amended complaint, PLAN constitutes the alleged racketeering "enterprise" for purposes of § 1962(c).

[The District Court] dismissed petitioners' RICO claims under § 1962(a) because the "income" alleged by petitioners consisted of voluntary donations from persons opposed to abortion which "in no way were derived from the pattern of racketeering alleged in the complaint." The District Court then concluded that petitioners failed to state a claim under § 1962(c) since "an economic motive requirement exists to the extent that some profit-generating purpose must be alleged in order to state a RICO claim." Finally, it dismissed petitioners' RICO conspiracy claim under § 1962(d) since petitioners' other RICO claims could not stand.

The Court of Appeals affirmed. As to the RICO counts, it agreed with the District Court that the voluntary contributions received by respondents did not constitute income derived from racketeering activities for purposes of § 1962(a). It adopted the analysis of the Court of Appeals for the Second Circuit in *United States v. Ivic*, 700 F.2d 51 (2d Cir. 1983), which found an "economic motive" requirement implicit in the "enterprise" element of the offense. The Court of Appeals determined that "non-economic crimes committed in furtherance of non-economic motives are not within the ambit of RICO." Consequently, petitioners failed to state a claim under § 1962(c). The Court of Appeals also affirmed dismissal of the RICO conspiracy claim under § 1962(d).

We granted certiorari to resolve a conflict among the courts of appeals on the putative economic motive requirement of 18 U.S.C. § 1962(c) and (d).

*   *   *

III.

We turn to the question of whether the racketeering enterprise or the racketeering predicate acts must be accompanied by an underlying economic motive. Section 1962(c) makes it unlawful "for any person employed by or associated with any enterprise engaged in, or the activities of which affect, interstate or foreign commerce, to conduct or participate, directly or indirectly, in the conduct of such enterprise's affairs through a pattern of racketeering activity or collection of unlawful debt." Section 1961(1) defines "pattern of racketeering activity" to include conduct that is "chargeable" or "indictable" under a host of state and federal laws. RICO broadly defines "enterprise" in § 1961(4) to "includ[e] any individual, partnership, corporation, association, or other legal entity, and any union or group of individuals associated in fact although not a legal entity." Nowhere in either § 1962(c), or in the RICO definitions in § 1961, is there any indication that an economic motive is required.

The phrase "any enterprise engaged in, or the activities of which affect, interstate or foreign commerce" comes the closest of any language in subsection (c) to suggesting a need for an economic motive. Arguably an enterprise engaged in interstate or foreign commerce would have a profit-seeking motive, but the language in § 1962(c) does not stop there; it includes enterprises whose activities "affect" interstate or foreign commerce. Webster's Third New International Dictionary 35 (1969) defines "affect" as "to have a detrimental influence on — used especially in the phrase affecting commerce." An enterprise surely can have a detrimental influence on interstate or foreign commerce without having its own profit-seeking motives.

The Court of Appeals thought that the use of the term "enterprise" in §§ 1962(a) and (b), where it is arguably more tied in with economic motivation, should be applied to restrict the breadth of use of that term in § 1962(c). Respondents agree, and point to our comment in *Sedima, S.P.R.L. v. Imrex Co.*, 473 U.S. 479, 489 (1985), regarding the term "violation," that "[w]e should not lightly infer that Congress intended the term [violation] to have wholly different meanings in neighboring subsections."

We do not believe that the usage of the term "enterprise" in subsections (a) and (b) leads to the inference that an economic motive is required in subsection (c). The term "enterprise" in subsections (a) and (b) plays a different role in the structure of those subsections than it does in subsection (c). Section 1962(a) provides that it "shall be unlawful for any person who has received any income derived, directly or indirectly, from a pattern of racketeering activity . . . to use or invest, directly or indirectly, any part of such income, or the proceeds of such income, in acquisition of any interest in, or the establishment or operation of, any enterprise which is engaged in, or the activities of which affect, interstate or foreign commerce." Correspondingly, § 1962(b) states that it "shall be unlawful for any person through a pattern of racketeering activity or through collection of an unlawful debt to acquire or maintain, directly or indirectly, any interest in or control of any enterprise which is engaged in, or the activities of which affect, interstate or foreign commerce." The "enterprise" referred to in subsections (a) and (b) is thus something acquired through the use of illegal activities or by money obtained from illegal activities. The enterprise in these subsections is the victim of unlawful activity and may very well be a "profit-seeking" entity that represents a property interest and may be acquired. But the statutory language in subsections (a) and (b) does not mandate that the enterprise be a "profit-seeking" entity; it simply requires that the enterprise be an entity that was acquired through illegal activity or the money generated from illegal activity.

By contrast, the "enterprise" in subsection (c) connotes generally the vehicle through which the unlawful pattern of racketeering activity is committed, rather than the victim of that activity. Subsection (c) makes it unlawful for "any person employed by or associated with any enterprise . . . to conduct or partici-pate . . . in the conduct of such enterprise's affairs through a pattern of racketeering activity . . . ." Consequently, since the enterprise in subsection (c) is not being acquired, it need not have a property interest that can be acquired nor an economic motive for engaging in illegal activity; it need only be an association in fact that engages in a pattern of racketeering activity. Nothing in subsections (a) and (b) directs us to a contrary conclusion.

The Court of Appeals also relied on the reasoning of *United States v. Bagaric*, 706 F.2d 42 (2d Cir. 1983), to support its conclusion that subsection (c) requires an economic motive. In upholding the dismissal of a RICO claim against a political terrorist group, the *Bagaric* court relied in part on the congressional statement of findings which prefaces RICO and refers to the activities of groups that " 'drain[] billions of dollars from America's economy by unlawful conduct and the illegal use of force, fraud, and corruption.' " 706 F.2d at 57 n.13 (quoting OCCA, 84 Stat. 922). The Court of Appeals for the Second Circuit decided that the sort of activity thus condemned required an economic motive.

We do not think this is so. Respondents and the two courts of appeals, we think, overlook the fact that predicate acts, such as the alleged extortion, may not benefit the protestors financially but still may drain money from the economy by harming businesses such as the clinics which are petitioners in this case.

We also think that the quoted statement of congressional findings is a rather thin reed upon which to base a requirement of economic motive neither expressed nor, we think, fairly implied in the operative sections of the Act. As we said in *H.J. Inc. v. Northwestern Bell Telephone Co.*, 492 U.S. 229, 248, (1989), "[t]he occasion for Congress' action was the perceived need to combat organized crime. But Congress for cogent reasons chose to enact a more general statute, one which, although it had organized crime as its focus, was not limited in application to organized crime."

In *United States v. Turkette*, 452 U.S. 576 (1981), we faced the analogous question of whether "enterprise" as used in § 1961(4) should be confined to "legitimate" enterprises. Looking to the statutory language, we found that "[t]here is no restriction upon the associations embraced by the definition: an enterprise includes any union or group of individuals associated in fact." *Id.* at 580. Accordingly, we resolved that § 1961(4)'s definition of enterprise "appears to include both legitimate and illegitimate enterprises within its scope; it no more excludes criminal enterprises than it does legitimate ones." *Id.* at 580–581. We noted that Congress could easily have narrowed the sweep of the term "enterprise" by inserting a single word, "legitimate." *Id.* at 581. Instead, Congress did nothing to indicate that "enterprise" should exclude those entities whose sole purpose was criminal.

The parallel to the present case is apparent. Congress has not, either in the definitional section or in the operative language, required that an "enterprise" in § 1962(c) have an economic motive.

The Court of Appeals also found persuasive guidelines for RICO prosecutions issued by the Department of Justice in 1981. The guidelines provided that a RICO indictment should not charge an association as an enterprise, unless the association exists " 'for the purpose of maintaining operations directed toward an economic goal . . . .' " The Second Circuit, in *United States v. Ivic, supra*, believed these guidelines were entitled to deference under administrative law principles. *See* 700 F.2d at 64. Whatever may be the appropriate deference afforded to such internal rules, for our purposes we need note only that the Department of Justice amended its guidelines in 1984. The amended guidelines provide that an association-in-fact enterprise must be "directed toward an economic or other identifiable goal."

Both parties rely on legislative history to support their positions. We believe the statutory language is unambiguous and find in the parties' submissions respecting legislative history no such "clearly expressed legislative intent to the contrary" that would warrant a different construction.

Respondents finally argue that the result here should be controlled by the rule of lenity in criminal cases. But the rule of lenity applies only when an ambiguity is present. We simply do not think there is an ambiguity here which would suffice to invoke the rule of lenity. . . .

We therefore hold that petitioners may maintain this action if respondents conducted the enterprise through a pattern of racketeering activity. The questions of whether the respondents committed the requisite predicate acts, and whether the commission of these acts fell into a pattern, are not before us.[e] We hold only that RICO contains no economic motive requirement.

The judgment of the Court of Appeals is accordingly reversed.

NOTES AND QUESTIONS

1. *The economic motive requirement.* What led the lower courts to apply an economic motive requirement to the enterprise element? Why did the Supreme Court reject that requirement? Is its reasoning persuasive? Is the result compelled by *Turkette*?

2. *The role of the enterprise.* According to the Court, what role does the enterprise play in a case brought under § 1962(a), (b), or (c)? Put another way, can you identify, under each subsection, the reason why Congress required that an enterprise be proven under that specific subsection?

3. *Prosecutorial guidelines.* The defendants relied on Department of Justice Guidelines in asserting their argument. How did the Court respond? Note that the United States Department of Justice requires that the Organized Crime and Racketeering Section of the DOJ's Criminal Division approve the initiation of any criminal RICO case or any civil RICO case brought by the government. *See* 4 Dep't of Justice Manual, tit. 9, §§ 9-110.101, 210. The DOJ provides the following guidelines for determining whether to bring a criminal RICO charge:

> Except as hereafter provided, a government attorney should seek approval for a RICO charge only if one or more of the following requirements is present:
>
> 1. RICO is necessary to ensure that the indictment adequately reflects the nature and extent of the criminal conduct involved in a way that prosecution only on the underlying charges would not;
>
> 2. A RICO prosecution would provide the basis for an appropriate sentence under all the circumstances of the case in a way that prosecution only on the underlying charges would not;

---

[e] The Court subsequently held that the predicate acts of extortion were not proven on these facts, and dismissed the case. Scheidler v. National Organization for Women, 537 U.S. 393 (2003). *See* Chapter 8, Extortion, *supra.* — eds.

3. A RICO charge could combine related offenses which would otherwise have to be prosecuted separately in different jurisdictions;

4. RICO is necessary for a successful prosecution of the government's case against the defendant or a codefendant;

5. Use of RICO would provide a reasonable expectation of forfeiture which is proportionate to the underlying criminal conduct;

6. The case consists of violations of State law, but local law enforcement officials are unlikely or unable to successfully prosecute the case, in which the federal government has a significant interest;

7. The case consists of violations of State law, but involves prosecution of significant or government individuals, which may pose special problems for the local prosecutor.

The last two requirements reflect the principle that the prosecution of state crimes is primarily the responsibility of state authorities. RICO should be used to prosecute what are essentially violations of state law only if there is a compelling reason to do so.

Id. at § 9-110.310. Why has the DOJ imposed these guidelines? Must courts defer to such guidelines? Why or why not? *See* Ellen S. Podgor, *Department of Justice Guidelines: Balancing "Discretionary Justice,"* 13 Cornell J.L. & Pub. Pol'y 167 (2004).

[2]   The Relationship Between the "Person" and the "Enterprise"

In the next case, the Court turned to the relationship between the enterprise and the "person" who conducts the enterprise under § 1962(c). As you read the case, consider whether the outcome comports with the purpose behind § 1962(c).

CEDRIC KUSHNER PROMOTIONS v. KING
533 U. S. 158 (2001)

JUSTICE BREYER delivered the opinion of the Court.

The Racketeer Influenced and Corrupt Organizations Act, 18 U.S.C. § 1961 et seq., makes it "unlawful for any person employed by or associated with any enterprise . . . to conduct or participate . . . in the conduct of such enterprise's affairs" through the commission of two or more statutorily defined crimes — which RICO calls "a pattern of racketeering activity." § 1962(c). The language suggests, and lower courts have held, that this provision foresees two separate entities, a "person" and a distinct "enterprise."

This case focuses upon a person who is the president and sole shareholder of a closely held corporation. The plaintiff claims that the president has conducted the corporation's affairs through the forbidden "pattern," though for present purposes it is conceded that, in doing so, he acted within the scope of his authority as the corporation's employee. In these circumstances, are there two entities, a "person" and a separate "enterprise"? Assuming, as we must given the posture of this case, that the allegations in the complaint are true, we conclude that the "person" and "enterprise" here are distinct and that the RICO provision applies.

Petitioner, Cedric Kushner Promotions, Ltd., is a corporation that promotes boxing matches. Petitioner sued Don King, the president and sole shareholder of Don King Productions, a corporation, claiming that King had conducted the boxing-related affairs of Don King Productions in part through a RICO "pattern," i.e., through the alleged commission of at least two instances of fraud and other RICO predicate crimes. The District Court, citing Court of Appeals precedent, dismissed the complaint, and the Court of Appeals affirmed that dismissal. 219 F.3d 115 (2d Cir. 2000) (per curiam). In the appellate court's view, § 1962(c) applies only where a plaintiff shows the existence of two separate entities, a "person" and a distinct "enterprise," the affairs of which that "person" improperly conducts. In this instance, "it is undisputed that King was an employee" of the corporation Don King Productions and also "acting within the scope of his authority." Under the Court of Appeals' analysis, King, in a legal sense, was part of, not separate from, the corporation. There was no "person," distinct from the "enterprise," who improperly conducted the "enterprise's affairs." And thus § 1962(c) did not apply.

Other circuits, applying § 1962(c) in roughly similar circumstances, have reached a contrary conclusion. We granted certiorari to resolve the conflict. We now agree with these circuits and hold that the Second Circuit's interpretation of § 1962(c) is erroneous.

We do not quarrel with the basic principle that to establish liability under § 1962(c) one must allege and prove the existence of two distinct entities: (1) a "person"; and (2) an "enterprise" that is not simply the same "person" referred to by a different name. The statute's language, read as ordinary English, suggests that principle. The Act says that it applies to "person[s]" who are "employed by or associated with" the "enterprise." In ordinary English one speaks of employing, being employed by, or associating with others, not oneself. In addition, the Act's purposes are consistent with that principle. Whether the Act seeks to prevent a person from victimizing, say, a small business, or to prevent a person from using a corporation for criminal purposes, *National Organization for Women v. Scheidler*, 510 U.S. 249, 259 (1994), the person and the victim, or the person and the tool, are different entities, not the same.

The Acting Solicitor General reads § 1962(c) "to require some distinctness between the RICO defendant and the RICO enterprise." And she says that this requirement is "legally sound and workable." We agree with her assessment, particularly in light of the fact that 12 Courts of Appeals have interpreted the statute as embodying some such distinctness requirement without creating discernible mischief in the administration of RICO. . . .

While accepting the "distinctness" principle, we nonetheless disagree with the appellate court's application of that principle to the present circumstances — circumstances in which a corporate employee, "acting within the scope of his authority," allegedly conducts the corporation's affairs in a RICO-forbidden way. The corporate owner/employee, a natural person, is distinct from the corporation itself, a legally different entity with different rights and responsibilities due to its different legal status. And we can find nothing in the statute that requires more "separateness" than that.

Linguistically speaking, an employee who conducts the affairs of a corporation through illegal acts comes within the terms of a statute that forbids any "person" unlawfully to conduct an "enterprise," particularly when the statute explicitly defines "person" to include "any individual . . . capable of holding a legal or beneficial interest in property," and defines "enterprise" to include a "corporation." 18 U.S.C. §§ 1961(3), (4). And, linguistically speaking, the employee and the corporation are different "persons," even where the employee is the corporation's sole owner. After all, incorporation's basic purpose is to create a distinct legal entity, with legal rights, obligations, powers, and privileges different from those of the natural individuals who created it, who own it, or whom it employs.

We note that the Second Circuit relied on earlier circuit precedent for its decision. But that precedent involved quite different circumstances which are not presented here. This case concerns a claim that a corporate employee is the "person" and the corporation is the "enterprise." It is natural to speak of a corporate employee as a "person employed by" the corporation. Section 1962(c). The earlier Second Circuit precedent concerned a claim that a corporation was the "person" and the corporation, together with all its employees and agents, were the "enterprise." *See Riverwoods Chappaqua Corp. v. Marine Midland Bank*, 30 F.3d 339, 344 (2d Cir. 1994) (affirming dismissal of complaint). It is less natural to speak of a corporation as "employed by" or "associated with" this latter oddly constructed entity. And the Second Circuit's other precedent also involved significantly different allegations compared with the instant case. We do not here consider the merits of these cases, and note only their distinction from the instant case.

Further, to apply the RICO statute in present circumstances is consistent with the statute's basic purposes as this Court has defined them. The Court has held that RICO both protects a legitimate "enterprise" from those who would use unlawful acts to victimize it, *United States v. Turkette*, 452 U.S. 576, 591 (1981), and also protects the public from those who would unlawfully use an "enterprise" (whether legitimate or illegitimate) as a "vehicle" through which "unlawful . . . activity is committed," *National Organization for Women*, 510 U.S. at 259. A corporate employee who conducts the corporation's affairs through an unlawful RICO "pattern . . . of activity," § 1962(c), uses that corporation as a "vehicle" whether he is, or is not, its sole owner.

Conversely, the appellate court's critical legal distinction — between employees acting within the scope of corporate authority and those acting outside that authority — is inconsistent with a basic statutory purpose. It would immunize from RICO liability many of those at whom this Court has said RICO directly aims — e.g., high-ranking individuals in an illegitimate criminal enterprise, who, seeking to further the purposes of that enterprise, act within the scope of their authority. . . .

In reply, King argues that the lower court's rule is consistent with (1) the principle that a corporation acts only through its directors, officers, and agents, (2) the principle that a corporation should not be liable for the criminal acts of its employees where Congress so intends, and (3) the Sherman Act principle limiting liability under 15 U.S.C. § 1 by excluding "from unlawful combinations or conspiracies the activities of a single firm," *Copperweld Corp. v. Independence Tube Corp.*, 467 U.S. 752, 769–770, n. 15 (1984). The alternative that we endorse, however, is no less consistent with these principles. It does not deny that a corporation acts through its employees; it says only that the corporation and its employees are not legally identical. It does not assert that ordinary respondeat superior principles make a corporation legally liable under RICO for the criminal acts of its employees; that is a matter of congressional intent not before us. Neither is it inconsistent with antitrust law's intracorporate conspiracy doctrine; that doctrine turns on specific antitrust objectives. Rather, we hold simply that the need for two distinct entities is satisfied; hence, the RICO provision before us applies when a corporate employee unlawfully conducts the affairs of the corporation of which he is the sole owner — whether he conducts those affairs within the scope, or beyond the scope, of corporate authority.

For these reasons, the Court of Appeals' judgment is reversed, and the case is remanded for further proceedings consistent with this opinion.

NOTES AND QUESTIONS

1. *RICO's purposes.* According to the Court, what is the purpose of § 1962(c)? Are these purposes served by allowing a sole shareholder to be charged under that section for conducting the affairs of a corporation that has no other owners or officers? Why or why not?

2. *The "person" and the "enterprise."* Under § 1962(c), the defendant is the "person" who conducted the enterprise through a pattern of racketeering activity. In *King*, the Supreme Court apparently agreed with lower courts that had held that the person and the enterprise must be distinct under § 1962(c). Thus, the *person*, not the enterprise, is the wrongdoer under that subsection. Under this reasoning, the enterprise cannot be named as the defendant in a case brought under § 1962(c). *See, e.g., Schofield v. First Commodity Corp. of Boston*, 793 F.2d 28, 29 (1st Cir. 1986).

3. *Sections 1962(a) and (b).* Does *King*'s reasoning apply to §§ 1962(a) and 1962(b)? In other words, could the enterprise be named as the defendant under subsection 1962(a) or (b)? Why or why not? *See Masi v. Ford City Bank and Trust Company*, 779 F.2d 397, 402 (7th Cir. 1985) (finding that the enterprise could be named as a defendant under § 1962(a)).

4. *Association-in-fact enterprises.* Could a plaintiff avoid the distinctiveness requirement under § 1962(c) by naming as the defendant an individual or entity that is part of an allegedly larger, association-in-fact enterprise? *See Riverwoods Chappaqua Corp. v. Marine Midland Bank*, 30 F.3d 339, 344 (2d Cir. 1994) ("where employees of a corporation associate together to commit a pattern of predicate acts in the course of their employment and on behalf of the corporation, the employees in association with the corporation do not form an enterprise distinct from the corporation"). *See generally* Paul Edgar Harold, Note, *Quo Vadis, Association in Fact? The Growing Disparity between How Federal Courts Interpret RICO's Enterprise Provision in Criminal and Civil Cases (With a Little Statutory Background to Explain Why)*, 80 Notre Dame L. Rev. 781 (2005).

5. *Parents and subsidiaries.* Are parent corporations and their wholly-owned subsidiaries distinct entities for purposes of § 1962(c)? Although courts have adopted varying approaches to this question, most courts conclude that parents and subsidiaries are not distinct entities. *See* Comment, William B. Ortman, *Parents, Subsidiaries, and RICO Distinctiveness*, 73 U. Chi. L. Rev. 377 (2006) (arguing that the courts' conclusion is not supported by the RICO statute and that parents and subsidiaries should be considered distinct entities under § 1962(c)).

[3]   Required Proof for the "Conduct" and "Enterprise" Elements

As the Supreme Court noted in the *King* case, under § 1962(c), the person who "conducts" the affairs of the enterprise must be separate from the enterprise. But, in such a case, what does it mean to "conduct" the affairs of the enterprise? The Supreme Court addressed this issue in the case that follows.

REVES v. ERNST & YOUNG
507 U.S. 170 (1993)

JUSTICE BLACKMUN delivered the opinion of the Court.

[The plaintiff alleged that the defendant, accounting firm Arthur Young (later known as Ernst & Young), had conducted and participated in the affairs of the alleged enterprise, a farmer's cooperative known as The Farmer's Cooperative of Arkansas and Oklahoma, Inc. (the "Co-Op"). The accounting firm had performed the annual financial audit for the Co-Op in 1981 and 1982. The accounting firm certified that the Co-Op's records adequately reflected its financial status, and relied upon those records, and a review of past Co-Op transactions, to prepare the audits. In completing these assignments, and without informing the Co-Op's board, the accounting firm utilized questionable measures to verify the Co-Op's solvency.

The audits failed to disclose the Co-Op's precarious financial condition. The Co-Op later filed for bankruptcy. The bankruptcy trustee, acting on behalf of the Co-Op and certain of its creditors, sued the accounting firm and others. All the defendants except the accounting firm settled. In the complaint, the plaintiffs alleged that the accounting firm had conducted or participated in the conduct of the Co-Op's affairs through a pattern of racketeering activity. The trial court granted summary judgment in favor of the accounting firm on the RICO claim, and the court of appeals affirmed. Both courts applied an "operation or management" test for determining when a person "conducts" an enterprise under § 1962(c). The courts concluded that the accounting firm's conduct did not "rise to the level of participation in the management or operation of the Co-Op." *See Arthur Young & Co. v. Reves*, 937 F.2d 1310, 1324 (8th Cir. 1991).]

* * *

III.

The narrow question in this case is the meaning of the phrase "to conduct or participate, directly or indirectly, in the conduct of such enterprise's affairs." The word "conduct" is used twice, and it seems reasonable to give each use a similar construction. As a verb, "conduct" means to lead, run, manage, or direct. Webster's Third New International Dictionary 474 (1976). Petitioners urge us to read "conduct" as "carry on," so that almost any involvement in the affairs of an enterprise would satisfy the "conduct or participate" requirement. But context is important, and in the context of the phrase "to conduct . . . [an] enterprise's affairs," the word indicates some degree of direction.

The dissent agrees that, when "conduct" is used as a verb, "it is plausible to find in it a suggestion of control." The dissent prefers to focus on "conduct" as a noun, as in the phrase "participate, directly or indirectly, in the conduct of [an] enterprise's affairs." But unless one reads "conduct" to include an element of direction when used as a noun in this phrase, the word becomes superfluous. Congress could easily have written "participate, directly or indirectly, in [an] enterprise's affairs," but it chose to repeat the word "conduct." We conclude, therefore, that as both a noun and a verb in this subsection "conduct" requires an element of direction.

The more difficult question is what to make of the word "participate." This Court previously has characterized this word as a "ter[m] . . . of breadth." *Russello v. United States*, 464 U.S. 16, 21–22 (1983). Petitioners argue that Congress used "participate" as a synonym for "aid and abet." That would be a term of breadth indeed, for "aid and abet" "comprehends all assistance rendered by words, acts, encouragement, support, or presence." Black's Law Dictionary 68 (6th ed. 1990). But within the context of § 1962(c), "participate" appears to have a narrower meaning. We may mark the limits of what the term might mean by looking again at what Congress did *not* say. On the one hand, "to participate . . . in the conduct of . . . affairs" must be broader than "to conduct affairs" or the "participate" phrase would be superfluous. On the other hand, as we already have noted, "to participate . . . in the conduct of . . . affairs" must be narrower than "to participate in affairs" or Congress' repetition of the word "conduct" would serve no purpose. It seems that Congress chose a middle ground, consistent with a common understanding of the word "participate" — "to take part in." Webster's Third New International Dictionary 1646 (1976).

Once we understand the word "conduct" to require some degree of direction and the word "participate" to require some part in that direction, the meaning of § 1962(c) comes into focus. In order to "participate, directly or indirectly, in the conduct of such enterprise's affairs," one must have some part in directing those affairs. Of course, the word "participate" makes clear that RICO liability is not limited to those with primary responsibility for the enterprise's affairs, just as the phrase "directly or indirectly" makes clear that RICO liability is not limited to those with a formal position in the enterprise, but *some* part in directing the enterprise's affairs is required. The "operation or management" test expresses this requirement in a formulation that is easy to apply.

IV.

A.

This test finds further support in the legislative history of § 1962. . . .

[T]he legislative history confirms what we have already deduced from the language of § 1962(c) — that one is not liable under that provision unless one has participated in the operation or management of the enterprise itself.

B.

RICO's "liberal construction" clause does not require rejection of the "operation or management" test. Congress directed that the "provisions of this title shall be liberally construed to effectuate its remedial purposes." This clause obviously seeks to ensure that Congress' intent is not frustrated by an overly narrow reading of the statute, but it is not an invitation to apply RICO to new purposes that Congress never intended. Nor does the clause help us to determine what purposes Congress had in mind. Those must be gleaned from the statute through the normal means of interpretation. In this case it is clear that Congress did not intend to extend RICO liability under § 1962(c) beyond those who participate in the operation or management of an enterprise through a pattern of racketeering activity.

V.

Petitioners argue that the "operation or management" test is flawed because liability under § 1962(c) is not limited to upper management but may extend to "any person employed by or associated with [the] enterprise." We agree that liability under § 1962(c) is not limited to upper management, but we disagree that the "operation or management" test is inconsistent with this proposition. An enterprise is "operated" not just by upper management but also by lower rung participants in the enterprise who are under the direction of upper management.[9] An enterprise also might be "operated" or "managed" by others "associated with" the enterprise who exert control over it as, for example, by bribery.

The United States also argues that the "operation or management" test is not consistent with § 1962(c) because it limits the liability of "outsiders" who have no official position within the enterprise. The United States correctly points out that RICO's major purpose was to attack the "infiltration of organized crime and racketeering into legitimate organizations," but its argument fails on several counts. First, it ignores the fact that § 1962 has four subsections. Infiltration of legitimate organizations by "outsiders" is clearly addressed in subsections (a) and (b), and the "operation or management" test that applies under subsection (c) in no way limits the application of subsections (a) and (b) to "outsiders." Second, § 1962(c) is limited to persons "employed by or associated with" an enterprise, suggesting a more limited reach than subsections (a) and (b), which do not contain such a restriction. Third, § 1962(c) cannot be interpreted to reach complete "outsiders" because liability depends on showing that the defendants conducted or participated in the conduct of the "*enterprise's* affairs," not just their *own* affairs. Of course, "outsiders" may be liable under § 1962(c) if they are "associated with" an enterprise and participate in the conduct of *its* affairs — that is, participate in the operation or management of the enterprise itself — but it would be consistent with neither the language nor the legislative history of § 1962(c) to interpret it as broadly as petitioners and the United States urge.

In sum, we hold that "to conduct or participate, directly or indirectly, in the conduct of such enterprise's affairs," § 1962(c), one must participate in the operation or management of the enterprise itself.

VI.

Both the District Court and the Court of Appeals applied the standard we adopt today to the facts of this case, and both found that respondent was entitled to summary judgment. Neither petitioners nor the United States have argued that

---

[9] At oral argument, there was some discussion about whether low-level employees could be considered to have participated in the conduct of an enterprise's affairs. We need not decide in this case how far § 1962(c) extends down the ladder of operation because it is clear that Arthur Young was not acting under the direction of the Co-Op's officers or board.

these courts misapplied the "operation or management" test. The dissent argues that by creating the Co-Op's financial statements Arthur Young participated in the management of the Co-Op because " 'financial statements are management's responsibility.' " Although the professional standards adopted by the accounting profession may be relevant, they do not define what constitutes management of an enterprise for the purposes of § 1962(c). . . .

The judgment of the Court of Appeals is affirmed.

JUSTICE SOUTER, with whom JUSTICE WHITE joins, dissenting.

In the word "conduct," the Court today finds a clear congressional mandate to limit RICO liability under 18 U.S.C. § 1962(c) to participants in the "operation or management" of a RICO enterprise. What strikes the Court as clear, however, looks at the very least hazy to me, and I accordingly find the statute's "liberal construction" provision not irrelevant, but dispositive. But even if I were to assume, with the majority, that the word "conduct" clearly imports some degree of direction or control into § 1962(c), I would have to say that the majority misapplies its own "operation or management" test to the facts presented here. I therefore respectfully dissent.

* * *

Even if I were to adopt the majority's view of § 1962(c), . . . I still could not join the judgment, which seems to me unsupportable under the very "operation or management" test the Court announces. If Arthur Young had confined itself in this case to the role traditionally performed by an outside auditor, I could agree with the majority that Arthur Young took no part in the management or operation of the Farmer's Cooperative of Arkansas and Oklahoma, Inc. (Co-Op). . . . Most importantly, Reves adduced evidence that Arthur Young took on management responsibilities, and Arthur Young itself conceded below that the alleged activity went beyond traditional auditing. Because I find, then, that even under the majority's "operation or management" test the Court of Appeals erroneously affirmed the summary judgment for Arthur Young, I would (again) reverse. . . .

NOTES AND QUESTIONS

1. *Employees and the "operation or management test."* What are the boundaries of the test the Court adopts? When do mid- or low-level employees of the enterprise meet the test? Note that the Court specifically avoided providing guidance on this issue.

2. *Outside advisors.* When do lawyers, accountants, or others "operate or manage" an enterprise?

* * *

In *Reves*, the Supreme Court adopted the "operation or management test." In the next case, the Eighth Circuit Court of Appeals applied the *Reves* test to an interesting set of facts. As you read the case, consider how you would advise a client concerning the circumstances in which an outsider's actions will amount to "conduct[ing]" an enterprise's affairs.

HANDEEN v. LEMAIRE
112 F.3d 1339 (8th Cir. 1997)

FLOYD R. GIBSON, CIRCUIT JUDGE.

Paul Handeen appeals the district court's order granting summary judgment in favor of the Orlins & Brainerd Law Firm and its principals (collectively the "Firm") on his claims under the Racketeer Influenced and Corrupt Organizations Act ("RICO"), 18 U.S.C. §§ 1961–1968. Given the procedural posture of this case, we find ourselves constrained to reverse the district court's dismissal of Handeen's RICO cause of action.

I. BACKGROUND

The appeal before us traces its genesis to a series of unfortunate events that has already been the subject of extensive litigation in this Court, *see Handeen v. LeMaire (In re LeMaire)*, 898 F.2d 1346, 1347–48 (8th Cir. 1990) (en banc) (*"LeMaire II"*) (describing underlying factual foundation), *rev'g* 883 F.2d 1373, 1375–76 (8th Cir. 1989) (containing further elaboration), and we see no present need to retell that sorry tale. Suffice it to say that Gregory Lemaire (individually referred to as "Gregory" or "Lemaire") set out to execute Handeen on July 9, 1978, and he very nearly succeeded.[2] As a result of this intentional deed, Lemaire pleaded guilty to a charge of aggravated assault and spent twenty-seven months in a Minnesota prison. Following his release, Lemaire resumed his graduate studies at the University of Minnesota and in January 1986 received a doctoral degree in, of all things, experimental behavioral pharmacology.

Handeen filed a civil suit against Lemaire and obtained a consent judgment in excess of $50,000. Lemaire used funds received from his father to pay an initial lump sum of $3,000 due under the judgment, but he failed to remit any agreed-upon monthly installments. This prompted Handeen to commence garnishment proceedings to collect the balance due him. Lemaire, who was represented by the Firm, filed a Chapter 13 bankruptcy petition shortly thereafter. . . .

---

[2] Lemaire represented himself *pro se* in the instant action, and one of the numerous documents he filed with the district court is a rambling, thirty-one page Answer recounting with chilling detail his version of the events which transpired on that summer day:

> The rifle was a semi-automatic, .22-calibre rifle that I had purchased many years before for the sole purpose of shooting at tin cans with my friends. The rifle was capable of holding 16 bullets. Prior to the shooting, I had loaded bullets into the gun in the front seat of my car; in checking that a bullet was in the chamber, I had ejected one bullet, which landed on the floor on the passenger's side of the front seat. When I began shooting at Mr. Handeen, it was from the car in which I sat, perhaps 150–200 feet away from him. I then left the car and ran toward him, continuing to shoot. At some point in my approach to him, there were no more bullets left in the gun. I ran back to the car, picked up the single remaining bullet from the floor of the car, placed it in the chamber of the rifle, and ran to Mr. Handeen. At the instant that I came to stand directly over Mr. Handeen, there was no thought involved: I clipped-on the safety mechanism of the rifle and placed it on the roof of Mr. Handeen's car, which was directly adjacent to us. From then on, I agitatedly paced back and forth in the street with raised hands, yelling to Mr. Handeen (who repeatedly attempted to rise), "Stay down![ ] Stay down! The ambulance is coming!" . . . I evidently did fire nine shots with the intent to execute Mr. Handeen; I did not fire the tenth shot, which would have done so.

Upon reading Lemaire's submissions to the district court, one comes away with the distinct impression that he considers himself the primary victim in this affair. This is a sentiment we do not share.

Handeen initiated this suit against the Firm and the Lemaires on October 16, 1992. The Complaint paints a sordid portrait of an intricate scheme through which Lemaire sought to fraudulently obtain a discharge of Handeen's judgment by manipulating the bankruptcy system.[3] As part of this plot, the Firm and the Lemaires contrived to minimize whatever reduced recovery Handeen might achieve via the bankruptcy process. To this end, the Firm instructed Gregory to inflate the amount of his debts by agreeing to pay his parents rent and by executing a false promissory note payable to the elder Lemaires.[4] Gregory listed his parents as creditors on schedules he filed with the bankruptcy court,[5] and the Firm relied on the parents' claims when preparing proposed repayment plans. Of course, to the extent the bankruptcy court recognized this "indebtedness," it would reduce Handeen's pro rata share of any Chapter 13 distributions. Indeed, the cabal enjoyed success in this venture, for the bankruptcy court in substantial measure approved the parents' petitions against the estate.[6] As such, Gregory's parents received a portion of the sums he paid under the approved plan, and they compounded the fraud by transferring much of this money back to Gregory.

The intrigue, however, does not end there. In 1989, while Handeen was appealing the bankruptcy court's confirmation of the Chapter 13 plan, Gregory found a new job which required him to relocate from Minneapolis to Houston, Texas. This employment significantly enhanced Lemaire's income. Nonetheless, presumably because a person who takes refuge in Chapter 13 must ordinarily devote to the repayment plan "all of the debtor's projected disposable income," Lemaire did not wish to reveal his increased wages to the bankruptcy trustee. Consequently, Lemaire, his parents, and the Firm formulated an artifice to avoid rousing the trustee's attention. Specifically, the ruse called for Lemaire to mail his father a parcel every month. Within that package would be an envelope addressed to the bankruptcy trustee and containing a check representing Lemaire's monthly payment under the plan. Lemaire's father would, in turn, place the enclosed envelope in the mails, and the trustee would thus receive a letter postmarked from Minneapolis rather than Houston. The object, it is clear, was to fool the trustee into believing that the status quo ante existed, and this exploitation of the postal service remained a monthly ritual until the court dismissed Lemaire's plan in July of 1990.

In his Complaint, Handeen charges that the Firm and the Lemaires, through their duplicitous association with Gregory's bankruptcy estate, violated 18 U.S.C. § 1962(c) by conducting a RICO enterprise (the estate) through a pattern of racketeering activity. Handeen also alleges that the group conspired to violate RICO in violation of 18 U.S.C. § 1962(d). On summary judgment, the district court dismissed these claims against the Firm based on its determination that Handeen

---

[3] As we explain below, at the current stage of these proceedings we must accept as true all of the allegations within the Complaint. We pay homage to this requirement during our recitation of the salient facts.

[4] Gregory had never before paid his mother and father rent for the privilege of living in their home. Furthermore, the promissory note was dated January 15, 1987, only one day prior to the date Gregory filed for bankruptcy protection.

[5] The Complaint also indicates that the Firm advised Gregory not to disclose on his schedules a contingent debt in the amount of $30,000 to $50,000 which he would have been obligated to repay to the United States Public Health Service if he failed to fulfill the terms of a fellowship stipend. This obscuration could have resulted in discrimination among creditors.

[6] The Firm also represented Henry and Patricia Lemaire before the bankruptcy court, and it therefore defended their claims against objections lodged by Handeen.

had failed to demonstrate "the existence of a pattern of racketeering separate and apart from the bankruptcy estate."

Handeen now appeals the district court's dismissal of his RICO cause of action. We reverse the court's grant of summary judgment on these claims.

II. DISCUSSION

* * *

Liability under § 1962(c) extends only to those persons associated with or employed by an enterprise who "conduct or participate, directly or indirectly, in the conduct of such enterprise's affairs through a pattern of racketeering activity." 18 U.S.C. § 1962(c). In *Reves v. Ernst & Young*, 507 U.S. 170, 185 (1993), the Supreme Court confirmed that this Circuit has correctly interpreted the "conduct" requirement to authorize recovery only against individuals who "participate in the operation or management of the enterprise itself." The Supreme Court clarified the scope of the operation or management test, observing:

> An enterprise is "operated" not just by upper management but also by lower rung participants in the enterprise who are under the direction of upper management. An enterprise also might be "operated" or "managed" by others "associated with" the enterprise who exert control over it as, for example, by bribery.
>
> Section 1962(c) cannot be interpreted to reach complete "outsiders" because liability depends on showing that the defendants conducted or participated in the conduct of the "enterprise's affairs," not just their own affairs. Of course, "outsiders" may be liable under § 1962(c) if they are "associated with" an enterprise and participate in the conduct of its affairs — that is, participate in the operation or management of the enterprise itself.

Reves, 507 U.S. at 184–85. Consonant with the dictate of *Reves*, it is not necessary that a RICO defendant have wielded control over the enterprise, but the plaintiff "must prove some part in the direction . . . of the enterprise's affairs." *Darden*, 70 F.3d at 1543.

The Supreme Court's approval and refinement of our operation or management test has had far-reaching implications, particularly in the area of professional liability under RICO. This is not especially surprising, given that *Reves* itself involved an attempt to impute liability to an accounting firm. There, the accounting firm certified that a co-op's records adequately reflected its financial status, and the firm relied upon those existing records, in combination with a review of past co-op transactions, to prepare audits for the organization. *Reves*, 507 U.S. at 173–75. In completing these assignments, and without informing the co-op's board, the firm utilized questionable measures to verify the co-op's solvency. The Supreme Court affirmed our decision finding that the accounting firm's activity did not constitute conduct of a RICO enterprise.

In our view, the *Reves* decision represents a fairly uncomplicated application of the operation or management test. This test, like *Reves* itself, is built upon a recognition that Congress did not mean for § 1962(c) to penalize all who are employed by or associated with a RICO enterprise, but only those who, by virtue of their association or employment, play a part in directing the enterprise's affairs. Furnishing a client with ordinary professional assistance, even when the client happens to be a RICO enterprise, will not normally rise to the level of participation sufficient to satisfy the Supreme Court's pronouncements in *Reves.* In acknowledgment of this certainty, a growing number of courts, including our own, have held that an attorney or other professional does not conduct an enterprise's affairs through run-of-the-mill provision of professional services . . . . By the same token, RICO is not a surrogate for professional malpractice actions.

Appreciation for the unremarkable notion that the operation or management test does not reach persons who perform routine services for an enterprise should not, however, be mistaken for an absolute edict that an attorney who associates with an enterprise can never be liable under RICO. An attorney's license is not an invitation to engage in racketeering, and a lawyer no less than anyone else is bound by generally applicable legislative enactments. Neither *Reves* nor RICO itself exempts professionals, as a class, from the law's proscriptions, and the fact that a defendant has the good fortune to possess the title "attorney at law" is, standing alone, completely irrelevant to the analysis dictated by the Supreme Court. It is a good thing, we are sure, that we find it extremely difficult to fathom any scenario in which an attorney might expose himself to RICO liability by offering conventional advice to a client or performing ordinary legal tasks (that is, by acting like an attorney). This result, however, is not compelled by the fact that the person happens to be a lawyer, but for the reason that these actions do not entail the operation or management of an enterprise. Behavior prohibited by § 1962(c) will violate RICO regardless of the person to whom it may be attributed, and we will not shrink from finding an attorney liable when he crosses the line between traditional rendition of legal services and active participation in directing the enterprise. The polestar is the activity in question, not the defendant's status.

Bearing these principles in mind, we are confident that Handeen's Complaint could support a verdict against the Firm. At the outset, we think it worthwhile to reflect upon the nature of a Chapter 13 bankruptcy estate. Chapter 13 affords to a debtor with a regular source of income or earnings, and with a relatively small debt load, an opportunity to obtain a discharge of debts after devoting to creditors disposable income received over a period not to exceed five years. Furthermore, the decision to seek Chapter 13 relief is wholly voluntary, and the debtor may, subject to exceptions not presently relevant, dismiss his case at any time. Finally, it is the debtor's exclusive prerogative to file a proposed repayment plan, and he enjoys many of the powers normally reserved to a bankruptcy trustee.

These examples illustrate, in pointed fashion, that the debtor exercises significant control over his Chapter 13 estate. Of current paramountcy is how much of that control the debtor, in this case Lemaire, may have relinquished to others. If the Complaint is to be believed, as it must, the Firm might have been the beneficiary of considerable abdication. In keeping with the contentions in that pleading, Handeen's proof could show that the Firm and the Lemaires joined in a collaborative undertaking with the objective of releasing Gregory from the financial encumbrance visited upon him by Handeen's judgment. To realize that goal, Lemaire sought the assistance of the Firm. The attorneys, in turn, may have suggested that Chapter 13 bankruptcy, which presented a real opportunity for Lemaire to obtain a discharge of the debt arising from infliction of "willful and malicious injury by the debtor to another entity," 11 U.S.C. § 523(a)(6), offered the most propitious opportunity to reach the desired result. While Lemaire, obviously, was the party on whose behalf the Chapter 13 petition was filed, the Complaint could support a showing that the Firm navigated the estate through the bankruptcy system. Under this postulation, the Firm directed Gregory and his parents to enter into a false promissory note and create other sham debts to dilute the estate, the Firm represented the elder Lemaires and defended their fraudulent claims against objections, the Firm prepared Lemaire's filings and schedules containing erroneous information, the Firm formulated and promoted fraudulent repayment plans, and the Firm participated in devising a scheme to conceal Gregory's new job from the bankruptcy trustee. In short, Handeen might prove that Lemaire, who was, after all, ultimately interested solely in ridding himself of the oppressive judgment, controlled his estate in name only and relied upon the Firm, with its legal acuity, to take the lead in making important decisions concerning the operation of the enterprise.

We underscore that we have no basis for speculating whether Handeen will, in the end, be able to substantiate this narrative. We merely include the above hypothetical to show that relief is available "under a[ ] set of facts that could be proved consistent with the allegations." *Hishon*, 467 U.S. at 73. If Handeen's evidence is up to this challenge, we are comfortable that he will have succeeded in proving that the attorneys conducted the bankruptcy estate. In that event, this would not be a case where a lawyer merely extended advice on possible ways to manage an enterprise's affairs. Nor would this be a situation where counsel issued an opinion based on facts provided by a client. Instead, if the Firm truly did associate with the enterprise to the degree encompassed by the Complaint, we would not hesitate to hold that the attorneys "participated in the core activities that constituted the affairs of the [estate]," *Napoli v. United States*, 32 F.3d 31, 36 (2d Cir. 1994), namely, the manipulation of the bankruptcy process to obtain a discharge for Lemaire. In that instance, the Firm would have played some "role in the conception, creation, or execution," *Azrielli*, 21 F.3d at 521, of the illegal scheme, and we could safely say that the lawyers participated in the operation or management of the estate by assuming at least "some part in directing the enterprise's affairs." *Reves*, 507 U.S. at 179. Therefore, we conclude that the Complaint could justify a finding that the Firm participated in the conduct of the alleged RICO enterprise.

*   *   *

For reasons expressed in the preceding pages, we reverse the district court's order to the extent it grants the Firm's motion for summary judgment on Handeen's RICO claims.

NOTES AND QUESTIONS

1. *The* Reves *test.* The issues litigated in *Handeen* recur often in RICO cases. When applying the operation or management test, the court in *Reves* found that the facts were not sufficient to show that the defendants had "conducted" the affairs of the enterprise. What were the key facts in *Reves* that led to this outcome? Why was the outcome different in *Handeen*?

2. *Proof of the enterprise.* What proof is required to demonstrate a RICO enterprise? This question raises two related issues. First, must the associated-in-fact enterprise have an ascertainable structure? (In *Handeen*, the court held that

proof of such structure is required. The court also found that the structure was inherent in the formal nature of a bankruptcy estate.) Second, must the enterprise's structure be distinct from the structure necessary for the underlying racketeering activity? These issues typically arise in connection with "association-in-fact" enterprises; formal entities, such as bankruptcy estates, generally have ascertainable, separate structures by their very nature.

As the Ninth Circuit noted in its *en banc* opinion in *Odom v. Microsoft Corp.*, 486 F.3d 541, 549 (9th Cir. 2007), the circuit courts are almost evenly split on both of these issues. The Third, Fourth, Eighth, and Tenth Circuits require proof that the enterprise had an ascertainable structure, and further require proof that the structure be distinct from the structure necessary for the underlying racketeering activity. The Seventh Circuit requires that there be an ascertainable structure, but it does not require that the structure be separate from the racketeering activity. *See id.* at 549–550 (citing cases). These circuits reason that, without the separate structure, the enterprise is not distinct from the racketeering activity itself. The First, Second, Eleventh, and D.C. Circuits, on the other hand, have declined to require proof of an ascertainable structure apart from the racketeering activity. *Id. Compare, e.g., United States v. Riccobene*, 709 F.2d 214, 223–224 (3d Cir. 1983) (plaintiff must allege and prove an enterprise structure distinct from the racketeering activity), *with United States v. Coonan*, 938 F.2d 1553, 1560 (2d Cir. 1991) (enterprise may consist solely of the illegal activity).

The Ninth Circuit in *Odom* sided with those circuits that decline to require proof that the enterprise had a separate or ascertainable structure. All that is required, the court held, is proof that the associated-in-fact enterprise (1) had a common purpose, (2) functioned as an ongoing organization, and (3) operated as a continuing unit. 486 F.3d at 552. The court reasoned that *Turkette* compels this result: "To require that an associated-in-fact enterprise have a structure beyond that necessary to carry out its racketeering activities would be to require precisely what the Court in *Turkette* held that RICO does *not* require. Such a requirement would necessitate that the enterprise have a structure to serve both illegal racketeering activities as well as legitimate activities." *Id.* at 551. Which side of the circuit split has the better of the argument? Why?

The Supreme Court has granted certiorari to resolve this issue. *Boyle v. United States*, 2007 U.S. App. LEXIS 26757 (2d Cir. Nov. 19, 2007), *cert. granted*, 129 S. Ct. 29, 171 L. Ed. 2d 931 (Oct. 01, 2008) (No. 07–1309) (granting certiorari to resolve whether an association-in-fact enterprise must have a separate, ascertainable structure distinct from the series of predicate acts).

PROBLEMS

14-1. Jimmy Suarez ran a business, Suarez Importing, that imported counterfeit DVDs. Jimmy arranged for private containers containing the DVDs to be shipped from overseas and off-loaded at his warehouse. Jimmy had numerous associates who worked for him in his business. Sammy Smith arranged for the shipping of the containers. Nick Flint was a forklift operator who removed the containers from the ships, relocated them to Jimmy's warehouse, and unpacked them for shipping. Barbara Richards acted as a security guard at the warehouse. Barbara mostly took directions from and did odd tasks for Jimmy.

After a search warrant was executed at the warehouse, all four were charged with and convicted of violating 18 U.S.C. § 1962(c) based on numerous predicate acts of trafficking in goods or services bearing counterfeit marks, 18 U.S.C. § 2320. At trial, the district court gave the jury the following instructions on the RICO charge:

> The government must prove that the defendant conducted or participated in the affairs of the enterprise, Suarez Importing. The terms conduct and participate in the affairs of an enterprise include the performance of acts, functions, or duties that are necessary or helpful to the operation of the enterprise.

> A person may participate in the affairs of an enterprise even though he or she had no part in the management or control of the enterprise and no share in any profits. But the participation must be willful and knowing.

All the defendants were convicted on all counts, and appeal, challenging sufficiency of the evidence and the jury instruction.

How should the court rule? Why?

14-2. Lewis ran M & M Associates ("M & M"), a check-cashing business, out of a small enclosed area that Lewis rented in the back of Keller's bar. M & M charged its customers a 1% or 1.5% commission on each check cashed. Lewis used some of the commission money to run the business and to buy computers and other office equipment. M & M is a sole proprietorship, and has no employees other than Lewis, although Lewis did retain an accountant who came to M & M once or twice a month to keep the books.

Bookmakers tended to frequent Keller's and to use M & M as a check-cashing service. Sometimes, M & M cashed bookmaker checks that banks would not accept. For example, some checks were neither made out by nor payable to the bookmakers (or bookmakers' agents) who were cashing them. Lewis neither asked about the names on the checks he cashed nor required that the checks be endorsed. And Lewis never filed a currency transaction report (CTR) notifying the Internal Revenue Service of his many currency transactions involving more than $10,000, thus violating civil and criminal laws. Lewis engaged in dozens of these transactions over a five-year period.

Assume that you are the Assistant United States Attorney in charge of an investigation into Lewis' activities, and that you believe you have sufficient evidence to charge Lewis with multiple counts of money laundering, 18 U.S.C. § 1956(a)(1), and failing to file CTRs, 31 U.S.C. §§ 5313(a) and 5322(b). You are also considering seeking a RICO charge against Lewis.

What RICO theory or theories would be viable? What arguments might the defense assert if you pursued a RICO charge? What is the likelihood of success at trial on the RICO charge? Why?

[C] THE RACKETEERING ACTIVITY

Any RICO case rests upon proof that the defendant committed the required "racketeering activity," consisting of at least two "predicate acts." Section 1961(1)(B) lists the dozens of federal crimes that qualify as "racketeering activity." Section 1961(1)(A) provides a short list of state offenses that also qualify. Under

§ 1961(1)(A), racketeering activity includes "any act or threat involving murder, kidnaping, gambling, arson, robbery, bribery, extortion, dealing in obscene matter, or dealing in a controlled substance or listed chemical . . . , which is chargeable under State law and punishable by imprisonment for more than one year."

[1]   State Crimes

In the following case, the defendants argued that the alleged state law predicate act did not qualify under the statute. As you read the case, be sure to identify the state statute that the government used and the reasons for the court's conclusions.

UNITED STATES v. GENOVA
333 F.3d 750 (7th Cir. 2003)

EASTERBROOK, CIRCUIT JUDGE.

After his election in 1993 as Mayor of Calumet City, Illinois, Jerome Genova appointed Lawrence Gulotta as City Prosecutor and arranged for his law firm, Gulotta & Kawanna, to get the lion's share of the City's legal business. Both a jury (with respect to Genova) and the judge (with respect to Gulotta, who elected a bench trial) concluded that Genova had a financial reason for this decision: Gulotta kicked back to Genova about 30% of all payments his firm received from the City. Genova diverted public resources to private ends in at least one other way: He induced Jerome Stack, the Public Works Commissioner, to make employees available for political duties. Stack gave employees leave (to provide the cover story that they were doing politics on their own) while providing each with a day of "comp time" for every day of political work. For some tasks, such as attending fundraisers, Stack gave the employees overtime credit, which immediately padded their paychecks — and always in an amount enough to cover the cost of tickets that the employees had purchased for themselves and their families.

For these machinations, Genova, Gulotta, and Stack have been convicted of violating the Racketeer Influenced and Corrupt Organizations Act (RICO); they operated the City (an "enterprise") through a pattern of racketeering (the predicate offenses are bribery and mail fraud).

*   *   *

Section 1961(1)(B) enumerates the federal crimes that are "racketeering activity," and § 1961(1)(A) has a shorter but more general list of state offenses:

> [A]ny act or threat involving murder, kidnapping, gambling, arson, robbery, bribery, extortion, dealing in obscene matter, or dealing in a controlled substance or listed chemical (as defined in [21 U.S.C. § 802]), which is chargeable under State law and punishable by imprisonment for more than one year[.]

The indictment charged that Stack's award of comp time for political work was "bribery" under Illinois law, which in 720 ILCS 5/33-1(a) says that a person commits that crime when, with intent to influence the performance of any act related to the employment or function of any public officer, [or] public employee . . . he promises or tenders to that person any property or personal advantage which he is not authorized by law to accept[.]

Stack's RICO conviction is valid only if the use of public money to pay for political assistance violates § 5/33-1(a). . . .

The prosecutor alleged that Genova, too, committed the predicate offense of bribery, but in his case the underlying acts concerned the Statements of Economic Interest that elected officials must make annually. Genova filed statements that did not disclose the money he received from Gulotta & Kawanna; this omission, according to the indictment, violated 720 ILCS 5/33-3, a statute covering several varieties of official misconduct. Relying on *United States v. Garner*, 837 F.2d 1404 (7th Cir. 1987), the district judge instructed the jury that official misconduct in violation of § 5/33-3 is a form of bribery, and the jury then convicted Genova of violating RICO. After trial the judge concluded that this instruction had been mistaken, but that Genova's RICO conviction could stand, because mail fraud (the mailing of these false and misleading forms, as part of a scheme to retain office and continue receiving kickbacks) still supplied the necessary pattern of racketeering activity. Mail fraud, in violation of 18 U.S.C. § 1341, *is* on the list in § 1961(1)(B). The prosecutor defends this decision and also contends that the jury instruction was correct and that all of the jury's findings thus should stand.

Although we understand the temptation to dilate criminal statutes so that corrupt officials get their comeuppance, people are entitled to clear notice of what the criminal law forbids, and courts must take care not to enlarge the scope of illegality. *See, e.g., Scheidler v. National Organization for Women, Inc.*, 537 U.S. 393 (2003) (rejecting an expansive interpretation of extortion designed to bring noxious activity within RICO); *Bailey v. United States*, 516 U.S. 137 (1995) (rejecting an expansive interpretation of "use" in a gun-control statute); *McNally v. United States*, 483 U.S. 350 (1987) (disapproving the creative "intangible rights" theory of mail fraud). Congress responded to *Bailey and McNally* by amending the statutes to provide a basis for the theories the courts had developed. Perhaps RICO should cover political corruption that does not entail bribery or extortion. But such a change should occur through legislation rather than prosecutorial and judicial creativity. [T]his principle leads us to conclude that neither misapplication of public funds nor concealment of illicit income is "bribery."

Let us start with Genova's situation. Gulotta bribed Genova, but Genova did not bribe anyone — certainly not the county bureaucrats who received and put on public view his Statements of Economic Interest. Genova did not pay anyone to perform any official duty. The idea that any violation of 720 ILCS 5/33-3 entails bribery comes from failure to distinguish among its subsections. It provides:

> A public officer or employee commits misconduct when, in his official capacity, he commits any of the following acts:
>
> (a) Intentionally or recklessly fails to perform any mandatory duty as required by law; or
>
> (b) Knowingly performs an act which he knows he is forbidden by law to perform; or
>
> (c) With intent to obtain a personal advantage for himself or another, he performs an act in excess of his lawful authority; or
>
> (d) Solicits or knowingly accepts for the performance of any act a fee or reward which he knows is not authorized by law.

A public officer or employee convicted of violating any provision of this Section forfeits his office or employment. In addition, he commits a Class 3 felony.

Garner dealt with subsection (d), which defines a species of bribery. 837 F.2d at 1417–19. Genova's misconduct, however, was alleged to violate subsection (c). Using § 5/33-3(c) is itself a stretch, for the law requiring officials to file Statements of Economic Interest has its own penalty clause. Someone who files a false or incomplete statement commits a Class A misdemeanor, *see* 5 ILCS 420/4A-107, and no misdemeanor is "racketeering activity" under RICO. We could not find any Illinois decision suggesting that any statute other than § 420/4A-107 applies to a false, incomplete, or misleading Statement of Economic Interest. At all events, § 5/33-3(c) does not read like a definition of bribery and therefore may not be used as a predicate offense under RICO.

Stack's conduct also is hard to see as bribery. . . . The United States concedes that no Illinois decision supports its view that using public funds to pay municipal employees for political labor is bribery under 720 ILCS 5/33-1, and it would deprive Stack of fair warning to put that statute to such a novel use in order to secure his conviction for violating RICO. Stack's RICO conviction cannot stand.

Whether Genova's RICO conviction is tenable depends on the mail fraud convictions (and the predicate acts based on mail fraud). Each count of mail fraud (and each parallel predicate act under the RICO charge) represented one annual Statement of Economic Interest that omitted the money Genova had received the prior year from Gulotta & Kawanna. Genova does not contest the jury's evident conclusion that the statements (and hence the mailings) were false. He does contend that they were not part of a scheme to defraud, but this goes nowhere. Keeping a lid on the kickbacks was essential to permit their continuation. Genova hoodwinked Calumet City out of the money he received as kickbacks; he also defrauded the voters out of their intangible right to his honest services — a theory of culpability resurrected by 18 U.S.C. § 1346, enacted soon after *McNally*. A jury sensibly could conclude that the false mailings were integral to this scheme, so that Genova violated § 1341. *See, e.g., Schmuck v. United States*, 489 U.S. 705 (1989). And because the scheme extended over several years, a jury also sensibly could find a pattern of racketeering. *See H.J., Inc. v. Northwestern Bell Telephone Co.*, 492 U.S. 229 (1989). Because the jury returned special verdicts identifying particular racketeering acts, we know that it determined beyond a reasonable doubt that Genova committed at least two mail frauds, and there is no good reason to think that the verdicts finding mail fraud predicates could have been influenced by the incorrect jury instruction about treating 720 ILCS 5/33-3 as a form of bribery. Both the mail fraud and the RICO convictions therefore are untainted by error.

* * *

Bottom line: Genova's and Gulotta's convictions and sentences are affirmed . . . . Stack's RICO conviction is reversed . . . .

NOTES AND QUESTIONS

1. *Defining state law predicate acts.* Why did the court in *Genova* find that the state law violations in that case — 720 ILCS 5/33-1(a) and 720 ILCS 5/33-3(c) — did not qualify as RICO predicates? Be as specific as you can when answering this

question. With respect to Genova's liability, could the prosecutor have alleged another theory of bribery that would have satisfied the court?

With respect to the latter question, consider *United States v. Garner*, 837 F.2d 1404 (7th Cir. 1987), cited by the *Genova* court. The court in *Garner* noted that § 1961(1)(A) describes state crime predicate acts by *substance* rather than by the *title* of the state crime. With respect to the predicate act of state law bribery, the court in *Garner* stated that "Congress intended for 'bribery' to be defined generically when it included bribery as a predicate act. Thus, any statute that proscribes conduct which could be generically defined as bribery can be the basis for a predicate act . . . ." *Id.* at 1418. The state "official misconduct" crime at issue in *Garner* was in effect a gratuity statute; the crime did not require the proof of a quid pro quo that is the essence of bribery under federal law. And "gratuity" is not listed as a state law predicate. However, 18 U.S.C. § 201 sets forth the distinct crimes of bribery and gratuity, both of which are *federal* predicate acts under RICO. Thus, the court in *Garner* concluded, "We see no reason why Congress would have defined bribery more broadly for federal officials than for state officials, particularly when it is remembered that Congress intended for RICO to 'be liberally construed to effectuate its remedial purpose.' " *Id.* Given that bribery and gratuity are distinct crimes under 18 U.S.C. § 201, why did the court in *Garner* conclude that the receipt of an illegal gratuity qualifies as state law "bribery" under § 1961(1)(A)?

2. *Double jeopardy.* The RICO statute presents potentially complicated double jeopardy issues. For example, may the government (1) prosecute a defendant under RICO based upon the specified predicate acts necessary for a RICO conviction, *and* (2) later prosecute that same defendant for the predicate criminal acts themselves? In an analogous circumstance, a plurality of the Supreme Court concluded that, under the facts of the particular case, the defendant could be punished in successive prosecutions for both operating a "continuing criminal enterprise" and for the underlying offenses. *Garrett v. United States*, 471 U.S. 773 (1985).

[2] Federal Crimes

As noted above, § 1961(1) includes dozens of federal crimes. Many of these statutes apply in the white collar context. These include bribery, extortion, financial institution fraud, obstruction of justice, money laundering, securities fraud, and — most significantly — mail and wire fraud. But how far can the government go in using the mail and wire fraud statutes to incorporate other offenses that are *not* listed as RICO predicates? For example, perjury is listed neither as a state RICO predicate nor as a federal RICO predicate. But if a defendant used the mail in order to suborn perjury in a fraud scheme, would that act qualify as a RICO predicate under the mail fraud statute? That is the issue in the next case.

UNITED STATES v. EISEN
974 F.2d 246 (2d Cir. 1992)

JON O. NEWMAN, CIRCUIT JUDGE:

This is an appeal of RICO convictions arising from a law firm's fraudulent conduct of civil litigation as plaintiff's counsel in personal injury cases. . . .

Morris J. Eisen, P.C. ("the Eisen firm") was a large Manhattan law firm that specialized in bringing personal injury suits on behalf of plaintiffs. The defendants, seven of the Eisen firm's attorneys, investigators, and office personnel, were tried jointly on two counts of conducting and conspiring to conduct the affairs of the Eisen firm through a pattern of racketeering activity, in violation of 18 U.S.C. §§ 1962(c), (d). The indictment alleged, as the underlying acts of racketeering, that each of the defendants committed, among other crimes, numerous acts of mail fraud, in violation of 18 U.S.C. § 1341; and bribery of witnesses, in violation of New York Penal Law § 215.00.

Eisen was the founder, sole shareholder, and principal attorney of the Eisen firm. Napoli was associated with the Eisen firm in an "of counsel" capacity, and he was the main trial attorney for the firm. Fishman, a trial attorney, was also "of counsel" to the firm. The Eisen firm regularly used investigators to assist attorneys in the trial preparation of personal injury cases, and defendants Weinstein, Gabe, and Rella were private investigators affiliated with the firm. Morganti was the office administrator of the Eisen firm with responsibility for managing the daily affairs of the firm, including assigning attorneys and investigators to particular cases, monitoring the firm's daily calendar, and managing the financial and personnel operations of the firm.

The evidence at trial established that the defendants conducted the affairs of the Eisen law firm through a pattern of mail fraud and witness bribery by pursuing counterfeit claims and using false witnesses in personal injury trials, and that the Eisen firm earned millions in contingency fees from personal injury suits involving fraud or bribery. The methods by which the frauds were accomplished included pressuring accident witnesses to testify falsely, paying individuals to testify falsely that they had witnessed accidents, paying unfavorable witnesses not to testify, and creating false photographs, documents, and physical evidence of accidents for use before and during trial. The government's proof included the testimony of numerous Eisen firm attorneys and employees as well as Eisen firm clients, defense attorneys, and witnesses involved in the fraudulent personal injury suits. Transcripts, correspondence, and trial exhibits from the fraudulent personal injury suits were also introduced.

The racketeering acts considered by the jury related to the defendants' conduct with regard to 18 fraudulent personal injury lawsuits in which the plaintiff was represented by the Eisen firm. . . . The jury convicted all seven defendants of RICO substantive and conspiracy offenses after three weeks of deliberations.

* * *

[W]einstein contends that permitting the mail fraud offenses charged in the Eisen indictment to serve as RICO predicate acts conflicts with the deliberate decision made by Congress in omitting perjury as one of the enumerated RICO predicate offenses within the definition of "racketeering activity." *See* 18 U.S.C. § 1961(1). Contrary to the government's abrupt dismissal of this argument as "baseless," we recognize that there is some tension between the congressional decision to include federal mail fraud as a predicate offense and to exclude perjury, whether in violation of federal or state law. That tension is illustrated by this prosecution in which the fraudulent scheme consists primarily of arranging for state court witnesses to commit perjury.

Though the tension exists, we do not believe it places the indictment in this case beyond the purview of RICO. Congress did not wish to permit instances of federal or state court perjury as such to constitute a pattern of RICO racketeering acts. Apparently, there was an understandable reluctance to use federal criminal law as a back-stop for all state court litigation. Nevertheless, where, as here, a fraudulent scheme falls within the scope of the federal mail fraud statute and the other elements of RICO are established, use of the mail fraud offense as a RICO predicate act cannot be suspended simply because perjury is part of the means for perpetrating the fraud. We do not doubt that where a series of related state court perjuries occurs, it will often be possible to allege and prove both a scheme to defraud within the meaning of the mail fraud statute as well as the elements of a RICO violation. But in such cases, it will not be the fact of the perjuries alone that suffices to bring the matter within the scope of RICO. In any event, we cannot carve out from the coverage of RICO an exception for mail fraud offenses that involve state court perjuries.

* * *

The judgments of conviction appealed from are all affirmed.

NOTES AND QUESTIONS

1. *Federalism issues.* Because the mail and wire fraud statutes are included as RICO predicates, and because those statutes are so far-reaching, RICO applies to a huge range of circumstances. Many RICO cases may look like ordinary state criminal or civil cases that have been federalized by RICO. What was the Second Circuit's concern about the government's theory of the case in *Eisen*? Given those concerns, why did the court affirm the conviction?

2. *Mail and wire fraud.* How much latitude does the government have in applying RICO through the mail and wire fraud statutes? For example, tax fraud is not listed as a RICO predicate. But, if a taxpayer submits a fraudulent tax return via mails or wires, may that lead to potential RICO liability? The government employed this controversial theory in one high-profile case, *United States v. Regan*, 937 F.2d 823 (2d Cir. 1991), *modified*, 946 F.2d 188 (2d Cir. 1991). At least in part because of the controversy over *Regan*, the Department of Justice later issued guidelines restricting the use of tax fraud/mail fraud as a RICO predicate. *See* U.S. Department of Justice, United States Attorneys' Manual, § 6-4.210. Does that mean that the government could not again bring a case on this theory? *See* Ellen S. Podgor, *Department of Justice Guidelines: Balancing "Discretionary Justice,"* 13 Cornell J.L. & Pub. Pol'y 167 (2004).

3. *Securities fraud.* Under § 1961(1), a defendant generally need not be charged with or convicted of the predicate acts; the statute only requires that the alleged acts be "chargeable," "indictable," or "punishable" under the applicable state or federal statute. As discussed more fully below, however, there is an exception to this rule in private RICO suits alleging securities fraud as the predicate acts.

PROBLEM

14-3. Defendant Grosser was "Of Counsel" to the law firm of Simon and Garcia, and was one of the four main trial attorneys for the firm. Simon and Garcia were the principals of the firm, which had six other partners and 18 associates. Grosser was the only attorney who acted as "Of Counsel" to the firm. Grosser was tried along with Simon under RICO.

The evidence at trial established that Grosser participated in a pattern of paying off court personnel to fix cases, and that the firm earned millions in contingency fees from these cases. The government's proof included the testimony of numerous firm attorneys, employees, and clients, as well as defense attorneys and witnesses involved in the fraudulent personal injury suits. Transcripts, correspondence, and trial exhibits from the fraudulent personal injury suits were also introduced. Grosser was found guilty under RICO based upon racketeering acts involving four personal injury cases in which he paid substantial sums of money to court clerks to divulge secret jury deliberations. The government's theory was that Grosser conducted the law firm's affairs through a pattern of racketeering activity in violation of § 1962(c).

As "Of Counsel" to the firm, Grosser had an office within the firm's offices, for which Grosser paid rent. Grosser assisted the firm on an "as-needed" basis, but was not employed by or a partner in the firm. There was evidence presented to the jury that Grosser handled approximately five percent of the firm's caseload and produced approximately five percent of the firm's income through jury verdicts and settlements. There was no evidence that Grosser participated in firm policy decisions, such as hiring, benefits, or salary decisions. He did not attend firm partnership meetings, but did regularly attend the annual firm retreat of all firm lawyers at which general firm policy was discussed.

The indictment alleged that the four pay-offs violated each of the following state statutes, which the government charged as the eight predicate acts in the case:

Penal Code § 100 (Bribery):

A person is guilty of bribery, a felony of the third degree, if he offers, confers, agrees to offer or confer upon another, or solicits, accepts or agrees to accept from another:

(1) any pecuniary benefit as consideration for the decision, opinion, recommendation, vote or other exercise of discretion as a public servant, party official or voter by the recipient;

(2) any benefit as consideration for the decision, vote, recommendation or other exercise of official discretion by the recipient in a judicial, administrative or legislative proceeding; or

(3) any benefit as consideration for a violation of a known legal duty as a public servant or party official.

A violation of this section is punishable by imprisonment up to one year.

Penal Code § 300 (Corrupt Compensation):

Whoever follows the occupation or practice of providing public officers of the State or of any political subdivision thereof with any compensation or thing of value otherwise than as provided for by the law of the state or political subdivision is guilty of the practice of corrupt compensation, a misdemeanor, and upon conviction thereof, shall be sentenced to pay a fine not exceeding one thousand dollars ($1,000), or to undergo imprisonment not exceeding two (2) years, or both.

Defendant appeals the conviction. Should he prevail? Why or why not?

[D]   THE PATTERN REQUIREMENT

In a RICO case, the government or private plaintiff must allege and prove that the defendant committed or entered into a conspiracy to commit a "pattern of racketeering activity."[f] Under § 1961(5), a RICO pattern "requires at least two acts of racketeering activity, one of which occurred after the effective date of this chapter and the last of which occurred within ten years . . . after the commission of a prior act of racketeering activity." In the next case, the Supreme Court turned its attention to the pattern requirement. As you read the case, pay particular attention to Justice Scalia's concurring opinion. The second case in the section illustrates how lower courts have applied the approach adopted by the Supreme Court for determining the existence of a RICO pattern.

H.J. INC. v. NORTHWESTERN BELL TELEPHONE CO.
492 U.S. 229 (1989)

JUSTICE BRENNAN delivered the opinion of the Court.

The Racketeer Influenced and Corrupt Organizations Act (RICO or Act), imposes criminal and civil liability upon those who engage in certain "prohibited activities." Each prohibited activity is defined in 18 U.S.C. § 1962 to include, as one necessary element, proof either of "a pattern of racketeering activity" or of "collection of an unlawful debt." "Racketeering activity" is defined in RICO to mean "any act or threat involving" specified state-law crimes, any "act" indictable under various specified federal statutes, and certain federal "offenses," 18 U.S.C. § 1961(1); but of the term "pattern" the statute says only that it "requires at least two acts of racketeering activity" within a 10-year period, 18 U.S.C. § 1961(5). We are called upon in this civil case to consider what conduct meets RICO's pattern requirement.

I.

*   *   *

Petitioners, customers of respondent Northwestern Bell Telephone Co., filed this putative class action in 1986 in the District Court for the District of Minnesota. Petitioners alleged violations of §§ 1962(a), (b), (c), and (d) by Northwestern Bell and the other respondents — some of the telephone company's officers and employees, various members of the Minnesota Public Utilities Commission (MPUC), and other unnamed individuals and corporations — and sought an injunction and treble damages under RICO's civil liability provisions, §§ 1964(a) and (c).

---

[f] An individual may also violate § 1962 through "collection of an unlawful debt," as defined by 18 U.S.C. § 1961(6).

The MPUC is the state body responsible for determining the rates that Northwestern Bell may charge. Petitioners' five-count complaint alleged that between 1980 and 1986 Northwestern Bell sought to influence members of the MPUC in the performance of their duties — and in fact caused them to approve rates for the company in excess of a fair and reasonable amount — by making cash payments to commissioners, negotiating with them regarding future employment, and paying for parties and meals, for tickets to sporting events and the like, and for airline tickets. Based upon these factual allegations, petitioners alleged in their first count a pendent state-law claim, asserting that Northwestern Bell violated the Minnesota bribery statute, Minn. Stat. § 609.42, as well as state common law prohibiting bribery. They also raised four separate claims under § 1962 of RICO. Count II alleged that, in violation of § 1962(a), Northwestern Bell derived income from a pattern of racketeering activity involving predicate acts of bribery and used this income to engage in its business as an interstate "enterprise." Count III claimed a violation of § 1962(b), in that, through this same pattern of racketeering activity, respondents acquired an interest in or control of the MPUC, which was also an interstate "enterprise." In Count IV, petitioners asserted that respondents participated in the conduct and affairs of the MPUC through this pattern of racketeering activity, contrary to § 1962(c). Finally, Count V alleged that respondents conspired together to violate §§ 1962(a), (b), and (c), thereby contravening § 1962(d).

The District Court granted respondents' Federal Rule of Civil Procedure 12(b)(6) motion, dismissing the complaint for failure to state a claim upon which relief could be granted. The court found that "[e]ach of the fraudulent acts alleged by [petitioners] was committed in furtherance of a single scheme to influence MPUC commissioners to the detriment of Northwestern Bell's ratepayers." It held that dismissal was therefore mandated by the Court of Appeals for the Eighth Circuit's decision in *Superior Oil Co. v. Fulmer*, 785 F.2d 252 (8th Cir. 1986), which the District Court interpreted as adopting an "extremely restrictive" test for a pattern of racketeering activity that required proof of "multiple illegal schemes." The Court of Appeals for the Eighth Circuit affirmed the dismissal of petitioners' complaint, confirming that under Eighth Circuit precedent "[a] single fraudulent effort or scheme is insufficient" to establish a pattern of racketeering activity, and agreeing with the District Court that petitioners' complaint alleged only a single scheme. Most Courts of Appeals have rejected the Eighth Circuit's interpretation of RICO's pattern concept to require an allegation and proof of multiple schemes, and we granted certiorari to resolve this conflict. We now reverse.

II.

In *Sedima, S.P.R.L. v. Imrex Co.*, 473 U.S. 479 (1985), this Court rejected a restrictive interpretation of § 1964(c) that would have made it a condition for maintaining a civil RICO action both that the defendant had already been convicted of a predicate racketeering act or of a RICO violation, and that plaintiff show a special racketeering injury. In doing so, we acknowledged concern in some quarters over civil RICO's use against "legitimate" businesses, as well as "mobsters and organized criminals" — a concern that had frankly led to the Court of Appeals' interpretation of § 1964(c) in *Sedima*. But we suggested that RICO's expansive uses "appear to be primarily the result of the breadth of the predicate offenses, in particular the inclusion of wire, mail, and securities fraud, and the failure of

Congress and the courts to develop a meaningful concept of 'pattern' " — both factors that apply to criminal as well as civil applications of the Act. *Id.* at 500. Congress has done nothing in the interim further to illuminate RICO's key requirement of a pattern of racketeering; and as the plethora of different views expressed by the Courts of Appeals since *Sedima* demonstrates, developing a meaningful concept of "pattern" within the existing statutory framework has proved to be no easy task.

It is, nevertheless, a task we must undertake in order to decide this case. Our guides in the endeavor must be the text of the statute and its legislative history. We find no support in those sources for the proposition, espoused by the Court of Appeals for the Eighth Circuit in this case, that predicate acts of racketeering may form a pattern only when they are part of separate illegal schemes. Nor can we agree with those courts that have suggested that a pattern is established merely by proving two predicate acts, or with *amici* in this case who argue that the word "pattern" refers only to predicates that are indicative of a perpetrator involved in organized crime or its functional equivalent. In our view, Congress had a more natural and commonsense approach to RICO's pattern element in mind, intending a more stringent requirement than proof simply of two predicates, but also envisioning a concept of sufficient breadth that it might encompass multiple predicates within a single scheme that were related and that amounted to, or threatened the likelihood of, continued criminal activity.

A.

We begin, of course, with RICO's text, in which Congress followed a "pattern [of] utilizing terms and concepts of breadth." *Russello v. United States*, 464 U.S. 16, 21 (1983). As we remarked in *Sedima, supra,* 473 U.S. at 496 n.14,[g] the section of the statute headed "definitions," 18 U.S.C. § 1961, does not so much define a pattern of racketeering activity as state a minimum necessary condition for the existence of such a pattern. Unlike other provisions in § 1961 that tell us what various concepts used in the Act "mean," 18 U.S.C. § 1961(5) says of the phrase "pattern of racketeering activity" only that it "requires at least two acts of racketeering activity, one of which occurred after [October 15, 1970,] and the last of which occurred within ten years (excluding any period of imprisonment) after the

---

[g] Here is the footnote to which the Court refers:

As many commentators have pointed out, the definition of a "pattern of racketeering activity" differs from the other provisions in § 1961 in that it states that a pattern *"requires* at least two acts of racketeering activity," § 1961(5) (emphasis added), not that it "means" two such acts. The implication is that while two acts are necessary, they may not be sufficient. Indeed, in common parlance two of anything do not generally form a "pattern." The legislative history supports the view that two isolated acts of racketeering activity do not constitute a pattern. As the Senate Report explained: "The target of [RICO] is thus not sporadic activity. The infiltration of legitimate business normally requires more than one 'racketeering activity' and the threat of continuing activity to be effective. It is this factor of *continuity plus relationship* which combines to produce a pattern." S. Rep. No. 91-617, p. 158 (1969) (emphasis added). Similarly, the sponsor of the Senate bill, after quoting this portion of the Report, pointed out to his colleagues that "[t]he term 'pattern' itself requires the showing of a relationship . . . . So, therefore, proof of two acts of racketeering activity, without more, does not establish a pattern . . . ." 116 Cong. Rec. 18940 (1970) (statement of Sen. McClellan). Significantly, in defining "pattern" in a later provision of the same bill, Congress was more enlightening: "[C]riminal conduct forms a pattern if it embraces criminal acts that have the same or similar purposes, results, participants, victims, or methods of commission, or otherwise are interrelated by distinguishing characteristics and are not isolated events." 18 U.S.C. § 3575(e). This language may be useful in interpreting other sections of the Act.

commission of a prior act of racketeering activity." It thus places an outer limit on the concept of a pattern of racketeering activity that is broad indeed.

Section 1961(5) does indicate that Congress envisioned circumstances in which no more than two predicates would be necessary to establish a pattern of racketeering — otherwise it would have drawn a narrower boundary to RICO liability, requiring proof of a greater number of predicates. But, at the same time, the statement that a pattern "requires at least" two predicates implies "that while two acts are necessary, they may not be sufficient." *Sedima*, 473 U.S. at 496 (Powell, J., dissenting). Section 1961(5) concerns only the minimum *number* of predicates necessary to establish a pattern; and it assumes that there is something to a RICO pattern *beyond* simply the number of predicate acts involved. The legislative history bears out this interpretation, for the principal sponsor of the Senate bill expressly indicated that "proof of two acts of racketeering activity, without more, does not establish a pattern." 116 Cong. Rec. 18940 (1970) (statement of Sen. McClellan). Section 1961(5) does not identify, though, these additional prerequisites for establishing the existence of a RICO pattern.

In addition to § 1961(5), there is the key phrase "pattern of racketeering activity" itself, from § 1962, and we must "start with the assumption that the legislative purpose is expressed by the ordinary meaning of the words used." *Richards v. United States*, 369 U.S. 1, 9 (1962). In normal usage, the word "pattern" here would be taken to require more than just a multiplicity of racketeering predicates. A "pattern" is an "arrangement or order of things or activity," 11 Oxford English Dictionary 357 (2d ed. 1989), and the mere fact that there are a number of predicates is no guarantee that they fall into any arrangement or order. It is not the number of predicates but the relationship that they bear to each other or to some external organizing principle that renders them "ordered" or "arranged." The text of RICO conspicuously fails anywhere to identify, however, forms of relationship or external principles to be used in determining whether racketeering activity falls into a pattern for purposes of the Act.

It is reasonable to infer, from this absence of any textual identification of sorts of pattern that would satisfy § 1962's requirement, in combination with the very relaxed limits to the pattern concept fixed in § 1961(5), that Congress intended to take a flexible approach, and envisaged that a pattern might be demonstrated by reference to a range of different ordering principles or relationships between predicates, within the expansive bounds set. For any more specific guidance as to the meaning of "pattern," we must look past the text to RICO's legislative history, as we have done in prior cases construing the Act.

The legislative history, which we discussed in *Sedima*, 473 U.S. at 496 n.14, shows that Congress indeed had a fairly flexible concept of a pattern in mind. A pattern is not formed by "sporadic activity," S. Rep. No. 91-617 at 158 (1969), and a person cannot "be subjected to the sanctions of title IX simply for committing two widely separated and isolated criminal offenses," 116 Cong. Rec. at 18940 (1970) (Sen. McClellan). Instead, "[t]he term 'pattern' itself requires the showing of a relationship" between the predicates, *id.*, and of " 'the threat of continuing activity,' " *id.*, quoting S. Rep. No. 91-617, at 158. "It is this factor of *continuity plus relationship* which combines to produce a pattern." *Id.* (emphasis added). RICO's legislative history reveals Congress' intent that to prove a pattern of racketeering activity a plaintiff or prosecutor must show that the racketeering predicates are related, *and* that they amount to or pose a threat of continued criminal activity.

B.

For analytic purposes these two constituents of RICO's pattern requirement must be stated separately, though in practice their proof will often overlap. The element of relatedness is the easier to define, for we may take guidance from a provision elsewhere in the Organized Crime Control Act of 1970 (OCCA), Pub.L. 91-452, 84 Stat. 922, of which RICO formed Title IX. OCCA included as Title X the Dangerous Special Offender Sentencing Act, 18 U.S.C. § 3575 *et seq.* (now partially repealed). Title X provided for enhanced sentences where, among other things, the defendant had committed a prior felony as part of a pattern of criminal conduct or in furtherance of a conspiracy to engage in a pattern of criminal conduct. As we noted in *Sedima,* Congress defined Title X's pattern requirement solely in terms of the *relationship* of the defendant's criminal acts one to another: "[C]riminal conduct forms a pattern if it embraces criminal acts that have the same or similar purposes, results, participants, victims, or methods of commission, or otherwise are interrelated by distinguishing characteristics and are not isolated events." Section 3575(e). We have no reason to suppose that Congress had in mind for RICO's pattern of racketeering component any more constrained a notion of the relationships between predicates that would suffice.

RICO's legislative history tells us, however, that the relatedness of racketeering activities is not alone enough to satisfy § 1962's pattern element. To establish a RICO pattern it must also be shown that the predicates themselves amount to, or that they otherwise constitute a threat of, *continuing* racketeering activity. As to this continuity requirement, § 3575(e) is of no assistance. It is this aspect of RICO's pattern element that has spawned the "multiple scheme" test adopted by some lower courts, including the Court of Appeals in this case. But although proof that a RICO defendant has been involved in multiple criminal schemes would certainly be highly relevant to the inquiry into the continuity of the defendant's racketeering activity, it is implausible to suppose that Congress thought continuity might be shown *only* by proof of multiple schemes. The Eighth Circuit's test brings a rigidity to the available methods of proving a pattern that simply is not present in the idea of "continuity" itself; and it does so, moreover, by introducing a concept — the "scheme" — that appears nowhere in the language or legislative history of the Act. We adopt a less inflexible approach that seems to us to derive from a commonsense, everyday understanding of RICO's language and Congress' gloss on it. What a plaintiff or prosecutor must prove is continuity of racketeering activity, or its threat, *simpliciter.* This may be done in a variety of ways, thus making it difficult to formulate in the abstract any general test for continuity. We can, however, begin to delineate the requirement.

"Continuity" is both a closed- and open-ended concept, referring either to a closed period of repeated conduct, or to past conduct that by its nature projects into the future with a threat of repetition. It is, in either case, centrally a temporal concept — and particularly so in the RICO context, where *what* must be continuous, RICO's predicate acts or offenses, and the *relationship* these predicates must bear one to another, are distinct requirements. A party alleging a RICO violation may demonstrate continuity over a closed period by proving a series of related predicates extending over a substantial period of time. Predicate acts extending over a few weeks or months and threatening no future criminal conduct do not satisfy this requirement: Congress was concerned in RICO with long-term criminal conduct. Often a RICO action will be brought before continuity can be established in this way. In such cases, liability depends on whether the *threat* of continuity is demonstrated.

Whether the predicates proved establish a threat of continued racketeering activity depends on the specific facts of each case. Without making any claim to cover the field of possibilities — preferring to deal with this issue in the context of concrete factual situations presented for decision — we offer some examples of how this element might be satisfied. A RICO pattern may surely be established if the related predicates themselves involve a distinct threat of long-term racketeering activity, either implicit or explicit. Suppose a hoodlum were to sell "insurance" to a neighborhood's storekeepers to cover them against breakage of their windows, telling his victims he would be reappearing each month to collect the "premium" that would continue their "coverage." Though the number of related predicates involved may be small and they may occur close together in time, the racketeering acts themselves include a specific threat of repetition extending indefinitely into the future, and thus supply the requisite threat of continuity. In other cases, the threat of continuity may be established by showing that the predicate acts or offenses are part of an ongoing entity's regular way of doing business. Thus, the threat of continuity is sufficiently established where the predicates can be attributed to a defendant operating as part of a long-term association that exists for criminal purposes. Such associations include, but extend well beyond, those traditionally grouped under the phrase "organized crime." The continuity requirement is likewise satisfied where it is shown that the predicates are a regular way of conducting defendant's ongoing legitimate business (in the sense that it is not a business that exists for criminal purposes), or of conducting or participating in an ongoing and legitimate RICO "enterprise."

The limits of the relationship and continuity concepts that combine to define a RICO pattern, and the precise methods by which relatedness and continuity or its threat may be proved, cannot be fixed in advance with such clarity that it will always be apparent whether in a particular case a "pattern of racketeering activity" exists. The development of these concepts must await future cases, absent a decision by Congress to revisit RICO to provide clearer guidance as to the Act's intended scope.

III.

Various *amici* urge that RICO's pattern element should be interpreted more narrowly than as requiring relationship and continuity in the senses outlined above, so that a defendant's racketeering activities form a pattern only if they are characteristic either of organized crime in the traditional sense, or of an organized-crime-type perpetrator, that is, of an association dedicated to the repeated commission of criminal offenses. Like the Court of Appeals' multiple scheme rule, however, the argument for reading an organized crime limitation into RICO's pattern concept, whatever the merits and demerits of such a limitation as an initial legislative matter, finds no support in the Act's text, and is at odds with the tenor of its legislative history. . . .

[T]he occasion for Congress' action was the perceived need to combat organized crime. But Congress for cogent reasons chose to enact a more general statute, one which, although it had organized crime as its focus, was not limited in application to organized crime. In Title IX, Congress picked out as key to RICO's application broad concepts that might fairly indicate an organized crime connection, but that it fully realized do not either individually or together provide anything approaching a perfect fit with "organized crime."

It seems, moreover, highly unlikely that Congress would have intended the pattern requirement to be interpreted by reference to a concept that it had itself rejected for inclusion in the text of RICO at least in part because "it is probably impossible precisely and definitively to define." *Id.* at 35204 (Rep. Poff). Congress realized that the stereotypical view of organized crime as consisting in a circumscribed set of illegal activities, such as gambling and prostitution — a view expressed in the definition included in the Omnibus Crime Control and Safe Streets Act, and repeated in the OCCA preamble — was no longer satisfactory because criminal activity had expanded into legitimate enterprises. Congress drafted RICO broadly enough to encompass a wide range of criminal activity, taking many different forms and likely to attract a broad array of perpetrators operating in many different ways. It would be counterproductive and a mismeasure of congressional intent now to adopt a narrow construction of the statute's pattern element that would require proof of an organized crime nexus.

As this Court stressed in *Sedima*, in rejecting a pinched construction of RICO's provision for a private civil action, adopted by a lower court because it perceived that RICO's use against non-organized-crime defendants was an "abuse" of the Act, "Congress wanted to reach both 'legitimate' and 'illegitimate' enterprises." 473 U.S. at 499. Legitimate businesses "enjoy neither an inherent incapacity for criminal activity nor immunity from its consequences"; and, as a result, § 1964(c)'s use "against respected businesses allegedly engaged in a pattern of specifically identified criminal conduct is hardly a sufficient reason for assuming that the provision is being misconstrued." *Id.* If plaintiffs' ability to use RICO against businesses engaged in a pattern of criminal acts is a defect, we said, it is one "inherent in the statute as written," and hence beyond our power to correct. RICO may be a poorly drafted statute; but rewriting it is a job for Congress, if it is so inclined, and not for this Court. . . .

IV.

We turn now to the application of our analysis of RICO's pattern requirement-. . . . Petitioners' complaint alleges that at different times over the course of at least a six-year period the noncommissioner respondents gave five members of the MPUC numerous bribes, in several different forms, with the objective — in which they were allegedly successful — of causing these commissioners to approve unfair and unreasonable rates for Northwestern Bell. RICO defines bribery as a "racketeering activity," 18 U.S.C. § 1961(1), so petitioners have alleged multiple predicate acts.

Under the analysis we have set forth above, and consistent with the allegations in their complaint, petitioners may be able to prove that the multiple predicates alleged constitute "a pattern of racketeering activity," in that they satisfy the requirements of relationship and continuity. The acts of bribery alleged are said to be related by a common purpose, to influence commissioners in carrying out their duties in order to win approval of unfairly and unreasonably high rates for Northwestern Bell. Furthermore, petitioners claim that the racketeering predicates occurred with some frequency over at least a six-year period, which may be sufficient to satisfy the continuity requirement. Alternatively, a threat of continuity of racketeering activity might be established at trial by showing that the alleged bribes were a regular way of conducting Northwestern Bell's ongoing business, or a regular way of conducting or participating in the conduct of the alleged and ongoing RICO enterprise, the MPUC.

The Court of Appeals thus erred in affirming the District Court's dismissal of petitioners' complaint for failure to plead "a pattern of racketeering activity." The judgment is reversed, and the case is remanded for further proceedings consistent with this opinion.

JUSTICE SCALIA, with whom THE CHIEF JUSTICE, JUSTICE O'CONNOR, and JUSTICE KENNEDY join, concurring in the judgment.

Four Terms ago, in *Sedima, S.P.R.L. v. Imrex Co.*, 473 U.S. 479 (1985), we gave lower courts the following four clues concerning the meaning of the enigmatic term "pattern of racketeering activity" in the Racketeer Influenced and Corrupt Organizations Act (RICO or Act). First, we stated that the statutory definition of the term in 18 U.S.C. § 1961(5) implies "that while two acts are necessary, they may not be sufficient." *Sedima*, 473 U.S. at 496 n.14. Second, we pointed out that "two isolated acts of racketeering activity," "sporadic activity," and "proof of two acts of racketeering activity, without more" would not be enough to constitute a pattern. *Id.* Third, we quoted a snippet from the legislative history stating "[i]t is this factor of *continuity plus relationship* which combines to produce a pattern." *Id.* Finally, we directed lower courts' attention to 18 U.S.C. § 3575(e), which defined the term "pattern of conduct which was criminal" used in a different title of the same Act, and instructed them that "[t]his language may be useful in interpreting other sections of the Act," 473 U.S. at 496 n.14. Thus enlightened, the District Courts and Courts of Appeals set out "to develop a meaningful concept of 'pattern,' " *id.* at 500, and promptly produced the widest and most persistent Circuit split on an issue of federal law in recent memory. Today, four years and countless millions in damages and attorney's fees later (not to mention prison sentences under the criminal provisions of RICO), the Court does little more than repromulgate those hints as to what RICO means, though with the caveat that Congress intended that they be applied using a "flexible approach."

Elevating to the level of statutory text a phrase taken from the legislative history, the Court counsels the lower courts: " 'continuity plus relationship.' " This seems to me about as helpful to the conduct of their affairs as "life is a fountain." Of the two parts of this talismanic phrase, the relatedness requirement is said to be the "easier to define," *id.*, yet here is the Court's definition, *in toto:* " '[C]riminal conduct forms a pattern if it embraces criminal acts that have the same or similar purposes, results, participants, victims, or methods of commission, or otherwise are interrelated by distinguishing characteristics and are not isolated events.' " . . .

It hardly closes in on the target to know that "relatedness" refers to acts that are related by "purposes, results, participants, victims, . . . methods of commission, *or* [just in case that is not vague enough] *otherwise.*" Is the fact that the victims of both predicate acts were women enough? Or that both acts had the purpose of enriching the defendant? Or that the different coparticipants of the defendant in both acts were his coemployees? I doubt that the lower courts will find the Court's instructions much more helpful than telling them to look for a "pattern" — which is what the statute already says.

The Court finds "continuity" more difficult to define precisely. "Continuity," it says, "is both a closed- and open-ended concept, referring either to a closed period of repeated conduct, or to past conduct that by its nature projects into the future with a threat of repetition." I have no idea what this concept of a "closed period of repeated conduct" means. Virtually all allegations of racketeering activity, in both civil and criminal suits, will relate to past periods that are "closed" (unless one expects plaintiff or the prosecutor to establish that the defendant not only committed the crimes he did, but is still committing them), and all of them *must* relate to conduct that is "repeated," because of RICO's multiple-act requirement. Since the Court has rejected the concept of separate criminal "schemes" or "episodes" as a criterion of "threatening future criminal conduct," I think it must be saying that at least a few months of racketeering activity (and who knows how much more?) is generally for free, as far as RICO is concerned. The "closed period" concept is a sort of safe harbor for racketeering activity that does not last *too* long, no matter how many different crimes and different schemes are involved, so long as it does not otherwise "establish a threat of continued racketeering activity." A gang of hoodlums that commits one act of extortion on Monday in New York, a second in Chicago on Tuesday, a third in San Francisco on Wednesday, and so on through an entire week, and then finally and completely disbands, cannot be reached under RICO. I am sure that is not what the statute intends, but I cannot imagine what else the Court's murky discussion can possibly mean . . . .

It is, however, unfair to be so critical of the Court's effort, because I would be unable to provide an interpretation of RICO that gives significantly more guidance concerning its application. Today's opinion has added nothing to improve our prior guidance, which has created a kaleidoscope of Circuit positions, except to clarify that RICO may in addition be violated when there is a "threat of continuity." It seems to me this increases rather than removes the vagueness. . . . There is no reason to believe that the Courts of Appeals will be any more unified in the future, than they have in the past, regarding the content of this law.

That situation is bad enough with respect to any statute, but it is intolerable with respect to RICO. For it is not only true, as JUSTICE MARSHALL commented in *Sedima, S.P.R.L. v. Imrex Co.*, 473 U.S. 479 (1985), that our interpretation of RICO has "quite simply revolutionize[d] private litigation" and "validate[d] the federalization of broad areas of state common law of frauds," *id.* at 501 (dissenting opinion), so that clarity and predictability in RICO's civil applications are particularly important; but it is also true that RICO, since it has criminal applications as well, must, even in its civil applications, possess the degree of certainty required for criminal laws. No constitutional challenge to this law has been raised in the present case, and so that issue is not before us. That the highest Court in the land has been unable to derive from this statute anything more than today's meager guidance bodes ill for the day when that challenge is presented.

However unhelpful its guidance may be, however, I think the Court is correct in saying that nothing in the statute supports the proposition that predicate acts constituting part of a single scheme (or single episode) can never support a cause of action under RICO. Since the Court of Appeals here rested its decision on the contrary proposition, I concur in the judgment of the Court reversing the decision below.

NOTES AND QUESTIONS

1. *Defining a "pattern."* In *H.J. Inc.*, the Supreme Court acknowledged a number of possible approaches to defining a "pattern." One approach would be to require proof of some sort of "organized" criminal activity. Another approach, used by the Court of Appeals in *H.J. Inc.*, requires multiple schemes. Why did the Court reject these approaches? What exactly is required under the Court's holding? Would two predicate acts within 10 years ever be sufficient? Why or why not?

2. *Fair notice.* If you were advising a client, how would you define the term "pattern"? Could you do so in a way that would be comprehensible to a lay person? Was Justice Scalia correct in concluding the vagueness of the term is "intolerable"? Why or why not?

* * *

In the next case, the court of appeals applied the test from *H.J. Inc.* As you read the case, consider why the trial court dismissed the case and whether its decision was justified.

LIBERTAD v. WELCH
53 F.3d 428 (1st Cir. 1995)

TORRUELLA, CHIEF JUDGE.

A group of individuals and organizations representing women who have sought or will seek family planning services in Puerto Rico ("Appellants") brought this action against certain individuals and organizations ("Appellees") who oppose abortion and coordinate anti-abortion demonstrations at women's health clinics in Puerto Rico. The Appellants appeal from the district court's grant of summary judgment disposing of their claims brought under §§ 1962(c) and (d) of the Racketeer Influenced and Corrupt Organizations Act ("RICO"). In granting summary judgment for Appellees, the district court ruled that Appellants' claims brought under §§ 1962(c) and (d) of RICO failed because Appellants did not show either the existence of an enterprise or a pattern of racketeering activity. . . .

I. BACKGROUND

A. *The Parties*

Appellants initiated this action on behalf of women seeking reproductive health services and their health care providers. Among the named plaintiffs are two women using the pseudonyms "Lydia Libertad" and "Emilia Emancipación." Both Libertad and Emancipación are Puerto Rico residents and have sought reproductive health services on the island. Another plaintiff, Rosa Cáceres, is the Clinic Administrator at the Women's Metropolitan Clinic ("WMC") in Río Piedras, Puerto Rico, which provides a range of reproductive health services including abortion. WMC is owned in turn by plaintiff Oficinas Médicas. Plaintiff Mary Rivera is the Clinic Supervisor and Director of Counselling at the Clínica Gineco-Quirúrgica, ("Clínica") which also provides reproductive health services including abortion. Plaintiffs Ana E. González-Dávila ("González") and Dr. Rafael E. Castro-De Jesús ("Castro") are, respectively, the administrator and the medical director of plaintiff Ladies Medical Center ("LMC"), which also provides reproductive health services including abortion. The Grupo Pro Derechos Reproductivos, an abortion rights organization, is also a plaintiff.

Defendant Father Patrick Welch is the head of the anti-abortion rights organization Pro-Life Rescue Team ("PLRT"), also a named defendant. Defendants Donald Treshman and Reverend Ed Martin are, respectively, the National Director and the Executive Director of defendant Rescue America, a nationwide anti-abortion rights group based in Houston. Defendant Norman Weslin is the director of the defendant anti-abortion rights group the Sacrificial Lambs of Christ ("SLC"). Defendant Carlos Sánchez is a member of the anti-abortion rights group Pro-Vida.

B. *Events Leading to this Action*

We present the facts here in the light most favorable to the Appellants. Some or all of the Appellees staged protest demonstrations, which they refer to as "rescues," at the plaintiff clinics on five occasions: September 26, 1992; September 28, 1992; December 17, 1992; December 24, 1992; and January 8, 1993. During each of the five protests, Appellees blockaded the clinics so that clinic personnel and patients could not enter. Each blockade was carried out in a similar manner. Typically, the protests began before the clinics opened, with Appellees blocking access to the clinics and parking lots by physically obstructing the entrances, linking their arms tightly together and refusing to allow anyone to pass through. Outside, the protesters shouted slogans through megaphones to clinic personnel and patients, told patients that they were "murderers," screamed insults at clinic personnel, and videotaped or photographed people as they attempted to enter and leave the clinics. The protesters also defaced the clinic property by affixing difficult-to-remove stickers depicting fetuses on the walls and entrances, and by scrawling graffiti on the clinic walls. During these blockades, litter was strewn around clinic property and on the properties of surrounding businesses. In addition to effectively shutting down the clinics for all or part of a day, these protests caused extensive and costly property damage to the clinics.

Appellee Welch and some of the minor children who protest with him have on occasion entered the clinics and intimidated or harassed patients and staff. On September 26, 1992, Welch invaded the LMC and pushed plaintiff González from the clinic entrance all the way through the waiting room to the back office, trapping her there for a number of hours. On September 28, 1992, Welch and a young girl entered one of the clinics and remained in the waiting room, despite being told to leave by clinic staff. Patients with appointments would enter and then leave when they recognized Welch in the waiting room. Eventually, the police had to come and remove Welch and the young girl.

The record indicates that of the five protests at issue in this case, the January 8, 1993 protest is the only one at which all of the Appellees, not just Welch and his followers, participated. The tactics employed on January 8 were considerably more aggressive. In addition to the above-mentioned blockade methods, Appellees also blocked clinic access by parking buses in front of clinic entrances and then refusing to move them when instructed to do so by the police. Appellees chain-locked a clinic entrance and then covered the lock with tape to prevent it from being pried open. One clinic supporter received a death threat from a protester. The clinic suffered considerable property damage as well; locks were filled with glue or gum, and gates were broken or otherwise damaged to prevent entry.

*   *   *

C. *Procedural History*

On January 8, 1993, Appellants filed the instant action seeking a temporary restraining order, a preliminary injunction, and a permanent injunction enjoining Appellees from using unlawful force, harassment, intimidation, and physical obstruction during their protests in front of Puerto Rico clinics. The district court denied the motion for a temporary restraining order, but held a hearing from February 4–9, 1993 on Appellants' request for a preliminary injunction, during which extensive testimonial and documentary evidence was presented by both parties. at the end of the procedural history par., add: [The district court ultimately granted summary judgment to the Appellees.]

*   *   *

III. ANALYSIS

A. *Appellants' RICO claims*

*   *   *

2. *Have Appellants established a "pattern of racketeering activity"?*

Under the terms of the RICO statute, a "pattern of racketeering activity requires at least two acts of racketeering activity." 18 U.S.C. § 1961(5). The definitional section "does not so much define a pattern of racketeering activity as state a minimum necessary condition for the existence of such a pattern." *H.J. Inc. v. Northwestern Bell Telephone Co.*, 492 U.S. 229, 237 (1989). The two predicate acts of racketeering activity must be acts chargeable or indictable under any one or more of certain specified criminal laws. These acts include "extortion" as it is defined in the Hobbs Act, 18 U.S.C. § 1951(b)(2).[13] In addition, a RICO plaintiff must demonstrate that the predicate acts are related, and that they amount to or pose a threat of continued criminal activity. *H.J. Inc.*, 492 U.S. at 237.

a. *Relatedness*

We have noted that "the relatedness test is not a cumbersome one for a RICO plaintiff." *Feinstein*, 942 F.2d 34, 44 (1st Cir. 1991). A RICO plaintiff establishes that predicate acts are related by demonstrating that they "have the same or similar purposes, results, participants, victims, or methods of commission, or otherwise are interrelated by distinguishing characteristics and are not isolated events." *H.J. Inc.*, 492 U.S. at 240. A fact-specific allegation of a single common

---

[13] As we explained above, this provision defines extortion as "the obtaining of property from another, with his consent, induced by wrongful use of actual or threatened force, violence, or fear." The intangible right to freely conduct one's lawful business constitutes "property" for purposes of this section. [In Scheidler v. National Organization for Women, 537 U.S. 393 (2003), the United States Supreme Court rejected this theory of extortion and reversed a finding of RICO liability. *See* Chapter 8, Extortion, *supra* — eds.]

scheme can be used to satisfy the relatedness requirement. As the district court succinctly and correctly noted, there is little doubt in this case that the alleged predicate acts are related. . . .

b. *Continuity*

In order to establish the continuity of the predicate acts, a plaintiff must show either (1) that the acts amount to continued criminal activity, in that the related acts extend over a period of time; or (2) that the predicate acts, though not continuous, pose a threat of continued activity. *H.J. Inc.*, 492 U.S. at 242. Because RICO was intended by Congress to apply only to enduring criminal conduct, predicate acts extending over a few weeks or months do not generally satisfy this requirement. *Feinstein*, 942 F.2d at 45. Under the second, "threat" approach, however, even where the predicate acts occur in a narrow time frame, the requirement can still be satisfied by demonstrating "a realistic prospect of continuity over an open-ended period yet to come." *Id.* This approach "necessitates a showing that 'the acts themselves include a specific threat of repetition extending indefinitely into the future, [or] . . . are part of an ongoing entity's regular way of doing business.' " *Id.* (quoting *H.J. Inc.*, 492 U.S. at 242).

Under the first method of establishing continuity, the district court found, we think correctly, that the five blockades over a three-month period did not constitute a closed-end period of continued criminal conduct. Appellants do not specifically contest this finding here. Rather, they challenge the district court's finding that the record does not reveal "a realistic prospect that the activity challenged in this suit will resume with enduring effects," and that therefore, no continuity was established.

Appellants point out that the predicate acts involved in this case — the blockades, vandalism, and the threatening harassment of clinic personnel and patients — are part of the regular way that the defendants conduct their ongoing activities. The entire purpose of Rescue America, the PLRT, and their leaders, contend the Appellants, is preventing abortions, and they do this by regularly using unlawful as well as lawful tactics. Appellants further argue, and the record shows, that part of the Appellees' strategy is to strike randomly with little or no warning of which clinic they will target, making it inherently difficult or impossible to determine whether and when they will blockade again. There is also evidence that Rescue America has been conducting protests and blockades for several years, and shows no signs of abating or changing its unlawful tactics. Indeed, the March 4, 1994 press release, quoted in relevant part above, strongly indicates that the Appellees plan to continue their activities in Puerto Rico, lawful and unlawful.

Appellees contend that there is nothing about the challenged conduct that by its nature projects into the future with a threat of repetition. The January 8, 1993 blockade, they claim, was a "special gathering," an event unlikely to be repeated. They point out that Treshman left Puerto Rico after the blockade and has "no immediate plans to return." It is not the nature of the conduct itself, however, that suggests a threat of continuing; it is the fact that the Appellees' regular way of conducting their affairs involves the illegal acts conducted at that blockade, and that the Appellees have admitted that they plan to "continue their efforts." Moreover, Treshman's physical presence in Puerto Rico is not necessary for Appellees to plan or threaten future unlawful blockade activities in furtherance of the alleged conspiracy. We therefore find that sufficient evidence in the record raises a genuine issue of material fact as to whether the Appellees' conduct posed a threat of continuing activity, and that the district court thus erred in granting summary judgment against the Appellants on this basis.

Accordingly, we remand the Appellants' RICO claims against Appellees Welch, Treshman, Rescue America, and the PLRT only, for further proceedings to determine whether Appellants can prove the elements of their RICO causes of action. . . .

NOTES AND QUESTIONS

1. *Alleging and proving a "pattern."* With respect to the pattern requirement, what does the government or a private plaintiff need to allege to survive a motion to dismiss? As a practical matter, the burden may be higher on private plaintiffs. As discussed in the introductory notes and shown in the *Libertad* case, federal trial courts are often hostile towards civil RICO actions, which clog the federal dockets with cases that otherwise would be brought in state court.

What if an appeals court determines that some predicate acts were not proven at trial? May a RICO conviction survive nonetheless? *Compare United States v. Regan*, 937 F.2d 823 (2d Cir. 1991) (reversing bulk of predicate acts and reversing RICO convictions), *with United States v. Genova*, 333 F.3d 750 (7th Cir. 2003) (reversing state law predicate act conviction, but affirming RICO conviction based on two counts of mail fraud).

2. *Due process and notice.* As in so many other areas of white collar crime, due process and notice issues abound in RICO cases. The majority in *H.J. Inc.* acknowledged that RICO is a poorly drafted statute, and Justice Scalia in concurrence invited a vagueness challenge. Note, however, that such challenges are very rarely successful. Is RICO unconstitutionally vague? Is it appropriate for the Court to attempt to clarify the statute, or should that task be left to Congress?

PROBLEMS

14-4. Tom Hivers was the elected district attorney for the city of Oakville. He worked closely with fellow deputy district attorney Wilma Katz. While both were working in the prosecutor's office, the federal government had a program providing supplemental funds to state and local prosecutors who did drug enforcement work. Hivers, however, was not eligible for any grant money because of his elected position.

Hivers appointed Katz as his deputy. In several grant applications mailed to the government, Hivers represented that Katz was primarily responsible for the drug enforcement cases. It was Hivers, however, who prosecuted all the drug cases and did all work in connection with the cases. Nevertheless, Katz signed her name on the monthly contractor reports detailing the drug enforcement work. For two years, Katz received monthly checks from the state and deposited the checks into her bank account. She subsequently wrote Hivers checks for the same amounts. Katz funneled approximately $90,000 in federal grant money to Hivers in this way. Katz and Hivers engaged in a similar scheme with money provided through state grants during the same period.

Hivers and Katz were indicted on crimes related to the district attorney's office over the last two years. Count 1 was a substantive RICO count, alleging a pattern of racketeering activity stemming from predicate acts including mail and wire fraud. Both defendants were convicted of two mail fraud counts in connection with the federal grant program and two mail fraud counts relating to the state grant program, and RICO based on those predicate acts. One mailing occurred per program in each of the two years in question.

The defendants appeal their RICO conviction, arguing that a pattern was not proven. How should the court rule? Why?

14-5. Joe Knight was the Mayor of Williamstown for three years. After a public outcry that his administration was corrupt, an extensive investigation took place. Two months later, Knight was charged with RICO based on the federal predicate acts of mail fraud (eight counts) and extortion (one count), and on the state law predicate act of bribery. Each of the federal predicate acts was also charged as a substantive count. The extortion and bribery allegations were based upon an incident during which Knight extorted a payment from a city contractor in exchange for granting a city contract to the contractor.

The jury convicted Knight on all counts. On appeal, the court reversed the mail fraud convictions on the grounds of insufficient evidence. Knight now argues that the RICO count must be dismissed for lack of a pattern. In response, the government argues that the federal extortion count and the state bribery predicate act are sufficient.

How should the court of appeals rule? Why?

14-6. The law firm of Simon and Garcia, P.C., is a Philadelphia firm noted for its work on behalf of personal injury plaintiffs. The senior partner, Seth Simon, is known locally as the "King of Torts," and has successfully sued on behalf of thousands of plaintiffs who have recovered millions of dollars from insurance companies, hospitals, and the like. The firm has also made a name for itself by successfully recovering in dozens of law suits brought against the City of Philadelphia.

Simon is something of a hero in the local legal community and among his clients for his ability to gain judgments against or settlements from powerful businesses and corporations on behalf of down-and-out individual plaintiffs. This success has not hurt the firm's or Simon's financial standing, given the firm's typical one-third contingency fee.

In one recent case, Simon brought a suit against the City on behalf of Imma Jones, whose husband, Irving, was killed in an accident on a Philadelphia street. At trial, the main plaintiff's witness was a truck driver named Helen Haley. Haley testified that she had noticed a crack in the pavement a week before the accident, which occurred in January of last year. The crack, everyone agreed, contributed to the accident. The testimony was critical because the plaintiff had to prove that the City was or should have been on notice of the condition in order to recover. The trial was held the following July, and resulted in an award to Jones of $2,000,000.

The next month, Simon tried another suit on behalf of Imma, this time against the driver of the other car. Once again, Haley testified at the trial. She stated that she happened to be driving by at the time of the accident, and noticed that the other driver was speeding just prior to the accident. After the testimony, the case settled for $50,000.

Shortly after the second trial, Haley was arrested and charged with transportation of stolen property. During plea negotiations, Haley admitted that a paralegal with the Simon firm had paid her $5,000 for the first trial and $7,000 for the second trial to testify as she did at both trials. The paralegal told the investigator that Simon had instructed him to make the payment to Haley.

Haley also told investigators that they might want to talk to her friend Keith Carp. Carp, who had his own history of troubles with the police, had worked as a private investigator for the Simon firm. In two of his cases, he admitted to having been instructed by Simon's secretary to pay the court clerk $500 in each of the cases to divulge the progress of jury deliberations. The secretary told the investigators that Simon instructed her to make the payments. When it appeared that the juries were about to find for the defendant in each case, Simon's associate, who was handling the trials, promptly settled the cases for $100,000 and $75,000, respectively. The trials occurred in November and December four years ago.

The government asserts that there were four instances of state law bribery, each punishable by more than a year in prison. The state bribery statute contains a three-year statute of limitations.

a. Assume that you are the defense attorney in the case. The prosecutor tells you that the government can prove the above facts at trial. *How would you argue that, even assuming the facts, the government should not bring a RICO case? What arguments can you make based upon the law? Based upon the wise exercise of prosecutorial discretion?*

b. Now assume that, based upon the foregoing facts, Simon has been convicted under 18 U.S.C. § 1962(c) for conducting the enterprise (the law firm) through a pattern of racketeering activity. *What are the defendant's likely arguments on appeal? Should he succeed? Why or why not?*

[E]   RICO CONSPIRACY

As discussed in Chapter 3, Conspiracy, *supra*, the United States criminal code contains a number of specific conspiracy provisions. One of those is set forth in § 1962(d). In the next case, the Supreme Court discussed the elements of RICO conspiracy.[h]

SALINAS v. UNITED STATES
522 U.S. 52 (1997)

JUSTICE KENNEDY delivered the opinion of the Court.

I.

This federal prosecution arose from a bribery scheme operated by Brigido Marmolejo, the Sheriff of Hidalgo County, Texas, and petitioner Mario Salinas, one

---

[h] Another aspect of the *Salinas* case is discussed in Chapter 7, Bribery & Gratuities, *supra*, at Section 7[C][2].

of his principal deputies. In 1984, the United States Marshals Service and Hidalgo County entered into agreements under which the county would take custody of federal prisoners. In exchange, the Federal Government agreed to make a grant to the county for improving its jail and also agreed to pay the county a specific amount per day for each federal prisoner housed. Based on the estimated number of federal prisoners to be maintained, payments to the county were projected to be $915,785 per year. . . .

Homero Beltran-Aguirre was one of the federal prisoners housed in the jail under the arrangement negotiated between the Marshals Service and the county. He was incarcerated there for two intervals, first for 10 months and then for 5 months. During both custody periods, Beltran paid Marmolejo a series of bribes in exchange for so-called "contact visits" in which he remained alone with his wife or, on other occasions, his girlfriend. Beltran paid Marmolejo a fixed rate of six thousand dollars per month and one thousand dollars for each contact visit, which occurred twice a week. Petitioner Salinas was the chief deputy responsible for managing the jail and supervising custody of the prisoners. When Marmolejo was not available, Salinas arranged for the contact visits and on occasion stood watch outside the room where the visits took place. In return for his assistance with the scheme, Salinas received from Beltran a pair of designer watches and a pickup truck.

Salinas and Marmolejo were indicted and tried together, but only Salinas' convictions are before us. Salinas was charged with one count of violating RICO, 18 U.S.C. § 1962(c), one count of conspiracy to violate RICO, § 1962(d), and two counts of bribery in violation of § 666(a)(1)(B). The jury acquitted Salinas on the substantive RICO count but convicted him on the RICO conspiracy count and the bribery counts. A divided panel of the Court of Appeals for the Fifth Circuit affirmed.

* * *

III.

Salinas directs his challenge to his conviction for conspiracy to violate RICO. There could be no conspiracy offense, he says, unless he himself committed or agreed to commit the two predicate acts requisite for a substantive RICO offense under § 1962(c). Salinas identifies a conflict among the Courts of Appeals on the point. Decisions of the First, Second, and Tenth Circuits require that, under the RICO conspiracy provision, the defendant must himself commit or agree to commit two or more predicate acts. Eight other Courts of Appeals, including the Fifth Circuit in this case, take a contrary view.

* * *

The Government's theory was that Salinas himself committed a substantive § 1962(c) RICO violation by conducting the enterprise's affairs through a pattern of racketeering activity that included acceptance of two or more bribes, felonies punishable in Texas by more than one year in prison. *See* Tex. Penal Code Ann. § 36.02(a)(1) (1994). The jury acquitted on the substantive count. Salinas was convicted of conspiracy, however, and he challenges the conviction because the jury was not instructed that he must have committed or agreed to commit two predicate acts himself. His interpretation of the conspiracy statute is wrong.

The RICO conspiracy statute, simple in formulation, provides: "It shall be unlawful for any person to conspire to violate any of the provisions of subsection (a), (b), or (c) of this section." 18 U.S.C. § 1962(d). There is no requirement of some overt act or specific act in the statute before us, unlike the general conspiracy provision applicable to federal crimes, which requires that at least one of the conspirators have committed an "act to effect the object of the conspiracy." § 371. The RICO conspiracy provision, then, is even more comprehensive than the general conspiracy offense in § 371.

In interpreting the provisions of § 1962(d), we adhere to a general rule: When Congress uses well-settled terminology of criminal law, its words are presumed to have their ordinary meaning and definition. The relevant statutory phrase in § 1962(d) is "to conspire." We presume Congress intended to use the term in its conventional sense, and certain well-established principles follow.

A conspiracy may exist even if a conspirator does not agree to commit or facilitate each and every part of the substantive offense. The partners in the criminal plan must agree to pursue the same criminal objective and may divide up the work, yet each is responsible for the acts of each other. *See Pinkerton v. United States*, 328 U.S. 640, 646 (1946) ("And so long as the partnership in crime continues, the partners act for each other in carrying it forward"). If conspirators have a plan which calls for some conspirators to perpetrate the crime and others to provide support, the supporters are as guilty as the perpetrators. As Justice Holmes observed: "[P]lainly a person may conspire for the commission of a crime by a third person." *United States v. Holte*, 236 U.S. 140, 144 (1915). A person, moreover, may be liable for conspiracy even though he was incapable of committing the substantive offense.

The point Salinas tries to make is in opposition to these principles, and is refuted by *Bannon v. United States*, 156 U.S. 464 (1895). There the defendants were charged with conspiring to violate the general conspiracy statute, which requires proof of an overt act. One defendant objected to the indictment because it did not allege he had committed an overt act. We rejected the argument because it would erode the common-law principle that, so long as they share a common purpose, conspirators are liable for the acts of their co-conspirators. We observed in *Bannon*: "To require an overt act to be proven against every member of the conspiracy, or a distinct act connecting him with the combination to be alleged, would not only be an innovation upon established principles, but would render most prosecutions for the offence nugatory." *Id.* at 469. The RICO conspiracy statute, § 1962(d), broadened conspiracy coverage by omitting the requirement of an overt act; it did not, at the same time, work the radical change of requiring the Government to prove each conspirator agreed that he would be the one to commit two predicate acts.

Our recitation of conspiracy law comports with contemporary understanding. When Congress passed RICO in 1970, the American Law Institute's Model Penal Code permitted a person to be convicted of conspiracy so long as he "agrees with such other person or persons that they or one or more of them will engage in conduct that constitutes such crime." American Law Institute, Model Penal Code § 5.03(1)(a) (1962). As the drafters emphasized, "so long as the purpose of the agreement is to facilitate commission of a crime, the actor need not agree 'to commit' the crime." American Law Institute, Model Penal Code, Tent. Draft No. 10,

p. 117 (1960). The Model Penal Code still uses this formulation. *See* Model Penal Code § 5.03(1)(a), 10 U.L.A. 501 (1974).

A conspirator must intend to further an endeavor which, if completed, would satisfy all of the elements of a substantive criminal offense, but it suffices that he adopt the goal of furthering or facilitating the criminal endeavor. He may do so in any number of ways short of agreeing to undertake all of the acts necessary for the crime's completion. One can be a conspirator by agreeing to facilitate only some of the acts leading to the substantive offense. It is elementary that a conspiracy may exist and be punished whether or not the substantive crime ensues, for the conspiracy is a distinct evil, dangerous to the public, and so punishable in itself.

It makes no difference that the substantive offense under subsection (c) requires two or more predicate acts. The interplay between subsections (c) and (d) does not permit us to excuse from the reach of the conspiracy provision an actor who does not himself commit or agree to commit the two or more predicate acts requisite to the underlying offense. True, though an "enterprise" under § 1962(c) can exist with only one actor to conduct it, in most instances it will be conducted by more than one person or entity; and this in turn may make it somewhat difficult to determine just where the enterprise ends and the conspiracy begins, or, on the other hand, whether the two crimes are coincident in their factual circumstances. In some cases the connection the defendant had to the alleged enterprise or to the conspiracy to further it may be tenuous enough so that his own commission of two predicate acts may become an important part of the Government's case. Perhaps these were the considerations leading some of the Circuits to require in conspiracy cases that each conspirator himself commit or agree to commit two or more predicate acts. Nevertheless, that proposition cannot be sustained as a definition of the conspiracy offense, for it is contrary to the principles we have discussed.

In the case before us, even if Salinas did not accept or agree to accept two bribes, there was ample evidence that he conspired to violate subsection (c). The evidence showed that Marmolejo committed at least two acts of racketeering activity when he accepted numerous bribes and that Salinas knew about and agreed to facilitate the scheme. This is sufficient to support a conviction under § 1962(d).

As a final matter, Salinas says his statutory interpretation is required by the rule of lenity. The rule does not apply when a statute is unambiguous or when invoked to engraft an illogical requirement to its text.

The judgment of the Court of Appeals is Affirmed.

NOTES AND QUESTIONS

1. *RICO conspiracy and § 371.* What was the defendant's contention in *Salinas*? Why did the Court reject the argument? According to the Court, how does § 1962(d) compare with the general conspiracy statute, § 371?

2. *Double jeopardy.* If you were a prosecutor, and believed that the elements of both RICO conspiracy and another federal conspiracy statute could be proven, which would you employ? Would you have to choose? Could a defendant be convicted and punished under both sections for the same act or acts? Why or why not? Similarly, could the government prosecute a defendant for RICO based upon a predicate act that the government later used as the basis for a separate prosecution? *See United States v. Luong,* 393 F.3d 913, 917 (9th Cir. 2004)

(concluding that "the government was not barred from successively prosecuting [defendants] for violations of RICO and for conspiracy to commit a Hobbs Act robbery when one of the RICO predicate acts was a conspiracy to commit Hobbs Act robberies").

[F] CIVIL RICO

As seen in the above materials, RICO allows for private parties and for the government to bring civil RICO actions. It is RICO's use in private actions — with the possibility of treble damages and attorneys' fees — that has engendered the most controversy. In the next case, the Supreme Court addressed two substantial restrictions that lower courts had placed upon plaintiffs in RICO cases.

[1]   Breadth of Civil RICO

SEDIMA, S.P.R.L. v. IMREX CO.
473 U.S. 479 (1985)

JUSTICE WHITE delivered the opinion of the Court.

The Racketeer Influenced and Corrupt Organizations Act (RICO), 18 U.S.C. §§ 1961–1968, provides a private civil action to recover treble damages for injury "by reason of a violation of" its substantive provisions. 18 U.S.C. § 1964(c). The initial dormancy of this provision and its recent greatly increased utilization[1] are now familiar history. In response to what it perceived to be misuse of civil RICO by private plaintiffs, the court below construed § 1964(c) to permit private actions only against defendants who had been convicted on criminal charges, and only where there had occurred a "racketeering injury." While we understand the court's concern over the consequences of an unbridled reading of the statute, we reject both of its holdings. . . .

In 1979, petitioner Sedima, a Belgian corporation, entered into a joint venture with respondent Imrex Co. to provide electronic components to a Belgian firm. The buyer was to order parts through Sedima; Imrex was to obtain the parts in this country and ship them to Europe. The agreement called for Sedima and Imrex to split the net proceeds. Imrex filled roughly $8 million in orders placed with it through Sedima. Sedima became convinced, however, that Imrex was presenting inflated bills, cheating Sedima out of a portion of its proceeds by collecting for nonexistent expenses.

In 1982, Sedima filed this action in the Federal District Court for the Eastern District of New York. The complaint set out common-law claims of unjust enrichment, conversion, and breach of contract, fiduciary duty, and a constructive trust. In addition, it asserted RICO claims under § 1964(c) against Imrex and two of its officers. Two counts alleged violations of § 1962(c), based on predicate acts of mail and wire fraud. A third count alleged a conspiracy to violate § 1962(c). Claiming injury of at least $175,000, the amount of the alleged overbilling, Sedima

---

[1] Of 270 District Court RICO decisions prior to this year, only 3% (nine cases) were decided throughout the 1970s, 2% were decided in 1980, 7% in 1981, 13% in 1982, 33% in 1983, and 43% in 1984. Report of the Ad Hoc Civil RICO Task Force of the ABA Section of Corporation, Banking and Business Law 55 (1985) (hereinafter ABA Report).

sought treble damages and attorney's fees.

The District Court held that for an injury to be "by reason of a violation of § 1962," as required by § 1964(c), it must be somehow different in kind from the direct injury resulting from the predicate acts of racketeering activity. 574 F. Supp. 963 (1983). While not choosing a precise formulation, the District Court held that a complaint must allege a "RICO-type injury," which was either some sort of distinct "racketeering injury," or a "competitive injury." It found "no allegation here of any injury apart from that which would result directly from the alleged predicate acts of mail fraud and wire fraud," *id.* at 965, and accordingly dismissed the RICO counts for failure to state a claim.

A divided panel of the Court of Appeals for the Second Circuit affirmed. 741 F.2d 482 (1984). After a lengthy review of the legislative history, it held that Sedima's complaint was defective in two ways. First, it failed to allege an injury "by reason of a violation of § 1962." In the court's view, this language was a limitation on standing, reflecting Congress' intent to compensate victims of "certain specific kinds of organized criminality," not to provide additional remedies for already compensable injuries. Analogizing to the Clayton Act, which had been the model for § 1964(c), the court concluded that just as an antitrust plaintiff must allege an "antitrust injury," so a RICO plaintiff must allege a "racketeering injury" — an injury "different in kind from that occurring as a result of the predicate acts themselves, or not simply caused by the predicate acts, but also caused by an activity which RICO was designed to deter." Sedima had failed to allege such an injury.

The Court of Appeals also found the complaint defective for not alleging that the defendants had already been criminally convicted of the predicate acts of mail and wire fraud, or of a RICO violation. This element of the civil cause of action was inferred from § 1964(c)'s reference to a "violation" of § 1962, the court also observing that its prior-conviction requirement would avoid serious constitutional difficulties, the danger of unfair stigmatization, and problems regarding the standard by which the predicate acts were to be proved.

The decision below was one episode in a recent proliferation of civil RICO litigation within the Second Circuit and in other Courts of Appeals. In light of the variety of approaches taken by the lower courts and the importance of the issues, we grant certiorari. We now reverse.

*   *   *

The language of RICO gives no obvious indication that a civil action can proceed only after a criminal conviction. The word "conviction" does not appear in any relevant portion of the statute. To the contrary, the predicate acts involve conduct that is "chargeable" or "indictable," and "offense[s]" that are "punishable," under various criminal statutes. As defined in the statute, racketeering activity consists not of acts for which the defendant has been convicted, but of acts for which he could be. Thus, a prior conviction-requirement cannot be found in the definition of "racketeering activity." Nor can it be found in § 1962, which sets out the statute's substantive provisions. Indeed, if either § 1961 or § 1962 did contain such a requirement, a prior conviction would also be a prerequisite, nonsensically, for a criminal prosecution, or for a civil action by the Government to enjoin violations that had not yet occurred.

The Court of Appeals purported to discover its prior-conviction requirement in the term "violation" in § 1964(c). However, even if that term were read to refer to a criminal conviction, it would require a conviction under RICO, not of the predicate offenses. That aside, the term "violation" does not imply a criminal conviction. It refers only to a failure to adhere to legal requirements. This is its indisputable meaning elsewhere in the statute. Section 1962 renders certain conduct "unlawful"; § 1963 and § 1964 impose consequences, criminal and civil, for "violations" of § 1962. We should not lightly infer that Congress intended the term to have wholly different meanings in neighboring subsections. . . .

The Court of Appeals was of the view that its narrow construction of the statute was essential to avoid intolerable practical consequences. First, without a prior conviction to rely on, the plaintiff would have to prove commission of the predicate acts beyond a reasonable doubt. This would require instructing the jury as to different standards of proof for different aspects of the case. To avoid this awkwardness, the court inferred that the criminality must already be established, so that the civil action could proceed smoothly under the usual preponderance standard.

We are not at all convinced that the predicate acts must be established beyond a reasonable doubt in a proceeding under § 1964(c). In a number of settings, conduct that can be punished as criminal only upon proof beyond a reasonable doubt will support civil sanctions under a preponderance standard. There is no indication that Congress sought to depart from this general principle here. That the offending conduct is described by reference to criminal statutes does not mean that its occurrence must be established by criminal standards or that the consequences of a finding of liability in a private civil action are identical to the consequences of a criminal conviction. But we need not decide the standard of proof issue today. For even if the stricter standard is applicable to a portion of the plaintiff's proof, the resulting logistical difficulties, which are accepted in other contexts, would not be so great as to require invention of a requirement that cannot be found in the statute and that Congress, as even the Court of Appeals had to concede, did not envision.

The court below also feared that any other construction would raise severe constitutional questions, as it "would provide civil remedies for offenses criminal in nature, stigmatize defendants with the appellation 'racketeer,' authorize the award of damages which are clearly punitive, including attorney's fees, and constitute a civil remedy aimed in part to avoid the constitutional protections of the criminal law." 741 F.2d at 500 n.49. We do not view the statute as being so close to the constitutional edge. As noted above, the fact that conduct can result in both criminal liability and treble damages does not mean that there is not a bona fide civil action. The familiar provisions for both criminal liability and treble damages under the antitrust laws indicate as much. Nor are attorney's fees "clearly punitive." As for stigma, a civil RICO proceeding leaves no greater stain than do a number of other civil proceedings. Furthermore, requiring conviction of the predicate acts would not protect against an unfair imposition of the "racketeer" label. If there is a problem with thus stigmatizing a garden variety defrauder by means of a civil action, it is not reduced by making certain that the defendant is guilty of *fraud* beyond a reasonable doubt. Finally, to the extent an action under § 1964(c) might be considered quasi-criminal, requiring protections normally applicable only to criminal proceedings, the solution is to provide those protections, not to ensure that they were previously afforded by requiring prior convictions.

Finally, we note that a prior-conviction requirement would be inconsistent with Congress' underlying policy concerns. Such a rule would severely handicap potential plaintiffs. A guilty party may escape conviction for any number of reasons — not least among them the possibility that the Government itself may choose to pursue only civil remedies. Private attorney general provisions such as § 1964(c) are in part designed to fill prosecutorial gaps. This purpose would be largely defeated, and the need for treble damages as an incentive to litigate unjustified, if private suits could be maintained only against those already brought to justice. . . .

In considering the Court of Appeals' second prerequisite for a private civil RICO action — "injury . . . caused by an activity which RICO was designed to deter" — we are somewhat hampered by the vagueness of that concept. Apart from reliance on the general purposes of RICO and a reference to "mobsters," the court provided scant indication of what the requirement of racketeering injury means. It emphasized Congress' undeniable desire to strike at organized crime, but acknowledged and did not purport to overrule Second Circuit precedent rejecting a requirement of an organized crime nexus. The court also stopped short of adopting a "competitive injury" requirement; while insisting that the plaintiff show "the kind of economic injury which has an effect on competition," it did not require "actual anticompetitive effect." 741 F.2d at 496. . . .

[W]e perceive no distinct "racketeering injury" requirement. Given that "racketeering activity" consists of no more and no less than commission of a predicate act, § 1961(1), we are initially doubtful about a requirement of a "racketeering injury" separate from the harm from the predicate acts . . . . There is no room in the statutory language for an additional, amorphous "racketeering injury" requirement.

A violation of § 1962(c), the section on which Sedima relies, requires (1) conduct (2) of an enterprise (3) through a pattern (4) of racketeering activity. The plaintiff must, of course, allege each of these elements to state a claim. Conducting an enterprise that affects interstate commerce is obviously not in itself a violation of § 1962, nor is mere commission of the predicate offenses. In addition, the plaintiff only has standing if, and can only recover to the extent that, he has been injured in his business or property by the conduct constituting the violation. . . .

But the statute requires no more than this. Where the plaintiff alleges each element of the violation, the compensable injury necessarily is the harm caused by predicate acts sufficiently related to constitute a pattern, for the essence of the violation is the commission of those acts in connection with the conduct of an enterprise. Those acts are, when committed in the circumstances delineated in § 1962(c), "an activity which RICO was designed to deter." Any recoverable damages occurring by reason of a violation of § 1962(c) will flow from the commission of the predicate acts. . . .

Underlying the Court of Appeals' holding was its distress at the "extraordinary, if not outrageous," uses to which civil RICO has been put. 741 F.2d at 487. Instead of being used against mobsters and organized criminals, it has become a tool for everyday fraud cases brought against "respected and legitimate 'enterprises.' " Id. Yet Congress wanted to reach both "legitimate" and "illegitimate" enterprises. The former enjoy neither an inherent incapacity for criminal activity nor immunity from its consequences. The fact that § 1964(c) is used against respected businesses allegedly engaged in a pattern of specifically identified criminal conduct is hardly a sufficient reason for assuming that the provision is being misconstrued. Nor does it reveal the "ambiguity" discovered by the court below. "[T]he fact that RICO has been applied in situations not expressly anticipated by Congress does not demonstrate ambiguity. It demonstrates breadth." *Haroco, Inc. v. American National Bank & Trust Co. of Chicago*, 747 F.2d 384, 398, *aff'd*, 473 U.S. 606 (1984).

It is true that private civil actions under the statute are being brought almost solely against such defendants, rather than against the archetypal, intimidating mobster.[16] Yet this defect — if defect it is — is inherent in the statute as written, and its correction must lie with Congress. It is not for the judiciary to eliminate the private action in situations where Congress has provided it simply because plaintiffs are not taking advantage of it in its more difficult applications.

We nonetheless recognize that, in its private civil version, RICO is evolving into something quite different from the original conception of its enactors. Though sharing the doubts of the Court of Appeals about this increasing divergence, we cannot agree with either its diagnosis or its remedy. The "extraordinary" uses to which civil RICO has been put appear to be primarily the result of the breadth of the predicate offenses, in particular the inclusion of wire, mail, and securities fraud, and the failure of Congress and the courts to develop a meaningful concept of "pattern." We do not believe that the amorphous standing requirement imposed by the Second Circuit effectively responds to these problems, or that it is a form of statutory amendment appropriately undertaken by the courts. . . .

The judgment below is accordingly reversed, and the case is remanded for further proceedings consistent with this opinion.

It is so ordered.

JUSTICE MARSHALL, with whom JUSTICE BRENNAN, JUSTICE BLACKMUN, and JUSTICE POWELL join, dissenting.

* * *

The Court today recognizes that "in its private civil version, RICO is evolving into something quite different from the original conception of its enactors." The Court, however, expressly validates this result, imputing it to the manner in which the statute was drafted. I fundamentally disagree both with the Court's reading of the statute and with its conclusion.

The Court's interpretation of the civil RICO statute quite simply revolutionizes private litigation; it validates the federalization of broad areas of state common law of frauds, and it approves the displacement of well-established federal remedial provisions. We do not lightly infer a congressional intent to effect such fundamental changes. To infer such intent here would be untenable, for there is no indication that Congress even considered, much less approved, the scheme that the Court today defines.

---

[16] The ABA Task Force found that of the 270 known civil RICO cases at the trial court level, 40% involved securities fraud, 37% common-law fraud in a commercial or business setting, and only 9% "allegations of criminal activity of a type generally associated with professional criminals." ABA Report, at 55–56. Another survey of 132 published decisions found that 57 involved securities transactions and 38 commercial and contract disputes, while no other category made it into double figures. American Institute of Certified Public Accountants, *The Authority to Bring Private Treble-Damage Suits Under "RICO" Should be Removed* 13 (Oct. 10, 1984).

The single most significant reason for the expansive use of civil RICO has been the presence in the statute, as predicate acts, of mail and wire fraud violations. Prior to RICO, no federal statute had expressly provided a private damages remedy based upon a violation of the mail or wire fraud statutes, which make it a federal crime to use the mail or wires in furtherance of a scheme to defraud. Moreover, the Courts of Appeals consistently had held that no implied federal private causes of action accrue to victims of these federal violations. The victims normally were restricted to bringing actions in state court under common-law fraud theories.

Under the Court's opinion today, two fraudulent mailings or uses of the wires occurring within 10 years of each other might constitute a "pattern of racketeering activity," leading to civil RICO liability. The effects of making a mere two instances of mail or wire fraud potentially actionable under civil RICO are staggering, because in recent years the Courts of Appeals have tolerated an extraordinary expansion of mail and wire fraud statutes to permit federal prosecution for conduct that some had thought was subject only to state criminal and civil law.

* * *

In summary, in both theory and practice, civil RICO has brought profound changes to our legal landscape. Undoubtedly, Congress has the power to federalize a great deal of state common law, and there certainly are no relevant constraints on its ability to displace federal law. Those, however, are not the questions that we face in this case. What we have to decide here, instead, is whether Congress in fact intended to produce these far-reaching results. . . .

NOTES AND QUESTIONS

1. *Breadth of civil RICO.* RICO is a controversial statute, nowhere more so than in its civil application. As the dissent noted, "civil RICO has brought profound changes to our legal landscape." Why is this so? Why didn't these concerns sway the majority of the Court? Despite considerable pressure from business lobbyists and others, and subject to a qualification discussed below, Congress has failed to narrow the reach of civil RICO. Why do you think this is so?

2. *Securities fraud as a predicate act in civil RICO cases.* The Supreme Court in *Sedima* declined to require civil RICO plaintiffs to show that the defendants had been convicted of the predicate acts. This remains the law, with one exception. In 1995, Congress added the following language to the civil RICO statute, § 1964:

[N]o person may rely upon any conduct that would have been actionable as fraud in the purchase or sale of securities to establish a violation of § 1962. The exception contained in the preceding sentence does not apply to an action against any person that is criminally convicted in connection with the fraud, in which case the statute of limitations shall start to run on the date on which the conviction becomes final.

Pub. L. No. 104-67, 109 Stat. 758 (1995), amending 18 U.S.C. § 1964(c). In your opinion, why did Congress add this language?

3. *Burden of proof.* Although the Court did not decide the issue in *Sedima*, lower courts have held that a civil RICO plaintiff must prove the elements by a preponderance of the evidence standard, rather than by the reasonable doubt standard applicable to criminal cases. *See, e.g., United States v. Local 560,*

International Brotherhood of Teamsters, 780 F.2d 267, 279 n.12 (3d Cir. 1985).

[2]   Standing

As in other civil contexts, a private RICO plaintiff must show an injury caused by the defendant's acts. What must a plaintiff allege in order to demonstrate standing in a RICO case? The United States Supreme Court has addressed this issue in a series of cases.

Note on *Holmes v. Securities Investor Protection Corp.*

In one of the leading RICO standing cases, *Holmes v. Securities Investor Protection Corp.*, 503 U.S. 258 (1992), the Supreme Court addressed the issue of the proof required to demonstrate standing. Plaintiff Securities Investor Protection Corp. (SIPC) is a non-profit corporation of which most securities brokers and dealers are members. In certain circumstances, SIPC is financially responsible for paying claims that the member broker/dealers' customers have filed against the broker/dealers. SIPC thus operates to insure the customers of member broker/dealers.

SIPC sued the defendants for securities fraud, and under RICO based upon the securities fraud predicate acts. SIPC alleged that the defendants illegally manipulated stock prices, causing those prices to appear to be artificially high. When the stock prices collapsed, the member broker/dealers who had invested in the stocks became insolvent and therefore unable to meet their obligations to their customers. The allegedly injured customers included customers who had not bought or sold the manipulated securities, but who were injured because of the illegal scheme's effect upon the customers' broker/dealers. Because of the harm to the member broker/dealers, SIPC was obliged to pay $13 million in claims to those customers.

The trial court granted the defendants' summary judgment motion. The court held that SIPC did not have standing to seek damages under RICO.

The Supreme Court affirmed on the ground that SIPC had not sufficiently alleged that the defendants proximately caused SIPC's injury. The Court focused on the language of § 1964(c), which provides that "[a]ny person injured in his business or property *by reason of* a violation of § 1962 of this chapter may sue therefor." The Court then rejected a "but for" test for standing, instead imposing a proximate cause requirement. The Court defined this test as requiring "some direct relation between the injury asserted and the injurious conduct alleged." *Id.* at 268. Applying this test to the facts, the Court held that the plaintiff had not alleged proximate causation. The plaintiff's injury resulted entirely from the member broker/dealers' insolvency, not directly from the alleged manipulation of stock by the defendants. Thus, the alleged injury was too attenuated from the securities fraud to sustain a RICO action.

NOTES AND QUESTIONS

1. *The test for standing.* What was the precise injury that the plaintiff asserted in *Holmes*? But for the defendants' actions, would the injury have occurred? If not, why wasn't this injury sufficient under the Court's reasoning?

2. *First-party reliance.* In *Bridge v. Phoenix Bond and Indem. Co.*, 128 S. Ct. 2131, 2138 (2008), the plaintiffs sued defendants under RICO, alleging that the defendants engaged in a bid-rigging scheme during a local government's auction of certain assets. The defendants mailed false documents to the local government in furtherance of this scheme, thus committing numerous counts of mail fraud. With respect to injury, the complaint alleged that the scheme gave the defendants an unfair advantage in the auction process, depriving plaintiffs of the opportunity to purchase the assets.

The trial court dismissed the complaint on the grounds that the local government, not the plaintiffs, was deceived by the scheme. The plaintiffs therefore lacked standing, the court held, because they had not actually relied upon the defendants' misrepresentations. The court of appeals reinstated the case, and the Supreme Court affirmed. The Court held that first-party reliance is not an element of a RICO case based on mail fraud. The Court further found that the plaintiffs had standing because they had sufficiently alleged that their injuries were proximately caused by defendants' actions.

3. *Overt acts and RICO conspiracy.* May a plaintiff recover in a civil RICO action where the alleged injury resulted from an overt act that was in furtherance of a RICO conspiracy but was not itself a RICO predicate or otherwise unlawful under the statute? In *Beck v. Prupis*, 529 U.S. 494 (2000), the plaintiff claimed that he was fired because he had refused to participate in RICO violations, and that his termination was an overt act giving rise to liability under RICO's conspiracy provision. The Supreme Court held that, because the termination was not itself unlawful under RICO, the plaintiff was not injured by a RICO violation.

PROBLEM

14-7. Plaintiff Metal Supply Corp. has sued Anzara Corp., a business competitor, under RICO. Plaintiff alleges that defendant committed mail and wire fraud when Anzara Corp. submitted state tax returns that fraudulently failed to reveal that it had not charged cash-paying customers state sales tax. The plaintiff alleged that this practice allowed the defendant to lower its prices and increase its market share, thus injuring the plaintiff by taking away business, in violation of § 1962(c).

The jury found for the plaintiff, and the appeals court affirmed. The defendant now appeals to the United States Supreme Court, arguing that the plaintiff lacked standing.

How should the court rule? Why?

Chapter 15

INTERNAL INVESTIGATIONS AND COMPLIANCE PROGRAMS

[A] INTRODUCTORY NOTES

The recent explosion in business crimes has prompted corporations to increase efforts to comply with the law and to institute measures to ensure that their corporate climate is ethical, legal, and profitable. Efforts to ensure that corporate behavior is legal and ethical require that corporations both adhere to applicable laws and regulations and foster responsible corporate cultures. The spotlight on corporate behavior has significantly heightened the fiduciary responsibilities of corporate officers and directors.

Recent, highly publicized business failures have also motivated all branches of state and federal governments to utilize creative avenues to address the public's concerns and fears. Agency regulators, along with prosecutors and private lawyers, have used many tools to pursue corporations and individuals in an effort to prevent and punish economic crime. In addition, Congress has created new laws to address business crime. The combination of these efforts has resulted in a new day for corporate crime, as the scandals of recent years demonstrate.

New enforcement tools and aggressive efforts have compelled businesses to implement internal investigations to ensure compliance with all legal requirements. In this chapter, we will examine the practical realities and risks associated with internal investigations and compliance programs.

[B] INTERNAL INVESTIGATIONS

[1] Determining Whether and How to Investigate

Because of the increased civil and criminal enforcement efforts against corporations, and the government's willingness to treat favorably those companies that make efforts to ferret out misconduct, internal investigations have become increasingly frequent. Corporations have begun aggressively to investigate claims that, if true, would subject them to criminal and/or civil liability. Although internal investigations have been instituted since the 1970s, their role today takes on renewed significance. Because internal investigations often provide a roadmap for government investigators, such investigations are fraught with risks. Thus, a corporation must proceed with caution when designing and managing an internal investigation.

One of the most practical initial considerations is whether to institute an investigation in situations where the government is already pursuing its own inquiry. In these circumstances, the corporation should seriously consider the impact of an internal investigation and should consider whether such action will enable it to respond adequately to the government and to defend itself.

In situations where there is no pending government investigation, the question becomes more acute: if the corporation is aware of wrongdoing and does nothing about it, it bears the risk of adverse government reaction should the conduct become public or result in a full-scale criminal investigation. Corporations must determine whether the activity would potentially subject the company to criminal investigation or civil lawsuits, or both.

The intricacies of an internal investigation are many, including the hiring of outside counsel or conducting the investigation with in-house counsel. A thorough investigation will assist the company in developing defense strategies, promoting detection, and halting illegal or improper conduct by employees at an early stage. Companies reviewing the results of an internal investigation can weigh the benefits and detriments of disclosing any discovered wrongdoing to the government. Red flags should be evident when the improper conduct is widespread or involves high-level corporate management.

Public reaction to an internal investigation, including shareholder awareness, can be a two-edged sword. On the one hand, the investigation demonstrates that the corporation is serious about ferreting out misbehavior and it may reduce adverse publicity. Conversely, the action can negatively affect stock prices and the market value of the company.

Depending on the nature of the wrongdoing, the scope of the fact-gathering necessary for a complete investigation can be very wide. Fiscal realities dictate that an appropriately conducted investigation will divert attention away from the day-to-day operations of the company and drain some corporate resources. Despite these risks, most large businesses today regularly conduct voluntary internal investigations.

[2]   Privilege and Related Issues

Attorney-client privilege. Attorney-client issues often arise during internal investigations. This privilege protects communications between the lawyer and the client in the context of rendering legal advice. One court defined the privilege as follows:

> (i) [w]hen legal advice of any kind is sought (ii) from a professional legal advisor in his or her capacity as such, (iii) the communications relating to that purpose, (iv) made in confidence (v) by the client, (vi) are, at the client's instance, permanently protected (vii) from disclosure by the client or by the legal advisor (viii) unless the protection be waived.

United States v. Martin, 278 F.3d 988, 999 (9th Cir. 2002) (quoting 8 Wigmore, Evidence § 2292, at 554 (McNaughton rev. 1961)).

Corporate investigations raise issues on the proper role between the attorney for the corporation and the attorney for the individual employees in the corporation. In most situations, the attorney cannot serve the professional interests of both the corporation and the employees because of inherent conflicts.

Moreover, the government will often seek to have a corporation waive the attorney-client privilege in order to assemble evidence against corporate agents.

Conversely, the very evidence against the corporation comes from the corporate agents or employees.

While individuals can claim a valid Fifth Amendment privilege, a corporation does not have the right to assert the privilege. The government has the right to obtain certain corporate documents over a Fifth Amendment objection. However, employees are the ones who will ultimately assemble and transfer the information to the government agents. Thus, attorneys who represent the corporation must gather information from the individual employees of the corporation acting on behalf of the corporation. The employees have personal rights, including Fifth Amendment rights, that the corporation lacks.

Work product doctrine. Closely related to the attorney-client privilege is the work product doctrine. This doctrine protects the confidentiality of materials generated during an internal investigation that includes the attorney's mental opinions and legal theories. The work product doctrine is designed to prevent adversaries from obtaining the benefit of the attorney's labor in anticipation of litigation. The Supreme Court originally acknowledged this doctrine in *Hickman v. Taylor*, 329 U.S. 495, 510–511 (1947):

> In performing his various duties . . . it is essential that a lawyer work with a certain degree of privacy, free from unnecessary intrusion by opposing parties and their counsel. Proper preparation of a client's case demands that he assemble information, sift what he considers to be the relevant from the irrelevant facts, prepare his legal theories and plan his strategy without undue influence and needless interference. . . . This work is reflected, of course, in interviews, statements, memoranda, correspondence, briefs, mental impressions, personal beliefs, and countless other tangible and intangible ways — aptly . . . termed . . . the "work product of the lawyer." Were such materials open to opposing counsel on mere demand, much of what is now put down in writing would remain unwritten.

This reasoning is applied both in civil cases, *see* Fed. R. Civ. P. 26(b)(3), and in criminal cases, *see* Fed. R. Crim. P. 16(a)(2) (discussing government's nondisclosure); Fed. R. Crim. P. 16(b)(2) (discussing defendant's nondisclosure).

The application of the work product doctrine raises complex questions concerning the scope of the doctrine. *See, e.g., Gray v. Oracle Corp.*, 2006 U.S. Dist. LEXIS 33439, at *5–*6 (D. Utah May 24, 2006) (tape recordings are not protected work product under *Hickman* because they do not involve the " 'mental impressions, opinions, or legal theories of an attorney,' — within the meaning of Rule 26(b)(3)").

*   *   *

During the course of a corporate criminal investigation, work product and attorney-client issues can create tremendous challenges to counsel both for the government and the defense. In the following case, pay close attention to the representational challenges the attorneys faced. Also, consider the company's reasons for granting the government access to the company's internal documents.

UNITED STATES v. BERGONZI
216 F.R.D. 487 (N.D. Cal. 2003)

Jenkins, District Judge:

Before the Court are a motion to intervene filed by nonparty McKesson Corporation ("McKesson") and motions to produce materials provided to the Government pursuant to agreements filed by both Defendants Albert Bergonzi ("Bergonzi") and Jay Gilbertson ("Gilbertson"). McKesson's motion to intervene requires the Court to determine whether the Company may intervene in the instant action to challenge Defendants' request for the production of documents on grounds of privilege. Defendants' motions for the production of materials provided to the Government pursuant to agreements require the Court to determine whether the Government is required to produce certain documents pursuant to Rule 16 of the Federal Criminal Rules of Evidence ("Rule 16") and *Brady v. Maryland*, 373 U.S. 83 (1963), and whether the documents at issue are privileged. In connection with the motions, the Court also considers the brief of the Securities and Exchange Commission ("SEC") and a recent decision issued by the Court of Chancery of the State of Delaware. Having read and considered the papers, and having heard the parties at oral argument, the Court GRANTS McKesson's motion and GRANTS Defendants' motions.

FACTUAL BACKGROUND

On September 27, 2000, a grand jury returned an indictment charging Defendants, former executives of HBO & Company ("HBOC"), with seventeen counts of securities, and mail and wire fraud. On January 20, 2001, the grand jury returned a superseding indictment alleging additional fraudulent activity. The indictment alleges that between 1997 and April 1999, Defendants and others deliberately engaged in a variety of fraudulent practices that resulted in the intentional misstatement of the publicly reported financial results of HBOC and McKesson HBOC ("McKesson HBOC" or "Company"). The latter entity, McKesson HBOC, was formed through the January 1999 acquisition of HBOC by McKesson.

The investigations of Defendants began shortly after McKesson's April 28, 1999 public disclosure that its auditors discovered accounting irregularities. Private actions alleging securities fraud began to be filed on the same day of the announcement. In light of these accounting problems, the Company's Board of Directors authorized an Audit Committee to review the circumstances surrounding them and to make recommendations regarding the Company's accounting policies, procedures and controls. The Audit Committee retained the firm of Skadden, Arps, Slate, Meagher & Flom ("Skadden") to provide legal advice. Skadden, in turn, retained the accounting firm of Price Waterhouse Coopers ("PWC") to assist with the review.

On May 10, 1999, Skadden and PWC met with SEC investigators. On May 27, 1999, the Company and the SEC entered into a confidentiality agreement ("SEC Agreement"), which stated that the Company was conducting an internal investigation, likely culminating in the preparation of a report ("Report"), and that the Company would provide this Report to the SEC when completed. The SEC Agreement professes that the Company has a "common interest" with the SEC "in obtaining information contained in the Report and Back-up Materials if it is able to do so without losing protection from further disclosure." It further states that, for its part, the SEC "has recognized that obtaining access to the Report and Back-up Materials can assist the [SEC] in carrying out its law enforcement responsibilities." In providing the "Report and Back-up Materials," the Company purported not to waive work product or applicable attorney-client privilege, and the SEC agreed that it would not argue that the voluntary submission of the information would constitute a waiver of any privilege. The SEC also agreed to maintain confidentiality of the information "except to the extent that the [SEC] determines that disclosure is otherwise required by federal law."

On May 28, 1999, Skadden, acting as counsel for the Company, and the United States Attorneys' Office ("USAO" or "Government") entered into a separate and similar confidentiality agreement ("USAO Agreement"), by which the USAO would receive a copy of the Report and Back-up Materials prepared as a result of the Company's internal investigation. The USAO Agreement provided that the Company was, based on information known to the USAO and prior to investigation, not the subject or target of any investigation. It further stated, however, the USAO could use any documentation produced in any criminal proceeding, including prosecution of the Company.

As part of the internal review, Skadden conducted fifty-five (55) interviews of thirty-seven (37) present and former employees of McKesson and HBOC, preparing an interview memoranda for each of those interviewed ("Interview Memoranda"). Based upon the information obtained and the conclusions reached, Skadden prepared the Report and presented it to the Audit Committee on July 26, 1999.

Between July 27, 1999, and August 5, 1999, Skadden provided the Report and Back-up Materials, including the Interview Memoranda, to both the SEC and the USAO. Prior to receipt of the Report and the Back-up Materials, and on July 19, 1999, the SEC issued a Formal Order of Investigation of the Company.

Skadden continued to provide documents to the SEC and the USAO and, on November 19, 1999, the SEC and Skadden entered into a supplemental agreement of confidentiality ("Supplemental Agreement"). Although the SEC has yet to charge the Company, staff from the SEC has filed a "Wells Letter," advising McKesson HBOC of its intent to seek authorization from the SEC to file charges against the Company. The Wells Letter was issued on June 29, 2001.

On January 10, 2002, during McKesson's review of materials the USAO had produced to Defendants, McKesson discovered that the USAO had produced four Interview Memoranda. That same day, McKesson called the Government to advise it of the inadvertent production and asked that it follow up with Defendants. By letter dated January 31, 2002, the Government sought the return of the four Interview Memoranda from Defendants. On February 7, 2002, McKesson learned that while Bergonzi returned the documents, Gilbertson refused. McKesson further learned that the USAO produced an additional Interview Memoranda to Gilbertson, and Gilbertson again refused to return the document.

ANALYSIS

I. *Motion to Intervene*

McKesson seeks to intervene in the instant action on grounds that the documents sought by Defendants are privileged. The motion is not opposed by the Government or either Defendant.

Third parties may intervene in a criminal trial to challenge the production of subpoenaed documents on the ground of privilege. Here, McKesson is challenging the production of the Report and Back-up Materials sought by Defendants from the USAO in the instant criminal action on grounds that production of the documents is precluded by its claim of attorney-client privilege and work product protection.

Because the privilege claimed belongs to McKesson, intervention is appropriate. Moreover, the parties to the criminal action do not oppose the intervention. As such, the Court GRANTS McKesson's motion to Intervene.

II. *Motion for Production*

Defendants seek production of the Report and Back-up Materials, including the Interview Memoranda. Defendants argue the Company waived any claim of privilege by producing the material to the Government. They also contend that the Government's subsequent production of the documents to Defendants effects a waiver of any applicable privileges. Defendants further contend they are entitled to the documents under Rule 16 and *Brady*. This entitlement, Defendants claim, exists even if the Court finds that the privilege attaches. The Court addresses each of the arguments in turn below. In resolving the motion, however, the Court reaches the issue of privilege first, as the Company argues that its claim of privilege precludes production of documents under either Rule 16 or *Brady*.

A. *Privilege*

Defendants contend neither the attorney-client privilege nor the protection under the work product doctrine precludes production of the Report and Back-up Materials they now seek where (1) the Company did not have the documents prepared to assist in providing legal advice but instead prepared them for the Government in an effort to obtain lenience; (2) the Company voluntarily produced the material to both the SEC and the USAO; and (3) the USAO produced portions of the allegedly privileged documents to Gilbertson. The Company counters that the documents sought by Defendants enjoy protection from disclosure under the attorney-client privilege and the work product doctrine and that it waived neither privilege through its disclosure of the documents to the Government, or the Government's disclosure of the documents to Defendants. The Government joins the opposition on grounds that McKesson did not waive protection under the work product doctrine. The SEC, with its *amicus* brief, joins the Government's position, relying on the doctrine of selective waiver articulated by the Eight Circuit in *Diversified Indus., Inc. v. Meredith*, 572 F.2d 596 (8th Cir. 1977).

1. *Attorney-Client Privilege*

a. *Applicability*

The parties do not dispute that the Audit Committee retained Skadden to gather relevant facts and to develop an effective legal strategy for responding to potential claims of securities fraud based upon the accounting irregularities discovered in connection with the merger of HBOC. Moreover, there is no dispute that both the Report and the Interview Memoranda contained the results of that query and that before the documents had been prepared, McKesson agreed to turn over the Report and Interview Memoranda to the Government, pursuant to the SEC Agreement and USAO Agreement (collectively "Agreements"). The question before the Court, therefore, is whether the attorney-client privilege attaches to the documents where McKesson HBOC agrees, prior to the creation of the documents, to disclose them to the Government on condition that the Government acknowledge and make efforts to maintain the confidential nature of the documents unless it determines, in its discretion, that it must disclose them.

The party asserting the privilege must make a *prima facie* showing the privilege protects the information the party intends to withhold. *In re Grand Jury Invest.*, 974 F.2d 1068, 1071 (9th Cir. 1992). The privilege applies where legal advice of any kind is sought from a professional legal adviser in his capacity as such, and the communication relates to that purpose, is made in confidence, by or for the client.

In order for the privilege to apply, the communication sought to be protected must be, among other things, made in confidence. Here, and as argued by the Company, the Agreements are replete with language which would support a finding the Company intended the documents now sought by Defendants to be confidential. Specifically, the Company stated that the documents were created "solely for the purposes of providing legal advice to the Company and the Audit Committee . . . " and would contain and reflect "communications protected by the work-product doctrine and attorney-client privilege. . . . " The Agreements also indicated that the Company did not want to or intend to waive the protection from further disclosure. The Company further sought and obtained agreement by the Government for efforts to maintain the confidentiality of the documents produced.

Having said that, communications between client and attorney for the purpose of relaying communication to a third party is not confidential and not protected by the attorney-client privilege. Here, the Agreements make clear that prior to preparation of the Report and Back-up Materials, the Company agreed to disclose the documents to the Government. . . .

The communication between Skadden and the Company, therefore, was made with the intent to relay the communication to the Government.

Moreover, certain terms in the same Agreements weigh against a finding that any of the advice contained therein was made in confidence. Specifically, the Company authorized the SEC to, in its discretion, "determine that disclosure is otherwise required by federal law or in furtherance of [either entities'] discharge of its duties and responsibilities." Likewise, the Company "consent[ed] to the disclosure of the [documents] to a federal grand jury as the [USAO] deems appropriate, and in any criminal prosecution that may result from the [USAO's] investigation." By giving the Government, whether the SEC or the USAO, full discretion to disclose the Report and Interview Memoranda in certain circumstances, the terms of the Agreements run counter to the Company's assertion the communication was intended to remain confidential.

As such, the Court is not persuaded that the Company intended the communications to remain confidential, as it must have in order for the privilege to apply in the first instance, and finds that the Company failed to meet its burden of persuading the Court that the attorney-client privilege applies to the documents sought by Defendants.

2. *Work Product Doctrine*

a. *Applicability*

The work product doctrine protects from discovery materials prepared by an attorney in anticipation of litigation. *See generally Hickman v. Taylor*, 329 U.S. 495, 511 (1947). The privilege is intended to allow an attorney to "work with a certain degree of privacy, free from unnecessary intrusion by opposing parties and their counsel." Materials that contain the impressions, conclusions or theories of counsel constitute work product.

Defendants argue that the work product protection never applied on grounds that both the Report and the Back-up Material were created with the intent to disclose. Although Defendants' argument makes logical sense, there is no requirement, when determining whether the protection applies, that the attorney and client intend to maintain the material in confidence. The work product doctrine extends beyond confidential communications between the attorney and client to "any document prepared in anticipation of litigation by or for the attorney." *In re Columbia/HCA Healthcare*, 293 F.3d 289, 304 (6th Cir. 2002).

Here, Skadden prepared the Report and Back-up Materials in response to the securities fraud suits being filed against the Company and certain employees, whether former employees or not. Because the Report and Back-up Materials were prepared in anticipation of actual litigation and constitute Skadden's mental impressions and legal analyses, the Court finds that the documents sought herein fall within the protection of the work product doctrine.

b. *Waiver*

Having found protection under the work product doctrine applies, the Government argues the Company did not waive the protection with its production of the material to the Government because the Company entered into valid confidentiality agreements with the Government before production. Moreover, the Government argues it could not waive the protection by having produced some of the interview memoranda to Gilbertson because the production was inadvertent and because the privilege was not the Government's to waive. McKesson HBOC makes the same arguments, but adds that it shared a common interest with the Government. The Court addresses each of the arguments in turn below.

(1) Common Interest Exception

As stated above, McKesson HBOC argues, *inter alia*, that it did not waive its privilege with its production to the Government because the Ninth Circuit recognizes that there is no waiver of the privilege where a party discloses privileged material to another with which it shares common interests and because McKesson HBOC entered into valid confidentiality agreements with the Government before production. Moreover, it argues the Government could not waive the Company's privilege by having produced some of the Interview Memoranda to Gilbertson because the production was inadvertent. The Court finds, as more fully explained below, that McKesson has failed to establish the existence of a common interest between itself and the Government and according finds that the applicable privilege has been waived and said waiver was not inadvertent.

The common interest privilege, frequently referred to as the joint defense privilege, applies where (1) the communication is made by separate parties in the course of a matter of common interest; (2) the communication is designed to further that effort; and (3) the privilege has not been waived. The privilege does not require a complete unity of interests among the participants, and it may apply where the parties' interests are adverse in substantial respects.

Here, the Company argues that in engaging Skadden to conduct a review to determine, among other things, whether any individuals violated the federal securities laws in connection with merger, it shared common interests with the Government. In support of its position, the Company points to the Agreements which specifically state that the production of the Report and Interview Memoranda could "assist the [Government] in carrying out its law enforcement responsibilities." The Company also asserts that its status as a potential adversary does not lessen the applicability of the common interest privilege.

Defendants, in response, argue that the Company and the Government were indeed adversaries, specifically pointing to language in the USAO Agreement which contemplated future prosecution of the Company. In addition, according to Gilbertson at least, the Government believed that it was adverse to the Company, as evidenced by its discussion of the materiality of the Report and Back-up Materials in the context of whether production is due under *Brady*. . . .

[T]he Company here voluntarily disclosed privileged material to a government agency. Although McKesson HBOC may have had a "common interest" in the investigation of the alleged securities fraud committed by its officers, the "common interest" alleged is not like the interest shared by allied lawyers and clients who are working together in prosecuting or defending a lawsuit. Indeed, the Company and the Government did not have a true common goal, as it could not have been the Company's goal to impose liability onto itself, a consideration always maintained by the Government.

Although McKesson entered into what it fashions to be confidentiality agreements with the Government entities involved, the agreement made by the Government to keep the documents was not unconditional. As such, the Court finds McKesson HBOC failed to demonstrate the common interest exception to the waiver of the work product privilege applies. Accordingly, the production of the Report and Back-up Materials to the Government and the SEC constituted waiver of the privilege.

(2) Disclosure to Government

Work product protection is waived where disclosure of the otherwise privileged documents is made to a third party, and that disclosure enables an adversary to gain access to the information. The question for the Court with respect to the Government is whether the Company's disclosure to the Government constituted a disclosure to an adverse party.

Likewise, here, McKesson HBOC disclosed the Report and the Back-up Materials to the Government despite the fact that the Government was investigating the Company. Indeed, as a result of that investigation, the SEC issued a Wells Letter against the Company in June 2001. As such, the Court finds that neither the Company nor the Government has successfully met its burden of establishing that the Government was not an adversary. Its disclosure of the Report and Back-up Materials to the Government, therefore, constitutes waiver of the protection under the work product doctrine.

(3) Disclosure to Defendants

Once a party has disclosed work product to one adversary, it waives work product protection as to all other adversaries. *See McMorgan*, 931 F. Supp. at 709. As discussed above, the Court finds that disclosure of the Report and Back-up Materials to the Government constitutes a disclosure of the documents to an adversary. Therefore, any work product protection claimed against production to the Defendants is also waived.

[The court then considered challenges to the disclosures under Rule 16 of the Federal Rules of Criminal Procedure and the *Brady* rule requiring the government to disclose "exculpatory information that is either admissible or reasonably likely to lead to admissible evidence." The court found that *Brady* "compel[ed] production of the Report." Rule 16 requires the government to allow the defendant to inspect and copy or photograph documents the government possesses. The Jencks Act, 18 U.S.C. § 3500(3), precludes disclosure of witness statements until after the witness has testified on direct examination. The court found that the reports and the interview memoranda were both material and discoverable under Rule 16.]

CONCLUSION

For the foregoing reasons, the Court GRANTS McKesson's motion to intervene and GRANTS Defendants' motions for the production of the Report and Interview Memoranda under the following condition:

Prior to production, the parties are to submit to the Court a protective order governing the production and use of the material ordered produced by this Court. To the extent the parties are unable to agree on a form of protective order, each party is to submit their proposed order to the Court, on or before January 23, 2003, along with an explanation as to the necessity for submission of a separate agreement.

IT IS SO ORDERED.

NOTES AND QUESTIONS

1. *Similar interests.* In conducting an internal investigation, a company is seeking evidence of wrongdoing. If such evidence is discovered, companies sometimes disclose the information to the government in order to forestall a criminal prosecution. McKesson argued that it had a similar interest with the government in this investigation. Do you agree? The court said, "The company and the government did not have a true common goal as it could not have been the company's goal to impose liability onto itself, a consideration always maintained by the government." Did the company and the government ever have any similar goal? If so, what was that goal?

2. *Premise of work product doctrine.* As stated by the majority in *In re Columbia/HCA Healthcare,* "The ability to prepare one's case in confidence, which is the chief reason articulated in *Hickman* for the work product protections, has little to do with talking to the Government." 293 F.3d 289, 306 (6th Cir. 2002). What is the premise behind the work product and attorney-client privileges?

3. *Well letters.* A Wells Notice is a letter sent by an SEC regulator to a prospective respondent, providing the substance of charges that the regulator intends to bring against the respondent, and affording the respondent the opportunity to submit a written statement to the ultimate decision maker. The Wells letter is a term derived from 17 C.F.R. § 202.5(c). The SEC outlines the significance of a submission to that agency:

> (c) Persons who become involved in preliminary or formal investigations may, on their own initiative, submit a written statement to the Commission setting forth their interests and position in regard to the subject matter of the investigation. Upon request, the staff, in its discretion, may advise such persons of the general nature of the investigation, including the indicated violations as they pertain to them, and the amount of time that may be available for preparing and submitting a statement prior to the presentation of a staff recommendation to the Commission for the commencement of an administrative or injunction proceeding. Submissions by interested persons should be forwarded to the appropriate Division Director, Regional Director, or District Administrator with a copy to the staff members conducting the investigation and should be clearly referenced to the specific investigation to which they relate. In the event a recommendation for the commencement of enforcement proceeding is presented by the staff, any submissions by interested persons will be forwarded to the Commission in conjunction with the staff memorandum.

17 C.F.R. § 202.5(c) (1994).

4. *Documents and objects.* Former Federal Rule of Criminal Procedure 16(a)(1)(C) has been relettered and is now Rule 16(a)(1)(E). Although the case law cited by this court references Rule 16(a)(1)(C), the decisions are referring to the following provision:

> Documents and Objects: Upon request of the defendant, the government must permit the defendant to inspect and to copy or photograph books, papers, documents, data, photographs, tangible objects, buildings or places, or copies or portions of any of these items, if the item is within the government's possession, custody, or control and
>
> (i)   the item is material to preparing the defense;
> (ii)   the government intends to use the item in its case-in-chief at trial, or
> (iii) the item was obtained from or belongs to the defendant.

Fed. R. Crim. P. 16(a)(1)(E).

5. *Federal Rules of Evidence — Rule 502.* During extensive and complex litigation, private communications can be inadvertently disclosed. If the information contains matters protected by the attorney-client privilege or the work product doctrine, the disclosures can have an adverse impact on the litigation. Congress enacted Rule 502 of the Federal Rules of Evidence, which limits the consequences

of inadvertent and mistaken disclosures that occur during litigation. The rule provides that any waiver of a privilege applies only to the matters waived, and not the broader subject matter. Any inadvertent disclosure does not constitute a waiver of the privilege, as long as the holder of the privilege took reasonable steps to prevent the disclosure or to minimize its impact.

6. *Selective waivers.* Selective waivers would allow corporations to aid government investigation without waiving the privilege as to future civil litigants. This is a recurring issue. Courts have traditionally rejected attempts to make selective waivers, though a few courts have recognized such waivers. What benefits might there be to the public in allowing such waivers? For further discussion of selective waivers and the attorney-client privilege, see Michael H. Dore, *A Matter of Fairness: The Need For a New Look at Selective Waiver in SEC Investigations*, 89 Marq. L. Rev. 761 (2006); and Zach Dostart, *Selective Disclosure: The Abrogation of the Attorney-Client Privilege and the Work Product*, 33 Pepp. L. Rev. 723 (2005/2006).

7. *Department of Justice policies.*

a. *Waivers of the attorney-client privilege.* The Department of Justice previously adopted controversial policies that had major implications for the conduct of internal investigations. For example, in the "Thompson Memorandum," issued by then-Deputy Attorney General Larry Thompson, entitled *Principles of Federal Prosecution of Business Organizations*, available at http://www.usdoj.gov/dag/cftf/corporate_guidelines.htm, the DOJ adopted policies that penalized entities that declined to waive the attorney-client privilege during a criminal investigation. Among other things, the Memorandum stated that an entity's decision to waive, or not to waive, the attorney-client privilege may affect the government's decision to prosecute the entity. For an analysis of the Thompson Memorandum, *see* Peter J. Henning, *Overcriminalization: The Politics of Crime*, 54 Am. U. L. Rev. 669 (2005).

The Thompson Memorandum was replaced by the "McNulty Memorandum," issued by former Deputy Attorney General Paul J. McNulty, which left many of the earlier policies in place. *See* http://lawprofessors.typepad.com/whitecollarcrime_blog/files/mcnulty_memo.pdf. Commentators speculated that the McNulty Memorandum was designed to forestall Congressional reaction to controversial policies put into place by the Thompson Memorandum. *See* John J. Carney and Dennis O. Cohen, *McNulty Memo: Changes Game Or Keeps Congress Out?*, N.Y. L.J, Jan. 3, 2007, at 3, col. 4. Most commentators concluded, however, that the changes were "too little, too late," and Congress continued to threaten to overturn aspects of the DOJ's policies by statute. *See* Elkan Abramowitz & Barry A. Bohrer, *The Defense of Corporate America: The Year in Review*, N.Y. L.J., Jan. 2, 2007, at 6, col. 3.

In response, the DOJ rescinded the McNulty Memorandum, replacing it in August 2008 with the Filip Memorandum. The new memorandum prohibits federal prosecutors, when assessing the degree of an entity's cooperation, from considering the entity's decision not to waive the attorney-client privilege. Now, "prosecutors must measure cooperation by the extent to which the organization voluntarily discloses 'relevant facts and evidence.'" Khizar A. Sheikh and Matthew M. Oliver, *SEC Prohibits Staff Attorneys from Seeking Privilege Waivers During Investigations*, N.Y.L.J., Feb. 9, 2009. The SEC adopted a similar policy shortly thereafter. *Id.*

The degree to which privilege waivers will, to some degree, affect the exercise of prosecutorial discretion remains to be seen. As commentators have noted, severe risks remain for business organizations conducting internal investigations:

- The SEC has not done away with privilege waivers. Instead, while SEC staff attorneys are prohibited from seeking privilege waivers as a matter of course, they may still do so with approval from supervising attorneys.
- The SEC still expects that business organizations will timely disclose facts relevant to an investigation, including 'factual information' garnered from witnesses during an internal investigation. Despite the new prohibition against privilege waivers, the SEC's expectations continue to implicate privilege considerations. It is unclear how the SEC expects counsel to disclose facts generated during an internal investigation without compromising privilege.
- Business organizations are still expected to (i) voluntarily produce relevant factual information the SEC did not directly request and otherwise might not have uncovered; (ii) request that corporate employees cooperate with the SEC and make all reasonable efforts to secure such cooperation; (iii) make witnesses available for interviews when it might otherwise be difficult or impossible for the staff to interview the witnesses; and (iv) assist in the interpretation of complex business records.

Id. What dangers remain for business organizations when conducting internal investigations? Why?

b. *The KPMG case.*

The attorneys' fees issue. The Thompson and McNulty Memorandums set forth a policy that penalized entities, in the government's charging decision, when the entities paid employees' attorneys' fees in connection with the criminal investigation or prosecution. As the court stated in *United States v. Stein*, 435 F. Supp. 2d 330 (S.D.N.Y. 2006), under the Thompson Memorandum, "all United States Attorneys are obliged to consider the advancing of legal fees by business entities, except such advances as are required by law, as at least possibly indicative of an attempt to protect culpable employees and as a factor weighing in favor of indictment of the entity." *Id.* at 338. This decision was handed down in the massive tax fraud case involving KPMG, one of the world's largest accounting firms. According to the decision, KPMG avoided prosecution by declining to pay its indicted employees' legal fees. The court concluded that this policy violated the defendants' Fifth and Sixth Amendment rights, stating that the government "let its zeal get in the way of its judgment" and thus violated "the Constitution it is sworn to defend." The judge ultimately dismissed the case against 13 of the 18 defendants. *United States v. Stein*, 495 F. Supp. 2d 390 (S.D.N.Y. 2007). The judge stated that he was reluctant to dismiss the case, but was compelled to do so because the government's violations of the defendants' constitutional rights "shock[ed] the conscience." *See* Kathy M. Kristof, *KPMG Fraud Case Wilts*, L.A. Times, July 17, 2007, at C1, C9.

The Second Circuit affirmed, holding that KPMG's actions amounted to state action that deprived the defendants of their Sixth Amendment right to the effective assistance of counsel; the court thus did not reach the Fifth Amendment issue. *United States v. Stein*, 541 F.3d 130, 136 (2d Cir. 2008). Note that the DOJ later changed its policy and instructed prosecutors " 'generally' not to consider whether a corporation was indemnifying an employee under investigation." Greg Saikin,

SEC, DOJ Clarify 'Cooperation,' Tex. Lawyer, Jan. 26, 2009.

Coerced Statements. In the KPMG case, the district judge also suppressed certain of the defendants' statements on the grounds that the statements were coerced in violation of the Fifth Amendment privilege against compelled self-incrimination. *United States v. Stein*, 440 F. Supp. 2d 315 (S.D.N.Y. 2006). The court held that government pressure on KPMG to cooperate led KPMG to coerce its employees into waiving their Fifth Amendment rights and making incriminating statements. The court concluded:

> Many companies faced with allegations of wrongdoing are under intense pressure to avoid indictment, as an indictment — especially of a financial services firm — threatens to destroy the business regardless of whether the firm ultimately is convicted or acquitted. That is precisely what happened to Arthur Andersen & Co., one of the world's largest accounting firms, which collapsed almost immediately after it was indicted — and the Supreme Court's eventual reversal of its conviction did not undo the damage. So any entity facing such catastrophic consequences must do whatever it can to avoid indictment.

> The DOJ and other federal agencies have capitalized on this, in part by altering the manner in which suspected corporate crime has been investigated, prosecuted, and, when proven, punished. The Thompson Memorandum is a part of this change. In cases involving vulnerable companies, the pressure exerted by it and by the prosecutors who apply it inevitably sets in motion precisely what occurred here — the exertion of enormous economic power by the employer upon its employees to sacrifice their constitutional rights.

> In this case, the pressure that was exerted on the [defendants] was a product of intentional government action. The government brandished a big stick — it threatened to indict KPMG. And it held out a very large carrot. It offered KPMG the hope of avoiding the fate of Arthur Andersen if KPMG could deliver to the [United States Attorneys Office] employees who would talk, notwithstanding their constitutional right to remain silent, and strip those employees of economic means of defending themselves. In two instances, that pressure resulted in statements that otherwise would not have been made. In seven, the evidence does not warrant that conclusion. The coerced statements and their fruits must be suppressed.

> It is no answer for the government to say that these aspects of the Thompson Memorandum are needed to fight corporate crime. Those responsible should be prosecuted and, if convicted, punished. But the end does not justify the means.

Id. at 37–38. Do you agree with the court's conclusions? Why or why not? As noted above, the Second Circuit affirmed the partial dismissal in the case on Sixth Amendment grounds, and did not reach the Fifth Amendment issue. *Stein*, 541 F.3d at 136. As also noted above, the government has now retreated from some aspects of the Thompson Memorandum. It remains to be seen whether and to what degree the government will continue to use a company's payment of employees' legal fees in deciding whether to investigate or charge the company.

* * *

In complex litigation, individuals and entities who are parties to the litigation often share common interests. A joint defense agreement may create a privilege, also known as the common interest privilege, which protects the free flow of information among such parties. The privilege provides that communications among the parties are protected when the communications are designed to establish a common litigation strategy. As you read the next case, consider what problems the joint defense agreement presents for both the individuals and the corporation.

UNITED STATES v. LECROY
348 F. Supp. 2d 375 (E.D. Pa. 2004)

BAYLSON, DISTRICT JUDGE.

Defendants LeCroy and Snell are charged with wire fraud under 18 U.S.C. §§ 1343 and 2, for allegedly soliciting and obtaining from Philadelphia attorney Ronald White (originally a named co-defendant in this case but now deceased) a false $50,000 invoice presented to J.P. Morgan Chase ("JPMC") for legal services purportedly performed by White's law firm.

The issue presented is whether this Court should preclude the government from using certain notes and memoranda it has in its possession, which were taken by JPMC counsel during interviews held with JPMC employees LeCroy and Snell by JPMC counsel, or whether these notes and interviews are protected by either the attorney-client privilege and/or a joint defense agreement entered into by counsel for LeCroy, Snell and JPMC.

I. PROCEDURAL HISTORY

During the grand jury investigation which preceded the return of the indictment in this case on June 29, 2004, JPMC, as well as Defendants LeCroy and Snell, received grand jury subpoenas. As set forth in further detail below, JPMC's internal counsel questioned LeCroy and Snell about their knowledge of the facts underlying the grand jury subpoena, recognized their need for individual counsel, and JPMC itself retained outside counsel in Philadelphia. LeCroy and Snell were then given recommendations for lawyers and retained their own individual counsel. A Joint Defense Agreement arose, and during the discussions among counsel for JPMC, LeCroy and Snell, JPMC counsel indicated a desire to interview LeCroy and Snell at various times. As the government had requested, JPMC subsequently decided that it would produce, pursuant to its grand jury subpoena, the notes and/or memoranda of the meetings between JPMC counsel and LeCroy and Snell.

Following the return of the indictment, LeCroy and Snell asserted claims of privilege with respect to notes and memoranda of interviews created by counsel for JPMC. The government designated two attorneys who were not connected with the prosecution of the indictment to maintain custody and control of these notes and memoranda, and constructed a "Chinese wall" between the government attorneys who were the prosecutors on the indictment, and the government attorneys designated to represent the government in connection with the claims of privilege by LeCroy and Snell.

II. FACTUAL BACKGROUND

Defendant Snell was served with a grand jury subpoena at his JPMC office in Atlanta, GA on or about October 17, 2003, and promptly advised Scott Campbell, JPMC's Senior Vice President and Associate General Counsel. Campbell was aware that JPMC itself had received a grand jury subpoena at or about the same time. Campbell had discussions with Snell and his supervisor, LeCroy, on October 20, 2003. At that time, the Court finds Snell and LeCroy were speaking to Campbell in their capacity as JPMC employees. Campbell was acting as JPMC counsel, and there were no discussions about either Snell or LeCroy having individual counsel.

As a result of further discussions with Snell on the following day, October 21, 2003, and with both Snell and LeCroy on October 27, 2003, JPMC recognized the need for both of these individuals to have individual counsel and so advised them of this fact. At this time JPMC itself retained outside counsel, Dodds, a Philadelphia lawyer with experience as both a prosecutor and a defense counsel. Up to and including October 27, 2003, Snell and LeCroy did not seek personal legal advice from Campbell; they had no expectation of getting personal legal advice from Campbell and they did not ask for it. JPMC made recommendations to LeCroy and Snell of certain Philadelphia attorneys to represent them in connection with the grand jury investigation. JPMC agreed to pay the legal fees of Snell and LeCroy.

Snell retained his counsel, Suddath, on or about October 30, 2003. LeCroy retained his counsel, Recker, in the time period of November 10-13, 2003. Both Suddath and Recker are Philadelphia lawyers experienced in grand jury investigations.

The Court finds that JPMC intended to form a Joint Defense Agreement ("JDA") prior to LeCroy and Snell retaining personal counsel. Campbell's handwritten notes for the meeting of October 27, 2003, state "we will work going forward on a joint defense basis." Campbell testified that at the October 27 meeting he informed LeCroy and Snell that he was speaking to them in his capacity as counsel for JPMC and that he was going to "recommend counsel to represent their personal interests." As soon as Suddath and Recker were retained, they confirmed the existence of the JDA with Dodds.

The government does not dispute the existence of a JDA in this case. The JDA was verbal, and although its terms were never specifically articulated, Recker accurately described her understanding of the JDA as follows:

> The joint defense arrangement, primarily the focus is twofold. One, that the lawyers are able to investigate facts and share the results of their investigation with each other, keeping everything under the cloak of privilege. The second important part in the understanding of a joint defense arrangement is that none of that information that has been shared pursuant to the privilege can be disclosed to a third party without the consult-consent of all the parties involved.

[Counsel] testified [to a] similar understanding of the JDA. From these facts, the Court concluded that the discussions which took place between JPMC counsel and LeCroy and Snell after October 27, 2003, specifically on October 29, 2003 as to both, and on December 11, 2003 with LeCroy, are protected by the JDA. During these meetings, both LeCroy and Snell had reason to believe that their discussions with either their own counsel or JPMC counsel were protected from disclosure. . . .

The testimony is undisputed that Dodds, on behalf of JPMC, was consistent and insistent that if the government pushed, JPMC would turn over the interview notes taken by JPMC counsel, to the government. Despite this clear warning, LeCroy and Snell went to New York on separate dates in January 2004 and were interviewed by JPMC counsel with their own counsel present.

The March 4, 2004 interviews of Snell and LeCroy were taken without their individual counsel present, and they did not know that the meeting was going to occur.

III. LEGAL PRINCIPLES OF A JOINT DEFENSE AGREEMENT

Although the Third Circuit has not specifically ruled on the applicability of a joint defense agreement in any similar factual situation, it has described a joint defense agreement. . . .

"Because the privilege sometimes may apply outside the context of actual litigation, what the parties call a 'joint defense' privilege is more aptly termed the 'common interest' rule." *In re Grand Jury Subpoena, A. Nameless Lawyer,* 274 F.3d 563, 572 (1st Cir. 2001). The burden of demonstrating the existence of a joint defense agreement falls on the person claiming it. A party seeking to assert the joint defense privilege must demonstrate that: 1) the communications were made in the course of a joint defense effort; 2) the statements were made in furtherance of that effort; and 3) the privilege has not been waived. Likewise, the party asserting privilege, both in the context of joint defense agreements and otherwise, bears the burden of proving the applicability of the privilege. In the absence of a JDA, when the party asserting privilege is a corporate officer, the individual corporate officer's assertion of attorney-client privilege cannot prevent the disclosure of corporate communications with corporate counsel when the corporation's privilege has been waived.

Although "privileges should be narrowly construed and expansions cautiously extended," *Weissman,* 195 F.3d at 100, courts have found that an oral joint defense agreement may be valid. *See Nameless Lawyer,* 274 F.3d at 569-70. A person need not be a litigant to be a party to a joint defense agreement.

It is axiomatic that in order for a communication to be privileged that communication must be made in confidence. Even in the context of joint defense agreements, in order for privilege to attach to a communication, the party asserting the privilege bears the burden of demonstrating that "the communication was given in confidence and that the client *reasonably understood it to be so given." United States v. Schwimmer,* 892 F.2d 237, 244 (2d Cir. 1989) (emphasis added). Additionally, the burden is on the party asserting a joint defense privilege to demonstrate that the clients reasonably believed that their statements were being made within the context and in furtherance of their joint defense.

IV. APPLICATION OF LEGAL PRINCIPLES
TO THE FACTS OF THIS CASE

A JDA is not an escape-proof prison. Indeed, public policy mandates that a participant in a JDA must be free to withdraw from it, unilaterally, but the withdrawal or waiver must be prospective only-and the duty of the Court in the present dispute is to determine whether there was such a withdrawal or waiver, and if so, precisely what notes and memoranda the government is entitled to retain and use at trial, and which notes and memoranda are protected by the JDA that was in existence.

A JDA without the right of prospective withdrawal would be void, if only because it would prevent one party to the JDA determining, as JPMC did in this case, that its own interests required it to cooperate with the government, rather than cooperate exclusively with its employees and their counsel. A participant in a JDA may also decide that it wants to "go it alone" and that doing so outweighs the benefits of continuing in the JDA. One party may decide that he, she or it wants to plead guilty to the charges that appear inevitable and that continuance in the JDA would deprive that party of the benefits which would come from negotiating an early plea agreement with the government.

A. *Waiver*

As to the issue of waiver of the attorney-client privilege, there is no waiver of the individual privilege between LeCroy and his counsel, and Snell and his counsel. The only issue of waiver relates to certain protections of the JDA. The leading case in the Third Circuit on waiver of privilege is *Westinghouse v. Republic of the Philippines*, 951 F.2d 1414, 1423 (3d Cir. 1991), holding that voluntary disclosure to a third party of purportedly privileged communications has long been considered inconsistent with the privilege. It is well settled that when a party voluntarily discloses privileged communications to a third party, the privilege is waived. Similarly, when a party discloses a portion of otherwise privileged material but withholds the remainder, the privilege is waived only as to those communications actually disclosed, unless a partial waiver would be unfair to the party's adversary. Disclosure alone, without intent, may constitute waiver of the attorney-client privilege.

Defendants rely on *In re Grand Jury Subpoenas (89-3 and 89-4)*, 902 F.2d 244, 248 (4th Cir. 1990), for the proposition that the joint defense privilege cannot be waived without the consent of all the parties to the joint defense agreement. That case involved a dispute between a parent company and its wholly owned subsidiary-both of whom had been summoned before a grand jury-regarding the production of records. The Fourth Circuit held that the subsidiary could not unilaterally waive a joint defense privilege, and that the joint defense privilege may attach irrespective of whether an action is criminal or civil, and regardless of whether an action is ongoing or contemplated.

The First Circuit recently made the following observation: "[T]he existence of a joint defense agreement does not increase the number of parties whose consent is needed to waive the attorney-client privilege; it merely prevents disclosure of a communication made in the course of preparing a joint defense by the third party to whom it was made." *Nameless Lawyer*, 274 F.3d at 572–73.

Applying these waiver principles to the present case, the Court finds that LeCroy and Snell waived some protections of the JDA by proceeding with the interviews with JPMC counsel in January 2004 and March 2004. Specifically, they voluntarily and knowingly waived the protection of the JDA to the extent that JPMC would be allowed to turn over the notes of those interviews to the government.

B. *Withdrawal*

. . . . [I]t is clearly contemplated by the parties to a JDA that one party could withdraw prospectively. Similarly, as the Court has noted above, any prohibition on withdrawal would be decidedly contrary to the public interest. There are some cases where courts have discussed the necessity of one party being able to withdraw from a JDA on a prospective basis.

In *United States v. Stepney*, 246 F.Supp.2d 1069, 1086 (N.D.Cal.2003), the court required that each joint defense agreement entered into by the defendants "must explicitly allow withdrawal upon notice to the other defendants." The court in *Stepney* elaborated on the risks inherent in a joint defense arrangement and emphasized that the protections afforded therein are not identical to the protections generally enjoyed under the attorney-client privilege:

> Although a limitation on confidentiality between a defendant and his own attorney would pose a severe threat to the true attorney-client relationship, making each defendant somewhat more guarded about the disclosures he makes to the joint defense effort does not significantly intrude on the function of joint defense agreements. . . . Co-defendants may eliminate inconsistent defenses without the same degree of disclosure that would be required for an attorney to adequately represent her client. *Id.*

C. *Modification*

As to modification, there can be no dispute that parties to an agreement have the right to modify it. While one party to a contract cannot modify its terms without the assent of the other parties, the fact of agreement as to a modification may be implied from a course of conduct in accordance with its existence.

D. *Analysis*

[T]he Court also finds partial withdrawal by JPMC and a partial waiver by LeCroy and Snell. The Court is not obliged to shoehorn its decision into any particular single legal doctrine, but rather, to pragmatically apply the law to the facts and make a decision as to what evidence may be used by the government at the trial.

It is also important to note that although the Court finds that there was a significant modification of the JDA as of January 2004, the JDA nonetheless continued in existence, as modified, throughout the balance of the investigation and indeed continues in existence today, during the pretrial preparation stages.

JPMC had determined for its own good and sufficient reasons-one of which is the fact that it is a highly regulated financial institution, and another may have been that it realized it may have been a victim of a fraudulent scheme-that it would, if the government "pushed," turn over the notes and memoranda of its meetings with LeCroy and Snell. JPMC thought it had the right to do so because LeCroy and Snell had their own counsel, and thus their meetings with JPMC counsel were not covered by their own personal attorney-client privilege. However, the Court finds that JPMC counsel was mistaken in this belief, because having joined the JDA, JPMC was bound by it until and unless it withdrew.

The Court believes that the most important facts on this issue relate to the discussions which Dodds had with Recker and Suddath *prior* to the January meetings in which Dodds explained to them that JPMC was retaining the right to turn over the notes of the interviews. Also significant is the fact that Recker and Suddath clearly made JPMC's intent known to their clients, LeCroy and Snell, respectively. With these facts, there is no dispute that LeCroy and Snell, and their counsel, were thoroughly advised of JPMC's intent and nonetheless decided to proceed with the January 2004 interviews with JPMC counsel. LeCroy and Snell had the option, knowing in advance that these notes may be turned over to the government by JPMC counsel pursuant to the grand jury subpoena, to decline to be interviewed by JPMC counsel. . . . . There are risks for every decision in a grand jury investigation, but the right of the grand jury to get the facts, and the right of JPMC, as a recipient of a grand jury subpoena, to decide to cooperate with the grand jury, are paramount. . . .

The grand jury may compel the production of evidence or the testimony of witnesses as it considers appropriate, and its operation generally is unrestrained by the technical procedural and evidentiary rules governing the conduct of criminal trials.

V. CONCLUSION

The facts of this case demonstrate that although entering into a JDA is often, indeed generally, beneficial to its participants, like skating on thin ice, dangers lurk below the surface. When JPMC insisted on its right of turning over the notes of its interviews with Snell and LeCroy to the government, Snell and LeCroy had the option to reject JPMC's terms and refuse to submit to the interviews. By proceeding the way they did, LeCroy and Snell waived the protections they had under the existing JDA and, by their conduct, agreed to a modification of the JDA. For this Court to refuse the government use of the interview notes which JPMC turned over to the grand jury would amount to judicial suppression of evidence that the recipient of a grand jury subpoena legitimately turned over to the grand jury. . . .

[For these reasons, the Court entered the Order protecting the interview notes while the JDA existed, and refused to protect the interview notes under the modification of the JDA proposed by JPMC and accepted by the conduct of LeCroy and Snell.]

NOTES AND QUESTIONS

1. *Strategy for counsel.* The *LeCroy* court noted that "[t]here were good and abundant reasons why LeCroy and Snell, with the advice of their counsel, rationally, intelligently and knowingly decided to allow JPMC and its counsel to interview them, knowing that the notes of the interviews may be turned over to the

government, but also knowing the JDA would continue, as modified. . . . " What are some of the reasons why counsel would allow the interviews to proceed with the knowledge that the information might be turned over to the government? If you were representing the defendants in *LeCroy*, would you have given different advice? Why or why not?

2. *Responsible corporation*. As corporate counsel, what are the implications of entering into a joint defense agreement? What benefits might exist for your client? What risks? *See* Ed Magarian and Surya Saxena, Commentary, *Joint Defense Agreements: What is a Responsible Company To Do?*, 22 White-Collar Crime Rep., No. 12, 1 (Sept. 2008).

3. *Disclosure to the government*. There are numerous implications in the decision to conduct an internal investigation. Many of these are positive. However, as a strategic matter, should the corporation disclose to the government the results of its internal investigation? In advising a company about the ramifications of this decision, how would you explain the advantages and disadvantages of each strategy?

4. *Non-waiver agreements*. Some United States Attorneys offices will enter into "non-waiver" agreements with a corporation under investigation. Questions remain, however, as to the extent to which the courts will recognize such agreements. Given the potential ramifications of disclosure to the government, corporations should consider approaches that lessen the consequences of any waivers. As one commentary stated, in conducting an investigation, attorneys should proceed

> with the expectation that any documents they generate may ultimately be discovered or even published in newspapers. . . . Any such documents should be carefully prepared. . . . Negotiate with regulators and prosecutors about the particular materials to be disclosed . . . [and] when a corporation does elect to provide privileged materials to the government, it can attempt to frame a non-waiver agreement in ways that will maximize the chances of the agreement being honored. For example, if a company can negotiate for disclosure to occur after or simultaneously with the company's settlement or other resolution of proceedings with the government, then the company will have a stronger argument that it and the government are not adversaries and that the disclosure is being made to further a common interest in fully investigating the alleged wrongdoing.

Robert C. Myers & Seth C. Farber, Commentary, *Corporate Internal Investigations in the Age of Cooperation: Strategies for Limiting Disclosure of Confidential Information*, 18 White-Collar Crime Rep., No. 6, 1 (March 2004).

PROBLEM

15-1. Last year, the United States Securities and Exchange Commission (SEC) began an inquiry into whether certain accounting practices at an accounting firm, Delta Corp., were not in accordance with applicable law and regulations, and requested production of documents from Delta Corp.

As Delta Corp. reviewed the documents to be produced, it discovered documents suggesting that certain employees might have engaged in improper practices. Accordingly, Delta Corp.'s Board of Directors resolved to conduct its own independent investigation of the disputed accounting practices and retained outside counsel, Felicia Franklin, to advise it.

Franklin reviewed thousands of documents and interviewed dozens of current and former employees. During Franklin's investigation, she was contacted by the SEC. The SEC informed Franklin that it, too, was investigating accounting practices at Delta Corp. The SEC invited Franklin to share her findings, including determinations as to whether any wrongdoing had occurred, and, if so, the identities of the persons responsible. After consulting with her client, Franklin agreed to share her documents and findings. The SEC, in turn, agreed to advise Franklin of its own findings. To govern Franklin's production of documents, the SEC entered into a written confidentiality agreement with Delta Corp. and Franklin.

After the above events, Paula Pailey sued Delta Corp., alleging that it improperly handled her accounts. At Pailey's request, the court in the civil case issued a subpoena demanding that Delta Corp. produce all documents created or collected during the internal investigation.

Delta Corp. has moved to quash the subpoena. How should the court rule? Why?

[C]   COMPLIANCE PROGRAMS

In today's business climate, there is a high premium on corporate compliance programs. Good corporate citizenship through self-policing requires that corporations tailor compliance programs to meet a company's legal requirements, while at the same time considering the company's needs and corporate culture. The development of compliance programs is one way that corporations have responded to highly-publicized corporate financial scandals in order to demonstrate their integrity and social responsibility. Moreover, a company receives powerful government incentives from establishing and following an effective compliance policy.

[1]   Sarbanes-Oxley Act of 2002[a]

Among the key effects of the Sarbanes-Oxley Act was to focus attention on corporate governance issues and to prompt the establishment of changes to the organizational sentencing guidelines. The primary intent of the changes was to provide greater guidance to organizations and to encourage "effective programs to prevent and detect violations of law." Most observers will agree that the Sarbanes-Oxley Act is the most significant piece of legislation affecting corporate governance, financial accounting, and public disclosure since the securities laws of the 1930s. The Act was the impetus for revision of the Sentencing Guidelines, which were amended for organizations effective November 1, 2004.

The revised organizational sentencing guidelines encourage a corporate culture that is both ethical and committed to compliance with applicable laws and regulations. In the "Effective Compliance and Ethics Program," U.S.S.G. § 8B2.1, the Sentencing Commission clearly stated that the purpose is to prevent and deter criminal conduct. The existence of a robust compliance policy can be used to

---

[a] Pub. L. No. 104-204, 116 Stat. 745. Section 805 directed the Sentencing Commission to review the guidelines to ensure that they are sufficient to deter and punish organizational misconduct.

attempt to persuade the prosecution to forego criminal charges. Note that the new organizational sentencing guidelines were not at issue in the recent decision on the sentencing guidelines for individuals announced in the *United States v. Booker*, 543 U.S. 220 (2005).

[2]　Department of Justice Policies

The Department of Justice issued its revised Principles of Federal Prosecution of Business Organizations, which are incorporated for the first time in the United States Attorneys' Manual (USAM) and are binding on all federal prosecutors. (The memorandum announcing the new policy is available at http://www.usdoj.gov/dag/readingroom/dag-memo-08282008.pdf.) USAM § 9-28.300 provides:

Factors to Be Considered

A. *General Principle*: Generally, prosecutors apply the same factors in determining whether to charge a corporation as they do with respect to individuals. See USAM § 9-27.220, *et seq.* Thus, the prosecutor must weigh all of the factors normally considered in the sound exercise of prosecutorial judgment: the sufficiency of the evidence; the likelihood of success at trial; the probable deterrent, rehabilitative, and other consequences of conviction; and the adequacy of noncriminal approaches. *However, due to the nature of the corporate "person," some additional factors are present.* In conducting an investigation, determining whether to bring charges, and negotiating plea or other agreements, prosecutors should consider the following factors in reaching a decision as to the proper treatment of a corporate target:

1. the nature and seriousness of the offense, including the risk of harm to the public, and applicable policies and priorities, if any, governing the prosecution of corporations for particular categories of crime;

2. the pervasiveness of wrongdoing within the corporation, including the complicity in, or the condoning of, the wrongdoing by corporate management;

3. the corporation's history of similar misconduct, including prior criminal, civil, and regulatory enforcement actions against it;

4. the corporation's timely and voluntary disclosure of wrongdoing and its willingness to cooperate in the investigation of its agents;

5. the existence and effectiveness of the corporation's pre-existing compliance program;

6. the corporation's remedial actions, including any efforts to implement an effective corporate compliance program or to improve an existing one, to replace responsible management, to discipline or terminate wrongdoers, to pay restitution, and to cooperate with the relevant government agencies;

7. collateral consequences, including whether there is disproportionate harm to shareholders, pension holders, employees, and others not proven personally culpable, as well as impact on the public arising from the prosecution;

8. the adequacy of the prosecution of individuals responsible for the corporation's malfeasance; and

9. the adequacy of remedies such as civil or regulatory enforcement actions.

B. *Comment*: The factors listed in this section are intended to be illustrative of those that should be evaluated and are not an exhaustive list of potentially relevant considerations. . . . Of course, prosecutors must exercise their thoughtful and pragmatic judgment in applying and balancing these factors, so as to achieve a fair and just outcome and promote respect for the law. In making a decision to charge a corporation, the prosecutor generally has substantial latitude in determining when, whom, how, and even whether to prosecute for violations of federal criminal law. . . . *[P]rosecutors should ensure that the general purposes of the criminal law — assurance of warranted punishment, deterrence of further criminal conduct, protection of the public from dangerous and fraudulent conduct, rehabilitation of offenders, and restitution for victims and affected communities — are adequately met, taking into account the special nature of the corporate "person."*

USAM § 9-28.300 (emphasis added). Do these principles provide adequate guidance for prosecutors? Why or why not?

[3]   Critical Aspects of Effective Compliance Programs

Compliance programs also go hand-in-hand with internal investigations because such programs frequently reveal the internal wrongdoing committed by employees. Compliance programs are especially important at sentencing, and the government also now regards the existence of a sound compliance program as relevant at the early stage of a criminal investigation. Despite the rise of compliance programs, they are not an insurance policy. While such programs often give the company ammunition to address governmental investigations and provide strategies for reduced charges or for defenses, they do not guarantee that the government will not institute criminal action.

The hallmarks of an effective corporate compliance program vary according to the type of organization and the specific nature of the corporation. For example, a corporation's structure can dictate that its compliance program be relaxed and centralized. Some organizations will need to have several compartmentalized programs that address different aspects of the business, while other companies must have rigid structures in place with little room for deviation.

One commentator has noted that, from the defense perspective, companies should observe 10 factors when handling sensitive corporate investigations:

1. Consider whether an outside law firm with little or no relationship to the company will better serve the objectives of an independent investigation.

2. Carefully define the scope of the investigation at the outset of the engagement.

3. Promptly take steps to secure all relevant documents.

4. Be sure to make clear to employees that investigating counsel does not represent them.

5. Ensure that investigating counsel avoid or at least minimize public statements about the internal investigation.

6. Keep in mind that a written report will in many cases be appropriate.

7. Assume that any written report may ultimately be released to the public.

8. Understand that a report should be written for multiple audiences.

9. Investigating counsel must be ever mindful of process when representing a Board of Directors, Audit Committee or Special Committee.

10. Counsel and client must follow through on recommendations to remedy problems at hand and prevent reoccurrence of the problem(s) that led to the investigation.

Robert W. Tarun, *Ten Tips for Handling Sensitive Corporate Investigations: Practical Advice in the Sarbanes-Oxley Era* (2004), *in* ABA-CLE Publication on White Collar Crime 2004, at D-83.

NOTES AND QUESTIONS

1. *Relevance of compliance program.* The government will consider the particulars of a corporate compliance program in deciding on whether to charge an organization. Should an effective compliance policy be a barrier to prosecution? Is a corporate compliance program relevant for any other evidentiary purpose during the criminal proceedings and if so, for what purpose(s)?

2. *Defense risks.* Can the presence of a corporate compliance policy work to the detriment of the company? How?

3. *Hilton Hotels.* Should a corporation be held criminally liable for conduct that is contrary to its compliance policies and procedures? *See United States v. Hilton Hotels Corp.*, 467 F.2d 1000 (9th Cir. 1972).

4. *Government policies.* Based on your readings in this chapter, are the changes in the law encouraging prosecutors to pursue more criminal indictments against corporations? Why or why not? *See* Charles J. Walsh & Alissa Pyrich, *Corporate Compliance Programs as a Defense to Criminal Liability: Can a Corporation Save Its Soul?*, 47 Rutgers L. Rev. 605, 666 (1995) (discussing prosecutorial discretion in bringing charges against a corporation). How does corporate counsel, conducting an internal investigation, react to these changes in the law? "[C]ounsel and the employees of a corporation must consider that the questions asked, the answers received and the advice rendered may soon be in the hands of a prosecutor, competitors and civil litigants. This possibility has the effect of chilling the inquiry from the outset. . . . " David M. Zornow & Keith D. Krakaur, *Essay: On the Brink of a Brave New World: The Death of Privilege in Corporate Criminal Investigations*, 37 Am. Crim. L. Rev. 147, 156 (2000).

5. Is it ethical for a corporation to refrain from investigating possible misconduct brought to its attention because it fears that the government might eventually ask for the results of the investigation? *See* Shirah Neiman, *Hallmark*

of an Effective Corporate Compliance Program and Waiver of the Privilege Under the Principles of Federal Prosecution of Business Organizations (2004), *in* ABA-CLE Publication on White Collar Crime 2004, at D-1.

PROBLEMS

15-2. You are in-house counsel to a large multi-state corporation, ByGone Industries, Inc. ("ByGone"). ByGone employs over 15,000 employees and is located in every state. ByGone is subject to regulatory governance because it produces widgets. You have instituted a wide-ranging and very effective internal compliance program. All employees have been informed of the program and trained on the rules and procedures that pertain to the specifics of the program. In its business, ByGone is required by law to release certain information to state agencies in order to comply with the various state rules and regulations. One state has sent an inquiry to ByGone regarding its materials used in the assembling of the widgets because there have been some reports of defects. In complying with this request and turning over the documents, ByGone has maintained its attorney-client privilege as to these documents. You discover that the federal government has opened a criminal investigation related to the matters contained in the documents you turned over to the state. You assert the privilege with respect to the released documents.

Will you have to comply with the criminal grand jury subpoena for the documents? Why or why not?

15-3. In Problem 15-1 above, does it matter if you were aware of the pending criminal investigation? Suppose the Assistant United States Attorney had not yet divulged the existence of the grand jury investigation. The AUSA was present at the hearings where the testimony and documents were turned over to the state agency.

Would this person's presence make a difference in your conclusion?

15-4. You are attending a meeting with the senior executives of ByGone. The board and executives are discussing the benefits and risks associated with disclosure of the internal investigation to the government. One of the participants remarked, "if the government is going to ask us to waive the privilege all the time then we should conduct a different kind of investigation of misconduct. For example, we might not want to investigate too thoroughly or probe too deeply."

Is it ethical for a corporation to refrain from investigating possible misconduct brought to its attention because it fears that the government might eventually ask for the results of the investigation?

15-5. The principals at the meeting decide not to reveal the details of the internal investigation to the government, even though the government has made the request. The executives begin to discuss this strategy after the meeting and ask your opinion.

What do you tell them and why?

Chapter 16

THE GRAND JURY

"The war on white collar crime is frequently waged, and often won or lost, at the grand jury stage of the criminal process."[a]

[A] INTRODUCTORY NOTES

Grand juries conduct the investigation and issue the charges in the vast majority of federal white collar cases. It is therefore critical for students and practitioners in the white collar field, and in corporate law in general, to have a thorough understanding of the grand jury system. Issues may arise, for example, with respect to possible criminal charges, related civil and/or investigative matters, and the representation of witnesses before grand juries.[b]

The Fifth Amendment of the United States Constitution provides that "[n]o person shall be held to answer for a capital, or otherwise infamous crime, unless on a presentment or indictment of a Grand Jury."[c] Rule 7(a) of the Federal Rules of Criminal Procedure further provides that, unless the defendant waives the right to a grand jury indictment, charges for any crime punishable by more than a year must be issued by a grand jury. As the Supreme Court has stated, the grand jury serves the "dual function of determining if there is probable cause to believe that a crime has been committed and of protecting citizens against unfounded criminal prosecutions." *Branzburg v. Hayes*, 408 U.S. 665, 686–687 (1972). When the grand jury finds probable cause that a crime has occurred, it issues the formal charge in the form of an indictment.

In terms of investigative functions, the grand jury has broad subpoena powers. The Assistant United States Attorney or Attorneys assigned to a particular matter will lead the grand jury's investigation. Various government agencies, including the Federal Bureau of Investigation, do the legwork in gathering and presenting evidence to the grand jury. Because the grand jury has such broad powers and generally operates in secret, defense counsel face many challenges when representing a grand jury witness, subject, or target.[d]

---

[a] John R. Wing & Harris J. Yale, *Grand Jury Practice, in* White Collar Crime: Business and Regulatory Offenses § 8.02 (Otto Obermaier & Robert Morvillo eds., 2009).

[b] Grand jury issues are also discussed *infra*, Chapter 17 (Self-Incrimination — Witness Testimony and Document Production) and Chapter 18 (Civil Actions, Civil Penalties, and Parallel Proceedings).

[c] The federal right to a grand jury does not apply to the states although many states do provide a right to a grand jury indictment in certain circumstances.

[d] A grand jury "witness" is a person with information generally related to the matter under investigation. The "subject" of a grand jury investigation is one about whom the grand jury seeks more specific information and who may at some point become a focal point of the investigation. A grand jury "target" is "a person as to whom the prosecutor or the grand jury has substantial evidence linking him or her to the commission of a crime and who, in the judgment of the prosecutor, is a putative defendant."

Rule 6 of the Federal Rules of Criminal Procedure governs the operation of the federal grand jury. A grand jury consists of between 16 and 23 people drawn from across the judicial district, and must represent a fair cross-section of the community. At least 12 grand jurors must sign the indictment.[e]

The grand jury operates in secret. Prior to trial, only grand jury witnesses may disclose matters occurring before the grand jury, and public discussion of the criminal investigation must await the actual filing of an indictment. Confidentiality protects the innocent by shielding the release of information that might fail to rise to the level of probable cause. Nonetheless, leaks do occur in grand jury investigations and may raise significant issues, including the defendant's right to a fair trial.

This chapter discusses some of the most important issues relating to grand juries. These issues include the scope of the grand jury's investigative powers, the role of the grand jury in assessing evidence, grand jury secrecy, and practical considerations in grand jury practice.

[B] SCOPE OF THE GRAND JURY'S INVESTIGATION

[1] Relevancy, Admissibility, and Specificity

Many of the issues regarding the scope of the grand jury's investigation are addressed in the first case, a leading case on the investigative powers of the federal grand jury.

UNITED STATES v. R. ENTERPRISES
498 U.S. 292 (1991)

JUSTICE O'CONNOR delivered the opinion of the Court.

This case requires the Court to decide what standards apply when a party seeks to avoid compliance with a subpoena *duces tecum* issued in connection with a grand jury investigation.

I.

Since 1986, a federal grand jury sitting in the Eastern District of Virginia has been investigating allegations of interstate transportation of obscene materials. In early 1988, the grand jury issued a series of subpoenas to three companies [Model, R. Enterprises and MFR, each distributing sexually oriented and adult materials]. . . . All three companies are wholly owned by Martin Rothstein. The grand jury subpoenas sought a variety of corporate books and records and, in Model's case, copies of 193 videotapes that Model had shipped to retailers in the Eastern District of Virginia. All three companies moved to quash the subpoenas,

---

U.S.A.M. § 9-11.151. *See* Chapter 17, Self-Incrimination — Witness Testimony and Document Production, at § 17[A], *infra.*

[e] Grand jurors, once empanelled, typically sit for 18 months or until discharged by the court, and hear evidence concerning a variety of criminal cases within the jurisdictional district. In many districts, a grand juror's obligations will be scheduled to recur every six weeks or so, when the jurors are called in for two to three days at a time to sit and receive evidence. In other, busier judicial districts, the grand jury members appear weekly according to the schedule of the United States Attorney.

arguing that the subpoenas called for production of materials irrelevant to the grand jury's investigation and that the enforcement of the subpoenas would likely infringe their First Amendment rights.

The District Court, after extensive hearings, denied the motions to quash. . . . The court concluded that the subpoenas in this case were "fairly standard business subpoenas" and "ought to be complied with." Notwithstanding these findings, the companies refused to comply with the subpoenas. The District Court found each in contempt and fined them $500 per day, but stayed imposition of the fine pending appeal.

The Court of Appeals for the Fourth Circuit upheld the business records subpoenas issued to Model, but remanded the motion to quash the subpoena for Model's videotapes. Of particular relevance here, the Court of Appeals quashed the business records subpoenas issued to R. Enterprises and MFR. In doing so, it applied the standards set out by this Court in *United States v. Nixon*, 418 U.S. 683, 699–700 (1974). The court recognized that *Nixon* dealt with a trial subpoena, not a grand jury subpoena, but determined that the rule was "equally applicable" in the grand jury context. Accordingly, it required the Government to clear the three hurdles that *Nixon* established in the trial context — relevancy, admissibility, and specificity — in order to enforce the grand jury subpoenas. The court concluded that the challenged subpoenas did not satisfy the *Nixon* standards, finding no evidence in the record that either company had ever shipped materials into, or otherwise conducted business in, the Eastern District of Virginia. The Court of Appeals specifically criticized the District Court for drawing an inference that, because Rothstein owned all three businesses and one of them had undoubtedly shipped sexually explicit materials into the Eastern District of Virginia, there might be some link between the Eastern District of Virginia and R. Enterprises or MFR. It then noted that "any evidence concerning Mr. Rothstein's alleged business activities outside of Virginia, or his ownership of companies which distribute allegedly obscene materials outside of Virginia, would most likely be inadmissible on relevancy grounds at any trial that might occur," and that the subpoenas therefore failed "to meet the requirements [*sic*] that any documents subpoenaed under [Federal] Rule [of Criminal Procedure] 17(c) must be admissible as evidence at trial." *Nixon, supra*, at 700. The Court of Appeals did not consider whether enforcement of the subpoenas *duces tecum* issued to respondents implicated the First Amendment.

We granted certiorari to determine whether the Court of Appeals applied the proper standard in evaluating the grand jury subpoenas issued to respondents. We now reverse.

II.

The grand jury occupies a unique role in our criminal justice system. It is an investigatory body charged with the responsibility of determining whether or not a crime has been committed. Unlike this Court, whose jurisdiction is predicated on a specific case or controversy, the grand jury "can investigate merely on suspicion that the law is being violated, or even just because it wants assurance that it is not." *United States v. Morton Salt Co.*, 338 U.S. 632 (1950). The function of the grand jury is to inquire into all information that might possibly bear on its investigation until it has identified an offense or has satisfied itself that none has occurred. As a necessary consequence of its investigatory function, the grand jury paints with a broad brush. "A grand jury investigation 'is not fully carried out until every available clue has been run down and all witnesses examined in every proper way to find if a crime has been committed.'" *Branzburg v. Hayes*, 408 U.S. 665, 701 (1972).

A grand jury subpoena is thus much different from a subpoena issued in the context of a prospective criminal trial, where a specific offense has been identified and a particular defendant charged. "[T]he identity of the offender, and the precise nature of the offense, if there be one, normally are developed at the conclusion of the grand jury's labors, not at the beginning." *Blair v. United States*, 250 U.S. 273 (1919). In short, the Government cannot be required to justify the issuance of a grand jury subpoena by presenting evidence sufficient to establish probable cause because the very purpose of requesting the information is to ascertain whether probable cause exists.

This Court has emphasized on numerous occasions that many of the rules and restrictions that apply at a trial do not apply in grand jury proceedings. This is especially true of evidentiary restrictions. The same rules that, in an adversary hearing on the merits, may increase the likelihood of accurate determinations of guilt or innocence do not necessarily advance the mission of a grand jury, whose task is to conduct an *ex parte* investigation to determine whether or not there is probable cause to prosecute a particular defendant. In *Costello v. United States*, 350 U.S. 359 (1956), this Court declined to apply the rule against hearsay to grand jury proceedings. Strict observance of trial rules in the context of a grand jury's preliminary investigation "would result in interminable delay but add nothing to the assurance of a fair trial." *Id.* at 384. In *United States v. Calandra*, 414 U.S. 338 (1974), we held that the Fourth Amendment exclusionary rule does not apply to grand jury proceedings. Permitting witnesses to invoke the exclusionary rule would "delay and disrupt grand jury proceedings" by requiring adversary hearings on peripheral matters, *id.* at 349, and would effectively transform such proceedings into preliminary trials on the merits, 414 U.S. 338 at 349–50. The teaching of the Court's decisions is clear: A grand jury "may compel the production of evidence or the testimony of witnesses as it considers appropriate, and its operation generally is unrestrained by the technical procedural and evidentiary rules governing the conduct of criminal trials." *Id.* at 343.

This guiding principle renders suspect the Court of Appeals' holding that the standards announced in *Nixon* as to subpoenas issued in anticipation of trial apply equally in the grand jury context. The multifactor test announced in *Nixon* would invite procedural delays and detours while courts evaluate the relevancy and admissibility of documents sought by a particular subpoena. We have expressly stated that grand jury proceedings should be free of such delays. "Any holding that would saddle a grand jury with minitrials and preliminary showings would assuredly impede its investigation and frustrate the public's interest in the fair and expeditious administration of the criminal laws." *United States v. Dionisio*, 410 U.S. 1, 17 (1973). Additionally, application of the *Nixon* test in this context ignores that grand jury proceedings are subject to strict secrecy requirements. Requiring the Government to explain in too much detail the particular reasons underlying a subpoena threatens to compromise "the indispensable secrecy of grand jury proceedings." *United States v. Johnson*, 319 U.S. 503 (1943). Broad disclosure also affords the targets of investigation far more information about the grand jury's internal workings than the Federal Rules of Criminal Procedure appear to contemplate.

III.

A.

The investigatory powers of the grand jury are nevertheless not unlimited. *See Branzburg, supra,* 408 U.S. at 688. Grand juries are not licensed to engage in arbitrary fishing expeditions, nor may they select targets of investigation out of malice or an intent to harass. In this case, the focus of our inquiry is the limit imposed on a grand jury by Federal Rule of Criminal Procedure 17(c), which governs the issuance of subpoenas *duces tecum* in federal criminal proceedings. The Rule provides that "[t]he court on motion made promptly may quash or modify the subpoena if compliance would be unreasonable or oppressive."

This standard is not self-explanatory. As we have observed, "what is reasonable depends on the context." *New Jersey v. T.L.O.,* 469 U.S. 325, 337 (1985). In *Nixon,* this Court defined what is reasonable in the context of a jury trial. We determined that, in order to require production of information prior to trial, a party must make a reasonably specific request for information that would be both relevant and admissible at trial. But, for the reasons we have explained above, the *Nixon* standard does not apply in the context of grand jury proceedings. In the grand jury context, the decision as to what offense will be charged is routinely not made until after the grand jury has concluded its investigation. One simply cannot know in advance whether information sought during the investigation will be relevant and admissible in a prosecution for a particular offense.

To the extent that Rule 17(c) imposes some reasonableness limitation on grand jury subpoenas, however, our task is to define it. In doing so, we recognize that a party to whom a grand jury subpoena is issued faces a difficult situation. As a rule, grand juries do not announce publicly the subjects of their investigations. A party who desires to challenge a grand jury subpoena thus may have no conception of the Government's purpose in seeking production of the requested information. Indeed, the party will often not know whether he or she is a primary target of the investigation or merely a peripheral witness. Absent even minimal information, the subpoena recipient is likely to find it exceedingly difficult to persuade a court that "compliance would be unreasonable." As one pair of commentators has summarized it, the challenging party's "unenviable task is to seek to persuade the court that the subpoena that has been served on [him or her] could not possibly serve any investigative purpose that the grand jury could legitimately be pursuing." 1 S. Beale & W. Bryson, *Grand Jury Law and Practice* § 6:28 (1986).

Our task is to fashion an appropriate standard of reasonableness, one that gives due weight to the difficult position of subpoena recipients but does not impair the strong governmental interests in affording grand juries wide latitude, avoiding minitrials on peripheral matters, and preserving a necessary level of secrecy. We begin by reiterating that the law presumes, absent a strong showing to the contrary, that a grand jury acts within the legitimate scope of its authority. Consequently, a grand jury subpoena issued through normal channels is presumed to be reasonable, and the burden of showing unreasonableness must be on the recipient who seeks to avoid compliance. Indeed, this result is indicated by the language of Rule 17(c), which permits a subpoena to be quashed only "on motion" and "if *compliance* would be unreasonable" (emphasis added). To the extent that the Court of Appeals placed an initial burden on the Government, it committed error. Drawing on the principles articulated above, we conclude that where, as here, a subpoena is challenged on relevancy grounds, the motion to quash must be denied unless the district court determines that there is no reasonable possibility that the category of materials the Government seeks will produce information relevant to the general subject of the grand jury's investigation. Respondents did not challenge the subpoenas as being too indefinite nor did they claim that compliance would be overly burdensome. The Court of Appeals accordingly did not consider these aspects of the subpoenas, nor do we.

B.

It seems unlikely, of course, that a challenging party who does not know the general subject matter of the grand jury's investigation, no matter how valid that party's claim, will be able to make the necessary showing that compliance would be unreasonable. After all, a subpoena recipient "cannot put his whole life before the court in order to show that there is no crime to be investigated." *Marston's Inc. v. Strand*, 114 Ariz. 260, 270 (1977). Consequently, a court may be justified in a case where unreasonableness is alleged in requiring the Government to reveal the general subject of the grand jury's investigation before requiring the challenging party to carry its burden of persuasion. We need not resolve this question in the present case, however, as there is no doubt that respondents knew the subject of the grand jury investigation pursuant to which the business records subpoenas were issued. In cases where the recipient of the subpoena does not know the nature of the investigation, we are confident that district courts will be able to craft appropriate procedures that balance the interests of the subpoena recipient against the strong governmental interests in maintaining secrecy, preserving investigatory flexibility, and avoiding procedural delays. For example, to ensure that subpoenas are not routinely challenged as a form of discovery, a district court may require that the Government reveal the subject of the investigation to the trial court *in camera*, so that the court may determine whether the motion to quash has a reasonable prospect for success before it discloses the subject matter to the challenging party.

IV.

Applying these principles in this case demonstrates that the District Court correctly denied respondents' motions to quash. It is undisputed that all three companies — Model, R. Enterprises, and MFR — are owned by the same person, that all do business in the same area, and that one of the three, Model, has shipped sexually explicit materials into the Eastern District of Virginia. The District Court could have concluded from these facts that there was a reasonable possibility that the business records of R. Enterprises and MFR would produce information relevant to the grand jury's investigation into the interstate transportation of obscene materials. Respondents' blanket denial of any connection to Virginia did not suffice to render the District Court's conclusion invalid. A grand jury need not accept on faith the self-serving assertions of those who may have committed criminal acts. Rather, it is entitled to determine for itself whether a crime has been committed.

Both in the District Court and in the Court of Appeals, respondents contended that these subpoenas sought records relating to First Amendment activities, and that this required the Government to demonstrate that the records were particularly relevant to its investigation. The Court of Appeals determined that the subpoenas did not satisfy Rule 17(c) and thus did not pass on the First Amendment issue. We express no view on this issue and leave it to be resolved by the Court of Appeals.

The judgment is reversed insofar as the Court of Appeals quashed the subpoenas issued to R. Enterprises and MFR, and the case is remanded for further proceedings consistent with this opinion.

It is so ordered.

Justice Stevens, with whom Justice Marshall and Justice Brennan join, concurring in part and concurring in the judgment. [Omitted.]

Notes and Questions

1. *Responding to a grand jury subpoena.* How should defense counsel advise a client who is served with a grand jury subpoena? Given the Court's concern about the potential for an "arbitrary fishing expedition," how should the defense counsel ensure that the government is *not* engaged in such prohibited information-gathering activities?

2. *Subpoenas to third parties.* The grand jury has issued a subpoena *duces tecum* to a third party who possesses your client's documents. The third party says that he is willing to comply with the subpoena. What steps can you take to protect your client's interests? *See Perlman v. United States*, 247 U.S. 7, 12–13 (1918).

3. *Challenging a subpoena.* Does the Supreme Court provide clear standards for determining the validity of a subpoena *duces tecum*? What evidence must be presented in order to challenge such a subpoena successfully? When and how must such a motion be presented to the court? *See United States v. Under Seal (In re Grand Jury Doe No. G.J. 2005–2)*, 478 F.3d 581 (4th Cir. 2007) (upholding district court's granting of motion to quash subpoena and discussing parties' burdens and unreasonableness and oppressiveness under Rule 17(c)).

4. *Scope.* Rule 17(c) governing grand jury subpoenas appears to be unlimited in scope. After *R. Enterprises*, what limitations exist on the power of the government to obtain testimony and documentation through the issuance of a grand jury subpoena? What specific approach should a defense attorney take in order to be successful in protecting his or her client prior to the appearance? What dangers flow from the testimonial aspect of producing documents? *See* Chapter 17, Self-Incrimination — Witness Testimony and Document Production, *infra*.

5. *Confidentiality and grand jury subpoenas.* How does the decision in *United States v. R. Enterprises*, 498 U.S. 292 (1991), apply to a subpoena for confidential information? In *In re United States v. Doe*, 434 F. Supp. 2d 377 (E.D. Va. 2006), the United States subpoenaed statements made by several police officers to the city's internal affairs office. The city moved to quash the subpoena on the grounds that the city had guaranteed that the statements would be confidential. The court quashed the subpoena, holding that the grand jury could avoid destroying the confidentiality guarantee by subpoenaing witnesses directly. *Id.* at 382–383.

Is there a valid argument that some information held by third parties should not be subject to grand jury subpoena powers? *See* Christopher Slobogin, *Subpoenas and Privacy*, 54 DePaul L. Rev. 805 (2005). Professor Slobogin argues that a relevance standard "ought to be inadequate when personal information is sought from the subject (in which case a warrant should be required or immunity granted) or from a third-party record holder such as a bank, hospital, or Internet Service Provider." *Id.* at 836. Do you agree or disagree with this conclusion?

[2]   Exculpatory Evidence

One of the major criticisms of the grand jury system is its one-sidedness. The only individuals who are permitted to be present during the course of a grand jury investigation are the federal grand jurors, the court reporter, the witness, and the prosecutor who directs questioning. A witness may leave the grand jury room to consult with counsel as questions arise. Everyone except the grand jurors themselves must exit the room when the grand jury begins its deliberations to consider the issuance of an indictment. As you read the next case, consider what difference the presence of defense counsel would have made to the outcome.

UNITED STATES v. WILLIAMS
504 U.S. 36 (1992)

JUSTICE SCALIA delivered the opinion of the Court.

The question presented in this case is whether a district court may dismiss an otherwise valid indictment because the Government failed to disclose to the grand jury "substantial exculpatory evidence" in its possession.

I.

On May 4, 1988, respondent John H. Williams, Jr., a Tulsa, Oklahoma, investor, was indicted by a federal grand jury on seven counts of "knowingly mak[ing] [a] false statement or report . . . for the purpose of influencing . . . the action [of a federally insured financial institution]," in violation of 18 U.S.C. § 1014. According to the indictment, between September 1984 and November 1985 Williams supplied four Oklahoma banks with "materially false" statements that variously overstated the value of his current assets and interest income in order to influence the banks' actions on his loan requests.

Williams' misrepresentation was allegedly effected through two financial statements provided to the banks, a "Market Value Balance Sheet" and a "Statement of Projected Income and Expense." The former included as "current assets" approximately $6 million in notes receivable from three venture capital companies. Though it contained a disclaimer that these assets were carried at cost rather than at market value, the Government asserted that listing them as "current assets" — *i.e.*, assets quickly reducible to cash — was misleading, since Williams knew that none of the venture capital companies could afford to satisfy the notes in the short term. The second document — the Statement of Projected Income and Expense — allegedly misrepresented Williams' interest income, since it failed to reflect that the interest payments received on the notes of the venture capital companies were funded entirely by Williams' own loans to those companies. The Statement thus falsely implied, according to the Government, that Williams was deriving interest income from "an independent outside source." Brief for United States 3.

Shortly after arraignment, the District Court granted Williams' motion for disclosure of all exculpatory portions of the grand jury transcripts. Upon reviewing this material, Williams demanded that the District Court dismiss the indictment, alleging that the Government had failed to fulfill its obligation under the Tenth Circuit's prior decision in *United States v. Page*, 808 F.2d 723, 728 (1987), to present "substantial exculpatory evidence" to the grand jury (emphasis omitted). His contention was that evidence which the Government had chosen not to present to the grand jury — in particular, Williams' general ledgers and tax returns, and Williams' testimony in his contemporaneous Chapter 11 bankruptcy proceeding — disclosed that, for tax purposes and otherwise, he had regularly accounted for the "notes receivable" (and the interest on them) in a manner consistent with the Balance Sheet and the Income Statement. This, he contended, belied an intent to mislead the banks, and thus directly negated an essential element of the charged offense.

The District Court initially denied Williams' motion, but upon reconsideration ordered the indictment dismissed without prejudice. It found, after a hearing, that the withheld evidence was "relevant to an essential element of the crime charged, created 'a reasonable doubt about [respondent's] guilt,'" App. to Pet. for Cert. 239–249, and thus "render[ed] the grand jury's decision to indict gravely suspect." App. Pet. for Cert. 269. Upon the Government's appeal, the Court of Appeals affirmed the District Court's order, following its earlier decision in *Page, supra*. It first sustained as not "clearly erroneous" the District Court's determination that the Government had withheld "substantial exculpatory evidence" from the grand jury. *See* 899 F.2d 898, 900–03 (10th Cir. 1990). It then found that the Government's behavior "'substantially influence[d]'" the grand jury's decision to indict, or at the very least raised a "'grave doubt that the decision to indict was free from such substantial influence.'" *Id.* at 903 (quoting *Bank of Nova Scotia v. United States*, 487 U.S. 250, 263 (1988)); *see* 899 F.2d at 903–04. Under these circumstances, the Tenth Circuit concluded, it was not an abuse of discretion for the District Court to require the Government to begin anew before the grand jury. We granted certiorari.

*   *   *

III.

Respondent does not contend that the Fifth Amendment itself obliges the prosecutor to disclose substantial exculpatory evidence in his possession to the grand jury. Instead, building on our statement that the federal courts "may, within limits, formulate procedural rules not specifically required by the Constitution or the Congress," *United States v. Hasting*, 461 U.S. 499, 505 (1983), he argues that imposition of the Tenth Circuit's disclosure rule is supported by the courts' "supervisory power." We think not. *Hasting*, and the cases that rely upon the principle it expresses, deal strictly with the courts' power to control their *own* procedures. That power has been applied not only to improve the truth-finding process of the trial, but also to prevent parties from reaping benefit or incurring harm from violations of substantive or procedural rules (imposed by the Constitution or laws) governing matters apart from the trial itself. Thus, *Bank of Nova*

Scotia v. United States, 487 U.S. 250 (1988), makes clear that the supervisory power can be used to dismiss an indictment because of misconduct before the grand jury, at least where that misconduct amounts to a violation of one of those "few, clear rules which were carefully drafted and approved by this Court and by Congress to ensure the integrity of the grand jury's functions," *United States v. Mechanik*, 475 U.S. 66, 74 (1986) (O'CONNOR, J., concurring in judgment).

We did not hold in *Bank of Nova Scotia*, however, that the courts' supervisory power could be used, not merely as a means of enforcing or vindicating legally compelled standards of prosecutorial conduct before the grand jury, but as a means of *prescribing* those standards of prosecutorial conduct in the first instance — just as it may be used as a means of establishing standards of prosecutorial conduct before the courts themselves. It is this latter exercise that respondent demands. Because the grand jury is an institution separate from the courts, over whose functioning the courts do not preside, we think it clear that, as a general matter at least, no such "supervisory" judicial authority exists, and that the disclosure rule applied here exceeded the Tenth Circuit's authority.

A.

"[R]ooted in long centuries of Anglo-American history," the grand jury is mentioned in the Bill of Rights, but not in the body of the Constitution. It has not been textually assigned, therefore, to any of the branches described in the first three Articles. It "is a constitutional fixture in its own right." In fact the whole theory of its function is that it belongs to no branch of the institutional Government, serving as a kind of buffer or referee between the Government and the people. Although the grand jury normally operates, of course, in the courthouse and under judicial auspices, its institutional relationship with the Judicial Branch has traditionally been, so to speak, at arm's length. Judges' direct involvement in the functioning of the grand jury has generally been confined to the constitutive one of calling the grand jurors together and administering their oaths of office.

The grand jury's functional independence from the Judicial Branch is evident both in the scope of its power to investigate criminal wrongdoing and in the manner in which that power is exercised. "Unlike [a] [c]ourt, whose jurisdiction is predicated upon a specific case or controversy, the grand jury 'can investigate merely on suspicion that the law is being violated, or even because it wants assurance that it is not.'" *United States v. R. Enterprises, Inc.*, 498 U.S. 292, 297 (1991). It need not identify the offender it suspects, or even "the precise nature of the offense" it is investigating. The grand jury requires no authorization from its constituting court to initiate an investigation, nor does the prosecutor require leave of court to seek a grand jury indictment. And in its day-to-day functioning, the grand jury generally operates without the interference of a presiding judge. . . .

True, the grand jury cannot compel the appearance of witnesses and the production of evidence, and must appeal to the court when such compulsion is required. And the court will refuse to lend its assistance when the compulsion the grand jury seeks would override rights accorded by the Constitution, or even testimonial privileges recognized by the common law. Even in this setting, however, we have insisted that the grand jury remain "free to pursue its investigations unhindered by external influence or supervision so long as it does not trench upon the legitimate rights of any witness called before it." *United States v. Dionisio*, 410

U.S. 1, 17–18 (1973). Recognizing this tradition of independence, we have said that the Fifth Amendment's "constitutional guarantee *presupposes* an investigative body 'acting independently of either prosecuting attorney *or judge*'. . . . " *Id.* at 16.

No doubt in view of the grand jury proceeding's status as other than a constituent element of a "criminal prosecutio[n]," U.S. Const., Amdt. 6, we have said that certain constitutional protections afforded defendants in criminal proceedings have no application before that body. The Double Jeopardy Clause of the Fifth Amendment does not bar a grand jury from returning an indictment when a prior grand jury has refused to do so. We have twice suggested, though not held, that the Sixth Amendment right to counsel does not attach when an individual is summoned to appear before a grand jury, even if he is the subject of the investigation. And although "the grand jury may not force a witness to answer questions in violation of [the Fifth Amendment's] constitutional guarantee" against self-incrimination, *United States v. Calandra*, 414 U.S. 338, 346 (1974), our cases suggest that an indictment obtained through the use of evidence previously obtained in violation of the privilege against self-incrimination "is nevertheless valid." *Id.* at 346.

Given the grand jury's operational separateness from its constituting court, it should come as no surprise that we have been reluctant to invoke the judicial supervisory power as a basis for prescribing modes of grand jury procedure.

* * *

B.

Respondent argues that the Court of Appeals' rule can be justified as a sort of Fifth Amendment "common law," a necessary means of assuring the constitutional right to the judgment "of an independent and informed grand jury," *Wood v. Georgia*, 370 U.S. 375, 390 (1962). Respondent makes a generalized appeal to functional notions: Judicial supervision of the quantity and quality of the evidence relied upon by the grand jury plainly facilitates, he says, the grand jury's performance of its twin historical responsibilities, *i.e.*, bringing to trial those who may be justly accused and shielding the innocent from unfounded accusation and prosecution. We do not agree. The rule would neither preserve nor enhance the traditional functioning of the institution that the Fifth Amendment demands. To the contrary, requiring the prosecutor to present exculpatory as well as inculpatory evidence would alter the grand jury's historical role, transforming it from an accusatory to an adjudicatory body.

It is axiomatic that the grand jury sits not to determine guilt or innocence, but to assess whether there is adequate basis for bringing a criminal charge. . . . As a consequence, neither in this country nor in England has the suspect under investigation by the grand jury ever been thought to have a right to testify or to have exculpatory evidence presented. Imposing upon the prosecutor a legal obligation to present exculpatory evidence in his possession would be incompatible with this system. If a "balanced" assessment of the entire matter is the objective, surely the first thing to be done — rather than requiring the prosecutor to say what he knows in defense of the target of the investigation — is to entitle the target to tender his own defense. To require the former while denying (as we do) the latter would be quite absurd. It would also be quite pointless, since it would merely invite the target to circumnavigate the system by delivering his exculpatory evidence to the prosecutor, whereupon it would *have* to be passed on to the grand jury — unless the prosecutor is willing to take the chance that a court will not deem the evidence important enough to qualify for mandatory disclosure.

Respondent acknowledges (as he must) that the "common law" of the grand jury is not violated if the *grand jury itself* chooses to hear no more evidence than that which suffices to convince it an indictment is proper. Thus, had the Government offered to familiarize the grand jury in this case with the five boxes of financial statements and deposition testimony alleged to contain exculpatory information, and had the grand jury rejected the offer as pointless, respondent would presumably agree that the resulting indictment would have been valid. Respondent insists, however, that courts must require the modern prosecutor to alert the grand jury to the nature and extent of the available exculpatory evidence, because otherwise the grand jury "merely functions as an arm of the prosecution." We reject the attempt to convert a nonexistent duty of the grand jury itself into an obligation of the prosecutor. The authority of the prosecutor to seek an indictment has long been understood to be "coterminous with the authority of the grand jury to entertain [the prosecutor's] charges." If the grand jury has no obligation to consider all "substantial exculpatory" evidence, we do not understand how the prosecutor can be said to have a binding obligation to present it.

There is yet another respect in which respondent's proposal not only fails to comport with, but positively contradicts, the "common law" of the Fifth Amendment grand jury. Motions to quash indictments based upon the sufficiency of the evidence relied upon by the grand jury were unheard of at common law in England. And the traditional American practice was described by Justice Nelson, riding circuit in 1852, as follows: "No case has been cited, nor have we been able to find any, furnishing an authority for looking into and revising the judgment of the grand jury upon the evidence, for the purpose of determining whether or not the finding was founded upon sufficient proof, or whether there was a deficiency in respect to any part of the complaint. . . . " *United States v. Reed*, 27 F. Cas. 727, 738 (No. 16,134) (CCNDNY 1852).

We accepted Justice Nelson's description in *Costello v. United States*, where we held that "[i]t would run counter to the whole history of the grand jury institution" to permit an indictment to be challenged "on the ground that there was inadequate or incompetent evidence before the grand jury." 350 U.S. at 363–64. And we reaffirmed this principle recently in *Bank of Nova Scotia*, where we held that "the mere fact that evidence itself is unreliable is not sufficient to require a dismissal of the indictment," and that "a challenge to the reliability or competence of the evidence presented to the grand jury" will not be heard. 487 U.S. at 261. It would make little sense, we think, to abstain from reviewing the evidentiary support for the grand jury's judgment while scrutinizing the sufficiency of the prosecutor's presentation. A complaint about the quality or adequacy of the evidence can always be recast as a complaint that the prosecutor's presentation was "incomplete" or "misleading." Our words in *Costello* bear repeating: Review of facially valid indictments on such grounds "would run counter to the whole history of the grand jury institution[,] [and] [n]either justice nor the concept of a fair trial requires [it]." 350 U.S. at 364.

* * *

Echoing the reasoning of the Tenth Circuit in *United States v. Page*, 808 F.2d at 728, respondent argues that a rule requiring the prosecutor to disclose exculpatory evidence to the grand jury would, by removing from the docket unjustified prosecutions, save valuable judicial time. That depends, we suppose, upon what the ratio would turn out to be between unjustified prosecutions eliminated and grand jury indictments challenged — for the latter as well as the former consume "valuable judicial time." We need not pursue the matter; if there is an advantage to the proposal, Congress is free to prescribe it. For the reasons set forth above, however, we conclude that courts have no authority to prescribe such a duty pursuant to their inherent supervisory authority over their own proceedings. The judgment of the Court of Appeals is accordingly reversed, and the cause is remanded for further proceedings consistent with this opinion.

So ordered.

JUSTICE STEVENS, with whom JUSTICE BLACKMUN and JUSTICE O'CONNOR join, and with whom JUSTICE THOMAS joins as to Parts II and III, dissenting.

*   *   *

Like the Hydra slain by Hercules, prosecutorial misconduct has many heads. Some are cataloged in Justice Sutherland's classic opinion for the Court in *Berger v. United States*, 295 U.S. 78 (1935):

> That the United States prosecuting attorney overstepped the bounds of that propriety and fairness which should characterize the conduct of such an officer in the prosecution of a criminal offense is clearly shown by the record. He was guilty of misstating the facts in his cross-examination of witnesses; of putting into the mouths of such witnesses things which they had not said; of suggesting by his questions that statements had been made to him personally out of court, in respect of which no proof was offered; of pretending to understand that a witness had said something which he had not said and persistently cross-examining the witness upon that basis; of assuming prejudicial facts not in evidence; of bullying and arguing with witnesses; and in general, of conducting himself in a thoroughly indecorous and improper manner. . . .
>
> The prosecuting attorney's argument to the jury was undignified and intemperate, containing improper insinuations and assertions calculated to mislead the jury. *Id.* at 84–85.

This, of course, is not an exhaustive list of the kinds of improper tactics that overzealous or misguided prosecutors have adopted in judicial proceedings.

*   *   *

Justice Sutherland's identification of the basic reason why that sort of misconduct is intolerable merits repetition:

> The United States Attorney is the representative not of an ordinary party to a controversy, but of a sovereignty whose obligation to govern impartially is as compelling as its obligation to govern at all; and whose interest, therefore, in a criminal prosecution is not that it shall win a case, but that justice shall be done. As such, he is in a peculiar and very definite sense the servant of the law, the twofold aim of which is that guilt shall not escape or innocence suffer. He may prosecute with earnestness and vigor

— indeed, he should do so. But, while he may strike hard blows, he is not at liberty to strike foul ones. It is as much his duty to refrain from improper methods calculated to produce a wrongful conviction as it is to use every legitimate means to bring about a just one.

Berger v. United States, 295 U.S. at 88.

It is equally clear that the prosecutor has the same duty to refrain from improper methods calculated to produce a wrongful indictment. Indeed, the prosecutor's duty to protect the fundamental fairness of judicial proceedings assumes special importance when he is presenting evidence to a grand jury. As the Court of Appeals for the Third Circuit recognized, "the costs of continued unchecked prosecutorial misconduct" before the grand jury are particularly substantial because there

the prosecutor operates without the check of a judge or a trained legal adversary, and virtually immune from public scrutiny. The prosecutor's abuse of his special relationship to the grand jury poses an enormous risk to defendants as well. For while in theory a trial provides the defendant with a full opportunity to contest and disprove the charges against him, in practice, the handing up of an indictment will often have a devastating personal and professional impact that a later dismissal or acquittal can never undo. Where the potential for abuse is so great, and the consequences of a mistaken indictment so serious, the ethical responsibilities of the prosecutor, and the obligation of the judiciary to protect against even the appearance of unfairness, are correspondingly heightened.

United States v. Serubo, 604 F.2d 807, 817 (3d Cir. 1979).

*   *   *

The standard for judging the consequences of prosecutorial misconduct during grand jury proceedings is essentially the same as the standard applicable to trials.

*   *   *

Unquestionably, the plain implication of that discussion is that if the misconduct, even though not expressly forbidden by any written rule, had played a critical role in persuading the jury to return the indictment, dismissal would have been required. In an opinion that I find difficult to comprehend, the Court today repudiates the assumptions underlying these cases and seems to suggest that the court has no authority to supervise the conduct of the prosecutor in grand jury proceedings so long as he follows the dictates of the Constitution, applicable statutes, and Rule 6 of the Federal Rules of Criminal Procedure. The Court purports to support this conclusion by invoking the doctrine of separation of powers and citing a string of cases in which we have declined to impose categorical restraints on the grand jury. Needless to say, the Court's reasoning is unpersuasive.

*   *   *

Explaining why the grand jury must be both "independent" and "informed," the Court wrote in *Wood v. Georgia*, 370 U.S. 375 (1962):

Historically, this body has been regarded as a primary security to the innocent against hasty, malicious and oppressive persecution; it serves the invaluable function in our society of standing between the accuser and the accused, whether the latter be an individual, minority group, or other, to determine whether a charge is founded upon reason or was dictated by an intimidating power or by malice and personal ill will.

Id. at 390.

It blinks reality to say that the grand jury can adequately perform this important historic role if it is intentionally misled by the prosecutor — on whose knowledge of the law and facts of the underlying criminal investigation the jurors will, of necessity, rely.

Unlike the Court, I am unwilling to hold that countless forms of prosecutorial misconduct must be tolerated — no matter how prejudicial they may be, or how seriously they may distort the legitimate function of the grand jury — simply because they are not proscribed by Rule 6 of the Federal Rules of Criminal Procedure or a statute that is applicable in grand jury proceedings. Such a sharp break with the traditional role of the federal judiciary is unprecedented, unwarranted, and unwise. Unrestrained prosecutorial misconduct in grand jury proceedings is inconsistent with the administration of justice in the federal courts and should be redressed in appropriate cases by the dismissal of indictments obtained by improper methods.

III.

What, then, is the proper disposition of this case? I agree with the Government that the prosecutor is not required to place all exculpatory evidence before the grand jury. . . . But that does not mean that the prosecutor may mislead the grand jury into believing that there is probable cause to indict by withholding clear evidence to the contrary. I thus agree with the Department of Justice that "when a prosecutor conducting a grand jury inquiry is personally aware of substantial evidence which directly negates the guilt of a subject of the investigation, the prosecutor must present or otherwise disclose such evidence to the grand jury before seeking an indictment against such a person." U.S. Dept. of Justice, United States Attorneys' Manual ¶ 9-11.233, at 88 (1988).

Although I question whether the evidence withheld in this case directly negates respondent's guilt, I need not resolve my doubts because the Solicitor General did not ask the Court to review the nature of the evidence withheld. Instead, he asked us to decide the legal question whether an indictment may be dismissed because the prosecutor failed to present exculpatory evidence. Unlike the Court and the Solicitor General, I believe the answer to that question is yes, if the withheld evidence would plainly preclude a finding of probable cause. I therefore cannot endorse the Court's opinion. . . .

NOTES AND QUESTIONS

1. *Exculpatory evidence.* The Department of Justice has been criticized for failing to present exculpatory evidence to grand juries. If such evidence need only be presented at the trial stage, does this create the potential for prosecutorial misconduct before the grand jury? Has the *Williams* case provided sufficient guidance as to how to avoid unfairness in this situation?

2. *The functioning of the grand jury.* The *Williams* Court stated that "the Fifth Amendment's constitutional guarantee *presupposes* an investigative body 'acting independently of either prosecuting attorney *or judge*' . . . . " *United States v. Williams*, 504 U.S. 36, 49 (1992). How can a grand jury operate without a prosecuting attorney? What did the Court intend by this statement?

More generally, what role does the grand jury serve in the criminal justice system? What role should it serve? *See* Roger A. Fairfax, Jr., *Grand Jury Discretion and Constitutional Design*, 93 Cornell L. Rev. 703 (2008) (arguing that a grand jury's discretion whether to bring criminal charges serves as an important check on government powers); Kevin K. Washburn, *Restoring the Grand Jury*, 76 Fordham L. Rev. 2333 (2008) (arguing that the current grand jury system undermines respect for the grand jury, and that the reforms are needed so that the grand jury can serve an important role in promoting the criminal justice system's popular legitimacy).

3. *State practice.* Some states do require that the prosecutors present exculpatory evidence to the grand jury. *See* R. Michael Cassidy, *Toward a More Independent Grand Jury: Recasting and Enforcing the Prosecutor's Duty to Disclose Exculpatory Evidence*, 13 Geo. J. Legal Ethics, 361 (2000). The Department of Justice requires disclosure as a matter of policy; however, this policy creates no substantive rights for the defendant. U.S. Dept. of Justice, Department of Justice Manual ¶ 9-11.233. Thus, failure to present such evidence forms no basis for dismissal of the indictment. Given the potential for prosecutorial abuses, should this rule be codified by Congress? Why or why not?

4. *The courts' role. Williams* held that an indictment may not be dismissed merely because the prosecutor failed to present substantial exculpatory evidence. In addition, courts have allowed the grand jury to consider a broad range of evidence, including evidence based on hearsay, evidence containing inconsistencies, evidence obtained from illegal searches and seizures, and evidence based on impeached testimony. The Supreme Court has held that the grand jury is entitled to a presumption of regularity. In *United States v. Mechanik*, 475 U.S. 66, 70 (1986), the Court held that a Rule 6(d) violation (limiting those individuals present in the grand jury room) was harmless error in light of the guilty verdict. Prejudice will be presumed, however, in those circumstances where the "structural protections of the grand jury have been so compromised as to render the proceedings fundamentally unfair. . . . " *Bank of Nova Scotia v. United States*, 487 U.S. 250, 257–258 (1988) (the district court exercised its supervisory power over the grand jury where there were allegations of prosecutorial grand jury abuses; the court dismissed 27 counts of a tax fraud, obstruction of justice, and mail fraud indictment).

[3]   Irregularities and Abuse

The grand jury is the primary investigative tool in federal white collar and corporate criminal investigations. If there has been an irregularity in the grand jury process, what recourse does a putative defendant have prior to or after the indictment? The next case discusses the defense's options and addresses the limitations on the government's use of the grand jury after an indictment has been issued.

UNITED STATES v. ARTHUR ANDERSEN, L.L.P.
Crim. Action No. H-02-0121 (S.D. Tex. Apr. 9, 2002)

[HARMON, DISTRICT JUDGE.]

Pending before the Court in the above referenced action is Defendant Arthur Andersen L.L.P.'s motion to quash subpoenas and limit grand jury proceedings.

Defendant contends that once an indictment has been returned, the government is prohibited from using the grand jury to conduct discovery or otherwise prepare its case for trial. Defendant charges that the government is abusing the grand jury process by seeking to use the grand jury to assist in its trial preparation and to conduct discovery and "freeze" testimony. Defendant complains that only now, after obtaining the indictment on March 7, 2002, charging it with obstruction of justice and after Defendant refused to plead guilty, is the government impermissibly subpoenaing Arthur Andersen personnel as fact witnesses to testify under oath about evidence relating to the obstruction of justice charge to strengthen its case, to "lock in — for trial purposes — those witnesses previously furnished through their voluntary interview." Defendant argues that not only the timing of these delayed subpoenas, but also the implausibility of the government's claim that it is now seeking to investigate whether to indict individuals in addition to the accounting institution, its subpoenas for Arthur Andersen witnesses whose testimony might constitute admissions attributable to their employer at trial support Defendant's charge of abuse by the government. Moreover, urges Defendant, the imminence of the trial setting eliminates any need to place witnesses before the grand jury now. Finally, Defendant asserts that "the government . . . made this bed; having rushed to indict on an extraordinarily expedited schedule, the Justice Department is in no position to complain if temporary restrictions on the grand jury are necessary to prevent the government from obtaining an unfair and improper advantage at trial."

In its memorandum in opposition, the government reiterates a point made in open court, i.e., that Andersen urged the Department of Justice to expedite a decision about whether to indict the firm for obstruction of justice based on document destruction; then after Defendant was indicted, Andersen reversed its position and asked the government to delay investigating individual employees, including those that Andersen has publicly blamed for the destruction of documents. The government further complains that in light of Andersen's campaign to enlist public sympathy by slanted statements and demonstrations, to influence the potential jury pool, and to signal its desired factual stance to current and former employees, including potential targets, subjects or witnesses in the grand jury investigation, expeditious investigation by the grand jury of current and former employees is necessary.

Emphasizing that the grand jury . . . is a separate entity from the courts, which have only a "very limited" supervisory power over grand jury proceedings, *United States v. Williams*, 504 U.S. 36 (1992), also underscores that grand jury proceedings are entitled to a presumption of regularity. The government points to the long settled principle that "where either primary purpose of the investigation is to determine whether others not indicted were involved in the same criminal activity, or whether the indicted party committed still other crimes, the government may go forward with the inquiry even though one result may be the production of evidence that could then be used at the trial of the pending indictment." Thus a grand jury subpoena may issue to assist the grand jury in its investigation even where the incidental effect might be that the prosecutor will use any information obtained for purposes other than that grand jury's investigation. Furthermore, the government's primary purpose for proceeding before the grand jury is not to collect evidence relating to the pending indictment against Arthur Andersen L.L.P. . . .

In support of its response, the government submits two declarations from attorneys working with the Enron Task Force, investigating all criminal matters associated with the collapse of Enron Corporation. The first, filed *ex parte* and under seal, was made by an Assistant United States Attorney and explains in detail that the challenged subpoenas were issued by a different grand jury than the one that indicted Defendant and were properly issued to investigate uncharged criminal conduct by individuals and entities. A second, unsealed declaration [was filed] by AUSU Leslie Caldwell delineating the procedural steps and negotiations between the government and Defendant up to the unsealing of the indictment for the instant case on March 14, 2002.

The Court has reviewed the applicable law and the record before it. A court should not intervene in the grand jury process absent a compelling reason. The existence of a pending indictment does not per se bar the government from using the grand jury to make a good faith, continuing inquiry into charges not included in that pending indictment. Abuse of the grand jury process occurs only when the government's sole or dominant purpose in convening a grand jury is to gather evidence for an already pending litigation. This sole or dominant purpose rule serves obvious purposes. It allows grand juries to continue investigations without having to wait to indict individuals or entities against which sufficient information to indict has already been uncovered, as well as to investigate additional individuals or entities who become suspects only after the indictment has been returned.

The government has explained with particularity and with documentary support that the government's expedited indictment was due to Arthur Andersen's urging. Thus the timing of the subpoena is not a factor bolstering Defendant' argument. Other than conclusory statements, Defendant has failed to show that the government's investigation in subpoenaing the Defendant's employees as witnesses is for the sole and dominant purpose of developing evidence for trial of its pending destruction-of-documents obstruction charge against Arthur Anderson L.L.P. The Court finds that the government's affidavits have shown it is acting in good faith to investigate unindicted charges against individuals and entities. As anyone following the news is fully aware, the collapse of Enron has spawned a complex and seemingly ever expanding investigation involving a wide range of parties and potential causes of action. The Court finds that there has been no abuse of grand jury process here. For these reasons the Court ORDERS that Defendant's motion to quash subpoenas and limit grand jury proceedings is DENIED.

NOTES AND QUESTIONS

1. *Motion to quash.* The motion to quash is a party's principal means for challenging grand jury irregularities. A motion to quash is directed to the federal district court supervising the grand jury. This court performs a limited supervisory

role when considering motions to quash because grand jury proceedings are presumptively valid.

2. *Timing.* In the *Andersen* case, the pre-indictment negotiations worked to the disadvantage of the government. By presenting its case prior to the completion of the evidence-gathering process, it risked not securing all of the witnesses and evidence. On the other hand, a defendant will typically seek to delay an indictment. Why did Andersen seek an expedited decision in this case? Why would a corporate defendant seek expedited resolution as a matter of defense strategy?

3. *Multiple grand juries.* This case grew out of the Enron corporate fraud scheme, a complex scheme involving multi-district civil proceedings and criminal investigations. In such situations, more than one grand jury may be conducting an investigation. This was the situation in the *Arthur Andersen* case, which was coordinated by the Enron Task Force that was investigating matters arising from Enron's collapse. What particular dangers are presented for defendants in the case of multiple investigations?

PROBLEMS

16-1. Five former local police officers were being investigated by a federal grand jury for civil rights violations. The government called 16 witnesses before the grand jury, including the alleged victim, and thereafter issued an indictment against all the defendants. It was later revealed that the alleged victim in the case perjured himself before the grand jury. There is no evidence that the government knew, at the time of the victim's testimony, that it was perjurious, although there is evidence that the government suspected that some of the testimony might have been fabricated. The defendants sought to dismiss the indictment on the grounds that the alleged victim's "entire testimony before the grand jury is severely tainted by his perjury." The district court dismissed the indictment on the basis of the false testimony.

The government appeals. How should the court rule? Why?

16-2. Defendants were indicted for fraud, bribery, and extortion. Three separate grand juries had investigated the allegations leading to the indictment, but the indictment came from the third grand jury. The defendants alleged that government attorneys leaked secret grand jury information relating to the second grand jury investigation, leading to news reports that discussed the identity, testimony, and demeanor of witnesses before the second grand jury. The defendants also alleged that the government eavesdropped on conversations by members of the second grand jury showing that they were not inclined to indict, which led the prosecution to engage in "grand jury shopping" when it chose to present the charges for indictment to a third grand jury. The government investigated all leaks of grand jury information that had allegedly been made, but found no misconduct, and said it did not engage in eavesdropping. The government also argued that its reasons for presenting the indictment to a third grand jury were not a proper subject for judicial inquiry. The district court stayed the trial indefinitely, pending completion of its own investigation into the alleged misconduct before the second grand jury.

The government appeals. How should the court rule? Why?

[C] GRAND JURY SECRECY AND RELATED ISSUES

The secrecy surrounding grand jury proceedings invites criticism and suspicions. While the premise is that grand jury secrecy operates to protect the innocent as well as the government, the reality is that secrecy is sometimes perceived as a potential shield for abuse. The public, through the media, clamors to know who is under investigation and for what offenses. Because of its secrecy and wide scope of authority, the grand jury has been much criticized for its almost unlimited power. Once the grand jury has been empanelled by the district court, it operates solely under the direction of the prosecutor.[f]

Grand jurors do not hear both sides of a case. This is a critical point because the defense counsel has no right to accompany the client into the grand jury room, to ask questions, or to submit evidence for the grand jury to consider. During the course of a long-running criminal investigation, as can frequently occur in complex white collar cases, the defense has a limited ability to discern the details of the criminal investigation. Absent a court order or other authorization, only the witness may disclose the substance of the witness' testimony before the grand jury. Secrecy is designed to promote freedom of deliberation and honest testimony. In addition, secrecy helps to prevent flight of those under investigation, to encourage the appearance of recalcitrant witnesses, and to protect innocent individuals under investigation.

In high-profile investigations, a witness can take a proactive, aggressive approach by striking the first public blow and granting media interviews both pre- and post-grand jury appearance. By doing so, a witness can hope to "spin" the facts and generate public sympathy and support. Moreover, communication with the prosecutor early on in the investigation may persuade the prosecutor to label what would otherwise be a target or subject as a witness. *See* Chapter 17, Self-Incrimination — Witness Testimony and Document Production, *infra*, for a definition of targets and subjects. Defendants have also claimed that the government agents and prosecutors have leaked grand jury information in order to prejudice the public and potential jurors.

Because secrecy rules are often unclear, issues involving grand jury secrecy can create havoc in investigations conducted by the Department of Justice. When in doubt, prosecutors should err on the side of caution and maintain secrecy.

[1]   Leaks

The following case provides an example of the complex issues that can arise under Rule 6. Did the players in this case have any motivation for attempting to "spin" the facts?

IN RE SEALED CASE No. 99-3091
192 F.3d 995 (D.C. Cir. 1999)

Opinion for the court filed PER CURIAM.

---

[f] Case law permits a witness to file a motion to quash a grand jury subpoena with the district court if the witness believes that the prosecutor is exceeding her authority.

ON A MOTION FOR SUMMARY REVERSAL OR STAY

Per Curiam:

The Office of Independent Counsel (OIC) seeks summary reversal of the district court's order to show cause why OIC should not be held in contempt for violating the grand jury secrecy rule. . . .

On January 31, 1999, while the Senate was trying President William J. Clinton on articles of impeachment, the *New York Times* published a front page article captioned "Starr is Weighing Whether to Indict Sitting President." As is relevant here, the article reported:

> Inside the Independent Counsel's Office, a group of prosecutors believes that not long after the Senate trial concludes, Mr. Starr should ask the grand jury of 23 men and women hearing the case against Mr. Clinton to indict him on charges of perjury and obstruction of justice, the associates said. The group wants to charge Mr. Clinton with lying under oath in his Jones deposition in January 1998 and in his grand jury testimony in August, the associates added.

The next day, the Office of the President (the White House) and Mr. Clinton jointly filed in district court a motion for an order to show cause why OIC, or the individuals therein, should not be held in contempt for disclosing grand jury material in violation of Federal Rule of Criminal Procedure 6(e). The White House and Mr. Clinton pointed to several excerpts from the article as evidence of OIC's violations of the grand jury secrecy rule.

OIC responded that the matters disclosed in the article merely rehashed old news reports and, in any event, did not fall within Rule 6(e)'s definition of "matters occurring before the grand jury. . . . "

Notwithstanding the foregoing, Independent Counsel Kenneth W. Starr asked the Federal Bureau of Investigation to provide OIC assistance in conducting an internal leak investigation.

Troubled by these developments, the district court ordered OIC to show cause why they should not be held in civil contempt for a violation of Rule 6(e), concluding that the portion of the *New York Times* article quoted above revealed grand jury material and constituted a *prima facie* violation of Rule 6(e).

* * *

Because OIC has withdrawn its argument that none of its attorneys was the source of the disclosures in the *New York Times* article at issue here, the only remaining issue is whether those disclosures qualify as "matters occurring before the grand jury." Fed. R. Crim. P. 6(e)(2).

The district court concluded that only one excerpt from the *New York Times* article constituted a *prima facie* violation of Rule 6(e). That excerpt disclosed the desire of some OIC prosecutors to seek, not long after the conclusion of the Senate trial, an indictment of Mr. Clinton on perjury and obstruction of justice charges, including lying under oath in his deposition in the Paula Jones matter and in his grand jury testimony. These statements, according to the district court, reveal a specific time frame for seeking an indictment, the details of a likely indictment, and the direction a group of prosecutors within OIC believes the grand jury investigation should take. Not surprisingly, Mr. Clinton and the White House agree with the district court's expansive reading of Rule 6(e). OIC takes a narrow view of the Rule's coverage, arguing that matters occurring outside the physical presence of the grand jury are covered only if they reveal grand jury matters. DOJ generally supports OIC with respect to the Rule's coverage, but emphasizes the importance of the context and concreteness of disclosures.

The key to the district court's reasoning is its reliance on this court's definition of "matters occurring before the grand jury." In *In re Motions of Dow Jones & Co.*, 142 F.3d 496, 500 (D.C. Cir. 1998), we noted that this phrase encompasses "not only what has occurred and what is occurring, but also what is likely to occur," including "the identities of witnesses or jurors, the substance of testimony as well as actual transcripts, the strategy or direction of the investigation, the deliberations or questions of jurors, and the like." *Id.* Despite the seemingly broad nature of the statements in *Dow Jones*, we have never read Rule 6(e) to require that a "veil of secrecy be drawn over all matters occurring in the world that happen to be investigated by a grand jury." *Securities and Exchange Comm'n v. Dresser Indus.*, 628 F.2d 1368, 1382 (D.C. Cir. 1980). Indeed, we have said that "[t]he disclosure of information 'coincidentally before the grand jury [which can] be revealed in such a manner that its revelation would not elucidate the inner workings of the grand jury' is not prohibited." *Senate of Puerto Rico v. United States Dept. of Justice*, 823 F.2d 574, 582 (D.C. Cir. 1987). Thus, the phrases "likely to occur" and "strategy and direction" must be read in light of the text of Rule 6(e) — which limits the Rule's coverage to "matters occurring before the grand jury" — as well as the purposes of the Rule.

These purposes, as well as the text of the Rule itself, reflect the need to preserve the secrecy of the *grand jury* proceedings themselves. It is therefore necessary to differentiate between statements by a prosecutor's office with respect to its own investigation, and statements by a prosecutor's office with respect to a *grand jury's* investigation, a distinction of the utmost significance upon which several circuits have already remarked.

Information actually presented to the grand jury is core Rule 6(e) material that is afforded the broadest protection from disclosure. Prosecutors' statements about their investigations, however, implicate the Rule only when they directly reveal grand jury matters. To be sure, we have recognized that Rule 6(e) would be easily evaded if a prosecutor could with impunity discuss with the press testimony about to be presented to a grand jury, so long as it had not yet occurred. Accordingly, we have read Rule 6(e) to cover matters "likely to occur." And even a discussion of "strategy and direction of the investigation" could include references to not yet delivered but clearly anticipated testimony. But that does not mean that *any* discussion of an investigation is violative of Rule 6(e). Indeed, the district court's Local Rule 308(b)(2), which governs attorney conduct in grand jury matters, recognizes that prosecutors often have a legitimate interest in revealing aspects of their investigations "to inform the public that the investigation is underway, to describe the general scope of the investigation, to obtain assistance in the apprehension of a suspect, to warn the public of any dangers, or otherwise aid in the investigation."

It may often be the case, however, that disclosures by the prosecution referencing its own investigation should not be made for tactical reasons, or are in fact prohibited by other Rules or ethical guidelines. For instance, prosecutors may be prohibited by internal guidelines, *see, e.g.*, United States Attorney Manual § 1-7.530, from discussing the strategy or direction of their investigation before an indictment is sought. This would serve one of the same purposes as Rule 6(e): protecting the reputation of innocent suspects. But a court may not use Rule 6(e) to generally regulate prosecutorial statements to the press. The purpose of the Rule is only to protect the secrecy of grand jury proceedings.

*   *   *

For these reasons, the disclosure that a group of OIC prosecutors "believe" that an indictment should be brought at the end of the impeachment proceedings does not on its face, or in the context of the article as a whole, violate Rule 6(e). We acknowledge, as did OIC, that such statements are troubling, for they have the potential to damage the reputation of innocent suspects. But bare statements that some assistant prosecutors in OIC wish to seek an indictment do not implicate the grand jury; the prosecutors may not even be basing their opinion on information presented to a grand jury.

The fact that the disclosure also reveals a time period for seeking the indictment of "not long after the Senate trial concludes" does not in any way indicate what is "likely to occur" before the grand jury within the meaning of Rule 6(e). That disclosure reflects nothing more than a desire on the part of some OIC prosecutors to seek an indictment at that time, not a decision to do so. The general uncertainty as to whether an indictment would in fact be sought (according to the article, only some prosecutors in OIC thought one should be) leads us to conclude that this portion of the article did not reveal anything that was "occurring before the grand jury."

Nor does it violate the Rule to state the general grounds for such an indictment — here, lying under oath in a deposition and before the grand jury — where no secret grand jury material is revealed. In ordinary circumstances, Rule 6(e) covers the disclosure of the names of grand jury witnesses. Therefore, the statement that members of OIC wished to seek an indictment based on Mr. Clinton's alleged perjury before a grand jury would ordinarily be Rule 6(e) material. In this case, however, we take judicial notice that the President's status as a witness before the grand jury was a matter of widespread public knowledge well before the *New York Times* article at issue in this case was written; the President himself went on national television the day of his testimony to reveal this fact. Where the general public is already aware of the information contained in the prosecutor's statement, there is no additional harm in the prosecutor referring to such information.

*   *   *

Similarly, it would ordinarily be a violation of Rule 6(e) to disclose that a grand jury is investigating a particular person. Thus, the statement that a grand jury is "hearing the case against Mr. Clinton" would be covered by Rule 6(e) if it were not for the fact that the *New York Times* article did not reveal any secret, for it was already common knowledge well before January 31, 1999, that a grand jury was investigating alleged perjury and obstruction of justice by the President. Once again, the President's appearance on national television confirmed as much.

*   *   *

[W]e reverse and remand with instructions to dismiss the Rule 6(e) contempt proceedings against OIC. . . .

NOTES AND QUESTIONS

1. *Scope of disclosure.* Rule 6(e)(2) governs disclosure of grand jury material. Although the government attorneys, personnel, and grand jurors are prohibited from disclosing matters occurring before the grand jury, the Supreme Court has held that the government may not prevent witnesses from discussing their own testimony before a grand jury. Rule 6(e)(2) allows for disclosure in certain circumstances including at trial and where there is a "particularized need." In situations where the prosecutor has disclosed matters to persons who are authorized recipients, such as federal agents, what obligations do such persons have to maintain secrecy?

2. *Witness testimony.* Does a witness have a right to review a transcript of the witness's own grand jury testimony? The circuits are split on this issue. *See In re: Grand Jury*, 490 F.3d 978, 986–988 (D.C. Cir. 2007) (reviewing circuit split and listing cases). In one decision, the D.C. Circuit reversed an order denying the witness such access, concluding that:

> In sum, grand jury witnesses have a strong interest in reviewing the transcripts of their own grand jury testimony. The government has little good reason to prevent witnesses from reviewing their transcripts. Weighing the interests of witnesses and the government, we therefore hold that the grand jury witnesses are entitled under Rule 6(e)(3)(E)(i) to review transcripts of their own grand jury testimony in private at the U.S. Attorney's Office or a place agreed to by the parties or designated by the district court.

Id. at 990. Was this the correct outcome? What are the competing interests in this situation? For an excellent overview of these and other issues relating to representation of a grand jury witness, see Jon May, *Advising the Grand Jury Witness: When Talk is Not Cheap*, 16 Crim. Just. 16, 17 (2008).

3. *Judicial notice.* The court was quite willing to relax Rule 6 by taking judicial notice that the "President's status as a witness before the grand jury was a matter of widespread public knowledge. . . . " *In re Sealed Case*, 192 F.3d 995, 1004 (D.C. Cir. 1999). Does this approach thwart the intention of Rule 6 to protect innocent citizens by prohibiting such disclosures? Would the answer be any more troubling if the witness were not a prominent public figure such as the President?

Assume that in a small community, everyone knows that the local bank executive has been subpoenaed by the grand jury and that the prosecutor states (as reported in the news media), "We are conducting an investigation into the criminal activities of the Bank President." Has Rule 6 been violated?

4. *Leaks.* Leaks of grand jury materials to the press pose special dangers. Rule 6(e) is designed to prevent such dangers. Do you favor a rule that prohibits the disclosure that occurred in this case? Why or why not? Can a prosecutor leak grand jury material and later claim that the matter is no longer secret? The court discussed this scenario in footnote 13: "Of course, a prosecutor is not free to leak grand jury material and then make a self serving claim that the matter is no longer secret. *Cf. In re North*, 16 F.3d 1234, 1245 (D.C. Cir. 1994) ('We do not intend to

formulate a rule that once a leak of Rule 6(e) material has occurred, government attorneys are free to ignore the pre-existing bond of secrecy.')." *In re Sealed Case*, 192 F.3d at 1004 n.13.

5. *Parallel civil and criminal proceedings.* Complex issues relating to grand jury secrecy also arise in the context of parallel proceedings. For example, in a civil case brought by the government, may the government gain access to grand jury information? May a private civil litigant gain access to such information? These issues are addressed in the next section and in Chapter 18, Civil Actions, Civil Penalties, and Parallel Proceedings, *infra.*

[2]   Disclosure to Government Attorneys

Frequently, in the performance of their duties, federal government attorneys seek to have access to grand jury material in order to further an investigation. Because of the long-standing rule that grand jury matters are secret and not generally subject to disclosure, codified in Rule 6, any such disclosures must be made within the confines of the rule or pursuant to court order. Two provisions of Rule 6 govern disclosures. Section 6(e)(3)(A)(i) states that "[d]isclosure of a grand-jury matter — other than the grand jury's deliberations or any grand juror's vote — may be made to: (i) an attorney for the government for use in performing that attorney's duty." By contrast, section 6(e)(3)(E)(i) [formerly 6(e)(C)(i)] states that disclosure is permissible "— at a time, in a manner, and subject to any other conditions that it directs — of a grand-jury matter: (i) preliminarily to or in connection with a judicial proceeding."

The Supreme Court in *United States v. Sells Engineering*, 463 U.S. 418 (1983), established the standard applicable to the disclosure of grand jury materials to government attorneys. In *Sells*, the investigation began as a combined civil and criminal matter handled by the Internal Revenue Service. The federal grand jury investigated charges of fraud and tax evasion by Sells Engineering in connection with certain governmental contracts. Sells Engineering reached an agreement with the government, and entered a plea of guilty to one count in the indictment; all other charges were dismissed.

After the dismissal, the government sought disclosure of the grand jury material in connection with their civil fraud investigation under the False Claims Act. The district court granted the motion for disclosure, finding that the matter fell within section 6(e)(3)A)(i), and that the civil attorneys within the Department of Justice were entitled to the material "as a matter of right." The Court of Appeals reversed, finding that the disclosure was only authorized if the government could demonstrate a "particularized need" under 6(e)(C)(i) [currently 6(3)(E)(i)].

The Supreme Court acknowledged the need for disclosure of grand jury materials in order to assist with further governmental investigations and business. The Court stated that "[i]t does not follow, however, that any Justice Department attorney is free to rummage through the records of any grand jury in the country, simply by right of office. Disclosure under (A)(i) is permitted only 'in the performance of such attorney's duty.' The heart of the primary issue in this case is whether performance of duty, within the meaning of (A)(i), includes preparation and litigation of a civil suit by a Justice Department attorney who had no part in conducting the related criminal prosecution." 463 U.S. at 428.

The Court first recognized that governmental disclosures serve many investigative purposes. In reconciling the different disclosure sections of Rule 6, the Court ultimately concluded that "[n]one of these considerations, however, provides any support for breaching grand jury secrecy in favor of government attorneys *other than prosecutors* — either by allowing them into the grand jury room, or by granting them uncontrolled access to grand jury materials. An attorney with only civil duties lacks both the prosecutor's special role in supporting the grand jury, and the prosecutor's own crucial need to know what occurs before the grand jury." *Id.* at 431. In deciding to limit the grand jury's extraordinary investigative powers, the Court held that "*no* disclosure of grand jury materials for civil use should be permitted without a court order." *Id.* at 440. Further, the Court held that the standard for this type of disclosure required the moving party to demonstrate a "particularized need," prior to any disclosure under Rule 6.

PROBLEMS

16-3. Doris Dern has been mayor of the town of Oakville for the last four years. Chris Chang, the President and sole shareholder of Construction Corp., is a political ally of Dern. Construction Corp. is regularly awarded contracts with the town of Oakville. Dern owns ten percent of Construction Corp. A federal grand jury has been convened to explore indictment, with Dern and Chang as targets of the investigation. The government believes that Dern failed to disclose her ownership interest in Construction Corp., in violation of state and local conflict of interest laws. The government also believes that this failure to disclose provides strong circumstantial evidence that Chang bribed Dern in connection with the award of the contracts.

The grand jury has seen documents and heard evidence from a number of witnesses, including Construction Corp. employees who testified that two years ago, Chang gave Dern an ownership interest in Construction Corp. in return for the award of city contracts. Chang mailed checks to Dern that represented Dern's interest in Construction Corp.'s profits. During the investigation, Anderson Andrews, the Assistant U.S. attorney in charge of the investigation received information showing that two years earlier, Dern filed documents that supplemented Dern's official conflict-of-interest disclosures and that fully revealed the arrangement between Construction Corp. and Dern. Andrews did not present this evidence to the grand jury.

During the grand jury's deliberations, Andrews gave a press conference during which Andrews made the following statement:

> A federal grand jury has been convened to explore wrongdoing at the highest levels of city government. We have information from witnesses that the mayor has taken kickbacks in return for awarding city business to a political ally, which is a crime under state and federal law, including the federal mail fraud and RICO statutes. We will vigorously pursue this investigation, and see to it that those responsible are brought to justice.

The day after the news conference, a local newspaper reported that Andrews had decided to ask the grand jury to return an indictment charging the mayor with mail fraud and RICO based upon the alleged kickback scheme.

Two weeks after the newspaper report, the grand jury returned an indictment against Dern under the RICO statute and mail fraud statutes.

(1) Argue for the defense that the government's conduct in this case was inappropriate, and for the prosecution that it was not.

(2) Assuming that the government's conduct was not appropriate, what recourse should the defense seek? How should the government respond to the defense's request for a remedy?

16-4. Baker & Tyler, Inc. ("B & T"), a wholesale bookseller, allegedly engaged in fraudulent pricing practices. Prior to the criminal grand jury proceedings at issue, former B & T employees initiated a civil suit alleging that B & T fraudulently overcharged institutional customers, including federally funded libraries, in violation of the civil provisions of the False Claims Act. The government also conducted a parallel civil investigation, "under seal," to determine whether or not to intervene in the action. The Department of Justice then commenced a criminal investigation.

During the parallel investigations, members of the government's civil and criminal teams met to exchange information and discuss how to proceed in the criminal case. In the meantime, discovery in the civil case had been stayed due to motions unrelated to the criminal case. Upon this occurrence, the government then decided to convene a grand jury. Several subpoenas were issued to B & T seeking "all business documents" for the five years in question. This request encompassed many of the same documents that were requested in discovery in the civil case prior to the stay.

B & T has filed a motion to quash the subpoenas. How should the court rule? Why?

Chapter 17

SELF-INCRIMINATION — WITNESS TESTIMONY AND DOCUMENT PRODUCTION

[A] INTRODUCTORY NOTES

The Fifth Amendment protection against compelled self-incrimination allows an individual witness to remain silent in the face of government questioning. If the government determines that the witness' testimony or documents are critical to the success of the investigation, the government can seek a grant of immunity with a corresponding court order to compel the testimony or production of the documents. The statutory provisions governing this procedure are found in 18 U.S.C. §§ 6001–6005.

Individuals suspected of engaging in white collar criminal activity are often respected members of their business and professional communities and occupy positions of prominence. Because they wish to maintain their reputations, such persons often strongly desire to speak with government investigators in an effort to convince the government that they are not culpable. As a result, when this type of "storytelling" is offered to the prosecutor in an effort to persuade the government that there was no wrongdoing, testimonial and documentary matters of self-incrimination arise.

The Fifth Amendment establishes that "[n]o person . . . shall be compelled in any criminal case to be a witness against himself. . . . " in white collar investigations because the unique nature of the case frequently centers on documentary evidence and proffered explanations, questions of the testimonial privilege are particularly complex. The witness can assert the privilege against self-incrimination when compelled to appear and give testimony before a grand jury, in a trial court, in a civil deposition, or before Congress. In order for the government to compel the testimony, it must first serve a subpoena *ad testificandum* for testimony or a subpoena *duces tecum* for documentary evidence. If the witness can assert a valid Fifth Amendment claim of privilege, then the government must resort to other measures in order to gain the information. It is most likely that a witness will first confront the Fifth Amendment dilemma in a white collar investigation during the grand jury stage of the proceedings.

[B] TESTIMONY

[1] Witnesses, Subjects, and Targets

Defense counsel representing witnesses, subjects, or targets before the grand jury have different concerns.

A witness is simply one with information generally related to the matter under investigation. For example, a records custodian, a victim of a crime, or a federal investigative agent can each be a witness subpoenaed to appear before the grand jury panel. Counsel representing a witness called before the grand jury will have to ascertain whether that witness falls within the category of either subject or target.

A subject is one about whom the grand jury seeks general information of a more specific nature, although not approaching the threshold of a potential defendant. Some defense counsel will allow a subject to appear, especially where the appearance will be beneficial in establishing the non-involvement of the witness and the potential to eliminate that person from the roster of those of interest to the government. A subject is a witness "whose conduct is within the scope of the grand jury's investigation." U.S.A.M. § 9-11.151. Advice of Rights of Grand Jury Witnesses. Subjects can sometimes turn into targets, and it is often as a result of the grand jury appearance that this transformation occurs.

By way of comparison, a target is "a person as to whom the prosecutor or the grand jury has substantial evidence linking him or her to the commission of a crime and who, in the judgment of the prosecutor, is a putative defendant." *Id.* A target is one who is the focus of the investigation for purposes of an indictment. As a matter of sound defense practice, counsel should generally not allow a target to appear before a federal grand jury for obvious reasons. In particular, a witness appears before a grand jury without counsel present. Because there is no opportunity for examination by the witness's attorney, the witness can be questioned by the prosecutor without any opportunity to clarify the testimony. Further, the testimony will give the government both an opportunity to learn information that it otherwise might not possess and a transcribed record that can be used to impeach the witness at a later proceeding.

[2] Immunity

Whenever a witness is subpoenaed to appear before a grand jury (or at trial) and provide sworn testimony, counsel for the witness must consider the witness' status prior to the appearance. In situations where the witness has information that would tend to incriminate if offered, and the government desires the testimony of a witness who invokes his or her Fifth Amendment protections, it must first offer immunity for such testimony.

There are two types of immunity: transactional and use/derivative use. Transactional immunity shields an individual from prosecution for any matter concerning the transaction about which the testimony relates. This immunity includes protection from prosecution even where the evidence on which a prosecution would be based is from a source wholly unrelated to the witness. Although some states allow transactional immunity, the Supreme Court has held that use/derivative use immunity is all that the Fifth Amendment requires. *Kastigar v. United States*, 406 U.S. 441 (1972).

Transactional immunity is much broader than use/derivative use immunity because it grants the witness full immunity from prosecution for any crimes about which the witness testifies. The federal government has eliminated transactional immunity in favor of use/derivative use immunity, codified in 18 U.S.C. § 6002–6003:

> [N]o testimony or other information compelled under the order (or any information directly or indirectly derived from such testimony or other information) may be used against the witness in any criminal case, except

in a prosecution for perjury, giving a false statement, or otherwise failing to comply with the order.

18 U.S.C. § 6002.

This category of immunity protects a witness against any adverse governmental use of the immunized testimony or documents in subsequent proceedings. Use/derivative use immunity allows the government to prosecute the witness if the government has an independent source for the information on which the prosecution is based. In *Kastigar*, the Court held that use/derivative use immunity is coextensive with Fifth Amendment guarantees in that nothing from the witness' own mouth can be used against the witness, but other, independent evidence can be used to prosecute the witness. 406 U.S. at 453–454.

When the government initiates an investigation, it does not always know at the outset what wrongdoing occurred and who was involved in the wrongdoing. The government must seek testimony of individuals to provide evidence that will assist in the development of the theory of the case. Many, if not most, of these witnesses will not have any valid Fifth Amendment rights to assert. They neither have any potential criminal exposure nor any reason to resist testifying. On the other hand, individuals more closely associated with the investigation certainly could have reason to hesitate before responding to a subpoena or making an appearance at the grand jury.

It is imperative for defense counsel who is representing a witness in receipt of a grand jury subpoena to ascertain that witness' status by contacting the prosecutor handling the investigation. If it is determined that the client is a subject or target and faces criminal exposure, then the best defense strategy is to secure a favorable deal for the client. There are many "deals" that can favor a witness, but the most favorable for a subject or target is to obtain immunity from prosecution.

In addition, issues arise when a litigant in a civil proceeding seeks to gain access to immunized testimony. These issues are addressed in the Chapter 18, Civil Actions, Civil Penalties, and Parallel Proceedings, *infra*.

[3]   Prosecuting the Immunized Witness

Although the Department of Justice is the entity most likely to seek immunity during the course of a criminal investigation, the legislative branch of government also has this power and can grant immunity in order to obtain testimony for Congressional hearings. Such was the case during the "Iran-Contra" investigation, which arose from the following facts. During President Reagan's first term in office, Congress supported covert activity by the Central Intelligence Agency to aid the military and paramilitary activities of a counter-revolutionary group in Nicaragua, the Nicaraguan Contras. The President viewed the Contras as necessary to counter the communist-leaning government of Nicaragua. Congress eventually terminated the CIA's authority to assist the Contras, but the President deployed his national security advisor, Robert McFarlane, to assist the Contras. McFarlane recruited Lt. Col. Oliver North to coordinate the secret mission.

Later, the President undertook an effort to obtain the release of seven U.S. hostages who were being held in Lebanon. Despite the official position of non-negotiation with terrorists, the President dealt indirectly with the kidnappers to gain the release of the hostages. The United States sold arms to Iran, which was at that time at war with Iraq, and Iran then negotiated with the kidnappers for the release of the hostages.

North and his colleagues secretly funneled money to the Contras by selling weapons to Iran and secretly diverting the excess profits through private Swiss bank accounts.

When these events were discovered, they led to a six-year investigation, including the appointment of an Independent Counsel, Congressional hearings, and multiple criminal prosecutions, all known as the "Iran-Contra" affair. Congressional immunity was granted to Lt. Col. Oliver North and others during the course of a Congressional investigation into matters that were simultaneously being investigated by the Independent Counsel. Despite this grant of immunity, the Independent Counsel prosecuted North and others. North was convicted, and appealed.

UNITED STATES v. NORTH
910 F.2d 843 (D.C. Cir. 1990), *modified*, 920 F.2d 940 (D.C. Cir. 1991)

[In the first *North* decision, the D.C. Circuit held, *inter alia*, that the district court erred by failing to hold a full hearing to determine whether North's immunized testimony had in any way been used during his criminal trial. The court remanded the case to the district court to conduct a hearing required by *Kastigar v. United States*, 406 U.S. 441 (1972), "to ensure that the IC (Independent Counsel) made no use of North's immunized congressional testimony." After issuing its original order, the D.C. Circuit court granted the petition for rehearing and issued the ruling that follows.]

Per Curiam:

* * *

In its petition for rehearing, the Independent Counsel ("IC") has raised several new issues regarding our original disposition. As we explain below, we believe that all but one of the IC's claims lack merit. We therefore grant in part and deny in part the petition for rehearing and modify our original opinion, accordingly.

I. Immunized Testimony at Trial

The IC claims that we misapplied *United States v. Rinaldi*, 808 F.2d 1579 (D.C. Cir. 1987), in remanding "for a massive inquiry into 'the taint of the testimony and the derivation of the testimony.' " Petition for Rehearing at 7–8 ("Pet. for Reh'g"). The IC's argument rests on the *ipse dixit* that "the prosecution's freedom from taint establishes that its evidence was necessarily derived independently" and therefore that the inquiry mandated by *Rinaldi* would be "superfluous." Pet. For Reh'g at 8. This bold proposition, however, would convert *Kastigar*'s total prohibition on use, *Kastigar v. United States*, 406 U.S. 441 (1973), to a mere ban on significant prosecutorial exposure to the immunized testimony. It simply does not follow that insulating prosecutors from exposure automatically proves that immunized testimony was not used against the defendant. *Kastigar* is instead violated whenever the prosecution puts on a witness whose testimony is shaped, directly or indirectly, by compelled testimony, regardless of *how or by whom* he was exposed to that compelled testimony. Were the rule otherwise, a private lawyer for a witness sympathetic to the government could listen to the compelled testimony and use it to prepare the witness for trial. The government would presumably thereby gain the advantage of use of the immunized testimony so long as it did not actually cooperate in that effort. This interpretation of *Kastigar* ("Look ma, no hands") pressed by the IC, if accepted, would enormously increase the risk of providing immunized testimony. To reject it, it is unnecessary to decide whether, as North asserts, particular significance should be placed on the fact that other government personnel in the legislative and executive branches outside the Independent Counsel's office were, after exposure to immunized testimony, actively involved in preparing witnesses.

Indeed, *Rinaldi* explicitly recognizes that witnesses' exposure to immunized testimony can taint their trial testimony irrespective of the prosecution's role in the exposure and that an inquiry is therefore necessary into whether the content of witnesses' testimony was derived from or motivated by the immunized testimony. It specifically mandates an inquiry into what a witness knew prior to exposure to the immunized testimony and what information she gleaned from that exposure- . . . . And even where the witness testifies from personal knowledge, use within the meaning of *Kastigar* may occur, if the immunized testimony influenced the witness' decision to testify. . . . Our opinion is thus entirely consistent with *Rinaldi* in calling for an inquiry on remand into the content and circumstances of witnesses' testimony.

Our dissenting colleague does not disagree with us on this central point so vigorously disputed by the IC — that the content and circumstances of testimony given by a witness exposed to the defendant's immunized testimony may constitute "use" of the immunized testimony in violation of a defendant's constitutional rights regardless of the prosecutor's "fault." But she does contend that we have extended *Rinaldi* by insisting that the testimony of any witness exposed to the immunized testimony be "pre-recorded" in much the same way as prosecutors memorialize their investigative material, including witnesses' statements, so as to be able to prove in a *Kastigar* hearing that the government has obtained no leads from the immunized testimony. . . .

To be sure, if such steps are not taken, it may well be extremely difficult for the prosecutor to sustain its burden of proof that a witness exposed to immunized testimony has not shaped his or her testimony in light of the exposure, or as the *Rinaldi* court observed, been motivated to come forward and testify in light of the immunized testimony. But we surely did not mean to preclude the use of any techniques of which we are not aware, nor did we mean to even suggest that the prosecutor was barred from trying to show in any fashion that a witness' testimony was not influenced by the immunized testimony.

What we did insist upon, however — and here we quite definitely part company with the Chief Judge — is that the prosecutor has to *prove* that witnesses who testified against the defendant did not draw upon the immunized testimony to use it against the defendant; the burden of disproving use cannot, under *Kastigar*, be shifted onto the defendant, nor can the defendant be required to assume the burden of going forward with evidence that puts in issue the question of use. Most important, the defendant is entitled to a *hearing* at which he would be able to challenge the prosecution's case for non-use.

*   *   *

If the prosecutor were to demonstrate through testimony that a particular witness exposed to the immunized testimony had not been affected by the exposure, for example, by showing that the witness had set down his story before exposure, then the burden of going forward would shift to the defendant to challenge that version. . . .

The IC (and the district court) obviously wished to avoid cross-examination of the exposed witnesses. Some might convincingly testify that their exposure had no effect on their trial or grand jury testimony. Others might well testify that they simply were unable to determine just how much exposure affected their testimony, in which case that uncertainty would surely be a grave problem for the party with the burden of proof — the prosecutor.

*   *   *

Government officials are subject to greater restraints on their behavior than private individuals. The Ethics in Government Act requires the Department of Justice to cooperate with an Independent Counsel. Other executive departments are expected to cooperate with the Department of Justice, the chief law enforcement arm of the executive. Moreover, the IC presumably has the power to bring charges of obstruction of justice against anyone who attempts to sabotage the investigation. We are not aware that the Independent Counsel made any efforts to prevent government officials who were to testify or who had already testified from exposing themselves to immunized testimony. . . .

Finally, and perhaps at the heart of the dissent's concerns, is the argument that a straightforward application of *Kastigar* in cases where a witness testifies before Congress, after Congress grants immunity under section 6005, unduly restricts Congress' role in exposing wrongdoing in the nation — including wrongdoing in the executive branch. . . . We do not think Congress would be so naive as lightly to grant use immunity to such prospective defendants. Surely Congress does so only when its perception of the national interest justifies this extraordinary step. When Congress grants immunity before the prosecution has completed preparing its "case," the prosecutor, whoever that may be, can warn that the grant of immunity has its institutional costs; in this case, the IC indeed warned Congress that "any grant of use and derivative use immunity would create serious — and perhaps insurmountable — barriers to the prosecution of the immunized witness." Memorandum of the Independent Counsel Concerning Use Immunity (Jan. 13, 1987) [Submitted to the Joint Congressional Iran Contra Committee J.A. at 2502]. . . . The political needs of the majority, or Congress, or the President never, never, never, should trump an individual's explicit constitutional protections.

II. Immunized Testimony Before the Grand Jury

The IC renews its argument that presentation of immunized testimony to the grand jury is permissible and that *no* inquiry into whether the grand jury considered evidence based upon North's congressional testimony is therefore appropriate. . . . The IC thus continues to miss the fundamental distinction between the presentation to the grand jury of evidence that has previously been unconstitutionally obtained and that of constitutionally-obtained evidence whose exposure to the grand jury amounts to a constitutional violation in and of itself. . . .

[T]he prosecution obtains the immunized testimony legally, but only by promising that neither the testimony or information itself nor any information directly or indirectly derived from it will "be used against [the defendant] in any criminal case." 18 U.S.C. § 6002. And it is only this promise that compels the defendant to testify in spite of his constitutional privilege: "immunity from use and derivative use is coextensive with the scope of the privilege against self-incrimination . . . [because i]t prohibits the prosecutorial authorities from using the compelled testimony in *any* respect." *Kastigar*, 406 U.S. at 453 (emphasis in original). When the prosecution reneges on this constitutionally-mandated bargain and presents the immunized testimony to the grand jury, the constitutional violation is part and parcel of the grand jury process. The presentation — "use" — of the testimony is precisely the proscribed act. The issue is thus not one of "derivative use . . . by the grand jury" and of the exclusionary rule (indeed, any use of the testimony is *per se* excluded under the statute and *Kastigar*). Rather, the situation is no different than if the grand jury had itself forced the defendant to give incriminating answers and any indictment based upon immunized evidence is no less tainted.

[The court then held that a *Kastigar* hearing was required into the content and circumstances of any testimony given by witnesses who were exposed to the defendant's immunized testimony.]

* * *

WALD, CHIEF JUDGE, dissenting as to Parts I, II, & III:

In his petition for rehearing, the Independent Counsel ("IC") argues that the prohibitions of the use-immunity statute, 18 U.S.C. § 6002, do not extend to the government's use of witnesses who have independently exposed themselves to immunized testimony. Although the claim that the statute does not cover any such witness exposure is problematical, I do agree, as my earlier dissent reflects, that the statute does not require that independent witness exposure and prosecutorial exposure be treated identically for prophylactic purposes. Since, as the IC's petition forcefully points out, my colleagues' original opinion effectively transformed a limited use immunity into a sweeping transaction immunity, I would grant the IC's petition for rehearing on the *Kastigar* issue. By exalting form over substance, the original *per curiam* eviscerates both the use-immunity and independent-counsel statutes; its consequences for future cases of public import are ominous.

III. *Kastigar* Requirements

A. *The Problem with the Original Opinion*

The Supreme Court has recognized that use immunity is coextensive with the Fifth Amendment privilege. Accordingly, restrictions on the use of immunized testimony are exacting.

> [T]he prosecution [bears] the affirmative duty to prove that the evidence it proposes to use is derived from a legitimate source wholly independent of the compelled testimony.

Kastigar at 460.

This "very substantial protection," *id.* at 461, while reflecting the importance of the constitutional values at stake, was not meant to make the prosecution's burden an impossible one. The use-immunity statute makes a precise accommodation between the privilege against self-incrimination and the public's legitimate interest in securing testimony; use immunity thus exists in a delicate tension with the Fifth Amendment.

By mandating additional — and practically unattainable — requirements not found in *Kastigar* itself, my colleagues have upset this tension. They have rendered impossible in virtually all cases the prosecution of persons whose immunized testimony is of such national significance as to be the subject of congressional hearings and media coverage. In their opinions, my colleagues have ruled that *Kastigar* requires at least *four* distinct showings, only the first two of which can be derived from *Kastigar* itself. First, the prosecutors must demonstrate that they avoided "significant exposure" to the immunized testimony. Majority Opinion ("Maj. op.") at 860. Second, the prosecution must demonstrate that its identification and questioning of witnesses was based solely on "independent leads" — without the use of immunized testimony. Maj. op. at 863. Third — a new requirement, appearing for the first time in the opinion denying rehearing — the prosecution must demonstrate that the immunized testimony did not "*motivate*" its witnesses to testify. And fourth, the prosecution must demonstrate that the testimony of witnesses "exposed" to immunized matter has been "canned" by the prosecution before such exposure. Maj. op. at 872.

The last and most stringent of these requirements — that witness testimony be pre-recorded — is certainly an unwarranted departure from current law.

*   *   *

My colleagues invoke *United States v. Rinaldi*, 808 F.2d 1579 (D.C. Cir. 1987), to support that radical extension of current law. Yet *Rinaldi* does not even suggest that the witness' original knowledge need be or was pre-recorded. Instead, the *Rinaldi* court indicated a far more lenient rule of inevitable discovery — the prosecution need only show that "the police *would* inevitably have learned the [facts] from [the witness]." 808 F.2d at 1583 (emphasis supplied).

*   *   *

A uniform requirement of pre-recording witness knowledge in exquisite detail is unworkable. As even the greenest trial lawyer knows, the accrual of evidence is interactive — the statements of one witness often suggest new questions for earlier witnesses. Pre-recording of every line of every witness' trial testimony in every prosecution in which a defendant might publicly offer immunized testimony would ultimately prove unfeasible.

The consequences of a pre-recording requirement are both predictable and troubling. Prospective targets of grand juries in national scandals would line up to testify before Congress, in exchange for what is effectively transaction immunity. A requirement of "nonuse" would be converted into a guarantee of nonprosecution.

*   *   *

The majority is correct in noting that, if *Kastigar* is read only to apply to exposure of *prosecutors*, then "a private lawyer for a witness sympathetic to the government could listen to the compelled testimony and use it to prepare the witness." Opinion on Petition for Rehearing at 942. But it is also true that if *Kastigar* is read to require pre-recording of all government-witness testimony, then a witness *hostile* to the government could "listen to the compelled testimony and use it" to insulate himself from testifying.

There must be a middle ground, and I believe the case should be reheard (by the panel or *en banc*) to find it. The significance of these issues for the prosecution of future governmental scandals and for the effective functioning of separation of powers is too great to let the overreach of the original opinion (or my colleagues' undefined backtracking) stand.

* * *

NOTES AND QUESTIONS

1. *Tainted prosecutors.* In the *North* prosecution, the defendants testified under a grant of immunity before Congress in a widely-viewed national broadcast that spanned several weeks during the summer of 1987. The independent counsel unsuccessfully sought to have Congress delay the public testimony until after the filing of the criminal charges. Members of the Office of Independent Counsel avoided exposure to this immunized public testimony through a variety of extreme measures in order to remain "untainted." Attorneys who were subsequently hired, including Professor Sandra Jordan (one of the co-authors of this text), were exposed to this immunized testimony and deemed to be "tainted" by this exposure.

2. *Exposure to immunized testimony.* Ultimately, individuals were deemed "tainted" in the following situations: those who had watched some or all of the immunized testimony in the preceding summer months before joining the office as an associate independent counsel; individuals exposed to news stories that were publicized with regularity in national and international media; and members of the public who did not take extraordinary steps to protect against exposure to immunized testimony. For example, Professor Jordan watched, along with the majority of the country, the Congressional hearings some nine months before she joined the Independent Counsel's prosecution team.

3. *Challenges to avoid taint.* The structure of the Independent Counsel's office was unique in almost every way. Those staff members who had taken great steps to insulate themselves from taint were only permitted to read news clippings that had been redacted (with objectionable sections blackened out); they were also instructed to avoid any commercial news broadcasts and to not receive information or communications directly from the tainted members of the staff. Thus, tainted members were one-way recipients of information from all sources, but the information and leads could not flow in the opposite direction to the untainted attorneys and investigators.

4. *Threat to evidence gathering.* Given the court's ruling, what can a prosecutor's office do to maintain the separation of material gathered pursuant to an order of immunity? If the extraordinary measures taken in the *North* case were insufficient to overcome the hurdle, what is the answer to the tension between immunized testimony and evidence gathering? *See* Sandra D. Jordan, *Classified*

Information and Conflicts: Balancing the Scales of Justice After Iran-Contra, 91 Colum. L. Rev. 1651 (1991).

5. *Benefits of immunity.* Immunity is not the only benefit available to a witness. Other advantageous bargains include cooperation agreements, informal immunity, dismissal of charges, sentencing recommendations, and outright declination of the prosecution.

6. *Prosecuting an immunized witness.* The United States Department of Justice has imposed strict procedures for situations where it is considering prosecution of an immunized witness. Although § 6002 immunity suggests the possibility of prosecuting an immunized witness, the United States Attorneys' Manual provides additional safeguards beyond the simple fact of the origin of the "independent evidence." U.S. Department of Justice, U.S.A.M. § 9-23.400. In addition to written authorization from the Attorney General, the prosecutor must "indicate the circumstances justifying prosecution and the method by which the government will be able to establish that the evidence it will use against the witness will meet the government's burden under *Kastigar v. United States.*" *Id.* Once a witness has testified under a grant of immunity, the witness has met the threshold requirement as long as the current prosecution is related to the immunized testimony. At this point, the burden shifts to the government to establish that its evidence was derived from an independent source. These hearings are commonly known as "*Kastigar* hearings" and are conducted at any point during the proceedings when the issue of the use of the immunized testimony arises.

PROBLEMS

17-1. The defendant, an FBI agent, was charged with knowingly and willfully making a materially false statement on his federal disclosure report (DR) regarding gifts given to him by a cooperating witness. Because of his position in the FBI, the defendant was responsible for training other agents on the impropriety of accepting gifts in connection with their official duties. The defendant allegedly received several free trips to Las Vegas provided by a cooperating witness, and these trips were not reported on his annual DR.

In an internal government investigation, the lead investigator obtained a statement that the defendant had been compelled to give in during a hearing "in an unrelated administrative investigation." In this unrelated statement, the defendant was under oath and was advised that none of the information obtained via the statement could be used against him in a later criminal or administrative proceeding. In the statement, the defendant described his role in "advising the other agents about the propriety of accepting free gifts."

The pertinent timeline shows the following:

- Defendant completed the DR in December Year 00;
- Defendant gave the statement in the administrative hearing in February Year 01;
- The investigation into the false statements in the DR was initiated in July Year 01;
- That July, the investigator requested a copy of the February statement;

- For a period of a year after the investigator requested the February statement, the investigator interviewed witnesses, reviewed the financial documentation supporting the Las Vegas trips, and began to construct a case theory;

- After this year-long investigation, the investigator received the copy of the February Year 01 statement in July Year 02. The investigator read the file of the administrative investigation, and sent an email summarizing its contents to other investigators in the office. One of them replied, "Thanks. Have we looked for other instances where defendant gave advice on free gifts?"

- Two months later, in September Year 02, the investigator presented the case to the United States Attorney's Office for possible prosecution. The defendant was indicted the following month.

The defendant has filed a motion for a *Kastigar* hearing, which the court granted.

a. You represent the defendant. What specific questions do you ask your client in preparation for the Kastigar *hearing? What legal standard must you meet to be successful?*

b. You are the Assistant U. S. Attorney assigned to this case. After interviewing the chief investigative agent, what questions do you ask the agent in preparation for the Kastigar *hearing? Are there any other witnesses you should interview? What legal standard must you meet to be successful?*

c. Argue both the defense and government positions at the hearing.

d. How should the court rule? Why?

17-2. You represent a defendant who is serving five years probation for possessing child pornography in violation of federal law. One of the conditions of his probation was that he submit to periodic and random polygraph examinations. Defendant raised a Fifth Amendment challenge, but the judge ruled that he had to submit to the polygraph on the ground that he was not entitled to immunity before he made incriminating statements. Defendant refused to submit to the polygraph without a grant of immunity, and the court revoked his probation.

Defendant appeals. What arguments should the defendant make? How should the government respond? How should the court rule? Why?

17-3. Robert is a real-estate agent who was involved in real-estate transactions with members of a real-estate fraud scheme. The United States Attorney wrote a letter to Robert's attorney granting Robert "informal immunity" for his testimony regarding the scheme. Robert was interviewed by the U.S. Attorney's office on two occasions, after which the government decided to seek formal use/derivative use immunity for Robert and to call him to testify before the grand jury. Robert then testified before the grand jury.

One year later, the government is considering charging Robert with bank fraud, mail fraud, and money laundering in connection with the real-estate fraud scheme. The U.S. Attorney sought the authority to prosecute from the Department of Justice, providing a summary of the immunized grand jury testimony and stating that the government believed that Robert testified falsely. The government did not have sufficient evidence to prosecute Robert for perjury. The U.S. Attorney's office listed several independent sources from which it received evidence that Robert was involved in criminal activity in connection with the fraud scheme:

a. Testimony from several of the fraud scheme leaders indicating that Robert had aided them in fraudulently purchasing real estate.

b. Documents obtained from Robert after he testified under immunity as to their existence.

c. Testimony from Robert's wife that ever since Robert appeared before the grand jury, she has suspected that Robert was involved in criminal activity because she heard him make incriminating statements on the phone.

d. Testimony from Robert's assistant, whose identity was revealed by Robert's testimony before the grand jury.

Assume that you work for the Department of Justice and must approve the prosecution. Would you do so? Why or why not?

[C] DOCUMENTS

Because of the nature of white collar criminal investigations, the wrongdoing is frequently proven through documents. The paper trail often establishes both the mens rea and the actus reus. The money trail might be found in financial institution documents as well as business and personal records. Thus, an issue of critical importance in these types of paper investigations is the proper handling and production of documents, especially where the production of the documents can be incriminating.

Business records may provide critical evidence to prosecutors in a white collar case. Because the Fifth Amendment does not extend to artificial entities like corporations, there are no legitimate objections to the production of corporate documents pursuant to the grand jury subpoena. Because a corporation is entitled to no Fifth Amendment protection, when a subpoena is served on the corporation for documents, the corporation must comply with the subpoena absent some other legal objection. Once a grand jury subpoena is properly issued to the holder of the records, the custodian must come forth and produce the records to the grand jury. A custodian of records can typically be an employee insulated from any allegations of criminal wrongdoing and, as a result, such subpoena *duces tecum* sparks no personal Fifth Amendment concerns. Examples of these types of witnesses are bank employees or corporate employees who work in the records divisions. The question takes on a different character when the grand jury subpoena seeks the records of a sole proprietor who has a personal Fifth Amendment claim.

UNITED STATES v. DOE (Doe I)
465 U.S. 605 (1984)

JUSTICE POWELL delivered the opinion of the Court.

This case presents the issue whether, and to what extent, the Fifth Amendment privilege against compelled self-incrimination applies to the business records of a sole proprietorship.

Respondent is the owner of several sole proprietorships. In late 1980, a grand jury, during the course of an investigation of corruption in the awarding of county and municipal contracts, served five subpoenas on respondent. The first two demanded the production of the telephone records of several of respondent's companies and all records pertaining to four bank accounts of respondent and his companies. The subpoenas were limited to the period between January 1, 1977 and the dates of the subpoenas. The third subpoena demanded the production of a list of virtually all the business records of one of respondent's companies for the period between January 1, 1976, and the date of the subpoena. The fourth subpoena sought production of a similar list of business records belonging to another company. The final subpoena demanded production of all bank statements and cancelled checks of two of respondent's companies that had accounts at a bank in the Grand Cayman Islands.

Respondent filed a motion in Federal District Court seeking to quash the subpoenas. The District Court for the District of New Jersey granted his motion except with respect to those documents and records required by law to be kept or disclosed to a public agency. In reaching its decision, the District Court noted that the Government had conceded that the materials sought in the subpoena were or might be incriminating. The court stated that, therefore, "the relevant inquiry is . . . whether the *act* of producing the documents has communicative aspects which warrant Fifth Amendment protection." *In re Grand Jury Empanelled March 19, 1980*, 541 F. Supp. 1, 3 (D.C.N.J. 1981). The court found that the act of production would compel respondent to "admit that the records exist, that they are in his possession, and that they are authentic." While not ruling out the possibility that the Government could devise a way to ensure that the act of turning over the documents would not incriminate respondent, the court held that the Government had not made such a showing.

The Court of Appeals for the Third Circuit affirmed. It first addressed the question whether the Fifth Amendment ever applies to the records of a sole proprietorship. After noting that an individual may not assert the Fifth Amendment privilege on behalf of a corporation, partnership, or other collective entity, the Court of Appeals reasoned that the owner of a sole proprietorship acts in a personal rather than a representative capacity. As a result, the court held that respondent's claim of the privilege was not foreclosed.

The Court of Appeals next considered whether the documents at issue in this case are privileged. The court noted that the contents of business records ordinarily are not privileged because they are created voluntarily and without compulsion. The Court of Appeals nevertheless found that respondent's business records were privileged under either of two analyses. First, the court reasoned that, the business records of a sole proprietorship are no different from the individual owner's personal records. Noting that Third Circuit cases had held that private papers, although created voluntarily, are protected by the Fifth Amendment, the court accorded the same protection to respondent's business papers. Second, it held that respondent's act of producing the subpoenaed records would have "communicative aspects of its own." *In re Grand Jury Empanelled March 19, 1980*, 680 F.2d 327, 335 (3d Cir. 1982). The turning over of the subpoenaed documents to the grand jury would admit their existence and authenticity. Accordingly, respondent was entitled to assert his Fifth Amendment privilege rather than produce the subpoenaed documents.

The Government contended that the court should enforce the subpoenas because of the Government's offer not to use respondent's act of production against respondent in any way. The Court of Appeals noted that no formal request for use immunity under 18 U.S.C. §§ 6002 and 6003 had been made. In light of this failure, the court held that the District Court did not err in rejecting the Government's attempt to compel delivery of the subpoenaed records.

We granted certiorari to resolve the apparent conflict between the Court of Appeals holding and the reasoning underlying this Court's holding in *Fisher v. United States*, 425 U.S. 391 (1976). We now affirm in part, reverse in part, and remand for further proceedings.

The Court in *Fisher* expressly declined to reach the question whether the Fifth Amendment privilege protects the contents of an individual's tax records in his possession. The rationale underlying our holding in that case is, however, persuasive here. As we noted in *Fisher*, the Fifth Amendment protects the person asserting the privilege only from *compelled* self-incrimination. 425 U.S. at 396. Where the preparation of business records is voluntary, no compulsion is present.[8] A subpoena that demands production of documents "does not compel oral testimony; nor would it ordinarily compel the taxpayer to restate, repeat, or affirm the truth of the contents of the documents sought." *Id.* at 409. Applying this reasoning in *Fisher*, we stated:

> [T]he Fifth Amendment would not be violated by the fact alone that the papers on their face might incriminate the taxpayer, for the privilege protects a person only against being incriminated by his own compelled testimonial communications. *The accountant's workpapers are not the taxpayer's. They were not prepared by the taxpayer, and they contain no testimonial declarations by him. Furthermore, as far as this record demonstrates, the preparation of all of the papers sought in these cases was wholly voluntary, and they cannot be said to contain compelled testimonial evidence, either of the taxpayers or of anyone else. The taxpayer cannot avoid compliance with the subpoena merely by asserting that the item of evidence which he is required to produce contains incriminating writing, whether his own or that of someone else.*

Id. at 409–410.

This reasoning applies with equal force here. Respondent does not contend that he prepared the documents involuntarily or that the subpoena would force him to restate, repeat, or affirm the truth of their contents. The fact that the records are in respondent's possession is irrelevant to the determination of whether the creation of the records was compelled. We therefore hold that the contents of those records are not privileged.

Although the contents of a document may not be privileged, the act of producing the document may be. A government subpoena compels the holder of the document to perform an act that may have testimonial aspects and an incriminating effect.

---

[8] Respondent's principal argument is that the Fifth Amendment should be read as creating a "zone of privacy which protects an individual and his personal records from compelled production." Brief for Respondent 15. This argument derives from language in Boyd v. United States, 116 U.S. 616 (1886). This Court addressed substantially the same argument in *Fisher*:

> Within the limits imposed by the language of the Fifth Amendment, which we necessarily observe, the privilege truly serves privacy interests; but the Court has never on any ground, personal privacy included, applied the Fifth Amendment to prevent the otherwise proper acquisition or use of evidence which, in the Court's view, did not involve compelled testimonial self-incrimination of some sort.

425 U.S. at 399.

* * *

In *Fisher*, the Court explored the effect that the act of production would have on the taxpayer and determined that the act of production would have only minimal testimonial value and would not operate to incriminate the taxpayer. Unlike the Court in *Fisher*, we have the explicit finding of the District Court that the act of producing the documents would involve testimonial self-incrimination. The Court of Appeals agreed. We therefore decline to overturn the finding of the District Court in this regard, where, as here, it has been affirmed by the Court of Appeals.

The Government, as it concedes, could have compelled respondent to produce the documents listed in the subpoena. Sections 6002 and 6003 of Title 18 provide for the granting of use immunity with respect to the potentially incriminating evidence. The Court upheld the constitutionality of the use immunity statute in *Kastigar v. United States*, 406 U.S. 441 (1972).

The Government did state several times before the District Court that it would not use respondent's act of production against him in any way. But counsel for the Government never made a statutory request to the District Court to grant respondent use immunity. We are urged to adopt a doctrine of constructive use immunity. Under this doctrine, the courts would impose a requirement on the Government not to use the incriminatory aspects of the act of production against the person claiming the privilege even though the statutory procedures have not been followed.

We decline to extend the jurisdiction of courts to include prospective grants of use immunity in the absence of the formal request that the statute requires-. . . . The decision to seek use immunity necessarily involves a balancing of the Government's interest in obtaining information against the risk that immunity will frustrate the Government's attempts to prosecute the subject of the investigation. Congress expressly left this decision exclusively to the Justice Department. If, on remand, the appropriate official concludes that it is desirable to compel respondent to produce his business records, the statutory procedure for requesting use immunity will be available.

We conclude that the Court of Appeals erred in holding that the contents of the subpoenaed documents were privileged under the Fifth Amendment. The act of producing the documents at issue in this case is privileged and cannot be compelled without a statutory grant of use immunity pursuant to 18 U.S.C. §§ 6002 and 6003. The judgment of the Court of Appeals is, therefore, affirmed in part, reversed in part, and the case is remanded to the District Court for further proceedings in accordance with this decision.

It is so ordered.

JUSTICE O'CONNOR, concurring. [Omitted.]

JUSTICE MARSHALL, with JUSTICE BRENNAN joins, concurring in part and dissenting in part. [Omitted.]

JUSTICE STEVENS, concurring in part and dissenting in part. [Omitted.]

NOTES AND QUESTIONS

1. *Delivery of records.* If John Doe had given the records to another individual to deliver to the grand jury, could the issue that concerned the Court have been avoided? Why or why not?

2. *Immunity guarantees.* During the oral argument, the Court questioned the government as to why it never requested the official use immunity pursuant to the statutory authority. The government "gave no plausible explanation," but simply promised that the documents would not be used against Doe after production. Why is this guarantee insufficient?

3. *Collective entity doctrine.* In *Amato v. United States*, 450 F.3d 46 (1st Cir. 2006), the court established the rule in the First Circuit for the collective entity doctrine and its application to a corporation consisting of only one person. In *Amato*, the defendant was the "sole shareholder, director, officer and employee" of two corporations. *Id.* at 47. The U.S. Attorney's office served subpoenas on Amato for the corporation's records because he was the "records custodian." *Id.* at 47–48. The defendant moved to quash the subpoenas, arguing "that the act-of-production doctrine protects production of the records because the testimonial aspects of the production would incriminate him." *Id.* He asserted that the "collective-entity doctrine" did not apply to his case because "a footnote in *Braswell v. United States* . . . left open the question of whether the collective-entity doctrine would apply if the custodian of corporate records is 'able to establish, by showing for example that he is the sole employee and officer of the corporation, that the jury would inevitably conclude that he produced the records.' " *Id.* at 48. (*Braswell* held that "[a] corporation does not enjoy the privilege against self incrimination guaranteed by the Fifth Amendment, as the privilege is a personal privilege enjoyed by natural individuals." *Id.* at 49). The magistrate judge refused to accept Amato's argument because "the First Circuit has rejected such an exception" and "*Braswell*'s footnote does not contradict the First Circuit's holdings." *Id.* at 48. The district court upheld the magistrate judge's decision. *Id.* at 49.

The First Circuit did not find the footnote in *Braswell* to be controlling, and instead relied on its holding in *In re Grand Jury Proceedings (The John Doe Company, Inc.)*, 838 F.2d 624 (1st Cir. 1988). *Amato*, 450 F.3d at 51. In *John Doe Company*, the First Circuit held that "the act-of-production doctrine is not an exception to the collective-entity doctrine even when the corporate custodian is the corporation's sole shareholder, officer and employee." 838 F.2d at 627 n.3. *John Doe* held that " 'production, including implied authentication, can be required of a corporation through a corporate officer regardless of the potential for self-incrimination.' " *Amato*, 450 F.3d at 52 (quoting *John Doe Company*, 838 F.2d at 626). Even though Amato was the sole employee and officer of the corporation, he still did not qualify for an "act of production" exception to the "collective-entity" doctrine. *Id.* at 51.

PROBLEMS

17-4. You represent a real-estate firm, Howdy Real Estate, with one local office in your town. The firm is a sole proprietorship and you discover that the government is investigating the illegal funneling of monies through certain bank accounts in a widespread money laundering scheme.

Your client, Howdy, owns Howdy Real Estate. Howdy was your college roommate. The federal authorities serve a grand jury subpoena on the office receptionist requesting that records for the previous three fiscal years be produced for the grand jury. Howdy's wife Happy is the receptionist for the firm. There are no more employees in the office because all of the other real-estate agents are independent contractors and maintain their offices in their homes.

You oppose the production of these business records. What motion do you file and what legal basis do you offer for your opposition?

17-5. Your motion has been denied. You now face the prospect of having Howdy or Happy appear before the grand jury with the records.

What other steps can you take to protect your client? Does your answer depend on whether Howdy or his wife appears with the records? Why or why not?

17-6. Depending on how you analyzed question 17.2, your client is now ready to make the appearance before the grand jury. You know that you cannot accompany him into the grand jury room.

What precautions do you take to fully represent him at this critical stage of the investigation?

*   *   *

The next case involves the Whitewater investigation. Twenty years before President Clinton was elected, he and Hillary Clinton joined a partnership with James and Susan McDougal called the Whitewater Development Corp. The partnership purchased 220 acres of land in Arkansas. James McDougal owned a savings and loan association which became insolvent in the 1980s as a result of a series of fraudulent loans. Hillary Clinton performed legal services for the savings and loan.

During the 1980s, there were investigations of many savings and loans failures. The McDougals were both found guilty of fraud. An independent counsel, Kenneth Starr, was appointed, and the Whitewater investigation grew to include the Clintons' financial and legal activities associated with the savings and loan as well as the Clintons' response to questions about the transactions and improprieties in the White House travel office. The next case arose from the Whitewater investigation, and centers on document production and the Fifth Amendment privilege against self incrimination.

UNITED STATES v. HUBBELL
530 U.S. 27 (2000)

JUSTICE STEVENS delivered the opinion of the Court.

The two questions presented concern the scope of a witness' protection against compelled self-incrimination: (1) whether the Fifth Amendment privilege protects a witness from being compelled to disclose the existence of incriminating documents that the Government is unable to describe with reasonable particularity; and (2) if the witness produces such documents pursuant to a grant of immunity, whether 18 U.S.C. § 6002 prevents the Government from using them to prepare criminal charges against him.

This proceeding arises out of the second prosecution of respondent, Webster Hubbell, commenced by the Independent Counsel appointed in August 1994 to investigate possible violations of federal law relating to the Whitewater Development Corporation. The first prosecution was terminated pursuant to a plea bargain. In December 1994, respondent pleaded guilty to charges of mail fraud and tax evasion arising out of his billing practices as a member of an Arkansas law firm from 1989 to 1992, and was sentenced to 21 months in prison. In the plea agreement, respondent promised to provide the Independent Counsel with "full, complete, accurate, and truthful information" about matters relating to the Whitewater investigation.

The second prosecution resulted from the Independent Counsel's attempt to determine whether respondent had violated that promise. In October 1996, while respondent was incarcerated, the Independent Counsel served him with a subpoena *duces tecum* calling for the production of 11 categories of documents before a grand jury sitting in Little Rock, Arkansas. On November 19, he appeared before the grand jury and invoked his Fifth Amendment privilege against self-incrimination. In response to questioning by the prosecutor, respondent initially refused "to state whether there are documents within my possession, custody, or control responsive to the Subpoena." Thereafter, the prosecutor produced an order, which had previously been obtained from the District Court pursuant to 18 U.S.C. § 6003(a) directing him to respond to the subpoena and granting him immunity "to the extent allowed by law." Respondent then produced 13,120 pages of documents and records and responded to a series of questions that established that those were all of the documents in his custody or control that were responsive to the commands in the subpoena, with the exception of a few documents he claimed were shielded by the attorney-client and attorney work-product privileges.

The contents of the documents produced by respondent provided the Independent Counsel with the information that led to this second prosecution. On April 30, 1998, a grand jury in the District of Columbia returned a 10-count indictment charging respondent with various tax-related crimes and mail and wire fraud. The District Court dismissed the indictment relying, in part, on the ground that the Independent Counsel's use of the subpoenaed documents violated § 6002 because all of the evidence he would offer against respondent at trial derived either directly or indirectly from the testimonial aspects of respondent's immunized act of producing those documents. . . .

The Court of Appeals vacated the judgment and remanded for further proceedings. The majority concluded that the District Court had incorrectly relied on the fact that the Independent Counsel did not have prior knowledge of the contents of the subpoenaed documents. The question the District Court should have addressed was the extent of the Government's independent knowledge of the documents' existence and authenticity, and of respondent's possession or control of them. It explained:

> On remand, the district court should hold a hearing in which it seeks to establish the extent and detail of the [G]overnment's knowledge of Hubbell's financial affairs (or of the paperwork documenting it) on the day the subpoena issued. It is only then that the court will be in a position to assess the testimonial value of Hubbell's response to the subpoena. Should the Independent Counsel prove capable of demonstrating with reasonable particularity a prior awareness that the exhaustive litany of documents

sought in the subpoena existed and were in Hubbell's possession, then the wide distance evidently traveled from the subpoena to the substantive allegations contained in the indictment would be based upon legitimate intermediate steps. To the extent that the information conveyed through Hubbell's compelled act of production provides the necessary linkage, however, the indictment deriving therefrom is tainted.

United States v. Hubbell, 167 F.3d 552, 581 (D.C. Cir. 1999).

In the opinion of the dissenting judge, the majority failed to give full effect to the distinction between the contents of the documents and the limited testimonial significance of the act of producing them. In his view, as long as the prosecutor could make use of information contained in the documents or derived therefrom without any reference to the fact that respondent had produced them in response to a subpoena, there would be no improper use of the testimonial aspect of the immunized act of production. In other words, the constitutional privilege and the statute conferring use immunity would only shield the witness from the use of any information resulting from his subpoena response "beyond what the prosecutor would receive if the documents appeared in the grand jury room or in his office unsolicited and unmarked, like manna from heaven." *In re Minarik*, 166 F.3d 591, 602 (3d Cir. 1999).

On remand, the Independent Counsel acknowledged that he could not satisfy the "reasonable particularity" standard prescribed by the Court of Appeals and entered into a conditional plea agreement with respondent. In essence, the agreement provides for the dismissal of the charges unless this Court's disposition of the case makes it reasonably likely that respondent's "act [of] production immunity" would not pose a significant bar to his prosecution. The case is not moot, however, because the agreement also provides for the entry of a guilty plea and a sentence that will not include incarceration if we should reverse and issue an opinion that is sufficiently favorable to the Government to satisfy that condition. . . . We now affirm.

It is useful to preface our analysis of the constitutional issue with a restatement of certain propositions that are not in dispute. The term "privilege against self-incrimination" is not an entirely accurate description of a person's constitutional protection against being "compelled in any criminal case to be a witness against himself."

*   *   *

More relevant to this case is the settled proposition that a person may be required to produce specific documents even though they contain incriminating assertions of fact or belief because the creation of those documents was not "compelled" within the meaning of the privilege. Our decision in *Fisher v. United States*, 425 U.S. 371 (1976), dealt with summonses issued by the Internal Revenue Service (IRS) seeking working papers used in the preparation of tax returns. Because the papers had been voluntarily prepared prior to the issuance of the summonses, they could not be "said to contain compelled testimonial evidence, either of the taxpayers or of anyone else." Accordingly, the taxpayer could not "avoid compliance with the subpoena merely by asserting that the item of evidence which he is required to produce contains incriminating writing, whether his own or that of someone else." 425 U.S. at 409–10. It is clear, therefore, that respondent Hubbell could not avoid compliance with the subpoena served on him merely because the demanded documents contained incriminating evidence, whether written by others or voluntarily prepared by himself.

On the other hand, we have also made it clear that the act of producing documents in response to a subpoena may have a compelled testimonial aspect. We have held that "the act of production" itself may implicitly communicate "statements of fact." By "producing documents in compliance with a subpoena, the witness would admit that the papers existed, were in his possession or control, and were authentic." *United States v. Doe*, 465 U.S. 605, 613 (1984). Moreover, as was true in this case, when the custodian of documents responds to a subpoena, he may be compelled to take the witness stand and answer questions designed to determine whether he has produced everything demanded by the subpoena. . . .

Finally, the phrase "in any criminal case" in the text of the Fifth Amendment might have been read to limit its coverage to compelled testimony that is used against the defendant in the trial itself. It has, however, long been settled that its protection encompasses compelled statements that lead to the discovery of incriminating evidence even though the statements themselves are not incriminating and are not introduced into evidence. . . .

Compelled testimony that communicates information that may "lead to incriminating evidence" is privileged even if the information itself is not inculpatory. *Doe v. United States*, 487 U.S. 201, 208 n.6 (1988). It is the Fifth Amendment's protection against the prosecutor's use of incriminating information derived directly or indirectly from the compelled testimony of the respondent that is of primary relevance in this case.

Acting pursuant to 18 U.S.C. § 6002, the District Court entered an order compelling respondent to produce "any and all documents" described in the grand jury subpoena and granting him "immunity to the extent allowed by law." In *Kastigar v. United States*, 406 U.S. 441 (1972), we upheld the constitutionality of § 6002 because the scope of the "use and derivative-use" immunity that it provides is coextensive with the scope of the constitutional privilege against self-incrimination. . . .

We also rejected the petitioners' argument that derivative-use immunity under § 6002 would not obviate the risk that the prosecutor or other law enforcement officials may use compelled testimony to obtain leads, names of witnesses, or other information not otherwise available to support a prosecution. That argument was predicated on the incorrect assumption that the derivative-use prohibition would prove impossible to enforce. But given that the statute contains a "comprehensive safeguard" in the form of a "sweeping proscription of any use, direct or indirect, of the compelled testimony and any information derived therefrom," we concluded that a person who is prosecuted for matters related to testimony he gave under a grant of immunity does not have the burden of proving that his testimony was improperly used. Instead, we held that the statute imposes an affirmative duty on the prosecution, not merely to show that its evidence is not tainted by the prior testimony, but "to prove that the evidence it proposes to use is derived from a legitimate source wholly independent of the compelled testimony." 406 U.S. at 460. Requiring the prosecution to shoulder this burden ensures that the grant of immunity has "le[ft] the witness and the Federal Government in substantially the same position as if the witness had claimed his privilege in the absence of a grant of immunity." 406 U.S. at 458–59.

The "compelled testimony" that is relevant in this case is not to be found in the contents of the documents produced in response to the subpoena. It is, rather, the testimony inherent in the act of producing those documents. The disagreement between the parties focuses entirely on the significance of that testimonial aspect.

The Government correctly emphasizes that the testimonial aspect of a response to a subpoena *duces tecum* does nothing more than establish the existence, authenticity, and custody of items that are produced. We assume that the Government is also entirely correct in its submission that it would not have to advert to respondent's act of production in order to prove the existence, authenticity, or custody of any documents that it might offer in evidence at a criminal trial; indeed, the Government disclaims any need to introduce any of the documents produced by respondent into evidence in order to prove the charges against him. It follows, according to the Government, that it has no intention of making improper "use" of respondent's compelled testimony.

The question, however, is not whether the response to the subpoena may be introduced into evidence at his criminal trial. That would surely be a prohibited "use" of the immunized act of production. But the fact that the Government intends no such use of the act of production leaves open the separate question whether it has already made "derivative use" of the testimonial aspect of that act in obtaining the indictment against respondent and in preparing its case for trial. It clearly has.

It is apparent from the text of the subpoena itself that the prosecutor needed respondent's assistance both to identify potential sources of information and to produce those sources. . . . The documents did not magically appear in the prosecutor's office like "manna from heaven." They arrived there only after respondent asserted his constitutional privilege, received a grant of immunity, and — under the compulsion of the District Court's order — took the mental and physical steps necessary to provide the prosecutor with an accurate inventory of the many sources of potentially incriminating evidence sought by the subpoena. It was only through respondent's truthful reply to the subpoena that the Government received the incriminating documents of which it made "substantial use . . . in the investigation that led to the indictment." Brief for United States 3.

For these reasons, we cannot accept the Government's submission that respondent's immunity did not preclude its derivative use of the produced documents because its "possession of the documents [was] the fruit *only* of a simple physical act — the act of producing the documents." *Id.* at 29. It was unquestionably necessary for respondent to make extensive use of "the contents of his own mind" in identifying the hundreds of documents responsive to the requests in the subpoena. . . .

In sum, we have no doubt that the constitutional privilege against self-incrimination protects the target of a grand jury investigation from being compelled to answer questions designed to elicit information about the existence of sources of potentially incriminating evidence. . . . On appeal and again before this Court, however, the Government has argued that the communicative aspect of respondent's act of producing ordinary business records is insufficiently "testimonial" to support a claim of privilege because the existence and possession of such records by any businessman is a "foregone conclusion" under our decision in *Fisher v. United States*, 425 U.S. at 411. This argument both misreads *Fisher* and ignores our subsequent decision in *United States v. Doe*, 465 U.S. 605 (1984). . . .

Given our conclusion that respondent's act of production had a testimonial aspect, at least with respect to the existence and location of the documents sought by the Government's subpoena, respondent could not be compelled to produce those documents without first receiving a grant of immunity under § 6003. As we construed § 6002 in *Kastigar*, such immunity is coextensive with the constitutional privilege. *Kastigar* requires that respondent's motion to dismiss the indictment on immunity grounds be granted unless the Government proves that the evidence it used in obtaining the indictment and proposed to use at trial was derived from legitimate sources "wholly independent" of the testimonial aspect of respondent's immunized conduct in assembling and producing the documents described in the subpoena. The Government, however, does not claim that it could make such a showing. Rather, it contends that its prosecution of respondent must be considered proper unless someone — presumably respondent — shows that "there is some substantial relation between the compelled testimonial communications implicit in the act of production (as opposed to the act of production standing alone) and some aspect of the information used in the investigation or the evidence presented at trial." Brief for United States at 9. We could not accept this submission without repudiating the basis for our conclusion in *Kastigar* that the statutory guarantee of use and derivative-use immunity is as broad as the constitutional privilege itself. This we are not prepared to do.

Accordingly, the indictment against respondent must be dismissed. The judgment of the Court of Appeals is affirmed.

JUSTICE THOMAS, with whom JUSTICE SCALIA joins, concurring. [Omitted.]

NOTES AND QUESTIONS

1. *"Communicative aspect" of production.* The Court rejected the government's argument that "the communicative aspect of respondent's act of producing ordinary business records is insufficiently 'testimonial' to support a claim of privilege because the existence and possession of such records by any businessman is a 'foregone conclusion' under our decision in *Fisher* [and *Doe*]." How did the government's conclusion misread *Fisher* and *Doe*?

2. *Scope of act of production immunity.* Despite the clarification the Court hoped to provide with *Fisher* and *Doe*, there remains a great deal of confusion as to the proper extent and scope of the act of production immunity. Does *Hubbell* offer any clear guidance? For an analysis of the issues arising from the assertion of the Fifth Amendment privilege in response to grand jury subpoenas, see Sara Sun Beale & James E. Felman, *The Fifth Amendment and the Grand Jury*, Crim. Justice 4 (Spring 2007).

Many uncertainties remain in this context. For example, what protection, if any, does a corporate employee have if the employee has terminated the employment, but still possesses corporate records? In *In Re three Grand Jury Subpoenas Duces tecum*, 191 F.3d 173 (2d Cir. 1999), for example, former corporate officers were in possession of corporate records and received a federal grand jury subpoena. Did the employees have a valid Fifth Amendment right to refuse production because the documents were in their personal possession? Or, were the records corporate records that must be produced by the individuals as corporate representatives?

3. *Prior awareness.* In *United States v. Arizechi*, 2006 U.S. Dist. LEXIS 41012 (D.N.J. June 20, 2006), the government sought records relating to possible tax violations from two corporations of which Arizechi was the sole director, officer, shareholder, and employee. The government served a subpoena on Arizechi as custodian of records of the companies. Arizechi moved to quash, arguing that the government's request for records was "deficient because the government failed to demonstrate any 'prior awareness' of the documents sought." *Id.* at 13. He argued that *Hubbell* requires the government to prove a prior awareness that the documents existed and that the individual possessed them. *Id.* at 13–14. The court held that because Arizechi's corporation had no Fifth Amendment privilege, the government did not need to prove that "possession of the documents sought is a foregone conclusion" or that "production of those documents is not testimony." *Id.* at 14.

4. *Applying the* Hubbell *decision.* Courts are applying the *Hubbell* holding, with varying results. *See United States v. Ponds*, 454 F.3d 313 (D.C. Cir. 2006) (finding that *Hubbell* did not apply with respect to some subpoenaed documents because the government had prior knowledge of the existence and location of several types of documents subpoenaed, but that the government did not meet the particularity/ prior knowledge requirements for many of the other document types listed in the subpoena); *United States v. Marra*, 2005 U.S. Dist. LEXIS 23411, at *14 (D.N.J. 2005) (accountant for client under investigation was required to produce and authenticate documents as custodian of record, but could not be compelled to give further testimony without implicating the Fifth Amendment). Also, in *Armstrong v. Guccione*, 470 F.3d 89 (2d Cir. 2006), the Second Circuit found that *Hubbell* did not undermine *Braswell v. United States*, 487 U.S. 99 (1988) (holding that a corporate custodian could not invoke the Fifth Amendment as a basis for refusing to produce corporate records, even though the act of producing those records has independent testimonial significance that might incriminate the custodian personally).

5. *Defense witness immunity.* What should defense counsel do when one of the witnesses asserts the Fifth Amendment privilege and refuses to testify (favorably) for the defense? Assume that the witness will not testify without immunity, that the government refuses to immunize the witness, and that the defendant, as a result, cannot call the witness. Should the government be required to grant immunity? If so, why and under what circumstances? If not, what policy reasons support your conclusions?

In the article by Reid H. Weingarten & Brian M. Heberlig, *The Defense Witness Immunity Doctrine: The Time Has Come to Give it Strength to Address Prosecutorial Overreaching*, 43 Am. Crim. L. Rev. 1189 (2006), the authors argue that it is extremely difficult for a defendant to obtain immunity for defense witnesses because the prosecutors can manipulate the system in their favor through the guise of "prosecutorial discretion" and use of the co-conspirator exception to the hearsay rule. The authors argue that it should be easier for a defendant to show that the government has used immunity to gain a tactical advantage. *Id.* at 1192–1195. Also, they argue that "exculpatory evidence" should be defined broadly, especially in white collar cases, and that defendants should not have a hard time demonstrating that the testimony is unavailable from another source. *Id.* at 1196–1198. Do you agree?

In the Enron prosecution, *United States v. Skilling*, 2006 U.S. Dist. LEXIS 42664 (S.D. Tex. June 23, 2006), defendants Skilling and Lay filed a motion requesting court-ordered use immunity for proposed witnesses who had asserted their Fifth Amendment rights. The court denied the motion, finding a lack of authority under 18 U.S.C. § 6001 to grant immunity against the wishes of the government. The court held that the defendants had failed to show that the government had used its immunity privileges to unfairly skew the facts before the jury or that the government had no legitimate reason for refusing to immunize. The defendants also failed to show that the proposed witnesses would offer exculpatory testimony or that the government coerced the witnesses into asserting their Fifth Amendment rights.

In a Third Circuit case, the court recognized a Sixth Amendment right to immunization of witnesses who would provide exculpatory testimony for the defense. The defendant made the required showing that he was entitled to judicial use immunity by establishing that he was "prevented from presenting exculpatory evidence which is critical to his case." *United States v. Herman*, 589 F.2d 1191, 1204 (3d Cir. 1978). The court found that it had "inherent remedial power to require that the distortion be redressed by requiring a grant of use immunity to defense witnesses as an alternative to dismissal." Id.

Problems

17-7. As an Assistant United States Attorney, you are handling the Howdy Real Estate investigation. You decide to offer immunity to one of the independent real-estate agents who works with the firm. During your investigation, you become aware of information leading you to believe that Howdy Real Estate is funneling monies through Caribbean bank accounts in an effort to hide revenue that should be taxable. Based on your investigation thus far, you believe that individuals may have committed the crimes of tax fraud, money laundering, and conspiracy.

One of the independent associates, Knowall, has been to several real-estate closings where she assisted in the handling of the settlement of funds from the transactions. Knowall witnessed the division of the settlement accounts in such a way that she realized that the Howdys had created a separate account for the deposit of settlement proceeds. Although she is not sure where this account is located, she is willing to testify that the settlement records will show that monies were diverted into accounts other than the business account of the real-estate firm. The main real-estate account is the one from which she is paid her commissions, as is the case with the other agents working with Howdy Real Estate. The defense counsel says that Knowall will not testify without immunity. You do not know why she needs immunity.

Do you agree to seek immunity for her? What are the risks associated with this?

17-8. You have made the decision that Knowall is more valuable as a witness than as a subject or target, so you agree to proceed with the immunity request. Once you receive the approval to seek the court order granting immunity to Knowall, you take her into your office to prep her for the grand jury appearance. She tells you that she learned during conversations with the principals in the Howdy investigation that the money being used for mortgages "represents the proceeds of some form of unlawful activity." 18 U.S.C. § 1956(a)(1). Knowall denies having any direct connection with the diversion of the money to the Caribbean account or any other accounts. Once in the grand jury room, you begin to ask her questions related to separate bank accounts maintained by Mr. Howdy. During her testimony, it becomes evident to you that she was, in fact, the person who assisted in the funneling of the monies from the local agency bank to a bank account in the Caribbean. This directly contradicts her statement to you in your office as a proffer for the immunity request.

a. *Because she told the grand jury a story that differs from what she told you in your office, could you prosecute her for perjury or false statements? What do you say as you discuss this situation with your superiors?*

b. *If Ms. Knowall's involvement is more extensive that you had originally envisioned, should you use her as a witness in your case against Mr. and Mrs. Howdy? Why or why not?*

Chapter 18

CIVIL ACTIONS, CIVIL PENALTIES, AND PARALLEL PROCEEDINGS

[A] INTRODUCTORY NOTES

[1] Issues in Parallel Proceedings

This chapter builds upon the materials in Chapter 2, Corporate and Individual Liability, Chapter 16, The Grand Jury, and Chapter 17, Self-Incrimination — Witness Testimony and Document Production. The state and federal governments regulate white collar activities and impose civil penalties for a wide variety of business and other white collar conduct. Because federal and state agencies often impose civil penalties for regulatory wrongdoing, and then refer the matter for criminal investigation, astute counsel must closely monitor all civil and agency investigations. A corporation or individual may simultaneously confront parallel administrative, civil, and/or criminal actions based on the same or similar facts.

Compliance programs, internal investigations, and global settlements (i.e., settlements of pending administrative, civil, and/or criminal actions) demonstrate that corporate culture is adapting to the needs of the times. As law enforcement investigators target businesses, evidence preservation and employee loyalties become critical factors in many investigations. In addition, parallel proceedings present important issues concerning the right against self-incrimination, stays of parallel civil proceedings, and discovery. This chapter will explore the principal ethical and legal challenges resulting from the interplay between civil and criminal accountability.

[2] Civil and Agency Investigations

Specific federal agencies have primary responsibility for enforcing the laws related to their respective zones of authority. The investigative power is located within the specific agency's Office of Inspector General (OIG). The OIG and its staff monitor agency compliance, conduct audits, and supervise investigations regarding the laws specific to that agency. 5 U.S.C. app. 3 § 4(a). Many OIG investigations focus on fraud and abuse in government programs.

Agencies have the power to issue subpoenas. These subpoenas are very similar to grand jury subpoenas in that they compel the production of evidence in connection with the agencies' investigations. In addition, the Internal Revenue Service issues summonses, which are the equivalents of subpoenas. Courts have authority to review both the scope and propriety of subpoenas and summonses issued by federal agencies. A court exercises only limited review of an agency's actions in a subpoena enforcement proceeding, and does not normally consider the merits of a party's claim that it has not violated a statute or regulation administered by the agency.

Federal agencies depend on the courts for enforcement of both subpoenas and summonses. As a general rule, a court will enforce an administrative subpoena if: (1) it reasonably relates to an investigation within the agency's authority, (2) the specific inquiry is relevant to that purpose and is not too indefinite, (3) the proper administrative procedures have been followed, and (4) the subpoena does not demand information for an illegitimate purpose. *See CFTC v. Tokheim*, 153 F.3d 474, 477 (7th Cir. 1998); *EEOC v. Quad/Graphics, Inc.*, 63 F.3d 642, 645 (7th Cir. 1995).

Standing alone, federal agencies cannot institute criminal actions. Instead, they must refer matters to the Department of Justice for a determination of whether criminal charges may be appropriate.

[3] Deferred Prosecution

The government has begun to use pretrial diversion as another tool to address corporate wrongdoing. Corporate diversion agreements — deferred and non-prosecution agreements — allow the government to impose terms of probation before or without conviction. This controversial procedure permits corporations to avoid criminal prosecution during a probationary period, and at the same time, gives the prosecutor extensive control over determining whether the corporation has complied with the terms and conditions of the probation. Such agreements have affected the attorney-client privilege, the work-product protections, restitution, parallel proceedings, fines, compliance, and individual rights within the corporation. Because of their importance, deferred prosecution agreements are addressed in this chapter.

[B] CIVIL REMEDIES

[1] Fines

Conduct that gives rise to criminal liability will often also subject the corporation or individual to civil fines and regulations. A legal matter may be resolved civilly with remedies including injunctions, forfeitures, restitution, and/or fines. When a corporation is obligated to pay a civil penalty, many of the constitutional protections that accompany criminal penalties do not apply. The question whether a civil penalty is sufficiently punitive to be equivalent to a criminal penalty has plagued the courts. In the next case, the Supreme Court addressed this issue under the Double Jeopardy Clause.

HUDSON v. UNITED STATES
522 U.S. 93 (1997)

CHIEF JUSTICE REHNQUIST delivered the opinion of the Court.

The Government administratively imposed monetary penalties and occupational debarment on petitioners for violation of federal banking statutes, and later criminally indicted them for essentially the same conduct. We hold that the Double Jeopardy Clause of the Fifth Amendment is not a bar to the later criminal prosecution because the administrative proceedings were civil, not criminal. Our reasons for so holding in large part disavow the method of analysis used in *United States v. Halper*, 490 U.S. 435, 448 (1989), and reaffirm the previously established rule exemplified in *United States v. Ward*, 448 U.S. 242, 248–49 (1980).

During the early and mid-1980's, petitioner John Hudson was the chairman and controlling shareholder of the First National Bank of Tipton (Tipton) and the First National Bank of Hammon (Hammon). During the same period, petitioner Jack Rackley was president of Tipton and a member of the board of directors of Hammon, and petitioner Larry Baresel was a member of the board of directors of both Tipton and Hammon.

An examination of Tipton and Hammon led the Office of the Comptroller of the Currency (OCC) to conclude that petitioners had used their bank positions to arrange a series of loans to third parties in violation of various federal banking statutes and regulations. According to the OCC, those loans, while nominally made to third parties, were in reality made to Hudson in order to enable him to redeem bank stock that he had pledged as collateral on defaulted loans.

On February 13, 1989, OCC issued a "Notice of Assessment of Civil Money Penalty." The notice alleged that petitioners had violated 12 U.S.C. §§ 84(a)(1) and 375b (1982 ed.) and 12 C.F.R. §§ 31.2(b) and 215.4(b) (1986) by causing the banks with which they were associated to make loans to nominee borrowers in a manner that unlawfully allowed Hudson to receive the benefit of the loans. The notice also alleged that the illegal loans resulted in losses to Tipton and Hammon of almost $900,000 and contributed to the failure of those banks. However, the notice contained no allegation of any harm to the Government as a result of petitioners' conduct. "After taking into account the size of the financial resources and the good faith of [petitioners], the gravity of the violations, the history of previous violations and other matters as justice may require, as required by 12 U.S.C. §§ 93(b)(2) and 504(b)," OCC assessed penalties of $100,000 against Hudson and $50,000 each against Rackley and Baresel. *Id.* at 89a. [App. to Pet. for Cert.] On August 31, 1989, OCC also issued a "Notice of Intention to Prohibit Further Participation" against each petitioner. These notices, which were premised on the identical allegations that formed the basis for the previous notices, informed petitioners that OCC intended to bar them from further participation in the conduct of "any insured depository institution." *Id.* at 100a.

In October 1989, petitioners resolved the OCC proceedings against them by each entering into a "Stipulation and Consent Order." These consent orders provided that Hudson, Baresel, and Rackley would pay assessments of $16,500, $15,000, and $12,500 respectively. In addition, each petitioner agreed not to "participate in any manner" in the affairs of any banking institution without the written authorization of the OCC and all other relevant regulatory agencies.

In August 1992, petitioners were indicted in the Western District of Oklahoma in a 22-count indictment on charges of conspiracy, 18 U.S.C. § 371, misapplication of bank funds, §§ 656 and 2, and making false bank entries, § 1005. The violations charged in the indictment rested on the same lending transactions that formed the basis for the prior administrative actions brought by OCC. Petitioners moved to dismiss the indictment on double jeopardy grounds, but the District Court denied the motions. The Court of Appeals affirmed the District Court's holding on the nonparticipation sanction issue, but vacated and remanded to the District Court on the money sanction issue. The District Court on remand granted petitioners' motion to dismiss the indictments. This time the Government appealed, and the Court of Appeals reversed. That court held, following *Halper*, that the actual fines imposed by the Government were not as grossly disproportional to the proved damages to the Government as to render the sanctions "punishment" for double jeopardy purposes. We granted certiorari because of concerns about the wide variety of novel double jeopardy claims spawned in the wake of *Halper*. We now affirm, but for different reasons.

The Double Jeopardy Clause provides that no "person [shall] be subject for the same offence to be twice put in jeopardy of life or limb." We have long recognized that the Double Jeopardy Clause does not prohibit the imposition of all additional sanctions that could, "in common parlance," be described as punishment. *United States ex rel. Marcus v. Hess*, 317 U.S. 537, 549 (1943). The Clause protects only against the imposition of multiple criminal punishments for the same offense, *Helvering v. Mitchell*, 303 U.S. 391, 399 (1938).

Whether a particular punishment is criminal or civil is, at least initially, a matter of statutory construction. A court must first ask whether the legislature, "in establishing the penalizing mechanism, indicated either expressly or impliedly a preference for one label or the other." *Ward*, 448 U.S. at 248. Even in those cases where the legislature "has indicated an intention to establish a civil penalty, we have inquired further whether the statutory scheme was so punitive either in purpose or effect," as to "transfor[m] what was clearly intended as a civil remedy into a criminal penalty," *Rex Trailer Co. v. United States*, 350 U.S. 148, 154 (1956).

In making this latter determination, the factors listed in *Kennedy v. Mendoza-Martinez*, 372 U.S. 144, 168–169 (1963), provide useful guideposts, including:

> (1) [w]hether the sanction involves an affirmative disability or restraint; (2) whether it has historically been regarded as a punishment; (3) whether it comes into play only on a finding of *scienter*; (4) whether its operation will promote the traditional aims of punishment-retribution and deterrence; (5) whether the behavior to which it applies is already a crime; (6) whether an alternative purpose to which it may rationally be connected is assignable for it; and (7) whether it appears excessive in relation to the alternative purpose assigned.

It is important to note, however, that "these factors must be considered in relation to the statute on its face," *id.* at 164, and "only the clearest proof" will suffice to override legislative intent and transform what has been denominated a civil remedy into a criminal penalty, *Ward, supra*, at 249.

Our opinion in *United States v. Halper* marked the first time we applied the Double Jeopardy Clause to a sanction without first determining that it was criminal in nature. In that case, Irwin Halper was convicted of, *inter alia*, violating the criminal false claims statute, 18 U.S.C. § 287, based on his submission of 65 inflated Medicare claims each of which overcharged the Government by $9. He was sentenced to two years' imprisonment and fined $5,000. The Government then brought an action against Halper under the civil False Claims Act, 31 U.S.C. §§ 3729–3731. The remedial provisions of the False Claims Act provided that a violation of the Act rendered one "liable to the United States Government for a civil penalty of $2,000, an amount equal to 2 times the amount of damages the Government sustains because of the act of that person, and costs of the civil action." *Id.* § 3729. Given Halper's 65 separate violations of the Act, he appeared to be liable for a penalty of $130,000, despite the fact he actually defrauded the Government of less than $600. However, the District Court concluded that a penalty of this magnitude would violate the Double Jeopardy Clause in light of Halper's previous criminal conviction. While explicitly recognizing that the statutory damages provision of the Act "was not itself a criminal punishment," the District Court nonetheless concluded that application of the full penalty to Halper would constitute a second "punishment" in violation of the Double Jeopardy Clause. 490 U.S. at 438–439.

On direct appeal, this Court affirmed. As the *Halper* Court saw it, the imposition of "punishment" of any kind was subject to double jeopardy constraints, and whether a sanction constituted "punishment" depended primarily on whether it served the traditional "goals of punishment," namely, "retribution and deterrence." *Id.* at 448. Any sanction that was so "overwhelmingly disproportionate" to the injury caused that it could not "fairly be said solely to serve [the] remedial purpose" of compensating the Government for its loss, was thought to be explainable only as "serving either retributive or deterrent purposes." *See id.* at 448–449.

The analysis applied by the *Halper* Court deviated from our traditional double jeopardy doctrine in two key respects. First, the *Halper* Court bypassed the threshold question: whether the successive punishment at issue is a "criminal" punishment. Instead, it focused on whether the sanction, regardless of whether it was civil or criminal, was so grossly disproportionate to the harm caused as to constitute "punishment." In so doing, the Court elevated a single *Kennedy* factor — whether the sanction appeared excessive in relation to its nonpunitive purposes — to dispositive status. But as we emphasized in *Kennedy* itself, no one factor should be considered controlling as they "may often point in differing directions." 372 U.S. at 169. The second significant departure in *Halper* was the Court's decision to "asses[s] the character of the actual sanctions imposed," 490 U.S. at 447, rather than, as *Kennedy* demanded, evaluating the "statute on its face" to determine whether it provided for what amounted to a criminal sanction, 372 U.S. at 169.

We believe that *Halper*'s deviation from longstanding double jeopardy principles was ill considered. As subsequent cases have demonstrated, *Halper*'s test for determining whether a particular sanction is "punitive," and thus subject to the strictures of the Double Jeopardy Clause, has proved unworkable. We have since recognized that all civil penalties have some deterrent effect. If a sanction must be "solely" remedial (*i.e.*, entirely nondeterrent) to avoid implicating the Double Jeopardy Clause, then no civil penalties are beyond the scope of the Clause. Under *Halper*'s method of analysis, a court must also look at the "sanction actually imposed" to determine whether the Double Jeopardy Clause is implicated. Thus, it will not be possible to determine whether the Double Jeopardy Clause is violated until a defendant has proceeded through a trial to judgment. But in those cases where the civil proceeding follows the criminal proceeding, this approach flies in the face of the notion that the Double Jeopardy Clause forbids the government from even "*attempting* a second time to punish criminally." *Helvering*, 303 U.S. at 399 (emphasis added).

Finally, it should be noted that some of the ills at which *Halper* was directed are addressed by other constitutional provisions. The Due Process and Equal Protection Clauses already protect individuals from sanctions which are downright irrational. *Williamson v. Lee Optical of Okla., Inc.*, 348 U.S. 483 (1955). The Eighth Amendment protects against excessive civil fines, including forfeitures. *Alexander v. United States*, 509 U.S. 544 (1993); *Austin v. United States*, 509 U.S. 602 (1993). The additional protection afforded by extending double jeopardy protections to proceedings heretofore thought to be civil is more than offset by the confusion created by attempting to distinguish between "punitive" and "nonpunitive" penalties.

Applying traditional double jeopardy principles to the facts of this case, it is clear that the criminal prosecution of these petitioners would not violate the Double Jeopardy Clause. It is evident that Congress intended the OCC money penalties and debarment sanctions imposed for violations of 12 U.S.C. §§ 84 and 375b to be civil in nature. As for the money penalties, both §§ 93(b)(1) and 504(a), which authorize the imposition of monetary penalties for violations of §§ 84 and 375b respectively, expressly provide that such penalties are "civil." While the provision authorizing debarment contains no language explicitly denominating the sanction as civil, we think it significant that the authority to issue debarment orders is conferred upon the "appropriate Federal banking agenc[ies]." §§ 1818(e)(1)-(3). That such authority was conferred upon administrative agencies is prima facie evidence that Congress intended to provide for a civil sanction.

Turning to the second stage of the *Ward* test, we find that there is little evidence, much less the clearest proof that we require, suggesting that either OCC money penalties or debarment sanctions are "so punitive in form and effect as to render them criminal despite Congress' intent to the contrary." *United States v. Ursery*, 518 U.S. 267, 290 (1996). First, neither money penalties nor debarment has historically been viewed as punishment. We have long recognized that "revocation of a privilege voluntarily granted," such as a debarment, "is characteristically free of the punitive criminal element." *Helvering*, 303 U.S. at 399, and n.2. . . . Second, the sanctions imposed do not involve an "affirmative disability or restraint," as that term is normally understood. While petitioners have been prohibited from further participating in the banking industry, this is "certainly nothing approaching the 'infamous punishment' of imprisonment." *Flemming v. Nestor*, 363 U.S. 603, 617 (1960). Third, neither sanction comes into play "only" on a finding of scienter. The provisions under which the money penalties were imposed, 12 U.S.C. §§ 93(b) and 504, allow for the assessment of a penalty against any person "who violates" any of the underlying banking statutes, without regard to the violator's state of mind.

Fourth, the conduct for which OCC sanctions are imposed may also be criminal (and in this case formed the basis for petitioners' indictments). This fact is insufficient to render the money penalties and debarment sanctions criminally punitive, *Ursery, supra,* at 292 (slip op., at 24–25), particularly in the double jeopardy context, *see United States v. Dixon,* 509 U.S. 688, 704 (1993) (rejecting "same-conduct" test for double jeopardy purposes).

Finally, we recognize that the imposition of both money penalties and debarment sanctions will deter others from emulating petitioners' conduct, a traditional goal of criminal punishment. But the mere presence of this purpose is insufficient to render a sanction criminal, as deterrence "may serve civil as well as criminal goals." *Ursery*, 518 U.S. at 292. For example, the sanctions at issue here, while intended to deter future wrongdoing, also serve to promote the stability of the banking industry. To hold that the mere presence of a deterrent purpose renders such sanctions "criminal" for double jeopardy purposes would severely undermine the Government's ability to engage in effective regulation of institutions such as banks.

In sum, there simply is very little showing, to say nothing of the "clearest proof" required by *Ward*, that OCC money penalties and debarment sanctions are criminal. The Double Jeopardy Clause is therefore no obstacle to their trial on the pending indictments, and it may proceed.

The judgment of the Court of Appeals for the Tenth Circuit is accordingly affirmed.

[Concurring opinions omitted.]

NOTES AND QUESTIONS

1. *Successive punishments and successive prosecutions.* Is there a practical distinction between successive punishments and successive prosecutions? Is the Court's test for determining whether or not a sanction is punitive defensible? Why was the *Halper* test unworkable? Note that the Court in *Hudson* relied upon its earlier decision in *United States v. Ursery*, 518 U.S. 267 (1996), a forfeiture case discussed in Chapter 20, Forfeitures, *infra.*

2. *Post-Halper concerns.* The Court spoke of post-*Halper* "concerns about the wide variety of novel double jeopardy claims spawned in the wake of" the case. Justice Stevens pointed out in his concurrence, however, that there were only seven such cases, and that in each of those cases, the Court rejected the double jeopardy claim. 522 U.S. at 106 (Stevens, J., concurring in the judgment.) Stevens questioned the Court's need to revisit *Halper* to reach the conclusion in *Hudson.* Why did the Court seemingly go out of its way to overturn *Halper*?

3. *Punitive civil fines.* Are some civil fines so punitive that they should preclude further prosecution? If so, in what circumstances?

PROBLEM

18-1. Dana Doe was a stock broker. The Commodity Futures Trading Commission (the "Commission") entered an order revoking Doe's floor brokerage registration, barring Doe from trading in any market regulated by the Commission, and imposing a $10,000 fine. The order stemmed from an earlier investigation by the Commission into the possibility that Doe engaged in insider trading. Doe argues that this administrative sanction violates the Double Jeopardy Clause of the Fifth Amendment because it followed a criminal sentence for the same conduct.

Is Doe correct? Why or why not?

[2]   *Qui Tam* Actions

The False Claims Act, 31 U.S.C. §§ 3729–3733 (FCA), is based on the theory that "one of the least expensive and most effective means of preventing frauds on the Treasury is to make the perpetrators of them liable to actions by private persons acting, if you please, under the strong stimulus of personal ill will or the hope of gain." *United States v. Griswold*, 24 F. 361, 366 (D. Or. 1885) (quoted, *inter alia*, in *U.S. ex rel. Springfield Terminal Ry. Co. v. Quinn*, 14 F.3d at 649)). Through the FCA, the government has established incentives to promote enforcement of the laws. The FCA supplements governmental efforts by utilizing and rewarding the citizenry for investigative purposes. *Qui tam* is shorthand for the Latin phrase "*qui tam pro domino rege quam pro seipse*," meaning "he who sues for the king as for himself."

The individual who brings a case under the FCA is called the relator. The next case discusses the standing of a private individual to bring an action under the FCA as a relator.

VERMONT AGENCY OF NATURAL RESOURCES v. UNITED STATES ex rel. STEVENS
529 U.S. 765 (2000)

Justice Scalia delivered the opinion of the Court:

This case presents the question whether a private individual may bring suit in federal court on behalf of the United States against a State (or state agency) under the False Claims Act, 31 U.S.C. §§ 3729–3733.

I.

Originally enacted in 1863, the False Claims Act (FCA) is the most frequently used of a handful of extant laws creating a form of civil action known as *qui tam*. As amended, the FCA imposes civil liability upon "[a]ny person" who, *inter alia*, "knowingly presents, or causes to be presented, to an officer or employee of the United States Government . . . a false or fraudulent claim for payment or approval." 31 U.S.C. § 3729(a). The defendant is liable for up to treble damages and a civil penalty of up to $10,000 per claim. An FCA action may be commenced in one of two ways. First, the Government itself may bring a civil action against the alleged false claimant. § 3730(a). Second, as is relevant here, a private person (the relator) may bring a *qui tam* civil action "for the person and for the United States Government" against the alleged false claimant, "in the name of the Government." § 3730(b)(1).

If a relator initiates the FCA action, he must deliver a copy of the complaint, and any supporting evidence, to the Government, § 3730(b)(2), which then has 60 days to intervene in the action, §§ 3730(b)(2), (4). If it does so, it assumes primary responsibility for prosecuting the action, § 3730(c)(1), though the relator may continue to participate in the litigation and is entitled to a hearing before voluntary dismissal and to a court determination of reasonableness before settlement, § 3730(c)(2). If the Government declines to intervene within the 60-day period, the relator has the exclusive right to conduct the action, § 3730(b)(4), and the Government may subsequently intervene only on a showing of "good cause," § 3730(c)(3). The relator receives a share of any proceeds from the action — generally ranging from 15 to 25 percent if the Government intervenes (depending upon the relator's contribution to the prosecution), and from 25 to 30 percent if it does not (depending upon the court's assessment of what is reasonable) — plus attorney's fees and costs. § 3730(d)(1)-(2).

Respondent Jonathan Stevens brought this *qui tam* action in the United States District Court for the District of Vermont against petitioner Vermont Agency of Natural Resources, his former employer, alleging that it had submitted false claims to the Environmental Protection Agency (EPA) in connection with various federal grant programs administered by the EPA. Specifically, he claimed that petitioner had overstated the amount of time spent by its employees on the federally funded projects, thereby inducing the Government to disburse more grant money than petitioner was entitled to receive. The United States declined to intervene in the action. . . .

II.

We first address the jurisdictional question whether respondent Stevens has standing under Article III of the Constitution to maintain this suit.

As we have frequently explained, a plaintiff must meet three requirements in order to establish Article III standing. First, he must demonstrate "injury in fact" — a harm that is both "concrete" and "actual or imminent, not conjectural or hypothetical." *Whitmore v. Arkansas*, 495 U.S. 149, 155 (1990). Second, he must establish causation — a "fairly . . . trace[able]" connection between the alleged injury in fact and the alleged conduct of the defendant. *Simon v. Eastern Kentucky Welfare Rights Organization*, 426 U.S. 26, 41 (1976). And third, he must demonstrate redressability — a "substantial likelihood" that the requested relief will remedy the alleged injury in fact. *Id.* at 45. These requirements together constitute the "irreducible constitutional minimum" of standing, which is an "essential and unchanging part" of Article III's case-or-controversy requirement, and a key factor in dividing the power of government between the courts and the two political branches. *See Lujan v. Defenders of Wildlife*, 504 U.S. 555, 559–60 (1992).

Respondent Stevens contends that he is suing to remedy an injury in fact suffered by the United States. It is beyond doubt that the complaint asserts an injury to the United States — both the injury to its sovereignty arising from violation of its laws (which suffices to support a criminal lawsuit by the Government) and the proprietary injury resulting from the alleged fraud. But "[t]he Art. III judicial power exists only to redress or otherwise to protect against injury *to the complaining party*." *Warth v. Seldin*, 422 U.S. 490, 499 (1975). It would perhaps suffice to say that the relator here is simply the statutorily designated agent of the United States, *in whose name* (as the statute provides, *see* 31 U.S.C. § 3730(b)) the suit is brought — and that the relator's bounty is simply the fee he receives out of the United States' recovery for filing and/or prosecuting a successful action on behalf of the Government. This analysis is precluded, however, by the fact that the statute gives the relator himself an interest *in the lawsuit*, and not merely the right to retain a fee out of the recovery. Thus, it provides that "[a] person may bring a civil action for a violation of section 3729 *for the person and for the United States Government*," § 3730(b) (emphasis added); gives the relator "the right to continue as a party to the action" even when the Government itself has assumed "primary responsibility" for prosecuting it, § 3730(c)(1); entitles the relator to a hearing before the Government's voluntary dismissal of the suit, § 3730(c)(2)(A); and prohibits the Government from settling the suit over the relator's objection without a judicial determination of "fair[ness], adequa[cy] and reasonable[ness]," § 3730(c)(2)(B). For the portion of the recovery retained by the relator, therefore, some explanation of standing other than agency for the Government must be identified.

There is no doubt, of course, that as to this portion of the recovery — the bounty he will receive if the suit is successful — a *qui tam* relator has a "concrete private interest in the outcome of [the] suit." *Lujan, supra*, at 573. But the same might be said of someone who has placed a wager upon the outcome. An interest unrelated to injury in fact is insufficient to give a plaintiff standing. The interest must consist of obtaining compensation for, or preventing, the violation of a legally protected right. A *qui tam* relator has suffered no such invasion — indeed, the "right" he seeks to vindicate does not even fully materialize until the litigation is completed and the relator prevails. This is not to suggest that Congress cannot define new legal rights, which in turn will confer standing to vindicate an injury caused to the claimant. *See Worth, supra*, at 500. As we have held in another context, however, an interest that is merely a "byproduct" of the suit itself cannot give rise to a cognizable injury in fact for Article III standing purposes. *See Steel Co. v. Citizens for Better Environment*, 523 U.S. 83, 93–102 (1998).

We believe, however, that adequate basis for the relator's suit for his bounty is to be found in the doctrine that the assignee of a claim has standing to assert the injury in fact suffered by the assignor. The FCA can reasonably be regarded as effecting a partial assignment of the Government's damages claim. Although we have never expressly recognized "representational standing" on the part of assignees, we have routinely entertained their suits. . . .

We conclude, therefore, that the United States' injury in fact suffices to confer standing on respondent Stevens.

We are confirmed in this conclusion by the long tradition of *qui tam* actions in England and the American Colonies. That history is particularly relevant to the constitutional standing inquiry since, as we have said elsewhere, Article III's restriction of the judicial power to "Cases" and "Controversies" is properly understood to mean "cases and controversies of the sort traditionally amenable to, and resolved by, the judicial process." *Steel Co.*, 523 U.S. at 102; *see also Coleman v. Miller*, 307 U.S. 433, 460 (1939).

Qui tam actions appear to have originated around the end of the 13th century, when private individuals who had suffered injury began bringing actions in the royal courts on both their own and the Crown's behalf. Suit in this dual capacity was a device for getting their private claims into the respected royal courts, which generally entertained only matters involving the Crown's interests. Starting in the 14th century, as the royal courts began to extend jurisdiction to suits involving wholly private wrongs, the common-law *qui tam* action gradually fell into disuse, although it seems to have remained technically available for several centuries.

*   *   *

Qui tam actions appear to have been as prevalent in America as in England, at least in the period immediately before and after the framing of the Constitution-. . . . Moreover, immediately after the framing, the First Congress enacted a considerable number of informer statutes. Like their English counterparts, some of them provided both a bounty and an express cause of action; others provided a bounty only.

We think this history well nigh conclusive with respect to the question before us here: whether *qui tam* actions were "cases and controversies of the sort tradition-ally amenable to, and resolved by, the judicial process." *Steel Co.*, 523 U.S. at 102. When combined with the theoretical justification for relator standing discussed earlier, it leaves no room for doubt that a *qui tam* relator under the FCA has Article III standing.

*   *   *

Justice Breyer, concurring. [Omitted.]

Justice Ginsberg, with whom Justice Breyer joins, concurring in the judgment. [Omitted.]

Justice Stevens, with whom Justice Souter joins, dissenting. [Omitted.]

NOTES AND QUESTIONS

1. *Whistleblowers.* *Qui tam* actions enable the government to discover fraudulent conduct by using the eyes and ears of citizens and by encouraging insiders to "blow the whistle" on government corruption, fraud, and abuse. Both the relator and the government share in the proceeds of the lawsuit.

2. *History.* The *qui tam* law dates back to the Civil War, and it has brought billions of dollars in recovery to the government. In 1986, the law was strengthened to make it easier for individuals to sue and recover. While *qui tam* actions can be brought in many types of cases, this area of law has exploded in recent years in the health care field. Why has this occurred?

3. *Monetary recovery.* The relator is entitled to a percentage of the potentially large monetary recovery as a reward for exposing the wrongdoing. The government seeks to protect its interest in the integrity of the claim by joining the *qui tam* action and handling the negotiations in order to assure a successful outcome. However, the government does not always join a *qui tam* action. This decision can present ethical issues. For example, is it proper for the government to fail to promote litigation when the government is on notice that fraud is occurring? In addition, these cases can produce tension between the relators, the defendant, and the government. Why might the relationship between DOJ and the relator be strained? *See United States ex rel. Taxpayers Against Fraud v. General Electric Company,* 41 F.3d 1032 (6th Cir. 1994).

4. *The original source requirement.* Under the FCA, a relator must be an "original source" of the information that forms the basis for the suit, that is, the relator must have "direct and independent knowledge of the information on which the allegations are based." 31 U.S.C. § 3730(e)(4)(B). In *Rockwell International Corp. v. United States,* 549 U.S. 457, 473–475 (2007), the Supreme Court found that the relator, a former employee of Rockwell, was not an original source as to events that occurred at Rockwell in 1987 and 1988. Because the relator had left Rockwell's employ in 1986, he had no personal knowledge of the events that occurred during 1987 and 1988, the timeframe upon which the *qui tam* action was based.

5. *Claims made to private entities.* Are false claims not made directly to the government for payment by the government actionable under the FCA? The Supreme Court addressed this issue in *Allison Engine Co., Inc. v. U.S. ex rel. Sanders,* 128 S. Ct. 2123, 2126 (2008). In that case, the Navy had entered into contracts with shipyards to build destroyers. The shipyards subcontracted with a components subcontractor, which in turn subcontracted with two other subcontractors. The subcontracts required that the components be accompanied by a certificate of conformance (COC) certifying that the components were manufactured according to Navy specifications. The contracts and subcontracts were paid with funds from the federal government.

Former employees of the initial subcontractor brought a *qui tam* suit seeking damages from the subcontractors under the FCA. At trial, the plaintiffs showed that the defendants had issued COCs falsely stating that their work complied with Navy specifications, and presented invoices for payment to the shipyards. The proof did not, however, include the invoices the shipyards submitted to the Navy. The district court granted defendants summary judgment, concluding that, absent proof that false claims were presented with the purpose of obtaining payment by the government, the evidence was legally insufficient under the FCA. The Sixth Circuit reversed, holding that FCA claims do not require proof of an intent to cause a false claim to be paid by the government; proof of an intent to cause such a claim to be paid by a private entity using government funds was sufficient.

Agreeing with the district court that an FCA claim does not lie in such circumstances, the Supreme Court reversed. The Court held that:

> If a subcontractor or another defendant makes a false statement to a private entity and does not intend the government to rely on that false statement as a condition of payment, the statement is not made with the purpose of inducing payment of a false claim "by the government." In such a situation, the direct link between the false statement and the government's decision to pay or approve a false claim is too attenuated to establish liability.

Id. at 2130. Reconsider the false statements statute, 18 U.S.C. § 1001, discussed in Chapter 9, False Statements, *supra.* Would the defendants be guilty of making false statements under § 1001? Why or why not?

[C] PARALLEL PROCEEDINGS

Parallel proceedings exist when the government pursues simultaneous or successive civil and criminal investigations and/or cases relating to the same parties and activities. At the conclusion of a civil matter, the federal agency frequently turns the matter over to the Department of Justice for possible criminal proceedings. If the government has reasonable suspicion to believe that the federal criminal laws have been violated, then the matter may be referred to the appropriate U.S. Attorney's office for further investigation.

[1] Fifth Amendment Risks

When civil matters threaten to become criminal matters, the risks for defendants are tremendous. A critical dilemma for the defendant involves the Fifth Amendment — should a defendant facing a possible criminal action refrain from testifying at a civil proceeding based on the right against self-incrimination?

UNITED STATES v. KORDEL
397 U.S. 1 (1970)

Mr. JUSTICE STEWART delivered the opinion of the Court.

The respondents are the president and vice president, respectively, of Detroit Vital Foods, Inc. They were convicted in the United States District Court for the Eastern District of Michigan, along with the corporation, for violations of the Federal Food, Drug, and Cosmetic Act. The Court of Appeals for the Sixth Circuit reversed the respondents' convictions on the ground that the Government's use of interrogatories to obtain evidence from the respondents in a nearly contemporaneous civil condemnation proceeding operated to violate their Fifth Amendment privilege against compulsory self-incrimination. We granted certiorari to consider the questions raised by the Government's invocation of simultaneous civil and criminal proceedings in the enforcement of federal law.

In March 1960 the Division of Regulatory Management of the Food and Drug Administration (hereafter FDA) instructed the agency's Detroit office to investigate the respondents' possible violations of the Food, Drug, and Cosmetic Act. Within a month the Detroit office recommended to the Division a civil seizure of two of the respondents' products, Korleen and Frutex; within another month the Division similarly recommended seizure to the FDA's General Counsel. On June 6, 1960, the General Counsel requested the United States Attorney for the Eastern District of Michigan to commence an in rem action against these products of the corporation, and the United States Attorney filed a libel three days later. The corporation, appearing as the claimant, answered the libel on September 12, 1960. An FDA official in the Division of Regulatory Management then prepared extensive interrogatories to be served on the corporation in this civil action. The United States Attorney filed the agency's interrogatories on January 6, 1961, pursuant to Rule 33 of the Federal Rules of Civil Procedure.

After the Division official had drafted the interrogatories, he recommended that pursuant to the Food, Drug, and Cosmetic Act the FDA serve upon the corporation and the respondents a notice that the agency contemplated a criminal proceeding against them with respect to the transactions that were the subject of the civil action. On January 9, 1961, three days after the filing of the interrogatories in the civil action, the Detroit office received an instruction from the Division to serve the statutory notice. The Detroit office complied 10 days later, and on March 8, 1961, the agency held a hearing on the notice.

On April 10, the corporation, having received the FDA's interrogatories but not yet having answered them, moved to stay further proceedings in the civil action or, in the alternative, to extend the time to answer the interrogatories until after disposition of the criminal proceeding. . . . Permitting the Government to obtain proof of violations of the Act by resort to civil discovery procedures, the movant urged, would be "improper" and would work a "grave injustice against the claimant;" it would also enable the Government to have pretrial discovery of the respondents' defenses to future criminal charges. Counsel expressly disavowed any "issue of a self-incrimination privilege in favor of the claimant corporation." And nowhere in the moving papers did counsel raise a claim of the Fifth Amendment privilege against compulsory self-incrimination with respect to the respondents.

On June 21, 1961, the District Court denied the motion upon finding that the corporation had failed to demonstrate that substantial prejudice and harm would result from being required to respond to the interrogatories. The court reasoned that the notice did not conclusively indicate the Government would institute a criminal proceeding, that six to 12 months could elapse from the service of the statutory notice to initiation of a criminal prosecution, and that the Government could obtain data for a prosecution from the testimony in the civil action or by subpoenaing the books and records of the corporation. Accordingly, the court concluded, the interests of justice did not require that the Government be denied the information it wanted simply because it had sought it by way of civil-discovery procedures. On September 5, 1961, in compliance with the court's directive, the corporation, through the respondent Feldten, answered the Government's interrogatories.

On July 28, 1961, five weeks after the District Court's order but more than a month before receipt of the answers to the interrogatories, the Director of the FDA's Detroit office recommended a criminal prosecution to the Division. The Division forwarded the recommendation to the General Counsel on August 31, 1961, still prior to receipt of Feldten's answers. While the matter was pending in the General Counsel's office, the Division officer who had originally drafted the proposed interrogatories recommended that additional violations of the statute be alleged in the indictment. On June 13, 1962, the Department of Health, Education, and Welfare requested the Department of Justice to institute a criminal proceeding, and about two months after that the latter department instructed the United States Attorney in Detroit to seek an indictment. The civil case, still pending in the District Court, proceeded to settlement by way of a consent decree in November 1962, and eight months later the Government obtained the indictment underlying the present judgments of conviction.

At the outset, we assume that the information Feldten supplied the Government in his answers to the interrogatories, if not necessary to the proof of the Government's case in the criminal prosecution, as the Court of Appeals thought, at least provided evidence or leads useful to the Government. . . .

The Court of Appeals thought the answers to the interrogatories were involuntarily given. The District Judge's order denying the corporation's motion to defer the answers to the interrogatories, reasoned the court, left the respondents with three choices: they could have refused to answer, thereby forfeiting the corporation's property that was the subject of the libel; they could have given false answers to the interrogatories, thereby subjecting themselves to the risk of a prosecution for perjury; or they could have done just what they did — disclose the requested information, thereby supplying the Government with evidence and leads helpful in securing their indictment and conviction.

In this analysis we think the Court of Appeals erred. For Feldten need not have answered the interrogatories. Without question he could have invoked his Fifth Amendment privilege against compulsory self-incrimination. Surely Feldten was not barred from asserting his privilege simply because the corporation had no privilege of its own, or because the proceeding in which the Government sought information was civil rather than criminal in character.

To be sure, service of the interrogatories obliged the corporation to appoint an agent who could, without fear of self-incrimination, furnish such requested information as was available to the corporation. The corporation could not satisfy its obligation under Rule 33 simply by pointing to an agent about to invoke his constitutional privilege. It would indeed be incongruous to permit a corporation to select an individual to verify the corporation's answers, who because he fears self-incrimination may thus secure for the corporation the benefits of a privilege it does not have. Such a result would effectively permit the corporation to assert on its own behalf the personal privilege of its individual agents.

*   *   *

The respondents press upon us the situation where no one can answer the interrogatories addressed to the corporation without subjecting himself to a real and appreciable risk of self-incrimination. For present purposes we may assume that in such a case the appropriate remedy would be a protective order under Rule 30(b), postponing civil discovery until termination of the criminal action. But we need not decide this troublesome question. For the record before us makes clear that even though the respondents had the burden of showing that the Government's interrogatories were improper, they never even asserted, let alone demonstrated, that there was no authorized person who could answer the interrogatories without the possibility of compulsory self-incrimination. To the contrary, the record shows that nobody associated with the corporation asserted his privilege at all. The respondents do not suggest that Feldten, who answered the interrogatories on behalf of the corporation, did so while unrepresented by counsel or without appreciation of the possible consequences. His failure at any time to assert the constitutional privilege leaves him in no position to complain now that he was compelled to give testimony against himself.

Kordel's claim of compulsory self-incrimination is even more tenuous than Feldten's. Not only did Kordel never assert the privilege; he never even answered any interrogatories.

The respondents urge that even if the Government's conduct did not violate their Fifth Amendment privilege against compulsory self-incrimination, it nonetheless reflected such unfairness and want of consideration for justice as independently to require the reversal of their convictions. On the record before us, we cannot agree that the respondents have made out either a violation of due process or a departure from proper standards in the administration of justice requiring the exercise of our supervisory power. The public interest in protecting consumers throughout the Nation from misbranded drugs requires prompt action by the agency charged with responsibility for administration of the federal food and drug laws. But a rational decision whether to proceed criminally against those responsible for the misbranding may have to await consideration of a fuller record than that before the agency at the time of the civil seizure of the offending products. It would stultify enforcement of federal law to require a governmental agency such as the FDA invariably to choose either to forgo recommendation of a criminal prosecution once it seeks civil relief, or to defer civil proceedings pending the ultimate outcome of a criminal trial.

We do not deal here with a case where the Government has brought a civil action solely to obtain evidence for its criminal prosecution or has failed to advise the defendant in its civil proceeding that it contemplates his criminal prosecution; nor with a case where the defendant is without counsel or reasonably fears prejudice from adverse pretrial publicity or other unfair injury; nor with any other special circumstances that might suggest the unconstitutionality or even the impropriety of this criminal prosecution.

Overturning these convictions would be tantamount to the adoption of a rule that the Government's use of interrogatories directed against a corporate defendant in the ordinary course of a civil proceeding would always immunize the corporation's officers from subsequent criminal prosecution. The Court of Appeals was correct in stating that the Government may not use evidence against a defendant in a criminal case which has been coerced from him under penalty of either giving the evidence or suffering a forfeiture of his property. But on this record there was no such violation of the Constitution, and no such departure from the proper administration of criminal justice.

Accordingly, the judgment of the Court of Appeals is reversed, and the case is remanded to that court for further proceedings consistent with this opinion.

It is so ordered.

NOTES AND QUESTIONS

1. *Civil testimony.* Notice the timing of the legal proceedings in the *Kordel* case. *Kordel* raises the very real dilemma faced by litigants who are considering testifying in a civil proceeding while the potential for criminal prosecution looms. What are the precise dilemmas a defendant faces when considering whether or not to testify in the civil proceeding?

2. *Fifth Amendment risks.* Identify the risks a civil litigant faces if the litigant wants to assert the Fifth Amendment in a civil case and the criminal prosecution is likely to occur in the future. What are the implications in the civil case? In the upcoming criminal case?

3. *Adverse inferences*: Baxter v. Palmigiano. The law is well established that the Fifth Amendment protects a defendant from having a judge or jury draw an adverse inference from the failure to testify. In civil proceedings, however, a witness's assertion of the Fifth Amendment right to silence may have serious negative consequences. In *Baxter v. Palmigiano*, 425 U.S. 308 (1976), for example, a prison inmate was brought before a disciplinary board on charges of inciting a disturbance in the prison. During the proceedings, he was told that the state might bring criminal charges against him. He was advised that if he chose to remain silent in the face of questioning by the board, his silence could be used against him in any subsequent criminal action. When he refused to answer questions based on his Fifth Amendment privilege, he was punished based on the assumption that his silence was equivalent to affirmative answers to the questions. The Supreme Court found that this use of the incriminating inference was proper and did not violate the Fifth Amendment. Lower courts have limited *Baxter* to those situations where there is independent evidence of the underlying facts.

[2]   Immunized Evidence

During the course of a civil matter, a litigant may seek to obtain evidence that has been produced in a prior proceeding. When a plaintiff seeks immunized evidence, several impediments exist. How can a civil attorney obtain information that is protected under a grant of immunity? Can civil attorneys offer immunity to a witness in order to secure the testimony of a deponent in a civil case? The Supreme Court addressed this and related questions in the next case. (Refer to Chapter 17, Self-Incrimination — Witness Testimony and Document Production, *supra*, for a discussion of principles of immunity.)

PILLSBURY CO. v. CONBOY
459 U.S. 248 (1983)

JUSTICE POWELL delivered the opinion of the Court.

Pursuant to the federal use immunity provisions, 18 U.S.C. §§ 6001–6005, a United States Attorney may request an order from a federal court compelling a witness to testify even though he has asserted his privilege against self-incrimination. Section 6002 provides, however, that "no testimony or other information compelled under the order (or any information directly or indirectly derived from such testimony or other information) may be used against the witness in any criminal case. . . . " The issue presented in this case is whether a deponent's civil deposition testimony, repeating verbatim or closely tracking his prior immunized testimony, is immunized "testimony" that can be compelled over the valid assertion of his Fifth Amendment privilege.

Respondent John Conboy is a former executive of a defendant in the *In re Corrugated Container Antitrust Litigation*, M.D.L. 310 (S.D. Tex.). In January 1978, United States Department of Justice attorneys interviewed Conboy following a promise of use immunity. Conboy subsequently appeared before a grand jury investigating price-fixing activities and, pursuant to 18 U.S.C. § 6002, was granted formal use immunity for his testimony.

Following the criminal indictment of several companies, numerous civil antitrust actions were filed in various United States district courts. . . . The District Court ordered that portions of the immunized government interview and grand-jury testimony of certain witnesses, including that of Conboy, be made available to lawyers for the class and opt-outs.

Pursuant to a subpoena issued by the District Court for the Northern District of Illinois, Conboy appeared in Chicago for a deposition at which he, his counsel, and petitioners' counsel had copies of his immunized testimony. The transcripts were marked as deposition exhibits so that all could follow the intended examination. The questioning fell into the following pattern: a question was read from the transcript; it then was rephrased to include the transcript answer (*i.e.*, "Is it not the fact that. . . . "); finally, Conboy was asked if he had "so testified" in his immunized interview and grand-jury examination. Conboy refused to answer each question, asserting his Fifth Amendment privilege against self-incrimination.

The District Court granted petitioners' motion to compel Conboy to answer the questions.

When Conboy continued to claim his privilege, the District Court held him in contempt, but stayed its order pending appeal. A panel of the Court of Appeals for the Seventh Circuit affirmed the contempt order, holding that, "[b]ecause the questions asked in this deposition were taken verbatim from or closely tracked the transcript of Conboy's grand jury testimony, we believe that his answers at the deposition would be 'derived from' the prior immunized [testimony] and therefore unavailable for use in any subsequent criminal prosecution." *In re Corrugated Container Antitrust Litigation*, 655 F.2d 748, 751 (1981).

On rehearing *en banc*, the Court of Appeals reversed the District Court. It first determined that Conboy's alleged fear of prosecution was more than "fanciful," and that Conboy therefore was entitled to assert his Fifth Amendment privilege unless his deposition testimony could not be used against him in a subsequent criminal action. The court then held that under § 6002, absent a separate and independent grant of immunity, a deponent's civil deposition testimony that repeats verbatim or closely tracks his prior immunized testimony is not protected. While acknowledging that verbatim questions "of course [would be] derived" from the immunized testimony, the court reasoned that the answers to such questions "are derived from the deponent's current, independent memory of events" and thus "necessarily create a new source of evidence" that could be used in a subsequent criminal prosecution against Conboy. 661 F.2d 1145, 1155 (1981).

We granted certiorari to resolve the conflict in the Courts of Appeals, and now affirm.

* * *

It is not disputed that the *questions* asked of Conboy were directly or indirectly derived from his immunized testimony. The issue as presented to us is whether the causal connection between the questions and the *answers* is so direct that the answers also are derived from that testimony and therefore should be excluded under the grant of immunity.

Petitioners' argument is based on the language of § 6002 and on a common understanding of the words "derived from." The questions formulated on the basis of immunized testimony are clearly "derived from" the prior testimony. Thus, the answers that repeat verbatim or closely track a deponent's testimony are necessarily also "derived from" and "tainted by" such testimony. Petitioners therefore find no basis for the distinction made by the Court of Appeals between questions and answers responsive to those same questions. An answer by its very nature is evoked by and responds to information contained in a question.

Conboy's position is also straightforward: Questions do not incriminate; answers do. Unlike the questions, answers are not directly or indirectly derived from the immunized grand jury or interview transcripts, but from the deponent's current, independent memory of events. Even when a deponent's deposition answers are identical to those he gave to the grand jury, he is under oath to tell the truth, not necessarily as he told it before the grand jury, but as he knows it now. Each new statement of the deponent creates a new "source." In sum, the initial grant of immunity does not prevent the prosecutor from prosecuting; it merely limits his sources of evidence.

Although the parties make their arguments in terms tracking those of the statute — whether the deposition testimony is "derived from" the prior testimony — it is clear that the crux of their dispute is whether the earlier grant of immunity itself compelled Conboy to talk. Petitioners contend that the prior grant of immunity *already* had supplanted Conboy's Fifth Amendment privilege at the time of the civil deposition. Petitioners would limit this immunity, of course, to testimony that "closely tracks" his prior immunized testimony. It is argued that this would not threaten the Government's need for admissible evidence or the individual's interest in avoiding self-incrimination. In the absence of such a threat, admissible evidence should be available to civil antitrust plaintiffs. But we cannot accept the assumptions upon which petitioners' conclusion rests. In our view, a District Court cannot compel Conboy to answer deposition questions, over a valid assertion of his Fifth Amendment right, absent a duly authorized assurance of immunity at the time.

We note at the outset that although there may be practical reasons for not testifying, as far as the deponent's Fifth Amendment right is concerned he should be indifferent between the protection afforded by silence and that afforded by immunity. A deponent's primary interest is that the protection be certain. The Government's interest, however, may be affected seriously by whether the deponent relies at the civil deposition on his Fifth Amendment privilege or on his prior grant of immunity. With due recognition of petitioners' need for admissible evidence, our inquiry then is whether this need can be met without jeopardizing the Government's interest in limiting the scope of an immunity grant or encroaching upon the deponent's certainty of protection.

Questions taken verbatim from a transcript of immunized testimony could evoke one of several responses from a deponent: (i) he could repeat or adopt his immunized answer; (ii) he could affirm that the transcript of his immunized answers accurately reflects his prior testimony; (iii) he could recall additional information responsive to the question but not disclosed in his immune testimony; or (iv) he could disclose information that is not responsive to the question. Petitioners do not contend, nor could they, that the prior grant of use immunity affords protection for all self-incriminating information disclosed by the immunized witness on any occasion after the giving of the immunized testimony. Rather, petitioners argue that only the first three responses would be "derived from" his immune testimony and therefore would be unavailable for use against the deponent in any subsequent criminal prosecution.

*　*　*

But even if the direct examination is limited to the questions and answers in the immunized transcript, there remains the right of cross examination, a right traditionally relied upon expansively to test credibility as well as to seek the truth. Petitioners recognize this problem, but maintain that the antitrust defendants "would be entitled to test the accuracy and truthfulness of Conboy's repeated immunized testimony without going beyond the confines of that testimony." Reply Brief for Petitioners 14–15. Regardless of any limitations that may be imposed on its scope, however, cross examination is intended to and often will produce information not elicited on direct. We must assume that, to produce admissible evidence, the scope of cross examination at the deposition cannot easily be limited to the immunized testimony. This assumption implicates both the Government's and the individual's interests embodied in § 6002.

Use immunity was intended to immunize and exclude from a subsequent criminal trial only that information to which the Government expressly has surrendered future use. If the Government is engaged in an ongoing investigation of the particular activity at issue, immunizing new information (*e.g.*, the answers to questions in a case like this one) may make it more difficult to show in a subsequent prosecution that similar information was obtained from wholly independent sources. If a District Court were to conclude in a subsequent civil proceeding that the prior immunity order extended to civil deposition testimony closely tracking the immunized testimony, it in effect could invest the deponent with transactional immunity on matters about which he testified at the immunized proceedings. This is precisely the kind of immunity Congress intended to prohibit. The purpose of § 6002 was to limit the scope of immunity to the level that is constitutionally required, as well as to limit the use of immunity to those cases in which the Attorney General, or officials designated by him, determine that gaining the witness's testimony outweighs the loss of the opportunity for criminal prosecution of that witness.

Petitioners' interpretation of § 6002 also places substantial risks on the deponent. Unless the grant of immunity assures a witness that his incriminating testimony will not be used against him in a subsequent criminal prosecution, the witness has not received the certain protection of his Fifth Amendment privilege that he has been forced to exchange. No court has authority to immunize a witness. That responsibility, as we have noted, is peculiarly an executive one, and only the Attorney General or a designated officer of the Department of Justice has authority to grant use immunity. Nor should a court, at the time of the civil testimony, pre-determine the decision of the court in a subsequent criminal prosecution on the question whether the Government has met its burden of proving "that the evidence it proposes to use is derived from a legitimate source wholly independent of the compelled testimony." *Kastigar*, 406 U.S. 441, 460 (1972). Yet in holding Conboy in contempt for his Fifth Amendment silence, the District Court below essentially predicted that a court in any future criminal prosecution of Conboy will be obligated to protect against evidentiary use of the deposition testimony petitioners seek. We do not think such a predictive judgment is enough.

* * *

We hold that a deponent's civil deposition testimony, closely tracking his prior immunized testimony, is not, without duly authorized assurance of immunity at the time, immunized testimony within the meaning of § 6002, and therefore may not be compelled over a valid assertion of his Fifth Amendment privilege. The judgment of the Court of Appeals accordingly is *Affirmed.*

[Concurring opinions omitted.]

JUSTICE STEVENS, with whom JUSTICE O'CONNOR joins, dissenting. [Omitted.]

NOTES AND QUESTIONS

1. *The power of immunity.* Civil litigants do not have the authority to offer immunity to witnesses in order to secure their testimony. Immunity is solely a prerogative of the government. Why is this so?

2. *Alternatives to immunity.* If the government does not offer immunity, how can a civil litigant obtain the testimony of a witness who asserts a valid Fifth Amendment claim?

3. *Benefits from civil testimony.* Prosecutors do not have the opportunity to depose subjects and targets of grand jury investigations or defendants in criminal proceedings. Thus, if a criminal defendant has testified in a civil matter, this provides the prosecutor with desirable evidence that is otherwise not available. A prosecutor can determine whether the civil testimony is at odds with the trial testimony and use any testimonial discrepancies in cross-examination. Evidence is also useful to corroborate or discredit other witnesses in the case. What other benefits can the government derive from the civil matter testimony?

[3] Grand Jury Risks

When a private civil litigant seeks disclosure of grand jury material, what standard must be met? In addition, logistical venue questions can be critical to the outcome, as the next cases demonstrate. (Refer to Chapter 16, The Grand Jury, *supra*, for principles relating to grand jury secrecy.)

DOUGLAS OIL CO. v. PETROL STOPS NORTHWEST
441 U.S. 211 (1979)

Mr. JUSTICE POWELL delivered the opinion of the Court.

This case presents two intertwined questions concerning a civil litigant's right to obtain transcripts of federal criminal grand jury proceedings. First, what justification for disclosure must a private party show in order to overcome the presumption of grand jury secrecy applicable to such transcripts? Second, what court should assess the strength of this showing — the court where the civil action is pending, or the court that acts as custodian of the grand jury documents?

Respondent Petrol Stops Northwest is a gasoline retailer unaffiliated with any major oil company. In 1973, it operated 104 service stations located in Arizona, California, Oregon, Washington, and several other States. On December 13, 1973, respondent filed an antitrust action in the District of Arizona against 12 large oil companies, including petitioners Douglas Oil Co. of California and Phillips Petroleum Co. In its complaint, respondent alleged that on January 1, 1973, there had been a sharp reduction in the amount of gasoline offered for sale to it, and that this reduction had resulted from a conspiracy among the oil companies to restrain trade in gasoline, in violation of §§ 1 and 2 of the Sherman Act. As a part of this conspiracy, respondent charged, petitioners and their codefendants had fixed the prices of gasoline at the retail and wholesale distribution levels in California, Oregon and Washington.

Respondents Gas-A-Tron of Arizona and Coinoco also independently sell gasoline through service stations they own or lease. Unlike respondent Petrol Stops Northwest, however, their operations are limited to the vicinity of Tucson, Ariz. On November 2, 1973, Gas-A-Tron and Coinoco filed an antitrust complaint in the District of Arizona naming as defendants nine large oil companies, including petitioner Phillips Petroleum Co. Like respondent Petrol Stops Northwest, Gas-A-Tron and Coinoco alleged that as of January 1, 1973, their supply of gasoline had been sharply reduced, and attributed this reduction to a conspiracy to restrain trade in violation of the Sherman Act. The specific charges of illegal behavior asserted by the two retailers substantially paralleled those made by Petrol Stops Northwest in its complaint, and included an allegation that the defendants had fixed the price of gasoline at the wholesale and retail levels.

Although the issues and defendants in the two actions were substantially the same, the cases were assigned to two different judges in the District of Arizona. In February 1974, respondents served upon petitioners a set of interrogatories which included a request that petitioners state whether either of their companies at any time between January 1, 1968, and December 14, 1974, had had any communication with any of their competitors concerning the wholesale price of gasoline to be sold to unaffiliated retailers. Petitioners also were asked to produce any documents they had concerning such communications. Petitioners responded that they were aware of no such communications, and therefore could produce no documents pertinent to the request.

In the meantime, the Antitrust Division of the Department of Justice had been investigating since 1972 the pricing behavior on the west coast of several major oil companies, including petitioners. As part of this investigation, employees of petitioners were called to testify before a grand jury empaneled in the Central District of California. The Government's investigation culminated on March 19,

1975, when the grand jury returned an indictment charging petitioners and four other oil companies with having conspired to fix the price of "rebrand gasoline" in California, Oregon, Washington, Nevada, and Arizona. The indictment alleged that the price-fixing conspiracy had begun in July 1970 and had continued at least until the end of 1971.

Although initially all six defendants charged in the criminal indictment pleaded not guilty, by December 1975, each had pleaded *nolo contendere* and was fined $50,000. Before changing their pleas, petitioners asked the District Court for the Central District of California to give them copies of the transcripts of testimony given by their employees before the grand jury. Their request was granted, and it appears that petitioners continue to possess copies of these transcripts.

In October 1976, respondents served upon petitioners requests for production of the grand jury transcripts in petitioners' possession. Petitioners objected to the requests for production, arguing that the transcripts were not relevant to the private antitrust actions and that they were not likely to lead to any admissible evidence. Respondents did not pursue their discovery requests by making a motion in the Arizona trial court to compel discovery. Rather, they filed a petition in the District Court for the Central District of California asking that court, as guardian of the grand jury transcripts to order them released to respondents. An attorney from the Antitrust Division of the Department of Justice appeared and indicated that the Government had no objection to respondents' receiving the transcripts already made available to petitioners. He suggested to the court, however, that the real parties in interest were petitioners, and therefore that they should be given an opportunity to be heard. The California District Court accepted this suggestion, and petitioners participated in the proceedings as parties adverse to respondents.

After briefing and oral argument, the court ordered the Chief of the Antitrust Division's Los Angeles Office "to produce for [respondents'] inspection and copying all grand jury transcripts previously disclosed to Phillips Petroleum Company or Douglas Oil Company of California or their attorneys relating to the indictment in *United States v. Phillips*." App. 48–49. The production order was subject, however, to several protective conditions. The transcripts were to "be disclosed only to counsel for [respondents] in connection with the two civil actions" pending in Arizona. Furthermore, under the court's order the transcripts of grand jury testimony "may be used . . . solely for the purpose of impeaching that witness or refreshing the recollection of a witness, either in deposition or at trial" in the Arizona actions. Finally, the court forbade any further reproduction of the matter turned over to respondents, and ordered that the material be returned to the Antitrust Division "upon completion of the purposes authorized by this Order."

On appeal, the Ninth Circuit affirmed the disclosure order. The Court of Appeals noted that under *United States v. Procter & Gamble Co.*, 356 U.S. 677 (1958), a party seeking access to grand jury transcripts must show a "particularized need." In evaluating the strength of the need shown in the present case, the Ninth Circuit considered two factors: the need for continued grand jury secrecy and respondents' need for the requested material. The court found the former need to be insubstantial, as the grand jury proceeding had concluded three years before and the transcripts already had been released to petitioners. As to respondents' claim, the court conceded that it knew little about the Arizona proceedings, but speculated that the transcripts would facilitate the prosecution of respondents' civil suits: Petitioners' answers to the 1974 interrogatories concerning price communications with competitors appeared to be at odds with their pleas of *nolo contendere* in the California criminal action.

Petitioners contend that the courts below erred in holding that, because the grand jury had dissolved and the requested material had been disclosed already to the defendants, respondents had to show only a "slight need" for disclosure. According to petitioners, this approach to disclosure is contrary to prior decisions of this Court indicating that "a civil litigant must demonstrate a compelling necessity for specified grand jury materials before disclosure is proper." Brief for Petitioners at 16.

We consistently have recognized that the proper functioning of our grand jury system depends upon the secrecy of grand jury proceedings. . . .

At the same time, it has been recognized that in some situations justice may demand that discrete portions of transcripts be made available for use in subsequent proceedings. Indeed, recognition of the occasional need for litigants to have access to grand jury transcripts led to the provision in Fed. R. Crim. Proc. 6(e)(2)(C)(i) that disclosure of grand jury transcripts may be made "when so directed by a court preliminarily to or in connection with a judicial proceeding."

In *United States v. Procter & Gamble Co.*, the Court sought to accommodate the competing needs for secrecy and disclosure by ruling that a private party seeking to obtain grand jury transcripts must demonstrate that "without the transcript a defense would be greatly prejudiced or that without reference to it an injustice would be done." 356 U.S. at 682. Moreover, the Court required that the showing of need for the transcripts be made "with particularity" so that "the secrecy of the proceedings [may] be lifted discretely and limitedly." *Id.* at 683.

In *Dennis v. United States*, 384 U.S. 855 (1966), the Court considered a request for disclosure of grand jury records in quite different circumstances. It was there held to be an abuse of discretion for a District Court in a criminal trial to refuse to disclose to the defendants the grand jury testimony of four witnesses who some years earlier had appeared before a grand jury investigating activities of the defendants. The grand jury had completed its investigation, and the witnesses whose testimony was sought already had testified in public concerning the same matters.

* * *

From *Procter & Gamble* and *Dennis* emerges the standard for determining when the traditional secrecy of the grand jury may be broken: Parties seeking grand jury transcripts under Rule 6(e) must show that the material they seek is needed to avoid a possible injustice in another judicial proceeding, that the need for disclosure is greater than the need for continued secrecy, and that their request is structured to cover only material so needed. Such a showing must be made even when the grand jury whose transcripts are sought has concluded its operations, as it had in *Dennis*. For in considering the effects of disclosure on grand jury proceedings, the courts must consider not only the immediate effects upon a particular grand jury, but also the possible effect upon the functioning of future grand juries. Persons called upon to testify will consider the likelihood that their testimony may one day be disclosed to outside parties. Fear of future retribution or social stigma may act as powerful deterrents to those who would come forward and aid the grand jury in the performance of its duties. Concern as to the future consequences of frank and full testimony is heightened where the witness is an employee of a company under investigation. Thus, the interests in grand jury secrecy, although reduced, are not eliminated merely because the grand jury has ended its activities.

It is clear from *Procter & Gamble* and *Dennis* that disclosure is appropriate only in those cases where the need for it outweighs the public interest in secrecy, and that the burden of demonstrating this balance rests upon the private party seeking disclosure. It is equally clear that as the considerations justifying secrecy become less relevant, a party asserting a need for grand jury transcripts will have a lesser burden in showing justification. In sum, as so often is the situation in our jurisprudence, the court's duty in a case of this kind is to weigh carefully the competing interests in light of the relevant circumstances and the standards announced by this Court. And if disclosure is ordered, the court may include protective limitations on the use of the disclosed material, as did the District Court in this case. Moreover, we emphasize that a court called upon to determine whether grand jury transcripts should be released necessarily is infused with substantial discretion.

Applying these principles to the present case, we conclude that neither the District Court nor the Court of Appeals erred in the standard by which it assessed the request for disclosure under Rule 6(e). . . .

Petitioners contend, irrespective of the legal standard applied, that the District Court for the Central District of California was not the proper court to rule on respondents' motion for disclosure. Petitioners note that the Court of Appeals and the District Court both purported to base their decisions in part upon the need for use of the requested material in the civil antitrust proceedings pending in Arizona. This determination necessarily involved consideration of the nature and status of the Arizona proceedings, matters peculiarly within the competence of the Arizona District Court.

Although the question is an important one, this Court heretofore has had no occasion to consider which court or courts may direct disclosure of grand jury minutes under Fed. Rule Crim. Proc. 6(e). The federal courts that have addressed the question generally have said that the request for disclosure of grand jury minutes under Rule 6(e) must be directed toward the court under whose auspices the grand jury was empaneled. Indeed, those who seek grand jury transcripts have little choice other than to file a request with the court that supervised the grand jury, as it is the only court with control over the transcripts.

Quite apart from practical necessity, the policies underlying Rule 6(e) dictate that the grand jury's supervisory court participate in reviewing such requests, as it is in the best position to determine the continuing need for grand jury secrecy- . . . . Where, as in this case, the request is made for use in a case pending in another district, the judges of the court having custody of the grand jury transcripts will have no firsthand knowledge of the litigation in which the transcripts allegedly are needed, and no practical means by which such knowledge can be obtained. In such a case, a judge in the district of the grand jury cannot weigh in an informed manner the need for disclosure against the need for maintaining grand jury secrecy. Thus, it may well be impossible for that court to apply the standard required by the decisions of this Court, reiterated above, for determining whether the veil of secrecy should be lifted.

* * *

In the present case, the District Court for the Central District of California was called upon to make an evaluation entirely beyond its expertise. The District Judge readily conceded that he had no knowledge of the civil proceedings pending several hundred miles away in Arizona. Nonetheless, he was asked to rule whether there was a "particularized need" for disclosure of portions of the grand jury transcript and whether this need outweighed the need for continued grand jury secrecy. Generally we leave it to the considered discretion of the district court to determine the proper response to requests for disclosure under Rule 6(e). We have a duty, however, to guide the exercise of discretion by district courts, and when necessary to overturn discretionary decisions under Rule 6(e).

We find that the District Court here abused its discretion in releasing directly to respondents the grand jury minutes they requested. Appreciating that it was largely ignorant of the Arizona civil suits, the court nonetheless made a judgment concerning the relative needs for secrecy and disclosure. The court based its decision largely upon the unsupported assertions of counsel during oral argument before it, supplemented only by the criminal indictment returned by the grand jury, the civil complaints, and petitioners' response to a single interrogatory that appeared to be inconsistent with petitioners' *nolo contendere* plea in the criminal case. Even the court's comparison of the criminal indictment and the civil complaints did not indicate unambiguously what, if any, portions of the grand jury transcripts would be pertinent to the subject of the Arizona actions, as only some of the same parties were named and only some of the same territory was covered.

The possibility of an unnecessary breach of grand jury secrecy in situations such as this is not insignificant. A court more familiar with the course of the antitrust litigation might have seen important differences between the allegations of the indictment and the contours of the conspiracy respondents sought to prove in their civil actions — differences indicating that disclosure would likely be of little value to respondents, save perhaps as a mechanism for general discovery. Alternatively, the courts where the civil proceedings were pending might have considered disclosure at that point in the litigation to be premature; if there were to be conflicts between petitioners' statements and their actions in the criminal proceedings, the court might have preferred to wait until they ripened at depositions or even during testimony at trial.

Under these circumstances, the better practice would have been for the District Court, after making a written evaluation of the need for continued grand jury secrecy and a determination that the limited evidence before it showed that disclosure might be appropriate, to send the requested materials to the courts where the civil cases were pending. The Arizona court, armed with their special knowledge of the status of the civil actions, then could have considered the requests for disclosure in light of the California court's evaluation of the need for continued grand jury secrecy. In this way, both the need for continued secrecy and the need for disclosure could have been evaluated by the courts in the best position to make the respective evaluations. . . .

Our decision today therefore is restricted to situations, such as that presented by this case, in which the district court having custody of the grand jury records is unlikely to have dependable knowledge of the status of, and the needs of the parties in, the civil suit in which the desired transcripts are to be used.

The judgment of the Court of Appeals is reversed, and the case is remanded for further proceedings consistent with this opinion.

It is so ordered.

JUSTICE REHNQUIST, concurring. [Omitted.]

JUSTICE STEVENS, with whom THE CHIEF JUSTICE and JUSTICE STEWART join, dissenting. [Omitted.]

NOTES AND QUESTIONS

1. *Secrecy interests.* What are the particular interests served by safeguarding the release of grand jury material? How are these interests adversely affected by simultaneous litigation in various courts? Do the interests in safeguarding the grand jury adequately take into account the interests of the litigants needing grand jury information for a legal proceeding?

2. *Standard for release of grand jury material.* In *Douglas Oil*, the Supreme Court adopted a standard for allowing a civil litigant access to grand jury materials:

> a. The material is needed to avoid a possible injustice in a judicial proceeding;

> b. The need for disclosure is greater than the need for continued secrecy; and

> c. The disclosure required is structured to cover only necessary materials.

3. *Availability to DOJ civil attorneys.* The Court in *United States v. Sells Engineering, Inc.*, 463 U.S. 418 (1983), addressed the standard by which grand jury material could be released to attorneys in the civil division of DOJ. Although the government argued that the Rule 6 disclosure exemptions applied to all government attorneys, the Supreme Court held that it was limited to only those government attorneys who were engaged in the criminal investigation. The Court held that the standard is a "highly flexible one, adaptable to different circumstances and sensitive to the fact that the requirements of secrecy are greater in some situations than in others." DOJ civil attorneys may receive grand jury information only via court order based on a showing of particularized need.

On the same day the Court decided the *Sells* case, it also refined the limits on the disclosure of grand jury information in connection with an IRS investigation. The Court considered whether a tax audit is "preliminary to or in connection with a judicial proceeding" in order to come within the protection of Rule 6(e). The Court in *United States v. Baggot*, 463 U. S. 476 (1983), held that administrative agencies cannot inspect grand jury materials unless the "primary purpose" of disclosure is to "assist in preparation or conduct of a judicial proceeding." The Court concluded that the IRS proposed to use the materials to perform the "non-litigative function of assessing taxes rather than to prepare for or to conduct litigation," and thus that the rules of grand jury secrecy prohibited the disclosure of the materials in these circumstances.

4. *Benefits for civil attorneys.* Why might a civil attorney want access to grand jury material? What are some of the ways in which a prior criminal litigation can

assist a civil claimant? The *Douglas Oil* Court reasoned that civil attorneys were not in the same class as criminal attorneys who were conducting the investigation at hand. Why is this so?

[4] Timing of Parallel Proceedings

The sequence of parallel proceedings has the potential to affect both the government and defense. A defendant, for example, may face a choice between asserting the Fifth Amendment privilege in the civil matter — and allowing an adverse inference to be drawn — or providing testimony in the civil case that could be used in a later criminal case. On the other hand, the government may have its own reasons for delaying a civil case, which might provide the defendant with depositions and other forms of discovery that would not be available in a criminal case. The government may also fear loss of evidence and witness tampering if the civil case is allowed to proceed. Parallel proceedings thus raise important tactical and legal questions.

In the following case, the government conducted an extensive civil investigation with the cooperation of persons who were later charged in a related criminal case. The district court dismissed the criminal indictment, holding that the government's conduct had violated the defendants' constitutional rights. As you read the appeals court's decision, consider whether the government's conduct created the potential for unfairness or abuse.

UNITED STATES v. STRINGER
521 F.3d 1189 (9th Cir. 2008)

SCHROEDER, CIRCUIT JUDGE:

I. INTRODUCTION

The United States appeals from a final order of the district court dismissing criminal indictments against three individual defendants charging counts of criminal securities violations. The dismissal was premised on the district court's conclusion that the government had engaged in deceitful conduct, in violation of defendants' due process rights, by simultaneously pursuing civil and criminal investigations of defendants' alleged falsification of the financial records of their high-tech camera sales company.

We vacate the dismissal of the indictments because in a standard form it sent to the defendants, the government fully disclosed the possibility that information received in the course of the civil investigation could be used for criminal proceedings. There was no deceit; rather, at most, there was a government decision not to conduct the criminal investigation openly, a decision we hold the government was free to make. There is nothing improper about the government undertaking simultaneous criminal and civil investigations, and nothing in the government's actual conduct of those investigations amounted to deceit or an affirmative misrepresentation justifying the rare sanction of dismissal of criminal charges or suppression of evidence received in the course of the investigations. . . .

II. BACKGROUND

A. *The concurrent SEC civil and U.S. Attorney criminal investigations*

Prior to the criminal action that forms the basis of this appeal, the SEC began investigating the defendants, J. Kenneth Stringer, III, J. Mark Samper, and William N. Martin, and their company for possible civil securities fraud violations. The company was FLIR Systems, Inc. ("FLIR"), an Oregon corporation headquartered in Portland that sells infrared and heat-sensing cameras for military and industrial use. The SEC began the investigation on June 8, 2000. About two weeks later, the SEC held the first of a series of meetings with the Oregon United States Attorney's Office ("USAO") to coordinate the ongoing SEC investigation with a possible criminal investigation. An SEC Assistant Director and an SEC Staff Attorney met with the supervisor of the white collar crime section of the USAO to discuss the possibility of opening a criminal investigation. The meeting apparently convinced the USAO supervisor to investigate. Within days, the USAO and the Federal Bureau of Investigation ("FBI") opened a criminal investigation.

Federal securities laws authorize the SEC to transmit evidence it has gathered to the USAO to facilitate a criminal investigation by the USAO. To gather evidence for its criminal investigation, the Oregon USAO in June of 2000 sent a letter to the SEC (the "Access Letter") requesting access to the SEC's non-public investigative files, and the SEC promptly granted access.

The civil and criminal investigations proceeded in tandem and the SEC continued to meet and communicate with the USAO and FBI. The SEC turned over documents the SEC collected through its civil investigation.

At the beginning of the criminal investigation, the USAO identified two of the three defendants, FLIR's former CEO, Stringer, and former CFO, Samper, as possible targets, and named them in the USAO's Access Letter to the SEC.

The district court concluded that the third defendant, Martin, former VP of Sales, was also an early potential target of the criminal investigation. During a January 2001 meeting, the SEC advised the USAO and FBI that FLIR was blaming Stringer and Martin for the fraudulent conduct at the heart of the investigation.

Early in the criminal investigation, the USAO decided the investigation should remain confidential. At an October 2000 meeting between the SEC, USAO, and FBI, the AUSA advised that the evidence collected by the SEC might support criminal wire fraud charges. Nonetheless, an internal FBI memo issued in late October stated that the AUSA had concluded, based on the defendants' cooperation with the SEC at that point, that the SEC should investigate "without the assistance or inclusion of the FBI." At the January 2001 meeting between the SEC, FBI, and USAO, the SEC revealed that FLIR was cooperative and was providing evidence that was damaging to Stringer and Martin.

By June 2001, the USAO was not yet ready to convene a grand jury and issue indictments. The SEC and USAO believed that FLIR and defendant Samper would settle with the SEC so long as the U.S. Attorney was not directly involved. During a December 2001 phone conversation between the AUSA assigned to the case and the SEC Assistant Director, the AUSA continued to believe it was "premature [sic] to surface" and that the presence of an AUSA would "impede" a meeting between the SEC and defendants. During a December 2002 phone call, the SEC and USAO decided that the USAO would not "surface", i.e., convene a grand jury and issue indictments, until the "end of Jan/early Feb" 2003.

The SEC facilitated the criminal investigation in a number of ways. The SEC offered to conduct the interviews of defendants so as to create "the best record possible" in support of "false statement cases" against them, and the AUSA instructed the SEC Staff Attorney on how best to do that. The AUSA asked the relevant SEC office, located in Los Angeles, to take the depositions in Oregon so that the Portland Office of the USAO would have venue over any false statements case that might arise from the depositions, and the SEC did so. Both the SEC and USAO wanted the existence of the criminal investigation kept confidential.

The SEC, however, did not hide from the defendants the possibility — even likelihood — of such an investigation. The SEC sent each of the defendants subpoenas in the summer of 2001, and attached to each was Form 1662, a form sent to all witnesses subpoenaed to testify before the SEC. Under the header "Routine Uses of Information," the four-page form states that "[t]he Commission often makes its files available to other governmental agencies, particularly the United States Attorneys and state prosecutors. There is a likelihood that information supplied by you will be made available to such agencies where appropriate."

Form 1662 also advises witnesses of their Fifth Amendment rights. After the heading "Fifth Amendment and Voluntary Testimony," the form states that:

> Information you give may be used against you in any federal . . . civil or criminal proceeding brought by the Commission of any other agency. You may refuse, in accordance with the rights guaranteed to you by the Fifth Amendment of the Constitution of the United States, to give any information that may tend to incriminate you or subject you to fine, penalty, or forfeiture.

None of the defendants invoked his right against self-incrimination during his deposition, and all proceeded to testify in compliance with the subpoena. Each of the defendants was represented by counsel when he testified.

During the course of Stringer's deposition, taken in Portland in October 2001, Stringer's attorney actually questioned the SEC Staff Attorney about the involvement of the USAO. In response to those questions, the SEC Staff Attorney answered as follows:

MR. MARTSON: My first question is whether Mr. Stringer is a target of any aspect of the investigation being conducted by the SEC.

STAFF ATTORNEY: The SEC does not have targets in this investigation.

MR. MARTSON: The other questions I have relate to whether or not, in connection with your investigation, the SEC is working in conjunction with any other department of the United States, such as the U.S. Attorney's Office in any jurisdiction, or the Department of Justice.

STAFF ATTORNEY: As laid out in the 1662 form, in the "routine use of" section there are routine uses of our investigation, and it is the agency's policy not to respond to questions like that, but instead, to direct you to the other agencies you mentioned.

MR. MARTSON: And which U.S. Attorney's Office might I inquire into?

STAFF ATTORNEY: That would be a matter up to your discretion.

The record does not show the SEC did anything to impede an inquiry, nor does it disclose that any inquiry was made. The record reflects that the government never furnished defendants with any false information concerning the existence of a criminal investigation.

In September 2002, a year before the criminal indictments, defendants Samper and Martin entered into consent decrees in the civil action, agreeing to pay penalties, disgorgement, and pre-judgment interest. . . .

III. DISCUSSION

A. *The Parallel Investigations*

The Supreme Court has held that the government may conduct parallel civil and criminal investigations without violating the due process clause, so long as it does not act in bad faith. *See United States v. Kordel*, 397 U.S. 1, 11 (1970). The Court suggested that the government may act in bad faith if it brings a civil action solely for the purpose of obtaining evidence in a criminal prosecution and does not advise the defendant of the planned use of evidence in a criminal proceeding.

In this case, the district court concluded that the government should have told defendants of the criminal investigation and that it violated the standards laid down in *Kordel* when it failed to "advise defendants that it anticipated their criminal prosecution." *Stringer*, 408 F.Supp.2d at 1088. It held that the government engaged in "trickery and deceit" when the SEC staff attorney instructed court reporters to refrain from mentioning the AUSA's involvement. When the SEC staff attorney responded to Stringer's attorney's question, during Stringer's deposition, by directing him to the U.S. Attorney, the district court concluded that the SEC attorney "evaded the question." *Id.* at 1089.

In its appeal, the government argues that it had no legal duty to make any further disclosure of the existence of the pending criminal investigation. It points to the warnings in Form 1662 in which the government disclosed the possibility of criminal prosecution, and it stresses that it did not make any affirmative misrepresentations. It maintains the SEC attorney's answer was appropriate and truthful. . . .

The defendants contend that the district court properly concluded that the government used the civil investigation solely to obtain evidence for a subsequent criminal prosecution, in violation of due process. . . . In this case, the government argues that it did not violate defendants' due process rights because the civil investigation was not commenced solely to obtain evidence for a criminal prosecution.

It is significant to our analysis that the SEC began its civil investigation first and brought in the U.S. Attorney later. This tends to negate any likelihood that the government began the civil investigation in bad faith, as, for example, in order to obtain evidence for a criminal prosecution. . . .

United States v. Posada Carriles, 486 F. Supp.2d 599, 619–21 (W.D. Tex. 2007), on the other hand, is a clear example of government bad faith. The district court dismissed an indictment because the U.S. Citizenship and Immigration Services ("USCIS") interviewed the defendant solely to collect evidence in support of a criminal case against him. The defendant, a Cuban national, filed an application for naturalization. Although USCIS had already determined that the defendant was not eligible for citizenship, the agency nonetheless invited him to a pre-citizenship interview in order to collect evidence for a criminal false statements case. The interview protocol was altered in so many ways to serve the needs of the criminal investigation that it became an interrogation. The court described the "interview" as follows:

> (1) it lasted eight hours over the course of two days as opposed to the usual maximum of thirty minutes, (2) it involved two interviewers, (3) the [g]overnment provided an interpreter, (4) there were a total of four attorneys present-two defense attorneys and two Government attorneys, and (5) it was both audio and videotaped.

Id. Because the "entire interview was . . . a pretext for a criminal investigation," the district court dismissed the indictment. *Id.* at 629–20.

Our case is not remotely similar to *Posada Carriles*. In this case the SEC's civil investigation was opened first, led to SEC sanctions and was conducted pursuant to the SEC's own civil enforcement jurisdiction. It was not a pretext for the USAO's criminal investigation of defendants. Congress has expressly authorized the SEC to share information with the Department of Justice to facilitate the investigation and prosecution of crimes. We must conclude the SEC interviewed the defendants in support of a bona fide civil investigation. There was no violation of due process.

*   *   *

IV. CONCLUSION

For the foregoing reasons, we conclude that there was no deception or affirmative misconduct on the part of the government in the course of the SEC and U.S. Attorney investigations that warranted dismissal of the indictment or suppression of any of the evidence in question.

NOTES AND QUESTIONS

1. *Potential for abuse.* Was the district court correct that the government used "trickery and deceit" in this case? Was the manner in which the government conducted the parallel investigations unfair to the defendants? Why or why not? Even if so, did the unfairness amount to a due process violation? For a critical analysis of the *Stringer* decision, see W. Warren Hamel & Danette R. Edwards, *Parallel Investigations — 'Pay No Attention to the Man Behind the Curtain:'* United States v. Stringer *and the Government's Obligations to Disclose*, White Collar Crime Rep. (BNA) Vol. 3, No. 11, at 367 (May 23, 2008).

For a case raising similar issues, see *United States v. Scrushy*, 366 F. Supp. 2d 1134 (N.D. Ala. 2005). In that case, the court found that the government's criminal investigation was too closely connected with its civil action. The government did not appeal this decision. *See* Eli Ewing, Comment: *Too Close for Comfort:* United States v. Stringer *and* United States v. Scrushy *Impose a Stricter Standard on SEC/DOJ Parallel Proceedings*, 25 Yale L. & Pol'y Rev. 217 (2006).

2. *Priority of litigation.* When there are common facts between the parallel civil and criminal proceedings, courts give judicial deference to the criminal proceeding. A criminal prosecution will have priority in scheduling because of the constitutional right to a speedy trial. When a civil litigant seeks a stay of an administrative or civil proceeding, the district court will have discretion to grant the stay pending the outcome of the criminal action. What specific risks does a litigant face if the requested stay is not granted?

3. *The Fifth Amendment and stays of civil proceedings.* The challenges facing a defendant confronted with parallel proceedings were illustrated in *Keating v. Office of Thrift Supervision*, 45 F.3d 322 (9th Cir. 1995), a case arising out of a major savings and loan scandal. In that case, the Office of Thrift Supervision (OTS) instituted a civil proceeding against Keating and refused to stay that proceeding while Keating faced parallel state and federal criminal proceedings. Because of the criminal proceedings, Keating asserted his Fifth Amendment privilege in the civil OTS matter. Keating argued on appeal in that matter that the failure to stay the OTS case violated his due process rights. The Ninth Circuit disagreed. The court found that Keating had sufficient time to prepare for the OTS proceeding, and had no absolute right to a stay. The court therefore concluded that there was no abuse of discretion in denying the stay.

4. *Benefits to litigants.* The government will often assert that its investigation would be impeded if civil discovery proceeds. Why is this? What are the possible costs and benefits for the government if the civil discovery proceeds? What are the possible costs and benefits for the criminal defendant if civil discovery proceeds?

5. *Martha Stewart.* Martha Stewart was indicted, found guilty, and served five months in prison for four counts of lying to federal agents and obstructing justice. While her criminal case was pending, a consolidated class action was filed against her and some of the directors of her company, Martha Stewart Living Omnimedia, Inc. *Semon v. Martha Stewart Living Omnimedia, Inc.*, 02 Civ. 6273 (S.D.N.Y. Sept. 30, 2003).

The parties sought a stay regarding some of the witnesses who were expected to testify in the criminal case. The government argued that, if the individuals were deposed, Stewart's lawyers would gain an unfair discovery advantage. The rules of criminal procedure do not provide for pre-trial depositions of witnesses. The court denied the government's request, finding that the government made numerous public pronouncements about the case. In addition, the court discredited the government's assertion that it would be unfairly disadvantaged, saying that it did not want the civil case to "hang[] in the air" for years, while the criminal proceedings were ongoing. *Id.* at 22. Courts are willing to consider allegations of unfair discovery and prejudice when ruling on motions such as these.

[D] DEFERRED AND NON-PROSECUTION AGREEMENTS

Background. Since early in the last century, pre-trial diversion had been used by the government as a way to ferret out of the criminal justice system those individuals who were minor offenders. Traditionally used for juveniles, it allowed the government to divert offenders after completion of a term of probation. One of the goals was to assist in case management so that judges could concentrate on more serious crimes. Upon successful completion of the probationary period, the offender was able to avert stigmatization for life by having the charges dropped.

Beginning in 2003, after the post-indictment collapse of Arthur Andersen, the government began to shift its tactics by using pre-trial diversion for corporate offenders. In its Thompson/McNulty memoranda (discussed in Chapter 15, Internal Investigations and Compliance Programs, *supra* at § 15[B][2]), the DOJ signaled that pre-trial diversion might be an option for corporations under investigation. As a result, a tool that was intended to clear the courts of minor cases is now being used to benefit large multinational corporations.

A corporate deferred prosecution agreement (DPA) or non-prosecution agreement (NPA) allows a company to submit to a term of probation before conviction and possibly to avoid conviction altogether. By focusing on cooperation, DOJ signaled to corporate America that the government could possibly defer prosecution through satisfactory cooperation with the investigation in a timely fashion. Under a DPA, a company is given a certain time period during which DOJ will hold the indictment in abeyance. In exchange, the corporation acknowledges that the government can prove its case, and agrees to fully cooperate with the investigation. If a corporation shows that it has engaged in corporate reform, including compliance with Sarbanes-Oxley obligations, then the charges are dismissed at the end of the probationary period. With the NPA, there is no indictment, and charges are never filed. (DPA will be used to refer to both types of agreements.)

Today, the use of DPAs has skyrocketed in white collar and corporate criminal cases, with more than 100 agreements just since 2003. A running compilation is maintained   at: http://www.law.virginia.edu/html/librarysite/ garrett_bycompany.htm. The continued use of DPAs raises many concerns for the criminal justice system. *See* Eric Lichtblau, *In Justice Shift, Corporate Deals Replace Trials*, N.Y. Times, Apr. 9, 2008.

Supervision. Traditionally, once an individual or company is convicted and placed on probation, the judicial branch, through the U.S. Probation and Pretrial Services Office, is the supervisory authority. In a twist of control, with a DPA, prosecutors are now in charge of both the prosecution and the probation. Because there is no judicial oversight, the conditions must be met to the satisfaction of the prosecutor. There is a great deal of debate over whether the government is the proper entity to monitor these DPAs, and DOJ has issued guidelines in this matter. *See* Memorandum for Heads of Department Components United States Attorneys: Selection and Use of Monitors in Deferred Prosecution Agreements and Non-Prosecution Agreements with Corporations. Morford Memorandum, http:// www.usdoj.gov/dag/morford-useofmonitorsmemo-03072008.pdf. DOJ is concerned that the appointed monitor avoid any conflict of interest with the corporation under DPA supervision. Questions remain whether the monitor should focus only on criminal allegations that were the subject of the investigation, or whether the monitor should investigate and report new allegations of wrongdoing.

Terms of Probation. The terms of the probationary period are as varied as a prosecutor's imagination. For example, probationary terms include fines, cooperation, maintenance or improvement of compliance programs, and restitution. Defendants have been required to waive procedural rights, such as the right to a speedy trial, and statutes of limitations. Noteworthy DPA terms include directing a corporation to donate money to the alma mater of the prosecutor, establishing an endowed chair at a university, creating thousands of jobs, and providing free health care. While these probationary conditions may be laudable, it remains to be seen whether their inclusion in a DPA serves the interests of justice. DOJ has issued new guidelines restricting the use of creative probationary terms. "Plea agreements, deferred prosecution agreements and non-prosecution agreements should not include terms requiring the defendant to pay funds to a charitable, educational, community, or other organization or individual that is not a victim of the criminal activity or is not providing services to redress the harm caused by the defendant's criminal conduct." U.S. Attorneys' Manual, 9–16.325 Plea Agreements, Deferred Prosecution Agreements, Non-Prosecution Agreements, and Extraordinary Restitution.

Attorney-client privilege waivers. Corporations have been placed under pressure to waive certain constitutional protections in order to gain a negotiating advantage with the government. *See* Chapter 15, Internal Investigations and Compliance Programs, *supra* at § 15[B][2]. Although the corporation has no Fifth Amendment rights, principals within the corporate structure and other key employees may be forced to choose between cooperating with the government and facing criminal prosecution. This dilemma is no different than the dilemma faced by individuals who come under scrutiny by the government. The matter takes on added significance in the corporate contact, however, because the corporation can only act through its agents. As a result, key individuals have been known to enter pleas on behalf of the corporation in order to avoid individual prosecution. After all, a corporation cannot be imprisoned.

Unresolved issues. Despite their historical limitations, DPAs are gaining in popularity and usage. These agreements raise a myriad of challenges and questions for defense counsel and corporations. Consider how a DPA differs from negotiating a civil resolution, ordinary probation, and restitution. Are the factors that motivate the government to pursue white collar and corporate crime more aggressively consistent with corporate DPAs? Is their use consistent with the war on corporate crime? What negative effects will the increased use of DPAs have on criminal justice? Consider these and other questions as you tackle the following problem.

PROBLEM

18-2. (a) You are working for the Deputy Attorney General at the Department of Justice. Your assignment is to draft a memorandum that will be issued to all United States attorneys concerning the use of deferred and non-prosecution agreements. Before you begin the draft of this memorandum for review, list the top five factors that weigh in favor of using these arrangements. Consider the benefits to the justice system, society, and the accused.

(b) You are connected with a national group of defense lawyers who practice in the area of corporate and white collar criminal defense. The group has asked you to advise them on the detriments of the deferred and non-prosecution agreements that the government is advocating. Prepare a short memorandum outlining the top five reasons why these arrangements are not in the best interests of the defense bar and criminal defendants.

NOTES ON RECURRING ISSUES

Other legal issues frequently arise in the context of the interplay between civil and criminal litigation. *See* Milton Pollack, *Parallel Civil and Criminal Proceedings*, 129 F.R.D. 201 (1989). Some of these are highlighted below.

1. *Settlements.* Settlement negotiations present another opportunity for the government to gain evidence for use in a criminal case. The subject of parallel proceedings has the opportunity to seek a global settlement in order to resolve criminal charges along with the civil claims simultaneously. Rule 408 of the Federal Rules of Evidence deals with settlement discussions and their use at trial. Rule 408 protects settlement discussions from disclosure at a subsequent trial or hearing. The rule's protection relates to civil matters but does not extend to criminal prosecutions. Most courts hold that settlement discussions can be used against a defendant in a criminal case. Why is this distinction made in the evidentiary rules?

2. *Admissions.* In addition, Rule 801(d)(2)(A) of the Federal Rules of Evidence allows party admissions to be offered against a litigant. *See United States v. Cohen*, 946 F.2d 430 (6th Cir. 1991) (SEC consent decree is admissible as party admission, not under Rule 408). The government does not have the opportunity to depose a criminal defendant or to obtain statements prior to the indictment or trial of a criminal case. Because the government does not know what the defendant's position will be on critical aspects of the criminal matter, the government benefits from any prior statements, especially those made under oath. If the government has available a deposition of the criminal defendant, the contents can be included in an indictment, and assist the prosecutor in crafting cross-examination questions. Whenever a party is engaged in discussions with the government preliminary to the filing of charges, during the course of a civil investigation, or during settlement negotiations, these statements or other documents can be admitted against the party as admissions.

PROBLEM

18-3. You have a corporate client who is engaged in retail activities. The company has a network of stores across the country, and also conducts sales on the Internet. During the past few years, you have assisted the client in much of its business and legal dealings. The client comes to you and tells you the following:

a. A former group of employees is suing the client for discriminatory dismissal, and seeks to depose the CEO.

b. The federal government has served a grand jury subpoena seeking the employment documents for the last five years.

c. The SEC is investigating improper activity with respect to the publicly-traded stock. In connection with this action, the SEC is holding a significant amount of the client's money in escrow.

The client's executives tell you that they have done nothing wrong, and are eager to get all of this behind them. The CEO wants to comply with the grand jury subpoena, and is eager to be deposed in the civil matter to "straighten this matter out." *Counsel this client with respect to the three situations above.*

Chapter 19

SENTENCING

[A] INTRODUCTORY NOTES

[1]   Sentencing Reform

Federal sentencing has undergone two profound changes since the mid-1980s. First, the adoption of the Federal Sentencing Guidelines ("Guidelines") in 1987 removed much of the sentencing discretion that trial judges had before that time. Second, beginning in 2005, the United States Supreme Court issued a series of decisions that restored substantial sentencing discretion to trial judges.

Prior to the adoption of the Guidelines, judges had wide discretion to sentence individual defendants anywhere between the minimum and maximum sentences that Congress specified for particular crimes. In addition, many defendants were granted parole before serving their full terms. This system resulted in widely disparate sentences for similarly situated defendants.

To reduce sentencing discretion and disparities, Congress passed the Sentencing Reform Act of 1984. The Act established the United States Sentencing Commission, which promulgated the Guidelines in 1987. The Guidelines effected a major overhaul of federal sentencing. Parole was eliminated, and judges were constricted in their ability to tailor sentences to the individual offenders. The Guidelines generally required sentencing judges to impose prison terms within a narrow range (for example, between 100 and 125 months) that the Guidelines specified.

The Sentencing Commission did provide for upward or downward "departures" from mandatory sentencing ranges in a limited set of circumstances. First, on motion by the government, the judges could depart downward where the defendant has provided "substantial assistance" to the government. Second, when the sentencing judge found the case to be outside "the heartland" of factors taken into account by the Sentencing Commission, the judge could employ an upward or downward departure from the Guidelines sentence. Nonetheless, the vast majority of sentences were within the mandatory ranges set by the Guidelines.

The mandatory nature of Guidelines-sentencing was highly controversial. Critics contended that this system did not allow defendants to be treated as individuals and was therefore unjust. Critics also argued that because sentences now depended largely on the charged offenses, the Guidelines provided prosecutors with enormous power to determine sentence ranges.[a]

---

[a] The critics were legion. *See, e.g,* Stephen J. Schulhofer & Ilene H. Nagel, *Plea Negotiations Under the Federal Sentencing Guidelines: Guideline Circumvention and Its Dynamics in the Post-*Mistretta *Period,* 91 Nw. U. L. Rev. 1284 (1997); Charles J. Ogletree, Jr., *The Death of Discretion? Reflections on the Federal Sentencing Guidelines,* 101 Harv. L. Rev. 1938 (1988).

[2]   The *Booker* Decision and Its Aftermath

Eighteen years after the Guidelines' enactment, the federal sentencing landscape again changed dramatically. In 2005, the United States Supreme Court issued its decision in *United States v. Booker*, 543 U.S. 220 (2005). The Court in *Booker* held that sentencing under the Guidelines may violate a defendant's Sixth Amendment right to a jury trial because such sentencing depends upon facts found by a judge rather than by a jury. The Court further held that the Guidelines can be constitutionally applied if they are considered merely *advisory* rather than mandatory. The Court also held that appellate courts should review sentences under a "reasonableness" standard.

The *Booker* opinion appeared to give sentencing courts substantially more discretion than they had previously under the mandatory sentencing scheme. Nonetheless, courts continued to impose Guidelines-range sentences on the vast majority of defendants. Many trial and appellate courts presumed that sentences outside the Guidelines range were unreasonable. The Court gave some support to that approach in *Rita v. United States*, 551 U.S. 338 (2007). In that case, the Court held that appeals courts may, but are not required to, presume that Guidelines-range sentences are reasonable.

Subsequent to *Rita*, however, the Supreme Court issued two decisions that reemphasized the discretionary nature of federal sentencing under *Booker*. First, in *Kimbrough v. United States*, 128 S. Ct. 558 (2007), the Court held that a district court may rely upon its own disagreement with policies underlying the Guidelines when imposing an outside-Guidelines-range sentence. Second, in *Gall v. United States*, 128 S. Ct. 586 (2007), the Court reiterated that neither trial nor appellate courts may presume that outside-Guidelines-range sentences are unreasonable. The Court further held that appellate courts may not require that "extraordinary" circumstances be present to justify non-Guidelines-range sentences.

The *Kimbrough* and *Gall* decisions should restore discretion to sentencing judges to impose non-Guidelines-range sentences. The degree to which sentencing judges will exercise the discretion remains to be seen. Also, it is unclear whether appellate courts will truly defer to trial judge's sentencing determinations.

This chapter evaluates the sentencing landscape in the wake of the recent United States Supreme Court decisions. Before turning to those cases, the chapter examines the Guidelines' sentencing scheme.

[B]   OVERVIEW OF THE SENTENCING COMMISSION AND GUIDELINES

Even after *Booker*, all federal sentencing begins with a calculation of the Guidelines' sentencing range. It therefore remains critical to understand how the Guidelines operate.

[1]   The Sentencing Commission

The Guidelines are promulgated by the Sentencing Commission, which is an independent body within the judicial branch of the federal government. The Commission consists of seven voting members, up to three of whom may be federal judges. The members are appointed by the President "after consultation with representatives of judges, prosecuting attorneys, defense attorneys, law enforcement officials [and others]" and "with the advice and consent of the Senate." 28 U.S.C. § 991(a). The Commission regularly reassesses and revises the Guidelines, subject to approval by Congress. *See* 28 U.S.C. § 994(o)–(p).

[2] The Sentencing Scheme

Sentencing under the Guidelines is intended to be based primarily upon the "real offense" that the defendant committed. Thus, the specific crime for which the defendant has been convicted does not solely determine the sentence range. Instead, the range will be determined by various facts relating to the crime.[b]

These facts produce the Guidelines-sentence range, which is set forth in the Sentencing Table (reproduced in the Casebook Statutory Supplement). The Table's vertical axis represents the "Offense Level," and the horizontal axis represents the defendant's "Criminal History Category." Once the Offense Level and Criminal History Category are determined, the sentence is a range determined by the intersection of the two. The actual sentence imposed cannot exceed the statutory maximum sentence, even where the Sentencing Table provides for a higher sentence.

Each federal offense is assigned a "base level" number of points. This number can be increased by various Guidelines factors, each of which will increase the base level by a specified number of points. The most important factor in many white collar cases is the "amount of loss" that the defendant's actions caused. Other important factors in white collar cases include the number of victims, the use of sophisticated means, the use of more than minimal planning, the abuse of a position of trust, and the role as an organizer in the criminal activity.

To determine a defendant's Criminal History, the sentencing judge must again make factual determinations. These include the number and length of prior sentences, and the commission of the offense while under any criminal sentence.

As discussed throughout this chapter, it is unclear whether and to what degree courts will adhere to Guidelines sentencing ranges in the wake of the *Booker* decision. The next section discusses constitutional issues relating to the Guidelines, sets forth the *Booker* decision, and concludes with the myriad of questions that the decision raises.

[3] Determining an Individual Sentence

As can be seen from the above summary, federal sentencing involves a technical determination of the sentencing range. This determination involves a number of specific steps.

---

[b] To arrive at the sentencing range, the United States Probation Office completes the Sentencing Worksheets (reproduced in the Statutory Supplement). The worksheets identify the specific offense characteristics, adjustments, and criminal history to determine the Guidelines range. The Probation Office also prepares a Pre-Sentence Report (PSR), which the Office provides to the trial judge prior to sentencing.

Federal sentencing law is both complex and rapidly changing. For more complete coverage, see Thomas W. Hutchison, *Federal Sentencing Law and Practice* (2006 ed.); Harry I. Subin, Barry Berke, & Eric Tirschwell, The Practice of Federal Criminal Law: Prosecution and Defense §§ 7.0–7.3 (2006). For the most recent sentencing data, see http://www.ussc.gov/bf.htm.

Base offense level. The base level offense must be determined. The Guidelines Manual sets forth hundreds of criminal offenses with base offense levels from one to forty-three. These are grouped together by offense type, and are ranked by severity.

Offense Characteristics. The court must determine the specific offense characteristics. These characteristics are also grouped by the type and severity of the offense. If these characteristics are present, the court will adjust the offense level to account for these factors. For example, the default offense level for economic offenses is six. U.S.S.G. § 2B1.1(a)(2). If the offense caused a loss of more than $200,000 but less than $400,000, 12 points are added to the offense level. U.S.S.G. § 2B1.1(b)(1). With a Criminal History Category of 1, the amount of loss results in an increase in the sentence range from 0–6 months to 27–33 months.

Aggravating or mitigating circumstances. After determining the offense level, the court will assess whether there are aggravating or mitigating circumstances present. Importantly in many white collar cases, a court may also impose an upward adjustment if the "defendant willfully obstructed or impeded, or attempted to obstruct or impede, the administration of justice during the course of the investigation, prosecution, or sentencing. . . . " U.S.S.G. § 3C1.1. An upward adjustment may also be made, for example, if the defendant organized or led criminal activity that involved five or more participants. Conversely, a court may adjust downward if the defendant played only a minor role in the offense. *See* U.S.S.G. Ch. 3 — Adjustments, Part B — Role in the Offense.

Grouping. If the defendant was convicted of multiple counts, the court may "group" those counts for sentencing if the counts involved substantially the same harm. Thus, multiple counts of mail fraud — each mailing can be a separate count — will be grouped together if they are part of the same fraudulent scheme. *See* U.S.S.G. § 3D1.2, Commentary — Application Notes (4). "Grouping" results in a "combined offense level."

Acceptance of responsibility. When the defendant accepts responsibility for the offense, the court may make a downward adjustment. This requires that the defendant "clearly demonstrate[] acceptance of responsibility." U.S.S.G. § 3E1.1(a).

Relevant conduct. In determining the offense level, the court may take "relevant conduct" into account. "Relevant conduct" includes "all acts and omissions . . . that occurred during the commission of the offense, in preparation for that offense, or in the course of attempting to avoid detection or responsibility for that offense. . . . " Further, relevant conduct includes "all acts and omissions that were part of the same course of conduct or common scheme or plan as the offense of conviction." U.S.S.G. § 1B1.3(a)(1). *See* § [E], *infra.*

Criminal history. Once the court calculates the offense level, it must then determine the criminal history category. The Guidelines rest on the assumption that a repeat offender poses a special danger to society and should be punished more severely. *See* U.S.S.G. Ch. 4 — Criminal History and Criminal Livelihood — Part A — Criminal History — Introductory Commentary. The sentencing judge adds points for each prior conviction and then calculates the criminal history category. U.S.S.G. § 4A1.1. The Guidelines also provide that the court may depart upward if the court has other information concerning the seriousness of the defendant's past criminal conduct or the likelihood that the defendant will commit future crimes. U.S.S.G. § 4A1.3.

Substantial assistance. As discussed in § [F], *infra,* a court may impose a below Guidelines-range sentence based upon a defendant's "substantial assistance" to the government in a criminal investigation or prosecution. U.S.S.G. § 5K1.1.

Section 3553(a) factors. The offense level and criminal history determine the sentencing range. After *Booker,* a court may not mechanically apply the Guidelines range, but must comply with the requirements of 18 U.S.C. § 3553(a). That section requires sentencing courts to consider:

(1)   the nature and circumstances of the offense and the history and characteristics of the defendant;

(2)   the need for the sentence imposed —

    (A)   to reflect the seriousness of the offense, to promote respect for the law, and to provide just punishment for the offense;

    (B)   to afford adequate deterrence to criminal conduct;

    (C)   to protect the public from further crimes of the defendant; and

    (D)   to provide the defendant with needed educational or vocational training, medical care, or other correctional treatment in the most effective manner;

(3)   the kinds of sentences available;

(4)   the advisory guideline range;

(5)   any pertinent policy statements issued by the Sentencing Commission;

(6)   the need to avoid unwarranted sentence disparities; and

(7)   the need to provide restitution to any victims of the offense.

18 U.S.C. § 3553(a). The statute further instructs sentencing courts to impose a sentence that is "sufficient but not greater than necessary" to satisfy the purposes of sentencing — just punishment, deterrence, protection of the public, and rehabilitation of the defendant. *Id.* The Supreme Court explained that this "parsimony" clause represents the "overarching provision" of the statute. *Kimbrough,* 128 S. Ct. at 570.

As discussed below in §§ [C]–[D], the post-*Booker, Rita, Kimbrough,* and *Gall* sentencing landscape will unfold in the years ahead. Before turning to current sentencing issues, the chapter will address the constitutional issues surrounding the Guidelines.

[C]   CONSTITUTIONAL CHALLENGES

[1]   Separation of Powers — The *Mistretta* Decision

Following the Guidelines' adoption in 1987, defendants challenged the constitutionality of the Guidelines and of the Sentencing Commission itself on two grounds. These challengers argued that (1) Congress' delegation of authority to the Commission was overly broad, and (2) the creation of the Commission violated the separation of powers doctrine.

In *Mistretta v. United States,* 488 U.S. 361 (1989), the Supreme Court rejected these challenges. Mistretta argued that the Guidelines were unconstitutional "on the grounds that the Sentencing Commission was constituted in violation of the established doctrine of separation of powers, and that Congress delegated excessive authority to the Commission to structure the guidelines." As to the excessive delegation argument, the Court found that Congress has the power to assign the task of formulating sentencing guidelines to a group of experts within the judicial branch who are guided by a very specific statutory mandate.

As to the separation of powers argument, the Court held that it was appropriate for the Commission to operate within the judicial branch because the judicial branch has general responsibility for sentencing. The Court also held that the judicial Commissioners' appointment by the President does not violate Article III because the Commission's judicial members act in an administrative rather than a judicial capacity. The Court also rejected the defendant's argument that presidential appointments to a judicial body violated the separation of powers, finding that the system does not prevent "the Judicial branch from performing its constitutionally assigned function of fairly adjudicating cases and controversies."

[2]   The Sixth Amendment Right to a Jury Trial — The *Booker* Decision

As seen from the introductory discussion, the Guidelines require the trial judge to find certain facts that will determine a defendant's sentence. In *Apprendi v. New Jersey*, 530 U.S. 466, 490 (2000), however, the Supreme Court held that "other than the fact of a prior conviction, any fact that increases the penalty for a crime beyond the prescribed statutory maximum must be submitted to a jury, and proved beyond a reasonable doubt." The *Apprendi* decision therefore called the Guidelines sentencing scheme into question.

Four years after the *Apprendi* decision, the Court held in *Blakely v. Washington*, 542 U.S. 296 (2004), that Washington state's sentencing system violated the defendant's Sixth Amendment right to a jury trial because the system allowed the judge to make factual findings that determined a defendant's sentence. The decision in *Blakely* set the stage for the consolidated cases of *United States v. Booker* and *United States v. Fanfan* (referred to in this text as *United States v. Booker* or *Booker*).

The *Booker* decision is lengthy, and is in effect two different decisions: (1) the "merits" decision on the Sixth Amendment issue; and (2) the "remedial" decision on how the Guidelines should be interpreted in light of the merits decision. As you read the decisions, pay particular attention to the role that white collar sentencing plays in the analysis underlying Justice Breyer's remedial opinion.

UNITED STATES v. BOOKER
543 U.S. 220 (2005)

STEVENS, J., delivered the [merits] opinion of the Court . . . , in which SCALIA, SOUTER, THOMAS, and GINSBURG, JJ., joined.

The question presented in each of these cases is whether an application of the Federal Sentencing Guidelines violated the Sixth Amendment. In each case, the courts below held that binding rules set forth in the Guidelines limited the severity of the sentence that the judge could lawfully impose on the defendant based on the facts found by the jury at his trial. In both cases the courts rejected, on the basis of our decision in *Blakely v. Washington*, 124 S. Ct. 2531 (2004), the Government's recommended application of the Sentencing Guidelines because the proposed sentences were based on additional facts that the sentencing judge found by a preponderance of the evidence. We hold that both courts correctly concluded that the Sixth Amendment as construed in Blakely does apply to the Sentencing Guidelines. In a separate opinion authored by Justice Breyer, the Court concludes that in light of this holding, two provisions of the Sentencing Reform Act of 1984 (SRA) that have the effect of making the Guidelines mandatory must be invalidated in order to allow the statute to operate in a manner consistent with congressional intent.

I.

Respondent Booker was charged with possession with intent to distribute at least 50 grams of cocaine base (crack). Having heard evidence that he had 92.5 grams in his duffel bag, the jury found him guilty of violating 21 U.S.C. § 841(a)(1). That statute prescribes a minimum sentence of 10 years in prison and a maximum sentence of life for that offense.

Based upon Booker's criminal history and the quantity of drugs found by the jury, the Sentencing Guidelines required the District Court Judge to select a "'base" sentence of not less than 210 nor more than 262 months in prison. See United States Sentencing Commission, Guidelines Manual §§ 2D1.1(c)(4), 4A1.1 (hereinafter USSG). The judge, however, held a post-trial sentencing proceeding and concluded by a preponderance of the evidence that Booker had possessed an additional grams of crack and that he was guilty of obstructing justice. Those findings mandated that the judge select a sentence between 360 months and life imprisonment; the judge imposed a sentence at the low end of the range. Thus, instead of the sentence of 21 years and 10 months that the judge could have imposed on the basis of the facts proved to the jury beyond a reasonable doubt, Booker received a 30-year sentence.

[T]he Court of Appeals for the Seventh Circuit held that this application of the Sentencing Guidelines conflicted with our holding in Apprendi v. New Jersey, 530 U.S. 466, 490 (2000). . . .

Respondent Fanfan was charged with conspiracy to distribute and to possess with intent to distribute at least 500 grams of cocaine in violation of 21 U.S.C. §§ 846, 841(a)(1), and 841(b)(1)(B)(ii). He was convicted by the jury after it answered "Yes" to the question "Was the amount of cocaine 500 or more grams?" Under the Guidelines, without additional findings of fact, the maximum sentence authorized by the jury verdict was imprisonment for 78 months.

A few days after our decision in Blakely, the trial judge conducted a sentencing hearing at which he found additional facts that, under the Guidelines, would have authorized a sentence in the 188-to-235 month range. Specifically, he found that respondent Fanfan was responsible for 2.5 kilograms of cocaine powder, and 261.6 grams of crack. He also concluded that respondent had been an organizer, leader, manager, or supervisor in the criminal activity. Both findings were made by a preponderance of the evidence. Under the Guidelines, these additional findings would have required an enhanced sentence of 15 or 16 years instead of the 5 or 6 years authorized by the jury verdict alone. Relying not only on the majority opinion in Blakely, but also on the categorical statements in the dissenting opinions and in the Solicitor General's brief in Blakely, the judge concluded that he could not follow the particular provisions of the Sentencing guidelines "which involve drug quantity and role enhancement." Expressly refusing to make "any blanket decision about the federal guidelines," he followed the provisions of the Guidelines that did not implicate the Sixth Amendment by imposing a sentence on respondent "based solely upon the guilty verdict in this case."

[T]he Government filed a notice of appeal in the Court of Appeals for the First Circuit, and a petition in this Court for a writ of certiorari before judgment. Because of the importance of the questions presented, we granted that petition, as well as a similar petition filed by the Government in Booker's case. In both petitions, the Government asks us to determine whether our *Apprendi* line of cases applies to the Sentencing Guidelines, and if so, what portions of the Guidelines remain in effect. . . .

II.

It has been settled throughout our history that the Constitution protects every criminal defendant "against conviction except upon proof beyond a reasonable doubt of every fact necessary to constitute the crime with which he is charged." *In re Kinship*, 397 U.S. 358, 364 (1970). It is equally clear that the "Constitution gives a criminal defendant the right to demand that a jury find him guilty of all the elements of the crime with which he is charged." *United States v. Gideon*, 515 U.S. 506 (1995). These basic precepts, firmly rooted in the common law, have provided the basis for recent decisions interpreting modern criminal statutes and sentencing procedures.

In *Jones v. United States*, 526 U.S. 227, 230 (1999), we considered the federal carjacking statute, which provides three different maximum sentences depending on the extent of harm to the victim: 15 years in jail if there was no serious injury to a victim, 25 years if there was "serious bodily injury," and life in prison if death resulted. In spite of the fact that the statute "at first glance has a look to it suggesting [that the provisions relating to the extent of harm to the victim] are only sentencing provisions," we concluded that the harm to the victim was an element of the crime. . . . Foreshadowing the result we reach today, we noted that our holding was consistent with a "rule requiring jury determination of facts that raise a sentencing ceiling" in state and federal sentencing guidelines systems.

In *Apprendi v. New Jersey*, 530 U.S. 466 (2000), the defendant pleaded guilty to second-degree possession of a firearm for an unlawful purpose, which carried a prison term of 5-to-10 years. Thereafter, the trial court found that his conduct had violated New Jersey's "hate crime" law because it was racially motivated, and imposed a 12-year sentence. This Court set aside the enhanced sentence. We held: "Other than the fact of a prior conviction, any fact that increases the penalty for a crime beyond the prescribed statutory maximum must be submitted to a jury, and proved beyond a reasonable doubt." . . .

In *Ring v. Arizona*, 536 U.S. 584 (2002), we reaffirmed our conclusion that the characterization of critical facts is constitutionally irrelevant. Here, we held that it was impermissible for "the trial judge, sitting alone" to determine the presence or absence of the aggravating factors required by Arizona law for imposition of the death penalty. . . .

In *Blakely v. Washington*, 124 S. Ct. 2531 (2004), we dealt with a determinate sentencing scheme similar to the Federal Sentencing Guidelines. There the defendant pleaded guilty to kidnapping, a class B felony punishable by a term of not more than 10 years. Other provisions of Washington law, comparable to the Federal Sentencing Guidelines, mandated a "standard" sentence of 49-to-53 months, unless the judge found aggravating facts justifying an exceptional sentence. Although the prosecutor recommended a sentence in the standard range, the judge found that the defendant had acted with " 'deliberate cruelty' " and sentenced him to 90 months.

For reasons explained in *Jones, Apprendi*, and *Ring*, the requirements of the Sixth Amendment were clear. The application of Washington's sentencing scheme violated the defendant's right to have the jury find the existence of " 'any particular fact' " that the law makes essential to his punishment. That right is implicated whenever a judge seeks to impose a sentence that is not solely based on "facts reflected in the jury verdict or admitted by the defendant." . . .

As the dissenting opinions in *Blakely* recognized, there is no distinction of constitutional significance between the Federal Sentencing Guidelines and the Washington procedures at issue in that case. This conclusion rests on the premise, common to both systems, that the relevant sentencing rules are mandatory and impose binding requirements on all sentencing judges.

If the Guidelines as currently written could be read as merely advisory provisions that recommended, rather than required, the selection of particular sentences in response to differing sets of facts, their use would not implicate the Sixth Amendment. We have never doubted the authority of a judge to exercise broad discretion in imposing a sentence within a statutory range. Indeed, everyone agrees that the constitutional issues presented by these cases would have been avoided entirely if Congress had omitted from the SRA the provisions that make the Guidelines binding on district judges; it is that circumstance that makes the Court's answer to the second question presented possible. For when a trial judge exercises his discretion to select a specific sentence within a defined range, the defendant has no right to a jury determination of the facts that the judge deems relevant.

The Guidelines as written, however, are not advisory; they are mandatory and binding on all judges. . . . Because they are binding on judges, we have consistently held that the Guidelines have the force and effect of laws. . . .

Booker's case illustrates the mandatory nature of the Guidelines. The jury convicted him of possessing at least 50 grams of crack based on evidence that he had 92.5 grams of crack in his duffel bag. Under these facts, the Guidelines specified an offense level of 32, which, given the defendant's criminal history category, authorized a sentence of 210-to-262 months. Booker's is a run-of-the mill drug case, and does not present any factors that were inadequately considered by the Commission. The sentencing judge would therefore have been reversed had he not imposed a sentence within the level 32 Guidelines range.

Booker's actual sentence, however, was 360 months, almost 10 years longer than the guidelines range supported by the jury verdict alone. To reach this sentence, the judge found facts beyond those found by the jury: namely, that Booker possessed 566 grams of crack in addition to the 92.5 grams in his duffel bag. The jury never heard any evidence of the additional drug quantity, and the judge found it true by a preponderance of the evidence. Thus, just as in *Blakely*, "the jury's verdict alone does not authorize the sentence. The judge acquires that authority only upon finding some additional fact." There is no relevant distinction between the sentence imposed pursuant to the Washington statutes in *Blakely* and the sentences imposed pursuant to the Federal Sentencing Guidelines in these cases.

* * *

III.

The Government advances three arguments in support of its submission that we should not apply our reasoning in *Blakely* to the Federal Sentencing Guidelines. It contends that *Blakely* is distinguishable because the Guidelines were promulgated by a commission rather than the Legislature; that principles of stare decisis require us to follow four earlier decisions that are arguably inconsistent with *Blakely*; and that the application of *Blakely* to the Guidelines would conflict with separation of powers principles reflected in *Mistretta v. United States*, 488 U.S. 361 (1989). These arguments are unpersuasive. . . .

IV.

All of the foregoing supports our conclusion that our holding in *Blakely* applies to the Sentencing Guidelines. We recognize, as we did in *Jones*, *Apprendi*, and *Blakely*, that in some cases jury factfinding may impair the most expedient and efficient sentencing of defendants. But the interest in fairness and reliability protected by the right to a jury trial — a common-law right that defendants enjoyed for centuries and that is now enshrined in the Sixth Amendment — has always outweighed the interest in concluding trials swiftly. Accordingly, we reaffirm our holding in *Apprendi*: Any fact (other than a prior conviction) which is necessary to support a sentence exceeding the maximum authorized by the facts established by a plea of guilty or a jury verdict must be admitted by the defendant or proved to a jury beyond a reasonable doubt.

Justice Breyer delivered the [remedial] opinion of the Court.*

* * *

We here turn to the second question presented, a question that concerns the remedy. We must decide whether or to what extent, "as a matter of severability analysis," the Guidelines "as a whole" are "inapplicable . . . such that the sentencing court must exercise its discretion to sentence the defendant within the maximum and minimum set by statute for the offense of conviction."

We answer the question of remedy by finding the provision of the federal sentencing statute that makes the Guidelines mandatory, 18 U.S.C.A. § 3553(b)(1), incompatible with today's constitutional holding. We conclude that this provision must be severed and excised, as must one other statutory section, § 3742(e), which depends upon the Guidelines' mandatory nature. So modified, the Federal Sentencing Act, makes the Guidelines effectively advisory. It requires a sentencing court to consider Guidelines ranges, but it permits the court to tailor the sentence in light of other statutory concerns as well.

---

* The Chief Justice, Justice O'Connor, Justice Kennedy, and Justice Ginsburg join this opinion.

I.

We answer the remedial question by looking to legislative intent. In this instance, we must determine which of the two following remedial approaches is the more compatible with the legislature's intent as embodied in the 1984 Sentencing Act.

One approach, that of Justice Stevens' dissent, would retain the Sentencing Act (and the Guidelines) as written, but would engraft onto the existing system today's Sixth Amendment "jury trial" requirement. The addition would change the Guidelines by preventing the sentencing court from increasing a sentence on the basis of a fact that the jury did not find (or that the offender did not admit).

The other approach, which we now adopt, would (through severance and excision of two provisions) make the Guidelines system advisory while maintaining a strong connection between the sentence imposed and the offender's real conduct — a connection important to the increased uniformity of sentencing that Congress intended its Guidelines system to achieve.

Both approaches would significantly alter the system that Congress designed. But today's constitutional holding means that it is no longer possible to maintain the judicial factfinding that Congress thought would underpin the mandatory Guidelines system that it ought to create and that Congress wrote into the Act in 18 U.S.C.A. §§ 3553(a) and 3661. Hence we must decide whether we would deviate less radically from Congress' intended system (1) by superimposing the constitutional requirement announced today or (2) through elimination of some provisions of the statute.

*   *   *

II.

Several considerations convince us that, were the Court's constitutional requirement added onto the Sentencing Act as currently written, the requirement would so transform the scheme that Congress created that Congress likely would not have intended the Act as so modified to stand. First, the statute's text states that "[t]he court" when sentencing will consider "the nature and circumstances of the offense and the history and characteristics of the defendant." 18 U.S.C.A. § 3553(a)(1). In context, the words "the court" mean "the judge without the jury," not "the judge working together with the jury." . . .

This provision is tied to the provision of the Act that makes the Guidelines mandatory. They are part and parcel of a single, unified whole — a whole that Congress intended to apply to all federal sentencing.

This provision makes it difficult to justify Justice Stevens' approach, for that approach requires reading the words "the court" as if they meant "the judge working together with the jury." Unlike Justice Stevens, we do not believe we can interpret the statute's language to save its constitutionality, because we believe that any such reinterpretation, even if limited to instances in which a Sixth Amendment problem arises, would be "plainly contrary to the intent of Congress." *United States v. X-Citement Video, Inc.*, 513 U.S. 64, 78 (1994). . . .

Second, Congress' basic statutory goal — a system that diminishes sentencing disparity — depends for its success upon judicial efforts to determine, and to base punishment upon, the real conduct that underlies the crime of conviction. That determination is particularly important in the federal system where crimes defined as, for example, "obstruct[ing], delay[ing], or affect[ing] commerce or the movement of any article or commodity in commerce, by . . . extortion," 18 U.S.C. § 1951(a), or, say, using the mail "for the purpose of executing" a "scheme or artifice to defraud," § 1341, can encompass a vast range of very different kinds of underlying conduct. But it is also important even in respect to ordinary crimes, such as robbery, where an act that meets the statutory definition can be committed in a host of different ways. Judges have long looked to real conduct when sentencing. Federal judges have long relied upon a presentence report, prepared by a probation officer, for information (often unavailable until after the trial) relevant to the manner in which the convicted offender committed the crime of conviction.

*   *   *

To engraft the Court's constitutional requirement onto the sentencing statutes, however, would destroy the system. It would prevent a judge from relying upon a presentence report for factual information, relevant to sentencing, uncovered after the trial. In doing so, it would, even compared to pre-Guidelines sentencing, weaken the tie between a sentence and an offender's real conduct. It would thereby undermine the sentencing statute's basic aim of ensuring similar sentences for those who have committed similar crimes in similar ways.

Several examples help illustrate the point. Imagine Smith and Jones, each of whom violates the Hobbs Act in very different ways. *See* 18 U.S.C. § 1951(a) (forbidding "obstruct[ing], delay[ing], or affect[ing] commerce or the movement of any article or commodity in commerce, by . . . extortion"). Smith threatens to injure a co-worker unless the co-worker advances him a few dollars from the interstate company's till; Jones, after similarly threatening the co-worker, causes far more harm by seeking far more money, by making certain that the coworker's family is aware of the threat, by arranging for deliveries of dead animals to the co-worker's home to show he is serious, and so forth. The offenders' behavior is very different; the known harmful consequences of their actions are different; their punishments both before, and after, the guidelines would have been different. But, under the dissenters' approach, unless prosecutors decide to charge more than the elements of the crime, the judge would have to impose similar punishments. . . .

Consider, too, a complex mail fraud conspiracy where a prosecutor may well be uncertain of the amount of harm and of the role each indicted individual played until after conviction — then the offenders may turn over financial records, when it becomes easier to determine who were the leaders and who the followers, when victim interviews are seen to be worth the time. In such a case the relation between the sentence and what actually occurred is likely to be considerably more distant under a system with a jury trial requirement patched onto it than it was even prior to the Sentencing Act, when judges routinely used information obtained after the verdict to decide upon a proper sentence.

This point is critically important. Congress' basic goal in passing the Sentencing Act was to move the sentencing system in the direction of increased uniformity. That uniformity does not consist simply of similar sentences for those convicted of violations of the same statute — a uniformity consistent with the dissenters' remedial approach. It consists, more importantly, of similar relationships between sentences and real conduct, relationships that Congress' sentencing statutes helped to advance and that Justice Stevens' approach would undermine. . . .

Third, the sentencing statutes, read to include the Court's Sixth Amendment requirement, would create a system far more complex than Congress could have intended. How would courts and counsel work with an indictment and a jury trial that involved not just whether a defendant robbed a bank but also how? Would the indictment in a mail fraud case have to allege the number of victims, their vulnerability, and the amount taken from each? How could a judge expect a jury to work with the Guidelines' definitions of, say, "relevant conduct," which includes "all acts and omissions committed, aided, abetted, counseled, commanded, induced, procured, or willfully caused by the defendant; and [in the case of a conspiracy] all reasonably foreseeable acts and omissions of others in furtherance of the jointly undertaken criminal activity"? How would a jury measure "loss" in a securities fraud case — a matter so complex as to lead the Commission to instruct judges to make "only . . . a reasonable estimate"? How would the court take account, for punishment purposes, of a defendant's contemptuous behavior at trial — a matter that the Government could not have charged in the indictment?

Fourth, plea bargaining would not significantly diminish the consequences of the Court's constitutional holding for the operation of the Guidelines. Rather, plea bargaining would make matters worse. Congress enacted the sentencing statutes in major part to achieve greater uniformity in sentencing, i.e., to increase the likelihood that offenders who engage in similar real conduct would receive similar sentences. The statutes reasonably assume that their efforts to move the trial-based sentencing process in the direction of greater sentencing uniformity would have a similar positive impact upon plea-bargained sentences, for plea bargaining takes place in the shadow of (i.e., with an eye towards the hypothetical result of) a potential trial. . . .

For all these reasons, Congress, had it been faced with the constitutional jury trial requirement, likely would not have passed the same Sentencing Act. It likely would have found the requirement incompatible with the Act as written. Hence the Act cannot remain valid in its entirety. Severance and excision are necessary.

III.

We now turn to the question of which portions of the sentencing statute we must sever and excise as inconsistent with the Court's constitutional requirement. Although, as we have explained, see Part II, supra, we believe that Congress would have preferred the total invalidation of the statute to the dissenters' remedial approach, we nevertheless do not believe that the entire statute must be invalidated. Most of the statute is perfectly valid. And we must "refrain from invalidating more of the statute than is necessary." *Regan v. Time, Inc.*, 468 U.S. 641, 652 (1984) (plurality opinion). Indeed, we must retain those portions of the Act that are (1) constitutionally valid, (2) capable of "functioning independently," and (3) consistent with Congress' basic objectives in enacting the statute.

Application of these criteria indicates that we must sever and excise two specific statutory provisions: the provision that requires sentencing courts to impose a sentence within the applicable Guidelines range (in the absence of circumstances that justify a departure), see 18 U.S.C. § 3553(b)(1), and the provision that sets forth standards of review on appeal, including de novo review of departures from the applicable Guidelines range, see § 3742(e). With these two sections excised (and statutory cross-references to the two sections consequently invalidated), the remainder of the Act satisfies the Court's constitutional requirements. . . .

The remainder of the Act "function[s] independently." *Alaska Airlines v. Brock*, 480 U.S. 678, 684 (1987). Without the "mandatory" provision, the Act nonetheless requires judges to consider the Guidelines "sentencing range established for . . . the applicable category of offense committed by the applicable category of defendant," § 3553(a)(4), the pertinent Sentencing Commission policy statements, the need to avoid unwarranted sentencing disparities, and the need to provide restitution to victims. And the Act nonetheless requires judges to impose sentences that reflect the seriousness of the offense, promote respect for the law, provide just punishment, afford adequate deterrence, protect the public, and effectively provide the defendant with needed educational or vocational training and medical care.

Moreover, despite the absence of § 3553(b)(1), the Act continues to provide for appeals from sentencing decisions (irrespective of whether the trial judge sentences within or outside the Guidelines range in the exercise of his discretionary power under § 3553(a)). We concede that the excision of § 3553(b)(1) requires the excision of a different, appeals-related section, namely § 3742(e), which sets forth standards of review on appeal. That section contains critical cross-references to the (now-excised) § 3553(b)(1) and consequently must be severed and excised for similar reasons.

Excision of § 3742(e), however, does not pose a critical problem for the handling of appeals. That is because, as we have previously held, a statute that does not explicitly set forth a standard of review may nonetheless do so implicitly. . . . We infer appropriate review standards from related statutory language, the structure of the statute, and the "sound administration of justice." And in this instance those factors, in addition to the past two decades of appellate practice in cases involving departures, imply a practical standard of review already familiar to appellate courts: review for "unreasonable[ness]." 18 U.S.C. § 3742(e)(3).

*   *   *

As we have said, the Sentencing Commission remains in place, writing Guidelines, collecting information about actual district court sentencing decisions, undertaking research, and revising the Guidelines accordingly. The district courts, while not bound to apply the Guidelines, must consult those Guidelines and take them into account when sentencing. The courts of appeals review sentencing decisions for unreasonableness. These features of the remaining system, while not the system Congress enacted, nonetheless continue to move sentencing in Congress' preferred direction, helping to avoid excessive sentencing disparities while maintaining flexibility sufficient to individualize sentences where necessary. We can find no feature of the remaining system that tends to hinder, rather than to further, these basic objectives. Under these circumstances, why would Congress not have preferred excision of the "mandatory" provision to a system that engrafts today's constitutional requirement onto the unchanged pre-existing statute — a system that, in terms of Congress' basic objectives, is counterproductive? . . .

Ours, of course, is not the last word: The ball now lies in Congress' court. The National Legislature is equipped to devise and install, long-term, the sentencing system, compatible with the Constitution, that Congress judges best for the federal system of justice.

* * *

V.

In respondent Booker's case, the District Court applied the Guidelines as written and imposed a sentence higher than the maximum authorized solely by the jury's verdict. The Court of Appeals held Blakely applicable to the Guidelines, concluded that Booker's sentence violated the Sixth Amendment, vacated the judgment of the District Court, and remanded for resentencing. We affirm the judgment of the Court of Appeals and remand the case. On remand, the District Court should impose a sentence in accordance with today's opinions, and, if the sentence comes before the Court of Appeals for review, the Court of Appeals should apply the review standards set forth in this opinion.

In respondent Fanfan's case, the District Court held Blakely applicable to the Guidelines. It then imposed a sentence that was authorized by the jury's verdict — a sentence lower than the sentence authorized by the Guidelines as written. Thus, Fanfan's sentence does not violate the Sixth Amendment. Nonetheless, the Government (and the defendant should he so choose) may seek resentencing under the system set forth in today's opinions. Hence we vacate the judgment of the District Court and remand the case for further proceedings consistent with this opinion.

As these dispositions indicate, we must apply today's holdings — both the Sixth Amendment holding and our remedial interpretation of the Sentencing Act — to all cases on direct review. That fact does not mean that we believe that every sentence gives rise to a Sixth Amendment violation. Nor do we believe that every appeal will lead to a new sentencing hearing. That is because we expect reviewing courts to apply ordinary prudential doctrines, determining, for example, whether the issue was raised below and whether it fails the "plain-error" test. It is also because, in cases not involving a Sixth Amendment violation, whether resentencing is warranted or whether it will instead be sufficient to review a sentence for reasonableness may depend upon application of the harmless-error doctrine.

It is so ordered.

JUSTICE STEVENS, with whom JUSTICE SOUTER joins, and with whom JUSTICE SCALIA joins except for Part III . . . , dissenting [from the Court's remedial opinion]. [Omitted.]

JUSTICE SCALIA, dissenting [from the Court's remedial opinion]. [Omitted.]

JUSTICE THOMAS, dissenting in part. I join JUSTICE STEVENS' [merits] opinion for the Court, but I dissent from JUSTICE BREYER'S [remedial] opinion for the Court. [Omitted].

JUSTICE BREYER, with whom THE CHIEF JUSTICE, JUSTICE O'CONNOR, and JUSTICE KENNEDY join, dissenting [from the Court's merits opinion]. [Omitted.]

NOTES AND QUESTIONS

1. *The merits decision.* Justice Stevens' merits majority opinion concluded that the *Apprendi* and *Blakely* decisions compelled the outcome. This conclusion rested on two assumptions: (1) *Apprendi* and *Blakely* were correctly decided; and (2) the

Federal Sentencing Guidelines are not distinguishable from the sentencing scheme at issue in *Blakely*. Do you agree with these assumptions? Why or why not?

The merits decision was decided by a five-to-four vote, with Justice Breyer authoring the dissent. How do you account for the split on the Court? Recall, as you consider this question, that then-Federal Appeals Court Judge Stephen Breyer was a member of the U.S. Sentencing Commission at the time the Guidelines were promulgated.

2. *The remedial decision.* The vote on the remedial decision was also five-to-four. What were the options available to the Court? Did the Court adopt the best remedy to the Sixth Amendment violation? Why or why not?

3. *The response to* Booker. The *Booker* decision produced a flood of criticism, commentary, and study. For example, the Sentencing Commission conducted hearings shortly after *Booker* was decided. During the hearings, one commentator characterized the decision as "incoherent and self-contradictory," while another commentator concluded that *Booker* established a "nearly perfect" sentencing scheme. *See U.S. Sentencing Commission Hears Views on How to Go Forward After Booker Ruling*, 73 U.S.L.W. No. 31, at 2486 (Feb. 22, 2005). Which of these characterizations hits closer to the mark? Why?

Many members of Congress were predictably angry that the Court had overturned the Guidelines' mandatory sentencing scheme. As the merits opinion noted, "The ball now lies in Congress' court." What are the possible Congressional responses to *Booker*? How should Congress respond, if at all? Why? Revisit this question after considering the *Rita, Gall,* and *Kimbrough* decisions discussed below.

4. *Plain error.* In the wake of *Booker*, the circuits have split as to whether the lower court's failure to adhere to the *Apprendi* rule constitutes a "plain error." Generally, if a defendant fails to raise an argument before the trial court, then the defendant waives the right to make the objection before the appeals court. An exception to this general rule exists when the trial judge committed "plain error." To determine whether a trial court error amounted to "plain error," appeals courts generally require appellants to show (a) there was error, (b) the error was obvious, and (c) the error affected the defendant's substantial rights. Some courts also require a fourth showing — that the error seriously affected the fairness of the judicial proceeding.

The First, Fifth, Eighth, Tenth, and Eleventh Circuits apply a strict standard, requiring the defendant to show a reasonable probability that the sentence would have been different had the lower court utilized the advisory guidelines correctly. *See, e.g., United States v. Marston*, 517 F.3d 996 (8th Cir. 2008). The Third, Fourth, and Sixth Circuits take a more defendant-friendly approach that results in a nearly automatic right to resentencing. *See, e.g., United States v. Brooks*, 524 F.3d 549 (4th. Cir. 2008). The D.C., Second, Seventh, and Ninth Circuits apply a "middle ground" approach. *See, e.g., Bulter v. Curry*, 528 F.3d 624, 648 (9th Cir. 2008) (explaining that the "relevant question is not what the trial court *would* have done, but what it legally *could* have done" when considering the severity of the error).

5. *Harmless error.* Is a *Booker* violation a "structural" violation that necessarily requires reversal? In *Washington v. Recuenco*, 548 U.S. 212 (2006), the Supreme

Court held six-to-three that *Booker* violations do not necessarily require reversal but instead are subject to harmless error analysis.

6. *Resentencing by the appeals court.* Assume that a sentencing judge imposes a lengthy sentence, and that the defendant appeals the sentence. In opposition to the appeal, the government notes that the defendant's sentence should have been even longer. The government does not cross-appeal, and makes this argument solely to counter the defendant's appeal. May the appeals court impose the correct, lengthier sentence even in the absence of a government appeal or cross-appeal? In *Greenlaw v. United States*, 128 S. Ct. 2559, 2564 (2008), the Court held not, and reversed the appeals court's imposition of the lengthier sentence. The Court stated that "an appellate court may not alter a judgment to benefit a nonappealing party."

[D] THE REASONABLENESS REVIEW

What does it mean for a sentence to be "unreasonable" under the *Booker* remedial decision? That decision stated that the advisory system will "maintain[] a strong connection between the sentence imposed and the offender's real conduct — a connection important to the increased uniformity of sentencing that Congress intended its Guidelines system to achieve."

Justice Stevens' dissent stated that "the Court does not explain how its proposed remedy will ensure that judges take real conduct into account." Justice Scalia's dissent further asserted that the "unreasonableness" standard "may lead some courts of appeals to conclude — may indeed be designed to lead courts of appeals to conclude — that little has changed."

The Court endeavored to provide guidance on the nature of the reasonableness review in *Rita*, *Gall*, and *Kimbrough*. After reviewing these holdings, consider whether the Court succeeded in that endeavor.

[1] The Reasonableness Presumption

When interpreting the *Booker* remedial opinion, the federal courts of appeal disagreed as to whether within-Guidelines-range sentences are presumptively reasonable. Some courts held that applying a reasonableness presumption would invoke the pre-*Booker* mandatory sentencing scheme and therefore would violate *Booker*. *See United States v. Fernandez*, 443 F.3d 19, 27–28 (2d Cir. 2006). Other courts held that Guidelines-range sentences are presumptively reasonable. *See United States v. Terrell*, 445 F.3d 1261 (10th Cir. 2006). The Supreme Court attempted to resolve this split in the case that follows. As you read the opinion, consider whether the Court has provided clear guidance as to the meaning of the reasonableness review.

RITA v. UNITED STATES
551 U.S. 338 (2007)

JUSTICE BREYER delivered the opinion of the Court.

The federal courts of appeals review federal sentences and set aside those they find "unreasonable." *See, e.g., United States v. Booker*, 543 U.S. 220, 261–263 (2005). Several Circuits have held that, when doing so, they will presume that a sentence imposed within a properly calculated United States Sentencing

Guidelines range is a reasonable sentence. The most important question before us is whether the law permits the courts of appeals to use this presumption. We hold that it does.

I.

The basic crime in this case concerns two false statements which Victor Rita, the petitioner, made under oath to a federal grand jury. The jury was investigating a gun company called InterOrdnance. Prosecutors believed that buyers of an InterOrdnance kit, called a "PPSH 41 machinegun 'parts kit,'" could assemble a machinegun from the kit, that those kits consequently amounted to machineguns, and that InterOrdnance had not secured proper registrations for the importation of the guns.

Rita had bought a PPSH 41 machinegun parts kit. Rita, when contacted by the Bureau of Alcohol, Tobacco, and Firearms and Explosives (ATF), agreed to let a federal agent inspect the kit. But before meeting with the agent, Rita called InterOrdnance and then sent back the kit. He subsequently turned over to ATF a different kit that apparently did not amount to a machinegun.

The investigating prosecutor brought Rita before the grand jury, placed him under oath, and asked him about these matters. Rita denied that the Government agent had asked him for the PPSH kit, and also denied that he had spoken soon thereafter about the PPSH kit to someone at InterOrdnance. The Government claimed these statements were false, charged Rita with perjury, making false statements, and obstructing justice, and, after a jury trial, obtained convictions on all counts.

The parties subsequently proceeded to sentencing. Initially, a probation officer, with the help of the parties, and after investigating the background both of the offenses and of the offender, prepared a presentence report. The completed report describes "offense characteristics," "offender characteristics," and other matters that might be relevant to the sentence, and then calculates a Guidelines sentence. The report also sets forth factors potentially relevant to a departure from the Guidelines or relevant to the imposition of an other-than-Guidelines sentence. It ultimately makes a sentencing recommendation based on the Guidelines.

In respect to "offense characteristics," for example, the report points out that the five counts of conviction all stem from a single incident. Hence, pursuant to the Guidelines, the report, in calculating a recommended sentence, groups the five counts of conviction together, treating them as if they amounted to the single most serious count among them (and ignoring all others). *See* USSG § 3D1.1. The single most serious offense in Rita's case is "perjury." The relevant Guideline, § 2J1.3(c)(1), instructs the sentencing court (and the probation officer) to calculate the Guidelines sentence for "perjury . . . in respect to a criminal offense" by applying the Guideline for an "accessory after the fact," as to that criminal offense. § 2X3.1. And that latter Guideline says that the judge, for calculation purposes, should take as a base offense level, a level that is "6 levels lower than the offense level for the underlying offense," (emphasis added) (the offense that the perjury may have helped someone commit). Here the "underlying offense" consisted of InterOrdnance's possible violation of the machinegun registration law. USSG § 2M5.2 (providing sentence for violation of 22 U.S.C. § 2778(b)(2), importation of defense articles without authorization). The base offense level for the gun registration crime is 26. See USSG § 2M5.2. Six levels less is 20. And 20, says the presentence report, is the base offense level applicable to Rita for purposes of Guidelines sentence calculation.

The presentence report next considers Rita's "Criminal History." Rita was convicted in May 1986, and sentenced to five years' probation for making false statements in connection with the purchase of firearms. Because this conviction took place more than 10 years before the present offense, it did not count against Rita. And because Rita had no other relevant convictions, the Guidelines considered him as having no "criminal history points." The report consequently places Rita in criminal history category I, the lowest category for purposes of calculating a Guidelines' sentence.

The report goes on to describe other "Offender Characteristics." The description includes Rita's personal and family data, Rita's physical condition (including a detailed description of ailments), Rita's mental and emotional health, the lack of any history of substance abuse, Rita's vocational and nonvocational education, and Rita's employment record. It states that he served in the Armed Forces for over 25 years, on active duty and in the Reserve. During that time he received 35 commendations, awards, or medals of different kinds. The report analyzes Rita's financial condition.

Ultimately, the report calculates the Guidelines sentencing range. The Guidelines specify for base level 20, criminal history category I, a sentence of 33-to-41 months' imprisonment. The report adds that there "appears to be no circumstance or combination of circumstances that warrant a departure from the prescribed sentencing guidelines."

At the sentencing hearing, both Rita and the Government presented their sentencing arguments. Each side addressed the report. Rita argued for a sentence outside (and lower than) the recommended Guidelines 33-to-41 month range.

The judge made clear that Rita's argument for a lower sentence could take either of two forms. First, Rita might argue within the Guidelines' framework, for a departure from the applicable Guidelines range on the ground that his circumstances present an "atypical case" that falls outside the "heartland" to which the United States Sentencing Commission intends each individual Guideline to apply. USSG § 5K2.0(a)(2). Second, Rita might argue that, independent of the Guidelines, application of the sentencing factors set forth in 18 U.S.C. § 3553(a) warrants a lower sentence.

Thus, the judge asked Rita's counsel, "Are you going to put on evidence to show that [Rita] should be getting a downward departure, or under 3553, your client would be entitled to a different sentence than he should get under sentencing guidelines?" And the judge later summarized:

> "[Y]ou're asking for a departure from the guidelines or a sentence under 3553 that is lower than the guidelines, and here are the reasons:

> "One, he is a vulnerable defendant because he's been involved in [government criminal justice] work which has caused people to become convicted criminals who are in prison and there may be retribution against him.

> "Two, his military experience. . . . "

Counsel agreed, while adding that Rita's poor physical condition constituted a third reason. And counsel said that he rested his claim for a lower sentence on "[j]ust [those] three" special Circumstances, "[p]hysical condition, vulnerability in prison and the military service." Rita presented evidence and argument related to these three factors. The Government, while not asking for a sentence higher than the report's recommended Guidelines range, said that Rita's perjury had interfered with the Government's potential "obstruction of justice" claim against InterOrdnance and that Rita, as a former Government criminal justice employee, should have known better than to commit perjury. The sentencing judge asked questions about each factor.

After hearing the arguments, the judge concluded that he was "unable to find that the [report's recommended] sentencing guideline range . . . is an inappropriate guideline range for that, and under 3553 . . . the public needs to be protected if it is true, and I must accept as true the jury verdict." The court concluded: "So the Court finds that it is appropriate to enter" a sentence at the bottom of the Guidelines range, namely a sentence of imprisonment "for a period of 33 months."

On appeal, Rita argued that his 33-month sentence was "unreasonable" because (1) it did not adequately take account of "the defendant's history and characteristics," and (2) it "is greater than necessary to comply with the purposes of sentencing set forth in 18 U.S.C. § 3553(a)(2)." The Fourth Circuit observed that it must set aside a sentence that is not "reasonable." The Circuit stated that "a sentence imposed within the properly calculated Guidelines range . . . is presumptively reasonable." It added that "while we believe that the appropriate circumstances for imposing a sentence outside the guideline range will depend on the facts of individual cases, we have no reason to doubt that most sentences will continue to fall within the applicable guideline range." The Fourth Circuit then rejected Rita's arguments and upheld the sentence.

Rita petitioned for a writ of certiorari. He pointed out that the Circuits are split as to the use of a presumption of reasonableness for within — Guidelines sentences.

We consequently granted Rita's petition. We agreed to decide whether a circuit court may afford a "presumption of reasonableness" to a "within-Guidelines" sentence. We also agreed to decide whether the District Court properly analyzed the relevant sentencing factors and whether, given the record, the District Court's ultimate choice of a 33-month sentence was "unreasonable."

II.

The first question is whether a court of appeals may apply a presumption of reasonableness to a district court sentence that reflects a proper application of the Sentencing Guidelines. We conclude that it can.

A.

For one thing, the presumption is not binding. It does not, like a trial-related evidentiary presumption, insist that one side, or the other, shoulder a particular burden of persuasion or proof lest they lose their case. Nor does the presumption reflect strong judicial deference of the kind that leads appeals courts to grant greater factfinding leeway to an expert agency than to a district judge. Rather, the presumption reflects the fact that, by the time an appeals court is considering a within-Guidelines sentence on review, both the sentencing judge and the Sentencing Commission will have reached the same conclusion as to the proper sentence in the particular case. That double determination significantly increases the likelihood that the sentence is a reasonable one.

Further, the presumption reflects the nature of the Guidelines-writing task that Congress set for the Commission and the manner in which the Commission carried out that task. In instructing both the sentencing judge and the Commission what to do, Congress referred to the basic sentencing objectives that the statute sets forth in 18 U.S.C. § 3553(a). That provision tells the sentencing judge to consider (1) offense and offender characteristics; (2) the need for a sentence to reflect the basic aims of sentencing, namely (a) "just punishment" (retribution), (b) deterrence, (c) incapacitation, (d) rehabilitation; (3) the sentences legally available; (4) the sentencing Guidelines; (5) Sentencing Commission policy statements; (6) the need to avoid unwarranted disparities; and (7) the need for restitution. The provision also tells the sentencing judge to "impose a sentence sufficient, but not greater than necessary, to comply with" the basic aims of sentencing as set out above.

Congressional statutes then tell the Commission to write Guidelines that will carry out these same § 3553(a) objectives. Thus, 28 U.S.C. § 991(b) indicates that one of the Commission's basic objectives is to "assure the meeting of the purposes of sentencing as set forth in [§ 3553(a)(2)]." The provision adds that the Commission must seek to "provide certainty and fairness" in sentencing, to "avoi[d] unwarranted sentencing disparities," to "maintai[n] sufficient flexibility to permit individualized sentences when warranted by mitigating or aggravating factors not taken into account in the establishment of general sentencing practices," and to "reflect, to the extent practicable [sentencing-relevant] advancement in [the] knowledge of human behavior." Later provisions specifically instruct the Commission to write the Guidelines with reference to this statement of purposes, the statement that itself refers to § 3553(a).

The upshot is that the sentencing statutes envision both the sentencing judge and the Commission as carrying out the same basic § 3553(a) objectives, the one, at retail, the other at wholesale.

*　　*　　*

An individual judge who imposes a sentence within the range recommended by the guidelines thus makes a decision that is fully consistent with the Commission's judgment in general. Despite Justice Souter'S fears to the contrary, the courts of appeals' "reasonableness" presumption, rather than having independent legal effect, simply recognizes the real-world circumstance that when the judge's discretionary decision accords with the Commission's view of the appropriate application of § 3553(a) in the mine run of cases, it is probable that the sentence is reasonable. Indeed, even the Circuits that have declined to adopt a formal presumption also recognize that a Guidelines sentence will usually be reasonable, because it reflects both the Commission's and the sentencing court's judgment as to what is an appropriate sentence for a given offender.

We repeat that the presumption before us is an appellate court presumption. Given our explanation in Booker that appellate "reasonableness" review merely asks whether the trial court abused its discretion, the presumption applies only on appellate review. The sentencing judge, as a matter of process, will normally begin by considering the presentence report and its interpretation of the Guidelines. He may hear arguments by prosecution or defense that the Guidelines sentence should not apply, perhaps because (as the Guidelines themselves foresee) the case at hand falls outside the "heartland" to which the Commission intends individual Guidelines to apply, USSG § 5K2.0, perhaps because the Guidelines sentence itself fails properly to reflect § 3553(a) considerations, or perhaps because the case warrants a different sentence regardless. Thus, the sentencing court subjects the defendant's sentence to the thorough adversarial testing contemplated by federal sentencing procedure. In determining the merits of these arguments, the sentencing court does not enjoy the benefit of a legal presumption that the Guidelines sentence should apply.

B.

Rita and his supporting *amici* make two further arguments against use of the presumption. First, Rita points out that many individual Guidelines apply higher sentences in the presence of special facts, for example, brandishing a weapon. In many cases, the sentencing judge, not the jury, will determine the existence of those facts. A pro-Guidelines "presumption of reasonableness" will increase the likelihood that courts of appeals will affirm such sentences, thereby increasing the likelihood that sentencing judges will impose such sentences. For that reason, Rita says, the presumption raises Sixth Amendment "concerns."

In our view, however, the presumption, even if it increases the likelihood that the judge, not the jury, will find "sentencing facts," does not violate the Sixth Amendment. This Court's Sixth Amendment cases do not automatically forbid a sentencing court to take account of factual matters not determined by a jury and to increase the sentence in consequence. Nor do they prohibit the sentencing judge from taking account of the Sentencing Commission's factual findings or recommended sentences.

The Sixth Amendment question, the Court has said, is whether the law forbids a judge to increase a defendant's sentence unless the judge finds facts that the jury did not find (and the offender did not concede).

A nonbinding appellate presumption that a Guidelines sentence is reasonable does not require the sentencing judge to impose that sentence. Still less does it forbid the sentencing judge from imposing a sentence higher than the Guidelines provide for the jury-determined facts standing alone. As far as the law is concerned, the judge could disregard the Guidelines and apply the same sentence (higher than the statutory minimum or the bottom of the unenhanced Guidelines range) in the absence of the special facts (say, gun brandishing) which, in the view of the Sentencing Commission, would warrant a higher sentence within the statutorily permissible range. Thus, our Sixth Amendment cases do not forbid appellate court use of the presumption.

*   *   *

Rita may be correct that the presumption will encourage sentencing judges to impose Guidelines sentences. But we do not see how that fact could change the constitutional calculus. Congress sought to diminish unwarranted sentencing disparity. It sought a Guidelines system that would bring about greater fairness in sentencing through increased uniformity. The fact that the presumption might help achieve these congressional goals does not provide cause for holding the presumption unlawful as long as the presumption remains constitutional. And, given our case law, we cannot conclude that the presumption itself violates the Sixth Amendment.

The fact that we permit courts of appeals to adopt a presumption of reasonableness does not mean that courts may adopt a presumption of unreasonableness. Even the Government concedes that appellate courts may not presume that every variance from the advisory Guidelines is unreasonable. However, a number of circuits adhere to the proposition that the strength of the justification needed to sustain an outside-Guidelines sentence varies in proportion to the degree of the variance. We will consider that approach next Term in United States v. Gall, No. 06-7949.

Second, Rita and his amici claim that use of a pro-Guidelines presumption on appeal conflicts with Congress' insistence that sentencing judges apply the factors set forth in 18 U.S.C. § 3553(a) (and that the resulting sentence be "sufficient, but not greater than necessary, to comply with the purposes" of sentencing set forth in that statute). We have explained above, however, why we believe that, where judge and Commission both determine that the Guidelines sentences is an appropriate sentence for the case at hand, that sentence likely reflects the § 3553(a) factors (including its "not greater than necessary" requirement). This circumstance alleviates any serious general conflict between § 3553(a) and the Guidelines, for the purposes of appellate review. And, for that reason, we find that nothing in § 3553(a) renders use of the presumption unlawful.

III.

We next turn to the question whether the District Court properly analyzed the relevant sentencing factors. In particular, Rita argues that the court took inadequate account of § 3553(c), a provision that requires a sentencing judge, "at the time of sentencing," to "state in open court the reasons for its imposition of the particular sentence." In our view, given the straightforward, conceptually simple arguments before the judge, the judge's statement of reasons here, though brief, was legally sufficient.

The statute does call for the judge to "state" his "reasons." And that requirement reflects sound judicial practice. Judicial decisions are reasoned decisions. Confidence in a judge's use of reason underlies the public's trust in the judicial institution. A public statement of those reasons helps provide the public with the assurance that creates that trust.

That said, we cannot read the statute (or our precedent) as insisting upon a full opinion in every case. The appropriateness of brevity or length, conciseness or detail, when to write, what to say, depends upon circumstances. Sometimes a judicial opinion responds to every argument; sometimes it does not; sometimes a judge simply writes the word "granted," or "denied" on the face of a motion while relying upon context and the parties' prior arguments to make the reasons clear. The law leaves much, in this respect, to the judge's own professional judgment.

*   *   *

In the present case the sentencing judge's statement of reasons was brief but legally sufficient. Rita argued for a downward departure from the 33to-41 month Guidelines sentence on the basis of three sets of special circumstances: health, fear of retaliation in prison, and military record. He added that, in any event, these same circumstances warrant leniency beyond that contemplated by the Guidelines.

The record makes clear that the sentencing judge listened to each argument. The judge considered the supporting evidence. The judge was fully aware of defendant's various physical ailments and imposed a sentence that takes them into account. The judge understood that Rita had previously worked in the immigration service where he had been involved in detecting criminal offenses. And he considered Rita's lengthy military service, including over 25 years of service, both on active duty and in the Reserve, and Rita's receipt of 35 medals, awards, and nominations.

The judge then simply found these circumstances insufficient to warrant a sentence lower than the Guidelines range of 33 to 45 months. He said that this range was not "inappropriate." (This, of course, is not the legal standard for imposition of sentence, but taken in context it is plain that the judge so understood.) He immediately added that he found that the 33 month sentence at the bottom of the Guidelines range was "appropriate." He must have believed that there was not much more to say.

We acknowledge that the judge might have said more. He might have added explicitly that he had heard and considered the evidence and argument; that (as no one before him denied) he thought the Commission in the Guidelines had determined a sentence that was proper in the mine run of roughly similar perjury cases; and that he found that Rita's personal circumstances here were simply not different enough to warrant a different sentence. But context and the record make clear that this, or similar, reasoning, underlies the judge's conclusion. Where a matter is as conceptually simple as in the case at hand and the record makes clear that the sentencing judge considered the evidence and arguments, we do not believe the law requires the judge to write more extensively.

IV.

We turn to the final question: Was the Court of Appeals, after applying its presumption, legally correct in holding that Rita's sentence (a sentence that applied, and did not depart from, the relevant sentencing Guideline) was not "unreasonable"? In our view, the Court of Appeals' conclusion was lawful. . . .

Rita argued at sentencing that his circumstances are special. He based this argument upon his health, his fear of retaliation, and his prior military record. His sentence explicitly takes health into account by seeking assurance that the Bureau of Prisons will provide appropriate treatment. The record makes out no special fear of retaliation, asserting only that the threat is one that any former law enforcement official might suffer.

Similarly, though Rita has a lengthy and distinguished military record, he did not claim at sentencing that military service should ordinarily lead to a sentence more lenient than the sentence the Guidelines impose. Like the District Court and the Court of Appeals, we simply cannot say that Rita's special circumstances are special enough that, in light of § 3553(a), they require a sentence lower than the sentence the Guidelines provide. . . .

For the foregoing reasons, the judgment of the Court of Appeals is *Affirmed.*

JUSTICE STEVENS, with whom JUSTICE GINSBURG joins as to all but Part II, concurring. [Omitted.]

JUSTICE SCALIA, with whom JUSTICE THOMAS joins, concurring in part and concurring in the judgment. [Omitted.]

JUSTICE SOUTER, dissenting.

* * *

Without a powerful reason to risk reversal on the sentence, a district judge faced with evidence supporting a high subrange Guidelines sentence will do the appropriate factfinding in disparagement of the jury right and will sentence within the high subrange. This prediction is weakened not a whit by the Court's description of within-Guidelines reasonableness as an "appellate" presumption. What works on appeal determines what works at trial, and if the Sentencing Commission's views are as weighty as the Court says they are, a trial judge will find it far easier to make the appropriate findings and sentence within the appropriate Guideline, than to go through the unorthodox factfinding necessary to justify a sentence outside the Guidelines range. The upshot is that today's decision moves the threat to the practical value of the Sixth Amendment jury right closer to what it was when this Court flagged it in Jones, and it seems fair to ask just what has been accomplished in real terms by all the judicial labor imposed by Apprendi and its associated cases.

NOTES AND QUESTIONS

1. *An appellate presumption only?* The majority insisted that a presumption of reasonableness is only an appellate presumption and should not be applied at the trial level. What is the significance of this holding?

2. *The meaning of the presumption.* What exactly is the reasonableness presumption? The majority terms the issue on appeal of a sentence as "whether the trial court abused its discretion."

3. *The Sixth Amendment revisited.* In his concurring opinion, Justice Scalia stated that the majority "has reintroduced the constitutional defect that *Booker* purported to eliminate." What did Justice Scalia mean? Was he correct? Why or why not?

NOTE ON THE *SCOOTER LIBBY* SENTENCE

Shortly after the Supreme Court issued the *Rita* decision, former President George W. Bush issued a statement commuting the prison sentence of former Vice President Dick Cheney's chief-of-staff, Lewis "Scooter" Libby. Libby had been sentenced to imprisonment for a term of 30 months for perjury and obstruction of justice in connection with the investigation into the leaking of the identity of Central Intelligence Agency employee Valerie Plame. The commutation left in place a sentence of two years' supervised release and a $250,000 fine.

In the "Statement by the President on Executive Clemency for Lewis Libby," the President gave his reasons for commuting the prison sentence:

> [C]ritics point out that neither Mr. Libby nor anyone else has been charged with violating the Intelligence Identities Protection Act or the Espionage Act, which were the original subjects of the investigation. Finally, critics say the punishment does not fit the crime: Mr. Libby was a first-time offender with years of exceptional public service and was handed

a harsh sentence based in part on allegations never presented to the jury.

Pundits were quick to point out the parallels between the *Rita* and *Libby* cases: (1) the sentences were similar — Rita was sentenced to 33 months in prison, Libby to 30 months; (2) both defendants were convicted only of cover-up crimes; (3) in both instances, the judge enhanced the sentence based on the underlying offense that the obstructive acts were intended to hide (in Rita's case, InterOrdnance's possible violation of the machinegun registration law; in Libby's case, the laws criminalizing revealing the identity of undercover government operatives); (4) neither defendant had a criminal history for Guidelines purposes; (5) both defendants had (in the President's words) "years of exceptional public service;" and (6) both defendants were given sentences, again in the President's words, "based in part on allegations never presented to the jury." *See* Adam Liptak, *Bush Rationale on Libby Stirs Legal Debate*, N.Y. Times, July 4, 2007, at A1.

Commentators also noted that the Department of Justice criticized the flexibility that *Booker* provided to sentencing judges and called for stricter, more rigid sentencing guidelines. The President's statement thus may seem inconsistent with the DOJ's own policies. *See id.*

After the commutation, the sentencing judge approved the remaining sentence of supervised release. In his opinion, the judge — who was appointed by President Bush — made many of the points outlined above:

> In commuting [Libby's] thirty-month term of incarceration, the President stated that the sentence imposed by this Court was "excessive" and that two years of supervised release and a $250,000 fine alone are a "harsh punishment" for an individual convicted on multiple counts of perjury, obstruction of justice, and making false statements to federal investigators. [T]he Court notes that the term of incarceration imposed in this case was determined after a careful consideration of each of the requisite statutory factors, and was consistent with the bottom end of the applicable sentencing range as properly calculated under the United States Sentencing Guidelines.

> Indeed, only recently the President's Attorney General called for the passage of legislation to "restore the binding nature of the sentencing guidelines so that the bottom of the recommended sentencing range would be a minimum for judges, not merely a suggestion," a stance that is fully consonant with the policies of this Administration as a whole. In light of these considerations, and given the indisputable importance of "provid[ing] certainty and fairness in sentencing . . . [and] avoid[ing] unwarranted sentencing disparities," *Rita*, 127 S. Ct. at 2463, it is fair to say that the Court is somewhat perplexed as to how its sentence could accurately be characterized as "excessive."

United States v. Libby, 495 F.Supp. 2d 49 at 51 n. 1 (D.D.C. 2007) (Walton, J.).

Evaluate Rita's sentence and the sentence originally imposed on Libby. Was either sentence "excessive" or "harsh"? Were the sentences reasonable? Why or why not?

[2]   The Justification Required for Non-Guidelines Sentences

After *Rita*, would it be valid for a court of appeals to review sentences under a presumption that "the strength of the justification needed to sustain an outside-Guidelines sentence varies in proportion to the degree of the variance?" A number of courts followed this approach, sometimes termed a "sliding scale" approach. *See, e.g., United States v. Crisp*, 454 F.3d 1285, 1291 (11th Cir. 2006) (holding that "[a]n extraordinary reduction must be supported by extraordinary circumstances"). The Court decided this issue in the case that follows.

GALL v. UNITED STATES
128 S. Ct. 586 (2007)

JUSTICE STEVENS delivered the opinion of the Court.

I.

In February or March 2000, petitioner Brian Gall, a second-year college student at the University of Iowa, was invited by Luke Rinderknecht to join an ongoing enterprise distributing a controlled substance popularly known as "ecstasy." Gall — who was then a user of ecstasy, cocaine, and marijuana — accepted the invitation. During the ensuing seven months, Gall delivered ecstasy pills, which he received from Rinderknecht, to other conspirators, who then sold them to consumers. He netted over $30,000.

A month or two after joining the conspiracy, Gall stopped using ecstasy. A few months after that, in September 2000, he advised Rinderknecht and other co-conspirators that he was withdrawing from the conspiracy. He has not sold illegal drugs of any kind since. He has, in the words of the District Court, "self-rehabilitated." He graduated from the University of Iowa in 2002, and moved first to Arizona, where he obtained a job in the construction industry, and later to Colorado, where he earned $18 per hour as a master carpenter. He has not used any illegal drugs since graduating from college.

After Gall moved to Arizona, he was approached by federal law enforcement agents who questioned him about his involvement in the ecstasy distribution conspiracy. Gall admitted his limited participation in the distribution of ecstasy, and the agents took no further action at that time. On April 28, 2004 — approximately a year and a half after this initial interview, and three and a half years after Gall withdrew from the conspiracy — an indictment was returned in the Southern District of Iowa charging him and seven other defendants with participating in a conspiracy to distribute ecstasy, cocaine, and marijuana, that began in or about May 1996 and continued through October 30, 2002. The Government has never questioned the truthfulness of any of Gall's earlier statements or contended that he played any role in, or had any knowledge of, other aspects of the conspiracy described in the indictment. When he received notice of the indictment, Gall moved back to Iowa and surrendered to the authorities. While free on his own recognizance, Gall started his own business in the construction industry, primarily engaged in subcontracting for the installation of windows and doors. In his first year, his profits were over $2,000 per month.

Gall entered into a plea agreement with the Government, stipulating that he was "responsible for, but did not necessarily distribute himself, at least 2,500 grams of [ecstasy], or the equivalent of at least 87.5 kilograms of marijuana." In the agreement, the Government acknowledged that by "on or about September of 2000," Gall had communicated his intent to stop distributing ecstasy to Rinderknecht and other members of the conspiracy. The agreement further provided that recent changes in the Guidelines that enhanced the recommended punishment for distributing ecstasy were not applicable to Gall because he had withdrawn from the conspiracy prior to the effective date of those changes.

In her presentence report, the probation officer concluded that Gall had no significant criminal history; that he was not an organizer, leader, or manager; and that his offense did not involve the use of any weapons. The report stated that Gall had truthfully provided the Government with all of the evidence he had concerning the alleged offenses, but that his evidence was not useful because he provided no new information to the agents. The report also described Gall's substantial use of drugs prior to his offense and the absence of any such use in recent years. The report recommended a sentencing range of 30 to 37 months of imprisonment.

The record of the sentencing hearing held on May 27, 2005, includes a "small flood" of letters from Gall's parents and other relatives, his fiancé, neighbors, and representatives of firms doing business with him, uniformly praising his character and work ethic. The transcript includes the testimony of several witnesses and the District Judge's colloquy with the Assistant United States Attorney (AUSA) and with Gall. The AUSA did not contest any of the evidence concerning Gall's law-abiding life during the preceding five years, but urged that "the Guidelines are appropriate and should be followed," and requested that the court impose a prison sentence within the Guidelines range. He mentioned that two of Gall's co-conspirators had been sentenced to 30 and 35 months, respectively, but upon further questioning by the District Court, he acknowledged that neither of them had voluntarily withdrawn from the conspiracy.

The District Judge sentenced Gall to probation for a term of 36 months. In addition to making a lengthy statement on the record, the judge filed a detailed sentencing memorandum explaining his decision, and provided the following statement of reasons in his written judgment:

> The Court determined that, considering all the factors under 18 U.S.C. 3553(a), the Defendant's explicit withdrawal from the conspiracy almost four years before the filing of the Indictment, the Defendant's post-offense conduct, especially obtaining a college degree and the start of his own successful business, the support of family and friends, lack of criminal history, and his age at the time of the offense conduct, all warrant the sentence imposed, which was sufficient, but not greater than necessary to serve the purposes of sentencing.

At the end of both the sentencing hearing and the sentencing memorandum, the District Judge reminded Gall that probation, rather than "an act of leniency," is a "substantial restriction of freedom." In the memorandum, he emphasized:

> [Gall] will have to comply with strict reporting conditions along with a three-year regime of alcohol and drug testing. He will not be able to change or make decisions about significant circumstances in his life, such as where to live or work, which are prized liberty interests, without first seeking

authorization from his Probation Officer or, perhaps, even the Court. Of course, the Defendant always faces the harsh consequences that await if he violates the conditions of his probationary term.

Finally, the District Judge explained why he had concluded that the sentence of probation reflected the seriousness of Gall's offense and that no term of imprisonment was necessary:

> Any term of imprisonment in this case would be counter effective by depriving society of the contributions of the Defendant who, the Court has found, understands the consequences of his criminal conduct and is doing everything in his power to forge a new life. The Defendant's post-offense conduct indicates neither that he will return to criminal behavior nor that the Defendant is a danger to society. In fact, the Defendant's post-offense conduct was not motivated by a desire to please the Court or any other governmental agency, but was the pre-Indictment product of the Defendant's own desire to lead a better life.

II.

The Court of Appeals reversed and remanded for resentencing. Relying on its earlier opinion in *United States v. Claiborne*, 439 F.3d 479 (8th Cir. 2006), it held that a sentence outside of the Guidelines range must be supported by a justification that " 'is proportional to the extent of the difference between the advisory range and the sentence imposed.' " 446 F.3d 884, 889 (8th Cir. 2006). Characterizing the difference between a sentence of probation and the bottom of Gall's advisory Guidelines range of 30 months as "extraordinary" because it amounted to "a 100% downward variance," the Court of Appeals held that such a variance must be — and here was not — supported by extraordinary circumstances.

Rather than making an attempt to quantify the value of the justifications provided by the District Judge, the Court of Appeals identified what it regarded as five separate errors in the District Judge's reasoning: (1) He gave "too much weight to Gall's withdrawal from the conspiracy"; (2) given that Gall was 21 at the time of his offense, the District Judge erroneously gave "significant weight" to studies showing impetuous behavior by persons under the age of 18; (3) he did not "properly weigh" the seriousness of Gall's offense; (4) he failed to consider whether a sentence of probation would result in "unwarranted" disparities; and (5) he placed "too much emphasis on Gall's post-offense rehabilitation." As we shall explain, we are not persuaded that these factors, whether viewed separately or in the aggregate, are sufficient to support the conclusion that the District Judge abused his discretion. As a preface to our discussion of these particulars, however, we shall explain why the Court of Appeals' rule requiring "proportional" justifications for departures from the Guidelines range is not consistent with our remedial opinion in *United States v. Booker*, 543 U.S. 220 (2005).

III.

In *Booker* we invalidated both the statutory provision, 18 U.S.C. § 3553(b)(1), which made the Sentencing Guidelines mandatory, and § 3742(e), which directed appellate courts to apply a *de novo* standard of review to departures from the Guidelines. As a result of our decision, the Guidelines are now advisory, and appellate review of sentencing decisions is limited to determining whether they are "reasonable." Our explanation of "reasonableness" review in the *Booker* opinion made it pellucidly clear that the familiar abuse-of-discretion standard of review now applies to appellate review of sentencing decisions.

It is also clear that a district judge must give serious consideration to the extent of any departure from the Guidelines and must explain his conclusion that an unusually lenient or an unusually harsh sentence is appropriate in a particular case with sufficient justifications. For even though the Guidelines are advisory rather than mandatory, they are, as we pointed out in *Rita*, the product of careful study based on extensive empirical evidence derived from the review of thousands of individual sentencing decisions.[2] In reviewing the reasonableness of a sentence outside the Guidelines range, appellate courts may therefore take the degree of variance into account and consider the extent of a deviation from the Guidelines. We reject, however, an appellate rule that requires "extraordinary" circumstances to justify a sentence outside the Guidelines range. We also reject the use of a rigid mathematical formula that uses the percentage of a departure as the standard for determining the strength of the justifications required for a specific sentence.

As an initial matter, the approaches we reject come too close to creating an impermissible presumption of unreasonableness for sentences outside the Guidelines range. Even the Government has acknowledged that such a presumption would not be consistent with *Booker*.

The mathematical approach also suffers from infirmities of application. On one side of the equation, deviations from the Guidelines range will always appear more extreme — in percentage terms — when the range itself is low, and a sentence of probation will always be a 100% departure regardless of whether the Guidelines range is 1 month or 100 years. Moreover, quantifying the variance as a certain percentage of the maximum, minimum, or median prison sentence recommended by the Guidelines gives no weight to the "substantial restriction of freedom" involved in a term of supervised release or probation.

We recognize that custodial sentences are qualitatively more severe than probationary sentences of equivalent terms. Offenders on probation are nonetheless subject to several standard conditions that substantially restrict their liberty. Probationers may not leave the judicial district, move, or change jobs without notifying, and in some cases receiving permission from, their probation officer or the court. They must report regularly to their probation officer, permit unannounced visits to their homes, refrain from associating with any person convicted of a felony, and refrain from excessive drinking. Most probationers are also subject to individual "special conditions" imposed by the court. Gall, for instance, may not patronize any establishment that derives more than 50% of its revenue from the sale of alcohol, and must submit to random drug tests as directed by his probation officer.

---

[2] Notably, not all of the Guidelines are tied to this empirical evidence. For example, the Sentencing Commission departed from the empirical approach when setting the Guidelines range for drug offenses, and chose instead to key the Guidelines to the statutory mandatory minimum sentences that Congress established for such crimes. This decision, and its effect on a district judge's authority to deviate from the Guidelines range in a particular drug case, is addressed in *Kimbrough v. United States*, 128 S. Ct. 558 (2007).

On the other side of the equation, the mathematical approach assumes the existence of some ascertainable method of assigning percentages to various justifications. Does withdrawal from a conspiracy justify more or less than, say, a 30% reduction? Does it matter that the withdrawal occurred several years ago? Is it relevant that the withdrawal was motivated by a decision to discontinue the use of drugs and to lead a better life? What percentage, if any, should be assigned to evidence that a defendant poses no future threat to society, or to evidence that innocent third parties are dependent on him? The formula is a classic example of attempting to measure an inventory of apples by counting oranges.[5]

Most importantly, both the exceptional circumstances requirement and the rigid mathematical formulation reflect a practice — common among courts that have adopted "proportional review" — of applying a heightened standard of review to sentences outside the Guidelines range. This is inconsistent with the rule that the abuse-of-discretion standard of review applies to appellate review of all sentencing decisions-whether inside or outside the Guidelines range.

As we explained in *Rita*, a district court should begin all sentencing proceedings by correctly calculating the applicable Guidelines range. As a matter of administration and to secure nationwide consistency, the Guidelines should be the starting point and the initial benchmark. The Guidelines are not the only consideration, however. Accordingly, after giving both parties an opportunity to argue for whatever sentence they deem appropriate, the district judge should then consider all of the § 3553(a) factors to determine whether they support the sentence requested by a party. In so doing, he may not presume that the Guidelines range is reasonable. He must make an individualized assessment based on the facts presented. If he decides that an outside-Guidelines sentence is warranted, he must consider the extent of the deviation and ensure that the justification is sufficiently compelling to support the degree of the variance. We find it uncontroversial that a major departure should be supported by a more significant justification than a minor one. After settling on the appropriate sentence, he must adequately explain the chosen sentence to allow for meaningful appellate review and to promote the perception of fair sentencing.

The third factor pertains to "the kinds of sentences available," § 3553(a)(3); the fourth to the Sentencing Guidelines; the fifth to any relevant policy statement issued by the Sentencing Commission; the sixth to "the need to avoid unwarranted sentence disparities," § 3553(a)(6); and the seventh to "the need to provide restitution to any victim," § 3553(a)(7). Preceding this list is a general directive to "impose a sentence sufficient, but not greater than necessary, to comply with the purposes" of sentencing described in the second factor. § 3553(a). The fact that § 3553(a) explicitly directs sentencing courts to consider the Guidelines supports the premise that district courts must begin their analysis with the Guidelines and remain cognizant of them throughout the sentencing process.

Regardless of whether the sentence imposed is inside or outside the Guidelines range, the appellate court must review the sentence under an abuse-of-discretion standard. It must first ensure that the district court committed no significant procedural error, such as failing to calculate (or improperly calculating) the Guidelines range, treating the Guidelines as mandatory, failing to consider the

---

[5] Notably, when the Court of Appeals explained its disagreement with the District Judge's decision in this case, it made no attempt to quantify the strength of any of the mitigating circumstances.

§ 3553(a) factors, selecting a sentence based on clearly erroneous facts, or failing to adequately explain the chosen sentence-including an explanation for any deviation from the Guidelines range. Assuming that the district court's sentencing decision is procedurally sound, the appellate court should then consider the substantive reasonableness of the sentence imposed under an abuse-of-discretion standard. When conducting this review, the court will, of course, take into account the totality of the circumstances, including the extent of any variance from the Guidelines range. If the sentence is within the Guidelines range, the appellate court may, but is not required to, apply a presumption of reasonableness. But if the sentence is outside the Guidelines range, the court may not apply a presumption of unreasonableness. It may consider the extent of the deviation, but must give due deference to the district court's decision that the § 3553(a) factors, on a whole, justify the extent of the variance. The fact that the appellate court might reasonably have concluded that a different sentence was appropriate is insufficient to justify reversal of the district court.

Practical considerations also underlie this legal principle. "The sentencing judge is in a superior position to find facts and judge their import under § 3553(a) in the individual case. The judge sees and hears the evidence, makes credibility determinations, has full knowledge of the facts and gains insights not conveyed by the record." Brief for Federal Public and Community Defenders et al. as *Amici Curiae* 16. "The sentencing judge has access to, and greater familiarity with, the individual case and the individual defendant before him than the Commission or the appeals court." *Rita*, 127 S. Ct. at 2469. Moreover, "[d]istrict courts have an institutional advantage over appellate courts in making these sorts of determinations, especially as they see so many more Guidelines sentences than appellate courts do." *Koon v. United States*, 518 U.S. 81, 98 (1996).

"It has been uniform and constant in the federal judicial tradition for the sentencing judge to consider every convicted person as an individual and every case as a unique study in the human failings that sometimes mitigate, sometimes magnify, the crime and the punishment to ensue." *Id.* at 113. The uniqueness of the individual case, however, does not change the deferential abuse-of-discretion standard of review that applies to all sentencing decisions. As we shall now explain, the opinion of the Court of Appeals in this case does not reflect the requisite deference and does not support the conclusion that the District Court abused its discretion.

IV.

As an initial matter, we note that the District Judge committed no significant procedural error. He correctly calculated the applicable Guidelines range, allowed both parties to present arguments as to what they believed the appropriate sentence should be, considered all of the § 3553(a) factors, and thoroughly documented his reasoning. The Court of Appeals found that the District Judge erred in failing to give proper weight to the seriousness of the offense, as required by § 3553(a)(2)(A), and failing to consider whether a sentence of probation would create unwarranted disparities, as required by § 3553(a)(6). We disagree.

Section 3553(a)(2)(A) requires judges to consider "the need for the sentence imposed . . . to reflect the seriousness of the offense, to promote respect for the law, and to provide just punishment for the offense." The Court of Appeals concluded that "the district court did not properly weigh the seriousness of Gall's offense" because it "ignored the serious health risks ecstasy poses." 446 F.3d at 890. Contrary to the Court of Appeals' conclusion, the District Judge plainly did consider the seriousness of the offense. It is true that the District Judge did not make specific reference to the (unquestionably significant) health risks posed by ecstasy, but the prosecutor did not raise ecstasy's effects at the sentencing hearing. Had the prosecutor raised the issue, specific discussion of the point might have been in order, but it was not incumbent on the District Judge to raise every conceivably relevant issue on his own initiative.

The Government's legitimate concern that a lenient sentence for a serious offense threatens to promote disrespect for the law is at least to some extent offset by the fact that seven of the eight defendants in this case have been sentenced to significant prison terms. Moreover, the unique facts of Gall's situation provide support for the District Judge's conclusion that, in Gall's case, "a sentence of imprisonment may work to promote not respect, but derision, of the law if the law is viewed as merely a means to dispense harsh punishment without taking into account the real conduct and circumstances involved in sentencing."

Section 3553(a)(6) requires judges to consider "the need to avoid unwarranted sentence disparities among defendants with similar records who have been found guilty of similar conduct." The Court of Appeals stated that "the record does not show that the district court considered whether a sentence of probation would result in unwarranted disparities." 446 F.3d at 890. As with the seriousness of the offense conduct, avoidance of unwarranted disparities was clearly considered by the Sentencing Commission when setting the Guidelines ranges. Since the District Judge correctly calculated and carefully reviewed the Guidelines range, he necessarily gave significant weight and consideration to the need to avoid unwarranted disparities.

. . . [I]t is perfectly clear that the District Judge considered the need to avoid unwarranted disparities, but also considered the need to avoid unwarranted *similarities* among other co-conspirators who were not similarly situated. The District Judge regarded Gall's voluntary withdrawal as a reasonable basis for giving him a less severe sentence than the three codefendants who neither withdrew from the conspiracy nor rehabilitated themselves as Gall had done. We also note that neither the Court of Appeals nor the Government has called our attention to a comparable defendant who received a more severe sentence.

Since the District Court committed no procedural error, the only question for the Court of Appeals was whether the sentence was reasonable — *i.e.*, whether the District Judge abused his discretion in determining that the § 3553(a) factors supported a sentence of probation and justified a substantial deviation from the Guidelines range. As we shall now explain, the sentence was reasonable. The Court of Appeals' decision to the contrary was incorrect and failed to demonstrate the requisite deference to the District Judge's decision.

V.

The Court of Appeals gave virtually no deference to the District Court's decision that the § 3553(a) factors justified a significant variance in this case. Although the Court of Appeals correctly stated that the appropriate standard of review was abuse of discretion, it engaged in an analysis that more closely resembled *de novo* review of the facts presented and determined that, in its view, the degree of variance was not warranted.

The Court of Appeals thought that the District Court "gave too much weight to Gall's withdrawal from the conspiracy because the court failed to acknowledge the significant benefit Gall received from being subject to the 1999 Guidelines."[10] This criticism is flawed in that it ignores the critical relevance of Gall's voluntary withdrawal, a circumstance that distinguished his conduct not only from that of all his codefendants, but from the vast majority of defendants convicted of conspiracy in federal court . . .

The Court of Appeals thought the District Judge "gave significant weight to an improper factor" when he compared Gall's sale of ecstasy when he was a 21-year-old adult to the "impetuous and ill-considered" actions of persons under the age of 18. The appellate court correctly observed that the studies cited by the District Judge do not explain how Gall's "specific behavior in the instant case was impetuous or ill-considered."

In that portion of his sentencing memorandum, however, the judge was discussing the "character of the defendant," not the nature of his offense. He noted that Gall's criminal history included a ticket for underage drinking when he was 18 years old and possession of marijuana that was contemporaneous with his offense in this case. In summary, the District Judge observed that all of Gall's criminal history "including the present offense, occurred when he was twenty-one-years old or younger" and appeared "to stem from his addictions to drugs and alcohol." . . .

Given the dramatic contrast between Gall's behavior before he joined the conspiracy and his conduct after withdrawing, it was not unreasonable for the District Judge to view Gall's immaturity at the time of the offense as a mitigating factor, and his later behavior as a sign that he had matured and would not engage in such impetuous and ill-considered conduct in the future. Indeed, his consideration of that factor finds support in our cases.

Finally, the Court of Appeals thought that, even if Gall's rehabilitation was dramatic and permanent, a sentence of probation for participation as a middleman in a conspiracy distributing 10,000 pills of ecstasy "lies outside the range of choice dictated by the facts of the case." If the Guidelines were still mandatory, and assuming the facts did not justify a Guidelines-based downward departure, this would provide a sufficient basis for setting aside Gall's sentence because the Guidelines state that probation alone is not an appropriate sentence for comparable offenses.[11] But the Guidelines are not mandatory, and thus the "range of choice dictated by the facts of the case" is significantly broadened. Moreover, the Guidelines are only one of the factors to consider when imposing sentence, and § 3553(a)(3) directs the judge to consider sentences other than imprisonment.

We also note that the Government did not argue below, and has not argued here, that a sentence of probation could never be imposed for a crime identical to Gall's. Indeed, it acknowledged that probation could be permissible if the record contained

---

[10] The Court of Appeals explained that under the current Guidelines, which treat ecstasy more harshly, Gall's base offense level would have been 32, eight levels higher than the base offense level imposed under the 1999 Guidelines.

[11] Specifically, probation is not recommended under the Guidelines when the applicable Guidelines range is outside Zone A of the sentencing table as it is here. USSG § 5B1.1.

different — but in our view, no more compelling — mitigating evidence.

The District Court quite reasonably attached great weight to Gall's self-motivated rehabilitation, which was undertaken not at the direction of, or under supervision by, any court, but on his own initiative. This also lends strong support to the conclusion that imprisonment was not necessary to deter Gall from engaging in future criminal conduct or to protect the public from his future criminal acts.

The Court of Appeals clearly disagreed with the District Judge's conclusion that consideration of the § 3553(a) factors justified a sentence of probation; it believed that the circumstances presented here were insufficient to sustain such a marked deviation from the Guidelines range. But it is not for the Court of Appeals to decide *de novo* whether the justification for a variance is sufficient or the sentence reasonable. On abuse-of-discretion review, the Court of Appeals should have given due deference to the District Court's reasoned and reasonable decision that the § 3553(a) factors, on the whole, justified the sentence. Accordingly, the judgment of the Court of Appeals is reversed.

It is so ordered.

Justice Scalia, concurring. [Omitted.]

Justice Souter, concurring. [Omitted.]

Justice Thomas, dissenting. [Omitted.]

Justice Alito, dissenting.

* * *

Read fairly, the opinion of the Court of Appeals holds that the District Court did not properly exercise its sentencing discretion because it did not give sufficient weight to the policy decisions reflected in the Guidelines. Petitioner was convicted of a serious crime, conspiracy to distribute "ecstasy." He distributed thousands of pills and made between $30,000 and $40,000 in profit. Although he eventually left the conspiracy, he did so because he was worried about apprehension. The Sentencing Guidelines called for a term of imprisonment of 30 to 37 months, but the District Court imposed a term of probation. . . .

If the question before us was whether a reasonable jurist could conclude that a sentence of probation was sufficient in this case to serve the purposes of punishment set out in 18 U.S.C. § 3553(a)(2), the District Court's decision could not be disturbed. But because I believe that sentencing judges must still give some significant weight to the Guidelines sentencing range, the Commission's policy statements, and the need to avoid unwarranted sentencing disparities, § 3553(a)(3), (4), and (5) (2000 ed. and Supp. V), I agree with the Eighth Circuit that the District Court did not properly exercise its discretion.

* * *

Notes and Questions

1. *The Significance of the* Gall *decision.* How much discretion does the decision give to trial judges? To what degree should appeals courts defer to trial judges? In one post-*Gall* decision, the Court reversed a Guidelines sentence because the district judge had presumed such a sentence to be reasonable. *See Nelson v.*

United States, ___U.S.___ (2009) ("The Guidelines are not only not mandatory on sentencing courts; they are also not to be presumed reasonable.").

2. *The* Kimbrough *decision*. Is a policy disagreement a "reasonable" basis for a departure? For example, if a judge disagrees with the policy underlying the Guidelines' 100-to-1 crack-to-powder cocaine sentencing ratio — treating each gram of crack cocaine as the equivalent to 100 grams of powder cocaine — may the judge use that disagreement to justify a below-Guidelines sentence? The disparity was based upon an initial assessment that crack cocaine was more dangerous and addictive than powder cocaine. This policy came under widespread attack, however, largely because of racial disparities between powder and crack cocaine sentencing; the vast majority of defendants in crack cocaine cases are African-American. *See Kimbrough v. United States*, 128 S. Ct. 558, 566–568 (2008).

In *Kimbrough*, the trial judge had issued a below-Guidelines sentence based on such a disagreement, and the appeals court reversed, holding that a sentence "outside the guidelines range is per se unreasonable when it is based on a disagreement with the sentencing disparity for crack and powder cocaine offenses." The Supreme Court reversed the appeals court, holding that sentencing judges have the discretion to consider the 100-to-1 sentencing disparity in crack-cocaine cases to ensure that a sentence for a cocaine conviction is "sufficient but not greater than necessary" under the Guidelines. Because the Guidelines are advisory, and because a judge may consider sentences within the statutory maximum and minimum sentences, a judge may consider policy disagreements among other factors when imposing a sentence. In a subsequent case, the Court reiterated district judges' discretion to disagree with policies reflected in the Guidelines. *See Spears v. United States*, ___U.S.___ (2009) (overturning reversal of sentence that was based on disagreement with crack cocaine guidelines).

3. *Booker's impact*. Statistics have shown a small but noticeable increase in both above-and below-Guidelines-range sentences after *Booker*. *See* http://www.ussc.gov/sc_cases/. From 2002 to 2005, within-range sentences averaged from roughly 65% to 72% of all sentences. Since *Booker* was decided in 2005, the percentages of all sentences within the Guidelines-range sentences have averaged around 60%. *See id.* at 10. Judges have issued both above- and below-Guidelines-range sentences. From 2005 to 2008, for example, the number of such above-Guidelines sentences doubled from 0.8% to 1.6% of all sentences.

Is this trend towards more outside-Guidelines-range sentences likely to continue after *Rita*, *Gall*, and *Kimbrough*? Why or why not?

PROBLEM

19-1. Defendant worked as a property manager for Mallow Properties. As part of his duties, he was authorized to approve invoices for work performed on the properties under his supervision. For two years, defendant used his position to steal from Mallow. His scheme worked in two ways. First, he took payment checks for legitimate invoices and deposited them into several bank accounts at his disposal. He then took the same invoices, broke them down into several smaller invoices, and resubmitted them for payment, using the smaller checks to pay the vendors. Second, he created fraudulent invoices for work never performed. In some cases, the listed contractor on these invoices did not even exist. He then deposited the payment checks into various bank accounts to which he had access.

Defendant stole a total of $180,000. As a result, Mallow had to institute new policies and procedures to verify invoice payments. Based on these facts, defendant has pleaded guilty to bank fraud.

Defendant has stated that, at the time of the offense, he was going through a difficult divorce and was concerned about providing for his children. He also admitted to living beyond his means. Defendant was 47 years old and had no prior criminal record. He was a divorced father of two sons, ages 15 and 13, and was by all accounts an excellent parent. Despite strained relations with his ex-wife, she had agreed to allow the youngest son to live with defendant. Other family members also made positive statements about defendant's character.

Defendant's mental and physical health appeared to be sound, and he had no substance abuse issues. A high-school graduate with some college education, defendant compiled a solid work history. Following his termination by Mallow, he obtained a well-paying job as a property manager for another company, but that employer terminated defendant when it learned about this offense via an anonymous phone call. The loss of this job clearly affected defendant's ability to make restitution. Defendant intended to re-pay Mallow and, shortly after the offense was discovered, signed over a motorcycle worth about $18,000 as a sign of good faith. He also took up residence in his office at his new work place in an effort to save money. Once he lost the property manager job, he became a self-employed contractor performing remodeling and drywall work, earning much less. Further, because his child support payments were based on his old salary, he quickly amassed arrears and was unable to make restitution.

The probation office indicated that defendant had, since being charged with this offense, complied with the conditions of release and been truthful in his dealings with that office. The supervising officer confirmed that he worked hard as a contractor, often reporting to her office covered in dust. He also sat down with his two sons and admitted to them what he had done, and expressed genuine remorse for his crime, indicating that he was humiliated by his downfall.

This case is now before the trial judge for sentencing.

(A) Calculate the Guidelines sentence range, assuming a base level of 7, U.S.S.G. § 2B1.1(a)(1) and a criminal history category of I.

(B) For the prosecution and the defense, please (1) determine the sentence that you believe should be imposed and (2) make the arguments in support of your recommended sentence.

(C) Now assume that you are the trial judge. What sentence would you impose? Why?

[E] RELEVANT CONDUCT

Whatever the long-term impact of the *Booker* decision and its progeny, it appears that most sentencing courts will continue to follow the Guidelines closely. One of the most important tasks of the sentencing judge under the Guidelines is to determine the defendant's "relevant conduct."

Note on *Witte v. United States* and *United States v. Watts*

In two cases, the Supreme Court rejected Double Jeopardy Clause challenges to the Guidelines' relevant conduct provisions. In *Witte v. United States*, 515 U.S. 389, 395–399 (1995), the defendant had been found guilty of narcotics charges relating to marijuana transactions that occurred in 1991 (the "1991 transactions"). At his sentencing on that charge, the court took into account 1990 cocaine transactions (the "1990 transactions") — with which the defendant had *not* been charged — as relevant conduct that increased the defendant's sentence on the charges arising from the 1991 transactions.

The defendant was later charged in a separate indictment with crimes arising from the 1990 transactions. The defendant moved to dismiss the charges based on the 1990 transactions on the grounds that he had already been punished for the 1990 transactions, i.e, the 1990 transactions had been considered as "relevant conduct" at sentencing for the 1991 transactions.

The Supreme Court rejected the defendant's argument, finding no Double Jeopardy violation because the defendant did not face consecutive charges for the same offense:

> Under *Blockburger v. United States*, 284 U.S. 299, 304 (1932), 'where the same act or transaction constitutes a violation of two distinct statutory provisions, the test to be applied to determine whether there are two offenses or only one, is whether each provision requires proof of a fact which the other does not.' Under the *Blockburger* test, the indictment in this case did not charge the same offense to which petitioner formerly had pleaded guilty.

Following this reasoning, the Court concluded that considering the defendant's prior conduct when deciding a sentence "does not constitute punishment for that conduct," and, therefore, does not violate the Double Jeopardy Clause's bar on imposing multiple punishments for the same offense. *Witte*, 515 U.S. at 406.

In *United States v. Watts*, 519 U.S. 148 (1997), the Supreme Court rejected another Double Jeopardy Clause challenge to the Guidelines' relevant conduct provisions. In *Watts*, the Court held that a sentencing court may consider conduct relating to a criminal charge even if the jury acquitted the defendant of that charge, so long as the government has proven the conduct by a preponderance of the evidence.

NOTES AND QUESTIONS

1. *The* Witte *decision*. Was the result in this case fair? Shouldn't a defendant be punished only once for the relevant conduct? If a defendant can be punished for relevant conduct more than once, as the Court held, what is to prevent the prosecutor from filing multiple charges and gaining enhanced sentences? How does *Booker* affect the answers to these questions?

2. *The* Watts *decision*. Is this outcome fair? Why or why not? Again, how does *Booker* affect your answers to these questions? Courts have continued to consider acquitted conduct after *Booker*. *See United States v. Brown*, 516 F.3d 1047, 1050 (D.C. Cir. 2008) (allowing the court to consider acquitted conduct because the sentence did not exceed the statutory limit); *United States v. Tyndall*, 521 F.3d

877, 884 (8th Cir. 2008) (explaining that conduct that is proven by a preponderance of the evidence may be considered when sentencing within the statutory limits); *United States v. Faust*, 456 F.3d 1342, 1348 (11th Cir. 2006) (affirming sentence where acquitted conduct was considered in the face of a Due Process challenge).

[F] DEPARTURES AND SUBSTANTIAL ASSISTANCE

[1] Substantial Assistance Motions

Under § 5K1.1 of the Guidelines, the government has the discretion to file a motion for a downward departure based upon a defendant's substantial assistance to the government in an ongoing criminal investigation or prosecution. In *Wade v. United States*, 504 U.S. 181 (1992), the Supreme Court held that the defendant has no recourse when the government declines to file a 5K1.1motion, unless the government's decision was based upon an impermissible ground such as race or religion.

Even if the government files a §5K1.1 motion, courts have held that the sentencing judge is not required to grant the motion. *See, e.g., United States v. Mariano*, 983 F.2d 1150, 1155 (1993) ("[t]he district court is not obliged to depart downward simply because a grateful prosecutor prefers a grateful sentence"). Nonetheless, substantial assistance departures account for most downward departures and are the principal reason for below-Guidelines departures. The United States Sentencing Commission maintains the most up-to-date sentencing information. *See* http://www.ussc.gov/.

Following the *Booker* decision, courts have held that judges now have the flexibility to order §5K1.1 downward departures even in the absence of a government motion. As the Second Circuit stated in *United States v. Fernandez*, 443 F.3d 19, 33 (2d Cir. 2006):

> [I]n formulating a reasonable sentence a sentencing judge must consider 'the history and characteristics of the defendant' within the meaning of 18 U.S.C. § 3553(a)(1), as well as the other factors enumerated in § 3553(a), and should take under advisement any related arguments, including the contention that a defendant made efforts to cooperate, even if those efforts did not yield a government motion for a downward departure pursuant to U.S.S.G. § 5K1.1.

And in *United States v. Lazenby*, 439 F.3d 928, 933–934 (8th Cir. 2006), the Eighth Circuit reversed the sentence because the trial court had failed to consider its post-*Booker* discretion to find grounds for a substantial assistance departure even in the absence of a government motion.

[2] Substantial Assistance and Reasonableness Review

Whatever the sentence, it will now be subject to review for reasonableness. One frequently litigated issue after *Booker* is the reasonableness of downward departures. The next case grew out of a high-profile accounting fraud scandal. In the case, the trial judge ordered a substantial assistance downward departure far greater than the government requested. As you read the case, consider whether the appeals court was correct in concluding that the district court's sentencing decision was unreasonable.

UNITED STATES v. LIVESAY
525 F.3d 1081 (11th Cir. 2008)

This case is before us on remand from the United States Supreme Court for reconsideration in light of *Gall v. United States*, 128 S. Ct. 586 (2007). In this $1.4 billion fraud scheme, defendant-appellee Kenneth K. Livesay, the former Assistant Controller and Chief Information Officer ("CIO") of HealthSouth Corporation who played a major role in the fraud, was sentenced to 60 months' probation, with the first 6 months to be served as home detention. This panel previously vacated Livesay's non-custodial sentence. *See United States v. Livesay (Livesay II)*, 484 F.3d 1324, 1325–26 (11th Cir.2007).[1] After reconsideration in light of *Gall* and affording substantial deference to the district court's sentencing determinations, we conclude that the district court committed *Gall* procedural error, and thus we must vacate Livesay's sentence and remand.

I. FACTUAL BACKGROUND

At some point in the early to mid-1990s, HealthSouth officials realized that HealthSouth's financial results were failing to produce sufficient earnings-per-share to meet the expectations of Wall Street analysts. Various HealthSouth officials, including Livesay, became aware that the earnings shortfall created a substantial risk that, unless the earnings-per-share were artificially inflated, the earnings would fail to meet analyst expectations, and the market price of HealthSouth's securities would decline.

Therefore, from at least 1994 until March 2003, a group of HealthSouth officials "conspired to artificially inflate HealthSouth's reported earnings and earnings per share, and to falsify reports about HealthSouth's overall financial condition." *United States v. Martin*, 455 F.3d 1227, 1230 (11th Cir.2006). The officials "made, and directed accounting personnel to make, false and fraudulent entries in HealthSouth's books and records for the purpose of falsely reporting HealthSouth's assets, revenues, and earnings per share and in order to defraud investors, banks, and lenders." *Id.*

For over ten years from April 1989 to November 1999, Livesay was the Assistant Controller in HealthSouth's accounting department.[3] During his time as Assistant Controller, Livesay had access to all of the financial information on HealthSouth's balance sheets and income statements. As Assistant Controller, Livesay directly assisted the Controller and the Chief Financial Officer in preparing the financial statements and reports that HealthSouth was required to file with the Securities and Exchange Commission ("SEC"). Senior executives issued instructions to defendant Livesay regarding the desired earnings-per-share, and Assistant Controller Livesay and HealthSouth's accounting staff met to discuss ways to meet Wall Street's earnings-per-share expectations.

---

[1] Our *Livesay II* decision was this Court's second review of Livesay's sentence. In *United States v. Livesay (Livesay I)*, 146 Fed. Appx. 403, 405 (11th Cir. 2005), we vacated and remanded Livesay's sentence of probation after concluding that the record provided a "scant basis to assess" the reasonableness of that sentence. On remand after *Livesay I*, the district court again sentenced Livesay to probation, and we again reversed, determining the sentence to be unreasonable. Livesay appealed from our decision in *Livesay II*, and the Supreme Court remanded to us for this reconsideration in light of *Gall*.

[3] In late 1999, Livesay became the CIO of HealthSouth.

More specifically, Livesay, as Assistant Controller, made false entries in HealthSouth's books and records to artificially inflate the company's earnings-per-share. Livesay also managed and supervised others in manipulating HealthSouth's books and records, instructing HealthSouth's accounting staff to alter certain accounts so as to inflate HealthSouth's earnings-per-share. Livesay participated in the preparation of HealthSouth's 1998 quarterly and annual reports that were filed with the SEC, and Livesay fully knew that the reports materially misstated HealthSouth's net income, revenue, earnings-per-share, assets, and liabilities. For example, HealthSouth's pre-tax income was overstated by approximately $440,000,000 in 1997 and $635,000,000 in 1998.

This massive fraud, in which Livesay directly participated for over five years, impacted many victims. After the conspiracy was uncovered in March 2003 and the SEC temporarily suspended trading in HealthSouth stock, the total drop in the value of outstanding HealthSouth stock was approximately $1.4 billion. Many shareholders had invested their life savings in HealthSouth stock, which plummeted to pennies per share. This fraud also affected many others, including: (1) HealthSouth employees, many of whom were long-time employees close to retirement, who suffered by either losing their job or their retirement savings that was invested in the company's stock ownership plan or pension fund; (2) employees of contractors who were dependent on HealthSouth contracts for income; (3) banks and other lenders who loaned money to HealthSouth based on false financial information; (4) health-service competitors who lost business or financing due to HealthSouth's false financial representations; and (5) members of the community who benefited from HealthSouth's charitable activities.

II. PROCEDURAL HISTORY

A. Guilty Plea and Advisory Guidelines Range

Livesay pled guilty to an information charging him with: (1) conspiracy to commit wire and securities fraud, in violation of 15 U.S.C. §§ 78m(a), (b)(2)(A)-(B) and (b)(5), and 78ff and 18 U.S.C. §§ 371 and 1343, et al. (Count One); and (2) falsification of financial information, in violation of 15 U.S.C. §§ 78m(b)(2)(A), 78m(b)(5), 78ff, and 18 U.S.C. § 2 (Count Two). The information also included a forfeiture count.

The presentence report set Livesay's base offense level at 6, pursuant to U.S.S.G. § 2F1.1(a). Livesay's adjusted offense level was 28, however, due to four enhancements reflecting the magnitude of the fraud and his significant role in it. The enhancements were: (1) 18 levels, pursuant to U.S.S.G. § 2F1.1(b)(1)(S), because the loss amount exceeded $80 million; (2) 2 levels, pursuant to U.S.S.G. § 2F1.1(b)(2)(A), because the offense involved more than minimal planning; (3) 2 levels, pursuant to U.S.S.G. § 2F1.1(b)(5)(C), because the offense involved sophisticated means; and (4) 3 levels, pursuant to U.S.S.G. § 3B1.1(b), for Livesay's role in the offense as a manager or supervisor. After a 3-level reduction for acceptance of responsibility under U.S.S.G. § 3E1.1, Livesay's adjusted offense level was 28. With an offense level of 28 and a criminal history category of I, Livesay's advisory Guidelines range was 78 to 97 months' imprisonment.

The government filed a U.S.S.G. § 5K1.1 motion for downward departure, based on Livesay's cooperation and substantial assistance. The government noted that

Livesay: (1) met whenever needed with several government agencies, each of which had a substantial need for his assistance; (2) met with the forensic auditor reconstructing HealthSouth's books and records; (3) spent many hours reviewing financial statements and other documents; (4) provided the government with critical documents evidencing the fraud; (5) helped quantify the fraud; and (6) facilitated guilty pleas from other co-conspirators and the prosecution of others yet to be convicted.

B. First Sentencing in June 2004

At Livesay's first sentencing, the government's § 5K1.1 motion recommended a downward departure of 3 levels (from 28 to 25) and a sentence of 60 months' imprisonment. The district court granted the government's § 5K1.1 motion, but departed downward *18 levels*, to an offense level of 10. Offense level 10, combined with Livesay's criminal history category of I, yielded an advisory Guidelines range of 6 to 12 months' imprisonment. Because Livesay's Guidelines range of 6 to 12 months' imprisonment fell within "Zone B" of the sentencing table, the Guidelines gave the district court the option of sentencing Livesay to probation and 6 months' home detention without any additional Guidelines departures. The government objected to the reasonableness of the § 5K1.1 departure.

Alternatively, the government asked that Livesay at least be sentenced to the maximum sentence in that range (12 months' imprisonment). The district court nevertheless sentenced Livesay to 60 months' probation, with the first 6 months to be served on home detention, pursuant to U.S.S.G. §§ 5B1.1(a)(2) and 5C1.1(c)(3).[5] The district court imposed a $10,000 fine and forfeiture of $750,000.

The government appealed, which resulted in our *Livesay I* decision. In *Livesay I*, this Court vacated Livesay's sentence and remanded Livesay's case to the district court for resentencing. This Court concluded that the sentencing court "failed entirely to address specifically the § 5K1.1 factors or otherwise to state reasons supporting the extent of its departure."

C. Resentencing in December 2005

This brief transcript shows that the district court actually began Livesay's resentencing hearing with "preliminary remarks," in which the district court commented that "[l]urking not too far in the background of this sentencing is the jury's verdict in the *Richard Scrushy* case." Richard Scrushy was the Chief Executive Officer of HealthSouth at all times pertinent, and he was acquitted by the jury in his trial. The district court, speaking "not as one of twelve Article III judges of the court, but as the Chief Judge of the Northern District of Alabama," observed that he knew of no allegations that the jury in the *Scrushy* case had been in any way compromised. The district court publicly thanked the *Scrushy* jury for its "tremendous public service," and observed that before attacking the jury's

---

[5] After departing downward to an offense level of 10, the district court was able to sentence Livesay to 60 months' probation and 6 months' home detention without any additional Guidelines departures because U.S.S.G. §§ 5B1.1(a)(2) and 5C1.1(c)(3) permit a sentence of probation, subject to certain conditions inapplicable here, if a defendant's applicable advisory Guidelines range is within "Zone B" of the sentencing table. Because Livesay's offense level was 10 and criminal history category was I, Livesay fell within "Zone B" on the sentencing table. Thus, by imposing 6 months' home detention, the district court was able to sentence Livesay to 60 months' probation. *See* U.S.S.G. §§ 5B1.1(a)(2), 5C1.1(c)(3).

verdict, "it is important to reflect on the fact that we did not sit here in the courtroom and hear and consider all of the evidence, as the jurors did."

The district court then noted that, in Livesay's case, this Court had directed the district court to outline in some detail the factors on which it relied in giving the § 5K1.1 departure and its reasons for the extent of the departure. The government renewed its § 5K1.1 motion, but in light of Livesay's continued substantial assistance since the first sentencing, recommended 20 months' imprisonment (i.e., less than its recommendation for 60 months' imprisonment at the first sentencing).

The district court again granted the government's § 5K1.1 motion and said it was "basically reimposing the original sentence." The district court did make specific § 5K1.1 findings that the significance and truthfulness of Livesay's information and testimony, as well as the nature and extent of his assistance, was "extraordinarily high" and warranted an "extraordinary departure." The district court further found that Livesay's assistance was "very timely" and warranted "extraordinary consideration." The district court acknowledged that Livesay's "actions were not sufficient to meet the legal standards for withdrawing from a conspiracy," but nevertheless stated that it was "impressed with the fact that from just an ordinary, common sense understanding, [Livesay] did substantially withdraw from the conspiracy."

The district court then repeated the same earlier § 5K1.1 downward departure and departed downward 18 levels to an offense level of 10, which once again left Livesay with an advisory Guidelines range of 6 to 12 months' imprisonment.

At that point, the government asked to be heard before the district court imposed its final sentence. While the government acknowledged that Livesay was "well deserving of a downward departure," the government stressed that Livesay also "was a key player, a significant cog, in the operation of this fraud at HealthSouth for a number of years." The government emphasized that although Livesay "did come forward early," he nevertheless "didn't come forward until the fraud itself was revealed." The government further observed that Livesay's "handiwork as one of the mechanics" of the fraud was reflected in the fraudulent forms that HealthSouth filed with the SEC. The government stressed the "need for deterrence" in sentencing Livesay, and stated its belief that some prison "sentence of significance" was necessary in light of the sentencing factors found in 18 U.S.C. § 3553(a). The government renewed its request for a sentence of 12 months' imprisonment under the adjusted Guidelines range found by the district court.

The district court then summarily stated, "If I'm wrong on the extent of the departure which I have just made, I believe that the sentence I'm about to impose is the most appropriate sentence in this case in consideration of the *Booker* case." In other words, even without the § 5K1.1 departure, the district court would have made the same variance under *United States v. Booker*, 543 U.S. 220 (2005), from the advisory Guidelines range of 78 to 97 months' imprisonment. The district court proceeded to sentence Livesay to 60 months' probation (the first 6 months to be served on home detention, which Livesay already had done). The district court reimposed the $10,000 fine and forfeiture of $750,000, both of which Livesay had already paid.

With regard to the sentencing factors in § 3553(a), the district court stated that it viewed the sentence as "appropriate" based on the "nature and circumstances" of Livesay's crimes; Livesay's "history and personal characteristics"; the "need for this sentence to reflect the seriousness" of the crimes to which Livesay pled guilty; the need to "promote respect for the law, and to provide just punishment"; "and to afford adequate deterrence." The district court further stated that it considered the sentence "justified in order to avoid unwarranted sentencing disparities among defendants with similar records who have been found guilty of similar conduct," and listed the sentences imposed on twelve other HealthSouth co-conspirators as follows:

> In the cases arising out of this conduct, Weston Smith received 27 months [imprisonment]; William Owens, 27 months [imprisonment]; Emery Harris, five months [imprisonment]; Angela Ayers, 48 months of probation; Cathy Edwards, 48 months of probation; Rebecca Morgan, 48 months of probation; Virginia Valentine, 48 months of probation; Michael Martin, seven days [imprisonment]; Aaron Beam, three months [imprisonment]; Richard Botts, 60 months of probation; Will Hicks, 24 months of probation; and Catherine Fowler, 24 months of probation.

This appeal followed.

III. DISCUSSION

A. District Court's Post-Gall Duties at Sentencing

After the Supreme Court's decisions in *Booker* and *Gall*, the district courts are still required to correctly calculate the advisory Guidelines range. *Gall* also instructs that the district court "must make an individualized assessment based on the facts presented." 128 S. Ct. at 597. If the district court decides that a sentence outside of the Guidelines is warranted, it "must consider the extent of the deviation and ensure that the justification is sufficiently compelling to support the degree of the variance." *Id.* at 597.

In addition, *Gall* admonishes that the district court "must adequately explain the chosen sentence to allow for meaningful appellate review and to promote the perception of fair sentencing." *Id.* at 597. The Supreme Court in *Rita* recognized that the requirement that a district court explain the reasons for its chosen sentence "reflects sound judicial practice" because "[c]onfidence in a judge's use of reason underlies the public's trust in the judicial institution" and a statement of the judge's reasoning "helps provide the public with the assurance that creates that trust." *Rita*, 127 S. Ct. at 2468.

The length and amount of detail of the judge's reasoning required depends on the circumstances. A statement of reasons for a criminal sentence is particularly important.

B. Appellate Review

. . . [U]nder *Gall*, we must engage in a two-step process of sentencing review. *See id.* First, we must " 'ensure that the district court committed no significant procedural error, such as failing to calculate (or improperly calculating) the Guidelines range, treating the Guidelines as mandatory, failing to consider the § 3553(a) factors, selecting a sentence based on clearly erroneous facts, *or failing to adequately explain the chosen sentence-including an explanation for any devia-*

tion from the Guidelines range.' " Id. (quoting *Gall*, 128 S. Ct. at 597) (emphasis added). Second, we must consider the " 'substantive reasonableness of the sentence imposed, under an abuse-of-discretion standard,' " taking into account the " 'totality of the circumstances.' " *Id.* (quoting *Gall*, 128 S. Ct. at 597). . . .

C. The Section 5K1.1 Departure

It remains true that after the government has made a motion for downward departure pursuant to U.S.S.G. § 5K1.1, the government has no control over whether and to what extent the district court will depart from the Guidelines. The district court's downward departure need only be reasonable. And after *Gall*, of course, we must review the district court's § 5K1.1 departure under a deferential abuse-of-discretion standard.

Applying *Gall* and affording substantial deference to the district court here, we are once again constrained to conclude that the district court legally erred in its § 5K1.1 downward departure. More specifically, the district court committed prong one, or "procedural," *Gall* error in its § 5K1.1 departure, because the district court based the extent of its § 5K1.1 departure on an impermissible consideration.

[I]n determining the extent of a § 5K1.1 departure, the district court must consider the five non-exclusive § 5K1.1 factors, which are: (1) the usefulness of the defendant's assistance; (2) the truthfulness and completeness of the defendant's information and testimony; (3) the nature and extent of the defendant's assistance; (4) any injury suffered or risk of injury or danger to the defendant and his family as a result of his assistance; and (5) the timeliness of the assistance. The district court may consider factors beyond those five, *"but only if the factors relate to the assistance provided by the defendant." Martin*, 455 F.3d at 1235, 1239 (concluding that the district court committed legal error by considering, in its § 5K1.1 analysis, the threat of future civil liability, which was not assistance-related). . . .

Here, the resentencing transcript makes clear that the district court, in determining the extent of its § 5K1.1 departure, considered "the fact that [Livesay] repudiated the conspiracy at an early time and no longer participated in it." The district court even explained in its § 5K1.1 ruling that "[a]lthough [Livesay's] actions were not sufficient to meet the legal standards for withdrawing from a conspiracy, the Court [was] impressed with the fact that from just an ordinary, common sense understanding, [Livesay] did substantially withdraw from the conspiracy." However, Livesay's repudiation of or "common sense" withdrawal from the conspiracy simply does not relate to the assistance that Livesay provided to the government. Accordingly, the district court should not have considered Livesay's repudiation of or withdrawal from the conspiracy in determining the extent of its § 5K1.1 departure. As such, the district court committed prong one or "procedural" *Gall* error when it departed 18 levels under § 5K1.1.

Nonetheless, it is unnecessary to remand for resentencing if the § 5K1.1 procedural error did not affect the ultimate sentence imposed. In fact, the district court here clearly indicated that it would have imposed the same sentence even if its § 5K1.1 downward departure was erroneous. In other words, even without any § 5K1.1 departure, the district court still would have varied under *Booker* from the advisory Guidelines range of 78 to 97 months' imprisonment to impose a sentence of 60 months' probation (with 6 months' home detention) based on the § 3553(a) factors. Thus, we also review the district court's alternative *Booker* variance from the advisory Guidelines range of 78 to 97 months' imprisonment.

D. The Alternative Variance Sentence

As to the alternative sentence, we conclude that another *Gall* procedural error occurred because the district court failed to adequately explain its variance from the advisory Guidelines range to its chosen sentence in a way that allows for any meaningful appellate review.

Here, the district court, for the second time, failed to give any explanation of its reasons for imposing a sentence of 60 months' probation (with 6 months' home detention). After imposing its sentence, the district court did proceed to list certain § 3553(a) factors. So far, so good. However, the district court then gave no reasoning or indication of what facts justified such a significant variance from the advisory Guidelines range under its alternative sentence.

Although the district court stated that it would exercise its discretion to impose the same sentence even if its § 5K1.1 departure was erroneous, it simply failed to explain its reasons for why it would do so in a way that allows for meaningful appellate review and promotes the perception of fair sentencing. Thus, there is also procedural error under *Gall* in the district court's alternative sentence of a *Booker* variance from the advisory Guidelines range of 78 to 97 months' imprisonment to the imposed sentence of 60 months' probation (with 6 months' home detention).

For example, the district court offered no explanation or reasoning of how a sentence of 60 months' probation (with 6 months' home detention) for an individual who pled guilty to knowingly playing an active and crucial supervisory role in a massive $1.4 billion fraud for at least five years reflected the seriousness of the offense or the nature and circumstances of the crime. The district court did not state or explain in any way why it rejected the government's argument that, notwithstanding Livesay's timely assistance, Livesay should receive "some sentence of significance" in this $1.4 billion fraud scheme because he was a "key player, a significant cog, in the operation of this fraud at HealthSouth for a number of years." Furthermore, as this Court noted in *Martin*, the legislative history of § 3553 reveals that Congress "viewed deterrence as 'particularly important in the area of white collar crime.'" *Martin*, 455 F.3d at 1240 (citation omitted). However, the district court provided nothing more than a conclusory statement that a variance from the advisory Guidelines range of 78 to 97 months' imprisonment to the ultimate sentence of 60 months' probation (with 6 months' home detention) satisfied Congress's important concerns of deterrence.

The district court did summarily list twelve other individuals convicted in the HealthSouth fraud and their respective sentences, which ranged from 24 months' probation to 60 months' imprisonment. However, the district court gave no description of the criminal conduct committed by these twelve defendants, much less any explanation of how Livesay's criminal conduct was similar to that of the co-conspirators who received probation. . . . In sum, the district court's list of sentences received by other defendants involved in the HealthSouth fraud provides no indication or explanation as to how Livesay's sentence serves the needs described in § 3553(a)(6).

In contrast, the district court in *Gall* discussed with the government at sentencing the circumstances of two of Gall's codefendants who had already been sentenced and, specifically, whether they also had voluntarily withdrawn from the conspiracy. The district court and the government also discussed another codefendant who engaged in comparable conduct, but had several circumstances that distinguished him from the defendant Gall. The Supreme Court was able to determine from this colloquy that the district court had considered the needs reflected in § 3553(a)(6) and ascertain why the district court had imposed a lesser sentence on Gall than these other codefendants received. While we do not mean to imply that such a colloquy is necessary in every case, we reference the sentencing in *Gall* as an example of what type of record evidence aids appellate courts in assessing whether the sentencing court considered the § 3553(a) factors and why it imposed the chosen sentence.

Therefore, even though the district court stated that it would exercise its discretion to impose the same sentence even if its § 5K1.1 departure was erroneous, it committed *Gall* procedural error by failing to adequately explain why it would do so in order to allow for meaningful appellate review.

IV. CONCLUSION

For all of the foregoing reasons, we vacate Livesay's sentence and remand this case for resentencing in a manner consistent with this opinion.[10]

NOTES AND QUESTIONS

1. *Reasonableness.* Consider the reasons the district judge employed for awarding the downward departure. Were these reasons valid? Was the sentence reasonable? Why or why not?

2. *The Scrushy trial.* As the court noted, a jury acquitted the HealthSouth founder and chief executive officer of all charges. *See* Kyle Whitmire, *Jurors Doubted Scrushy's Colleagues*, N.Y. Times p. 5 (July 2, 2005). Should this result be relevant to Livesay's sentence? Why or why not?

3. *Defining "substantial" assistance.* Frequently there is a genuine disagreement between the defense and the government on the level of assistance that a defendant can provide. In some cases, the defendant is not able to provide any assistance. For example, a low-level defendant in a criminal scheme may not be able to provide any information about higher-ups in the scheme. Alternatively, a defendant may have good investigative information, but the government may already possess that information.

How should courts evaluate substantial assistance? *Compare United States v. Haack*, 403 F.3d 997 (8th Cir. 2005) (the district court granted a greater substantial assistance departure than the government requested; the appeals court reversed the sentence as unreasonable), *with United States v. Pizano*, 403 F.3d 991 (8th Cir. 2005) (the district court granted a greater substantial assistance departure than the government requested; the appeals court affirmed the sentence as reasonable).

---

[10] As to the government's request that this case be reassigned to a different district judge on remand, we observe that the district judge has already recused himself from further participation in this matter. Thus, we need not address this request.

PROBLEM

19-2. Casey Madden was a bank teller at Central Federal Credit Union, a federally insured credit union. He was approached by Danielle Roberts, who worked for an identity theft ring in the area. Roberts offered Madden $100 for each set of 10 names, Social Security numbers, and account numbers that Madden provided to her.

Madden retrieved the information for 80 customers from the credit union's computer, and gave the information to Roberts. Roberts then gave the information to Darrel Park, who was the mastermind behind the identity theft ring. Park used the personal information obtained from the customers to defraud them of over $500,000.

After receiving complaints from numerous Central Federal Credit Union customers, federal agents launched an investigation. They soon determined that Madden was involved in the scheme. The agents approached Madden and offered him a plea bargain in exchange for his cooperation. Thereafter, Madden cooperated fully with the government's investigation of Roberts and Park. Park was the principal target of the investigation. Because Roberts had also agreed to plead guilty and cooperate, and because Madden had never met Park and could not provide any information as to Park, the government determined that Madden was unable to provide substantial assistance in the investigation.

Madden has pleaded guilty to one count of computer fraud in violation of 18 U.S.C. § 1030(a)(2)(A). The government has declined to bring a substantial assistance motion.

(a) Calculate Madden's Guidelines sentence.

(b) Evaluate the Guidelines sentence under the reasonableness standard.

[G] ORGANIZATIONAL SENTENCING GUIDELINES

[1] Overview

As white collar prosecutions have escalated in recent years, the government has aggressively enforced the laws against both organizations and individuals. The Organizational Guidelines governing the sentencing of corporations became effective in 1991 and are located in Chapter Eight of the Federal Sentencing Manual. The Organizational Guidelines have since been amended on a number of occasions. The Organizational Guidelines are designed to regulate sentencing of corporations and other organizations, and apply to "all organizations for felony and Class A misdemeanor offenses." § 841.1. An "organization" under these guidelines includes publicly and privately held entities such as corporations, partnerships, labor unions, pension funds, trusts, non-profit entities, and governmental units. This group of offenses includes many of the white collar and corporate offenses such as fraud, tax violations, money laundering, and bribery.

There are many similarities between the Guidelines for individuals and those for organizations, such as the determination of a base offense level, culpability of the defendant, and the allowances for departures. In addition, the *Booker* opinion will affect organizational sentencing to the extent that courts view the Organizational Guidelines as advisory and not mandatory.[c]

The Organizational Guidelines have affected corporations' conduct and have fostered corporate compliance programs. The Guidelines give organizations incentives for being good corporate citizens by setting forth lower penalties for organizations convicted of federal offenses if they have implemented effective compliance programs prior to the commission of the offense.

Under the Organizational Guidelines, four factors can increase the punishment: (1) involvement in or tolerance of criminal activity; (2) prior violations, including civil and administrative dispositions; (3) violation of an earlier court order during the occurrence of the offense which is being prosecuted; and (4) obstruction of justice. Punishment can be mitigated in two situations: (1) when the organization had an effective compliance and ethics program; and (2) when the organization engaged in self-reporting, cooperated with the authorities, or accepted responsibility.

[2]   Compliance Programs

The significance of corporate compliance programs cannot be overstated. An organization convicted of a criminal offense can be sentenced to restitution, community service, and/or fines. The existence of a corporate compliance program allows for a three-point reduction in a corporation's culpability score if the "offense occurred despite an effective program to prevent and detect violations." § 8C2.5(f)(1).

In October 2003, the Sentencing Commission released a special report which was a "culmination of an 18-month process to review the effectiveness of the Organizational Guidelines and solicit suggestions for their improvement." U.S. Sentencing Commission, *Panel on the Sentencing Guidelines for Organizations Issues Final Report* (Oct. 8, 2003), available at http://www.ussc.gov/press/rel100803b.htm. The Commission strengthened the criteria for compliance programs and incorporated some of the recent changes in administrative and regulatory law, including the Sarbanes-Oxley Act of 2002. Based on this report, in May 2004, the Sentencing Commission recommended to Congress that the Organizational Guidelines be revised, and the revisions became effective in November 2004.

The revision led to the adoption of a new guideline, § 8B2.1, which was designed to "strengthen[] the existing criteria an organization must follow" to prevent

---

[c] It appears likely that *Booker* will apply to the Organizational Guidelines:

> While both *Booker* and *Fanfan* involve application of the federal sentencing guidelines to individuals, it seems likely that these cases would also govern the sentencing of organizations. It is possible that courts would apply different reasoning to a challenge to the constitutionality of the federal sentencing guidelines for organizations. The Supreme Court has never squarely addressed the question of whether a corporation has a Sixth Amendment right to a jury trial, and the *Booker* decision was based on that constitutional right. However, while the law on this issue is unclear, precedent seems to point to a finding that a corporation does have a Sixth Amendment right to a jury trial in criminal proceedings. It therefore seems likely that the holding in *Booker* and *Fanfan* would extend to the sentencing guidelines for organizations.

Rebecca Walker, *Impact of United States v. Booker and United States v. Fanfan on Compliance*, Practicing Law Institute, Corporate Law and Practice Course Handbook Series 170–171 (March-June, 2005).

criminal activity. *United States Sentencing Guidelines, Effective Compliance and Ethics Programs in Chapter Eight, Synopsis of Amendment* (May 1, 2004), available at http://www.ussc.gov. *See* Robert G. Morvillo and Robert J. Anello, *Corporate Compliance Programs: No Longer Voluntary*, N.Y.L.J., Dec. 7, 2004, at 3.

As the first substantial change to the Guidelines since their inception, these standards are designed to encourage corporate compliance efforts. The highlights of the revisions include:

- Placing more responsibility on boards and top management. The new requirements impose more onerous obligations on board members, high-level management, and the individual with daily responsibility for the program.
- Requiring discipline and incentives. Companies must establish "appropriate incentives to perform in accordance with the compliance and ethics program." Personnel decisions now are required to include background checks and determination whether the individual has engaged in "other conduct inconsistent with an effective program."
- Requiring ethics training. Training is now more than a suggestion. Instead, companies are required to engage in compliance activities.

[3] Sanctions

Organizations can be sentenced to a variety of punishments and penalties depending on the nature of the offense and the harm. The most common penalty is a civil or criminal fine. The determination of a fine is similar to that used in calculating an individual sentence under the Guidelines — base offense level coupled with any adjustments. To reach the correct base fine, the court must consider the largest amount from among the following: the offense level fine table based upon the organization's offense level; the pecuniary gain to the organization from the offense; or the pecuniary loss caused by the organization. U.S.S.G. § 8C2.4. Once the base fine is determined, the court adjusts for aggravating or mitigating circumstances and subsequent culpability.

Once the base fine is determined, the court next assigns a culpability score using a five-point system. At this juncture, the court examines any preventive steps taken by the organization to prevent and detect criminal conduct prior to the offense (such as compliance programs); the level and extent of high-level involvement; and the conduct by the organization's agents once the offense was detected. If the organization has turned a blind eye toward the criminal conduct or sanctioned it in any way, the culpability score will increase. On the other hand, effective compliance programs will benefit the organization with downward adjustments.

After the court calculates the base score, the court sets the fine within the Guidelines range. The court must consider the "need for the sentence to reflect the seriousness of the offense, promote respect for the law, provide just punishment, afford adequate deterrence, and protect the public from further crimes of the organization." U.S.S.G. § 8C2.8(a)(1).

In addition to fines, the court must order an organization to pay restitution for the full amount of the victim's loss or impose a term of probation conditioned on the payment of restitution. In addition, courts may order that the organization engage in community service, which effectively imposes on the employees the obligation to engage in service voluntarily or with corporate pay. Any probationary sentence "shall include the condition that the organization not commit another federal, state, or local crime during the term of probation." U.S.S.G. § 8D1.3(a).

[4]   Sarbanes-Oxley

The Sarbanes-Oxley Act of 2002 affects organizational criminal sentencing in areas including obstruction of justice, securities fraud, and certification of financial reports. In addition, the Sentencing Commission issued directives that seek to address securities, accounting, and pension fraud. A January 2003 series of amendments made significant changes in the ways organizations are sentenced under the Guidelines. Section 2B1.1(b)(2)(c) provides for a six-level enhancement for offenses involving more than 250 victims. Section 2B1.1(b)(12)(B) provides punishment for any offense that endangers (i) a publicly traded corporation, (ii) an organization that employs 1000 or more employees, or (iii) 100 or more individual victims. This provision requires a four-level enhancement and/or a minimum offense level of 24. A new amendment adds four levels for officers and directors of publicly traded companies who commit securities violations, and recalculates the loss tables in § 2B1.1(b)(1). If the loss is over $200 million, the offense is categorized in level 28. When the loss reaches $400 million, the punishment increases to level 30.

Chapter 20

FORFEITURES

[A] INTRODUCTORY NOTES

[1] The Policy Tension

Federal forfeiture statutes provide the government with the power to both seize and obtain ownership of private property that is related to criminal activity, including such white collar crimes as money laundering and RICO violations.[a] Congress enacted the forfeiture laws with the express purposes of deterring illegal activity and depriving wrongdoers of the fruits of their acts. The statutes have not only generated substantial revenues for the government, but have also produced significant controversy.[b] Critics have argued that "the forfeiture laws . . . are producing self-financing, unaccountable law enforcement agencies divorced from any meaningful oversight." *See* Eric D. Blumenson & Eva Nilsen, *Policing for Profit: The Drug War's Hidden Economic Agenda*, 65 U. Chi. L. Rev. 35, 41 (1998). Correspondingly, property owners have raised a number of constitutional challenges to forfeitures, and the United States Supreme Court has addressed a number of such constitutional challenges. Congress has also taken heed of the controversy, enacting the Civil Asset Forfeiture and Reform Act (CAFRA). As discussed more fully below, CAFRA does provide some protections to property owners, including a uniform "innocent owner" defense and certain procedural safeguards.

---

[a] Although most states also have their own forfeiture laws, this chapter focuses primarily on federal forfeiture proceedings.

[b] Much of the controversy over forfeitures arises from the government's financial stake in these proceedings. In United States v. James Daniel Good Real Property, 510 U.S. 43, 56 n.2 (1993), the Supreme Court tacitly acknowledged the potential for a conflict between the government's budgetary needs and property owners' rights:

> The extent of the government's financial stake in drug forfeiture is apparent from a 1990 memo, in which the Attorney General urged United States Attorneys to increase the volume of forfeitures in order to meet the Department of Justice's annual budget target: "We must significantly increase production to reach our budget target. Failure to achieve the $470 million projection would expose the Department's forfeiture program to criticism and undermine confidence in our budget projections. Every effort must be made to increase forfeiture income during the remaining three months of [fiscal year] 1990."

The U.S. Department of Justice issues annual reports listing the total value of the property subject to seizure and forfeiture. For the fiscal year ending 2006, the amount was over $1.5 billion. *See* http://www.usdoj.gov/jmd/afp/01programaudit/index.htm.

At the state level, some efforts are being made to alleviate this potential conflict between governments' budgetary objectives and property owners' rights. *See* Eric D. Blumenson & Eva Nilsen, *The Next Stage of Forfeiture Reform*, 14 Fed. Sent. R. 76 (2001) (describing state reform efforts to direct that proceeds of state forfeitures be used not for general law enforcement purposes but instead for such purposes as narcotics treatment).

[2]   The Statutory Provisions

[a]   Overview

The forfeiture statutes apply to virtually all types of property, whether the property was actually used in the illegal activity or was purchased with the proceeds of such activity. For the purposes of this text, the most important avenues of federal forfeitures are the financial crimes statutes and the RICO statute. Although many of the forfeitures discussed in the cases below did not arise in the context of white collar crime, the legal principles in those cases apply equally in the white collar context.

Depending upon the statute used in the particular case, the forfeiture may occur as part of a criminal case or a civil proceeding. Criminal forfeitures did not come into widespread use at the federal level until the enactment of the RICO statute in 1970. Such forfeitures occur as part of the sentencing in a criminal case. The principal criminal forfeiture provisions are set forth in the financial crimes statutes, the RICO statute, and the narcotics statutes. *See* 18 U.S.C. §§ 982, 1963; 21 U.S.C. § 853.

Unlike criminal forfeitures, civil forfeitures have a long history in Anglo-American law. A civil forfeiture case is an in rem proceeding in which the property itself is named as the defendant. Such a case is based upon the legal fiction that the property itself is the wrongdoer. Thus, a civil forfeiture proceeding may be brought even where the alleged wrongdoer has not been convicted of or even charged with a crime.

[b]   Civil Forfeitures

The most important federal civil forfeiture statutes relate to financial crimes, 18 U.S.C. § 981, and narcotics offenses, 21 U.S.C. § 881. The provisions of 18 U.S.C. § 981(a)(1)(A) make forfeitable all real and personal property related to money laundering, currency transaction reporting crimes, and dozens of other crimes involving financial transactions, financial institutions, or fraud against the United States. Under 21 U.S.C. § 881, the government may obtain forfeiture of a wide range of property, including materials used to manufacture narcotics, conveyances, and all proceeds of a controlled substances transaction, whether direct or indirect, as well as "all moneys, negotiable instruments, and securities used or intended [for use] . . . " in the facilitation of such a transaction. Under subsection 881(a)(7), all real property used or intended for use in committing, or facilitating the commission of, a federal drug law violation is also subject to forfeiture.

These statutes contain provisions allowing the government, in certain circumstances, to seize or otherwise assume control over property prior to obtaining forfeiture. Such a seizure must be supported by probable cause that the property is subject to forfeiture.

The government files a civil complaint to initiate the forfeiture proceeding, at which the government must prove by a preponderance of the evidence that the property is forfeitable. As seen in § [C] below, a bona fide purchaser or seller of the property may have standing to contest the forfeiture, as may those who use the property as a primary residence.

[c]   Criminal Forfeitures

A criminal forfeiture occurs as an in personam proceeding against the defendant, and the property is forfeited as part of the penalty phase of the case. As seen in § [C] below, however, criminal forfeitures may affect the property interests of innocent persons.

Since 1970, Congress has adopted an increasingly broad range of criminal forfeiture provisions. Three forfeiture statutes provide the basis for most of the federal criminal forfeitures. First, § 982 of the federal criminal code focuses on property involved in financial crimes. That statute covers property related to violations of the currency transaction reporting statutes, the money laundering statutes, and other specified crimes. *See* 18 U.S.C. § 982. Second, the RICO statute contains a broad forfeiture provision. *See* 18 U.S.C. § 1963. Finally, violations of the federal drug laws can also give rise to forfeitures under 21 U.S.C. § 853. The criminal forfeiture statues, like their civil counterparts, allow the government to assume control over the potentially forfeitable property prior to determination of forfeitability at trial. The statutes allow this in order to preserve the property for forfeiture.

Under § 982, the government may obtain forfeiture of property involved in, or traceable to, an offense that violates one of the currency transaction reporting or money laundering statutes, as well as property constituting or derived from the proceeds of additional specified crimes. Under § 853, the government likewise may obtain forfeiture of a broad range of property, including real property and tangible and intangible personal property interests. Section 1963 similarly covers a broad range of property, and makes such property forfeitable when the defendant has been convicted for violating one of the RICO provisions.

All three criminal forfeiture statutes allow forfeiture of "substitute" assets. *See* 21 U.S.C. § 853(p); 18 U.S.C. § 982(b); 18 U.S.C. § 1963(m). This occurs when, for example, the specific assets subject to forfeiture cannot be located. This may occur, for example, when assets have been transferred or sold to a third party, or when such assets have been commingled with non-forfeitable property and cannot be easily separated.

Under 28 U.S.C. § 2461(c), a provision enacted as part of CAFRA and amended in 2006, whenever civil forfeiture is authorized, the government may seek criminal forfeiture based upon the civil forfeiture provision. Courts have rejected restrictive interpretations of this statute, and have held that the full range of civil forfeiture provisions now may be employed in criminal cases. *See, e.g., United States v. Schlesinger*, 514 F.3d 277, 278 (2d Cir. 2008) (finding that mail fraud may give rise to criminal forfeiture due to operation of § 2461(c)); *United States v. Vampire Nation*, 451 F.3d 189 (3d Cir. 2006) (same).

[B]   THE SCOPE OF FORFEITABLE PROPERTY

[1]   Statutory Scope

[a]   Civil Forfeitures

Prior to the enactment of CAFRA, the courts had adopted a number of approaches for determining the extent of forfeitable property. Congress resolved this conflict by codifying the approach that had been adopted by a number of courts. Thus, CAFRA requires the government to establish a "substantial connection" between the illegal activity and the property. As you read the next case, (a) identify the alternative theories of forfeiture that the government employed, and (b) consider whether the court correctly analyzed each theory.

UNITED STATES v. ONE 1998 TRACTOR
288 F. Supp. 2d 710 (W.D. Va. 2003)

JONES, DISTRICT JUDGE.

The claimant in this in rem civil forfeiture proceeding is Karapet Shimshiryan, a truck driver who transports goods in his tractor-trailer for a living. Shimshiryan's tractor and the trailer are the defendant property. Shimshiryan has previously pleaded guilty to violating the federal criminal laws that prohibit transporting, concealing, or possessing contraband cigarettes.[1] In the present action, the government seeks the forfeiture of Shimshiryan's tractor and trailer pursuant to the statute permitting the forfeiture of "an aircraft, vehicle, or vessel involved in" transporting, concealing, or possessing contraband cigarettes. 49 U.S.C. § 80303. I agree with Shimshiryan that the trailer is not subject to forfeiture because it was his tractor and not his trailer that carried the contraband and because the government has failed to establish that the trailer was substantially connected to the offense, as required under the Civil Asset Forfeiture Reform Act of 2000 ("CAFRA"), 18 U.S.C.A. § 983. I reject Shimshiryan's argument that the forfeiture is barred on constitutional grounds.

A bench trial has been held on the government's complaint for forfeiture. . . .

The basic facts are not in dispute. On September 6, 2002, while returning to California after having delivered his trailer's cargo of produce to its destination in New York, driver-owner Shimshiryan and a companion stopped at a tobacco sales outlet in Virginia in this judicial district. The two men purchased and loaded approximately twenty-three half cases of cigarettes (approximately 282,400 cigarettes) into the cab of the tractor and went on their way. Shimshiryan intended to take the cigarettes back to California and from there send them to his brother in Armenia who in turn would sell them for a profit. The sales outlet had been under

---

[1] *See* 18 U.S.C.A. § 2342 ("It shall be unlawful for any person knowingly to ship, transport, receive, possess, sell, distribute, or purchase contraband cigarettes."); 49 U.S.C.A. § 80302(b) ("A person may not — (1) transport contraband in an aircraft, vehicle, or vessel; (2) conceal or possess contraband on an aircraft, vehicle, or vessel; or (3) use an aircraft, vehicle or vessel to facilitate the transportation, concealment, receipt, possession, purchase, sale, exchange, or giving away of contraband."). "Contraband cigarettes" are a quantity in excess of 60,000 cigarettes, which bear no evidence of the payment of applicable State cigarette taxes in the State where such cigarettes are found, if such State requires a stamp, impression, or other indication to be placed on packages or other containers of cigarettes to evidence payment of cigarette taxes. 18 U.S.C.A. § 2341(2).

surveillance by law enforcement officers and Shimshiryan was followed a few miles into the neighboring state of Tennessee. Agents from the Bureau of Alcohol, Tobacco, and Firearms, along with state and local law enforcement officers, stopped the tractor-trailer in Tennessee and recovered the cigarettes from the tractor. These cigarettes did not bear Tennessee state tax stamps as required by law. Shimshiryan's criminal prosecution and this in rem forfeiture action followed.

The government has two arguments as to why the trailer should be subject to forfeiture, even though the contraband cigarettes were never transported there. First, the government argues that the tractor-trailer constitutes a single "vehicle" under 49 U.S.C.A. § 80303. Second, the government claims that even if the tractor-trailer does not constitute a single vehicle for the purposes of § 80303, the trailer should still be subject to forfeiture because it provided the illegal activity with an air of legitimacy and thus shielded it from the government's suspicion.

Section 80303 permits the forfeiture of "an aircraft, vehicle, or vessel involved in" transporting contraband. The government argues that the trailer should be forfeited even though it did not carry the contraband because it should not be viewed as separate from the tractor — the tractor-trailer should be considered one vehicle. Section 80303 does not define "vehicle." There are two cases applicable to this issue, *The Dolphin*, 3 F.2d 1 (1st Cir. 1925), and *United States v. Santoro*, 866 F.2d 1538 (4th Cir. 1989).

The Dolphin addressed the issue of what constitutes a "vessel" for the purposes of what was then a forfeiture statute directed at vessels delivering foreign cargo to the United States without a government permit. In that case, a tugboat towed a barge that delivered foreign liquor to a Brooklyn pier without the requisite permit. The applicable forfeiture statute permitted the forfeiture of "the vessel, tackle, apparel, and furniture" that illegally unloaded the cargo. The district court had construed the term "vessel" to include the tug as well as the barge, even though the contraband had not been unloaded from the tug. In holding that the tugboat was not subject to forfeiture, the court of appeals found that (1) there was no applicable law to support the assertion that "the tug and its tow constitute one vessel" and (2) the tugboat was not part of the "tackle" attached to the barge.

A Fourth Circuit case that also provides guidance in interpreting § 80303 answered the question of whether a twenty-six acre lot that was separated by a road into two parts should be wholly forfeited when the criminal activity only occurred on one part of the land. In *United States v. Santoro*, five acres of the land at issue lay across the road from the other nineteen acres, and it was on the five-acre parcel that the claimant had sold drugs. The claimant challenged the forfeiture on the basis that the two parcels were separate, and only the smaller parcel should be forfeited because her illegal activity was confined to that area.

First, the court looked to the language of the statute, which permitted the forfeiture of "[a]ll real property, including any right, title, and interest *in the whole of any lot or tract of land* and any appurtenances or improvements." *Id.* at 1543 (alteration in original). The court of appeals then adopted the reasoning of the trial court and held that the " 'whole of any lot or tract of land' must be determined from the duly recorded instruments and documents filed in the county offices where the defendant property is located." *Id.* at 1543. Because the property's deed described it as a single, undivided tract, the court held that the twenty-six acre lot was subject to forfeiture in its entirety, even though it was taxed as two separate parcels.

Shimshiryan's tractor and trailer were purchased separately, had separate titles, and separate vehicle identification numbers. Based on the First Circuit's holding in *The Dolphin* and the Fourth Circuit's reasoning in *Santoro*, I hold that the tractor and the trailer do not constitute one vehicle.

The government's second argument for forfeiture of the trailer is that § 80303 permits the forfeiture of a vehicle "involved in" a violation of the federal laws that prohibit transportation, concealment, or possession of contraband cigarettes. CAFRA provides that if the government's theory of forfeiture is that the property was "involved in the commission of a criminal offense," then the government must show, "by a preponderance of the evidence," that there was a "substantial connection between that property and the offense." 18 U.S.C.A. § 983(c). Therefore, in order for the government to gain forfeiture of the trailer on the basis that it was "involved in" Shimshiryan's violation, CAFRA requires that it establish, by a preponderance of the evidence, that there was a substantial connection between the trailer and the offense.

Although the Fourth Circuit has yet to apply CAFRA's "substantial connection" test, *see United States v. Mondragon*, 313 F.3d 862, 865 (4th Cir. 2002) (discussing CAFRA in the context of the sufficiency of pleading), its pre-CAFRA decisions in civil forfeiture cases are still instructive in applying that test because the only change in this circuit in that area of civil forfeiture law is in the government's burden of proof. Before the passage of CAFRA in 2000, "the government's trial burden was to show probable cause for forfeiture; the burden of proof then shifted to the claimant. Now, after CAFRA's enactment, the government must prove by a preponderance of the evidence that the property is subject to forfeiture." *Mondragon*, 313 F.3d at 865. Thus, the only difference between the Fourth Circuit's pre-CAFRA case law determining whether property involved with transporting contraband should be forfeited and the current test under CAFRA is in the government's heightened burden of proof — the government must now establish a substantial connection by a preponderance of the evidence, and not just probable cause.

In *United States v. Two Tracts of Real Property*, 998 F.2d 204 (4th Cir. 1993), the defendant in the underlying criminal case permitted marijuana to be transported by boat to his father's marina. After it was delivered, it was driven from the marina across another lot of land, also owned by the defendant's father, in order to access a public road. Crossing that lot of land was the only means by which the smugglers could reach the public road. The government sought the forfeiture of the land with access to the public road because it was allegedly substantially connected to the criminal activity on the basis that (1) it provided access to a public road following the unloading of the marijuana and (2) it tended to shield the illegal activity from public view. As for the first claim, the court found that it was "physically impossible" for the smugglers to reach the road from the marina without crossing the land in question, but it held that this "geographic fact" did not establish a substantial connection. *Id.* at 212.

As for the second argument that the property's shielding effect created a substantial connection to the activity, the court held that the "mere fact that a physical obstruction tends to conceal crime does not, without more, make the obstruction forfeitable." *Id.* In further explaining its decision, the court of appeals distinguished the facts of a case it decided three years earlier, *United States v. Schifferli*, 895 F.2d 987 (4th Cir. 1990), in which it upheld the forfeiture of a dental office used by the dentist to write illegal prescriptions.[4] It stated that the "use of an office building to commit crimes that closely resemble the owner's or tenant's lawful work is a far cry from a natural object's inherent, irrepressible ability to conceal whatever lies behind it" because in the former case "the guilty owner's intent establishes a sufficient connection with crime to render the property forfeitable." *Id.* at 212.

The decision in *Two Tracts of Real Property* establishes that when the government seeks the forfeiture of property on the basis that it was substantially connected to the crime by shielding the illegal activity from public view, it must show "more" than that the property "tends to conceal" the crime. Furthermore, proof of the owner's intent to use the property for the purpose of shielding his or her criminal activity qualifies as the something "more" required to establish a substantial connection. In this case, the government merely alleges that the trailer shielded the criminal activity from detection by creating the appearance that the claimant was engaged in a legitimate trucking business. Because the government has not provided any evidence indicating that Shimshiryan's trucking business was a sham, or that he operated it with the intent of concealing his criminal activity, it has not met its burden of proof. The government has failed to establish a substantial connection between the trailer and the offense, as required by CAFRA, and the trailer is not subject to forfeiture. . . .

NOTES AND QUESTIONS

1. *The government's theories.*

a. *The conveyance theory.* Why did the court conclude that the trailer did not qualify as a "vehicle"? Did the court correctly apply the reasoning from *The Dolphin* and *Santoro*?

b. *The substantial connection theory.* Based on the case above and the precedent it discusses, what is required for a "substantial connection"? Can you divine factors to use in making this determination? Do the cases that the court cites (*Two Tracts of Real Property* and *Schifferli*) support its conclusion? According to the court, what more did the government need to show?

If the contraband had been in the trailer, would the tractor have been forfeitable under either theory? Why or why not?

2. *The burden of proof.* As noted in the opinion, prior to CAFRA, the government could obtain forfeiture merely by establishing probable cause. Now, the government must meet the preponderance test generally applicable in civil proceedings.

---

[4] In *Schifferli*, the claimant was a dentist who had used his office over forty times during a four-month period to write illegal prescriptions for eight individuals. 895 F.2d at 989. *Schifferli* is like many other cases in that forfeiture of the office was upheld on the basis that it was the situs of the illegal prescription writing. It is well settled that the use of property as a situs for conducting illegal activities establishes a substantial connection between the property and the underlying criminal activity.

3. *The USA PATRIOT Act.* The USA PATRIOT Act added a new forfeiture statute that provides for forfeiture of:

(G) *All assets, foreign or domestic —*

(i) *of any individual, entity, or organization engaged in planning or perpetrating any act of domestic or international terrorism* . . . against the United States, citizens or residents of the United States, or their property, and *all assets, foreign or domestic, affording any person a source of influence over any such entity or organization*;

(ii) acquired or maintained by any person *with the intent and for the purpose of supporting, planning, conducting, or concealing an act of domestic or international terrorism* . . . against the United States, citizens or residents of the United States, or their property; or

(iii) *derived from, involved in, or used or intended to be used to commit any act of domestic or international terrorism* . . . against the United States, citizens or residents of the United States, or their property.

18 U.S.C. § 981(a)(1)(G) (emphasis added). What is the scope of forfeitable property under this section? What connection is required between a specific act of terrorism and the property at issue? Are there dangers from this approach? Why or why not?

[b]   Criminal Forfeitures

Federal Rule of Criminal Procedure 32.2(b) governs the determination of the scope of forfeitable property. Under that rule, upon a determination of the defendant's guilt, the court or jury identifies the property subject to forfeiture and determines whether the "requisite nexus between the property and the offense" has been established by the government. The following case examines the scope of forfeitable property under the narcotics and money laundering forfeiture provisions.

UNITED STATES v. HALL
434 F.3d 42 (1st Cir. 2006)

Howard, Circuit Judge.

A federal grand jury in Maine returned an indictment against Kevin Hall charging him with one count of conspiring to distribute marijuana, 21 U.S.C. §§ 841(A)(1) & 846; 163 counts of money laundering, 18 U.S.C. § 1956(a)(1)(B)(i), for his use of the conspiracy proceeds; and four counts of tax evasion, 26 U.S.C. § 7201, for failing to pay income tax on the drug-related income. The government also brought two forfeiture counts to obtain assets related to Hall's illegal conduct, 21 U.S.C. § 853; 18 U.S.C. § 982. After a ten-day jury trial, Hall was convicted on all counts. He was sentenced to 151 months of imprisonment on the conspiracy and money laundering convictions, to be served concurrently with 60 months of imprisonment on each of the tax evasion convictions. He also was ordered to forfeit his illegally obtained assets.

After finding Hall guilty on all counts, the jury returned forfeiture findings concerning Hall's drug trafficking and money laundering activities. *See* 21 U.S.C. § 853 (forfeiture for drug trafficking); 18 U.S.C. § 982 (forfeiture for money laundering). After the jury returned these findings, the court entered a forfeiture order pursuant to Fed. R. Crim. P. 32.2. In regard to the drug trafficking forfeiture, the court imposed a money judgment in the amount of $511,321.22 and ordered the forfeiture of specific items of personal and real property which the jury found were connected [to] Hall's drug activities. The money laundering forfeiture order commanded Hall to turn over specific items of property (in accord with the jury's findings) but did not impose an additional money judgment. Both orders permitted the government to seize "substitute property" under certain circumstances to satisfy the forfeiture amount.[1]

Hall's first challenge concerns the district court's entry of a money judgment as part of the drug trafficking forfeiture. A money judgment permits the government to collect on the forfeiture order in the same way that a successful plaintiff collects a money judgment from a civil defendant. Thus, even if a defendant does not have sufficient funds to cover the forfeiture at the time of the conviction, the government may seize future assets to satisfy the order. Relying on *United States v. Croce*, 334 F. Supp. 2d 781(E.D. Pa. 2004), Hall argues that a court may not issue a money judgment as part of a forfeiture order.

Croce is at odds with the law of this circuit. In *Candelaria-Silva*, 166 F.3d at 42, we ruled that a "criminal forfeiture may take several forms [including] an in personam judgment against the defendant for the amount of money the defendant obtained as proceeds of the offense." This position accords with the several appellate decisions that have addressed the question. *See United States v. Huber*, 404 F.3d 1047, 1056 (8th Cir. 2005); *United States v. Baker*, 227 F.3d 955, 970 (7th Cir. 2000); *United States v. Lester*, 85 F.3d 1409, 1413 (9the Cir. 1996); *United States v. Robilotto*, 828 F.2d 940, 948–49 (2d Cir. 1987); *United States v. Ginsburg*, 773 F2d 798, 801–03 (7th Cir. 1985) (en banc).

There are two primary reasons for permitting money judgments as part of criminal forfeiture orders. First, criminal forfeiture is a sanction against the individual defendant rather than a judgment against the property itself. Because the sanction "follows the defendant as a part of the penalty," the government need not prove that the defendant actually has the forfeited proceeds in his possession at the time of conviction. *Robilotto*, 828 F.2d at 948–49. Second, permitting a money judgment, as part of a forfeiture order, prevents a drug dealer from ridding himself of his ill-gotten gains to avoid the forfeiture sanction. In rejecting an argument against the use of money judgments pursuant to the RICO forfeiture statute, the Seventh Circuit explained:

> What the defendant's argument overlooks is the fact that a racketeer who dissipates profits or proceeds of his racketeering activity on wine, women, and song has profited from organized crime to the same extent as if he had put the money in his bank account. Every dollar that the racketeer derives from illicit activities and then spends on such items as food, entertainment, college tuition, and charity, is a dollar that should not have been available for him to spend for those purposes. In order to truly separate the racketeer from his dishonest gains, therefore, the statute requires him to forfeit to the United States the total amount of the proceeds of his racketeering activity, regardless of whether the specific

---

[1] Substitute property may be seized by the government to satisfy a forfeiture order where, by an act or omission, the defendant has prevented the government from tracing his illegally obtained assets. *See United States v. Candelaria-Silva*, 166 F.3d 42 (1st Cir. 1999).

dollars received from that activity are still in his possession.

Ginsburg, 773 F2d at 802. The policy rationale for permitting a money judgment as part of a forfeiture in a racketeering case applies equally to a forfeiture in a drug case. *See Nava*, 404 F.3d at 1124 n.1 (stating that RICO forfeiture cases are useful in interpreting the drug forfeiture statute because the statutes are "substantially identical"). The district court did not err in entering a money judgment as part of the drug trafficking forfeiture.[2]

Hall next contends that the forfeiture orders wrongly permit the government to seize substitute property. He argues that the power to forfeit substitute property rests exclusively with the court.

Federal Rule of Criminal Procedure 32.2(e) provides the procedure for the forfeiture of substitute property. It states: "On the government's motion, the court may at anytime enter an order of forfeiture or amend an existing order of forfeiture to include property . . . " that is substitute property under an applicable statute. The forfeiture orders in this case state that the government may "forfeit" substitute property. It is not clear whether this means that the government may move for forfeiture or may seize the substitute property without any action by the court.

The government acknowledges that only the court can order the forfeiture of substitute property. In light of this acknowledgment and the plain language of Fed. R. Crim. P. 32(e)(1), we interpret the forfeiture orders in this case to permit the government to *move* for substitute property but to reserve for the court the authority to order the property forfeited.[3]

For the reasons set forth, we *affirm* the forfeiture orders . . . .

Notes and Questions

1. *Money judgments.* Other circuit courts appear to agree that money judgments are appropriate in criminal forfeiture cases. Why did the court affirm the entry of a money judgment in the case above? According to the court, what is the principal purpose behind criminal forfeiture statutes? Would a money judgment be appropriate in a *civil* forfeiture case? Why or why not?

2. *Substitute assets.* Many statutes allow the government to obtain forfeiture of "substitute assets" when the forfeitable assets cannot be located, have been transferred or sold to a third party, are beyond the court's jurisdiction, have been reduced in value, or were commingled with non-forfeitable property and cannot be easily separated. *See* 21 U.S.C. § 853(p); 18 U.S.C. § 982(b); 18 U.S.C. § 1963(m). In such a case, and subject to certain statutory limitations, the court will order the forfeiture of substitute assets up to the value of the otherwise forfeitable assets.

---

[2] Hall also contends that, even if the court could enter a money judgment, it could not enter both a money judgment and a forfeiture of specific assets as part of the same order. Hall has cited no authority for this proposition, and there are several cases in which such hybrid orders have been entered.

[3] Hall also asserts that the forfeiture of his real property holdings was erroneous because there was insufficient evidence for the jury to have found a nexus between his real estate holdings and his drug trafficking and money laundering activities. We disagree. The jury could have found that Hall renovated his property with drug proceeds and that he used one of the properties to receive a shipment of drugs. This evidence is sufficient to support the jury's forfeiture finding.

Why did Congress allow for the forfeiture of substitute assets? Are there dangers in this approach?

3. *The nexus requirement.* The defendant argued that there was insufficient evidence of the required nexus between his illegal acts and his real-estate holdings. Why did the court reject the argument? How much does the government have to show to establish the nexus?

4. Apprendi. In *Apprendi v. New Jersey*, 530 U.S. 466 (2000), the United States Supreme Court held that any fact that increases the penalty for a crime beyond the prescribed statutory maximum must be submitted to a jury and proven beyond a reasonable doubt. Does this rule apply to determinations of the scope of criminal forfeitures? The circuit courts have held not. *See, e.g., United States v. Shryock*, 342 F.3d 948, 989 (9th Cir. 2003); *United States v. Keene*, 341 F.3d 78, 85–86 (1st Cir. 2003); *United States v. Vera*, 278 F.3d 672, 673 (7th Cir. 2002); *United States v. Najjar*, 300 F.3d 466, 485–486 (4th Cir. 2002); *United States v. Cabeza*, 258 F.3d 1256, 1257 (11th Cir. 2001) (per curiam); *United States v. Corrado*, 227 F.3d 543, 550–551 (6th Cir. 2000).

Does the outcome in *United States v. Booker*, 125 S. Ct. 738 (2005), discussed in the Chapter 19, Sentencing, *supra*, affect this result? Why or why not? *See* Comment, Matthew R. Ford, *Criminal Forfeiture and the Sixth Amendment's Right to Jury Trial Post-Booker*, 101 Nw. U. L. Rev. 1371 (2007) (arguing that *Booker* should apply to forfeiture proceedings in some circumstances).

PROBLEM

20-1. Defendant Clarissa Clement was addicted to the prescription pain killer hydrocodone. To support her addiction, she called in phony prescriptions to pharmacies, using numerous aliases. Last January, a pharmacist informed the police that he suspected defendant of fraud. The pharmacist gave the police a physical description of defendant and of the defendant's vehicle, which Ms. Clement used to pick up the prescription. In April, another pharmacist from a different pharmacy contacted police about suspected fraud. On that occasion, defendant picked up the prescription using the pharmacy's drive-thru window, and the pharmacist identified the customer as Ms. Clement using a police photograph. The pharmacist also described the defendant's vehicle and gave its license plate number. The police were able to document five other such occasions when defendant used the vehicle to pick up hydrocodone with phony prescriptions.

In May, police arrested defendant for obtaining drugs with fraudulent prescriptions. The government now seeks civil forfeiture of the vehicle under 21 U.S.C. § 881(a)(4). The vehicle is a minivan that served as the sole family vehicle for Ms. Clement and her three children. The evidence shows that driving related to the prescription drug scheme constituted only about two percent of the vehicle's use over the relevant time period.

Is the vehicle subject to forfeiture? Why or why not?

[2]   Constitutional Limitations

[a]   Civil Forfeitures

After long declining to place constitutional constraints on civil forfeitures, *see Calero-Toledo v. Pearson Yacht Leasing Co.*, 416 U.S. 663, 680–690 (1974), the Supreme Court in the next case squarely addressed the issue whether the Eighth Amendment's Excessive Fines Clause potentially limits the scope of such forfeitures. As you read the case, pay particular attention to the majority and concurring opinions' views on the history of civil forfeitures.

AUSTIN v. UNITED STATES
509 U.S. 602 (1993)

JUSTICE BLACKMUN delivered the opinion of the Court.

In this case, we are asked to decide whether the Excessive Fines Clause of the Eighth Amendment applies to forfeitures of property under 21 U.S.C. §§ 881(a)(4) and (a)(7). We hold that it does and therefore remand the case for consideration of the question whether the forfeiture at issue here was excessive.

On August 2, 1990, petitioner Richard Lyle Austin was indicted on four counts of violating South Dakota's drug laws. Austin ultimately pleaded guilty to one count of possessing cocaine with intent to distribute and was sentenced by the state court to seven years' imprisonment. On September 7, the United States filed an *in rem* action in the United States District Court for the District of South Dakota seeking forfeiture of Austin's mobile home and auto body shop under 21 U.S.C. §§ 881(a)(4) and (a)(7). Austin filed a claim and an answer to the complaint.

On February 4, 1991, the United States made a motion, supported by an affidavit from Sioux Falls Police Officer Donald Satterlee, for summary judgment. According to Satterlee's affidavit, Austin met Keith Engebretson at Austin's body shop on June 13, 1990, and agreed to sell cocaine to Engebretson. Austin left the shop, went to his mobile home, and returned to the shop with two grams of cocaine which he sold to Engebretson. State authorities executed a search warrant on the body shop and mobile home the following day. They discovered small amounts of marijuana and cocaine, a .22 caliber revolver, drug paraphernalia, and approximately $4,700 in cash. In opposing summary judgment, Austin argued that forfeiture of the properties would violate the Eighth Amendment.[2] The District Court rejected this argument and entered summary judgment for the United States. The United States Court of Appeals for the Eighth Circuit "reluctantly agree[d] with the government" and affirmed. We granted certiorari to resolve an apparent conflict with the Court of Appeals for the Second Circuit over the applicability of the Eighth Amendment to *in rem* civil forfeitures.

Austin contends that the Eighth Amendment's Excessive Fines Clause applies to *in rem* civil forfeiture proceedings. The United States now argues that "any claim that the government's conduct in a civil proceeding is limited by the Eighth Amendment generally, or by the Excessive Fines Clause in particular, must fail unless the challenged governmental action, despite its label, would have been

---

[2] "Excessive bail shall not be required, nor excessive fines imposed, nor cruel and unusual punishments inflicted." U.S. Const., Amdt. 8.

recognized as a *criminal* punishment at the time the Eighth Amendment was adopted." It further suggests that the Eighth Amendment cannot apply to a civil proceeding unless that proceeding is so punitive that it must be considered criminal under *Kennedy v. Mendoza-Martinez*, 372 U.S. 144 (1963), and *United States v. Ward*, 448 U.S. 242 (1980). We disagree.

Some provisions of the Bill of Rights are expressly limited to criminal cases. The Fifth Amendment's Self-Incrimination Clause, for example, provides: "No person . . . shall be compelled in any criminal case to be a witness against himself." The protections provided by the Sixth Amendment are explicitly confined to "criminal prosecutions." The text of the Eighth Amendment includes no similar limitation.

Nor does the history of the Eighth Amendment require such a limitation. . . .

The purpose of the Eighth Amendment, putting the Bail Clause to one side, was to limit the government's power to punish. The Cruel and Unusual Punishments Clause is self-evidently concerned with punishment. The Excessive Fines Clause limits the government's power to extract payments, whether in cash or in kind, "as *punishment* for some offense." "The notion of punishment, as we commonly understand it, cuts across the division between the civil and the criminal law." *United States v. Halper*, 490 U.S. 435, 447–448 (1989). "It is commonly understood that civil proceedings may advance punitive as well as remedial goals, and, conversely, that both punitive and remedial goals may be served by criminal penalties." *Id.* at 447. Thus, the question is not, as the United States would have it, whether forfeiture under §§ 881(a)(4) and (a)(7) is civil or criminal, but rather whether it is punishment.

In considering this question, we are mindful of the fact that sanctions frequently serve more than one purpose. We need not exclude the possibility that a forfeiture serves remedial purposes to conclude that it is subject to the limitations of the Excessive Fines Clause. We, however, must determine that it can only be explained as serving in part to punish. . . .

Our cases . . . have recognized that statutory *in rem* forfeiture imposes punishment. The same understanding of forfeiture as punishment runs through our cases rejecting the "innocence" of the owner as a common-law defense to forfeiture. In these cases, forfeiture has been justified on two theories — that the property itself is "guilty" of the offense, and that the owner may be held accountable for the wrongs of others to whom he entrusts his property. Both theories rest, at bottom, on the notion that the owner has been negligent in allowing his property to be misused and that he is properly punished for that negligence. . . .

In sum, even though this Court has rejected the "innocence" of the owner as a common-law defense to forfeiture, it consistently has recognized that forfeiture serves, at least in part, to punish the owner. More recently, we have noted that forfeiture serves "punitive and deterrent purposes," *Calero-Toledo*, 416 U.S. at 686, and "impos[es] an economic penalty," *id.* at 687. We conclude, therefore, that forfeiture generally and statutory *in rem* forfeiture in particular historically have been understood, at least in part, as punishment.

We turn next to consider whether forfeitures under 21 U.S.C. §§ 881(a)(4) and (a)(7) are properly considered punishment today. We find nothing in these provisions or their legislative history to contradict the historical understanding of forfeiture as punishment. Unlike traditional forfeiture statutes, §§ 881(a)(4) and (a)(7) expressly provide an "innocent owner" defense. These exemptions serve to focus the provisions on the culpability of the owner in a way that makes them look more like punishment, not less.

The legislative history of § 881 confirms the punitive nature of these provisions. When it added subsection (a)(7) to § 881 in 1984, Congress recognized "that the traditional criminal sanctions of fine and imprisonment are inadequate to deter or punish the enormously profitable trade in dangerous drugs." S.Rep. No. 98-225, p. 191 (1983). It characterized the forfeiture of real property as "a powerful deterrent." *Id.* at 195.

The government argues that §§ 881(a)(4) and (a)(7) are not punitive but, rather, should be considered remedial in two respects. First, they remove the "instruments" of the drug trade "thereby protecting the community from the threat of continued drug dealing." Second, the forfeited assets serve to compensate the government for the expense of law enforcement activity and for its expenditure on societal problems such as urban blight, drug addiction, and other health concerns resulting from the drug trade.

In our view, neither argument withstands scrutiny. Concededly, we have recognized that the forfeiture of contraband itself may be characterized as remedial because it removes dangerous or illegal items from society. The Court, however, previously has rejected government's attempt to extend that reasoning to conveyances used to transport illegal liquor. *See One 1958 Plymouth Sedan v. Pennsylvania*, 380 U.S. 693, 699 (1965). In that case it noted: "There is nothing even remotely criminal in possessing an automobile." The same, without question, is true of the properties involved here, and the government's attempt to characterize these properties as "instruments" of the drug trade must meet the same fate as Pennsylvania's effort to characterize the 1958 Plymouth sedan as "contraband."

The government's second argument about the remedial nature of this forfeiture is no more persuasive. We previously have upheld the forfeiture of goods involved in customs violations as "a reasonable form of liquidated damages." *One Lot Emerald Cut Stones v. United States*, 409 U.S. 232, 237 (1972). But the dramatic variations in the value of conveyances and real property forfeitable under §§ 881(a)(4) and (a)(7) undercut any similar argument with respect to those provisions.

Fundamentally, even assuming that §§ 881(a)(4) and (a)(7) serve some remedial purpose, the government's argument must fail. "[A] civil sanction that cannot fairly be said *solely* to serve a remedial purpose, but rather can only be explained as also serving either retributive or deterrent purposes, is punishment, as we have come to understand the term." *Halper*, 490 U.S. at 448 (emphasis added). In light of the historical understanding of forfeiture as punishment, the clear focus of §§ 881(a)(4) and (a)(7) on the culpability of the owner, and the evidence that Congress understood those provisions as serving to deter and to punish, we cannot conclude that forfeiture under §§ 881(a)(4) and (a)(7) serves solely a remedial purpose. We therefore conclude that forfeiture under these provisions constitutes "payment to a sovereign as punishment for some offense," *Browning-Ferris*, 492 U.S. at 265, and, as such, is subject to the limitations of the Eighth Amendment's Excessive Fines Clause.

Austin asks that we establish a multifactor test for determining whether a forfeiture is constitutionally "excessive." We decline that invitation.

The judgment of the Court of Appeals is reversed, and the case is remanded to that court for further proceedings consistent with this opinion.

JUSTICE SCALIA, concurring in part and concurring in the judgment.

We recently stated that, at the time the Eighth Amendment was drafted, the term "fine" was "understood to mean a payment to a sovereign as punishment for some offense." *Browning-Ferris Industries of Vt. v. Kelco Disposal, Inc.*, 492 U.S. 257, 265 (1989). It seems to me that the Court's opinion obscures this clear statement, and needlessly attempts to derive from our sparse case law on the subject of *in rem* forfeiture the questionable proposition that the owner of property taken pursuant to such forfeiture is always blameworthy.

In order to constitute a fine under the Eighth Amendment, however, the forfeiture must constitute "punishment," and it is a [close] question whether statutory *in rem* forfeitures, as opposed to *in personam* forfeitures, meet this requirement. The latter are assessments, whether monetary or in kind, to punish the property owner's criminal conduct, while the former are confiscations of property rights based on improper use of the property, regardless of whether the owner has violated the law. Statutory *in rem* forfeitures have a long history. The theory of *in rem* forfeiture is said to be that the lawful property has committed an offense.

However the theory may be expressed, it seems to me that this taking of lawful property must be considered, in whole or in part, punitive. Its purpose is not compensatory, to make someone whole for injury caused by unlawful use of the property. Punishment is being imposed, whether one quaintly considers its object to be the property itself, or more realistically regards its object to be the property's owner.

The Court apparently believes, however, that only actual culpability of the affected property owner can establish that a forfeiture provision is punitive, and sets out to establish that such culpability exists in the case of *in rem* forfeitures. In my view, however, the case law is far more ambiguous than the Court acknowledges. We have never held that the Constitution requires negligence, or any other degree of culpability, to support such forfeitures.

JUSTICE KENNEDY, with whom THE CHIEF JUSTICE and JUSTICE THOMAS join, concurring in part and concurring in the judgment.

In recounting the law's history, we risk anachronism if we attribute to an earlier time an intent to employ legal concepts that had not yet evolved. I see something of that in the Court's opinion here, for in its eagerness to discover a unified theory of forfeitures, it recites a consistent rationale of personal punishment that neither the cases nor other narratives of the common law suggest. For many of the reasons explained by JUSTICE SCALIA, I am not convinced that all *in rem* forfeitures were on account of the owner's blameworthy conduct.

NOTES AND QUESTIONS

1. *History of in rem forfeitures.* The majority opinion concludes that "forfeiture generally and statutory in rem forfeiture in particular historically have been understood, at least in part, as punishment." The concurring opinions — perhaps with some justification — call this historical analysis into question. What is the true debate between the majority and concurring opinions on this matter? Is the debate significant? Why or why not?

2. *Purposes of in rem forfeitures.* According to the Court, what are the purposes behind in rem forfeitures? Why does the Court reject the government's argument that such forfeitures are purely remedial? Do you agree with the Court's conclusion? Why or why not?

3. *Double jeopardy.* The Court in *Austin* unanimously held that civil forfeitures constitute punishment and therefore are subject to Excessive Fines Clause analysis. Does that mean that it would violate the Double Jeopardy Clause to subject a defendant both to (a) punishment in a criminal case and (b) civil forfeiture arising out of the same act? In *United States v. Ursery*, 518 U.S. 267 (1996), the Supreme Court held not. The Court concluded that the definition of "punishment" under the Double Jeopardy Clause is narrower than the definition of "punishment" under the Excessive Fines Clause. Therefore, the Double Jeopardy Clause is not triggered by civil forfeitures. Only Justice Stevens dissented, stating that "the Court today stands *Austin* on its head — a decision rendered only three years ago, with unanimity on the pertinent points." Are these two decisions in fact inconsistent? Can you explain the considerations that might have produced the outcome in *Ursery*? Is it fair to subject a person both to criminal punishment for an offense, and to civil forfeiture for the same offense? Why or why not?

Of course, the government need not obtain a criminal conviction in order to seek civil forfeiture. But in *Ursery*, the government, in two different instances, initiated both a civil in rem forfeiture proceeding and a criminal proceeding against the property owner. Why would the government choose to initiate a civil forfeiture proceeding, rather than simply obtain criminal forfeiture as part of the penalty phase of its criminal case?

4. *The* Halper *and* Hudson *decisions.* The *Austin* majority relied upon *United States v. Halper*, 490 U.S. 435, 448 (1989) ("[A] civil sanction that cannot fairly be said *solely* to serve a remedial purpose, but rather can only be explained as also serving either retributive or deterrent purposes, is punishment, as we have come to understand the term"). In *Hudson v. United States*, 522 U.S. 93, 99–104 (1997), however, the Court rejected the *Halper* test, relying in part on *Ursery*. As discussed more fully in Chapter 18, Civil Actions, Civil Penalties, and Parallel Proceedings, *supra*, the Court in *Hudson* stated that "the Double Jeopardy Clause does not prohibit the imposition of any additional sanction that could . . . be described as punishment" but "only protects against the imposition of multiple criminal punishments for the same offense." In order for a civil penalty to trigger the Double Jeopardy Clause under *Hudson*, then, a court must first determine whether the civil penalty is either (a) explicitly criminal or (b) "so punitive in form and effect as to render [it] criminal despite Congress' intent to the contrary. . . . "

[b]   Criminal Forfeitures

The same year it decided *Austin*, the Court held in *Alexander v. United States*, 509 U.S. 544, 558–559 (1993), that criminal forfeitures under the RICO statute, 18 U.S.C. § 1963, are also subject to the Eighth Amendment's Excessive Fines Clause. The Court did not provide guidance, in either *Austin* or *Alexander*, for applying the Excessive Fines Clause to forfeiture cases. The Court finally turned to that task in the case that follows.

UNITED STATES v. BAJAKAJIAN
524 U.S. 321 (1998)

JUSTICE THOMAS delivered the opinion of the Court.

Respondent Hosep Bajakajian attempted to leave the United States without reporting, as required by federal law, that he was transporting more than $10,000 in currency. Federal law also provides that a person convicted of willfully violating this reporting requirement shall forfeit to the Government "any property . . . involved in such offense." 18 U.S.C. § 982(a)(1). The question in this case is whether forfeiture of the entire $357,144 that respondent failed to declare would violate the Excessive Fines Clause of the Eighth Amendment. We hold that it would, because full forfeiture of respondent's currency would be grossly disproportional to the gravity of his offense.

On June 9, 1994, respondent, his wife, and his two daughters were waiting at Los Angeles International Airport to board a flight to Italy; their final destination was Cyprus. Using dogs trained to detect currency by its smell, customs inspectors discovered some $230,000 in cash in the Bajakajians' checked baggage. A customs inspector approached respondent and his wife and told them that they were required to report all money in excess of $10,000 in their possession or in their baggage. Respondent said that he had $8,000 and that his wife had another $7,000, but that the family had no additional currency to declare. A search of their carry-on bags, purse, and wallet revealed more cash; in all, customs inspectors found $357,144. The currency was seized and respondent was taken into custody.

A federal grand jury indicted respondent on three counts. Count One charged him with failing to report, as required by 31 U.S.C. § 5316(a)(1)(A), that he was transporting more than $10,000 outside the United States, and with doing so "willfully," in violation of § 5322(a). Count Two charged him with making a false material statement to the United States Customs Service, in violation of 18 U.S.C. § 1001. Count Three sought forfeiture of the $357,144 pursuant to 18 U.S.C. § 982(a)(1).

Respondent pleaded guilty to the failure to report in Count One; the government agreed to dismiss the false statement charge in Count Two; and respondent elected to have a bench trial on the forfeiture in Count Three. After the bench trial, the District Court found that the entire $357,144 was subject to forfeiture because it was "involved in" the offense. The court also found that the funds were not connected to any other crime and that respondent was transporting the money to repay a lawful debt. The District Court further found that respondent had failed to report that he was taking the currency out of the United States because of fear stemming from "cultural differences": Respondent, who had grown up as a member of the Armenian minority in Syria, had a "distrust for the government."

Although § 982(a)(1) directs sentencing courts to impose full forfeiture, the District Court concluded that such forfeiture would be "extraordinarily harsh" and "grossly disproportionate to the offense in question," and that it would therefore violate the Excessive Fines Clause. The court instead ordered forfeiture of $15,000, in addition to a sentence of three years of probation and a fine of $5,000 — the maximum fine under the Sentencing Guidelines — because the court believed that the maximum Guidelines fine was "too little" and that a $15,000 forfeiture would "make up for what I think a reasonable fine should be."

The United States appealed, seeking full forfeiture of respondent's currency as provided in § 982(a)(1). The Court of Appeals for the Ninth Circuit affirmed. Applying Circuit precedent, the court held that, to satisfy the Excessive Fines Clause, a forfeiture must fulfill two conditions: The property forfeited must be an "instrumentality" of the crime committed, and the value of the property must be proportional to the culpability of the owner. A majority of the panel determined that the currency was not an "instrumentality" of the crime of failure to report because "[t]he crime [in a currency reporting offense] is the withholding of information, . . . not the possession or the transportation of the money." The majority therefore held that § 982(a)(1) could never satisfy the Excessive Fines Clause in cases involving forfeitures of currency and that it was unnecessary to apply the "proportionality" prong of the test. Although the panel majority concluded that the Excessive Fines Clause did not permit forfeiture of *any* of the unreported currency, it held that it lacked jurisdiction to set the $15,000 forfeiture aside because respondent had not cross-appealed to challenge that forfeiture. Because the Court of Appeals' holding — that the forfeiture ordered by § 982(a)(1) was *per se* unconstitutional in cases of currency forfeiture — invalidated a portion of an Act of Congress, we granted certiorari.

The Eighth Amendment provides: "Excessive bail shall not be required, nor excessive fines imposed, nor cruel and unusual punishments inflicted." U.S. Const., Amdt. 8. This Court has had little occasion to interpret, and has never actually applied, the Excessive Fines Clause. We have, however, explained that at the time the Constitution was adopted, "the word 'fine' was understood to mean a payment to a sovereign as punishment for some offense." *Browning-Ferris Industries of Vt. v. Kelco Disposal, Inc.*, 492 U.S. 257, 265 (1989). The Excessive Fines Clause thus "limits the government's power to extract payments, whether in cash or in kind, as punishment for some offense." *Austin v. United States*, 509 U.S. 602, 609–610 (1993) (emphasis deleted). Forfeitures — payments in kind — are thus "fines" if they constitute punishment for an offense.

We have little trouble concluding that the forfeiture of currency ordered by § 982(a)(1) constitutes punishment. The statute directs a court to order forfeiture as an additional sanction when "imposing sentence on a person convicted of" a willful violation of § 5316's reporting requirement. The forfeiture is thus imposed at the culmination of a criminal proceeding and requires conviction of an underlying felony, and it cannot be imposed upon an innocent owner of unreported currency, but only upon a person who has himself been convicted of a § 5316 reporting violation.[3]

---

[3] [T]the dissent's speculation about the effect of today's holding on "kingpins" and "cash couriers" is misplaced. Section 982(a)(1)'s criminal *in personam* forfeiture reaches only currency owned by someone who himself commits a reporting crime. It is unlikely that the government, in the course of criminally

The United States argues, however, that the forfeiture of currency under § 982(a)(1) "also serves important remedial purposes." The government asserts that it has "an overriding sovereign interest in controlling what property leaves and enters the country." It claims that full forfeiture of unreported currency supports that interest by serving to "dete[r] illicit movements of cash" and aiding in providing the government with "valuable information to investigate and detect criminal activities associated with that cash." Deterrence, however, has traditionally been viewed as a goal of punishment, and forfeiture of the currency here does not serve the remedial purpose of compensating the Government for a loss. Although the government has asserted a loss of information regarding the amount of currency leaving the country, that loss would not be remedied by the government's confiscation of respondent's $357,144.

The United States also argues that the forfeiture mandated by § 982(a)(1) is constitutional because it falls within a class of historic forfeitures of property tainted by crime. In so doing, the Government relies upon a series of cases involving traditional civil *in rem* forfeitures that are inapposite because such forfeitures were historically considered nonpunitive. . . .

The theory behind such forfeitures was the fiction that the action was directed against "guilty property," rather than against the offender himself. Historically, the conduct of the property owner was irrelevant; indeed, the owner of forfeited property could be entirely innocent of any crime. . . . [6]

The forfeiture in this case does not bear any of the hallmarks of traditional civil *in rem* forfeitures. The Government has not proceeded against the currency itself, but has instead sought and obtained a criminal conviction of respondent personally. The forfeiture serves no remedial purpose, is designed to punish the offender, and cannot be imposed upon innocent owners.

The government specifically contends that the forfeiture of respondent's currency is constitutional because it involves an "instrumentality" of respondent's crime.[8] According to the government, the unreported cash is an instrumentality because it "does not merely facilitate a violation of law," but is "the very *sine qua non* of the crime." The government reasons that "there would be no violation at all without the exportation (or attempted exportation) of the cash.

Acceptance of the government's argument would require us to expand the traditional understanding of instrumentality forfeitures. This we decline to do.

---

indicting and prosecuting a cash courier, would not bother to investigate the source and true ownership of unreported funds.

[6] It does not follow, of course, that all modern civil *in rem* forfeitures are nonpunitive and thus beyond the coverage of the Excessive Fines Clause. Because some recent federal forfeiture laws have blurred the traditional distinction between civil *in rem* and criminal *in personam* forfeiture, we have held that a modern statutory forfeiture is a "fine" for Eighth Amendment purposes if it constitutes punishment even in part, regardless of whether the proceeding is styled *in rem* or *in personam*. See *Austin v. United States, supra*, at 621–622 (although labeled *in rem*, civil forfeiture of real property used "to facilitate" the commission of drug crimes was punitive in part and thus subject to review under the Excessive Fines Clause).

[8] Although the term "instrumentality" is of recent vintage, it fairly characterizes property that historically was subject to forfeiture because it was the actual means by which an offense was committed. "Instrumentality" forfeitures have historically been limited to the property actually used to commit an offense and no more. A forfeiture that reaches beyond this strict historical limitation is *ipso facto* punitive and therefore subject to review under the Excessive Fines Clause.

Instrumentalities historically have been treated as a form of "guilty property" that can be forfeited in civil *in rem* proceedings. In this case, however, the Government has sought to punish respondent by proceeding against him criminally, *in personam*, rather than proceeding *in rem* against the currency. It is therefore irrelevant whether respondent's currency is an instrumentality; the forfeiture is punitive, and the test for the excessiveness of a punitive forfeiture involves solely a proportionality determination.[9]

Because the forfeiture of respondent's currency constitutes punishment and is thus a "fine" within the meaning of the Excessive Fines Clause, we now turn to the question whether it is "excessive."

The touchstone of the constitutional inquiry under the Excessive Fines Clause is the principle of proportionality: The amount of the forfeiture must bear some relationship to the gravity of the offense that it is designed to punish. Until today, however, we have not articulated a standard for determining whether a punitive forfeiture is constitutionally excessive. We now hold that a punitive forfeiture violates the Excessive Fines Clause if it is grossly disproportional to the gravity of a defendant's offense.

The text and history of the Excessive Fines Clause demonstrate the centrality of proportionality to the excessiveness inquiry; nonetheless, they provide little guidance as to how disproportional a punitive forfeiture must be to the gravity of an offense in order to be "excessive." Excessive means surpassing the usual, the proper, or a normal measure of proportion. The constitutional question that we address, however, is just how proportional to a criminal offense a fine must be, and the text of the Excessive Fines Clause does not answer it.

Nor does its history. The Clause was little discussed in the First Congress and the debates over the ratification of the Bill of Rights. . . .

We must therefore rely on other considerations in deriving a constitutional excessiveness standard, and there are two that we find particularly relevant. The first, which we have emphasized in our cases interpreting the Cruel and Unusual Punishments Clause, is that judgments about the appropriate punishment for an offense belong in the first instance to the legislature. The second is that any judicial determination regarding the gravity of a particular criminal offense will be inherently imprecise. Both of these principles counsel against requiring strict proportionality between the amount of a punitive forfeiture and the gravity of a criminal offense, and we therefore adopt the standard of gross disproportionality articulated in our Cruel and Unusual Punishments Clause precedents.

In applying this standard, the district courts in the first instance, and the courts of appeals, reviewing the proportionality determination *de novo*, must compare the amount of the forfeiture to the gravity of the defendant's offense. If the amount of the forfeiture is grossly disproportional to the gravity of the defendant's offense, it is unconstitutional.

---

[9] The currency in question is not an instrumentality in any event. The Court of Appeals reasoned that the existence of the currency as a "precondition" to the reporting requirement did not make it an "instrumentality" of the offense. We agree; the currency is merely the subject of the crime of failure to report. Cash in a suitcase does not facilitate the commission of that crime as, for example, an automobile facilitates the transportation of goods concealed to avoid taxes. In the latter instance, the property is the actual means by which the criminal act is committed. *See* Black's Law Dictionary 801 (6th ed. 1990) ("Instrumentality" is "[s]omething by which an end is achieved; a means, medium, agency").

Under this standard, the forfeiture of respondent's entire $357,144 would violate the Excessive Fines Clause.[11] Respondent's crime was solely a reporting offense. It was permissible to transport the currency out of the country so long as he reported it. Section 982(a)(1) orders currency to be forfeited for a "willful" violation of the reporting requirement. Thus, the essence of respondent's crime is a willful failure to report the removal of currency from the United States.[12] Furthermore, as the District Court found, respondent's violation was unrelated to any other illegal activities. The money was the proceeds of legal activity and was to be used to repay a lawful debt. Whatever his other vices, respondent does not fit into the class of persons for whom the statute was principally designed: He is not a money launderer, a drug trafficker, or a tax evader.[13] And under the Sentencing Guidelines, the maximum sentence that could have been imposed on respondent was six months, while the maximum fine was $5,000. Such penalties confirm a minimal level of culpability.[14]

The harm that respondent caused was also minimal. Failure to report his currency affected only one party, the government, and in a relatively minor way. There was no fraud on the United States, and respondent caused no loss to the public fisc. Had his crime gone undetected, the government would have been deprived only of the information that $357,144 had left the country. The government and the dissent contend that there is a correlation between the

---

[11] The only question before this Court is whether the full forfeiture of respondent's $357,144 as directed by § 982(a)(1) is constitutional under the Excessive Fines Clause. We hold that it is not. The government petitioned for certiorari seeking full forfeiture, and we reject that request. Our holding that full forfeiture would be excessive reflects no judgment that "a forfeiture of even $15,001 would have suffered from a gross disproportion," nor does it "affir[m] the reduced $15,000 forfeiture on *de novo* review." Those issues are simply not before us. Nor, indeed, do we address in *any* respect the validity of the forfeiture ordered by the District Court, including whether a court may disregard the terms of a statute that commands full forfeiture: respondent did not cross-appeal the $15,000 forfeiture ordered by the District Court. The Court of Appeals thus declined to address the $15,000 forfeiture, and that question is not properly presented here either.

[12] Contrary to the dissent's contention, the nature of the nonreporting offense in this case was not altered by respondent's "lies" or by the "suspicious circumstances" surrounding his transportation of his currency. A single willful failure to declare the currency constitutes the crime, the gravity of which is not exacerbated or mitigated by "fable[s]" that respondent told one month, or six months, later. The government indicted respondent under 18 U.S.C. § 1001 for "lying," but that separate count did not form the basis of the nonreporting offense for which § 982(a)(1) orders forfeiture. Further, the District Court's finding that respondent's lies stemmed from a fear of the government because of "cultural differences," does not mitigate the gravity of his offense. The dissent's charge of ethnic paternalism on the part of the District Court finds no support in the record, nor is there any indication that the District Court's factual finding that respondent "distrust[ed] . . . the government," was clearly erroneous.

[13] Nor, contrary to the dissent's repeated assertion, is respondent a "smuggl[er]." Respondent owed no customs duties to the government, and it was perfectly legal for him to possess the $357,144 in cash and to remove it from the United States. His crime was simply failing to report the wholly legal act of transporting his currency.

[14] In considering an offense's gravity, the other penalties that the Legislature has authorized are certainly relevant evidence. Here, as the government and the dissent stress, Congress authorized a maximum fine of $250,000 plus five years' imprisonment for willfully violating the statutory reporting requirement, and this suggests that it did not view the reporting offense as a trivial one. That the maximum fine and Guideline sentence to which respondent was subject were but a fraction of the penalties authorized, however, undercuts any argument based solely on the statute, because they show that respondent's culpability relative to other potential violators of the reporting provision — tax evaders, drug kingpins, or money launderers, for example — is small indeed. This disproportion is telling notwithstanding the fact that a separate Guideline provision permits forfeiture if mandated by statute. That Guideline, moreover, cannot override the constitutional requirement of proportionality review.

amount forfeited and the harm that the government would have suffered had the crime gone undetected. We disagree. There is no inherent proportionality in such a forfeiture. It is impossible to conclude, for example, that the harm respondent caused is anywhere near 30 times greater than that caused by a hypothetical drug dealer who willfully fails to report taking $12,000 out of the country in order to purchase drugs.

Comparing the gravity of respondent's crime with the $357,144 forfeiture the government seeks, we conclude that such a forfeiture would be grossly disproportional to the gravity of his offense. It is larger than the $5,000 fine imposed by the District Court by many orders of magnitude, and it bears no articulable correlation to any injury suffered by the government.

For the foregoing reasons, the full forfeiture of respondent's currency would violate the Excessive Fines Clause. The judgment of the Court of Appeals is affirmed.

JUSTICE KENNEDY, with whom THE CHIEF JUSTICE, JUSTICE O'CONNOR, and JUSTICE SCALIA join, dissenting.

For the first time in its history, the Court strikes down a fine as excessive under the Eighth Amendment. The decision is disturbing both for its specific holding and for the broader upheaval it foreshadows. At issue is a fine Congress fixed in the amount of the currency respondent sought to smuggle or to transport without reporting. If a fine calibrated with this accuracy fails the Court's test, its decision portends serious disruption of a vast range of statutory fines. The Court all but says the offense is not serious anyway. This disdain for the statute is wrong as an empirical matter and disrespectful of the separation of powers.

Turning to the question of excessiveness, the majority states the test: A defendant must prove a gross disproportion before a court will strike down a fine as excessive. This test would be a proper way to apply the Clause, if only the majority were faithful in applying it. The Court does not, however, explain why in this case forfeiture of all of the cash would have suffered from a gross disproportion. The offense is a serious one, and respondent's smuggling and failing to report were willful. The cash was lawful to own, but this fact shows only that the forfeiture was a fine; it cannot also prove that the fine was excessive.

The majority illuminates its test with a principle of deference. Congress deems the crime serious, but the Court does not. Under the congressional statute, the crime is punishable by a prison sentence, a heavy fine, and the forfeiture here at issue. As the statute makes clear, the government needs the information to investigate other serious crimes, and it needs the penalties to ensure compliance.

Congress considered currency smuggling and non-reporting a serious crime and imposed commensurate penalties. It authorized punishments of five years' imprisonment, a $250,000 fine, plus forfeiture of all the undeclared cash. Congress found the offense standing alone is a serious crime, for the same statute doubles the fines and imprisonment for failures to report cash "while violating another law of the United States." Congress experimented with lower penalties on the order of one year in prison plus a $1,000 fine, but it found the punishments inadequate to deter lucrative money laundering. The Court today rejects this judgment.

The Court rejects the congressional judgment because, it says, the Sentencing Guidelines cap the appropriate fine at $5,000. The purpose of the Guidelines, however, is to select punishments with precise proportion, not to opine on what is a gross disproportion. In addition, there is no authority for elevating the Commission's judgment of what is prudent over the congressional judgment of what is constitutional. The majority, then, departs from its promise of deference in the very case announcing the standard.

The Court's argument is flawed, moreover, by a serious misinterpretation of the Guidelines on their face. The Guidelines do not stop at the $5,000 fine the majority cites. They augment it with this vital point: "Forfeiture is to be imposed upon a convicted defendant as provided by statute." United States Sentencing Commission, Guidelines Manual § 5E1.4 (Nov.1995). The fine thus supplements the forfeiture; it does not replace it. Far from contradicting congressional judgment on the offense, the Guidelines implement and mandate it.

The crime of smuggling or failing to report cash is more serious than the Court is willing to acknowledge. The drug trade, money laundering, and tax evasion all depend in part on smuggled and unreported cash. Congress enacted the reporting requirement because secret exports of money were being used in organized crime, drug trafficking, money laundering, and other crimes. Likewise, tax evaders were using cash exports to dodge hundreds of millions of dollars in taxes owed to the government.

The Court does not deny the importance of these interests but claims they are not implicated here because respondent managed to disprove any link to other crimes. Here, to be sure, the government had no affirmative proof that the money was from an illegal source or for an illegal purpose. This will often be the case, however. By its very nature, money laundering is difficult to prove; for if the money launderers have done their job, the money appears to be clean. The point of the statute, which provides for even heavier penalties if a second crime can be proved, is to mandate forfeiture regardless. It is common practice, of course, for a cash courier not to confess a tainted source but to stick to a well-rehearsed story. The kingpin, the real owner, need not come forward to make a legal claim to the funds. He has his own effective enforcement measures to ensure delivery at destination or return at origin if the scheme is thwarted. He is, of course, not above punishing the courier who deviates from the story and informs. The majority is wrong, then, to assume *in personam* forfeitures cannot affect kingpins, as their couriers will claim to own the money and pay the penalty out of their masters' funds. Even if the courier confessed, the kingpin could face an *in personam* forfeiture for his agent's authorized acts, for the kingpin would be a co-principal in the commission of the crime.

In my view, forfeiture of all the unreported currency is sustainable whenever a willful violation is proved. The facts of this case exemplify how hard it can be to prove ownership and other crimes, and they also show respondent is far from an innocent victim. For one thing, he was guilty of repeated lies to government agents and suborning lies by others.

Respondent told these lies, moreover, in most suspicious circumstances. His luggage was stuffed with more than a third of a million dollars. All of it was in cash, and much of it was hidden in a case with a false bottom.

The majority ratifies the District Court's see-no-evil approach. It dismissed the lies as stemming from "distrust for the Government" arising out of "cultural differences." While the majority is sincere in not endorsing this excuse, it nonetheless affirms the fine tainted by it. This patronizing excuse demeans millions of law-abiding American immigrants by suggesting they cannot be expected to be as truthful as every other citizen. Each American, regardless of culture or ethnicity, is equal before the law. Each has the same obligation to refrain from perjury and false statements to the government.

In short, respondent was unable to give a single truthful explanation of the source of the cash. The multitude of lies and suspicious circumstances points to some form of crime. Yet, though the government rebutted each and every fable respondent proffered, it was unable to adduce affirmative proof of another crime in this particular case.

Given the severity of respondent's crime, the Constitution does not forbid forfeiture of all of the smuggled or unreported cash. Congress made a considered judgment in setting the penalty, and the Court is in serious error to set it aside. . . .

In these circumstances, the Constitution does not forbid forfeiture of all of the $357,144 transported by respondent. I dissent.

NOTES AND QUESTIONS

1. *A split court.* As is so often true in white collar cases, the Court in *Bajakajian* was sharply split; the dissent is written in particularly vehement terms. Note that the dissent does not quarrel with the test for determining whether a fine is excessive, but does dispute the outcome in the case. Can you explain why the issue divided the Court so narrowly? The majority and dissent have very different views both of the seriousness of the crime at issue and of Bajakajian's individual culpability. Which side has the better of the debate? Why?

2. *Application to civil forfeitures.* In CAFRA, Congress codified the *Bajakajian* rule for civil forfeitures. That provision, codified at 18 U.S.C § 983(g) (General Rules for Civil Forfeiture Proceedings), provides:

(g) Proportionality.

(1) The claimant . . . may petition the court to determine whether the forfeiture was constitutionally excessive.

(2) In making this determination, the court shall compare the forfeiture to the gravity of the offense giving rise to the forfeiture.

(3) The claimant shall have the burden of establishing that the forfeiture is grossly disproportional by a preponderance of the evidence at a hearing conducted by the court without a jury.

(4) If the court finds that the forfeiture is grossly disproportional to the offense it shall reduce or eliminate the forfeiture as necessary to avoid a violation of the Excessive Fines Clause of the Eighth Amendment of the Constitution.

3. *The "cultural" defense.* What role did the defendant's background play in the decision? What was the dissent's point in this regard? Is the dissent right? Why or why not?

4. *The congressional response to* Bajakajian.

a. *The "cash smuggling" statute.* As part of the "USA PATRIOT Act" of 2001, Congress enacted a law, entitled "Bulk Cash Smuggling into or out of the United States." 31 U.S.C. § 5332. That statute makes it a criminal offense to knowingly conceal more than $10,000 in cash and to transport or attempt to transport that cash in or out of the country with the intent to evade the currency reporting requirements.

b. *Forfeitures.* In addition to imprisonment of not more than five years, the statute provides for both criminal and civil forfeiture of all property "involved in" or "traceable to" the crime. The statute further provides that "any currency or other monetary instrument that is concealed or intended to be concealed in violation of . . . *shall be considered property involved in the offense.*" 31 U.S.C. § 5332 (emphasis added). The preamble to the statute states that prior statutes forced criminals to eschew traditional financial institutions in favor of carrying bulk cash and "only the confiscation of [this cash] can effectively break the cycle of criminal activity" of which it is a part, requiring a new crime so that the cash can be "confiscated as the *corpus delicti*" of the offense.

This language appears to respond to language in *Bajakajian* concluding that (1) cash is not an "instrumentality" of the crime of failing to report currency, and (2) merely failing to report, as part of the "gross proportionality" analysis, does not cause substantial harm to the government. In particular, the *Bajakajian* majority had rejected the dissent's conclusion that the defendant was a "smuggler." In response, the preamble to § 5332 states that carrying and failing to report the currency "is the equivalent of, and creates the same harm as, the smuggling of goods."

In light of this language, are civil and criminal forfeitures based upon violations of § 5332 subject to Excessive Fines Clause analysis? District courts have held that, despite apparent Congressional intent to the contrary, § 5332 forfeitures *are* subject to Excessive Fines Clause review. *See United States v. $120,856*, 394 F. Supp. 2d 687, 695–696 (D.V.I. 2005) (holding that forfeiture under § 5332 of $120,856 that legal immigrant attempted to bring into United States "would be extraordinarily harsh and grossly disproportionate to the offense," and reducing the forfeiture to $7,500); *United States v. $293,316 in United States Currency*, 349 F. Supp. 2d 638, 650–651 (S.D.N.Y. 2004) (Weinstein, J.) (reducing forfeiture under § 5332 on facts similar to those presented in *Bajakajian*, and rejecting the government's argument that § 5332 compels forfeiture of the entire amount). *Cf. United States v. Jose*, 499 F.3d 105, 111–114 (1st Cir. 2007) (holding that the forfeiture on the facts of the case was not excessive, and declining to decide the threshold question whether the Excessive Fines Clause even applies to § 5332 forfeitures).

PROBLEM

20-2. Robert Prince appeals from a judgment of civil forfeiture against his 29.6 acres of property, including his own barn-residence, another residence, and outbuildings. Prince argues that forfeiture of his interest in the entire property violates the Eighth Amendment.

The police arrested Robert Prince after they discovered 20 marijuana plants being grown in a barn on Prince's property. Prince lived in a small apartment in the loft area of the barn. Prince was charged with cultivation of marijuana under applicable state law. Prince pleaded guilty to possession and cultivation of marijuana. Although subject to a possible maximum five-year prison term, he was sentenced to two years' imprisonment because he had no prior criminal record.

Almost seven months after Prince's guilty plea, the United States entered the case and filed a complaint in the United States district court for in rem forfeiture of Prince's property under 21 U.S.C. § 881(a)(7). Both the United States and Prince moved for summary judgment. The district court granted the government's motion for summary judgment, denied Prince's motion, and entered a judgment of forfeiture against Prince's 29.6 acres of property and structures.

In ordering the forfeiture, the court made the following factual findings: the barn and curtilage are worth $100,000; the remaining property is worth $200,000; the barn is the defendant's home; the defendant owns all the property in full (i.e., there is no mortgage); the defendant is employed and has earned an average of approximately $50,000 a year for the last 20 years as a hospital nurse; the defendant is 45 years old, and his only other asset is $25,000 in a retirement account; the defendant bought the entire property five years ago for $150,000; he inherited $100,000 of that amount from his parents, and the remaining $50,000 came from savings; the 20 marijuana plants had a market value of $450,000; the defendant grew the marijuana for personal use, and also gave marijuana to friends and acquaintances who suffer from illnesses, including cancer, glaucoma, and HIV/ AIDS. The maximum statutory sentence for the defendant's crime was five years in prison and a $100,000 fine.

Does the forfeiture violate the Eighth Amendment? Why or why not? If there is an Eighth Amendment violation, what level of forfeiture would pass constitutional muster?

[C]   THIRD-PARTY INTERESTS

Issues relating to ownership interests of potentially innocent third parties — that is, those who are not the suspected wrongdoers — frequently arise in civil forfeitures, where there is no requirement that the property owner be convicted of or even charged with a crime. Criminal forfeitures, on the other hand, *do* depend upon the determination of the defendant's guilt before the defendant's property can be seized or forfeited. People other than the defendant may also have an interest in the potentially forfeitable property, however. The following cases deal with these "third party" interests.

[1]   Civil Forfeitures

NOTE ON UNITED STATES v. 92 BUENA VISTA AVENUE

Civil forfeiture statutes provide that title to forfeitable property "vests" with the federal government at the time that the underlying crime occurs. *See* 21 U.S.C. § 881(h). Federal forfeiture statutes provide, however, that property belonging to innocent third parties is not forfeitable. Are these provisions reconcilable? In other words, how could an innocent property owner retain title to property that already belongs to the government?

The United States Supreme Court confronted this issue in *United States v. 92 Buena Vista Avenue,* 507 U.S. 111 (1993). In *Buena Vista*, the third party claimant purchased her home with cash generated from drug sales. Even though the claimant asserted that she did not know the origin of the cash, the government sought forfeiture of the home. The government argued that the claimant was not the owner of the house because title vested with the government at the moment the house was purchased with drug money. *Id.* at 124. The Court rejected the government's argument, holding that title does not pass to the government until a court enters a forfeiture order and that a third party may assert an innocent owner defense to forfeiture.

As discussed in the notes below, this holding had the effect of encouraging those who possessed proceeds of illegal activity to transfer those proceeds to "innocent," unknowing third parties in order to avoid forfeiture. In response, Congress amended the innocent owner provisions, severely limiting third parties' ability to assert innocent ownership as to property acquired *after* the illegal activity.

NOTES AND QUESTIONS

1. *A uniform innocent owner defense.* Prior to the passage of CAFRA, federal civil forfeiture statutes varied widely in the degree to which they provided an innocent ownership defense. CAFRA provides an innocent owner defense applicable to all federal civil forfeitures. 18 U.S.C. § 983(d).

2. *Property owned at the time of the illegal activity.* With respect to property owned at the time of the illegal activity, under CAFRA, the third party claimant has the burden of proving by a preponderance of the evidence that the claimant

> (i) did not know of the conduct giving rise to forfeiture; or

> (ii) upon learning of the conduct giving rise to the forfeiture, did all that reasonably could be expected under the circumstances to terminate such use of the property.

The statute provides examples of the latter, including giving timely notice to law enforcement of the illegal activity, or revoking or attempting to revoke permission for the wrongdoer to use the property. Is the defense too narrow? Too broad? Why?

3. *Property acquired after the illegal activity.*

a. *The bone fide purchaser or seller requirement.* After the *92 Buena Vista Avenue* decision, those who possessed proceeds from criminal activity began to transfer property to family members to avoid potential forfeiture. In an attempt to deal with this practice, CAFRA limits third-party "innocent owner" claims in situations where the third party acquired the property interest *after* the conduct giving rise to forfeiture took place. In such a circumstance, the third party must show (1) that the claimant was "a bona fide purchaser or seller for value (including a purchaser or seller of goods or services for value)," and (2) that the claimant "did not know and was reasonably without cause to believe that the property was subject to forfeiture."

b. *The exclusion for primary residences.* In an attempt to avoid overly harsh results from the foregoing provision, CAFRA also provides that:

> An otherwise valid claim . . . shall not be denied on the ground that the claimant gave nothing of value in exchange for the property if —

> (i) the property is the *primary residence* of the claimant;

(ii) depriving the claimant of the property would deprive the claimant of the *means to maintain reasonable shelter* in the community for the claimant and all dependents residing with the claimant;

(iii) the property *is not, and is not traceable to, the proceeds of any criminal offense*; and

(iv) the claimant acquired his or her interest in the property through *marriage, divorce, or legal separation*, or the claimant was *the spouse or legal dependent of a person whose death resulted in the transfer of the property to the claimant* through inheritance or probate, except that the court shall limit the value of any real property interest for which innocent ownership is recognized under this subparagraph to the value necessary to maintain reasonable shelter in the community for such claimant and all dependents residing with the claimant. . . .

18 U.S.C. § 983(d)(3)(B)(i) (emphasis added). This exclusion only provides to property used to facilitate a criminal offense, and does not apply to property purchased with proceeds from illegal activity. Also note that this exclusion does not apply to criminal forfeitures under the narcotics laws, which requires any third-party claimant to be a bona fide purchaser for value. *See* 21 U.S.C. § 853(n)(6)(B).

What would have been the result in *92 Buena Vista Avenue* under CAFRA? Is this provision unnecessarily limited? What competing policy concerns are at issue? For a history and analysis of this section of CAFRA, see Stefan D. Cassella, *The Uniform Innocent Owner Defense to Civil Asset Forfeiture: The Civil Asset Forfeiture Reform Act of 2000 Creates a Uniform Innocent Owner Defense to Most Civil Forfeiture Cases Filed by the Federal Government*, 89 Ky. L.J. 653 (2001).

In *92 Buena Vista Avenue*, the Supreme Court interpreted a federal statute that contained an "innocent owner" provision. After CAFRA, all federal civil forfeiture statutes are subject to such a provision. As seen above, however, the federal innocent owner defense is subject to substantial limitations. Further, many state civil forfeiture statutes contained no innocent owner defenses at all. Does a third party have a constitutional right to an innocent owner defense? That is the issue in the case that follows.

BENNIS v. MICHIGAN
516 U.S. 442 (1996)

CHIEF JUSTICE REHNQUIST delivered the opinion of the Court.

Petitioner was a joint owner, with her husband, of an automobile in which her husband engaged in sexual activity with a prostitute. A Michigan court ordered the automobile forfeited as a public nuisance, with no offset for her interest, notwithstanding her lack of knowledge of her husband's activity. We hold that the Michigan court order did not offend the Due Process Clause of the Fourteenth Amendment or the Takings Clause of the Fifth Amendment.

Detroit police arrested John Bennis after observing him engaged in a sexual act with a prostitute in the automobile while it was parked on a Detroit city street. Bennis was convicted of gross indecency. The State then sued both Bennis and his wife, petitioner Tina B. Bennis, to have the car declared a public nuisance and abated as such under Sections 600.3801² and 600.3825³ of Michigan's Compiled Laws.

Petitioner defended against the abatement of her interest in the car on the ground that, when she entrusted her husband to use the car, she did not know that he would use it to violate Michigan's indecency law. The Wayne County Circuit Court rejected this argument, declared the car a public nuisance, and ordered the car's abatement. In reaching this disposition, the trial court judge recognized the remedial discretion he had under Michigan's case law. He took into account the couple's ownership of "another automobile," so they would not be left "without transportation." He also mentioned his authority to order the payment of one-half of the sale proceeds, after the deduction of costs, to "the innocent co-title holder." He declined to order such a division of sale proceeds in this case because of the age and value of the car (an 11-year-old Pontiac sedan recently purchased by John and Tina Bennis for $600); he commented in this regard: "[T]here's practically nothing left minus costs in a situation such as this."

The gravamen of petitioner's due process claim is not that she was denied notice or an opportunity to contest the abatement of her car; she was accorded both. Rather, she claims she was entitled to contest the abatement by showing she did not know her husband would use it to violate Michigan's indecency law. But a long and unbroken line of cases holds that an owner's interest in property may be forfeited by reason of the use to which the property is put even though the owner did not know that it was to be put to such use.

In *Calero-Toledo v. Pearson Yacht Leasing Co.*, 416 U.S. 663 (1974), the most recent decision on point, the Court concluded that "the innocence of the owner of property subject to forfeiture has almost uniformly been rejected as a defense."

Petitioner relies on a passage from *Calero-Toledo*, that "it would be difficult to reject the constitutional claim of . . . an owner who proved not only that he was uninvolved in and unaware of the wrongful activity, but also that he had done all that reasonably could be expected to prevent the proscribed use of his property."

---

² Section 600.3801 states in pertinent part:

> Any building, vehicle, boat, aircraft, or place used for the purpose of lewdness, assignation or prostitution or gambling, or used by, or kept for the use of prostitutes or other disorderly persons, . . . is declared a nuisance, . . . and all . . . nuisances shall be enjoined and abated as provided in this act and as provided in the court rules.

> Any person or his or her servant, agent, or employee who owns, leases, conducts, or maintains any building, vehicle, or place used for any of the purposes or acts set forth in this section is guilty of a nuisance.

³ Section 600.3825 states in pertinent part:

> (1) Order of abatement. If the existence of the nuisance is established in an action as provided in this chapter, an order of abatement shall be entered as a part of the judgment in the case, which order shall direct the removal from the building or place of all furniture, fixtures and contents therein and shall direct the sale thereof in the manner provided for the sale of chattels under execution. . . .

> (2) Vehicles, sale. Any vehicle, boat, or aircraft found by the court to be a nuisance within the meaning of this chapter, is subject to the same order and judgment as any furniture, fixtures and contents as herein provided.

> (3) Sale of personalty, costs, liens, balance to state treasurer. Upon the sale of any furniture, fixtures, contents, vehicle, boat or aircraft as provided in this section, the officer executing the order of the court shall, after deducting the expenses of keeping such property and costs of such sale, pay all liens according to their priorities . . . , and shall pay the balance to the state treasurer to be credited to the general fund of the state. . . .

416 U.S. at 689. But she concedes that this comment was *obiter dictum.* And the *holding* of *Calero-Toledo* on this point was that the interest of a yacht rental company in one of its leased yachts could be forfeited because of its use for transportation of controlled substances, even though the company was "in no way . . . involved in the criminal enterprise carried on by [the] lessee" and "had no knowledge that its property was being used in connection with or in violation of [Puerto Rican Law]." 416 U.S. at 668. Petitioner has made no showing beyond that here.

[Petitioner] argues that our holding in *Austin v. United States,* 509 U.S. 602 (1993), that the Excessive Fines Clause limits the scope of civil forfeiture judgments, "would be difficult to reconcile with any rule allowing truly innocent persons to be punished by civil forfeiture."

Forfeiture of property prevents illegal uses "both by preventing further illicit use of the [property] and by imposing an economic penalty, thereby rendering illegal behavior unprofitable." *Calero-Toledo, supra* at 687.

Petitioner also claims that the forfeiture in this case was a taking of private property for public use in violation of the Takings Clause of the Fifth Amendment, made applicable to the States by the Fourteenth Amendment. But if the forfeiture proceeding here in question did not violate the Fourteenth Amendment, the property in the automobile was transferred by virtue of that proceeding from petitioner to the State. The government may not be required to compensate an owner for property which it has already lawfully acquired under the exercise of governmental authority other than the power of eminent domain.

The State here sought to deter illegal activity that contributes to neighborhood deterioration and unsafe streets. The Bennis automobile, it is conceded, facilitated and was used in criminal activity. Both the trial court and the Michigan Supreme Court followed our longstanding practice, and the judgment of the Supreme Court of Michigan is therefore

Affirmed.

JUSTICE THOMAS, concurring.

* * *

This case is ultimately a reminder that the Federal Constitution does not prohibit everything that is intensely undesirable. . . .

The limits on *what* property can be forfeited as a result of what wrongdoing — for example, what it means to "use" property in crime for purposes of forfeiture law — are not clear to me. Those limits, whatever they may be, become especially significant when they are the sole restrictions on the state's ability to take property from those it merely suspects, or does not even suspect, of colluding in crime. It thus seems appropriate, where a constitutional challenge by an innocent owner is concerned, to apply those limits rather strictly, adhering to historical standards for determining whether specific property is an "instrumentality" of crime.

In this case, the trial judge apparently found that the sales price of the car would not exceed by much the "costs" to be deducted from the sale; and he took that fact into account in determining how to dispose of the proceeds of the sale of the car. The state statute has labeled the car a "nuisance" and authorized a procedure for preventing the risk of continued criminal use of it by Mr. Bennis (forfeiture and sale); under a different statutory regime, the State might have authorized the destruction of the car instead, and the State would have had a plausible argument that the order for destruction was "remedial" and thus noncompensable. That it chose to order the car sold, with virtually nothing left over for the State after "costs," may not change the "remedial" character of the State's action substantially. And if the forfeiture of the car here (and the State's refusal to remit any share of the proceeds from its sale to Mrs. Bennis) can appropriately be characterized as "remedial" action, then the more severe problems involved in punishing someone not found to have engaged in wrongdoing of any kind do not arise. . . .

JUSTICE GINSBURG, concurring.

I join the opinion of the Court and highlight features of the case key to my judgment.

The dissenting opinions target a law scarcely resembling Michigan's "red light abatement" prescription, as interpreted by the State's courts. First, it bears emphasis that the car in question belonged to John Bennis as much as it did to Tina Bennis. At all times he had her consent to use the car, just as she had his. And it is uncontested that Michigan may forfeit the vehicle itself. The sole question, then, is whether Tina Bennis is entitled not to the car, but to a portion of the proceeds (if any there be after deduction of police, prosecutorial, and court costs) as a matter of constitutional right.

Second, it was "critical" to the judgment of the Michigan Supreme Court that the nuisance abatement proceeding is an "equitable action." That means the State's Supreme Court stands ready to police exorbitant applications of the statute. It shows no respect for Michigan's high court to attribute to its members tolerance of, or insensitivity to, inequitable administration of an "equitable action."

Nor is it fair to charge the trial court with "blatant unfairness" in the case at hand. That court declined to order a division of sale proceeds, as the trial judge took pains to explain, for two practical reasons: the Bennises have "another automobile," and the age and value of the forfeited car (an 11-year-old Pontiac purchased by John and Tina Bennis for $600) left "practically nothing" to divide after subtraction of costs.

Michigan, in short, has not embarked on an experiment to punish innocent third parties. Nor do we condone any such experiment. Michigan has decided to deter johns from using cars they own (or co-own) to contribute to neighborhood blight, and that abatement endeavor hardly warrants this Court's disapprobation.

JUSTICE STEVENS, with whom JUSTICE SOUTER and JUSTICE BREYER join, dissenting.

For centuries prostitutes have been plying their trade on other people's property. Assignations have occurred in palaces, luxury hotels, cruise ships, college dormitories, truck stops, back alleys and back seats. A profession of this vintage has provided governments with countless opportunities to use novel weapons to curtail its abuses. As far as I am aware, however, it was not until 1988 that any State decided to experiment with the punishment of innocent third parties by confiscating property in which, or on which, a single transaction with a prostitute has been consummated.

The logic of the Court's analysis would permit the States to exercise virtually unbridled power to confiscate vast amounts of property where professional criminals have engaged in illegal acts. Some airline passengers have marijuana cigarettes in their luggage; some hotel guests are thieves; some spectators at professional sports events carry concealed weapons; and some hitchhikers are prostitutes. The State surely may impose strict obligations on the owners of airlines, hotels, stadiums, and vehicles to exercise a high degree of care to prevent others from making illegal use of their property, but neither logic nor history supports the Court's apparent assumption that their complete innocence imposes no constitutional impediment to the seizure of their property simply because it provided the locus for a criminal transaction. . . .

Petitioner has done nothing that warrants punishment. She cannot be accused of negligence or of any other dereliction in allowing her husband to use the car for the wholly legitimate purpose of transporting himself to and from his job. She affirmatively alleged and proved that she is not in any way responsible for the conduct that gave rise to the seizure. If anything, she was a *victim* of that conduct. In my opinion, these facts establish that the seizure constituted an arbitrary deprivation of property without due process of law. . . .

I therefore respectfully dissent.

JUSTICE KENNEDY, dissenting.

This forfeiture cannot meet the requirements of due process. Nothing in the rationale of the Michigan Supreme Court indicates that the forfeiture turned on the negligence or complicity of petitioner, or a presumption thereof, and nothing supports the suggestion that the value of her co-ownership is so insignificant as to be beneath the law's protection.

For these reasons, and with all respect, I dissent.

NOTES AND QUESTIONS

1. *CAFRA and state forfeitures.* As discussed above, CAFRA provides a uniform innocent owner defense for federal civil forfeitures. Would Ms. Bennis likely have prevailed under CAFRA? Why or why not? Do you need additional facts in order to answer this question? Many states, like Michigan, have forfeiture statutes that do not provide any innocent owner defenses. Should such a defense be constitutionally compelled? Was the outcome in this case fair? Why or why not?

2. *The Court's historical analysis.* How did the Court in *Bennis* characterize the historical significance of a property owner's innocence in connection with in rem forfeitures? Recall that in *Austin*, the majority claimed that in rem forfeitures historically were based upon the owner's culpability. The Court appeared to retreat from this view in both *Bajakajian* and in *Bennis*. What explains this apparent inconsistency? What is the significance for the way the Court is likely to treat constitutional challenges to in rem forfeitures in the future?

3. *The import of* Bennis. Once again, the Court in *Bennis* split by the narrowest of margins. The concurring Justices either seem to place limitations on the grounds for their concurrences, or to question the result itself. Do these concurrences mean that an innocent owner defense might be constitutionally compelled in circumstances different from those in *Bennis*? If so, what facts might produce a different result?

PROBLEM

20-3. Acting on an anonymous tip, a United States customs official stopped and questioned Linda as she was about to board her flight at Los Angeles International Airport en route to visit her sister in London, England. The official advised Linda of the relevant currency reporting requirements, and told her that she must declare any currency, travelers' checks, and other negotiable monetary instruments totaling more than $10,000.00. Linda stated that she was carrying $9,000.00 in cash. The customs official offered Linda the opportunity to amend her declaration, and specifically advised her of the need to report the transportation of monetary instruments on behalf of others. Linda, however, declined this invitation, and again stated that she was carrying only $9,000.00 in cash. Upon searching Linda's purse, Clark discovered $8,900 in cash, along with six negotiable checks totaling nearly $200,000.

Linda stated that the negotiable checks were the proceeds of a sale of certain land in Florida. These checks were made out to, and appeared to be endorsed by, Linda's husband, Armando. According to the customs official, Linda claimed that she had forged the signatures on these checks, and that Armando was not aware that she had these checks in her possession or that she planned to take them out of the country.

Customs agents then telephoned Armando. Armando contradicted his wife on a number of points, stating that he had, in fact, signed the checks bearing his name, and that he was aware that his wife had these checks in her possession as she left the United States. According to Armando, his wife kept the checks so that he would not, in her absence and without her final approval, invest these funds in the purchase of another parcel of property in Florida.

Linda was charged with violating the reporting requirements of 31 U.S.C. § 5316 and making false statements to the customs official. The government also seeks civil forfeiture of the cash and negotiable checks under 18 U.S.C. § 981(a)(1)(A). The cash and checks are the joint property of Linda and Armando.

Armando and Linda both assert an innocent owner defense. Will either likely succeed? Why or why not?

[2] Criminal Forfeitures

As noted above, under Federal Rule of Criminal Procedure 32.2, the court is required to promptly enter a preliminary forfeiture order once the "requisite nexus between the property and the offense" has been established, regardless of the property interests of those other than the defendant. Once that nexus has been established, the order may be entered *regardless* of any such existing third-party interests. After such order has been entered, however, Rule 32.2(b)(3) authorizes the Attorney General "to commence proceedings that comply with any statutes governing third-party rights." Thus, the statutes allow for protection of third-party interests, but only after the criminal forfeiture proceeding has been concluded. As discussed below, some courts allow third parties to intervene prior to the conclusion of the case.

NOTE ON *UNITED STATES V. REGAN*

In *United States v. Regan*, 858 F.2d 115 (2d Cir. 1988), the first RICO case to be brought against a major securities firm, the government alleged that the defendant/executives of Princeton/Newport Partners, L.P. ("PNP") violated RICO by operating several companies, owned and controlled by PNP, through a pattern of racketeering activity. The trial judge entered an order restraining PNP from disposing of its assets, even though PNP was not a defendant in the criminal RICO case. The court entered this order to ensure that the companies' assets were not dissipated and that the assets would thus be available for forfeiture.

PNP appealed the restraining order, arguing that it was improper to apply such an order to an unindicted third party. The Second Circuit rejected PNP's argument. The court reasoned that an order restraining third-party assets may be imposed under § 1963(d)(1), which allows the court to "take any other action to preserve the availability of property." The court then considered the specifics of the order imposed in the case. The court held that there were less burdensome alternatives to the restraining order, such as requiring PNP to post a bond in the amount of the defendants' forfeitable interests or ordering restraint of a defendant's own substitute assets. The court remanded, directing the trial court to determine whether a less onerous restraint could be imposed.

Shortly after the *Regan* decision, PNP filed for bankruptcy and ceased to exist. Can you imagine why this happened? Note that the amount ultimately ordered forfeited in the case was a small fraction of the amount that the government originally sought to obtain control over. Was prosecutorial discretion wisely exercised in this case? For an example of another highly-publicized criminal RICO case in which third-party interests were at issue, see *United States v. BCCI Holdings (Luxembourg)*, S.A., 69 F. Supp. 2d 36 (D.D.C. 1999).

[D] THE SIXTH AMENDMENT

Recall that, in a criminal case, the government may obtain an order freezing a defendant's assets prior to trial in order to preserve the assets for possible forfeiture. Do the criminal forfeiture statutes allow the government to obtain such an order even where the defendant needs the frozen property to pay attorneys' fees? Even if so, would such a result violate the Sixth Amendment's right to counsel?

As to the statutory construction issue, the Supreme Court held five-to-four in *United States v. Monsanto*, 491 U.S. 600, 606 (1989), that the criminal forfeiture provisions of the federal narcotics laws applied to property even when the defendant intended to use that property to pay attorney's fees. The Court stated that the statute's plain meaning requires that "all assets falling within its scope . . . be forfeited upon conviction, with no exception existing for the assets used to pay attorney's fees — or anything else, for that matter." The Court turned to the constitutional issue in the companion case set forth below.

CAPLIN & DRYSDALE v. UNITED STATES
491 U.S. 617 (1989)

JUSTICE WHITE delivered the opinion of the Court.

A.

Petitioner's first claim is that the forfeiture law makes impossible, or at least impermissibly burdens, a defendant's right "to select and be represented by one's preferred attorney." *Wheat v. United States*, 486 U.S. 153, 159 (1988). Petitioner does not, nor could it defensibly do so, assert that impecunious defendants have a Sixth Amendment right to choose their counsel. The Amendment guarantees defendants in criminal cases the right to adequate representation, but those who do not have the means to hire their own lawyers have no cognizable complaint so long as they are adequately represented by attorneys appointed by the courts. "[A] defendant may not insist on representation by an attorney he cannot afford." *Wheat, supra* at 159. Petitioner does not dispute these propositions. Nor does the Government deny that the Sixth Amendment guarantees a defendant the right to be represented by an otherwise qualified attorney whom that defendant can afford to hire, or who is willing to represent the defendant even though he is without funds. Applying these principles to the statute in question here, we observe that nothing in § 853 prevents a defendant from hiring the attorney of his choice, or disqualifies any attorney from serving as a defendant's counsel. Thus, unlike *Wheat*, this case does not involve a situation where the Government has asked a court to prevent a defendant's chosen counsel from representing the accused. Instead, petitioner urges that a violation of the Sixth Amendment arises here because of the forfeiture, at the instance of the Government, of assets that defendants intend to use to pay their attorneys.

Even in this sense, of course, the burden the forfeiture law imposes on a criminal defendant is limited. The forfeiture statute does not prevent a defendant who has nonforfeitable assets from retaining any attorney of his choosing. Nor is it necessarily the case that a defendant who possesses nothing but assets the Government seeks to have forfeited will be prevented from retaining counsel of choice. Defendants like Reckmeyer may be able to find lawyers willing to represent them, hoping that their fees will be paid in the event of acquittal, or via some other means that a defendant might come by in the future. The burden placed on defendants by the forfeiture law is therefore a limited one.

Nonetheless, there will be cases where a defendant will be unable to retain the attorney of his choice, when that defendant would have been able to hire that lawyer if he had access to forfeitable assets, and if there was no risk that fees paid by the defendant to his counsel would later be recouped under § 853(c). It is in these cases, petitioner argues, that the Sixth Amendment puts limits on the forfeiture statute.

This submission is untenable. Whatever the full extent of the Sixth Amendment's protection of one's right to retain counsel of his choosing, that protection does not go beyond "the individual's right to spend his own money to obtain the advice and assistance of . . . counsel." *Walters' v. National Assn. of Radiation Survivors*, 473 U.S. 305, 370 (1985) (Stevens, J., dissenting). A defendant has no Sixth Amendment right to spend another person's money for services rendered by an attorney, even if those funds are the only way that that defendant will be able to retain the attorney of his choice. A robbery suspect, for example, has no Sixth Amendment right to use funds he has stolen from a bank to retain an attorney to defend him if he is apprehended. The money, though in his possession, is not rightfully his; the Government does not violate the Sixth Amendment if it seizes the robbery proceeds and refuses to permit the defendant to use them to pay for his defense. "[N]o lawyer, in any case, . . . has the right to . . . accept stolen property, or . . . ransom money, in payment of a fee. . . . The privilege to practice law is not a license to steal." *Laska v. United States*, 82 F.2d 672, 677 (10th Cir. 1936). . . .

There is no constitutional principle that gives one person the right to give another's property to a third party, even where the person seeking to complete the exchange wishes to do so in order to exercise a constitutionally protected right. While petitioner and its supporting *amici* attempt to distinguish between the expenditure of forfeitable assets to exercise one's Sixth Amendment rights, and expenditures in the pursuit of other constitutionally protected freedoms, *see, e.g.,* Brief for American Bar Association as *Amicus Curiae* 6, there is no such distinction between, or hierarchy among, constitutional rights. If defendants have a right to spend forfeitable assets on attorney's fees, why not on exercises of the right to speak, practice one's religion, or travel? The full exercise of these rights, too, depends in part on one's financial wherewithal; and forfeiture, or even the threat of forfeiture, may similarly prevent a defendant from enjoying these rights as fully as he might otherwise. Nonetheless, we are not about to recognize an antiforfeiture exception for the exercise of each such right; nor does one exist for the exercise of Sixth Amendment rights. . . .

B.

Petitioner's second constitutional claim is that the forfeiture statute is invalid under the Due Process Clause of the Fifth Amendment because it permits the Government to upset the "balance of forces between the accused and his accuser." *Wardius v. Oregon*, 412 U.S. 470 (1973).

Forfeiture provisions are powerful weapons in the war on crime; like any such weapons, their impact can be devastating when used unjustly. But due process claims alleging such abuses are cognizable only in specific cases of prosecutorial misconduct (and petitioner has made no such allegation here) or when directed to a rule that is inherently unconstitutional. Petitioner's claim — that the power available to prosecutors under the statute *could* be abused — proves too much, for many tools available to prosecutors can be misused in a way that violates the rights of innocent persons. . . .

The Constitution does not forbid the imposition of an otherwise permissible criminal sanction, such as forfeiture, merely because in some cases prosecutors may abuse the processes available to them, *e.g.,* by attempting to impose them on persons who should not be subjected to that punishment. Cases involving particular abuses can be dealt with individually by the lower courts, when (and if) any such cases arise.

JUSTICE BLACKMUN, with whom JUSTICE BRENNAN, JUSTICE MARSHALL, and JUSTICE STEVENS join, dissenting.

Those jurists who have held forth against the result the majority reaches in these cases have been guided by one core insight: that it is unseemly and unjust for the Government to beggar those it prosecutes in order to disable their defense at trial.

* * *

The right to retain private counsel serves to foster the trust between attorney and client that is necessary for the attorney to be a truly effective advocate. Not only are decisions crucial to the defendant's liberty placed in counsel's hands, but the defendant's perception of the fairness of the process, and his willingness to acquiesce in its results, depend upon his confidence in his counsel's dedication, loyalty, and ability. When the Government insists upon the right to choose the defendant's counsel for him, that relationship of trust is undermined: counsel is too readily perceived as the Government's agent rather than his own. . . .

The right to retain private counsel also serves to assure some modicum of equality between the Government and those it chooses to prosecute. The Government can be expected to "spend vast sums of money . . . to try defendants accused of crime," *Gideon v. Wainwright*, 372 U.S. at 344, and of course will devote greater resources to complex cases in which the punitive stakes are high. Precisely for this reason, "there are few defendants charged with crime, few indeed, who fail to hire the best lawyers they can get to prepare and present their defenses." *Id.* But when the Government provides for appointed counsel, there is no guarantee that levels of compensation and staffing will be even average. Where cases are complex, trials long, and stakes high, that problem is exacerbated. "Despite the legal profession's commitment to *pro bono* work," *United States v. Bassett*, 632 F. Supp. 1308, 1316 (D. Md. 1986), even the best intentioned of attorneys may have no choice but to decline the task of representing defendants in cases for which they will not receive adequate compensation. Over the long haul, the result of lowered compensation levels will be that talented attorneys will "decline to enter criminal practice- . . . . This exodus of talented attorneys could devastate the criminal defense bar." Winick, *Forfeiture of Attorneys' Fees under RICO and CCE and the Right to Counsel of Choice: The Constitutional Dilemma and How to Avoid It*, 43 U. Miami L. Rev. 765, 781 (1989). Without the defendant's right to retain private counsel, the Government too readily could defeat its adversaries simply by outspending them. . . .

In sum, our chosen system of criminal justice is built upon a truly equal and adversarial presentation of the case, and upon the trust that can exist only when counsel is independent of the Government. Without the right, reasonably exercised, to counsel of choice, the effectiveness of that system is imperiled.

Had it been Congress' express aim to undermine the adversary system as we know it, it could hardly have found a better engine of destruction than attorney's-fee forfeiture. The main effect of forfeitures under the Act, of course, will be to deny the defendant the right to retain counsel, and therefore the right to have his defense designed and presented by an attorney he has chosen and trusts. If the Government restrains the defendant's assets before trial, private counsel will be unwilling to continue, or to take on, the defense. Even if no restraining order is entered, the possibility of forfeiture after conviction will itself substantially diminish the likelihood that private counsel will agree to take the case. The "message [to private counsel] is 'Do not represent this defendant or you will lose your fee.' That being the kind of message lawyers are likely to take seriously, the defendant will find it difficult or impossible to secure representation." *United States v. Badalamenti*, 614 F. Supp. at 196.

The resulting relationship between the defendant and his court-appointed counsel will likely begin in distrust, and be exacerbated to the extent that the defendant perceives his new-found "indigency" as a form of punishment imposed by the Government in order to weaken his defense. If the defendant had been represented by private counsel earlier in the proceedings, the defendant's sense that the Government has stripped him of his defenses will be sharpened by the concreteness of his loss. Appointed counsel may be inexperienced and undercompensated and, for that reason, may not have adequate opportunity or resources to deal with the special problems presented by what is likely to be a complex trial. The already scarce resources of a public defender's office will be stretched to the limit. Facing a lengthy trial against a better armed adversary, the temptation to recommend a guilty plea will be great. The result, if the defendant is convicted, will be a sense, often well grounded, that justice was not done.

Perhaps most troubling is the fact that forfeiture statutes place the Government in the position to exercise an intolerable degree of power over any private attorney who takes on the task of representing a defendant in a forfeiture case. The decision whether to seek a restraining order rests with the prosecution, as does the decision whether to waive forfeiture upon a plea of guilty or a conviction at trial. The Government will be ever tempted to use the forfeiture weapon against a defense attorney who is particularly talented or aggressive on the client's behalf — the attorney who is better than what, in the Government's view, the defendant deserves. The specter of the Government's selectively excluding only the most talented defense counsel is a serious threat to the equality of forces necessary for the adversarial system to perform at its best. An attorney whose fees are potentially subject to forfeiture will be forced to operate in an environment in which the Government is not only the defendant's adversary, but also his own.

The long-term effects of the fee-forfeiture practice will be to decimate the private criminal-defense bar. As the use of the forfeiture mechanism expands to new categories of federal crimes and spreads to the States, only one class of defendants will be free routinely to retain private counsel: the affluent defendant accused of a crime that generates no economic gain. As the number of private clients diminishes, only the most idealistic and the least skilled of young lawyers will be attracted to the field, while the remainder seek greener pastures elsewhere.

In short, attorney's-fee forfeiture substantially undermines every interest served by the Sixth Amendment right to chose counsel, on the individual and institutional levels, over the short term and the long haul.

NOTES AND QUESTIONS

1. *The policy debate.* The majority stated that, under the relation-back doctrine, the forfeitable property belongs to the government and that a wrongdoer (such as a robber) has no right to use ill-gotten property. The dissent, on the other hand, concluded in harsh language that "it is unseemly and unjust for the government to beggar those it prosecutes in order to disable their defense at trial." Which side has the better of the argument? Does the dissent persuasively argue that the result does not bode well for effective representation of criminal defendants? Why or why not?

2. *Procedural protections.* The majority specifically declined to determine whether a judicial hearing must be held before the government can assume control of the defendant's property before trial in circumstances where the property is necessary to pay for defense counsel's fees. What are the competing concerns in such a circumstance? What is the appropriate resolution?

3. *The split on the Supreme Court.* As seen throughout this text, many of the most important white collar cases have been decided by the barest of majorities. Nowhere is this more true than in the context of forfeitures. Why should this be so?

[E]   PROCEDURAL DUE PROCESS

Recall that both civil and criminal forfeiture statutes allow for the government to assume control of the property prior to the civil forfeiture trial or the criminal trial of the defendant. When evaluating the constitutionality of such pre-trial restraints, federal courts have struggled to balance the government's need to maintain the property for forfeiture and the defendant's due process rights.

[1]   Restraints on Real Property

Note on *James Daniel Good Real Property*

In what circumstances may the government seize property prior to a trial without notice or a hearing? In *Calero-Toledo v. Pearson Yacht Leasing Co.*, 416 U.S. 663, 680 (1974), a civil forfeiture case, the Court approved such seizures in "extraordinary" circumstances. Such circumstances may exist, for example, when there is a risk that the property could be hidden or destroyed. *Id.*

In 1993, the Supreme Court addressed the issue of *ex parte* seizures of *real* property in *United States v. James Daniel Good Real Property*, 510 U.S. 43 (1993).

In *James Daniel Good Real Property*, the government sought forfeiture of the defendant's home and land because the property had been used to violate the federal drug laws. Without notice or a hearing, a federal magistrate found probable cause that the property was subject to forfeiture under § 881(a)(7). The magistrate issued a warrant of arrest in rem that authorized the seizure of the property. By a five-to-four majority, the Court found that the owner's due process rights had been violated. The Court stated that notice and a hearing are generally required by due process, acknowledging that such notice and hearing may not be required in exceptional circumstances. Such circumstances are not present, the Court held, with respect to real property, which cannot be moved or hidden.

Congress codified this decision in CAFRA, 18 U.S.C. § 985, which provides in part that "real property that is the subject of a civil forfeiture action shall not be seized before entry of an order of forfeiture" pursuant to hearing, and that the government must notify the property owner before seeking such an order. The statute provides an exception to the notice and hearing requirement where the court "makes an *ex parte* determination that there is probable cause for the forfeiture and that there are exigent circumstances that permit the Government to seize the property without prior notice and an opportunity for the property owner to be heard. . . . [T]o establish exigent circumstances, the Government shall show that less restrictive measures such as a *lis pendens*, restraining order, or bond would not suffice to protect the Government's interests in preventing the sale, destruction, or continued unlawful use of the real property."

NOTES AND QUESTIONS

Why did Congress provide special protections for seizures of real property? Are such protections justified? What sort of "exigent circumstances" might warrant seizure of real property without notice and a hearing?

[2] Pre-Trial Seizures and Attorneys' Fees

As the next case shows, the statutes allowing for pre-trial seizures of a criminal defendant's property raise important constitutional and tactical issues. As you read the case, carefully identify these issues.

UNITED STATES v. E-GOLD, LTD
521 F.3d 411 (D.C. Cir. 2008)

SENTELLE, CHIEF JUDGE:

I. BACKGROUND

On April 24, 2007, a grand jury indicted [the corporate and individual defendants]. The indictment alleged one count of conspiracy to operate an unlicensed money transmitting business in violation of 18 U.S.C. § 371, two counts of operation of an unlicensed money transmitting business, and one count of money transmitting without a license. On April 25, 2007, while the indictment remained sealed, the United States filed an *ex parte* application and a supporting affidavit with the United States District Court seeking to seize for forfeiture to the United States property held in two E-Gold digital currency accounts, one in the name of E-Gold and the other of GSR. The application alleged that the accounts constituted "property involved in an unlicensed money transmitting business" in violation of 18 U.S.C. § 1960. The district court properly issued the seizure warrant upon a finding that "there is probable cause to believe that the property at issue . . . may become worthless property for purposes of its forfeitures . . . and that, at this time, conversion of property valued as E-Gold into gold or funds denominated as United States currency . . . is reasonable and necessary." The court further ordered GSR to "exchange/convert the E-Gold held in the E-Gold account[s] at issue into gold or into the funds denominated as United States currency . . . within twenty-four (24) hours of the execution of this warrant and to provide that gold or currency through the federal law enforcement officers serving the warrant." The post-indictment restraining order also imposed restrictions on further transactions by the defendants. The government obtained $1,481,976.38 from appellants under the seizure warrant.

Appellants move to vacate the civil seizure warrant and modify the restraining order to permit, *inter alia*, the use of the seized assets for the purpose of retaining counsel in defense of the action. In their motion, appellants sought an evidentiary hearing as to the propriety of the seizure of assets, and specifically as to the existence of probable cause to believe that the defendants had committed an offense warranting the issuance of the seizure warrant and restraining order. In a bench ruling, the district court denied appellants' motion, and in so doing, ruled the defendants were not entitled to a post-seizure evidentiary hearing.

Appellants filed the instant appeal, arguing that the seizure without a post-seizure evidentiary hearing violated their due process rights in violation of the

Fifth Amendment. Appellants further argue the seizure violates the Sixth Amendment's right to counsel because they were unable to afford counsel of their choice without the seized assets. During the pendency of this appeal, a magistrate judge ruled that the individual defendants had made a showing of financial inability to retain counsel and were eligible for appointed counsel . . . .

II. ANALYSIS

To begin with, we repair to first principles. In ascertaining the requirements of the due process clause in affording a hearing to those whose assets are the subject of seizure, we look first to the Supreme Court's declarations in *Mathews v. Eldridge*, 424 U.S. 319 (1976). That case commands that "the fundamental requirement of due process is the opportunity to be heard 'at a meaningful time and in a meaningful manner.'" *Id.* at 333.

In *Mathews v. Eldridge*, the Supreme Court set forth three elements of inquiry which the courts must apply in determining the due process rights of citizens who were subjected to the seizure of their property or other constitutionally protected interests:

> First, the private interest that will be affected by the official action; second, the risk of an erroneous deprivation of such interest through the procedures used, and the probable value, if any, of additional or substitute procedural safeguards; and finally, the Government's interest, including the function involved and the fiscal and administrative burdens that the additional or substitute procedural requirement would entail.

424 U.S. at 335.

We have previously employed the *Mathews v. Eldridge* three-part analysis in determining the constitutional necessity of a post-deprivation hearing to invasions of constitutionally protected interests occurring pretrial where circumstances may compel protective seizure before merits adjudication. We have not, however, applied that analysis to civil seizure under 18 U.S.C. § 1960 or similar statutes. But as we noted above, other circuits have.

In *United States v. Monsanto*, 924 F.2d 1186 (2d Cir.1991), the Second Circuit considered just the question before us on circumstances paralleling those we review. In *Monsanto*, the Second Circuit, en banc, reviewed the case on remand from the Supreme Court's decision in *United States v. Monsanto*, 491 U.S. 600 (1989) [which] left open for the circuit's decision on remand the question "whether the Due Process Clause requires a hearing before a pretrial restraining order can be imposed." *Id.* at 615 n.10. The Second Circuit then determined the question before us in the present case, and we find its reasoning most instructive.

On remand, the en banc court first considered whether notice and a hearing were required before the initial seizure. The Second Circuit held, and we agree, that because the seizure "'operates to remove the assets from the control of the defendant on the claim of the government that it has a higher right to those assets,' *Moya-Gomez*, 860 F.2d at 725," even though the seizure is potentially temporary, the "deprivation of property" is "subject to the constraints of due process." *Id.* at 1192 (quoting *North Georgia Finishing, Inc. v. Di-Chem, Inc.*, 419 U.S. 601, 606 (1975)). Thus, faced with the underlying principle that "[t]he due process clause of the fifth amendment generally requires notice and an opportunity to be heard," a pre-deprivation hearing would normally be in order. *Id.* at 1192. However, the Second Circuit noted, and again we agree, that in " 'extraordinary situations-' . . . notice and a hearing [may] be postponed until after the deprivation." *Id.* (quoting *Fuentes v. Shevin*, 407 U.S. 67, 90(1972)).

The extraordinary circumstances for the postponement of the due process hearing are satisfied where

> [f]irst, . . . the seizure has been directly necessary to secure an important governmental or general public interest. Second, there has been a special need for very prompt action. Third, the State has kept strict control over its monopoly of legitimate force: the person initiating the seizure has been a government official responsible for determining, under the standards of a narrowly drawn statute, that it was necessary and justified in the particular instance.

Id. (quoting *Fuentes*, 407 U.S. at 91).

Like the Second Circuit, we hold that the circumstances giving rise to the seizure of assets upon probable cause that the assets were used in violation of specified criminal statutes meets the "extraordinary circumstances" three-part test for seizure without a predeprivation hearing. . . .

However, this leaves open the question then before the *Monsanto* court and presently before us: "whether a hearing is required *after* the entry of such an order, but before trial." *Id.* at 1193 (emphasis in original).

The *Monsanto* court went on to consider, as we must, the three *Mathews v. Eldridge* factors. That court concluded, and we agree, that the first factor — that is, the private interests to be affected by the official action — weighs particularly heavily. There, as here, "[t]he private interest at stake is not merely a defendant's wish to use his property in whatever manner he sees fit." *Id.* While that interest by itself is of course weighty, it is, as the Second Circuit noted, "augmented by an important liberty interest: the qualified right, under the sixth amendment, to counsel of choice." *Id.* As we noted above, that need is clearly established in the case before us where a magistrate judge has found that the defendants are not financially capable of retaining counsel of choice without the seized property. While the deprivation is nominally temporary, it is "in that respect effectively a permanent one." *Id.* "The defendant needs the attorney *now* if the attorney is to do him any good." *Moya-Gomez*, 860 F.2d at 726 (emphasis in the original).

Therefore, the first *Mathews v. Eldridge* factor weighs heavily in favor of a conclusion that the owners of the seized property are entitled to a post-deprivation pretrial opportunity to be heard. It would seem apparent that a successful showing by defendants at such a hearing provides potential protection against the quasi-temporary but effectively permanent deprivation of assets required by the defendants for an effective exercise of their Sixth Amendment right to counsel.

As did the *Monsanto* court, we must move then to the second *Mathews v. Eldridge* factor: the risk of an erroneous deprivation of a defendant's interest in retaining counsel of choice, and the probable value of procedural alternatives. Based as it is on a grand jury's finding of probable cause, a seizure warrant is the product of an *ex parte* proceeding. The defendants have had no opportunity to be heard.

The inherent risk in allowing the deprivation of a property interest through ex parte proceedings accounts for the general rule that a prior adversary hearing is required, absent special circumstances . . . .

As to the third element of the *Mathews v. Eldridge* inquiry — the government's interest, including the burden to be imposed by a pretrial probable cause hearing — we certainly find weight in favor of the government's position, but not sufficient weight to offset the due process rights of the defendant as established under the totality of the *Mathews v. Eldridge* inquiry. It is true that the grand jury proceeding is not only *ex parte* but subject to orders of secrecy for compelling reasons. Certainly, it is important to protect, *inter alia*, the identity and location of witnesses who might be subject to threat or interference. But it is not necessarily the case that affording indicted defendants a right to be heard before the deprivation of their property rights and liberty interests under the Fifth and Sixth Amendments entails an invasion of grand jury secrecy or an evisceration of the important goals of that secrecy. As the *Monsanto* court noted, the district court, in such a post-indictment pretrial hearing, would need only to require the government to "establish probable cause as to the defendant's guilt and the forfeitability of the specified assets." *Monsanto*, 924 F.2d at 1195. In such an adversary hearing, the court could use limitations on the disclosure of evidence, such as *in camera* hearings and appropriate application of the normal rules of evidence to protect the grand jury proceedings against unwarranted invasion.[4]

Thus, while we recognize the weightiness of the government's concern in grand jury secrecy, we find nothing that outweighs the defendant's constitutional rights to due process and to counsel under the Fifth and Sixth Amendments. We thus join the Second Circuit in holding that defendants have a right to an adversary post-restraint, pretrial hearing for the purpose of establishing whether there was probable cause "as to the defendant[s'] guilt and the forfeitability of the specified assets" needed for a meaningful exercise of their rights to counsel. *Monsanto*, 924 F.2d at 1195.

We note that in addition to the Second Circuit's decision in *Monsanto*, there are several other circuit decisions addressing similar constitutional issues. We join the majority of those circuits in holding that the adversarial hearing sought by the appellants is constitutionally required.

We note that in briefing the government alluded to the proposition which it asserted specifically at oral argument that if a grand jury finding of probable cause is adequate to deprive a person of liberty interests, as it historically has been, then surely it should be sufficient to survive due process examination of the invasion of the "lesser" interest in access to their property. This might perhaps be a more compelling argument if the interest invaded were not only lesser, but included. However, the interests of the defendants in their property stand independent of their interests in their freedom. Defendants deprived of liberty pending trial either by imprisonment or by limitation under bail bond normally have full property rights in whatever they owned before indictment and in many, if not most, cases will retain those interests even if convicted. And they may use such property to retain counsel. Absent criminal statutes of the sort invoked in this case and in others such as *Monsanto*, the indicted but unconvicted defendant remains a citizen free to hold

---

[4] We note that when asked directly at oral argument, the government could not identify any harm to its law enforcement efforts in the Second Circuit that has resulted from the *Monsanto* standard.

property, retain counsel, and indeed to exercise the mass of rights available to other citizens not so indicted. The historic power, indeed the necessary power, of the state to limit liberty interests of those persons as to whom probable cause exists warranting a criminal trial are normally irrelevant to other constitutional or even statutory or common law rights. . . .

Neither the need to assure the presence of the defendant at trial nor any of the other historic reasons recognized by the Supreme Court for the *ex parte* secret nature of the grand jury proceedings compels the deprivation of property rights without due process pending a trial to determine whether the defendant is in fact guilty of the crimes charged and the property properly forfeitable.

It is true that in the due process hearing on the question of the seizure of the defendants' assets, the government risks the premature disclosure of otherwise undiscoverable evidence before trial on the merits. It is also true, however, that at such a hearing the trial court may invoke whatever protections are necessary to protect such evidence. It is further true that the defendant may have access to evidence not presented to the grand jury which the defendant may choose to offer the court in support of the proposition that there is no probable cause supporting the seizure of the assets.

CONCLUSION

In short, we hold that where the government has obtained a seizure warrant depriving defendants of assets pending a trial upon the merits, the constitutional right to due process of law entitles defendants to an opportunity to be heard at least where access to the assets is necessary for an effective exercise of the Sixth Amendment right to counsel. We need not determine, nor do we determine, whether the due process rights of the defendants compel such a hearing when the assets are not necessary to obtaining counsel of choice.

This case is remanded to the district court for further proceedings consistent with this opinion.

NOTES AND QUESTIONS

1. *Pre-seizure hearings.* The court agreed with the district court that the defendants did not have a right to notice and a hearing prior to the initial seizure. Other courts have generally agreed with this conclusion. Why have the courts reached this conclusion? What policy considerations are at play in such circumstances?

2. *Post-seizure hearings.* As the court noted, the circuits are split as to whether a property owner is entitled to a post-seizure hearing. Most courts appear to allow such hearings only where the defendant can show that Sixth Amendment rights are affected and that there is no probable cause for forfeiture.

What are the competing concerns? What constitutional rights are at play in such cases? *See* Ricardo J. Bascuas, *Of Defense Lawyers and Pornographers: Pretrial Asset Seizures and the Fourth Amendment*, 62 U. Miami L. Rev. 1159, 1162–1163 (2008) (reviewing Sixth Amendment challenges and arguing that the Fourth Amendment provides a more appropriate avenue for challenging pre-trial seizures).

3. *The role of the grand jury.* The government argued strongly that a pre-trial hearing would require an inappropriate inquiry into the grand jury proceedings. How did the court respond? Do you agree with its conclusion? Why or why not?

PROBLEMS

20-4. A man, Jim Jarman, and his two small children live in a rent-controlled, one-bedroom apartment in Chicago. Mr. Jarman has a part-time job as a waiter, and barely makes ends meet. Without a rent-controlled apartment, he and his children would not be able to afford housing. Mr. Jarman's younger brother, Sam, is a truck-driver who spends an average of a couple of nights a week sleeping on a fold-out couch in the living room. Sam does not contribute to the rent, but does buy food for members of the household. Jim is much older than Sam, and raised Sam from the time Sam was 12 years old when their parents were killed in a car accident.

The apartment building and its grounds are known to the police and the residents as the location of narcotics sales. The sales are often accompanied by violence; within the past year, 15 residents who were innocent bystanders, including four small children, have been wounded in shootings associated with drug sales. Six residents, including two small children, died from the gunshot wounds. The police have strong hearsay evidence that Sam was responsible for at least several of the shootings, and are continuing their investigation in the hopes of obtaining sufficient evidence to arrest him on that charge.

While residing at Jim's apartment, Sam, on occasion, brings in small packages from his truck and keeps them in the closet in the living room. When Jim asked Sam about the contents of the packages, Sam told Jim to mind his own business. Jim has also seen Sam take the packages down to the street below, where Sam sometimes meets with and takes cash from people Jim does not know. Jim advised Sam in no uncertain terms that he never wanted any drugs brought into his household.

Jim told his neighbor, Martha Mills, that he wondered what Sam was doing when he left the apartment with the packages. Martha told Jim that she did not know what Sam was up to, but that she had a friend, Alice, whose apartment had been used by Alice's son to store drugs that he sold. Martha also told Jim that, if Jim thought Sam was selling drugs, he should kick Sam out of the apartment because Jim could lose his lease just like Alice did. Jim told Martha that he had helped raise Sam, and could never bring himself to kick Sam out. Martha advised Jim to retain an attorney.

Assume that you are a criminal defense attorney with a great deal of experience in civil and criminal forfeitures. Jim has come to you for advice about the foregoing. He is adamant that his brother remain in the apartment, but wants to know how to protect himself. How do you advise him?

20-5. Please incorporate the facts from the preceding problem. Early in the morning of the Monday after Jim met with his attorney, there were several drug-related shootings at Jim's building, resulting in one death. Federal agents arrived at Jim's apartment at 2:00 a.m. and broke down the door. They entered the bedroom, where Jim and the children were sleeping. The agents had their guns drawn. Terrified, Jim demanded that they leave. The agents refused to do so, and informed Jim that they had a warrant issued by a United States magistrate one hour earlier authorizing them to seize the apartment under 21 U.S.C. § 881. The agents gave Jim 15 minutes to pack his belongings and leave with his children; Sam was not present. Jim and his children spent the following week in a shelter.

The government then entered into an occupancy agreement that allowed the family to return to the apartment, but required them to obtain prior governmental approval for any guests that visited the apartment. Jim and his children have returned and are abiding by the occupancy agreement; they have not seen or heard from Sam since the evening the agents appeared. The government has initiated a civil forfeiture proceeding under 21 U.S.C. § 881(a)(7).

Assume that the government has established by a preponderance of the evidence that the lease is a forfeitable property interest. Jim argues both that (1) the lease cannot be forfeited because the seizure was invalid under the Due Process Clause, and (2) in any event he is an innocent holder of the lease. Should Jim prevail on either of his arguments? Why or why not?

TABLE OF CASES

[References are to pages]

[References are to pages]

[References are to pages]

[References are to pages]

[References are to pages]

[References are to pages]

[References are to pages]

TABLE OF STATUTES

[References are to pages]

[References are to pages]

[References are to pages]

[References are to pages]

[References are to pages]

INDEX

[References are to page numbers.]

[References are to page numbers.]

[References are to page numbers.]

[References are to page numbers.]

[References are to page numbers.]